Cretney & Lush on Lasting
and Enduring Powers of Attorney

Eighth Edition

While every care has been taken to ensure the accuracy of this work, no responsibility for loss or damage occasioned to any person acting or refraining from action as a result of any statement in it can be accepted by the authors, editors or publishers.

Cretney & Lush on Lasting and Enduring Powers of Attorney

Eighth Edition

Caroline Bielanska LLB (Hons), TEP, Solicitor
Caroline Bielanska Consultancy

Denzil Lush BA, MA, LLM
Former Senior Judge of the Court of Protection

Members of the LexisNexis Group worldwide

United Kingdom	RELX (UK) Limited, trading as LexisNexis, Lexis House, 30 Farringdon Street, London EC4A 4HH
Australia	LexisNexis Butterworths, Chatswood, New South Wales
Austria	LexisNexis Verlag ARD Orac GmbH & Co KG, Vienna
Benelux	LexisNexis Benelux, Amsterdam
Canada	LexisNexis Canada, Markham, Ontario
China	LexisNexis China, Beijing and Shanghai
France	LexisNexis SA, Paris
Germany	LexisNexis Deutschland GmbH, Munster
Hong Kong	LexisNexis Hong Kong, Hong Kong
India	LexisNexis India, New Delhi
Italy	Giuffrè Editore, Milan
Japan	LexisNexis Japan, Tokyo
Malaysia	Malayan Law Journal Sdn Bhd, Kuala Lumpur
New Zealand	LexisNexis NZ Ltd, Wellington
Singapore	LexisNexis Singapore, Singapore
South Africa	LexisNexis Butterworths, Durban
USA	LexisNexis, Dayton, Ohio

First Published in 1987

© RELX (UK) Limited 2017

Published by LexisNexis

A CIP Catalogue record for this book is available from the British Library.

ISBN for this volume: 9781784733766

Printed and bound by Hobbs the Printers Ltd, Totton, Hampshire

Visit LexisNexis at www.lexisnexis.co.uk

Foreword

I began preparing Enduring Powers of Attorney for clients on Monday 10 March 1986 – the day that the Enduring Powers of Attorney Act 1985 came into force – and must have drawn up hundreds of them while I was still a solicitor in private practice.

In April 1996 I was appointed as Master of the Court of Protection. My job title changed to Senior Judge when the Mental Capacity Act 2005 (MCA) was implemented in October 2007, and I retired in July 2016. During those 20 years at the court I adjudicated on issues relating to over 1,000 Enduring Powers of Attorney (EPAs) and over 5,000 Lasting Powers of Attorney (LPAs).

In addition to 30 years' experience of dealing with powers of attorney, both as a practitioner and a judge, I have also been one of the authors of this book, but I have never made an EPA or LPA myself, and an explanation is both due and overdue.

In a nutshell, I have seen so much of the pathology associated with powers of attorney and the causes and effects when things go pear-shaped, that I find it difficult to recall cases where powers have operated smoothly and to the credit of everyone involved.

During the financial year 2016/17, there were 648,318 applications to the Office of the Public Guardian ('OPG') to register LPAs and EPAs and the year ended with 2,478,758 current instruments on the register.

LPAs are clearly popular. Their popularity is the result of a vigorous and effective campaign by the OPG and the Ministry of Justice to promote them, but I am sorry to say that this crusade has involved demonising the appointment of deputies by the Court of Protection.

For example, LPA9, one of the leaflets published by the OPG, asks the question, 'What could happen if I don't create an LPA?' and gives the following answer:

'If you lose mental capacity, through illness or injury, and haven't created an LPA:

- you'll no longer be able to decide who makes decisions for you (you can only make your LPA while you still have mental capacity)
- people you don't know could end up making crucial decisions for you instead – such as whether to accept medical treatment to keep you alive, or about what you eat and wear and where you live
- your family or friends might have to go to court to make decisions on your behalf – which can be a lot more expensive and time-consuming than making an LPA.

If you still have mental capacity, LPAs are a simple and legally robust way of giving someone you trust power to make decisions for you – temporarily or for a longer time.'

In mentioning only the problems that can arise if you don't make an LPA, this leaflet is disingenuous because it fails to mention the risks if you do make one, or to inform you that, if something does go wrong, putting it right will be significantly more expensive and time-consuming than applying to the court for the appointment of a deputy in the first place.

One of the reasons why I haven't made an LPA personally is that I have greater confidence in deputyship as a means of managing someone's property and financial affairs. I accept that deputyship is more costly, more onerous and more time-consuming than making an LPA, but there are other entries on the balance sheet, which, in my opinion, are factors of magnetic importance:

(1)   The autonomy principle whereby 'you decide' who to appoint has consistently been overstated. Unless there is a cogent reason why someone should not be your deputy, it is likely that the Court of Protection will appoint as your deputy the person whom you would have appointed to be your attorney, if you had the capacity to do so. In deciding what is in your best interests, the court has a duty under the MCA to consider your past and present wishes and feelings, beliefs and values, and any other factors that you would be likely to consider. The true beneficiaries of the autonomy principle are the attorneys, who can basically do as they please.

(2)   A deputy is required to account annually to the OPG and a deputyship usually starts with the preparation of an inventory of assets and liabilities, which acts as a focal point on which to base and audit all future accounts. Attorneys are also expected to keep accounts, receipts, invoices, bank statements and other financial documents, but generally speaking nobody ever calls for them or routinely scrutinises them, so most attorneys don't bother to maintain proper records. I was astonished by how few of them were able to produce accounts when they were asked to do so by the court or the OPG. This is unacceptable.

(3)   Deputyship is more structured and disciplined than attorneyship. The Public Guardian has a statutory duty to supervise deputies, but he is under no obligation to supervise attorneys. Supervision involves more than just checking accounts. It includes educating, supporting and visiting deputies and, if necessary, admonishing them. No comparable service exists for attorneys, who have exactly the same need as deputies for instruction, back-up and the occasional reprimand.

(4)   A deputy is generally required to give security to cover the possibility that he or she could act incompetently or dishonestly. A few years ago, there was a notorious case which illustrates this point perfectly. It was widely reported in the national press and also appeared in the formal law reports under the titles *Re GM* [2013] COPLR 290 and *Re Gladys Meek; Jones v Parkin and Others* [2014] COPLR 535. Gladys Meek was a 94-year-old widow who lived in Heanor, Derbyshire. Her late husband's niece and great niece were appointed as her deputies for property and affairs and they went on a spending spree with her money. They bought themselves a Mini Countryman, a Ford Fiesta, an Apple laptop computer, a Sony laptop, Rolex and Omega watches, handbags

by Vivienne Westwood, Alexander McQueen and Mulberry, season tickets to watch Derby County Football Club and expensive rings and perfume, and then started buying presents for other members of their families. The court was able to call in a security bond for £275,000, which just about covered the extent of their defalcation. This would not have been possible if they had been Gladys Meek's attorneys, because a security bond would neither have been required nor available.

(5)   For all the talk of deputyship being costly and time-consuming, the average life-expectancy of a case in the Court of Protection is only 3½ years. The OPG's annual deputy supervision fee is currently £320, so in most cases the expenditure on supervision fees is likely to be around the £1,000 mark, to which should be added, of course, the application fee to the court and the annual premium payable in respect of the security bond. Hence, for a relatively modest outlay over a fairly short period of time, a person's property and financial affairs can be more adequately safeguarded than if he or she made an LPA.

(6)   Finally, it has been suggested – and I fully understand why – that the main problem with deputyship is the time it takes to obtain an order appointing a deputy, which can cause difficulties if there is an urgent need to access someone's funds. Judges of the Court of Protection have power to make interim orders instantly in an emergency because the rules allow them to shorten or extend any time limits. The Public Guardian has no comparable powers to reduce the period for registering an LPA, so in theory, at least, obtaining an order from the Court of Protection should be quicker than applying to the OPG to register an LPA.

There is another key reason why I haven't made an LPA, and that's the devastating effect it can have on family relationships. The lack of transparency and accountability causes suspicions and concerns, which tend to rise in a crescendo and eventually explode. I have seen it happen in a family related to mine by marriage.

In October 2016, Dr Gillian Dalley and her colleagues at Brunel University presented a report to the Dawes Trust on *Financial Abuse of People Lacking Mental Capacity*. In chapter 4 of the report they analysed 34 of my judgments, which had been published on the BAILII website in 2015, and came up with the following observations:

(1)   'Having to take responsibility for the property and financial affairs of a relative, often a parent, seems to have one or other of two negative aspects – that it poisons pre-existing relationships further, or that it precipitates bad feeling where none existed in the past.'

(2)   'Misuse of a donor's funds did not, it appears, always result from a fraudulent impulse; sometimes it was grounded in naïve incompetence, bitter intra-family disputes, or the pressure of personal problems.'

(3)   'It was striking to see that in a number of cases, attorneys, who had been appointed jointly, or jointly and severally, failed to observe their co-operative responsibilities. The tensions that are shown time and time again to exist within families do not necessarily sit comfortably with their duties to work jointly often imposed by the deputyship. And those self-same arrangements may exacerbate pre-existing tensions that had not surfaced before.'

(4)   'Reports of cases often included statements from the attorneys involved in tones that ranged through contrition, faux surprise, apparent amazement, brazen self-justification to argumentative contestation of the judge's view.'

(5)   'The assumptions often embedded in public discourse about the "family" – goodwill, mutual support, blood being thicker than water – are often challenged by behaviour and attitudes revealed in court.'

I know precisely whom I would appoint as my attorney, if I had any intention of making an LPA for property and financial affairs. She is a family member and a practising solicitor and the most honest person I know, but I would rather she acted as my deputy than as my attorney. This would ensure that there is accountability on her part and that she gets all the support she needs from the OPG, but the main advantage is that there is a greater likelihood that her relationship with her siblings will remain cordial, rather than turn sour.

I haven't made an LPA for health and welfare because, in most cases, I don't think they're necessary. The people, who, according to LPA9, 'don't know you' and 'could end up making crucial decisions for you, such as whether to accept medical treatment to keep you alive' are usually qualified health-care professionals, who will make these decisions in your best interests after consulting you and your nearest and dearest.

Mr Justice Jonathan Baker expressed this elegantly in *G v E* [2010] COPLR Con Vol 470, at paragraph [57]. When describing health and welfare decision making, where the issues that need to be addressed are quite different from those relating to the management of someone's property and financial affairs, he said:

> 'The Act and the Code are therefore constructed on the basis that the vast majority of decisions concerning incapacitated adults are taken informally and collaboratively by individuals or groups of people working together. It is emphatically not part of the scheme underpinning the Act that there should be one individual who as a matter of course is given special legal status to make decisions about incapacitated persons.'

When I retired from the Court of Protection, I was invited to become a trustee of the national charity Action on Elder Abuse. Its chief executive, Gary Fitzgerald, has expressed his concern that what safeguards there are in respect of LPAs have been consistently eroded in recent years because of the Public Guardian's drive towards creating and registering LPAs online. Caroline Bielanska raises similar concerns in the Preface and I agree with her and Gary Fitzgerald.

I apologise if this has been a rant rather than a heart-warming homily, but I need to voice these concerns, which I suppressed in the past because they were difficult to express while I was in office. I hope that in future the media, the Ministry of Justice, the OPG, and professional advisers will be more judicious when advising people to make an LPA. There is a perfectly viable alternative, which is by no means as unattractive as they have hitherto portrayed it.

I am delighted that Caroline Bielanska has agreed to edit the eighth edition of this book. I have known her for many years and appreciate the estimable efforts she has put into keeping another work that is dear to my heart, *Elderly*

Clients: A Precedent Manual, up-to-date and accessible to the legal profession and the general public.

Denzil Lush
July 2017

Preface

I intend this to complement Denzil's Foreword, which at first blush may appear to fly in the face of a book about enduring and lasting powers of attorney.

I have concerns about the path the Office of the Public Guardian (OPG) is travelling. The 2015 lasting power of attorney prescribed forms marked a sharp deviation in direction for the OPG: moving away from the Law Commission's vision for the replacement to the enduring power regime.

The Law Commission identified that most enduring powers were registered within a few weeks of their creation, as the attorney believed that either the donor lacked mental capacity or was becoming mentally incapable of managing his property and affairs, which begged the question, whether the donor understood what they were signing. It was for this reason the Mental Capacity Act 2005 requires an independent person to counter sign the donor's signature: to confirm that in his opinion the donor understands what he is signing and there is no fraud or undue pressure being used to get the donor to grant the power.

The role of the certificate provider is a vital safeguard at the point of creation of the power. Unfortunately, the 2015 prescribed forms have watered down this safeguard. It is unlikely the OPG would be able to identify whether the certificate provider is disqualified. Certificate providers may not know they cannot act as such, as the font size setting out those who are disqualified is so small; only those with perfect vision could possibly read it. No doubt the change has made the OPG's work easier.

The OPG no longer have any guidance aimed at the certificate provider to help him work out how to form his opinion. The legislation specifically requires the certificate provider to form an 'opinion', which I would suggest requires him to take some positive action in this regard. Yet, the 2015 prescribed forms do not require an opinion but rather passively state that this is, 'so far as I'm aware'. To quote District Judge Eldergill, in *The Public Guardian's Severance Applications (Rev 1)* [2017] EWHC COP 10, 'It is always risky to depart from the statutory language when drafting forms'. It has the potential for being misleading.

According to statistics published by the Ministry of Justice in March 2017, the single largest group of registered LPAs are for people aged between 81–90, followed not far behind by those aged between 71–80. The incidence of disability and cognitive impairment increases with age, and so statistically there is a high chance that many of these donors already had such difficulties when they made their lasting power. It is not uncommon in practice for family members to contact a professional adviser, to 'get' a power over their relative's money: rather than wishing to be 'given' the power by their relative. The donor is rarely initiating the need to have the power. It is for this reason, I believe that professional advisers act as an important safeguard. They are able to provide impartial advice about the donor's choice of attorney and how best to include appropriate provisions to ensure the attorney makes good decisions which are tailored to the donor's needs and wishes.

The OPG intend to move forward with their plan to make the process fully digital: completing the creation and registration of the power without any wet signatures. I am not convinced that this provides any benefit for the donor, and may increase the risk of their personal data being used without their authority and without their knowledge to create a power. Whist I appreciate this can happen now, the current practical obstacles are such that it acts as a deterrent.

The OPG have redesigned their deputyship supervision regime, utilising the 'Nudge Theory'. Nudge Theory is usually credited to Richard Thaler, Professor of Behavioural Science and Economics at the University of Chicago Booth School of Business and Daniel Kahneman, an American psychologist. Nudge Theory argues that positive reinforcement and indirect suggestions to try to achieve non-forced compliance can influence the motives, incentives and decision making of groups and individuals alike, at least as effectively – if not more effectively – than direct instruction, legislation, or enforcement.

In effect, most people are compliant when they are told the rules; some need to understand the reasons behind the rules, before they are compliant; and a small number will ignore the rules, regardless of the consequences. If the Nudge Theory were applied to lasting powers, nearly all attorneys would make legally compliant decisions.

It is noticeable that there is very little useful information provided to attorneys at the point of creating the power. The prescribed forms make no reference to the need to consult the donor, co-attorney and those interested in the donor's welfare when making decisions; and for financial attorneys, the need to keep accounts and the limited power to make gifts. It simply refers the parties to the legislation and its Code. There is a high risk that attorneys will exceed their authority and fail to follow the law.

Court of Protection cases which involve the removal of an attorney because they have unlawfully used the donor's money, contain four common assertions made by the attorney. In many cases, the attorney is convinced they were acting appropriately.

Assertion 1: 'Mum had capacity and said I could have the money'.

Although capacity is to be presumed, it is rebuttable where there is evidence to the contrary. Capacity to make a gift is complex, as it varies depending on the size of the gift and how the gift leaves the donor financially. Ideally, assessing capacity should be a simple and straightforward process, but as court judgments demonstrate – they can be anything but. How likely is it that the attorney has the skills to make that judgment?

The limited power to make gifts under s 12 of the Mental Capacity Act 2005, allows the attorney to make gifts to people associated with the donor (which includes himself), on customary occasion so long as the gift is reasonable both in relation to its size and the circumstances. The attorney can make gifts where the donor lacks mental capacity, or if it is unrestricted, when the donor has mental capacity. Indeed, the donor may have wanted to make a gift beyond the sum allowed under s 12. The attorney cannot seek the court's approval to the gift, as the court lacks jurisdiction if the donor possesses mental capacity. Meaning, the donor is denied the ability to make the gift, through the vehicle of a lasting power. The nuance of this point tests specialist professionals – what chance has the lay attorney?

Assertion 2: 'Mum would have wanted me to have this money, if she had mental capacity'.

Families work in their own way and it may very well be the case that this assertion is the truth. There is nothing in the 2015 prescribed forms which draw to the attention of the attorney the limited powers to make gifts. The OPG have in recent years published specific guidance, but this must be drawn to the attorney's attention, by some mechanism, and before they make any gifts.

A best interest decision requires the attorney to take into account the donor's views, wishes and beliefs. If they were unaware of their limited power, it's easy to see an attorney concluding that making the gift is a best interest decision because they believe that's what the donor would have wanted.

Assertion 3: 'It will all be mine eventually'.

This is particularly likely, where the attorney is the only child of the donor and the only residuary beneficiary and may be linked to assertion 2 above. The attorney sees the use of the donor's funds as an advance on their eventual inheritance, and where they have pressing needs, do not consider it wrong.

Assertion 4: 'I deserve this for the sacrifice I am making'.

This assertion can arise where there is a primary attorney making most, if not all decisions. They can become resentful of the time and effort it takes to manage the donor's affairs, especially where other people will eventually inherit to the same extent as they do from the donor's estate. The attorney 'restores the equity' by utilising the donor's funds for their own benefit.

I believe it is possible to have the equivalent benefits of a deputyship by including appropriate conditions in the power, and by providing robust support and information to the attorney. For example:

(i)   Including a supervision clause, such as requiring the attorney to provide copies of financial statements to a non-attorney.
(ii)   Expressly providing for accounts to be produced.
(iii)   Expressly requiring the attorney to consult with the donor, co-attorneys and other named individuals.
(iv)   Arranging for financial statements to be sent to the less active or dormant attorney.
(v)   Providing information to the attorney about how they work with the donor to support decision making and working with their co-attorney in partnership to make good decisions.
(vi)   Explaining the consequence of poor decisions, such as the risk of their removal and publicity in the media.
(vii)   Identifying events, which trigger the need to get expert advice.

(viii) Notifying interested people after the registration of the power with details of how to raise any concern they might have with the OPG.

Although there is no alternative to the advantage of the security bond under the deputyship regime, if the risk of things going wrong under the LPA is reduced, the benefit of the deputyship security bond over attorneyship is also reduced.

I am a fan of the health and welfare LPA. Medical professionals are not always fully aware of the complex health issues with which the patient lives. Whilst the attorney does not have any power to force a health professional to provide treatment, the LPA gives the attorney standing to be consulted and if the attorney considers it appropriate, the power to refuse consent to treatment.

I have been a welfare attorney for both my parents, which allowed me to ensure they continued to live and die in their home. I refused consent to my late father being given CPR, when he went into cardiac and respiratory failure. My father had severe dementia, various cancers and was extremely frail. CRP was unlikely to be successful and would have involved significant pain and injury to him, followed by an admission to hospital, where he was likely to die. When the paramedics arrived at his home, I refused consent for them to perform CPR so he could die in the comfort of his own bed, in his own home surrounded by his family.

The success of decision making under an LPA, relies on the donor making a good choice of attorney and the attorney knowing how to correctly go about the business of making decisions. Advisers must consider their advice in the context of the donor's circumstances, drafting the instrument and providing advice and support which will keep the attorney on the straight and narrow. I hope the updated edition of this book will help professionals achieve this.

Caroline Bielanska
June 2017

Contents

Contents

Chapter 3   Capacity to Create a Lasting Power of Attorney

Chapter 4   Attorneys

Contents

Contents

Contents

Contents

Contents

Contents

Contents

PART II   ENDURING POWERS OF ATTORNEY

Chapter 16   Granting an Enduring Power of Attorney
Introduction

Contents

Contents

tered

Chapter 19   The Court of Protection and Enduring Powers of Attorney

Contents

Contents

Contents

Contents

Contents

Table of Cases

J

K

L

M

N

O

W

Y

Table of Statutes

Table of Statutory Instruments

59

Part I

LASTING POWERS OF ATTORNEY

Chapter 1

THE HISTORY OF ENDURING AND LASTING POWERS OF ATTORNEY

INTRODUCTION

The automatic revocation rule at common law

1.1 A power of attorney is a deed in which one person (called 'the donor') gives another person (called 'the attorney' or 'the donee') authority to act on his behalf and in his name.

1.2 An ordinary power of attorney is automatically revoked when the donor becomes mentally incapacitated:*Drew v Nunn* (1878) 4 QBD 661. There is a narrow exception to this rule, namely, that the donor's loss of mental capacity (or even his death) will not revoke a power given to the attorney to secure a proprietary interest of the attorney or the performance of an obligation owed to him. These so-called irrevocable powers are sometimes given by a mortgagor to a mortgagee to facilitate the power of sale, should it prove necessary (Powers of Attorney Act 1971, s 4).

1.3 The automatic revocation of the power when the donor loses capacity is highly inconvenient. At the very time when the attorney's assistance has become not simply desirable but essential, the attorney no longer has the authority to act. The need for the donor's affairs to be managed properly continues, but the attorney's authority does not. In such circumstances, an application has to be made to the Court of Protection for the appointment of a deputy to manage the property and financial affairs of an incapacitated adult (P).

1.4 An enduring power of attorney (EPA) or lasting power of attorney (LPA) is a power of attorney that continues to remain in operation notwithstanding the donor's supervening incapacity. EPAs and LPAs are subject to the common law of agency, insofar as it has not been affected by subsequent legislation, and to the provisions of the Powers of Attorney Act 1971 with regard to execution (s 1), proof of instruments creating powers of attorney (s 3), and the protection of the donee and third parties where a power of attorney is revoked (s 5).

Avoiding court proceedings

1.5 The primary purpose of EPAs and LPAs is to avoid Court of Protection proceedings, which are often complicated, time-consuming and expensive. In some cases, they can even be humiliating and embarrassing. Relatives have to ask the court to make an order declaring that P is no longer capable of managing his own property and financial affairs. If the judge decides that the appointment of a deputy is necessary, there is no guarantee that the person he appoints will be someone whom P would have chosen. Although the judge will generally take into account P's preferences, he is not bound by such preferences, especially if there is a dysfunctional family and the members do not trust each other, or where P's preferred choice of deputy has a history of dishonesty or financial ineptitude, or where various matters need to be investigated. Where family members argue about who should be appointed, the proceedings are often acrimonious and end in stalemate whereby the court appoints a professional deputy from a panel of solicitors. As a result, legal costs escalate, and they are usually payable from P's estate (Court of Protection Rules 2007 (SI 2007/1744), r 156).

1.6 EPAs and LPAs, or durable powers of attorney, as they are known in the United States of America:

- a relatively cheap, simple procedure whereby the donor is able to prepare in advance for the possibility that he might become mentally incapacitated at some time in the future;
- respect the donor's autonomy by allowing him to choose the person or persons he wishes to manage his affairs;
- allow a smooth and seamless transition in the management of the donor's affairs from the time when he is fully in command of his faculties, through the twilight stage when he is becoming incapacitated, to the time when he is incapable of managing his affairs. It is often difficult to determine the point at which the donor lacks capacity to do various things. An elderly person with mild to moderate Alzheimer's dementia may have fluctuating periods of lucidity and periods of confusion, or 'good days' and 'bad days';
- legitimise community practice. Before it was possible to make an EPA, it was common practice for attorneys to continue using an ordinary power of attorney even though it had been revoked by the donor's supervening incapacity. In doing so, the attorneys were running a considerable risk, because technically they did not have any legal authority or effective protection if their acts were subsequently challenged;
- avoid the stigma of having a formal assessment of capacity, and the bureaucracy, delay, and expense of court proceedings; and
- give greater freedom of action to the attorney. The argument that EPAs and LPAs provide greater autonomy for the donor has generally been overstated. The person who really does benefit from enhanced autonomy is the attorney, because of the absence of the constraints that would be imposed upon him if he were a court-appointed deputy.

DURABLE POWERS OF ATTORNEY IN THE UNITED STATES OF AMERICA

Early prototypes of durable powers of attorney

1.7 There were two prototypes of durable power of attorney in the United States of America. In 1954, the state of Virginia enacted the first statute that enabled an agent to continue acting under a power of attorney after the principal had become mentally incapacitated. In 1964, the National Conference of Commissioners on Uniform State Laws (NCCUSL) promulgated the Model Special Power of Attorney for Small Property Interests Act.

Uniform Probate Code (1969)

1.8 In 1969, the NCCUSL approved and promulgated the Uniform Probate Code. Two sections of the Code (5-501 and 5-502) simply abolished the 'automatic revocation rule' – the rule which says that a power of attorney is automatically revoked on the supervening incapacity of the donor – and provided that the authority of an attorney to act under a power of attorney could continue despite the donor's incapacity. After the promulgation of the Uniform Probate Code, the use of durable powers of attorney became widespread throughout the United States.

1.9 In 1979, the NCCUSL added to the Uniform Probate Code three more sections on durable powers of attorney and approved the Uniform Durable Powers of Attorney Act, a freestanding Act designed as an alternative to the Uniform Probate Code. By the middle of the 1980s all 50 states and the District of Columbia had enacted statutes authorising durable powers of attorney for financial decision-making. In 1978, the Uniform Law Conference of Canada produced a draft Uniform Powers of Attorney Act, based on the American model, which was subsequently adopted to a greater or lesser extent by British Columbia, Ontario and Manitoba.

1.10 In 1982, the Pennsylvania legislature was the first to amend its durable power of attorney statute specifically enabling the agent to give directions regarding medical and surgical procedures. The amendment merely permitted the agent to consent to treatment, and not to refuse treatment on the principal's behalf. California's Uniform Durable Power of Attorney Act, which was amended in 1983 to cover health care decisions, was the first specifically to authorise an agent to refuse life-sustaining treatment on behalf of an incapacitated principal.

1.11 In 1988, the NCCUSL approved a Uniform Statutory Form of Power of Attorney Act. This was similar in concept to the English prescribed form, which had been introduced in 1986, although it was quite different in design. The American statutory form of power of attorney is simply intended to define the scope of the agent's authority. The principal is required to place his initials next to any one or more transactions on a list of 13 different types of transaction. If he wishes to confer general authority on the agent, he must place his initials next to the final, fourteenth box. The Uniform Statutory Power of Attorney Act has not been particularly popular and has only been adopted in a few states.

THE LAW COMMISSION'S RECOMMENDATIONS

Report on Powers of Attorney (1970)

1.12 In England and Wales in 1970, as part of the consultation process leading up to the enactment of the Powers of Attorney Act 1971, there was some discussion of the possibility that a power might be granted under which the attorney would be entitled to carry on handling the donor's affairs notwithstanding the donor's incapacity. However, the Law Commission concluded at that time that this was not a matter that could be dealt with properly 'in isolation from a complete review of the present procedure for dealing with the property of persons of unsound mind' (Law Com No 30 (Cmnd 4473), para 27).

The Incapacitated Principal (1983)

1.13 In 1973, the Lord Chancellor asked the Law Commission to 'consider the law and practice governing powers of attorney and other forms of agency in relation to the mental incapacity of the principal, and to make recommendations'. The Commission's report, *The Incapacitated Principal* (Law Com No 122, Cmnd 8977), published in 1983 contained a draft Bill, which formed the basis of the Enduring Powers of Attorney Act 1985.

1.14 The Law Commission considered – but rejected – proposals that would simply have abolished the common law rule that the donor's mental incapacity terminates the attorney's power. But it found overwhelming support for a new sort of power of attorney that would, subject to conditions and safeguards, continue in force despite the donor's subsequent incapacity. However, its consultation was by no means unanimous as to the detailed provisions that should be made for such a power. In particular, there was no general consensus about the safeguards needed to protect the donor against the danger of exploitation. There were two conflicting needs that had to be balanced:

> 'First, the need to provide a simple, effective and inexpensive method of allowing powers to continue despite the donor's incapacity. Secondly, the need to protect the donor's interests against exploitation. Both needs are perfectly valid. Unfortunately they are not easily reconciled.' (Law Com No 122, para 3.9).

1.15 In seeking to balance these conflicting needs, the Law Commission investigated a number of EPA schemes in other parts of the Commonwealth and in the United States. It concluded that these schemes were generally popular. They were seen as fulfilling a previously unmet need, particularly by providing an inexpensive and useful alternative to receivership proceedings. However, 'there was no such thing as an internationally accepted form of EPA scheme'. (Law Com No 122, para 3.16).

1.16 Most of the foreign schemes examined by the Law Commission contained some basic provisions designed to protect the donor's interests. For example:

(1)   a requirement that the enduring power contain a statement by the donor showing his intention that the power should survive his mental incapacity;

(2)   a requirement that the donor's signature be witnessed by someone other than the attorney; and

(3)   machinery whereby the power could be terminated or controlled by the intervention of a court or some other official body.

Some schemes contained more extensive protective measures.

1.17 In the light of this examination the Law Commission concluded that it could not recommend the adoption of a scheme that had only the basic level of protection outlined above (Law Com No 122, para 3.21). It considered that such a scheme would fail to provide sufficient protection for the donor. In particular, it was concerned by the fact that many enduring powers would be granted by elderly donors whose mental state was already beginning to deteriorate. Such people were likely to be highly suggestible and do whatever the prospective attorney said was best, perhaps without even appreciating the effect of granting an enduring power.

ENDURING POWERS OF ATTORNEY ACT 1985

Principal features of the Enduring Powers of Attorney Act 1985

1.18 The scheme originally embodied in the Enduring Powers of Attorney Act 1985, and now re-enacted as Sch 4 to the Mental Capacity Act 2005 (MCA 2005), contains a number of provisions specifically designed to protect the donor. Indeed, it has been said that the exercise of the power 'is hedged about on all sides with statutory protection for the donor' (*Re K, Re F* [1988] 2 FLR 15, at 20, per Hoffmann J).

1.19 The principal features of the EPA scheme are as follows:

- *The donor's capacity.* In order to be valid, an EPA must have been granted by someone who was able to understand the nature and effect of the power. The legislation did not actually define the capacity required to create such a power. This was decided later in *Re K, Re F* [1988] 2 FLR 15.
- *The form and contents of the document.* An EPA had to be in the form prescribed by the Lord Chancellor, containing explanatory information about the effect of creating or accepting an EPA (MCA 2005, Sch 4, para 2(1)).
- *Registration.* When the attorney has reason to believe that the donor is, or is becoming, mentally incapable, he must apply to the Office of the Public Guardian (OPG) for the power to be registered (Sch 4, paras 4(1) and (2)).
- *Notification of relatives.* Immediately before applying to the OPG, the attorney must give notice of his intention to apply for registration to the donor and to at least three of the donor's nearest relatives (Sch 4, para 4(3) and Part 3).
- *The right to object to registration.* Within five weeks of receiving the notice of intention to apply for registration, the donor or his relatives can object to the registration of the power on any one or more of five grounds. These are:
  - (a)   the power is not valid as an enduring power of attorney, usually because the donor did not have the mental capacity to make it;

(b)   the power no longer exists, because the donor has revoked it;
(c)   the application to register the power is premature because the donor is not yet becoming mentally incapable;
(d)   fraud or undue pressure was used to induce the donor to create the power; and
(e)   having regard to all the circumstances, the attorney is unsuitable to be the attorney of this particular donor (Sch 4, para 13(9)).

• *Gifts.* The attorney only has authority to make gifts to charities or to persons who are related to or connected with the donor. Gifts to family and friends can only be made on birthdays or wedding anniversaries or on seasonal occasions. The value of gifts must be 'not unreasonable having regard to all the circumstances, and in particular the size of the donor's estate' (Sch 4, para 3(3)). Any larger gifts, intended to be part of a tax-planning exercise, must be approved by the Court of Protection before they are made (Sch 4, para 16(2)(e)).

• *The role of the Court of Protection.* The Law Commission considered that the existence of the Court of Protection would be and would remain the ultimate safeguard (*The Incapacitated Principal* (1983), para 3.38), though it envisaged that the court's involvement in the running of any EPA would be very much more the exception, rather than the rule and that the court would only become involved if a problem arose. Nevertheless, the court has various corrective functions and is able to order an investigation into the attorney's conduct and, if necessary, bring the EPA to an end (Sch 4, para 16(4)).

Reaction in other jurisdictions to the Enduring Powers of Attorney Act 1985

1.20 The EPA scheme introduced in England and Wales by the 1985 Act was initially criticised elsewhere in the common law world, and particularly in Australia, for being 'so complicated that it is virtually impossible to use one without professional legal help'. It was also suggested that the effect of the Act's requirements was to produce 'a cumbersome, public, bureaucratic system, which can cause distress to those involved and which is little different from a formal guardianship or property management scheme' (Australian Law Reform Commission, *Enduring Powers of Attorney* (ALRC 47) (1988), para 14).

1.21 In fact, the Law Commission for England and Wales consciously avoided tackling a number of important issues because it was aware that its proposals were already complicated enough and did not want to make them even more elaborate. It also was anxious to ensure that the legislation encouraged people to accept appointment as agents under an EPA, and did not contain a list of duties, responsibilities and sanctions that might deter them from acting (Law Com No 122, para 4.68).

1.22 Ironically, despite these criticisms, several features of the English scheme, such as the mandatory use of a prescribed form, the requirement to register the instrument with a registration authority, and the right to object to registration, have subsequently been adopted in several other jurisdictions.

The impact of the Enduring Powers of Attorney Act 1985

1.23 It would be impossible to assess the number of enduring powers that have been executed since the Enduring Powers of Attorney Act 1985 came into force on 10 March 1986, until it ceased to be possible to create an EPA when the Mental Capacity Act 2005 came into force on 1 October 2007, as many will not need to be registered, but the number of applications for registration grew steadily, but has been declining since the introduction of the Mental Capacity Act 2005 as the following table shows.

Number of applications for registration each year

Year	No of applications	Year	No of applications
1986	605	2001	12,677
1987	1,476	2002	13,670
1988	2,215	2003	14,624
1989	2,842	2004	16,314
1990	3,649	2005	19,776
1991	4,309	2006	21,751
1992	5,189	2007	25,314
1993	5,767	2008/09	20,000
1994	6,637	2009/10	18,000
1995	7,562	2011/12	18,000
1996	8,921	2012/13	18,000
1997	9,548	2013/14	16,000
1998	10,726	2014/15	14,970
1999	11,337	2015/16	13,792
2000	12,340	2016/17	12,778

1.24 The Mental Capacity Act 2005 applies to four main client groups:

- older people, mainly with dementia of the vascular type or Alzheimer's type;
- people with mainstream psychiatric illnesses, such as schizophrenia or bipolar disorder;
- people with learning difficulties; and
- people who have suffered a head injury as a result of a car accident, or an accident at work, or an assault, or who have suffered brain damage as a result of clinical negligence, and have been awarded damages.

1.25 For various reasons, the uptake of EPAs was almost exclusively confined to older people, and it is doubtful whether EPAs were really suitable for the other client groups. People with learning difficulties often lacked the capacity to create an EPA in the first place. Where people suffer from mainstream 'revolving door' mental illnesses, the problems of registering the power, cancelling registration on recovery, re-registering, etc, may have been a disincentive to the creation of an EPA. In addition, people who are mentally ill may fall out with their attorney and seek to revoke the power. The issue of suitability also arguably applies to Lasting Powers of Attorney (LPAs).

1.26 People who have suffered brain damage in an accident or assault often lack the capacity to create a power after the accident, and most of the leading personal injury and clinical negligence lawyers consider that, as a matter of policy, EPAs or LPAs are unsuitable for the management and administration of a substantial damages award because of the lack of accountability and security. Indeed, damages awards often contain a specific order that an application be made to the Court of Protection for the appointment of a deputy.

Enduring Powers of Attorney: A Report to the Lord Chancellor (1991)

1.27 The Law Commissioner who produced the report, *The Incapacitated Principal*, in 1983 was Dr Stephen Cretney, and, when his term of office as a commissioner came to an end, he was appointed as a professor of law at the University of Bristol. In 1990 the Lord Chancellor's Department commissioned him and a team of colleagues from Bristol (Gwynn Davies, Roger Kerridge and Andrew Borkowski) to report on various aspects of the efficacy of the Enduring Powers of Attorney Act 1985. Their result of their research, *Enduring Powers of Attorney: A Report to the Lord Chancellor*, was published by the Lord Chancellor's Department in June 1991, and was enormously influential in shaping policy on the procedures that would apply in future legislation on lasting powers of attorney.

1.28 Their main findings and conclusions were as follows:

- *Registration should be mandatory*. There was what they described as a 'widespread failure to register' EPAs. 'The evidence of non-registration which we have gathered, although imprecise, renders us somewhat sceptical about the effectiveness of the limited protective mechanism built into the EPA procedure' (para 2.19).
- *Registration should not be linked to supervening incapacity*. Where EPAs were being registered, 'the timing of the registration process seems something of a lottery and we can hardly be surprised that registration is not effected in many cases where it ought to be' (para 2.38).
- Notification of an application to register the power should be to persons selected by the donor, rather than the nearest relatives.

   'The donor (who would of course be mentally capable) could choose the people who know him best, or who have a genuine interest in the conduct of his financial affairs. This would be consistent with the principle maintaining the donor's control over his affairs and ensuring that his wishes are followed. . . . We are not entirely convinced that notification of relatives is the most appropriate safeguard of the donor's interests, but if there is to be notification we think that this proposal deserves further examination.' (para 2.39)

- *Certification of capacity at the time of creating the power.*

   'We believe there is a case for focusing more narrowly upon the question of the donor's capacity when creating the power, and we consider that the interpretation put on the laws in *Re K* reinforces the view that there is a case for requiring medical evidence of capacity and for requiring registration of the EPA in order for it to become legally effective' (p 76). 'Despite the weaknesses of such a procedure, which we acknowledge, we think it might be a more effective safeguard than the present system of notifying the donor and relatives upon registration. It would inevitably make the creation of an EPA more expensive, but perhaps this is a reasonable additional expenditure'. (para 2.40)

- Separating the administrative, protective and adjudicative roles of the Court of Protection.

THE LAW COMMISSION'S PROJECT ON MENTALLY INCAPACITATED ADULTS AND DECISION-MAKING

Consultation papers

1.29 In 1989, the Law Commission embarked upon an investigation into the adequacy of legal and other procedures for decision-making on behalf of mentally incapacitated adults. The law commissioner in charge of the project was Professor Brenda Hoggett QC (now the Right Honourable Baroness Hale of Richmond, DBE).

1.30 An initial consultation paper, *Mentally Incapacitated Adults and Decision-Making: An Overview* (Consultation Paper No 119), was circulated in 1989, followed by three further consultation papers in 1993:

- *Mentally Incapacitated Adults and Decision-Making: A New Jurisdiction* (Consultation Paper No 128);
- *Mentally Incapacitated Adults and Decision-Making: Medical Treatment and Research* (Consultation Paper No 129); and
- *Mentally Incapacitated Adults and Decision-Making: Public Law Protection* (Consultation Paper No 130).

Mental Incapacity (1995)

1.31 The Law Commission's investigation concluded with a report, *Mental Incapacity* (Law Com No 231), which was published on 28 February 1995. It recommended the introduction of a single piece of legislation to make new provision for people who lack mental capacity (para 2.51), and that the legislation should be based on 'two fundamental concepts', lack of capacity and best interests (para 3.1). This involved a new statutory definition of 'lack of capacity', and a requirement that, once it is established that a person lacks capacity in relation to a particular matter at the material time, anything done for him, or any decision made on his behalf, should be done or made in his best interests. A draft Mental Incapacity Bill, which in essence forms the basis of the Mental Capacity Act 2005, appeared in the appendix to the report.

The prime policy aim is to encourage anticipatory decision-making

1.32 At para 7.1 of its report on *Mental Incapacity* (Law Com No 123 (1995)) the Law Commission said:

'Our prime policy aim is to encourage people to take for themselves those decisions which they are able to take. This should cover "anticipatory decisions" by people who, knowing or fearing that their decision-making facilities may fail, wish to make plans for what is to happen at that time. Respondents to our consultation papers repeatedly asserted that any judicial process of substitute decision-making should be a last resort, reserved for serious or disputed cases. Anticipatory decision-making or advance planning may well obviate the need for any decision or action imposed by the state. As always, however, endorsement of the autonomy principle must be balanced with the requirements of protection. A law which allows and encourages private arrangements intended to outlast the capacity of the maker to change or cancel them must also provide adequate safeguards for that person.'

Donors should be permitted to delegate authority to make personal welfare and health care decisions

1.33 At para 7.7 of its report on *Mental Incapacity* (Law Com No 123 (1995)) the Law Commission said:

'As the law now stands, the donor of an EPA can only delegate continuing decision-making authority over his or her "property and affairs". In Consultation Paper No 128 we suggested that donors should be permitted to delegate authority over "personal welfare" decisions, while in Consultation Paper No 129 we extended the proposal to health care decisions. Our consultees almost universally supported the proposal that a donor should be able to delegate non-financial decision-making in advance, in such a way that the authority would outlast any supervening incapacity of the donor. It was said that the great advantage of appointing an attorney to take health care decisions is the ability of the attorney to respond to new situations as they arise. For this reason, some respondents who expressed reservations about the advisability of "advance directives" for health care were nonetheless enthusiastic about allowing people to appoint proxy decision-makers. . . . In our view, the appointment of an attorney with a range of powers should be one option available to those who wish to plan for the possibility of future incapacity. As under the present law, it should always be open to a donor to impose specific conditions or restrictions on the attorney.'

The need for a different description from 'enduring' power of attorney

1.34 At para 7.5 of its report on *Mental Incapacity* (Law Com No 123 (1995)) the Law Commission said:

'Our draft Mental Incapacity Bill incorporates an improved statutory scheme for powers of attorney to continue in effect after a donor has lost capacity. Documents executed after the bringing into force of the new legislation will be able to give attorneys authority over whole new areas of decision-making, and should therefore be distinguished from those executed under the 1985 Act by the use of a new label. New safeguards, consistent with the policy aims of this project and with the lessons learned since the introduction of the 1985 Act, are provided.'

Accordingly, the Law Commission recommended that a new form of power of attorney, to be called a 'continuing power of attorney' should be introduced: *Mental Incapacity*, para 7.6.

The Law Commission's specific recommendations on continuing powers of attorney

1.35 As regards continuing powers of attorney, the Law Commission made the following recommendations:

- A new form of power, to be called a 'continuing power of attorney' (CPA) should be introduced. The donee of a CPA should have authority to make and implement decisions on behalf of the donor that the donor is without capacity to make (paras 7.1 to 7.6, and cl 12(1) and (2) of the draft Bill).
- Where an instrument purports to create a CPA but does not comply with the statutory requirements it should confer no powers on the donee (para 7.9, and cl 12(4) of the draft Bill).
- An attorney acting under a CPA should act in the best interests of the donor, having regard to the statutory factors (para 7.10, and cl 3 of the draft Bill).
- The restriction against coercion or confinement should apply equally to attorneys as to other decision-makers (para 7.13, and cl 16(4) and (5) of the draft Bill).
- No attorney may consent to or refuse any treatment unless the donor is, or is reasonably believed by the donor to be, without capacity to give or refuse personal consent to that treatment (para 7.14, and cl 16(3)(a) of the draft Bill).
- No attorney should have power to consent to the donor's admission to hospital for assessment or treatment for mental disorder. Where such admission is against the will of the donor (para 7.15, and cl 16(3)(b) of the draft Bill).
- No attorney should be authorised to withhold basic care from the donor or refuse consent to its provision (para 7.16, and cls 16(4)(3)(c) and 9(8) of the draft Bill).
- Unless expressly authorised to do so, no attorney may consent to any treatment refused by the donor by an advance refusal of treatment (para 7.17, and cl 16(3)(d)(i) of the draft Bill).
- Unless expressly authorised to do so, no attorney may consent on a donor's behalf to:
  — a procedure requiring court approval;
  — a procedure requiring a certificate from an independent medical practitioner;
  — discontinuance of artificial nutrition or hydration;
  — procedures for the benefit of others; or
  — participation in non-therapeutic research (para 7.18, and cl 16(3)(d)(ii) and (5) of the draft Bill).
- Unless expressly authorised to do so, no attorney may refuse consent to any treatment necessary to sustain life (para 7.19, and cl 16(3)(d)(iii) of the draft Bill).
- A CPA may only be created by an individual who has attained the age of 18 (para 7.20, and cl 14(1) of the draft Bill).
- An individual donee of a CPA may be described as the holder for the time being of a specified office or position (para 7.21, and cl 14(3) of the draft Bill).
- A donor may, in a CPA, appoint a person to replace the donee in the event of the donee disclaiming, dying, becoming bankrupt or becoming divorced from the donor (para 7.22, and cl 20(1) of the draft Bill).

- A CPA must contain a statement by the donee that he or she understands the duty to act in the best interests of the donor in relation to any decision which the donor is, or is reasonably believed by the donee to be, without capacity to make (para 7.24, and cl 13(3)(b)(ii) of the draft Bill).
- A CPA may be expressed to confer general authority on a donee (para 7.25, and cl 16(2) of the draft Bill).
- No document should create a CPA until it has been registered in the prescribed manner (paras 7.28 to 7.31, and cl 15(1) of the draft Bill).
- A registration authority appointed by the Lord Chancellor should register CPAs (para 7.32, and cl 15(1) of the draft Bill).
- If a donor objects to registration of a CPA then the registration authority should inform the donee and should not register the document unless the court directs it to do so (para 7.34, and cl 15(4) of the draft Bill).
- Once a CPA has been registered the registration authority should give notice of that fact in the prescribed form to a maximum of two people (not including the donee) as specified in the CPA (para 7.38, and cl 15(6)(b) of the draft Bill).
- No disclaimer of a registered CPA should be valid unless notice is given to the donor and the registration authority (para 7.41, and cl 12(4) of the draft Bill).
- There should be an express provision that nothing in the legislation should preclude the donor of a CPA from revoking it at any time when he or she has the capacity to do so (paras 7.42 and 7.43, and cl 12(3) of the draft Bill).
- Section 5 of the Powers of Attorney Act 1971 should apply to CPAs (para 7.44, and cl 19(6) of the draft Bill).
- Any part of a CPA which relates to matters other than property and financial affairs should not be revoked by the donor's bankruptcy (para 7.47, and cl 16(6) of the draft Bill).
- In the absence of a contrary intention, the appointment of the donee's spouse as an attorney under a CPA should be revoked by the subsequent dissolution or annulment of the parties' marriage (para 7.48, and cl 14(5) of the draft Bill).
- The registration authority should cancel the registration of a CPA on receipt of a revocation by the donor, a disclaimer by the donee or evidence that the power has expired or been revoked by death, bankruptcy, winding up or the dissolution of the parties' marriage (para 7.9, and cl 18(1) of the draft Bill).
- The registration authority should attach an appropriate note to any registered CPA which has been partially revoked, or in relation to which a replacement donee has gained power to act (para 7.49, and cl 18(2) and (5) of the draft Bill).
- The court should have power to declare that a document not in the prescribed form shall be treated as if it were in that form if the court is satisfied that the persons executing it intended to create a CPA (para 7.55, and cl 17(1) of the draft Bill).

- Subject to any contrary intention expressed in the document, the court should have power to appoint a donee in substitution for or in addition to the donee mentioned in the CPA. The court may act where the donor is without capacity to act and the court thinks it desirable to do so (para 7.56, and cl 17(3)(c)(i) of the draft Bill).
- Subject to any contrary intention expressed in the document, the court should have power to modify or extend the scope of the donee's power to act. The court may act where the donor is without capacity to act and the court thinks it desirable to do so (para 7.57, and cl 17(3)(c)(ii) of the draft Bill).
- The court may, on behalf of a donor without capacity to do so, either direct that a purported CPA should not be registered or revoke a CPA where the donee or intended donee has behaved, is behaving or proposes to behave in a way that (1) contravenes or would contravene the authority granted in the CPA or (2) is not or would not be in the donor's best interests (para 7.58, and cl 17(6)(b) of the draft Bill).
- No EPA should be created after the coming into force of the new law in relation to CPAs. Transitional provisions should apply to EPAs made prior to the repeal of the 1985 Act (para 7.59, and cl 21(1) and (3) of the draft Bill).
- An unregistered EPA may be converted into a CPA by the donor and donee executing a prescribed form and by registration (para 7.61, and cl 21(2) of the draft Bill).

Most, though by no means all, of these recommendations found their way into the Mental Capacity Act 2005.

DEVELOPMENTS BETWEEN 1995 AND 2005

Making Decisions (1999)

1.36 In December 1997 the Lord Chancellor's Department issued a consultation paper, *Who Decides?* (Cm 3808), followed by a policy statement, *Making Decisions* (Cm 4465), on 27 October 1999, which set out the Government's response to the proposals in the Law Commission's report on *Mental Incapacity*. In it, the Government announced that it had decided that:

- As with EPAs, there will be a mandatory prescribed form of CPA.
- The form must be accompanied by evidence that the donor was mentally capable at the time that it was created. That evidence could be provided by either a separate medical certificate or a signed statement by a doctor in the CPA form itself.
- Donors will be able to appoint substitute attorneys in case their first choice of attorney loses mental capacity or dies. The Court of Protection will not, however, have the power to appoint a substitute attorney, as had originally been proposed by the Law Commission.
- It will not be possible to convert an existing financial EPA into a CPA, as was originally proposed by the Law Commission. The legislation will contain appropriate transitional arrangements in respect of EPAs to ensure a smooth transition.

• There will be a compulsory registration system and a registration authority. All CPAs must be registered before the attorney can use them.

The Government pledged to introduce the necessary legislation 'when Parliamentary time allows' (*Making Decisions*, para 7).

Quinquennial Review of the Public Trust Office (1999)

1.37 The Public Trust Office was established under the Public Trustee and Administration of Funds Act 1986, and operated as the administrative arm of the Court of Protection from 1 January 1987 until it was abolished and replaced by the Public Guardianship Office on 1 April 2001. It became an executive agency within the Lord Chancellor's Department in July 1994. The Quinquennial Review of the Public Trust Office was carried out between May and October 1999 by Miss Ann Chant CB, whose report was published in November 1999.

1.38 The Chant report stated that:

'An EPA bestows virtually unfettered control of someone's financial assets once it is brought into force. While its objective (to put someone's financial affairs in the hands of an individual they have pre-selected, rather than surrendering them to the Court of Protection) fits entirely with the objective of keeping the state out of family affairs unless there is no alternative, if an EPA goes wrong the results can be catastrophic for the person concerned. Although comparatively rare, there are plenty of instances where the system has been deliberately or accidentally abused and getting the position rectified through the court is a long and difficult process'. (para 47)

The report went on to propose that there should be various enhancements to the existing system to instigate essential regulation and oversight.

'It is the lack of them which prevents current EPA arrangements being confidently recommended to the public by Ministers as a practical alternative for some people to the Court of Protection.' (para 48)

Draft Mental Incapacity Bill (2003)

1.39 On 27 June 2003 the Secretary of State for Constitutional Affairs presented to Parliament a draft Mental Incapacity Bill (Cm 5859), based largely on the Law Commission's report in 1995. The Bill proposed a new system of Lasting Powers of Attorney (LPAs), rather than continuing powers of attorney, and it is not entirely clear why the name of the new-style powers of attorney was changed.

Joint Committee on the Draft Mental Incapacity Bill (2003)

1.40 On 11 July 2003 an all-party pre-legislative scrutiny committee of Members of Parliament and peers was appointed to examine and report on the draft bill. The chairman was Lord Carter and the members – eight from the House of Lords and eight from the House of Commons. The committee received over 1,200 written submissions and took evidence from 61 witnesses, including Government ministers. It published its report in two volumes on

28 November 2003 (Session 2002–03, HL Paper 189, HC 1083), and made 99 recommendations: the final one being that 'consideration be given to changing the Bill's title to the Mental Capacity Bill'. It was felt that this would send a more positive message about the enabling ethos of the Bill.

1.41 Specifically with regard to LPAs, the joint committee said:

'46. Whilst we support the intention of the draft Bill to allow individuals the freedom to choose their donee(s) when making an LPA, we recommend that further guidance is provided to warn donors of the potential for conflict. Furthermore, we recommend the inclusion, in Codes of Practice, of an additional safeguard mechanism by which the Court of Protection or Public Guardian could monitor LPAs with a view to preventing the abuse and exploitation of a donee's powers (Paragraph 150).

47. We strongly recommend that an express duty of care is incorporated into the draft Bill in respect of donees acting under an LPA (and for court appointed deputies). We consider that a greater degree of accountability is required from those groups in order to limit the potential for abuse of their powers and, therefore, we recommend the exploration of effective methods to achieve that end. In particular, we recommend that specific requirements in the form of a standard of conduct should be included in the Codes of Practice, aimed at those exercising formal powers under the draft Bill (Paragraph 154).

48. We have concluded that the proposed system requiring the registration of LPAs before use will assist in monitoring the use of LPAs and detecting possible abuse. However, we recommend that donees should be placed under an obligation to notify both the donor and the Public Guardian that the donor is, or is becoming incapacitated, thereby putting this information on the public record and opening it up to challenge. We further recommend that guidance should be provided to assist financial institutions to deal with the operational realities of LPAs (Paragraph 157).

49. We believe that the additional safeguard of requiring two additional persons to witness the certification of capacity should be included where there are no named persons for notification of the registration of an LPA (Paragraph 159).'

The Government's response to the Scrutiny Committee's report (2004)

1.42 In February 2004, the Lord Chancellor presented to Parliament *The Government Response to the Scrutiny Committee's Report on the draft Mental Incapacity Bill* (Cm 6121). The responses to the joint committee's specific recommendations on LPAs were as follows:

'46. We recognise that there may be potential for conflict of interest in an LPA and we agree that donors should be given information about this and more generally about the seriousness of making an LPA. All financial LPAs will be under the supervision of the Public Guardian in any case. It may be possible for a higher level of monitoring of an LPA to be offered to donors who are concerned about the potential for a conflict of interest or who foresee other difficulties.

47. Duties of care generally across the Bill have been discussed above at Recommendation 28. There we noted that LPAs and deputies under the Bill will be acting as agents of the person who lacks capacity. This is the same as EPAs and receivers at present although with the additional requirement of having to action the donor's best interests. Therefore they will be subject to the fiduciary duties of an agent. We will consider whether it would be helpful to state this expressly in the Bill.

We will also consider how we can best use the Codes of Practice in explaining the nature and extent of fiduciary duties, and how these interact with the new statutory duty to act in P's best interests.

48. We welcome the Committee's conclusion that registration of LPAs prior to use will be beneficial. Further notification by the donee at a notional point of incapacity could bring difficulties though. We consider that this runs contrary to the functional approach to capacity. It would be wrong to rely on blanket levels of incapacity to avoid the complexities of assessing capacity in relation to the particular decision at the particular time. We have already begun work with financial institutions because we want to ensure they are assisted with their new responsibilities under the Bill and we will continue this work through to implementation and beyond.

49. The requirement for a certification of capacity is at the time of making an LPA not registration. We agree, however, that it makes sense to have additional safeguards for the registration of an LPA where there are no named persons. We are looking at the best way to achieve this and it may be that additional notification or other formal requirements may be appropriate.'

Legislative passage of the Mental Capacity Act 2005

1.43 The Mental Capacity Bill was introduced in the House of Commons on 17 June 2004 by David Lammy MP, the Parliamentary Under-Secretary at the Department for Constitutional Affairs, and finally received Royal Assent on Thursday, 7 April 2005 in what is known in Westminster parlance as the 'wash up'. On Tuesday, 5 April, the Prime Minister, Tony Blair, announced that a general election would take place on 5 May, and that parliament would be dissolved on Monday, 11 April. Accordingly, the government entered into negotiations on this and several other bills in an attempt to get Royal Assent before the dissolution of parliament.

DEVELOPMENTS SINCE THE IMPLEMENTATION OF THE MENTAL CAPACITY ACT 2005

Commencement of the Mental Capacity Act 2005

1.44 It was originally intended that the Mental Capacity Act 2005 would come into force in its entirety on 1 April 2007, and with this deadline in sight the Department of Health laid The Mental Capacity Act 2005 (Commencement No 1) Order (SI 2006/2814 (C.95)) before parliament in October 2006. This order brought into effect from 1 November 2006 ss 35–41 on independent mental capacity advocates (IMCAs) and from 1 April 2007 the sections relating to research (ss 30–34), codes of practice (ss 42–43), and ill-treatment or neglect (s 44).

1.45 The remainder of the Mental Capacity Act 2005, including ss 9 to 14 and Sch 1 on LPAs and Sch 4 on EPAs, came into force on 1 October 2007 by virtue of The Mental Capacity Act 2005 (Commencement No 2) Order (SI 2007/1897 (C.72)).

Revision of the 2007 prescribed forms of LPA

1.46 On 23 October 2008 the Ministry of Justice published a consultation paper (CP 26/08) called *Reviewing the Mental Capacity Act 2005: forms, supervision and fees*. The consultation ended on 15 January 2009 and the Ministry of Justice published its response to consultation (CP(R) 26/08) on 11 March 2009.

1.47 In its conclusion to the response, the Ministry of Justice stated, at pages 54–56:

'LPA forms

4.   The content of the responses will inform the format and content of the revised LPA forms and guidance. Many respondents gave lengthy, detailed technical responses to which we will continue to give consideration as we work to finalise the new forms and guidance. It is our intention that the LPA forms, including revised guidance literature and supporting regulations, will be ready to be introduced into Parliament at the beginning of July 2009, in order to be ready for introduction on 1 October 2009. We are particularly keen to ensure that practitioners and financial institutions have sufficient time to prepare for the changes. The regulations in which these forms are prescribed are subject to the negative resolution procedure.

5.   The responses to the proposed form design changes were on the whole very supportive, indicating it is right for the forms to be improved and that the majority of changes are helpful and uncontroversial. There was strong support for incorporating guidance notes into the margins of the form, and we will consider suggestions on re-wording or making additions to some of that guidance.

6.   We will consider the suggestions for the use of continuation sheets and whether those sheets ought to be of a prescribed design issued by the OPG along with other design suggestions which may help reduce the overall length of the forms, which for many was an area of primary importance and concern. However, many respondents also acknowledged the difficulties in finding a balance, which will suit the majority of users, whilst incorporating the requirements and safeguards laid down in the MCA such as the inclusion of certificate providers, which inevitably leads to a from that is longer than the EPA form it replaced. Where we can reduce length, we will look to do so, especially where re-design allows for the removal of blank or unused spaces.

7.   There were many recurring themes that emerged from the responses, outside of the questions contained in the consultation. The most common being:

- The forms should be shorter.
- The forms should contain specific information/guidance other than that in the proposed revised versions (42 respondents offered suggestions).
- Guidance needs to be better/clearer around/for:
  — Certificate providers and substitute attorneys.
  — How to cancel an LPA.
  — What is meant by life-sustaining treatment.
  — Signatures and the order they are required to be completed.
  — Clearer distinction between the 3 parts of the forms (some suggested different coloured parts/headings).
- Scope for fraud on optional continuation pages and suggestions on how this could be avoided including comparisons to other forms such as tax returns.
- Unworkable conditions and restrictions.
- The method used to validate LPAs (i.e. the holographic stickers).

- New forms should be widely tested.

The OPG will use professional accessibility experts to help with the re-design work it will now undertake to further improve LPAs. It has been decided that the new forms should be introduced in October 2009 so as to allow time to make the changes and allow users to prepare. The timing will not allow for further widespread consultation but the OPG will work with stakeholders during this process.'

1.48 New prescribed forms of LPA were contained in the Lasting Powers of Attorney, Enduring Powers of Attorney and Public Guardian (Amendment) Regulations 2009 (SI 2009/1884), which were made on 14 July 2009, laid before Parliament on 15 July 2009, and came into force on 1 October 2009.

United Nations Convention on the Rights of Persons with Disabilities

1.49 On 13 December 2006, the United Nations General Assembly adopted the Convention on the Rights of Persons with Disabilities. Following ratification by 20 States Parties, the Convention came into force on 3 May 2008 and, as at 1 September 2013, the Convention had had 156 signatories and 133 ratifications. The Convention was ratified by the United Kingdom on 8 June 2009.

1.50 Article 12 of the Convention is titled 'Equal recognition before the law' and Article 12.3 expressly provides that: 'States Parties shall take appropriate measures to provide access by persons with disabilities to the support they may require in exercising their legal capacity.' Essentially, the Convention seeks to promote 'supported decision-making', where the person with disabilities is given support to help them make a decision for themselves, as distinct from 'substitute decision-making', where someone else makes the decision for them. It is anticipated that during the next few years there will be an increasing call for 'supported decision-making agreements' to be made available for persons with learning difficulties. This change of emphasis, sometimes described as a 'paradigm shift', can be seen in the title of the Assisted Decision-Making (Capacity) Bill 2013, which was published in the Republic of Ireland on 17 July 2013, passed into law in 2015 and partially brought into force on 11 October 2016.

Digitalisation of the OPG's services

1.51 The Government Digital Service (GDS) is a team in the Cabinet Office which was established following the publication of the report of the UK Digital Champion, Martha Lane Fox, *Directgov 2010 and beyond: revolution not evolution*, on 23 October 2010. The aim of the GDS is to encourage as many people as possible to go online, and thereby improve the efficiency of public services by driving online delivery. The OPG is working closely with the GDS to deliver new services that take advantage of digital technology in the creation and registration of Lasting Powers of Attorney.

1.52 On 27 July 2012, the Ministry of Justice published a consultation paper on transforming the services of the OPG. The consultation lasted until 19 October 2012, and on 22 January 2013 the ministry published its response,

CP(R) 23/2012, *Transforming the Services of the Office of the Public Guardian*. The conclusion and next steps are as follows:

- 'In April 2013, the OPG will launch the new digital tool which will make it easier for customers to complete the current LPA forms online. This will help to eradicate many of the errors that currently occur during the completion of the LPA form and will reduce inefficiencies in the current processes. We will also reduce the current statutory waiting period from six to four weeks in order to make the process quicker for customers, whilst still retaining adequate safeguards.

- The Ministry of Justice has identified the OPG transformation programme as an 'exemplar' for digital transformation of services. The OPG's online services are being developed to meet customer needs, in line with the new Government digital service standard, as well as ensuring assisted digital support is in place for those who cannot access digital services independently.

- Throughout 2013 we will take further steps to revise the LPA forms and guidance, including shortening the LPA002 'application to register', and consider in more detail how a 'hybrid' LPA might look and operate. We will consult about these changes as appropriate.

- As part of its continuing programme to transform the way in which it delivers its services, the OPG has also commenced a fundamental review of the way the Public Guardian exercises his statutory duty to supervise deputies appointed by the Court of Protection. If required, we will consult on any proposals in 2013.

- The suggestions and feedback we have received in relation to the questions regarding certificate providers, named persons and the statutory waiting period will be used to inform the ongoing work that is being undertaken as part of the transformation of OPG services. Some of these changes, if they were to be adopted may require primary legislation. We will consult further on these areas as necessary.'

House of Lords Select Committee on the Mental Capacity Act 2005

1.53 On 16 May 2013 the House of Lords set up a post-legislative scrutiny committee on the Mental Capacity Act 2005 under the chairmanship of Lord Hardie, the former Lord Advocate of Scotland.

1.54 The context in which this committee was convened was described as follows:

'The Mental Capacity Act has been in force since 2007, and the time is right to scrutinise the legislation to see if it is working as Parliament intended. The Act provides protection for some of the most vulnerable members of our society and it is critical to understand whether implementation has delivered on what was promised in legislation.

We will be examining whether the Government's implementation programme was effective in embedding the guiding principles of the Act in every day practice, and whether there has been a noticeable change in the culture of care. We need to know how well the Act is understood by those who are affected by it. And we are very interested to hear about whether the safeguards contained in the Act are sufficient:

are people able effectively to challenge decisions made under the Act? Is the Court of Protection accessible to those affected?'

1.55 The committee published a call for evidence in June 2013, in which it sought written responses to 27 questions, including the following three on LPAs:

'10.   Are those directly affected by the Act being enabled and supported to make decisions for themselves to a greater or lesser extent than they would have been in the past? Does the means by which the decision is made – 'general authority', Lasting Power of Attorney, deputyship, Court of Protection – affect the quality of decision-making?

19.   What has been the impact of the introduction of Lasting Powers of Attorney (LPA), especially with regard to decision making on matters of personal care and welfare?

20.   What concerns, if any, are there regarding the costs associated with registering an LPA, or with making an application to the Court of Protection?'

1.56 The Committee published its report on 25 February 2014. Paragraphs 191–192 of the report contained recommendations on LPAs:

'191.   As with other aspects of the Mental Capacity Act, low levels of awareness have affected implementation of the provisions relating to Lasting Powers of Attorney. Awareness needs to be raised among the general public of the benefits of Lasting Powers of Attorney in order to encourage greater take-up, especially for Health and Welfare matters. We support the initiatives of the Public Guardian to improve take-up by simplifying the forms and reducing the cost of registration, as well as identifying other barriers to take-up.

192.   We recommend that the Government, working with the independent oversight body recommended in CHAPTER 4, and the Office of the Public Guardian:

- address the poor levels of understanding of LPAs among professional groups, especially in the health and social care sector, paying specific attention to the status of Lasting Powers of Attorney in decision-making;
- consider how best to ensure that information concerning registered Lasting Powers of Attorney can be shared between public bodies, and where appropriate with private sector bodies such as banks and utilities;
- issue guidance to local authorities that their new responsibilities for provision of information in relation to care contained in the Care Bill should include information on Lasting Powers of Attorney;
- consider how attorneys and deputies faced with non-compliance by public bodies or private companies can be supported in the absence of specific sanctions;
- review the apparent anomalies in the current arrangements with regard to successive replacement attorneys, and the status in England of Scottish Powers of Attorney.'

The future of Lasting Power of Attorney research

1.57 In March 2014, a research report for the OPG, *The Future of Lasting Power of Attorney* was published by Ipsos MORI. To increase LPA applications, the OPG needs to better understand the shape of the potential LPA customer market and identify factors which could inhibit or enhance LPA uptake. The report makes interesting reading:

- The research revealed a lack of awareness of LPA amongst potential customers: 45% had never heard of it, or knew nothing about it.
- Of those who were interested in applying for an LPA, 33% thought they would wait until they were diagnosed with a condition that affected their mental capacity to get their LPA(s).
- The qualitative research among those who were recently diagnosed suggested that diagnosis often did not act as a trigger in the same way that undiagnosed potential customers thought it would, arguing that it was more emotionally difficult to accept than others may consider.
- The research revealed a number of barriers which may prevent take-up of LPA or may mean that people put off applying until they need it. Of those who were not interested in an LPA:
  (i) 40% did not believe that they would lose capacity or cared if they did, or did not want to give someone else the power to make decisions on their behalf.
  (ii) 29% said they did not need an LPA because they believed their relatives would be able to manage without one.
  (iii) 26% did not having someone they could currently nominate as an attorney.
  (iv) 26% stated they did not know enough about an LPA or had never thought about it.
  (v) 17% were put off by the cost of registering an LPA or felt it would be too complicated.

OPG's digital LPA tool

1.58 In May 2014, the OPG, working with the Government Digital Service (GDS), launched its digital tool which enables customers to complete most the LPA process online. The digital tool has continued to be developed and improved as a direct result of user feedback. In the OPG's Annual Report and Accounts for 2015/2016, published on 7 July 2016, the Public Guardian reported that of those who applied to register an LPA during the year, over 26% did so using the online LPA digital service. The service has maintained a steady user satisfaction score with 93% of those surveyed saying that they were satisfied or very satisfied with the service. However, there is concern amongst the legal profession and some judges with the ease at which an LPA can be created. In *JL (Revocation of Lasting Power of Attorney)* [2014] EWCOP 36, Senior Judge revoked an LPA which had been created using the OPG's digital tool. He said,

'. . . . . it gives rise to additional concern about the circumstances in which the LPA was created. If AS failed to read Part C, it makes it hard to believe her assertion that she had carefully read and explained to her mother the contents of Part A of the LPA – the part that the donor is required to complete.'

Proposal for new forms

1.59 On 15 October 2013, the Ministry of Justice published a further consultation paper *Transforming the services of the Office of the Public Guardian: enabling digital by default*. The consultation lasted until 26 November 2013. The consultation included proposals for a revision to the LPA prescribed forms, fees for a new combined form and improvement to access the OPG Registers. More controversially, it included proposals for the delivery of a fully digital method of creating and registering LPAs (e-LPAs), which will require primary legislation to take it forward. The response to the Consultation (CP(R) 26/11/2013) was published on 21 August 2014 and confirmed the following plans:

- a redesign of the prescribed forms;
- retaining separate health & welfare and property & financial affairs LPA forms;
- encourage donors to state when they wish their property & financial affairs LPA to come into effect;
- include new language aimed at making the LPA easier to complete for lay donors;
- remove the requirement for a second certificate provider;
- amalgamate the revised 'application to register' form with the main LPA form; and
- expand the range of cases for which a reduced application fee is applicable to include those cases where the LPA can only be made capable of registration by an application being made to the Court of Protection.

1.60 The OPG would start to take forward work to:

- launch a digital tool for second tier searches of the OPG's register; and
- provide intermediate access to the register for accredited parties.

The consultation identified that there are a number of points which need to be resolved before a fully digital LPA can be implemented.

1.61 The Lasting Powers of Attorney, Enduring Powers of Attorney and Public Guardian (Amendment) Regulations 2015 (SI 2015/899), were laid before Parliament on 26 March 2015 and came into force on 1 July 2015, and implemented the recommendations made by the *enabling digital by default* consultation response (CP(R) 26/11/2013).

The National Mental Capacity Forum

1.62 The House of Lords Select Committee post legislative scrutiny report of 2014 highlighted the MCA 2005 had not met the expectations that it raised and there was a need for a body to champion the Act. In response, the Government established the National Mental Capacity Forum (NMCF) in September 2015. Professor Baroness Finlay of Llandaff is the Chair of the NMCF, with the aim of identifying and driving local actions to improve awareness; improving understanding and implementation of the MCA; and making possible improved outcomes and benefits for individuals who may (or may in the future) lack mental capacity.

1.63 In her first report, published on 1 March 2017, Baroness Finlay said that health and social care professionals reported not knowing how to recognise whether a health and welfare LPA is valid, and whether it has been specifically created to include the power to consent to or refuse life sustaining treatments. These issues have been addressed by a guide with images hosted on the gov.uk website. Details about the membership and activities of the NMCF can be found on http://www.scie.org.uk/mca-directory/forum/

Statistics

1.64 The following statistics are taken from the OPG's Annual Report and Accounts 2010/11 (page 10), 2011/2012 (page 8), 2012/2013 (page 5), 2013/2014 (page 10), 2014/15 (page 13), and 2015/2016 (page 8) and show the number of LPAs that were actually registered during those accounting years. The figures are rounded to the nearest 1,000.

Accounting year 1 April – 31 March	LPAs registered
2009–2010	98,400
2010–2011	162,000
2011–2012	183,000
2012–2013	229,000
2013–2014	295,000
2014–2015	395,000
2015–2016	533,000
2016–2017	635,540

The digital future

1.65 Mental Capacity Act 2005:Office of the Public Guardian:annual report

The OPG's Annual Report for 2015/16 confirmed that it continues to work with the Ministry of Justice to take forward work on a fully digital LPA without the need for wet signatures. Whilst technology may be available to achieve this outcome, it remains a concern that donors of LPAs are in the main, older people, with many being prompted to make an LPA due to a crisis. Such donors may be vulnerable and not fully aware of the powers that they are granting. Evidence from Court of Protection judgments demonstrates that attorneys continue to misuse their authority. Although the OPG has updated its supporting guidance for attorneys to ensure they are carrying out their duties within the requirements of the MCA 2005, the onus is on the attorney to seek it out.

Chapter 2

DIFFERENCES BETWEEN ENDURING POWERS OF ATTORNEY AND LASTING POWERS OF ATTORNEY

ENDURING POWERS OF ATTORNEY

Effective date

It has not been possible to make an EPA since 30 September 2007 (MCA 2005, s 66(1)(b)).

An EPA made before 30 September 2007 remains in full force and an application to register it should be made to the Public Guardian when the duty to apply for registration arises (MCA 2005, Sch 4, para 4(1) and (2)).

Creating an EPA

An EPA must:

- have been in the prescribed form; and have been executed in the prescribed manner by the donor and the attorney.
  (MCA 2005, Sch 4, para 2(1)(a) and (b)).

LASTING POWERS OF ATTORNEY

Effective date

It was not possible to create an LPA before 1 October 2007 (MCA 2005 (Commencement No 2) Order 2007 (SI 2007/1897)).

Creating an LPA

An LPA:

- must be in the prescribed form (MCA 2005, Sch 1, para 1(1)). There are two prescribed forms: one for property and financial affairs, and one for health and welfare (LPA, EPA & PG (Amendment) Regs 2015 (SI 2015/899), Sch 1).

- may contain the names of up to five 'named persons' or 'people to notify', whom the donor wishes to be notified of any application to register the LPA, or it must contain a statement that there are no such persons (MCA 2005, Sch 1, para 2(1)(c)).

- must contain a certificate by a person of a prescribed description that the donor understands the purpose of the LPA and the scope of the authority conferred under it. (MCA 2005, Sch 1, para 2(1)(e)). Until 30 June 2015, where the donor chose to have no named persons, two persons of a prescribed description had to each give a certificate (MCA 2005, Sch 1, para 2(2)(b)). This requirement was removed by SI 2015/899.

ENDURING POWERS OF ATTORNEY

More than one attorney

Where two or more persons are appointed as attorneys under an EPA, the instrument must appoint them to act either:

- jointly, or
- jointly and severally.

(MCA 2005, Sch 4, para 20(1)).

LASTING POWERS OF ATTORNEY

More than one attorney

Where two or more persons are appointed as attorneys under an EPA, the instrument may appoint them to act:

- jointly,
- jointly and severally, or
- jointly in respect of some matters and jointly and severally in respect of other matters.

(MCA 2005, s 10(4)).

To the extent that the LPA fails to specify whether the attorneys are to act jointly or jointly and severally, the instrument is to be assumed to appoint them to act jointly (MCA 2005, s 10(5)).

Successive attorneys

There was no provision for the appointment of successive attorneys in the EPA legislation, but see *Re J (Enduring Power of Attorney)* [2009] COPLR Con Vol, 753

Successive attorneys

A donor can appoint a replacement attorney to replace the original attorney (or if more than one, any of them) on the occurrence of an event mentioned in s 13(6) of the MCA 2005 (MCA 2005, s 10(8)(b)).

When an EPA comes into operation

Unless the donor expressly stated that the EPA would not come into operation until he or she has become mentally incapable, an EPA can be used as soon as it has been executed by the donor and the attorney(s).

The attorney(s) will continue to have authority to act under the EPA after the donor has become incapable by reason of mental disorder of managing and administering his or her property and affairs, provided the EPA is registered (MCA 2005, Sch 4, para 1(1)(a) and 23(1)).

When an LPA comes into operation

An LPA cannot be used until it has been registered by the OPG (MCA 2005, s 9(3)).

An LPA can be registered by the Public Guardian before the donor becomes mentally incapacitated, but the attorney(s) can only make personal welfare decisions that the donor is mentally incapable of making himself or herself (MCA 2005, s 11(7)(a)).

The duty of the attorney(s)

Attorneys under an EPA have a duty to apply to the OPG to register the instrument if they have reason to believe that the donor is, or is becoming, mentally incapable of managing and administering his or her property and affairs (MCA 2005, Sch 4, para 4).

The duty of the attorney(s)

Attorneys under an LPA have no statutory duty to apply to the OPG to register the instrument: indeed, the donor may apply to register the instrument himself or herself (MCA 2005, Sch 1, para 4(2)).

ENDURING POWERS OF ATTORNEY

Attorneys under an EPA are not required to follow the principles in s 1, (MCA 2005, Sch 4, para 1(1)). Notwithstanding this, the exercise of the attorney's powers made under Schedule 4 of the MCA 2005 mean the duties imposed by ss 4(1)–(7) apply when the attorney reasonably believes the donor lacks mental capacity and so requires the attorney to act in the donor's best interests (MCA 2005, s 4(8)(b)).

The attorney(s) must comply with the fiduciary duties described in paragraphs 7.58–7.68 of the Mental Capacity Act 2005 Code of Practice (Code of Practice, para 7.79).

An attorney acting under an EPA, who has the care of a donor who lacks capacity, is guilty of an offence if he or she ill-treats or wilfully neglects the donor (MCA 2005, s 44).

Decisions the attorney(s) can make

Unless the donor has put in any restrictions or conditions, the attorneys can do anything with the donor's property and affairs that the donor can lawfully do by an attorney, but the attorneys cannot make decisions about the donor's personal welfare (MCA 2005, Sch 4, para 3(1)).

- the attorneys can (subject to any further restrictions and conditions in the power) make the following limited gifts:

LASTING POWERS OF ATTORNEY

Attorneys under an LPA have a statutory duty:

- to act in accordance with the principles in s 1 of the Mental Capacity Act 2005 (MCA 2005, s 9(4));
- to act in the donor's best interests (MCA 2005, s 1(5) and 9(4)); and
- to have regard to the guidance in the Mental Capacity Act 2005 Code of Practice (MCA 2005, s 42(4)(a)).

The fiduciary duties of attorneys are set out in the Code of Practice, and it is the duty of any attorney acting under an LPA to have regard to them (Code of Practice, paras 7.58–7.68).

An attorney acting under an LPA, who has the care of a donor who lacks capacity, is guilty of an offence if he or she ill-treats or wilfully neglects the donor (MCA 2005, s 44).

Decisions the attorney(s) can make

Unless the donor puts in any restrictions or conditions:

- the attorneys appointed in an LPA for property and financial affairs can make decisions about all or any of the donor's property affairs or specified matters concerning the donor's property and affairs (MCA 2005, s 9(1)).
- the attorneys appointed in an LPA for health and welfare can make decisions about all matters or specified matters concerning the donor's health and welfare, but can only make decisions when the donor lacks, or the attorney reasonably believes that the donor lacks, the mental capacity to make such decisions himself or herself at the time the decision has to be made (MCA 2005, ss 9(1) and 11(7)(a)).
- the attorneys appointed in an LPA for property and financial affairs have the following limited power to make gifts (subject to any further restrictions and conditions in the power):

ENDURING POWERS OF ATTORNEY

(a) those of a seasonal nature or at a time, or on an anniversary, of a birth, a marriage or the formation of a civil partnership, to the attorney or persons who are related to or connected with the donor, and

(b) to any charity to whom the donor made or might be expected to make gifts,

provided that the value of each such gift is not unreasonable having regard to all the circumstances and in particular the size of the donor's estate (MCA 2005, Sch 4, para 3(3)).

• the attorneys (subject to any further restrictions and conditions in the power) have an express power to provide for the needs of the attorney or a third party for whom the donor might be expected to provide (MCA 2005, Sch 4, para 3(2)).

Decisions the donor can make

Until the EPA is registered, both the donor and the attorneys have concurrent authority to manage and administer the donor's property and financial affairs.

In theory, when the EPA is registered, the donor can still make decisions about his property and financial affairs, if he is mentally capable of making such decisions at the time. However, once the EPA is registered, the donor cannot extend or restrict the scope of the authority conferred on the attorneys, and no instruction or consent given by the donor confers any right or obligation on the attorney(s) or other persons.

(MCA 2005, Sch 4, para 15(c), but see *Day v Harris and Anor* [2013] COPLR 254, CA).

LASTING POWERS OF ATTORNEY

(a) on customary occasions to persons (including himself) who are related to or connected with the donor, or

(b) to any charity to whom the donor made or might have been expected to make gifts,

If the value of each such gift is not unreasonable having regard to all the circumstances and, in particular, the size of the donor's estate.

'Customary occasion' means the occasion or anniversary of a birth, a marriage or the formation of a civil partnership, or any other occasion on which presents are customarily given within families or among friends or associates. (MCA 2005, s 12).

Decisions the donor can make

The donor can carry on making decisions, provided he has the capacity to do so, even though the LPA is registered.

The attorneys can only make personal welfare decisions that the donor is incapable of making, or which the attorneys reasonably believe the donor is incapable of making, for himself at that time (MCA 2005, s 11(7)(a)).

ENDURING POWERS OF ATTORNEY

Registering the EPA

The attorneys have a duty to apply to the OPG to register the EPA if they have reason to believe that the donor is, or is becoming, mentally incapable of managing his property and affairs (MCA 2005, Sch 4, para 4(1) and (2)).

Before making the application to the OPG, the attorneys must give written notice, on form EP1PG, of their intention to apply for registration to:

- the donor personally,
- any co-attorney, and
- at least three of the donor's relatives from a list which specifies an order of priority (MCA 2005, Sch 4, Part 3).

The attorneys apply to register the EPA on form EP2PG.

- There is a fee of £82 for application to register an EPA (The Public Guardian (Fees, etc) (Amendment) Regs 2017 (SI 2017/503), reg 5(a)).

Powers pending registration

Pending registration and until the EPA is registered, the attorney may maintain the donor or take action to prevent loss to the donor's estate, or maintain the attorney or a third party for whom the donor might be expected to provide (MCA 2005, Sch 4, para 1(2)).

Objections to the registration of an EPA

LASTING POWERS OF ATTORNEY

Registering the LPA

The application can be made before the onset of the donor's incapacity.
Either the donor or the attorney(s) can apply to the OPG to register the LPA (MCA 2005, Sch 1, para 4(2)).

Before making the application to register, the applicant must give notice, on form LP3, to the persons who the donor has named as being entitled to receive notice of intention to apply for registration of the LPA (MCA 2005, Sch 1, paras 6-9).

The applicant applies to register the LPA by completion of Sections 12 and 13, the relevant parts of Section 14 and Section 15 of each 2015 prescribed form. Registration of a pre-July 2015 prescribed form must be made by using form LP2 (LPA, EPA & PG Regs 2007, reg 11(1) and Sch 3).

The following fees apply:

- a fee of £82 for an application to register an LPA, and
- a reduced fee of £41 for a repeat application to register an LPA (The Public Guardian (Fees, etc) (Amendment) Regs 2017 (SI 2017/503), reg 5(b) and (c)).

The Public Guardian will give notice that the application has been received to:

- the attorneys on form LPA 003A, and
- the donor on form LPA 003B.

(LPA, EPA & PG Regs 2007, reg 13).

None

Objections to the registration of an LPA

ENDURING POWERS OF ATTORNEY

Those who have received notice of the attorney's intention to apply for registration can object to the application on the grounds that:

- the power purported to have been created by the instrument was not valid as an EPA;

- the power created by the instrument no longer subsists;

- the application is premature because the donor is not yet becoming mentally incapable;

- fraud or undue pressure was used to induce the donor to create the power; and

- having regard to all the circumstances, and in particular the attorney's relationship to or connection with the donor, the attorney is unsuitable to be the donor's attorney.
  (MCA 2005, Sch 4, para 13(9)).

LASTING POWERS OF ATTORNEY

The donor's relatives will not be automatically notified of the application to register the LPA, unless the donor has named them as persons who are entitled to receive notice of the application to register.

If the donor objects to the registration of any LPA he or she is not required to specify any grounds of objection and the Public Guardian must not register the LPA unless the Court of Protection is satisfied that the donor lacks capacity to object and directs the Public Guardian to register the LPA (MCA 2005, Sch 1, para 14).

The attorneys and the named persons may object to the OPG about the registration of the LPA on the following 'factual grounds':

- the donor is dead;

- the attorney is dead;

- the marriage or civil partnership between the donor and the attorney has been dissolved or annulled (unless the LPA provided that such an event should not affect the instrument);

- the attorney lacks the capacity to be an attorney under an LPA;

- the attorney(s) have disclaimed their appointment.

(MCA 2005, Sch 1, para 13).

The attorneys, and the named persons may object to the OPG about the registration of an LPA for property and financial affairs only on the following 'factual grounds':

- the donor is bankrupt or interim bankrupt;

- the attorney is bankrupt or interim bankrupt;

- the attorney is a trust corporation which is wound up or dissolved.

(MCA 2005, Sch 1, para 13).

The attorneys, and the named persons may object to the Court of Protection about the registration of the LPA on the grounds that:

- the power purported to be created by the instrument is not valid as an LPA;

- the power created by the instrument no longer exists;

ENDURING POWERS OF ATTORNEY

LASTING POWERS OF ATTORNEY

- fraud or undue pressure was used to induce the donor to create the power; and
- the attorney has behaved or proposes to behave in a way that would contravene his authority or is not or would not be in the donor's best interests.

(MCA 2005, s 22(2) and (3)).

Revocation of an EPA by the donor

If the EPA is registered, no revocation of the power by the donor is valid unless and until the Court of Protection confirms the revocation (MCA 2005, Sch 4, para 15(1)(a)).

The court must confirm the revocation if it is satisfied that the donor:

- has done whatever is necessary in law to effect an express revocation of the power, and
- was mentally capable of revoking a power of attorney when he did so (whether or not he is so when the court considers the application) (MCA 2005, Sch 4, para 16(3)).

On confirming the revocation, the court must direct the OPG to cancel the registration of the EPA (MCA 2005, Sch 4, para 16(4)(a)).

Revocation of an LPA by the donor

The donor may, at any time when he has the capacity to do so, revoke an LPA (MCA 2005, s 13(2)).

The donor who revokes an LPA must (a) notify the Public Guardian that he has done so and (b) notify the donee (or, if more than one, each of them) of the revocation of the LPA (LPA, EPA & PG Regs 2007, reg 21(1)).

The Court of Protection may determine any question relating to whether an LPA has been revoked or has otherwise come to an end (MCA 2005, s 22(2)(b)).

Revocation of an EPA by the court

The Court of Protection must by order revoke the EPA and direct the OPG to cancel registration on being satisfied that:

- fraud or undue pressure was used to induce the donor to create the power; or
- having regard to all the circumstances, and in particular the attorney's relationship to or connection with the donor, the attorney is unsuitable to be the donor's attorney (MCA 2005, Sch 4, para 16(5)).

The Court of Protection can revoke an EPA if:

Revocation of an LPA by the court

The Court of Protection may revoke an LPA, if the donor lacks the capacity to do so (MCA 2005, s 22(4)(b)), but only if it is satisfied that:

- fraud or undue pressure was used to induce the donor to create the LPA, or
- the attorney has behaved, is behaving, or proposes to behave in a way that would contravene his or her authority or would not be in the donor's best interests (MCA 2005, s 22(3)).

ENDURING POWERS OF ATTORNEY

- it exercises a power under ss 16 to 20 of the MCA 2005 in relation to the donor, and

- directs that the EPA is to be revoked (MCA 2005, Sch 4, para 2(9)).

LASTING POWERS OF ATTORNEY

Chapter 3

CAPACITY TO CREATE A LASTING POWER OF ATTORNEY

AGE

3.1 A lasting power of attorney (LPA) is not created unless, at the time when the donor executes the instrument, the donor has reached 18 and has capacity to execute it (Mental Capacity Act 2005 (MCA 2005), s 9(2)(c)). There was no age restriction on the donors of enduring powers of attorney (EPAs), and, at paragraph 7.20 of its report on *Mental Incapacity* (Law Com No 231 (1995)), the Law Commission gave the following reasons for deciding to impose an age limit on the persons wishing to create an LPA:

'Under the current law, a donor of an EPA must be an individual with capacity to create the power. There are no other restrictions on donors, and it was stated in Law Com No 122 that minors and undischarged bankrupts would be able to create EPAs, albeit that this would be unusual and that any attorney's authority might be restricted by the general law. The general law as to the effect of a minor appointing an attorney remains complex, and it may be that the appointment itself is voidable by the minor if it is not for his or her benefit. Where [LPAs] are concerned, it would not be satisfactory to rely on the fact that a minor has power to "avoid" transactions by an attorney. There may be physical, emotional or psychological consequences of a personal welfare or health care decision which cannot easily be reversed by the payment of a compensatory sum of money. Since [an LPA] may cover personal welfare matters and health care decisions, there would also be very significant complications with the law in relation to parental responsibility and the inherent jurisdiction of the High Court if [an LPA] could be created by a minor. We think it entirely appropriate that the right to create a document with such far-reaching legal consequences as a [Lasting] Power of Attorney should be restricted to adults. We recommend that [an LPA] may only be created by an individual who has attained the age of eighteen.'

STATUTORY DEFINITION OF LACK OF CAPACITY

3.2 The Law Commission was of the view that there should be a single statutory definition of incapacity. At paragraph 3.7 of its report on *Mental Incapacity* (Law Com No 231 (1995)), it said:

'The present law offers a number of tests of capacity depending on the type of decision in issue. Case-law has offered answers to some problems put to it; individual statutes include occasional definitions; the Mental Health Act Code of Practice deals in some detail with capacity to make medical decisions; and Part VII of the 1983 Act addresses capacity in relation to the management of "property and affairs". For the purposes of our new legislative scheme, a single statutory definition should be adopted.'

3.3 Section 2 of the MCA 2005 defines 'people who lack capacity' as follows:

'(1)   For the purposes of this Act, a person lacks capacity in relation to a matter if at the material time he is unable to make a decision for himself in relation to the matter because of an impairment of, or a disturbance in the functioning of, the mind or brain.

(2)   It does not matter whether the impairment or disturbance is permanent or temporary.'

FUNCTIONAL APPROACH TO CAPACITY

3.4 The legislation has adopted what is known as the 'functional approach' to capacity, as distinct from the 'status approach' and 'outcome approach'. The status approach excludes people from participating in a range of activities or transactions because of their age, gender, religion, ethnic origin, mental health status, etc, and is quite out of line with contemporary policy objectives of empowering people to make decisions for themselves that they have the capacity to make. The outcome approach focuses on the content of an individual's decision, and there is a danger that any decision which is inconsistent with mainstream conventional values, or with which the assessor disagrees, could be classed as incompetent. It would be wrong, however, to assume that the outcome of a decision is entirely irrelevant. In *Masterman-Lister v Brutton & Co* [2003] 3 All ER 162, at para 54, Kennedy LJ suggested that, although the role of the court was the investigation of capacity not outcomes, outcomes 'can often cast a flood of light on capacity'.

3.5 The functional approach, which for centuries has been applied by English courts in several discrete tests of capacity – such as the capacity to make a will, or to marry or enter into a contract – examines whether the individual understands the nature and effect of a transaction at the time he enters into it. An individual's capacity is, therefore, both decision-specific and time-specific, and this message is reinforced in the MCA 2005 Code of Practice, where every chapter is prefaced by the following words:

'In this chapter, as throughout the Code, a person's capacity (or lack of capacity) refers specifically to their capacity to make a particular decision at the time it needs to be made.'

Accordingly, if one were to apply the statutory definition of lack of capacity to the creation of an LPA, a donor would lack the capacity to create an LPA if, at the material time, he was unable to make a decision for himself in relation to that matter because of an impairment of, or a disturbance in the functioning of, the mind or brain.

THE DIAGNOSTIC THRESHOLD

3.6 The statutory definition of lack of capacity includes what is often referred to as a 'diagnostic threshold'. A person's inability to make a decision must be caused by either an impairment of, or a disturbance in the functioning of, the mind or brain. A diagnostic threshold already exists for registering an EPA. An attorney has a duty to register the power if he 'has reason to believe that the donor is or is becoming mentally incapable' (MCA 2005, Sch 4, para 4(1)). 'Mentally incapable' means 'incapable, by reason of mental disorder (within the meaning of the Mental Health Act 1983) of managing and administering his property and affairs' (MCA 2005 Sch 4, para 23(1)). 'Mental disorder' now means 'any disorder or disability of the mind' which has been changed from the previous definition of 'mental illness, arrested or incomplete development of mind, psychopathic disorder, and any other disorder or disability of mind' following amendments as a result of the Mental Health Act 2007 (Mental Health Act 1983, s 1(2)). Accordingly, for the registration of an EPA the diagnostic threshold is a mental disorder.

3.7 In its Consultation Paper 128, *Mentally Incapacitated Adults and Decision-Making: A New Jurisdiction*, published in 1993, at paragraphs 3.9–3.14, the Law Commission considered in depth the various arguments, both for and against retaining a diagnostic threshold and, ultimately, in its report on *Mental Incapacity* (Law Com No 231 (1995)), at paragraph 3.8, decided to retain one for the following reasons:

> 'In the consultation papers we suggested that a person (other than someone unable to communicate) should not be found to lack capacity unless he or she is first found to be suffering from "mental disorder" as defined in the Mental Health Act 1983. The arguments for and against such a diagnostic hurdle are very finely balanced and they are set out in full in Consultation Paper No 128. In the event, most respondents agreed with our preliminary view that a diagnostic hurdle did have a role to play in any definition of incapacity, in particular in ensuring that the test is stringent enough *not* to catch large numbers of people who make unusual or unwise decisions. There may also be a small number of cases where a finding of incapacity could lead to action which could amount to "detention" as defined in the European Convention on Human Rights. The case-law of the European Court of Human Rights requires that any such detention should be pursuant to a finding of unsoundness of mind based on "objective medical expertise". Although we gave very careful consideration to the arguments against the inclusion of any diagnostic threshold, we have concluded that such a threshold would provide a significant protection and would in no sense prejudice or stigmatise those who are in need with help in decision-making.'

3.8 Although it decided to retain a diagnostic threshold, at paragraph 3.11 of its report on *Mental Incapacity*, the Law Commission chose to replace the existing diagnostic threshold of 'mental disorder' with one of 'an impairment of, or a disturbance in the functioning, of the mind or brain'. It gave the following reasons for doing so:

> 'Many respondents to our medical treatment consultation paper were concerned to ensure that all the conditions which can result in incapacity to take medical decisions should be included in the new definition. Some of these will have very little in common with psychiatric illnesses or congenital impairments of the kind addressed by the provisions of the 1983 Act. It was argued that some relevant conditions might not qualify as disorders or disabilities "of mind" at all. Temporary toxic confusional states (whether resulting from prescription or illicit drugs, alcohol or other toxins) and neurological disorders were given as examples. Some doctors would argue that these are properly labelled disorders of *brain* rather than mind. One respondent pointed out that women can lack capacity to take obstetric decisions after prolonged labour, and queried whether the effects of pain and exhaustion were a disability "of mind". We are persuaded that there are many good reasons for departing from the 1983 Act definition.'

THE STATUTORY PRINCIPLES

3.9 Section 1 of the MCA 2005 sets out five principles, which are referred to in the Code of Practice as the 'statutory principles' and are the fundamental values that underpin the legal requirements in the Act. They aim to assist and support people who may lack capacity to make particular decisions, not to restrict or control their lives (Code of Practice, para 2.1).

3.10 None of the principles is new. Each one has its antecedents in the common law or equity. The first three relate to capacity, and the final two relate to the action that should be taken once it is established that someone lacks the capacity to make a specific decision at a specific time.

3.11 Section 1 provides as follows:

'(1)   The following principles apply for the purposes of this Act.
(2)   A person must be assumed to have capacity unless it is established that he lacks capacity.
(3)   A person is not to be treated as unable to make a decision unless all practicable steps to help him do so have been taken without success.
(4)   A person is not to be treated as unable to make a decision merely because he makes an unwise decision.
(5)   An act done, or decision made, under this Act for or on behalf of a person who lacks capacity must be done, or made, in his best interests.
(6)   Before the act is done, or the decision is made. Regard must be had to whether the purpose for which it is needed can be as effectively achieved in a way that is less restrictive of the person's rights and freedom of action.'

Chapter 2 of the Code of Practice – *What are the statutory principles and how should they be applied?* – considers the principles in much greater detail than is possible here.

PRESUMPTION OF CAPACITY

3.12 Section 1(2) of the MCA 2005 establishes the fundamental principle that all persons over the age of 16 (s 2(5)) are presumed to be capable of making their own decisions. This presumption can only be overridden if it is established that the person concerned lacks the capacity to make a particular decision at the material time (s 2(1)). In proceedings under the MCA 2005 or any other enactment, any question as to whether a person lacks capacity must be decided on the balance of probabilities (s 2(4)).

3.13 In the law of evidence, the presumption of capacity was traditionally accompanied by the presumption of continuance. The effect of this was that, once it had been established that a person lacked capacity, the incapacity was presumed to continue until the contrary was proved: *Attorney-General v Parnther* (1792) 3 Bro CC 440. However, in view of the decision of the Court of Appeal in *Masterman-Lister v Brutton & Co* [2003] 3 All ER 162, at para 17, it would appear that one can no longer rely on the presumption of continuance in cases involving incapacity. Certainly, there is no reference to it in the MCA 2005, and perhaps the presumption of capacity is now as inviolate as the presumption of innocence in criminal law.

ALL PRACTICABLE STEPS

3.14 The MCA 2005 Code of Practice states, at paragraphs 2.6 and 2.7 that:

'It is important to do everything practical (the Act uses the term 'practicable') to help a person make a decision for themselves before concluding that they lack capacity to do so. People with an illness or disability affecting their ability to make a decision should receive support to help them make as many decisions as they can. This principle aims to stop people being automatically labelled as lacking capacity to make particular decisions. Because it encourages individuals to play as big a role as possible in decision-making, it also helps prevent unnecessary interventions in their lives.

The kind of support people might need to help them make a decision varies. It depends on personal circumstances, the kind of decision that has to be made and the time available to make the decision. It might include:
- using a different form of communication (for example non-verbal communication)
- providing information in a more accessible form (for example, photographs, drawings or tapes)
- treating a medical condition which may be affecting the person's capacity, or
- having a structured programme to improve a person's capacity to make particular decisions (for example, helping a person with learning disabilities to learn new skills).'

Chapter 3 of the Code of Practice gives more information on ways to help people make decisions for themselves.

3.15 The requirement to take all practicable steps to help a person make a decision now must also be interpreted in the context of the United Nations Convention on the Rights of Persons with Disabilities (UNCRPD), which post-dates the MCA 2005. On 13 December 2006 the United Nations General Assembly adopted the UNCRPD and, following ratification by twenty States Parties, it came into force on 3 May 2008. The United Kingdom signed the convention on 30 March 2007 and ratified it on 8 June 2009. The UNCRPD is binding on the UK as a matter of international law. Although it does not form part of domestic law, it may have an interpretative influence, particularly in human rights cases, and before the European Court of Human Rights and the European Court of Justice. Article 12.3 of the UNCRPD requires States Parties to take appropriate measures to provide access by persons with disabilities to the support they may require in exercising their legal capacity.

UNWISE DECISIONS

3.16 In an equity case, *Bird v Luckie* (1850) 8 Hare 301, at p 306, the Vice-Chancellor, Sir James Lewis Knight-Bruce remarked that, although the law insists that individuals should be capable of understanding the nature and effects of their actions, it does not require them to behave 'in such a manner as to deserve approbation from the prudent, the wise, or the good'. He went on to say that 'a testator is permitted to be capricious and improvident, and is, moreover, at liberty to conceal the circumstances and motives by which he has been actuated in his dispositions'.

3.17 In its consultation papers, the Law Commission invited views on whether there was any need for a provision stipulating that a person should not be regarded as lacking capacity because the decision would not have been made by a person of ordinary prudence, and it initially doubted that there was such a need. However, those who responded to its consultation programme overwhelmingly urged it to include such a stipulation in the legislation itself in order to emphasise the fact that the 'outcome approach' to capacity had been rejected, even though it is almost certainly in daily use (*Mental Incapacity* (1995), para 3.19). The right to make mistakes is central to a person's self-determination and to his development as an individual.

3.18 In recent years there have been some valuable judicial insights into unwise decisions. For example, in *Re S; D v R and S* [2012] COPLR Con Vol 1112, at para 43, Henderson J remarked that:

'The significance of section 1(4) must not, however, be exaggerated. The fact that a decision is unwise or foolish may not, without more, be treated as conclusive, but it remains, in my judgment, a relevant consideration for the court to take into account in considering whether the criteria of inability to make a decision for oneself in section 3(1) are satisfied. This will particularly be the case where there is a marked contrast between the unwise nature of the impugned decision and the person's former attitude to the conduct of his affairs when his capacity was not in question.'

3.19 In the Court of Appeal in the case of *PC v City of York Council* [2013] COPLR 409, at para 54, McFarlane commented that:

'There is a space between an unwise decision and one which an individual does not have the mental capacity to take and . . . . It is important to respect that space and to ensure that it is preserved, for it is within that space that an individual's autonomy operates.'

UNJUSTIFIED ASSUMPTIONS

3.20 Section 2(3) of the MCA 2005 provides that:

'A lack of capacity cannot be established merely by reference to
(a)   a person's age or appearance, or
(b)   a condition of his, or an aspect of his behaviour, which might lead others to make unjustified assumptions about his capacity.'

3.21 This subsection, and an almost identical one for determining what is in someone's best interests (MCA 2005, s 4(1)), were last-minute additions to the Mental Capacity Bill. During the report stage in the House of Lords on 15 March 2005 (*Hansard* HL Vol 670, col 1319), Baroness Andrews said:

'I want to reinforce the belief shared across the House that no one should be assumed to lack capacity, excluded from decision-making, discriminated against or given substandard care and treatment simply, for example, as a result of disability. . . .

I turn to the first concern over the non-prejudicial assessment of capacity. . . . It would be completely wrong and contrary to the Bill's spirit if preconceptions or prejudicial assumptions were to influence an assessment of capacity in the first instance; for example, "He's got a learning disability, so why should we assume that he can make any decisions?" The Bill's assumptions of capacity and its decision-making approach mean that that should never happen. People should be assumed to have capacity until it is established that they lack it, and all practical steps have been taken to enable them to make their decision.

We want to be 100 per cent clear and to know that people understand that. That is why we have tabled Amendment No. 5 to Clause 2, which provides that a lack of capacity cannot be established merely by reference to a person's age or appearance, or a condition of his, or an aspect of his behaviour, which might lead others to make unjustified assumptions about his capacity. That makes it abundantly clear. It also gives further emphasis to the Bill's principle that everyone should be assumed to have capacity until it is shown that they do not. For example, it is not acceptable to say, on the assumption that someone has a learning disability, that he cannot or will not want to make decisions about where to live.'

INABILITY TO MAKE DECISIONS

3.22 At paragraph 3.15 of its report on *Mental Incapacity* (Law Com No 231 (1995)), the Law Commission said:

'It would defeat our aim of offering clarity and certainty were no further guidance given as to the meaning of the phrase "unable to make a decision". In the consultation papers we identified two broad sub-sets within this category, one based on inability to understand relevant information and the other based on inability to make a "true choice". Although many respondents expressed disquiet about the elusiveness of the concept of "true choice", there was broad agreement that incapacity cannot in every case be ascribed to an inability to understand information. It may arise from an inability to negotiate information which has been understood. In most cases an assessor of capacity will have to consider both the ability to understand information and the ability to use it in exercising choice, so that the two "sub-sets" should not be seen as mutually exclusive.'

3.23 Accordingly, s 3(1) of the MCA 2005 sets out the following guidance on the meaning of the phrase 'unable to make a decision':

'For the purposes of section 2, a person is unable to make a decision for himself if he is unable:
(a)   to understand the information relevant to the decision,
(b)   to retain that information,
(c)   to use or weigh that information as part of the process of making the decision, or
(d)   to communicate his decision (whether by talking, using sign language or any other means).'

3.24 In *RT v LT and A Local Authority* [2010] COPLR Con Vol 1061, the President, Sir Nicholas Wall, said at paragraph 40:

'In my judgment, section 3 of the Act is at the heart of the case. The use of the word "or" in section 3(1)(c) demonstrates that the individual capacities set out in section 3(1) are not cumulative. A person lacks capacity if any one of the sub-sections (a) to (d) applies. In the instant case, I am satisfied that section 3(1)(c) applies.'

3.25 A person is not to be regarded as unable to understand the information relevant to a decision if he is able to understand an explanation of it given to him in a way that is appropriate to his circumstances (using simple language, visual aids or any other means) (MCA 2005, s 3(2)).

3.26 The fact that a person is able to retain the information relevant to a decision for a short period only does not prevent him from being regarded as able to make the decision (MCA 2005, s 3(3)). In cases where the donor has borderline or fluctuating capacity, where his or her ability to retain the relevant information is in doubt, it is advisable to choose a certificate provider who has appropriate skills to assess capacity and that he also acts as the witness to satisfy the assessment is contemporaneous to the donor signing. On this issue, in respect of an elderly man who had mild vascular dementia, Hedley J in *A, B and C v X and Z* [2012] EWHC 2400 (COP) gave a warning at paragraph 38:

' . . . . I am unwilling to make, on the evidence, a general declaration that he lacks capacity, but qualify that immediately by saying that the exercise of such a power, unless accompanied by contemporary medical evidence of capacity, would give rise to a serious risk of challenge or of refusal to register.'

RELEVANT INFORMATION

3.27 The information relevant to decisions in general includes information about the reasonably foreseeable consequences of:

- deciding one way or another (MCA 2005, s 3(4)(a)); or
- failing to make the decision (MCA 2005, s 3(4)(b)).

Accordingly, in the context of creating an LPA, the relevant information should include information about the consequences of not executing an LPA.

3.28 The information specifically relevant to the execution of an LPA includes the prescribed information about the purpose of the instrument and the effect of LPA (MCA 2005, Sch 1, para 2(1)(a)), which is contained in the prescribed form of LPA itself.

3.29 A person is not to be regarded as unable to understand the relevant information if he is able to understand an explanation of it given to him in a way that is appropriate to his circumstances, such as using simple language, visual aids or any other means (MCA 2005, s 3(2)).

3.30 The fact that a person is able to retain the relevant information for a short period only does not prevent him from being regarded as able to make the decision (MCA 2005, s 3(3)).

3.31 There have been some recent judicial pronouncements on the relevant information an individual is expected to understand, retain, and use and weigh when making a decision.

3.32 In *CC v KK and STCC* [2012] COPLR 637, at para 69, Baker J stated that:

'It is not necessary for a person to demonstrate a capacity to understand and weigh up every detail of the respective options, but merely the salient factors.'

3.33 In *Heart of England NHS Foundation Trust v JB* [2014] EWCOP 342, at paras 25 and 26, Peter Jackson J commented that:

'What is required here is a broad, general understanding of the kind that is expected from the population at large. JB is not required to understand every last piece of information about her situation and her options. . . . We should not ask more of people whose capacity is questioned that those whose capacity is undoubted.'

STANDARD OF PROOF

3.34 In proceedings under the MCA 2005 or any other enactment, any question whether a person lacks capacity within the meaning of the Act must be decided on the balance of probabilities (MCA 2005, s 2(4)).

CERTIFICATION

3.35 The MCA 2005, Sch 1, para 2(1)(e) expressly requires an LPA to include a certificate by a person of a prescribed description that, at the time when the donor executes the instrument:

- the donor understands the purpose of the instrument and the scope of the authority conferred under it;
- no fraud or undue pressure is being used to induce the donor to create an LPA; and
- there is nothing else which would prevent an LPA from being created by the instrument.

The role of the certificate provider is considered in detail in CHAPTER 6.

FURTHER GUIDANCE ON ASSESSING CAPACITY

3.36 Further guidance for persons assessing whether a person has capacity can be found in the MCA 2005 Code of Practice, and in particular at chapters:

2: What are the statutory principles and how should they be applied?
3: How should people be helped to make their own decisions?
4: How does the Act define a person's capacity to make a decision and how should capacity be assessed?

3.37 The Office of the Public Guardian has produced guidance for LPA donors: *Make and register your lasting power of* attorney (LP12) which does not contain any specific guidance for the certificate provider on how to assess capacity. Page 5 contains the following guidance:

'To work out whether someone lacks the mental capacity to make a decision, you need to answer 'yes' to these two questions:
1. Do they have a mental or brain problem that stops their brain or mind from working properly?
2. Is that problem causing them such difficulty now that they are unable to make this particular decision at the time it needs to be made?'

It is notable there is no reference to case-law or suggestions of any questions which could be used to be satisfied the donor has capacity. The role of the certificate provider is considered in more detail in CHAPTER 6 and 7.60–7.63 which sets out how the certificate provider should form his opinion.

THE CRITERIA IN *RE K, RE F* AND LPAS

3.38 The statutory definition of capacity in s 2(1) of the MCA 2005 is prefaced by the words 'for the purposes of this Act'. Accordingly, it does not affect the existing common law definitions of capacity, such as those for making a will (*Banks v Goodfellow* (1870) LR 5 QB 549), or for revoking a will (*Re Sabatini* (1970) 114 SJ 35), or for making a substantial lifetime gift (*Re Beaney (Deceased)* [1978] 2 All ER 595).

3.39 The MCA 2005 Code of Practice suggests, at para 4.33, that:

'The Act's new definition of capacity is in line with the existing common law tests, and the Act does not replace them. When cases come before the court on the above issues, judges can adopt the new definition if they think it appropriate.'

3.40 The capacity required to create an EPA was considered in *Re K, Re F (Enduring Power of Attorney)* [1988] 2 FLR 15, in which Hoffmann J gave, at p 20, the following summary of the matters which should ordinarily be explained to the donor, and which the evidence should show that he had understood:

'First (if such be the terms of the power), that the attorney will be able to assume complete authority over the donor's affairs. Secondly (if such be the terms of the power), that the attorney will in general be able to do anything with the donor's property which he himself could have done. Thirdly that the authority will continue if the donor should be or become mentally incapable. Fourthly, that if he should be or become mentally incapable, the power will be irrevocable without confirmation by the court.'

3.41 In *Re Collis* (October 27, 2010), Lush SJ held that the criteria in *Re K, Re F* was not applicable to LPAs because of the fairly major differences between EPAs and LPAs, and would need to be adapted in several respects. In particular:

- The donor would need to understand that the LPA cannot be used until it is registered by the Public Guardian.
- One would expect to see a change of emphasis between the creation of an LPA for health and welfare and an LPA for property and financial affairs; and, in particular, the donor would need to understand that the attorney under an LPA for health and welfare can only make decisions that the donor is contemporaneously incapable of making for himself (MCA 2005, s 11(7)(a)).
- Unlike an EPA, the donor can revoke an LPA at any time when he has capacity to do so (MCA 2005, s 13(2)), without the court having to confirm the revocation.
- The authority conferred by an LPA, unlike an EPA, is subject to the provisions of the MCA 2005 and, in particular, s 1 (the principles) and s 4 (best interests) (MCA 2005, s 9(4)).
- The statutory definition of capacity specifically requires the donor to be aware of the foreseeable consequences of not executing an LPA (MCA 2005, s 3(4)), whereas Hoffmann J did not include an understanding of the effect of not making an EPA in his summary of the matters which should ordinarily be explained to the donor.

Chapter 4

ATTORNEYS

WHO MAY BE AN ATTORNEY?

Introduction

4.1 Sections 10(1) and (2) of the Mental Capacity Act 2005 (MCA 2005) provide that:

> '(1)   A donee of a lasting power of attorney must be –
>   (a)   an individual who has reached 18, or
>   (b)   if the power relates only to P's property and affairs, either such an individual or a trust corporation.
> (2)   An individual who is bankrupt may not be appointed as donee of a lasting power of attorney in relation to P's property and affairs.'

The primary and secondary legislation on lasting powers of attorney (LPAs) refer to 'donees', rather than 'attorneys', perhaps to distinguish LPAs from enduring powers of attorney (EPAs). The Enduring Powers of Attorney Act 1985, most of which now appears as Sch 4 to the MCA 2005, referred to the person appointed by the donor as the 'attorney'. The prescribed forms of LPA and the publications on LPAs issued by the Office of the Public Guardian (OPG), however, use the word 'attorneys' instead of donees, and in this book, the two terms are used interchangeably.

Minors

4.2 A person under the age of 18 cannot be a donee of an LPA (MCA 2005, s 10(1)(a)). The position with regard to EPAs was slightly different. A power of attorney could not be an EPA unless, when he executed the instrument creating it, the attorney was an individual who had reached 18 (MCA 2005, Sch 4, para 2(5)(a)). In theory, therefore, the donor could have appointed a minor to be his attorney, and the minor would have needed to wait until he was of full age before he could execute the instrument (see para **16.16**). With LPAs, however, there is an absolute prohibition on the appointment of a minor as a donee.

Trust corporations

4.3 The effect of MCA 2005, s 10(1)(b) is that a trust corporation can be a donee of an LPA for property and affairs, but cannot be a donee of an LPA for personal welfare. In its report on *Mental Incapacity* (1995), at para 7.21, the Law Commission stated that:

> 'The 1985 Act specifically provided that the donee executing an EPA must be either an individual (over eighteen and not bankrupt) or a trust corporation. It would not be appropriate for a trust corporation to exercise personal health care powers, but apart from that there is no need for any change in the law.'

4.4 *Trust corporation* has the meaning given in s 68(1) of the Trustee Act 1925 (MCA 2005, s 64(1)), namely:

> 'the Public Trustee or a corporation either appointed by the court in any particular case to be a trustee, or entitled by rules made under subsection (3) of section four of the Public Trustee Act 1906 to act as custodian trustee.'

On 1 April 2001, the offices of the Public Trustee and the Official Solicitor were combined, and on 1 April 2007 they merged again to form the Offices of Court Funds, Official Solicitor and Public Trustee. On 1 April 2009, the Court Funds Office demerged from the Official Solicitor and the Public Trustee.

4.5 The relevant rules under s 4(3) of the Public Trustee Act 1906 are the Public Trustee Rules 1912 (SR&O 1912/348), r 30, as substituted by SI 1975/1189 and amended by SIs 1976/836, 1981/358, 1984/109, 1985/132, and 1994/2519. There have also been amendments enacted by changes to health and social care legislation, such as SI 2015/643.

4.6 Rule 30(1): The following corporations are currently entitled to act as custodian trustees:

> '(a) the Treasury Solicitor;
> (b) any corporation which –
> > (i) is constituted under the law of the United Kingdom or of any part thereof, or under the law of any other Member State of the European Economic Union or of any part thereof;
> > (ii) is empowered by its constitution to undertake trust business (which for the purpose of this rule means the business of acting as trustee under wills and settlements and as executor and administrator) in England and Wales;
> > (iii) has one or more of its places of business in the United Kingdom; and
> > (iv) is –
> > > — a company incorporated by special Act of Parliament or Royal Charter, or
> > > — a company registered (whether with or without limited liability) in the United Kingdom under the Companies Act 1948 (*repealed- see now the Companies Act 2006*) or under the Companies Act (Northern Ireland) 1960 or in another Member State of the European Economic Union and having a capital (in stock or shares) for the time being issued of not less than £250,000 (or its equivalent in the currency of the State where the company is registered), of which not less than £100,000 (or its equivalent) has been paid up in cash, or
> > > — a company registered without limited liability in the United Kingdom under the Companies Act 1948 (*repealed- see now the Companies Act 2006*) or the Companies Act (Northern Ireland) 1960 or in another Member State of the European

Economic Union and of which one of the members is a company within any of the classes defined in this sub-paragraph;

(c) any corporation which is incorporated by special Act or Royal Charter or under the Charitable Trustees Incorporation Act 1872 [now Part 12 of the Charities Act 2011] which is empowered by its constitution to act as a trustee for any charitable purposes, but only in relation to trusts in which its constitution empowers it to act;

(d) any corporation which is constituted under the law of the United Kingdom or of any part thereof and having its place of business there, and which is either –

    (i) established for the purpose of undertaking trust business for the benefit of Her Majesty's Navy, Army, Air Force or Civil Service or of any unit, department, member or association of members thereof, and having among its directors or members any persons appointed or nominated by the Defence Council or any Department of State or any one or more of those Departments, or

    (ii) authorised by the Lord Chancellor to act in relation to any charitable ecclesiastical or public trusts as a trust corporation, but only in connection with any such trust as is so authorised;

    (i) any NHS Trusts, Foundation Trusts, Local Health Boards, Strategic [*replaced by the NHS Board, known as NHS England*] or special health authority, but only in relation to any trust which the authority is authorised to accept or hold by virtue of section 90 of the National Health Service Act 1977 (*now repealed and consolidated in National Health Service Act 2006 or National Health Service (Wales) Act 2006*);

    (ii) any preserved Board as defined by section 15(6) of the National Health Service Reorganisation Act 1973, but only in relation to any trust which the Board is authorised to accept or hold by virtue of an order made under that section;

[*(f) and (g)* deal with pension funds administered by the British Gas Corporation *(now dissolved) and the London Transport Executive*]

(h) any of the following, namely -
    (i) . . . ,
    (ii) the corporation of any London borough (acting by the council),
    (iii) a county council, district council, parish council or community council,
    (iv) the Council of the Isles of Scilly,
but only in relation to charitable or public trusts (and not trust for an ecclesiastical charity or a charity for the relief of poverty) for the benefit of the inhabitants of the area of the local authority concerned and its neighbourhood, or any part of that area;

(i) any of the following, namely -
    (i) a metropolitan district council or a non-metropolitan county council,
    (ii) the corporation of any London borough (acting by the council),
    (iii) the Common Council of the City of London,
    (iv) the Council of the Isles of Scilly,
but only in relation to any trust under which property devolves for the sole benefit of a person who occupies residential accommodation provided under Part 1 of the Care Act 2014 (care and support) or Part 1 of the Social Services and Well-being (Wales) Act 2014 by the local authority concerned or is in the care of that authority; and a corporation acting as a custodian trustee by virtue of this paragraph in relation to any trust shall be entitled to continue so to act in relation to that trust, and until a new custodian trustee

is appointed, notwithstanding that the person concerned ceases to occupy such accommodation or be in the care of that authority, as the case may be;

(j) The British Coal Corporation or any subsidiary of the British Coal Corporation, but only in relation to a scheme or arrangements established under regulations made under section 37 of the Coal Industry Nationalisation Act 1946;

(k) deals with pension funds administered by the British Broadcasting Corporation;

(l) any corporation appointed by the Secretary of State as a trustee of any scheme having effect by virtue of regulations made under section 37 of the Coal Industry Nationalisation Act 1946 for purposes relating to pensions, gratuities or other like benefits and in relation to which provision is, or has been, made by regulations made under paragraph 2(1) of schedule 5 to the Coal Industry Act 1994 for the scheme to continue in force notwithstanding the repeal by the Coal Industry Act 1994 of section 37 of the Coal Industry Nationalisation Act 1946 and of the enactments modifying that section, but only in relation to such a scheme.'

Bankrupts

4.7 Section 10(2) of the MCA 2005 provides that an individual who is bankrupt may not be appointed as donee of an LPA in relation to the donor's property and affairs. An individual who is bankrupt may, however, be appointed as an attorney in relation to the donor's personal welfare. The policy objectives behind these provisions can be found in the Law Commission's report on *Mental Incapacity* (1995), at para 7.45:

'The rules about bankruptcy in relation to [LPAs] need to distinguish between the grant of powers over "property and affairs" and the grant of powers over personal and health care matters. Although the existing rules whereby a bankrupt cannot act as an attorney should continue to apply to any powers over "property and affairs", we see no reason for an absolute rule that a bankrupt may not act as an attorney in relation to personal and health care matters.'

Section 10(2) disqualifies 'an individual who is bankrupt' from acting as an attorney under an LPA for property and affairs. It does not disqualify someone who has been bankrupt in the past.

The Tribunals, Courts and Enforcement Act 2007 (Consequential Amendments) Order 2012 (SI 2012/2404), Sch 2, Art 53(2), provides that MCA 2005, s 10(2) also applies to a person to whom a debt relief order has been made under Part 7A of the Insolvency Act 1986.

Office-holders

4.8 In its report, *Mental Incapacity* (1995) Law Com No 231, at para 7.21, the Law Commission commented:

'In the consultation papers we provisionally proposed that it should never be possible for a public official in his or her official capacity to be appointed attorney. However, we were influenced by the views of the Public Trustee and the Association of Directors of Social Services (among others) that there might be occasions when a public official should be available to act as attorney of last resort. This would not require specific provision, since all the likely candidates will be either "individuals" or trust corporations. For the avoidance of doubt, we think the legislation should specify that an individual can be identifiable by reference to an office or position (eg, the manager for the time being of X branch of the Y Bank, or the Director of Social Services of Z region). The person fulfilling the description at the time of execution would have to execute the [LPA] as donee of the power, even though a successor might subsequently act as attorney. Appointing an office-holder is probably possible under the existing law, but is uncommon. Where it is not intended to put the [LPA] into immediate effect, there will often be good reasons for avoiding the appointment of an office-holder. The result of local government or NHS re-organisation, or of business changes to a solicitors' firm or a financial institution, might be that there is no person fulfilling the description of the attorney when a time arrives when the [LPA] is needed. In such cases where the [LPA] is to be registered and put into effect at once, however, the appointment of an office-holder might be a useful facility. We recommend that an individual donee of [an LPA] may be described as the holder for the time being of a specified office or position.'

Notwithstanding this recommendation, the MCA 2005 does not allow an office-holder to be appointed as a donee of an LPA, although, by contrast, s 19(2) of the Act enables the court to appoint an individual as deputy 'by appointing the holder for the time being of a specified office or position'.

4.9 *Make and register your lasting power of attorney – a guide* (LP12), issued by the OPG – states on page 11 in respect of the appointment of a property and financial affairs attorney:

'If you appoint a professional attorney for a property and financial affairs LPA, such as a solicitor, you must name an individual, you can't just give a job title or the name of a firm.'

On page 12, in respect of health and welfare attorneys, the guidance is less specific, which states:

'An attorney for a health and welfare LPA must be a person not a company.'

4.10 In *Re McGreen* (Unreported: The Senior Judge, 19 April 2012) the donor appointed A as attorney and B as replacement attorney and stated on the continuation sheet A2 that 'if my replacement attorney is no longer a partner in the firm of XYZ Solicitors, I appoint in his place a suitably qualified partner of that firm or the firm which has succeeded to that firm and carries on its practice, to be my replacement attorney.' The OPG applied for severance of the provision, which the court duly granted on the basis that there is no provision in the MCA 2005 that permits the donor of an LPA to appoint an office holder to be an attorney or replacement attorney.

MORE THAN ONE ATTORNEY

Number of attorneys

4.11 There is no limit to the number of donees a donor may appoint, though for practical reasons the greater the number appointed, the more cumbersome it can become to make decisions on the donor's behalf and to manage his affairs efficiently. The OPG's guide *Make and register your lasting power of attorney* (LP12) states at page 10:

'If you want more than four attorneys, mark the "More attorneys" box on this page with an "X". Take a copy of Continuation sheet 1, called "Additional people". For each extra attorney, mark the "Attorney" box on the sheet and add their details'.

It goes on to state:

'You must have at least one attorney. There's no upper limit but too many attorneys could make things difficult, as they'll need to work together'.

Joint and joint and several appointments

4.12 Section 10(4) of the MCA 2005 states that, where two or more persons are to act as donees of an LPA:

'The instrument may appoint them to act –
(a)   jointly,
(b)   jointly and severally, or
(c)   jointly in respect of some matters and jointly and severally in respect of others.'

4.13 The essential difference between attorneys appointed to act jointly, and those who are appointed to act jointly and severally, is that the authority of joint attorneys can only be exercised collectively, whilst an attorney who is appointed to act jointly and severally may act either together with his co-attorneys or entirely independently. Consequently, a joint power will automatically come to an end when any one of the attorneys dies, disclaims, or lacks the capacity to act ('a terminating event'), because it is no longer possible for all of the attorneys to act together, but a joint and several power will continue to operate in these circumstances.

4.14 In *Miles v The Public Guardian and Beattie v The Public Guardian* [2015] EWHC 2960 (Ch), Judge Nugee, confirmed that a terminating event will result in a joint power ending, unless a replacement is appointed. However, there is nothing in the MCA 2005 which precludes the reappointment on a terminating event, of an originally appointed joint attorney. The MCA 2005 should be construed in a way which gives flexibility to donors to set out how they wish their affairs to be dealt, provided that the wording is sufficiently clear and transparent that the donor, the attorneys and the OPG can see precisely how it is intended to operate.

4.15 The original LPA forms, prescribed by the Lasting Powers of Attorney, Enduring Powers of Attorney and Public Guardian Regulations 2007 (SI 2007/1253), Schedule 1, avoided the use of the terms 'jointly' and 'jointly and severally', and referred instead to attorneys acting 'together' or 'together and independently.'

4.16 In its consultation paper, *Reviewing the Mental Capacity Act 2005: forms, supervision and fees*, CP 26/08, published on 23 October 2008, the Ministry of Justice asked, as question 3, 'Do you agree that we should change the wording of "together" or "together and independently" to "jointly" or "jointly and severally" or is the former wording acceptable?'

4.17 In its response to the consultation, CP(R) 26/08, published on 11 March 2009, the Ministry of Justice said at page 13:

'63 of 76 respondents answered question 3. Almost three quarters of respondents to this question (46) agreed that the wording should be changed from "together" or "together and independently" to "jointly" or "jointly and severally". 14 respondents did not agree that we should change the wording and 3 respondents neither agreed nor disagreed. Some noted that the current "together" or "together and independently" formulation was itself unclear and that the alternative was to be preferred on grounds of common usage elsewhere. Many respondents recognised that the change of wording may not result in terms immediately understood by the layperson, but in expressing their agreement to the proposed changes also mentioned that they felt that the accompanying guidance should clearly explain the meaning. We will adopt the wording "jointly" or "jointly and severally".'

Accordingly, the forms of LPA prescribed by the LPA, EPA & PG (Amendment) Regulations 2009 (SI 2009/1884), which came into force on 1 October 2009, and subsequently replaced by the prescribed forms under the LPA, EPA & PG (Amendment) Regulations 2015 (SI 2015/899), which came into force on 1 July 2015 contain the terms 'jointly' and 'jointly and severally'.

Failure to specify whether joint or joint and several

4.18 Section 10(5) of the MCA 2005 provides that, where two or more persons are to act as donees of an LPA, 'to the extent to which it does not specify whether they are to act jointly or jointly and severally, the instrument is to be assumed to appoint them to act jointly'.

4.19 The provenance of this subsection was the dismay arising from defective EPAs, where the donor had failed to cross out one of the two alternatives, 'jointly' or 'jointly and severally', as a result of which the court, which was then the registration authority for EPAs, was obliged to reject the application to register.

4.20 This subsection is possibly now otiose because of the box design of the prescribed form of LPA. In Section 3 of the instrument the donor is required to state how he or she wishes the attorneys to act:

'How do you want your attorneys to work together? (tick one only)

Jointly and severally

Attorneys can make decisions on their own or together. Most people choose this option because it's the most practical. Attorneys can get together to make important decisions if they wish, but can make simple or urgent decisions on their own. It's up to the attorneys to choose when they act together or alone. It also means that if one of the attorneys dies or can no longer act, your LPA will still work.

If one attorney makes a decision, it has the same effect as if all the attorneys made that decision.

Jointly

Attorneys must agree unanimously on every decision, however big or small. Remember, some simple decisions could be delayed because it takes time to get the attorneys together. If your attorneys can't agree a decision, then they can only make that decision by going to court.

Be careful – if one attorney dies or can no longer act, all your attorneys become unable to act. This is because the law says a group appointed 'jointly' is a single unit.

Your LPA will stop working unless you appoint at least one replacement attorney (in section 4).

Jointly for some decisions, jointly and severally for other decisions

Attorneys must agree unanimously on some decisions, but can make others on their own. If you choose this option, you must list the decisions your attorneys should make jointly and agree unanimously on Continuation sheet 2. The wording you use is important. There are examples in the Guide, part A3.

Be careful – if one attorney dies or can no longer act, none of your attorneys will be able to make any of the decisions you've said should be made jointly. Your LPA will stop working for those decisions unless you appoint at least one replacement attorney (in section 4). Your original attorneys will still be able to make any of the other decisions alongside your replacement attorneys.'

Effect of one attorney failing to satisfy the qualifications for appointment

4.21 Sections 10(6) and 10(7) of the MCA 2005 cover the situation where the donor appoints more than one attorney, and there is a failure on the part of any one of them to comply with the following provisions:

- s 10(1), which says that the donee of an LPA must be an individual who has reached 18 or, in the case of an LPA for property and affairs, either such an individual or a trust corporation;
- s 10(2), which says that an individual who is bankrupt may not be appointed as a donee of an LPA for property and affairs; and
- Parts 1 or 2 of Sch 1 to the Act. Part 1 governs the formalities of making an LPA, and Part 2 governs the formalities of registration.

Joint appointment

4.22 Section 10(6) of the MCA 2005 states that, where the attorneys have been appointed to act jointly, a failure, as respects one of them, to comply with these requirements will prevent an LPA from being created. This is relevant at the point of the creation of the instrument and is in contrast to a subsequent terminating event where the donor has expressly reappointed a joint attorney to continue to act (see **4.14**).

Joint and several appointment

4.23 Section 10(7) of the MCA 2005 states that, where the attorneys have been appointed to act jointly and severally, a failure, as respects one of them, to comply with these requirements:

- will prevent the appointment taking effect in his case; but
- will not prevent an LPA from being created in respect of the other or others.

Application for registration where there is more than one attorney

Joint appointment

4.24 If the attorneys have been appointed to act jointly, all of them must join in the application to register the instrument.

Joint and several appointment

4.25 If the attorneys have been appointed to act jointly and severally in respect of any matter, the application to register the instrument may be made by any of the donees (MCA 2005, Sch 1, para 4(2)(c)).

4.26 As soon as practicable after receiving an application by a joint and several attorney to register an LPA, the Public Guardian must notify the donor and the donees who did not join in making the application, that the application has been received (MCA 2005, Sch 1, para 8(2)(b)).

Objection to registration where there is more than one attorney

4.27 The court can direct that an instrument purporting to create an LPA is not to be registered (MCA 2005, s 22(4)(a)) and, if the donor lacks the capacity to do so, revoke the instrument (MCA 2005, s 22(4)(b)), if it is satisfied that:

- fraud or undue pressure was used to induce the donor to create the LPA (MCA 2005, s 22(3)(a)); or
- an attorney has behaved, or is behaving, in a way that contravenes his authority or is not in the donor's best interests (MCA 2005, s 22(3)(b)(i)); or
- an attorney proposes to behave in a way that would contravene his authority or would not be in the donor's best interests (MCA 2005, s 22(3)(b)(ii)).

Joint appointment

4.28 Section 22(5) of the MCA 2005 provides that 'if there is more than one donee, the court may under subsection 22(4)(b) revoke the instrument or the LPA so far as it relates to any one of them'. Although this subsection fails expressly to state that this would only apply if the attorneys had been appointed to act jointly and severally, it is submitted that, because joint attorneys must act together, the revocation of the appointment of any one attorney who had been appointed to act jointly would result in the revocation of the entire instrument.

Joint and several appointment

4.29 Section 22(5) of the MCA 2005 provides that 'if there is more than one donee, the court may under subsection 22(4)(b) revoke the instrument or the lasting power of attorney so far as it relates to any one of them'.

Effect of termination of one attorney's authority

4.30 Section 13(6) of the MCA 2005 lists various events, which have the effect of terminating the appointment of an individual attorney. They are:

'(a) the disclaimer of the appointment by the donee in accordance with such requirements as may be prescribed for the purposes of this section in regulations made by the Lord Chancellor,

(b) subject to subsections (8) and (9), the death or bankruptcy of the donee or, if the donee is a trust corporation, its winding-up or dissolution,

(c) subject to subsection (11), the dissolution or annulment of a marriage or civil partnership between the donor and the donee,

(d) the lack of capacity of the donee.'

Joint appointment

4.31 The occurrence of any of the events listed in MCA 2005, s 13(6) will revoke the power (s 13(5)), unless the donee is replaced under the terms of the instrument (s 13(7)): but see the discussion under the heading replacement attorney at **4.51** and the possibility of reappointing a joint attorney at **4.14**.

4.32 In an LPA for property and financial affairs, where the attorney is bankrupt merely because an interim bankruptcy order has effect in respect of him, his appointment (and that of his co-attorneys) and the power are suspended for so long as the order has effect (MCA 2005, s 13(9)). The Tribunals, Courts and Enforcement Act 2007 (Consequential Amendments) Order 2012 (SI 2012/2404), Sch 2, Art 53(2), provides that MCA 2005, s 13(9) also applies to a person to whom a debt relief order has been made under Part 7A of the Insolvency Act 1986.

Joint and several appointment

4.33 The occurrence of any of the events listed in MCA 2005, s 13(6) will revoke the power (s 13(5)), unless:

- the donee is replaced under the terms of the instrument; or
- he is one of two or more persons appointed to act as donees jointly and severally in respect of any matter and, after the event, there is at least one remaining donee (s 13(7)).

4.34 Where the attorney is bankrupt merely because an interim bankruptcy order has effect in respect of him, his appointment and the power are suspended, so long as they relate to the donor's property and affairs, for so long as the order has effect (MCA 2005, s 13(9)).

4.35 In an LPA for property and financial affairs, where the attorney is bankrupt merely because an interim bankruptcy order has effect in respect of him, his appointment (but not that of his co-attorneys) is suspended for so long as the order has effect (MCA 2005, s 13(10)).

REPLACEMENT ATTORNEYS

Section 10(8)

4.36 Section 10(8) of the MCA 2005 states that:

'An instrument used to create a lasting power of attorney –
(a)   cannot give the donee (or, if more than one, any of them) power to appoint a substitute or successor, but
(b)   may itself appoint a person to replace the donee (or, if more than one, any of them) on the occurrence of an event mentioned in section 13(a) to (d) which has the effect of terminating the donee's appointment.'

The donee cannot appoint his own replacement

4.37 The provision in MCA 2005, s 10(8)(a) is similar in wording to what was formerly s 2(9) of the Enduring Powers of Attorney Act 1985 (now the MCA 2005, Sch 4, para 2(6)). The reasons for prohibiting an attorney from appointing someone to succeed or replace him were explained by the Law Commission in paragraph 4.22 of its report, *The Incapacitated Principal* (1983) (Law Com No 122), as follows:

'We would not wish, however, the attorney to be enabled to appoint a substitute or successor to himself: i.e. thereby irrevocably parting with his authority under the power (as opposed to mere delegation). This would be contrary to the special relationship of trust subsisting between the EPA donor and attorney and would undermine some of the safeguards we recommend in this Report. We accordingly recommend that no power that enabled the attorney to appoint a substitute or successor should be capable of being an EPA.'

Policy considerations

4.38 In 1983, when it was drafting the enduring powers of attorney legislation, the Law Commission was opposed to providing facilities whereby the donor might himself, in the instrument, appoint a person to replace the attorney if he should be unable to act for any reason. In a footnote – number 214 – to its report *The Incapacitated Principal*, the Law Commission stated:

'We do not recommend that an instrument should be able to provide for successive EPAs; that is, one or more attorneys who would replace the original attorney or attorneys should he or they cease to act. Our main reason for this is that the benefit to be gained by including successive EPAs in our proposals would be out of all proportion to the complexity that such powers would create in relation to some of the more detailed areas of our scheme. In any event, successive EPAs are rendered largely unnecessary because a joint and several EPA would permit the continuation of the EPA in the event of one of the attorneys ceasing to act. It would, however, be possible to create the effect of successiveness by a donor granting EPAs in separate instruments so that the authority of an attorney under one power could commence only upon the termination of the authority of an attorney under another power.'

4.39 However, the Law Commission later changed its mind and, in paragraph 7.22 of its report on *Mental Incapacity* (1995), said as follows:

'The present law makes special provision for multiple attorneys, specifically allowing "joint" or "joint and several" attorneys. We suggested in the consultation papers that, in contrast with the present law, donors should also be permitted to appoint an "alternate" attorney to act if the original fails or ceases to act for some reason. Respondents agreed that there would be advantages in allowing for such a possibility. In order to ensure consistency with the registration system we describe below, replacement attorneys should only be available in circumstances where the original donee has ceased to act for a reason which can be established by objective evidence. We recommend that a donor may, in [an LPA], appoint a person to replace the donee in the event of the donee disclaiming, dying, becoming bankrupt or becoming divorced from the donor.'

4.40 This recommendation was implemented as s 10(8)(b) of the MCA 2005. However, for reasons that will become apparent in the following paragraphs, the legislators failed properly to address the issues that caused the Law Commission to reject making a similar recommendation in *The Incapacitated Principal* on the grounds that any benefit to be gained would be out of all proportion to the complexities it would create.

Events causing the replacement of a donee

4.41 The donor himself may appoint a person, known as a 'replacement attorney', to replace the original attorney on the occurrence of an event mentioned in s 13(6) of the MCA 2005, which has the effect of terminating the original attorney's appointment (MCA 2005, s 10(8)(b)).

4.42 Section 13(6) of the MCA 2005 sets out the events as follows:

'(a) the disclaimer of the appointment by the donee in accordance with such requirements as may be prescribed for the purposes of this section in regulations made by the Lord Chancellor,

(b) subject to subsections (8) and (9), the death or bankruptcy of the donee or, if the donee is a trust corporation, its winding-up or dissolution,

(c) subject to subsection (11), the dissolution or annulment of a marriage or civil partnership between the donor and the donee,

(d) the lack of capacity of the donee.'

4.43 These events do not include the revocation of a donee's appointment by the Court of Protection if, for example, it is satisfied that the original donee (or, if more than one, any of them) has behaved, or is behaving, or proposes to behave in a way that contravenes his authority or is not in the donor's best interests (MCA 2005, s 22(4)). Nor do they include a revocation by the donor of the original attorney's appointment.

4.44 Nor do the events in MCA 2005, s 13(6) include the replacement of the original donee in the event that he had failed to execute Part C or Section 11 of the LPA properly. Nor is it possible for the donor to specify additional events, on the occurrence of which the replacement attorney will replace the original donee. In one case, for example, the donor specified that the replacement attorney could act in the event of the original attorney 'being not available through travel or living abroad or any other circumstances that may prevent or restrict his capacity to act on my behalf as attorney'. The Public Guardian applied to the Court of Protection for this provision to be severed, and the application was duly granted (*Jenkins* (unreported) 2 September 2008, the Senior Judge).

Number of replacement attorneys

4.45 The donor can appoint as many replacement attorneys as he wishes, but can only appoint a replacement for an original attorney, not a replacement for a replacement attorney. Although the prescribed forms of LPA make provision for the appointment of two replacement attorneys, the donor can appoint additional replacement attorneys by using continuation sheet 1.

Replacement sequence

4.46 In the absence of any specific directions to the contrary, the default position is that the replacement attorney will replace the first attorney who needs to be replaced. Specific directions to the contrary might include:

- the replacement attorney should only step in when all the original attorneys are unable to act (where more than one original attorney);
- the replacement attorney should only replace a specific named attorney; or
- the replacement attorney can replace any attorney except a specific named attorney.

Practical problems with replacement attorneys

4.47 A replacement attorney cannot:

- be a 'named person'. The persons who may be named persons do not include a person who is appointed as a donee under the instrument (MCA 2005, Sch 1, para 2(3));
- be a 'certificate provider'. A donee of the power is disqualified from giving an LPA certificate in respect of any instrument intended to create an LPA (Lasting Powers of Attorney, Enduring Powers of Attorney and Public Guardian Regulations 2007 (SI 2007/1253), reg 8(3)(b));
- 'witness any signature required for the power apart from that of another donee' (reg 9(8)).

4.48 The inability of a replacement attorney to be a named person has given rise to problems in several cases in which the replacement attorney was the only named person.

4.49 The current practice of the Public Guardian is that, when the donor or attorney makes an application to register the LPA, the named persons are not notified of the identity of the replacement attorney. Nor is the Public Guardian required to notify the replacement attorney that he has received an application to register the LPA.

4.50 There is no facility whereby a named person can object to the appointment of a replacement attorney, either when the initial application is made to register the instrument, or when an event under MCA 2005, s 13(6) activates the replacement.

4.51 A replacement attorney can replace an attorney who was appointed to act jointly with one or more co-attorneys, but in most cases the outcome is not what the donor would have anticipated. For example, where the donor appoints A and B to act jointly, and appoints C as a replacement attorney, if one of the events mentioned in MCA 2005, 13(6) terminates the appointment of either of the joint attorneys, the joint appointment fails entirely, and the replacement attorney, C, steps in as the sole attorney. To avoid this, the donor should expressly reappoint the originally appointed attorney (see **4.14** and Chapter 15 of this book, which contains precedents).

CHOOSING AN ATTORNEY

Guidance for donors

4.52 The OPG has published guidance for potential donors: (LP12) *Make and register your lasting power of attorney.* Pages 10–11 state:

'Make sure that each person agrees to be your attorney before you name them in your LPA. When selecting attorneys, think about:
- how many you want to appoint and if they'll be able to work together
- whether you trust them to act in your best interests
- how well you know each other and how well they understand you
- how willing they'll be to make decisions for you
- how well they organise their own affairs, such as how well they look after their own money.

Don't feel you have to choose someone just because you don't want to offend them. If you want them to feel involved, you could make them a "person to notify" instead.'

It goes on to state:

'Attorneys don't need to be solicitors. Most people choose family members, friends and other people they trust with no legal background. If an attorney is not a professional, the important thing is that you know each other well and they respect your views and will act in your best interests.

You can ask anyone with mental capacity aged 18 or over to be your attorney, including:
- your wife, husband, civil partner or partner
- a family member
- a close friend
- a professional, such as a solicitor.'

4.53 At paragraph 149 of volume 1 of its report on the Draft Mental Incapacity Bill (Session 2002–03, HL Paper 189–1, HC 1083–1, para 137), the Joint Committee picked up on the comments of the then Health Minister, Ms Rosie Winterton, who had acknowledged that there was a need, in some cases, to appoint different donees in relation to different affairs. She had suggested that:

'From the health care side it may be that people might want different attorneys for different decisions. Somebody that you trust with your finances may not be the same as somebody that you wanted to make decisions about your health and welfare.'

Appointing a spouse or civil partner

4.54 If the donor intends to appoint their spouse or civil partner as an attorney, they should consider the effect of any future breakdown in the relationship. The Enduring Powers of Attorney Act 1985 made no specific provision for cases where the donor and attorney were married when the power was created but subsequently divorced. The Law Commission considered this in paragraph 7.48 of its report on *Mental Incapacity* (1995), and said:

> 'Since [an LPA] cannot take effect immediately, but must first be registered, we think it appropriate to provide for such circumstances. The law already makes provision for the situation where a testator appointed a divorced spouse executor of beneficiary under his or her will. A donor of [an LPA] may be equally unable to remedy the original, now inappropriate, appointment.
>
> We recommend that, in the absence of a contrary intention, the appointment of the donor's spouse as an attorney under [an LPA] should be revoked by the subsequent dissolution or annulment of the parties' marriage.
>
> A reminder might helpfully be placed on the standard form decree absolute of divorce. By analogy with the case where one attorney becomes bankrupt but multiple attorneys have been appointed to act jointly and severally, the divorce between the donor and one of multiple joint and several attorneys should not terminate the powers of the other donees to act.'

4.55 Since publication of the Law Commission's report in 1995, the Civil Partnership Act 2004 has come into force, and s 13 of the MCA 2005 provides that the dissolution or annulment of a marriage or civil partnership between the donor and the donee will terminate the appointment of the donee, unless the instrument provided that it was not to do so. The termination of the appointment will also revoke the power, unless the donor appointed a replacement attorney, or had appointed more than one attorney to act jointly and severally, and there is at least one remaining attorney.

4.56 The authorities for these propositions are subsections 13(5), (6) and (7), which provide as follows:

> '(5)   The occurrence in relation to a donee of an event mentioned in subsection (6) –
>
>   (a)   terminates his appointment, and
>
>   (b)   except in the cases given in subsection (7), revokes the power.
>
> (6)   The events are –
>
>   . . .
>
>   (c)   subject to subsection (11), the dissolution or annulment of a marriage or civil partnership between the donor and the donee.
>
> (7)   The cases are –
>
>   (a)   the donee is replaced under the terms of the instrument,
>
>   (b)   he is one of two or more persons appointed to act as donees jointly and severally in respect of any matter and, after the event, there is at least one remaining donee.'

4.57 Subsection (11) of MCA 2005, s 13 provides that:

> 'The dissolution or annulment of a marriage or civil partnership does not terminate the appointment of a donee or revoke the power, if the instrument provided that it was not to do so.'

4.58 It is unclear how useful or effective these provisions are. In practice, as soon as a relationship has broken down irretrievably, there can be a potential conflict of interests between the donor and any attorney who is their spouse or civil partner. The actual dissolution or annulment of the marriage or civil partnership is merely the end of what is sometimes a long and acrimonious process.

4.59 A donor may wish their child's spouse or civil partner to act as an attorney or replacement attorney. Whilst it is possible to make the appointment conditional on their being married or in a civil partnership, once the attorney is acting, it is not possible for the appointment to be terminated on a subsequent dissolution or annulment of their marriage or civil partnership. It is not possible to extend the statutory terminating events. In effect, a conditional appointment can only be included for a replacement attorney.

Chapter 5

NAMED PERSONS

SUMMARY

5.1 A donor may name up to five persons – excluding the donee(s) of the power – who are entitled to be notified of an application to register a lasting power of attorney (LPA). The MCA 2005, Schedule 1, paragraph 2(4) defines this person as a 'named person', yet the 2009 prescribed forms used the term 'People to be told' and the 2015 prescribed forms and amendments made to the Lasting Powers of Attorney, Enduring Powers of Attorney and Public Guardian Regulations 2007 (LPA, EPA & PG Regulations 2007) refers to them as 'People to notify'. In this chapter, the person concerned is referred to in accordance with the MCA 2005.

5.2 Until 1 July 2015, where the donor did not name anyone to be notified when an application is made to register the LPA, two people had to provide a separate certificate in Part B of the either the 2007 or 2009 prescribed form of LPA, which certifies that at the time of signing the LPA the donor understands the purpose of the instrument and the scope of the authority conferred under it, and that no fraud or undue pressure is being used to induce the donor to create an LPA.

5.3 A donor or donee who is about to make an application to register the LPA must notify the named persons using form LP3. Under the LPA, EPA & PG Regs 2007 the form was known as 'LPA 001'. The LPA, EPA & PG (Amendment) Regs 2015 made changes to the notification form, renaming it 'LPA3'. The Office of the Public Guardian (OPG) have headed it 'LP3'; presumably so as not to confuse it with LPA003A or LPA003B, which are prescribed notices sent by the OPG to non-applicants to inform them of the application to register the LPA.

5.4 The named persons have a right to object to the proposed registration of the LPA, and may do so within three weeks from the day on which the notice in form LP3 was given to them.

5.5 On the application of the donor or donee who is about to make an application to register the power, the Court of Protection may dispense with the requirement to notify any named person, if it is satisfied that no useful purpose would be served by giving the notice.

61

POLICY AND LEGISLATIVE HISTORY

5.6 This section examines the reasons for the shift in policy from a duty under the Enduring Powers of Attorney Act 1985 (EPAA 1985) to notify certain close relatives of the donor to a requirement under the Mental Capacity Act 2005 (MCA 2005) to notify only those persons selected by the donor himself.

The Incapacitated Principal (1983)

5.7 In paragraph 4.36 of its report, *The Incapacitated Principal* (1983), which led to the EPAA 1985, The Law Commission said:

'Under our scheme the initial responsibility for the selection of the attorney rests with the donor. Since, however, for a variety of reasons the attorney may not be suitable to act on the donor's behalf without supervision, our scheme would ensure that the donor's relatives would have an opportunity to consider whether it would be safe to allow the attorney to continue acting once the donor's capacity was in doubt.'

5.8 Accordingly, under the EPAA 1985, an attorney had a duty to apply for registration of the enduring power of attorney (EPA) if he had reason to believe that the donor was or was becoming mentally incapable: (ss 4(1) and 4(2) EPAA 1985, now MCA 2005, Sch 4, paras 4(1) and 4(2)). Before making an application for registration, the attorney was required to comply with the provisions as to notice set out in Sch 1 to that Act: EPAA 1985, s 4(3). This required giving notice of intention to apply for registration (form EP1) to the donor personally, and to at least three of the donor's relatives. These provisions still apply to the registration of EPAs, and are set out in paras 4 to 6 of Sch 4 to the MCA 2005.

Enduring Powers of Attorney: A Report to the Lord Chancellor (1991)

5.9 The need for an attorney to notify the donor's relatives when he was about to make an application to register an EPA was reconsidered by Stephen Cretney, Gwynn Davis, Roger Kerridge, and Andrew Borkowski in *Enduring Powers of Attorney: A Report to the Lord Chancellor*, which was published by the Lord Chancellor's Department in June 1991. At paragraph 2.39 the report stated:

'Having discussed the purpose and timing of registration, we now turn to a consideration of what that registration process should involve. We here consider one interesting suggestion which was put to us by one of the solicitors whom we interviewed. It relates to the notification of relatives – an aspect of the procedure criticised by many solicitors. There was widespread agreement that the list of relatives to be named was inappropriate in many instances and, in general, did not take account of the complexity of relationships within present-day families. One solicitor suggested that, rather than try to devise a new set of categories, so that we have yet another list of relatives who need to be notified on registration (albeit one that includes girlfriends, homosexual lovers, and toy-boys), the donor should simply be invited, upon creating the Power, to specify those people whom he or she wished to have informed at the point when the EPA came to be registered. In other words, the donor (who would of course be mentally capable) could choose the people who know him best, or have a genuine interest in the conduct of his financial affairs. This would be consistent with the principle of maintaining the donor's control over his affairs and of ensuring that his wishes are followed. It would bring to an end the present practice of informing distant relatives who really have no interest in the donor.

For reasons that will by now have become apparent, we are not entirely convinced that the notification of relatives is the most appropriate safeguard of the donor's interests, but if there *is* to be notification we think that this proposal deserves further examination. We are not, of course, unmindful of the problems to be encountered where the donor is starting to lose mental capacity at the time of creation of the EPA. If we fear that a donor may be put under pressure by an unscrupulous attorney, there is a risk, presumably, that this pressure could extend to the choice of named relatives. There might also, on this proposal, be difficulties if, come registration, all the named relatives were dead or incapacitated.'

The Law Commission's consultation paper (1992)

5.10 In 1989 the Law Commission began an investigation into the adequacy of the legal and other procedures for making decisions on behalf of mentally incapacitated adults. In December 1992 it published a consultation paper, *Mentally Incapacitated Adults and Decision-Making: A New Jurisdiction* (Consultation Paper No 128), in which it revisited the need to notify the donor's relatives of the attorney's intention to apply for registration of an EPA. Paragraphs 7.16 to 7.18 of that consultation paper stated as follows:

'Under our present financial EPA scheme, an attorney is under a duty to notify the donor and specified relatives when he or she believes the donor to be or be becoming mentally incapable. In the context of the principle of "least restrictive intervention", the requirement of notification is hard to justify. If a person, presumed competent, chooses to appoint a proxy decision-maker we are not sure why the law should require that proxy to notify often distant family members that the person's faculties are failing. A family member with any involvement with the person would find out that the proxy was acting. If there is legitimate concern, they can have access to the court. This appears preferable to the law determining who is to be told that a person is becoming incapable, and literally inviting them to object to the person's choice of proxy. At the same time, we are mindful of the principle of protection and the public interest in ensuring that proxy decision-making, especially in relation to personal welfare, with all its ethical complexities, be properly regulated.

If safeguards for the donor are to be shifted from the point of incapacity to the point of executing the document, it can be argued that any notification should take place then. A standard form could ask the donor to state the names and addresses of two persons who are to be sent copies of the document, together with an explanation of its nature and effect and why they are being notified of it. The attorney might then be prohibited from acting until an acknowledgement was received from each of them. If no acknowledgement is received, directions would have to be sought from the court or other judicial authority.

Alternatively, if registration is to continue, we would propose that the standard form ask the donor to state who should be notified of the attorney's belief that the donor is or is becoming incapable of decision-making. Again, the names and addresses of a minimum of two persons should be required. We therefore provisionally propose that a donor should name in an EPA the two (or more) persons who are to be notified of its execution and no action should be taken by an attorney under the power unless and until an acknowledgment has been received from the persons so named.'

The Law Commission's report on *Mental Incapacity* (1995)

5.11 In 1995, at the conclusion of its investigation into the adequacy of legal and other procedures for making decisions on behalf of mentally incapacitated adults, the Law Commission published a report, *Mental Incapacity* (Law Com No 231). The report recommended that EPAs be replaced by a 'continuing power of attorney' (CPA), which could enable an attorney to make personal welfare decisions on behalf of the donor in addition to making decisions about the donor's property and financial affairs. The CPA was later renamed 'lasting power of attorney'. At paragraphs 7.37 to 7.39 of that report, the Law Commission expressed its opinion regarding the notification process:

> 'In Consultation Paper No 128 we suggested that requiring an attorney to notify listed relatives of the donor was hard to justify in the context of "least restrictive intervention". Many respondents endorsed this view. There was particular concern about the fact that the statutory list makes no acknowledgment that close and important relationships may exist outside of legal marriage and blood ties. It conflicts with the autonomy principle to require, regardless of the donor's wishes, that certain relatives must be notified of a private arrangement to govern future decision-making. Our respondents strongly supported the idea that a donor should be able to choose who might be notified about his or her attorney.
>
> We see a place for the notification of relatives or others as part of the "publicity" facet of the new registration scheme. It should, however, differ in two marked respects from the present notification scheme. First, it should be a notification that a CPA *has been* registered rather than a notification of an intention to register. We see no reason for the law to assume that the donor's actions are such that his or her relatives should have a right to object. The assumption should be that the donor has made valid arrangements, although properly concerned relatives will be able to take positive steps to challenge those arrangements. Secondly, it is for the donor to say who should be notified and not for statute to lay down a list.
>
> *We recommend* that once a CPA has been registered the registration authority should give notice of that fact in the prescribed form to a maximum of two people (not including the donee) as specified in the CPA. (Draft Bill, clause 15(6)(b)).
>
> Although some respondents expressed concern about donors who had no friends or relatives to name for the purposes of notification, the same problem arises under the present statutory list arrangements. Notification can only ever be one small part of the protection afforded to donors. We note that more than one respondent to Consultation Paper No 129 suggested that a GP would be an appropriate person to be notified about a health care power of attorney.'

The Joint Committee's report on the Draft Mental Incapacity Bill (2003)

5.12 The House of Lords and House of Commons Joint Committee on the Draft Mental Incapacity Bill published its report on 28 November 2003 (HL Paper 189-1, HC 1083-1). In volume 1, paragraph 158, the committee said:

> 'Schedule 1 of the draft Bill contains the requirements for executing LPA instruments. The donor of an LPA must state, *inter alia*, the names of a person or persons he wishes to be notified of any application to register the instrument, or that there are no such persons. The Law Society have expressed concern that 'extreme caution should be taken where there are no named persons for notification' as it could be an indication that the LPA was not made or registered with the donor's own free will. Although there is a requirement that, on registration, an LPA must be accompanied

by a certificate from a prescribed person as to the capacity of the donor, that safeguard would not necessarily preclude the presence of duress. Accordingly the Law Society have recommended that: "An application for registration without persons named for notification should be witnessed in the presence of the person who certifies capacity and two other persons."

We believe that the additional safeguard of requiring two additional persons to witness the certification of capacity should be included where there are no named persons for notification of the registration of an LPA.'

The Report Stage of the Mental Capacity Bill (2005)

5.13 On 15 March 2005, during the first day of the Report Stage on the Mental Capacity Bill in the House of Lords, Lord Christopher of Leckhampton introduced an amendment seeking to impose a duty on anyone applying to register an LPA to notify members of the donor's family, as is the case with an application to register EPAs. His amendment was opposed by Baroness Ashton of Upholland, the Parliamentary Under-Secretary of State at the Department for Constitutional Affairs. The debate is recorded in *Hansard*, 15 March 2005, cols 1313 to 1316:

'Lord Christopher of Leckhampton:

I question whether it is wrong to leave out families. I suppose that in practice families would largely be written in anyway by the person making the act. But it is not always like that. The practitioners tell me that it is the ones that do not fit the norm that cause the real problems unless one ensures that something is done about it. That is especially important where the family is driven away. I am told that that is far more common than is imagined. Manipulative people seeking undue influence will, one way or another, drive families and friends away. I have personal experience of that.

I have produced a list. The noble Baroness is not keen on lists – neither am I when it comes to European elections. But the list follows that for intestacy. It seems to me that if that is what the law would say on intestacy, perhaps the law should say it when there may not be – or someone is seeking to do something to replace a person's capacity.

Baroness Ashton of Upholland:

We know that there have to be safeguards for the vulnerable. I know that my noble friend's fears for the elderly vulnerable are the motivation behind the amendments to Schedule 1 and the desire to preserve the entitlement of relatives to receive notice of the application to register the LPA. I was grateful that my noble friend corrected himself.

I said that families are different. I did not say that they were not very important. I simply said that families are not what they used to be. We have lots of different kinds of families. People have many strong relationships—for example, half-siblings, step-children, and different situations within families. I would like my noble friend to accept that his amendment would make this quite difficult. As noble Lords who have heard me speak on any previous Bill will know, I have a difficulty with lists, as they inevitably mean that people are left out and things are not dealt with appropriately.

I am also very clear that this provision is about the donor making a choice. Ultimately, the donor should say who they would like to have notified. It could be a relative, but there may not be any relatives around or the donor may be estranged from his or her family – so there would be little point in notifying a relative. Just because someone is related does not necessarily mean that he will care anything for the donor. He may even have his own selfish motives for showing an interest in trying to object to the donor's chosen attorney.

So the Bill provides freedom of choice, but it does not lose sight of protection. My noble friend has made it clear that he is worried about the coercion or pressure that could be put on someone to give a decision-making power to a person through a lasting power of attorney.

That is why the Bill provides that all applications to register a lasting power of attorney must be accompanied by a certificate from a person of prescribed description that, in his opinion, the donor understands what he is doing and that no fraud or undue pressure is being used to induce the donor to create that lasting power of attorney. It goes one step further than that. Where there is no named person, regulations may require two certificates of that kind to be provided. This is the balance that I feel we have struck within the Bill: freedom and protection working in tandem.'

Transforming the Services of the Office of the Public Guardian (2012)

5.14 In 2012 the Ministry of Justice published a consultation paper, CP10/2012, called *Transforming the Services of the Office of the Public Guardian: A Consultation*. The consultation period began on 27 July 2012 and ended on 19 October 2012. On pages 11 and 12 the paper stated:

'Legislation currently provides that the person making the LPA can name up to five people whom they wish to be notified that the LPA is about to be registered. These are known as named persons. Once notified of the impending LPA registration, the named persons are able to object to the appointment of the attorney if they feel that the individual who has made the LPA lacked the capacity to do so, or that the LPA was made under duress, or that the attorney may not act in the best interests of the individual. Currently, it is the responsibility of the person applying to notify the named person(s) of their intention to register the LPA. On receipt of an application to register, it is also then the responsibility of the OPG to notify either the donor or the attorney of the application (whoever did not make the application).

The Mental Capacity Act (MCA) 2005 intends for named persons to act as another safeguarding measure. However, we wish to understand in more detail the protection their role offers to the LPA process. Evidence suggests that, for the majority of the LPA applications made, only one or two named persons are given. Therefore, we are seeking views on whether we should reduce the maximum number of named persons allowed.

In the future, we may also wish to consider whether the notification process could be revisited. This could include removing the notification process in its entirety, or limiting the persons notified to just the attorney and the donor. We would welcome your views on this and any other changes that could be made to the notification process.

If the notification process is retained in its current form, we seek your views on whether the OPG should assume responsibility for notifying all parties of the application to register the LPA. This would be irrespective of whether the application had been made digitally or on paper.

Question 12. Do you think the maximum number of persons should be reduced from five? If you do, what do you think the maximum number should be?

Question 13. What other changes to the notification process could we consider?

Question 14. If the facility to notify named persons is retained, do you agree the OPG should send notifications of the application to register to the named persons, rather than the onus being on the donor/attorney?'

5.15 The Ministry of Justice published its response to the consultation on 22 January 2013, *Transforming the Services of the Office of the Public Guardian*, CP(R) 23/2012. On page 17 the author of the response stated:

'We have decided not to change the current number of named persons at the present time. However, we intend to undertake further work on issues around the notification process, including assessing the additional amount of operational work that sending out notifications may involve for the OPG. Any future changes are likely to require primary legislation.

Response to specific questions
12.   Do you think the maximum number of persons should be reduced from five? If you do, what do you think the maximum number should be?

The majority of respondents replied to this question. Around a third of respondents felt that the number should be reduced, but were divided on the question of what the maximum number of named persons should be, with no clear consensus reached. A similar number of respondents agreed that it should not be reduced and that the option of five people should remain:

"Should be optional as named persons do not add any value to the process."

"There's more to notifying persons than just their ability to object. It can allow you to ensure that those who you feel should be aware are made aware."

"The donor should have as much choice as possible."

As there was no clear view from respondents about whether they were in favour or reducing the number of named persons or not, we have decided not to change the current number of named persons at the present time. We will, however, undertake further work into the role of named persons and this may form part of a future consultation.
13.   What other changes to the notification process could we consider?

All respondents replied to this question. Many agreed that the notification process should remain as it is, whilst others made some suggestions for improvements:

"Get rid of the process entirely."

"Notifiable person to acknowledge receipt of notification."

"It would be safer if the notice was served by the OPG."

14.   If the facility to notify named persons is retained, do you agree the OPG should send notifications of the application to register to the named persons, rather than the onus being on the donor/attorney?

The majority of respondents answered this question. Around two thirds agreed that the OPG should send notifications of the application to register to the named persons, with a small minority stating that they did not favour the OPG taking on this role:

"A good way to prevent fraud, a good audit trail."

"Might induce panic in people who do not know what to do with it."

"I see no reason to put the burden on the OPG."

We have considered the comments made by respondents in relation to the removal of the notification process and the possibility of the OPG taking on the notification responsibility. We agree that this proposal is a sensible way forward. However, concerns were also expressed about the OPG's ability to send out notifications in a timely manner, as well as the impact that this additional role may have on registration times. As any changes will require primary legislation, we therefore intend to undertake further work on the issues around the notification process, including assessing the additional workload that sending out notifications may involve for the OPG, whilst ensuring that the registration process is not affected.'

TABLE OF POLICY CHANGES IN RELATION TO NAMED PERSONS

Publication	Date	Recommendation or requirement
Law Commission Report No 123 *The Incapacitated Principal*, paragraph 4.36	1983	'Our scheme would ensure that the relatives would have an opportunity to consider whether it would be safe to allow the attorney to continue acting once the donor's capacity was in doubt.'
Enduring Powers of Attorney Act 1985, s 4 and Sch 1	1985	Before making an application for registration the attorney must comply with the provisions as to notice set out in Schedule 1, and give notice to relatives of the donor who are entitled to receive notice in a prescribed order of priority.
Stephen Cretney, Gwynn Davis, Roger Kerridge and Andrew Borkowski, *Enduring Powers of Attorney: A Report to the Lord Chancellor*, paragraph 2.39	1991	'We are not entirely convinced that the notification of relatives is the most appropriate safeguard of the donor's interests. . . . The donor should simply be invited, upon creating the power, to specify those people whom he or she wished to have informed at the point when the EPA came to be registered.'
Law Commission Consultation Paper No 128, *Mentally Incapacitated Adults and Decision-Making: A New Jurisdiction*, paragraph 7.18	1992	'We therefore provisionally propose that a donor should name in an EPA the two (or more) persons who are to be notified of its execution and no action should be taken by an attorney under the power unless and until an acknowledgment has been received from the persons so named.'

Publication	Date	Recommendation or requirement
Law Commission report no 231, *Mental Incapacity*, paragraphs 7.37-7.39	1995	'It conflicts with the autonomy principle to require, regardless of the donor's wishes, that certain relatives must be notified of a private arrangement to govern future decision-making. Our respondents strongly supported the idea that a donor should be able to choose who might be notified about his or her attorney . . . It is for the donor to say who should be notified and not for statute to lay down a list. We recommend that once a CPA has been registered the registration authority should give notice of the fact to a maximum of two people (not including the donee) as specified in the CPA.'
Lord Chancellor's Department consultation paper, *Who Decides? Making Decisions on Behalf of Mentally Incapacitated Adults*, paragraphs 6.48 and 6.49	1997	'The Law Commission also recommended that there should be notification to others once the CPA *had been* registered rather than *when there is an intention* to register. The people to be notified would be left to the donor but there would be a limit of two people. The Government has a number of practical concerns about this proposal, on which views are sought.'
Report of the House of Lords, House of Commons Joint Committee on the Draft Mental Incapacity Bill, recommendation 49	2003	'We believe that there should be an additional safeguard of requiring two additional persons to witness the certification of capacity where there are no named persons for notification of the registration of an LPA.'
Department for Constitutional Affairs, *The Government Response to the Scrutiny Committee's Report on the draft Mental Incapacity Bill*	2004	'We agree that it makes sense to have additional safeguards for the registration of an LPA where there are no named persons. We are looking at the best way to achieve this and it may be that additional notification or other formal requirements may be appropriate.'
MCA 2005, Sch 1, para 2(1)(c)	2005	The instrument must include . . . a statement by the donor naming a person or persons whom the donor wishes to be notified of any application for registration of the instrument, or stating that there are no persons whom he wishes to be notified of any such application.

Publication	Date	Recommendation or requirement
MCA 2005, Sch 1, para 2(2)		Regulations may (a) prescribe a maximum number of named persons, and (b) provide that where [there are no persons whom the donor wishes to be notified of any application for registration of the instrument], two persons of a prescribed description must each give a certificate under sub-paragraph 1(e).
MCA 2005, Sch 1, para 2(3)		The persons who may be named persons do not include a person who is appointed as donee under the instrument.
Department for Constitutional Affairs, *Lasting Powers of Attorney – forms and guidance* Consultation Paper CP 01/06, page 14	2006	'The Act provides for "named persons" to be notified when an application to register the form is made. We consider this an important safeguard. In the draft forms we have proposed that the donor can nominate up to 5 "named persons" who they would like to be notified at the time an application to register the LPA is made. Q14. Is five an appropriate number of named persons to be notified?"
Department for Constitutional Affairs, *Lasting Powers of Attorney – forms and guidance* Response to consultation CP(R) 01/06, page 34	2006	'73 respondents answered this question compared with 45 who did not. A majority agreed with the proposal for five named persons. 42 (over half of the respondents) thought that 5 was an appropriate number of people to be notified when registration is sought and 31 did not.'
Lasting Powers of Attorney, Enduring Powers of Attorney and Public Guardian Regulations 2007 (SI 2007/1253), reg 6	2007	The maximum number of named persons that the donor of a lasting power of attorney may specify in the instrument intended to create the power is 5.
Ministry of Justice consultation paper CP10/2012, *Transforming the Services of the Office of the Public Guardian: A Consultation*	2012	Seeking views on whether: • the maximum number of named persons should be reduced from five; • any other changes should be made to the notification process; and • the OPG should notify the named persons
Ministry of Justice response to consultation CP(R)23/2012, *Transforming the Services of the Office of the Public Guardian,* page 17		'We have decided not to change the current number of named persons at the present time. However, we intend to undertake further work on issues around the notification process.'

Publication	Date	Recommendation or requirement
Ministry of Justice Consultation paper CP 10/2013, *Transforming the Services of the Office of the Public Guardian Enabling: Digital by Default*	2013	Seeking views on whether there should be a change of name to 'People to be notified'.
Ministry of Justice response to consultation CP(R) 26/11/2013, *Transforming the Services of the Office of the Public Guardian: Enabling Digital by Default*	2014	It was confirmed that the next revised prescribed form would refer named persons as 'People to be notified'.

REQUIREMENTS OF THE ACT REGARDING NAMED PERSONS

5.16 MCA 2005, Sch 1, para 2(1)(c) provides that the instrument creating an LPA must include:

'a statement by the donor –
(i)   naming a person or persons whom the donor wishes to be notified of any application for the registration of the instrument, or
(ii)   stating that there are no persons whom he wishes to be notified of any such application.'

5.17 MCA 2005, Sch 1, para 2(2)(a) states that Regulations may prescribe a maximum number of named persons.

Maximum number of five named persons

5.18 Schedule 1, para 2(2)(a) to the MCA 2005 provides that Regulations may prescribe a maximum number of named persons. The relevant regulation is Lasting Powers of Attorney, Enduring Powers of Attorney and Public Guardian Regulations 2007 (LPA, EPA & PG Regs 2007) (SI 2007/1253), reg 6, which states that:

'The maximum number of persons that the donor of the power may specify in the instrument intended to create the power is 5.'

5.19 The MCA 2005 received the Royal Assent on 7 April 2005, and on 20 January 2006 the Department for Constitutional Affairs (DCA) issued a consultation paper, CP01/06, *Lasting Powers of Attorney – forms and guidance*. This included two draft prescribed forms of LPA, and the explanatory information relating to them. It was proposed that the donor could nominate up to five 'named persons' to be notified at the time an application to register the LPA was made, and question 14 in the consultation paper asked whether five was an appropriate number of persons to be notified.

5.20 The consultation lasted from 20 January 2006 until 14 April 2006, and 118 responses were received. On 17 July 2006 the DCA published a summary of responses, CP(R) 01/06. At page 34 it stated:

'73 respondents answered this question compared with 45 who did not. A majority agreed with the proposal for five named persons. 42 (over half of the respondents) thought that 5 was an appropriate number of people to be notified when registration is sought and 31 did not. Some respondents who disagreed said that having a maximum number of five or any maximum numbers was not necessary. Some respondents were not keen on limiting the numbers because they saw this as simply being about form design rather than donor choice. One respondent questioned what would happen if the named persons were uncontactable or deceased at the time that notification was due to take place. There were some responses that used this question to give a more detailed opinion on the notification process and also the question of changes to the form if notifiable parties' details changed.'

An attorney may not be a named person

5.21 Schedule 1, para 2(3) to the MCA 2005 provides that persons who may be named persons do not include a person who is appointed as donee under the instrument.

5.22 In *Re Howarth* (Senior Judge Lush, 29 July 2008), the donor named the replacement attorney as the only person who was to be notified of an application to register the LPA. If there was no effective named person, the LPA could only be valid if it contained two Part B certificates but in this case there was only one such certificate. On the application of the Public Guardian, the court severed the appointment of the replacement attorney on the ground that a replacement attorney was person 'appointed as donee under the instrument', and could not, therefore, be a named person. As the appointment of the replacement attorney was severed, the named person was no longer a donee under the instrument, and so it could be registered.

5.23 The same principle was applied in *Re McAdam* (Senior Judge Lush, 29 March 2010), where the donor appointed X and Y jointly and severally to be his attorneys, and named X as the only named person. On being informed of the nature of the problem, the donor consented to X's appointment being severed so that the LPA could be registered with Y acting as the sole attorney.

5.24 As a result of the decision in *Re Howarth*, the prescribed forms of LPA introduced in 2009 made it much clearer that an attorney or a replacement attorney could not be a named person. This remains the case with the 2015 prescribed forms.

Where there are no named persons

5.25 MCA 2005, Sch 1, para 2(2) states that:

'Regulations may –
  (a)   prescribe a maximum number of named persons;
  (b)   provide that, where the instrument includes a statement under sub-para-
        graph (1)(c)(ii), two persons of a prescribed description must each give a
        certificate under sub-paragraph (1)(e).'

5.26 Regulation 7 of the LPA, EPA & PG Regs 2007 stated that:

'Where an instrument intended to create a lasting power of attorney includes a statement by the donor that there are no persons whom he wishes to be notified of any application for the registration of the instrument –

(a) the instrument must include two LPA certificates, and

(b) each certificate must be completed and signed by a different person.'

Regulation 7 was removed by reg 6 of the LPA, EPA & PG (Amendment) Regs 2015, with the effect that LPAs made after 1 July 2015 require the certificate of only one person.

The contents of the instrument relating to named persons

5.27 The OPG has published *Make and register a lasting power of attorney – a guide* (LP12). In Part A6 *People to notify when the LPA is registered* limited guidance is given on the choice to be made by the donor. It advises:

'These should be people who know you well and would be willing to raise concerns about your LPA. They can object to the LPA if they think you were under pressure to make it or if they think fraud was involved.'

It omits to mention that the named persons can object on the basis the donor did not understand what they were signing. The guidance is focused on form filling, rather than the purpose of the named person and what they can do if they have concerns. However, it does suggest:

'Letting people know about your LPA just before it's registered protects you. It's especially important if there's a long time between making your LPA and registering it.'

It states:

'You can choose up to five people to notify but they can't be your attorneys or replacement attorneys. Many donors choose family members or close friends' and 'you don't have to choose people to notify'.

5.28 In the prescribed form of LPA for property and financial affairs the opportunity to choose named persons appears in Section 6. The wording is identical in both forms and states as follows:

'You can let people know that you're going to register your LPA. They can raise any concerns they have about the LPA – for example, if there was any pressure or fraud in making it.

When the LPA is registered, the person applying to register (you or one of your attorneys) must send a notice to each 'person to notify'.

You can't put your attorneys or replacement attorneys here.

People to notify can object to the LPA, but only for certain reasons (listed in the notification form LP3). After that, they are no longer involved in the LPA.

Choose people who care about your best interests and who would be willing to speak up if they were concerned.'

5.29 There are boxes for inserting the titles (Mr, Mrs, etc), full names, addresses and postcodes, of up to four people to notify that the LPA is to be registered. If the donor wishes to choose an additional person to notify, the person's details need to be included on continuation sheet 1. The box at the bottom of Section 6, which states, 'I want to appoint another person to notify' needs to be ticked. It is arguable, that the donor is merely making a choice, rather than an appointment and the wording is erroneous, but the intention is nevertheless clear.

5.30 Section 9 of the prescribed forms of LPA state:

'I have either appointed people to notify (in section 6) or I have chosen not to notify anyone when the LPA is registered.'

5.31 The pre- 2015 OPG guidance in LPA 111 (p 26) and 112 (p 25) suggested that 'if contact details for any of your people to be told change after you have completed your LPA and before it is registered, do not make any changes to your LPA. This would make it invalid. Instead, record any changes on a separate sheet of paper, and keep this with your LPA. Your people to be told could die, or move away – this is a good reason to register your LPA straightaway.' Post 2015 OPG guidance, *Make and register your LPA – a guide (LP12)* makes no reference to what to do in the event of changes to the named person's details.

Notifying the named persons

5.32 MCA 2005, Sch 1, para 4 requires an application to be made to the Public Guardian for the registration of an instrument intended to create an LPA. Paragraph 4(2) provides that the application may be made by the donor or the donee(s), or, if the instrument appoints two or more donees to act jointly and severally in respect of any matter, by any of the donees.

5.33 MCA 2005, Sch 1, para 6, states that a donor or donee(s) about to make an application to register the instrument must notify any named persons that he is or they are about to do so.

5.34 Regulation 10 (as amended by SI 2015/899) of the LPA, EPA & PG Regs 2007 states that:

'Schedule 2 to these Regulations sets out the form of notice ("LPA3") which must be given by a donor or donee who is about to make an application for the registration of an instrument intended to create a lasting power of attorney.'

NOTICE OF INTENTION TO APPLY FOR REGISTRATION OF A LASTING POWER OF ATTORNEY: LP3

5.35 The notice of intention to apply for registration of an LPA is referred to as form LP3, and is set out in Sch 2 to the LPA, EPA & PG Regs 2007 (as amended by SI 2015/899).

5.36 Form LP3 states:

'When you apply to register the LPA you must tell the people to notify that the LPA will be registered.

You must send a copy of this form to each of the people to notify, before you send the LPA to be registered. You can send them this form or hand it to them in person.

You can save time by filling in pages 2 and 3 and making a photocopy to send to each person.

The donor's relatives are not entitled to be notified unless they have been named in the LPA.'

5.37 The form then provides space for inserting details of the name of each person to notify, their address and postcode, and explains the purpose of an LPA – followed by this statement:

'When they made the LPA, the donor decided you should be told about it before it's registered. This is so you can raise any concerns you may have. If you do have concerns, you can only object to the registration of the LPA for the reasons listed on page 4 of this form.'

5.38 The form then provides boxes for inserting details of the donor and the attorneys, who is the applicant, the type of LPA, the date the donor signed the LPA and whether the attorneys are authorised to act solely, jointly, jointly and severally, or jointly in some matters and jointly and severally in others. The notice explains how a named person can object to the registering of an LPA and is considered in CHAPTER 9.

Practical points

5.39 If the applicant is applying to register both types of LPA (ie for property and financial affairs and health and welfare), and the same named persons are contained in each, they are treated as separate applications and the applicant must send notices for each of the LPAs he or she is applying to register. The reason for this apparent duplication of effort is that the named person may be content for the registration of one type of LPA to go ahead, but may wish to object to the other application.

5.40 The applicant may have to show the OPG that he has made all reasonable attempts to contact the named person, but has been unable to contact them. In such circumstances, the OPG would expect to see proof of posting or a returned notice from the last address.

Where the named persons have died or cannot be contacted

5.41 The OPG's pre- 2015 booklet, LPA 110, *How to register your lasting power of attorney*, stated, on page 4 of 11:

'If it is not possible to establish contact with any of the people to be told, you must keep proof of posting slips, or returned-to-sender evidence, to demonstrate that you have made reasonable efforts.'

The OPG's post 2015, *Make and register an LPA – a guide* (LP12) makes no mention of what to do in these circumstances.

Dispensing with the requirement to notify

5.42 MCA 2005, Sch 1, para 10, states that:

'The court may –
(a)   on the application of the donor, dispense with the obligation to notify under paragraph 6(1), or

(b)   on the application of the donee or donees concerned, dispense with the requirement to notify under paragraph 6(2),

if satisfied that no useful purpose would be served by giving the notice.'

5.43 Slightly different provisions exist whereby the court can dispense with the requirement to give notice of an attorney's intention to apply for the registration of an EPA to a relative of the donor, to the donor himself, and to any co-attorney: MCA 2005, Sch 4, paras 7(2), 8(2) and 11(1) respectively. The attorney, before applying for registration, may make an application to the court to be dispensed from the requirement to give notice, and the court must grant the application if it is satisfied (a) that it would be undesirable or impracticable for the attorney to give him notice, or (b) that no useful purpose is likely to be served by giving him notice.

5.44 In relation to EPAs, Sch 4 to the MCA 2005 provides that the donor's relatives (para 6(2)), and any co-attorney of the attorney applying to register an instrument (para 11(2)) are not entitled to receive notice if:

* their address is not known to the applying attorney and cannot reasonably be ascertained by him; or
* the applying attorney has reason to believe that he has not reached 18 or is mentally incapable.

5.45 There is no similar provision for persons applying to register an LPA. Where a named person's address is not known and cannot reasonably be ascertained, or when a named person has become mentally incapable, the applicant could either:

* send the form LPA 3 to the named person at the address show in the instrument; or
* apply to the Court of Protection to dispense with the requirement to notify pursuant to para 10 of Sch 1 to the MCA 2005.

THE CODE OF PRACTICE AND THE NAMED PERSONS

5.46 The named persons are not included in the list of persons, set out in s 42(4) of the MCA 2005, who have a duty to have regard to the code when acting in relation to a person who lacks capacity. Nevertheless, any named person who wished to object to the registration of an instrument would be well advised to read relevant parts of the Code of Practice for the purpose of setting out his or her reasons for objecting.

Chapter 6

CERTIFICATE PROVIDERS

INTRODUCTION

6.1 A lasting power of attorney (LPA) must include a certificate (an LPA certificate) by a person of a prescribed description that, in his opinion, at the time when the donor executes the instrument:

- the donor understands the purpose of the instrument and the scope of the authority conferred under it;
- no fraud or undue pressure is being used to induce the donor to create an LPA; and
- there is nothing else which would prevent an LPA from being created by the instrument.

6.2 There are two categories of persons of a prescribed description who may give an LPA certificate, namely:

- Category A – Knowledge certification; someone who has known the donor personally for a period of at least 2 years; or
- Category B – Skills certification; someone who reasonably considers that he has the relevant professional skills and expertise to certify such matters. The regulations and the prescribed forms contain a non-exhaustive list of persons who may have such skills.

6.3 Certain persons – such as family members, and care home proprietors and staff – are expressly disqualified from giving an LPA certificate.

6.4 It is a requirement for LPAs made before 1 July 2015, where the donor has not named anyone who is to be notified when an application is made to register the LPA, that two persons of a prescribed description must each provide a separate LPA certificate (LPA, EPA & PG Regs 2007, reg 7). Regulation 7 was removed by reg 6 of the LPA, EPA & PG (Amendment) Regs 2015, with the effect that LPAs made after 1 July 2015 require the certificate of only one person.

6.5 Until July 2015, The Office of the Public Guardian (OPG) published guidance about the certificate provider's role and responsibilities in CHAPTER 4 of:

- *Guidance for people who want to make a lasting power of attorney for health and welfare* (LPA 111).
- *Guidance for people who want to make a lasting power of attorney for property and financial affairs* (LPA 112).

However, the guidance ceased to be published after the introduction of the 2015 prescribed forms. In its place, Section 10A of *Make and Register your LPA – a guide* (LP12) contains limited guidance.

6.6 In addition to completing and signing the LPA certificate in Section 10 of the prescribed form, a certificate provider may also witness the donor's signature in Section 9 of the prescribed form.

POLICY AND LEGISLATIVE HISTORY

The purpose of the certificate

6.7 The purpose of a formal document certifying the donor's capacity to create a LPA is twofold. The first is to remedy the situation in which a potentially vulnerable person with borderline capacity signs a power of attorney without adequate safeguards in place. The second is to provide evidence that may assist the court in the event of there being any future challenge to the validity of the instrument.

An overview

6.8 The policy underlying the need for a formal certificate of the donor's capacity at the time of the creation of the power had a long and tortuous history, with several spectacular U-turns, and aroused more controversy and debate than any other issue involving LPAs. The following table gives an overview of the legislative history of the LPA certificate, and the subsequent sections contain a more detailed analysis of the reasons why particular policy decisions were made.

Publication	Year	Requirement, proposal or recommendation
Law Commission Report No 123, *The Incapacitated Principal*	1983	There is no need for formal certification of the donor's capacity to create an EPA.
Enduring Powers of Attorney Act 1985	1985	No requirement for formal certification of the donor's capacity to create an EPA.
Stephen Cretney, Gwynn Davis, Roger Kerridge and Andrew Borkowski, *Enduring Powers of Attorney: A Report to the Lord Chancellor*	1991	Formal medical certification at the time of creation of the EPA might be a more effective safeguard than the notification process on application to register the EPA.
Law Commission Consultation Paper No 128, *Mentally Incapacitated Adults and Decision-Making: A New Jurisdiction*	1992	The donor's capacity to create an EPA must be certified by both a solicitor and a registered medical practitioner.
Law Commission Report No 231, *Mental Incapacity*	1995	There is no need for formal certification of the donor's capacity to create a Continuing Power of Attorney.

Publication	Year	Requirement, proposal or recommendation
Lord Chancellor's Department consultation paper, *Who Decides? Making Decisions on Behalf of Mentally Incapacitated Adults*	1997	Certification by a solicitor and a medical practitioner might help unnecessary abuse of these powers.
Lord Chancellor's Department report issued in response to the consultation paper *Who Decides? Making Decisions: The Government's proposals for making decisions on behalf of mentally incapacitated adults*	1999	The form must be accompanied by evidence that the donor was mentally capable at the time that it was created. That evidence could be provided by either a separate medical certificate or a signed statement by a doctor in the prescribed form itself.
Department for Constitutional Affairs, *Draft Mental Incapacity Bill*, Sch 1, para 2(1)(e)	2003	The instrument must include a certificate signed by a person of a prescribed description as to the capacity of the donor.
Report of the House of Lords, House of Commons Joint Committee on the Draft Mental Incapacity Bill, recommendation 49	2003	There should be an additional safeguard of requiring two additional persons to witness the certification of capacity where there are no named persons for notification of the registration of an LPA.
Department for Constitutional Affairs, *The Government Response to the Scrutiny Committee's Report on the draft Mental Incapacity Bill*	2004	'We agree that it makes sense to have additional safeguards for the registration of an LPA where there are no named persons.'
MCA 2005, Sch 1, para 2(1)(e)	2005	The instrument must include a certificate by a person of a prescribed description, or two such certificates where there are no named persons to be notified, that (i) the donor understands the purpose of the instrument and the scope of the authority conferred under it; (ii) no fraud or undue pressure is being used to induce the donor to create an LPA; and (iii) there is nothing else that would prevent an LPA being created by the instrument.
Department for Constitutional Affairs consultation paper, CP01/06, *Lasting Powers of Attorney – forms and guidance*	2006	The certificate provider must either (a) have known the donor for a period of at least 2 years, or (b) have a specified occupation, and must not be disqualified from giving an LPA certificate.
Lasting Powers of Attorney, Enduring Powers of Attorney and Public Guardian Regulations 2007 (SI 2007/1253), reg 8	2007	The person of a prescribed description must fall within either Category A – Knowledge certification, or Category B – Skills certification, provided he is not disqualified from giving an LPA certificate.

Publication	Year	Requirement, proposal or recommendation
Ministry of Justice consultation paper CP10/2012, *Transforming the Services of the Office of the Public Guardian: A Consultation*	2012	Seeking views on: • whether the requirement for an additional certificate provider, in circumstances where the donor has not specified any named persons, should be removed; • how well the role of the certificate provider is operating and whether it is in the way that the MCA 2005 intended; and • what the role of the certificate provider might be in a digital context.
Ministry of Justice response to consultation CP(R)23/2012, *Transforming the Services of the Office of the Public Guardian*, pages 13 and 14		'We agree that the role of the certificate provider remains an important safeguard and we intend to undertake further work as to how this role might continue to provide the appropriate safeguards in a digital context.'
Ministry of Justice Consultation paper CP 10/2013, *Transforming the Services of the Office of the Public Guardian: Enabling Digital by Default*	2013	Seeking views on: • whether there should be a change of name for the certificate provider to 'People to Certify'; • again: whether the requirement for an additional certificate provider, in circumstances where the donor has not specified any named persons, should be removed; and • the proposal to introduce legislation to create a fully digital LPA without physical signatures, including that of the certificate provider.

Publication	Year	Requirement, proposal or recommendation
Ministry of Justice response to consultation CP(R) 26/11/2013, *Transforming the Services of the Office of the Public Guardian: Enabling Digital by Default*	2014	• It was confirmed that the phrase 'certificate providers' is appropriate and will be retained. • The requirement to have two certificate providers, where there was no one to be notified of the registration was to be removed. • In respect of a fully digital LPA: 'We are confident that a fully digital LPA will provide benefits for donors. However, as the consultation has identified, there are a number of points which need to be resolved before a fully digital LPA can be implemented. We will build on the feedback received and work with key stakeholders to refine our proposal for a fully digital LPA and consult with the public when we have a fuller picture of how the digital tool will operate.'

The Incapacitated Principal (1983)

6.9 There was no requirement in the Enduring Powers of Attorney Act 1985 for formal certification of the donor's capacity to create an enduring power. The reason for this is given at paragraph 4.19 of the Law Commission's report, *The Incapacitated Principal*, (Law Com No 122, Cmnd 8977), which was published in 1983, and contained a draft of the 1985 Act:

'We would mention at this point that we have given careful consideration to the question whether the witness should be a "special" witness – a solicitor or doctor, for example – for the purpose of assessing the donor's capacity to create an EPA. Some of our consultees would have favoured such a rule but we have come down, on balance, against it. It is true that if the donor's solicitor or doctor knew the donor sufficiently well to be able to judge whether he had sufficient capacity to create the EPA, his attestation (which might incorporate some form of certificate) would go a long way towards proving that the EPA was not void at the time of creation on the ground of incapacity. But the attestation of a solicitor or doctor who was not familiar with the donor should not, we think, carry such additional weight; and problems would certainly arise if the witness were required to furnish any form of certificate, because a person's degree of understanding is notoriously difficult to judge on short acquaintance. By contrast, the persons who would be far more likely to be able to make that judgment would be the relatives who would be notified under the proposed notification procedure and we think that this aspect of the matter would be better left to them. Indeed it could be argued that the existence of a special witness would tend to eclipse the views of the relatives on this point and we think that this would be undesirable. An additional objection to a requirement

81

of a special witness is that donors might be reluctant to approach the necessary solicitor or doctor.'

Enduring Powers of Attorney: A Report to the Lord Chancellor (1991)

6.10 The need for formal certification of the donor's capacity at the time of creating an enduring power of attorney was reconsidered by Stephen Cretney, Gwynn Davis, Roger Kerridge, and Andrew Borkowski in *Enduring Powers of Attorney: A Report to the Lord Chancellor*, which was published by the Lord Chancellor's Department in June 1991. Stephen Cretney had been the Law Commissioner responsible for producing the report, *The Incapacitated Principal*, in 1983 and, when his term of office came to an end, he took up an appointment as Professor of Law at the University of Bristol. In 1990 the Lord Chancellor's Department commissioned him and a team of colleagues from the Faculty of Law at the University of Bristol to report on various aspects of the efficacy of the Enduring Powers of Attorney Act 1985.

6.11 Their report was highly influential in shaping policy on the procedures that would apply in future legislation on lasting powers of attorney. Although they acknowledged that there were inherent weaknesses in such a process, on balance, the authors of the report considered that the formal medical certification of the donor's capacity at the time of creating the power of attorney 'might provide a more effective safeguard than the present system of notifying the donor and relatives upon registration'. At paragraph 2.40 of the report, Cretney and his colleagues set out the following arguments both for and against certification:

'An alternative protective mechanism would be to require that every EPA be supported by medical authority concerning the donor's capacity to create the Power. (The EPA could be registered immediately, or at some point in the future – that is to say, whenever it was proposed that it become a working document). If the donor wished to revoke the Power, this would likewise require medical confirmation of the donor's capacity at that time. The suggestion might be that we should rely upon medical evidence, rather than notification of relatives, to protect the donor. Just as with a will (where there is of course no question of notifying relatives when the document is prepared) the real issue is that of capacity.

We gained the impression that most solicitors, where they had some doubts about the donor's capacity to create the Power, would seek medical opinion. One solicitor who had experienced an objection to registration which revolved around the question of capacity told us that this, and the leading cases of *Re K* and *Re F*, had led him and his colleagues always to get a doctor as a witness wherever there was the slightest doubt about the donor's capacity. He said that he asked the doctor to write to him, indicating whether he was satisfied on the four points outlined by Hoffmann J in the cases of *Re K* and *Re F*. Needless to say, this is not something that solicitors are required to do; but most thought that it was good practice in circumstances where they had reason to doubt the donor's capacity.

We asked some of the more experienced solicitors whom we interviewed whether they would favour a requirement that medical evidence be produced in every case. One solicitor advised against. He made the point that he routinely created EPAs for people who were young and fit. For instance, he and his wife both had EPAs; so did his son and daughter, who were only in their early twenties. He obviously thought that it would be excessively burdensome to require medical evidence in every case.

(He also did not consider it realistic – and nor would we – to define, by age or some other factor, when medical evidence should be required).

A further difficulty raised by some solicitors was that, in their experience, doctors – certainly non-specialists – appeared to vary in their judgment of capacity. One solicitor observed that "a lot of the doctors in this area seem to be bending over backwards to say that people do have capacity". Another solicitor told us of an elderly client who had been in a nursing home for many years. He decided to visit the client and he formed the view, as a layman, that he probably wasn't capable of creating a Power of Attorney. In this case the GP certified that the potential donor *was* capable; so the Power was created. But as this solicitor put it: "One has one's nagging doubts". A couple of solicitors referred to the Guidance Note drawn up by the Court which sets out the criteria for capacity upon executing the EPA. The first solicitor regarded the Guidance Note as "very helpful". He always sent it to the GP, so that he could visit the patient armed with the Guidance Note.

The second solicitor who referred to the Guidance Note took an entirely opposite view. He claimed that GPs had told him that it was worse than useless – they were more confused than they had been to start with. He referred in particular to the difficulty involved in the nebulous state of "becoming incapable". It was one thing to define someone as incapable – certainly a psychiatrist should be able to do that – but there was no sensible medical definition of "becoming incapable". In this solicitor's view, the tests advanced by Hoffmann J in *Re K* and *Re F* were not the answer. He referred to one case in which the donor had been seen by four different doctors; two had said one thing and two had said the other . . . "and I can't blame them – it depends on the time of day, the place, and so on".

A great deal of fun is poked at the concept of the "lucid interval" – probably most of it justified – but if we accept that there is such a thing as a lucid interval (or a relatively lucid interval) then one has to accept that it is difficult to define, on the basis of one consultation with a GP, whether a potential donor has capacity. Thus, one solicitor described a client who "understood what she was doing at the time, but she tends to be very forgetful, so a couple of days later she didn't remember she'd done it. So if somebody else told her something different, she might change it again. Obviously there is that problem with people in that type of state – they're swayed by whoever they last spoke to".

There is also the fact that a medical test of capacity would not cover the possibility of duress (although it is difficult to devise any effective safeguard in respect of this). Several solicitors speculated that pressure was sometime put on donors by their children. One solicitor mentioned a case where the donor was brought into the office by his daughter to sign the EPA, but refused to do so. Another solicitor told us of a case which had caused her considerable unease, where a son had consulted her with a view to creating both a Deed of Gift and an EPA. She had spoken to the donor over the telephone. She had no doubts about her capacity, but she had been worried about the possibility of duress. Nevertheless, the EPA had been created in favour of the son. In this case the solicitor anticipated problems in the shape of objections from other relatives when the EPA came to be registered. She was sure that they would not be happy with what had occurred.

We have set out all these counter-arguments because, given that we are attracted to a protective mechanism which focuses upon the key issue of capacity, we thought it important to examine counter-arguments. Despite the weakness of such a procedure, which we acknowledge, we think it might provide a more effective safeguard than the present system of notifying the donor and relatives upon registration. It would inevitably make the creation of an EPA more expensive, but perhaps this is a reasonable additional expenditure.'

Law Commission consultation paper *Mentally Incapacitated Adults and Decision-Making: A New Jurisdiction* (1992)

6.12 Following the publication of Stephen Cretney's report, *Enduring Powers of Attorney: A Report to the Lord Chancellor*, the Law Commission issued a consultation paper in December 1992, *Mentally Incapacitated Adults and Decision-Making: A New Jurisdiction* (Consultation Paper No 128), in which it suggested, at paragraph 7.15, that the donor's capacity to create an enduring power of attorney should be certified by both a solicitor and a registered medical practitioner at the time of execution. The reasoning behind this proposal was as follows:

'At present, both donor and attorney under an EPA must execute in the presence of a witness. The donor certifies that he or she has read the explanatory notes. Other jurisdictions require certifications from witnesses as to the ability of the donor to act. The Scottish Law Commission tended to the view that a solicitor should certify that he or she has explained the nature and effect of the document to the donor. The research report commissioned by the Lord Chancellor's Department suggested that a system for certification by a medical practitioner of the donor's capacity on execution would be a "more effective safeguard" than the existing notification and registration scheme. It can be argued that the capacity of the donor to execute the document is of much greater significance than supervening incapacity. If the existing notification and registration requirements are felt unnecessary or ineffective, we would propose that a certificate at the time of execution (together with a more complicated standard form) would be one way of replacing them. However, although capacity is a legal rather than a strictly medical concept, it appears that most EPAs are drafted by solicitors acting for the donor; we would therefore suggest that there should be certificates from both the solicitor and a registered medical practitioner, that each has seen the donor recently, and explained the nature and effect of the document, and that he or she appears to understand it. We invite comments on this matter and suggest that the donor's capacity to execute an EPA should be certified by a solicitor and a registered medical practitioner at the time of execution.'

Law Commission report, *Mental Incapacity* (1995)

6.13 However, following consultation paper number 128, the Law Commission revised its opinion and rejected the need for any kind of certification. In paragraph 7.27 of its final report, *Mental Incapacity* (Law Com No 231, 1995), it said:

'In the consultation papers, we proposed creating much more stringent formalities for execution than those which have been imposed in relation to EPAs. The 1985 Act stipulates that an EPA must be executed in the prescribed manner. At present, the relevant regulations require signature by both donor and donee, each in the presence of a single witness. Our provisional proposal that the donor's capacity to execute should be certified by a solicitor and a doctor at the time of execution did not commend itself to the majority of consultees. Numerous respondents said that any such requirement would present practical difficulties and force donors to incur extra costs. Concern focused on the idea that both a doctor and a lawyer need be involved in every case. It should in any event be a matter of good practice for all health professionals not to witness a signature without considering the question of the person's capacity to execute the document. Lawyers involved in drawing up powers of attorney should also, as a matter of good practice, be very clear that the client to whom the duty of care is owed is the donor of the power and no-one else.

In appropriate cases good practice already demands that an appropriate medical certificate should be obtained and/or appropriate records kept on file. The provisional proposal for a certification procedure was a corollary to the proposed abolition of any form of registration, which, as we explain below, we are no longer pursuing. In those circumstances, the draft Bill simply provides that a CPA (like an EPA) must be executed in the prescribed manner by both donor and donee.'

Who Decides? (1997)

6.14 In December 1997 the Lord Chancellor's Department published the consultation paper, *Who Decides? Making Decisions on Behalf of Mentally Incapacitated Adults* (ISBN 0-10-138032-1), which favoured formal certification of a donor's capacity to create an LPA. It stated, at paragraphs 6.39 and 6.40:

'The Law Commission's provisional proposal that a donor's capacity to execute should be subject to a certificate from a doctor and solicitor was regarded as overly intrusive by respondents to their consultation.

Although the Law Commission revised its view, and rejected a requirement for certification, the Government considers that a system for certification by a solicitor and a medical practitioner might help prevent unnecessary abuse of these powers.'

Department for Constitutional Affairs, Consultation Paper CP 01/06

6.15 The Mental Capacity Act 2005 (MCA 2005) received the Royal Assent on 7 April 2005, and on 20 January 2006 the Department for Constitutional Affairs (DCA) issued a consultation paper, CP01/06, *Lasting Powers of Attorney – forms and guidance*, which included two draft prescribed forms of LPA, and the explanatory information relating to them. It was proposed that the certificate provider would be a person who:

'Either

Has known the donor for at least two years

Or is one of the people in the list below:
- a local business person or shopkeeper
- a registered social worker
- a General Practitioner (GP) or any other registered Medical Health Care Professional
- a police officer
- a bank or building society officer
- a solicitor, barrister, magistrate or Justice of the Peace
- a librarian
- a minister of religion
- a professionally qualified person, for example, a teacher or engineer
- a local authority councillor
- a civil servant
- a Member of Parliament (MP) or Member of the European Parliament (MEP)

And is NOT
- a relative of the donor
- a husband, wife or civil partner of the donor

- a person who has lived with the donor as husband and wife or as civil partner for two years or more
- an attorney appointed under this form or any other LPA or any other enduring power of attorney
- a current paid carer
- the manager or an employee of the care home where the donor resides; and
- a person named on the form to be notified of an application to register this LPA.'

Response to Consultation Paper CP 01/06

6.16 The consultation period lasted from 20 January 2006 until 14 April 2006, and the Department for Constitutional Affairs published a summary of responses, CP(R) 01/06, on 17 July 2006. A total of 118 responses were received, 96 of which related to questions raised about the certificate provider. At pages 7 and 8, the summary stated:

'The certification process was the area where most respondents voiced the strongest opinions. Respondents emphasised the mischief that the role of certificate provider was intended to remedy and that they did not think the current list of certificate providers addressed this. They highlighted the skills, expertise and knowledge they thought were necessary to be a certificate provider and for the role to be a meaningful safeguard against abuse. Some respondents suggested that only certain professions should be able to be a certificate provider. Respondents suggested specific detailed guidance for the certificate provider on how to carry out their role and the consequences of not paying adequate attention to the nature of the role and requirements upon the certificate provider. They also raised issues around the timing of the certification within the process of making an LPA.'

6.17 At page 44 of the response to consultation, the DCA concluded:

'We know that we will need to revisit aspects of the certification process and we welcome the extensive input we have received on this. This is an area where consultees expressed the greatest desire for change and greater clarity. We will need to look again at who can be a certificate provider and, in particular, the skills necessary to perform the role. We do not think the certificate provider is a role which should be undertaken exclusively by certain professions. We will reconsider the categories of person who should be excluded from being a certificate provider and make sure that certain categories of people who are closely acquainted with the attorney are not able to fulfil the role. We will make it clearer that it is attorneys for the donor in question who should not be certificate providers rather than attorneys generally.

We agree that we will need to provide further guidance for the certificate provider on the nature of the undertaking that they are making and assessing capacity and undue influence. We will also need to make it clear at what point the certificate should be signed. We also intend to signpost the existence and relevance of the Code of Practice as a source of information and guidance for certificate providers, donors and attorneys.'

6.18 In the event, the government opted for two categories of 'person of a prescribed description', one based on the certificate provider's personal knowledge of the donor, and the other based on the certificate provider's experience in assessing mental capacity in cases of this kind.

Transforming the Services of the Office of the Public Guardian (2012)

6.19 In 2012 the Ministry of Justice published a consultation paper, CP10/2012, called *Transforming the Services of the Office of the Public Guardian: A Consultation*. The consultation period began on 27 July 2012 and ended on 19 October 2012. On page 10 the paper stated:

'A certificate provider is an independent person who is able to confirm that the person making the LPA understands its significance. They must have known the individual for at least two years or have the relevant professional skills to confirm that the person making the LPA understands its significance. They also need to certify that no undue pressure or fraud was involved in the making of the LPA application. If the donor has not chosen any named person to be notified on registration of the LPA, a second certificate provider is required for the donor's added protection.

The certificate providers, therefore, provide an important safeguarding role. We are aware, however, of the difficulties that can be caused in donors needing to find a second certificate provider where they have not specified any named persons to be notified of their intention to register an LPA. We are, therefore, considering whether the requirement for an additional certificate provider remains necessary and should be removed. One certificate provider would still be required.

Beyond this, we would also like to explore whether the certificate provider role is operating as the Mental Capacity Act (MCA) 2005 intended and how it might operate in the future in a digital context. While any changes to the requirements for certificate providers would be for the future, we would welcome your views now on any amendments that could be made.

Question 7. Should the requirement for an additional certificate provider, in circumstances where the donor has not specified any named persons, be removed?

Question 8. How well do you think that the role of the certificate provider is operating and is it in the way that the MCA legislation intended?

Question 9. What value do you think the role of the certificate provider might add to the process for making an LPA within a digital context?'

6.20 The Ministry of Justice published its response to the consultation on 22 January 2013, *Transforming the Services of the Office of the Public Guardian*, CP(R) 23/2012. On pages 13 and 14 the author of the response stated:

'We have carefully considered the responses provided. Many respondents consider a second certificate provider remains an important additional safeguard, although they also flagged up the difficulties that donors face in practice in identifying a second certificate provider. We will, therefore, retain the requirement for a second certificate provider, although we intend to consider further how much additional protection they provide in practice and the difficulties donors experience in identifying them.

In addition, we do not intend to specify that the certificate provider must be a professional. Whilst we acknowledge the benefits that their involvement can bring, we continue to advocate that individuals should be able to complete the LPA forms without having to seek assistance from a professional. We also intend to undertake further work to explore how the certificate provider role might continue to provide the appropriate safeguards in a digital context.

Response to specific questions

7. Should the requirement for an additional certificate provider, in circumstances where the donor has not specified any named persons, be removed?

Most respondents replied to this question. Of those, around half felt that the requirement should not be removed, as this is regarded as a necessary and important safeguard to protect the donor. Comments included:

"The protection is appropriate."

"If you remove the second certificate provider, it means that it is easier to get a power signed and therefore easy to abuse."

A minority felt that the additional certificate provider should be removed. Comments included:

"If the first certificate provider is undertaking their role properly, in particular ensuring that the donor has capacity . . . then the second certificate provider's role is superfluous."

"The requirement for an additional certificate provider should be removed. It is comparatively rare."

Other comments suggested that if the certificate provider were a professional person i.e. a solicitor or the donor's GP, this would alleviate the need to have two certificate providers.

As outlined above, we are aware that this is an area of significant concern. Consequently, as a second certificate provider remains an important safeguard to ensure that the donor understands the significance of the LPA and is not under any undue pressure or that any fraud is involved in the making of the LPA application, we consider that this requirement should remain.

We do not, however, agree that the certificate provider must be a professional. Whilst we acknowledgment the benefits that their involvement can bring, all individuals should be able to complete the LPA forms and application process without having to seek assistance from a professional. Constraining the role of the certificate provider to only those who are professionals would force individuals to use their services and, most likely, to incur a cost.

8. How well do you think that the role of the certificate provider is operating and is it in the way that the MCA legislation intended?

Two thirds of respondents replied to this question. Of those, nearly half felt that the role of the certificate provider was effective and operating as the Mental Capacity Act had intended it to, while an equal number thought that the role was not working well, with the potential for fraud being cited as the main issue. Comments included:

"I think it is working well and as the MCA intended. It makes people stop and think which needs to be done when making an LPA."

"It provides valuable contemporaneous evidence of the donor's state of mind at the time of the making of the LPA."

A range of comments were made about how well the role of the certificate provider was operating, with some respondents feeling that the role was difficult for lay persons to undertake as they did not understand it fully and would be leading themselves open to criticism if the LPA was challenged. Others felt that lay certificate providers do carry out this role effectively. Some respondents also commented that the role should be combined with that of the witness to the donor's signature, thereby providing a more up-to-date assessment of the donor's capacity at the time the LPA is executed.

9.   What value do you think the role of the certificate provider might add to the process for making an LPA within a digital context?

Many respondents replied that the role of the certificate provider is no less important in a digital context than it is in a paper based one. It was queried how this role would work in a digital context:

"It will be imperative to identify the donor and ensure that their wishes are being accorded with."

"We are concerned that it will make it more difficult to ensure that the donor is fully involved in the process."

"The same protection that it adds is needed in a non digital form."

We agree that the role of the certificate provider remains an important safeguard and we intend to undertake further work to explore how this role might continue to provide the appropriate safeguards in a digital context. Any changes to the requirements for a certificate provider will be for the future and would require primary legislation.'

TRANSFORMING THE SERVICES OF THE OFFICE OF THE PUBLIC GUARDIAN: ENABLING DIGITAL BY DEFAULT (2013)

6.21 Just a year later, the Ministry of Justice published a further consultation paper, CP10/2013, *Transforming the Services of the Office of the Public Guardian: Enabling Digital by Default*. The consultation period began on 15 October 2013 and ended on 26 November 2013. A total of 424 responses to the consultation paper were received from a range of Ministry of Justice and OPG stakeholders, professional bodies, interested parties and members of the public. Most responses came from legal professionals, in the main solicitors, or organisations representing them. The response was published on 21 August 2014. In relation to the role of the certificate provider, the consultation paper asked the following questions and had the following responses:

'Q9. Do you agree that the renaming of 'certificate providers' and 'named persons' helps to clarify their roles?'

6.22 The majority of respondents answered 'yes' to this question. Where opinion was divided, respondents were more positive about the renaming of named persons than certificate providers, which some thought was already suitable.

In the end the recommendation was that there was to be no change to the term 'certificate provider'.

6.23

'Q12. Do you agree with the proposal that the requirement for a second certificate provider should be dispensed with?

Despite the majority of respondents not agreeing with the proposal, the Ministry of Justice recommended on page 20:

'the OPG's own examination of data informs us that of 993,500 live LPAs on their register only 12% have two certificate providers. Other respondents confirm the difficulties in trying to find a second certificate provider, particularly if the proposed donor is elderly and isolated, and the fact that this sometimes leads to additional costs for the donor if the second certificate provider is another professional. Having considered all of the above we will remove the requirement for the second certificate provider . . . '

6.24

'Q29. Are you in favour of the proposal to introduce legislation to create a fully digital LPA without physical signatures?';

'Q31. Are you in favour of the proposal to use online identity assurance to verify the identities of those involved in making an LPA?;

Q32. Are you in favour of the proposal that 'signing' the document would be completed in a digital context by each individual logging on securely with an assured ID and formally agreeing that they understand the nature of their role and agree to act in that capacity?; and

Q33. If you foresee any potential issues with implementing a fully digital approach, do you have any suggestions about how they might be addressed?'

The majority of respondents who replied were not in favour of the proposals to go fully digital. The major concerns were the potential for fraud and discrimination against the elderly. Fifty five respondents provided the following statement:

'The donor's wet signature is the best and probably only conclusive way of establishing his identity and intention, and is evidence of such. Although fraud can occur within the current system, the requirement for a wet signature enables a challenge to be made where there are concerns, through handwriting experts and contemporaneously, witnessed and signed by the certificate provider who has seen the donor execute the deed. This would not be possible within a digitally created power. Furthermore it would dilute the safeguarding function of the certificate provider who by seeing the donor is able to make a better judgment to complete the certificate. Safeguarding should never be a tick box exercise.'"

The Ministry of Justice confirmed that the OPG will continue to explore ways in which the development of a fully digital LPA can be made as safe and as secure as possible and they will consult on this once it has further proposals.

THE REQUIREMENT FOR A CERTIFICATE

6.25 MCA 2005, Sch 1, para 2(1)(e) provides that the instrument creating an LPA must include:

'a certificate by a person of a prescribed description that, in his opinion, at the time when the donor executes the instrument:
(i)   the donor understands the purpose of the instrument and the scope of the authority conferred under it,
(ii)   no fraud or undue pressure is being used to induce the donor to create a lasting power of attorney, and
(iii) there is nothing else which would prevent a lasting power of attorney from being created by the instrument.'

This is satisfied in the 2007 and 2009 prescribed forms by reference to the certificate provider forming an 'opinion', whereas the 2015 prescribed form frames this differently, so that the certificate states, 'as far as I'm aware'. It is submitted that the former implies some positive steps have been taken to ascertain the opinion, whereas the latter is a general expression indicating a level of awareness, where no positive steps may have been taken. Section 10 of the 2015 prescribed form states that in signing, the certificate provider confirms 'they've discussed the lasting power of attorney (LPA) with the donor, that the donor understands what they're doing and that nobody is forcing them to do it'. There is no longer any OPG guidance on what sort of questions the certificate provider should discuss with the donor. See **7.60–7.63** for more information on how the certificate provider should form his opinion.

PERSONS WHO MAY PROVIDE THE CERTIFICATE

6.26 The Lasting Powers of Attorney, Enduring Powers of Attorney and Public Guardian Regulations 2007 (LPA, EPA & PG Regs 2007), reg 8 states who can and cannot give an LPA certificate.

6.27 Regulation 8(1) says that, subject to reg 8(3), the following persons may give an LPA certificate:

'(a)   a person chosen by the donor as being someone who has known him personally for the period of at least two years which ends immediately before the date on which that person signs the LPA certificate;

(b)   a person chosen by the donor who, on account of his professional skills and expertise, reasonably considers that he is competent to make the judgments necessary to certify the matters set out in paragraph (2)(1)(e) of Schedule 1 to the Act.'

These are respectively referred to in the remainder of this chapter as Category A – Knowledge certification, and Category B – Skills certification.

The certificate provider must be chosen by the donor

6.28 The LPA, EPA & PG Regs 2007, reg 8(1) provides that the person providing the certificate, whether by way of knowledge certification or skills certification, must be chosen by the donor.

Category A – Knowledge certification

6.29 Regulation 8(1)(a) says that, subject to reg 8(3), the following persons may give an LPA certificate:

'a person chosen by the donor as being someone who has known him personally for the period of at least two years which ends immediately before the date on which that person signs the LPA certificate.'

6.30 The certificate itself in Section 10 of the prescribed form of LPA requires the certificate provider to confirm that, 'the donor has chosen me as someone who has known them personally for at least 2 years'. In contrast the 2009 prescribed form required the following confirmation, 'I have known the donor for at least two years and as more than an acquaintance. My personal knowledge of the donor is:'. The certificate provider was then required to describe the nature of their personal knowledge of the donor. The OPG's former guidance to certificate providers in CHAPTER 4 of LPA 111 and LPA112 stated:

'If you are forming your opinion as someone who has known the donor personally, personal knowledge of the donor could include:

- "I have been a neighbour for 5 years, and I have frequently talked at length with the donor."
- "We attend the same congregation at church every week."
- "I am a close friend who meets the donor in the pub every fortnight. I've known him since 1932".'

The OPG's publication, *Making and registering your LPA – a guide* (LP12), at Part 10A advises the Category A certificate provider can be 'a friend, colleague or someone you've known well for at least two years – they must be more than just an acquaintance.' The 2015 prescribed form gives the following examples, 'a friend, neighbour, colleague or former colleague', but there is no requirement to expressly set out the nature of the personal knowledge, so there is no method to check whether this requirement has been satisfied.

6.31 Regulation 9(4) provides that the certificate provider must complete the LPA certificate at Section 10 of the instrument and sign it 'as soon as reasonably practicable' after the donor has completed Sections 1 to 7 of the form that apply to him, sign Section 9, and Section 5 in respect of a health and welfare LPA in the presence of a witness. Although the whole point of completing a capacity assessment is that capacity is 'time-specific' as well as 'decision-specific', it is conceivable that, in some cases, there could be a delay between the completion and signing of Section 9, and the completion and signing of Section 10. In such a case, the relevant date for the purposes of qualifying for Category A – Knowledge certification is the period of 2 years ending immediately before the date on which the certificate provider completes and signs Section 10, rather than the date on which the donor completed and signed Section 9. The certificate provider's opinion should be based on the date the donor signed Section 9, and not the date the certificate provider signs Section 10.

6.32 It is submitted that the following persons would *not* be competent to give an LPA certificate under Category A – Knowledge certification:

- anyone who has known the donor for a period of less than 2 years;
- anyone who has known the donor during the last 2 years but is disqualified from giving an LPA certificate by virtue of reg 8(3);
- an 'in-law' – for example, brother-in-law, sister-in-law, son-in-law, daughter-in-law – of the donor or a donee, on the basis that they are a 'family member' for the purposes of reg 8(3);
- a 'step' relative – such as a stepson, stepdaughter, stepbrother, stepsister, etc – of the donor or a donee, on the basis that they also are a 'family member' for the purposes of reg 8(3).

6.33 It is unclear whether the following persons would be competent to give an LPA certificate:

- a former spouse or civil partner of the donor or a donee; or
- a former spouse or civil partner of a blood relative of the donor or a donee.

6.34 It is submitted that the following persons would be competent to give an LPA certificate under Category A – Knowledge certification, even though, in some cases, it may be inadvisable for the donor to choose them for that purpose:

- a former business partner or former employee of the donor or attorney;
- the owner, director, manager or employee of any care home in which the donor lived before he moved to the care home in which he is currently living – provided that they continued to remain in contact with him during the period of 2 years immediately before they complete and sign the LPA certificate.

Category B – Skills certification

6.35 The LPA, EPA & PG Regs 2007, reg 8(1)(b) states that the certificate provider may be someone chosen by the donor who, on account of his professional skills and expertise, reasonably considers that he is competent to make the judgments necessary to certify the matters he is required to certify.

6.36 Regulation 8(2) provides that:

'The following are examples of persons within paragraph 1(b) –
(a)   a registered health care professional,
(b)   a barrister, solicitor, or advocate called or admitted in any part of the United Kingdom,
(c)   a registered social worker, or
(d)   an independent mental capacity advocate.'

6.37 Regulation 8(2) simply gives examples of persons who may, on account of their professional skills and expertise, reasonably consider that they are competent to make the judgments necessary to give an LPA certificate. The list is not exhaustive, and there are other persons who may have the relevant skills and expertise, but whose professional qualifications are not included in this list. Obvious examples are members and fellows of the Chartered Institute of Legal Executives, or members of STEP (the Society of Trust and Estate Practitioners), who are neither barristers nor solicitors. Such people may, nevertheless, give an LPA certificate. The 2009 prescribed form itself states:

'I have relevant professional skills. (Please state your profession – for example, a GP or solicitor – and then the particular skills that are relevant to you forming your opinion – for example, a consultant specialising in geriatric care.)

My profession and particular skills are:'.

The requirement to qualify the Category B certificate provider's skills and expertise has been removed in the 2015 prescribed form, which merely contains a general confirmation that 'the donor has chosen me as a person with relevant professional skills and expertise.' The consequence is that there is no method to check whether the Category B certificate provider meets the statutory requirements.

6.38 It is submitted that, although the list in reg 8(2) is not exhaustive, the legislation anticipates that skills certification will be carried out by a member of a profession, with 'the relevant professional skills and expertise', and that, by and large, this requirement will be construed *eiusdem generis* with the occupations contained in reg 8(2) to restrict the ability to give an LPA certificate under Category B – Skills certification to professional persons who have relevant experience or training, or a combination of experience or training in:

* dealing with people who lack capacity to make a decision for themselves because of an impairment of, or a disturbance in the functioning of, their mind or brain; or
* preparing and advising clients on legal documents, and in particular LPAs.

Registered health care professionals

6.39 The LPA, EPA & PG Regs 2007, reg 8(4) states that a 'registered health care professional' means a person who is a member of a profession regulated by a body mentioned in s 25(3) of the National Health Service Reform and Health Care Professions Act 2002. The bodies mentioned in that subsection are:

'(a) the General Medical Council,
(b) the General Dental Council,
(c) the General Optical Council,
(d) the General Osteopathic Council,
(e) the General Chiropractic Council,
(f) subject to section 26(5), the Royal Pharmaceutical Society of Great Britain,
(g) subject to section 26(6), the Pharmaceutical Society of Northern Ireland,
(h) until their abolition by virtue of section 60(3) of the Health Act 1999 –
    (i) the United Kingdom Central Council for Nursing, Midwifery and Health Visiting, and each of the National Boards for Nursing, Midwifery and Health Visiting, and
    (ii) the Council for Professions Supplementary to Medicine and each Board established by or by virtue of the Professions Supplementary to Medicine Act 1960,
(i) any regulatory body (within the meaning of Schedule 3 to the 1999 Act) established by an Order in Council under section 60 of that Act as a successor to a body mentioned in paragraph (h), and
(j) any other regulatory body (within that meaning) established by an Order in Council under that section.'

Barristers, solicitors or advocates

6.40 The LPA, EPA & PG Regs 2007, reg 8(2)(b) gives 'barristers, solicitors or advocates called or admitted in any part of the United Kingdom' as an example of persons who may, on account of their professional skills and expertise, reasonably consider that they are competent to make the judgments necessary to provide an LPA certificate.

6.41 Regulation 8(2)(b) refers to barristers, solicitors or advocates who have been 'called or admitted in any part of the United Kingdom', and it is submitted that the reference to 'called or admitted' limits the scope of this example to persons who are legally qualified, thus excluding 'advocates' in the usual sense of the term. Such persons may, nevertheless, be competent to give an LPA certificate, but will need to describe their relevant professional skills and expertise in the certificate itself. As stated in **6.37**, reg 8(2)(b) does not expressly include legal executives, or members of the Society of Trust and Estate Practitioners, professional will writers and various other persons who may have the relevant legal skills and expertise to provide an LPA certificate.

Registered social workers

6.42 The LPA, EPA & PG Regs 2007, reg 8(4) states that:

'"registered social worker" means a person registered as a social worker in a register maintained by:
(a)   the Health and Care Professional Council,
(b)   Social Care Wales,
(c)   the Scottish Social Services Council, or
(d)   the Northern Ireland Social Care Council.'

Independent mental capacity advocates

6.43 Sections 35 to 41 of the MCA 2005 deal with the appointment and functions of independent mental capacity advocates (IMCAs), whose function is to provide support and present the views of any person, who has no family or friends to support him, and who lacks the capacity to consent to proposals where:

- an NHS body is proposing to provide serious medical treatment for him (s 37(1)); or
- he is being placed in NHS accommodation, or arrangements are being made for a change in his accommodation to another hospital or care home (s 38); or
- he is being placed in residential accommodation provided by a local authority, or arrangements are being made for a change in his residential accommodation (s 39).

6.44 The Mental Capacity Act 2005 (Independent Mental Capacity Advocate) (Expansion of Role) Regulations 2006 in England (SI 2006/2883) and The Mental Capacity Act 2005 (Independent Mental Capacity Advocates) (Wales) Regulations 2007 (SI 2007/852) (w.77) in Wales gives local authorities and NHS bodies additional powers to instruct IMCAs in care reviews and in adult protection cases, and reg 8(2)(d) of the LPA, EPA & PG Regs 2007 provides that an IMCA may be a Category B certificate provider.

6.45 The Mental Capacity Act 2005 (Independent Mental Capacity Advocate) (General) Regulations 2006 (SI 2006/1832) in England and The Mental Capacity Act 2005 (Independent Mental Capacity Advocates) (Wales) Regulations 2007 (SI 2007/852) (w.77) set out the details on how an IMCA is appointed, and his functions, including his role in challenging the decision maker, and provide definitions of 'serious medical treatment' and 'NHS body'. Regulation 5 of the English Regulations provides for the appointment of IMCAs as follows:

'(1)   No person may be appointed to act as an IMCA for the purposes of sections 37 to 39 of the Act, or regulations made by virtue of section 41 of the Act, unless –

        (a)   he is for the time being approved by a local authority on the grounds that he satisfies the appointment requirements,

        (b)   he belongs to a class of persons which is for the time being approved by a local authority on the grounds that all persons in that class satisfy the appointment requirements.

(2)   The appointment requirements, in relation to a person appointed to act as an IMCA, are that –

        (a)   he has appropriate experience or training or an appropriate combination of experience and training;

        (b)   he is a person of integrity and good character; and

        (c)   he is able to act independently of any person who instructs him.

(3)   Before a determination is made in relation to any person for the purposes of paragraph (2)(b), there must be obtained in respect of that person –

        (a)   an enhanced criminal record certificate issued pursuant to section 113B of the Police Act 1997; or

        (b)   if the purpose for which the certificate is required is not one prescribed under subsection (2) of that section, a criminal record certificate issued pursuant to section 113A of that Act.'

The Welsh Regulations are not identical, although the meaning and effect is the same.

When should professionals be involved?

6.46 Paragraphs 4.51 to 4.54 of the Mental Capacity Act 2005 Code of Practice give the following guidance on when there may be a need to get a professional opinion when assessing a person's capacity to make complex or major decisions.

'4.51   Anyone assessing someone's capacity may need to get a professional opinion when assessing a person's capacity to make complex or major decisions. In some cases this will simply involve contacting the person's general practitioner (GP) or family doctor. If the person has a particular condition or disorder, it may be appropriate to contact a specialist (for example, consultant psychiatrist, psychologist, or other professional with experience of caring for patients with that condition). A speech and language therapist might be able to help if there are communication difficulties. In some cases, a multi-disciplinary approach is best. This means combining the skills and expertise of different professionals.

4.52   Professionals should never express an opinion without carrying out a proper examination and assessment of the person's capacity to make a decision. They must apply the appropriate test of capacity. In some cases, they will need to meet the person more than once – particularly if the person has communication difficulties. Professionals can get background information from a person's family and carers. But the personal views of these people about what they want for the person who lacks capacity must not influence the outcome of that assessment.

4.53   Professional involvement might be needed if:
- the decision that needs to be made is complicated or has serious consequences.
- an assessor concludes a person lacks capacity, and the person challenges the finding.
- family members, carers and/or professionals disagree about a person's capacity.

- there is a conflict of interest between the assessor and the person being assessed.
- the person being assessed is expressing different views to different people – they may be trying to please everyone or telling people what they think they want to hear.
- somebody might challenge the person's capacity to make a decision – either at the time of the decision or later (for example, a family member might challenge a will after a person has died on the basis that the person lacked capacity when they made the will.
- somebody has been accused of abusing a vulnerable adult who may lack capacity to make decisions that protect them.
- a person repeatedly makes decisions that put them at risk or could result in suffering or damage.

4.54   In some cases, it may be a legal requirement, or good professional practice, to undertake a formal assessment of capacity. These cases include:

- where a person's capacity to sign a legal document (for example, a will) could later be challenged, in which case an expert should be asked for an opinion (*Kenward v Adams, The Times*, 29 November 1975).
- to establish whether a person who might be involved in a legal case needs the assistance of the Official Solicitor or other litigation friend (somebody to represent their views to a court and give instructions to their legal representative) and there is doubt about the person's capacity to instruct a solicitor or take part in the case (Civil Procedure Rules 1998, r 21.1).
- whenever the Court of Protection has to decide if a person lacks capacity in a certain matter.
- if the courts are required to make a decision about a person's capacity in other legal proceedings (*Masterman-Lister v Brutton & Co* [2002] EWCA Civ 1889, CA at 54).
- If there may be legal consequences of a finding of capacity (for example, deciding on financial compensation following a claim for personal injury).'

PERSONS WHO ARE DISQUALIFIED FROM GIVING A CERTIFICATE

6.47 The LPA, EPA & PG Regs 2007, reg 8(3) states that:

'A person is disqualified from giving an LPA certificate in respect of any instrument intended to create a lasting power of attorney if that person is –
(a)   a family member of the donor;
(b)   a donee of that power;
(c)   a donee of –
   (i)   any other lasting power of attorney, or
   (ii)   an enduring power of attorney,
which has been executed by the donor (whether or not it has been revoked);
(d)   a family member of a donee within sub-paragraph (b);
(e)   a director or employee of a trust corporation acting as a donee within sub-paragraph (b);
(f)   a business partner or employee of –
   (i)   the donor,
   (ii)   a donee within sub-paragraph (b);
(g)   an owner, director, manager or employee of any care home in which the donor is living when the instrument is executed; or
(h)   a family member of a person within sub-paragraph (g).'

Regulation 8(4) states that 'care home' has the meaning given in s 3 of the Care Standards Act 2000, as amended by the Health and Social Care Act 2008, which provides that:

'(1)   For the purposes of this Act, an establishment is a care home if it provides accommodation, together with nursing or personal care, for any of the following persons.

(2)   They are –
   (a)   persons who are or have been ill;
   (b)   persons who have or have had a mental disorder;
   (c)   persons who are disabled or infirm;
   (d)   persons who are or have been dependent on alcohol or drugs.

(3)   But an establishment is not a care home in Wales if it is –
   (a)   a hospital;
   (b)   an independent clinic; or
   (c)   a children's home
   or if it is of a description excepted by regulations.'

(4)   And an establishment in England is not a care home if it is –
   (a)   a hospital (within the meaning of the National Health Service Act 2006; or
   (b)   a children's home
   or if it is of a description excepted by regulations.'

6.48 Regulation 8(3)(f) of the LPA, EPA & PG Regs 2007 is particularly significant in the context of a solicitors' practice. It is not possible for a member of staff to act as a certificate provider and witness if a partner in the firm is being appointed as an attorney.

FORMER REQUIREMENT FOR TWO CERTIFICATES WHERE THE INSTRUMENT HAS NO NAMED PERSONS

6.49 Schedule 1, para 2(1)(c) of the MCA 2005 states that:

'2
(1)   The instrument must include . . .
   (c)   a statement by the donor –
      (i)   naming a person or persons whom the donor wishes to be notified of any application for the registration of the instrument, or
      (ii)   stating that there are no persons whom he wishes to be notified of any such application.'

Schedule 1, para 2(2) states that:

'Regulations may –
   (a)   prescribe a maximum number of named persons;
   (b)   provide that, where the instrument includes a statement under sub-paragraph (1)(c)(ii), two persons of a prescribed description must each give a certificate under sub-paragraph (1)(e).'

6.50 Until removed by reg 6 of the 2015 Amendment Regulations, The LPA, EPA & PG Regs 2007, reg 7 provided as follows:

'Where an instrument intended to create a lasting power of attorney includes a statement by the donor that there are no persons whom he wishes to be notified of any application for the registration of the instrument –
   (a)   the instrument must include two LPA certificates; and
   (b)   each certificate must be completed and signed by a different person.'

For LPAs made before 1 July 2015, it does not matter whether the two certificates were provided under Category A – Knowledge certification, or under Category B – Skills certification, or a combination of the two categories.

THE ROLE AND RESPONSIBILITIES OF A CERTIFICATE PROVIDER

The certificate provider must act independently

6.51 The 2007 and 2009 prescribed forms for creating an LPA, required the certificate provider to confirm that they were acting independently. This was an additional requirement to not being disqualified by regulation 8. In the prescribed form introduced by the LPA, EPA & PG (Amendment) Regs 2009, the certificate provider is required to make the following 'statement of acting independently':

> 'I confirm that I act independently of the attorneys and of the donor and I am aged 18 or over.'

The 2015 prescribed form contains no reference to acting independently, presumably because the meaning of 'acting independently' in this context is not entirely clear. However, the OPG publication *Make and Register your LPA – a guide* (LP12) in Part 10A states 'A certificate provider is an impartial person'.

6.52 In response to enquiries from solicitors who regularly prepare LPAs for clients and were concerned that they may not be construed as 'acting independently' of their clients, The Law Society expressed the view that, as long as the solicitor is not a donee of the power, and not someone who falls within classes of disqualified persons set out in reg 8(3) of the LPA, EPA and PG Regulations 2007, then they can act as the certificate provider. The Law Society interprets the reference to 'acting independently' as simply reinforcing the provisions of reg 8(3): namely, that someone is acting independently if they are unconnected with the donor in terms of a family relationship, and is not a donee of the power, or associated with the donee as a family member, employee, director, business partner, etc.

Guidance

6.53 Until July 2015, the OPG produced two booklets for potential donors: LPA111, *Guidance for people who want to make a lasting power of attorney for health and welfare,* and LPA112, *Guidance for people who want to make a lasting power of attorney for property and financial affairs.* Chapter 4 of each booklet provided important guidance to certificate providers. For the guidance on how certificate providers should assess the donor's capacity, see **7.60-7.63.**

6.54 The first paragraph of Part B of the 2009 prescribed forms of LPA expressly refers to the guidance in LPA111 and LPA112 in the following terms:

> 'Please refer to separate guidance for certificate providers. If the guidance is not followed, this lasting power of attorney may not be valid and could be rejected when an application is made to register it'.

The OPG's guidance, *Making and registering your LPA – a guide* (LP12) at Part 10A is aimed at the donor so unless this is provided to the certificate provider, he may not be aware of the full extent of what is required of the role and its responsibilities.

6.55 Further discussion on the certificate provider's functions can be found in paras **7.54-7.66**.

CASE-LAW ON THE ELIGIBILITY OF CERTIFICATE PROVIDERS

6.56 The OPG website previously contained summaries of three decisions of the Senior Judge of the Court of Protection relating to the eligibility of a certificate provider. All case digests have since been removed, following the consolidation of public departments and agencies websites into www.gov.uk.

'1.   *Re Kittle* (1 December 2009). A cousin is not a 'family member for the purposes of the LPA, EPA & PG Regs 2007, reg 8(3).
      On 29 December 2008 Mrs Kittle executed an LPA for property and affairs. A legal executive witnessed her signature and on 5 January 2009 a man called Roy completed the certificate in Part B of the prescribed form. In response to the question 'How do you know the donor?' Roy said, 'We are cousins.' The OPG refused to register the LPA because the certificate provider was 'a family member of the donor' and the attorneys applied to the Court of Protection to determine the matter under MCA 2005 s 22(2)(a).
      HELD the Court of Protection, which was presented with a variety of authorities that decided the matter either way, chose to apply the decision of the Court of Appeal in a Rent Act case, *Langdon v Horton* [1951] 1 All ER 60, and held that a cousin should not be regarded as 'a family member of the donor' or, for that matter, a family member of the donee or a care home owner for the purposes of the LPA, EPA & PG Regs 2007, reg 8(3).

2.   *Re Putt* (22 March 2011). An employee of a limited liability partnership, in which two of the partners were appointed as attorneys, was ineligible to act as a certificate provider.
      On 5 August 2010 Mrs Putt executed an LPA for property and financial affairs and an LPA for health and welfare, in which she appointed a family member and two solicitors to be her attorneys. The solicitors are partners in M Solicitors LLP. An associate solicitor with M Solicitors LLP witnessed her signature and provided the certificate in Part B of both LPAs. Regulation 8(3)(f) of the Lasting Powers of Attorney, Enduring Powers of Attorney and Public Guardian Regulations 2007 provides that: "A person is disqualified from giving an LPA certificate in respect of any instrument intended to create a lasting power of attorney if that person is a business partner or employee of (i) the donor, (ii) a donee within sub-paragraph (b)."
      HELD: the wording of regulation 8(3)(f) cannot be construed as distinguishing between a partnership under the Partnership Act 1890 and the Limited Liability Partnership Act 2000 for the purpose of providing an LPA certificate and that, as the associate solicitor was an employee of M Solicitors LLP, she was ineligible to provide the certificates in Mrs Putt's LPAs.

3.   *Re Phillips* (16 May 2012). A certificate provider who described himself as the attorney's 'partner' was a member of the attorney's family and was accordingly ineligible to act as a certificate provider.
      On 26 January 2011 Mrs Phillips signed an LPA for property and financial affairs, in which she appointed three attorneys, including her daughter A, and named nobody to be notified when an application was made to register

the instrument. S witnessed her signature and acted as one of the two Part B certificate providers. In describing how he knew the donor, he said, "I am the partner of [A], and have known the donor for 3 years." The OPG refused to register the LPA because the certificate provider was a member of the attorney's family. A applied to the court for a direction to register the LPA and the Public Guardian was joined as respondent.

HELD: that S was to be regarded as a member of A's family, and so he was ineligible to be a certificate provider and the LPA could not be registered. The judge said: "The OPG currently receives in the region of 175,000 applications to register Lasting Powers of Attorney each year and . . . anything that would require it to investigate and examine the nature, duration and intimacy of a relationship between an attorney and an LPA certificate provider would be impracticable and disproportionate. . . . In my judgment, anyone who describes himself in this context as the attorney's partner is courting trouble and automatically disqualifies himself from being a person who can give an LPA certificate. This applies regardless of whether he describes himself as the attorney's partner intentionally or inadvertently, whether they live at the same address or at separate locations, whether the relationship is intimate or platonic, and whether the statement is true or false".'

Chapter 7

EXECUTION OF A LASTING POWER OF ATTORNEY

SUMMARY

7.1 An instrument intended to create a lasting power of attorney (LPA) must be:

- in the prescribed form; and
- executed in accordance with reg 9 of the Lasting Powers of Attorney, Enduring Powers of Attorney and Public Guardian Regulations 2007 (LPA, EPA & PG Regs 2007).

7.2 There are two prescribed forms:

- one for property and financial affairs; and
- one for health and welfare.

7.3 Each current prescribed form contains:

- Section 8 which contains prescribed information headed, 'Your legal rights and responsibilities;
- Section 9 – Declaration by the donor;
- Section 10 – Declaration by the certificate provider; and
- Section 11 – Declaration by each attorney or replacement attorney.

7.4 There are two additional pages at the front of the form which are not part of the prescribed form and give limited guidance on how to complete the form and to make notes of the names of people who will be involved in the making of the LPA.

7.5 In addition to the prescribed information in the LPA itself, the Office of the Public Guardian (OPG) has produced *Make and register your lasting power of attorney: a guide* (LP12), aimed at the donor. This is referred to as 'the Guide' within the margin notes throughout each prescribed form. The guidance provides an explanation of how to complete each Section of the prescribed form.

7.6 Before signing or marking the LPA, the donor must have read (or have read to him):

- Section 8 in the prescribed form headed 'Your legal rights and responsibilities'; and

- all the information contained in Sections 1–7 and Section 9 and any continuation sheet.

7.7 The donor must sign Section 9 and any continuation sheets to the LPA in the presence of a witness and in the case of an LPA for health and welfare, the donor must also sign Option A or Option B, in Section 5, in the presence of a witness. Option A says, 'I give my attorneys authority to give or refuse consent to life-sustaining treatment on my behalf.' Option B is where the donor does not want to give the attorneys such authority.

7.8 The person who witnesses the donor's signature:

- must be 18 or over;
- cannot be an attorney or replacement attorney;
- can be the certificate provider;
- can be a named person, or people to notify when an application is made to register the LPA; and
- must initial any changes made in Sections 1–7.

7.9 The regulations and the prescribed forms make allowances for where the donor is unable to sign or make a mark. In such a case:

- the LPA can be signed by someone else at the donor's direction, in the donor's presence, and in the presence of two witnesses;
- the person signing must be at least 18 years of age, and must not be an attorney, replacement attorney or the certificate provider; and
- the two witnesses must be at least 18, must not be an attorney or replacement attorney but may be the certificate provider.

7.10 As soon as reasonably practicable after the above steps, the certificate provider(s) should:

- consider whether there is a restriction which prevents him from acting as a certificate provider;
- understand his role as a certificate provider;
- read Sections 1–7 of the LPA so he can discuss with the donor the scope of the authority being granted and its purpose;
- where possible, discuss the LPA with the donor in private, and away from the attorney(s);
- read 'Your legal rights and responsibilities' on Section 8;
- have no doubt about the donor's identity;
- assess the donor's capacity to create the LPA;
- (optional) keep a record of their assessment; and
- complete the certificate in Section 10 of the instrument, and sign it.

7.11 As soon as reasonably practicable after the above steps, the attorney(s) must:

- read Sections 1–7 of the LPA;
- read (or have read to them) 'Your legal rights and responsibilities' in Section 8;
- read and complete Section 11 of the instrument; and
- sign it in the presence of a witness.

7.12 The person who witnesses the attorney's signature:

- must be at least 18 years of age;

- can be another attorney or replacement attorney;
- can be the certificate provider;
- can be a named person, or person to notify when an application is made to register the LPA; but
- cannot be the donor.

THE PRESCRIBED FORM

An LPA must be in the prescribed form

7.13 Section 9 of the Mental Capacity Act 2005 (MCA 2005) states that:

'(1)   A lasting power of attorney is a power of attorney under which the donor ("P") confers on the donee (or donees) authority to make decisions about all or any of the following –

(a)   P's personal welfare or specified matters concerning P's personal welfare, and

(b)   P's property and affairs or specified matters concerning P's property and affairs.

and which includes authority to make such decisions in circumstances where P no longer has capacity.

(2)   A lasting power of attorney is not created unless –

(a)   section 10 is complied with,

(b)   an instrument conferring authority of the kind mentioned in subsection (1) is made and registered in accordance with Schedule 1, and

(c)   at the time when P executes the instrument, P has reached 18 and has the capacity to execute it.

(3)   An instrument which –

(a)   purports to create a lasting power of attorney, but

(b)   does not comply with this section, section 10, or Schedule 1, confers no authority.'

7.14 Schedule 1, para 1 states that:

'(1)   An instrument is not made in accordance with this Schedule unless –

(a)   it is in the prescribed form,

(b)   it complies with paragraph 2, and

(c)   any prescribed requirements in connection with its execution are satisfied.

(2)   Regulations may make different provision according to whether –

(a)   the instrument relates to personal welfare or to property and affairs (or to both);

(b)   only one or more than one donee is to be appointed (and if more than one, whether jointly or jointly and severally).

(3)   In this Schedule –

(a)   "prescribed" means prescribed by regulations, and

(b)   "regulations" means regulations made for the purposes of this Schedule by the Lord Chancellor.'

7.15 There are three versions of the prescribed forms, set out in Regulations:

- The first (the 2007 forms) set out in the original Lasting Power of Attorney, Enduring Power of Attorney and Public Guardian Regulations 2007 (LPA, EPA & PG Regs 2007), are 25 pages long and are known as 'property and affairs' and 'personal welfare' powers respectively. These prescribed forms could be made between 1 October 2007 until 31 March 2011. The donor must have executed the LPA before the 1 April 2011.

- The second (the 2009 forms) were laid in the Lasting Powers of Attorney, Enduring Powers of Attorney and Public Guardian (Amendment) Regulations 2009. The 2009 forms were renamed as a 'property and financial affairs lasting power' and a 'health and welfare lasting power'. Named persons were renamed 'people to be notified'. The 2009 forms could be granted from 1 October 2009 until 31 December 2015. The 2009 form was amended slightly on 1 April 2013, to change the period in which an objection to the registration can be made from five weeks to three weeks, calculated from the date the objector was notified of the application to register the power.

  The 2009 forms are 12 pages long, contain guidance and come with a number of separate continuation sheets, which are explained in more detail in **7.28**.

  Each LPA form is divided into three parts:

  (i) **Part A** – a donor's statement that includes details of the attorney(s) being appointed, how they are to act, the persons to be notified when an application to register is made and a statement by the donor confirming his understanding of the power.

  (ii) **Part B** – a certificate by an independent person confirming no undue pressure or fraud is involved in the decision to make an LPA and that the donor understands the scope and power of the LPA.

  (iii) **Part C** – a statement by the attorney(s) confirming that they understand their duties and obligations as an attorney.

- The third (the 2015 forms) were laid in the Lasting Powers of Attorney, Enduring Powers of Attorney and Public Guardian (Amendment) Regulations 2015 and can be granted by the donor from 1 July 2015. The forms are simplified to make it easier to make and are available to complete on-line using the OPG's digital tool, although they still need to be printed off and signed with wet signatures by all parties. The LPA for property and financial affairs is identified as 'LP1F' and the LPA for health and welfare is identified as 'LP1H'. Both run to 15 pages. In addition, the registration application form follows on from each LPA. There are separate continuation sheets, which are generic so can be used regardless of the type of power being made. See **7.29** below.

7.16 The 2015 LPA forms are no longer divided into three distinct parts, instead:

- what was previously Part A is now contained in Sections 1–7;
- what was previously Part B is now contained in Section 10; and
- what was previously Part C is contained in Section 11.

The prescribed information which the donor, certificate provider, attorneys, and replacement attorneys must read before signing, which was historically always on the first page, is now in Section 8 of the form. There is no longer a need to have two independent certificates of understanding if the donor chooses to tell nobody of the registration of the LPA.

7.17 The LPA, EPA & PG (Amendment) Regs 2009, reg 6 contained a transitional provision whereby an instrument executed by the donor before 1 April 2011 in one of the forms prescribed in the 2007 Regs would be capable of being an LPA. In *Re Lane* (Senior Judge Lush, 24 January 2011), Mrs Lane executed two LPAs in the forms prescribed by the 2007 Regs on 3 May 2011, five weeks after the transitional period in reg 6 had expired. In both LPAs she envisaged that the survivor of two jointly appointed replacement attorneys would be able to act. The Public Guardian applied to the court to sever the invalid provisions and at the same time drew the court's attention to the date on which the LPAs were executed, submitting that the 'old' forms were not materially different from the 'new' forms. The court accepted that the difference was immaterial and accordingly it fell within the MCA 2005, Sch 1, para 3(1), which provides that, if an instrument differs in an immaterial respect in form or mode of expression from the prescribed form, it is to be treated as sufficient in point of form and expression. The LPA, EPA & PG (Amendment) Regulations 2015, reg 17 contains a similar transitional provision whereby an instrument executed by the donor before 1 January 2016 in one of the 2009 prescribed forms would be capable of being an LPA.

Two prescribed forms

7.18 The LPA, EPA & PG Regs 2007, reg 5 states:

'The forms set out in Parts 1 and 2 of Schedule 1 to these Regulations are the forms which, in the circumstances to which they apply, are to be used for instruments intended to create a lasting power of attorney.'

7.19 Schedule 1, Part 1 is the form for the instrument intended to create a property and financial affairs LPA. Schedule 1, Part 2 is the form for the instrument intended to create a health and welfare LPA. Schedule 1 in the 2007 Regulations was most recently substituted by the Schedule to the LPA, EPA & PG (Amendment) Regs 2015, reg 11.

7.20 In its consultation paper on *Lasting Powers of Attorney – forms and guidance* (CP 01/06), published on 20 January 2006, the Department for Constitutional Affairs gave the following reasons for prescribing two forms, rather than one or three:

'The Act says that an LPA must be in the prescribed form though it does not specify how many forms there should be. Prescribed form means that the format of the form is set down in regulations.

In a prescribed form there must be 'prescribed information' and a 'certificate' to confirm the donor (the person making the LPA) understands the LPA.

We propose to create two prescribed forms – one for making an LPA in relation to property and affairs and one for making an LPA in relation to personal welfare. We accept that there will be people who wish the same person to act in relation to both their personal welfare and their property and affairs. Under these proposals two separate forms (and two separate certificates) would be required, one for each area.

We consider that a single form would be too cumbersome in practice and confusing for those simply wishing to make an LPA in relation to one area or the other. A single form for both types of LPA could be misleading as an LPA for property and affairs can be used when the donor has capacity and when the donor lacks capacity, whereas an LPA for personal welfare can only be used when the donor lacks capacity.

We considered creating a third form for use when someone wishes to appoint the same person as an LPA with powers in respect of their personal welfare and property and affairs. However we do not think that this is desirable. For example, a donor may want to include particular instructions about his or her healthcare on their personal welfare LPA but they would not wish this information to be seen by financial institutions who are following the property and affairs LPA.'

7.21 The consultation paper invited views on this issue, and specifically asked 'Is creating two separate forms, one for personal welfare and one for property and affairs, the most appropriate way forward?' 84 out of 118 respondents answered this question, and in its response to consultation, *Lasting Powers of Attorney – forms and guidance* (CP(R) 01/06), published on 17 July 2006, the Department for Constitutional Affairs said, at page 42:

'We will implement the proposal for two forms: one for personal welfare and one for property and affairs. We are not going to change the names of the forms because they mirror the provisions of section 9 of the Mental Capacity Act. We will, however, give more thought to how we can show what matters donors can cover under each of the different types of form.'

7.22 In 2012 the Ministry of Justice published a consultation paper, CP10/2012, called *Transforming the Services of the Office of the Public Guardian: A Consultation*. The consultation period began on 27 July 2012 and ended on 19 October 2012. On page 9 the following question was asked, 'Are there any reasons why a "hybrid LPA form", covering both property and affairs and health and welfare, should not be introduced?'

7.23 The Ministry of Justice published a response to the consultation on 22 January 2013, *Transforming the Services of the Office of the Public Guardian*, CP(R) 23/2012. On page 10 the response stated:

'Overall, the responses to the changes in the LPA forms and the possible introduction of a "hybrid" form (covering both property and affairs and health and welfare) were broadly positive. Many respondents wanted to see a prototype of the proposed hybrid form in order to give a more informed response. We agree that this is the most appropriate way forward.

We intend to develop a draft "hybrid" form, taking on board all the detailed and technical comments made during the consultation. We are also mindful that many responses were concerned that a "hybrid" form would not become the default option. We will therefore consult on a potential "hybrid" form alongside any revisions to the existing forms in more detail in 2013.'

Meaning of 'in the prescribed form'

7.24 An instrument which appears to correspond with the form set out in the Regulations may not necessarily be 'in the prescribed form'. The 2007 and 2009 prescribed forms required, among other things, the inclusion of numerous confirmatory statements. If the legislation had not adopted the 'place a cross in the box' approach, then it would have been the case that an instrument including all these statements would have been in the prescribed form. However, the confirmatory statements are included only if they are complete.

They are incomplete if they have not been crossed by way of confirmation. If any of these statements have not been completed, the position is the same as if the instrument did not include such a statement at all. An instrument which does not include an essential confirmatory statement cannot be regarded as made in the prescribed form. The question then arises as to whether the instrument differs in an immaterial respect in form or mode of expression from the prescribed form, so that para 3(2) of Sch 1 to MCA 2005 may apply. To avoid complications, the 2015 prescribed forms have removed the need to expressly indicate acceptance of confirmatory statements.

Continuation sheets

7.25 In the guidance notes to the forms prescribed by the LPA, EPA & PG Regs 2007, donors were advised that:

> 'If there is not enough room for you to express your intentions in any Part or paragraph of the LPA, you should continue on a separate sheet and attach it securely at the back of the LPA. You should sign and date any continuation sheets and note clearly which Part and paragraph of the LPA they relate to.'

7.26 Additional appointments, restrictions or guidance were set out on separate sheets of paper, which were not part of the prescribed form itself, and there was a risk that a fraud could be committed by additions being inserted after the donor had signed the instrument but before an application had been made to register it.

7.27 The prescribed forms of LPA were reviewed in 2009, and in *Reviewing the Mental Capacity Act 2005: forms, supervision and fees*, the response to consultation CP(R) 26/08, published on 11 March 2009, the Ministry of Justice recommended, at page 23, 'that there are prescribed continuation sheets to reduce fraud and to ensure the acceptance of the power by third parties.'

7.28 Accordingly, the LPA, EPA & PG (Amendment) Regs 2009 introduced six prescribed continuation sheets:

- Continuation sheet A1 – Additional people: additional attorneys, replacement attorneys or people to be told.
- Continuation sheet A2 – how your attorneys make decisions jointly and severally, restrictions & conditions, guidance, payment.
- Continuation sheet A3 PFA – if you cannot sign or make a mark. This applies to LPAs for property and financial affairs, and makes provision for the person executing the instrument on the donor's behalf to do so in the presence of the donor and two witnesses.
- Continuation sheet A3 HW – if you cannot sign or make a mark. This applies to health and welfare LPAs and makes additional provision for the person signing on the donor's behalf to sign Option A or Option B.
- Continuation sheet B – declaration by your second certificate provider: certificate to confirm understanding.
- Continuation sheet C – appointing a trust corporation as attorney or replacement attorney. This can apply only to LPAs for property and financial affairs by virtue of s 10(1)(b) of the MCA 2005.

7.29 For instruments created after 1 July 2015, the continuation sheets were replaced by the LPA, EPA & PG (Amendment) Regs 2015, which can be used for either type of LPA:

- Form 1 – continuation sheet for adding additional original and replacement attorneys and people to be notified.
- Form 2 – continuation sheet to extend conditions, restrictions and guidance where more space is needed than the form provides.
- Form 3 – continuation sheet for donors unable to sign or make a mark and need to sign at their direction.
- Form 4 – for the appointment of trust corporations, which can apply only to LPAs for property and financial affairs by virtue of s 10(1)(b) of the MCA 2005.

7.30 The prescribed form contains four Section 11 pages, which cater for the majority of preferences made by donors of LPAs. Where a donor appoints more than four original and replacement attorneys, they are advised to photocopy Section 11 before it is filled in and signed so that each attorney and replacement has a copy to fill in and sign.

7.31 Continuation sheets cannot be added after Sections 1–7 have been filled in and Section 9 has been signed by the donor.

Welsh language versions

7.32 The LPA, EPA & PG Regs, reg 3(1) provides that:

'(1)   In these Regulations, any reference to a form –
  (a)   in the case of a form set out in Schedules 1 to 7 to these Regulations, is to be regarded as including a Welsh version of that form; and
  (b)   in the case of a form set out in Schedules 2 to 7 to these Regulations, is to be regarded as also including –
    (i)   a form to the same effect but which differs in am immaterial respect in form or mode of expression;
    (ii)   a form to the same effect but with such variations as the circumstances may require or the court or the Public Guardian may approve; or
    (iii) a Welsh version of a form within (i) or (ii).'

All prescribed forms are available in Welsh, via the OPG portal of www.gov.uk.

Large print versions

7.33 It is possible to download from the OPG's website large print versions of the following documents:

- Lasting power of attorney – property and financial affairs.
- Lasting power of attorney – health and welfare.
- Continuation sheets for an LPA.
- Make and register your LPA; a guide (LP12).
- People to notify forms (LP3).
- Remission or exemption from fee form (LPA120).

FILLING IN THE FORM

Before filling in the form

7.34 On each page of both prescribed forms of the LPA are margin notes, headed with the word 'Help?', that refer the person drafting the instrument to the relevant part of 'the Guide'. This is a reference to *Making and registering your LPA: a guide* (LP12), available at www.gov.uk. In addition, on the top right-hand corner of each page, is printed the Helpline telephone number: 0300 456 0300.

The people involved in your LPA

7.35 The second page of the LPA is not part of the prescribed form, and is headed 'the people involved in your LPA'. It asks for the names of the attorney(s), the replacement attorney(s), the people to notify, the certificate provider and the independent witnesses. It explains the role of the certificate provider, and who that person may be. It signposts the person drafting the LPA to the list of people who cannot be a certificate provider.

Guidance

7.36 The OPG has published *Making and registering your LPA: a guide* (LP12), available at www.gov.uk.

7.37 The guide LP12 contains four distinct parts (A, B, C and D) with completion tips and examples of acceptable wording:

Part A Make your lasting power of attorney (LPA)

Part A1 The donor

Part A2 The attorneys

Part A3 How should your attorneys make decisions?

Part A4 Replacement attorneys

Part A5 When can your attorneys make decisions? (LPA for financial decisions only)

Part A5 Life-sustaining treatment (LPA for health and care decisions only)

Part A6 People to notify when the LPA is registered

Part A7 Preferences and instructions

Part A8 Your legal rights and responsibilities

Part A9 Signature: donor

Part A10 Signature: certificate provider

Part A11 Signature: attorney or replacement attorney

Part B1 Register your lasting power of attorney (LPA)

Part B2 Register your lasting power of attorney

Part B3 Who do you want to receive the LPA?

Part B4 Application fee

Part B5 Signature

Part C People to notify

Part D Cancelling your LPA, concerns about attorneys, privacy policy and contacting the Office of the Public Guardian

Filling in the form

7.38 The first page of each form, which is not part of the prescribed form provides limited instructions on how to fill in the form and states as follows:

- Please write in capital letters using a black Pen.
- Mark your choice with an X.
- If you make a mistake, fill in the box and then mark the correct choice with an X.

Continuation sheets

7.39 There are four continuation sheets: 1, 2, 3 and 4. The information sheet (LPC) describes how they should be used as follows:

'Continuation sheet 1 – Additional people
- Use this sheet if you need space to write more names for sections 2, 4 or 6 of the LPA form.
- You must sign and date this continuation sheet before you sign section 9 of the LPA, or on the same day.

Continuation sheet 2 – Additional information

- Use this sheet if you need more space to write information for sections 3, 4 or 7 of the LPA form.
- If you have to write extra information for more than one of those sections, use a fresh copy of the sheet for each one.
- You must sign and date this continuation sheet before you sign section 9 of the LPA, or on the same day.

Continuation sheet 3 – If the donor cannot sign or make a mark

- Use this sheet if you can't sign or make a mark yourself.
- You will need someone else to sign on your behalf and two people must witness their signature.
- If you're making an LPA for health and care decisions, the person signing for you must also sign section 5 of the LPA on the same day as they sign this sheet.

Continuation sheet 4 – Trust corporation appointed as an attorney
- Use this sheet if you appointed a trust corporation as an attorney or replacement attorney.
- Someone from the trust corporation must sign this sheet instead of signing section 11 of the LPA form.
- They must sign this sheet after your 'certificate provider' has signed section 10 of the LPA form.'

EXECUTION BY THE DONOR

The donor must read (or have read to him) all the prescribed information

7.40 Schedule 1, para 2(1)(a) of the MCA 2005 stipulates that 'the instrument must include the prescribed information about the purpose of the instrument and the effect of a lasting power of attorney'.

7.41 The LPA, EPA & PG Regs 2007, reg 9(2) states that 'the donor must read (or have read to him) all the prescribed information.' Regulation 2 provides that:

> '"prescribed information", in relation to an instrument intended to create a lasting power of attorney, means the information contained in the form used for the instrument which appears under the heading "Section 8- your legal rights and responsibilities".'

7.42 In its consultation paper on *Lasting Powers of Attorney – forms and guidance* (CP 01/06), published on 20 January 2006, the Department for Constitutional Affairs said, at pages 12 and 13:

> 'The first section on each form will contain what we consider should be the "prescribed information". This is information that will feature as an integral part of the form and which is essential for someone considering making an LPA. The prescribed information will remain part of the form even after it has been registered, for example when shown to a bank when a person is seeking to use it.

> Creating an LPA is a very significant decision and it may involve some complex considerations. A balance needs to be struck between providing essential information to be contained in the form and keeping the form to a manageable length. We consider it best to put only the essential information on the forms and to publish alongside them more detailed guidance.'

7.43 The Ministry of Justice consultation paper, *Transforming the Services of the Office of the Public Guardian Enabling Digital by Default* (CP 10/13), published on the 15 October 2013, annexed draft revised prescribed forms. Without an explanation contained in the consultation document, the prescribed information was retitled, 'your legal rights and responsibilities' and was placed in Section 8, just before the donor signs the instrument. The Ministry of Justice also gave no explanation when it responded to the consultation CP(R) 26/11/2013.

7.44 The current (2015 Regs) prescribed form contains a confirmation by the donor that:

> 'By signing on this page I confirm all of the following:
> * I have read this lasting power of attorney (LPA) including section 8 "Your legal rights and responsibilities", or I have had it read to me
> * I appoint and give my attorneys authority to make decisions about my property and financial affairs, including when I cannot act for myself because I lack mental capacity, subject to the terms of this LPA and to the provisions of the Mental Capacity Act 2005' (*property and financial affairs LPA only*)
> * I appoint and give my attorneys authority to make decisions about my health and welfare, when I cannot act for myself because I lack mental capacity, subject to the terms of this LPA and to the provisions of the Mental Capacity Act 2005' (*health and welfare LPA only*)

'• I confirm I have chosen either Option A or Option B about life sustaining treatment in section 5 of this LPA' (*health and welfare LPA only*)

'• I have either appointed people to notify (in section 6) or I have chosen not to notify anyone when the LPA is registered

• I agree to the information I've provided being used by the Office of the Public Guardian in carrying out its duties.'

The donor must complete Sections 1-7 of the instrument, and sign Section 9 of it in the presence of a witness

7.45 The LPA, EPA & PG Regs 2007, reg 9(3) says that:

'As soon as reasonably practicable after the steps required by paragraph (2) have been taken, the donor must –
(a) complete the provisions of Sections 1 to 7 of the instrument that apply to him (or direct another person to do so); and
(b) subject to paragraph (7), sign Section 9 of the instrument in the presence of a witness.'

Signature or mark

7.46 The LPA, EPA & PG Regs 2007, reg 9(10) says:

'Any reference in this regulation to a person signing an instrument (however expressed) includes signing it by means of a mark made on the instrument at the appropriate place.'

The witness of the donor's signature

7.47 The person who witnesses the donor's signature at the end of Section 9 of the prescribed form:

• must be at least 18 years of age;
• must not be one of the attorneys or replacement attorneys being appointed;
• can be the certificate provider.

7.48 The LPA, EPA & PG Regs 2007, reg 9(8) and (9) states:

'(8) For the purposes of this regulation –
(a) the donor may not witness any signature required for the power;
(b) a donee may not witness any signature required for the power apart from that of another donee.
(9) A person witnessing a signature must –
(a) sign the instrument; and
(b) give his full name and address.'

7.49 The prescribed form of LPA itself contains the additional requirement that the witness must be aged 18 or over. *Making and registering your LPA: a guide* (LP12) at page 36 requires that 'There must be an independent witness to watch you signing your LPA.' This is explained as someone other than the appointed attorney or replacement attorney or the employee of any trust corporation named as an attorney or replacement attorney.

Execution at the direction of the donor

7.50 Regulation 9(7) of the LPA, EPA & PG Regs 2007 provides that:

'If the instrument is to be signed by any person at the direction of the donor, or at the direction of any donee, the signature must be done in the presence of two witnesses.'

7.51 *Making and registering your LPA: a guide* (LP12) states on page 37:

'If you can't sign or make a mark, someone can sign for you using Continuation sheet 3. You must be present and must tell the person to sign. That person's signature must be witnessed by two people. The two witnesses can't be:
- under 18
- your attorneys
- your replacement attorneys
- employees of a trust corporation that that is your attorney or replacement attorney (LPA for financial decisions only).'

7.52 In Section 9, where the donor should sign or make a mark, if he were able, the prescribed form states, 'If you can't sign or make a mark you can instruct someone else to sign for you, using Continuation sheet 3'. The consequence is that Section 9 remains blank and must not be struck through to comply with reg 9(3)(b).

7.53 Continuation sheets 3 states that:

'You must:
- sign in the donor's presence and in the presence of 2 witnesses
- sign in your own name
- not also be a witness to this LPA
- sign any copies of Continuation Sheet 1 and 2 used in this LPA at the same time

If the LPA is for health and care decisions:
- you must also sign and date either Option A or Option B of Section 5, as directed by the donor
- your signature in Section 5 must be witnessed.'

THE CERTIFICATE PROVIDER

The certificate provider must read Sections 8 and 10 of the LPA

7.54 *Making and registering your LPA: a guide* (LP12) states at Part A10 on page 38: 'The certificate provider must read LPA Sections 8 and 10 before they sign your LPA.' However, the LPA, EPA & PG Regs 2007, reg 9(4) does not expressly require the certificate provider to read all the prescribed information, in contrast to the donor and attorney(s) who are required to read the prescribed information.

The certificate provider should read the LPA

7.55 Given that the certificate is signing to confirm the donor understands the scope and authority of the power they have signed, it is implicit that the certificate provider will need to have read Sections 1-7 to form his opinion.

Despite this not being a regulatory requirement, the prescribed form requires the certificate provider to confirm he has read the LPA.

The certificate provider should discuss the form with the donor in private, if possible

7.56 For details on who can and cannot be a certificate provider, see Chapter 6.

7.57 The first LPA forms, prescribed in 2007, required the certificate provider to tick the following boxes:

☐ I confirm that I have discussed the contents of this LPA with the donor and that the attorney(s) was not present.

☐ I understand that I should make efforts to discuss this LPA with the donor without anyone present, and

☐ I have discussed this LPA with the donor without anyone else present or

☐ I have discussed this LPA with the donor in the presence of: because

7.58 The former form LPA107, Lasting Powers of Attorney: A guide for Certificate Providers and Witnesses, stated, at page 8, in response to the question 'What are my responsibilities as Certificate Provider?'

'You will need to talk to the donor in private and away from his or her attorney(s) and you will need to confirm in the certificate that you have done so. The certificate is not valid if the attorney is present when you discuss the LPA with the donor.

There may be circumstances where someone needs to be present with the donor when you discuss the LPA with him or her. For example, if the donor is deaf and you need someone to translate sign language for you. You should state on the certificate if someone else was present and why. This person must never be the attorney(s).'

7.59 The declarations in 7.57 do not appear in the forms prescribed by the LPA, EPA & PG (Amendment) Regulations 2009 or the LPA, EPA & PG (Amendment) Regulations 2015. There was no comparable guidance to that contained in 7.57, until the OPG published *Making and registering your LPA: a guide* (LP12), which is aimed at the donor rather than the certificate provider, but states in Part A10 on page 36:

'When if possible, they should discuss your LPA with you in private, without attorneys or other people present, before they sign to 'certify' their part of the LPA.'

The certificate provider must form an opinion on the donor's capacity

7.60 Prior to the introduction of the 2015 prescribed forms, the OPG produces two booklets for LPA donors: LPA111, *Guidance for people who want to make a lasting power of attorney for health and welfare*, and LPA112, *Guidance for people who want to make a lasting power of attorney for property and financial affairs*. Chapter 4 of each booklet, at pages 32 and 31 respectively, provided the following guidance to certificate providers:

'Being a certificate provider is an important role. In carrying out the role in a professional capacity you should have no doubt about the person's identity.

You need to fully understand what the role involves before agreeing to take it on – and you can refuse to do it if you do not feel able to confirm everything that you are being asked to certify.

In completing part B of the donor's LPA, you are confirming that in your opinion the donor understands:

- what an LPA is;
- the contents of their LPA;
- the powers they are giving to their attorney(s); and that
- the donor is not being put under pressure, being tricked or being forced by someone else to make the LPA; or
- nothing else exists that would prevent the donor's LPA being created.

To establish the donor's capacity and understanding, here are some suggested topics to discuss:

- What is your understanding of what an LPA is?
- What are your reasons for making an LPA?
- Why have you chosen me to be your certificate provider?
- Who have you chosen to be your attorneys?
- Why them?
- What powers are you giving them?
- In what circumstances should the power be used by your attorneys?
- What types of decision would you like them to make, and what (if any) should they not take?
- If there are any restrictions in the LPA, what do you believe they achieve?
- What is the difference between any restrictions and any guidance made in the LPA?
- Have the chosen attorneys provided you with answers to any of these questions?
- Do you have any reason to think they could be untrustworthy?
- Do you know when you could cancel the LPA?
- Are there any other reasons why the LPA should not be created?'

7.61 There is now little guidance about how the certificate provider should go about forming his opinion in order to sign the certificate in Section 10 of the LPA. *Making and registering your LPA: a guide* (LP12) explains it simply as:

'A certificate provider is an impartial person who confirms that you understand what you're doing and that nobody is forcing you to make an LPA.

They must confirm that:
- you understand the significance of the LPA
- you have not been put under pressure to make it
- there has been no fraud involved in making the LPA
- there is no other reason for concern'

7.62 The introduction to *Making and registering your LPA: a guide* (LP12) on page 3 informs the donor:

'You don't have to read it now. You can start filling in your LPA form and look at the guide if you need more information.'

This is not particularly helpful, as there is no prompt for the donor to refer the guidance to the certificate provider.

7.63 The introduction on page 5 of *Making and registering your LPA: a guide* (LP12) contains generic information about the meaning of 'mental capacity' and states:

'A person with mental capacity has at least a general understanding of:
- the decision they need to make
- why they need to make it
- any information relevant to the decision
- what is likely to happen when they make it

They should be able to communicate their decision through speech, signs, gestures or in other ways.

People can sometimes make certain decisions but don't have the mental capacity to make others. For example, someone may be able to decide what to buy for dinner but be unable to understand and arrange their home insurance.

Assessing mental capacity

To work out whether someone lacks the mental capacity to make a decision, you need to answer 'yes' to these two questions:
1.	Do they have a mental or brain problem that stops their brain or mind from working properly?
2.	Is that problem causing them such difficulty now that they are unable to make this particular decision at the time it needs to be made?

Being 'unable to make this particular decision' means that the person can't:
- understand relevant information about the decision that needs making
- keep that information in their mind long enough to make the decision
- weigh up the information in order to make the decision
- communicate their decision – this could be by talking, using sign language, pictures or even just squeezing a hand or blinking.'

The certificate provider should keep a record of the assessment

7.64 There is no current guidance to the certificate provider to keep a record of his assessment. This is a marked departure from Chapter 4, of the 2009 Guidance for certificate providers, in the booklets LPA111 and LPA112, *Guidance for people who want to make a lasting power of attorney*, which stated at pages 32 and 31 respectively:

'It is advisable to keep a record of the questions and answers in case someone challenges the donor's capacity to make an LPA. You could be asked to explain to the Court of Protection how you formed your opinion.'

It clearly is best practice to keep a record, as the certificate provider might be called to account for his opinion if there is an objection made to the registration of the LPA. See CHAPTER 9 for more details on objecting to the registration of an LPA.

7.65 This was reiterated in Part B of the 2009 prescribed form of LPA which stated:

'If someone challenges this lasting power of attorney, you may need to explain how you formed your opinion.'

No such warning is contained in the 2015 prescribed forms.

7.66 Where someone applies to the Court of Protection objecting to the registration of an LPA on the ground that the power purported to be created by the instrument is not valid as an LPA, the standard directions order made by the court requires the certificate provider to explain:

- the questions he asked the donor in order to assess his capacity to create the lasting power of attorney;
- the measures he took to ascertain that the donor had understood all the relevant information;
- the measures he took to ascertain that the donor had been able to retain all the relevant information;
- how he was satisfied that the donor was able to use or weigh that information as part of the process of making the decision to create the lasting power of attorney;
- how the donor communicated the decision to him as certificate provider;
- why he came to the conclusion that the donor had the capacity to make the lasting power of attorney and that no fraud or undue pressure was being used to induce the donor to create the lasting power of attorney; and
- what record he kept of the assessment.

The certificate provider must complete the certificate in Section 10 of the instrument and sign it

7.67 The LPA, EPA & PG Regs 2007, reg 9(4) says that:

'As soon as reasonably practicable after the steps required by paragraph (3) have been taken –
(a)   the person giving an LPA certificate,

must complete the LPA certificate at Section 10 of the instrument and sign it.'

7.68 The current prescribed forms of LPA state at Section 10:

'Only sign this section after the donor has signed Section 9.'

7.69 The Regulations do not define 'as soon as reasonably practicable' in reg 9(4) and there has not been any judicial decision on its meaning. Part A10 on page 38 of the *Making and registering your LPA: a guide* (LP12) states, 'The certificate provider must sign after you and can sign on the same day as you (the donor) or as soon as possible afterwards.' Schedule 1, paragraph 2(c) of MCA 2005, sets out the requirements of the core certificate, which is worded in the present tense, ie the donor understands the purpose of the instrument and the scope of the authority conferred under it at the time he signs Section 9. However, the 2015 prescribed form frames this in the past tense, ie at the time the donor signed he understood the purpose of the LPA etc. This raises the question of whether it matters if there has been a delay between the donor signing Section 9 and the certificate provider signing Section 10. The certificate provider's opinion is based on when the donor signed Section 9, so where there has been a delay there is a risk it might undermine the purpose of the certificate, particularly if the donor has fluctuating capacity and/or undue pressure was used to induce the donor to sign. It is highly unlikely a certificate provider could provide as robust an opinion if he was not there when the instrument was signed by the donor.

7.70 In *Re Hurren* (Senior Judge Lush, 28 September 2011) the certificate provider, a professional will writer, completed part B on 25 September 2009, and the donor, Mr Hurren, executed part A two days later on 27 September

2009. The Public Guardian refused to register the instrument because the certificate provider had signed part B before the donor had signed part A, in contravention of reg 9 of the LPA, EPA & PG Regs 2007. The donor subsequently lost capacity and the attorney applied to the Court of Protection for a declaration under paragraph 3(2) of Schedule 1 to the MCA 2005 that the instrument was to be treated as if it were in the prescribed form. The court dismissed the application and confirmed that its discretion under paragraph 3(2) applies only to an instrument which is not in the prescribed form, and does not apply to any prescribed requirements in connection with its execution.

EXECUTION BY THE ATTORNEY

The attorney must read all the prescribed information in Section 8

7.71 Schedule 1, para 2(1)(d) of the MCA 2005 states that:

'The instrument must include . . . (d) a statement by the donee (or, if more than one, each of them) to the effect that he –
(i)   has read the prescribed information or a prescribed part of it (or has had it read to him), and
(ii)   understands the duties imposed on a donee of a lasting power of attorney under sections 1 (the principles) and 4 (best interests).'

7.72 The LPA, EPA & PG Regs 2007, reg 9(5) says that:

'As soon as reasonably practicable after the steps required by paragraph (4) have been taken –
(a)   the donee, or
(b)   if more than one, each of the donees,

must read (or have read to him) all the prescribed information.'

7.73 Section 11 of the prescribed form alerts the attorneys to:

'only sign this section after the certificate provider has signed section 10',

which is supported by Part A11 of *making and registering your LPA: a guide* (LP12), which states,

'attorneys and replacement attorneys must sign after the certificate provider.'

7.74 It is not a requirement of either the Act or the Regulations that an attorney should read the completed Sections 1–7. The attorney's statutory obligation is limited to reading the prescribed information in Section 8 and completing and signing Section 11 of the prescribed form of LPA. However, Section 11 requires the attorney to confirm that:

'I have read this lasting power of attorney (LPA) including section 8 'Your legal rights and responsibilities', or I have had it read to me.'

An attorney is not required to read the certificate provider's declaration in Section 10 of the LPA.

The attorney must complete Section 11 of the instrument, and sign and date it in the presence of a witness

7.75 The LPA, EPA & PG Regs 2007, reg 9(6) says that:

'As soon as reasonably practicable after the steps required by paragraph (5) have been taken, the donee or, if more than one, each of them –
(a)   must complete the provisions of Section 11 of the instrument that apply to him (or direct another person to do so); and
(b)   subject to paragraph (7), must sign Section 11 in the presence of a witness.'

7.76 Paragraph (7) provides that, 'if the instrument is to be signed by any person . . . At the direction of the donee, the signature must be done in the presence of two witnesses.' The procedure is the same as for the execution of the instrument at the direction of the donor: see 7.50–7.53.

7.77 If the date on any attorney declaration is earlier than the date of the donor's signature in Section 9 or the certificate provider's signature in Section 10, the LPA will be rejected.

7.78 There has been no judicial pronouncement on the meaning of 'as soon as reasonably practicable' in regulation 9(6). Guidance on the time scale to sign Section 11 is contained in *Making and registering your LPA: a guide* (LP12) in Part A11 on page 40, which states:

'Attorneys and replacements should sign as soon as possible after the certificate provider – it's preferable if they all sign on the same day.'

The witness of the attorney's signature

7.79 Each 2015 prescribed form of LPA states that:

'The witness must not be the donor of this LPA, and must be aged 18 or over.'

7.80 The LPA, EPA & PG Regs 2007, reg 9(8) and (9) state:

'(8)   For the purposes of this regulation –
(a)   the donor may not witness any signature required for the power;
(b)   a donee may not witness any signature required for the power apart from that of another donee.
(9)   A person witnessing a signature must –
(a)   sign the instrument; and
(b)   give his full name and address.'

Part A11 on page 40 of *Making and registering your LPA: a guide* (LP12) reminds the donor of this requirement. A failure to include the full name of the witness will result in the rejection of the LPA by the OPG at registration. This is a common problem where the witness merely writes the initials of their first name. Similarly, if the same person is witnessing more than one parties' signature, they must include their full name and address on each occasion to satisfy reg 9(9). Merely stating 'as before' may result in the instrument being rejected by the OPG as non-compliant.

Execution by a trust corporation

7.81 The law relating to the execution of powers of attorney by companies is governed by The Regulatory Reform (Execution of Deeds and Documents) Order 2005, which came into force on 15 September 2005, and implemented recommendations made by the Law Commission in its report on *The Execution of Deeds and Documents by and on behalf of Bodies Corporate* (Law Com 253).

7.82 'Continuation sheet 4 – trust corporation appointed as an attorney' is provided for the execution of Section 11 of an LPA for property and financial affairs by a trust corporation. At least one authorised person (unless the company requires two authorised persons) must sign and date the right-hand column. The company registration number also needs to be inserted. This does not require separate witnessing.

Execution by a replacement attorney

7.83 The execution requirements for a replacement attorney are the same as those for any other individual attorney. Section 11 of the prescribed form is headed 'Signature: attorney or replacement attorney.'

7.84 Section 11 does, however, contain the following provision which, applies specifically to replacement attorneys and not to the original attorneys:

> 'I understand that I have the authority to act under this LPA only after an original attorney's appointment is terminated. I must notify the Public Guardian if this happens.'

7.85 There is no requirement that the replacement attorney must execute the instrument after it has been executed by the original attorney. Section 11 of the prescribed form simply states that:

> 'Only sign this section after the certificate provider has signed section 10.'

Re-execution

7.86 The Public Guardian does not consider that defects in the prescribed form or in the execution of the prescribed form can be remedied by returning the instruments to the donor, certificate provider, or attorneys for completion and re-submission. Regulation 9 lays down a very specific order for executing an instrument. Section 9 must be completed and executed first. Section 10 must be completed and executed next. Finally, Section 11 must be completed and executed. Even if a deed could be amended after execution under the general law, nothing could be completed or amended after the final stage of execution by the attorneys. If an amended instrument were to be returned to the Public Guardian, he would have no power to register it because the defect would be one of execution, falling outside the scope of paragraph 3(1) of Schedule 1 to the Act. Nor could the Public Guardian register the instrument on being provided with extrinsic evidence supplying essential missing information, because the instrument itself would remain defective. Such extrinsic evidence may be accepted only by the Court of

Protection in the exercise of its jurisdiction under paragraph 3(2) of Schedule 1.

CONSEQUENCES OF FAILURE TO COMPLY WITH THE FORMALITIES

An instrument which does not comply with the statutory requirements confers no authority

7.87 Section 9(3) of the MCA 2005 states that:

'An instrument which –
(a)   purports to create a lasting power of attorney, but
(b)   does not comply with this section, section 10 or Schedule 1,

confers no authority.'

An unregistered LPA cannot operate as an ordinary power of attorney

7.88 The Law Commission, in paragraph 7.9 of its report on *Mental Incapacity* (1995), said:

'The general law in relation to powers of attorney will continue to underlie our proposed scheme for [lasting] powers of attorney. It would, however, be confusing and unhelpful if a document intended to take effect as [an LPA], but which failed to meet some of the specific statutory requirements, could be taken to operate as an ordinary power of attorney. (There has been some debate as to whether a 'would be' enduring power of attorney can take effect as a valid ordinary power of attorney: R T Oerton, *EPAs as ordinary powers?* (1987) 131 SJ 1645). Nor does this possibility fit with the simplified procedures which we recommend, whereby registration of the [LPA] will act as a trigger to its effectiveness. We take the view that express provision to rule out any question of an unregistered (and therefore ineffective) [LPA] operating as an ordinary power would be helpful. We recommend that where an instrument purports to create [an LPA] but does not comply with the statutory requirements it should confer no powers on the donee.'

Immaterial differences

7.89 Paragraph 3(1) of Sch 1 to the MCA 2005 provides that:

'If an instrument differs in an immaterial respect in form or mode of expression from the prescribed form, it is to be treated by the Public Guardian as sufficient in point of form and expression.'

7.90 This provision is limited in scope. The Public Guardian has no power to register an instrument (unless directed to do so by the Court of Protection), if it departs from the prescribed form in the matter of content, or if it has not been executed in accordance with the statutory requirements.

The court may declare that an LPA that is not in the prescribed form is to be treated as if it were

7.91 Paragraph 3(2) of Sch 1 to the MCA 2005 provides that:

'The court may declare that an instrument which is not in the prescribed form is to be treated as if it were, if it is satisfied that the persons executing the instrument intended it to create a lasting power of attorney.'

This provision is considered in detail at **11.28 ff.**

Omissions

7.92 There has been some case-law on the omission of certain information in the prescribed form. For example,*Re Cretney* (Senior Judge Lush, 24 February 2011) and *Re Baker* (Senior Judge Lush, 4 February 2011), the details of which are contained in Annex H of this publication.

Severance of ineffective or invalid provisions

7.93 The Court of Protection has power to determine any question as to the meaning or effect of a lasting power of attorney or an instrument purporting to create one (s 23(1)). If it appears to the Public Guardian that an instrument contains a provision which would be ineffective as part of an LPA, or would prevent the instrument from operating as a valid LPA, the Public Guardian must apply to the court to determine the matter and, if necessary, sever the offending provision (MCA 2005, Sch 1, para 11).

Chapter 8

APPLICATION TO REGISTER A LASTING POWER OF ATTORNEY

INTRODUCTION

Summary

8.1 If there are no defects in the lasting power of attorney (LPA), and no defects in the application form, and no objections to registration, the registration of an LPA is a straightforward process:

- The applicant, who can be the donor or the attorney, sends form LP3 – Notice of intention to register a lasting power of attorney – to the named persons: referred to in the 2009 prescribed forms as 'people to be told' and the 2015 LPA prescribed forms as 'people to notify'.
- The applicant then sends the original LPA, which contains the application to register the power to the Office of the Public Guardian (OPG). If the LPA is made either on a 2007 or 2009 prescribed form, the applicant must instead send form LP2 – Register your lasting power of attorney.
- The OPG sends the attorney a form LPA 003A – Notice to an attorney of receipt of an application to register a lasting power of attorney.
- The OPG sends the donor a form LPA 003B – Notice to donor of receipt of an application to register a lasting power of attorney.
- At the end of the prescribed period of four weeks beginning with the latest date on which forms LPA 003A and LPA 003B were sent out, the OPG may register the instrument.
- The OPG sends the donor and the attorney a form LPA 004 – Notice of registration of a lasting power of attorney.

An LPA must be registered

8.2 An LPA must be registered with the OPG before it can be used. The Mental Capacity Act 2005 (MCA 2005), s 9(2)(b) provides that an LPA is not created unless the instrument conferring authority on the attorney(s) is registered in accordance with Sch 1. Section 9(3)(b) reinforces this, and states that an unregistered instrument confers no authority on the attorney. This is in contrast to an enduring power of attorney, where a failure to comply with the requirements for its creation, whilst not taking effect as an enduring power, can still operate as an ordinary power (see **16.2**).

Obtaining the registration forms

8.3 The forms required for registering an LPA can be obtained from the OPG, PO Box 16185, Birmingham B2 2WH, or downloaded from the Government website: https://www.gov.uk/government/collections/lasting-power-of-attorne y-forms or completed digitally via https://www.lastingpowerofattorney.servic e.gov.uk/home.

8.4 The forms and guidance to create and register a LPA are contained in a combined pack which includes the following forms and booklets relating to the registration:

- LP3 – Notice of intention to apply to register a lasting power of attorney.
- LP12 – Make and register your lasting power of attorney (parts B and C).
- LPA120 – EPA and LPA Fees.
- LPA 120A – Application for exemption or remission of EPA/LPA Application to register fees.

8.5 A separate registration pack is available for LPAs made on either the 2007 or 2009 prescribed forms, which contains:

- LP3 – Notice of intention to register a lasting power of attorney.
- LP2 – Register your lasting power of attorney.
- LP13 – Register your lasting power of attorney – a guide.
- LPA120 – EPA and LPA Fees.
- LPA 120A – Application for exemption or remission of EPA/LPA Application to register fees.

The applicant

8.6 Unlike an enduring power of attorney (EPA), there is no necessary link between the intention to register an LPA and any incipient incapacity of the donor. Accordingly, there is no reason why the donor cannot apply to register the instrument himself and the MCA 2005, Sch 1, para 4(2) provides that:

'The application may be made –
(a)   by the donor;
(b)   by the donee or donees; or
(c)   if the instrument appoints two or more donees to act jointly and severally in respect of any matter, by any of the donees.'

8.7 Where the attorneys have been appointed to act jointly, both or all must make the application. A replacement attorney is not required to join in making the application, unless he has replaced an original attorney on the occurrence of an event mentioned in s 13(6) of the MCA 2005, which has the effect of terminating the original attorney's appointment.

FORM LP3

Form LP3: Notice of intention to register a Lasting Power of Attorney

8.8 The donor or attorney who is applying to register the LPA must notify any named persons of his intention to apply for registration in the prescribed form LP3 (Lasting Powers of Attorney, Enduring Powers of Attorney and Public Guardian Regulations 2007 (SI 2007/1253) (LPA, EPA & PG Regs 2007), reg 10 and Sch 2).

8.9 Form LP3, which is reproduced in Appendix C, sets out:

- Details of the person to notify: his title, name, address and postcode, and advises him that 'When they made the LPA, the donor decided you should be told about it before it's registered. This is so you can raise any concerns you may have. If you do have concerns, you can only object to the registration of the LPA for the reasons listed on page 4 of this form. If you want to object you must do so within 3 weeks of the date of this notice'.
- Details of the donor: his title, name, address and postcode.
- Details of the LPA: whether it is the donor or the attorney who is applying to register; whether it is a property and financial affairs LPA or a health and welfare LPA that is being registered; and the date on which the donor signed the LPA.
- Details of the attorney: his title, name, address, and postcode; and whether he is acting solely, jointly, jointly and severally, or jointly in some matters and severally in others. Altogether, there is space for the details of four attorneys. The applicant is informed 'You don't need to list replacement attorneys appointed in the LPA (if any).' There is no express mention that where a replacement attorney has replaced the attorney in an unregistered lasting power of attorney, they can also register it.
- Details of how to object to the registering of an LPA on factual grounds and prescribed grounds.

8.10 Where an application is being made to register both types of LPA – Property and Financial Affairs, and Health and Welfare – and the same people to notify are named in each instrument, the applicant must send the people to notify a separate form LP3 for each LPA. A person to notify may be content for the registration of one type of LPA to go ahead, but may wish to object to the other type.

There is no need for the applicant to notify anyone other than named persons or people to notify

8.11 Unlike an application to register an EPA, there is no legal requirement for an attorney who is applying to register an LPA to give notice of intention to register (LP3) to the donor; to any co-attorney who has been appointed to act jointly and severally with the applicant attorney; or any replacement attorney. The OPG will formally give notice of receipt of the application to register the LPA to the donor (on form LPA 003B) and any co-attorneys (on form LPA 003A). The OPG does not notify a replacement attorney, the consequence of which is that the replacement attorney may be unaware when an application to register the LPA has been made and if successful, when it is eventually registered.

8.12 LP12 Make and register your lasting power of attorney – a guide, makes no mention that it is a good idea to discuss the application to register the LPA with the non-applicant donor or attorney beforehand. This is particularly important if there has been a delay between completion of the signing of the power and the application to register.

8.13 In paragraph 7.34 of its report on *Mental Incapacity* (Law Com No 231 (1995)), the Law Commission emphasised the importance of letting the donor know that the attorney intends to register the power:

'We favour the retention of a requirement that a donee must notify a donor of his or her intention to register [an LPA]. It may be some time since the document was executed and, in any event, the act of registration will significantly alter matters by triggering the attorney's power to act. The donor must be warned that this is in prospect and given an opportunity to prevent registration.'

8.14 Similarly, there is no legal requirement for a donor who is applying to register an LPA to give notice of intention to apply for registration (LP3) to the attorney(s). The OPG will formally give notice of receipt of the application to register the LPA to them on form LPA 003A.

Where the applicant is unable to locate a named person

8.15 The OPG's post 2015 guidance LP12 – Make and register your lasting power of attorney, makes no mention of what to do if the person applying to register the power is unable to locate a named person (person to notify or person to be told). The OPG's pre-2015 guidance, LPA110, How to register your lasting power of attorney, stated at page 4:

'If it is not possible to establish contact with any of the people to be told, you must keep proof of posting slips, or returned-to-sender evidence, to demonstrate that you have made reasonable efforts.'

Dispensing with the requirement to notify a named person

8.16 On the application of either the donor or the attorney who is about to make an application to register the power, the Court of Protection may dispense with the requirement to notify any named person, if it is satisfied that no useful purpose would be served by giving the notice (MCA 2005, Sch 1, para 10).

8.17 Any application to dispense with the requirement to notify must be made to the court on form COP 1. A fee of £400 is payable on such an application (Court of Protection Fees Order 2007 (SI 2007/1745 (L.13)), art 4(1)).

8.18 The court's powers to dispense with the requirement to notify a named person of an intended application to register an LPA are slightly different from its powers in respect of dispensing with the requirement of an attorney to notify the donor's relatives of his intention to apply for registration of an EPA. Where an application is being made to register an EPA, in addition to being satisfied that no useful purpose would be served in giving a particular relative notice, the court can also dispense with notification if it is satisfied that 'it would be undesirable or impracticable for the attorney to give him notice' (MCA 2005, Sch 4, para 7(2)(a)). The reason for the change in procedure is explained in paragraph 7.35 of the Law Commission's report on *Mental Incapacity* (Law Com No 231 (1995)), although the discussion was primarily in the context of notifying the donor. The EPA legislation also enables the court to dispense with the requirement to notify the donor (MCA 2005, Sch 4, para 8(2)). There is no equivalent provision in relation to LPAs.

SECTIONS 12–15 OF THE LPA FORM OR FORM LP2

Application to register a Lasting Power of Attorney

8.19 MCA 2005, Sch 1, para 4(1) provides that:

> 'An application to the Public Guardian for the registration of an instrument intended to create a lasting power of attorney –
> (a)   must be made in the prescribed form, and
> (b)   must include any prescribed information.'

8.20 The application to register is contained in Sections 12–15 of the 2015 prescribed LPA form, or if the power is a 2007 or 2009 prescribed form, the application is prescribed Form LP2 (LPA, EPA & PG Regs 2007, reg 11(1) and Sch 3). The OPG provides guidance for those wishing to register a power made on a 2015 prescribed form; LP12 – Make and register you lasting power of attorney- a guide (part B). Separate guidance for those wishing to register either a 2007 or 2009 prescribed form is contained in LP13 – Register your lasting power of attorney – a guide.

8.21 The application for registration must be completed in block capitals using a black pen.

8.22 If the applicant is registering an LPA for property and financial affairs and an LPA for health and welfare, for each power of attorney, he must complete Sections 12–15 of the 2015 prescribed LPA forms or a separate form LP2 if the power was made on a 2007 or 2009 prescribed form.

8.23 The registration of a LPA on a 2015 prescribed form is contained within the following Sections:

- Section 12 – The applicant. The applicant is required to tick the box stating whether the donor is applying to register the LPA, or whether the attorney(s) are applying to register it. Each applicant attorney must complete their title, name and date of birth. It is not necessary to include the names of non- applicant attorneys.
- Section 13 – Who do you want to receive the LPA. The applicant can choose who the OPG should correspond with regarding the application and where the power should be sent once it has been registered. It can be the donor, an attorney or another person or company, such as a professional legal adviser or practice. As the power contains the addresses of the donor and attorney there is no need to repeat these, unless there has been a change since the LPA was signed. The applicant can also choose their preferred method of contact.

- Section 14 – Application fee. If the applicant wishes to apply for an exemption or remission of the application to register fee, he will need to mark the appropriate box. He will also need to complete the exemption or remission application form (LPA120A). If the applicant wishes to pay by credit card or debit card, he must tick the relevant box and provide a telephone number so that an agent can call him to arrange payment when the application has been received. The applicant may qualify for a reduction in fee (half the full fee, which is currently £41) when making a repeat application. This applies in circumstances where a previous application was made to register a LPA and it was rejected by the Public Guardian.
- Section 15 – Signature. The applicant must sign and date this Section. By signing, the applicant confirms that he has notified the named persons or people to notify (if any) and that the information is correct to the best of his knowledge and belief.

8.24 There are six Sections to form LP2, for the registration of a 2007 or 2009 prescribed form:

- Section 1 – About the lasting power. This requires completion of the donor's title and full name. The applicant is required to also state whether he is applying to register an LPA for property and financial affairs or an LPA for health and welfare.
- Section 2 – The applicant. This is identical to Section 12 of the 2015 prescribed form (see **8.23**).
- Section 3 – This is identical to Section 13 of the 2015 prescribed form (see **8.23**).
- Section 4 – Application fee. This is identical to Section 14 of the 2015 prescribed form (see **8.23**), except there is no provision for the repeat registration fee, because if the application for registration is rejected, a fresh LPA will have to be made on the 2015 prescribed form.
- Section 5 – Signature. This is almost identical to Section 15 of the 2015 prescribed form (see **8.23**) save that numbers references are different.

Offences

8.25 A person who, in an application for the registration of an LPA, makes a statement which he knows to be false in a material particular, is guilty of an offence and is liable:

- on summary conviction, to imprisonment for a term not exceeding 12 months or a fine not exceeding the statutory maximum or both (MCA 2005, Sch 1, para 4(4)(a));
- on conviction on indictment, to imprisonment for a term not exceeding 2 years or a fine or both (Sch 1, para 4(4)(b)).

Documents to be sent to the Office of the Public Guardian

8.26 As soon as practicable after giving any notices in form LP3, the donor or attorney who is applying to register the instrument must send the following papers to the OPG:

- the application to register the instrument in Sections 12–15 of the 2015 LPA prescribed forms or prescribed form LP2;
- the original instrument creating the LPA; and
- a cheque for the application fee of £82 (or if a repeat application: a fee of £41) or a form LPA 120A if the applicant is applying for exemption, or remission of the fee.

8.27 The OPG will send a notice confirming that it has received the application to register the LPA:

- to the attorney(s) on form LPA 003A (LPA, EPA & PG Regs 2007, reg 13(1)); and
- to the donor on form LPA 003B (LPA, EPA & PG Regs 2007, reg 13(1)).

Where the original LPA is missing

8.28 If the original instrument is unavailable for any reason, the Public Guardian may register a certified copy of it (LPA, EPA & PG Regs 2007, reg 11(2)). 'Certified copy' means a photographic or other facsimile copy which is certified as an accurate copy by the donor or a solicitor or notary (LPA, EPA & PG Regs 2007, reg 11(3)).

8.29 The LPA, EPA & PG Regs 2007, reg 11 states that:

> '(2)   Where the instrument to be registered which is sent with the application is neither –
>   (a)   the original instrument intended to create the power, nor
>   (b)   a certified copy of it,
>   the Public Guardian must not register the instrument unless the court directs him to do so.
> (3)   In paragraph (2) "a certified copy" means a photographic or other facsimile which is certified as an accurate copy by –
>   (a)   (the donor); or
>   (b)   a solicitor or notary.'

8.30 Accordingly, it will be necessary for any applicant seeking to register an uncertified copy of an LPA to apply to the Court of Protection for an order directing the Public Guardian to register it.

8.31 The application should be made on form COP 1 and there will be an application fee of £400. The court will require:

- a witness statement relating to the circumstances of the execution of the LPA;
- evidence as to the contents of the LPA;
- evidence relating to the loss or destruction of the original instrument; and
- evidence that the power had not been revoked by the donor.

FORMS LPA 003A AND LPA 003B

Form LPA 003A: Notifying the attorney

8.32 The LPA, EPA & PG Regs 2007, reg 13(1) says that Part 1 of Sch 4 to the Regulations sets out the prescribed form of notice (LPA 003A) which the Public Guardian must give to the attorney or attorneys when he receives an application for the registration of an LPA. This provision in the 2007 Regulations was amended, with effect from 1 July 2015, by the LPA, EPA & PG (Amendment) Regs 2015, reg 11.

8.33 Form LPA 003A – Notice to an attorney of receipt of an application to register a lasting power of attorney – which is reproduced at APPENDIX C, states:

'You have received this notice because:
- ('the donor') made a Lasting Power of Attorney (LPA) for
- they named you as attorney in that LPA
- the person(s) named below has applied to register the LPA

Person(s) who applied to register the LPA

The following person(s) applied to register the LPA:

Your right to object

You can object to the proposed registration of the LPA.

You have 3 weeks from to object. Page 2 of this notice tells you how to object.'

Page 2 of form LPA 003A sets out details of how to object to registration on either factual grounds or prescribed grounds.

Form LPA 003B: Notifying the donor

8.34 The LPA, EPA & PG Regs 2007, reg 13(2) says that Part 2 of Sch 4 to the Regulations sets out the prescribed form of notice (LPA 003B) which the Public Guardian must give to the donor when he receives an application for the registration of an LPA. This provision in the 2007 Regulations was amended, with effect from 1 July 2015, by the LPA, EPA & PG (Amendment) Regs 2015, reg 12.

8.35 Form LPA 003B – Notice to donor of receipt of an application to register a lasting power of attorney – is different from form LPA 003A and, in particular, does not contain details of how to object to the registration on either factual or prescribed grounds. It states:

'You have received this notice because:
- You made a Lasting Power of Attorney (LPA) for
- the person(s) named below has applied to register the LPA

Person(s) who applied to register the LPA

The following person(s) applied to register the LPA:

Your right to object

You can object to the proposed registration of the LPA.

You have 3 weeks from to object.

How to object

Complete form LPA006 and send it to the Office of the Public Guardian or get the form from www.gov.uk/object-registration or by calling 0300 456 0300.'

Duty of the Public Guardian to provide the donor with an explanation of form LPA 003B

8.36 The LPA, EPA & PG Regs 2007, reg 13 provides that, in addition to sending the donor a notice in form LPA 003B, where it appears to the Public Guardian that there is good reason to do so, the Public Guardian must also provide (or arrange for the provision of) an explanation to the donor of the notice in form LPA 003B, and what the effect of it is, and why it is being brought to his attention (reg 13(3)). Any such explanation must be provided to the donor personally (reg 13(4)(a)), and in a way that is appropriate to the donor's circumstances: for example, using simple language, visual aids, or other appropriate means (reg 13(4)(b)).

PROCESSING THE APPLICATION

8.37 When it receives an application to register an LPA, the OPG will:

- check whether the LPA has been enclosed and whether it is in the prescribed form;
- check whether the application form has been enclosed and whether it has been correctly completed. This will either be Sections 12 to 15 of the 2015 LPA prescribed form or LP2 if registration is in respect of a 2007 or 2009 prescribed form;
- check that a cheque for the correct fee of £82 (or £41 if a repeat application) made payable to 'Office of the Public Guardian' has been enclosed, or whether the applicant has submitted a request on form LPA 120A for a fee exemption or remission;
- check to see whether a deputy has already been appointed, or whether there is an existing enduring power of attorney;
- check the instrument for any ineffective provisions that may affect its validity;
- notify the attorney on form LPA 003A and the donor on form LPA 003B that the application has been received; and
- wait for the prescribed period of four weeks to elapse during which an objection to the registration of the instrument may be made. The prescribed period was six weeks in the LPA, EPA & PG Regs 2007, reg 12. This was amended by The LPA, EPA & PG (Amendment) Regs 2013, reg 3, which substituted four weeks for six weeks with effect from 1 April 2013.

Defects in the LPA

8.38 If the instrument intended to create an LPA is defective, the OPG will send a letter to the applicant informing him of the problem. Common defects include:

- Pages of the LPA have been omitted.

- The signatories to the LPA have failed to sign in the correct order; or failed to enclose the completed Section 9,10, or 11, if a 2015 prescribed form; or Part A, B or C if a 2007 or 2009 prescribed form.
- The donor's or attorney's full name, address, or date of birth has been omitted.
- The donor and attorney(s) signature(s) has not been witnessed.
- The witness has not included their full name and/or address.
- The donor has failed to sign the LPA, particularly Section 5 (life sustaining treatment option) of a health and welfare LPA.

Defects in the application

8.39 If the application for registration is defective, the OPG will send a letter to the applicant informing him so. When the OPG was first established, it sent the following standard letter to applicants, which is reproduced below because it still serves as a useful checklist.

'Thank you for your application to register the Lasting Power of Attorney (LPA). Unfortunately, we are unable to register the LPA for the following reason(s):
- Please confirm in writing the date on which notice was given to all [or the following] named persons, as this information was missing on the application form LPA 002.
- It appears from the LPA 002 that one or more of the named persons have not been notified of the application to register the LPA. Please explain why notification has not occurred.
- One or more attorneys have not signed the application form. The attorneys should sign and return the form.
- Please let us know why the co-attorney has not been notified of the application. If the co-attorney has died, please send us the death certificate.
- If you do not intend registration to be limited to the attorney(s) named above, please let us know, and also let us know whether the notices (form LPA001) sent to the named persons showed both or all the attorneys names.
- We have noted a clause in the LPA relating to the attorney's powers, which appear to exceed an attorney's authority. [Insert details]. We propose to remove the clause from the LPA and may need to refer this to the Court of Protection for a direction on how to proceed. Before we do this we would like to know if you have any comments.'

Repeat applications to register

8.40 The Public Guardian (Fees, etc.) (Amendment) Regulations 2011 introduced a reduced fee for a repeat application to register an LPA in the following circumstances:

- the initial application to register an LPA is made on or after 1 October 2011;
- the initial application is returned to the applicant as invalid; and
- the repeat application to register is submitted within three months of the date on which the invalid application was returned to the applicant.

8.41 Section 14 of the 2015 prescribed LPA form should be completed to have the benefit of the reduced registration fee.

8.42 The repeat application fee is £41, is payable upon the submission of the repeat application to register.

8.43 The policy considerations underlying the repeat application fee were discussed at page 12 of the Ministry of Justice's response to consultation, CP(R) 16/10, *Office of the Public Guardian: Fees 2011/2012*, as follows:

> 'LPAs that are "imperfect" – that is correctable without requiring a fresh instrument to be made and a new submission to the OPG – are currently accepted once corrected free of charge. This is because, with the provision of additional information, or with invalid parts replaced, they can become valid instruments and be registered. This approach will continue. This proposal concerns only invalid LPAs, which are currently returned to the donor as unregistered because the faults contained with them are so significant that they cannot be corrected within the terms of the legislation to allow for registration.'

The prescribed period to elapse before registration

8.44 The 'prescribed period' is the period at the end of which the Public Guardian *must* register an instrument unless there is an objection or defect. Regulation 12 of the LPA, EPA & PG Regs 2007 (as amended by the LPA, EPA & PG (Amendment) Regs 2013, reg 3) stipulates that the prescribed period is four weeks beginning with:

- the date on which the OPG gave the notices, LPA 003A and LPA 003B, confirming receipt of the application; or
- if those notices were given on different dates, the latest of those dates.

Circumstances in which the Public Guardian must not register

8.45 The circumstances in which the Public Guardian must not register an instrument are considered in more detail at **10.39** , but, by way of a summary, at the end of the prescribed period the Public Guardian must register the instrument (MCA 2005, Sch 1, para 5), unless:

- the LPA is not in the prescribed form, or has not been properly executed (Sch 1, para 11);
- it contains a provision which would be ineffective as part of an LPA, or would prevent it from operating as a valid LPA (Sch 1, para 11(2));
- the Court of Protection has appointed a deputy for the donor, and the powers conferred on the deputy would conflict with those conferred on the attorney(s) (Sch 1, para 12);
- within the prescribed period, an attorney or a named person objects to the registration on a 'factual ground' (Sch 1, para 13(1) and (2));
- within the prescribed period, an attorney or a named person makes an application to the Court of Protection objecting to the registration on a 'prescribed ground', and notifies the OPG of the application (Sch 1, para 13(3) and (4)); or
- the donor objects (Sch 1, para 14).

REGISTRATION

8.46 The LPA, EPA & PG Regs 2007, reg 17(1) states that, where the Public Guardian registers an LPA, he must:

- retain a copy of the instrument; and
- return to the person(s) who applied for registration the original instrument, or the certified copy of it which accompanied the application.

Form LPA 004: Notice of registration of an LPA

8.47 The OPG must give notice to the donor and the attorney(s) in the prescribed form LPA 004 to confirm the registration of the LPA (MCA 2005, Sch 1, para 15, and LPA, EPA & PG Regs 2007, reg 17(2) and Sch 5). The form simply states the case number, the name of the donor, the names of the attorneys, and the date on which the LPA was entered into the register.

8.48 Where it appears to the Public Guardian that there is good reason to do so, the Public Guardian must also provide (or arrange for the provision of) an explanation to the donor of the notice in form LPA 004, and what the effect of it is, and why it is being brought to his attention (LPA, EPA & PG Regs 2007, reg 17(3)). Any such explanation must be provided to the donor personally (reg 17(4)(a)), and in a way that is appropriate to the donor's circumstances: for example, using simple language, visual aids, or other appropriate means (reg 17(4)(b)).

The appearance of a registered LPA

8.49 The appearance of a registered LPA, in the form prescribed by the LPA, EPA & PG (Amendment) Regs 2015, is as follows:

- on the front page, in the bottom centre, there is a box for official use by the OPG only stating the registration date and the OPG reference number;
- at the bottom of each page is a box marked 'Only valid with the official stamp here'. In a registered LPA this box is perforated with the words 'VALIDATED – OPG';
- inside the LPA there is a rubber stamp on each page or box that was blank at the time of registration recording the fact that the page or box was blank at the time of registration.

8.50 Various other official stamps may appear on a registered LPA, for example:

- 'The words . . . . have been severed from this instrument by order of the Court of Protection.'
- 'Office of the Public Guardian has been notified of the death/ disclaimer/ bankruptcy/ mental incapacity of this attorney on (*date on which the OPG received notification*).'
- 'Under the terms of this instrument (*replacement attorney*) is now entitled to act as an attorney.'

Office copies of the registered LPA

8.51 The OPG will produce an office copy of an LPA for a fee of £35 if a registered LPA is lost or in other exceptional circumstances. The fee is payable by the person requesting the document, and there is no remission or exemption available on this fee. If the OPG is responsible for the loss of the original LPA, the Public Guardian will provide office copies without charge.

8.52 A document purporting to be an office copy of a registered LPA is, in any part of the United Kingdom, evidence of the contents of the instrument, and the fact that it has been registered (MCA 2005, Sch 1, para 16(1)).

APPLICATION TO REGISTER A REPLACEMENT ATTORNEY

8.53 Where one of the events listed in MCA 2005, s 13(6) has occurred, and the replacement attorney has replaced an original attorney prior to an application to register the LPA, the application for registration will proceed in the usual way, although the OPG will require evidence of the relevant event under s 13(6). Where a replacement attorney becomes entitled to replace an original attorney after the LPA has been registered, no formal application or fee is required to register the replacement attorney. All that is required is to send a letter to the OPG enclosing the original registered instrument and evidence of the relevant event under s 13(6). The OPG will amend the register accordingly and will stamp the former attorney's declaration in Section 11 (if it relates to a 2015 prescribed form) or Part C (if it relates to a 2007 or 2009 prescribed form) of the instrument as follows: 'Office of the Public Guardian has been notified of the death/disclaimer/bankruptcy/mental incapacity of this attorney on *(date)*.' It will stamp the replacement attorney's Part C declaration with the words 'Under the terms of this instrument *(replacement attorney's name)* is now entitled to act as an Attorney.'

Chapter 9

OBJECTIONS TO REGISTRATION OF A LASTING POWER OF ATTORNEY

INTRODUCTION

9.1 The procedure for applying to register a lasting power of attorney (LPA) is described Chapter 8. Either the donor or the attorney(s) can apply for registration.

9.2 The person who is applying to register the LPA must notify any named persons (referred in the 2015 prescribed forms as 'people to notify' or the 2009 prescribed forms as 'people to be told') of his intention to apply for registration on form LP3, which informs the named person of the grounds on which he can object to the registration, and the procedure to be followed if he wishes to object.

9.3 The person who is applying to register the LPA then sends the application to register, by completing Sections 12–15 of the 2015 prescribed form or if the power was made on a 2007 or 2009 prescribed form on form LP2, to the Office of the Public Guardian (OPG), PO Box 16185, Birmingham B2 2WH.

9.4 The OPG will send a notice of receipt of the application to register the LPA on form:

- LPA 003A to the attorney(s); and
- LPA 003B to the donor.

9.5 Form LPA 003A informs the recipient of the grounds on which he can object to the registration, and the procedure to be followed. LPA 003B informs the donor that he has a right to object to the registration and the procedure to be followed. In the donor's case, however, no grounds of objection are specified.

9.6 An attorney or named person can object to the registration of the LPA on either:

- factual grounds – in which case, the objection must be made to the OPG on form LPA 007; or
- prescribed grounds – in which case, the objection must be made to the OPG on form LPA 008 and a separate application made to the Court of Protection on form COP 7 issued by the court.

9.7 An attorney or named person who wishes to object to the registration on factual grounds must give notice of his objection to the OPG within three weeks from the date of the form LP3 (in the case of a named person) or LPA 003A (in the case of the attorney(s)).

9.8 An attorney or a named person who objects to registration on any of the prescribed grounds must give notice of his objection to the Court of Protection within three weeks from the date of the form LP3 or LPA 003A, as the case may be. The objector must also notify the OPG on form LPA 008 that he has made an application to the court. The Public Guardian must not register the instrument unless the court directs him to do so.

9.9 If the Public Guardian is satisfied that a factual ground for making the objection is established, he must not register the instrument unless the court, on the application of the person applying for the registration:

- is satisfied that the ground is not established; and
- directs the Public Guardian to register the instrument.

9.10 The procedure is different where the donor is the objector. Although form LPA 003B informs him that he has a right to object to registration, there is no need for him to specify the grounds on which he objects. However, he must inform the OPG of his objection within 3 weeks from the date on which he received form LPA 003B, and preferably he should use form LPA 006 for that purpose. The Public Guardian must not register the instrument, unless the court, on the application of the attorney(s):

- is satisfied that the donor lacks the capacity to object to the registration; and
- directs the Public Guardian to register the instrument.

FACTUAL GROUNDS OF OBJECTION

List of factual grounds

9.11 The factual grounds of objection, which are mainly set out in s 13(3) and (6) and para 13 of Sch 1 to the Mental Capacity Act 2005 (MCA 2005), are as follows:

- the donor is bankrupt, interim bankrupt or the subject of a debt relief order (for property and financial affairs LPAs only);
- the attorney is bankrupt, interim bankrupt or the subject of a debt relief order (for property and financial affairs LPAs only);
- the donor is dead;
- the attorney is dead;
- there has been a dissolution or annulment of a marriage or civil partnership between the donor and the attorney (except if the LPA provided that such an event should not affect the instrument);
- the attorney lacks the capacity to be an attorney under the LPA;
- the attorney has disclaimed the appointment.

Donor's bankruptcy

9.12 Section 13(3) of the MCA 2005 provides that 'P's bankruptcy revokes the power so far as it relates to P's property and affairs'. Section 13(4) adds:

'But where P is bankrupt merely because an interim bankruptcy restrictions order has effect in respect of him, the power is suspended, so far as it relates to P's property and affairs, for so long as the order has effect.'

9.13 Section 64(3) of the MCA 2005, the interpretation section, provides that: 'In this Act, references to the bankruptcy of an individual include a case where a bankruptcy restrictions order under the Insolvency Act 1986 has effect in respect of him.' Section 64(4) provides that 'bankruptcy restrictions order' includes an interim bankruptcy restrictions order.

9.14 The Tribunals, Courts and Enforcement Act 2007 introduced debt relief orders and debt relief restrictions orders into the Insolvency Act 1986. Once a debtor has entered into such an order, he or she is subject to a number of restrictions that are similar to those imposed on people declared bankrupt. With effect from 1 October 2012 amendments were introduced into the MCA 2005 by the Tribunals, Courts and Enforcement Act 2007 (Consequential Amendments) Order 2012 (SI 2012/2404) Sch 2, para 53, in order to exclude from the category of people eligible to be donors of an LPA persons made subject to a debt relief order under Part 7A of the Insolvency Act 1986 and, where a donor is made subject to such an order, to revoke the LPA insofar as it relates to the donor's property and affairs, or suspend it if the order is an interim one.

Attorney's bankruptcy

9.15 Subsections 13(5) and (6)(b) of the MCA 2005 provide that the bankruptcy of an attorney will terminate his appointment. The attorney's bankruptcy will also revoke the power, unless one of the exceptions set out in s 13(7) applies, namely where he is:

- replaced under the terms of the instrument; or
- one of two or more persons appointed to act as donees jointly and severally in respect of any matter and, after his bankruptcy, there is at least one remaining.

9.16 Subsections 13(8) and (9) of the MCA 2005 provide that:

'(8)   The bankruptcy of a donee does not terminate his appointment, or revoke the power, in so far as his authority relates to P's personal welfare.

(9)   Where the donee is bankrupt merely because an interim bankruptcy restrictions order has effect in respect of him, his appointment and the power are suspended, so far as they relate to P's property and personal affairs, for so long as the order has effect.'

9.17 Where a donee of an LPA is made the subject of a debt relief order, the order revokes the power in so far as it relates to the donor's property and affairs, or suspends it if the order is an interim one: MCA 2005, ss 13(6) and (8) as amended by the Tribunals, Courts and Enforcement Act 2007 (Consequential Amendments) Order 2012, Sch 2, para 53.

Dissolution or winding-up of a trust corporation

9.18 Subsections 13 (5) and (6)(b) of the MCA 2005 also provide that, if the attorney is a trust corporation, its winding-up or dissolution will terminate its appointment. The winding-up or dissolution of a trust corporation which is an attorney will also revoke the power, unless one of the exceptions set out in s 13(7) applies, namely where the trust corporation:

- is replaced under the terms of the instrument; or
- is one of two or more persons appointed to act as donees jointly and severally in respect of any matter and, after its winding-up or dissolution, there is at least one donee remaining.

Donor's death

9.19 The donor's death revokes a lasting power of attorney. Where the instrument is registered, the Public Guardian must cancel the registration if he is satisfied that the power has been revoked as a result of the donor's death (Lasting Powers of Attorney, Enduring Powers of Attorney and Public Guardian Regulations 2007 (LPA, EPA & PG Regs 2007), reg 22(1)), and notify the donee or, if more than one, each donee (reg 22(2)).

Attorney's death

9.20 Subsections 13 (5) and (6)(b) of the MCA 2005 provide that the death of a donee terminates his appointment. His death will also revoke the power, unless one of the exceptions set out in s 13(7) applies, namely where:

- he is replaced under the terms of the instrument; or
- he is one of two or more persons appointed to act as donees jointly and severally in respect of any matter and, after his death, there is at least one remaining.

Dissolution or annulment of marriage or civil partnership

9.21 The dissolution or annulment of a marriage or civil partnership between the donor and the donee terminates the appointment of the donee, and revokes the power, unless the donee is replaced under the terms of the instrument, or he is one of two or more persons appointed to act jointly and severally and, after the dissolution or annulment, there is at least one remaining donee (MCA 2005, s 13(5), (6)(c) and (7)).

9.22 However, the dissolution or annulment of a marriage or civil partnership will not terminate the appointment of a donee or revoke the power, if the instrument expressly provided that it was not to do so (MCA 2005, s 13(11)).

Attorney's incapacity

9.23 Section 13(5) and (6)(d) of the MCA 2005 provide that the lack of capacity of a donee terminates his appointment. His lack of capacity will also revoke the power, unless one of the exceptions set out in s 13(7) applies, namely where:

- he is replaced under the terms of the instrument; or
- he is one of two or more persons appointed to act as donees jointly and severally in respect of any matter and, after he has become incapacitated, there is at least one remaining.

9.24 When considering the role of the registration authority, now the Public Guardian, at paragraph 7.49 of the report on *Mental Incapacity* (1995), the Law Commission stated:

'The role of the registration authority should simply be (1) to register [LPAs] and give notice of registration, (2) to cancel registrations and (3) to amend registrations in cases of partial revocation or the appointment of replacement attorneys. Since the registration authority will be an administrative rather than a judicial body, cancellation or amendment should only be effected on the receipt of specified types of objective evidence.'

9.25 A doctor's letter or other medical evidence of the attorney's incapacity will usually be sufficient and, if there is any doubt or dispute, the Public Guardian will consider asking a Court of Protection Special Visitor to visit the attorney. He has the authority to do so by virtue of s 58(1)(d) of the MCA 2005.

Attorney's disclaimer

9.26 Section 13(5) and (6)(a) of the MCA 2005 provide that the disclaimer of the appointment by a donee, 'in accordance with such requirements as may be prescribed for the purposes of the section in regulations made by the Lord Chancellor', terminates his appointment. The requirements for disclaimer are set out in reg 20 of the LPA, EPA & PG Regs 2007. Disclaimer is considered in more detail at **14.10–14.24**.

9.27 The attorney's disclaimer will also revoke the power, unless one of the exceptions set out in MCA 2005, s 13(7) applies, namely where:

- he is replaced under the terms of the instrument; or
- he is one of two or more persons appointed to act as attorneys jointly and severally in respect of any matter and, after he has become incapacitated, there is at least one remaining.

OBJECTION ON FACTUAL GROUNDS

The objection must be sent to the Office of the Public Guardian

9.28 The LPA, EPA & PG Regs 2007, reg 14(1) provides that:

'This regulation deals with any objection to the registration of an instrument as a lasting power of attorney which is made to the Public Guardian.'

Time limit of three weeks

9.29 There is a time limit of three weeks in which a person can object to the registration of an instrument. Reg 14(2) of the LPA, EPA & PG Regs 2007, as amended by reg 4 of the LPA, EPA & PG (Amendment) Regs 2013 provides that:

'Where any person –
   (a)   is entitled to receive notice under paragraph 6, 7 or 8 of Schedule 1 to the Act of an application for the registration of the instrument, and
   (b)   wishes to object to registration on a ground set out in paragraph 13(1) of Schedule 1 to the Act,

he must do so before the end of the period of 3 weeks beginning with the date on which the notice is given.'

LPA 007: Notice of objection

9.30 Regulation 14(3) of the LPA, EPA & PG Regs 2007 provides that:

'A notice of objection must be given in writing, setting out –
   (a)   the name and address of the objector;
   (b)   if different, the name and address of the donor of the power;
   (c)   if known, the name and address of the donee (or donees); and
   (d)   the ground for making the objection.'

9.31 Although it is not officially a prescribed form, the OPG issues a form LPA 007, Objection to the Office of the Public Guardian, of a proposed registration of a Lasting Power of Attorney on factual grounds, which can be downloaded from the Government's website: https://www.gov.uk/government /publications/object-to-registration-of-a-lasting-power-of-attorney

9.32 This form can only be used by attorneys and named persons, and, in addition to the requirements of LPA, EPA & PG Regs 2007, reg 14(3), the objector is required to list the evidence on which the objection is based and attach a copy to the form LPA 007 when sending it to the OPG.

Notice that the ground of objection is established

9.33 Regulation 14(4) of the LPA, EPA & PG Regs 2007 provides that:

'The Public Guardian must notify the objector as to whether he is satisfied that the ground of objection is established.'

Request for further information

9.34 Regulation 14(5) of the LPA, EPA & PG Regs 2007 states that:

'At any time after receiving the notice of objection and before giving the notice required by paragraph (4), the Public Guardian may require the objector to provide such further information, or produce such documents, as the Public Guardian reasonably considers necessary to enable him to determine where the ground for making the objection is established.'

Notice that, although the ground of objection is established, the instrument is not revoked

9.35 Regulation 14(6) of the LPA, EPA & PG Regs 2007 stipulates that:

'Where –
(a)   the Public Guardian is satisfied that the ground of objection is established, but
(b)   by virtue of section 13(7) of the Act, the instrument is not revoked,

the notice under paragraph (4) must contain a statement to that effect.'

9.36 Section 13(7) of the MCA 2005 provides that the occurrence in relation to a donee of an event mentioned in subsection (6) terminates his appointment, except where:

• the donee is replaced under the terms of the instrument; or
• he is one of two or more persons appointed to act as donees jointly and severally in respect of any matter and, after the event, there is at least one remaining donee.

Right to make further objection

9.37 Regulation 14(7) of the LPA, EPA & PG Regs 2007 provides that:

'Nothing in this regulation prevents an objector from making a further objection under paragraph 13 of Schedule 1 to the Act where –
(a)   the notice under paragraph (4) indicates that the Public Guardian is not satisfied that the particular ground of objection to which that notice relates is established; and
(b)   the period specified in paragraph (2) has not expired.'

Effect of successful objection on factual grounds

9.38 Paragraph 13(2) of Sch 1 to the MCA 2005 provides that:

'If the Public Guardian is satisfied that the ground for making the objection is established, he must not register the instrument unless the court, on the application of the person applying for the registration –
(a)   is satisfied that the ground is not established, and
(b)   directs the Public Guardian to register the instrument.'

OBJECTION BY DONOR

Introduction

9.39 Where the donor objects to the registration of an LPA, the procedure is entirely different from the procedure that applies when:

• the donor objects to the registration of an EPA; or
• named persons or attorneys object to the registration of an LPA.

9.40 The reasoning behind this was explained in the following terms by the Law Commission, at paragraph 7.34 of its report, *Mental Incapacity* (Law Com Report No 231 (1995)):

'We favour the retention of a requirement that a donee must notify a donor of his or her intention to register [an LPA]. It may be some time since the document was executed and, in any event, the act of registration will significantly alter matters by triggering the attorney's power to act. The donor must be warned that this is a prospect and be given an opportunity to prevent registration. The registration authority will have no power to determine disputes and such matters will always have to go to the court. Thus, if the registration authority is informed by a donor that he or she objects to registration of [an LPA] then the registration authority will have no power to register it in the absence of a direction from the court. There is no need to specify any particular grounds on which a donor may object to registration. We recommend that if a donor objects to registration of [an LPA] then the registration authority should inform the donee and should not register the instrument unless the court directs it to do so.'

Schedule 1, paragraph 14

9.41 Paragraph 14 of Sch 1 to the MCA 2005 states that:

'(1) This paragraph applies if the donor –
   (a) receives a notice under paragraph 8 of an application for the registration of an instrument, and
   (b) before the end of the prescribed period, gives notice to the Public Guardian of an objection to the registration.
(2) The Public Guardian must not register the instrument unless the court, on the application of the donee or, if more than one, any of them –
   (a) is satisfied that the donor lacks capacity to object to the registration, and
   (b) directs the Public Guardian to register the instrument.'

9.42 The notice under para 8 is form LPA 003B, which is prescribed by reg 13(2) and Part 2 of Sch 4 to the LPA, EPA & PG Regs 2007.

Time limit of three weeks

9.43 The donor is bound by the same time limit of three weeks in which to object to the registration of an instrument, though in his case he must give notice of objection before the end of the period of three weeks beginning with the date on which notice in form LPA 003B was given (LPA, EPA & PG Regs 2007, reg 14A(2)(d), as amended by the 2013 Regulations).

LPA 006: Objection by the donor

9.44 Although it is not officially prescribed in the LPA, EPA & PG Regs 2007, the OPG issues a form LPA 006, Objection by the donor to the registration of a lasting power of attorney, which can be accessed from the Government website: https://www.gov.uk/government/publications/object-to-registration-of-a-lasting-power-of-attorney

9.45 Form LPA 006, which is reproduced at APPENDIX C, states:

'If you (the donor) **do not want** your lasting power of attorney(s) (LPA) to be registered then you need to complete and sign this form and return it to the Office of the Public Guardian (OPG). You can use this form to object to registration of up to two LPAs; please provide below the case number and LPA type for each LPA you want to object to.

(*There follows a space in which the donor is required to state the reason(s) for his objection*).

Note: The OPG will suspend your LPA(s) when we receive this form. Your attorney(s) will then not be able to use the LPA(s), unless they apply to the Court of Protection and the court orders the LPA(s) to be registered.(*The donor is required to give his full name, address, date of birth, and the case number(s) (if known). He must sign the form to confirm the objection, and date it*)

(the donor must provide the full names, addresses of all the attorneys (if known).)'

The attorney must apply to the court to direct the Public Guardian to register

9.46 The donor's objection will automatically suspend the registration of the LPA and, if the attorney wishes to resolve this impasse, he will need to apply to the Court of Protection for an order directing the Public Guardian to register the instrument (MCA 2005, Sch 1, para 14(2)(b)), which the court will only do if it is satisfied that the donor lacks capacity to object to the registration (para 14(2)(a)).

9.47 There is no application fee. Article 4(3) of the Court of Protection Fees Order 2007 (L.13) exempts attorneys from the requirement to pay an application fee of £400 in relation to any objection to the registration of an LPA.

9.48 Rule 67(5) of the Court of Protection Rules 2007 (COP Rules 2007) (SI 2007/1744 (L.12)) states that:

'Where the applicant knows or has reasonable grounds to believe that the donor of the power lacks capacity to make a decision in relation to any matter that is the subject of the application, he must notify the donor in accordance with Part 7 (of the Court of Protection Rules 2007).'

Capacity to object to registration

9.49 In reality, most donors who are faced with an application to register an LPA, to which they object, will simply revoke the LPA, if they have the capacity to do so (MCA 2005, s 13(2)). Although there is no case-law on this subject yet, it is likely that the court would regard the criteria for capacity to object to the registration of the LPA as slightly different from the criteria to revoke the LPA, and possibly less demanding.

9.50 SAD and ACD v SED, DJ Glentworth, case no. 12791319

Under the EPA regime, occasionally cases came before the court in which the donor had taken a dislike to his attorneys, and objected to their continued involvement, but formally lacked the capacity to revoke the instrument: perhaps, for example, because he did not fully understand the scope of the attorneys' authority, or he did not appreciate the foreseeable consequences of revoking the instrument. In such circumstances, where there was evidence that it was likely that the continued involvement of the attorneys would cause distress to the donor, the court would usually find the attorneys are not acting in the best interests to be the donor's attorneys, and revoke the power. As an example, see the decisions of District Judge Glentworth, *SAD and ACD v SED*, case no 12791319.

OBJECTION ON A PRESCRIBED GROUND

List of prescribed grounds

9.51 Regulation 15 of the LPA, EPA and PG Regs 2007 governs any objection to the registration of an instrument as a lasting power of attorney, which is to be made to the Court of Protection (reg 15(1)).

9.52 LPA, EPA & PG Regs 2007, reg 15(2) provides:

'The grounds for making an application to the court are –
  (a) that one or more of the requirements for the creation of a lasting power of attorney have not been met;
  (b) that the power has been revoked, or has otherwise come to an end, on a ground other than the grounds set out in paragraph 13(1) of Schedule 1 to the Act;
  (c) any of the grounds set out in paragraph (a) or (b) of section 22(3) of the Act.'

9.53 The list of prescribed grounds given in forms LP3 and LPA 003A to the named persons and attorneys respectively is expressed in a way that a lay person would find easier to understand, but is slightly different. The forms state:

'   Prescribed objections:
  •   the LPA isn't legally valid – for example, you don't believe the donor had mental capacity to make an LPA
  •   the donor cancelled their LPA when they had mental capacity to do so
  •   there was fraud or the donor was pressured to make the LPA
  •   an attorney is acting above their authority or against the donor's best interests (or you know that they intend to do this)'.

That one or more of the requirements for creating an LPA have not been met

9.54 The LPA, EPA & PG Regs 2007, reg 15(2)(a) provides that one of the prescribed grounds for making an application to the Court of Protection objecting to the registration of an LPA is 'that one or more of the requirements for the creation of a lasting power of attorney have not been met'.

9.55 This is similar to the ground on which an objection can be made to the registration of an EPA, namely, 'that the power purported to have been created by the instrument was not valid as an enduring power of attorney' (MCA 2005, Sch 4, para 13(9)(b)). As stated in that paragraph, an objection on this ground is likely to be based on arguments that:

  •   the donor lacked capacity to create an LPA when he purported to do so; and
  •   the instrument creating the power is formally defective in some way.

9.56 Objections on this ground were rarely successful in the case of EPAs, and are even less successful in respect of LPAs for two reasons. The first is the requirement that an LPA must include a certificate of a person of a prescribed description that, in his opinion, at the time when the donor executes the instrument, the donor understands the purpose of the instrument and the scope of the authority conferred under it, etc (MCA 2005, Sch 1, para 2(1)(e)). The second reason is that, because of the obligations imposed on him by Sch 1, para 11, the Public Guardian has to scrutinise each instrument for any provision that might be ineffective as part of an LPA, or would prevent it from operating as a valid LPA.

That the power has been revoked or has otherwise come to an end

9.57 The LPA, EPA & PG Regs 2007, reg 15(2)(b) provides that one of the prescribed grounds for making an application to the Court of Protection objecting to the registration of an LPA is that 'the power has been revoked, or has otherwise come to an end on a ground other than the grounds set out in paragraph 13(1) of Schedule 1 to the Act'.

9.58 The grounds set out in MCA 2005, Sch 1, para 13(1) are the events mentioned in s 13(3) or (6)(a) to (d) of the Act; events such as death, bankruptcy, and disclaimer. An objection that the power has been revoked on one of these grounds should not be made to the Court of Protection, but to the Public Guardian as an objection based on factual grounds (see **9.26**). Accordingly, that leaves a potential objector with only one basis on which to sustain an objection on this ground, namely that the donor has validly revoked the power.

That fraud or undue pressure was used to induce the donor to create an LPA

9.59 The LPA, EPA & PG Regs 2007, reg 15(2)(c) provides that the prescribed grounds for making an application to the Court of Protection objecting to the registration of an LPA include 'any of the grounds set out in paragraph (a) or (b) of section 22(3) of the Act'.

9.60 Referring to the donor as P, MCA 2005, s 22(3) provides that:

'Subsection (4) applies if the court is satisfied –
   (a)   that fraud or undue pressure was used to induce P –
      (i)   to execute an instrument for the purpose of creating a lasting power of attorney, or
      (ii)   to create a lasting power of attorney, or
   (b)   that the donee (or, if more than one, any of them) of a lasting power of attorney –
      (i)   has behaved, or is behaving, in a way that contravenes his authority or is not in P's best interests, or
      (ii)   proposes to behave in a way that would contravene his authority or would not be in P's best interests.'

The 'fraud or undue pressure' ground is the same as the ground in MCA 2005, Sch 4, para 13(9)(d) for objecting to the registration of an EPA, and this is discussed in detail at **17.83-17.89**.

9.61 Although objectors objected fairly often to the registration of an EPA on this ground, they were rarely successful, and in over 20 years the court has upheld an objection on this ground on only three occasions. Two of them were where the attorney had fraudulently used a prescribed form which was post-dated, and was not in existence at the time when the power was purported to have been created by the donor. The other occasion was when the witness to the donor's signature, who was acting on instructions from the attorney, had concealed the contents of the prescribed form, and had persuaded the donor that the document was of an entirely different nature.

The attorney's behaviour contravenes his authority, or is not in the donor's best interests

9.62 By expressly referring to s 22(3)(b) of the MCA 2005, the LPA, EPA & PG Regs 2005, reg 15(2)(c) provides that one of the prescribed grounds for making an application to the Court of Protection objecting to the registration of an LPA is 'that the donee (or, if more than one, any of them) of a lasting power of attorney, has behaved, or is behaving, in a way that contravenes his authority or is not in P's best interests, or proposes to behave in a way that would contravene his authority or would not be in P's best interests'.

9.63 This final ground of objection is notably different from its equivalent in the EPA legislation, namely, 'that, having regard to all the circumstances and in particular the attorney's relationship to or connection with the donor, the attorney is unsuitable to be the donor's attorney' (MCA 2005, Sch 4, para 13)(9)(e)), on which there have been several reported decisions.

9.64 In its report on *Mental Incapacity* (Law Com No 231) (1995), at paragraph 7.58, the Law Commission recommended that the Court of Protection should have power to direct that an LPA should not be registered, where the donee has behaved, is behaving, or proposes to behave in a way that would contravene his authority, or is not or would not be in the donor's best interests. It gave the following reasons for making this recommendation:

'The 1985 Act provides that the court shall cancel the registration of, and revoke, an EPA if "the attorney is unsuitable to be the donor's attorney". In Consultation Paper No 129 we suggested that this power to revoke should be linked to the question of whether the attorney was acting in the donor's best interests. Respondents supported this proposal, with some seeking reassurance that the court should not be able to override a patient's advance decisions about health care by revoking the appointment of an attorney. We have already recommended that an attorney under [an LPA] should be under a duty to act in the donor's best interests. It is therefore logical to use this terminology, rather than that of "unsuitability", in relation to the court's power to displace an attorney. Express provisions should also be made for revocation by the court where an attorney's acts contravene the terms of the authority granted by the donor. We recommend that the court may, on behalf of a donor without capacity to do so, either direct that a purported [LPA] should not be registered or revoke [an LPA] where the donee or intended donee has behaved, is behaving or proposes to behave in a way that (1) contravenes or would contravene the authority granted in the [LPA] or (2) is not or would not be in the donor's best interests.'

9.65 The Mental Capacity Act Code of Practice, at paragraph 7.70, gives several examples of behaviour that might constitute the contravention of an attorney's authority or a failure to act in the donor's best interests, though the list is by no means exhaustive.

'Signs that an attorney may be exploiting the donor (or failing to act in the donor's best interests) include:
- stopping relatives or friends contacting the donor – for example, the attorney may prevent contact or the donor may suddenly refuse visits or telephone calls from family and friends for no reason.
- sudden unexplained changes in living arrangements (for example, someone moves in to care for a donor they've had little contact with).
- not allowing healthcare or social care staff to see the donor.
- taking the donor out of hospital against medical advice, while the donor is having necessary medical treatment.
- unpaid bills (for example, residential care or nursing home fees).
- an attorney opening a credit card account for the donor.
- spending money on things that are not obviously related to the donor's needs.
- the attorney spending money in an unusual or extravagant way.
- transferring financial assets to another country.'

9.66 There has been surprisingly little case-law on objections to the registration of an LPA. In *Re J* [2011] COPLR Con Vol 716, Her Honour Judge Hazel Marshall QC considered an objection to the registration of an LPA on the grounds that it was not valid and that the attorney proposed to behave in a way that would contravene his authority or not be in the donor's best interests. The circumstances were rather unusual insofar as the attorneys were partners in a firm of solicitors who were acting on her behalf in a family rift; hence, the reference to acting 'in any other capacity'. At para [75] she held that:

'In my judgment, the key to giving proper effect to the distinction between an attorney's behaviour as attorney and his behaviour in any other capacity lies in considering the matter in stages. First, one must identify the allegedly offending behaviour or prospective behaviour. Secondly, one looks at all the circumstances and context and then decides whether, taking everything into account, it really does amount to behaviour which is not in P's best interests, or can be fairly characterised as such. Finally, one must decide whether, taking everything into account including the fact that it is behaviour in some other capacity, it also gives good reason to take the very serious step of revoking the LPA.'

OBJECTION TO THE COURT OF PROTECTION

Introduction

9.67 A named person should have received from the applicant a form LP3 (Notice of Intention to Apply for Registration of a Lasting Power of Attorney), and an attorney should have received from the OPG a form LPA 003A (Notice of Receipt of an Application to Register a Lasting Power of Attorney). The notices are similar but not identical.

Form LPA 003A states:

'You can object to the proposed registration of the LPA. You have 3 weeks from [ ] to object. Page 2 of this notice tells you how to object.'

In comparison, LP3 explains to the recipient that:

'When they made the LPA, the donor decided you should be told about it before it's registered. This is so you can raise any concerns you may have. If you do have concerns, you can only object to the registration of the LPA for the reasons listed on page 4 of this form.

If you want to object, you must do so within 3 weeks of the date of this notice.

If you don't want to object you don't have to do anything.'

(*Page 2 of form LPA 003 and page 4 of form LP3 states the following* :)

'To make a prescribed objection:
*   complete form COP7 and send it to the Court of Protection. Get the form from www.gov.uk/object-registration or by calling 0300 456 4000 AND
*   complete form LPA008 and send it to the Office of the Public Guardian.

Get the form from www.gov.uk/object-registration or by calling 0300 456 0300

If you are objecting to a specific attorney, it may not prevent registration if other attorneys or a replacement attorney have been appointed.'

Permission

9.68 Section 50 of the MCA 2005 (Applications to the Court of Protection) imposes a general requirement to obtain the court's permission to make an application, but exempts certain people from that requirement. Rule 51 of the COP Rules 2007 includes even more exemptions, and specifically provides that permission of the court is not required where an application concerns a lasting power of attorney (r 51(2)(b)).

Obtaining the forms

9.69 Anyone wishing to object to the registration of an LPA on one or more of the prescribed grounds should obtain the forms from the Court of Protection, First Avenue House, 42–49 High Holborn, London WC1V 6NP or via: http://hmctsformfinder.justice.gov.uk

9.70 The following forms are to be used for applications that relate to an objection to the registration of an LPA on prescribed grounds, and includes:

*   COP 1 – Application form.
*   COP 7 – Application to object to the registration of a lasting power of attorney.
*   COP 24 – Witness statement.
*   COP 42 – Making an application to the Court of Protection.
*   LPA 008 – Notice to the Office of the Public Guardian of an application to object to the registration of a lasting power of attorney made to the Court of Protection.

COP 7: Application to object to the registration of an LPA

9.71 The applicant (objector) is asked to read first the preliminary information on the front page of COP 7 before completing the form. Among other things, this states that:

- The applicant can only object by using this form if he is an intended attorney or a named person who received an LP3 notice of intention to apply for registration of the LPA.
- There is no fee for filing this form with the court.
- Any application to object must be made within three weeks from the day on which the applicant received the LP3 notice.
- If the applicant is not one of the named persons who received an LP3 notice, but wishes to object, he may do so, but he needs to file a COP 1 application form, instead of the COP 7, and pay the specified fee. He also needs to notify the Public Guardian of his application to the court.
- If the objector is the donor, he should not use form COP 7, but complete a form LPA 006 instead, and sent it to the OPG.
- The applicant is warned that he may have to pay any costs he incurs during the proceedings, and if the court considers that he has acted unreasonably, it can order him to pay any costs incurred by the other parties.

9.72 Form COP 7 itself consists of four sections:

- Section 1– Your details (the applicant). The applicant must state his full name and contact details, and whether a solicitor is representing him and, if so, the solicitor's name and contact details. He is also required to state whether he is an attorney or a named person.
- Section 2 – Objection to the registration of an LPA. The applicant is required to provide the full names of the donor and intended attorneys; the date on which the donor signed the LPA; the date on which the applicant was given notice of the application to register the LPA; and the prescribed ground(s) on which the applicant objects to the proposed registration.
- Section 3 – Attending court hearings. The applicant is asked whether he needs any special assistance or facilities if the court requires him to attend a hearing.
- Section 4 – Statement of truth.

9.73 At the back of form COP 7 are four guidance notes:

- Notifying the Public Guardian. The applicant must notify the OPG on form LPA 008.
- If the applicant needs special assistance or facilities for a disability or impairment (for example documents to be supplied in Braille or in large print, a hearing loop, wheelchair access, or a sign language interpreter), he is asked to set out his requirements in full.
- What the applicant needs to do next. The court requires two copies (ie the original plus one copy) of each of the documents the applicant files. He is told to send the original completed forms documents and copies to the Court of Protection, First Avenue House, 42–49 High Holborn, London WC1V 6NP.
- What happens next? The court will notify him when his application form has been issued and will return a sealed copy of the application form. He is informed that he will need to serve a copy on the donor and each attorney of the LPA.

LPA 008: Notice to the Office of the Public Guardian of an application to object to the registration of an LPA made to the Court of Protection

9.74 Where a person applies to the Court of Protection to object to the registration of an LPA, he must give notice to the Public Guardian on form LPA 008. This form requires the applicant (objector) to state:

- The case number (if known).
- The donor's name, address, postcode, and telephone number.
- The applicant objector's name, address, postcode, and telephone number.
- The reasons for making the objection ('Why are you making the objection').
- The date on which the objection was sent to the Court of Protection.

Issue of application form

9.75 The general rule is that proceedings are started when the court issues an application form at the request of the applicant (COP Rules 2007, r 62 – When proceedings are started).

9.76 When the court receives the application form COP 7 and any supporting documentation, it will issue the application by sealing the application form and returning it to the applicant with the following forms:

- COP 5 – Acknowledgment of service/notification.
- COP 14 – Proceedings about you in the Court of Protection.
- COP 14A – Guidance notes for completing COP14.
- COP 15 – Notice that an application form has been issued.
- COP 15A – Guidance notes for completing COP 15.
- COP 20A – Certificate of notification/non-notification of the person to whom the proceedings relate.
- COP20B – Certificate of service/non-service, and certificate of notification. This form must be filed with the court to confirm that a document has been served on respondents or notification has been provided to interested persons.

Service of documents

9.77 The COP Rules 2007, r 67, requires that, as soon as practicable, and in any event within 14 days of the date on which the court issued the application form, the applicant must serve on the donor and every donee of the power the following documents:

- a copy of the application form;
- copies of any documents filed with the application form; and
- a form COP 5 acknowledging service.

9.78 The COP Rules 2007, r 70 requires that, as soon as practicable, and in any event within 14 days of the date on which the court issued the application form, the applicant must notify the persons specified ('interested persons') in the relevant practice direction. Practice Direction 9B: Notification of others than an application has been issued, sets out the class of people who should be notified. If the application for objection is made by an attorney or certificate provider, these persons are not required to be notified (COP Rules, r 67(2)).

9.79 Interested persons should be notified that an application has been made and sent the following documents:

- Form COP 15; and
- form COP 5 acknowledging service.

9.80 Practice Direction 7A: Notifying P, sets out the manner and detail of how the donor should be notified about the application. The donor must be notified personally by the applicant, his agent or such other person as the court directs (COP Rules 2007, r 41 and r 46) and must be provided with the following information set out in form COP 14, in a way that is appropriate to his circumstances (for example, using simple language, visual aids or any other appropriate means):

(a) who the applicant is;
(b) what the application is about;
(c) what will happen if the court makes the order or direction that has been applied for; and
(d) that P may seek advice and assistance in relation to any matter of which he is notified.

Certificate of service

9.81 Within 7 days of the service of documents, the applicant must complete and return to the court the forms COP 20A (in respect of the donor) and COP 20B (in respect of respondents or interested persons: Certificate of service/non-service and certificate of notification/non-notification (COP Rules 2007, r 67(4)).

Responding to the application

9.82 The persons who have been served or notified of the application have 14 days to file with the court their acknowledgement of service on form COP 5.

Dealing with applications

9.83 Part 12 (rr 84–89) of the COP Rules 2007 sets out the manner in which the court may deal with the application. A pilot case management scheme (as set out in the Pilot Case Management Practice Direction) is in operation until 30 November 2017 which includes a property and financial affairs case management pathway. The intention is that by the end of 2017, new Court of Protection Rules will be laid with supporting Practice Directions, which will incorporate the pilot. Objection to the registration of a LPA falls within the scope of this project. The judge will list the case for a Dispute Resolution Hearing or transfer the case to the most appropriate regional court outside the Central Office and Registry for listing of the Dispute Resolution Hearing and future case management. The judge may also order the respondent to file further evidence if the grounds are not clear from the submitted form COP 5. A Dispute Resolution Hearing is a form of judicial mediation, to enable the court to determine whether the case can be resolved and avoid unnecessary litigation. If the parties reach agreement to settle the case, the court will make a final order if it considers it in the donor's best interests. If the parties do not reach agreement, the court will give directions for the management of the case. Subject to this, Rule 84 provides that, as soon as practicable after any application has been issued, the court may decide to:

- make a decision based on the application without a court hearing;
- give directions about the application, and the next steps to be taken; or
- fix a date for the application to be heard by the court at an attended hearing.

Decisions based on the application without a court hearing

9.84 The court usually disposes of applications involving LPAs without a hearing in cases where no one objects to the application or proposes that a different order is made: for example, in applications:

- by the Public Guardian to sever an ineffective or invalid provision in an instrument pursuant to MCA 2005, Sch 1, para 11; and
- for declarations that an instrument which is not in the prescribed form is to be treated as if it were, pursuant to MCA 2005, Sch 1, para 3(2).

9.85 When the court decides that it can deal with the matter without a hearing, it will do so, and serve a copy of its order on the parties and on any other person it directs (COP Rules 2007, r 84(5)).

Reconsideration of orders made without a hearing

9.86 Where the court makes an order without a hearing, the donor, any party to the proceedings, or anyone else who is affected by the order may apply to the court for reconsideration of the order made (COP Rules 2007, r 89(2)). An application for reconsideration must be made in accordance with Part 10 of the COP Rules 2007, using a COP 9: Application notice, within 21 days of the order being served (COP Rules 2007, r 89(3)).

Directions about the application

9.87 Subject to the pilot case management project, where there is an objection to the registration of an LPA, the court usually makes a preliminary directions order defining the parties and setting out a timetable for the filing of evidence in anticipation of the final hearing. In some cases, the judge may require the papers to be referred to him at a later date after additional evidence has been filed, to decide whether to deal with the application without a hearing or to list it for a final hearing. In clearly contentious cases, the matter is listed for hearing in the initial directions order.

Section 49 reports

9.88 The court may require a report to be made, pursuant to s 49 of the MCA 2005 by the Public Guardian, a Court of Protection Visitor, a local authority, or an NHS body (s 49(2) and (3)).

9.89 In cases where the donor's capacity to revoke the LPA or to object to its registration is an issue, the court may decide to obtain a report from a Court of Protection Special Visitor. A Special Visitor is a registered medical practitioner, or someone who has special knowledge of and experience in cases of impairment of or disturbance in the functioning of the mind or brain, or someone whom the Lord Chancellor considers to have other suitable qualifications or training (MCA 2005, s 61(2)). In cases where it is alleged that the attorney has contravened his authority or is not acting in the donor's best interests, the court may decide to obtain a report from the Public Guardian.

9.90 Further information on s 49 reports can be found in COP Rules 2007, rr 117 and 118, and Practice Direction 14E, which supplements Part 14 of the Rules.

Decision to hold an attended hearing

9.91 In considering whether it is necessary to hold a hearing, r 84(3) of the COP Rules 2007 requires the court to have regard to:

'(a)   the nature of the proceedings and the orders sought;
(b)   whether the application is opposed by a person who appears to the court to have an interest in matters relating to the donor's best interests;
(c)   whether the application involves a substantial dispute of fact;
(d)   the complexity of the facts and the law;
(e)   any wider public interest in the proceedings;
(f)   the circumstances of the donor and any party, in particular as to whether their rights would be adequately protected if a hearing were not held;
(g)   whether the parties agree that the court should dispose of the application without a hearing; and
(h)   any other matter specified in the relevant practice direction.'

9.92 If the court decides to hold an attended hearing, the applicant and all others involved in the proceedings will receive either a directions order or a letter from the court setting out the date, time and location of the hearing, and whether it is for directions only, or disposing of the matter, or for any other purpose.

9.93 Within 14 days of receiving the notice of hearing, and no later than 14 days before the date of the hearing, the applicant, or the person effecting notification on his behalf, must personally inform the donor of the date of the hearing using form COP 14: Proceedings about you in the Court of Protection (COP Rules 2007, r 42(1)). The person effecting notification must also inform the donor that he may seek legal advice and assistance in relation to the hearing (r 42(4)). The applicant must then complete and return the form COP 20A: Certificate of service/non-service within 7 days of making that notification.

Hearings

9.94 The general rule is that a Court of Protection hearing is held in private (COP Rules 2007, r 90(1)), and that the only persons entitled to attend are:

(a) the parties;

(b) the donor (whether or not a party);

(c) any person acting in the proceedings as litigation friend;

(d) any legal representatives of the above; and

(e) any court officer (r 90(2)).

9.95 However, the court may make an order:

• authorising any person, or class of persons to attend the hearing or part of it; or exclude any person, or class of persons, from attending a hearing or part of it (COP Rules 2007, r 90(3));

• authorising the publication of such information relating to the proceedings as it may specify, or the publication of the text or summary of the whole or part of a judgment or order made by the court (r 91(2)); and

• for the hearing, or part of it, to be held in public, and excluding any person or class of persons from attending a public hearing (r 92(1)).

9.96 Further information about hearings, including reporting restrictions, can be found in Practice Direction 13A, which supplements Part 13 of the COP Rules 2007. A pilot project is taking place to create greater transparency in the court. A Practice Direction – Transparency Pilot – sets out the factors the court should consider in allowing all or part of the hearing to be conducted in public. It contains a standard template order, which will protect the donor's identity.

9.97 Rules 90 to 93 of the COP Rules 2007 were considered in detail by the Court of Appeal in *Independent News & Media v A* in the context of whether the media are to be permitted to attend a hearing.

9.98 Attended hearings take place either at the central registry of the court at First Avenue House, 42–49 High Holborn, London WC1V 6NP, or at one of the designated regional hearing venues. Arrangements have been made with HM Courts and Tribunals Service for judges nominated under s 46(1) of the MCA 2005 to hear contested Court of Protection applications in Birmingham, Bradford, Bristol, Cardiff, Leeds, Liverpool, Manchester, Newcastle upon Tyne, Nottingham, Oxford, Preston, Southampton and Swindon.

Burden of proof

9.99 As in the case of enduring powers of attorney, the burden of proof is generally on the person who is objecting to the registration of an LPA (*Re W (Enduring Power of Attorney)* [2001] 1 FLR 832). However, where the Public Guardian is prevented from registering an LPA, the burden of proof is generally on the person who is seeking the registration of the instrument. The circumstances in which the Public Guardian is prevented from registering an instrument are discussed in detail in CHAPTER 10.

Notifying the donor of the final order

9.100 The donor must be notified of the final order of the court (COP Rules 2007, r 44(1)) within 14 days of its being made (r 46(3)). The person effecting notification must explain to the donor the effect of the order, and inform the donor that he may seek advice and assistance in relation to the order (r 44(2) and (3)). This is done using form COP 14: Proceedings about you in the Court of Protection. The person effecting notification must complete and return a COP 20: Certificate of service/non-service within 7 days of making the notification (r 48). The court can, however, dispense with this requirement (r 49).

Appeals

9.101 The legislation governing rights of appeal in Court of Protection cases can be found in s 53 of the MCA 2005, Part 20 (rr 169–182) of the COP Rules 2007, and Practice Direction 20A, which supplements Part 20 of the Rules.

9.102 An appeal against any decision of the court may not be made without permission (COP Rules 2007, r 172(1)), unless the appeal is against an order for committal to prison (r 172(8)).

9.103 The persons who may apply for permission to appeal are the parties to the proceedings (COP Rules 2007, r 73) and any persons who are bound as if parties (r 74), namely:

- the applicant;
- any person who is named as a respondent in the application form and who has filed an acknowledgment of service (COP 5) in respect of the application form;
- any person whom the court has joined as a party;
- the donor; and
- any person who has been served with or notified of an application form.

9.104 An application for permission to appeal may be made to the first instance judge at the hearing at which the decision being appealed was made, or, if the first instance judge refuses to give permission, an appeal judge (COP Rules 2007, r 172(4)). Rule 173 provides that permission will only be granted where the court considers that the appeal would have a real prospect of success, or there is some other compelling reason why the appeal should be heard.

9.105 The appellant must complete form COP 35: Appellant's notice, and file it with the court within the time limit set by the first instance judge, or, if he did not set a time limit, within 21 days of the date of the decision being appealed (COP Rules 2007, r 175(2)).

9.106 The appellant should file the following documents with the court:

- form COP 35: Appellant's notice, plus one copy of the COP 35;
- one copy of COP 37: Skeleton argument;
- a sealed (or stamped by the court) copy of the order being appealed;
- a suitable record of the judgment of the first instance judge;

- a copy of any order giving or refusing permission to appeal, together with the judge's reasons for allowing or refusing permission to appeal;
- any witness statements or affidavits in support of any other applications included in the COP 35: Appellant's notice;
- the application form and any application notice or response (where relevant to the subject of the appeal);
- in cases where the decision itself was made on appeal, the order of the first instance judge, the reasons given, and the appellant's notice used to appeal from that order;
- any other documents which the appellant reasonably considers necessary to enable the court to reach its decision on the hearing of the application or appeal;
- such other documents as the court may direct; and
- the appeal fee of £400, payable in accordance with art 5 of the Court of Protection Fees Order 2007 (SI 2007/1745 (L.13)).

9.107 Further information on the procedure on an appeal can be found in the relevant practice direction (COP Rules 2007, r 174), Practice Direction 20A, which supplements Part 20 of the Rules.

9.108 An appeal lies to a prescribed higher judge of the Court of Protection, who has been nominated under s 46 of the MCA 2005. Essentially, the higher judges of the court are:

- a circuit judge, where the first instance decision was made by a district judge (MCA 2005, s 53(3)(b)); and
- the President, Vice-President, or a puisne judge of the High Court, where the first instance decision was made by a district judge or circuit judge (s 53(3)(c)).

9.109 Subject to the above provisions, an appeal lies to the Court of Appeal from any decision of the Court of Protection (MCA 2005, s 53(1)). However, where a higher judge of the court has made a decision on an appeal, no appeal may be made to the Court of Appeal from that decision unless the Court of Appeal considers that:

- the appeal would raise an important point of principle or practice; or
- there is some other compelling reason for the Court of Appeal to hear it (MCA 2005, s 53(4)(d)).

Chapter 10

FUNCTIONS OF THE PUBLIC GUARDIAN

INTRODUCTION

The Public Guardian

10.1 Section 57 of the Mental Capacity Act 2005 (MCA 2005) provides for an office-holder, known as the Public Guardian, to be appointed by the Lord Chancellor. The Lord Chancellor may provide the Public Guardian with such officers and staff as the Lord Chancellor thinks necessary for the proper discharge of the Public Guardian's functions, or he may enter into contracts with other persons for the provision by them, or their sub-contractors, of such officers, staff or services.

The functions of the Public Guardian in relation to LPAs

10.2 The functions of the Public Guardian are set out in s 58 of the MCA 2005. So far as they relate to lasting powers of attorney (LPAs), his functions are as follows:

- establishing and maintaining a register of LPAs (s 58(1)(a));
- directing a Court of Protection Visitor to visit a donee of an LPA, and to make a report to the Public Guardian on such matters as he may direct (s 58(1)(d)(i));
- directing a Court of Protection Visitor to visit the person granting the LPA, and to make a report to the Public Guardian on such matters as he may direct (s 58(1)(d)(iii));
- receiving reports from donees of LPAs (s 58(1)(f));
- dealing with representations (including complaints) about the way in which a donee of an LPA is exercising his powers (s 58(1)(h));
- publishing in any manner the Public Guardian thinks appropriate, any information which he thinks appropriate about the discharge of his functions (s 58(1)(i)); and
- making applications to the Court of Protection in connection with his functions under the Act in such circumstances as he considers it necessary or appropriate to do so (the Lasting Powers of Attorney, Enduring Powers of Attorney and Public Guardian Regulations 2007 (LPA, EPA & PG Regs 2007) (SI 2007/1253), reg 43).

10.3 The Lord Chancellor may by regulations make provision conferring on the Public Guardian other functions in connection with the MCA 2005 (s 58(3)(a)), and in connection with the discharge by the Public Guardian of his functions (s 58(3)(b)), including:

- the fees which may be charged (s 58(4)(b));
- the way in which and funds from which such fees are to be paid (s 58(4)(c));
- exemptions from and reductions in such fees (s 58(4)(d)); and
- remission of such fees in whole or in part (s 58(4)(e)).

10.4 The regulations relating to fees are the Public Guardian (Fees etc) Regulations 2007 (SI 2007/2051), as amended, which are considered in detail in CHAPTER 12.

Annual report

10.5 Section 60 of the MCA 2005 requires the Public Guardian to make an annual report about his work to the Lord Chancellor, who must within one month of receipt lay a copy of the report before both Houses of Parliament.

FUNCTIONS RELATING TO ESTABLISHING AND MAINTAINING THE REGISTER OF LPAS

The purpose of registration

10.6 The purpose of keeping a register of powers of attorney was described by the Law Commission, in its report on *Mental Incapacity* (1995), at paragraph 7.30, as follows:

'A straightforward administrative registration procedure can have the merit of bringing a document into the public domain and establishing its formal validity. A mark of validity can be of benefit to both donor and donee. A process of registration involving a public body will undoubtedly discourage some people who might abuse powers which remain in the private domain and will provide a point of reference for those who have queries or concerns about the status of a particular document.'

Registration is compulsory

10.7 To be effective, the registration of powers of attorney needs to be:

- compulsory;
- in a single national register open to public inspection;
- accurate and kept up to date; and
- kept by a public authority, which is under a duty to investigate complaints or circumstances giving rise to concern, and to pass on information to other investigating bodies on request.

10.8 The registration of LPAs is compulsory. The donee has no authority unless the instrument is registered. Section 9(2)(b) of the MCA 2005 states that 'a lasting power of attorney is not created unless . . . an instrument conferring authority of the kind mentioned in subsection (1) is made and registered in accordance with Schedule 1,' and s 9(3) states that 'an instrument which purports to create a lasting power of attorney, but does not comply with this section, s 10 or Schedule 1, confers no authority'.

Registration is a purely administrative function

10.9 The Enduring Powers of Attorney Act 1985 conferred on the Court of Protection numerous administrative, as well as judicial, functions in relation to the registration of enduring powers of attorney. The Law Commission, in its report on *Mental Incapacity* (1995), at paragraph 7.32 and 7.33, states as follows:

> 'The registration scheme we now recommend will be purely administrative in nature and we would expect it to be operated by the Public Trust Office, many of whose staff have been performing administrative functions in relation to EPAs for the past eight years. It will, however, be for the Lord Chancellor to determine which administrative body should discharge the functions described in our Bill.

> Any donee of [an LPA] who seeks to use the powers granted in the document will be obliged to apply for registration of the document. Questions about the donor's capacity will not concern the registration authority, which will register the power upon the donee making an application for registration in the prescribed form, subject only to the [LPA] complying with the prescribed formalities.'

10.10 The Law Commission considered the role of the registration authority at paragraph 7.49 of the report on *Mental Incapacity* (1995):

> 'The role of the registration authority should simply be (1) to register [LPAs] and give notice of registration, (2) to cancel registrations and (3) to amend registrations in cases of partial revocation or the appointment of replacement attorneys. Since the registration authority will be an administrative rather than a judicial body, cancellation or amendment should only be effected on the receipt of specified types of objective evidence. If a change to the registration requires a determination of some disputed fact, or the exercise of discretion, then the court will make the necessary determination and give instructions to the registration authority.'

The Public Guardian's duty to establish and maintain the register

10.11 Section 58(1)(a) of the MCA 2005 states that one of the functions of the Public Guardian is to establish and maintain a register of LPAs.

10.12 The LPA, EPA & PG Regs 2007, reg 30, which deals with establishing and maintaining the registers, provides that:

> '(1) In this Part "the registers" means –
>   (a) the register of lasting powers of attorney;
>   (b) the register of enduring powers of attorney;
>   (c) the register of court orders appointing deputies;
>   which the Public Guardian must establish and maintain.
> (2) On each register the Public Guardian may include –
>   (a) such descriptions of information about a registered instrument or a registered order as the Public Guardian considers appropriate; and
>   (b) entries which relate to an instrument or order for which registration has been cancelled.'

Contents of the register

10.13 At pages 15 and 16 of its consultation paper on *Lasting Powers of Attorney – forms and guidance* (CP 01/06), published on 20 January 2006, the Department for Constitutional Affairs proposed that the register should contain the following details:

- the name of the donor;
- the date of birth of the donor;
- the nature of the LPA (whether it is for property and affairs or personal welfare);
- the date that the LPA was created;
- the date that the LPA was registered;
- the name(s) and address(es) of the attorneys;
- the nature of their appointment (joint or joint and several);
- whether or not the LPA contains conditions or restrictions; and
- whether a health and welfare LPA contains provision for the attorney to give or refuse consent to life-sustaining treatment.

Accessibility of register and confidentiality

10.14 On page 16 of its consultation paper on *Lasting Powers of Attorney – forms and guidance* (CP 01/06), published on 20 January 2006, the Department for Constitutional Affairs ('DCA') mentioned that:

'We are working towards making the register searchable online on payment of a fee. For those without internet access it will be possible to apply to the Public Guardian for the register to be searched.'

10.15 However, it later retreated from this position, and on page 8 of its response to consultation, CP(R) 01/06, published on 17 July 2006, the DCA said:

'A number of respondents were concerned about confidentiality, data protection and privacy issues in relation to public searching of the register of LPAs. They mentioned items of information they thought should not be accessed by members of the public. This was particularly the case in relation to the contents of personal welfare LPAs.'

10.16 The response to consultation, CP(R) 01/06, concluded on page 45 with the following assurances:

'We will revise the suggested fields for the register of LPAs. We will consider carefully the concerns about accessibility of the register and online searching of the register for a fee. It was never our intention to make the entire contents of either the register or individual LPAs open for blanket searching either online or in any other context and we recognise that this may not have been sufficiently clear in the consultation paper. We simply wanted to explore the possibility of accessing the register online in the future, subject to safeguards, rather than contacting the Public Guardian in any other matter.

Our intention is to ensure that people can find out if an LPA has been registered. We think, and consultees agreed, that in some circumstances, relevant people will need to know if an LPA is registered and in some circumstances they will need to know what the LPA says. This would be similar to the approach taken in Scotland and with Enduring Powers of Attorney currently. Any further information disclosed would be on a "need to know" basis at the discretion of the Public Guardian, depending on the purpose for which the person wanted this information. We accept that we will need to consider the circumstances under which information is disclosed, the level of confidentiality appropriate to the different types of information in an LPA of either type and ensure that our proposals comply with the Data Protection Act 1998.'

Search by the Public Guardian

10.17 The LPA, EPA & PG Regs 2007, reg 31 deals with the disclosure of information on the register:

'(1) Any person may, by an application made under paragraph (2), request the Public Guardian to carry out a search of one or more of the registers.

(2) An application must –
    (a) state –
        (i) the register or registers to be searched,
        (ii) the name of the person to whom the application relates, and
        (iii) such other details about that person as the Public Guardian may require for the purpose of carrying out the search; and
    (b) be accompanied by any fee provided for under section 58(4)(b) of the Act.

(3) The Public Guardian may require the applicant to provide such further information, or produce such documents, as the Public Guardian reasonably considers necessary to enable him to carry out the search.

(4) As soon as reasonably practicable after receiving the application –
    (a) the Public Guardian must notify the applicant of the result of the search;
    (b) and in the event that it reveals one or more entries on the register, the Public Guardian must disclose to the applicant all the information appearing on the register in respect of each entry.'

10.18 Where a search is carried out under LPA, EPA & PG Regs 2007, reg 31, the Public Guardian must disclose to the applicant 'all the information appearing on the register'; he has no discretion to withhold any of this information. However, under reg 32, which is considered in the following paragraph, the Public Guardian has discretion to withhold any additional information requested by the applicant.

Disclosure of additional information

10.19 The LPA, EPA & PG Regs 2007, reg 32 provides that:

'(1) This regulation applies in any case where, as a result of a search made under regulation 31, a person has obtained information relating to a registered instrument or a registered order which confers authority to make decisions about matters concerning a person ("P").

(2) On receipt of an application made in accordance with paragraph (4), the Public Guardian may, if he considers that there is good reason to do so, disclose to the applicant such additional information as he considers appropriate.

(3) "Additional information" means any information relating to P –
    (a) which the Public Guardian has obtained in exercising the functions conferred on him under the Act; but
    (b) which does not appear on the register.

(4)   An application must state –
  (a)   the name of P;
  (b)   the reasons for making the application; and
  (c)   what steps, if any, the applicant has taken to obtain the information from P.

(5)   The Public Guardian may require the applicant to provide such further information, or produce such documents, as the Public Guardian reasonably considers necessary to enable him to determine the application.

(6)   In determining whether to disclose any additional information to P, the Public Guardian must, in particular, have regard to –
  (a)   the connection between P and the applicant;
  (b)   the reasons for requesting the information (in particular, why the information cannot or should not be obtained directly from P);
  (c)   the benefit to P, or any detriment he may suffer, if a disclosure is made; and
  (d)   any detriment that another person may suffer if a disclosure is made.'

10.20 This rule is based largely on the former r 75 of the Court of Protection Rules 2001 (SI 2001/824) – or, to be precise, its predecessor, r 77 of the Court of Protection Rules 1994 (SI 1994/3046) – which was considered judicially by Jonathan Parker J (as he then was) in the case of *Re Y* ((unreported) 13 February 1997). The trustees of two substantial trust funds sought disclosure of two documents lodged with the Court of Protection in connection with an application for the appointment of a receiver for the patient. The documents in question were the medical certificate, form CP3, and the certificate of family and property, form CP5. In his judgment, Jonathan Parker J said:

> 'There is plainly on the wording of the sub-rule a two-stage process involved. Firstly, the applicants have to show "good reason". In that respect I derived assistance from some dicta of Lindley LJ in the case of *H. W. Strachan* [1895] 1 Ch 439. The facts of that case were different from the instant case in that the patient was dead, and the applicant was a party to a probate action in which the patient's state of mind was directly in issue. Nevertheless, it seems to me that Lindley LJ's dicta are of general application and I find them of assistance in the instant case . . .

> I take the words "good reason" in rule 77(3) of the Court of Protection Rules as synonymous for present purposes with "reasonable and proper purpose". On that basis, the first question is whether the applicants have demonstrated a reasonable and proper purpose in seeking disclosure. In my judgment they have. There is nothing improper in the application, and it is, in all the circumstances, reasonable that they should seek disclosure. But that is not the end of the matter. Indeed, it is the beginning of it, in the sense that at this point that the discretion arises.

> [Counsel] accepts, as he must, that in considering whether or not to exercise this discretion I must have regard to the interests of the patient. In so doing, I am not, as I read the rule, required to undertake a process of weighing the risk of prejudice against the reasonableness or propriety of the applicants' purpose in seeking disclosure. The question which I have to consider is whether, having regard to the patient's interests, disclosure ought in all the circumstances to be allowed. In this respect I am, I must say, unable to discern any material or relevant difference between the word "benefit" and the word "interest". If something is for the patient's benefit it is, by the same token, in his interest and vice versa. However, in case there be some difference which I have failed to detect, I am content to frame my decision in terms of the patient's interests.

In my judgment it is quite impossible to say at this stage that the disclosure of any of the information in the documents in question is in the patient's interests. On the contrary, there appears to me to be a clear risk of prejudice to the patient; that is to say, a clear risk that disclosure may operate against his interests. So far as the action is concerned, it is not possible to foresee at this stage to what use the applicants may perfectly properly seek to put information disclosed to them, but in so far as such disclosure influences their conduct of the action, there must be a clear risk that the patient's position may thereby be weakened ins some way. Nor, in my judgment, is it feasible or practical to attempt to set up machinery designed to preserve confidentiality or restrict dissemination of information. The action will inevitably be fought in the full glare of publicity and, the world being what it is, however hard the applicants and their advisers try to prevent it, the risk of leaks must be very high. Similarly, redaction of the documents in my judgment is not feasible either.

Looking at the matter more widely, the views of Dr Isaacs . . . provide further support for the conclusion that it is not in the patient's interests that the documents be disclosed. That being the conclusion which I have reached, I accordingly decline to exercise my discretion in favour of allowing the application. It follows that the application is refused.'

Procedure on applying for a search

10.21 Guidance on searching the register can be found in the Office of the Public Guardian's booklet, LPA 109 – *Office of the Public Guardian Registers: Register of Lasting Powers of Attorney, Register of Enduring Powers of Attorney, Register of Court orders appointing Deputies.*

10.22 The search procedure described in LPA, EPA & PG Regs 2007, reg 31 is what is known as a 'first tier search', whereby anyone may apply to the Office of the Public Guardian (OPG) to find out whether an LPA has been registered. The applicant should send to the Office of the Public Guardian, PO Box 16185, Birmingham B2 2WH or email customerservices@publicguardia n.gsi.gov.uk:

- a completed application form OPG 100: Application for a search of the Public Guardian registers.

10.23 A fee was formerly payable in respect of an application to the OPG to search the register, but this was abolished with effect from 1 October 2011 by the Public Guardian (Fees, etc.) (Amendment) Regulations 2011, reg 5.

10.24 The information the applicant will obtain from a 'first tier search' includes:

- the allocated case number;
- known other names of the donor;
- date of birth of the donor;
- name(s) of any attorney(s);
- whether the LPA relates to 'property and affairs' or 'personal welfare';
- the date on which the LPA was made;
- the date on which the LPA was registered;
- the date on which the LPA was revoked (if applicable);
- name(s) of any replacement attorney(s);
- whether any replacement attorney(s) are active;
- whether the attorneys are appointed jointly;

- whether the attorneys are appointed jointly and severally; and
- whether there are any conditions or restrictions on the LPA (but not details about the conditions or restrictions).

10.25 If the applicant requires further information, he should apply for a 'second tier' search, which is governed by reg 32 of LPA, EPA & PG Regs 2007: see **10.18**.

10.26 The procedure for a 'second tier search' is to write to the OPG with the following information:

- the name of the donor;
- the specific information the applicant requires;
- the reasons why the applicant requires this information; and
- why the applicant has been unable to obtain the information from the person themselves or from another source.

10.27 Any information provided in response to a second tier search is at the discretion of the OPG, and will vary according to the individual circumstances of the case.

FUNCTIONS RELATING TO THE REGISTRATION OF LPAS

Registration procedure

10.28 Guidance on the registration procedure can be found in the OPG's booklet, LP13 – Register your lasting power of attorney: a guide, for powers made before 1 July 2015 or LP12 – Make and register your lasting power of attorney, for powers made on or after 1 July 2015.

10.29 An application may be made by the donor or attorney(s) to the Public Guardian for the registration of an instrument intended to create an LPA (MCA 2005, Sch 1, para 4(1)).

10.30 As soon as is reasonably practical after receiving an application:

- if the application was made by the donor, the Public Guardian must notify the attorney(s), in form LPA 003A (LPA, EPA & PG Regs 2007, reg 13(1)), that the application has been received (MCA 2005, Sch 1, para 7));
- if the application was made by the attorney(s), the Public Guardian must notify the donor, in form LPA 003B (reg 13(2)), and any attorney who did not join in making the application, that the application has been received (MCA 2005, Sch 1, para 8)).

10.31 Where it appears to the Public Guardian that there is good reason to do so, he must also provide (or arrange for the provision of) an explanation to the donor of:

- form LPA 003B, and what the effect of it is; and
- why it is being brought to his attention (LPA, EPA & PG Regs 2007, reg 13(3)).

10.32 This explanation must be provided to the donor personally, and in a way that is appropriate to his circumstances (for example, using simple language, visual aids or other appropriate means) (LPA, EPA & PG Regs 2007, reg 13(4)).

10.33 Except in the circumstances described below, where he is prevented from registering an instrument, the Public Guardian *must* register the instrument as an LPA at the end of the prescribed period (MCA 2005, Sch 1, para 5) The prescribed period is 4 weeks beginning with the date on which the Public Guardian gave the notices of receipt of an application for registration (forms LPA 003A and LPA 003B), or, if those notices were given on more than one date, the latest of those dates.

10.34 When the Public Guardian registers an instrument:

- he must retain a copy of the instrument (LPA, EPA & PG Regs 2007, reg 17(1)(a));
- he must return the original instrument, or certified copy of it, to the person(s) who applied for registration (reg 17(1)(b)); and
- he must give notice of the fact in the prescribed form, LPA 004 (reg 17(2)), to the donor and the attorney(s) (MCA 2005, Sch 1, para 15).

10.35 Where it appears to the Public Guardian that there is good reason to do so, he must also provide (or arrange for the provision of) an explanation to the donor of:

- form LPA 004, and what the effect of it is; and
- why it is being brought to his attention (LPA, EPA & PG Regs 2007, reg 17(3)).

10.36 This explanation must be provided to the donor personally, and in a way that is appropriate to his circumstances (for example using simple language, visual aids or other appropriate means) (LPA, EPA & PG Regs 2007, reg 17(4)).

Immaterial differences from the prescribed form

10.37 The only circumstances in which the Public Guardian must register an imperfect instrument is under para 3(1) of Sch 1 to the MCA 2005, which provides that:

> 'If an instrument differs in an immaterial respect in form or mode of expression from the prescribed form, it is to be treated by the Public Guardian as sufficient in point of form and expression.'

10.38 This provision is limited in scope. The Public Guardian has no power to register an instrument (unless directed to do so by the Court of Protection) if it departs from the prescribed form in the matter of content, or if it has not been executed in accordance with the statutory requirements.

Circumstances in which the Public Guardian is prevented from registering an instrument

10.39 The circumstances in which the Public Guardian must not register the instrument are as follows.

(1)   **The LPA is not in the prescribed form, or has not been properly executed**
      If it appears to the Public Guardian that the instrument has not been made in accordance with Schedule 1 to the MCA 2005, he must not register the instrument unless the Court of Protection directs him to do so (MCA 2005, Sch 1, para 11(1)). However, if an instrument differs in an immaterial respect in form or mode of expression from the prescribed form of LPA, it is to be treated by the Public Guardian as sufficient in point of form and expression (Sch 1, para 3(1)).

(2)   **Where the instrument which is sent with the application to register is neither the original instrument nor a certified copy of it**
      The Public Guardian must not register the instrument unless the Court of Protection directs him to do so (LPA, EPA & PG Regs 2007, reg 11(2)).

(3)   **The Public Guardian applies to the Court of Protection for a determination as to the meaning or effect of a provision in the instrument**
      If it appears to the Public Guardian that the instrument contains a provision which would be ineffective as part of an LPA (MCA 2005, Sch 1, para 11(2)(a)), or would prevent the instrument from operating as a valid LPA (Sch 1, para 11(2)(b)), the Public Guardian must apply to the Court of Protection for a determination as to the meaning or effect of the provision (Sch 1, para 11(3)(a)), and, pending the determination by the court, he must not register the instrument (Sch 1,para 11(3)(b)). If the court notifies him that it has severed the provision, the Public Guardian must register the instrument with a note to that effect attached (Sch 1, para 11(6)). Technically, the application to the Court of Protection is for it to determine any question as to the meaning or effect of the instrument under the MCA 2005, s 23(1).

(4)   **The Court of Protection has already appointed a deputy for the donor**
      If it appears to the Public Guardian that there is a deputy appointed by the court for the donor (MCA 2005, Sch 1, para 12(1)(a)), and the powers conferred on the deputy would, if the instrument were registered, to any extent conflict with the powers conferred on the attorney (MCA 2005, Sch 1, para 12(1)(b)), the Public Guardian must not register the instrument unless the court directs him to do so.

(5)   **Within the prescribed period, an attorney or a named person objects to the registration of the instrument on a 'factual ground'**
      If the Public Guardian is satisfied that the ground for making the objection is established, he must not register the instrument unless the Court of Protection – on the application of the person applying for registration – is satisfied that the ground is not established, and directs the Public Guardian to register the instrument (MCA 2005, Sch 1, para 13(2)). The Public Guardian must notify the objector as to whether he is satisfied that the ground of objection is established (LPA, EPA & PG Regs 2007, reg 14(4)), and may at any time require the objector to provide such further information or produce such documents as the Public Guardian reasonably considers necessary to enable him to determine whether the ground for making the objection is established (reg 14(5)).

(6)   **Within the prescribed period, an attorney or a named person makes an application to the Court of Protection objecting to the registration of the instrument on a 'prescribed ground'**
The Public Guardian must not register the instrument unless the court directs him to (MCA 2005, Sch 1, para 13(3) and (4)).

(7)   **Within the prescribed period, the donor objects to the registration of the instrument**
The Public Guardian must not register the instrument unless the Court of Protection – on the application of the attorney(s) – is satisfied that the donor lacks the capacity to object to the registration, and directs the Public Guardian to register the instrument (MCA 2005, Sch 1, para 14).

Provision of court order to Public Guardian

10.40 Any order of the court requiring the Public Guardian to register the instrument or not to register the instrument must be served by the court on the Public Guardian as soon as practicable and, in any event, not later than 7 days after the order was made (Court of Protection Rules 2007 (SI 2007/1744 (L.12)), r 21)).

Notifying applicants of non-registration of an instrument

10.41 Where the Public Guardian is prevented from registering an instrument as an LPA for any of the above reasons, he must notify the person(s) who applied for registration of that fact (LPA, EPA & PG Regs 2007, reg 16).

FUNCTIONS ON CANCELLATION OF REGISTRATION

Circumstances in which registration must be cancelled

10.42 The Public Guardian must cancel the registration of an LPA:

- on being satisfied that the power has been revoked as a result of the donor's bankruptcy or a debt relief order (under Part 7A of the Insolvency Act 1986) having been made in respect of the donor (MCA 2005, Sch 1, para 17(1)(a) as amended by SI 2012/2404);
- on being satisfied that the power has been revoked on the occurrence of any of the events mentioned in s 13(6) of the MCA 2005 (eg disclaimer, the attorney's bankruptcy, etc) (MCA 2005, Sch 1, para 17(1)(b));
- on receiving a notice that the donor has revoked the LPA, on being satisfied that the donor has taken such steps as are necessary in law to revoke it (LPA, EPA & PG Regs 2007, reg 21(2)). The regulations provide that the Public Guardian may require the donor to provide such further information, or produce such documents, as the Public Guardian considers necessary to enable him to determine whether the steps necessary for revocation have been taken (reg 21(3));
- if the Court of Protection directs him to cancel the registration, having determined that a requirement for creating the power was not met (MCA 2005, Sch 1, para 18(a));

- if the Court of Protection directs him to cancel the registration, having determined that the power has been revoked or has otherwise come to an end (MCA 2005, Sch 1, para 18(b));
- if the Court of Protection directs him to cancel the registration, having revoked the instrument under MCA 2005, s 22(4)(b) (eg fraud, undue pressure, etc) (MCA 2005, Sch 1, para 18(c));
- if the Court of Protection directs him to cancel the registration of an LPA which contains a provision that it has determined is ineffective as an LPA or prevents the instrument from operating as a valid LPA, but has not severed the provision (MCA 2005, Sch 1, para 19(1) and (2)).

Duty to notify on cancellation

10.43 On the cancellation of the registration of an LPA:

- the Public Guardian must notify the donor and the attorney(s) (MCA 2005, Sch 1, para 17(2));
- the instrument and any office copies of it must be delivered up to the Public Guardian to be cancelled (MCA 2005, Sch 1, para 20).

RECORDING ALTERATIONS IN REGISTERED POWERS

10.44 As was suggested at **10.7**, to be effective, a register of powers of attorney needs to be accurate and kept up to date. Accordingly, any changes need to be entered on the register as soon as possible.

10.45 The Public Guardian must attach a note to the instrument:

- if it appears that an LPA is partially revoked or suspended as a result of bankruptcy (MCA 2005, Sch 1, para 21);
- if an event has occurred which has terminated the appointment of the attorney but which has not revoked the instrument (MCA 2005, Sch 1, para 22);
- if the attorney has been replaced under the terms of the LPA (MCA 2005, Sch 1, para 23);
- if the Court of Protection notifies him that it has severed a provision of the instrument (MCA 2005, Sch 1, para 24).

10.46 If the Public Guardian is required to attach such a note to the instrument, he must give notice to the donee(s) of the power (MCA 2005, Sch 1, para 25), and the donor (LPA, EPA & PG Regs 2007, reg 18(2)), requiring him to deliver to the Public Guardian:

- the original of the instrument which was sent to the Public Guardian for registration (reg 18(2)(a));
- any office copy of that registered instrument (reg 18(2)(b)); and
- any certified copy of that registered instrument (reg 18(2)(c)).

10.47 On receipt of the document, the Public Guardian must:

- attach the required note (LPA, EPA & PG Regs 2007, reg 18(3)(a)); and
- return the document to the person from whom it was obtained (reg 18(3)(b)).

COMPLAINTS AND INVESTIGATIONS

Identifying and tackling possible abuse

10.48 In its report on *Mental Incapacity* published in 1995, The Law Commission made no mention of a Public Guardian, but merely recommended that the Lord Chancellor should appoint a registration authority to register powers of attorney (paragraph 7.32).

10.49 However, the draft Mental Incapacity Bill, published in 2003, proposed that there be a Public Guardian, with the functions now set out in s 58(1) of the MCA 2005. In its evidence to the joint pre-legislative scrutiny committee on the draft Mental Incapacity Bill, the Department for Constitutional Affairs submitted a memorandum (MIB 1222), in which it said that:

'There would be a new Office of the Public Guardian (OPG), replacing the existing Public Guardianship Office. Both the new Court and the Office of the Public Guardian would build on the existing court and office structures. The OPG would liaise and work closely with other agencies in financial, health and welfare areas.

As now the OPG would have partly an administrative function and partly a supervisory function. It would be responsible for registering LPAs and for supporting the Court. Its supervisory function would be mainly focused on financial decision-making (see below). However, it would have a role in identifying and tackling possible abuse with other agencies by providing a focus for concerns and fielding them to the appropriate agency.

Under the Bill, the Public Guardian has a supervisory role in monitoring LPAs and Deputies. The OPG's supervisory role would be geared to risk and would intrude as little as possible. The focus would be on supervision of Deputies. Deputies would have a new and unique relationship with the person lacking capacity under the Bill and further work is being undertaken to understand how this will affect the monitoring requirements.

Where there are allegations of possible abuse (of any kind) Office of the Public Guardian would liaise closely with all of the agencies and individuals involved, including social services, the police, voluntary organisations and Adult Protection Committees. The existing Public Guardianship Office is already establishing and developing partnerships with local authorities and other bodies to ensure that any concerns about a person lacking capacity are highlighted and acted upon. Work is also in progress to establish an investigation unit.

The OPG is supported by the currently named Lord Chancellor's Visitors. Visitors would be able to visit attorneys and Deputies if so directed and provide an independent and impartial report on circumstances to the Court.'

Dealing with representations (including complaints) about an attorney

10.50 One of the functions specifically conferred on the Public Guardian under the MCA 2005 is to deal with representations (including complaints) about the way in which a donee of an LPA is exercising his powers (MCA 2005, s 58(1)(h)).

10.51 An LPA is a private arrangement between the donor and the attorney (Code of Practice, para 14.12). The Public Guardian will not usually get involved once somebody has registered an LPA – unless someone is worried about how the attorney is carrying out their duties. If concerns are raised about an attorney, the OPG works closely with organisations such as local authorities and NHS Trusts to carry out investigations (Code of Practice, para 14.14).

10.52 The functions conferred on the Public Guardian by s 58 of the MCA 2005 may be discharged in co-operation with any other person who has functions in relation to the care or treatment of the person concerned (s 58(2)). So far as the record relates to any person who is alleged to lack capacity, for the purpose of enabling him to carry out his functions, the Public Guardian may, at all reasonable times, examine and take copies of:

- any health record (s 58(5)(a));
- any record of, or held by, a local authority and compiled in connection with a social services function (s 58(5)(b));
- any record held by a person registered under Part 2 of the Care Standards Act 2000 (s 58(5)(c)).

10.53 The Public Guardian does not have any specific power to obtain the donor's financial records direct from a financial institution or third party and has to seek them from the attorney. However, the OPG has established working relationships with many financial institutions which if they exercise their discretion can disclosure confidential information.

10.54 The Public Guardian may also interview in private any person who is alleged to lack capacity (s 58(6)).

Making applications to the Court of Protection

10.55 The Public Guardian has the function of making applications to the Court of Protection in connection with his functions under the Act in such circumstances as he considers necessary or appropriate to do so (LPA, EPA & PG Regs 2007, reg 43).

Visits by the Public Guardian or by Court of Protection Visitors at his direction

10.56 The Public Guardian may visit, or direct a Court of Protection Visitor to visit, any person under any provision of the MCA 2005 or the LPA, EPA & PG Regs 2007 (MCA 2005, s 58(1)(d) and (6), and LPA, EPA & PG Regs 2007, reg 44(1)).

10.57 The Public Guardian must notify (or make arrangements to notify) the person to be visited of:

- the date(s) on which it is proposed that the visit is to take place (LPA, EPA & PG Regs 2007, reg 44(2)(a));
- to the extent that it is practicable to do so, any specific matters likely to be covered in the course of the visit (reg 44(2)(b)); and
- any proposal to inform any other person that the visit is to take place (reg 44(2)(c)).

10.58 Where the visit is to be carried out by a Court of Protection Visitor, the Public Guardian may give such directions to the Visitor, and provide him with such information about the person to be visited, as the Public Guardian considers necessary for the purposes of enabling the visit to take place and the Visitor to prepare any report that the Public Guardian may require (LPA, EPA & PG Regs 2007, reg 44(3)(a)).

10.59 The Visitor must seek to carry out the visit and take all reasonable steps to obtain such other information as he considers necessary for the purpose of preparing a report (LPA, EPA & PG Regs 2007, reg 44(3)(b)).

10.60 A Court of Protection Visitor must submit any report requested by the Public Guardian in accordance with any timetable specified by the Public Guardian (LPA, EPA & PG Regs 2007, reg 44(4)).

10.61 If he considers it appropriate to do so, the Public Guardian may, in relation to any person interviewed in the course of preparing a report:

- disclose the report to him (LPA, EPA & PG Regs 2007, reg 44(5)(a)); and
- invite him to comment on it (reg 44(5)(b)).

Power to require information from attorneys

10.62 The LPA, EPA & PG Regs 2007, reg 46 gives the Public Guardian power to require information where it appears to him that there are circumstances suggesting that the attorney of an LPA may:

- have behaved, or may be behaving, in a way that contravenes his authority or is not in the best interests of the donor of the power (reg 46(1)(a));
- be proposing to behave in a way that could contravene that authority or would not be in the donor's best interests (reg 46(1)(b)); or
- have failed to comply with the requirements of an order made, or directions given, by the Court of Protection (reg 46(1)(c)).

10.63 In such circumstances, the Public Guardian may require the attorney:

- to provide specified information or information of a specified description (LPA, EPA & PG Regs 2007, reg 46(2)(a)); or
- to produce specified documents or documents of a specified description (reg 46(2)(b)).

10.64 'Specified' means specified in a notice in writing given by the Public Guardian to the attorney (LPA, EPA & PG Regs 2007, reg 46(5)).

10.65 The information or documents must be provided or produced:

- before the end of such reasonable period as may be specified (LPA, EPA & PG Regs 2007, reg 46(3)(a)); and
- at such place as may be specified (reg 46(3)(b)).

10.66 The Public Guardian may require:

- any information provided to be verified in such manner as he may reasonably require (LPA, EPA & PG Regs 2007, reg 46(4)(a)); or
- any document produced to be authenticated in such manner as he may reasonably require (reg 46(4)(b)).

10.67 These powers are, in many respects, similar to those of the Court of Protection under MCA 2005, s 23(3)(a) and (b).

PUBLICATIONS

10.68 One of the functions expressly conferred on the Public Guardian by the MCA 2005 is to publish in any manner the Public Guardian thinks appropriate, any information which he thinks appropriate about the discharge of his functions (MCA 2005, s 58(1)(i)).

10.69 The OPG publishes the following guidance notes, which can be downloaded from https://www.gov.uk/government/publications?departments %5B%5D=office-of-the-public-guardian:

EPA 101	A guide to Enduring Powers of Attorney
EP2PG Notes	Guidance notes for completing form EP2PG: Application to register an Enduring Power of Attorney
LP9	What happens when I can't make decisions for myself?
LP12	Make and register your lasting power of attorney: a guide (*for LPAs made on or after 1 July 2015*)
LP13	Register your lasting power of attorney: a guide (*for LPAs made before 1July 2015*)
LP10	Getting started as a health and welfare attorney
LP11	Getting started as a Property and financial attorney
LP14	How to be a Property and financial attorney
LP15	How to be a health and welfare attorney
OPG2	Giving gifts for someone else: A guide for attorneys and deputies
British Bankers Association	Guidance for people wanting to manage a bank account for someone else
LPA 120	EPA and LPA fees, exemption and remission guidance

10.70 The OPG publishes the following practice notes, which can be downloaded from its website http:

02/2011	Notification of death
02/2012	Gifts: Deputies and EPA/LPA Attorneys
02/2013	Avoiding invalid provisions in a lasting power of attorney
SD8	Safeguarding policy: protecting vulnerable adults
SD14	OPG's approach to family care payments
PN1	Agreeing to act as a professional attorney – a good practice guide

10.71 Some guidance is also available in the Welsh language at: https://www. gov.uk/guidance/ffurflenni-a-chanllawiau-ar-gyfer-atwrneiaeth-a-dirprwyon

10.72 The following are general booklets relating to making decisions published by the Public Guardian:

OPG601	Making decisions about your health, welfare or finances. Who decides when you can't?
OPG603	Making decisions: a guide for people who work in health and social care
OPG604	Making decisions: a guide for advice workers
OPG606	Making decisions: the Independent Mental Capacity Advocate service

Chapter 11

FUNCTIONS OF THE COURT OF PROTECTION

INTRODUCTION

11.1 The Court of Protection may determine any question as to the meaning and effect of an instrument creating a lasting power of attorney (LPA), regardless of whether it is registered or unregistered (Mental Capacity Act 2005 (MCA 2005), s 23(1)).

11.2 The Court of Protection has the following powers in relation to an application to register an LPA:

- to consider applications to register instruments which are neither the original instrument nor a certified copy of it (Lasting Powers of Attorney, Enduring Powers of Attorney and Public Guardian Regulations 2007 (LPA, EPA & PG Regs 2007) (SI 2007/1253), reg 11(2));
- to declare that an instrument which is not in the prescribed form is to be treated as if it were in the prescribed form (MCA 2005, Sch 1, para 3(2));
- to dispense with the requirement for the applicant to notify the named persons (MCA 2005, Sch 1, para 10);
- to sever any provision that is ineffective or invalidates an LPA (MCA 2005, Sch 1, para 11);
- to consider applications to register an LPA where a deputy has already been appointed by the court for the donor (MCA 2005, Sch 1, para 12);
- to consider objections to the registration of an LPA on one or more of the 'prescribed grounds'(LPA, EPA & PG Regs 2007, reg 15).

11.3 The Court of Protection has the following powers where the donor of an LPA lacks the capacity to do so himself:

- to give directions with respect to decisions which the attorney of an LPA has authority to make, and which the donor lacks capacity to make (MCA 2005, s 23(2)(a));
- to give any consent or authorisation to act which the attorney would have to obtain from the donor if he had the capacity to give it (MCA 2005, s 23(2)(b));
- to give directions to the attorney with respect to the rendering by him of reports or accounts, and the production of records kept by him for that purpose (MCA 2005, s 23(3)(a));

- to require the attorney to supply information or to produce documents or things in his possession as attorney (MCA 2005, s 23(3)(b));
- to give directions with respect to the remuneration or expenses of the attorney (MCA 2005, s 23(3)(c));
- to relieve the attorney wholly or partly from any liability which he has or may have incurred on account of a breach of his duties as attorney (MCA 2005, s 23(3)(d));
- to authorise the making of gifts which are not permitted in accordance with the parameters set out in s 12(2) of the MCA 2005 (s 23(4));
- to make an order or give directions requiring or authorising a person to execute a will on behalf of the donor (MCA 2005, s 18(1)(i), and Sch 2, paras 1–4).

THE STRUCTURE OF THE COURT

The Court of Protection

11.4 Section 45 of the MCA 2005 abolished the former office of the Supreme Court, known as the Court of Protection, and replaced it with a new court, also known as the Court of Protection, which deals with all areas of decision-making for people who lack capacity. The court combines the personal welfare and healthcare jurisdiction, which was formerly exercised by High Court judges of the Family Division, with the property and financial decision-making jurisdiction of the former Court of Protection.

11.5 Section 45(4) of the MCA 2005 provides that the court is to have a central office and registry at a place appointed by the Lord Chancellor. The central office and registry of the court is at First Avenue House, 42–49 High Holborn, London WC1V 6NP, where all the paperwork is processed. In addition, arrangements have been made with HM Courts and Tribunals Service for judges nominated under s 46(1) of the MCA 2005 to hear contested Court of Protection applications in the parties' local court.

Judges of the Court of Protection

11.6 Section 46 of the MCA 2005 describes the judges of the Court of Protection. There are a President, Vice-President, and Senior Judge. Other judges have been nominated from various levels of the judiciary, through High Court judges to circuit judges and district judges. All the puisne judges of the Family Division and Chancery Division have been nominated to exercise the jurisdiction of the Court of Protection.

Appeals

11.7 Section 53 of the MCA 2005 allows the court rules to provide that an appeal in respect of a decision of the Court of Protection may be heard by a higher judge of the Court of Protection, rather than being heard by the Court of Appeal. Rule 180 of the Court of Protection Rules 2007 provides that an appeal from a decision of a district judge shall be heard by a circuit judge, and that a first instance decision of a circuit judge shall be heard by the President,

Vice-President, or a puisne judge of the High Court. Rule 181 provides that, where the decision sought to be appealed is a decision of the President, Vice-President, or a puisne judge, an appeal will lie only to the Court of Appeal. Rule 182 provides that a decision of a judge which was itself made on appeal from a judge of the court may only be appealed further to the Court of Appeal.

Functions of the court

11.8 The main functions of the Court of Protection are to:

- make declarations as to whether or not someone has the capacity to make a particular decision (MCA 2005, s 15(1));
- make declarations as to the lawfulness or otherwise or any act done, or yet to be done, in relation to a person (MCA 2005, s 15(1)(c));
- make single, one-off orders (MCA 2005, s 16(2)(a)); for example, an order authorising the execution of a statutory will, or an order for the sale of a house and the investment of the net proceeds of sale;
- appoint a deputy to make decisions in relation to the matter(s) in which a person lacks the capacity to make a decision (MCA 2005, s 16(2)(b));
- resolve various issues involving LPAs (MCA 2005, ss 22 and 23), and EPAs (MCA 2005, Sch 4);
- make a declaration as to whether an advance decision to refuse treatment exists, is valid, or is applicable to a particular treatment (MCA 2005, s 26(4));
- exercise an appellate jurisdiction in 'deprivation of liberty safeguards' (DOLS) cases, where someone who has not been formally sectioned under the Mental Health Act 1983 has been deprived of his or her liberty, in a care home or hospital. These safeguards were introduced in the Mental Health Act 2007 as a result of the decision on 5 October 2004 of the European Court of Human Rights in *HL v United Kingdom* [2005] Lloyds Rep Med 169, which is often referred to as the *Bournewood* case, after the hospital in Surrey in which HL was deprived of his liberty in 1997. The Mental Health Act 2007 made various amendments to the MCA 2005, notably a new Sch A1, and a new s 21A, which defines the court's powers in relation to Sch A1. If a person is to be deprived of his or her liberty in a place other than a care home or hospital, the court can make a single order under s 16(2)(a) for authorisation under s 4A(3) and (4).

Court of Protection Rules 2007

11.9 Section 51 of the MCA 2005 empowers the Lord Chancellor to make rules of court with respect to the practice and procedure of the court. The Court of Protection Rules 2007 (SI 2007/1744 (L.12)) came into force on 1 October 2007 (as amended) and their contents can be summarised as follows:

- Part 1 of the Rules revokes the Court of Protection Rules 2001 (SI 2001/824) and Court of Protection (Enduring Powers of Attorney) Rules 2001 (SI 2001/825).

- Part 2 sets out the overriding objective enabling the court to deal with a case justly, having regard to the principles contained in the Act, when it exercises any power under the Rules, or interprets any rule or practice direction.
- Part 3 contains provisions for interpreting the Rules, and for the Civil Procedure Rules 1998 and the Family Procedure Rules 2010 to be applied in default (r 9).
- Part 4 makes provision as to court documents, including the requirement for certain documents to be verified by a statement of truth (r 11).
- Part 5 sets out the court's general case management powers, and includes the power to dispense with the requirement of any rule (r 26).
- Part 6 deals with the service of documents generally.
- Part 7 sets out the procedure for notifying 'P', the person who lacks, or is alleged to lack, capacity.
- Part 8 relates to cases where the court's permission is required before proceedings can be started.
- Part 9 describes how to start proceedings; how to file an application; the steps to be taken following the issue of an application; responding to an application; and who the parties to the proceedings are.
- Part 10 is about applications within proceedings, and Part 11 contains a single rule (r 83), which applies whenever anyone seeks to invoke the Human Rights Act 1998.
- Part 12 describes how the court will deal with applications, including the allocation of cases (r 86), and Part 13 is about hearings.
- Parts 14, 15 and 16 set out the procedure in relation to evidence, experts, and disclosure respectively.
- Parts 17 and 18 deal with the appointment of litigation friends, and change of solicitor.
- Parts 19, 20 and 21 relate to costs, appeals, and the enforcement of orders.
- Part 22 covers transitory and transitional matters, the detail of most of which will be provided in separate practice directions.
- Part 23, contains some miscellaneous provisions, including one (r 201) relating to objections to the registration of an enduring power of attorney.
- Part 24, the final part, covers the international protection of adults (rr 204–209).

Practice directions

11.10 Section 52 of the MCA 2005 authorises the President of the Court of Protection, with the concurrence of the Lord Chancellor, to give directions as to the practice and procedure of the court. Forty-six practice directions have been made. In addition, three 'pilot' practice directions have been made on transparency, case management and s 49 reports. The aim of the pilot project is to test how the court process can be improved and whether the default position should change so all final hearings are held in public. The pilot project will continue at least until 30 November 2017. The intention is that by the end of 2017, new Court of Protection Rules will be laid with supporting Practice Directions, which will incorporate the pilot.

Court forms

11.11 The following court forms, guidance and practice notes can be down-loaded from http://hmctsformfinder.justice.gov.uk/HMCTS/GetForms.do?cour t_forms_category=court%20of%20protection

COP 1	Application form
COP 1	Guidance notes for use with COP 1, COP 1A, COP 1B, and COP 4
COP 1A	Annex A: Supporting information for property and affairs applications
COP 1B	Annex B: Supporting information for health and welfare applications
COP 1C	Annex C: Supporting information for statutory will, codicil, gift(s), deed of variation or settlement of property
COP 1D	Annex D: Supporting information for applications to appoint or discharge a trustee
COP 1E	Annex E: Supporting information for an application by existing deputy or attorney
COP 1F	Annex F: Supporting information relating to validity or operation of enduring power of attorney or lasting power of attorney
COP 3	Assessment of capacity
COP 3	Guidance notes
COP 4	Deputy's declaration
COP 5	Acknowledgment of service/notification
COP 5A	Guidance notes
COP 7	Application to object to the registration of a lasting power of attorney
COP 8	Application relating to the registration of an enduring power of attorney
COP 8	Guidance notes
COP 9	Application notice
COP 10	Application notice for applications to be joined as a party
COP 12	Special undertaking by trustees
COP 14	Proceedings about you in the Court of Protection
COP 14A	Guidance notes on completing COP 14
COP 15	Notice that an application form has been issued
COP 15A	Guidance notes for completing form COP 15
COP 17	Request for directions relating to an objection to the registration of an enduring power of attorney
COP 20A	Certificate of notification/non-notification of the person to whom the proceedings relate
COP 20A	Guidance notes for completing COP 20A
COP 20B	Certificate of service/non-service, Certificate of notification/non-notification
COP 20B	Guidance notes for completing COP 20B

COP 22	Certificate of suitability of litigation friend
COP 23	Certificate of failure or refusal of witness to attend before an examiner
COP 24	Witness statement
COP 25	Affidavit
COP 29	Notice of hearing for committal order
COP 30	Notice of change of solicitor
COP 31	Notice of intention to file evidence by deposition
COP 35	Appellant's notice
COP 35	Guidance notes for completing COP 35
COP 36	Respondent's Notice
COP 36	Guidance notes for completing COP 36
COP 37	Skeleton Argument
COP 37	Guidance notes for completing COP 37
COP DLA	Deprivation of Liberty Application Form - For urgent consideration
COP DLB	Deprivation of Liberty - Declaration of exceptional urgency
COP DLD	Deprivation of Liberty Certificate of service non-service Certificate of notification non-notification
COP DLE	Acknowledgment of service/notification
COP DOL10	Application to authorise a deprivation of liberty
COP GN1	Applications for the appointment of a deputy for property and financial affairs
COP GN2	Guidance on the sale of jointly owned property
COP GN3	Applications by existing deputies - Guidance note
COP GN4	Making a personal welfare application to the Court of Protection
COP GN5	Coming for a hearing at the Court of Protection in London or at one of our regional courts
COP GN8	Applications for statutory wills, gifts, settlements and other dealings with P's property
COP FAQ	Making an application to the Court of Protection - Frequently asked questions

SEPARATION OF SUPERVISORY FUNCTIONS BETWEEN THE COURT AND THE PUBLIC GUARDIAN

Separation of functions

11.12 Under the Enduring Powers of Attorney Act 1985, the Court of Protection carried out several different functions in relation to enduring powers of attorney, namely:

- administering the registration process;
- providing a limited supervisory or protective mechanism; and
- adjudicating disputes.

11.13 The Law Commission considered that it was appropriate to transfer the purely administrative functions to a separate registration authority. In paragraph 7.49 of its report on *Mental Incapacity* (Law Com No 231 (1995)), it said:

> 'The role of the registration authority should simply be (1) to register [LPAs] and give notice of registration, (2) to cancel registrations and (3) to amend registrations in cases of partial revocation or the appointment of replacement attorneys. Since the registration authority will be an administrative rather than a judicial body, cancellation or amendment should only be effected on the receipt of specified types of objective evidence. If a change to the registration requires a determination of some disputed fact, or the exercise of discretion, then the court will make the necessary determination and then give instructions to the registration authority.'

11.14 However, s 58 of the MCA 2005 gives the registration authority, the Public Guardian, wider powers and functions than were originally envisaged in relation to LPA attorneys, some of which overlap with the powers and functions of the court. The functions of the Public Guardian are considered in CHAPTER 10.

The court has no jurisdiction to review decisions of the Public Guardian

11.15 The Court of Protection has no jurisdiction to review the decisions of the Public Guardian. Only the High Court has such jurisdiction by way of judicial review proceedings.

POWERS OF COURT IN RELATION TO THE VALIDITY OF LPAS

11.16 Section 22 of the MCA 2005, which is headed 'Powers of court in relation to validity of lasting powers of attorney', states that:

'(1) This section and section 23 apply if –
    (a) a person (P) has executed or purported to execute an instrument with a view to creating a lasting power of attorney, or
    (b) an instrument has been registered as a lasting power of attorney conferred by P.
(2) The court may determine any question relating to –
    (a) whether one or more of the requirements for the creation of a lasting power of attorney have been met;
    (b) whether the power has been revoked or has otherwise come to an end.
(3) Subsection (4) applies if the court is satisfied –
    (a) that fraud or undue pressure was used to induce P –
        (i) to execute an instrument for the purpose of creating a lasting power of attorney; or
        (ii) to create a lasting power of attorney, or
    (b) that the donee (or, if more than one, any of them) of a lasting power of attorney –
        (i) has behaved, or is behaving, in a way that contravenes his authority or is not in P's best interests, or
        (ii) proposes to behave in a way that would contravene his authority or would not be in P's best interests.
(4) The court may –

(a)   direct that an instrument purporting to create a lasting power of attorney is not to be registered, or

(b)   if P lacks capacity to do so, revoke the instrument or the lasting power of attorney.

(5)   If there is more than one donee, the court may under subsection (4)(b) revoke the instrument or the lasting power of attorney so far as it relates to any of them.'

POWERS OF COURT IN RELATION TO APPLICATIONS TO REGISTER AN LPA

Summary of powers in relation to applications to register LPAs

11.17 The Court of Protection has the following powers in relation to an application to register an LPA:

- to consider applications to register instruments which are neither the original instrument nor a certified copy of it (LPA, EPA & PG Regs 2007, reg 11(2));
- to declare that an instrument which is not in the prescribed form is to be treated as if it were in the prescribed form (MCA 2005, Sch 1, para 3(2));
- to dispense with the requirement for the applicant to notify the named persons (MCA 2005, Sch 1, para 10);
- to sever any provision that is ineffective or invalidates an LPA (MCA 2005, Sch 1, para 11);
- to consider applications to register an LPA where a deputy has already been appointed by the court for the donor (MCA 2005, Sch 1, para 12);
- to consider objections to the registration of an LPA on one or more of the 'prescribed grounds'(LPA, EPA & PG Regs 2007, reg 15).

Where the instrument is neither the original nor a certified copy of it

11.18 The Office of the Public Guardian (OPG) require the original LPA to be submitted with the application to register the instrument. If the original is missing a certified copy may be accepted. In the event there is no certified copy, an application can be made to the court for an order that the Public Guardian register a copy.

11.19 The LPA, EPA & PG Regs 2007, reg 11 states that:

'(2)   Where the instrument to be registered which is sent with the application is neither –

(a)   the original instrument intended to create the power, nor

(b)   a certified copy of it,

the Public Guardian must not register the instrument unless the court directs him to do so.

(3)   In paragraph (2) "a certified copy" means a photographic or other facsimile which is certified as an accurate copy by –

(a)   (the donor); or

(b)   a solicitor or notary.'

11.20 In the absence of even a certified copy of the original power, the court will require a witness statement relating to the circumstances of the execution of the LPA; evidence as to the contents of the LPA; evidence relating to the loss or destruction of the original instrument; and evidence that the power had not been revoked by the donor.

11.21 The case of *Smith* ((unreported) 22 February 2007) is a good illustration of the circumstances in which an application might be made to register a certified copy, or even an uncertified copy, of an LPA. Mrs Smith was born in 1925 and lived in Wales. She had two daughters from her first marriage, who also lived in Wales, and two sons from her second marriage, who lived in the Midlands. On 27 July 2005, she executed an EPA appointing all four of her children jointly and severally to be her attorneys. The daughters executed Part C of the instrument shortly afterwards, and on 1 August 2005 the solicitor who had drawn up the EPA sent it to one of Mrs Smith's sons to execute. The sons refused to act as attorneys if their half-sisters were also appointed as attorneys, and were unwilling to return the original instrument to the solicitor, despite several requests to do so. In June 2006 Mrs Smith's daughters applied for the registration of a certified copy of the instrument that had been made before the original had been sent to the sons. An affidavit setting out the circumstances was filed and, following an attended hearing, the application was granted.

Dispensing with the requirement to notify named persons

11.22 MCA 2005, Sch 1, para 10, provides that, on the application of the donor or donee who is about to make an application to register the power, the Court of Protection may dispense with the requirement to notify any named person, 'if it is satisfied that no useful purpose would be served by giving the notice'.

11.23 The court's power to dispense with notification of an intention to apply for registration of an LPA differs in two respects from its power to dispense with notification of an intention to apply for registration of an EPA. First, the court has discretion to dispense with notification of an application to register an LPA, whereas the EPA legislation requires the court to dispense with notice. And secondly, the grounds on which the court can dispense with notification of an application to register an EPA are slightly wider. An attorney, before applying to register an EPA, may make an application to the court to be dispensed from the requirement to give notice to a relative (MCA 205, Sch 4, para 7(2)), or co-attorney (para 11(1)), or the donor (para 8(2)), and the court must grant the application if it is satisfied:

- that it would be undesirable or impracticable for the attorney to give him notice; or
- that no useful purpose is likely to be served by giving him notice.

11.24 In addition to the court's power to dispense with notification of an intention to apply for registration of an EPA, Sch 4 of the MCA 2005 provides that the donor's relatives (Sch 4, para 6(2)), and any co-attorney of the attorney applying to register an instrument (Sch 4, para 11(2)) are not entitled to receive notice if:

- their address is not known to the applying attorney and cannot reasonably be ascertained by him; or
- the applying attorney has reason to believe that he has not reached 18 or is mentally incapable.

11.25 However, there is no similar provision in the LPA legislation disentitling anyone from receiving notice if their address is unknown, or if they are under 18, or mentally incapable. The OPG no longer provide any guidance on what to do in such circumstance. Its former guidance LPA 110, How to register your lasting power of attorney, stated on page 4: 'If it is not possible to establish contact with any of the people to be told, you must keep proof of posting slips, or returned-to-sender evidence, to demonstrate that you have made reasonable efforts'.

Declaration that an LPA, which is not in the prescribed form, is to be treated as if it were

11.26 The practical difficulties encountered following the introduction of LPAs have been similar to those encountered when EPAs were introduced in 1986. The following paragraph from Gwynn Davis's article, 'Research into enduring powers of attorney', published in *Family Law* in July 1991, could apply almost verbatim to LPAs:

'Some solicitors were disenchanted with the procedural requirements associated with registration and with what they saw as the deficiencies of the EPA form (this was, in fact, amended shortly after we conducted our interviews). Many of the EPAs for which registration was sought proved to be defective in one way or another. Also, some of the early applications to register were inept. The standard improved as the procedure became better known, but there continued to be a large number of failures and abandonments. Those few solicitors who had much experience of registration admitted that they had made mistakes in creating powers and had had applications rejected. Indeed, one firm told us that all the applications which they had made to register to date had been rejected. They had since reverted to the standard law stationer's forms. As our informant put it: "I'm looking forward to the first registration with one of these to score a win for a change."'

11.27 In order to solve such problems, the Law Commission recommended that the Court of Protection should have a 'dispensing power', enabling it to declare that a document which is not in the prescribed form is to be treated as if it were, provided that the court is satisfied that the persons executing the instrument intended it to create an LPA. In paragraph 7.55 of its report, *Mental Incapacity* (1995), the Law Commission said:

'A number of our respondents expressed concern about the rejection of EPAs on "pettifogging" technical grounds. In some cases the donor will have suffered irreversible loss of capacity by the time the rejection of registration is made, with the result that a technically valid EPA can no longer be executed. The 1985 Act does provide that a document which "differs in an immaterial respect" from the prescribed form shall be treated as sufficient. This is a useful provision of general application and we have retained it in our draft Bill. Respondents did, however, give an enthusiastic welcome to our provisional proposal for a wider power whereby a judicial forum could "cure" technical defects in a document. This would enable the court to look at the intention of the donor in executing any document which fails to conform to all the prescribed formalities. We recommend that the court should have power to declare that a document not in the prescribed form shall be treated as if it were in that form if the court is satisfied that the persons executing it intended to create [an LPA].'

11.28 Accordingly, the MCA 2005, Sch 1, para 3, which is headed 'Failure to comply with prescribed form', provides that:

'(1)   If an instrument differs in an immaterial respect in form or mode of expression from the prescribed form, it is to be treated by the Public Guardian as sufficient in point of form and expression.

(2)   The court may declare that an instrument which is not in the prescribed form is to be treated as if it were, if it is satisfied that the persons executing the instrument intended it to create a lasting power of attorney.'

11.29 The provision in MCA 2005, Sch 1, para 3(2) needs to be considered in conjunction with Sch 1, para 11(1) of the Act, which provides that:

'If it appears to the Public Guardian that an instrument accompanying an application under paragraph 4 is not made in accordance with this Schedule, he must not register the instrument unless the court directs him to do so.'

11.30 The following case *Nazran* ((unreported: Senior Judge) 27 June 2008) was the first occasion on which the court exercised this discretion, and the circumstances epitomise the whole raison d'être of MCA 2005, Sch 1, para 3(2):

'Mr Nazran was born in 1974. In June 2007 he was diagnosed as having Creutzfeld-Jakob Disease, which he appears to have contracted as a result of hormone injections he received in childhood. On 24 October 2007 he signed an LPA for property and affairs in which he appointed his mother and wife jointly and severally to be his attorneys. The Part B certificate provider was a consultant neurologist, who unfortunately omitted to cross the two boxes prefacing the certificate provider's statement. In November 2007 the attorneys applied to register the LPA, and on 31 January 2008 the Office of the Public Guardian wrote to the attorneys rejecting the application because the instrument had not been made in accordance with Schedule 1. By that time Mr Nazran had lost the capacity to create a new LPA.

On 5 June 2008 the attorneys applied to the Court of Protection for:

(1)   a declaration that the instrument executed by the donor on 24 October 2007 was a valid LPA, or alternatively

(2)   a declaration that the instrument executed by the donor on 24 October 2007 was to be treated as if it were a valid LPA pursuant to MCA 2005, Schedule 1 paragraph 3(2).

The attorneys produced counsel's opinion, in which it was submitted that "when the MCA 2005 and the Lasting Powers of Attorney, Enduring Powers of Attorney & Public Guardian Regulations 2007 are considered as a whole, a valid LPA simply requires a certificate in the form set out at Sched 1 para 2(e) MCA 2005 from someone with requisite qualifications to provide it. The only boxes in the prescribed form relating to a certificate provider which the regulations require to be completed are those on page 17."

The court did not wish to make a declaration that the instrument was a valid LPA for two reasons. The first was that, on balance, it preferred the Public Guardian's argument that the failure of the certificate provider to confirm that he was not disqualified from providing such a certificate meant that the instrument was not made in accordance with the general requirements as to making instruments set out in paragraph 1 of Schedule 1 to the Act.

The second and main reason was based on Mr Nazran's best interests. Although it would have been useful to the profession in terms of precedent to have held a hearing, from which there would probably have been an appeal, to consider the merits of the arguments on either side, and to have made a declaration one way or the other on the validity of the instrument, the delay and uncertainty caused by such proceedings would not have been in Mr Nazran's best interests. He had a very short life expectancy, and until the LPA was registered his attorneys were unable to access an interim compensation payment of £25,000 that had been awarded by the Department of Health. There was also a litigation risk that, if his application for a declaration that the instrument was a valid LPA were unsuccessful, the costs of the proceedings would erode most of the compensation he has received.

In the circumstances, a declaration that the instrument executed by the donor was to be treated as if it were a valid LPA pursuant to paragraph 3(2) of Schedule 1 to the Mental Capacity Act 2005 was a more attractive proposition. It also allowed the court to exercise a broad discretion, and the decision was less vulnerable to appeal. The solicitor who had drawn up the instrument was able to produce a witness statement that satisfied the court that the persons executing the instrument had intended it to create a lasting power of attorney, and the court duly made a declaration that the instrument was to be treated as if it were in the prescribed form and directed the Public Guardian to register it forthwith.'

Severance of ineffective or illegal provisions

11.31 Section 23(1) of the MCA 2005 states that, 'the court may determine any question as to the meaning or effect of a lasting power of attorney or an instrument purporting to create one'.

11.32 Schedule 1, paragraph 11 of the MCA 2005 provides that:

'(1)   . . .
(2)   Sub-paragraph (3) applies if it appears to the Public Guardian that the instrument contains a provision which –
    (a)   would be ineffective as part of a lasting power of attorney, or
    (b)   would prevent the instrument from operating as a lasting power of attorney.
(3)   The Public Guardian –
    (a)   must apply to the court for it to determine the matter under section 23(1), and
    (b)   pending the determination by the court, must not register the instrument.
(4)   Sub-paragraph (5) applies if the court determines under section 23(1) (whether or not on an application by the Public Guardian) that an instrument contains a provision which –
    (a)   would be ineffective as part of a lasting power of attorney, or
    (b)   would prevent the instrument from operating as a valid lasting power of attorney.
(5)   The court must –
    (a)   notify the Public Guardian that it has severed the provision, or
    (b)   direct him not to register the instrument.
(6)   Where the court notifies the Public Guardian that it has severed a provision, he must register the instrument with a note to that effect attached to it.'

11.33 Similar provisions relate to the severance of provisions in LPAs that have already been registered. MCA 2005, Sch 1, para 19 provides that:

'(1) Sub-paragraph (2) applies if the court determines under section 23(1) that a lasting power of attorney contains a provision which –
    (a) is ineffective as part of a lasting power of attorney, or
    (b) prevents the instrument from operating as a lasting power of attorney.
(2) The court must –
    (a) notify the Public Guardian that it has severed the provision, or
    (b) direct him to cancel the registration of the instrument as a lasting power of attorney.'

11.34 Since 1 October 2007 the Public Guardian has made numerous applications to the Court of Protection to sever ineffective or invalid provisions. So far, these applications have been with the consent of the donors, who have applied to register their own LPAs. Although these donors have been perfectly capable of creating new LPAs, the cost of doing so, and the need to re-notify the named persons, and pay a further application fee have been a deterrent, and an application by the Public Guardian to the court to sever the offending provision has been the preferred course of action. Consequently, the clauses have been severed on the paper submissions of the Public Guardian alone, rather than at an attended hearing. For examples of provisions that have been severed see APPENDIX H.

Application to register an LPA where a deputy has been appointed

11.35 MCA 2005, Sch 1, para 12 states that:

'(1) Subparagraph (2) applies if it appears to the Public Guardian that –
    (a) there is a deputy appointed by the court for the donor, and
    (b) the powers conferred on the deputy would, if the instrument were registered, to any extent conflict with the powers conferred on the attorney.
(2) The Public Guardian must not register the instrument unless the court directs him to do so.'

Objections to the registration of an LPA

11.36 Any objection to the registration of an LPA on any of the following grounds must be made to the Court of Protection:

- that one of the requirements for the creation of an LPA has not been met;
- that the power has been revoked, or has otherwise come to an end, other than on the donor's bankruptcy, the donee's bankruptcy, winding up or dissolution, disclaimer by the donee, the dissolution or annulment of a marriage or civil partnership between the donor and donee, or the lack of capacity of the donee;
- that fraud or undue pressure was used to induce the donor to create the power; or
- the donee has behaved, is behaving, or proposes to behave in a way that contravenes his authority or is not in the donor's best interests.

For further discussion, see CHAPTER 9 on objections.

SUPERVISORY POWERS WHERE THE DONOR LACKS CAPACITY

Policy and legislative history

11.37 In paragraphs 7.50 to 7.53 of its report, *Mental Incapacity* (1995), the Law Commission put forward the following arguments for separating the administrative and judicial functions:

'Under the 1985 Act, the Court of Protection was given some judicial control over attorneys acting under registered EPAs, and over attorneys where the donor is or is becoming mentally incapable. Although our scheme for [LPAs] distinguishes very clearly between the administrative powers of the registration authority and the judicial powers of the court, many of the court's powers over [LPAs] will mirror the powers of the Court of Protection in relation to EPAs. We will simply mention here such powers for the sake of completeness.

The court should have power to determine any question as to the meaning or effect of [an LPA], whether the donor had the capacity to create or revoke it, and whether it has effectively been revoked.

It will be remembered that the fact that [an LPA] has been registered will in future signify only that the attorney expects to seek to use it, rather than that the donor is losing capacity. The powers of the court to direct or control the attorney should only arise in relation to matters where the donor no longer has capacity, and the draft Bill therefore provides that the court should have power to give directions to the attorney and to give any consent to authorisation which the donor might have given had he or she had capacity.

The court should also retain some supervisory powers where donors of [LPAs] lack capacity. Thus, the court should have power to give directions to an attorney in relation to reports, accounts and records; to require attorneys to produce information, documents or things; to give directions to an attorney in relation to remuneration or expense; and to relieve an attorney from liability for breach of duty. Where the court finds that fraud or undue pressure was used to induce the donor to create a purported [LPA], it should have power to direct that the document shall not be registered, or to revoke it if it has been registered. Where it follows from the decision of the court that the registration of the [LPA] should be cancelled, then the court should have power to direct the registration authority to cancel the registration.'

Summary of powers of the court in relation to the operation of LPAs

11.38 The Court of Protection has the following powers where the donor of an LPA lacks the capacity to do so himself:

- to give directions with respect to decisions which the attorney of an LPA has authority to make, and which the donor lacks capacity to make (MCA 2005, s 23(2)(a));
- to give any consent or authorisation to act which the attorney would have to obtain from the donor if he had the capacity to give it (MCA 2005, s 23(2)(b));
- to give directions to the attorney with respect to the rendering by him of reports or accounts, and the production of records kept by him for that purpose (MCA 2005, s 23(3)(a));
- to require the attorney to supply information or to produce documents or things in his possession as attorney (MCA 2005, s 23(3)(b));

- to give directions with respect to the remuneration or expenses of the attorney (MCA 2005, s 23(3)(c));
- to relieve the attorney wholly or partly from any liability which he has or may have incurred on account of a breach of his duties as attorney (MCA 2005, s 23(3)(d));
- to authorise the making of gifts which are not permitted in accordance with the parameters set out in s 12(2) of the MCA 2005 (MCA 2005, s 23(4));
- to make an order or give directions requiring or authorising a person to execute a will on behalf of the donor (MCA 2005, s 18(1), and Sch 2, paras 1–4).

Directions with respect to decisions which the attorney has authority to make and which the donor lacks capacity to make

11.39 Section 23(2)(a) of the MCA 2005 provides that 'the court may give directions with respect to decisions (i) which the donee of a lasting power of attorney has authority to make, and (ii) which P lacks capacity to make'. In respect of property and affairs LPAs, this function is similar to the court's function under Sch 4, para 16(2)(b)(i) in relation to EPAs, where the court may give directions with respect to the management or disposal by the attorney of the property and affairs of the donor. The power under s 23(2)(a) is, of course, much wider because it also extends to giving directions in respect of personal welfare decisions. Section 23(2)(a) of the MCA does not provide the court with an express power to suspend an LPA, pending a final determination concerning the actions of an attorney. Suspension of the attorney's powers can be achieved by the court giving directions that the attorney makes no decisions. An interim deputy may be appointed pending the final determination. As an example, see *Re YW (The Public Guardian v TW, KW, HF and SC)* [2016] EWCOP 18.

Consent or authorisation to act which the attorney would have to obtain from the donor if he had the capacity to give it

11.40 MCA 2005, s 23(2)(b) states that 'the court may . . . (b) give any consent or authorization to act which the donee would have to obtain from P if P had capacity to do it'.

11.41 This discretion is useful where there is a conflict of interest between the donor and the attorney in the exercise of a power. An example of such a conflict might be where the attorney wishes to buy the donor's property, albeit at full value, for himself or for a member of his family (see, generally, *Re Thompson's Settlement* [1985] 2 All ER 720). In such cases, as a matter of general agency law, the consent of the principal would be required to such a transaction, but an incapable donor could not give a valid consent.

Directions to the attorney with respect to the rendering by him of reports or accounts, and the production of records

11.42 Section 23(3)(a) of the MCA 2005 states that 'the court may, if P lacks the capacity to do so, . . . (a) give directions to the donee with respect to the rendering by him of reports or accounts and the production of records kept by him for that purpose'.

Requiring the attorney to supply information or to produce documents or things in his possession

11.43 MCA 2005, s 23(3)(b) states that 'the court may, if P lacks the capacity to do so, . . . (b) require the donee to supply information or produce documents or things in his possession as donee'.

11.44 This power enables the Court of Protection to carry out any investigation which it considers appropriate. It also empowers the court to require the attorney to hand over the donor's property. When the MCA 2005 came into force, on 1 October 2007, most of the court's investigative functions were transferred to the Public Guardian, though the court still retains powers of its own.

Directions with respect to the remuneration or expenses of the attorney

11.45 Section 23(3)(c) of the MCA 2005 states that 'the court may, if P lacks the capacity to do so, . . . (c) give directions with respect to the remuneration or expenses of the donee'.

11.46 The OPG's guidance Make and register your lasting power of attorney (LP12), makes clear at pages 32-33, that professional attorneys, such as solicitors or accountants, charge for their services. Non-professional attorneys are probably happy to act without being paid. If the donor agrees to pay a fee, this must be set out in the instructions box of the LPA, otherwise the attorney cannot be paid. For non-professional attorneys, fees are often set as a payment each year.

11.47 The comparable provisions relating to EPAs seem, at first sight, to be more extensive, though in practical terms the court's powers are probably identical. MCA 2005, Sch 4, which governs EPAs, provides at para 16(2)(b)(iii) that 'the court may . . . give directions with respect to . . . the remuneration or expenses of the attorney whether or not in default of or in accordance with any provision made by the instrument, including directions for the repayment of excessive or the payment of additional remuneration'.

Relieve the attorney from any liability that he has or may have incurred on account of a breach of his duties as attorney

11.48 MCA 2005, s 23(3)(d) states that 'the court may, if P lacks the capacity to do so, . . . (d) relieve the donee wholly or partly from any liability which he has or may have incurred on account of a breach of his duties as donee'. This is comparable to the power of the High Court under s 61 of the Trustee Act 1925 to relieve a trustee from liability. However, the Trustee Act only empowers the court to grant relief if the trustee 'has acted honestly and reasonably, and ought fairly to be excused the breach of trust and for omitting to obtain the directions of the court . . . ' The Court of Protection's powers in respect of attorneys are, by contrast, unrestricted.

Authorising the making of gifts which are not permitted by section 12(2)

11.49 The attorney authority has limited authority under MCA 2005, s 12(2) to make gifts on customary occasions to persons (including himself) who are related to or connected with the donor, or to any charity to whom the donor made or might have been expected to make gifts, if the value of each such gift is not unreasonable, having regard to all the circumstances and, in particular, the size of the donor's estate. The court may give the attorney more extensive powers and can authorise gifts intended to minimise the ultimate impact of Inheritance Tax on the donor's estate. The court's procedural requirements can be found in Practice Direction 9F – *Applications relating to statutory wills, codicils, settlements and other dealings with P's property.*

11.50 Although the case related to deputies appointed by the court, rather than attorneys, there is a detailed consideration of the extent to which both deputies and attorneys are authorized to make gifts in *Re GM* [2013] COPLR 290.

Authorising a person to execute a will on behalf of the donor

11.51 The powers conferred by an LPA cannot extend to the execution of a will on the donor's behalf. However, the MCA 2005, s 18(1)(i) empowers the court to authorise the execution of a statutory will or codicil for a person who lacks testamentary capacity.

11.52 An application for an order for the execution of a statutory will may be made by any of the persons listed in r 52(4) of the Court of Protection Rules 2007 (SI 2007/1744 (L.12)). Rule 52(4)(d) specifically includes 'an person who is a donee of a lasting power of attorney which has been registered in accordance with the Act.' See, generally, Practice Direction 9F – *Applications relating to statutory wills, codicils, settlements and other dealings with P's property.*

POWER TO CALL FOR REPORTS

11.53 Section 49 of the MCA 2005 enables the Court of Protection to call for reports to assist it in determining a case. Such reports can be commissioned from the Public Guardian, local authorities, NHS bodies or Court of Protection Visitors. Subsections (7) to (9) allow the Public Guardian or Court of Protection Visitor who is reporting to the court to have access to health, social services or care records relating to the person and interview him in private. Where a Court of Protection Visitor is a Special Visitor (ie a registered medical practitioner or someone with other suitable qualifications or training) he may, on the directions of the court, carry out medical, psychiatric or psychological examinations.

11.54 Rules 117 and 118 of the Court of Protection Rules 2007 (SI 2007/1744 (L.12)) contain further provisions relating to s 49 reports, and Practice Direction 14E, which supplements Part 14 of the Rules, specifically governs s 49 reports, and provides a draft order for commissioning a report.

11.55 Section 49 reports are commissioned for a variety of reasons. In the context of LPAs, typical scenarios include commissioning a report from:

- a Special Visitor if, an issue arose as to whether the donor had the capacity to revoke an LPA; and
- the Public Guardian, where an application has been made to the court for the cancellation of registration of an LPA, and there are allegations of financial abuse that need to be investigated.

REVOCATION OF AN LPA BY THE COURT

11.56 The MCA 2005, s 22(3)(b) states that: 'subsection (4) applies if the court is satisfied:

'(b) that the donee (or, if more than one, any of them) of a lasting power of attorney –
   (i) has behaved, or is behaving, in a way that contravenes his authority or is not in P's best interests, or
   (ii) proposes to behave in a way that would contravene his authority or would not be in P's best interests.'

11.57 The MCA 2005, s 22(4) provides that:

'The court may –
   (a) direct that an instrument purporting to create the lasting power of attorney is not to be registered, or
   (b) if P lacks capacity to do so, revoke the instrument or the lasting power of attorney.'

11.58 In *Re Harcourt: The Public Guardian v A* [2013] COPLR 69, the Senior Judge revoked an LPA in circumstances where the attorney, A, was deliberately obstructing an investigation by the OPG into the way in which she had managed the donor's property and financial affairs. At para 39 he said:

'Essentially, the Lasting Powers of Attorney scheme is based on trust and envisages minimal intervention by public authorities. Even where a donor lacks the capacity to ask the attorney to provide accounts and records, the court would not normally exercise its supervisory powers under section 23, unless it had reason to do so, possibly because of concerns raised by the OPG. The court's powers in this respect simply duplicate those of a capable donor.'

11.59
And at para 71 of *Re Harcourt* he held that:

'In the absence of appropriate safeguards, the revocation by the court of a Lasting Power of Attorney, which a donor executed when they had capacity and in which they chose a family member to be their attorney, would be a violation of their Article 8 rights. For this reason the Mental Capacity Act has been drafted in a labyrinthine manner to ensure that any decision by the court to revoke an LPA cannot be taken lightly.'

Chapter 12

FEES AND COSTS

FEES: THE STATUTORY FRAMEWORK

12.1 In this chapter:

- 'fees' means the charges payable to the Office of the Public Guardian (OPG) and the Court of Protection; and
- 'costs' mean the professional fees charged by solicitors and disbursements such as barristers' fees and experts' fees.

The Public Guardian's fees

12.2 Sections 58(3) and (4) of the Mental Capacity Act 2005 (MCA 2005) state that:

'(3) The Lord Chancellor may by regulations make provision –
   (a) conferring on the Public Guardian other functions in connection with this Act;
   (b) in connection with the discharge by the Public Guardian of his functions.
(4) Regulations made under subsection 3(b) may in particular make provision as to –
   (a) .
   (b) the fees which may be charged by the Public Guardian;
   (c) the way in which, and the funds from which, such fees are to be paid;
   (d) exemptions from and reductions in such fees;
   (e) remission of such fees in whole or in part.'

12.3 In exercise of the powers conferred by ss 58(3) and (4) and 65 of the MCA 2005, the Lord Chancellor has made the following statutory instruments regarding the fees chargeable by the Public Guardian:

Statutory Instrument	SI No	Came into force	LPA	EPA	Other provisions
The Public Guardian (Fees, etc.) Regulations 2007 (PG(F)R 2007)	2007/2051	1.10.2007	£150	£120	Search fee £25

Statutory Instrument	SI No	Came into force	LPA	EPA	Other provisions
The Public Guardian (Fees, etc.) (Amendment) Regulations 2009	2009/514	1.4.2009	£120	£120	Introduced a fee for office copies £25
The Public Guardian (Fees, etc.) (Amendment) Regulations 2010	2010/1062	1.5.2010	£120	£120	Amended the provisions relating to the reduction and remission of fees
The Public Guardian (Fees, etc.) (Amendment) Regulations 2011	2011/2189	1.10.2011	£130	£130	Repeat application to register an LPA £65Office copy LPA £35Office copy EPA £25Abolished search fee
The Public Guardian (Fees, etc.) (Amendment) Regulations 2013	2013/1748	1.10.2013	£110	£110	Repeat application to register an LPA £55
The Public Guardian (Fees, etc.) (Amendment) Regulations 2017	2013/503	1.4.2017	£82	£82	Reduced the registration fee to £81; and repeat application fee to £41

Court of Protection fees

12.4 Section 54 of the MCA 2005 provides that:

'(1)   The Lord Chancellor may with the consent of the Treasury by order prescribe fees payable in respect of anything dealt with by the court.

(2)   An order under this section may in particular contain provision as to –

(a)   scales or rates of fees;

(b)   exemptions from and reductions in fees;

(c)   remission of fees in whole or in part.

(3)   Before making an order under this section, the Lord Chancellor must consult –

(a)   the President of the Court of Protection,

(b)   the Vice-President of the Court of Protection, and

(c)   the Senior Judge of the Court of Protection.

(4)   The Lord Chancellor must take such steps as are reasonably practicable to bring information about fees to the attention of persons likely to have to pay them.

(5)   Fees payable under this section are recoverable summarily as a civil debt.'

12.5 Section 56 of the MCA 2005 contains the following supplementary provisions relating to fees and costs:

'(1)   Court of Protection Rules may make provision –

(a)   as to the way in which, and funds from which, fees and costs are to be paid;

(b)   for charging fees and costs upon the estate of the person to whom the proceedings relate;

(c)   for the payment of fees and costs within a specified time of the death of the person to whom the proceedings relate or the conclusion of the proceedings.

(2)   A charge on the estate of a person created by virtue of subsection (1)(b) does not cause any interest of the person in any property to fail or determine or to be prevented from recommencing.'

12.6 The following statutory instruments have been made in respect of the fees chargeable by the Court of Protection:

• the Court of Protection Fees Order 2007 (SI 2007/1745) (L.13), which came into force on 1 October 2009;
• the Court of Protection Fees (Amendment) Order 2009 (SI 2009/513) (L3), which came into force on 1 April 2009;
• the Courts and Tribunals Fee Remissions Order 2013 (SI 2013/2302) made amendments to eligibility for remission of fees from 7 October 2013; and
• the Courts and Tribunals Fees (Miscellaneous Amendments) Order 2014 (SI 2014/590) made minor changes to definitions from 6 April 2014.

THE PUBLIC GUARDIAN'S FEES

Fees payable to the Public Guardian

12.7 Five fees are payable to the Public Guardian in respect of powers of attorney, namely:

Fee	Amount
Application to register an EPA	£82
Application to register an LPA	£82
Repeat application to register an LPA	£41
Office copy of an LPA	£35
Office copy of an EPA	£25

Payment terms and methods

12.8 All fees are payable upon application and are not refundable, even if the power of attorney is not subsequently registered.

12.9 A separate fee is payable in respect of applications to register an LPA for property and financial affairs and an LPA for health and welfare.

12.10 The fee for an application to register an EPA or LPA is payable from the donor's funds or estate: PG(F)R 2007, reg 9(3) and (4).

12.11 The fee for an office copy is payable by the person requesting the document, and no remission or exemption is available: PG(F)R 2007, reg 9(5).

12.12 Fees can be paid by:

- Online payment. If the LPA is made using the OPG's digital LPA tool, the registration fee can be made online by credit or debit card.
- Debit or credit card. The applicant must indicate this clearly in the application form or in a covering letter and provide their telephone number so that an agent can call them to arrange payment when the application has been received.
- Cheque made payable to 'Office of the Public Guardian' with the donor's name written on the back.

Application to register an EPA

12.13 The PG(F)R 2007, reg 4, as amended by the 2011 fee regulations, provides as follows:

'Fee for application to register an enduring power of attorney

This section has no associated Explanatory Memorandum

4.(1) A fee for the registration of an enduring power of attorney shall be payable by the person seeking to register the enduring power of attorney under regulation 24 of the Lasting Powers of Attorney, Enduring Powers of Attorney and Public Guardian Regulations 2007 (application for registration).

(2) The fee prescribed by paragraph (1) shall be payable upon the application to register the enduring power of attorney.'

12.14 The 2011 fee regulations changed the name of the fee from 'enduring power of attorney registration fee' to 'fee for application to register an enduring power of attorney.' Reg 3(a) of the 2017 fee regulations sets the fee for an application to register an EPA at £82.

12.15 In the 2007 fee regulations, the fee for applying to register an LPA was pitched at a higher level than the fee for an application to register an EPA because of the additional verification work that needs to be undertaken by the OPG as part of the registration process, including notifying the parties involved. The fees for applications to register both types of power of attorney were set at the same level (£120) in 2009 following the Ministry of Justice's consultation *Reviewing the Mental Capacity Act 2005: forms, supervision and fees*, CP 26/08, and were subsequently increased to £130 by the 2011 fee regulations with the purpose of financing investment in the OPG's IT system. It was subsequently reduced to £110 by the 2013 fee Regulations and further reduced to £82 by the 2017 fee Regulations.

Application to register as an LPA

12.16 The PG(F)R 2007, reg 5, as amended, provides as follows:

'Fees for application to register a lasting power of attorney and repeat application to register

(1) A fee for the registration of a lasting power of attorney shall be payable by the person seeking to register the lasting power of attorney under regulation 11 of the Lasting Powers of Attorney, Enduring Powers of Attorney and Public Guardian Regulations 2007 (application for registration).

(2) The fee prescribed by –

(a)   paragraph (1) shall be payable upon the application to register the lasting power of attorney.'

12.17 Separate applications are required to register an LPA for property and financial affairs and an LPA for health and welfare, and a fee is payable in respect of each application. In its response to the consultation paper, CP(R) 23/06, issued on 30 April 2007, the Department for Constitutional Affairs said, at pages 18 and 19:

'The decision to use two separate forms, one for personal welfare and one for property and affairs LPAs was supported by the majority of respondents to the Lasting Powers of Attorney – Forms and Guidance consultation. As stated in the response to the above-mentioned consultation, we looked again at the work involved in registering two forms and whether any reduction was possible.

The approach of using two separate forms allows for someone to choose to make only one type of LPA, provides the freedom to appoint different attorneys for each type of LPA and to choose different persons to be notified when an application to register the LPA is made. Consequently, it is expected that the only common date across both types of LPAs may be the name and address of the applicant. OPG have to perform the same checks and notification requirements for each form, leading to little or no reduction in cost and effort. There will therefore remain a single fee for handling and registering each LPA.'

12.18 The fee is payable by 'the person seeking to register the lasting power of attorney' who may be either the donor or the attorney. Where the attorney is applying to register the LPA, he is liable to pay the application fee, but is entitled to claim reimbursement for it from the donor's estate.

12.19 The PG(F)(A)R 2017, reg 3(b) sets the fee for an application to register an LPA at £82.

Repeat application to register an LPA

12.20 The PG(F)R 2007, reg 5, as amended by the PG(F)(A)R 2011, provides as follows:

'(1A) A reduced fee for an application to register a lasting power of attorney shall be payable where the application is a repeat application in the following circumstances:
    (a)   the initial application to register a lasting power of attorney is made on or after 1st October 2011;
    (b)   the initial application is returned to the applicant as invalid; and
    (c)   the repeat application to register is submitted within 3 months of the date on which the invalid application was returned to the applicant.
(2)   The fee prescribed by –
    (a)   .'
    (b)   paragraph (1A) shall be payable upon the submission of the repeat application to register.'

12.21 The PG(F)(A)R 2011, reg 10(c) set the fee for a repeat application to register an LPA at £65. This was reduced to £55 by the PG(F)(A)R 2013, reg 5(c) and further reduced to £41 by the PG(F)(A)R 2017.

12.22 The repeat application fee was introduced following the Ministry of Justice's consultation on the OPG's fees in 2011. In its response to consultation, CP(R) 16/10, *Office of the Public Guardian: Fees 2011/2012*, the Ministry of Justice stated at pages 11 and 12:

'There was a degree of confusion amongst some respondents to this question who were unaware that a currently invalid LPA requires a fresh instrument to be made, together with a new application to the OPG incurring an additional £120 fee. Some respondents assumed such repeat applications do not attract a further fee at present and the proposal was therefore to charge a new fee that is not currently payable. This is not the case and the proposal was effectively for such further applications to see their cost halved, as compared to the current approach.

The main arguments against this proposal were either that the fee for further applications in such circumstances should be zero or, if a fee were to continue to be charged, that it be even lower than 50% and potentially only discretionary in nature.

It was also raised that the forms are too complex and people will not be able to afford multiple resubmission fees and that the level of work around a resubmitted LPA should not generate any further cost to the OPG.

LPAs are an exercise of choice and therefore a fee is required to cover business overheads. The perceived complexities of the form have also been discussed previously and we will continue to look at the forms as part of the continuous improvement processes within the OPG.

LPAs that are "imperfect" – that is correctable without requiring a fresh instrument and a new submission to the OPG – are currently accepted once corrected free of charge. This is because, with the provision of additional information, or with invalid parts replaced, they can become valid instruments and be registered. This approach will continue. This proposal concerns only invalid LPAs, which are currently returned to the donor as unregistered because the faults contained within them are so significant that they cannot be corrected within the terms of the legislation to allow for registration.

As outlined above, the proposed reduction to £65 for the resubmission fee represents a 50% saving to the applicant based on the current position. Once the resubmission has been made, the instrument will normally be registered provided the new LPA is valid. We will look to minimise the risk of multiple resubmission fees being payable by the applicant by providing clear guidance as to why the original LPA was found to be invalid.

If implemented, this proposal would benefit around 7000 customers each year (based on current numbers of LPAs received for registration) and has the potential to encourage more people to submit an LPA for registration, or have the confidence to do so without recourse to legal advice.

Given this proposal is of benefit to customers, and given that some fee is necessary to cover the additional costs of processing such applications, we will amend the Public Guardian Fees Regulations to introduce a "Repeat Application Fee" of £65 each time an LPA is resubmitted to the OPG within 3 months of the invalid application being sent back to the applicant.'

12.23 There was a separate prescribed form for a Repeat Application to Register a Lasting Power of Attorney: LPA 002R, which was prescribed by reg 12 of the 2011 fee regulations and was set out in the schedule to those regulations. Reg 14 of the Lasting Powers of Attorney, Enduring Powers of Attorney and Public Guardian (Amendments) Regulations 2015 (SI 2015/899), introduced new prescribed forms, which include the application to register the LPA, and removed the specific repeat application form contained in Schedule 3A of the 2007 Regulations. Section 14 of each form contains a box to select to pay the repeat application fee. For LPAs made on either the 2007 or 2009 prescribed forms, which if are subsequently rejected, a new LPA will need to be made on a 2015 prescribed form.

Office copies

12.24 The Explanatory Memorandum to the Public Guardian (Fees, etc.)(Amendment) Regulations 2009 stated that:

'A new fee relating to EPA and LPA office copies is to be introduced. The Office of the Public Guardian does not normally provide office copies of EPAs or LPAs as certified copies can usually be obtained from solicitors. On occasions where there is no alternative to an office copy being obtained, the Public Guardian will exceptionally provide an office copy. In those circumstances the fee will be payable to offset the cost of producing the office copy.'

Enduring Power of Attorney office copy fee

12.25 The PG(F)(A)R 2009, reg 4 provides as follows:

'Amendment of the Public Guardian (Fees, etc.) Regulations 2007

4. After regulation 4 (enduring power of attorney registration fee), insert –

"Enduring power of attorney office copy fee"

4A.(1)A fee for an office copy of an enduring power of attorney registered under paragraph 13 in Part 4 of Schedule 4 to the Mental Capacity Act 2005 shall be payable by the person requesting the office copy.

(2)   The fee prescribed by paragraph (1) shall be payable at the time the request for an office copy is made".'

12.26 The PG(F)(A)R 2009, reg 9(a) set the EPA office copy fee at £25 and it has remained at that level, notwithstanding the amendment to the fee for an office copy of an LPA in the 2011 fees regulations.

Lasting Power of Attorney office copy fee

12.27 The PG(F)(A)R 2009, reg 5 provided as follows:

'Amendment of the Public Guardian (Fees, etc.) Regulations 2007

This section has no associated Explanatory Memorandum

5. After regulation 5 (lasting power of attorney registration fee), insert –

"Lasting power of attorney office copy fee

5A.(1)A fee for an office copy of a lasting power of attorney registered under Part 2 of Schedule 1 to the Mental Capacity Act 2005(1) shall be payable by the person requesting the office copy.

(2)   The fee prescribed by paragraph (1) shall be payable at the time the request for an office copy is made.".'

12.28 In its consultation paper, *Office of the Public Guardian: Fees 2011/2012*, CP 16/10, the Ministry of Justice proposed to discontinue the production of LPA office copies by the OPG except in exceptional and limited circumstances for a £50 fee. In the response to consultation, CP(R) 16/20, the Ministry of Justice stated, at pages 13 and 14:

> 'The main arguments against this proposal were that office copies remain an important aspect of LPAs when dealing with multiple organisations, and although donors can obtain certified copies themselves, this is not always possible if the donor has lost capacity and the costs of the alternative – having a solicitor produce a certified copy – can be prohibitive.
>
> It was also pointed out that, whilst the production of office copies is not core to the business of the OPG, the proposed charge of £50 is too high and disproportionate to the equivalent fees in other organisations.
>
> The OPG maintains its position that as donors are already able to make their own certified copies for as long as they still have capacity to do so and attorneys can obtain office copies by other means, it will discontinue the production of free office copies at the registration stage and concentrate its resource on the core objective of LPA registration which in the long term will help expedite the process.
>
> As part of this change, there will be improved information to highlight alternative means of creating or obtaining certified copies.
>
> We accept that the proposed level of £50 for this fee seems disproportionate. We have reviewed the process of producing office copies, the level of resource involved, and the charges for similar operations in other parts of government. As a result we intend that the fee in such circumstances will be £35 per copy rather than the £50 fee consulted upon.
>
> The service will, however, still only be available where a registered LPA is lost or in other exceptional circumstances. There will be no remission or exemption available however as the fee has been set as low as can be and accurately reflects the cost of a bespoke production and the redirection of resource from the other areas of the business,
>
> Should the loss of the original LPA be due to the fault of the OPG, the Public Guardian will of course provide appropriate office copies without charge.'

12.29 The PG(F)(A)R 2011, reg 10(d) set the LPA office copy fee at £35.

Search fee (abolished)

12.30 From 1 October 2007 until 1 October 2011 a fee was payable to the Public Guardian for an application to search the registers under regulation 31 of the PG(F)R 2007, reg 6.

12.31 The search fee was abolished by the PG(F)(A)R 2011, reg 5, following a recommendation in the Ministry of Justice's consultation on the OPG's fees in 2011. In its response to consultation, CP(R) 16/10, *Office of the Public Guardian: Fees 2011/2012*, the Ministry of Justice stated at pages 15 and 16:

> 'There was little disagreement to this proposal although the main arguments were that abolishing this fee will cause other fee increases to compensate and given that other organisations make a charge for equivalent services, the fee should be left in place.
>
> OPG fees are individually set to cover the cost of resource involved in each specific process and bear no influence in fee increases in other areas. In this particular case, the administration and collection of the fee involves more resource than the activity

it covers. Although other organisations may make a charge for equivalent services, the OPG believes it does not need to as it is not cost effective.

In order to ensure that public bodies have sufficient access to data, it has always been the case that they are exempt from the fee which, in practice, means that only 30% of applicants to date would incur the current fee.

We have decided against implementing a fair usage policy at the present time but will reserve the right to do so in the future, depending on the number of applications which we will monitor over the coming year.

Given the above, the OPG will amend the Public Guardian Fees Regulations to remove this fee. This is also in line with the Government's transparency priorities to improve the accessibility of information.'

Exemptions

12.32 Certain people in receipt of qualifying means-tested benefits are eligible for an exemption from the OPG's fees. The PG(F)R 2007, reg 9, as amended, provides as follows:

'(1)   Subject to paragraphs (2) and (2A) no fee shall be payable under these regulations when, at the time when the fee would otherwise become payable, the relevant person is in receipt of any qualifying benefit.

(2)   Paragraph (1) does not apply to a person who has an award of damages in excess of £16,000 which has been disregarded for the purposes of determining eligibility for that benefit.

(2A)   Paragraph (1) does not apply to office copy fees prescribed by regulations 4A and 5A.

(3)   For the purposes of regulation 4 the relevant person is the donor of the enduring power of attorney.

(4)   For the purposes of regulation 5 the relevant person is the donor of the lasting power of attorney.

(5)   For the purposes of regulation 6 the relevant person is the person making the application,

(6)   For the purposes of regulations 7 and 8 the relevant person is P.

(7)   The following are qualifying benefits for the purposes of paragraph (1)—

(a)   income support under the Social Security Contributions and Benefits Act 1992;

(b)   working tax credit, provided that—

(i)   child tax credit is being paid to the relevant person, or to a couple (as defined in section 3(5)(A) of the Tax Credits Act 2002) which includes the relevant person; or

(ii)   there is a disability element or severe disability element (or both) to the tax credit received by the relevant person;

(c)   income-based job-seeker's allowance under the Jobseekers Act 1995;

(d)   guarantee credit under the State Pensions Credit Act 2002;

(e)   council tax benefit under the Social Security Contributions and Benefits Act 1992;

(f)   housing benefit under the Social Security Contributions and Benefits Act 1992; and

(g)   income-related employment and support allowance under Part 1 of the Welfare Reform Act 2007.'

12.33 Further information can be found in the leaflet published by the OPG, LPA 120, *EPA and LPA Fees*. The form of *Application for exemption or* *remission of EPA/LPA Application to register fees* is LPA 120A. The application must be supported by relevant documentary evidence.

Reductions and remissions in exceptional circumstances

12.34 Where the donor's gross annual income is less than £12,000, the donor is eligible for a 50% reduction of the fee. Gross annual income is the income received before the deduction of Income Tax and National Insurance contributions, and may come from employment, non-means-tested benefits (such as Attendance Allowance and Disability Living Allowance), pensions and interest from investments.

12.35 If the donor does not qualify for an exemption or reduction, and the payment of fees would cause undue hardship (for example, making it difficult to meet normal living expenses), the donor can apply to have the fees remitted by writing to the OPG. Proof of gross annual income must be submitted and the evidence should cover a period of at least three months and include wage slips, banks statements or statements from a pension provider.

12.36 Reductions and remissions are permitted on a discretionary basis, depending on the circumstances of the case. The PG(F)R 2007, reg 10, as amended, makes the following provisions for fee reductions and remissions in exceptional circumstances:

'(1)   Where it appears to the Public Guardian that the payment of any fee prescribed by these Regulations would, owing to the exceptional circumstances of the particular case, involve undue hardship, he may reduce or remit the fee in that case.

(1A)   Where, at the time that a fee under these Regulations is payable, the relevant person (or a couple which includes the relevant person) is in receipt of universal credit under the Welfare Reform Act 2012, the Public Guardian may reduce or remit that fee.

(1B)   Paragraph (1A) does not apply to the office copy fees prescribed by regulations 4A and 5A.

(1C)   In paragraph (1A) –

(a)   paragraphs (3) to (6) of regulation 9 apply for the purpose of determining who is the relevant person;

(b)   "couple" has the meaning given in section 39 of the Welfare Reform Act 2012".'

12.37 Further information on fee reductions and remissions can be found in the OPG's leaflet, LPA 120, *EPA and LPA Fees*. The form of *Application for exemption or remission of EPA/LPA Application to register fees* is LPA 120A.

12.38 Until 1 October 2011 the following remissions and partial remissions applied:

Gross annual income	% of fee remitted
Up to £12,000	No fee to pay
£12,001 to £13,000	75% remission
£13,001 to £14,000	50% remission
£14,001 to £16,000	25% remission
Over £16,000	No remission

12.39 In its consultation paper, *Office of the Public Guardian: Fees 2011/2012*, CP 16/10, the Ministry of Justice proposed to remove all the former remissions and partial remissions and introduce a 50% remission policy for those who have a gross income of up to £12,000 a year, and the removal of all remissions for incomes above this level. In the response to the consultation, CP(R) 16/20, the Ministry of Justice stated, at pages 21 and 22:

'The main argument against this proposal was that the change would negatively impact the elderly, vulnerable and poorer sections of society and preclude them from using OPG services. It was argued that the policy should remain as it is or be based on levels of capital rather than income.

As described in the consultation document, the OPG remission policy has always been discretionary but in the current economic climate, it is now unsustainable. If the remission policy were to remain, additional funding would be required from government to cover the cost of remissions and within the current climate this is not a viable option.

An income based remission policy (rather than capital) is consistent with Her Majesty's Courts and Tribunals Service (HMCTS) remissions policy and we would not look to change this at present. We have taken this point on board however and as part of our ongoing review of the implementation of the Mental Capacity Act, we will look to investigate the potential of moving to a capital based remissions scheme in the future. We will also feed this finding into any fee review process that may take place in the future across the wider MoJ family.

Whilst we recognise that this proposal will adversely impact around 22,000 customers who will see their remission reduced from 100% to 50% as discussed in the consultation document, the idea of removing remissions altogether was explored as part of the background work for this proposal but a decision was made to keep a remission for those with an income up to £12,000. We believe this to be the fairest way of moving forward in the current financial climate without overburdening other OPG fee payers or the taxpayer more generally.

Given the above reasons and the financial necessity that has driven this proposal we will proceed to amend the Public Guardian Fees Regulations to remove partial remissions and offer a 50% remission for those who have a gross income of up to £12,000 (who would previously have received a remission of 100%).'

Review

12.40 If an application for fee exemption or remission is unsuccessful, the applicant can request a review of the decision within four weeks by writing to the Head of Corporate Services, Office of the Public Guardian, PO Box 16185, Birmingham B2 2WH. If the original decision to refuse the remission or exemption is upheld, it will be referred to the Public Guardian and Chief Executive for confirmation.

COURT OF PROTECTION FEES

Fees payable to the Court of Protection

12.41 Four fees are payable to the Court of Protection in respect of applications relating to powers of attorney, namely:

Fee	Amount	When payable
Application fee	£400	On making an application to start court proceedings or on making an application for permission to start proceedings
Appeal fee	£400	On filing an appellant's notice (COP35) appealing a court decision or seeking permission to appeal a court decision
Hearing fee	£500	Where the court has held a hearing to decide the application and has made a final order, declaration or decision
Copy of a document fee	£5	On requesting a copy of a document filed during court proceedings

12.42 Applications and hearings relating to objections to the registration of an EPA or LPA will not incur a fee if the applicant is an attorney or a person entitled to receive notice of the application for registration. A person entitled to receive notice should have received either an LPA3 notice, in the case of an application to register an LPA, or an EP1PG notice in respect of an application to register an EPA.

Payment terms and methods

12.43 The application fee, appeal fee and hearing fee are payable by the person making the application or appeal. Unless they are applying for a fee exemption or remission, the applicant must send the fee with the application, even if they intend to recover the fee from the person to whom the proceedings relate.

12.44 The fee for a copy of a document is payable by the person requesting the copy document, and no remission or exemption is available.

12.45 Fees must be paid by a cheque made payable to 'HM Courts & Tribunal Service' or 'HMCTS'. Unlike the OPG's fees, there is currently no facility for the payment of court fees by debit or credit card.

Application fee

12.46 Article 4 of the CPFO 2007, when read in conjunction with the Schedule to that Order, provides for the payment of an application fee of £400 in the following circumstances. However, it will be noted that the application fee is not payable in respect of an objection to the registration of an LPA by an attorney or named person.

'(1) An application fee shall be payable by the applicant on making an application under Part 9 of the Rules (how to start proceedings) in accordance with the following provisions of this article.

(2) Where permission to start proceedings is required under Part 8 of the Rules (permission), the fee prescribed by paragraph (1) shall be payable on making an application for permission.

(3) The fee prescribed by paragraph (1) shall not be payable where the application is made under –

(a) rule 67 of the Rules (applications relating to lasting powers of attorney) by –

(i) the donee of a lasting power of attorney, or

(ii) a person named in a statement made by the donor of a lasting power of attorney in accordance with paragraph 2(1)(c)(i) of Part 1 of Schedule 1 to the Act,

and is solely in respect of an objection to the registration of a lasting power of attorney.'

12.47 Article 4(3) of the CPFO 2007 does not refer to any objection by the donor. This is because, where the donor objects to the registration of an LPA, the Public Guardian must not register the instrument unless the court, 'on the application of the donee or, if more than one, any of them' is satisfied that the donor lacks capacity to object to the registration, and directs the Public Guardian to register the instrument. Accordingly, the applicant will be the donee, instead of the donor.

12.48 At pages 15 and 16 of its consultation paper on *Court of Protection and Office of the Public Guardian Fees*, CP 23/06, issued on 7 September 2006, the Department for Constitutional Affairs gave the following reasons for setting the fee for any application to the Court of Protection at £400:

'As well as a new jurisdiction and increased number of judges sitting to hear cases in more locations, a new fee regime for applications to the Court of Protection is proposed. The proposed new fees reflect a change of legislation and operating processes. It is proposed that the current range of application fees is replaced with a single application fee of £400. The same would apply to an application for a further order making a change or variation to an order that the Court has made. The fee of £400 reflects the work which must be undertaken by the Court of Protection to process the application and the judge to make a decision on it. This includes interim considerations by a judge that may be necessary.

The proposed fee of £400 is also intended to cover the process of seeking the Court's permission to make an application to the Court (for those cases where permission to make an application to the Court is required). It is not proposed to charge a separate fee, in addition to the £400 fee, for the seeking of the Court's permission to apply.

The Court of Protection application fee is a flat fee which will cover the range of reasons for applying to the Court for a decision. It is recognised that some applications will not require as much work as others, however, implementing and employing a time recording system for each application would increase the cost for no significant benefit for the majority of cases.'

12.49 In its response to the consultation paper, CP(R) 23/06, issued on 30 April 2007, the DCA said, at pages 10 and 11:

'This fee attracted the most interest among respondents. Of the 25 who commented specifically on this fee, the following main concerns were raised. Firstly, as the proposed fee would apply across all applications, in some cases it would be disproportionate to the level of work carried out by the OPG of the Court. This would lead to simpler applications paying for more complex ones. Secondly, the level would deter applicants. Thirdly, it was inappropriate to impose a fee of £400 for all types of applications, and finally the cumulative effect of this and other fees would be cost prohibitive. Some respondents suggested a lower fee category for simple applications, and many examples were provided.'

12.50 At page 20 of CP(R) 23/06, the DCA confirmed its original decision:

'The application fee of £400 will apply to a variety of decisions that the Court of Protection may be asked to make. Some applications will be dealt with on consideration of the application, some will require an attended oral hearing and some will require the commissioning of further information. As previously mentioned, only judges will decide on all new matters that come before the new Court, in contrast to existing arrangements.

As mentioned above, charging separate fees for each type of application would mean introducing so many fees that the whole process would be unmanageable, complicated and susceptible to economic change. Therefore an application fee of £400 will be charged for all applications and as a general rule, an application to vary an order will be charged at the same fee as the original application.

In response to concerns that this level of fee was inappropriate for simple types of applications, the general scope and extent of authority that could be provided to deputies upon appointment are being considered. This may enable some decisions to be made without further recourse to the Court.'

Appeal fee

12.51 Article 5 of the CPFO 2007, when read in conjunction with the Schedule to that Order, provides for the payment of an appeal fee of £400. There is no provision relieving an appellant from paying an appeal fee in respect of an appeal against a decision of a judge at first instance in relation to an objection to the registration of an LPA. Article 5 provides as follows:

'(1)   An appeal fee shall be payable by the appellant on the filing of an appellant's notice under Part 20 of the Rules (appeals) in accordance with the following provisions of this article.
(2)   The fee prescribed by paragraph (1) shall not be payable where the appeal is –
(a)   brought by the Public Guardian; or
(b)   an appeal against a decision of a nominated officer made under rule 197 of the Rules (appeal against a decision of a nominated officer).
(3)   The fee prescribed by paragraph (1) shall be refunded where P dies within five days of the appellant's notice being filed.'

Hearing fee

12.52 Article 6 of the CPFO 2007, when read in conjunction with the Schedule to that Order, provides for the payment of a hearing fee of £500 in addition to the application fee of £400, which will already have been paid under Article 4. However, it will be noted that, by virtue of Article 6(5), a hearing fee is not payable in respect of an objection to the registration of an LPA by an attorney or named person.

'(1)   A hearing fee shall be payable by the applicant where the court has –
    (a)   held a hearing in order to determine the case; and
    (b)   made a final order, declaration or decision.

(2)   A hearing fee shall be payable by the appellant in relation to an appeal where the court has –
    (a)   held a hearing in order to determine the appeal; and
    (b)   made a final order, declaration or decision in relation to the appeal.

(3)   The fees prescribed by paragraphs (1) and (2) shall not be payable where the hearing is in respect of an application or appeal brought by the Public Guardian.

(4)   The fee prescribed by paragraph (2) shall not be payable where the hearing is in respect of an appeal against a decision of a nominated officer made under rule 197 of the Rules (appeal against a decision of a nominated officer).

(5)   The fee prescribed by paragraph (1) shall not be payable where the applicant was not required to pay an application fee under Article 4(1) by virtue of Article 4(3).

(6)   The fees prescribed by paragraphs (1) and (2) shall be payable by the applicant or appellant as the case may be within 30 days of the date of the invoice for the fee.'

12.53 At page 16 of its consultation paper on *Court of Protection and Office of the Public Guardian Fees*, CP 23/06, issued on 7 September 2006, the Department for Constitutional Affairs gave the following reasons for setting a hearing fee in respect of any application to the Court of Protection at £500:

'In the majority of applications to the current Court of Protection, none of the parties attend at court and the application is decided on the basis of the papers. We consider that this will be the case for many applications to the new Court of Protection, with the majority decided on the basis of the judge's consideration of the papers without any of the parties attending.

Oral hearings to resolve matters at issue provide the opportunity for all parties to put forward their case and ask questions about the evidence and assertions put forward by other parties. Consequently they take time and require sufficient judicial and courtroom resources to be devoted to them. We consider that it would be unfair to ask the majority of people applying to the Court of Protection, whose cases do not require a substantive oral hearing, to pay a share of the costs of the oral hearings of a minority of applications. For this reason, it is proposed to charge an oral hearing fee only for those cases which require a substantive oral hearing. This fee will not apply to directions hearings. It will apply when a substantive oral hearing is needed to decide applications to vary an existing order.

It is proposed that this oral hearing fee is set at £500. This fee does not represent the full cost of having an oral hearing and so does not pass the full cost onto those paying it. It is estimated that in the majority of applications to the Court, an oral hearing will not be required as matters will be decided on the papers.'

Fees for copies of court documents

12.54 Article 7 of the CPFO 2007, when read in conjunction with the Schedule to that Order, provides for the payment of a fee of £5 for a copy of a court document.

'(1) A fee for a copy of a court document shall be payable by the person requesting the copy of the document.

(2) A fee for a certified copy of a court document shall be payable by the person requesting the certified copy of the document.

(3) The fees prescribed by paragraphs (1) and (2) shall be payable at the time the request for the copy is made to the court.'

12.55 The Court of Protection Fees (Amendment) Order 2009 abolished the fee for the provision of a certified copy of an order.

Consultation and report

12.56 On 18 April 2013, the Ministry of Justice issued a consultation paper CP 15/2012, *Fee remissions for courts and tribunals* (Cm 8608), and on 9 September 2013 it published its response to that consultation. It proposed a new remissions system, the key features of which are:

• a single system of remission across all courts and tribunals, which in theory should be easier for users to understand and access;

• a new disposable capital case to assess eligibility for remission, with some amendments to reflect concerns about the impact of the test on those of retirement age and to make clearer the types of capital that are considered or disregarded; and

• a new single income test, which should be simpler to use and will require a greater contribution from those who pay part of their fee.

The Courts and Tribunals Fee Remissions Order 2013

12.57 The new remissions system was introduced in the Courts and Tribunals Fee Remissions Order 2013 (SI 2013/2302 (L.21)) (CTFRO), which was laid before Parliament on 16 September 2013 and came into force on 7 October 2013. It provides that eligibility for remission or part remission of a fee is based on two new tests – a disposable capital test and a gross monthly income test. CTFRO article 5 makes various amendments to the CPFO 2007.

Disposable capital test

12.58 Paragraphs 3 and 4 of the Schedule to the CTFRO 2013 set out the disposable capital test. Parties who satisfy the disposable capital test will receive a full fee remission, pay a contribution to the fee, or have to pay the fee in full, as determined by the gross monthly income test set out in paragraphs 11 and 12 of the Schedule. If a party or their partner is aged 61 or over, they satisfy the test if their disposable capital is less than £16,000. In all other cases a party satisfies the disposable capital test if:

- the fee payable by the party and for which an application for remission is made, falls within a fee band set out in column 1 of the following table; and
- the party's disposable capital is less than the amount in the corresponding row of column 2.

Column 1 (fee band)	Column 2 (disposable capital)
Up to and including £1,000	£3,000
£1,001 to £1,335	£4,000
£1,336 to £1,665	£5,000
£1,666 to £2,000	£6,000
£2,001 to £2,330	£7,000
£2,331 to £4,000	£8,000
£4,001 to £5,000	£10,000
£5,001 to £6,000	£12,000
£6,001 to £7,000	£14,000
£7,001 or more	£16,000

Gross monthly income test

12.59 'Gross monthly income' means the total monthly income, for the month preceding that in which the application for remission is made, from all sources, other than receipt of any of the excluded benefits. The gross monthly income test applies a series of thresholds to single people or couples, with an allowance for the number of dependent children they have. Parties with a gross monthly income below a certain threshold will receive a full fee remission. Parties will be required to pay a contribution of £5 towards their fee for every £10 of gross monthly income they earn over the relevant threshold. Parties with income in excess of £4,000 above the relevant threshold will not be eligible for any remission or part remission of a fee.

COSTS

Sources of law

12.60 There are three sources of law relating to costs in the Court of Protection:

- Part 19 (ie rules 155–168) of the Court of Protection Rules 2007 (SI 2007/1744 (L.12));
- the Practice Directions – 19A and 19B – which supplement Part 19 of the Court of Protection Rules; and
- judicial precedent, whereby judges follow previously decided cases where there are similarities in the facts or points of law.

Rules 156 to 159

12.61 Rules 156 to 159 of the Court of Protection Rules 2007 (as amended by SI 2015/548) set out the general rule on costs, and the circumstances in which it is appropriate to depart from the general rule. In essence, these rules reflect a compromise between the practice of the former office of the Supreme Court called the Court of Protection in property and affairs cases, and the practice of the Family Division of the High Court in personal welfare cases.

'**156. Property and affairs – the general rule**

Where the proceedings concern P's property and affairs the general rule is that the costs of the proceedings, or of that part of the proceedings that concerns P's property and affairs, shall be paid by P or charged to his estate.

157. Personal welfare – the general rule

Where the proceedings concern P's personal welfare the general rule is that there will be no order as to the costs of the proceedings or of that part of the proceedings that concerns P's personal welfare.

158. Apportioning costs – the general rule

Where the proceedings concern both property and affairs and personal welfare the court, insofar as practicable, will apportion the costs as between the respective issues.

159. Departing from the general rule
(1)   The court may depart from rules 156 to 158 if the circumstances so justify, and in deciding whether departure is justified the court will have regard to all the circumstances, including:
  (a)   the conduct of the parties;
  (b)   whether a party has succeeded on part of his case, even if he has not been wholly successful; and
  (c)   the role of any public body involved in the proceedings.
(2)   The conduct of the parties includes:
  (a)   conduct before, as well as during, the proceedings;
  (b)   whether it was reasonable for a party to raise, pursue or contest a particular issue;
  (c)   the manner in which a party has made or responded to an application or a particular issue;
  (d)   whether a party who has succeeded in his application or response to an application, in whole or in part, exaggerated any matter contained in his application or response; and
  (e)   any failure by a party to comply with a rule, practice direction or court order.
(3)   Without prejudice to rules 156 to 158 and the foregoing provisions of this rule, the court may permit a party to recover their fixed costs in accordance with the relevant practice direction.'

Practice directions on costs

12.62 Practice Direction 19A is concerned primarily with modifications to the Civil Procedure Rules 1998. Practice Direction 19B is about fixed costs.

Case-law

12.63 Since the MCA 2005 came into force on 1 October 2007, costs in Court of Protection proceedings have been considered in the following cases:

- *Re AH (Costs): AH and others v Hertfordshire Partnership Foundation Trust* [2012] COPLR 327, CP.
- *B v B* [2012] COPLR 480, Fam.
- *Cheshire West and Cheshire Council v P* [2012] COPLR 76, CA.
- *Re D (Costs)* [2012] COPLR 499, CP.
- *Manchester City Council v G, E (by the O.S.) and F* [2012] COPLR 95, CA.
- *Re RC (Deceased)* COPLR Con Vol 1022.
- *Re S; D v R (the deputy of S) and S (Costs)* [2012] COPLR 154, CP.
- *Sharma and Judkins v Hunter* [2012] COPLR 166, CP.
- *Re G (Adult) (Costs)* [2014] EWCOP 7.
- *BIM & Ors v MD* [2014] EWCOP 39.
- *The Public Guardian v CT and EY* [2014] EWCOP 51.
- *Somerset County Council v MK* [2015] EWCOP B1.
- *Re G* [2015] EWCA Civ 446.
- *MR v SR & Anor (application for costs)* [2016] EWCOP 54.

12.64 Of these cases, the only decision on costs that has any bearing on LPAs was the decision in *Re RC (Deceased)* COPLR Con Vol 1022, in which Senior Judge Lush considered an appeal against a decision of a district judge in a case involving a challenge to the validity of an LPA for health and welfare. The Senior Judge held that the judge had been wrong to apply rule 157 of the COPR 2007, namely that there be 'no order as to the costs of the proceedings', and should have applied rule 156, namely that the costs 'shall be paid by P or charged to his estate.' Given that the format of both types of LPA were virtually the same, and that the procedures for both execution and registration and the grounds of objection were identical, as a general rule the incidence of costs in cases where there was an LPA for health and welfare should not necessarily differ from the general rule in property and affairs cases, subject of course to the provisions of rule 159, which allow the court to depart from the general rule if the circumstances justified this.

Chapter 13

THE SCOPE OF THE ATTORNEY'S AUTHORITY UNDER A LASTING POWER

INTRODUCTION

The attorney has no authority unless the instrument is registered

13.1 Unless the instrument creating it is registered with the Office of the Public Guardian (OPG) in accordance with Sch 1 to the Mental Capacity Act 2005 (MCA 2005), a lasting power of attorney (LPA) confers no authority (MCA 2005, s 9(2)(b) and 9(3)).

General authority

13.2 In relation to enduring powers of attorney (EPAs), which extend only to the donor's property and affairs, the MCA 2005, Sch 4, para 3(1) provides that:

'If the instrument which creates an enduring power of attorney is expressed to confer general authority on the attorney, the instrument operates to confer, subject to –
  (a)   the restriction imposed by sub-paragraph (3), and
  (b)   any conditions or restrictions contained in the instrument,

authority to do on behalf of the donor anything which the donor could lawfully do by an attorney at the time when the donor executed the instrument.'

13.3 The Law Commission considered whether it was appropriate to retain a general authority in the case of LPAs. At paragraph 7.25 of its 1995 report on *Mental Incapacity* (Law Com No 231), it stated:

'In Consultation Paper No 128 we expressed reservations about a "general" power of attorney being used in relation to personal welfare matters. Numerous respondents, however, saw disadvantages in requiring donors to use a more complex prescribed form. Few agreed that a more complex form would offer any significant protection to vulnerable donors. Some recalled the days before the 1971 Act, when every power of attorney had to specify the powers being granted and many of them ran into copious pages of small print. Respondents to Consultation Paper No 129 were in favour of a standard form which could be adapted as required by an individual donor. We are now persuaded that there is no objection in principle to donors granting wide "general" powers so long as the explanatory information makes clear the nature of the powers granted. As we have explained, donors can

219

impose their own restrictions and there will be certain conditions and restrictions imposed by law. We recommend that [an LPA] may be expressed to confer general authority on a donee.'

13.4 The Law Commission drafted a Mental Incapacity Bill, which appeared in the appendix to its report. Clause 16(2) of the draft Bill stated:

'Where the instrument creating a [lasting] power of attorney is expressed to confer general authority on the donee it shall, subject to the provisions of this section, be construed as extending to all the matters mentioned in subsection (1)(a) above but without prejudice to such conditions or restrictions (if any) as are specified in the instrument.'

13.5 However, this clause did not find its way into the MCA 2005, and the authority conferred on attorneys in the MCA 2005 and in the prescribed forms of LPA does not expressly confer 'general' authority.

Scope of authority under an LPA

13.6 Section 9 of the MCA 2005 provides as follows:

'(1) A lasting power of attorney is a power of attorney under which the donor ("P") confers on the donee (or donees) authority to make decisions about all or any of the following –
  (a) P's personal welfare or specified matters concerning P's personal welfare, and
  (b) P's property and affairs or specified matters concerning P's property and affairs,
and which includes authority to make such decisions in circumstances where P no longer has capacity.

(2) . . .
(3) . . .
(4) The authority conferred by a lasting power of attorney is subject to –
  (a) the provisions of this Act and, in particular, sections 1 (the principles) and 4 (best interests), and
  (b) any conditions or restrictions specified in the instrument.'

13.7 Regulation 5 of the Lasting Powers of Attorney, Enduring Powers of Attorney and Public Guardian Regulations 2007 (SI 2007/1253) (LPA, EPA & PG Regs 2007) as amended by the LPA, EPA & PG (Amendment) Regs 2015, provides that the forms set out in Parts 1 and 2 of Sch 1 to those Regulations are the prescribed forms to be used for instruments intended to create an LPA.

• Part 1 sets out the prescribed form for an instrument intended to create an LPA for property and financial affairs; and
• Part 2 sets out the prescribed form of instrument intended to create an LPA for health and welfare.

13.8 In both prescribed forms, the appointment clause is in Section 9 of the 2015 prescribed form, where the donor signs, or at the end of Part A of the 2007 and 2009 prescribed form. The appointment in the 2007 LPA prescribed form for property and financial affairs states, 'I confirm that I intend to give my attorney(s) authority to make decisions on my behalf, including in circumstances when I lack capacity subject to any restrictions I have made.' The health and welfare LPA simply states, 'I confirm I give my attorney(s) authority to make decisions on my behalf in circumstances when I lack capacity.' It is noted that there is no express appointment of the attorney; rather it appears to be implicit from the granting of powers. Both the 2009 and 2015 prescribed forms state: 'I appoint and give my attorneys authority to make decisions about my property and financial affairs, including when I cannot act for myself because I lack mental capacity, subject to the terms of this lasting power of attorney and to the provisions of the Mental Capacity Act 2005.' The wording in the LPA for health and welfare is virtually identical.

Meaning of 'property and affairs'

13.9 The expression 'property and affairs' is not defined in the MCA 2005, although the word 'property' is defined in s 64(1) as including 'anything in action and any interest in real or personal property' Lord Brandon in *Re F (Sterilisation: Mental Patient)* [1989] 2 FLR 376, at page 423, held that it extended to business matters, legal transactions and other dealings of a similar kind. The 2009 and 2015 prescribed forms changed the wording of the property and affairs power to 'property and financial affairs', to provide clarity to the word 'affairs'.

Examples of decisions relating to property and affairs

13.10 The MCA 2005 Code of Practice, paragraph 7.36 states that:

'If a donor does not restrict the decisions the attorney can make, the attorney will be able to decide on any or all of the person's property and financial affairs. This might include:

- buying or selling property.
- opening, closing or operating any bank, building society or other account.
- giving access to the donor's financial information.
- claiming, receiving and using (on the donor's behalf) all benefits, pensions, allowances and rebates (unless the Department for Work and Pensions has already appointed someone and everyone is happy for this to continue).
- receiving any income, inheritance or other entitlement on behalf of the donor.
- dealing with the donor's tax affairs.
- paying the donor's mortgage, rent and household expenses.
- insuring, maintaining and repairing the donor's property.
- investing the donor's savings.
- making limited gifts on the donor's behalf [in accordance with the provisions of section 12 of the Mental Capacity Act 2005].
- paying for private medical care and residential care or nursing home fees.
- applying for any entitlement to funding for NHS care, social care or adaptations.
- using the donor's money to buy a vehicle or any equipment or other help they need.
- repaying interest and capital on any loan taken out by the donor.'

Acting as a company director

13.11 The role of director is not a personal role but one where he acts on behalf of the company, which is a separate legal entity. The Articles of

Association may provide for a director to delegate his powers via a power of attorney, such as a property and financial affairs LPA. Whether this is possible and to what extent, will require sight of the Articles, and if not, then the Articles will need to be changed. A director may also be a shareholder. As the shares will be the shareholder's personal property, he can freely appoint an attorney to act in relation to the management of those shares. Where this situation arises, it is usual that separate LPAs are made, which separate the management of the donor's personal affairs from decision making as a director.

Meaning of 'personal welfare'

13.12 The term 'personal welfare' is not defined by the MCA 2005, although it does define 'life sustaining treatment' in s 4(10), as 'treatment in the view of the person providing health care for the person concerned is necessary to sustain life'. The 2009 and 2015 prescribed forms are retitled to 'health and welfare' to make it clearer as to what they cover.

Examples of health and welfare decisions

13.13 The MCA 2005 Code of Practice, paragraph 7.21 states that:

'LPAs can be used to appoint attorneys to make decisions about personal welfare which can include healthcare and medical treatment decisions. Personal welfare LPAs might include decisions about:
- where the donor should live and who they should live with.
- the donor's day-to-day care, including diet and dress.
- who the donor may have contact with.
- consenting to or refusing medical examination and treatment on the donor's behalf.
- arrangements for the donor to be given medical, dental or optical treatment.
- assessments for and provision of community care services.
- whether the donor should take part in social activities, leisure activities, education or training.
- the donor's personal correspondence and papers.
- rights of access to personal information about the donor.
- complaints about the donor's care or treatment.'

13.14 An attorney can only consent to, or refuse, life-sustaining treatment on the donor's behalf if, when making the health and welfare LPA, the donor has expressly stated in the LPA that he wants the attorney to have this authority (MCA 2005, s 11(8)). See **13.37**.

RESTRICTIONS ON THE SCOPE OF THE ATTORNEY'S AUTHORITY

General

13.15 The scope of the attorney's authority is subject to:

- the provisions of the MCA 2005 and, in particular, ss 1 (the principles) and 4 (best interests) (MCA 2005, s 9(4)(b));
- excluded decisions under the MCA 2005;
- the provisions of any other enactment;

- the common law of agency; and
- any conditions or restrictions contained in the instrument (MCA 2005, s 9(4)(b)).

Excluded decisions under the Mental Capacity Act 2005

13.16 An attorney cannot make excluded decisions on behalf of the donor. In its report on *Mental Incapacity* (Law Com No 231), at paragraph 4.29, the Law Commission explained that:

'One benefit of setting out a clear general authority institute is that the statute can then specify which matters fall outside the scope of that general authority. The general law already provides that certain acts can only be effected by a person acting for himself or herself. Examples would be entering in to a marriage or casting a vote at a public election. For the avoidance of doubt, our draft Bill lists certain matters which must be done by a person acting for him or herself.'

13.17 Excluded decisions specifically mentioned in the MCA 2005 are:

- decisions relating to family relationships, etc (MCA 2005, s 27);
- consenting to the donor being given treatment for mental disorder if his treatment is regulated by Part IV of the Mental Health Act 1983 (MCA 2005, s 28); and
- voting on behalf of the donor at an election for any public office or at a referendum (MCA 2005, s 29).

Excluded decisions relating to family relationships

13.18 Section 27(1) of the MCA 2005 provides that:

'Nothing in this Act permits a decision on any of the following matters to be made on behalf of a person:
(a)   consenting to marriage or a civil partnership.
(b)   consenting to have sexual relations.
(c)   consenting to a decree of divorce being granted on the basis of two years' separation.
(d)   consenting to a dissolution order being made in relation to a civil partner.
(e)   consenting to a child's being placed for adoption by an adoption agency.
(f)   consenting to the making of an adoption order.
(g)   discharging parental responsibilities in matters not relating to a child's property.
(h)   giving a consent order under the Human Fertilisation and Embryology Act 1990.
(i)   giving a consent under the Human Fertilisation and Embryology Act 2008.'

13.19 An 'adoption order' means an order within the Adoption and Children Act 2002, including a future adoption order, and an order under s 84 of that Act regarding parental responsibility prior to adoption abroad (MCA 2005, s 27(2)).

Excluded decisions relating to Mental Health Act matters

13.20 Section 28(1) of the MCA 2005 provides that:

'Nothing in this Act authorises anyone –
  (a)   to give a patient medical treatment for mental disorder, or
  (b)   to consent to a patient being given medical treatment for mental disorder,

if at the time when it is proposed to treat the patient, his treatment is regulated by Part 4 of the Mental Health Act.
  (1A)   Subsection (*1) does not apply in relation to any form of treatment to which section 58A of that Act (electro-convulsive therapy, etc.) applies if the patient comes within subsection (7) of that section (informal patient under 18 who cannot give consent).
  (1B)   Section 5 does not apply to an act to which section 64B of the Mental Health Act applies (treatment of community patients not recalled to hospital).'

13.21 The health and welfare attorney cannot give or refuse consent on behalf of the donor in relation to the treatment of the donor's mental disorder where the donor has been detained under the Mental Health Act 1983 for treatment. However, such an attorney can consent or refuse consent to medical treatment which is not for the treatment of the mental disorder, for which the donor is being detained, such as a physical disorder, provided the donor lacks mental capacity to make the decision. It should be noted; a person may be detained for the treatment of a mental disorder but retain mental capacity to make health and treatment decisions. For these purposes, 'medical treatment', 'mental disorder' and 'patient' have the same meaning as in the Mental Health Act 1983.

13.22 The MCA 2005 Code of Practice, chapter 13, considers in some detail the relationship between the MCA 2005 and the Mental Health Act 1983, and at paras 13.38–13.45, which sets out how it impacts on attorneys. The Deprivation of Liberty Safeguards (DOLS) Code of Practice, which supplements the main Code, should also be considered, as to the role of a health and welfare attorney in refusing to the donor's deprivation of liberty (see paragraph 5.11 of the DOLS Code).

Excluded decisions relating to voting rights

13.23 Section 29(1) of the MCA 2005 provides that: 'Nothing in this Act permits a decision on voting at an election for any public office, or at a referendum, to be made on behalf of a person.' 'Referendum' has the same meaning as in the Political Parties, Elections and Referendums Act 2000, s 101.

Decisions excluded by other enactments

13.24 An attorney has no authority to make decisions which statute requires the donor to make personally. For example, an attorney cannot make a will for the donor, or exercise the donor's functions as a trustee, or act as his litigation friend. The court controls its own procedure and the principles of agency do not apply. So, a power of attorney cannot confer a right to conduct litigation or a right of audience: *Gregory v Turner, R (on the application of Morris) v North Somerset Council* [2003] EWCA Civ 183; [2003] 1 WLR 1149 (CA).

Decisions excluded by the common law of agency

13.25 An LPA is a power of attorney, and is subject to the rules relating to powers of attorney in the common law of agency. An attorney has no authority to make decisions, which the law of agency requires the donor to make personally. These tend to be decisions:

- where statute requires the evidence of the donor's signature; or
- where the donor's competency to act arises by virtue of his holding an office, public or otherwise; or
- where the donor's ability to make the decision is of a personal nature, requiring special skill, knowledge, or discretion in exercising it. For example, in *Clauss v Pir* [1987] 2 All ER 752 it was held that the swearing of an affidavit is a duty requiring personal knowledge that cannot be delegated to an agent.

Acting for the donor as an administrator or executor

13.26 As with EPAs, an attorney of a property and financial affairs LPA may act for the donor as an administrator or executor, where the donor lacks mentally incapacity and is incapable of managing his affairs. The Non-Contentious Probate Rules 1987 (SI 1987/2024), r 35(2), set out the criteria and requirements and are covered at **18.12**.

SPECIFIC RESTRICTIONS IMPOSED BY THE MENTAL CAPACITY ACT 2005

Use of restraint

13.27 An attorney acting under an LPA can only use restraint in limited circumstances. 'Restraint' involves:

- the use of force – or threatening to use force – to make the donor do something that he is resisting (MCA 2005, s 11(5)(a));
- restricting the donor's freedom of movement, whether or not he is resisting (MCA 2005, s 11(5)(b)).

13.28 Restraint can only be used when:

- the donor lacks capacity to make a decision on the matter in question (MCA 2005, s 11(2));
- the attorney reasonably believes that it is necessary to use restraint in order to prevent harm to the donor (MCA 2005, s 11(3));
- the amount or type of restraint used, and the length of time it is used for, is a proportionate response to both the likelihood and seriousness of the harm (MCA 2005, s 11(4)); and
- it is in the donor's best interests to use necessary and proportionate restraint.

13.29 An attorney originally had no authority to deprive the donor of his liberty within the meaning of Article 5(1) of the European Convention on Human Rights (MCA 2005, s 11(6)). However, this subsection was repealed by the Mental Health Act 2007, ss 50(4)(b), 55 and 56 with effect from 1 April 2009.

13.30 The origins of these provisions can be found in the Law Commission's report on *Mental Incapacity* (1995), paragraph 7.13, which stated as follows:

> 'If an attorney under [an LPA] has powers in relation to personal health care matters then that attorney should be bound by the general restriction against acts of confinement or coercion which we have recommended as a qualification upon the general authority of informal decision-makers. It is a well-established fact of the general law in relation to powers of attorney that the donor may revoke the power either expressly or impliedly, by doing acts inconsistent with the continued existence of the power. The active objection of the donor is highly likely to be an act amounting to implied revocation. It might therefore be argued that no express restriction on the authority of the attorneys under [LPAs] to confine or coerce donors is needed. It appears to us, however, that the arguments in favour of express provision apply to attorneys as they apply to informal decision-makers.'

An attorney can only make personal welfare decisions which the donor does not have the capacity to make himself

13.31 There is a fundamental difference between LPAs for health and welfare and LPAs for property and financial affairs. An attorney for property and affairs can make decisions on the donor's behalf before the donor has lost the capacity to make such decisions himself, as in the case of an ordinary general power of attorney under the Powers of Attorney Act 1971, or an unregistered EPA. However, s 11(7)(a) of the MCA 2005 provides that acting under a personal welfare LPA can only make personal welfare decisions that the donor lacks, or the attorney reasonably believes that the donor lacks, capacity to make for himself. The exact wording of the subsection is as follows:

> 'Where a lasting power of attorney authorises the donee (or, if more than one, any of them) to make decisions about P's personal welfare, the authority –
>
> (a) does not extend to making such decisions in circumstances other than those where P lacks, or the donor reasonably believes that P lacks, capacity.'

13.32 Although the Law Commission originally intended to confine this provision to purely medical treatment decisions, rather than the broader range of personal welfare decisions, it described the rationale for this requirement in paragraph 7.14 of its report on *Mental Incapacity* (1995) as follows:

> 'The origins of the EPA scheme in the 1985 Act lie in the general law relating to powers of attorney and it is no part of that law that a donor or a principal must lack capacity before an attorney or agent may act. We suggested in the consultation papers, however, that while no such restriction need apply to personal welfare powers, an attorney should only have power to take a medical treatment decision if the donor lacks the capacity to take that decision for himself or herself. The difference in the health care context is that the health care provider is always under a personal obligation to assess the patient's capacity to consent to any treatment proposed. There is therefore nothing unduly burdensome in expecting both doctor

and attorney to investigate whether the donor can give or refuse personal consent to any particular treatment. Respondents supported our provisional views.'

Effect of an advance decision to refuse treatment

13.33 The authority of an attorney under a health and welfare LPA is subject to the provisions on advance decisions to refuse treatment contained in ss 24, 25 and 26 of the MCA 2005 (MCA 2005, s 11(7)(b)). For example, an attorney cannot consent to a particular treatment if the donor has made a valid and applicable advance decision to refuse that treatment.

13.34 The origin of this provision can be found in the Law Commission's report on *Mental Incapacity*, paragraph 7.17 of which said:

'It may be that people will wish to give written instructions about their future health care, as well as appointing another person under [an LPA]. It follows from our discussion of advance refusals of treatment in Part V above that an attorney can have no more power than any other person (or the court) to override a valid and applicable advance refusal. In Consultation Paper No 129 we suggested that an attorney might override an advance refusal if the refusal itself provided for this eventuality. An example might be "I refuse cardio-pulmonary resuscitation unless my attorney consents to it." There is, however, no need for any special provision to cover the possibility of such wording; the refusal will simply not "apply in the circumstances" of the attorney consenting. The situation may be less clear and easy to resolve where a donor has granted a general power over health care matters to an attorney, but *subsequently* makes an advance refusal. We think it would be helpful to specify that, in the absence of express provision to the contrary in the [LPA], the attorney may not consent to procedures covered by an advance refusal. In relation to advance statements which are not "advance refusals" the attorney, acting in the best interests of the donor, will be obliged to consider the donor's expressed wishes and feelings. An attorney will also be able to take into account such factors as changes in medical technology and changes in the donor's outlook and attitudes. In this way the appointment of an attorney will, importantly, allow a flexible and adaptable approach to future health care issues to be constructed by a donor.'

13.35 An advance decision to refuse treatment is not valid if, under a health and welfare LPA created after the advance decision was made, the donor conferred authority on the attorney(s) to give or refuse consent to treatment to which the advance decision relates (MCA 2005, s 25(2)(b)). It is an important reminder, that where an advance decision and health and welfare LPA are made on the same date, the point of creation is when it is registered with the Public Guardian.

Life-sustaining treatment

13.36 'Life-sustaining treatment' means treatment which, in the view of a person providing health care for the person concerned, is necessary to sustain life (MCA 2005, s 4(10)).

13.37 As mentioned briefly at **13.14**, an attorney can only consent to, or refuse, life-sustaining treatment on the donor's behalf if, when making an LPA for health and welfare, the donor has expressly stated in the LPA that he wants the attorney to have this authority (MCA 2005, s 11(8)). The exact wording of the Act is:

'(7)   Where a lasting power of attorney authorises the donee (or, if more than one, any of them) to make decisions about P's personal welfare, the authority –
. . .

(c)   extends to giving or refusing consent to the carrying out or continuation of a treatment by a person providing health care for P.

(8)   But subsection (7)(c) –

(a)   does not authorise the giving or refusing of consent to the carrying out or continuation of life-sustaining treatment, unless the instrument contains express provision to that effect, and

(b)   is subject to any conditions or restrictions in the instrument.'

13.38 In Section 5, on page 6 of the prescribed form of LPA for health and welfare, the donor is required to make a choice between Option A ('I want to give my attorney(s) authority to give or refuse consent to life-sustaining treatment on my behalf'), or Option B ('I do not want to give my attorney(s) authority to give or refuse consent to life-sustaining treatment on my behalf'), and to sign and date one of those alternatives in the presence of a witness, who should also sign and state his full name and address. The date, incidentally, should be the same as the date in the declaration in Section 10 of the prescribed form. The choice was contained in Section 6 of page 8 of the 2007 prescribed personal welfare LPA form.

13.39 The genesis of this provision can be found in the Law Commission's report on *Mental Incapacity* (Law Com No 231 (1995)), paragraph 7.19 of which stated:

'Many respondents agreed with our preliminary view that power over certain sorts of serious medical decision (and not only those requiring independent supervision) should require express authorisation by a donor. Such decisions would never be covered by a "general power" and would require express "opting-in" on the donor's part. In the consultation paper we suggested that a donor might be required to take a positive decision about granting power to refuse "life-saving treatment". It was clear on consultation that many people might want to appoint a health care attorney precisely so as to ensure that someone makes appropriate "treatment-limiting" decisions for them. While there is therefore no question of preventing donors from giving attorneys such powers, it is entirely appropriate to require that the donor should have made express provision in the [LPA].'

13.40 The MCA 2005 Code of Practice, at paragraph 7.28, summarising the position in common law, states that 'LPAs cannot give attorneys the power to demand specific forms of medical treatment that healthcare professionals do not believe are necessary or appropriate for the donor's particular condition'. The consequence is that either the attorney gives consent to treatment, which the health professionals have decided is necessary or appropriate, or they refuse such consent. A refusal would occur where the donor believes that it is the donor's best interest not to have the treatment. In the case of life sustaining treatment, the attorney must not be motivated by a desire to bring about the donor's death. See **13.80**.

13.41 An example of a case in which an attorney acting under an LPA for health and welfare for was demanding medical treatment that the healthcare professionals did not believe was in the patient's best interests can be found in the decision of the Court of Appeal in *AVS v NHS Foundation Trust and B PCT* [2011] COPLR Con Vol 219.

Gifts

13.42 The authority of an attorney acting under a property and affairs LPA does not extend to disposing of the donor's property by making gifts except to the extent permitted by s 12(2) of the MCA 2005, which provides that, subject to any conditions or restrictions in the instrument, the attorney may make gifts:

'(a)   on customary occasions to persons (including himself) who are related to or connected with the donor, or

(b)   to any charity to which the donor made or might have been expected to make gifts,

if the value of each such gift is not unreasonable having regard to all the circumstances and, in particular, the size of the donor's estate.'

13.43 MCA 2005, s 12(3) states that 'customary occasion' means:

'(a)   the occasion or anniversary of a birth, a marriage, or the formation of a civil partnership, or

(b)   any other occasion on which presents are customarily given within families or among friends or associates.'

13.44 The wording is very similar to the restriction that applies to attorneys acting under an EPA (MCA 2005, Sch 4, para 3(3)), though the EPA legislation refers to 'gifts of a seasonal nature' rather than to gifts 'on customary occasions'. The OPG have produced a number of publications in relation to gifts: OPG2 – Giving gifts for someone else: a guide for attorneys and deputies; Practice Note – Gifts: Deputies and EPA/LPA Attorneys (02/2012); and LP14 – How to be a property and finances attorney. For a more detailed analysis of the attorney's limited power to make gifts, see **18.32–18.40**.

13.45 In the case of *Re Buckley* (22 January 2013) Senior Judge Lush decided in an attempt to be both proportionate and pragmatic, and to prevent the court from being overwhelmed with applications, with which it does not have the resources to cope, that it is not necessary to seek authority where the gift is of de minimis; which can be construed as covering the annual Inheritance tax exemption of £3,000 and the annual small gifts exemption of £250 per person, up to a maximum of ten people in the following circumstances:

(i)   where the donor has a life expectancy of less than five years;

(ii)   the donor's estate exceeds the nil rate band for Inheritance Tax purposes;

(iii)   the gifts are affordable having regard to the donor's care costs and will not adversely affect the donor's standard of care and quality of life; and

(iv)   there is no evidence that the donor would be opposed to gifts of this magnitude being made on their behalf.

13.46 If the attorney wishes to make a more extensive gift of the donor's assets, perhaps as part of an inheritance tax-planning exercise, or wishes to make gifts on an unauthorised occasion, or for a non-charitable purpose, an application should be made to the Court of Protection for an order under MCA 2005, s 23(4), which provides that 'the court may authorize the making of gifts which are not within s 12(2) (permitted gifts)'. Details of the court's procedure and requirements on applications for the making of gifts of the donor's property are set out in Practice Direction 9F, which supplements

Part 9 of the Court of Protection Rules 2007 (SI 2007/1744), and is headed *Applications relating to statutory wills, codicils, settlements and other dealings with P's property.*

13.47 The OPG's publication LP12: Make and register a lasting power of attorney – a guide, states at page 31:

'Instructions about gifts often cause problems.

There are strict limits on the kinds of gifts that attorneys can give on your behalf.

They can give presents on 'customary occasions', including weddings, birthdays and religious holidays. They can donate to charities you've previously given to.

Any gifts should be reasonable and take into account how much money you have.

You can't give your attorneys instructions to go beyond these limits.

Here are some types of gifts you can't authorise:
- trust funds for grandchildren
- payment of school fees for grandchildren
- interest-free loans to family
- maintenance for any family member other than your wife, husband, civil partner or child under 18.'

Maintenance

13.48 There is no specific power under the MCA 2005 to maintain another person or any guidance in the Code of Practice. This is in contrast to the power of an attorney acting under an EPA, where there is authority in paragraph 3(2), Schedule 4 of the MCA 2005, to provide for another person's needs. See **18.20–18.29.** To plug this gap, some donors have included maintenance provisions in their LPA. Appendix H contains cases where the court has severed such provisions, as a prohibited attempt to increase the power conferred by MCA 2005, s 12.

13.49 In *Re Gee*, (22 August 2011) the Public Guardian referred the court to the view expressed by the Law Commission in its report, Mental Incapacity (Law Com. No. 231) to the effect that an LPA attorney could provide for the needs of others as part of his duty to act in the donor's best interests, even in the absence of an express provision such as is conferred on EPA attorneys. The Public Guardian asked the court to consider whether the view of the Law Commission could be relied on in cases where the donor contemplated that the attorneys could provide for the needs of others in circumstances outside the statutory gifting power. However, the court said the Law Commission's report was not the law and decided to sever the provision as it contravened the power to make gifts under MCA 2005, s 12.

13.50 The court has allowed maintenance clauses for the donor's spouse (*Re Bloom,* 16 March 2012). In *Re Strange,* 21 May 2012, Senior Judge Lush said:

'In the context of clauses in an LPA in which the donor makes provision for the maintenance of his or her spouse, there should be no distinction between male and female spouses and, in principle, such clauses should be treated as valid on the basis of the specific maintenance obligations imposed by statutes such as National Assistance Act 1948, section 24(1)(b) and Social Security Administration Act 1992, section 105(3), and the absence of any distinction between husband and wife in other legislation, such as the Matrimonial Causes Act 1973 and the Inheritance (Provision for Family and Dependants) Act 1975.'

13.51 In *the Public Guardian v Marvin* [2014] EWCOP 45, Senior Judge Lush said of the absence of any maintenance provision:

'Although the Mental Capacity Act is silent on this issue, the best interests test applies and, in most cases, making reasonable financial provision for their dependants is likely to be in the best interests of someone who lacks capacity to manage their own finances.'

13.52 The case of *the Public Guardian v Marvin* [2014] EWCOP 45 concerned an attorney using the donor's funds to maintain the donor's long-term cohabitee. The OPG published a Practice Note in 2012, *Gifts: Deputies and EPA/LPA Attorneys*, which has not been undated since the *Marvin* case and states on page 6:

'The Mental Capacity Act does not expressly permit an LPA attorney to benefit themselves or other persons by providing for their needs. However, the Court of Protection has confirmed that an LPA attorney may provide for the needs of family members if P is legally obliged to maintain them, as in the case of P's spouse, civil partner or minor child. An application to Court will be necessary if an attorney wishes to maintain anyone else.'

More specific guidance was provided by District Judge Eldergill in *Re PG* [2017] EWCOP 10 who said at para 152:

'Having regard to the above considerations, I would be of the view that the legal position is as follows:
   a)   An act done by an attorney is in general to be treated as one done by the person themselves.
   b)   An attorney's primary duty is to act only within the scope of the actual authority conferred by the power.
   c)   The extent of an attorney's authority turns primarily on the wording of the power and the authority given to them is a matter to be decided upon by the donor in consultation with the attorney.
   d)   There is nothing to prevent a donor who does not wish their estate to be used to meet the needs of family members or dependants from inserting in the instrument a condition or restriction to that effect. Likewise, a donor may impose conditions or restrictions in relation to gifting.
   e)   If a general power to manage the donor's property and financial affairs is granted to an attorney then the attorney has authority to make decisions about 'all or any' matters concerning the donor's property and affairs, including therefore meeting the needs of other persons and making gifts, subject to:
         i)   A statutory duty to comply with section 1 of the Act (principles) which, *inter alia*, requires an attorney to act in the best interests of an incapacitated donor;
         ii) A statutory duty to comply with section 4 of the Act (best interests) which, *inter alia*, requires an attorney before deciding that a decision or payment is in the best interests of an incapacitated donor to consider the donor's past and present wishes and feelings (and, in particular, any written statement made by them, including statements in the LPA itself), their beliefs and values, the factors which the donor would be likely to consider if s/he were able to do so, the views of any co-attorneys, the views of any non-professional carers, and any other relevant considerations such as the donor's current financial position and own needs.

iii) A statutory duty not to make gifts of the donor's property without court authority if they exceed the level permitted by section 12.

iv) A duty to act in good faith.

v) A fiduciary duty not to use the power for personal advantage in a way that is not in the donor's best interests upon a proper application of section 4.

vi) A duty to use such care and skill of care when carrying out their functions under the power of attorney as the attorney would in the management of their own affairs.

f) It is not possible to define precisely the boundary between a gift and a payment to meet a person's needs because each person's situation, circumstances and resources are unique. However, marriage and equivalent relationships typically create a relationship of interdependence and mutual support, and dependence is commonly created by the presence either of children or a family member with a significant disability. Such relationships commonly generate needs met by other loved ones within the circle. In very general terms, gifts lack the regularity of weekly, monthly and other periodic payments to meet the needs of family members and dependants, and often are not supported by a history of frequent similar periodic payments predating the onset of incapacity.

g) Where a spouse or partner attorney applies part of the donor's funds to meet their own continuing needs and those of other dependents in a way which —allowing for any reduction in family income and assets caused by care home fees or loss of earnings and any increase in the donor's own needs — is consistent with the donor's historical expenditure prior to the onset of incapacity then this is likely to be an indicator that it is a need that is being met, not a gift. Because the donor has entrusted such decisions to their attorney, rather than leave them to a court, the courts are likely to be reluctant to interfere without good evidence that the attorney has not applied the requirements of section 4 when making their best interests decision. Such expenditure is consistent with the donor's historical expenditure which acts as a barometer of their wishes, feelings, beliefs and values, and the lifestyle enjoyed prior to the onset of incapacity sets a benchmark that is relevant to the assessment of need. In order not to allow for any doubt at all, a prudent donor may wish to make the matter explicit by including a condition or statement in their LPA about future provision for the needs of specified persons.

h) Payments on customary occasions such as birthdays will generally be gifts, not payments to satisfy a need. Likewise, the making of one-off payments in the absence of good evidence of a sudden present need which historically the donor would have met or be likely to meet from their own funds may be construed by a court as a gift. Therefore, given that an attorney who breaches any of their duties is personally liable to compensate the donor for any loss thereby sustained to the donor's estate, the prudent course would be to apply for the court to authorise such a payment.'

Gratuitous care

13.53 It is common for family members and friends to provide some level of informal care for the donor, such as shopping, cooking and cleaning. This sort of care is usually done without any expectation of payment. However, on occasions the carer needs to receive a payment to ease their own financial situation and enable them to continue in their caring role. Such payments are commonly known as 'gratuitous care' or 'family care payments'. An attorney acting under a property and financial affairs power will usually have authority to make such payments, provided he believes it is in the best interests of the donor. However, where the attorney is also the person providing care, a conflict arises, as the attorney is not allowed to take advantage of their position. Where this occurs, the attorney should apply to the court for authorisation. The OPG has published a Practice Note: *Family care payments*, which set out factors which should be considered when deciding whether to make a gratuitous payment.

Substitutes or successors

13.54 Statutory authority granted to a particular person cannot normally be delegated and, generally, it is not possible for an attorney who is himself a delegate to further delegate his authority. The MCA 2005 expressly provides that an LPA attorney cannot appoint a substitute or successor (MCA 2005, s 10(8)).

CONDITIONS OR RESTRICTIONS IMPOSED BY THE DONOR

The prescribed form

13.55 The authority conferred by an LPA is subject to any conditions or restrictions specified in the instrument (MCA 2005, s 9(4)(b)).

13.56 Section 7 of the 2015 prescribed form of LPA for property and financial affairs, and for health and welfare states as follows:

'This section is optional

You can tell your attorneys how you'd **prefer** them to make decisions, or give them specific **instructions** which they must follow when making decisions.

Most people leave this page blank- you can just talk to your attorneys so they understand how you want them to make decision for you.

Preferences

Your attorneys don't have to follow your preferences but they should keep them in mind. For examples of preferences, see the Guide, part 7A.' [*This is a reference to LP12: Make and register your lasting power of attorney- a guide*].

[*The form then contains a box for preferences*]

'Instructions

Your attorneys will have to follow your instructions exactly. For examples of instructions, see the Guide, part A7.

Be careful - if you give instructions that are not legally correct they would have to be removed before your LPA could be registered.'

[*The form then contains a box for instructions*]

13.57 Examples of restrictions and conditions can be found in CHAPTER 15 on LPA precedents.

Guidance distinguished from conditions and restrictions

13.58 One of the lessons to be learned from the applications made by the Public Guardian to the Court of Protection to sever ineffective or invalid provisions from an LPA (see **13.61** below) is that donors should give greater thought to whether they wish to impose a legally binding restriction or condition on the attorney, or whether it would be more appropriate to give their instructions in the non-legally binding guidance section of the instrument. The OPG's guide, LP12: Make and register a lasting power of attorney, contains details of common problems and mistakes and states at part A7, on page 29:

> 'Instructions cause more problems than preferences. If you want to give instructions, read through the information below to find out about common problems and mistakes. It may be better to phrase them as preferences.'

13.59 The OPG's pre- 2015 publication, *Guidance for people who want to make a lasting power of attorney for property and financial affairs* (LPA112) gave more focused advice, which stated, at page 23:

> 'A requirement that cannot be incorporated as a restriction can often be achieved as guidance. For example, if you have 3 attorneys acting jointly and severally you cannot include a restriction and condition that two of them must act jointly in relation to decisions about selling your house. It is possible, however, to state in the "guidance for your attorneys" that you wish them to work together for transactions of this kind.'

13.60 Because the guidance is not legally binding, a situation could arise where, after considering the guidance, the attorney came to the conclusion that it would be in the donor's best interests not to follow the guidance.

Severance of ineffective or invalid provisions

13.61 The Court of Protection has power to determine any question as to the meaning or effect of an LPA or an instrument purporting to create one (MCA 2005, s 23(1)). If it appears to the Public Guardian that an instrument contains a provision which would be ineffective as part of an LPA, or would prevent the instrument from operating as a valid LPA, the Public Guardian must apply to the court to determine the matter, and must not register pending the determination by the court (MCA 2005, Sch 1, para 11(2) and (3)).

13.62 If the Court of Protection determines that an LPA contains a provision which is ineffective as part of an LPA, or prevents the instrument from operating as a valid LPA, the court must notify the Public Guardian that it has severed the provision, or direct him to cancel the registration of the instrument as a lasting power of attorney: MCA 2005, Sch 1, para 11(5).

13.63 Where the court notifies the Public Guardian that it has severed a provision of the instrument, the Public Guardian must attach a note to it to that effect (MCA 2005, Sch 1, para 11(6)).

Examples of provisions that the court has severed

13.64 There were numerous examples on the OPG's website of illegal or ineffective provisions that the Court of Protection has been asked to sever. These have been removed but can be found in Annex H of this publication. Those that most commonly occur in LPAs can be summarised as follows.

Severance in both kinds of LPA

Provisions that are incompatible with a 'joint' or 'joint and several' appointment

	Where the donor has appointed attorneys to act jointly and severally and subsequently inserts a provision that they are to act jointly for some decisions. The donor should have ticked the box appoint the attorneys to act
(1)	jointly for some decisions and jointly and severally for other decisions
(2)	Clauses that require a majority or a quorum to act
(3)	Clauses that allow the survivor of joint attorneys to carry on acting
(4)	Where the donor's spouse should have been appointed as sole attorney and the donor's children appointed as replacement attorneys
(5)	Where the donor fails to specify any joint and several functions in a hybrid appointment
(6)	Where the donor states that the decision of one attorney is to prevail

Replacement attorneys

(7)	Where a replacement attorney is the only named person
(8)	Allowing a replacement attorney to act in circumstances not prescribed by s 13(6) of the Act
(9)	Providing for a replacement attorney to replace a replacement attorney
(10)	Providing for succession when attorneys have been appointed to act jointly

Miscellaneous provisions

(11)	Requiring the attorney to obtain the consent of a third party
(12)	Ousting the jurisdiction of the court

Severance in LPAs for property and financial affairs

(13)	Attempts to confer greater gift-making powers than those conferred on attorneys by s 12 of the Act
(14)	Authorising the attorney to make financial provision for someone other than the donor
(15)	Cases where the donor should have made two LPAs: one for their business affairs and the other for their personal finances
(16)	Health and welfare decision-making powers in an LPA for property and financial affairs

Severance in LPAs for health and welfare

(17)	Clauses that authorise the attorney to make health and welfare decisions when the donor is only physically incapacitated
(18)	Restrictions that are incompatible with Option B
(19)	Clauses that authorise assisted suicide
(20)	Clauses that confer financial powers on the attorneys

DECISION-MAKING BY THE ATTORNEY

Introduction

13.65 In the MCA 2005, a person's capacity, or lack of capacity, refers specifically to his capacity to make a particular decision at the time it needs to be made (MCA 2005, s 2(1)).

13.66 If the donor still has the capacity to make a particular decision:

- a personal welfare attorney must not make the decision on the donor's behalf. A personal welfare attorney can only make a decision that the donor lacks the capacity to make himself (MCA 2005, s 11(7)(a)); but
- a property and affairs attorney may make the decision on the donor's behalf – a property and affairs LPA can operate as an ordinary power of attorney while the donor has mental capacity – but not if the donor objects.

13.67 Section 9(4)(a) of the MCA 2005 provides that the authority conferred on an attorney is subject to the provisions of the MCA 2005, and in particular:

- s 1, the principles; and
- s 4, best interests.

The principles

13.68 Attorneys are expected to pay special attention to chapter 2 of the MCA 2005 Code of Practice, which describes how the principles in s 1 of the Act should be applied (Code of Practice, paragraph 7.54).

13.69 Section 1 of the MCA 2005 sets out the five 'principles' that underpin the legal requirements in the Act. The Act is intended to be enabling and supportive of people who lack capacity, not restricting or controlling of their lives. It aims to protect people who lack capacity to make particular decisions, but also to maximise their ability to make decisions, or to participate in decision-making, as far as they are able to do so (Code of Practice, page 19).

13.70 The five principles are:

- A person must be assumed to have capacity unless it is established that he lacks capacity (MCA 2005, s 1(2)).
- A person is not to be treated as unable to make a decision unless all practical steps to help him do so have been taken without success (MCA 2005, s 1(3)).
- A person is not to be treated as unable to make a decision merely because he makes an unwise decision (MCA 2005, s 1(4)).
- An act done, or decision made, under this Act for or on behalf of a person who lacks capacity must be done, or made, in his best interests (MCA 2005, s 1(5)).
- Before the act is done, or the decision is made, regard must be had to whether the purpose for which it is needed can be as effectively achieved in a way that is less restrictive of the person's rights and freedom of action (MCA 2005, s 1(6)).

Assisting the donor to make his own decisions

13.71 Attorneys are expected to have regard to chapter 3 of the MCA 2005 Code of Practice, which gives guidance on how people can be helped to make their own decisions (Code of Practice, paragraph 7.54). The following is a brief summary of that chapter.

13.72 The attorney should make every effort to encourage and support the donor to make as many decisions as possible and in doing so should consider:

- whether the donor has all the relevant information needed to make the decision, and, if there is a choice, whether information has been given on the alternatives;
- whether the information could be explained or presented in a way that is easier for the donor to understand. Help should be given to communicate information wherever necessary, for example using pictures, photographs, videos, tapes, or sign language;
- whether there are particular times of the day when the donor's understanding is better, or whether there is a particular place where they feel more at ease and able to make a decision; and
- whether anyone else – for example, a relative or friend – who can help or support the donor to make a choice or express a view.

Assessing the donor's capacity

13.73 Attorneys are expected to have regard to chapter 4 of the MCA 2005 Code of Practice, which gives guidance on how capacity should be assessed (Code of Practice, paragraph 7.54). The following is a brief summary of that chapter.

13.74 The attorney is not expected to be an expert in assessing capacity, but, when deciding to make a decision on the donor's behalf, he must reasonably believe that the donor lacks the mental capacity to make that particular decision.

13.75 It is suggested that, when assessing the donor's mental capacity, the attorney will need to think about whether:

- the donor has a general understanding of what the decision is that needs to be made;
- the donor has a general understanding of the consequences of this decision;
- the donor can weigh up information and use it to make the decision;
- there is any way in which the donor could be assisted to make the decision for himself;
- there is any way in which the donor can be helped to communicate his decision or wishes and feelings.

Acting in the donor's best interests

13.76 If the donor is incapable of making a decision for himself, the attorney may make the decision on his behalf, but must do so in the donor's best interests (MCA 2005, s 1(5)). Attorneys are required to pay special attention to chapter 5 of the Code of Practice, which gives guidance on determining what is in the donor's best interests (Code of Practice, paragraph 7.54).

13.77 The MCA 2005 does not actually define 'best interests', but s 4 sets out a non-exhaustive checklist of things the attorney *must do* when determining what is in the donor's best interests. Section 4(8)(a) expressly states that the duties imposed by subsections (1) to (7) also apply in relation to the exercise of any powers which are exercisable under an LPA.

- He must not make the determination merely on the basis of the donor's age or appearance, or a condition of his, or an aspect of his behaviour, which might lead others to make unjustified assumptions about what might be in his best interests (MCA 2005, s 4(1)).
- He must consider all the relevant circumstances (MCA 2005, s 4(2)). 'Relevant circumstances' are those of which the attorney is aware, and which it would be reasonable to regard as relevant (MCA 2005, s 4(11)). In particular, he must take the following steps.
- He must consider whether it is likely that the donor will at some time have capacity in relation to the matter in question, and, if it appears likely that he will, when that is likely to be (MCA 2005, s 4(3)). This is in case the decision can be put off, until the donor can make it himself. Even if the decision cannot be put off, the decision is likely to be influenced by whether the donor will always lack capacity or is likely to regain capacity (Explanatory Notes to Mental Capacity Act 2005, paragraph 29).
- He must, so far as reasonably practicable, permit and encourage the donor to participate, or to improve his ability to participate, as fully as possible in any act done for him and any decision affecting him (MCA 2005, s 4(4)).
- He must not be motivated by a desire to bring about the donor's death, where the determination relates to life-sustaining treatment, and the attorney is considering whether the treatment is in the donor's best interests (MCA 2005, s 4(5)).
- He must consider, so far as is reasonably practical, the donor's past and present wishes and feelings, and, in particular, any relevant written statement made by him when he had capacity (MCA 2005, s 4(6)(a)).
- He must consider, so far as is reasonably practical, the donor's beliefs and values that would be likely to influence his decision if he had capacity (MCA 2005, s 4(6)(b)). These would include, for example, the donor's cultural background, religious beliefs, political convictions, and past behaviour and habits (Code of Practice, paragraph 5.46).
- He must consider, so far as is reasonably practical, the other factors that the donor would be likely to consider if he were able to do so (MCA 2005, s 4(6)(c)). This might include the effect of the decision on other people, obligations to dependants, or the duties of a responsible citizen (Code of Practice, paragraph 5.47).
- He must take into account, if it is practicable and appropriate to consult them, the views of anyone named by the donor as someone to be consulted on the matter in question or on matters of that kind, or anyone engaged in caring for the donor or who is interested in his

welfare, as to what would be in the donor's best interests, and as to what the donor's wishes and feelings, and beliefs and values would be (MCA 2005, s 4(7)(a) and (b)).

• He must take into account, if it is practicable and appropriate to consult them, the views of any other donee of an LPA granted by the donor, as to what would be in the donor's best interests, and what the donor's wishes and feelings, and beliefs and values would be (MCA 2005, s 4(7)(c)). This would include not only consulting any co-attorneys under the LPA, but would require a health and welfare attorney to consult a property and affairs attorney, and vice versa.

13.78 Best interests is not a test of 'substituted judgement' (what the donor would have wanted), but rather it requires a determination to be made by applying an objective test as to what would be in the donor's best interests. All the relevant circumstances, including the factors mentioned in MCA 2005, s 4 must be considered, but none carries any more weight or priority than another. They must all be balanced in order to determine what would be in the best interests of the person concerned. The factors in this section do not provide a definition of best interests and are not exhaustive.

13.79 There is sufficient compliance with the Act if, having complied with the above requirements, the attorney reasonably believes that what he does or decides is in the donor's best interests (MCA 2005, s 4(9)).

Making decisions about life-sustaining treatment

13.80 When the Mental Capacity Bill was at its Third Reading stage in the House of Lords, on 24 March 2005, Earl Howe proposed an amendment that would have denied an attorney acting under an LPA for personal welfare the authority to refuse life-sustaining treatment on the donor's behalf. The amendment was opposed by the government, and the Parliamentary Under-Secretary at the Department of Constitutional Affairs, Baroness Ashton of Upholland, made the following speech (*Hansard*, vol 671, no 59, cols 435 and 436), in which she described the attorney's role when making decisions about life-sustaining treatment:

'The fourth point is that the attorney has this power only if it is explicit and written in the lasting power of attorney. There can be no mistake about whether the donor of the lasting power of attorney really intended the attorney to make decisions about life-sustaining treatment; and the donor will have to discuss that aspect of the lasting power of attorney with the prospective attorney. I know that some people are concerned that people will not want to give their loved ones such an onerous duty as to make life or death decisions in what will undoubtedly be very distressing circumstances for them personally. That is a valid point, but we have to remember that they do not have to give them this power. It is not automatic. The fact that it needs to be an explicit provision in the lasting power of attorney must cause people to discuss it, and sign up only if both parties are content with what it includes and what it will involve. We shall ensure that there is guidance and information to help people be absolutely clear about that process.

Fifthly, attorneys do not make clinical decisions or decisions about medical best interests. I know that there have been concerns that it is not safe for attorneys to take over the medical decision-making role of the doctor. I can completely reassure your Lordships' House on that point. An attorney has only the same power as a patient who has capacity, so he can only give or refuse consent to treatment; he cannot take the medical decision. The doctor continues to have the professional duty of care to his patient and can be sued in negligence for breaching that duty.

In any given treatment decision, the doctor must make clinical judgments about which treatments of those available for a given condition would be accepted as proper by a responsible body of professional medical opinion. That is the so-called *Bolam* test. In many situations, there will be a range of medically appropriate options that are what might be called *Bolam* compliant. It is clear from case-law that doctors have a duty to advise patients of those alternative treatments when seeking consent. If the patient lacks capacity to make a decision on the basis of the advice, the doctor must then himself decide which of the possible treatment options would be in their best interests.

Under this Bill, patients have an attorney, if they want one. Then it will be the attorney's role to decide which of the treatment options is in the patient's best interests; but it will not be the attorney's role to take the medical decision of which treatment options to offer in the first place. I shall give a very short example. A doctor may believe that providing and withholding artificial nutrition and hydration in the last few days of a person's life are both *Bolam*-compliant treatment decisions. He may have doubts about whether the burdens outweigh the benefits of the treatment but the attorney knows that the patient, perhaps because of a very strong religious commitment, would definitely wish to receive artificial nutrition and hydration and believes that the option to give ANH is in the patient's best interests. The attorney ensures that treatment is continued for as long as it is *Bolam* compliant—in other words, that clinically it is not detrimental to the individual and is in the person's best interests. That would be removed by this amendment.

Sixthly, and finally, doctors must go to court if they disagree with attorney's assessment of best interests. We know that there are concerns about what happens when a doctor does not feel that the attorney is genuinely acting in the patient's best interests. The answer is very straightforward: if the issue cannot be resolved, the doctors must seek the guidance from the Court of Protection to ensure that a decision in the best interests of the patient is reached. We know that that works, because it is exactly the same as the sharing of responsibility between clinicians and parents when parents are giving or refusing consent on behalf of their children.'

Consulting others

13.81 The MCA 2005 Code of Practice suggests, at paragraph 5.51, that:

'Decision-makers must show that they have thought carefully about who to speak to. If it is practical and appropriate to speak to the people mentioned above, they must do so, and take their views into account. They must be able to explain why they did not speak to a particular person – it is good practice to have a clear record of their reasons. It is also good practice to give careful consideration to the views of family carers, if it is possible to do so.'

13.82 This endorses the comments made by the Law Commission in its report on *Mental Incapacity* (1995), at paragraph 3.34:

'It is inevitable, on this approach, that the consultee must be a person whom it is "practicable" and "appropriate" to consult. This is not to give absolute discretion to the decision-maker. If challenged, decision-makers will have to be prepared to explain why a consultation which they declined to carry out was either impracticable or inappropriate.'

13.83 In *Re A, D v B* [2009] COPLR Con Vol 1 Senior Judge Lush held that it would not have been in the donor's best interests for the attorney to consult her brother in circumstances where the consultation would have been unduly onerous, futile or would have served no useful purpose.

OTHER DUTIES

Regard to the Code

13.84 The Mental Capacity Act Code of Practice has been issued as guidance (MCA 2005, s 42(1)). The Code explains the extent of the legislation, the process to be applied when assessing whether an individual has capacity, the process by which a decision-maker is to come to a conclusion as to the decision or act being in an individual's best interests. Attorneys acting under an LPA have a specific duty to have regard to the Code (MCA 2005, s 42(4)(a)). Chapter 7 'What does the Act say about Lasting Powers of Attorney', is relevant to such attorneys. There are no specific sanctions for failing to follow the code, but where an attorney fails to follow it, this may be taken into account in any criminal or civil proceedings in a court or tribunal, if relevant in determining a question arising in those proceedings (MCA 2005, s 42(5)).

Fiduciary duties

13.85 Paragraphs 7.58–7.68 of the Code of Practice set out in detail other duties which an attorney acting under an LPA should follow. Paragraph 7.58 contains a brief but useful summary:

'An attorney appointed under an LPA is acting as the chosen agent of the donor and therefore, under the law of agency, the attorney has certain duties towards the donor. An attorney takes on a role which carries a great deal of power, which they must use carefully and responsibly.

They have a duty to:
- apply certain standards of care and skill (duty of care) when making decisions
- carry out the donor's instructions
- not take advantage of their position and not benefit themselves, but benefit the donor (fiduciary duty)
- not delegate decisions, unless authorised to do so
- act in good faith
- respect confidentiality
- comply with the directions of the Court of Protection
- not give up the role without telling the donor and the court.

In relation to property and affairs LPAs, they have a duty to:
- keep accounts
- keep the donor's money and property separate from their own.'

Court guidance on investments

13.86 How to invest is a best interest decision, and as such the attorney cannot simply so as he wishes. The attorney also has fiduciary responsibilities and must exercise such care and skill as is reasonable in the circumstances when investing the donor's assets and this duty of care is even greater where attorneys hold themselves out as having specialist knowledge or experience. All investments should be made in the donor's name. If, for any reason, it is not possible to register the investment in the donor's name, the attorney should execute a declaration of trust or some other formal record acknowledging the donor's beneficial interest in the asset.

13.87 Guidance about the attorney's approach to investment was given by Senior Judge Lush in *Re Buckley* (22 January 2013). Noting that the fiduciary obligations of an attorney are similar to those of trustees, the provisions of s 4 of the Trustee Act 2000, as regards the standard investment criteria, should be followed by attorneys, when exercising any power of investment. This requires consideration of:

(i)   the suitability of the investments;

(ii)   the need to diversify the investments, in so far as it is appropriate in the circumstances;

(iii)   the need to review the investments from time to time and consider whether, having regard to the standard investment criteria, they should be varied; and

(iv)   the need to take advice of a person who is reasonably believed by the attorney to be qualified to give it by his ability in and practical experience of financial and other matters relating to the proposed investment, unless the attorney reasonably concludes that it is unnecessary or inappropriate to do so.

13.88 Senior Judge Lush also recommend that for a donor with a life expectancy of less than 5 years, attorneys and their financial advisers should have regard to the criteria that were historically approved by the Court of Protection and the antecedents of the OPG titled, 'Investing for Patients', albeit with some allowance for updating. This can be summarised as follows:

(i)   Funds of up to £85,000 should be held in an easily accessible and safe investment, such as cash deposit that provides a competitive interest rate when compared with base rates and NS&I returns.

(ii)   Funds of over £85,000 should be held in an investment where all or part is available quickly – and with very little risk.

(iii)   An existing investment portfolio should be made available quickly but to reduce the exposed risk commensurate with the donor's requirements. Depending on the nature of the portfolio, a liquidation process should be adopted using the annual Capital Gains Tax allowance. The cash funds should be retained in cash deposits with different financial institutions that provides a competitive rate when compared with base rates and NS&I returns.

13.89 A family attorney who wishes to invest in high risk investments, which are made with the purpose of Inheritance tax savings on death, where they are a beneficiary or potential beneficiary under the donor's will, is likely to be in a position of conflict, and so should obtain the Court's permission before making the investment (see *Re MM* [September 2016] (unreported) (DJ Batten).

ATTORNEY'S LIABILITY FOR WRONGS OF CO-ATTORNEY

13.90 Although the legislation makes no specific provision in this respect, at common law an attorney is not liable for any loss or harm caused by the wrongful act or omission of a co-attorney, unless he authorised or was otherwise party or privy to such wrongful act or omission: (see *Bowstead and Reynolds on Agency*, 19th edn (Sweet & Maxwell, 2010)).

13.91 An attorney appointed under a joint and several power may find themselves 'a dormant attorney': only making decisions when the active attorney is for whatever reason, unable or unwilling to act. There is a danger that the dormant attorney is unaware that the active attorney has exceeded his or her authority or is not acting in the donor's best interests, particularly if the active attorney fails to consult the dormant attorney when making a best interest decision. In *Re MM* [2016] (unreported), District Judge Batten was highly critical of a professional attorney who was appointed to act with a family member, as the professional attorney had failed to put into place any safeguards, such as receiving bank statements and was unaware that the other attorney had made excessive gifts to his wife. In that case, both attorneys were removed and the LPA was revoked.

Chapter 14

REVOCATION, DISCLAIMER AND TERMINATION OF LASTING POWERS OF ATTORNEY

INTRODUCTION

14.1 Subject to the provisions relating to joint and several appointments and replacement attorneys, a lasting power of attorney (LPA) comes to an end when:

(1)   the donor revokes the power;
(2)   the attorney disclaims his appointment;
(3)   the power is terminated by operation of law – for example, on the death or bankruptcy of one of the parties;
(4)   the marriage or civil partnership between the donor and the attorney is dissolved or annulled, unless the instrument provides otherwise;
(5)   the Court of Protection directs that an instrument is not to be registered, which in effect renders it unusable; or
(6)   the Court of Protection revokes the power, but the court can only revoke a power if the donor is incapable of revoking it himself.

14.2 The Public Guardian cannot revoke an LPA, but in certain circumstances he must:

* not register the instrument;
* cancel the registration of the instrument; or
* attach a note to the instrument.

REVOCATION BY THE DONOR

The donor may revoke the power at any time when he has capacity to do so

14.3 Section 13(2) of the Mental Capacity Act 2005 (MCA 2005) states that 'P may, at any time when he has capacity to do so, revoke the power'. The reason for including an express provision to this effect in the Act was given by the Law Commission, in paragraphs 7.42 and 7.43 of its report on *Mental Incapacity* (1995):

'There is a common law principle that a donor of a power can revoke all or any of it, either expressly (for example by saying so, or by tearing up the document) or impliedly, by doing an act which is inconsistent with the continuation of the power (for example, concealing the whereabouts of all assets from the attorney). The general rule as to capacity applies to revocation and a donor's revocation is only effective if he or she has the capacity to revoke, in other words understands the nature and effect of the action being taken. The 1985 Act does not affect the common law position until the attorney makes an application for registration, whereupon it radically alters it. Our predecessors recommended that the ability of a donor of an EPA to deal in any way with a registered power should be curtailed, in order to preserve "the 'sanctity' of registration". The 1985 Act therefore provides that "no revocation of . . . [a registered] power by the donor shall be valid unless and until the court confirms the revocation."

We suggested in the consultation papers that a donor with capacity to do so should always be able to revoke a power of attorney. Respondents unanimously agreed with this policy and some of them mentioned that it was particularly important not to restrict, and not even to impose any delay upon, a donor's ability to revoke a health care power. In relation to [LPAs] covering health care decisions, we have explained that no attorney's authority will ever coincide with that of a donor who is still able personally to consent to or refuse any treatment offered. Where a donor does, however, lack capacity to take the decision in question, he or she may still have capacity to revoke the [LPA] ("I don't want X deciding things for me any more"). It would be most unappealing to require that a treatment provider must continue to honour the decision of an attorney when faced with a donor who is now revoking the authority granted. We therefore think it necessary to stress, by way of an explicit provision, that a donor should always retain the power to revoke his or her [LPA].'

Capacity to revoke an LPA

14.4 District Judge Glentworth held in *SAD and ACD v SED*, case no 12791319 (Unreported) (4 November 2016), that, in order to understand the information relevant to the decision, including the reasonably foreseeable consequences of deciding one way or another or failing to make the decision, the donor would need to understand:

- who the attorneys are;
- what authority they have;
- why it is necessary or expedient to revoke the power;
- the foreseeable consequences of revoking the power; and
- why he originally made the power.

14.5 One of the foreseeable consequences of revoking the power would be that the donor should understand revocation means he will not have anyone appointed to make property and financial decisions for him, which may result in the court appointing a deputy or if he has sufficient mental capacity, he may make a new LPA. This is despite the suggestion in paragraph 7.43 of the Law Commission's report on *Mental Capacity*, quoted above, that a statement by the donor that 'I don't want X deciding things for me any more' would be sufficient evidence of his capacity to revoke an LPA.

Steps necessary for revocation

14.6 A power of attorney is a deed (Powers of Attorney Act 1971, s 1), and preferably should be revoked by a deed of revocation. An attorney is an agent of the donor and, under the general law of agency, the authority of an agent may be revoked (a) by express notice given by the principal to the agent, and (b) by the conduct of the principal. To amount to revocation by conduct, the conduct must be inconsistent with the continuation of the agency. To be inconsistent, it must be unambiguous in its effect: *Re E (Enduring Power of Attorney)* [2000] 1 FLR 882 per Arden J. It would be unwise, however, for a donor to rely simply on revocation by conduct, and he should confirm it by an express revocation without delay.

14.7 Where the donor of a registered EPA revokes the instrument, the revocation is not valid unless and until the court confirms the revocation under MCA 2005, Sch 4, para 16(3). That paragraph states that 'the court must confirm the revocation of the power if it is satisfied that the donor (a) has done whatever is necessary in law to effect an express revocation of the power, and (b) was mentally capable of revoking a power of attorney when he did so (whether or not he is so when the court considers the application)'. There is no similar requirement for the court to confirm the revocation of an LPA.

Procedure following revocation by the donor

14.8 Regulation 21 of the Lasting Powers of Attorney, Enduring Powers of Attorney and Public Guardian Regulations 2007 (SI 2007/1253) (LPA, EPA & PG Regs 2007) sets out the following procedure for revocation of an LPA by the donor:

'(1)   A donor who revokes a lasting power of attorney must –
    (a)   notify the Public Guardian that he has done so; and
    (b)   notify the donee (or, if more than one, each of them) of the revocation.
(2)   Where the Public Guardian receives a notice under paragraph (1)(a), he must cancel the registration of the instrument creating the power if he is satisfied that the donor has taken such steps as are necessary in law to revoke it.
(3)   The Public Guardian may require the donor to provide such further information, or produce such documents, as the Public Guardian reasonably considers necessary to enable him to determine whether the steps necessary for revocation have been taken.
(4)   Where the Public Guardian cancels the registration of the instrument he must notify –
    (a)   the donor; and
    (b)   the donee or, if more than one each of them.'

The court may determine whether an LPA has been revoked

14.9 Section 22(2) of the MCA 2005 provides that:

'The court may determine any question relating to –
(a)   . . .
(b)   whether the power has been revoked or has otherwise come to an end.'

Disclaimer by the attorney

14.10 Disclaimer occurs where an attorney resigns or renounces his appointment. At common law the actual authority of an agent comes to an end when the agent gives a notice of renunciation to the principal and the principal accepts it. A problem arises where the donor is incapacitated and unable to accept the renunciation or disclaimer.

14.11 As regards LPAs, s 13 of the MCA 2005 provides that:

'(5) The occurrence in relation to a donee of an event mentioned in subsection (6) –
    (a)   terminates his appointment, and
    (b)   except in the cases given in subsection (7), revokes the power.
(6)   The events are –
    (a)   the disclaimer of the appointment by the donee in accordance with such requirements as may be prescribed for the purposes of this section in regulations made by the Lord Chancellor, . . .
(7)   The cases are –
    (a)   the donee is replaced under the terms of the instrument,
    (b)   he is one of two or more persons appointed to act as donees jointly and severally in respect of any matter and, after the event, there is at least one remaining donee.'

Prescribed form of disclaimer: LPA 005

14.12 Section 13(6)(a) of the MCA 2005 requires the disclaimer of the appointment by an attorney to be 'in accordance with such requirements as may be prescribed for the purposes of this section in regulations made by the Lord Chancellor'.

14.13 Regulation 20(1) of the LPA, EPA & PG Regs 2007 states that:

'Schedule 6 to these Regulations sets out the form ("LPA 005") which a donee of an instrument registered as a lasting power of attorney must use to disclaim his appointment as donee.'

14.14 The prescribed form was amended by the Lasting Powers of Attorney, Enduring Powers of Attorney and Public Guardian (Amendments) Regulations 2015. The use of the prescribed form is mandatory. A letter from the attorney saying he is resigning, or intends to resign, will not suffice.

14.15 The prescribed form LPA 005 is described as a 'Disclaimer by a proposed or acting attorney under a Lasting Power of Attorney'. Neither of the terms 'proposed' or 'acting' is defined. An 'acting attorney' is presumably one who is already acting under a registered LPA. A 'proposed attorney' could be either:

- an attorney who has been appointed by the donor, and who has accepted the appointment, but the instrument has not yet been registered; or
- a replacement attorney, where the instrument has been registered, but an event has not yet occurred which has the effect of terminating the appointment of the original attorney, whom the donor intended the replacement attorney to replace.

The completed form LPA 005 must be sent to the donor

14.16 Regulation 20(2) of the LPA, EPA & PG Regs 2007 states that:

'The donee must send –
(a)   the completed form to the donor.'

Copies of the completed form LPA 005 must be sent to the Public Guardian and to the other donee(s)

14.17 Regulation 20(2) of the LPA, EPA & PG Regs 2007 states that:

'The donee must send –
(a)   the completed form to the donor; and
(b)   a copy of it to –
   (i)   the Public Guardian; and
   (ii)   any other donee who, for the time being, is appointed under the power.'

14.18 The prescribed form of disclaimer (LPA 005) contains a footnote that says,

'If the Office of the Public Guardian (OPG) has registered the LPA, you should also:
•   send a copy of this form to the OPG
•   send any copes of the LPA that you have to the OPG

Address: Office of the Public Guardian, PO Box 16185, Birmingham B2 2WH.'

The inference is that, if the instrument has not been registered, there is no need to send a copy to the OPG at this stage.

14.19 The use of the words 'for the time being' in LPA, EPA & PG Regs 2007, reg 20(2)(b)(ii) would seem to suggest that a copy of the completed form LPA 005 does not need to be sent to a replacement attorney, even though the effect of the disclaimer may be to trigger the replacement attorney's authority to act.

14.20 In any event, the Public Guardian must:

• cancel the registration of the LPA on being satisfied that the power has been revoked by the attorney's disclaimer, and notify the donor and donee(s) – MCA 2005, Sch 1, paras 17(1) and (2); or
• attach to the instrument a note to the effect that an event has occurred which has terminated the appointment of the donee, but which has not revoked the instrument, and give notice of the note to the donor and donees – MCA 2005, Sch 1, paras 22 and 25.

The effect of a disclaimer

14.21 Sections 13(5)(a) and 13(6)(a) of the MCA 2005 provide that 'the disclaimer of the appointment by the donee in accordance with such requirements as may be prescribed for the purposes of this section in regulations prescribed by the Lord Chancellor' terminates the donee's appointment.

14.22 It follows that a failure to comply with the requirements prescribed in the regulations will not necessarily terminate the donee's appointment, for example:

- failure to use the prescribed form LPA 005;
- failure to send the completed form LPA 005 to the donor;
- failure to send a copy of the completed form LPA 005 to any other donee; and
- failure to send a copy of the completed form LPA 005 to the Public Guardian.

14.23 Sections 13(5)(b) and 13(7) provide that a disclaimer of the appointment by the donee will also revoke the power unless:

(a)   the donee is replaced under the terms of the instrument; or

(b)   he is one of two or more persons appointed to act as donees jointly and severally in respect of any matter and, after the event, there is at least one remaining donee.

14.24 Schedule 1, para 17(1) of the MCA 2005 requires the Public Guardian to cancel the registration of an instrument as an LPA on being satisfied that the power has been revoked on the occurrence of an event mentioned in s 13(6) of the Act.

REVOCATION BY OPERATION OF LAW

Donor's bankruptcy

14.25 Section 13(3) of the MCA 2005 (as amended) provides that 'P's bankruptcy, or the making of a debt relief order (under Part 7A of the Insolvency Act 1986) in respect of P, revokes the power so far as it relates to P's property and affairs'. Section 13(4) adds: 'But where P is bankrupt merely because an interim bankruptcy restrictions order has effect in respect of him, or where P is subject to an interim debt relief restrictions order (under Schedule 4ZB of the Insolvency Act 1986), the power is suspended, so far as it relates to P's property and affairs, for so long as the order has effect'.

14.26 Section 64(3), the interpretation section, provides that: 'In this Act, references to the bankruptcy of an individual include a case where a bankruptcy restrictions order under the Insolvency Act 1986 has effect in respect of him.' Section 64(3A) provides that: 'In this Act references to a debt relief order (under Part 7A of the Insolvency Act 1986) being made in relation to an individual include a case where a debt relief restrictions order under the Insolvency Act 1986 has effect in respect of him.' Section 64(4) provides: 'Bankruptcy restrictions order' includes an interim bankruptcy restrictions order, and s 64(4A) provides: 'Debt relief restrictions order' includes an interim debt relief restrictions order.

14.27 The origins of MCA 2005, s 13(3) can be found in the Law Commission's report on *Mental Incapacity* (1995), at paragraph 7.47, which said that:

'The authority of an attorney is revoked by the later bankruptcy of the donor: *Markwick v Hardingham* (1880) 15 Ch D 339. This rule applies to transactions relating to property of which the donor is divested by the vesting of it in the trustee in bankruptcy and it would not therefore apply to personal or health care matters. The 1985 Act did not give the rule a statutory form. In view of the fact that [LPAs] can extend beyond financial matters, express provision in the new legislation would be helpful. We recommend that any part of [an LPA] which relates to matters other than property and financial affairs should not be revoked by the donor's bankruptcy.'

14.28 All references to bankruptcy in the MCA 2005 were amended by The Tribunals, Courts and Enforcement Act 2007 (Consequential Amendments) Order 2012 (SI 2012/2404) Sch 2, para 53, which came into force on 1 October 2012.

Attorney's bankruptcy

14.29 Sections 13(5) and (6)(b) of the MCA 2005 (as amended) provide that the bankruptcy of an attorney or the making of a debt relief order will terminate his appointment. The attorney's bankruptcy will also revoke the power, unless one of the exceptions set out in s 13(7) applies, namely where he is:

- replaced under the terms of the instrument; or
- one of two or more persons are appointed to act as donees jointly and severally in respect of any matter and, after his bankruptcy, there is at least one remaining.

14.30 Sections 13(8) and (9) of the MCA 2005 (as amended) provide that:

'(8) The bankruptcy of a donee or the making of a debt relief order (under Part 7A of the Insolvency Act 1986) in respect of a donee does not terminate his appointment, or revoke the power, in so far as his authority relates to P's personal welfare.

(9) Where the donee is bankrupt merely because an interim bankruptcy restrictions order has effect in respect of him or where the donee is subject to an interim debt relief restrictions order (under Schedule 4ZB of the Insolvency Act 1986), his appointment and the power are suspended, so far as they relate to P's property and personal affairs, for so long as the order has effect.'

14.31 The origins of MCA 2005, s 13(8) can be found in the Law Commission's report on *Mental Incapacity* (1995), at paragraphs 7.45 and 7.46:

'The rules about bankruptcy in relation to [LPAs] need to distinguish between the grant of powers over "property and affairs" and the grant of powers over personal and health care matters. Although the existing rules whereby a bankrupt cannot act as an attorney should continue to apply to any powers over "property and affairs", we see no reason for an absolute rule that a bankrupt may not act as an attorney in relation to personal and health care matters. Those parts of an [LPA] which relate to personal or health care matters need not, therefore, be revoked by the donor's bankruptcy.

A bankrupt may not be appointed as a donee of powers over property and financial affairs in [an LPA]. The supervening bankruptcy of a donee revokes an EPA and so should the supervening donee of powers over the property and affairs in [an LPA] revoke his or her appointment as the donee of such powers. The 1985 Act provides that where two or more attorneys are appointed to act jointly then the bankruptcy of any one should revoke the powers of all; where they may act jointly and severally, however, the bankruptcy of any one of them does not revoke the powers of the others. Similar provision is made in the draft Bill.'

Dissolution or winding-up of a trust corporation attorney

14.32 Subsections 13(5) and (6)(b) of the MCA 2005 also provide that, if the attorney is a trust corporation, its winding-up or dissolution will terminate its appointment. The winding-up or dissolution of a trust corporation which is an attorney will also revoke the power, unless one of the exceptions set out in s 13(7) applies, namely where a trust corporation:

- is replaced under the terms of the instrument; or
- is one of two or more persons appointed to act as donees jointly and severally in respect of any matter and, after its winding-up or dissolution, there is at least one donee remaining.

Donor's death

14.33 Regulation 22 of the LPA, EPA & PG Regs 2007 states that:

'(1)   The Public Guardian must cancel the registration of an instrument as a lasting power of attorney if he is satisfied that the power has been revoked as a result of the donor's death.

(2)   Where the Public Guardian cancels the registration of an instrument he must notify the donee or, if more than one, each of them.'

Attorney's death

14.34 Subsections 13(5) and (6)(b) of the MCA 2005 provide that the death of a donee terminates his appointment. His death will also revoke the power, unless one of the exceptions set out in s 13(7) applies, namely where:

- he is replaced under the terms of the instrument; or
- he is one of two or more persons appointed to act as donees jointly and severally in respect of any matter and, after his death, there is at least one remaining.

Attorney's incapacity

14.35 Section 13(5) and (6)(c) of the MCA 2005 provide that the lack of capacity of a donee terminates his appointment. His lack of capacity will also revoke the power, unless one of the exceptions set out in s 13(7) applies, namely where:

- he is replaced under the terms of the instrument; or
- he is one of two or more persons appointed to act as donees jointly and severally in respect of any matter and, after he has become incapacitated, there is at least one remaining.

DISSOLUTION OR ANNULMENT OF A MARRIAGE OR CIVIL PARTNERSHIP BETWEEN THE DONOR AND THE ATTORNEY

14.36 The Enduring Powers of Attorney Act 1985 made no specific provision for cases where a donor and attorney were married to each other when the power was created but have subsequently divorced. The Law Commission considered this in paragraph 7.48 of its report on *Mental Incapacity* (1995), and said:

> 'Since [an LPA] cannot take effect immediately, but must first be registered, we think it appropriate to provide for such circumstances. The law already makes provision for the situation where a testator appointed a divorced spouse executor of beneficiary under his or her will. A donor of [an LPA] may be equally unable to remedy the original, now inappropriate, appointment.
>
> We recommend that, in the absence of a contrary intention, the appointment of the donor's spouse as an attorney under [an LPA] should be revoked by the subsequent dissolution or annulment of the parties' marriage.
>
> A reminder might helpfully be placed on the standard form decree absolute of divorce. By analogy with the case where one attorney becomes bankrupt but multiple attorneys have been appointed to act jointly and severally, the divorce between the donor and one of multiple joint and several attorneys should not terminate the powers of the other donees to act.'

14.37 Since publication of the Law Commission's report in 1995, the Civil Partnership Act 2004 has come into force. Accordingly, s 13 of the MCA 2005 provides that the dissolution or annulment of a marriage or civil partnership between the donor and the donee will terminate the appointment of the donee, unless the instrument provided that it was not to do so. The termination of the appointment will also revoke the power, unless the donor appointed a replacement attorney, or had appointed more than one attorney to act jointly and severally, and there is at least one remaining attorney.

REVOCATION BY THE COURT OF PROTECTION

14.38 Section 22(4) of the MCA 2005 provides that:

> 'The court may –
> (a)   direct that an instrument purporting to create the lasting power of attorney is not to be registered, or
> (b)   if P lacks the capacity to do so, revoke the instrument or the lasting power of attorney.'

14.39 Section 22(5) of the MCA 2005 provides that:

> 'If there is more than one donee, the court may under subsection 4(b) revoke the instrument or the lasting power of attorney so far as it relates to any of them.'

14.40 Section 22(3) of the MCA 2005 provides that s 22(4) applies if the court is satisfied that:

> '(a)   that fraud or undue pressure was used to induce P –
> (i)   to execute an instrument for the purpose of creating a lasting power of attorney, or
> (ii)   to create a lasting power of attorney, or
> (b)   that the donee (or, if more than one, any of them) of a lasting power of attorney –
> (i)   has behaved, or is behaving, in a way that contravenes his authority or is not in P's best interests, or
> (ii)   proposes to behave in a way that would contravene his authority or would not be in P's best interests.'

14.41 These provisions differ from those relating to EPAs in paras 13(11) and 16(5) of Sch 4 to the MCA 2005, which require the court to revoke a power where it is satisfied that fraud or undue pressure was used to induce the donor to create it, or that, having regard to all the circumstances, the attorney is unsuitable to be the donor's attorney. In the case of an LPA, however, the court has a discretion to revoke the power, and can only exercise that discretion if the donor lacks the capacity to revoke it himself.

14.42 The reason for this change in policy between the Enduring Powers of Attorney Act 1985 and the MCA 2005 can be found in the Law Commission's report on *Mental Incapacity* (1995). At paragraph 7.58 the report stated:

'The 1985 Act provides that the court shall cancel the registration of, and revoke, an EPA if "the attorney is unsuitable to be the donor's attorney". In Consultation Paper No. 129 we suggested that this power to revoke should be linked to the question of whether the attorney was acting in the donor's best interests. Respondents supported this proposal, with some seeking reassurance that the court should not be able to override a patient's advance decisions about health care by revoking the appointment of an attorney. We have already recommended that an attorney under [an LPA] should be under a duty to act in the donor's best interests. It is therefore logical to use this terminology, rather than that of "unsuitability", in relation to the court's power to displace an attorney. Express provision should also be made for revocation by the court where an attorney's acts contravene the terms of the authority granted by the donor.'

14.43 In *Re Harcourt; The Public Guardian v A* [2013] COPLR 69, Senior Judge Lush discussed in detail the circumstances in which the Court of Protection may consider revoking an LPA and, at para [71] of the judgment, commented as follows:

'In the absence of appropriate safeguards, the revocation by the court of a Lasting Power of Attorney, which a donor executed when they had capacity and in which they chose a family member to be their attorney, would be a violation of their Article 8 rights. For this reason the Mental Capacity Act has been drafted in a labyrinthine manner to ensure that any decision by the court to revoke an LPA cannot be taken lightly.'

14.44 There have been many occasions where the court has revoked a LPA on the basis that the attorney has contravened his authority or has not acted in the donor's best interest. Applications are usually made by the Public Guardian as part of his investigatory and supervisory powers (see **10.62–10.66**). However, there are occasions when an application is made by the attorneys for retrospective approval to their decisions, where the consequence has been the attorneys' removal.

See JL (Revocation of Lasting Power of Attorney) [2014] EWCOP 36 *Re Buckley*, case no. 12228697; the *Public Guardian v AW and DH* [2014] EWCOP 28; the *Public Guardian v DA, YS and ES* [2015] EWCOP 41; the *Public Guardian v PM and SH* [2016] EWCOP 25.

14.45 The court will remove the attorney and cancel the LPA where:

• the attorney exceeded their authority to make gifts under the MCA 2005, s 12, not paid bills, and kept the donor short of money (see *JL (Revocation of Lasting Power of Attorney)* [2014] EWCOP 36);

- the attorney has invested in their own business and not sought independent financial advice (see *Re Buckley*, case no 12228697);
- the attorney severely restricted contact between the donor and other family members (see the *Public Guardian v AW and DH* [2014] EWCOP 28);
- the attorney is not giving effect to the donor's current wishes and feelings (see *SAD and ACD v SED*, District Judge Glentworth, case no 12791319);
- the attorney has failed to keep accounts and has used the donor's funds to benefit himself (see *the Public Guardian v DA, YS and ES* [2015] EWCOP 41);
- there is hostility between the attorneys which impedes best interests decision making (see *the Public Guardian v PM and SH* [2016] EWCOP 25).

Suspension of the LPA

14.46 Section 23(2)(a) of the MCA 2005 provides that the court may give directions with respect to decisions which the attorney under an LPA has authority to make and which the donor lacks the capacity to make. Pursuant to this provision, the court may direct the attorney to make no decisions at all and thereby suspend his authority to act under the LPA. For examples of when the court has suspended the attorney's decision making see *Re MRJ (Reconsideration of an order)* [2014] EWHC B15 (COP) and *The Public Guardian v TW, KW, HF and SC* [2016] EWCOP 18.

Functions of the Public Guardian on revocation

14.47 MCA 2005, Sch 1, para 17 states that:

'(1)   The Public Guardian must cancel the registration of an instrument as a lasting power of attorney on being satisfied that the power has been revoked –

   (a)   as a result of the donor's bankruptcy, or
   (b)   on the occurrence of an event mentioned in section 13(6)(a) to (d).

(2)   If the Public Guardian cancels the registration of an instrument he must notify –
   (a)   the donor, and
   (b)   the donee or, if more than one, each of them.'

Schedule 1, para 18 provides:

'The court must direct the Public Guardian to cancel the registration of an instrument as a lasting power of attorney if it –
   (a)   determines under section 22(2)(a) that a requirement for creating the power was not met,
   (b)   determines under section 22(2)(b) that the power has been revoked or has otherwise come to an end, or
   (c)   revokes the power under section 22(4)(b) (fraud etc.).'

Functions of the Public Guardian on partial revocation

14.48 MCA 2005, Sch 1, paras 21–23 provide that in the following cases, the Public Guardian must attach to the instrument a note:

> '21   If in the case of a registered instrument it appears to the Public Guardian that under s 13 an LPA is revoked or suspended, in relation to the donor's property and affairs (but not in relation to other matters), the Public Guardian must attach to the instrument a note to that effect.
>
> 22   If in the case of a registered instrument it appears to the Public Guardian that an event has occurred –
> (a)   which has terminated the appointment of the donee, but
> (b)   which has not revoked the instrument,
> the Public Guardian must attach to the instrument a note to that effect.
>
> 23   If in the case of a registered instrument it appears to the Public Guardian that the donee has been replaced under the terms of the instrument the Public Guardian must attach to the instrument a note to that effect.'

Chapter 15

LASTING POWER OF ATTORNEY PRECEDENTS

Part 1: both kinds of LPA

Applicable law

15.1

'The law of [*territorial jurisdiction*] shall be the law applicable to the existence, extent, modification or extinction of this Lasting Power of Attorney.'

Note:

The Mental Capacity Act 2005 (MCA 2005), Sch 3, para 13(1) provides that if the donor of an LPA is habitually resident in England and Wales at the time of granting the LPA, the law applicable to the existence, extent, modification or extinction of the LPA is the law of England and Wales, or, if he specifies in writing the law of a connected country for the purpose, that law. For the meaning of 'connected country' see MCA 2005, Sch 3, para 13(3). This precedent should be inserted in the box at section 7 (instructions) or continuation sheet 2.

Consultation

15.2

'In determining what is in my best interests, my attorney(s) must take into account the views of [*name*], if it is practicable and appropriate to consult them.'

NOTE:

MCA 2005, s 4(2) states that when making the determination as to what is in the best interests of an individual who lacks capacity, the substitute decision-maker 'must consider all the relevant circumstances and, in particular, take the following steps'. These steps include s 4(7)(a), which provides that a decision-maker must take into account the views of anyone named by the person as someone to be consulted on the matter in question or on matters of that kind. For a discussion of the meaning of 'if it is practicable and appropriate to consult them', see *Re A; D v B* [2009] COPLR Con Vol, 1. This precedent should be inserted in the box at section 7 (preferences) or continuation sheet 2.

Dissolution or annulment of marriage or civil partnership

15.3

'The dissolution or annulment of my marriage to [*attorney*] shall [not] terminate [his][her] appointment as donee of this Lasting Power of Attorney.

The dissolution or annulment of my civil partnership with [*attorney*] shall [not] terminate [his][her] appointment as donee of this Lasting Power of Attorney.'

Note:

MCA 2005, s 13(11) provides that the dissolution or annulment of a marriage of civil partnership does not terminate the appointment of a donee, or revoke the LPA if the instrument provided that it was not to do so. This precedent should be inserted in the box at section 7 (instructions) or continuation sheet 2.

'[*insert name*] shall only act as my Replacement Attorney if [he][she] remains legally married to my [son][daughter] at the point [he][she] becomes unable to act as my Attorney.'

Note:

This precedent is a conditional appointment of a replacement attorney aimed at a donor who wishes to appoint their son or daughter in law as a replacement, but only wants then to act in the event they remain married. It is distinguished from the statutory termination of the appointment of an original attorney which occurs on dissolution or annulment of a marriage of civil partnership between the donor and that attorney. It is not possible to include this condition for the original appointment, as divorce between the attorneys is not a terminating event and it is not possible to extend the statutory provision. This precedent should be inserted in the box at section 7 (instructions) or continuation sheet 2.

Reappointment of original joint attorneys

15.4

'In the event that any of my original attorneys shall be unable to act due to the occurrence of an event set out in section 13(6)(a) to (d) of the Mental Capacity Act 2005 which has the effect of terminating the appointment, I expressly re-appoint the remaining of my original attorneys, as the case may be, to act as my attorney, and in the event, that there is only one of my original attorneys capable of acting I expressly reappoint that attorney to act alone.'

Note:

Nugee J in *Miles v The Public Guardian and Beattie v The Public Guardian* [2015] EWHC 2960 (Ch) held it is possible for joint authority to survive a terminating event, provided the power expressly provides for this. This precedent should be inserted in the box at section 7 (instructions) or continuation sheet 2.

Replacement attorneys – order of acting

15.5

'My replacement attorney(s) shall replace the first original attorney who is unable to act.'

Note:

If the donor has appointed more than one original attorney they should set out the order in which the replacements should act. For example, if the donor appoints their spouse and child as their original attorneys and their grandchildren as the replacements, it may be the donor wishes their grandchildren to replace the first original attorney who is unable to act or that they are to step in only when both original attorneys are unable to act. Note, however, that this really only works where the attorneys are appointed to act jointly and severally. The OPG would apply to the court to sever this clause if the attorneys were appointed to act jointly or jointly for some decisions and jointly and severally for others and in the latter case, it would only work in respect of the joint and several authority but not in respect of the joint authority. This precedent should be inserted in the box at section 7 (instructions) or continuation sheet 2.

or

'My two replacement attorneys are to replace both original attorneys only when they are both unable to act. I do not want either of my replacement attorneys to replace a single attorney who is unable to act.

Note:

As with the precedent above, it is really only suitable where the original attorneys were appointed to act jointly and severally.

or

'If my attorney [A] becomes unable to act under this power, I want replacement attorney [C] to step in and act in [his/her] place. If my attorney [B] becomes unable to act under this power, I want replacement attorney [D] to step in and act in [his/her] place.'

Note:

This precedent allows a specific replacement attorney to act in place of a named original attorney. This precedent should be inserted in the box at section 7 (instructions) or continuation sheet 2.

Replacement attorneys – how they are to act

15.6

'My replacement attorneys are appointed to act [jointly and severally] [jointly] [joint in respect of the following decisions [*insert type of decision*] and jointly and severally in respect of everything else].'

Note:

In many cases, the replacement will be acting with an original attorney under the authority set out in the LPA but it is uncertain as to whether the way they are appointed applies when the replacements step in when all original attorneys are unable to act. As the LPA prescribed form does not expressly provide how the replacements are to act, the default position of joint authority applies (MCA 2005, s10(5)). It is for this reason that the donor should expressly set out how the replacements should act. This also applies when a sole attorney is appointed and more than one replacement is appointed. This precedent should be inserted in the box at section 7 (instructions) or continuation sheet 2.

Revocation of registered LPA

15.7

'THIS DEED OF REVOCATION is made this . . . . . . day of . . . . 20[xx] by [*Insert donor's full name and address*]

I REVOKE the Lasting Power of Attorney ('LPA') made by me on [*date of LPA*] [and registered by the Public Guardian on [*registration date*].

I HEREBY GIVE NOTICE to the Public Guardian that I have revoked the LPA and invite him to cancel the registration of the LPA.

AND I HEREBY GIVE NOTICE of the revocation to the attorney(s) appointed in the LPA namely [*insert full name(s) and address(es) of the attorney(s)*].

SIGNED as a deed and delivered
In the presence of:
Full name of witness
Address of witness'

- - - - - - - - - - -

Note:

MCA 2005, s 13(2), which refers to the donor as 'P' states that 'P may, at any time when he has capacity to do so, revoke the power. The LPA, EPA & PG Regs 2007, reg 21(1) sets out the following procedure for the revocation of an LPA by the donor: 'A donor who revokes a lasting power of attorney must – (a) notify the Public Guardian that he has done so; and (b) notify the donee (or, if more than one, each of them) of the revocation.' MCA 2005, s 14(2) states that an attorney who acts in purported exercise of a power does not incur any liability because of the non-existence of the power unless at the time of acting he is aware of circumstances which would have terminated his authority. Accordingly, it is advisable that the donor gives the attorney(s) notice of the revocation immediately. This precedent can be adapted to provide for revocation of an unregistered LPA.

or

I REVOKE the enduring/lasting power of attorney made by me on [*insert date the power was made*] [*and in the case of an LPA, insert the date of registration with the Public Guardian*] [and registered with the Public Guardian on].

Note:

It is possible to revoke a previous enduring power of attorney or LPA, within the body of a new LPA. This may be effective immediately in relation to an EPA or on the registration of the LPA. This precedent fulfils the requirement of notifying the Public Guardian, which is done at registration of the power. The precedent should be inserted in the box at section 7 (instructions) or on continuation sheet 2. The donor will still separately need to notify the attorney of the revocation.

Revocation of one attorney in a joint and several registered LPA

15.8

'THIS DEED OF REVOCATION OF THE APPOINTMENT OF AN ATTORNEY is made this . . . . . . day of . . . . 20[xx] by [*insert donor's full name and address*]

I REVOKE the appointment of [*insert the name and address of the attorney who is removed*] as my attorney appointed by me under the [Property and Financial Affairs/ Health and Welfare Lasting Power of Attorney] (LPA) dated [xx] day of 20[xx] for the purposes of the Mental Capacity Act 2005 [and registered with the Public Guardian on [*registration date*]

I DECLARE that all power and authority conferred to [*insert the name and address of the attorney to be removed*] by the [Property and Financial Affairs/ Health and Welfare Lasting Power of Attorney is now revoked and withdrawn by me.

I HEREBY GIVE NOTICE to the Public Guardian that I have revoked the appointment of [*insert the name and address of the attorney who is removed*] and invite him to amend his records as to the removal of [*insert the name and address of the attorney who is removed*] on his register of LPAs and on the original LPA.

AND I HEREBY GIVE NOTICE of the revocation to [*insert the name and address of the attorney who is removed*] appointed in the LPA.

SIGNED as a deed and delivered
In the presence of:
Full name of witness
Address of witness'

Note:

To avoid the need to revoke the entire power, where the donor has appointed more than one attorney jointly and severally, and no longer wants one of those attorneys to act, the donor can revoke the appointment of that attorney. A replacement attorney is not able to step in to act, as revocation of an attorney's authority is not a terminating event under MCA, s 13(6).

Part 2: LPAs for property and financial affairs

Triggering event: evidence of mental incapacity

15.9

'My attorneys shall only act under this power if they have obtained a written medical opinion stating that I am no longer mentally capable of managing and administering my property and financial affairs. I give my attorneys authority to obtain a medical opinion for the purpose of establishing that they can act, and for the avoidance of doubt, I give my consent to the disclosure of confidential information to my attorneys.'

Note:

The 2015 prescribed property and financial affairs LPA form states in section 5, '**When do you want your attorneys to be able to make decisions?**' and allows the donor to tick the box 'Only when I don't have mental capacity'. It goes on to warn, '**Be careful**- this can make your LPA a lot less useful. Your attorneys may be asked to prove you do not have mental capacity each time they try to use this LPA.' As such, where the donor wishes to limit his authority, a suitable precedent should be included to confirm who is to decide when the donor lacks mental capacity, and if it is on the production of a medical opinion, it will need to give the attorney authority to obtain such opinion. The precedent should be inserted in the box at section 7 (instructions) or on continuation sheet 2. There is no need for such a triggering event in an LPA for health and welfare, because of the provisions of MCA 2005, s 11(7)(a).

Jointly for some decisions, and jointly and severally for other decisions

15.10

'My attorneys must act jointly in respect of decisions relating to:

(1) selling, charging, letting or otherwise disposing of my only or principal private residence;
(2) entering into an equity release scheme;
(3) investments;
(4) any transaction involving a sum or value of [£5,000] or more;
(5) making permitted gifts in accordance with section 12(2) of the Mental Capacity Act 2005;
(6) decisions each year on a maximum annual sum to be used for general household expenditure and care costs, and how this will be funded;
(7) the reimbursement of their own out-of-pocket expenses.

My attorneys may act jointly and severally in respect of all other decisions.'

Note:

MCA 2005, s 10(4) provides that an instrument appointing more than one attorney may appoint them to act '(a) jointly, or (b) jointly and severally, or (c) jointly in respect of some decisions and jointly and severally in respect of others.' There are two completed examples on page 15 of LP12, *Make and register your lasting power of attorney a guide*: 'My attorneys must act jointly for decisions about selling or letting my house, and may act jointly and severally for everything else'; and 'My attorneys must act jointly for decisions about investments in stocks and shares, and may act jointly and severally for everything else'. The precedent should be inserted in the box at section 7 (instructions) or on continuation sheet 2.

Business affairs

15.11

'My attorneys shall have general authority to act in relation to all my property and financial affairs except my business known as [*name of business*], in respect of which I have executed a separate Lasting Power of Attorney.'

And in a separate LPA

'My attorney(s) shall have general authority to act in relation to all my interest in my business known as [*name of business*]. For the avoidance of doubt, this does not extend to my personal property and affairs, in respect of which I have executed a separate Lasting Power of Attorney.'

Note:

On several occasions the Public Guardian has applied to the Court of Protection to sever a provision in an LPA in which the donor has sought to appoint different attorneys to make decisions regarding the donor's business affairs from the attorneys appointed to manage the donor's property and personal finances. In these circumstances, it is recommended that the donor creates two separate LPAs. Insert in the box at section 7 (instructions) of the LPA or continuation sheet 2.

Digital assets

15.12

'My attorney shall have:

(i)   authority to access, use and control my digital devices, including but not limited to, desktops, laptops, tablets, peripherals, storage devices, mobile telephones, smartphones, and any similar digital device which currently exists or may exist as technology develops or such comparable items as technology develops for the purpose of accessing, modifying, deleting, controlling or transferring my digital assets; and

(ii)   the authority to access, modify, delete, control and transfer my digital assets, including but not limited to, my emails received, email accounts, digital music, digital photographs, digital videos, software licenses, social network accounts, file sharing accounts, financial accounts, domain registrations, DNS service accounts, web hosting accounts, tax preparation service accounts, online stores, affiliate programs, other online accounts and similar digital items which currently exist or may exist as technology develops or such comparable items as technology develops.'

Note:

Although general authority to manage property and financial affairs is usually given within a property and financial affairs LPA, the aim of this clause is to provide clarity and avoid any gaps, particularly as the terms of service agreement entered into by the donor may not allow for access; or transfer of data or the account to a third party, without express authority. Digital assets include but are not limited to the following: on line savings and investment accounts, PayPal and Amazon accounts, reward cards, on line gaming, virtual currency such as bitcoins, digital media accounts and cloud storage. If including this clause, the donor will need to have prepared an inventory of his digital assets, with details of how the attorney can access these.

Record-keeping

15.13

'My attorney(s) shall keep accounts and records of all their dealings with my property and financial affairs and be ready on reasonable notice to produce them to me, or anyone appointed by me, or anyone with lawful authority to call for their production.'

Note:

MCA 2005, s 23(3) refers to the court's power, if the donor lacks capacity to do so, to give directions to the attorney 'with respect to the rendering by him of reports or accounts and the production of records kept by him for that purpose.' The LPA, EPA & PG Regs 2007, reg 46 gives a similar power to the Public Guardian to require information from donees of LPAs. Paragraph 7.67 of the Mental Capacity Act 2005 Code of Practice states that: 'Property and affairs attorneys must keep accounts of transactions carried out on the donor's behalf. Sometimes the Court of Protection will ask to see accounts. If the attorney is not a financial expert and the donor's accounts are relatively straightforward, a record of the donor's income and expenditure (for example, through bank statements) may be enough. The more complicated the donor's affairs, the more detailed the accounts may need to be.' Insert in the box at section 7 (instructions) of the LPA PFA or continuation sheet 2.

Disclosure of records to the attorney

15.14

'I authorise any person or organisation holding any records relating to my property or financial affairs to supply a copy of those records on request to my attorney(s).'

Note:

Insert in the box at section 7 (instructions) of the LPA PFA or continuation sheet 2.

Disclosure of the donor's will

15.15

'I authorise my solicitor to disclose to my attorney(s) a copy of my will and any other testamentary document executed by me [but not to release the original without an order of the Court of Protection].'

Note:

This is included for the avoidance of doubt. Joint guidance was published on the 1 March 2017, by the Law Society, Solicitors Regulation Authority, Legal Services Ombudsman and STEP which sets out the process to be followed in the event an attorney wishes to see the donor's will. See Annex I and at https://www.sra.org.uk/solicitors/code-of-conduct/guidance/guidance/Access-to-and-disclosure-of-an-incapacitated-persons-will.page

Sale of donor's residence

15.16

'My attorney(s) shall not sell my home unless there is no reasonable prospect of my ever returning to live there.'

Note:

Insert in the box at section 7 (instructions) of the LPA PFA or continuation sheet 2.

Gifts

15.17

'My attorneys may make gifts (1) on customary occasions to persons (including themselves) who are related to or connected with me, or (2) to any charity to which I made or might have been expected to make gifts, provided that the value of each such gift is not unreasonable having regard to all the circumstances, and in particular the size of my estate.'

Note:

Strictly speaking, there is no need to insert this provision in an LPA for property and financial affairs, because this authority is conferred on the attorney(s) anyway by virtue of MCA 2005, s 12(2). Nevertheless, it may be sensible to include it in the LPA itself as a reminder to the attorney(s) of the scope of their authority. Insert in the box at section 7 (instructions) of the LPA PFA or continuation sheet 2.

No gifts

15.18

'Notwithstanding the provisions of section 12 of the Mental Capacity Act 2005, my attorney(s) shall not make any gifts on my behalf.'

Note:

MCA 2005, s 12(2) confers a limited authority on the attorney to make gifts of the donor's assets. Section 12(4) provides that the limited authority to make gifts is subject to any conditions or restrictions in the instrument. Insert in the box at section 7 (instructions) of the LPA PFA or continuation sheet 2.

Specified limit

15.19

'My attorney(s) shall not make gifts on customary occasions to any person exceeding [£250] per year provided that a gift of that annual amount is affordable and not unreasonable having regard to all the circumstances and, in particular, the size of my estate.'

Note:

MCA 2005, s 12(2) and 12(4). Insert in the box at section 7 (instructions) of the LPA PFA or continuation sheet 2.

Guidance of gifts

15.20

'For the purpose of my attorney(s) ascertaining what is reasonable for gifts to be made on customary occasions:

(i)   it is my wish that my attorneys should not make gifts [exceeding £ . . . .] in total in any one calendar year out of my capital assets;

(ii)   it is my wish that no gift of my money to any one person or any charity should exceed £ . . . . in any one calendar year.'

Note:

Insert in the box at section 7 (preferences) of the LPA PFA or continuation sheet 2.

Application to court for greater authority

15.21

'My attorney(s) may to apply to the Court of Protection for authority to make gifts of my money or property, which are not permitted gifts within section 12(2) of the Mental Capacity Act 2005, if they consider that it would be in my best interests to do so.'

Note:

Section 23(4) of the Mental Capacity Act 2005 states that 'the court may authorise the making of gifts which are not within section 12(2) (permitted gifts).' This guidance puts the attorney on clear notice that he cannot make gifts other than those permitted without the court's approval. It also provides information to the court, that the donor would not generally be opposed to such gifts. Insert in the box at section 7 (preferences) of the LPA PFA or continuation sheet 2.

Personal chattels

15.22

'My attorney(s) shall not dispose of any items of my jewellery while I am still capable of using and enjoying them.

My attorney(s) may distribute any items of furniture and household effects to the persons to whom I have specifically bequeathed them in my will, subject to the recipient giving an undertaking that they will hold the items for safe custody and keep them fully insured and not dispose of them during my lifetime.'

Note:

It is unlikely that any outright distribution of furniture and household effects and other person chattels would be a permitted gift under MCA 2005, s 12(2). This clause is based on the undertaking as to furniture and effects which, prior to the implementation of the MCA 2005, the Court of Protection required persons to give under rule 72 of the Court of Protection Rules 2001 (SI 2001/824), which provided that: 'Where under a direction of the court any furniture or effects of a patient are allowed to remain in the possession of, or deposited wit, any person, that person shall, unless the court otherwise directs, sign and file a statement of the furniture or effects and an undertaking not to part with them except on a direction under seal.' Insert in the box at section 7 (instructions) of the LPA PFA or continuation sheet 2.

Consultation

15.23

'In determining what is in my best interests when making decisions regarding [*investments; repairs to the house, or as the case may be*], my attorney(s) must take into account, [if it is practicable and appropriate to consult them], the views of [*name*].'

Note:

MCA 2005, s 4(7)(a) provides that a decision-maker must take into account the views of anyone named by the person as someone to be consulted on the matter in question or on matters of that kind. Insert in the box at section 7 (preferences) of the LPA PFA or continuation sheet 2.

Consultation with health and welfare attorneys

15.24

'I would like my attorney(s) to consult with the attorney(s) acting under my Lasting Power of Attorney for health and welfare in order that they are kept up to date on any financial matters that could have an impact on my health and welfare.'

Note:

MCA 2005, s 4(7)(a) provides that a decision-maker must take into account the views of anyone named by the person as someone to be consulted on the matter in question or on matters of that kind. Insert in the box at section 7 (preferences) of the LPA PFA or continuation sheet 2.

Investments

Obtaining advice

15.25

'My attorney(s) shall not make any investment decisions without first obtaining professional advice.'

Note:

See, generally, *Re Buckley* [2013] COPLR 39, where the court gave guidance on the responsibilities of an attorney acting under an LPA when investing the donor's funds. Attorneys have fiduciary obligations similar to those of trustees. Until the OPG issues its own guidance, attorneys should comply with the provisions of the Trustee Act 2000 as regards the standard investment criteria and the requirement to obtain and consider proper advice. Insert in the box at section 7 (instructions) of the LPA PFA or continuation sheet 2.

Low risk investments

15.26

'Any savings or investments made on my behalf shall be restricted to the following:

* Bank or building society accounts.
* Bank or building society savings bonds.
* UK Government bonds (gilts).
* National Savings (NS&I) bonds or certificates.
* Investment grade corporate bonds.
* Investment grade corporate bond funds.'

Note:

Insert in the box at section 7 (instructions) of the LPA PFA or continuation sheet 2.

Delegation

15.27

'My attorneys may transfer my investments into a discretionary management scheme, even though this means that investment decisions will be made by the managers of the scheme and my investments will be held in the name of the managers of the scheme or their nominees.'

'If I already hold investments in a discretionary management scheme before I became unable to make financial decisions, I want the scheme to continue.'

Note:

Paragraph 7.38 of the Mental Capacity Act 2005 Code of Practice states that 'the attorney must make these decisions personally and cannot generally give someone else authority to carry out their duties. But if the donor wants the attorney to be able to give authority to a specialist to make specific decisions, they need to state this clearly in the LPA document (for example, appointing an investment manager to make particular investment decisions).' Insert in the box at section 7 (instructions) of the LPA PFA or continuation sheet 2.

Ethical investment

15.28

'I would like my attorneys to avoid investing, either directly or indirectly, in companies that are involved in the arms trade, animal testing, the fur trade, genetic engineering, the manufacture of pesticides, alcohol production, tobacco production, gambling, pornography, usury, or who use child labour or employ third parties who do so.

I would like my attorneys to invest in funds that seek to support companies that have a positive effect, such as recycling businesses, and where the fund managers are able to use the power and influence of their investment to lobby companies to change the way they operate.

I would like my attorneys to invest in companies which favour renewable energy resources and sustainable development.'

Note:

Insert in the box at section 7 (instructions) of the LPA PFA or continuation sheet 2.

ISAs

15.29

'I authorise my attorney(s) to make use of the total subscription limit for an individual savings account (ISA) in each tax year.'

Note:

Insert in the box at section 7 (instructions) of the LPA PFA or continuation sheet 2.

Minimum balance

15.30

'My attorney(s) should at all times maintain a minimum balance of [£3,000] on my current account [and any surplus cash should be placed in a savings account].'

Note:

Insert in the box at section 7 (instructions) of the LPA PFA or continuation sheet 2.

Employment of professional advisers

15.31

'My attorney(s) may employ any suitably qualified professional adviser to advise and assist in connection with any aspect of my property and financial affairs, and that adviser may be paid for their services, including services that would not normally require professional advice or assistance.'

Note:

Insert in the box at section 7 (instructions) of the LPA PFA or continuation sheet 2.

Accountability and transparency

15.32

'My attorney(s) must keep an account and submit it [annually][half yearly] to [name(s)].'

or

'My attorney(s) shall, within [two] months of the first anniversary of the registration of this power and each subsequent anniversary, have prepared [and audited] by a chartered accountant accounts of their dealings as my attorneys. [I further direct that the said accounts shall be disclosed by my attorneys to [name] within [xx weeks] of the date of their preparation].'

or

'If [*name*][any of my other children] ask(s) to see my bank statements or any paperwork concerning the management of my property and financial affairs my attorney(s) shall comply with such request as soon as is reasonably practicable.'

or

'I direct that my attorneys shall provide copies of my bank statements on a [monthly/quarterly/annual] basis to my [friend/brother/sister/daughter/son etc.].'

Note:

Paragraph 7.39 of the Mental Capacity Act 2005 Code of Practice suggests that 'donors may like to appoint someone (perhaps a family member or a professional) to go through their accounts with the attorney from time to time. This might help to reassure donors that somebody will check their financial affairs when they lack the capacity to do so. It may also be helpful for attorneys to arrange a regular check that everything is being done properly. The donor should ensure that the person is willing to carry out this role and is prepared to ask for the accounts if the attorney does not provide them. They should include this arrangement in the signed LPA document. The LPA should also say whether the person can charge a fee for this service.' Insert in the box at section 7 (instructions) of the LPA PFA or continuation sheet 2.

Restrictions and conditions

15.33

'My attorneys must not:

- make any investments without seeking professional advice;
- sell my home unless, in my doctor's opinion, I can no longer live independently;
- make any gifts.'

Note:

Insert in the box at section 7 (instructions) of the LPA PFA or continuation sheet 2.

Miscellaneous guidance

15.34

- I like to reinvest all interest from each year's investments into next year's ISA allowance.
- I like to maintain a minimum balance of £1,000 in my current account.
- I prefer to invest in ethical funds.
- I'd like my attorneys should consult my doctor if they think I don't have the mental capacity to make decisions about my house.
- I would like to donate £100 each year to Age UK'

Note:

These examples of 'guidance' appear on page 29 of LP12, Make and register your *lasting power of attorney– a guide*. Page 28 of LP12 states: 'Preferences are what you'd like all your attorneys to think about when they make decisions for you. Your attorneys don't have to follow them but should bear them in mind'. Insert in the box at section 7 (preferences) of the LPA PFA or continuation sheet 2.

Charge for services

15.35

'My attorneys may be paid a fee of [£500] each for their services, payable in arrears on 31 December each year, in addition to the reimbursement of their reasonable out of pocket expenses [in recognition of their own time they will have to give up to act on my behalf] [The fees will stop when my estate drops to below [£].

or

'Any attorney of mine who is a solicitor may charge for acting as my attorney at a rate of [£ per hour]/[the usual charging rate].'

or where an attorney is a trust corporation

'My attorney may charge for acting as my attorney in accordance with its published terms of business in force from time to time.'

Note:

Insert in the box at section 7 (instructions) of the LPA PFA or continuation sheet 2. The OPG Practice Note PN1, *Agreeing to act as a professional attorney – a good practice guide*, states at page 6, 'Remember you have no power to charge for your services if the LPA is silent on fees'. This is because an attorney is not allowed to benefit from his position unless specifically authorised by the donor or the court. The Mental Capacity Act 2005 Code of Practice at para 7.60 explains, 'A fiduciary duty means attorneys must not take advantage of their position. Nor should they put themselves in a position where their personal interests conflict with their duties. They also must not allow any other influences to affect the way in which they act as an attorney. Decisions should always benefit the donor, and not the attorney. Attorneys must not profit or get any personal benefit from their position, apart from receiving gifts where the Act allows it, whether or not it is at the donor's expense.'

Pets

15.36

'My attorneys should ensure that any pets I own are properly cared for and, if it is not feasible for them to remain at home, I authorise my attorneys find a suitable alternative home for them and for this purpose to spend a sum of money that is not unreasonable having regard to all the circumstances, and in particular, the size of my estate.'

Note:

Insert in the box at section 7 (preferences) of the LPA PFA or continuation sheet 2.

Part 3: LPAs for health and welfare

Jointly for some decisions, and jointly and severally for other decisions

15.37

'My attorneys must act jointly in respect of decisions relating to:

* where I live;
* whether I should have surgical treatment;
* whether I should receive life-sustaining treatment.

My attorneys may act jointly and severally in respect of all other decisions.'

Note:

MCA 2005, s 10(4) provides that an instrument appointing more than one attorney may appoint them to act (a) jointly, or (b) jointly and severally, or (c) jointly in respect of some decisions and jointly and severally in respect of others.' There are three completed examples on page 20 of LPA 111, *Guidance for people who want to make a lasting power of attorney for health and welfare*: 'My attorneys must act jointly in relation to decisions about where I live, and may act jointly and severally for everything else'; 'My attorneys must act jointly in relation to decisions I have authorised them to make about life-sustaining treatment, and may act jointly and severally for everything else'; and 'My attorneys must act jointly and severally when making decisions about whether I should have surgical treatment, and may act jointly and severally for everything else.'

Reappointment clause where life sustaining treatment decisions are made jointly

15.38

' My attorneys may act jointly and severally save with regard to any decision as to the withdrawal of life sustaining treatment when all attorneys shall act jointly insofar as there may be more than one of them able to do so but in the event that there is only one of them capable of acting I expressly re-appoint that attorney to act alone.'

Note:

Nugee J in *Miles v The Public Guardian and Beattie v The Public Guardian* [2015] EWHC 2960 (Ch) confirmed it was possible for the joint authority to survive a terminating event, provided the power expressly provides for this. This precedent should be inserted in the box at section 7 (instructions) or continuation sheet 2.

Access to health records

15.39

'I authorise and consent to the release to my attorney(s) of any information from my health records that my attorney(s) may require.'

Note:

Section 7 of the Data Protection Act 1998 gives an individual the right to see personal information that an organisation holds about them. They may also authorise someone else to access that information on their behalf. See, generally, the Mental Capacity Act 2005 Code of Practice, chapter 16, *What rules govern information about a person who lacks capacity?* This precedent should be inserted in the box at section 7 (instructions) or continuation sheet 2.

Consent to research

15.40

'I consent to participation in any clinical trial or intrusive research if my attorney is satisfied that the potential benefit to me outweighs the potential burden.'

Note:

For the participation of someone who lacks capacity in research or clinical trials, see generally MCA 2005, ss 30-34. This precedent should be inserted in the box at section 7 (instructions) or continuation sheet 2.

Consultation

15.41

'In determining what is in my best interests when making decisions regarding [*serious medical treatment*], my attorney(s) must take into account, if it is practicable and appropriate to consult them, the views of [*name*].'

Note:

MCA 2005, s 4(7)(a) provides that a decision-maker must take into account the views of anyone named by the person as someone to be consulted on the matter in question or on matters of that kind. . . . For a discussion of the meaning of 'if it is practicable and appropriate to consult them', see *Re A; D v B* [2009] COPLR Con Vol 1. This precedent should be inserted in the box at section 7 (preferences) or continuation sheet 2.

Consultation with attorneys for property and financial affairs

15.42

'I would like my attorney(s) to consult with the attorney(s) acting under my Lasting Power of Attorney for property and financial affairs in order that they are aware of any health and welfare issues that could have an impact on my financial affairs.'

Note:

MCA 2005, s 4(7)(a) provides that a decision-maker must take into account the views of anyone named by the person as someone to be consulted on the matter in question or on matters of that kind. This precedent should be inserted in the box at section 7 (preferences) or continuation sheet 2.

Contact

15.43

'The authority of my attorney does not extend to deciding who can contact me or visit me.'

Note:

This restriction is comparable to that imposed on deputies under the MCA 2005, s 20(2). A restriction of this kind is referred to in a scenario under the heading 'Denying attorneys the right to make certain decisions' on page 121 of the Mental Capacity Act 2005 Code of Practice. This precedent should be inserted in the box at section 7 (instructions) or continuation sheet 2.

Jewish law

15.44

'Any decisions regarding my health and welfare should be made in accordance with orthodox Jewish Law. In case of doubt, and if circumstances permit, a competent orthodox rabbinical authority should be consulted.'

Note:

MCA 2005, s 4 sets out a checklist of various matters that must be taken to account in determining what is in a person's best interests. These include, at s 4(6)(b), the beliefs and values that would be likely to influence the decision of the person who lacks capacity. This clause can easily be adapted to accommodate other beliefs and values. This precedent should be inserted in the box at section 7 (instructions) or continuation sheet 2.

Blood products

15.45

'My attorney(s) must not consent to any medical treatment involving blood products, as this would be contrary to my religious beliefs.'

Note:

This precedent should be inserted in the box at section 7 (instructions) or continuation sheet 2.

Special dietary requirements

15.46

'My attorneys must ensure that I have a [*specify*] diet.'

Note:

For example: diabetic, gluten-free, halal, Hindu, kosher, low-cholesterol, low salt/sodium, low lactose, low calorie, vegan, vegetarian. This precedent should be inserted in the box at section 7 (instructions) or continuation sheet 2.

Life-sustaining treatment: restriction

15.47

'My attorneys shall not consent to life-sustaining treatment on my behalf, even if life is at risk, if I have any one or more of the following conditions:

- advanced disseminated malignant disease;
- severe immune deficiency;
- advanced degenerative disease of the nervous system;
- vegetative state or minimally conscious state;
- severe and permanent brain damage as a result of injury, stroke, illness or any other cause;
- vascular, Alzheimer's, mixed or Lewy-Body dementia; or
- any other condition of comparable gravity.'

Note:

Unlike an advance decision to refuse medical treatment, decisions must be made in the donor's best interest applying s4 MCA 2005. This instruction makes clear to the attorney that they cannot consent to life sustaining treatment in specific situations. Option A in the health and welfare LPA should be selected. This precedent should be inserted in the box at section 7 (instructions) or continuation sheet 2.

Life-sustaining treatment: guidance

15.48

'(i)   If I am:
- (a)   Unconscious and it is unlikely that I shall ever regain consciousness; or
- (b)   Suffering from an incurable or irreversible condition that will result in my death within a relatively short time; or
- (c)   So severely physically or mentally disabled that I shall be totally dependent on others for the rest of my life;

THEN I would wish my Attorneys to ensure that any medical treatment (which is to be regarded as including artificial feeding/hydration and ventilation and all that these procedures involve) to be limited to keeping me comfortable and free from pain even though such treatment might unintentionally precipitate my death.

(ii)   I would wish my Attorneys refuse all other medical treatment or surgical treatment if:
- (a)   Its burdens and risks outweigh its potential benefits; or
- (b)   It involves any research or experimentation which is likely to be of little or no therapeutic value to me; or
- (c)   It will prolong my life or postpone the actual moment of my death with no further benefit to me.

(iii)   If I am on a life support machine I wish that the machine be switched off. If I am in a coma I do not wish to be resuscitated.'

Note:

Unlike an advance decision to refuse medical treatment, decisions must be made in the donor's best interest applying s4 MCA 2005. This is guidance to assist the attorney make end of life decisions, and is a clear expression of the donor's views, and so should be taken into account when the attorney makes a decision. Option A in the health and welfare LPA should be selected. This precedent should be inserted in the box at section 7 (instructions) or continuation sheet 2.

Life sustaining authority subject to earlier advance decision

15.49

'The authority for my attorneys to give or refuse consent to life sustaining treatment is subject to my advance decision to [*insert specific treatment, for example, refuse a blood transfusion*] made by me on [*insert date*].'

Note:

This would be relevant, for example, where the donor has made a prior advance decision for specific medical treatment not to be given, for example a blood transfusion. All other life sustaining treatment would be governed by the health and welfare LPA. This precedent is to be used when the donor has chosen Option A (authority giving or refusing consent to life sustaining treatment).

Advance decision to refuse treatment

15.50

'My wishes concerning medical treatment are as follows, even if life is at risk:

- If I have a physical illness from which there is no real likelihood of recovery and it is so serious that my life is near its end, I do not wish to have medical or surgical treatment purely for the purposes of keeping me alive for a temporary period only.
- If my mental functions have become permanently impaired and there is no likelihood of improvement and the impairment is so severe that I do not understand what is happening to me <u>and</u> I also have a physical illness, then I do not wish to be kept alive by medical or surgical treatment.
- If I become permanently unconscious with no real likelihood of regaining consciousness, I do not wish to be kept alive by medical or surgical treatment.
- If I am in any of the conditions described above I do not want:
  - cardiac resuscitation.
  - mechanical respiration.
  - tube feeding.
  - antibiotics.
- In all these cases I wish medical treatment to be limited to keeping me comfortable and free from pain and to feeding me and I consent to such treatment even though it may shorten my life.'

Note:

For advance decisions to refuse treatment, generally, see MCA 2005, ss 24-26. Section 25(5) provides that an advance decision is not applicable to life-sustaining treatment unless the decision is verified by a statement by the donor to the effect that it is to apply to that treatment even if life is at risk.

Palliative care only

15.51

'If I am suffering from [*condition or the following conditions*], and even if life is at risk, it is my wish that any medical treatment I receive be limited to palliative care and keeping me comfortable and free from pain: [*where appropriate, list conditions*].'

Note:

MCA 2005, s 25(5) provides that an advance decision to refuse treatment is not applicable to life-sustaining treatment unless the decision is verified by a statement by the donor to the effect that it is to apply to that treatment even if life is at risk.

Miscellaneous guidance

15.52

'•   I wish to maintain my independence for as long as possible.
•   I would prefer to be dressed in smart casual clothes.
•   I wish to have regular haircuts, manicures and pedicures.
•   I prefer to be prescribed generic medicines when they are available.
•   I would prefer to live no more than [*number*] miles from my daughter [*name*].
•   I have no particular religious beliefs and would prefer not to be included in any religious observance if I am no longer capable of understanding or expressing a view on the matter.
•   If my [*spouse or partner*] and I both require residential or nursing care, it is my wish that we be placed in the same home together and permitted to share a room, if possible.
•   I would like my pets to live with me for as long as possible- if I go into a care home I would like to take them with me.
•   I would like to take exercise at least three times a week whenever I am physically able to do so.'

Note:

Some of these examples of 'guidance' are based on those which appear on page 29 of LP12, Make and register your lasting power of attorney- a guide.

Part II

ENDURING POWERS
OF ATTORNEY

Chapter 16

GRANTING AN ENDURING POWER OF ATTORNEY

INTRODUCTION

Essentials of an enduring power of attorney

16.1 In order that a power of attorney can qualify as an enduring power of attorney (EPA):

- the donor must be an individual who had the capacity to grant the power;
- the donee must not be disqualified from acting as attorney under an enduring power;
- the instrument must be in the prescribed form, and must incorporate the prescribed explanatory information; and
- the power must not fall into one of those categories of powers of attorney which cannot be enduring powers.

Is a defective EPA valid as an ordinary power?

16.2 An instrument which does not satisfy the requirements of an enduring power may, nevertheless, take effect as an ordinary power. That this is what Parliament intended can be seen from the Mental Capacity Act 2005 (MCA 2005), Sch 4, para 20(4) which, in respect of joint and several powers, provides that:

'a failure, as respects any one attorney, to comply with the requirements for the creation of enduring powers –

(a) prevents the instrument from creating such a power in his case, but

(b) does not affect its efficacy for that purpose as respects the other or others or its efficacy in his case for the purpose of creating a power which is not an enduring power.'

This question was considered by Arden J in *Re E (Enduring Power of Attorney)* [2000] 1 FLR 882. In that case it was held that an EPA which was technically invalid because of an inconsistency in the appointment of joint attorneys took effect as an ordinary power even if it could not take effect as an enduring power.

THE DONOR

The donor must be an individual

16.3 Only an *individual* could create an enduring power of attorney (MCA 2005, Sch 4, para 1(1)). Partnerships, companies, and others who are not individuals could not do so.

The donor must have had mental capacity when creating the power

16.4 It is a fundamental principle that the donor must, at the time when he granted the power, have had the mental capacity to grant it. The Enduring Powers of Attorney Act 1985 (EPAA 1985) did not specify the capacity required to create an enduring power, unlike the MCA 2005, ss 2 and 3 which define lack of capacity and the inability to make decisions. In *Re K, Re F* [1988] 2 FLR 15, it was held that the relevant question is whether the donor had at the time the mental capacity, with the assistance of such explanation as he may have been given, to understand the nature and effect of the power. The validity of the power does not depend upon whether the donor would hypothetically have been able to perform all the acts that it authorises (at page 19, per Hoffmann J).

16.5 In that case, a power was held to have been validly granted by a woman who, at the date of execution, enjoyed a period during which she was able to understand that a named individual was to be her attorney under an EPA, and who understood what an enduring power was, even though she was at the time incapable by reason of mental disorder of managing her property and affairs.

16.6 Hoffmann J stated (at page 20):

> 'Plainly one cannot expect that [a] donor should have been able to pass an examination on the provisions of the Act. At the other extreme, I do not think that it would be sufficient if he realised only that it gave [the donee] power to look after his property.'

Hoffmann J went on to accept the following summary, put forward by counsel for the Official Solicitor acting as *amicus curiae*, as a statement of the matters which should ordinarily be explained to the donor and which the evidence should show that he had understood:

> 'First (if such be the terms of the power), that the attorney will be able to assume complete authority over the donor's affairs. Secondly (if such be the terms of the power), that the attorney will in general be able to do anything with the donor's property which he himself could have done. Thirdly that the authority will continue if the donor should be or become mentally incapable. Fourthly, that if he should be or become mentally incapable, the power will be irrevocable without confirmation by the court' (at page 20).

16.7 As a result, someone with limited capacity may, nevertheless, have executed a valid power, even though he may have been incapable, by reason of mental disorder, of managing and administering his property and affairs.

16.8 The decision in *Re K, Re F* has been criticised for being inconsistent with the common law rules affecting the creation of powers of attorney (Roderick Munday, *The Capacity to Execute and Enduring Power of Attorney in New*

Zealand and England: A Case of Parliamentary Oversight? (1989) 13 New Zealand Universities Law Review 253).

16.9 It has also been criticised for imposing too simple a test of capacity to create an EPA: see the discussion in S. Cretney, G. Davis, R. Kerridge and A. Borkowski, *Enduring Powers of Attorney: A Report to the Lord Chancellor* (Lord Chancellor's Department, June 1991, para 2.7). Whether the test is simple or hard, however, depends largely on the explanation given and the questions asked by the person assessing the donor's capacity. For example, if the four pieces of basic relevant information described by the judge in *Re K; Re F* were recited to the donor and he was asked 'Do you understand this?' in such a way as to encourage an affirmative reply, he would probably pass the test with flying colours and, arguably, it would be too simple. If, on the other hand, after an explanation about the nature and effect of the transaction had been given in broad terms and simple language, the assessor were specifically to ask, 'What will your attorney be able to do?' and 'What will happen if you become mentally incapable?', the test would be substantially harder.

16.10 Such matters were considered by the Court of Appeal in *Re W (Enduring Power of Attorney)* [2001] 2 WLR 957 at 962. Sir Christopher Staughton said:

> 'For my part, I would not be inclined to rely on evidence of one interview. No doubt it is right to ask questions when it is contemplated that a donor shall execute an enduring power, but that is not by any means the final way of determining whether there is the necessary capacity.'

Evidence of mental capacity

16.11 If the donor did not have capacity at the time of grant, an objection may subsequently be made to the registration of the power on the ground that it was not valid as an EPA (MCA 2005, Sch 4, para 13(9)(a)). If such an objection is established to the satisfaction of the court, the court must direct the Public Guardian not to register the instrument, and the instrument must be delivered up for cancellation (MCA 2005, Sch 4, para 13(10) and (12)). Moreover, the attorney may be liable to third parties for misrepresenting his authority; and dealings with third parties may be affected, since the power will never have existed.

16.12 Unlike the requirement for the execution of a lasting power of attorney (LPA), where a person of a prescribed description must certify that the donor understands the purpose of the instrument, there was no such requirement in the EPAA 1985, and there was no statutory requirement that the person who witnessed the donor's signature on an EPA should be specially qualified: for example, a solicitor or doctor. Indeed, the Law Commission specifically rejected proposals that there should be such a requirement (Law Com No 122, paragraph 4.19) (see **6.9**). However, it was generally recommended as a matter of good practice that, if there was any doubt about the donor's capacity to create an EPA, a formal assessment of his capacity should be carried out by a registered medical practitioner or other specialist at assessing capacity, who should record his examination and findings and, where appropriate, witness the donor's execution of the power.

Other incapacity

16.13 In theory, there seems to be no reason why a minor or undischarged bankrupt could not have granted an enduring power insofar as he could grant an ordinary power but, in practice, it is unlikely that such appointments were made (Law Com No 122, para 4.5, and fn 109).

THE ATTORNEY

16.14 A power of attorney cannot be an enduring power unless the attorney is a *trust corporation* or an *individual* who has attained the age of 18 (MCA 2005, Sch 4, para 2(5)). A donor cannot constitute a partnership or a company, other than a trust corporation, as an attorney under an enduring power.

Trust corporations

16.15 *The appointment of a trust corporation* is considered in more detail at **4.3–4.6**. See also **16.56**.

Individuals

Minors cannot be EPA attorneys

16.16 At the time when he executed the instrument creating the EPA, the attorney must have attained the age of 18 (MCA 2005, Sch 4, para 2(5)(a)). The fact that he was under 18 when the power was granted will not prevent it taking effect as an enduring power, provided that the attorney, having attained the age of 18, executes the power before the donor loses capacity. The Enduring Powers of Attorney (Prescribed Form) Regulations 1990 (SI 1990/1376), reg 3(1) provided that execution by the donor and attorney need not be contemporaneous.

Bankrupts cannot be EPA attorneys

16.17 The attorney, when he executed the instrument creating the EPA, must not have been bankrupt or subject to a debt relief order (MCA 2005, Sch 4, para 2(5)(a)). If he subsequently becomes bankrupt or a debt relief order is made in respect of him, the EPA is revoked (MCA 2005, Sch 4, para 2(7)), but where he is bankrupt merely because an interim bankruptcy restrictions order has effect in respect of him, the power is suspended for so long as the order has effect (MCA 2005, Sch 4, para 2(8)). All references to bankruptcy in the MCA 2005 were amended by The Tribunals, Courts and Enforcement Act 2007 (Consequential Amendments) Order 2012 (SI 2012/2404), Sch 2, para 53, which came into force on 1 October 2012.

Appointment of more than one attorney

16.18 Schedule 4, para 20 (1) MCA 2005 states:

'An instrument which appoints more than one person to be an attorney cannot create an enduring power unless the attorneys are appointed to act—
(a)   jointly, or
(b)   jointly and severally.'

16.19 Chapter 21 sets out in detail the consequence of the appointment of more than one attorney under an EPA.

Substitute and successor attorneys

16.20 A power of attorney which gives the attorney a right to appoint a substitute or successor cannot be an enduring power (MCA 2005, Sch 4, para 2(6)). However, the donor may have appointed a substitute or successor attorney, although the draftsman may have encountered difficulties with the rules relating to joint and joint and several attorneys (MCA 2005, Sch 4, para 20(1)). See **16.47**.

THE FORM OF THE POWER

16.21 The form and content of an EPA were intended to be matters of the greatest importance (*The Incapacitated Principal*, Law Com No 122, para 4.10). To ensure that both the donor and attorney appreciated the nature and effect of the instrument, the legislation provided that a power could not be an EPA unless it was in the prescribed form (EPAA 1985, s 2(1)(a), now MCA 2005, Sch 4, para 2(1)(a)).

16.22 The various Enduring Powers of Attorney (Prescribed Form) Regulations, which were made by the Lord Chancellor under powers conferred in s 2(2) of the EPAA 1985, gave detailed effect to the statutory requirement that a power of attorney must, if it is to qualify as an enduring power, be in the prescribed form and contain prescribed explanatory information. They also contained provisions about execution by the donor and attorney.

THE PRESCRIBED FORM

Use of prescribed form was mandatory

16.23 An instrument cannot be a valid EPA unless, when it was executed by the donor, it was in the form prescribed at that time by the Lord Chancellor (MCA 2005, Sch 4, para 2(1)(a)). The following prescribed form Regulations were made:

Enduring Powers of Attorney (Prescribed Form) Regulations 1986

16.24 The form prescribed by the 1986 Regulations (SI 1986/126) was drafted by the Law Commission: Law Com No 122, *The Incapacitated Principal*, Cmnd 8977 (HMSO, 1983), Appendix C, 'Specimen Form of Enduring Power of Attorney'. It is most readily identifiable by the fact that the explanatory information appears at the end. This was the prescribed form from 10 March 1986 to 30 June 1988 inclusive.

16.25 *Granting an Enduring Power of Attorney*

Enduring Powers of Attorney (Prescribed Form) Regulations 1987

16.25 The form prescribed by the 1987 Regulations (SI 1987/1612) was drafted by what was then the Public Trust Office in response to criticisms that the first form was difficult for a layman to follow and gave insufficient information as to its purpose: see P.D. Lewis, Assistant Public Trustee, 'Enduring Powers of Attorney Act 1985 – New Form and Regulations', *The Law Society's Gazette*, 28 October 1987, pp 3083–3085. This form is most easily identified by the fact that it is in three parts: 'Part A: About using this form'; 'Part B: To be completed by the donor'; and 'Part C: To be completed by the attorney(s)'. The instrument was under seal, and paragraph 8 of Part A referred to the 1987 Regulations. This form was the prescribed form for an EPA executed by the donor between 1 November 1987 and 30 July 1991 inclusive.

Enduring Powers of Attorney (Prescribed Form) Regulations 1990

16.26 The 1990 prescribed form was introduced because of the implementation of the Law of Property (Miscellaneous Provisions) Act 1989, s 1(1)(b) of which abolished any rule of law which required a seal for the valid execution of a deed. It also made provision for the execution of an EPA at the direction of the donor. The 1990 form is virtually identical to the 1987 form, except that paragraph 9 of Part A of the form refers to the Enduring Powers of Attorney (Prescribed Form) Regulations 1990 (SI 1990/1376), and the attestation clauses state that the EPA is 'Signed by me as a deed and delivered'. This form was prescribed for EPAs executed by the donor from 31 July 1990 until 30 September 2007.

16.27 Even though there were subsequent Prescribed Form (Amendment) Regulations, the amendments were merely to the form prescribed in the schedule to the 1990 Regulations, and the Regulations themselves remained in force until the MCA 2005 came into force on 1 October 2007.

Enduring Powers of Attorney (Welsh Language Prescribed Form)
Regulations 2000

16.28 A Welsh language prescribed form was prescribed by the Lord Chancellor, in exercise of the powers conferred upon him by s 2(2) of the EPAA 1985 as extended by s 26(3) of the Welsh Language Act 1993. The Welsh regulations (SI 2000/289) came into force on 1 March 2000.

Enduring Powers of Attorney (Prescribed Form) (Amendment)
Regulations 2005

16.29 This form was introduced because, in the marginal notes to Part B of the 1990 prescribed form, there was a reference to it being inadvisable for the donor's husband or wife to witness the donor's signature. In view of the provisions of the Civil Partnership Act 2004, it was felt necessary to amend the prescribed form of EPA to state that it was inadvisable for the donor's signature to be witnessed by the donor's spouse or civil partner. In the event, the advice in the marginal note was omitted entirely. The Civil Partnership Act

2004 came into force on 5 December 2005, as did the 2005 Prescribed Form Regulations (SI 2005/3116). Regulation 3 provided for transitional relief whereby the form prescribed by the Prescribed Form Regulations 1990 could continue to be used until 1 April 2007, which at that time was the anticipated date on which the MCA 2005 would come into force.

Enduring Powers of Attorney (Welsh Language Prescribed Form)
(Amendment) Regulations 2005

16.30 The same considerations as in SI 2005/3116 applied to the Welsh language prescribed form (SI 2005/3125).

The Enduring Powers of Attorney (Prescribed Form) (Amendment)
Regulations 2007

16.31 The MCA 2005 received the Royal Assent on 7 April 2005, and the original intention was that it would come into effect in its entirety on 1 April 2007. Because of a delay in drafting the Court of Protection Rules, a ministerial statement on commencement was made in the House of Commons on Monday, 18 December 2006 deferring the implementation of most of the Act until 1 October 2007 (*Hansard*, col 111WS). Accordingly, it was considered necessary to extend from 1 April 2007 to 1 October 2007 the period during which the 1990 prescribed form of EPA could still be used. The 2007 Amendment Regulations (SI 2007/548) came into force on 30 March 2007.

Enduring Powers of Attorney (Welsh Language Prescribed Form)
(Amendment) Regulations 2007

16.32 The Welsh language prescribed form regulations were amended (SI 2007/549) with effect from 30 March 2007 for the same reasons as the English language prescribed form regulations.

16.33 The relevant prescribed form had to be used if the power of attorney is an enduring power within the meaning of Sch 4 to the MCA 2005. In particular, the power must include all the explanatory information headed *About using this form* in Part A and the relevant marginal notes to Parts B and C (Enduring Powers of Attorney (Prescribed Form) Regulations 1990, reg 2(1)). Regulation 2(3) permitted the form of execution to be adapted to provide for cases where a party signs by means of a mark, and for cases where the attorney is a trust corporation. Regulation 2(2) required the exclusion, either by omission or deletion, from the prescribed form of one and only one of any pair of alternatives. For example, the references to *all my property and affairs* or *the following property and affairs*. The same regulation also permitted the exclusion of certain matters - for example, marginal notes corresponding to any words which have been excluded.

Permitted variations

16.34 Although reg 2(4) of the Enduring Powers of Attorney (Prescribed Form) Regulations 1990 provided that, in general, an instrument which sought to exclude any provisions contained in the Regulations was not a valid EPA, some freedom of choice was permitted. In particular, an enduring power could also include 'such additions (including paragraph numbers) or restrictions as the donor may decide' (reg 2(1)). The following are examples.

Additions

Authorising the attorney's remuneration

16.35 It is preferable that the instrument should contain an express power for a professional attorney or a trust corporation to make charges for acting if it is intended that such an attorney be appointed (*Frith v Frith* [1906] AC 254). The Law Commission suggested that it was desirable for an enduring power to state whether or not the attorney was to be remunerated, and if so on what basis (Law Com No 122, *The Incapacitated Principal*, paragraph 4.83(iv)). The prescribed forms of LPA contain a specific section 'About paying your attorneys' and state that 'if you do not record any agreement here they will only be able to recover reasonable out-of-pocket expenses'. However, even in the absence of an express charging clause in an EPA, it would seem that the attorney will be entitled to be indemnified from the donor's estate for costs and expenses which he incurs in execution of his responsibilities (*Curtis v Barclay* (1826) 5 B & C 141).

16.36 Section 3(4) of the EPAA 1985 (now re-enacted as the MCA 2005, Sch 4, para 3(2)) provided that an attorney under an enduring power may only benefit himself to meet his *needs*. It might be argued that a right for a professional or other attorney to charge for his services constitutes a more extensive power to benefit himself, and this view can be supported by reference to authorities on the effect of professional charging clauses in wills. See, for example, *Re Pooley* (1888) 40 Ch D 1. However, it can also be argued that other provisions of the MCA 2005 (notably Sch 4, para 16(2)(b)(iii)), clearly envisage that an EPA may validly provide for the attorney's remuneration. This view seems to be supported by paragraph 6 of the prescribed explanatory information in Part A of the old prescribed form, which said 'If your attorney(s) are professional people, for example solicitors or accountants, they may be able to charge for their professional services as well. You may wish to provide expressly for remuneration of your attorney(s) (although if they are trustees they may not be allowed to accept it).'

Authorising the attorneys to delegate the management of investments

16.37 As in the case of ordinary powers, an attorney acting under an enduring power has an implied power to delegate any of his functions which are not such that the donor would have expected him to have attended to personally. Any wider power to delegate must be expressly provided for in the instrument (Law Com No 122, paragraph 4.22). Where the donor has organised his finances to be managed via a discretionary management regime, some financial institutions will not allow the attorney to be involved in the arrangement unless the power has expressly empowered the attorney to do so. The same applies where the attorney would like to arrange funds via a discretionary management regime. In such circumstances, the attorney is expected to apply to the Court of Protection for specific authority to make such arrangements.

Authorising disclosure of the donor's will to the attorney

16.38 The donor could authorise a solicitor to disclose to his attorney the contents of his will, provided that the power is registered, and provided that the solicitor considers disclosure to be necessary or expedient for the proper exercise of the attorney's functions. The attorney may need to know about the donor's will in order to avoid acting in a manner contrary to his wishes.

16.39 In March 2017, the Solicitors' Regulation Authority, the Legal Services Ombudsman, the Law Society of England and Wales and the Society of Trust and Estate Practitioners published joint guidance, which help a solicitor to decide if he or she can disclose a copy of the donor's will to their attorney. It can be found in APPENDIX I.

Requiring the attorney to notify additional people of his intention to apply for registration

16.40 It was not possible to derogate from the statutory list of relatives who are entitled to receive notification of the attorney's intention to apply for registration of an EPA, but it was possible to add to the list. The donor may have wanted to include among those entitled to receive notice, say, a partner; friend; step-relation; brother- or sister-in-law; solicitor; GP; priest; social worker; home-help; next-door neighbour; or the proprietor of the residential care home or nursing home in which he was residing.

Requiring the attorney to keep accounts

16.41 An attorney has a common law duty to keep accounts and to be constantly ready to produce them. The explanatory information in Part A of the prescribed form omitted to mention this duty, though the Enduring Powers of Attorney (Prescribed Form) (Amendment) Regulations 2005 included in Part C of the form a statement by the attorney that 'I also understand that I have a duty to keep proper accounts and records and produce them to the Court when requested.'

Requiring the attorney to account periodically to a third party

16.42 Donors occasionally inserted a provision in the instrument requiring the attorney periodically to provide an account of his dealings under the power to a third party, such as a solicitor or accountant, or a member of the family.

Restrictions

16.43 The prescribed explanatory information warned the donor that an attorney who had been given general power in relation to all the donor's property and affairs would be able to deal with the donor's money and property and may be able to sell his house; and that if the donor did not want the attorney to have such wide powers the donor could 'include any restrictions you like': para 3 of Part A of the prescribed form. Among restrictions commonly found are the following.

Not to make gifts

16.44 A donor could restrict or exclude the power of the attorney to benefit himself and persons other than the donor, and to make gifts of the donor's property (s 3(4) and (5) of the EPAA 1985, now MCA 2005, Sch 4, para 3(2) and (3)). For an example, see *Re R (Enduring Power of Attorney)* [1991] 1 FLR 128, where the donor also provided that the attorney was not to have power in respect of an investment portfolio managed by a named person.

Not to dispose of specified property

16.45 The donor may like to include a restriction that the attorney should not be entitled to dispose of a specified property, such as the family home - an asset expressly referred to in para 2 of the explanatory information in Part A of the prescribed form.

Powers only effective on registration

16.46 The donor could have stipulated that the attorney is not to have any authority unless and until he has reason to believe that the donor is or is becoming mentally incapable (MCA 2005, Sch 4, para 4). It was preferable to express such a provision in the above terms, rather than state that the attorney is to have no authority unless and until the power has been registered, because pending registration of the power (which takes a minimum of 5 weeks) it may be necessary for the attorney to exercise his limited powers of maintenance and preventing loss to the donor's estate (MCA 2005, Sch 4, para 1(2)).

Appointment of alternative or successive attorneys

16.47 Ever since the EPAA 1985 came into force there had been differing opinions on whether it was possible to appoint successive or replacement attorneys in an EPA. This issue was finally resolved by Lewison J (as he then was) in *Re J (Enduring Power of Attorney)* [2009] EWHC (Ch); [2009] COPLR Con Vol 753. On 9 February 2007 J executed an EPA in which he appointed his wife, W, to be his sole attorney and, if she was unable to act for any reason, he appointed his sons jointly and severally to be his attorneys. The Office of the Public Guardian refused to register the instrument on the grounds that the donor of an EPA cannot appoint alternative or successive attorneys. The judge held that the EPA was valid. Provided an instrument makes it clear whether, in the event that they exercise the power, the attorneys must exercise it jointly or jointly and severally, such an instrument may appoint attorneys in the alternative or in succession. See **16.20**.

Short form of EPA

16.48 The omission of unused alternatives and corresponding marginal notes, permitted by reg 2(2) of the Enduring Powers of Attorney (Prescribed Form) Regulations 1990, made it possible to draw up a short and simple form of general, unrestricted power. Regulation 2(1) required all the explanatory information to be included in every case, but the donor was told in para 11 of Part A of the prescribed form that 'some of these explanatory notes may not apply to the form you are using if it has already been adapted to suit your particular requirements'.

EXECUTION OF THE POWER

16.49 Schedule 4, para 2(1)(b) of the MCA 2005 provides that the instrument which creates an EPA must be executed in the prescribed manner by the donor and the attorney. If there are joint attorneys, all must execute the power.

The requirements of execution and attestation

16.50 The Law of Property (Miscellaneous Provisions) Act 1989, which came into force on 31 July 1990, changed the law relating to deeds and their execution, and necessitated the making of the Enduring Powers of Attorney (Prescribed Form) Regulations 1990 (SI 1990/1376).

16.51 Regulation 3 provided that:

- an enduring power must be executed by both the donor and the attorney;
- execution by the donor and attorney need not necessarily take place at the same time. (Indeed, there is no reason why execution by an attorney should not be postponed, provided that it takes place before the donor becomes mentally incapable);
- execution by the donor and attorney(s) must take place in the presence of a witness, but not necessarily the same witness, who must sign the form and give his full name and address;
- the donor and an attorney must not witness each other's signature;
- one attorney must not witness the signature of another attorney.

16.52 In *Re R* ((unreported) 23 February 1988, Knox J) the donor, Mrs R, executed an EPA on 26 July 1986, 4 days after it had been executed by the attorney. The Master of the Court of Protection refused to register the power, holding that the donor must execute the instrument before the attorney because one cannot accept an obligation until it has been conferred. Allowing an appeal by the attorney, Knox J held that 'one has to find affirmatively in the Act or in the Regulations something which compels the conclusion that the order of execution has to be donor first, attorney second. I have come to the conclusion that there is no material from which that conclusion by way of implication can be reached.' The decision in *Re R* is now largely academic, because the Enduring Powers of Attorney (Prescribed Form) Regulations 1990 expressly stated in Part C, 'Don't sign this form before the donor has signed Part B'; nevertheless, the principle still applies to any instruments executed under the earlier prescribed form regulations.

Execution - special cases

16.53 The 1990 Regulations made provision for special cases. Regulation 2(3) allowed the prescribed form to be adapted to provide for a case where the donor or an attorney signs by means of a mark. Regulation 3 allowed an enduring power to be executed at the direction of the donor or attorney.

16.54 If the instrument was signed by someone else at the direction of the donor or attorney:

- it should have included, in Part B or Part C as appropriate, a statement that the instrument had been executed at the direction of the donor or attorney;
- the person signing should not be the donor, the attorney or any of the witnesses to the signature of either the donor or an attorney; and
- it must have been signed in the presence of two witnesses, each of whom must have signed the form and given their full names and addresses (regs 3(3) and (4)).

16.55 Although the Regulations did not specifically state that, when someone signed the power at the direction of the donor, he should do so *in the presence of* the donor, it is essential that the donor was present, otherwise the deed will not have been validly executed in accordance with the provisions of the Law of Property (Miscellaneous Provisions) Act 1989, s 1(3)(a)(ii).

16.56 Where the donor is blind, it was generally suggested that the attestation clause should have been amended to show the circumstances in which the donor executed the instrument, and that if the power was registered, the court would need an explanation from the attorney or his solicitors as to how the donor had been notified of the intention to apply for registration (P.D. Lewis (1987) LSG 1219). A blind person could not witness the donor's or attorney's signature. *Witness* means, with regard to things audible, someone who has the faculty of hearing, and, with regard to things visible, someone who has the faculty of sight. Because the execution of a deed is a visible transaction it cannot be signed *in the presence* of a blind person (*Re Gibson (Deceased)* [1949] P 434).

Trust corporations

16.57 Regulation 2(3) of the 1990 Regulations provided that the form of execution by an attorney of an enduring power could be adapted to provide for execution by a trust corporation (see the Companies Act 2006, s 44).

Attestation by spouse

16.58 The marginal notes in Part B of the form prescribed by the 1990 Regulations warned the donor that 'It is not advisable for your husband or wife to be your witness.' The reason for the inclusion of this warning was because the effect of s 14(1) of the Civil Evidence Act 1968 was that a spouse would not necessarily be a compellable witness if there were proceedings attacking the power. In view of the provisions of the Civil Partnership Act 2004, it was considered necessary to amend the prescribed form to state that it was inadvisable for the donor's signature to be witnessed by the donor's spouse or civil partner. In the event, in the Enduring Powers of Attorney (Prescribed Form) (Amendment) Regulations 2005 the advice in the marginal note was omitted entirely.

Alterations

16.59 The 1990 Regulations contained no requirement that alterations to the document be initialled, and there is a general presumption that alterations to a deed have been made before execution.

CONSEQUENCES OF FAILURE TO COMPLY WITH THE FORMALITIES

16.60 If the formal requirements set out above were not complied with, the instrument cannot take effect as an EPA. It may, of course, be effective as an ordinary power of attorney (see **16.2**), but such a power will be revoked by the donor's supervening mental incapacity. The MCA 2005, Sch 4, paras 2(3) and (4) contain contains two minor modifications to the general principle that failure to observe the prescribed formalities will prevent the power taking effect as an enduring power.

A presumption that the prescribed information was incorporated

16.61 If the instrument is in the prescribed form, and purports to have been executed in the prescribed manner, it shall, in the absence of any evidence to the contrary, be taken to be a document which incorporated at the time of execution by the donor the prescribed explanatory information (MCA 2005, Sch 4, para 2(3)). This provision is limited in scope. It does not provide a general presumption in favour of due compliance with the prescribed formalities but merely a presumption that one particular requirement - namely, that prescribed explanatory information be endorsed on the EPA - was satisfied at the relevant time.

Material and immaterial differences

16.62 Where an instrument differs in an immaterial respect in form or mode of expression from the prescribed form, the instrument shall be treated as sufficient in point of form and expression (MCA 2005, Sch 4, para 2(4)). The scope of this provision is slightly obscure, but guidance on its application was given in a couple of articles by the former Assistant Public Trustee, P.D. Lewis, ((1986) LSG 3455 and (1987) LSG 1219).

16.63 For example, when it was the registration authority for EPAs, the Court of Protection decided that:

- the omission of the prescribed statement by the donor – 'I intend that this power shall continue even if I become mentally incapable' – constituted a material difference, with the result that the instrument in question would be incapable of taking effect as an enduring power;
- leaving in both alternatives *jointly* and *jointly and severally* was a material difference and invalidated the instrument as an enduring power;
- crossing out both alternatives *all my property and affairs* and *the following property and affairs* was also a material difference. The earlier words *with general authority to act on my behalf* were not sufficient on their own;
- omitting the date on which the donor or attorney signed the instrument was immaterial, provided that it could be established by extraneous affidavit evidence;
- the omission of the witness's address was considered to be an immaterial difference. Extraneous evidence was acceptable.

16.64 When the MCA 2005 came into force on 1 October 2007, the authority responsible for registering EPAs ceased to be the Court of Protection and became the Public Guardian. Although the wording of MCA 2005, Sch 4, para 2(4) was not amended specifically to cover this point, if an instrument differs in an immaterial respect in form or mode of expression from the prescribed form, it is to be treated by the Public Guardian as sufficient in point of form and expression.

Severance of ineffective clauses

16.65 The Court of Protection may agree to the registration of an instrument subject to the severance of an offending clause, applying the common law doctrine that 'where you cannot sever the illegal from the legal part of a covenant, the contract is altogether void, but, where you can sever them, whether the illegality be created by statute or by the common law, you may reject the bad part and retain the good' (*Pickering v Ilfracombe Railway* (1868) LR 3 CP 235, 250). Examples of clauses which the court has severed from instruments include a provision that any two of three attorneys appointed jointly may act together; clauses in which the donor purports to authorise the attorney to make gifts without restriction; and clauses which purport to authorise the attorney to make medical treatment decisions on the donor's behalf.

16.66 The legislators approved the court's approach towards severance, and expressly made provision in the MCA 2005, Sch 1, para 11 for the severance of invalid or ineffective clauses from LPAs. If it appears to the Public Guardian that an LPA contains a provision which would be ineffective as part of an LPA or would prevent the instrument from operating as a valid LPA, then the Public Guardian must apply to the Court of Protection for it to determine the matter under MCA 2005, s 23(1), and if the court determines that the provision is invalid or ineffective, it may sever the provision (see **11.31–11.34**).

16.67 However, the Act did not amend the law to make express provision for the Court of Protection to sever offending clauses from EPAs, and in practice the procedure for severance is governed by MCA 2005, Sch 4, para 4(5). This says that the attorney may, before making an application for the registration of the instrument, refer to the court for its determination any question as to the validity of the power, and must comply with any direction given to him by the court on that determination.

16.68 Summaries of orders made by the Court of Protection in relation to EPAs, and these including a number of severance cases, where the principles applied have been identical to those relating to LPAs are contained in APPENDIX H.

Rectification of EPAs

16.69 Rectification is an equitable remedy, normally awarded in the Chancery Division. Section 47(1) of the MCA 2005 provides that 'The court has in connection with its jurisdiction the same powers, rights, privileges and authority as the High Court.' It is arguable, though perhaps not beyond doubt, that the combined effect of s 47(1) and the provisions set out in MCA 2005, Sch 4, paras 4(5) and 16(2)(a), is that the court's jurisdiction in respect of EPAs includes the exercise of the High Court's powers to award the equitable remedy of rectification.

16.70 There have been several instances in which the court has ordered rectification of an EPA. For example:

- *Re Portues* (6 January 2009). The donor appointed attorneys to act jointly and severally. She deleted the words 'with general authority to act on my behalf' but failed to give any directions beneath the words 'with authority to do the following on my behalf'. District Judge S E Rogers made an order directing that the instrument be construed as if the donor had granted general authority to act on her behalf, on being satisfied that the deletion of those words was a clerical error.
- *Re Sawyer* (31 March 2009). The donor appointed three attorneys but failed to specify whether they were to act jointly or jointly and severally. District Judge S E Rogers made an order directing that the instrument be read as if the word 'jointly' had been deleted, on being satisfied that the donor intended to appoint the attorneys to act jointly and severally.
- *Re Smith* (7 December 2009). The attorney deleted from Part C the prescribed words 'I also understand my limited power to use the donor's property to benefit persons other than the donor.' District Judge Mainwaring-Taylor made an order restoring the deleted words, on being satisfied that they had been deleted in error.

Chapter 17

ONSET OF MENTAL INCAPACITY AND FUNCTIONS OF THE PUBLIC GUARDIAN

THE SIGNIFICANCE OF THE ONSET OF MENTAL INCAPACITY

17.1 Provided the donor remains fully mentally capable of managing and administering his property and affairs, an enduring power of attorney (EPA) is operated in the same way as an ordinary power of attorney, and the duties of the attorney are largely the same as those of an attorney under an ordinary power. In particular, in the absence of any express or implied contractual obligation, the attorney owes no duty to the donor to operate the power.

17.2 The only significant difference between an ordinary and an enduring power at this stage lies in the fact that, if the power is an EPA, the extent to which the attorney may benefit himself and third parties and make gifts is governed by express statutory provisions to be found in paras 3(2) and (3) of Sch 4 to the Mental Capacity Act 2005 (MCA 2005). These provisions are fully explained at **18.20–18.54**.

17.3 An ordinary power will be revoked by the donor's incapacity, but it is expressly provided that an EPA shall not be revoked by the donor's subsequent mental incapacity (MCA 2005, Sch 4, para 1(1)(a)).

17.4 It does not follow from this that the donor's supervening mental incapacity is irrelevant in the case of an EPA. The onset of such incapacity has two important consequences. First, if the donor becomes incapable, the powers of the attorney are restricted until the power has been registered by the Public Guardian (MCA 2005, Sch 4, para 1(2)). Secondly, Sch 4, para 4 imposes special duties on the attorney 'if he has reason to believe that the donor is *or is becoming* mentally incapable' (para 4(1)). Since these special duties may, in point of time, arise before it becomes necessary to consider the effect of the donor's incapacity on the extent of the attorney's powers, they are examined first.

ATTORNEY'S DUTIES WHEN THE DONOR IS BECOMING MENTALLY INCAPABLE

17.5 If the attorney under an EPA has reason to believe that the donor is or is becoming mentally incapable, he has two specific duties:

- a duty to give notice to the donor and prescribed relatives; and
- a duty to apply to the Public Guardian for the registration of the instrument.

These duties arise in the context of the donor's mental incapacity, and MCA 2005, Sch 4, paras 23(1) and 23(1A) provides a definition of mental incapacity for this purpose.

Mental incapacity

17.6 MCA 2005, Sch 4, para 23(1) states that:

'"Mentally incapable" or "mental incapacity" . . . means, in relation to any person, that he is incapable by reason of mental disorder of managing and administering his property and affairs and "mentally capable" and "mental capacity" shall be construed accordingly.'

Mental disorder

17.7 It will be noted that the donor's inability to deal with his property and affairs must arise by reason of mental disorder. MCA 2005, Sch 4, Para 23 (1A) clarifies that:

'In sub-paragraph (1), "mental disorder" has the same meaning as in the Mental Health Act but disregarding the amendments made to that Act by the Mental Health Act 2007.'

17.8 Section 1(2) of the Mental Health Act 1983, defines this widely and states:

'"mental disorder" means any disorder or disability of the mind; and "mentally disordered" shall be construed accordingly.'

17.9 The Mental Health Act 2007 made amendments to the definition of 'mental disorder' with the effect that people with learning disabilities are excluded from falling within this definition unless their disability is associated with abnormally aggressive or seriously irresponsible behaviour. The consequence of MCA 2005, Sch 4, para 23(1A) is that people with learning disabilities fall within the definition of mental disorder for the purpose of the MCA 2005.

Incapable of managing his property and affairs

17.10 In *F v West Berkshire Health Authority* [1989] 2 FLR 376 at 423H, Lord Brandon stated that 'property and affairs' means 'business matters, legal transactions and other dealings of a similar kind'. It does not include matters relating to personal welfare (such as where the donor should live, or with whom he should have contact) or medical treatment. An attorney acting under an EPA has no authority to make personal or medical decisions on behalf of the donor, although inevitably power over the purse will confer some degree of power over the person.

17.11 The meaning of 'incapable . . . of managing and administering his property and affairs' was considered in detail at first instance by Wright J in *Masterman-Lister v Brutton & Co.* [2002] Lloyd's Reports Med. 239 (QBD), and his decision was subsequently upheld by the Court of Appeal in *Masterman-Lister v Brutton & Co. (Nos 1 and 2)* [2003] 1 WLR 1511.

17.12 The claimant, Martin Masterman-Lister, was born in 1963. In September 1980, while he was on his way to work on a motorbike, he collided with a milk float driven by Mr Jewell, and sustained various orthopaedic injuries and a severe closed head injury. Brutton & Co., Solicitors, Fareham, acted for him in the personal injury litigation, and in 1987, on counsel's advice, the claim was settled for £76,000 - half its value on full liability on account of contributory negligence. A few years later, the claimant felt aggrieved that his claim had been settled at an undervalue, and he sought to re-open it. His solicitors obtained a medical report from an expert in head injuries, and a report from a leading clinical neuropsychologist, both of whom were of the opinion that the claimant was a patient, and had been a patient continuously since the accident. The defendants, however, obtained reports from some equally eminent doctors and psychologists to support their contention that he was not a patient. Essentially, if he were a patient, time would not have run against him under the Limitation Act 1980, and the original settlement would have been a nullity because it had not been approved by the court. In March 2000, the court directed that the question be tried as a preliminary issue. The trial began before Wright J on 28 January 2002, and lasted 15 days. The judge decided that the claimant may have been a patient for the first 3 years after the accident; but that he had not been a patient since 1983; that he had survived for the last 20 years without any major or even minor catastrophe, and that his affairs had, in fact, been perfectly adequately managed. Accordingly, the claim was statute-barred.

17.13 In the course of his judgment, Wright J reviewed the previous case-law in this area, most of which had never been reported before. He held that, although the opinions of skilled and experienced medical practitioners were an important element in the evidence to be considered by the court, it was for the court to decide whether or not a person had capacity not the medical profession. The presumption of capacity applied in cases of this kind. In other words, a person must be assumed to be capable of managing his own affairs until the contrary was proved. The basic starting point in considering what was meant by capacity was the common-law rule to the effect that to have capacity the person concerned at the relevant time understood in broad terms what he was doing and the likely effects of his action. Legal capacity depended on understanding rather than wisdom, and the quality of the decision was irrelevant as long as the person understood what he was deciding.

17.14 The wording of s 94(2) of the Mental Health Act 1983 (which has been repealed following the coming in force of the MCA 2005) made it clear that the assessment of a person's capacity to manage and administer his property and affairs was a question of functional capacity, and was essentially a subjective matter. Under that Act the court was exercising its protective jurisdiction in respect of individuals, not just a class of persons. For that reason, the nature and extent of the property and affairs that a given individual had to administer were relevant when considering whether or not he had the capacity to manage and administer his affairs. To do otherwise would be to incur the risk of stripping an individual of the right to be the master of his own fate, a serious inroad into dignity and standing as a human being for no good reason. The environmental information to be ascertained included an examination of the value of the income and capital, the financial needs and responsibilities and the extent of the specialised knowledge and time that it might take to manage such affairs, the extent to which the person in question would be likely to seek, understand and act on appropriate advice where needed and the complexity of his affairs (considering *Assessment of Mental Capacity – Guidance for Doctors and Lawyers*, 4th edn (2015), at para 5.6). The personal information about the subject of the assessment which had to be taken into consideration included the conditions in which that person lived, his or her family background, family and social responsibilities and the degree of backup and support the person received or could expect to receive from others.

17.15 If too liberal a construction was applied to the words of s 94(2) of the Mental Health Act 1983 the Court of Protection was liable to find itself inundated with applications in respect of persons who needed no protection in the sense that the court could give it. That could be because they had no property or affairs that required a significant degree of management or because they were entirely capable, given explanation and advice, to take decisions for themselves for better or for worse on their business and financial affairs. The purpose of the court's jurisdiction was to declare a person to be a patient with the consequent involvement of the Court of Protection. It was not to protect the individual from the consequences of a wrong or imprudent decision. It was to take out of the hands of that individual his or her decision-making function in relation to property when it was shown that such a person did not have the capacity sufficiently to understand information relevant to the matters in question to enable them to make decisions based upon such information. The court was not concerned with the question whether such decisions when made were wise or unwise, or on good advice or bad. *Masterman-Lister* has subsequently been considered in a number of cases, including *Mitchell v Alasia* [2005] EWHC 11; *Bailey v Warren* [2006] EWCA Civ 51; *Lindsay v Wood* [2006] EWHC 2895 (QB); and *Folks v Faizey* [2006] EWCA Civ 381. *Saulle v Nouvet* [2007] EWHC 2902 (QB), which was the first decision of this kind after the MCA 2005 had come into force; and *Dunhill v Burgin* [2012] EWCA Civ 397; [2012] COPLR 679.

Becoming mentally incapable

17.16 There may be little difficulty in the attorney being able to decide that he has reason to believe that the donor *is* mentally incapable, but his duties under Sch 4 to the MCA 2005 arise at an earlier stage if he has reason to believe that the donor *is becoming mentally incapable.*

17.17 The MCA 2005 gives no help on the construction of this imprecise formula. In particular, it will be noted that the Act gives no indication of the proximity required to actual incapacity for the duties to arise.

17.18 In the circumstances, it is suggested that it should be construed in the way that ordinary sensible people would construe them. The view that this would be a correct interpretation derives some support from the following passage in the Law Commission's Report *The Incapacitated Principal* (1983) Law Com No 122, paragraph 4.35:

'The duty [to register] would operate only when the attorney had "reason to believe". The reason for this is the difficulty in deciding when a person has lost capacity: such decisions can be very much a matter of opinion. It would perhaps have been possible to require that the attorney should obtain an expert medical opinion; but medical evidence (which is required in receivership proceedings) is liable to cause embarrassment both to the donor and attorney and might detract from the acceptability of the proposed EPA scheme as a whole. In any event, our recommendation is intended to cover not only the incapable donor but also the donor who is *merely becoming* incapable. We feel that our choice of words would help prevent the risk that the conscientious attorney might delay his application until (perhaps years later) he was absolutely certain that the donor was incapable. Our proposal would also in many cases enable the attorney to register his EPA before his authority became inoperable by the donor's actual incapacity.'

See **17.80–17.82** which considers the meaning of *not yet becoming mentally incapable.*

Early registration is desirable

17.19 In practice, the prudent attorney will apply to register the EPA as soon as he has any grounds to suspect that incapacity could reasonably be alleged. Apart from anything else, once the registration process is under way, his powers are restricted (see MCA 2005, Sch 4, para 1(1)(b), and **18.51**). There may, however, be cases in which he will be deterred from timely registration because of embarrassment caused by the requirement that he must first notify the donor of his intention to apply for registration, and by the fact that the donor may object to registration on the ground that the application is premature (MCA 2005, Sch 4, para 13(9)(c); and see **17.80–17.82**).

THE NOTIFICATION REQUIREMENT

17.20 Before making an application for registration the attorney must give notice of his intention to do so to the donor and certain specified relatives of the donor (MCA 2005, Sch 4, paras 5 and 6).

Power to dispense with notification

17.21 Before applying for registration of the EPA, the attorney may apply to the Court of Protection to be dispensed from the requirement to give notice to the donor or to any of the specified relatives of the donor (MCA 2005, Sch 4, para 7(2) in respect of the relatives, and para 8(2) in respect of the donor). Such an application will be granted if the court is satisfied:

- that it would be undesirable or impracticable for the attorney to give him notice; or
- that no useful purpose is likely to be served by giving him notice.

17.22 Applications for dispensation may, perhaps, be made in two classes of case. First, the attorney may feel that, although the donor is or is becoming mentally incapable, he still retains sufficient understanding to be distressed by the service of a notice on him. Secondly, there may be cases in which the facts suggest that relatives who are entitled to be notified are unlikely to take a concerned interest in the matter. For example, the donor's wife may have long been separated from him.

17.23 It should be noted that there are circumstances (for example, the fact that a person's whereabouts cannot be discovered) in which it is not necessary to notify a relative who would otherwise be entitled (see MCA 2005, Sch 4, para 6(2)(a)). In such cases there is no need for any application to the Court of Protection for dispensation.

17.24 An application for dispensation should be made in the standard application form (COP 1). An application fee of £400 is payable by the applicant attorney (Court of Protection Fees Order 2007, art 4(1) and Schedule). The provisions of art 4(3)(b) of that Order provide for a fee exemption solely in respect of an objection to the registration of an EPA.

17.25 It has been said that an application to dispense with service on the donor on the grounds that he is incapable of understanding the registration procedure is unlikely to succeed. Moreover, applications on other grounds are 'unlikely to succeed unless there is clear medical evidence that service would be detrimental to the donor's health' (see P.D. Lewis (1986) LSG 3566, at p 3567). In the absence of a successful application for dispensation, notice must be given as stipulated in the EPAA 1985.

The notice to the donor

17.26 Unless the Court of Protection has dispensed him from the requirement, the attorney must give the donor notice of his intention to apply for registration in form EP1PG, which is set out in Sch 7 to the Lasting Powers of Attorney, Enduring Powers of Attorney and Public Guardian Regulations 2007 (LPA, EPA & PG Regs 2007). The notice must be given to the donor personally. Service by post is not sufficient.

17.27 Service of the notice on the donor is governed by the LPA, EPA & PG Regs 2007, regs 23(2) and (3), which state that the attorney must provide, or arrange for the provision of, an explanation to the donor of the notice and what the effect of it is, and why it is being brought to his attention. The information must be provided to the donor personally, and in a way that is appropriate to the donor's circumstances: for example, using simple language, visual aids or other appropriate means.

17.28 In *The Incapacitated Principal* (1983) the Law Commission gave the following reasons for requiring personal service on the donor:

> 'Whilst we appreciate that there might be cases where the sight of a formal letter of notification might cause the donor worry or distress it seems to us on balance more undesirable that the donor should be unaware of the proposed registration or learn of the proposed registration at second hand, perhaps from a notified relative. The donor's notice would merely inform him of the attorney's intention to apply for registration and of the fact that the donor, once the power was registered, would not be able to revoke the power effectively without the revocation being confirmed by the court.' (Law Com No 122, paragraph 4.42).

17.29 Although, as suggested above, there may be cases where the attorney will prefer to apply to the Court of Protection to dispense with the need to notify the donor on the ground that such notification would be undesirable or impracticable, or that it would be unlikely to serve any useful purpose, the prospects of such an application being successful are not very high.

The notice to relatives

17.30 The notification to relatives required by MCA 2005, Sch 4, paras 5 and 6 is the initial stage in the registration procedure which was said by the Law Commission to constitute 'the keystone of the protective part' of the EPA scheme. The Commission explained the importance that it attached to the registration requirement in these words:

> 'Under our scheme the initial responsibility for the selection of the attorney rests with the donor. Since, however, for a variety of reasons the attorney may not be suitable to act on the donor's behalf without supervision, our scheme would ensure that the donor's relatives would have an opportunity to consider whether it would be safe to allow the attorney to continue acting once the donor's capacity was in doubt.' (Law Com No 122, paragraph 4.36).

Power to dispense classes of attorney from notification requirement

17.31 Section 12 of the Enduring Powers of Attorney Act 1985 enabled the Lord Chancellor to make an order exempting attorneys of such description as he thinks fit from the requirements of that Act to give notice to relatives prior to registration. No such order was ever made, and the section has been omitted entirely from Sch 4 to the MCA 2005.

Who are the specified relatives?

17.32 Schedule 4, para 6(1) of the MCA 2005 specifies a list of relatives of the donor who are entitled to receive notice of an intended application for registration. However, Sch 4, para 6(2) provides that a person who falls within the definition is, nevertheless, not entitled to receive notice if, *either* his name and address is not known to the attorney and cannot be reasonably ascertained by him, *or* the attorney has reason to believe that the relative has not attained 18 years of age or is mentally incapable. A decision by the attorney to this effect may have the practical consequence that notice will have to be given to other relatives (see **17.35–17.37**, and compare the position where the Court of Protection dispenses with the requirement to give notice to a particular relative, discussed at **17.39**).

17.33 The Law Commission stated that the specified classes of relatives had been drawn up to reflect:

> '(in descending order) those relatives who will be most likely to know the donor best (and, perhaps, the attorney also) and have an interest in his well-being. As these relatives would also probably be the persons most nearly concerned in the donor's estate after his death, non-objection by them would be the best available

guarantee that the attorneyship would not be fraught with difficulties caused by friction within the family.' (Law Com No 122, paragraph 4.39).

17.34 The classes of relatives are set out in MCA 2005, Sch 4, para 6(1) as follows:

(a) The donor's spouse or civil partner. A separated spouse or civil partner would qualify under this head, but where the marriage or civil partnership has been finally dissolved or annulled there would be no need to notify the donor's former spouse or civil partner.

(b) The donor's children. A stepchild of the donor is not included in this or any other class. The EPAA 1985, Sch 1, para 8(1) provided that an illegitimate child was for these purposes to be treated as if he were the legitimate child of his mother and father, though this was not carried through to Sch 4 to the MCA 2005. Possibly, the legislators considered that there was no need to repeat this provision because of the effect of Article 14 of the European Convention on Human Rights, which states that the enjoyment of the rights and freedoms set forth in the Convention shall be secured without discrimination on any ground including birth or other status. However, there will, no doubt, be cases in which the existence or whereabouts of such a child are not known, and the child will, presumably, then not be entitled to be notified because of the rule set out above.

(c) The donor's parents. For the reasons stated above this expression includes the natural father of an illegitimate child. Once again, there will be many cases in which such a father will not have to be notified because his whereabouts are unknown.

(d) The donor's brothers and sisters, whether of the whole blood or half blood.

(e) The widow or widower of a child of the donor. It is not clear whether such a person ceases to be entitled to notice on remarriage, and it has been suggested that 'for safety's sake they should be notified, and anyone in the next class as well' (P.D. Lewis (1986) LSG 3566, at p 3567).

(f) The donor's grandchildren.

(g) The children of the donor's brothers and sisters of the whole blood.

(h) The children of the donor's brothers and sisters of the half blood.

(i) The donor's uncles and aunts of the whole blood.

(j) The children of the donor's uncles and aunts of the whole blood.

How many relatives have to be notified?

17.35 In principle, only *three* of the donor's relatives are entitled to receive notice, and those three come from the class appearing first in the list. Thus, if the donor is married, his spouse (even if separated from the donor) will always be entitled to receive notice unless either her whereabouts are not known to the attorney and cannot reasonably be ascertained, or the court has dispensed with notification under the procedure described at 17.21. If the donor has children, those children (if they are 18 or over, and subject to the same exceptions) are then entitled to be notified; and so on down the list.

17.36 Although, in principle, no more than three persons are entitled to be notified (MCA 2005, Sch 4, para 6(3)), it is provided that if there is any relative in a particular class who is entitled to be notified in order to make up the requirement of three, then every member of that class must be notified - even if that means notifying five, six or more relatives (MCA 2005, Sch 4, para 6(4)). The principle is that the attorney is not to be allowed to choose which relatives in a particular class should be notified. It should be noted that the legislation is couched in terms of giving certain relatives an entitlement to be notified of the application. It can never be wrong to notify a relative who is not so entitled. Accordingly, if there is any doubt as to entitlement it would be safer to notify.

17.37 If the donor has fewer than three relatives falling into the specified categories, only those relatives need to be notified. If he has no relatives within the specified categories, no notification need be given to any relative or friend - even if, for example, the donor has been sharing a common household with another person for many years. However, where there are no relatives entitled to be notified the Public Guardian must not register the instrument and must undertake such inquiries as he thinks appropriate (MCA 2005, Sch 4, para 13(7)).

Examples of notification requirement

17.38 Some examples may make the operation of the notification rules clearer:

- The donor has a wife and four surviving children, all of whom are 18 or over. Notice must be given to all five.
- The donor has one child, one parent and eight grandchildren. All ten relatives must be notified, unless any grandchild is under 18.
- The donor has a spouse and two adult children. These three relatives are entitled to notice. It is not necessary to notify anyone else.
- The donor has a wife from whom he has been separated for 20 years, and a 'common law' wife of 10 years' standing. He lives with her and the three children of her marriage. Only his lawful wife need be notified.
- The donor has a spouse, two children (one aged 16 and one aged 18) and a mentally incapable uncle who has three adult children. The spouse, the 18-year-old child and the three cousins are entitled to be notified. The 16-year-old child is not so entitled, nor is the uncle.
- The donor has a spouse, two children under 18, one parent and three adult brothers. The children are not entitled to receive notice. Hence the spouse, the surviving parent, and the donor's brothers are all entitled to receive notice.

Effect of the Court of Protection dispensing with notification

17.39 It seems that a successful application under the procedure explained at **17.21** to dispense with service on a relative does not have the consequential effect of adding to the class of relatives who must be notified in order that three or more will actually be notified. This is because the Act provides that 'no more than three persons are entitled to receive notice' (MCA 2005, Sch 4, para 6(3)(a)). In the situation under discussion the court has merely dispensed with the requirement to serve a person who is so entitled. It has not altered the fact that such a person falls within the statutory description of being a person 'entitled to receive notice'.

Attorney a specified relative

17.40 It will often happen that the attorney will himself be a member of one of the specified classes of relatives. Such an attorney is not required to notify himself (MCA 2005, Sch 4, para 7(1)(a)), but he continues to count as a person entitled to receive notice for the purpose of the rule that no more than three persons are entitled to receive notice. For example, if a donor who has a wife and two adult daughters appoints his wife as his attorney, it is necessary for the attorney to notify the daughters, but nobody else.

Notice must be in the prescribed form

17.41 The EPAA 1985 did not specify the contents of the notices, but the MCA 2005, Sch 4 does.

17.42 MCA 2005, Sch 4, para 9 provides that the notice to the donor's relatives must:

- be in the prescribed form;
- state that the attorney proposes to make an application to the Public Guardian for the registration of the instrument creating the EPA;
- inform the person to whom it is given of his right to object to the registration under MCA 2005, Sch 4, para 13(4); and
- specify, as the grounds on which an objection to registration may be made, the grounds set out in MCA 2005, Sch 4, para 13(9).

17.43 MCA 2005, Sch 4, para 10 provides that the notice to the donor must:

- be in the prescribed form;
- state that the attorney proposes to make an application to the Public Guardian for the registration of the instrument creating the EPA; and
- inform the donor that, while the instrument remains registered, any revocation of the power by him will be ineffective unless and until revocation is confirmed by the court.

17.44 The notices to be given under the provisions explained above must be in the prescribed form EP1PG, as set out in reg 23(1) of and Sch 7 to the LPA, EPA & PG Regs 2007. The prescribed form of notice explains that the attorneys intend to apply to the Public Guardian for registration of the EPA.

17.45 Paragraph 1 of form EP1PG advises the recipient that he may object to the proposed registration, and that to do so he must make an application to the Court of Protection under rule 68 of the Court of Protection Rules 2007 on one (or more) of the grounds set out in paragraph 2 of EP1PG, and then notify the Office of the Public Guardian (OPG) of that objection within 5 weeks from the date on which form EP1PG was given to him. Paragraph 2 summarises the grounds on which the objection may be made, and paragraph 3 tells the recipient that he can obtain the necessary forms to object by calling the court on 0300 456 4600 or by downloading them from www.jus tice.gov.uk/global/forms/hmcts/index.htm. The web link no longer exists but EP1PG can be found at https://www.gov.uk/government/publications/register-an-enduring-power-of-attorney. A marginal note explains that the OPG's staff will be able to assist with any questions the recipient may have regarding objections generally; however, they cannot provide advice about the recipient's particular objection.

17.46 Paragraph 4 reminds the donor that, while the EPA remains registered, the donor will not be able to revoke it until the Court of Protection confirms the revocation. The form of notice should be signed by all the attorneys who are applying to register the EPA. A marginal note informs attorneys that they must keep a record of the date on which notice was given to the donor and to relatives, because this information will be required from them when they apply to register the instrument.

Service on the donor

17.47 The notice of intention to apply for registration (form EP1PG) must be given to the donor personally. The attorney must also provide or arrange for the provision of an explanation to the donor of the notice, what the effect of it is, and why it is being brought to his attention. This information must be provided in a way that is appropriate to the donor's circumstances (for example, using simple language, visual aids or other appropriate means) (LPA, EPA & PG Regs 2007, reg 23(2) and 23(3)).

Service on relatives

17.48 The Court of Protection (Enduring Powers of Attorney) Rules 2001 (SI 2001/825), which were revoked by r 2(b) of the Court of Protection Rules 2007 (SI 2007/1744), provided at r 15(2) that notification to relatives could be effected by sending the prescribed notice of intention to apply for registration to the relative concerned:

- by first class post;
- through a document exchange;
- by fax; or
- by other electronic means.

17.49 The LPA, EPA & PG Regs 2007 contain no specific provision on the method of service. However, MCA 2005, Sch 4, para 12 states that ' . . . for the purposes of this Part of this Schedule a notice given by post it to be regarded as given on the date on which it is posted'.

Service on a solicitor

17.50 Rule 16 of the Court of Protection (Enduring Powers of Attorney) Rules 2001 provided that where a solicitor acting for the person to be given any document, other than the donor, endorses on that document, or on a copy of it, a statement that he accepts the document on behalf of that person, the document shall be deemed to have been duly given to that person and to have been received on the date that the endorsement was made. The 2001 rules were revoked by the Court of Protection Rules 2007, r 2(b), and the LPA, EPA & PG Regs 2007 make no provision for service on a solicitor. Although r 31 of the Court of Protection Rules 2007 contains provisions for service on solicitors, this rule does not apply to the service of a form EP1PG on a solicitor acting for a relative of the donor.

Substituted service

17.51 Rule 17 of the Court of Protection (Enduring Powers of Attorney) Rules 2001 made provision for substituted service. Where it appeared to the Court of Protection that it was impracticable for any document to be given to a person in accordance with r 15(2), the court could give such directions as it thought fit for the purpose of bringing the document to the notice of the person to whom it is addressed.

17.52 The 2001 rules were revoked by the Court of Protection Rules 2007, r 2(b), and the LPA, EPA & PG Regs 2007 make no provision for substituted service. Rule 34 of the Court of Protection Rules 2007 states that, where it appears to the court that it is impracticable for any reason to serve a document in accordance with any of the methods provided under r 31, the court may make an order for substituted service of the document by taking such steps as the court may direct to bring it to the notice of the person to be served. However, this rule does not apply to the substituted service of a notice of intention to apply for registration in form EP1PG.

Duty to give notice to other attorneys

17.53 MCA 2005, Sch 4, para 11(1) stipulates that, before making an application for registration, an attorney under a joint and several power must give notice of his intention to do so to any other attorney under the power who is not joining in making the application. No such notice need be given if the co-attorney's address is not known to the applying attorney and cannot reasonably be ascertained by him, or if the applying attorney has reason to believe that the co-attorney has not reached the age of 18 or is mentally incapable (MCA 2005, Sch 4, para 11(2)). The Court of Protection also has power, as in the case of notification of relatives and the donor, to dispense with the giving of notice to a co-attorney if it is satisfied that it would be undesirable or impracticable for the attorney to give him notice, or that no useful purpose is likely to be served by giving him notice (MCA 2005, Sch 4, paras 7(2) and 11(1)). The form of notice sent to the other attorney is identical to that given to the relatives and the donor – form EP1PG (MCA 2005, Sch 4, paras 9 and 11(1)).

No time limit

17.54 The Court of Protection (Enduring Powers of Attorney) Rules 2001, r 6(1) required the notices of the attorney's intention to register the power to be served on the donor, relatives and any co-attorney within 14 days of each other. There is no time limit in the LPA, EPA & PG Regs 2007.

THE APPLICATION FOR REGISTRATION

Must be made as soon as practicable

17.55 MCA 2005, Sch 4, para 4(2) provides that the attorney must make an application to the Public Guardian for the registration of the instrument as soon as practicable if he has reason to believe that the donor is, or is becoming, mentally incapable. However, the notification requirement must be dealt with as set out in the preceding paragraphs before the application can be made.

17.56 If the attorney is not sure whether the power is, in fact, valid as an EPA - for example, because he is uncertain whether the donor had the necessary mental capacity to grant it (see **16.4–16.10**) - he may, and perhaps should, apply to the Court of Protection to have the validity of the power determined rather than apply for registration. This facility is expressly provided for in MCA 2005, Sch 4, para 4(5), and the attorney must comply with any direction given to him by the court on such a determination.

No time limit

17.57 The Court of Protection (Enduring Powers of Attorney) Rules 2001, r 7 required an application to register an EPA to be made in form EP2 and to be lodged with the court office not later than 10 days after the date on which (a) notice had been given to the donor and every relative entitled to receive notice and every co-attorney; or (b) leave had been given to dispense with notice, whichever was the later. There is no time limit in the LPA, EPA & PG Regs 2007.

Form of application: EP2PG

17.58 The application for registration must be in the prescribed form - form EP2PG: LPA, EPA & PG Regs 2007, reg 24 and Sch 8. The form consists of 12 parts, and must be completed in block capitals using black ink:

- *Part One – The Donor*. The applicant is required to state the donor's title, full name, present address (as distinct from the donor's address on the EPA itself), postcode and date of birth.
- *Part Two – Attorney One*. The applicant is required to state the attorney's title, full name, present address, postcode and date of birth, and in addition the attorney's telephone number, e-mail address, occupation and relationship to the donor.
- *Part Three – Attorney Two*. The details required are the same as in Part Two of the form.
- *Part Four – Attorney Three*. The details required are the same as in Part Two of the form.

- *Part Five – The Enduring Power of Attorney.* In this part the applicants state that they are applying to register the EPA made by the donor, the original of which accompanies this application, and that the applicants have reason to believe that the donor is or is becoming mentally incapable. The applicants are required to state the date on which the donor signed the EPA, and whether they know of any other EPA made by the donor and, if so, to give details including the date of registration, if applicable.
- *Part Six – Notice of Application to Donor.* In this part the applicants state that they gave notice of the application to register the EPA (form EP1PG) to the donor personally on a particular date. If someone other than the applicant gave the notice to the donor personally, the applicant is required to state that person's name, address, and postcode.
- *Part Seven – Notice of Application to Relatives.* The applicants are required to state the full names and addresses and relationship to the donor of the relatives to whom they have given notice in form EP1PG, and the date on which they gave such notice.
- *Part Eight – Notice of Application to Co-Attorney.* The applicant is required to state whether all the attorneys are applying to register the instrument. If not, the applicants are required to state the full names and addresses of their co-attorneys and the date on which they gave them notice in form EP1PG.
- *Part Nine – Fees.* This part is a reminder to the applicants to enclose a cheque for the registration fee, or, if they wish to apply for postponement, exemption or remission of the fee, to complete and enclose the application for exemption or remission form.
- *Part Ten – Declaration.* The application form must be signed and dated by all attorneys who are making the application. This must not pre-date the dates on which the form EP1PG notices were given. The applicants certify that the above information is correct and that to the best of their knowledge they have complied with the provisions of the MCA 2005.
- *Part Eleven – Correspondence Address.* This is primarily for the benefit of solicitors, who are asked to note that the address to which the correspondence should be sent must be entered here if it is different from the address of Attorney One. The applicants are required to state the full name and postal address, or DX address, and company reference.
- *Part Twelve – Additional Information.* This final section invites the applicants to 'write down any additional information to support this application'. The guidance notes for completing the form suggest that, if there are more than three attorneys, the details of the additional attorneys should be inserted here.

17.59 The OPG issues Guidance notes for completing form EP2PG: *Application to register an Enduring Power of Attorney* and can be downloaded from: https://www.gov.uk/government/uploads/system/uploads/attachment_data/file /245534/EP2PG_Notes_completing_EP2PG_form.pdf.

17.60 The application should be submitted to the Office of the Public Guardian, PO Box 16185, Birmingham B2 2WH as soon as the required notifications have taken place, and should include:

- the completed form EP2PG;

- the original EPA or a certified copy of the EPA;
- a cheque for £82 made payable to 'Office of the Public Guardian' in respect of the prescribed fee or the application for exemption or remission of the fee by completing form LPA120A.

Reasons why EPAs are defective

17.61 If the instrument itself - rather than the application - is defective, the applicant or his solicitors will receive a letter from the OPG informing him that the application to register the power has been rejected. The main reasons for failure are:

- 'The power omits the donor's date of birth.' (This can be put right by sending a copy of the donor's birth certificate.)
- 'The explanatory information (Part A) has been omitted.'
- 'The marginal notes have been omitted.'
- 'The power fails to appoint the attorneys either 'jointly' or 'jointly and severally'.'
- 'The power fails to show the extent of the attorney(s) authority.'
- 'The power fails to show the extent of the property over which the attorney(s) have authority.'
- 'The power was not dated when it was executed by the donor/attorney.'

Reasons why applications to register are defective

17.62 If the application is defective the applicant will receive a letter from the OPG stating the reasons why. The commonest reasons are:

- 'The date(s) the notices (forms EP1PG) were given to the relatives or the donor is/are missing.'
- 'The attorney(s) signed the application for registration (form EP2PG) before giving the notices of intention to register (form EP1PG).'
- 'The attorney(s) have not signed the application for registration (form EP2PG).'
- 'No additional Part C was used for the second attorney.'
- 'The application to register has not been made by both or all the attorneys. If you intend registration to be limited to . . . . please confirm that the notice(s) of intention to register (form EP1PG) served on the donor and relatives showed that attorney's or those attorneys' names only.'
  or
- 'If you intend registration to be limited to the above-named attorney(s), please confirm that the notice(s) of intention to register (form EP1PG) served on the donor and relatives showed both or all the attorneys' names.'

FUNCTIONS OF THE PUBLIC GUARDIAN ON AN APPLICATION FOR REGISTRATION

17.63 In its report in 1983, which recommended legislation on EPAs, the Law Commission regarded it as an important feature of the EPA scheme that registration should normally be a simple administrative process. In the great majority of cases, applications for registration were to involve the registration authority in doing no more than checking that the relevant documents were in order and that no objections had been made. The Commission thought it essential to the success of the EPA scheme both in terms of resources and of public acceptability that the registration authority should be bound to grant the application and register the power 'in the absence of a valid objection or any other reason for not doing so'. In particular, the registration authority was to have no duty to make independent inquiries unless there were suspicious circumstances, and it would not normally be expected to check that those relatives whose names and addresses appeared in the registration application had actually been notified (*The Incapacitated Principal*, Law Com No 122, paragraph 4.46).

17.64 The Court of Protection was the registration authority until the MCA 2005 came into force on 1 October 2007, whereupon the purely administrative functions relating to the registration of powers of attorney were transferred to the Public Guardian.

The Public Guardian's duty to register if the application is formally correct

17.65 The MCA 2005, Sch 4, para 13(1) provides that the Public Guardian *must* register the instrument to which a formally correct application relates, save in two groups of exceptional cases. However, it is important to emphasise that the duty to register only arises in the case of an application that is made in accordance with the provisions relating to formality and notification discussed above. Thus, the Public Guardian could refuse to register an application if the donor's signature to the power were not attested, or if the power had not been executed by an attorney, or if it were apparent on the face of the application that the notification requirements had not been satisfied.

The Court of Protection may waive failure to notify relatives

17.66 There is one exception to the principle that the application must be formally correct. If it is apparent from the application that notice has not been given to a relative who is entitled to receive notice under the Act, the Court of Protection may, on the application of the attorney, direct the Public Guardian to register the instrument if it is satisfied:

- that it was undesirable or impracticable for the attorney to give notice to that person; or
- that no useful purpose is likely to be served by giving him notice (MCA 2005, Sch 4, para 13(3)).

These conditions are, in substance, identical to the grounds upon which the court could have dispensed with the notification requirement if an application in that behalf had been made before making the registration application (MCA 2005, Sch 4, para 7(2)).

Circumstances in which the Public Guardian is prevented from registering an EPA

17.67 The Public Guardian is prevented from registering an EPA, and must not register the instrument except in accordance with the court's directions in the following circumstances:

- where it appears to the Public Guardian that there is a deputy appointed for the donor of the power created by the instrument, and the powers conferred on the deputy would, if the instrument were registered, to any extent conflict with the powers conferred on the attorney (MCA 2005, Sch 4, para 13(2));
- if, before the end of the period of 5 weeks beginning with the date (or the latest date) on which the attorney gave notice of the application for registration, the Public Guardian receives a valid notice of objection to the registration from a person entitled to notice of the application (MCA 2005, Sch 4, para 13(4) and (5));
- where the Public Guardian is required to undertake appropriate inquiries, if there is no one notified of the application to register the EPA or he has reason to believe that such inquiries may bring to light evidence on which he could be satisfied that one of the grounds for objection as set out in para 13(9) could be established (MCA 2005, Sch 4, para 13(6) and (7));
- where the application for registration was not accompanied by either the original instrument or a certified copy (LPA, EPA & PG Regs 2007, reg 24(2)).

17.68 In all of these circumstances, the Public Guardian must notify the person or persons who applied for registration of the fact that he is prevented from registering the instrument except in accordance with the directions of the Court of Protection (LPA, EPA & PG Regs 2007, reg 26).

PUBLIC GUARDIAN MUST NOT REGISTER IF A DEPUTY HAS BEEN APPOINTED

17.69 If it appears to the Public Guardian that there is a deputy appointed for the donor of the power created by the instrument, and that the powers conferred on the deputy would, if the instrument were registered, to any extent conflict with the powers conferred on the attorney, the Public Guardian must not register the instrument except in accordance with the directions of the Court of Protection: MCA 2005, Sch 4, para 13(2).

17.70 Sometimes, applications to register an EPA appointing one person as attorney and requesting the appointment of someone else as a deputy under the MCA 2005 arrive simultaneously, or in quick succession. The traditional practice of the Court of Protection in such cases is to follow the EPA route as far as possible, only considering the appointment of a deputy if it proves impossible to register the EPA. The reasoning behind this is that, on the face of it, the donor chose to execute an EPA in preference to having his affairs handled by a deputy. If his wishes can be respected, they should be.

17.71 As a matter of procedure, it is possible that, once a conflict between two applications becomes apparent, the Court of Protection will arrange a directions' hearing in order to identify the issues and attempt to dispose of them, or may try to move the matter forward by encouraging the parties to correspond with each other and the court.

17.72 Traditionally, the principal exception to 'following the EPA route' has been in cases where an individual has sustained head injuries, perhaps as a result of a road traffic accident, and there is likely to be a substantial award of damages. Quite often in such cases an EPA, executed after the accident, is produced, and there are doubts as to whether the donor had the requisite capacity to create the power. Furthermore, it may be preferable for those responsible for managing a large award to be subject to the monitoring, accounting and security requirements imposed upon a deputy.

VALID NOTICE OF OBJECTION

Time-limits

17.73 If a valid notice of objection to the registration is received by the Public Guardian before the expiry of 5 weeks beginning with the date (or the latest date) on which the attorney gave notice in form EP1PG to any person entitled to receive notice under MCA 2005, Sch 4, Part 3, the Public Guardian must not register the instrument except in accordance with the directions of the Court of Protection (MCA 2005, Sch 4, para 13(4) and (5)). This creates an indefinite suspension of the registration and requires a separate application to be made to the court for the matter to be resolved.

Valid grounds for objection

17.74 MCA 2005, Sch 4, para 13(9) provides that a notice of objection is valid if the objection is made on one or more of the following five grounds, namely:

(a)   that the power purported to have been created by the instrument was not valid as an EPA;

(b)   that the power created by the instrument no longer subsists;

(c)   that the application is premature because the donor is not yet becoming mentally incapable;

(d)   that fraud or undue pressure was used to induce the donor to create the power;

(e)   that, having regard to all the circumstances and in particular the attorney's relationship to or connection with the donor, the attorney is unsuitable to be the donor's attorney.

At this stage it is immaterial whether the grounds are established

17.75 It should be emphasised that the question at this stage is whether the notice - rather than the objection itself - is valid, and such a notice will be valid if an objection is made on one or more of the specified grounds. If a valid notice is received by the Public Guardian within the specified 5-week period, he must not register the instrument except in accordance with the court's directions (MCA 2005, Sch 4, paras 13(4) and (5)). At this stage it is immaterial whether or not those grounds are ultimately made out.

Grounds for valid notice

17.76 The grounds on which a valid notice can be based must now be examined in detail.

Power not valid

17.77 It would seem that an objection made on this ground might be based on two main (and rather different) grounds. First, the objector might claim that at the date when the power was purportedly created the *donor already lacked capacity* to grant it. It is a fundamental principle that a power cannot be valid unless the donor had mental capacity at the date of grant (see **16.4**). If an objector can show that the donor then lacked sufficient mental capacity to understand the nature and effect of the power, it is not and never has been valid. The appropriate action in such a case may be for an application to be made to the Court of Protection for the appointment of a deputy for property and affairs purposes. The question of invalidity due to lack of capacity was considered in detail in *In re W (Enduring Power of Attorney)* [2000] 3 WLR 45.

17.78 The second ground on which the objector might claim would be that the instrument purportedly creating the power was *formally defective*. The objection might be that the power omitted the obligatory statements stipulated in the prescribed form; that it was not executed by the parties; or that it was not properly witnessed. Again, the objection could be that for some other reason the power fell outside the definition of an EPA contained in para 2 of Sch 4 to the MCA 2005 and the regulations made thereunder - for example, because the attorney was an undischarged bankrupt or a minor, or that the attorney was not an individual or trust corporation.

Power no longer subsists

17.79 This would cover cases where the donor had validly revoked the power, or the attorney had validly disclaimed it. Revocation and disclaimer are considered in CHAPTER 20.

The donor is not yet becoming mentally incapable

17.80 This head of objection is easy to state, but difficult to explain. Reference should be made to **17.16–17.18** above for comments on the elusive nature of the concept of 'becoming mentally incapable'.

17.81 The definition of mental incapacity in MCA 2005, Sch 4, para 23(1) contains two prerequisites. A person must:

- have a mental disorder; and
- be incapable, or be becoming incapable, by reason of that mental disorder, of managing and administering his property and affairs.

17.82 These two prerequisites do not always coincide. A person with a mental disorder might be more than capable of looking after his affairs, and may even be financially astute. On the other hand, a person who has no kind of mental disorder could be totally incapable of managing and administering his property and affairs, perhaps because he is physically ill or disabled, not interested, poorly educated, or just lazy. The gerund *becoming* applies to the incapacity, rather than the mental disorder, and the incapacity must be preceded by some form of mental disorder as defined in s 1(2) of the Mental Health Act 1983. In other words, to succeed in objecting to registration of the power on this ground, it must be shown that either (a) the donor is not suffering from mental disorder; or (b) even though he has a mental disorder, he is not yet becoming incapable, by reason of that disorder, of managing and administering his property and affairs.

Fraud or undue pressure was used to induce the donor to create the power

17.83 If objection is made on this ground, it is difficult to see how the objection could be dealt with other than at a hearing when the evidence could be fully considered. However, the mere making of the objection would, no doubt, almost invariably cause the court to defer a decision on registration pending further inquiries.

17.84 The existence of this ground of objection serves to emphasise the importance of keeping adequate records about the circumstances leading up to the grant of the power. It should be remembered that it will be possible to establish this ground of objection even if the attorney is a perfectly respectable person, and even if the 'pressure' in question had not been exercised by him but, for example, by well-intentioned relatives of the donor.

17.85 The burden of proof is on the objector to prove to the satisfaction of the court that:

- the donor was 'induced' to create the power;
- 'fraud' or 'pressure' was used to induce him to create it; and
- the pressure was 'undue'.

17.86 The word 'induce' should be construed in its ordinary meaning, that is 'to persuade or to prevail upon to bring about': *Commission of Racial Equality v Imperial Society of Teachers of Dancing* [1983] ICR 473. So, where, for example, the impetus or initiative to create an EPA comes from the donor personally, it can hardly be said that he or she had been induced to create the power.

17.87 The MCA 2005 does not define fraud, and it probably needs to be construed in an ordinary commonsense way. Fraud would include, for example, making a false statement to the donor, knowing it to be false, with the intention that the donor would be deceived by it into creating an EPA, which he or she would not otherwise have made, provided the donor is so deceived and does create the power on account of the false statement.

17.88 To use 'pressure' means to behave in a manner whereby the will of the donor is overborne by the will of another person, so that in creating the power the donor is not acting of his or her own free will. Pressure can assume various forms. It can be physical, psychological, emotional, and financial. Physical pressure constitutes any act or rough treatment directed towards the donor, whether or not actual physical injury results. Psychological or emotional pressure includes any behaviour that may diminish the donor's sense of identity, dignity and self-worth, including humiliation, intimidation, verbal abuse, threats, and isolation. Financial pressure includes the deliberate denial of the donor's access to his or her money or property.

17.89 The meaning of 'undue' has been considered judicially in the context of hardship and delay. For example, in *Liberian Shipping Corporation v A King & Sons Ltd* [1967] 1 All ER 934, 938, CA, Lord Denning MR said, 'undue' simply means excessive. It means greater hardship than the circumstances warrant.

The attorney is unsuitable to be the donor's attorney

17.90 This ground, as the Law Commission pointed out (*The Incapacitated Principal*, Law Com No 122, paragraph 4.49(e)), amounts, in effect, to a criticism of the donor's choice of attorney. It is, in practice, the ground that is most commonly alleged. As with the 'fraud or undue pressure' ground considered above, it will be an easy matter to lodge a valid objection to registration on this ground, and that will of itself serve to delay registration pending the making of inquiries, and usually, no doubt, the holding of a hearing.

17.91 The ground leaves a considerable element of discretion with the court in deciding what criteria are to be regarded as rendering an attorney 'unsuitable'. The statutory reference to the attorney's relationship to or connection with the donor suggests that the court might well find this ground made out if the attorney were connected with the residential care home or nursing home in which the donor was residing and there were some grounds for thinking that financial advantage might, in consequence, be taken of the donor (see *Re Davey (deceased)* [1980] 3 All ER 342). However, the Law Commission stated that it would not wish the ground to be sustained 'merely because the attorney was not the sort of person that a particular relative would have chosen'. The Commission said:

> 'It is our wish that the donor's choice of attorney should carry considerable weight. Thus, for example, a mother might be content to appoint her son as her EPA attorney despite being aware of a conviction for theft. We would not want her choice of attorney to be upset simply because a particular relative would not want the son to be his attorney. The question should be whether the particular attorney is suitable to act as an attorney for the particular donor. In short, the court should examine carefully all the circumstances - particularly the relationship between donor and attorney.' (Law Com No 122, paragraph 4.49(e)).

17.92 Generally speaking, any attorney acting under an EPA who has behaved, is behaving, or proposes to behave in a way that contravenes his authority or is not in the donor's best interests is likely to be unsuitable to be the donor's attorney, but the converse is not necessarily true. An attorney may be unsuitable to be the donor's attorney because the attorney has fallen out with them and no longer wishes them to act, even though their conduct as attorney has been exemplary. Unsuitability in the context of general hostility within the donor's family was considered in *Re W (Enduring Power of*

Attorney) [2001] 2 WLR 957, in *Re E (Enduring Powers of Attorney)* [2000] 3 WLR 1974, and in *Re F* [2004] 3 All ER 277. In *Re F*, at page 284f, Patten J said:

> 'It seems to me that to remove a chosen attorney because of hostility from a sibling or other relative, in the absence of any effective challenge to his competence or integrity, should require clear evidence either that the continuing hostility will impede the proper administration of the estate or will cause significant distress to the donor which would be avoided by the appointment of a receiver.'

17.93 To refuse registration of the power on the grounds of unsuitability, the court has to be satisfied not of the chosen attorney's suitability, but rather that he is unsuitable to be the attorney (see *Re E (Enduring Power of Attorney)* [2001] Ch 364 at page 376H). See **19.30-19.37** and **19.39-19.60** for the court procedure to apply to object to the registration of the EPA. The attorney's unsuitability may be considered by the court prior to registration, but more often after registration. Examples of cases where the court has considered the attorney's unsuitability include:

- Adverse transactions between the donor and attorney which pre-date the power in *Re C*, 21 December 1999 (unreported) Court of Appeal.
- The attorney had wholesale assumption of dominion over the donor's estate as if she had died and he had inherited in *Re Stapleton*(Decision of Senior Judge Lush, 2 July 2012).
- Challenge to the attorney's competence and integrity in *Re RG* [2015] EWCOP 2.

Notice of objection to registration

17.94 Form EP1PG – Notice of Intention to Apply for Registration of an Enduring Power of Attorney – informs the donor, donor's relatives and any co-attorneys that:

> 'You have the right to object to the proposed registration on one or more of the grounds set out below. You must notify the Office of the Public Guardian of your objection within five weeks from the day this notice was given to you. You may make an application to the Court of Protection under rule 68 of the Court of Protection Rules 2007 for a decision on the matter. No fee is payable for such an application. If you do not make such an application, the Public Guardian may ask for the court's directions about registration.'

17.95 The LPA, EPA & PG Regs 2007 do not require the use of a prescribed form for notifying the Public Guardian of an objection to the registration of an EPA. Regulation 25(2) does, however, specify the contents of the notice of objection. The OPG has created form EP3PG which satisfies the requirements that the notice of objection must be in writing and sets out:

- the name and address of the objector;
- if different, the name and address of the donor of the power;
- if known, the name and address of the attorney (or attorneys); and
- the ground for making the objection.

NO RELATIVE TO WHOM NOTICE HAS BEEN GIVEN

17.96 The Law Commission's protective scheme relies heavily on the specified relatives being likely to know the donor and to have an interest in his well-being. If a donor has no relatives within the specified classes, no notice can be given, and this element of protection will, accordingly, be absent. Yet it may be, perhaps, that it is those who have no relatives who are most likely to need some protection against unscrupulous attorneys. It was for this reason that the Law Commission proposed that, where no relative had been notified, the court should not register or refuse to register without 'first considering the possibility of making inquiries' (Law Com No 122, paragraph 4.48), and this proposal is implemented by MCA 2005, Sch 4, para 13(6)(a).

17.97 Such applications usually receive special scrutiny by the Public Guardian, who will generally ask for details of the donor's assets and liabilities, and income and expenditure, and, depending on the reply, may require this information to be verified.

APPROPRIATE INQUIRIES MIGHT PRODUCE EVIDENCE OF A GROUND FOR OBJECTION

17.98 MCA 2005, Sch 4, para 13(6)(b) and (7) provide that, if the Public Guardian has reason to believe that appropriate inquiries might bring to light evidence on which he could be satisfied that one of the grounds of objection was established, he must not register the instrument, and must undertake such inquiries as he thinks appropriate in all the circumstances.

17.99 This ground for deferring registration might cover cases where the Public Guardian knew that there were suspicious circumstances relating to a particular attorney, or where it had received information (perhaps by an anonymous letter) which indicated grounds for concern. It must again be emphasised that what is in issue at this stage is simply whether the case is one of the exceptions where registration is not a simple and automatic administrative act. The method and extent of those inquires is at the discretion of the Public Guardian. It may be that a third party who has concerns will need to make an application to the court. This is considered in **19.37**.

WHERE THE APPLICATION FOR REGISTRATION IS NOT ACCOMPANIED BY THE ORIGINAL INSTRUMENT OR A CERTIFIED COPY

17.100 If the original instrument is unavailable for any reason, the Public Guardian may register a certified copy of it. The LPA, EPA & PG Regs 2007, reg 24 states that:

'(2)   Where the instrument to be registered which is sent with the application is neither
    (a)   the original instrument intended to create the power, nor
    (b)   a certified copy of it,
        the Public Guardian must not register the instrument unless the court directs him to do so.

(3)   "Certified copy", in relation to an enduring power of attorney, means a copy certified in accordance with section 3 of the Powers of Attorney Act 1971.'

Accordingly, it will be necessary for any applicant seeking to register an uncertified copy of an EPA to apply to the Court of Protection for an order directing the Public Guardian to register it. The application should be made on form COP1 and there will be an application fee of £400. The court will require a sworn statement relating to the circumstances of the execution of the instrument; evidence as to the contents of the instrument; evidence relating to the loss or destruction of the original instrument; and evidence that the power had not been revoked by the donor.

WHERE THE PUBLIC GUARDIAN RECEIVES A NOTICE OF OBJECTION BUT THE COURT DOES NOT RECEIVE AN APPLICATION

17.101 Rule 201 of the Court of Protection Rules 2007 and Practice Direction 23A apply where:

•   the Public Guardian has received a notice of objection to the registra-tion of an EPA, and is therefore prevented by para 13(5) of Sch 4 to the MCA 2005 from registering the instrument except in accordance with the court's instructions; but
•   no application has been made to the Court of Protection.

17.102 After a specific time has elapsed, the Public Guardian can apply to the court for directions. The time limit is 5 weeks from the date, or the latest date, on which the attorney gave notice of his intention to apply for registration (form EP1PG) to the donor's relatives (Court of Protection Rules 2007, r 201(2)(a)). However, this period is extended if it would otherwise expire less than 14 days after the Public Guardian receives the notice of objection that prevents him from registering the instrument. In this case, the Public Guardian may not request directions from the court until the end of the 14-day period, which begins on the date on which he received the notice of objection (r 201(2)(b)). It should be noted that the Public Guardian is not compelled to apply to the court for directions, and may decide to leave it to the attorney to make an application for the matter to be resolved by the court (MCA 2005, Sch 4, para 13(8)).

17.103 The Public Guardian must make the request for directions on form COP17, which states:

•   the name and address of the attorney who has applied to register the EPA;
•   the name and address of the donor;
•   the name and address of the objector; and
•   the date on which the Public Guardian received the notice of objection.

17.104 The Public Guardian must attach copies of the following papers relating to the objection to the registration of the EPA:

•   the EPA instrument;
•   the application to register the EPA (EP2PG);
•   the notice of objection; and

- any other relevant papers.

17.105 As soon as practicable, and in any event within 21 days of the date on which the COP17 is filed:

- the court must notify the objector(s), and the attorney(s) (Court of Protection Rules 2007, r 201(4)); and
- the Public Guardian must notify the donor that the request for directions has been filed (r 201(5)).

17.106 Rule 201(6) of the Court of Protection Rules 2007 provides that the notice that the court sends to the objector(s) and attorney(s) must:

- state that the Public Guardian has requested the court's directions about registration;
- state that the court will give directions in response to the request unless an application under Part 9 of the Court of Protection Rules is made to it before the end of the period of 21 days commencing with the date on which the notice is issued; and
- set out the steps required to make such an application.

17.107 If anyone wishes to participate in the proceedings, he then has 21 days to file an application using form COP8. The application must be made in accordance with the detailed requirements for application relating to the registration of EPAs, which are set out in Practice Direction 9H, accompanying Part 9 of the Rules. If no such application is made, the court will proceed to consider the matter in response to the Public Guardian's request, and will give directions to the Public Guardian.

ESTABLISHING AND MAINTAINING A REGISTER OF EPAS

17.108 A note of the registration must be added to the register of EPAs which the Public Guardian is required to establish and maintain under MCA 2005, Sch 4, para 14. See **10.11-10.12** and **10.17-10.27** for detail of how to search the register and the contents.

17.109 On registration, the attorney's power to act under the EPA is fully restored. See **18.50-18.55** as to the attorney's authority and powers following registration.

Chapter 18

THE SCOPE OF THE ATTORNEY'S AUTHORITY UNDER AN ENDURING POWER

INTRODUCTION

18.1 Schedule 4, para 3(1) of the Mental Capacity Act 2005 (MCA 2005) provides that:

'If the instrument which creates an enduring power of attorney is expressed to confer general authority on the attorney, the instrument operates to confer, subject to –
(a) the restriction imposed by sub-paragraph (3), and
(b) any conditions or restrictions contained in the instrument,
authority to do on behalf of the donor anything which the donor could lawfully do by an attorney at the time when the donor executed the instrument.'

18.2 In effect, there are four options – or potentially eight, if one counts the alternatives 'with' or 'without' any restrictions or conditions. These four options are to confer:

- *general authority* in relation to all the donor's property and affairs;
- *general authority* in relation to a specified part of the donor's property and affairs;
- *specific authority* in relation to all the donor's property and affairs; and
- *specific authority* in relation to a specified part of the donor's property and affairs.

18.3 The expression 'property and affairs' extends only to business matters, legal transactions and other dealings of a similar kind, and an attorney acting under an enduring power has no authority to make any decision relating to the donor's health care or personal welfare, such as where to live and with whom to have contact (see *Re F (Sterilisation: Mental Patient)* [1989] 2 FLR 376, particularly at p 423, per Lord Brandon).

GENERAL AUTHORITY

The effect of conferring general authority

18.4 If the donor wished to confer general power authority on his attorney he must have used the words contained in the prescribed form, namely: 'I appoint *(name and address)* to be my attorney for the purpose of the Enduring Powers of Attorney Act 1985 with general authority to act on my behalf.' See **18.1** for definition of the expression 'general authority'.

18.5 The enduring power of attorney (EPA) is a creature of statute and is effective only if the instrument is *expressed to confer* such general authority. The requirement that a particular form of words be used should be contrasted with the position under the Powers of Attorney Act 1971, s 10(1) of which provides that ' . . . a general power of attorney in the form set out in Schedule 1 to this Act, or in a form to the like effect but expressed to be made under this Act, shall operate to confer on *(the donee(s))* authority to do on behalf of the donor anything which he can lawfully do by an attorney'.

18.6 It must also be remembered that the Enduring Powers of Attorney Act 1985 required the use of a prescribed form. Failure to have used that form will prevent the instrument from being an EPA within the meaning of MCA 2005, Sch 4, para 2(1). The Prescribed Form Regulations used the formula set out in the legislation, but a minor variation in wording (for example, general authority to act as my attorney) would possibly, by reason of the rule that an instrument may differ in an immaterial respect in form and mode of expression from the prescribed form, not prevent the instrument from taking effect as an EPA (MCA 2005, Sch 4, para 2(4)). On the other hand, failure to have used the words 'general authority' would, for the reasons given above, leave the extent of the attorney's powers in doubt.

What can a donor lawfully do by an attorney?

18.7 The extent of the authority conferred by an EPA giving the attorney general authority is a matter, first, for the general law. This is because the MCA 2005 provides that an instrument is expressed to confer general authority to do on behalf of the donor 'anything which the donor can lawfully do by an attorney' (MCA 2005, Sch 4, para 3(1)).

18.8 The meaning of this expression was considered in *Clauss v Pir* [1988] 1 Ch 267, where it was held that the attorney could not lawfully swear an affidavit on the donor's behalf. See also *Gregory v Turner* [2003] EWCA Civ 183; [2003] 2 All ER 1114, in which it was held that a person cannot by an EPA confer on the donee a right to appear in court as his representative as this right is personal to the litigant.

18.9 The donor can lawfully do most things by an attorney, but there are three important exceptions:

- where statute requires the evidence of the donor's signature; or
- where the donor's competency to do the act arises by virtue of holding some office, public or otherwise; or
- where the donor's own authority or duty to do the act is of a personal nature, requiring skill or discretion for its exercise.

18.10 Therefore, by virtue of the first exception, an attorney could not execute a will on behalf of the donor, because s 9 of the Wills Act 1837 provides that the will must be 'signed . . . by the testator or by some other person in his presence and by his direction' (but see **19.12** and **19.13**). Because of the second exception, the attorney of a bishop could not lawfully ordain a priest, and because of the third exception an attorney acting for a student could not lawfully sit an examination on the donor's behalf.

18.11 Statutory authority granted to a particular person cannot normally be delegated and, generally speaking, it is not possible for an attorney who is himself a delegate further to delegate his authority. And, as has already been noted, a power of attorney which gives the attorney a right to appoint a substitute or successor cannot be an EPA (MCA 2005, Sch 4, para 2(6)).

Acting for the donor as an administrator or executor

18.12 The attorney under an EPA is not automatically entitled to take over the powers of a donor who has been acting as an executor or administrator. The Non-Contentious Probate Rules 1987 (SI 1987/2024), r 35(2) provides that 'where a registrar is satisfied that a person entitled to a grant is by reason of mental incapacity incapable of managing his affairs, administration for his use and benefit, limited until further representation be granted' may be granted to the lawful attorney of the incapable person acting under a registered EPA or LPA. Only a person specifically authorised by the Court of Protection to apply for a grant has a higher priority to seek a grant. Notice of an intended application under r 35(2) must be given to the Court of Protection. This is commonly done by letter, which is acknowledged in writing by the court. A copy of the acknowledgment should be submitted to the Probate Registry when making an application for the grant of representation.

General authority over part of the donor's property and affairs

18.13 Most EPAs relate to all the donor's property. According to a survey conducted by Bristol University in 1990, in no less than 98.4% of applications to register an EPA, the EPA conferred on the attorney general authority to act in relation to all the donor's property and affairs: S Cretney, G Davis, R Kerridge and A Borkowski, *Enduring Powers of Attorney: A Report to the Lord Chancellor* (Lord Chancellor's Department, June 1991), p 27.

18.14 It was, however, possible to give the attorney general authority only in relation to specified property - for example, 'my property situated in England' or 'my Blackacre estate' or 'my bank account at the Royal Bank of Scotland, Oxford Branch'. The prescribed form made provision for the donor to give general authority in relation to not only 'all my property and affairs but also the following property and affairs'. In such a case the attorney may do anything an attorney can lawfully do in respect of that property, but he has no powers over any other property.

Specific authority

18.15 It was possible to limit the scope of the attorney's authority to the carrying out of specified transactions: for example, the transfer of a specific property. In such a case the prescribed form will state that the attorney has authority 'to do the following on my behalf . . . ' (for example, 'execute a transfer in relation to the following property and affairs, Blackacre'). If the power is limited to doing specified things on the donor's behalf it will be a matter of construction of the words used as to what authority is conferred on the donee.

Omission to delete general or specific authority

18.16 An omission to delete either the general or specific provision will be regarded by the Public Guardian as 'immaterial' within the meaning of paragraph 2(4), Schedule 4 of the MCA 2005, because if the donor has not set out any details in the space below the second option, it may be assumed that he intended to give the attorneys general authority to act.

Subject to any conditions or restrictions

18.17 An EPA, whether general or specific, may be granted subject to restrictions and conditions, which should be set out where indicated in the prescribed form. Some examples of restrictions which are occasionally imposed in practice are given at **16.43** ff.

18.18 An EPA is potentially extremely wide-ranging, and in some cases the right to impose conditions and restrictions may be important. However, the Law Commission, in its report *The Incapacitated Principal* (1983) Law Com No 122, para 4.31, sounded a note of caution about the excessive use of restricted powers. While accepting the general principle that people should be able to make such arrangements as they please for the management of their affairs, it emphasised that it would be important for the donor to ensure that the authority bestowed under his EPA effectively covered the whole of his property and affairs. As the Commission said:

> 'If he leaves a "gap" so that part of his property and affairs is not covered by an EPA, it may be necessary for the court to intervene and appoint a receiver. And whilst we would not wish to prevent the donor giving his attorney such limited authority as he thought fit, the fact remains that the less authority that is given to the attorney, the greater is the risk that he would be unable to act for the donor at a later date. If by that time the donor were incapable so that he could not create a new power, the court might have to take over.'

Scope of authority: the Act's provisions

18.19 The MCA 2005 contains two important provisions relating to the scope of the attorney's authority, which will apply, regardless of whether the power is general or limited, unless the instrument itself contains any relevant special conditions or restrictions. These are:

- the power to provide for the needs of persons other than the donor; and
- a circumscribed power to make gifts of the donor's money and property.

POWER TO PROVIDE FOR PEOPLE'S NEEDS

Schedule 4, paragraph 3(2)

18.20 MCA 2005, Sch 4, para 3(2) provides that:

'Subject to any conditions or restrictions contained in the instrument, an attorney under an enduring power, whether general or limited, may (without obtaining any consent) act under the power so as to benefit himself or other persons than the donor to the following extent but no further –

(a) he may so act in relation to himself or in relation to any other person if the donor might be expected to provide for his or that person's needs respectively; and

(b) he may do whatever the donor might be expected to do to meet those needs.'

18.21 Thus, in the absence of any express provision in the instrument creating the power, the attorney may provide for the *needs* of any person, including himself. Three questions need to be asked.

- First, is the provision in question required to meet a need of the person benefited?
- Secondly, might the donor be expected to provide for that person's needs?
- Thirdly, what might the donor be expected to do to meet those needs?

Needs

18.22 The authority is only to provide for needs. It is submitted that needs are not limited to maintenance in any narrow sense. The courts would probably adopt a reasonably generous view of what is comprised in this expression, extending it no doubt to the provision of suitable housing, clothing, holidays, etc. In this context, decisions on the Inheritance (Provision for Family and Dependants) Act 1975 and Matrimonial Causes Act 1973 may be relevant.

Might the donor be expected to provide for that person's needs?

18.23 Even if the provision in question is to satisfy someone's needs, the attorney may only act if the donor might be expected to provide for them. Suppose, for example, that the question is whether provision should be made towards the further education or training of the donor's adult child. First, it would have to be established that such provision constituted a need. Secondly, it would have to be asked whether this particular donor might be expected to provide for the needs of that child. And thirdly, it would have to be asked what this particular donor might have been expected to do to meet that need. For example, it might be clear that the donor had himself envisaged meeting the costs involved; conversely, it might be clear that he had decided against doing so.

18.24 MCA 2005, Sch 4, para 23(2) provides that any question as to what the donor might be expected to do shall be determined by assuming that he had full mental capacity at the time but otherwise by reference to the circumstances existing at that time. It would seem, therefore, that the donor's personality and preferences should be taken into account. For example, he may believe that adult children should be self-sufficient. However, matters stemming from the incapacity should be disregarded. For example, a delusion that the child in question has been neglectful or cruel. Again, an attorney could properly take account of the fact that the donor's means had much diminished, but should not take account of any delusional belief on the donor's part that he was extremely poor.

What might the donor be expected to do to meet those needs?

18.25 Some donors might be more generous than others in meeting needs. One might take the view that his wife should have the best that money can buy while convalescing after an illness and, thus, provide on an appropriately extensive scale. Another might take a more parsimonious view. The question for the attorney in all cases is: assuming that he had full mental capacity, what would *this particular donor* have done in the light of the facts as they are?

18.26 If the donor still has mental capacity the best way of answering this question would be to ask him. However, this statutory power will also be available, provided that the power has been registered, after the onset of incapacity.

Re Cameron (deceased)

18.27 The provisions of what is now MCA 2005, Sch 4, para 3(2) were considered by Lindsay J in *Re Cameron (deceased)* [1999] 2 All ER 924, the facts of which were as follows. Mrs Marjorie Cameron had four sons, Donald, Iain, Alastair and Hamish, all of whom were educated at fee-paying schools. In 1974, she executed a will leaving her residuary estate to her sons in equal shares. In March 1989, she executed an EPA appointing three of her sons (though not Donald) jointly to be her attorneys with general authority to act on her behalf in relation to all her property and affairs. The power was registered in July 1989. In 1991 the attorneys, exercising their powers to provide for someone's needs, paid £62,596 to trustees to provide for the private education of their brother Donald's son, Jamie. The payment was made on the basis that, as a portion, it would, by virtue of the rule against double portions, adeem *pro tanto* Donald's share of Mrs Cameron's residuary estate. At that time Donald was unemployed and living on state benefits. Mrs Cameron died in November 1992. Donald maintained that there had been no ademption of his share of the estate, contending, *inter alia,* that private education was not a 'need' within the meaning of what is now MCA 2005, Sch 4, para 3(2).

18.28 Lindsay J held that, for the purposes of para 3(2), the education of a child was a 'need', and the provision of private education for a grandson came within that section. Furthermore, in the circumstances, Mrs Cameron might have been expected to provide for her grandson's needs, and the provision that the attorneys had made on her behalf was of a kind which she might have been expected to make, both to confer some benefit on Donald and to meet the need to provide an education for his son. Accordingly, the payment of £62,596 was a valid exercise of the power of attorney. With regard to the rule against double portions, the judge held that a gift by a grandparent for the benefit of a grandchild could be treated as being for the benefit of the grandchild's parent. Accordingly, the payment adeemed Donald's share of his mother's residuary estate to the extent of that payment.

The effect of the donor's incapacity

18.29 The attorney's powers under MCA 2005, Sch 4, para 3(2) are not affected by the onset of the donor's incapacity. Schedule 4, para 1(2)(b) provides that, where the attorney has made an application for registration of the instrument, the attorney may still take action under the power to maintain himself or other persons in so far as para 3(2) permits him to do so.

POWER TO MAKE GIFTS

Schedule 4, paragraph 3(3)

18.30 The MCA 2005, Sch 4, para 3(3) states:

'Without prejudice to sub-paragraph (2) but subject to any conditions or restrictions contained in the instrument, an attorney under an enduring power, whether general or limited, may (without obtaining any consent) dispose of the property of the donor by way of gift to the following extent but no further -

(a) he may make gifts of a seasonal nature or at a time, or on an anniversary, of a birth, a marriage or the formation of a civil partnership, to persons (including himself) who are related to or connected with the donor, and

(b) he may make gifts to any charity to whom the donor made or might be expected to make gifts,

provided that the value of each such gift is not unreasonable having regard to all the circumstances and in particular the size of the donor's estate.'

Power to make gifts is in addition to the power to provide for needs

18.31 The power to make gifts operates 'without prejudice to' the power conferred by Sch 4, para 3(2) to provide for needs. The power to make gifts is, therefore, additional to the power to provide for needs and could be invoked if for some reason that power is inapplicable; for example, where no 'need' can be established. The power to make gifts is quite limited.

Four conditions must be satisfied

18.32 Four conditions have to be established before the power to make gifts in accordance with Sch 4, para 3(3) can be used:

* there must be *no restrictions* or conditions in the EPA itself which prohibit the attorney from making the gift;
* the *timing* of the gift must fall within the prescribed parameters;
* the *recipient* must either be a charity, or an individual who is related to or connected with the donor; and
* the *value* of the gift must be not unreasonable.

There must be no restrictions in the instrument

18.33 There must be no restrictions or conditions in the instrument which would prohibit the attorney from making a gift of the donor's property. Where the EPA specifically states that no gifts are to be made to the donor's friends or relatives, the powers of the Court of Protection under para 16(2) of Sch 4 to the MCA 2005 do not extend to directing the attorney to make provision for a third party by way of gift or in recognition of a moral obligation owed by the donor (*Re R (Enduring Power of Attorney)* [1991] 1 FLR 128).

The timing of the gift

18.34 A gift to charity can be made at any time of the year, but in the case of an individual, the gift must be either 'of a seasonal nature', or made 'at a time of a birth, a marriage or the formation of a civil partnership', or 'on an anniversary of a birth, a marriage or the formation of a civil partnership'. Seasonal gifts include, for example, presents given at Christmas, Diwali or Eid, but it is unclear whether *seasonal* means the end of one tax year and the beginning of another. If the donor was in the habit of making gifts of the annual exemption for inheritance tax purposes for the needs of one or more members of the family, then the gift would fall within the scope of MCA 2005, Sch 4, para 3(2) in any event. In *Re GM* [2013] COPLR 290 Senior Judge Lush gave guidance on the circumstances in which the use of the annual exemption and small gifts exemption for Inheritance Tax purposes may be regarded as falling within the provisions of para 3(2). The Act does not specify on whose birthday or anniversary the gift may be made, and for ethnic, cultural or other reasons the donor may have traditionally given presents on his own birthday, rather than the recipient's. Presents given on a christening, confirmation, barmitzvah, graduation, engagement or retirement are, effectively, excluded from the scope of MCA 2005, Sch 4, para 3(3).

The recipient of the gift

18.35 An individual recipient, as distinct from a charity, must be someone who is 'related to' or 'connected with' the donor. Neither of these expressions is defined. Although MCA 2005, Sch 4, para 6(1) lists certain 'relatives', in this context the word 'relatives' only applies to the persons who may be entitled to receive notice of the attorney's intention to register the instrument, and the expression 'related to' is wider and may include, for example, a parent-in-law, son- or daughter-in-law, step-parent and stepchild, none of whom fall within the definition of relatives in MCA 2005, Sch 4, para 6(1). In any event, these people are likely to be 'connected with' the donor.

18.36 The attorney may make gifts to any charity if the donor made or might be expected to make such gifts. The question whether or not the donor made such gifts is one of fact which should be comparatively easy to answer. The question whether he might be expected to do so is to be answered on the basis that he has full mental capacity (MCA 2005, Sch 4, para 23(2)). The older reported decisions on statutory wills before the MCA 2005 came into force give some useful guidance on the factors to be taken into account in ascertaining what an incapacitated person might be expected to do, assuming he had full mental capacity at the time (see *Re D(J)* [1982] Ch 237; *Re C (Spinster and Mental Patient)* [1992] 1 FLR 51; but compare *Re S (Gifts by Mental Patient)* [1997] 1 FLR 96). The wording of Sch 4, para 3(3) prima facie excludes any purposes which are not charitable: for example, political parties, animal rights groups, or Dignity in Dying (previously known as the Voluntary Euthanasia Society).

The value of the gift

18.37 Even if these conditions are satisfied, the gift must be of such an amount that it can properly be described as not unreasonable. This involves a consideration of all the circumstances, but particular reference is made to the size of the donor's estate. A millionaire might reasonably make larger gifts than a person who lives solely on a State retirement pension. Although the attorney is the arbiter of what is not unreasonable in this context, if the matter is brought before the Court of Protection in an application for relief under MCA 2005, Sch 4, para 16(2)(e), the court will decide whether what is proposed is reasonable.

18.38 In *In re W (Enduring Power of Attorney)* [2000] 3 WLR 45, at 51d, Jules Sher QC commented that 'the power of an attorney to make gifts of the donor's property is extremely limited, and certainly, without the authorization of the court after the power is registered, does not extend to the making of gifts as part of inheritance tax planning'.

No need to obtain consent

18.39 The attorney may exercise this power to make gifts of the donor's property without consulting the donor or, indeed, anyone else. If the donor still has mental capacity, he could either revoke the power or forbid the attorney to make a projected gift. The position would, of course, be different once the donor had lost capacity (see **18.51**).

Wider authority to make gifts cannot be conferred in the EPA

18.40 Any provision in an EPA which purports to give the attorney greater authority to make gifts is ineffective (Law Com No 122, p 29, fn 134). It has been suggested, however, that it may be possible for the donor, while he is still mentally capable, to execute an ordinary power of attorney authorising the attorney to benefit others without limitation (as above, fn 135).

The effect of registration on the power to make gifts

18.41 The attorney's power to dispose of the donor's property pending the registration of an EPA is considered at **18.48**, and the position once the power is registered is discussed at **18.53**.

THE ATTORNEY'S AUTHORITY AND POWER AT THE ONSET OF DONOR'S INCAPACITY

18.42 At common law, the power of attorney would have been revoked when the donor of the power became mentally incapable. MCA 2005, Sch 4, para 1(1)(a) prevents such automatic revocation taking place, but para 1(1)(b) provides that, once incapacity has supervened, the attorney may not do anything under the authority of the power, subject to two exceptions which only apply if the attorney has made an application for registration. The inability of an attorney validly to exercise the power once mental incapacity has supervened constitutes an incentive for the donor to register (*Re K; Re F (Enduring Powers of Attorney)* [1988] 2 FLR 15 per Hoffmann J).

Restricted powers pending registration

18.43 If the attorney has made an application for registration of the instrument, the attorney may take action under the power for two purposes only until it is registered, namely:

- to maintain the donor or prevent loss to his estate; or
- to maintain himself or other persons in so far as MCA 2005, Sch 4, para 3(2) permits him to do so (Sch 4, para 1(2)).

18.44 The scope of the attorney's authority under these powers is narrow. He may not take action - such as, for example, subscribing for shares under a rights issue - unless his failure to do so would cause actual loss to the donor's estate.

18.45 The restricted powers described above do not arise unless and until an application for registration has been made, and that can only be done after notification for registration has been given to the donor and specified relatives. If a donor were suddenly totally incapacitated (eg comatose) the attorney would not be able to take any action under the instrument at all until an application had been made to register it.

18.46 The Enduring Powers of Attorney Act 1985 formerly made limited provision for such an emergency situation. Section 5 provided that, if the Court of Protection had reason to believe that the donor of an EPA may be, or may be becoming, mentally incapable, it could exercise any power which would become exercisable on the registration of the power, provided that the court was of the opinion that it was *necessary* to do so before the power was registered. This provision was not re-enacted in Sch 4 to the MCA 2005. However, s 48 of that Act enables the court, pending the determination of an application to it, make an order or give directions in respect of any matter if –

- there is reason to believe that the person concerned lacks capacity in relation to the matter;
- the matter is one to which its powers under the Act extend; and
- it is in the best interests of the person concerned to make the order, or give the directions, without delay.

Authority only restricted when mental incapacity established

18.47 In many cases there will be no gaps between the onset of mental incapacity and the registration of the power. This is because the attorney's authority under the power is only restricted in the way described above in circumstances in which the power would have been revoked at common law (MCA 2005, Sch 4, paras 1(1) and 23(1)). That will not occur until the donor has, in fact, become mentally incapable, and in many cases the power will by then already have been registered. As we have seen at **17.19**, the attorney will have come under a duty to apply for registration at what will often be the earlier stage at which he had reason to believe the donor to be becoming mentally incapable.

No power to make gifts pending registration

18.48 As has been mentioned above, when an attorney has applied for registration of the power, then, until it is registered, the only action he can take is (a) to maintain the donor or prevent loss to his estate, or (b) to maintain himself or other persons in so far as MCA 2005, Sch 4, para 3(2) permits him to do so (Sch 4, para 1(2)). So, the attorney cannot make gifts in accordance with Sch 4, para 3(3) until the power has been registered.

The attorney may not disclaim without notifying the Public Guardian

18.49 MCA 2005, Sch 4, para 4(6) provides that, if the attorney has reason to believe that the donor is or is becoming mentally incapable, he may not disclaim his appointment under the power unless and until he gives notice of it to the Public Guardian. In contrast to the regulations regarding lasting powers of attorney, there is no prescribed form of disclaimer. The Public Guardian must notify the donor if he receives a notice of disclaimer from the attorney.

THE ATTORNEY'S AUTHORITY AND POWERS WHEN THE POWER IS REGISTERED

The attorney may act under power

18.50 Once a power has been registered, the attorney will, in principle, have the same powers as he had before the onset of the donor's mental incapacity. He may then act under the authority conferred by the power (MCA 2005, Sch 4, para 1(1)(b)).

The attorney cannot rely on the donor's further authorisation

18.51 MCA 2005, Sch 4, para 15(1)(c) provides that, once the power has been registered:

'the donor may not extend or restrict the scope of the authority conferred by the instrument and no instruction or consent given by him after registration, in the case of a consent, confers any right and, in the case of an instruction, imposes or confers any obligation or right on or creates any liability of the attorney or other persons having notice of the instruction or consent.'

Hence, whether or not he is in fact mentally incapable, the donor has no power to authorise the attorney to participate in transactions (such as making gifts) not authorised by the power. In effect, the legislation requires it to be assumed that the donor has no capacity even though he may still have capacity.

18.52 The meaning of MCA 2005, Sch 4, para 15(1)(c) (formerly the Enduring Powers of Attorney Act 1985, s 7(1)(c)) was considered by the Court of Appeal in *Day v Harris and another* [2013] COPLR 254. In June 1990 the composer, Sir Malcolm Arnold, made an EPA in which he appointed his factotum, Anthony Day, to be his sole attorney. The EPA was registered by the Court of Protection in 2002. Sir Malcolm and Mr Day also held a bank account in their joint names and, after registration of the EPA Mr Day, with Sir Malcolm's consent, signed five cheques making gifts to himself totalling £36,000. The Court of Appeal held by a majority (Lloyd and McFarlane LJ; Rix LJ dissenting) that where an EPA has been registered, what is now Sch 4, para 15(1)(c) does not regulate any other subsisting relationship between the principal and the attorney. Accordingly, Mr Day was entitled to continue to operate the joint bank account after registration of the EPA, as he had done before registration. He could not use it to benefit himself without the full free and informed consent of Sir Malcolm. However, if he had such consent, any gifts he made by drawing cheques on the joint account were not invalidated by the effect of para 15(1)(c). Rix LJ (dissenting) held that the effect of para 15(1)(c) is that after the registration of an EPA, the attorney is barred from acting upon the donor's instructions or consent to do something which is not authorised by the EPA, unless he obtains authorisation from the Court of Protection.

The attorney may apply to the Court of Protection

18.53 When the power has been registered, the attorney also has the right to apply to the Court of Protection to exercise its powers under MCA 2005, Sch 4, para 16(2), the provisions of which are considered in detail at **19.11**. For the present, it is sufficient to note that the court may authorise the attorney to take action which is not authorised by the power.

Gifts when the power is registered

18.54 When the power is registered, the attorney's power to make gifts of the donor's property in accordance with the provisions of MCA 2005, Sch 4, para 3(3) resumes. If the attorney wishes to make a more extensive gift of the donor's assets, perhaps as part of an inheritance tax-planning exercise, or wishes to make gifts on an unauthorised occasion, or for a non-charitable purpose, an application could be made to the Court of Protection for an order under MCA 2005, Sch 4, para 16(2)(e) which provides that, where an instrument has been registered:

'The court may . . . authorise the attorney to act so as to benefit himself or other persons than the donor otherwise than in accordance with paragraph 3(2) and (3) (but subject to any conditions or restrictions contained in the instrument).'

18.55 For details of the court's procedure and requirements on applications for the making of gifts of the donor's property, see Practice Direction 9F, which supplements Part 9 of the Court of Protection Rules 2007, and is headed *Applications relating to statutory wills, codicils, settlements and other dealings with P's property.*

Acting in the donor's best interests

18.56 Unlike an attorney acting under an LPA, the attorney acting under an EPA is expressly excluded from following the principles as set out in MCA 2005, s 1: Schedule 4, paragraph 1(1) (see **13.67**). However, the attorney must still make decisions in the donor's best interests (see **13.76–13.79** and **13.81–13.83**) and para 5.2 of the Code of Practice) and following the process set out in MCA 2005, s 4(1)–(7) by virtue of s 4(8)(a), which states,

'The duties imposed by subsection (1) to (7) in relation to the exercise of any powers which –
(a)   Are exercisable under a lasting power of attorney; or
(b)   Are exercisable by a person under this Act where he reasonably believes that another person lacks capacity.'

Guidance within the Code

18.57 An attorney acting under an EPA is not under a specific obligation to have regard to the code but the attorney can use it as guidance. Where a professional attorney is acting under an enduring power, it is arguably possible that he is under a duty to follow the code, as the duty would apply to him acting in a professional capacity. The code says very little specifically on EPAs, however the chapters on helping the person make his own decisions will be relevant (Chapter 3), assessing capacity (Chapter 4), best interests (Chapter 5) and paragraphs 7.58–7.64 of the Code of Practice, which set out the general fiduciary duties the attorney owes the donor. This is discussed in more detail within this publication at **13.71–13.72** (assisting the donor to make his own decisions); **13.75** (assessing capacity); **13.76–13.79**, **13.81–13.83** (best interests), **13.85** (fiduciary duties) and **13.86–13.89** (court guidance on investments).

Chapter 19

THE COURT OF PROTECTION AND ENDURING POWERS OF ATTORNEY

THE COURT OF PROTECTION

19.1 The Enduring Powers of Attorney Act 1985 conferred three functions on the Court of Protection:

- first, it was the registration authority for enduring powers of attorney (EPAs);
- secondly, it had functions as the ultimate safeguard for donors of EPAs; and
- thirdly, it was intended to provide support and assistance to attorneys when necessary.

19.2 The Mental Capacity Act 2005 (MCA 2005), s 66 and Sch 7 repealed the Enduring Powers of Attorney Act 1985, and the Public Guardian is now the registration authority for EPAs. In addition, many of the investigative functions, which were formerly vested in the court, have been transferred to the Public Guardian. However, the Court of Protection still has certain functions relating to the registration of EPAs, and the management and administration of the donor's property and affairs by an attorney acting under a registered EPA.

NO JURISDICTION TO REVIEW DECISIONS OF THE PUBLIC GUARDIAN

19.3 The Court of Protection has no jurisdiction to review decisions of the Public Guardian. Only the High Court has such jurisdiction by way of judicial review proceedings.

FUNCTIONS PRIOR TO REGISTRATION

Determining validity of power

19.4 An attorney under an EPA, who has reason to believe that the donor is or is becoming mentally incapable may, before making an application for the registration of the instrument, refer to the court for its determination any question as to the validity of the power (MCA 2005, Sch 4, para 4(5)(a)). The attorney must comply with any direction given to him by the court on that determination (Sch 4, para 4(5)(b)). The court will require forms COP1, COP1F: Supporting information relating to validity or operation of enduring power of attorney, COP 24 (witness statement in support), a copy of the EPA to be submitted, together with the court fee of £400.

19.5 This procedure may be useful in cases where the attorney is uncertain in his own mind as to whether the donor had mental capacity at the time when the power was granted. A reference to the court would avoid needless notification of relatives, and it would also avoid an attorney feeling obliged to seek to register a power if he had doubts about its validity.

19.6 Since the implementation of the MCA 2005, on 1 October 2007, this provision has been used as the means of severing ineffective or invalid provisions from EPAs, in the same way as the court can sever provisions in lasting powers of attorney (LPAs) pursuant to MCA 2005, Sch 1, para 11. The following case is an example:

> 'On 16 February 2006 NH executed an EPA in which she appointed her sister and nephew jointly and severally to be her attorneys. The instrument contained the following provision: 'In addition to the general authority conferred by this enduring power of attorney, I delegate all my trustee functions and powers whether conferred by statute general law or a trust instrument to my attorneys.'
>
> Her sister died in 2007 and the surviving attorneys, her nephews, referred the question of the validity of the trustee delegation clause in the EPA to the Court of Protection for its determination pursuant to para 4(5) of Sch 4 to the MCA 2005.
>
> The court determined that the provision would be ineffective as part of an EPA, because, since 1 March 2000, when the Trustee Delegation Act 1999 came into force, it has not been possible to create an EPA which enables the attorney to exercise any of the donor's functions as a trustee. Accordingly, the Court of Protection determined that the provision should be severed, and gave notice to the Public Guardian that it had severed the provision.'

Dispensing with the requirement to give notice of the attorney's intention to apply for registration

19.7 Before applying for registration, the attorney may make an application to the court to be dispensed from the requirement to give notice of his intention to apply for registration to:

- any relative of the donor who is entitled to receive notice by virtue of MCA 2005, Sch 4, para 6 (Sch 4, para 7(2));
- the donor (Sch 4, para 8(2)); and
- any other attorney who has been appointed to act jointly and severally and is not joining in making the application (Sch 4, para 11(1)).

19.8 The court must grant the application if it is satisfied that:

- it would be undesirable or impracticable for the attorney to give him notice (MCA 2005, Sch 4, para 7(2)(a)); or
- no useful purposes is likely to be served by giving him notice (Sch 4, para 7(2)(b)).

FUNCTIONS ON APPLICATION FOR REGISTRATION

19.9 The court's powers and duties on an application for registration of an instrument are as follows:

- on the application of the attorney, the court may direct the Public Guardian to register an instrument even though notice has not been given to a person who is entitled to receive it as required by para 4(3) and Part 3 of Sch 4 to the MCA 2005, if it is satisfied that it was undesirable or impracticable for the attorney to give notice to that person, or that no useful purpose is likely to be served by giving him notice (Sch 4, para 13(3));
- on the application of the attorney, the court may give directions in a case in which the Public Guardian has undertaken such inquiries as he thinks appropriate in all the circumstances, and as a result is satisfied that one of the grounds of objection in para 13(9) is established (Sch 4, para 13(8));
- on the application of the Public Guardian, the court may give directions regarding the registration of the instrument, if there is a deputy appointed for the donor of the power and the powers conferred on the deputy would conflict with the powers conferred on the attorney if the instrument were registered (Sch 4, para 13(2));
- on the application of the Public Guardian, the court may give directions regarding registration in any case where, before the end of the period of 5 weeks from the latest date on which the attorney gave notice in form EP1PG, the Public Guardian receives a valid notice of objection to the registration from a person entitled to receive notice of the application (Sch 4, para 13(4) and (5));
- on the application of the attorney, the court may give directions regarding the registration of an uncertified copy of the instrument (Lasting Powers of Attorney, Enduring Powers of Attorney and Public Guardian Regulations 2007 (LPA, EPA & PG Regs 2007) (SI 2007/1253), reg 24(2) and (3)).

FUNCTIONS WITH RESPECT TO REGISTERED POWERS

19.10 The Court of Protection needs to have powers after registration because the donor is no longer in a position to give instructions himself but, essentially, it is the attorney who is in charge. Registration will in most cases make little difference to the attorney's authority and duties (Law Com No 122, paragraph 4.59).

THE COURT'S FUNCTIONS AFTER REGISTRATION

The court's functions

19.11 MCA 2005, Sch 4, para 16 gives the Court of Protection wide powers to supervise the conduct of an attorney, and to see that he is exercising his powers of management and administration properly. It is specifically provided that:

(1) *The court may determine any question as to the meaning or effect of the instrument* (Sch 4, para 16(2)(a)).
This, in effect, gives the court power to rule on the true construction of the instrument.

(2) *The court may give certain directions*

(a) *Directions as to the management or disposal by the attorney of the property and affairs of the donor* (Sch 4, para 16(2)(b)(i)).
This is an important power which gives the court general authority to authorise transactions which could not otherwise be carried out, and to give directions in cases where the attorney is doubtful as to the propriety of any action - for example, if he is concerned that there is or may be a conflict of interest between himself and the donor.

(b) *Directions as to the rendering of accounts by the attorney and the production of records kept by him for the purpose* (Sch 4, para 16(2)(b)(ii)).
Technically, every attorney has a duty to keep accounts of transactions involving the donor's money (*Gray v Haig* (1854) 20 Beav 219). In practice, however, the parties may agree to other arrangements and this is no doubt common, for example, where the attorney is the donor's spouse. The scheme of the legislation is that the attorney under a registered EPA is not required as a matter of routine to prepare accounts in a special form. To impose such a requirement would, as the Law Commission recognised, not only be a burden to the attorney but also an expensive charge on the donor's estate. Accordingly, the matter is to be left to the discretion of the court. Consistent with its view that court involvement in the running of an EPA is to be 'very much more the exception than the rule' (Law Com No 122, paragraph 4.78), the Law Commission stated that it would not expect the court to call for accounts unless it had reason for believing that there was something wrong with the attorneyship, and that the attorney should certainly not be required to file annual accounts as a matter of routine (Law Com No 122, paragraph 4.83(iii)). In the light of these indications of the policy on which the legislation was based, it seems reasonable to believe that the court would be circumspect in ordering production of accounts.
The power of the court extends to requiring the attorney to produce records kept by him for the purpose of rendering accounts. An illustration of such an order can be found in *Re C (Power of Attorney)* [2000] 2 FLR 1.

(c) *Directions as to the remuneration or expenses of the attorney, whether or not in default of or in accordance with any provision made in the instrument, including directions for the repayment of excessive or the payment of additional remuneration* (Sch 4, para 16(2)(b)(iii)).
The Law Commission said that it was desirable that an EPA should state whether or not an attorney is to be remunerated and, if so, on what basis (Law Com No 122, paragraph 4.83(iv)); a view endorsed by The Law Society.

However, the court can authorise remuneration. Even if the instrument contains a charging clause, the court has power to authorise additional remuneration, or to direct remuneration at a lower level than is provided for in the instrument. Awarding a fixed annual fee might prove unsatisfactory in the event of inflation or, indeed, 'if it assumed a large volume of work which never materialised . . . ' (as above, paragraph 4.83(iv)).

Although the Law Commission accepted that an attorney who was authorised to charge might wish to apply to the court if there was a substantial and unforeseen increase in his duties, it expressed the view that the court should be circumspect in considering such requests. 'One relevant factor . . . would be the likelihood and relative desirability of the attorney disclaiming the power (in favour, perhaps, of receivership) if his request were rejected' (as above, paragraph 4.83(iv)).

The court is given a specific power to direct the repayment of excessive remuneration (Sch 4, para 16(2)(b)(iii)).

(3) *The court may require the attorney to furnish information or produce documents or things in his possession as attorney* (Sch 4, para 16(2)(c)). This power enables the Court of Protection to carry out any investigation which it considers appropriate. It also empowers the court to require the attorney to hand over the donor's property.

When the MCA 2005 came into force, on 1 October 2007, most of these investigative functions were transferred to the Public Guardian, though the Court of Protection retains residual powers of its own. Section 58(1) of the Act - the section which sets out the Public Guardian's functions - is silent on his functions with regard to EPAs, compared with LPAs. However, s 58(3) provides that the Lord Chancellor may by regulations make provision conferring on the Public Guardian other functions in connection with the Act. These regulations are LPA, EPA & PG Regs 2007.

Regulation 47 confers various powers on the Public Guardian, where it appears to him that there are circumstances suggesting that, having regard to all the circumstances (and in particular the attorney's relationship to or connection with the donor), the attorney under a registered EPA may be unsuitable to be the donor's attorney (LPA, EPA & PG Regs 2007, reg 47(1)).

In such a case the Public Guardian may require the attorney:

- to provide specified information or information of a specified description; or
- to produce specified documents or documents of a specified description. (LPA, EPA & PG Regs 2007, reg 47(2)).

'Specified' means specified in a notice in writing given to the attorney by the Public Guardian (LPA, EPA & PG Regs 2007, reg 47(5)). The information or documents must be provided or produced before the end of such reasonable period as may be specified, and at such place as may be specified (LPA, EPA & PG Regs 2007, reg 47(3)). In addition, the Public Guardian may require any information to be verified, or any document produced to be authenticated, in such manner as he may reasonably require (LPA, EPA & PG Regs 2007, reg 47(4)).

Another function of the Public Guardian is to deal with representations (including complaints) about the way in which an attorney under a registered EPA is exercising his powers (LPA, EPA & PG Regs 2007, reg 48(b)).

(4) *The court may give any consent or authorisation to act which the attorney would have to obtain from a mentally capable donor* (Sch 4, para 16(2)(d)).

This power is exercised in two main classes of cases. First, there are cases where the power itself requires that the donor's consent be obtained: for example, to the sale of the family home. In such a case, the donor himself could act prior to registration, but it is specifically provided that no consent given by him after registration shall confer any right (Sch 4, para 15(1)(c)). This is so, even if the power has been registered before the donor became mentally incapable.

The second case in which an application for the giving of consent may be brought under this head is where there is a conflict of interest between the donor and the attorney in the exercise of a power. An example of such a conflict might be where the attorney wished to buy the donor's property, albeit at full value, for himself or for a member of his family (see, generally, *Re Thompson's Settlement* [1985] 2 All ER 720). In such cases, as a matter of general agency law, the consent of the principal would be required to such a transaction, but an incapable donor could not give a valid consent (Law Com No 122, paragraph 4.83 and fn 195).

(5) *The court, may, subject to any conditions or restrictions in the instrument creating the power, authorise the attorney to act beyond the statutory powers relating to maintenance and gifts so as to benefit himself or persons other than the donor* (Sch 4, para 16(2)(e)).

The restrictions on the attorney's authority to benefit persons other than the donor himself have already been discussed at **18.30** ff. The court may, however, relax these restrictions, and give the attorney more extensive power to benefit others (including himself). In an appropriate case it could, for example, authorise gifts intended to minimise the ultimate impact of Inheritance Tax on the donor's estate.

The EPA itself cannot authorise the conferring of any benefit outside the scope of that permitted by the MCA 2005 and, even if it purports to do so, an application would still have to be made to the Court of Protection for leave to act on it.

The EPA may prohibit or restrict the exercise of the statutory powers, or make their exercise subject to conditions, and the court has no power in this jurisdiction to override the instrument in these respects (see *Re R (Enduring Power of Attorney)* [1991] 1 FLR 128).

The court's procedural requirements can be found in Practice Direction 9F – *Applications relating to statutory wills, codicils, settlements and other dealings with P's property.*

(6) *The court may relieve the attorney wholly or partly from any liability which he has or may have incurred on account of a breach of his duties as attorney* (Sch 4, para 16(2)(f)).

This power, which enables the Court of Protection to relieve an attorney from any liability for breach of duty, is comparable to the power of the court under s 61 of the Trustee Act 1925 to relieve a trustee from liability. The Trustee Act only empowers the court to grant relief if the trustee 'has acted honestly and reasonably, and ought fairly to be excused the breach of trust and for omitting to obtain the directions of the court . . . ' The Court of Protection's powers in respect of attorneys are, by contrast, unrestricted.

Wills

19.12 As already pointed out (at **18.1**) the powers conferred by a power of attorney cannot extend to the execution of a will on behalf of the donor. However, the MCA 2005, s 18(1)(i) empowers the court to authorise the execution of a statutory will or codicil for a person who lacks testamentary capacity. This power may be exercised to permit the execution of a will or codicil on behalf of the donor of an EPA, provided that the power is registered. Medical evidence must be produced to establish that the donor lacks testamentary capacity.

19.13 There is no restriction on who can bring an application for an order for the execution of a statutory will. As such the application may be made by an attorney appointed under the registered EPA; or existing beneficiaries under the donor's will; relatives who would be entitled on his intestacy; or any person for whom the donor might be expected to provide if he had capacity to do so. See, generally, Practice Direction 9F: *Applications relating to statutory wills, codicils, settlements and other dealings with P's property.*

CANCELLATION OF A REGISTERED POWER

19.14 Once a power has been registered the attorney may operate it, and third parties may deal with him, on the footing that both the power and the attorney's authority under it are valid and subsisting (MCA 2005, Sch 4, para 18). In effect, registration verifies the validity of the instrument as an EPA: (Law Com No 122, paragraph 4.88). In some cases it may be desirable to cancel the registration, and the MCA 2005 enables the court to do so in certain specified circumstances.

Confirmation of donor's revocation

19.15 Once the power has been registered, the donor, even if he then has the mental capacity to revoke the power, may not do so unless and until the court exercises its power to confirm the revocation (MCA 2005, Sch 4, paras 15(1)(a) and 16(3)). On confirming the revocation of the power, the court must direct the Public Guardian to cancel the registration of the power (Sch 4, para 16(4)(a)). Revocation is considered in detail in CHAPTER 20.

Exercise of powers under sections 16 to 20

19.16 The court must direct the Public Guardian to cancel the registration if it gives a direction revoking the power on exercising any of its functions under ss 16–20 of the MCA 2005 (Sch 4, paras 2(9)(b) and 16(4)(b)).

19.17 Occasionally an attorney under an EPA chooses to apply for his own appointment as a deputy. In such circumstances, the application will be accepted if the court considers him suitable to act in that capacity. It has been pointed out by the former Assistant Public Trustee, P.D. Lewis, at (1987) LSG 1219, that 'this may not be what the donor wished, but an attorney, even though he has executed the EPA, cannot be required to act as attorney under it'.

19.18 The fact that the court exercises its powers in relation to the donor under ss 16–20 of the MCA 2005 does not automatically mean that it will give a direction revoking the EPA. For example, when it authorises the execution of a statutory will on behalf of the donor, the court exercises its powers under s 18(1)(i) of the Act, but it is unlikely that it would order that the EPA be revoked. In an unreported decision *Re C*, on 23 January 1996 the nominated judge, Rattee J, considered a case where the donor of a registered EPA had imposed a restriction on the attorney, his wife, prohibiting her from entering into any individual transaction involving a sum exceeding £50,000. An opportunity arose for the donor to acquire the freehold of his home in central London, but the purchase price was in excess of £50,000. The judge granted the wife's application to be appointed as an *ad hoc* receiver under the Mental Health Act 1983 for the purpose of acquiring the freehold, without revoking the EPA.

Donor mentally capable

19.19 We have seen that a power may be registered even though the donor is, in fact, mentally capable, but is *becoming* mentally incapable (see **17.16**, **17.17**). However, if the court is subsequently satisfied that the donor *is and is likely to remain mentally capable*, then it must direct the Public Guardian to cancel the registration of the instrument (MCA 2005, Sch 4, para 16(4)(c)). The Law Commission suggested that 'this would involve a complete recovery rather than a return to, say, the *becoming incapable* level' (Law Com No 122, p 47).

19.20 The court will require:

- written confirmation from the donor (if he is not the applicant) that he agrees to the cancellation of the registration;
- written confirmation from the donor that he is not seeking to revoke the EPA; and
- the original of any medical report or certificate (it being a basic rule that primary evidence is preferred to secondary evidence, such as a photocopy). Medical evidence is required because the court needs to be *satisfied* that the donor is and is likely to remain mentally capable.

19.21 If the registration is cancelled under this provision, the power will remain operative unless and until the donor revokes it. Should the donor once again become incapable, the power may again be registered.

The power has expired or been revoked by the incapacity of the attorney

19.22 The court must direct the Public Guardian to cancel the registration of an instrument registered under MCA 2005, Sch 4, para 13:

' . . . on being satisfied that the power has expired or has been revoked by the mental incapacity of the attorney' (Sch 4, para 16(4)(d)).'

19.23 Once again, the court will require primary evidence of the event which has caused the power to be revoked. Expiration of an EPA is exceedingly unusual, and would occur, for example, where the donor placed a time limit of, say, 5 years on the attorney's exercise of his authority under the instrument, or if the EPA was granted for a specific purpose, such as a property sale, which has now been completed.

19.24 The wording of MCA 2005, Sch 4, para 16(4)(d) differs from that of s 8(4)(d) of the Enduring Powers of Attorney Act 1985, which it has replaced. The 1985 Act provided that the court should cancel the registration of an instrument:

' . . . on being satisfied that the power has expired or has been revoked by the death or bankruptcy of the donor or the death, mental incapacity or bankruptcy of the attorney or, if the attorney is a body corporate, its winding up or dissolution.'

19.25 The reason for the difference between these subsections is because MCA 2005, Sch 4, para 17 sets out various circumstances in which the Public Guardian must cancel the registration of an instrument creating an EPA. These are purely administrative and include cancellation:

' . . . if satisfied that the power has been revoked by the death or bankruptcy of the donor or attorney or, if the attorney is a body corporate, by its winding up or dissolution, . . .'

Power not valid at the time of registration

19.26 Registration, in effect, confirms that the power was valid and subsisting at the time when it was registered. If this assumption is subsequently found to be false, for example, by proof that the donor had effectively revoked the power prior to registration, the court must direct the Public Guardian to cancel the registration (MCA 2005, Sch 4, para 16(4)(e)).

Fraud or undue pressure

19.27 The court must direct the Public Guardian to cancel the registration if it is satisfied that fraud or undue pressure was used to induce the donor to create the power (MCA 2005, Sch 4, para 16(4)(f) and see **17.83–17.89**). The court must, also, by order, revoke the power (Sch 4, para 16(5)).

Attorney unsuitable

19.28 Finally, the court must direct the Public Guardian to cancel the registration of an instrument on being satisfied that, having regard to all the circumstances and in particular the attorney's relationship to or connection with the donor, the attorney is unsuitable to be the donor's attorney (MCA 2005, Sch 4, para 16(4)(g) and see **17.90–17.93**). Again, in such a case, the court must by order revoke the power (Sch 4, para 16(5)).

Delivering up the instrument to be cancelled

19.29 If the court directs the cancellation of the registration of an instrument under MCA 2005, Sch 4, para 16(4), unless the court directs otherwise, the instrument itself must be delivered up to the Public Guardian to be cancelled, except where the cancellation of registration is based on the court being satisfied of the donor's continuing capacity (Sch 4, para 16(6)).

COURT OF PROTECTION PROCEDURE

Introduction

19.30 The donor, his closest relatives, and any co-attorney who is not joining in making the application should have received from the applicant attorney a form EP1PG (Notice of Intention to Apply for Registration of an Enduring Power of Attorney) informing them that:

> 'You have the right to object to the proposed registration on one or more of the grounds set out below. You must notify the Office of the Public Guardian of your objection within five weeks from the day this notice was given to you. You may make an application to the Court of Protection under rule 68 of the Court of Protection Rules 2007 for a decision on the matter. No fee is payable for such an application. If you do not make such an application, the Public Guardian may ask for the court's directions about registration.'

Obtaining the forms

19.31 Anyone wishing to object to the registration of an EPA can obtain the relevant forms from the Court of Protection, First Avenue House, 42-49 High Holborn, London WC1V 6NP. The application forms can be:

- requested by phone – 0300 456 4600 from Monday to Friday, 9am to 5pm. The cost of the call depends on your phone provider and whether you use a landline or mobile;
- requested by email – courtofprotectionenquiries@hmcts.gsi.gov.uk;
- obtained from this website – https://www.gov.uk/object-registration

19.32 The applicant objecting to the registration of an EPA on prescribed grounds should refer to Practice Direction 9H: *How to start proceedings: Applications relating to the registration of an Enduring Powers of Attorney*.

The following forms will need to be completed and submitted to the court:

- COP 8 – Application relating to the registration of an enduring power of attorney with guidance notes.
- COP 24 – Witness statement.

COP 8: Application relating to the registration of an enduring power of attorney (EPA)

19.33 The applicant (objector) is asked to read first the preliminary information on the front page of COP 8 before completing the form. Among other things, this states that:

- The applicant can only use this form if he is the donor, an intended attorney or a relative of the donor who has received an EP1PG and wishes to object to the registration of the EPA or wishes to register the EPA where he has been notified by the Public Guardian that the registration has been suspended.
- There is no fee for filing this form with the court.
- Any application to object to the registration of the EPA must be filed as soon as reasonably possible after the applicant received the EP1PG notice.
- If the applicant is not one of the named persons who received an EP1PG notice, but wishes to object, he may do so, but he needs to file a COP 1 application form, instead of the COP 8, and pay the specified application fee. The applicant also needs to notify the Public Guardian of his application to the court (see **17.73-17.75**).
- The applicant is warned that he may have to pay any costs he incurs during the proceedings, and if the court considers that he has acted unreasonably, it can order him to pay any costs incurred by the other parties.

19.34 Form COP 8 itself consists of five Sections:

- *Section 1- Your details (the applicant).* The applicant must state his full name and contact details, and whether a solicitor is representing him and, if so, the solicitor's name and contact details. He is also required to state whether he is the donor, attorney or another person entitled to be notified of the application to register the EPA.
- *Section 2 – Details of the EPA.* The applicant is required to provide the full names of the donor and intended attorneys; the date on which the donor signed the EPA; and the date on which the applicant was given notice of the application to register the EPA.
- *Section 3 – Your application.* The applicant must state the directions he is seeking, and indicate his grounds for objecting to the proposed registration.
- *Section 4 – Attending court hearings.* The applicant is asked whether he needs any special assistance or facilities if the court requires him to attend a hearing.
- *Section 5 - Statement of truth.*

19.35 At the end of form COP 8 are four guidance notes:

- Notifying the Public Guardian. The applicant must notify the OPG within five weeks of receiving the EP1PG notice of his application to object by writing to: Office of the Public Guardian, PO Box 16185, Birmingham B2 2WH, or DX 744240, Birmingham 79. Upon notification, the Office of the Public Guardian will suspend the registration until the court provides further directions. If the Public Guardian is not notified there is a risk that the EPA will be registered.

- If the applicant needs special assistance or facilities for a disability or impairment (for example documents to be supplied in Braille or in large print, a hearing loop, wheelchair access, or a sign language interpreter), he is asked to set out his requirements in full.
- What the applicant needs to do next. The court requires two copies (ie the original plus one copy) of each of the documents the applicant files. He is told to send the original completed forms documents and copies to the Court of Protection, First Avenue House, 42–49 High Holborn, London WC1V 6NP.
- What happens next? The court will notify him when his application form has been issued and will return a sealed copy of the application form. He is informed that he will need to serve a copy on the donor and each attorney of the EPA.

Practice Direction 9H

19.36 Practice Direction 9H applies in respect of applications relating to the registration of an EPA. The application form COP 8 must be supported by evidence set out in either:

- a witness statement; or
- if it is verified by a statement of truth, the application form. The standard form COP8 is verified by a statement of truth.

THIRD PARTY OBJECTION TO REGISTRATION APPLICATIONS TO THE COURT

19.37 Court of Protection Rules 2007, r 68

Mental Capacity Act 2005, Sch 4, paras 2(9) and 16(4)

Mental Capacity Act 2005, s 49

Whilst an inquiry by the Public Guardian will suspend registration whilst those inquiries are being made, the Public Guardian has limited powers of investigation prior to registration. As such, a third party may seek an order from the court under rule 68 of the Court of Protection Rules 2007 on form COP1, with evidence in support, including COP1A, and a witness statement, to suspend registration; or if it has been registered, that the court revokes the EPA and directs the Public Guardian to cancel the registration: MCA 2005, Sch 4, paras 2(9) and 16(4). Ideally evidence of the donor's mental incapacity should be provided at the same time in form COP3, but where this is not possible; the applicant may ask the court for an order under s 49 MCA 2005 for a court visitor to attend the donor to ascertain his capacity. It is usually appropriate to make an application for a deputy to be appointed at the same time. Unlike an objection made by a statutory notified person, the third party will have to pay the court fee.

Other applications

19.38 Applications, other than objections to registration, relating to EPAs should generally be made by filing an application form COP 1 together with any evidence in support of the application. If the application is relating to the validity or operation of the EPA, form COP1F also needs to be submitted. In some cases, reference should be made to any relevant practice direction. For example, Practice Direction 9D, which supplements Part 9 of the COP Rules 2007, and sets out a slightly streamlined procedure which governs applications by currently appointed attorneys and donees in relation to the donor's property and affairs. Examples of applications which may be suitable for the procedure set out in Practice Direction 9D are:

- applications for regular payments from the donor's assets to an attorney in respect of remuneration;
- applications to make a gift from the donor's assets, provided that the sum in question is not disproportionately large when compared to the size of the donor's estate as a whole;
- applications to authorise a sale of the donor's property to the attorney, or a family member of the donor or attorney;
- applications for authority to obtain a copy of the donor's will;
- applications for the approval of equity releases; and
- applications for orders for sale pursuant to paras 8 and 9 of Sch 2 to the MCA 2005 (preservation of interests in property disposed of on behalf of a person lacking capacity).

Issue of application form to object to registration

19.39 The general rule is that proceedings are started when the court issues an application form at the request of the applicant (COP Rules 2007, r 62 - When proceedings are started).

19.40 When the court receives the application form COP 8 and any supporting documentation, it will issue the application by scaling the application form and returning it to the applicant with the following forms:

- COP 5 – Acknowledgment of service/notification.
- COP 14 – Proceedings about you in the Court of Protection.
- COP14A – Guidance notes for completing COP 14.
- COP 15 – Notice that an application form has been issued.
- COP15A – Guidance notes for completing COP 15.
- COP20A – Certificate of notification/non-notification of the person to whom the proceedings relate.
- COP 20B – Certificate of service/non-service, and certificate of notification. This form must be filed with the court to confirm that a document has been served or notification has been provided.

Service of documents

19.41 The COP Rules 2007, r 68(3), requires that, as soon as practicable, and in any event within 14 days of the date on which the court issued the application form, the applicant must serve on the donor and every donee of the power the following documents:

- a copy of the application form COP 8;
- copies of any documents filed with the application form; and
- an acknowledgment of service form COP 5.

19.42 The COP Rules 2007, r 68 requires that, as soon as practicable, and in any event within 14 days of the date on which the court issued the application form, the applicant must notify the persons specified ('interested persons') in the relevant practice direction. Practice Direction 9B: *Notification of others that an application has been issued*, sets out the class of people who should be notified. These are similar but not identical to the people who are to be notified of the registration of the EPA as set out in MCA 2005, para 6(1) of Sch 4. In particular, a person who is not a spouse or civil partner but who has been living with the donor as if they were, any step parents and any grandparent should be notified. If the application for objection is made by an attorney or certificate provider, the interested persons are not required to be notified (COP Rules, r 68(2)).

19.43 Interested persons should be notified that an application has been made and sent the following documents:

• form COP15; and
• form COP 5 acknowledging service.

19.44 Where the applicant knows or has reasonable grounds to believe that the donor of the power lacks capacity to make a decision in relation to any matter that is the subject of the application, he must notify the donor of the application in accordance with Part 7 of the COP Rules 2007. Practice Direction 7A: *Notifying P*, sets out the manner and detail of how the donor should be notified about the application. The donor must be notified personally by the applicant, his agent or such other person as the court directs (COP Rules 2007, r 41 and r 46) and must be provided with the following information set out in COP14, in a way that is appropriate to his circumstances (for example, using simple language, visual aids or any other appropriate means):

(a) who the applicant is;
(b) what the application is about;
(c) what will happen if the court makes the order or direction that has been applied for; and
(d) that the donor may seek advice and assistance in relation to any matter of which he is notified.

Certificate of service

19.45 Within seven days of the service of documents, the applicant must complete and return to the court the forms COP 20A (in respect of the donor) and COPB: Certificate of service/non-service and certificate of notification/non-notification (in respect of respondents (the donees) or interested persons) (COP Rules 2007, r 68(4)).

Responding to the application

19.46 The persons who have been served or notified of the application have 14 days to file their acknowledgement of service on form COP5.

Dealing with applications

19.47 Part 12 (rr 84–89) of the COP Rules 2007 sets out the manner in which the court may deal with the application. A pilot case management scheme (as set out in the Pilot Case Management Practice Direction) is in operation until 30 November 2017, which includes a property and financial affairs case management pathway. The intention is that by the end of 2017, new Court of Protection Rules will be laid with supporting Practice Directions, which will incorporate the pilot. Objections to the registration of an EPA fall within the scope of the pilot project. The judge will list the case for a Dispute Resolution Hearing or transfer the case to the most appropriate regional court outside the Central Office and Registry for listing of the Dispute Resolution Hearing and future case management. The judge may also order the respondent to file further evidence if the grounds are not clear from the submitted form COP5. A Dispute Resolution Hearing is a form of judicial mediation, to enable the court to determine whether the case can be resolved and avoid unnecessary litigation. If the parties reach agreement to settle the case, the court will make a final order if it considers it in the donor's best interests. If the parties do not reach agreement, the court will give directions for the management of the case. Subject to this, Rule 84 provides that, as soon as practicable after any application has been issued, the court may decide to:

- make a decision based on the application without a court hearing;
- give directions about the application, and the next steps to be taken; or
- fix a date for the application to be heard by the court at an attended hearing.

19.48 Subject to the pilot case management practice direction, when the court decides that it can deal with the matter without a hearing, it will do so, and serve a copy of its order on the parties and on any other person it directs (COP Rules 2007, r 84(5)).

19.49 Subject to the pilot case management practice direction, where there is an objection to the registration of an EPA, the court usually makes a preliminary directions order defining the parties and setting out a timetable for the filing of evidence in anticipation of the final hearing. In some cases, the judge may require the papers to be referred to him at a later date after additional evidence has been filed, to decide whether to deal with the application without a hearing or to list it for a final hearing. In clearly contentious cases, the matter is listed for hearing in the initial directions order.

19.50 The court may require a report to be made, pursuant to s 49 of the MCA 2005 by the Public Guardian, a Court of Protection Visitor, a local authority, or an NHS body (s 49(2) and (3)). Further information on s 49 reports can be found in rr 117 and 118, and Practice Direction 14E, which supplements Part 14 of the COP Rules 2007.

Reconsideration of orders made without a hearing

19.51 Where the court makes an order without a hearing, the donor, any party to the proceedings, or anyone else who is affected by the order may apply to the court for reconsideration of the order made (COP Rules 2007, r 89(2)).

An application for reconsideration must be made in accordance with Part 10 of the COP Rules 2007, using a COP 9: Application notice, within 21 days of the order being served (r 89(3)).

19.52 In *Re S & S (Protected Persons)* [2008] COPLR Con Vol 1074, at paras 61 and 62, Her Honour Judge Hazel Marshall QC described the procedure under rule 89 as follows:

'. . . Such a reconsideration is not an appeal. The processes in the Court of Protection are intended to give the court wide flexibility to reach a decision quickly, conveniently and cost effectively where it can, whilst still preserving a proper opportunity for those affected by its orders to have their views taken into account in full argument if necessary. To that end, on receiving an application, the court can make a decision on the papers, or direct a full hearing, or make any order as to how the application can best be dealt with. This will often lead to a speedy decision made solely on paper which everyone is content to accept, but any party still has the right to ask for a reconsideration.

If this occurs, the court should approach the matter as if making the decision afresh, not on the basis that the question is whether there is a justifiable attack on the first order. The party making the application has not had a proper opportunity to be heard, and should be allowed one without feeling that s/he suffers from the disadvantage of having been placed in the position of an appellant by an order made without full consideration of his points or his views.'

Decision to hold an attended hearing

19.53 In considering whether it is necessary to hold a hearing, r 84(3) of the COP Rules 2007 requires the court to have regard to:

(a)   the nature of the proceedings and the orders sought;

(b)   whether the application is opposed by a person who appears to the court to have an interest in matters relating to the donor's best interests;

(c)   whether the application involves a substantial dispute of fact;

(d)   the complexity of the facts and the law;

(e)   any wider public interest in the proceedings;

(f)   the circumstances of the donor and any party, in particular as to whether their rights would be adequately protected if a hearing were not held;

(g)   whether the parties agree that the court should dispose of the application without a hearing; and

(h)   any other matter specified in the relevant practice direction.

COP 28: Notice of hearing

19.54 If the court decides to hold an attended hearing, the applicant and all others involved in the application will receive a directions order made by a judge or a form COP 28: Notice of hearing. This form sets out the date, time, and location of the hearing, and states whether it is for directions only, disposing of the matter, or for any other purpose. In practice, the form is never used because any notice of hearing is given in a judge's directions order.

19.55 Within 14 days of receiving the directions order or COP 28, and no later than 14 days before the date of the hearing, the applicant, or the person effecting notification on his behalf, must inform the donor of the date of the hearing using form COP 14: Proceedings about you in the Court of Protection (COP Rules 2007, r 42(1)). The person effecting notification must also inform the donor that he may seek legal advice and assistance in relation to the hearing (r 42(4)). The applicant must then complete and return the form COP 20A: Certificate of service/non-service within seven days of making that notification.

Hearings

19.56 The general rule is that a Court of Protection hearing is held in private (COP Rules 2007, r 90(1)), and that the only persons entitled to attend are:

(a)   the parties;
(b)   the donor (whether or not a party);
(c)   any person acting in the proceedings as litigation friend;
(d)   any legal representatives of the above; and
(e)   any court officer (r 90(2)).

19.57 However, the court may make an order:

•   authorising any person, or class of persons to attend the hearing or part of it; or exclude any person, or class of persons, from attending a hearing or part of it (COP Rules 2007, r 90(3));
•   authorising the publication of such information relating to the proceedings as it may specify, or the publication of the text or summary of the whole or part of a judgment or order made by the court (r 91(2)); and
•   for the hearing, or part of it, to be held in public, and excluding any person or class of persons from attending a public hearing (r 92(1)).

19.58 The Court of Protection is running a 'Transparency Pilot' to increase access to the court for members of the public and media, which has altered the default position so hearings are held in public, subject to reporting restrictions, until 30 November 2017.The intention is that by the end of 2017, new Court of Protection Rules will be laid with supporting Practice Directions, which will incorporate the pilot. The Transparency Pilot Practice Direction, with a sample court order can be found at https://www.judiciary.gov.uk/publications/transp arency-pilot-court-of-protection/. Further information about hearings, including reporting restrictions, can be found in Practice Direction 13A, which supplements Part 13 of the COP Rules 2007.

19.59 Attended hearings take place either at the central registry of the Court of Protection at First Avenue House, 42–49 High Holborn, London WC1V 6NP, or at a regional hearing venue. Arrangements have been made with HM Courts & Tribunals Service for judges nominated under s 46(1) of the MCA 2005 to hear contested Court of Protection applications in courts in most of the major cities in England and Wales.

Notifying the donor of the final order

19.60 The donor must be notified of the final order of the court (COP Rules 2007, r 44(1)) within 14 days of its being made (r 46(3)). The person effecting notification must explain to the donor the effect of the order, and inform the donor that he may seek advice and assistance in relation to the order (r 44(2) and (3)). This is done using form COP 14: Proceedings about you in the Court of Protection. The person effecting notification must complete and return a COP 20: Certificate of service/non-service within seven days of making the notification (r 48). The court can, however, dispense with this requirement (r 49).

Chapter 20

REVOCATION, DISCLAIMER AND TERMINATION OF ENDURING POWERS

INTRODUCTION

The common law

20.1 At common law there are three main ways in which a power of attorney may come to an end.

(1) *Revocation by act of donor*
First, the power may be revoked by the donor. Normally, he may do so in any circumstances and without obtaining any consent. Revocation may be express (in which case it will usually be by deed), or it may be implied by the doing of an act which is incompatible with the continued operation of the power.

(2) *Disclaimer by attorney*
Secondly, the power may be revoked by renunciation or disclaimer on the part of the attorney. At common law the attorney is (in the absence of any provision to that effect in the instrument creating the power) under no duty to act and, in principle, may disclaim at any time.

(3) *Operation of law*
Thirdly, the power may come to an end by operation of law - for example, where the donor dies or becomes mentally incapable (*Drew v Nunn* (1879) 4 QBD 661).

The policy of the legislation

20.2 The fundamental principle underlying the Enduring Powers of Attorney Act 1985, most of which has been re-enacted and can now be found in Sch 4 to the Mental Capacity Act 2005 (MCA 2005), was that an enduring power of attorney (EPA) should not come to an end solely by reason of the donor's loss of mental capacity, and this aspect of revocation need not be further considered here. However, the Act had to make a number of special provisions dealing with disclaimer and revocation in other circumstances for two reasons. First, it is possible that the donor of a power will seek to revoke it at a time when the attorney believes that the donor has become or is becoming mentally incapable. Secondly, the attorney might wish to disclaim his appointment under the power, and this might leave the donor without anyone to look after his affairs in circumstances in which the donor could be exposed to risk.

20.3 We consider, first, the rules governing the revocation of an EPA by the donor; secondly, the rules governing disclaimer; and, finally, the position about termination by operation of law.

REVOCATION

20.4 An EPA may be revoked in one of three ways: first, automatically; secondly, by act of the donor; and thirdly, by the court. Despite being the registration authority, the Public Guardian can only not register an instrument or cancel the registration, and has no power to revoke an EPA.

Automatic revocation

20.5 An EPA is revoked by the bankruptcy of the donor or attorney or the making of a debt relief order (under Part 7A of the Insolvency Act 1986) in respect of the donor or attorney (MCA 2005, Sch 4, para 2(7), as amended by The Tribunals, Courts and Enforcement Act 2007 (Consequential Amendments) Order 2012 (SI 2012/2404), Sch 2, para 53). This reflects the position at common law (*Marwick v Hardingham* (1880) 15 Ch D 339). A power coupled with an interest is an exception to this rule. However, where the donor is bankrupt merely because an interim bankruptcy restrictions order has effect in respect of him, the power is suspended for so long as the order has effect (Sch 4, para 2(8)). In Sch 4, para 2(7), the reference to the making of a debt relief order (under Part 7A of the Insolvency Act 1986) in respect of the attorney is to be read as a reference to the making of a debt relief order in respect of the last remaining attorney under the power; and the making of a debt relief order in respect of any other attorney under the power causes that person to cease to be an attorney under the power.

Revocation by act of the donor

20.6 *Until an application for registration has been made*, the donor may revoke the power in exactly the same way as he can at common law. If he does so, and an application is subsequently made for the registration of the power, the fact that the power created by the instrument no longer subsists is a ground on which the donor or anyone else may validly object to registration (MCA 2005, Sch 4, para 13(9)(b)). If this ground of objection is established, the court must direct the Public Guardian not to register the instrument (Sch 4, para 13(10)).

20.7 *After registration* no revocation of a power by the donor is valid unless and until the court confirms the revocation under the procedure mentioned below (MCA 2005, Sch 4, para 15(1)(a)). The reason for this was explained by the Law Commission, in its report, *The Incapacitated Principal* (1983) Law Com No 122, paragraph 4.72, as follows:

'The significance of this recommendation lies in the importance we attach to the ability of the attorney and third parties to rely on the fact of registration as verifying the validity of the instrument. Much of this reliance would be jeopardised if the donor were permitted to make informal revocations of his registered power. The attorney and third parties would often be uncertain whether the revocations were effective; that is, whether the donor retained sufficient capacity to revoke. We suspect that in many cases third parties would play safe and refuse to deal with the attorney further. This might not be in the donor's interests especially since the third parties might be wary of dealing with him as well. We therefore feel that, in these cases, the attorney and third parties should be entitled to act on the strength of the registered power until such time as the donor's purported revocation had been confirmed by the court.'

20.8 This provision effectively deprives a donor who still retains mental capacity but is 'becoming incapable' of the right to revoke, even though he could have done so if the power had not been registered. The Law Commission said:

'A desire to revoke after registration might be perfectly legitimate but would, perhaps, be more likely to be attributable to a measure of mental incapacity rendering the continuation of the power more beneficial to the donor than its revocation.' (Law Com No 122, paragraph 4.73).

20.9 If a donor wishes to revoke a registered power, he must apply to the Court of Protection to confirm the revocation (MCA 2005, Sch 4, para 15(1)(a)). The court will only confirm the revocation if it is satisfied that the donor (a) has done whatever is necessary in law to effect an express revocation of the power, and (b) was mentally capable of revoking a power of attorney when he did so. It is immaterial whether or not he is still capable at the time when the court considers the application (Sch 4, para 16(3)).

20.10 The expression 'whatever is necessary in law to effect an express revocation of the power' is not defined in the MCA 2005. The most satisfactory way of expressly revoking a power is for the donor to execute a deed of revocation. However, what is important is not so much the method used to revoke the power, but the notice given to the attorney. On its own, revocation is insufficient because the attorney's authority under the power does not cease until he is given notice of the revocation (*Re Oriental Bank, ex parte Guillemin* (1884) 28 Ch D 634).

A later EPA does not necessarily revoke an earlier one

20.11 In *Re E (a donor)* [2000] 3 WLR 1974 it was held that the execution of a later EPA does not automatically revoke an earlier EPA. The facts were as follows. Mrs E had three daughters, X, Y and Z. In 1992 she made an EPA appointing Y and Z jointly to be her attorneys. In 1997 she executed another EPA appointing all three daughters to act jointly as her attorneys. However, the words 'save that any two of my attorneys may sign' were inserted by hand after the printed word 'jointly'. X applied unilaterally to register the 1997 power, but the application was rejected because the condition that two of the three attorneys could act was incompatible with a joint appointment for the purposes of s 11(1) of the Enduring Powers of Attorney Act 1985 (now MCA 2005, Sch 4, para 20(1)). Y and Z then applied to register the 1992 power. X, who was not on the best of terms with her sisters, objected to registration inter alia on the ground that the 1992 power no longer subsisted, having been revoked by the donor's mere execution of the 1997 power. The Master of the Court of Protection dismissed the objection because there was no evidence that the donor had *animus revocandi*, and that in the 1997 power the donor was confirming the appointment of Y and Z as her attorneys and attempting unsuccessfully to add another attorney. X appealed.

20.12 On 21 February 2000, Arden J (as she then was) dismissed the appeal and, held as follows:

'I accept the appellant's submission that the 1997 power takes effect as an ordinary power even if it cannot take effect as an EPA. The 1997 power is therefore capable of being used prior to the donor becoming mentally incapable. However, in my judgment, the 1992 power has not been revoked by the execution of the 1997 power and the reasons for my conclusion are as follows.

The general law of agency in my judgment shows that to amount to revocation by conduct, the conduct must be inconsistent with the continuation of the agency. Contrary to the appellant's submission, this in my judgment means more than that the conduct should be reasonably understood as amounting to revocation. To be *inconsistent*, it must be unambiguous in its effect. . . .

The onus is on the appellant to show that the 1992 power has been revoked. Accordingly, she has to show that the donor must have intended to revoke the 1992 power. It is not enough to show that the donor must have forgotten about the 1992 power or made no reference to it. Indeed if she had forgotten about it that would suggest that she did not intend to revoke it. As the passages cited by the Master from the Law Commission's report show, it is not the policy of the 1985 Act to prohibit successive EPAs. . . .

There is no contemporaneous evidence as to the donor's intentions, or even any later evidence from her as to what she intended. All that is known is that she did not expressly revoke the 1992 power when she executed the 1997 power. . . .

I do not consider that it is clear that the 1997 power revokes the 1992 power. There is no reason why the donor should not want to preserve the possibility that the 1992 power might be used if for some reason the 1997 power could not be used. She did not know that the 1997 power was not valid as an EPA when she signed it, but there is no reason why she should not have wanted to cover the situation that it might be invalid. To have several simultaneous powers would be a legitimate and understandable wish, and not an irrational one as suggested by the appellant.'

Capacity to revoke an EPA

20.13 The meaning of the expression 'mentally capable of revoking a power of attorney' is not entirely clear. It has been held that the same degree of capacity is required to revoke a will as to make one (*Re Sabatini* (1970) 114 SJ 35), and it could be argued that the same principle applies to an EPA. Indeed, in some common law jurisdictions, the relevant legislation provides that 'a person is capable of revoking a continuing power of attorney if he or she is capable of giving one' (Ontario, Substitute Decisions Act 1992, s 8(2)). Accordingly, if the donor of the power has *Re K, Re F* capacity (see **16.4–16.10**) at the time of revocation, he would be mentally capable of revoking the power of attorney, regardless of whether he is mentally capable of managing and administering his property and affairs generally.

20.14 However, it could also be argued that the revocation of an EPA is an entirely different transaction from the creation of such a power. 'The mental capacity required by the law in respect of any instrument is relative to the particular transaction which is being effected by means of the instrument, and may be described as the capacity to understand the nature of that transaction when it is explained.' (*Gibbons v Wright* (1954) 91 CLR 423, 438 per Dixon CJ).

20.15 The creation and revocation of an EPA are different transactions involving different thought processes. The discretion exercised by the court when initially appointing a person to manage the finances of an incapacitated person is different from the discretion it exercises when removing a manager who is already in place (*Holt v Protective Commissioner* (1993) 31 NSWLR 227, 241 (New South Wales Court of Appeal)). In such a case it has to be shown that either (a) the manager is incompetent or has acted unlawfully or improperly or that there is a conflict of interest or duty, or (b) it is otherwise in the protected person's best interests to remove the installed manager. The thought process behind the revocation of an EPA is similar, and usually involves a change in circumstances or some measure of dissatisfaction with the existing attorney or the manner in which he has performed his duties.

20.16 At first instance, the Court of Protection has preferred this second line of authority, and has held (in *Re S* (unreported), Master Lush, 13 March 1997 and more recently in *Re KJP* [2016] EWCOP 6) that for it to be satisfied that a donor understands the nature and effect of the transaction of revoking a power, it has to be shown that, having received in broad terms and simple language an explanation of the nature and effect of the transaction, the donor understands:

- who the attorneys are;
- what authority they have;
- why it is necessary or expedient to revoke the power; and
- the foreseeable consequences of revoking the power.

20.17 In contrast, to revoke a lasting power of attorney, the donor is expected to also understand why he originally made the power (see the decision of District Judge Glentworth in *SAD and ACD v SED*, Case no. 12791319 (Unreported) (4 November 2016)).

20.18 One of the foreseeable consequences of revoking the power would be, in a case where the power is already registered, that the revocation will not be valid unless and until it is confirmed by the Court of Protection. Another is that the donor should understand revocation means he will not have anyone appointed to make property and financial decisions for him, which may result in the court appointing a deputy or if he has sufficient mental capacity, he may make a lasting power of attorney.

20.19 In *Re Cloutt* (7 November 2008), Senior Judge Lush held that capacity to revoke an EPA is not necessarily the same as the capacity to create an LPA. Mrs Cloutt was born in 1921 and lived in County Durham. In October 2000, she made an EPA appointing NatWest Bank to be her attorney. The EPA was registered on 31 March 2008. A few days later, on 3 April 2008, the donor executed an LPA for property and affairs appointing as her attorney a distant cousin, who had been notified of the NatWest Bank's intention to register the EPA. At the same time, she executed a deed revoking the EPA. The certificate in Part B of the LPA was completed by a consultant in old age psychiatry, who confirmed that he was satisfied that Mrs Cloutt had the capacity to make an LPA, and in June 2008 the attorney under the LPA applied to the court for an order confirming the revocation of the EPA, pursuant to MCA 2005, Sch 4, para 16(3). The Senior Judge made a directions order requiring the submission of further evidence on the ground that the revocation of an EPA was a different transaction from the creation of an LPA, and that capacity to create an LPA was not necessarily the same as the capacity to revoke an EPA. Thus, a doctor's certification of an LPA is not of itself sufficient proof of capacity to revoke an EPA. On considering the further evidence provided by the doctor and the donor's solicitor, the court was satisfied that the donor had capacity to revoke the EPA, and a final order was made confirming the revocation of the EPA and directing the Public Guardian to cancel its registration.

Revocation by the court

20.20 The court may revoke an EPA in two circumstances:

(1) *Valid objection*
The Court of Protection is obliged by order to revoke the power created by the instrument if it is satisfied that (i) fraud or undue pressure was used to induce the donor to create the power, or (ii) having regard to all the circumstances, and in particular the attorney's relationship to or connection with the donor, the attorney is unsuitable to be the donor's attorney (MCA 2005, Sch 4, paras 13(9)(d) and (e) and 13(11), or, where the instrument has already been registered, Sch 4, paras 16(4)(f) and (g) and 16(5)). When doing so it must direct the Public Guardian not to register the instrument or to cancel the registration of the instrument (Sch 4, paras 13(10) and 16(5)). For consideration of what is meant by being 'unsuitable' see **17.90–17.93**. For the position regarding an 'unsuitable' attorney who has been appointed to act jointly and severally with others, see **21.30**.

(2) *On exercising powers under ss 16–20 of the MCA 2005*
The court may give a direction revoking the power on exercising any of its powers (principally that of appointing a deputy) under ss 16–20 of the MCA 2005 (Sch 4, para 2(9)), and directing the Public Guardian to cancel the registration of the instrument (Sch 4, para 16(4)(b)). The court does not always revoke the power on exercising its powers under ss 16–20 of the MCA 2005. For example, if the attorney applied to the court for a statutory will to be executed on behalf of the donor, although the order would be made under s 18(1)(i) of the Act, it is highly improbable that the court would direct that the EPA be revoked.

DISCLAIMER

20.21 An attorney normally has an unrestricted right to disclaim or renounce a power of attorney, but this is not true of an EPA. MCA 2005, Sch 4, para 2(10) provides that 'no disclaimer of an enduring power, whether by deed or otherwise, is valid unless and until the attorney gives notice of it to the donor or, where paragraph 4(6) or 15(1) applies, to the Public Guardian'.

20.22 As the Law Commission said, the reason for such notification is to 'alert the capable donor to the fact that he could no longer rely on the attorney to act for him: the donor would thereby be able to consider making alternative arrangements' (Law Com No 122, paragraph 4.32).

20.23 It is not necessary for a notice of disclaimer to be made by deed, and (unlike the position with regard to lasting powers of attorney) there is no prescribed form of disclaimer. Nor is it necessary for the attorney to give his or her reasons for disclaiming. If the attorney is one of two or more attorneys who have been appointed jointly (rather than jointly and severally) the remaining attorneys will no longer have the authority to act under the EPA. The Office of the Public Guardian has created a standard disclaimer form EP5, which can be downloaded from https://www.gov.uk/government/publications /disclaim-an-enduring-power-of-attorney.

Notice to the Public Guardian required after onset of incapacity

20.24 If an attorney has reason to believe that the donor is or is becoming mentally incapable, the attorney cannot disclaim simply by giving notice to the donor. Instead, the attorney must give notice of the disclaimer to the Public Guardian, and the disclaimer is not valid unless and until he has done so (MCA 2005, Sch 4, para 4(6)). The same is true if the power is registered (Sch 4, para 15(1)(b)). Where the Public Guardian receives a notice under Sch 4, para 4(6), he must notify the donor of the power. There is no requirement for the Public Guardian to notify the donor if the instrument is registered and he receives a notice of disclaimer under Sch 4, para 15(1)(b).

Right to disclaim is preserved

20.25 The effect of these provisions is not to prevent the attorney disclaiming. It is merely to ensure that the Public Guardian is notified. As the Law Commission said, 'the donor is not to be abandoned, once he is no longer capable, without alternative arrangements for his welfare being made . . . and it would be for the court to decide whether a receivership or other order should be made for the donor' (Law Com No 122, paragraph 4.55). The Law Commission envisaged that 'few attorneys would disclaim lightly . . . especially since they would often be close relatives and feel a strong moral obligation to continue' (as above, paragraph 4.56).

TERMINATION BY OPERATION OF LAW

20.26 An EPA will come to an end on the death of the donor, or on the death or mental incapacity of a sole attorney, or a joint attorney, or the surviving attorney of attorneys who were appointed to act jointly and severally.

20.27 An EPA is revoked by the bankruptcy of the donor or attorney (MCA 2005, Sch 4, para 2(7)). However, where the donor or attorney is bankrupt merely because an interim bankruptcy restrictions order has effect in respect of him, the power is suspended for so long as the order has effect (Sch 4, para 2(8)).

20.28 MCA 2005, Sch 4, para 17 stipulates that the Public Guardian must cancel the registration of an instrument creating an EPA if he is satisfied that 'the power has been revoked by the death or bankruptcy of the donor or attorney or, if the attorney is a body corporate, by its winding up or dissolution'.

20.29 The provisions of MCA 2005, Sch 4, paras 2(7), 2(8) and 17 were amended by The Tribunals, Courts and Enforcement Act 2007 (Consequential Amendments) Order 2012 (SI 2012/2404), Sch 2, Art 53, to include references to the making of a debt relief order under Part 7A of the Insolvency Act 1986.

20.30 The court must direct the Public Guardian to cancel the registration of an instrument if it is satisfied that the power has been revoked by the mental incapacity of the attorney (MCA 2005, Sch 4, para 16(4)(d)).

20.31 In contrast to lasting powers of attorney, there is no automatic revocation of the attorney's appointment if the donor's marriage or civil partnership to the attorney is dissolved or annulled. Unless the attorney was willing to disclaim, an application would need to be made to the court for the removal of the attorney on the basis that having regard to all the circumstances and in particular, the attorney's relationship to or connection with the donor, the attorney is unsuitable to be the donor's attorney. See **19.38** which contains detail of the court's procedure.

TERMINATION BY EFFLUXION OF TIME

20.32 If an EPA is granted for a limited period of time, it will come to an end on the expiry of that period. MCA 2005, Sch 4, para 16(4)(d) provides that the court must direct the Public Guardian to cancel the registration of the power if it is satisfied that the power has expired.

Chapter 21

APPOINTMENT OF MORE THAN ONE ATTORNEY

INTRODUCTION

Appointments under ordinary powers

21.1 Donors of powers of attorney commonly appoint two or more attorneys to act. The attorneys may be joint attorneys (in which case all of them must join together in a transaction), or they may be joint and several attorneys (in which case each attorney may act by himself, with the same effect as if all the attorneys had joined in the transaction).

21.2 Sometimes, a power of attorney appoints successive attorneys - for example, the instrument might appoint Adam to be the donor's attorney but provide that, if Adam ceased for any reason to be an attorney, then Ben should assume his powers instead. Alternatively, the instrument might give Adam the right to appoint another attorney to act in his place. It is possible (although the Law Commission thought that it was rarely done (Law Com No 122, fn 211)) to appoint an alternative attorney: someone who will act if the donor's first choice is unable to take up the appointment.

Application to enduring powers

21.3 The Mental Capacity Act 2005 (MCA 2005), Sch 4 contains a number of complicated provisions dealing with the appointment of more than one attorney. In particular, special provision has to be made because of the essential difference between joint powers on the one hand and joint and several powers on the other. As the Law Commission said:

'Any matter affecting the capacity of an attorney under a joint power to operate his power affects all his co-attorneys also since they cannot act without him. Where, however, the power is joint and several the incapacity of one will not, generally, prejudice the capacity of the other attorneys. This difference creates a measure of complexity for some aspects of our proposed EPA scheme since the validity of the power and the attorneys authority under it may differ according to whether the power is joint or joint and several. Furthermore, the very fact that more than one attorney has been appointed raises questions which cannot necessarily be answered by applying to such cases our recommendations as they apply to sole attorneys.' (Law Com No 122, paragraph 4.94).

ONLY JOINT OR JOINT AND SEVERAL APPOINTMENTS PERMITTED

Appointment of substitute attorneys

21.4 MCA 2005, Sch 4, para 20(1) provides that an instrument which appoints more than one person to be an attorney cannot create an EPA unless the attorneys are appointed to act (a) jointly or (b) jointly and severally. This provision was originally intended to prevent an instrument from qualifying as an EPA if it provides for one or more attorneys to replace the original attorneys should he or they cease to act.

21.5 Having identified three different types of appointment, namely (1) a sole attorney, (2) joint attorneys, and (3) joint and several attorneys, at footnote 211 of *The Incapacitated Principal* the Law Commission said:

'There is a fourth type of appointment, the alternative attorney, who can only act if the donor's first choice is unable to take up the attorneyship. This type does, however, appear to be used but rarely under the existing law and we would not envisage its use under our proposed EPA scheme.'

21.6 In footnote 214 the Law Commission went on to say:

' . . . We do not recommend that an instrument should be able to provide for successive EPAs; that is, one or more attorneys who would replace the original attorney or attorneys should he or they cease to act. Our main reason for this is that the benefit to be gained by including successive EPAs . . . would be out of all proportion to the complexity that such powers would create in relation to some of the more detailed areas of our scheme. In any event, successive EPAs are rendered largely unnecessary because a joint and several EPA would permit the continuation of the EPA in the event of one of the attorneys ceasing to act'. (Law Com No 122, p 50, fn 214).

21.7 The statute also expressly provides that a power of attorney which gives the attorney a right to appoint a substitute or successor cannot be an EPA (MCA 2005, Sch 4, para 2(6)).

21.8 It is not clear that the legislation has given effect to the Law Commission's view that it should not be possible within the EPA scheme to provide for the appointment of an alternative attorney: one who can only act if the donor's first choice is unable to take up the attorneyship. It would seem to be at least open to argument that an EPA which appoints 'A or, if A is unable to take up office as my attorney, B' is not 'an instrument which appoints more than one person to be an attorney' within the meaning of the prohibition contained in MCA 2005, Sch 4, para 20(1), and it would appear that the Court of Protection took this view from the early days of the implementation of the EPA scheme (see P.D. Lewis, formerly the Assistant Public Trustee, (1986) LSG 3566 at p 3567; see also Law Commission, *Mental Incapacity*, Law Com No 231 (1995), p 114, fn 55).

Attorneyship cannot run with title

21.9 Although, in general, a power of attorney given to secure a proprietary interest may be given to the person entitled to the interest and to persons deriving title under him (s 4(2) of the Powers of Attorney Act 1971), such a power could not be an enduring power because of the provisions of the MCA 2005, Sch 4, para 2(6). However, this is unlikely to be of practical importance, since such powers would not in any event be revoked by the incapacity of the donor.

A way of providing for a succession of attorneys

21.10 In the earlier editions of this book it was suggested that the most satisfactory way of creating what the Law Commission described (Law Com No 122, p 50, fn 214) as the 'effect of successiveness' within the EPA scheme was for the donor to make EPAs in separate instruments with the result that the authority of an attorney under one power would commence only upon the termination of the authority under another power.

21.11 In *Re J (Enduring Power of Attorney)* [2009] COPLR Con Vol 753, Lewison J (as he then was) could see no reason why the Public Guardian should not register an EPA in which there was the following successive appointment: 'I . . . appoint my wife [W] to be my Attorney for the purposes of the Enduring Powers of Attorney Act 1985 but if she shall have predeceased me or shall be unable to act or to continue to act as my attorney whether registered or unregistered then in the alternative I appoint my son [A] and my son [B] and my son [C] jointly and severally to be my attorney(s) for the purpose of the Enduring Powers of Attorney Act 1985 with general authority to act on my behalf in relation to all my property and affairs.'

21.12 In paragraph [25] of his judgment, Lewison J held that:

> 'The persons named in the instrument as actual or contingent attorneys are, I think, within the meaning of the word 'attorney' as used in par 20 of the Schedule. So para 20 is engaged where an enduring power purports to appoint successive attorneys. . . . . Provided that an instrument makes this clear it complies with para 20. If and so far as additional words need to be added to the prescribed form to repeat the designation of each set of attorneys, this is permitted by reg 2. In my judgment, this is a permissible reading of para 20, and I hold that it is the correct one. I further consider that this construction applies whether the power of attorney purports to appoint attorneys in the alternative or in succession. What is important is that the power makes clear whether, while they are acting, the attorneys are to act jointly, or jointly and severally.'

JOINT ATTORNEYS

21.13 The advantage of making the appointment joint is that the donor has an added measure of security against dishonesty or even imprudence. But the death, disclaimer or bankruptcy of any joint attorney will effectively terminate the power.

21.14 Generally speaking, the legislation applies to joint attorneys collectively as it applies to a single attorney (MCA 2005, Sch 4, para 20(2)). Hence, all the attorneys come under a duty to apply for registration if they have reason to believe that the donor is or is becoming mentally incapable (Sch 4, para 4(1)). Presumably, the duty arises if only one attorney has 'reason to believe', but it is not easy to see how the other attorneys could come under such a duty if they were unaware of the facts which have created it. The legislation is modified in its application to joint attorneys in a number of minor respects, and is considered below at **21.15–21.24.**

Time when attorney must satisfy conditions as to age and solvency

21.15 A power of attorney cannot be an EPA unless, when he executes the instrument creating it, the attorney is an individual who has reached 18 and is not bankrupt (MCA 2005, Sch 4, para 2(5)(a)). The relevant time for determining whether those conditions are satisfied in respect of joint appointments is the time when the second or last attorney executes the instrument (Sch 4, para 21(1)).

21.16 Thus, if the donor had appointed his wife and two children to be joint attorneys, the instrument would be capable of taking effect as an EPA, notwithstanding the fact that one child was under 18 at the time when his mother and the elder child executed it, provided that the younger child was eighteen or over when he executed it. However, it would seem that, unless and until he does execute the instrument, it cannot take effect as an EPA.

21.17 It has not been possible to create an EPA since the MCA 2005 came into force on 1 October 2007. The Office of the Public Guardian (OPG) will not register an EPA appointing joint attorneys, unless both or all of them had signed Part C of the prescribed form before 1 October 2007.

Substitute attorneys

21.18 If the power purports to give *any* of the joint attorneys the right to appoint a substitute or successor, it cannot be an EPA (MCA 2005, Sch 4, paras 2(6) and 21(2)).

Attorney's bankruptcy

21.19 An EPA will be revoked if *any* joint attorney becomes bankrupt (MCA 2005, Sch 4, paras 2(7) and 21(2)). It will not be saved as respects the attorneys who were not affected by the bankruptcy. Where an attorney is bankrupt merely because an interim bankruptcy restrictions order has effect in respect of him, the power is suspended for so long as the order has effect (Sch 4, paras 2(8) and 21(2)). The other attorney(s) cannot act under the power for so long as the interim bankruptcy restrictions order has effect.

21.20 The provisions of MCA 2005, Sch 4, paras 2(7), 2(8) and 17 were amended by The Tribunals, Courts and Enforcement Act 2007 (Consequential Amendments) Order 2012 (SI 2012/2404), Sch 2, Art 53, to include references to the making of a debt relief order under Part 7A of the Insolvency Act 1986.

Valid grounds of objection

21.21 The fact that *any* of the attorneys under a joint power is unsuitable to be the donor's attorney, having regard to all the circumstances and, in particular, the attorney's relationship to or connection with the donor, is a valid ground of objection (MCA 2005, Sch 4, paras 13(9)(e) and 21(3)). If this ground of objection is made out, the court must direct the Public Guardian not to register the instrument, notwithstanding the fact that the other named attorneys would still be perfectly good appointments. The court has no power to authorise the appointment of another attorney in place of the one found to be unsuitable.

Powers of the court once the power is registered

21.22 The powers of the court after registration (for example, the power to require the attorney to furnish information or produce documents) are exercisable in respect of any attorney under the power (MCA 2005, Sch 4, paras 16(2) and 21(4)). Similar provisions apply to the court's duty to direct the Public Guardian to cancel the registration of the instrument if, for example, the court is satisfied that, having regard to all the circumstances and in particular the attorney's relation to or connection with the donor, the attorney is unsuitable to be the donor's attorney (Sch 4, paras 16(4) and 21(5)).

Powers of the Public Guardian once the power is registered

21.23 As a result of the separation of functions between the Court of Protection and the Public Guardian, the Public Guardian has power to require the attorneys to provide specified information or produce specified documents (Lasting Powers of Attorney, Enduring Powers of Attorney and Public Guardian Regulations 2007 (LPA, EPA & PG Regs 2007) (SI 2007/1253), reg 47). Presumably, by analogy to MCA 2005, Sch 4, para 21(4), though it is not expressly stated in the regulations, this power is exercisable in respect of any attorney appointed to act jointly.

21.24 There are, however, express provisions relating to the Public Guardian's duty to cancel the registration of an instrument creating an EPA on receipt of a disclaimer, etc, where references to the attorney are to be read as including any attorney under the power (MCA 2005, Sch 4, paras 17 and 21(6)).

JOINT AND SEVERAL ATTORNEYS

21.25 The main advantage of the donor appointing joint and several attorneys is that action may have to be taken when one of the attorneys is for any reason unable or unwilling to act. Whilst such an appointment runs the risk that an attorney may be unaware of another attorney's dishonesty or imprudence, it has the advantage that the death, disclaimer or bankruptcy of any joint and several attorney will not terminate the power. The legislation cannot and does not adopt a general principle that it applies to joint and several attorneys collectively as it applies to a single attorney. For many purposes, each attorney must be considered separately, and Sch 4 to the MCA 2005 is modified in the following respects in the case of joint and several attorneys.

One attorney failing to satisfy qualifications for appointment

21.26 If one of a number of joint and several attorneys does not satisfy the requirements for the creation of an EPA, for example, because he is a minor at the time of execution, or if he executed Part C of the prescribed form after 1 October 2007, then the power will be invalid in his case, but valid in respect of the others (MCA 2005, Sch 4, para 20(4)). It would seem that, if a power is thereby invalidated in respect of an attorney, it may nevertheless be effective to create an *ordinary* power of attorney in his favour (Sch 4, para 20(4)) (see **16.2**).

Registration procedure

21.27 Whereas all attorneys under a joint power have to join in the application to register, it is open to attorneys under a joint and several power to make *either* a joint application *or* for one or more of them to make the application (MCA 2005, Sch 4, para 20(5)). The Law Commission described the policy behind this facility as follows:

'Whilst we propose that all attorneys under a *joint* power should have to join in the application to register we feel that it should be open to attorneys under a *joint and several* power to make either a joint application together or else leave it to one or more to make the application (though we envisage that in practice they will usually apply together jointly). Whichever choice is made by the joint and several attorneys, a successful application will have the effect of registration of the instrument for all of them. We therefore consider it important that all the attorneys are made aware of the proposed registration. Some of them might, for example, be aware of circumstances rendering it desirable that the application should be refused or not made at all. Accordingly, we recommend that any attorney under a joint and several power who is not applying for registration should be notified of the proposed registration by the attorney(s) who is applying. The notification would be similar to that sent to relatives.' (Law Com No 122, paragraph 4.97).

21.28 If the instrument is then registered, the registration will be effective in respect of all the attorneys.

Notice to co-attorneys

21.29 Where an attorney intends to register an EPA, notice of his intention (form EP1PG) must be given to any other attorney or attorneys who have not joined in the application (MCA 2005, Sch 4, para 20(5)(b)).

21.30 An attorney who is not an applicant for registration of the instrument (as well as one who is) may act as provided in MCA 2005, Sch 4, para 1(2) to maintain the donor or prevent loss to his estate, or to maintain himself or other persons in so far as Sch 4, para 3(2) permits him to do so (Sch 4, para 20(5)(a)).

Objections to registration not applying to all joint and several attorneys

21.31 An objection may validly be taken to the registration on a ground relating to an attorney who has not applied for registration as well as one who has (MCA 2005, Sch 4, para 20(5)(c)). However, the Public Guardian is not precluded from registering the instrument, and the court must not direct him not to do so under Sch 4, para 13(10) if an enduring power subsists as respects some attorney who is not affected. Where the Public Guardian registers an instrument in such a case, he must make against the registration an entry in the prescribed form (Sch 4, para 20(6)).

Revocation not applying to all joint and several attorneys

21.32 The court must direct the Public Guardian not to register an instrument and must by order revoke the power created by the instrument if it is satisfied that fraud or undue pressure was used to induce the donor to create the power, or that, having regard to all the circumstances, the attorney is unsuitable to be the donor's attorney (MCA 2005, Sch 4, para 13(9)(d) and (e), and para 11). However, the court must not revoke the EPA if it subsists as respects some attorney who is not affected by the ground or grounds in question (Sch 4, para 20(7)). For example, the court may be satisfied that one attorney is unsuitable to be the donor's attorney but not so satisfied as respects the others. Where the court directs the Public Guardian to register an instrument in such circumstances, he must make against the registration an entry in the prescribed form (Sch 4, para 20(6)).

Prescribed form of qualification of registration

21.33 In a case within paras 20(6) or (7) of Sch 4 to the MCA 2005, where an objection or revocation does not apply to all the joint and several attorneys, the Public Guardian 'must make against the registration an entry in the prescribed form'. Regulation 28 of the LPA, EPA & PG Regs 2007 provides that the form of entry to be made is a stamp bearing the following words:

'THE REGISTRATION OF THIS ENDURING POWER OF ATTORNEY IS QUALIFIED AND EXTENDS TO THE APPOINTMENT OF . . (insert name of attorney(s) not affected by ground(s) of objection or revocation) ONLY AS THE ATTORNEY(S) OF . . . . (insert name of donor).'

Bankruptcy of attorney

21.34 An EPA is revoked by the bankruptcy of the attorney (MCA 2005, Sch 4, para 2(7)). However, where the attorney is bankrupt merely because an interim bankruptcy order has effect in respect of him, the power is suspended for so long as the order has effect (Sch 4, para 2(8).

21.35 In the case of a joint and several power, the reference in MCA 2005, Sch 4, para 2(7) to the bankruptcy of the attorney is to be read as a reference to the bankruptcy of the last remaining attorney under the power, and the bankruptcy of any other attorney under the power causes that person to cease to be an attorney under the power (Sch 4, para 22(1)).

21.36 The reference in MCA 2005, Sch 4, para 2(8) to the suspension of the power is to be read as a reference to its suspension in so far as it relates to the attorney in respect of whom the interim bankruptcy restrictions order has effect (Sch 4, para 22(2)).

21.37 The provisions of MCA 2005, Sch 4, paras 2(7), 2(8), 22(1) and 22(2) were amended by The Tribunals, Courts and Enforcement Act 2007 (Consequential Amendments) Order 2012 (SI 2012 No 2404), Sch 2, Art 53, to include references to the making of a debt relief order under Part 7A of the Insolvency Act 1986

Disclaimer

21.38 Generally speaking, no disclaimer of a power is valid once an attorney has reason to believe that the donor is or is becoming mentally incapable unless and until the attorney gives notice of it to the Public Guardian (MCA 2005, Sch 4, paras 2(10) and 4(6)). As regards joint powers this applies to any attorney, but in the case of joint and several powers it applies only to those attorneys who have reason to believe that the donor is or is becoming mentally incapable (Sch 4, para 22(3)).

ATTORNEY'S LIABILITY FOR WRONGS OF CO-ATTORNEY

21.39 Although the legislation makes no specific provision in this respect, at common law an attorney is not liable for any loss or harm caused by the wrongful act or omission of a co-attorney, unless he authorised or was otherwise party or privy to such wrongful act or omission: (see *Bowstead and Reynolds on Agency*, 19th edn (Sweet & Maxwell, 2010)).

Chapter 22

PROTECTION OF THIRD PARTIES

INTRODUCTION

Consequences of revocation - the common law

22.1 There are two main risks arising from the possibility that a power of attorney may have been revoked or terminated. First, a third party dealing with the attorney may find that a transaction is invalid because the attorney no longer had authority to carry it out. Such invalidity may, of course, affect his title and that of others subsequently relying on the validity of the transaction. Secondly, an attorney who purports to act under the authority conferred by a power of attorney which is no longer valid may himself be liable to a third party who relied on that authority for breach of an implied warranty that he continued to have the authority conferred by the power (*Yonge v Toynbee* [1910] 1 KB 215).

Protection – the Powers of Attorney Act 1971

22.2 The Powers of Attorney Act 1971 (the 1971 Act), accordingly, conferred some protection on attorneys and those dealing with them. The policy of the Enduring Powers of Attorney Act 1985 was that attorneys and third parties acting pursuant to an EPA should, in principle, have the same protection as is conferred by law in the case of ordinary powers, but it was necessary to confer certain additional protection. This has been re-enacted in Sch 4 to the Mental Capacity Act 2005 (MCA 2005) in respect of an Enduring Powers of Attorney (EPA) and in MCA 2005, s 14 in respect of a lasting power of attorney (LPA).

APPLICATION OF 1971 ACT TO ENDURING AND LASTING POWERS

22.3 An EPA and an LPA is a power of attorney for the purposes of the protection conferred by ss 5 and 6 of the 1971 Act. The scope of this protection is as follows.

Protection for innocent attorney

22.4 An attorney who acts in pursuance of any power of attorney at a time when it has been revoked does not, by reason of the revocation, incur any liability to the donor of the power or to a third party for breach of an implied warranty of authority, provided that at that time he did not know that the donor had revoked the power, or that an event had occurred which caused it to be revoked (1971 Act, s 5(1) and (5)).

Protection for innocent third party

22.5 In favour of a third party dealing with the attorney, any transaction is as effective as if the power continued in operation, notwithstanding that it may have been revoked by the donor, or that he may have died or become incapable or bankrupt or, in the case of a body corporate, been wound up or dissolved, *unless* the third party at the time of the transaction had knowledge that the power had been revoked by the donor or of an event which caused it to be revoked (1971 Act, s 5(2) and (5)).

What constitutes knowledge of revocation of enduring or lasting power?

22.6 Whether or not there is knowledge of revocation is of crucial importance for the purpose of the protection discussed above. The donor's purported revocation of an EPA which has been registered will not be valid unless and until the court confirms the revocation (MCA 2005, Sch 4, para 15(1)(a)). For the purposes of the protection conferred by s 5 of the 1971 Act, knowledge of the confirmation of the revocation is knowledge of the revocation of the power, but knowledge of the unconfirmed revocation is not (Sch 4, para 18(5)). Unlike an EPA, the donor of a registered LPA can revoke the power provided he has mental capacity, without the need for confirmation of the court (MCA 2005, s13 (2)). The MCA 2005 makes no specific reference to what constitutes knowledge for the purposes of the protection conferred by s 5 of the 1971 Act in respect of an LPA.

Presumption that third party had no knowledge

22.7 For these purposes, where the interest of a purchaser (as defined in s 205(1) of the Law of Property Act 1925) depends on the third party's knowledge, it is to be conclusively presumed that the third party had no such knowledge if:

- the transaction by the attorney was completed within 12 months of the date on which the power came into operation; or
- before, or within 3 months after, the completion of the purchase the third party makes a statutory declaration that he had no such knowledge (1971 Act, s 5(4)).

FURTHER PROTECTION UNDER THE MENTAL CAPACITY ACT 2005 IN RESPECT OF ENDURING POWERS

22.8 The additional protection given by Sch 4, paras 18 and 19 to the MCA 2005 covers three situations:

- where an instrument was intended to create an EPA but failed to do so;

- where the attorney's powers are restricted pending the registration of the instrument; and
- where the donor never had capacity to grant a power of attorney.

Where the instrument fails to create an enduring power

22.9 The MCA 2005 provides protection for the attorney and persons dealing with him in cases where: (a) an instrument 'framed in a form prescribed as mentioned in paragraph 2(2)' of Sch 4 to the Act creates a power which is not a valid enduring power, and (b) the power is revoked by the mental incapacity of the donor (Sch 4, para 19(1)).

(1)   *Protection for attorney*
       In such a case, an attorney who acts in pursuance of the power does not, by reason of the revocation, incur any liability (either to the donor or to any other person) unless at the time of acting he knows: (a) that the instrument did not create a valid EPA, and (b) that the donor has become mentally incapable (Sch 4, para 19(2)).

(2)   *Protection for third parties*
       In these circumstances, and subject to the same two provisions, any transaction between the attorney and another person is, in favour of that person, as valid as if the power had then been in existence (Sch 4, para 19(3)).

(3)   *Presumption in favour of validity*
       For the purpose of determining whether a transaction was valid by virtue of these provisions, it is to be conclusively presumed in favour of the purchaser that the transaction was valid if: (a) the transaction between that person and the attorney was completed within 12 months of the date on which the instrument was registered, or (b) that person makes a statutory declaration, before or within 3 months after the completion of the purchase, that he had no reason at the time of the transaction to doubt that the attorney had authority to dispose of the property which was the subject of the transaction (Sch 4, para 18(4)). These provisions mirror those contained in the 1971 Act.

(4)   *Circumstances in which protection available*
       The Law Commission envisaged that an instrument intended to create an EPA might fail to do so by reason of a drafting error, and that the protection described in the preceding paragraphs would then be available (see *The Incapacitated Principal* (1983) Law Com No 122, p 49, fn 207). However, it will be noted that the protection only applies where an instrument is 'framed in' the prescribed form and, if an instrument is so framed, it is not easy to see how any drafting error could have the effect of creating an ordinary but not an enduring power. It seems more probable that the provisions would be applicable in cases in which the power cannot be an EPA for some reason not connected with the drafting - as, for example, where the attorney executes the power while he is a minor (Sch 4, para 2(5)(a)).

Protection where the attorney's powers are restricted pending registration

22.10 The protection conferred by s 5 of the 1971 Act arises only when the power has been revoked, and an EPA will not be revoked by the donor's supervening mental incapacity (MCA 2005, Sch 4, para 1(1)(a)). However, as explained in **18.43**, the donee's authority to act under the power will be severely restricted when such incapacity occurs unless and until the power is registered (MCA 2005, Sch 4, para 1(2)).

22.11 The MCA 2005 therefore provides that the protection for the attorney and persons dealing with him conferred by s 5 of the 1971 Act shall in those circumstances be available as it would if the power had been revoked (MCA 2005, Sch 4, para (1)(c)). For practical purposes, it can be said that the protection will be available if the third party concerned did not know of the incapacity.

22.12 The fact that the authority of an attorney is restricted pending registration could give rise to another difficulty. This is because a person dealing with an attorney must normally be concerned to ensure that the attorney is acting within the scope of his authority. Such a person might, in the absence of any provision dealing with the matter, have been put on inquiry as to whether or not the attorney's acts were within the powers to maintain and prevent loss conferred by MCA 2005, Sch 4, para 1(2). See **18.43**.

22.13 It is true that if the third party were unaware of the onset of the donor's mental incapacity he would be protected by the provision explained above, but the legislation provides some protection even if he does know. Provided that the third party does not know the attorney is acting otherwise than in accordance with his restricted authority, he is entitled to assume that the attorney is acting in accordance with it (MCA 2005, Sch 4, para 1(3)). In practice, therefore, a third party should not need to raise requisitions as to whether or not the action in question is within the attorney's statutory power to maintain the donor and others and to prevent loss to the donor's estate.

Protection where the donor never had capacity to grant a power of attorney

22.14 The protection conferred on attorneys and third parties by the 1971 Act is not available if the power never existed - for example, because the donor lacked capacity at the time when he purported to grant it. The Law Commission, therefore, proposed that a bona fide attorney and purchaser should be able to rely on the fact of registration as having 'verified the validity' of an instrument as an EPA once it had been registered as such (Law Com No 122, paragraph 4.88). Such persons should, in principle, be able to assume that the EPA was validly created and was still subsisting, and registration should confer protection against any irregularities that there might have been.

22.15 MCA 2005, Sch 4, para 18(2) accordingly provides that, where an instrument which did not create a valid EPA has been registered, an attorney who acts in pursuance of the power should not incur any liability (either to the donor or to any other person) by reason of the non-existence of the power unless at the time of acting he knows: (a) that the instrument did not create a valid EPA, (b) that an event had occurred which, if the instrument had created a valid EPA, would have had the effect of revoking it, or (c) that, if the instrument had created a valid EPA, it would have expired before that time.

22.16 Similar protection is available to those dealing with the attorney. MCA 2005, Sch 4, para 18(3) provides that any transaction between the attorney and another person shall, in favour of that person, be as valid as if the power had then been in existence, unless at the time of the transaction that person has knowledge of any of the matters mentioned above.

FURTHER PROTECTION UNDER THE MENTAL CAPACITY ACT 2005 IN RESPECT OF LASTING POWERS

22.17 The additional protection given by MCA 2005, s 14 covers where an instrument was intended to create an LPA but failed to do so.

Protection for the attorney

22.18 Where an LPA has been registered with the Public Guardian but was not validly created, the attorney does not incur any liability to the donor or any other person because of the non- existence of the power, unless he knows the LPA was not created, or is aware of circumstances, which if it had been created, would have terminated his authority (MCA 2005, s 14(1)–(2)). Although an LPA cannot be created unless it is registered with the Public Guardian (MCA 2005, s 9(2)(a)), registration is not a conclusive statement of its validity. For example, if the certificate provider falls within the list of persons who are prohibited from acting as such, the instrument will not be validly created, but it may not have been noticed by the Office of the Public Guardian during the registration process and may very well be registered. Another example is where the attorney is an undischarged bankrupt at the time of making a property and financial affairs power; the circumstances are such that if the power had been created, it would terminate his authority.

Protection for a third party

22.19 Any transaction between the attorney and another person (third party) is valid, as if the power had been created, unless the third party knows the LPA was not created, or is aware of circumstances, which if it had been created, would have terminated the attorney's authority. For example, if the third party knew the donor was an undischarged bankrupt (which terminates the LPA under MCA 2005, s 13(3)) and the attorney was operating under a property and financial affairs LPA, the transaction will not be valid.

Presumption in favour of validity

22.20 For the purpose of determining whether a transaction was valid by virtue of these provisions, it is to be conclusively presumed in favour of the purchaser that the transaction was valid if: (a) the transaction between that person and the attorney was completed within 12 months of the date on which the instrument was registered, or (b) that person makes a statutory declaration, before or within 3 months after the completion of the purchase, that he had no reason at the time of the transaction to doubt that the attorney had authority to dispose of the property which was the subject of the transaction (MCA 2005, s 14(4)). These provisions mirror those contained in the 1971 Act.

Part III

COMMON PROVISIONS

Chapter 23

THE CODE OF PRACTICE

INTRODUCTION

23.1 Section 42 of the Mental Capacity Act 2005 (MCA 2005) requires the Lord Chancellor to prepare and issue one or more codes of practice for the guidance of people with different duties and functions under the Act.

23.2 The code provides practical guidance on how the provisions of the Act should be applied in ordinary, everyday situations.

23.3 The MCA 2005 Code of Practice contains 16 chapters, most of which begin with a 'quick summary'. Each chapter is also prefaced with a reminder that a person's capacity (or lack of capacity) refers specifically to their capacity to make a particular decision at the time it needs to be made.

23.4 Certain categories of people – including the donees of a lasting power of attorney (LPA) – are required to 'have regard to' the relevant guidance in the Code of Practice. This means they must be aware of the Code of Practice when acting or making decisions on behalf of someone who lacks capacity to make a decision for him or herself.

23.5 Chapter 7 of the Code of Practice – *What does the Act say about Lasting Powers of Attorney?* – explains how people can plan ahead for the possibility that they might in future lack the capacity to make decisions for themselves by creating a lasting power of attorney naming individuals who can make certain decisions on their behalf. It also describes how the attorneys appointed under an LPA should act.

23.6 As well as having regard to chapter 7, attorneys should pay special attention to the following guidance set out in the code:

- chapter 2, which sets out how the Act's principles should be applied;
- chapter 3, which describes the steps which can be taken to try to help the person make decisions for him or herself;
- chapter 4, which describes the Act's definition of lack of capacity and gives guidance on assessing capacity; and
- chapter 5, which gives guidance on working out the donor's best interests.

23.7 In some circumstances, attorneys might also find it useful to refer to guidance in:

- chapter 6, which explains when attorneys who have caring responsibilities may have protection from liability and gives guidance on the few circumstances when the Act allows restraint in connection with care and treatment;
- chapter 8, which gives a summary of the Court of Protection's powers relating to LPAs;
- chapter 9, which explains how LPAs may be affected if the donor has made an advance decision to refuse treatment; and
- chapter 15, which describes ways to settle disagreements.

23.8 Although the MCA 2005 requires certain people, including the donees of LPAs, to 'have regard to' the code, it does not impose a legal duty upon them to 'comply with' it, or impose specific penalties if they fail to have regard to it.

23.9 However, s 42(5) of the MCA 2005 provides that, if it appears to a court or tribunal conducting any criminal or civil proceedings, that a provision of the code, or a failure to comply with the code, is relevant to a question arising in the proceedings, the provision or failure must be taken into account when deciding the question.

MENTAL CAPACITY ACT 2005 CODE OF PRACTICE

23.10 Section 42 of the MCA 2005 requires the Lord Chancellor to prepare and issue 'one or more codes of practice' for the guidance of a range of people with different duties and functions under the Act. Despite the reference to more than one code, it was originally intended that there would only be one code. In the summary of responses to its consultation paper on the code, which is referred to in greater detail in the paragraph below, the then Department for Constitutional Affairs said, at page 71:

> 'We think it is important that all the relevant material should be in one place and those who have a duty to have regard to the Code of Practice have one document with which to work rather than many.'

23.11 Section 43 of the MCA 2005 requires the Lord Chancellor to consult with various people before he prepares or revises a code of practice and, before it can be issued, it must have been laid before both Houses of Parliament for 40 days without either House voting against it; known as the 'negative resolution procedure'. The Department for Constitutional Affairs circulated a draft code for consultation on 9 March 2006. The consultation period ended on 2 June 2006, and a summary of the 161 responses received was published on 29 September 2006. The first edition of the MCA 2005 Code of Practice was issued on 23 April 2007.

23.12 Hard copies of the code can be obtained from TSO (The Stationery Office) and leading bookshops. Audio and large print versions will be made available in English and Welsh, and there will also be a Braille edition. The code can also be downloaded from the gov.uk website https://www.gov.uk/gov ernment/uploads/system/uploads/attachment_data/file/497253/Mental-capaci ty-act-code-of-practice.pdf

DEPRIVATION OF LIBERTY SAFEGUARDS CODE OF PRACTICE

23.13 Despite the government's original intention to have just one Code of Practice, there is also a Deprivation of Liberty Safeguards Code of Practice (DOLS Code), which supplements the main MCA 2005 Code of Practice and came into force on 3 November 2008. The need for the DOLS Code arose as a result of the amendments made to the MCA 2005 in the Mental Health Act 2007, and in particular the insertion of the new:

- section 4A – Restriction on deprivation of liberty;
- section 4B – Deprivation of liberty necessary for life-sustaining treatment etc.;
- section 16A – section 16 powers: Mental Health Act patients etc;
- section 21A – Powers of court in relation to Schedule A1;
- Sch A1, to be inserted before Sch 1 of the MCA 2005 – Hospital and care home residents: deprivation of liberty; and
- Schedule 1A, to be inserted after Sch 1 to the MCA 2005 – Persons ineligible to be deprived of liberty by this Act.

23.14 The DOLS Code is particularly intended to provide guidance for professionals involved in administering and delivering the safeguards who are under a duty to have regard to the code. The DOLS Code is also intended to provide information for people who are, or could become, subject to the deprivation of liberty safeguards, and for their families, friends and carers, as well as for anyone who believes that someone is being deprived of their liberty unlawfully. Attorneys acting under health and welfare lasting powers may need to refer to the DOLS Code, in relation to the donor. The DOLS Code is 124 pages long and can be purchased for £13 from TSO. It is only available on line from the National Archives website at http://webarchive.nationalarchives. gov.uk/20130107105354/http://www.dh.gov.uk/prod_consum_dh/groups/dh_ digitalassets/@dh/@en/documents/digitalasset/dh_087309.pdf

THE PURPOSE OF THE CODE

23.15 The purpose of the MCA 2005 Code of Practice is to complement the Act by considering a number of important issues, which relate to the provisions of the Act, but are not, in themselves, suitable matters for inclusion in the primary or secondary legislation. It provides practical guidance on how the provisions of the Act should be applied in ordinary, everyday situations. For example, it gives guidance on:

- how to assess whether a person has capacity in relation to making a particular decision;
- how to decide whether a particular course of action is in a person's best interests;
- acting as a carer or treatment provider not only in everyday situations but also in an emergency;
- acting as an attorney under an LPA, or as a court-appointed deputy;
- carrying out intrusive research on a patient who lacks the capacity to consent to such research.

THE CONTENTS OF THE CODE

23.16 The MCA 2005 Code of Practice is paperback, A4 size, 296 pages long, and contains 16 chapters, most of which begin with a 'quick summary'. Each chapter is also prefaced with the following reminder, which stands out like the government health warning on a packet of cigarettes, emphasising the fact that capacity is to be treated as both time-specific and issue specific: 'In this chapter, as throughout the Code, a person's capacity (or lack of capacity) refers specifically to their capacity to make a particular decision at the time it needs to be made.' At the end, instead of an index, there is a glossary of 'key words and phrases used in the Code', and an annex containing contact details for various organisations with an interest in this area.

23.17 Each chapter includes a number of 'scenarios'. These are vignettes or case studies designed to illustrate the meaning of the legislation described in the main text of the code. However, page 6 of the introduction to the code contains a rather unhelpful disclaimer, which says that, 'The scenarios should not in any way be taken as templates for decisions that need to be made in similar situations.'

THE CHAPTERS OF THE CODE

23.18 The 16 chapters of the Mental Capacity Act 2005 Code of Practice are as follows.

23.19 Chapter 1 – *What is the Mental Capacity Act 2005?* This introduces the Act; describes what decisions are covered by it, and what decisions are excluded; and briefly summarises what the Act says about the Code of Practice itself.

23.20 Chapter 2 – *What are the statutory principles and how should they be applied?* This describes the five principles set out in s 1 of the Act, and how they should be applied in practice.

23.21 Chapter 3 – *How should people be helped to make their own decisions?* This describes how the Act requires people to be given the right amount of help and support to enable them to make their own decisions. It considers providing relevant information, communicating in an appropriate way, and making the person feel at ease.

23.22 Chapter 4 – *How does the Act define a person's capacity to make a decision and how should capacity be assessed?* This explains what is meant by 'capacity' and 'lack of capacity', provides guidance on how to assess whether someone has the capacity to make a decision, and suggests when professional people should be involved in making the assessment (paragraph 4.53).

23.23 Chapter 5 – *What does the Act mean when it talks about 'best interests'?* This considers what acting in someone's best interests means, and discusses the checklist set out in s 4 of the Act.

23.24 Chapter 6 – *What protection does the Act offer for people providing care or treatment?* This chapter discusses ss 5–8 of the Act which allow carers, healthcare and social staff to carry out certain tasks without fear of civil or criminal liability.

23.25 Chapter 7 – *What does the Act say about Lasting Powers of Attorney?* This chapter explains how people can plan ahead for the possibility that they might in future lack the capacity to make decisions for themselves by creating an LPA naming individuals who can make certain decisions on their behalf. It also describes how the attorneys appointed under an LPA should act. The legislation described in this chapter can be found in MCA 2005, ss 9–14.

23.26 Chapter 8 – *What is the role of the Court of Protection and court-appointed deputies?* This describes the role of the Court of Protection to make a decision or appoint a decision-maker on someone's behalf when there is no alternative way of resolving the matter. The legislation described in this chapter can be found in MCA 2005, ss 15–21.

23.27 Chapter 9 – *What does the Act say about decisions to refuse treatment?* This chapter explains the procedures that must be followed if someone wishes to make an advance decision to refuse medical treatment, which will come into effect when he or she lacks contemporaneous capacity to refuse the specified treatment. The legislation described in this chapter can be found in MCA 2005, ss 24–26.

23.28 Chapter 10 – *What is the new Independent Mental Capacity Advocate service and how does it work?* This chapter describes the role of Independent Mental Capacity Advocates appointed under the Act to help and represent particularly vulnerable people who lack capacity to make certain significant decisions. It also sets out when they should be instructed. The legislation described in this chapter can be found in MCA 2005, ss 35–41.

23.29 Chapter 11 – *How does the Act affect research projects involving a person who lacks capacity?* This chapter gives guidance on what is meant by 'research'; the requirements that must be met if a research project involves someone who lacks capacity; and the specific responsibilities of researchers. The legislation described in this chapter can be found in MCA 2005, ss 30–34.

23.30 Chapter 12 – *How does the Act apply to children and young people?* The MCA 2005 does not generally apply to persons under the age of 16, and this chapter looks at the rare exceptions to that rule.

23.31 Chapter 13 – *What is the relationship between the Mental Capacity Act and the Mental Health Act 1983?* This chapter describes the circumstances in which it may be appropriate to detain someone under the Mental Health Act, rather than to rely on the MCA 2005; describes how the MCA 2005 affects people who are also subject to the Mental Health Act 1983; and explains when doctors cannot give certain treatments for a mental disorder to a person who lacks the capacity to consent to it.

23.32 Chapter 14 – *What means of protection exist for people who lack capacity to make decisions for themselves?* This chapter describes the functions of different agencies that exist to help make sure that adults who lack capacity to make decisions are protected from abuse.

23.33 Chapter 15 – *What are the best ways to settle disagreements and disputes about issues covered in the Act?* This chapter sets out the different options available for settling disagreements, including advocacy, mediation, formal and informal ways of complaining about health care or social care, contacting the Ombudsman, and applying to the Court of Protection.

23.34 Chapter 16 – *What rules govern access to information about a person who lacks capacity?* This chapter gives guidance on what personal information family members and carers have a right to see about someone who lacks capacity, and how they can get hold of that information.

PEOPLE WHO HAVE A DUTY TO HAVE REGARD TO THE CODE

23.35 Page 2 of the introduction to the Code of Practice says that:

'Certain categories of people are legally required to 'have regard to' relevant guidance in the Code of Practice. That means they must be aware of the Code of Practice when acting or making decisions on behalf of someone who lacks capacity to make a decision for themselves, and they should be able to explain how they have had regard to the Code when acting or making decisions.'

23.36 A list of the persons who are required to have regard to the Code of Practice can be found in s 42(4) of the MCA 2005, which states that:

'It is the duty of a person to have regard to any relevant code if he is acting in relation to a person who lacks capacity and is doing so in one or more of the following ways –
  (a)   as the donee of a lasting power of attorney,
  (b)   as a deputy appointed by the court,
  (c)   as a person carrying out research in reliance on any provision made by or under this Act (see sections 30 to 34),
  (d)   as an independent mental capacity advocate,
  (da) in the exercise of functions under Schedule A1,
  (db) as a representative appointed under Part 10 of Schedule A1,
  (e)   in a professional capacity,
  (f)   for remuneration.'

23.37 Page 2 of the Code of Practice gives the following examples of people acting 'in a professional capacity' or 'for remuneration':

• a variety of healthcare staff (doctors, dentists, nurses, therapists, radiologists, paramedics, etc);
• social care staff (social workers, care managers, etc);
• others who may occasionally be involved in the care of people who lack capacity to make the decision in question, such as ambulance crew, housing workers, or police officers.

23.38 People who are being paid for acts for or in relation to a person who lacks capacity may include:

• care assistants in a care home;
• care workers providing domiciliary care services; and
• others who have been contracted to provide a service to people who lack capacity to consent to that service.

23.39 However, the MCA 2005 applies more generally to everyone who looks after, or cares for, someone who lacks capacity to make particular decisions for themselves. This includes family carers or other carers. Although these carers are not legally required to have regard to the Code of Practice, the guidance given in the Code will help them understand the Act and apply it. They should follow the guidance in the Code as far as they are aware of it.

CHAPTERS THAT ATTORNEYS NEED TO BE AWARE OF

23.40 For the first time standards of good conduct have been formally imposed upon decision-makers appointed under a power of attorney or a court order. In addition to having regard to chapter 7 – *What does the Act say about Lasting Powers of Attorney?* – paragraphs 7.54 and 7.55 of the code say that:

'As well as this chapter, attorneys should pay special attention to the following guidance set out in the Code:
- chapter 2, which sets out how the Act's principles should be applied
- chapter 3, which describes the steps which can be taken to try to help the person make decisions for themselves
- chapter 4, which describes the Act's definition of lack of capacity and gives guidance on assessing capacity, and
- chapter 5, which gives guidance on working out the donor's best interests.

In some circumstances, attorneys might also find it useful to refer to guidance in:
- chapter 6, which explains when attorneys who have caring responsibilities may have protection from liability and gives guidance on the few circumstances when the Act allows restraint in connection with care and treatment
- chapter 8, which gives a summary of the Court of Protection's powers relating to LPAs
- chapter 9, which explains how LPAs may be affected if the donor has made an advance decision to refuse treatment, and
- chapter 15, which describes ways to settle disagreements.'

23.41 Legal advisers and others who prepare LPAs will need to draw to the attorney's attention their duty to have regard to the code, and in particular to the chapters mentioned in paragraphs 7.54 and 7.55. They should bear in mind that not all attorneys have access to the Internet, or to booksellers who stock copies of the code.

23.42 The obligation under s 42(4) of the MCA 2005 does not expressly extend to attorneys acting under an enduring power of attorney, whether registered or unregistered, presumably because of the effect of Article 7 of the European Convention on Human Rights, which guards against retrospective legislation, albeit criminal offences. However, paragraph 7.79 of the code states that:

'EPA attorneys may find guidance in this chapter helpful. In particular, all attorneys must comply with the duties described in paragraphs 7.58–7.68 above. EPA attorneys can also be found liable under section 44 of the new Act, which sets out the new criminal offences of ill treatment and wilful neglect. The OPG has produced guidance on EPAs.'

23.43 Paragraphs 8.52 and 8.53 of the code provide that court-appointed deputies should have regard to chapter 8 – *What is the role of the Court of Protection and court-appointed deputies?* – and to the same chapters as attorneys are advised to be aware of.

FAILURE TO COMPLY WITH THE CODE

23.44 Although the MCA 2005 requires certain people to 'have regard to' the code, it does not impose a legal duty upon them to 'comply with' it, or impose specific penalties if they fail to have regard to it. The code should be regarded as guidance, rather than instruction, but, if anyone who has a duty to have regard to the code fails to follow the relevant guidance contained in it, they may need to explain their reasons for departing from it.

23.45 Section 42(5) of the MCA 2005 provides that, if it appears to a court or tribunal conducting any criminal or civil proceedings, that a provision of the code, or a failure to comply with the code, is relevant to a question arising in the proceedings, the provision or failure must be taken into account when deciding the question. So, for example, if the Court of Protection is considering whether an attorney under an LPA has behaved in a way that is not in the donor's best interests, it can take into account any failure by the attorney to have regard to the code.

THE MUNJAZ CASE

23.46 A good example of the need to give a satisfactory explanation for departing from the guidance contained in a code of practice is the case of *R (Munjaz) v Mersey Care NHS Trust* [2005] UKHL 58, [2006] 2 AC 148, where the House of Lords considered the status of the code of practice issued under the Mental Health Act 1983, and the reasons why Ashworth Special Hospital had decided to depart from it. Ashworth, in Merseyside, is one of three special hospitals in England, which provide high security accommodation for particularly violent or dangerous patients. The others are Broadmoor and Rampton. In 2001 Ashworth implemented its own revised written policy on the use of seclusion, or solitary confinement, which differed in various ways from the code of practice issued by the Secretary of State for Health under s 118 of the Mental Health Act 1983. For example, it required fewer medical reviews of the period of seclusion.

23.47 Mr Munjaz, who was born in 1947 and had been an inpatient at Ashworth since 1994, complained about four periods of seclusion during 2001 and 2002 – the shortest being for 4 days, and the longest 18 days – and he applied for a judicial review of Ashworth's policy, alleging that it was unlawful under domestic law, and that it contravened his rights under the European Convention on Human Rights.

23.48 Sullivan J dismissed the application: [2002] EWHC 1521 (Admin). The Court of Appeal, however, upheld Mr Munjaz's appeal, and declared that the hospital's policy was, indeed, unlawful, and that it had violated his human rights: [2003] EWCA Civ 1036; [2003] 3 WLR 1505. In a majority decision, the House of Lords held that the Court of Appeal had given the code of practice a stronger effect than was permissible – a weight that Parliament had never intended to give it. The code is guidance, not instruction, and it was too strong to say that the hospital could not depart from it. Nevertheless, the circumstances in which the code was drawn up, and the high importance of protecting detained mental patients from abuse, showed that it should be given great weight. It was to be considered with great care, and any departure from it would require cogent reasons. Such reasons would be the subject of intense scrutiny by the court. However, the statutory scheme left the power and responsibility of making the final decision to those with the legal and practical responsibility and, on the particular evidence in this case, Ashworth Special Hospital had justified its policy. The section on seclusion in the code of practice was addressed to mental hospitals generally, and did not address the special needs of high security mental hospitals, and Ashworth had carefully considered the code before venturing to depart from it.

23.49 Mr Munjaz subsequently appealed to the European Court of Human Rights, which on 17 July 2012 held that, although his complaints under Articles 5 and 8 were admissible, there had been no violation of his rights in these circumstances: *Munjaz v The United Kingdom* [2012] ECHR 1704.

POSSIBLE REASONS FOR DEPARTING FROM THE CODE

23.50 In the first edition of his *Mental Capacity Act Manual* (Thomson: Sweet & Maxwell, 2005), at pages 9-91 and 9-92, Richard Jones has suggested that the following would constitute a good reason for justifying a departure from the guidance in the code:

(1)   The particular clinical or social care needs of P (or a group of persons who share particular well-defined characteristics) would not be satisfied if the guidance was followed.

(2)   There has been a determination of the High Court that a particular aspect of the guidance is not legally accurate.

(3)   Legal advice has been received which casts a significant doubt on the legal correctness of an aspect of the guidance.

(4)   Following the guidance would involve breaching P's rights under the European Convention on Human Rights.

(5)   A judgment is taken that a particular aspect of the guidance should not be followed for safety or other legitimate reasons.

CASE-LAW ON THE MCA 2005 CODE OF PRACTICE

23.51 In *SBC v PBA and others* [2011] COPLR Con Vol 1095, Roderic Wood J was considering whether to appoint deputies for personal welfare (including healthcare) for PBA, a 74-year-old man suffering from alcohol related dementia. Paragraph 8.38 of the MCA 2005 Code of Practice states that 'deputies for personal welfare decisions will only be required in the most difficult cases' and gives examples. Having decided to appoint personal welfare deputies, Roderic Wood J said as follows at paragraph [67] of his judgment:

'[Counsel] argues that I should look at the unvarnished words of the Statute consistent as that approach is with the contemporaneous practice of interpreting statutory provision and the law in general, but in doing so I can take account of the guidance in the Code in coming to my conclusions. . . . My reasons for preferring [counsel's] interpretation are as follows:
(i)   the words of the statute are the essential provisions laid down by Parliament;
(ii)   whatever its genesis and weight, the Code of Practice is indeed only guidance;
(iii)   there is a reasonable expectation in the Code that its provisions should be followed;
(iv)   departure from it, if undertaken, should require careful explanation;
(v)   as I have already said, it, it remains essentially guidance – however weighty and significant – and is not the source of the relevant power which is to be found in the statutory provision;
(vi)   in any event, I do not interpret (if I may respectfully say so) the careful and erudite discussion of this issue by Baker J or indeed His Honour Judge Turner QC (quoted above) as advocating a contrary approach.'

REVISING THE CODE

23.52 The MCA 2005 Code of Practice is a 'living instrument', which, presumably like that other living instrument, the European Convention on Human Rights, 'must be interpreted in the light of present day conditions': *Tyrer v United Kingdom* (1978) 2 EHRR 1, at para 31. The aim of Parliament was to create a maintained and accurate document that will grow and develop over time. Subsections 42(2) and (3) of the MCA 2005 state that the Lord Chancellor may from time to time revise the code, and that he may delegate the revision of the whole or any part of the code so far as he considers expedient. The Lord Chancellor has delegated the revision of the code to the Public Guardian, pursuant to s 58(3)(a) of the MCA 2005.

23.53 On 4 November 2004, when the Mental Capacity Bill was at the committee stage in parliament, David Lammy MP, the then Parliamentary Under-Secretary of State at the Department for Constitutional Affairs, informed the committee that:

'As case-law develops, we may revise sections of the code regularly – perhaps even several times a year. It would be very cumbersome for Parliament to have to debate each revision. The first revision of the code laid before Parliament will have been subject to extensive consultation. . . . Following Royal Assent, a fully revised draft code will be put out for formal public consultation in accordance with Government guidelines on consultations, and we will consult before each revision.'

23.54 The Select Committee of the House of Lords undertook a comprehensive post legislative scrutiny of the Mental Capacity Act 2005 and published its report on 13 March 2014 (HL Paper 139). The report highlighted the shortcoming of the Code, which stated,

'159. A wide range of audiences require information on the Act, ranging from medical practitioners to local authorities, legal professionals, families, carers and people who may lack capacity. Current methods of provision, principally the Codes of Practice, are not meeting the needs of all concerned.

160. We do not believe that a standard review of the Code of Practice is adequate to meet the information needs identified. A broader approach to meeting the diverse needs is required, with the possibility of several tailored resources being designed for different audiences. Some of these resources could be provided exclusively online in order to be updated in line with case law.'

23.55 Despite Mr Lammy's and the Select Committee's comments, the MCA 2005 Code of Practice has not been revised since it was originally published on 23 April 2007. However, the Social Care Institute for Excellence (SCIE) has developed a hub for mental capacity information, principally aimed at health and social care decisions for those who lack mental capacity, but useful to a wider audience. The hub can be found at http://www.scie.org.uk/mca/introduc tion/mental-capacity-act-2005-at-a-glance

RESEARCH RELATING TO THE CODE

23.56 The *Best Interests Decisions Study* was published on 31 January 2012. It was the first large scale national research to examine professional practices in best interests decisions made under the MCA 2005. The study was led by the Norah Fry Research Centre at Bristol University, in collaboration with the

University of Bradford and the Mental Health Foundation, and was funded by the Department of Health. The following were some of the key recommendations that emerged from the study:

- The MCA 2005 Code of Practice should be revised in relation to unwise decision-making how 'insight' relaters to mental capacity; and the relationship of best interests to adult safeguarding.
- New case studies should be produced for the MCA 2005 Code of Practice covering: more complex situations; consensus or joint decision-making; and how best interests processes are dealt with in teams and in care planning.
- Terms used in the MCA 2005 Code of Practice should better reflect roles identified by the research, such as 'best interests leader'.

CONCLUSION

23.57 The Code of Practice has the potential – perhaps more than any other feature of the MCA 2005 – to revolutionise the way we treat members of society who are unable to make their own decisions. Over time, the standards laid down in the code should permeate and influence good practice. However, the code will only be a success if people know about it, and read, mark, learn and inwardly digest it. It is essential that the government agencies involved, such as the Office of the Public Guardian and the Department of Health, put in place adequate mechanisms for ensuring that attorneys, court-appointed deputies, health and social care professionals, and paid carers are aware of and familiar with the contents of the code. Focused information as recommended by the House of Lords Select Committee on the Mental Capacity Act 2005 may be useful but should not undermine the more detailed and comprehensive statutory code.

Chapter 24

PRIVATE INTERNATIONAL LAW

INTRODUCTION

24.1 This chapter looks at the interaction between private international law and mental capacity law and considers the problems that can arise, for example, when someone who is habitually resident outside of England and Wales, who lacks mental capacity and has immovable or immovable property in England and Wales or when someone who is habitually resident in England and Wales:

- becomes mentally incapacitated in another country; or
- becomes mentally incapacitated in England and Wales, and has immovable or movable property in another country that needs to be safeguarded, managed, or dealt with.

24.2 In descending order, the rules that govern situations of this kind should be:

- any international agreement relating to the person or property of mentally incapacitated people; in the absence of which;
- any reciprocal agreement between the territories involved; failing which;
- the general principles of private international law; and
- domestic law.

THE HAGUE CONVENTION ON THE INTERNATIONAL PROTECTION OF ADULTS

24.3 The Hague Convention on Private International Law (*Conférence de La Haye de Droit International Privé*) was instituted in 1893 to work for the progressive unification of the rules of private international law. Currently there are 73 member states plus the European Union.

24.4 On 13 January 2000, The Hague Conference on Private International Law adopted convention number 35, a Convention on the International Protection of Adults (*Convention du 13 janvier 2000 sur la protection internationale des adultes*). The aim of the Convention is to create a mechanism to resolve questions as to which court has jurisdiction to take protection measures on behalf of a vulnerable adult and which law applies to those measures. It establishes a framework for the effective recognition and enforcement of such measures in other contracting states and to determine questions relating to powers of representation granted in advance by adults prior to the onset of incapacity and designed either to survive such incapacity or to take effect upon their incapacity. A system of central authorities should cooperate, locate vulnerable adults and give information on the status of vulnerable persons to other authorities, and provide certificates under Article 38 to confirm the status of a power of representation or other protective measure.

24.5 There is a difference between the adoption of a convention by the conference, its signing by member states, its ratification by member states and its entry into force. By signing a convention, a contracting state expresses in principle its intention to become a party to it. By ratifying a convention, a state places itself under a legal obligation to apply it. A convention finally enters into force when three instruments of ratification have been deposited with the Dutch Ministry of Foreign Affairs.

24.6 The Hague Convention on the International Protection of Adults entered into force on 1 September 2009. As at 1 February 2017 there were 18 contracting states. The table below sets out a list of the states that have signed and ratified the convention, the date on which the convention came into force within a particular state, and whether ratification was subject to a declaration or reservation.

Contracting State	Signed	Ratified	Entered into force	Reservations and Declarations
Netherlands	13.01.2000			
France	13.07.2001	18.09.2008	01.01.2009	D Art 32
United Kingdom	01.04.2003	05.11.2003	01.01.2009	D Arts 32 and 55
		(Scotland)	(Scotland)	
Germany	22.12.2003	03.04.2007	01.01.2009	R Arts 51 and 56
Switzerland	03.04.2007	27.03.2009	01.07.2009	
Finland	18.09.2008	19.11.2010	01.03.2011	
Greece	18.09.2008			
Ireland	18.09.2008			
Luxembourg	18.09.2008			
Poland	18.09.2008			
Italy	31.10.2008			
Cyprus	01.04.2009			
Czech Republic	01.04.2009	18.04.2012	01.08.2012	R Art 51
Estonia		13.12.2010	01.11.2011	D Art 32 R Art 51
Austria	10.07.2013	09.10.2013	01.02.2014	R Arts 51 and 56
Belgium	06.02.2017			
Latvia	15.12.2016			
Monaco	04.03.2016	04.03.2016	01.07.2016	

STATUS OF THE HAGUE CONVENTION IN ENGLAND AND WALES

24.7 As far as the United Kingdom is concerned, the Hague Convention is only in force in Scotland. The declaration made by the United Kingdom when it ratified the convention on 5 November 2003 specifically excluded England and Wales by stating that:

> 'The United Kingdom declares, in accordance with Article 55, that the Convention shall extend to Scotland only, and that it may modify this declaration by submitting another declaration at any time.'

24.8 Although the Hague Convention has not yet been ratified by the United Kingdom government in respect of England and Wales, the Mental Capacity Act 2005 (MCA 2005), s 63, which is headed 'International protection of adults', provides as follows:

> 'Schedule 3 –
> (a) gives effect in England and Wales to the Convention on the International Protection of Adults signed at the Hague on 13 January 2000 (Cm. 5881) (in so far as this Act does not otherwise do so), and
> (b) makes related provision as to the private international law of England and Wales.'

24.9 Section 63 and Schedule 3 came into force on 1 October 2007: Mental Capacity Act 2005 (Commencement No. 2) Order 2007, (C.72), art 2. In *Re M* [2012] COPLR 430 Mostyn J held that the Hague Convention is part of the domestic law of England and Wales, whether or not the foreign country whose order it is sought to be enforced has or has not ratified the Hague Convention. The consequence is that a foreign order made in any country, may be recognised and enforced in England and Wales.

24.10 However, paragraphs 15, 25, 31 and 32(1) of the MCA 2005, Sch 3, envisage that further action is necessary before the Hague Convention can be fully effective in England and Wales. No Orders in Council have been made, although amendments have been made to the Court of Protection Rules 2007 (see **24.35**). These paragraphs provide as follows:

> '15 Regulations may provide for Schedule 1 (lasting powers of attorney: formalities) to apply with modifications in relation to a lasting power which comes within Sch 3, para 13(6)(c).
> 25 Court of Protection Rules may make provision about an application under Sch 3, para 20 or 22.
> 31 Her Majesty may by Order in Council confer on the Lord Chancellor, the court or another public authority functions for enabling the Convention to be given effect in England and Wales.
> 32(1) Regulations may make provision (a) giving further effect to the Convention, or (b) otherwise about the private international law of England and Wales in relation to the protection of adults.'

24.11 In addition, paragraph 35 of MCA 2005, Sch 3 states that paragraphs 8, 9, 19(2), 19(5), and 30 and Part 5 will only have effect if the Convention is in force in accordance with Article 57. In *Re PO* [2013] EWCOP 3932, President Munby confirmed these provisions are accordingly treated as having no effect.

24.12 Article 38 of the Hague Convention envisages that each contracting state shall designate an authority that is competent to draw up a certificate indicating the capacity in which a person is entitled to act and the powers conferred on them. This has not yet been done in respect of England and Wales, although, as a default position, the MCA 2005, Sch 3, para 6(1) provides that 'any function under the Convention of a Central Authority is exercisable in England and Wales by the Lord Chancellor'.

24.13 As is apparent from the title of the convention, the Hague Convention and MCA 2005 relate to adults. An adult is defined in MCA 2005, Sch 3, para 4, as a person who has reached the age of 16 whereas the Hague Convention applies to adults aged 18 years or over. The MCA 2005 is concerned with those who may or do lack mental capacity, whereas the Hague Convention applies to those who 'as a result or insufficiency in his personal faculties, cannot protect his interests.'

DISTINCTION BETWEEN PROTECTIVE MEASURES AND POWERS OF REPRESENTATION

24.14 The Hague Convention draws a clear distinction between:

- 'measures of protection' (*mesures de protection*), to which the MCA 2005, Sch 3, para 5 refers as 'protective measures'; and
- 'powers of representation' (*pouvoirs de représentation*) to which the MCA 2005, Sch 3, para 13 confusingly refers as 'lasting powers'.

24.15 Essentially, protective measures are measures taken by administrative or judicial authorities, such as a court or tribunal, in contracting states, whereas powers of representation are arrangements made in advance by individuals for their care and representation in the event that they may become mentally incapacitated.

24.16 There is a significant difference between protective measures and lasting powers in terms of their recognition and enforcement. MCA 2005, Sch 3, paras 19 to 21, on recognition, and para 22 on enforcement, apply only to protective measures and do not apply to lasting powers.

24.17 MCA 2005, Sch 3, para 19 provides that a protective measure taken in relation to an adult under the law of a country other than England and Wales is to be recognised in England and Wales in certain circumstances.

24.18 MCA 2005, Sch 3, para 22 provides that an interested person may apply to the court for a declaration as to whether a protective measure taken under the law of, and enforceable in a country other than England and Wales is enforceable, or to be registered, in England and Wales in accordance with Court of Protection Rules.

POWERS OF REPRESENTATION

24.19 In relation to 'powers of representation' or 'lasting powers', MCA 2005, Sch 3, para 13(6) provides that Schedule 3 – and thereby the Hague Convention - applies to:

- a lasting power of attorney (as defined in MCA 2005, s 9);
- an enduring power of attorney (as defined in MCA 2005, Schedule 4); or
- any other power of like effect.

24.20 Rule 205(2) of the Court of Protection Rules 2007 provides:

'Notwithstanding the provisions of paragraph 13(6) of Schedule 3 to the Act, "lasting power" does not include—
(a)   a lasting power of attorney within the meaning of section 9 of the Act; or
(b)   an enduring power of attorney within the meaning of Schedule 4 to the Act.'

24.21 The effect of rule 205(2) is to limit the definition of a lasting power, to powers which have not been created under the MCA 2005, and as such are 'foreign powers'.

24.22 Many jurisdictions have powers of representation of like effect to an LPA in England and Wales, although the formalities relating to their creation or termination can vary considerably. MCA 2005, Sch 3, para 15 provides that regulations may provide for the formalities in relation to LPAs as set out in MCA 2005, Sch 1, to apply with modifications in relation to 'any other power of like effect' but, as yet, no such regulations have been made.

24.23 MCA 2005, Sch 3, Part 3, in which the provisions relating to lasting powers appear, is principally concerned with issues relating to 'applicable law', and it distinguishes between the applicable law regarding:

- the existence, extent, modification, or extinction of a lasting power; and
- the manner in which a lasting power is being exercised.

24.24 The applicable law in relation to the manner of the exercise of a lasting power is straightforward. It is the law of the country where it is exercised: MCA 2005, Sch 3, para 13(5).

24.25 The donor is given a choice (*dépeçage*) regarding the applicable law in relation to the existence, extent, modification, or extinction of a lasting power. The choice is between the law of:

- the donor's habitual residence; or
- a 'connected country', if the donor has specified in writing that the law of that country is to be the applicable law.

24.26 MCA 2005, Sch 3, para 13(3) provides that, in relation to the donor of a lasting power a 'connected country' is a country:

- of which he is a national;
- in which he was formerly habitually resident; or
- in which he has property – but only in relation to the property which the donor has in the connected country (MCA 2005, Sch 3, para 13(4)).

24.27 Accordingly, if the donor of a lasting power is habitually resident in England and Wales at the time of granting the power, the law applicable to the existence, extent, modification or extinction of the power is the law of England and Wales, unless the donor has specified in writing that the law of a 'connected country' shall be the applicable law, in which case it shall be that law: MCA 2005, Sch 3, para 13(1).

24.28 Similarly, if the donor is habitually resident outside England and Wales at the time of granting the power, but England and Wales is a connected country, the law applicable to the existence, extent, modification or extinction of the power is the law of the country in which the donor is habitually resident, unless the donor has specified in writing that the law of England and Wales shall be the applicable law, in which case it shall be that law: MCA 2005, Sch 3, para 13(2).

EXERCISE OF POWERS OF REPRESENTATION

24.29 It was stated above that the law applicable to the manner of exercise of a lasting power is the law of the country in which it is exercised: MCA 2005, Sch 3, para 13(5).

24.30 MCA 2005, Sch 3, para 14, which replicates Article 16 of the Hague Convention, implicitly refers to the exercise of a lasting power in England and Wales, and confers powers on 'the court', which, pursuant to MCA 2005, s 64(1) means the Court of Protection, where the donee of the power is acting inappropriately. Paragraph 14 provides that:

'(1)   Where a lasting power is not exercised in a manner sufficient to guarantee the protection of the person or property of the donor, the court, in exercising jurisdiction under this Schedule, may disapply or modify the power.

(2)   Where, in accordance with this Part of this Schedule, the law applicable to the power is, in one or more respects, that of a country other than England and Wales, the court must, so far as possible, have regard to the law of the other country in that respect (or those respects).'

24.31 These powers have not yet been exercised by the Court of Protection, but it is likely that the court would apply similar criteria to those in s 22 of the MCA 2005, and intervene only if the donee has behaved, or is behaving, or proposes to behave in a way that contravenes his authority or is not in the donor's best interests. The reference to disapplying the power probably falls short of actual revocation, though in practical terms disapplication may have the same effect.

24.32 MCA 2005, Sch 3, para 16 makes provision for the protection of third parties where a representative, in purported exercise of an authority to act on behalf of an adult enters into a transaction with them.

24.33 MCA 2005, Sch 3, para 17 provides that, where the Court of Protection is entitled to exercise its jurisdiction under Sch 3, the mandatory provisions of the law of England and Wales apply, regardless of any system of law which would otherwise apply in relation to the matter.

24.34 MCA 2005, Sch 3, para 18 provides that none of the provisions in the Schedule relating to applicable law requires or enables the application in England and Wales of a provision of the law in another country if its application would be manifestly contrary to public policy. An example might be assisting suicide, to which express reference is made in MCA 2005, s 62.

24.35 As foreign powers of attorney are not protective measures, they are not capable of being made the subject of applications for recognition and enforcement under the provisions of MCA 2005, Part 4 of Sch 3. Instead questions as to their validity and exercise fall for consideration by reference to Part 3 of Sch 3. The Court of Protection (Amendment) Rules 2017 (SI 2017/187) have inserted a new Part 24 into the Court of Protection Rules 2007. It is supported by Practice Direction 24A: *International Protection of Adults*, and sets out a new procedure to recognise and enforce foreign protective measures; disapply or modify a foreign LPA; and for a declaration as to the authority of an attorney of a foreign power, which is designed to oblige a public authority or financial institution to accept a foreign power of attorney that is valid according to its governing law.

CASE-LAW

24.36 There have been a limited number of reported cases on the operation of the MCA 2005, Sch 3, since the Act came into force on 1 October 2007:

- *Re MN (Recognition and Enforcement of Foreign Protective Measures)* [2010] COPLR Con Vol 893;
- *Re M* [2012] COPLR 430;
- *Re PO* [2014] Fam 197 (CP);
- *An English Local Authority v SW* [2014] EWCOP 43; and
- *DB v Worcestershire County Council and EC v Worcestershire County Council* [2016] EWCOP 30.

24.37 MN was born in 1921 and until 2009 had lived in California, where in 2004 she made an advance health care directive appointing her niece, PLH, to be her agent. In May 2009, PLH, who lives in Camberley, Surrey, arranged for MB to be flown over to England. Proceedings were commenced in California, and on 27 April 2010 Judge Cain revoked PLH's appointment as agent and ordered that MN be returned to California. His order was stayed pending an appeal in California and, in the meantime, proceedings were commenced in the Court of Protection in England. An expert psycho-geriatrician, Dr Peter Jefferys, was of the opinion that MN was capable of making the journey back to California, but he had serious reservations as to whether it was in her longer term best interests to do so.

24.38 In his judgment in *Re MN*, which was handed down on 30 July 2010, Hedley J considered in some detail the provisions on the international protection of adults in Sch 3 to the MCA 2005, and summarised the position in this case, at paragraph 38, as follows:

> 'The basis of jurisdiction is habitual residence. In this case the key to that decision is whether PLH's authority as agent permitted this removal to England. If it did not, MN remains habitually resident in California and the courts of that State should exercise primary jurisdiction. If, however, it did, I am likely to conclude that MN is now habitually resident in England and Wales and jurisdiction belongs to this court. If that is so, I could not enforce the order of the Californian court unless, having conducted a full best interests enquiry on evidence, I concluded that her best interests required a return to California. On the other hand if jurisdiction belongs to California, I am likely to recognise and enforce the Californian order (if un-amended and there is no stay) and to give directions for implementation unless the carrier or Dr Jefferys were to advise otherwise, My best interests enquiry would essentially be confined to the journey. However this court could adopt a full best interests jurisdiction at the invitation of the Californian court.'

24.39 *Re M* [2012] COPLR 430 involved a young man who is a national of and habitually resident in the Republic of Ireland. The High Court in Dublin made an order for him to be transferred to and detained and treated in a psychiatric institution in England; there being no suitable facility in Ireland.

The Health Services Executive in Ireland applied to the Court of Protection for recognition and enforcement of the order under Part 4 of Sch 3 to the MCA 2005.

24.40 In his judgment in *Re M*, Mostyn J held that the Hague Convention on the International Protection of Adults is part of the domestic law of England and Wales, whether or not the foreign country whose order it is sought to be enforced has or has not ratified the Convention. The Irish order was a 'protective measure' for the purposes of paragraph 19(1) of Schedule 3, and its recognition is mandatory subject to the limited exceptions in sub-paragraphs (3) and (4), none of which applied in this case.

24.41 In *Re PO* [2014] Fam 197 (CP), the court had to consider whether an elderly lady with dementia was habitually resident in England or Scotland. President Munby held that habitual residence can in principle be lost and another habitual residence can be acquired on the same day. Where the adult lacks mental capacity, this may be without the need for a court order or the appointment of a deputy. However, habitual residence will not change if removal has been wrongful or in breach of a court order.

24.42 In *an English Local Authority v SW* [2014] EWCOP 43, Mostyn J held that the definition of habitual residence should be kept free of analytical constructs and should be the same as other private family law instruments. The extent to which the adult had integrated into her current setting was a factor to consider but it was not determinative.

24.43 *DB v Worcestershire County Council and EC v Worcestershire County Council* [2016] EWCOP 30

In *Re DB and Re EC* [2016] EWCOP 30, Baker J, building on *Re SW* held that habitual residence is not a legal concept but is to be determined on the facts, but as a general rule it must have a certain duration which reflects an adequate degree of permanence and stability without requiring a minimum duration.

CONCLUSION

24.44 Although they contain some useful provisions regarding applicable law, neither the Hague Convention nor the MCA 2005, Sch 3 are satisfactory in terms of the recognition and enforcement of powers of representation. They assume that the rules on applicable law are sufficient, and as a consequence there is no direct mechanism for obtaining a court order under the Hague Convention or the MCA to authenticate a power of representation and facilitate its acceptance and enforcement in other territories. However, the recent change to the Court of Protection Rules does at least provide for a mechanism to obtain a declaration as to the authority of an attorney to act under a foreign power.

24.45 This unsatisfactory state of affairs is summarised in the following question and answer which appear on the FAQs pages on the website of the Office of the Public Guardian (Scotland):

'Q. Can a Scottish Power of Attorney (PoA) be used in England?

A. A Scottish PoA can be used in England if an organisation (e.g. a bank) accepts its authority but if they do not there are difficulties. What the organisation may require is an endorsement of the Scottish PoA from the English authorities [Public Guardian or Court of Protection] but the English legislation does not appear to permit these authorities to offer this endorsement. If a Scottish PoA can't be used without an endorsement but one cannot get such an endorsement the Scottish PoA becomes a worthless document. It is recognised that this is an unacceptable position and perhaps not what was intended. The matter rests with England to agree and make any changes that are required.'

Appendix A

STATUTES

POWERS OF ATTORNEY ACT 1971

Chapter 27

A1

1 Execution of powers of attorney

(1) An instrument creating a power of attorney shall be executed as a deed by the donor of the power.

(2) . . .

(3) This section is without prejudice to any requirement in, or having effect under, any other Act as to the witnessing of instruments creating powers of attorney and does not affect the rules relating to the execution of instruments by bodies corporate.

Amendment: substituted by the Law of Property (Miscellaneous Provisions) Act 1989, s 1, Sch 1, para 6(a).Sub-s (2): repealed by the Law of Property (Miscellaneous Provisions) Act 1989, ss 1, 4, Sch 1, para 6(b), Sch 2.

---

2 . . .

Amendment: Repealed by the Supreme Court Act 1981, s 152(4), Sch 7.

3 Proof of instruments creating powers of attorney

(1) The contents of an instrument creating a power of attorney may be proved by means of a copy which –

   (a)   is a reproduction of the original made with a photographic or other device for reproducing documents in facsimile; and

   (b)   contains the following certificate or certificates signed by the donor of the power or by a solicitor [*duly certificated notary public*] [, authorised person] or stockbroker, that is to say—

      (i)   a certificate at the end to the effect that the copy is a true and complete copy of the original; and

      (ii)   if the original consists of two or more pages, a certificate at the end of each page of the copy to the effect that it is a true and complete copy of the corresponding page of the original.

(2) Where a copy of an instrument creating a power of attorney has been made which complies with subsection (1) of this section, the contents of the instrument may also be proved by means of a copy of that copy if the further copy itself complies with that subsection, taking references in it to the original as references to the copy from which the further copy is made.

(3) In this section ['duly certificated notary public' has the same meaning as it has in the Solicitors Act 1974 by virtue of section 87(1) of that Act and] ['authorised person' means a person (other than a solicitor) who, for the purposes of the Legal Services Act 2007, is an authorised person in relation to any activity which constitutes a notarial

activity (within the meaning of that Act) and] 'stockbroker' means a member of any stock exchange within the meaning of the Stock Transfer Act 1963 or the Stock Transfer Act (Northern Ireland) 1963.

(4)   This section is without prejudice to section 4 of the Evidence and Powers of Attorney Act 1940 (proof of deposited instruments by office copy) and to any other method of proof authorised by law.

(5)   For the avoidance of doubt, in relation to an instrument made in Scotland the references to a power of attorney in this section and in section 4 of the Evidence and Powers of Attorney Act 1940 include references to a factory and commission.

Amendments: words prospectively substituted by the Legal Services Act 2007, s 208(1), Sch 21, para 26(a); inserted by Courts and Legal Services Act 1990,s 125(2), Sch 17, para 4(a); Sub-s (3): words from "duly certificated notary" to "that Act and" in italics prospectively repealed and subsequent words in square brackets substituted by the Legal Services Act 2007, s 208(1), Sch 21, para 26(b);.inserted by the Courts and Legal Services Act 1990, s 125(2), Sch 17, para 4(b).

4 Powers of attorney given as security

(1)   Where a power of attorney is expressed to be irrevocable and is given to secure –

- (a)   a proprietary interest of the donee of the power; or
- (b)   the performance of an obligation owed to the donee,

then, so long as the donee has that interest or the obligation remains undischarged, the power shall not be revoked –

- (i)   by the donor without the consent of the donee; or
- (ii)   by the death, incapacity or bankruptcy of the donor or, if the donor is a body corporate, by its winding up or dissolution.

(2)   A power of attorney given to secure a proprietary interest may be given to the person entitled to the interest and persons deriving title under him to that interest, and those persons shall be duly constituted donees of the power for all purposes of the power but without prejudice to any right to appoint substitutes given by the power.

(3)   This section applies to powers of attorney whenever created.

5 Protection of donee and third persons where power of attorney is revoked

(1)   A donee of a power of attorney who acts in pursuance of the power at a time when it has been revoked shall not, by reason of the revocation, incur any liability (either to the donor or to any other person) if at that time he did not know that the power had been revoked.

(2)   Where a power of attorney has been revoked and a person, without knowledge of the revocation, deals with the donee of the power, the transaction between them shall, in favour of that person, be as valid as if the power had then been in existence.

(3)   Where the power is expressed in the instrument creating it to be irrevocable and to be given by way of security then, unless the person dealing with the donee knows that it was not in fact given by way of security, he shall be entitled to assume that the power is incapable of revocation except by the donor acting with the consent of the donee and shall accordingly be treated for the purposes of subsection (2) of this section as having knowledge of the revocation only if he knows that it has been revoked in that manner.

(4)   Where the interest of a purchaser depends on whether a transaction between the donee of a power of attorney and another person was valid by virtue of subsection (2) of this section, it shall be conclusively presumed in favour of the purchaser that that person did not at the material time know of the revocation of the power if –

- (a)   the transaction between that person and the donee was completed within twelve months of the date on which the power came into operation; or
- (b)   that person makes a statutory declaration, before or within three months after the completion of the purchase, that he did not at the material time know of the revocation of the power.

(5) Without prejudice to subsection (3) of this section, for the purposes of this section knowledge of the revocation of a power of attorney includes knowledge of the occurrence of any event (such as the death of the donor) which has the effect of revoking the power.

(6) In this section 'purchaser' and 'purchase' have the meaning specified in section 205 (1) of the Law of Property Act 1925.

(7) This section applies whenever the power of attorney was created but only to acts and transactions after the commencement of this Act.

6 Additional protection for transferees under stock exchange transactions

(1) Without prejudice to section 5 of this Act, where –

    (a)   the donee of a power of attorney executes, as transferor, an instrument transferring registered securities; and

    (b)   the instrument is executed for the purposes of a stock exchange transaction,

it shall be conclusively presumed in favour of the transferee that the power had not been revoked at the date of the instrument if a statutory declaration to that effect is made by the donee of the power on or within three months after that date.

(2) In this section 'registered securities' and 'stock exchange transaction' have the same meanings as in the Stock Transfer Act 1963.

7 Execution of instruments etc by donee of power of attorney

(1) If the donee of a power of attorney is an individual, he may, if he thinks fit –

    (a)   execute any instrument with his own signature, and

    (b)   do any other thing in his own name,

by the authority of the donor of the power; and any [instrument executed or thing done in that manner shall, subject to subsection (1A) of this section, be as effective as if executed by the donee in any manner which would constitute due execution of that instrument by the donor or, as the case may be, as if done by the donee in the name of the donor.

(1A) Where an instrument is executed by the donee as a deed, it shall be as effective as if executed by the donee in a manner which would constitute due execution of it as a deed by the donor only if it is executed in accordance with section 1(3)(a) of the Law of Property (Miscellaneous Provisions) Act 1989.

(2) For the avoidance of doubt it is hereby declared that an instrument to which subsection (3) . . . of section 74 of the Law of Property Act 1925 applies may be executed either as provided in [that subsection] or as provided in this section.

(3) . . .

(4) This section applies whenever the power of attorney was created.

    Amendment: substituted by Law of Property (Miscellaneous Provisions) Act 1989; amended by SI 2005/1906 date in force 15 September 2005 (except in relation to any instrument executed before that date.

8 . . .

    Amendment: repealed by Statute Law (Repeals) Act 2004.

9 . . .

    Amendment: Repealed by the Trustee Delegation Act 1999, s 12.

10 Effect of general power of attorney in specified form

(1) Subject to subsection (2) of this section, a general power of attorney in the form set out in Schedule 1 to this Act, or in a form to the like effect but expressed to be made under this Act, shall operate to confer –

    (a)   on the donee of the power; or

(b)   if there is more than one donee, on the donees acting jointly or acting jointly or severally, as the case may be,

authority to do on behalf of the donor anything which he can lawfully do by an attorney.

(2)   Subject to section 1 of the Trustee Delegation Act 1999, this section does not apply to functions which the donor has as a trustee or personal representative or as a tenant for life or statutory owner within the meaning of the Settled Land Act 1925.

Amendment: Substituted by the Trustee Delegation Act 1999, s 3.

11 Short title, repeals, consequential amendments, commencement and extent

(1)   This Act may be cited as the Powers of Attorney Act 1971.

(2)   The enactments specified in Schedule 2 to this Act are hereby repealed to the extent specified in the third column of that Schedule.

(3)   . . .

(4)   . . .

(5)   Section 3 of this Act extends to Scotland and Northern Ireland but, save as aforesaid, this Act extends to England and Wales only.

Amendments:-Sub-s (3): in part amends the Law of Property Act 1925, s 125(2); remainder repealed by the Supreme Court Act 1981, s 152(4), Sch 7. Sub-s (4): repealed by the Statute Law (Repeals) Act 2004.

SCHEDULE 1
FORM OF GENERAL POWER OF ATTORNEY FOR PURPOSES OF SECTION 10

Section 10

This general power of Attorney is made this . . . day of . . . 19 . . . by AB of I appoint CD of (*or* CD of . . . and EF of . . . jointly *or* jointly and severally) to be my attorney(s) in accordance with section 10 of the Powers of Attorney Act 1971. In Witness etc,

TRUSTEE DELEGATION ACT 1999

Chapter 15

ATTORNEY OF TRUSTEE WITH BENEFICIAL INTEREST IN LAND

A2

1 Exercise of trustee functions by attorney

(1)   The donee of a power of attorney is not prevented from doing an act in relation to –

    (a)   land,

    (b)   capital proceeds of a conveyance of land, or

    (c)   income from land,

by reason only that the act involves the exercise of a trustee function of the donor if, at the time when the act is done, the donor has a beneficial interest in the land, proceeds or income.

(2)   In this section –

    (a)   'conveyance' has the same meaning as in the Law of Property Act 1925, and

    (b)   references to a trustee function of the donor are to a function which the donor has as trustee (either alone or jointly with any other person or persons).

(3)   Subsection (1) above –

    (a)   applies only if and so far as a contrary intention is not expressed in the instrument creating the power of attorney, and

    (b)   has effect subject to the terms of that instrument.

(4)   The donor of the power of attorney –

    (a)   is liable for the acts or defaults of the donee in exercising any function by virtue of subsection (1) above in the same manner as if they were acts or defaults of the donor, but

    (b)   is not liable by reason only that a function is exercised by the donee by virtue of that subsection.

(5)   Subsections (1) and (4) above –

    (a)   apply only if and so far as a contrary intention is not expressed in the instrument (if any) creating the trust, and

    (b)   have effect subject to the terms of such an instrument.

(6)   The fact that it appears that, in dealing with any shares or stock, the donee of the power of attorney is exercising a function by virtue of subsection (1) above does not affect with any notice of any trust a person in whose books the shares are, or stock is, registered or inscribed.

(7)   In any case where (by way of exception to section 3(1) of the Trusts of Land and Appointment of Trustees Act 1996) the doctrine of conversion continues to operate, any person who, by reason of the continuing operation of that doctrine, has a beneficial interest in the proceeds of sale of land shall be treated for the purposes of this section and section 2 below as having a beneficial interest in the land.

(8)   The donee of a power of attorney is not to be regarded as exercising a trustee function by virtue of subsection (1) above if he is acting under a trustee delegation power; and for this purpose a trustee delegation power is a power of attorney given under –

    (a)   a statutory provision, or

    (b)   a provision of the instrument (if any) creating a trust, under which the donor of the power is expressly authorised to delegate the exercise of all or any of his trustee functions by power of attorney.

(9)   Subject to section 4(6) below, this section applies only to powers of attorney created after the commencement of this Act.

2 Evidence of beneficial interest

(1)   This section applies where the interest of a purchaser depends on the donee of a power of attorney having power to do an act in relation to any property by virtue of section 1(1) above.

In this subsection 'purchaser' has the same meaning as in Part I of the Law of Property Act 1925.

(2)   Where this section applies an appropriate statement is, in favour of the purchaser, conclusive evidence of the donor of the power having a beneficial interest in the property at the time of the doing of the act.

(3)   In this section 'an appropriate statement' means a signed statement made by the donee –

> (a)   when doing the act in question, or
>
> (b)   at any other time within the period of three months beginning with the day on which the act is done,

that the donor has a beneficial interest in the property at the time of the donee doing the act.

(4)   If an appropriate statement is false, the donee is liable in the same way as he would be if the statement were contained in a statutory declaration.

3 General powers in specified form

In section 10(2) of the Powers of Attorney Act 1971 (which provides that a general power of attorney in the form set out in Schedule 1 to that Act, or a similar form, does not confer on the donee of the power any authority to exercise functions of the donor as trustee etc), for the words 'This section' substitute 'Subject to section 1 of the Trustee Delegation Act 1999, this section'.

4 . . .

> **Amendment:** Repealed by Mental Capacity Act 2005, s 67(2), Sch 7; SI 2007/1897.

TRUSTEE DELEGATION UNDER SECTION 25 OF THE TRUSTEE ACT 1925

5 Delegation under section 25 of the Trustee Act 1925

(1)   For section 25 of the Trustee Act 1925 substitute –

'25 DELEGATION OF TRUSTEE'S FUNCTIONS BY POWER OF ATTORNEY

> (1)   Notwithstanding any rule of law or equity to the contrary, a trustee may, by power of attorney, delegate the execution or exercise of all or any of the trusts, powers and discretions vested in him as trustee either alone or jointly with any other person or persons.
>
> (2)   A delegation under this section –
>
> > (a)   commences as provided by the instrument creating the power or, if the instrument makes no provision as to the commencement of the delegation, with the date of the execution of the instrument by the donor; and
> >
> > (b)   continues for a period of twelve months or any shorter period provided by the instrument creating the power.
>
> (3)   The persons who may be donees of a power of attorney under this section include a trust corporation.

(4) Before or within seven days after giving a power of attorney under this section the donor shall give written notice of it (specifying the date on which the power comes into operation and its duration, the donee of the power, the reason why the power is given and, where some only are delegated, the trusts, powers and discretions delegated) to –

    (a)   each person (other than himself), if any, who under any instrument creating the trust has power (whether alone or jointly) to appoint a new trustee; and

    (b)   each of the other trustees, if any;

but failure to comply with this subsection shall not, in favour of a person dealing with the donee of the power, invalidate any act done or instrument executed by the donee.

(5) A power of attorney given under this section by a single donor –

    (a)   in the form set out in subsection (6) of this section; or

    (b)   in a form to the like effect but expressed to be made under this subsection,

shall operate to delegate to the person identified in the form as the single donee of the power the execution and exercise of all the trusts, powers and discretions vested in the donor as trustee (either alone or jointly with any other person or persons) under the single trust so identified.

(6) The form referred to in subsection (5) of this section is as follows –
'THIS GENERAL TRUSTEE POWER OF ATTORNEY is made on [date] by [name of one donor] of [address of donor] as trustee of [name or details of one trust].
I appoint [name of one donee] of [address of donee] to be my attorney [if desired, the date on which the delegation commences or the period for which it continues (or both)] in accordance with section 25(5) of the Trustee Act 1925.
[To be executed as a deed]'.

(7) The donor of a power of attorney given under this section shall be liable for the acts or defaults of the donee in the same manner as if they were the acts or defaults of the donor.

(8) For the purpose of executing or exercising the trusts or powers delegated to him, the donee may exercise any of the powers conferred on the donor as trustee by statute or by the instrument creating the trust, including power, for the purpose of the transfer of any inscribed stock, himself to delegate to an attorney power to transfer, but not including the power of delegation conferred by this section.

(9) The fact that it appears from any power of attorney given under this section, or from any evidence required for the purposes of any such power of attorney or otherwise, that in dealing with any stock the donee of the power is acting in the execution of a trust shall not be deemed for any purpose to affect any person in whose books the stock is inscribed or registered with any notice of the trust.

(10) This section applies to a personal representative, tenant for life and statutory owner as it applies to a trustee except that subsection (4) shall apply as if it required the notice there mentioned to be given –

    (a)   in the case of a personal representative, to each of the other personal representatives, if any, except any executor who has renounced probate;

    (b)   in the case of a tenant for life, to the trustees of the settlement and to each person, if any, who together with the person giving the notice constitutes the tenant for life; and

    (c)   in the case of a statutory owner, to each of the persons, if any, who together with the person giving the notice constitute the statutory owner and, in the case of a statutory owner by virtue of section 23(1)(a) of the Settled Land Act 1925, to the trustees of the settlement.'

(2)   Subsection (1) above has effect in relation to powers of attorney created after the commencement of this Act.

(3)   In section 34(2)(b) of the Pensions Act 1995 (delegation by trustees of trustee scheme under section 25 of the Trustee Act 1925), for 'during absence abroad' substitute 'for period not exceeding twelve months'.

6 . . .

Amendment: Repealed by the Mental Capacity Act 2005, s 67(2), Sch 7; Si 2007/1897.

MISCELLANEOUS PROVISIONS ABOUT ATTORNEY ACTING FOR TRUSTEE

7 Two-trustee rules

(1)   A requirement imposed by an enactment –

  (a)   that capital money be paid to, or dealt with as directed by, at least two trustees or that a valid receipt for capital money be given otherwise than by a sole trustee, or

  (b)   that, in order for an interest or power to be overreached, a conveyance or deed be executed by at least two trustees,

is not satisfied by money being paid to or dealt with as directed by, or a receipt for money being given by, a relevant attorney or by a conveyance or deed being executed by such an attorney.

(2)   In this section 'relevant attorney' means a person (other than a trust corporation within the meaning of the Trustee Act 1925) who is acting either –

  (a)   both as a trustee and as attorney for one or more other trustees, or

  (b)   as attorney for two or more trustees,

and who is not acting together with any other person or persons.

(3)   This section applies whether a relevant attorney is acting under a power created before or after the commencement of this Act (but in the case of such an attorney acting under an enduring power created before that commencement is without prejudice to any continuing application of section 3(3) of the Enduring Powers of Attorney Act 1985 to the enduring power after that commencement.

Amendment:-Words repealed by Mental Capacity Act 2005, s 67(2), Sch 7.

8 Appointment of additional trustee by attorney

(1)   In section 36 of the Trustee Act 1925 (appointment of trustees), after subsection (6) (additional trustees) insert –

  '(6A)   A person who is either –

  (a)   both a trustee and attorney for the other trustee (if one other), or for both of the other trustees (if two others), under a registered power; or

  (b)   attorney under a registered power for the trustee (if one) or for both or each of the trustees (if two or three),

may, if subsection (6B) of this section is satisfied in relation to him, make an appointment under subsection (6)(b) of this section on behalf of the trustee or trustees.

  (6B)   This subsection is satisfied in relation to an attorney under a registered power for one or more trustees if (as attorney under the power) –

  (a)   he intends to exercise any function of the trustee or trustees by virtue of section 1(1) of the Trustee Delegation Act 1999; or

  (b)   he intends to exercise any function of the trustee or trustees in relation to any land, capital proceeds of a conveyance of land or income from land by virtue of its delegation to him under section 25 of this Act or the instrument (if any) creating the trust.

(6C)   In subsections (6A) and (6B) of this section "registered power" means a power of attorney created by an instrument which is for the time being registered under section 6 of the Enduring Powers of Attorney Act 1985.

(6D)   Subsection (6A) of this section –

(a)   applies only if and so far as a contrary intention is not expressed in the instrument creating the power of attorney (or, where more than one, any of them) or the instrument (if any) creating the trust; and

(b)   has effect subject to the terms of those instruments.'

(2)   The amendment made by subsection (1) above has effect only where the power, or (where more than one) each of them, is created after the commencement of this Act.

9 Attorney acting for incapable trustee

(1)   In section 22 of the Law of Property Act 1925 (requirement, before dealing with legal estate vested in trustee who is incapable by reason of mental disorder, to appoint new trustee or discharge incapable trustee), after subsection (2) insert –

'(3)   Subsection (2) of this section does not prevent a legal estate being dealt with without the appointment of a new trustee, or the discharge of the incapable trustee, at a time when the donee of an enduring power (within the meaning of the Enduring Powers of Attorney Act 1985) is entitled to act for the incapable trustee in the dealing.'

(2)   The amendment made by subsection (1) above has effect whether the enduring power was created before or after the commencement of this Act.

AUTHORITY OF ATTORNEY TO ACT IN RELATION TO LAND

10 Extent of attorney's authority to act in relation to land

(1)   Where the donee of a power of attorney is authorised by the power to do an act of any description in relation to any land, his authority to do an act of that description at any time includes authority to do it with respect to any estate or interest in the land which is held at that time by the donor (whether alone or jointly with any other person or persons).

(2)   Subsection (1) above –

(a)   applies only if and so far as a contrary intention is not expressed in the instrument creating the power of attorney, and

(b)   has effect subject to the terms of that instrument.

(3)   This section applies only to powers of attorney created after the commencement of this Act.

SUPPLEMENTARY

11 Interpretation

(1)   In this Act –

'land' has the same meaning as in the Trustee Act 1925, and

'enduring power' has the same meaning as in the Enduring Powers of Attorney Act 1985.

(2)   References in this Act to the creation of a power of attorney are to the execution by the donor of the instrument creating it.

12 Repeals

The enactments specified in the Schedule to this Act are repealed to the extent specified in the third column, but subject to the note at the end.

13 Commencement, extent and short title

(1)   The preceding provisions of this Act shall come into force on such day as the Lord Chancellor may by order made by statutory instrument appoint.

(2)   This Act extends to England and Wales only.

(3) This Act may be cited as the Trustee Delegation Act 1999.

MENTAL CAPACITY ACT 2005

2005 CHAPTER 9

PART 1   PERSONS WHO LACK CAPACITY

The principles

A3

1 The principles

(1)   The following principles apply for the purposes of this Act.

(2)   A person must be assumed to have capacity unless it is established that he lacks capacity.

(3)   A person is not to be treated as unable to make a decision unless all practicable steps to help him to do so have been taken without success.

(4)   A person is not to be treated as unable to make a decision merely because he makes an unwise decision.

(5)   An act done, or decision made, under this Act for or on behalf of a person who lacks capacity must be done, or made, in his best interests.

(6)   Before the act is done, or the decision is made, regard must be had to whether the purpose for which it is needed can be as effectively achieved in a way that is less restrictive of the person's rights and freedom of action.

Preliminary

2 People who lack capacity

(1)   For the purposes of this Act, a person lacks capacity in relation to a matter if at the material time he is unable to make a decision for himself in relation to the matter because of an impairment of, or a disturbance in the functioning of, the mind or brain.

(2)   It does not matter whether the impairment or disturbance is permanent or temporary.

(3)   A lack of capacity cannot be established merely by reference to—

    (a)   a person's age or appearance, or

    (b)   a condition of his, or an aspect of his behaviour, which might lead others to make unjustified assumptions about his capacity.

(4)   In proceedings under this Act or any other enactment, any question whether a person lacks capacity within the meaning of this Act must be decided on the balance of probabilities.

(5)   No power which a person ("D") may exercise under this Act—

    (a)   in relation to a person who lacks capacity, or

    (b)   where D reasonably thinks that a person lacks capacity,

is exercisable in relation to a person under 16.

(6)   Subsection (5) is subject to section 18(3).

3 Inability to make decisions

(1)   For the purposes of section 2, a person is unable to make a decision for himself if he is unable—

    (a)   to understand the information relevant to the decision,

    (b)   to retain that information,

    (c)   to use or weigh that information as part of the process of making the decision, or

    (d)   to communicate his decision (whether by talking, using sign language or any other means).

(2)   A person is not to be regarded as unable to understand the information relevant to a decision if he is able to understand an explanation of it given to him in a way that is appropriate to his circumstances (using simple language, visual aids or any other means).

(3)   The fact that a person is able to retain the information relevant to a decision for a short period only does not prevent him from being regarded as able to make the decision.

(4)   The information relevant to a decision includes information about the reasonably foreseeable consequences of—

    (a)   deciding one way or another, or

    (b)   failing to make the decision.

4 Best interests

(1)   In determining for the purposes of this Act what is in a person's best interests, the person making the determination must not make it merely on the basis of—

    (a)   the person's age or appearance, or

    (b)   a condition of his, or an aspect of his behaviour, which might lead others to make unjustified assumptions about what might be in his best interests.

(2)   The person making the determination must consider all the relevant circumstances and, in particular, take the following steps.

(3)   He must consider—

    (a)   whether it is likely that the person will at some time have capacity in relation to the matter in question, and

    (b)   if it appears likely that he will, when that is likely to be.

(4)   He must, so far as reasonably practicable, permit and encourage the person to participate, or to improve his ability to participate, as fully as possible in any act done for him and any decision affecting him.

(5)   Where the determination relates to life-sustaining treatment he must not, in considering whether the treatment is in the best interests of the person concerned, be motivated by a desire to bring about his death.

(6)   He must consider, so far as is reasonably ascertainable—

    (a)   the person's past and present wishes and feelings (and, in particular, any relevant written statement made by him when he had capacity),

    (b)   the beliefs and values that would be likely to influence his decision if he had capacity, and

    (c)   the other factors that he would be likely to consider if he were able to do so.

(7)   He must take into account, if it is practicable and appropriate to consult them, the views of—

    (a)   anyone named by the person as someone to be consulted on the matter in question or on matters of that kind,

    (b)   anyone engaged in caring for the person or interested in his welfare,

    (c)   any donee of a lasting power of attorney granted by the person, and

    (d)   any deputy appointed for the person by the court,

as to what would be in the person's best interests and, in particular, as to the matters mentioned in subsection (6).

(8)   The duties imposed by subsections (1) to (7) also apply in relation to the exercise of any powers which—

    (a)   are exercisable under a lasting power of attorney, or

    (b)   are exercisable by a person under this Act where he reasonably believes that another person lacks capacity.

(9)   In the case of an act done, or a decision made, by a person other than the court, there is sufficient compliance with this section if (having complied with the requirements of subsections (1) to (7)) he reasonably believes that what he does or decides is in the best interests of the person concerned.

(10)   "Life-sustaining treatment" means treatment which in the view of a person providing health care for the person concerned is necessary to sustain life.

(11)   "Relevant circumstances" are those—

    (a)   of which the person making the determination is aware, and

    (b)   which it would be reasonable to regard as relevant.

[4A   Restriction on deprivation of liberty]

[(1)   This Act does not authorise any person ("D") to deprive any other person ("P") of his liberty.

(2)   But that is subject to—

    (a)   the following provisions of this section, and

    (b)   section 4B.

(3)   D may deprive P of his liberty if, by doing so, D is giving effect to a relevant decision of the court.

(4)   A relevant decision of the court is a decision made by an order under section 16(2)(a) in relation to a matter concerning P's personal welfare.

(5)   D may deprive P of his liberty if the deprivation is authorised by Schedule A1 (hospital and care home residents: deprivation of liberty).]

[4B   Deprivation of liberty necessary for life-sustaining treatment etc]

[(1)   If the following conditions are met, D is authorised to deprive P of his liberty while a decision as respects any relevant issue is sought from the court.

(2)   The first condition is that there is a question about whether D is authorised to deprive P of his liberty under section 4A.

(3)   The second condition is that the deprivation of liberty—

    (a)   is wholly or partly for the purpose of—

        (i)   giving P life-sustaining treatment, or

        (ii)   doing any vital act, or

    (b)   consists wholly or partly of—

        (i)   giving P life-sustaining treatment, or

        (ii)   doing any vital act.

(4)   The third condition is that the deprivation of liberty is necessary in order to—

    (a)   give the life-sustaining treatment, or

    (b)   do the vital act.

(5)   A vital act is any act which the person doing it reasonably believes to be necessary to prevent a serious deterioration in P's condition.]

5   Acts in connection with care or treatment

(1)   If a person ("D") does an act in connection with the care or treatment of another person ("P"), the act is one to which this section applies if—

    (a)   before doing the act, D takes reasonable steps to establish whether P lacks capacity in relation to the matter in question, and

    (b)   when doing the act, D reasonably believes—

        (i)   that P lacks capacity in relation to the matter, and

        (ii)   that it will be in P's best interests for the act to be done.

(2)   D does not incur any liability in relation to the act that he would not have incurred if P—

    (a)   had had capacity to consent in relation to the matter, and

    (b)   had consented to D's doing the act.

(3)   Nothing in this section excludes a person's civil liability for loss or damage, or his criminal liability, resulting from his negligence in doing the act.

(4)   Nothing in this section affects the operation of sections 24 to 26 (advance decisions to refuse treatment).

6 Section 5 acts: limitations

(1)   If D does an act that is intended to restrain P, it is not an act to which section 5 applies unless two further conditions are satisfied.

(2)   The first condition is that D reasonably believes that it is necessary to do the act in order to prevent harm to P.

(3)   The second is that the act is a proportionate response to—

    (a)   the likelihood of P's suffering harm, and

    (b)   the seriousness of that harm.

(4)   For the purposes of this section D restrains P if he—

    (a)   uses, or threatens to use, force to secure the doing of an act which P resists, or

    (b)   restricts P's liberty of movement, whether or not P resists.

(5)   . . .

(6)   Section 5 does not authorise a person to do an act which conflicts with a decision made, within the scope of his authority and in accordance with this Part, by—

    (a)   a donee of a lasting power of attorney granted by P, or

    (b)   a deputy appointed for P by the court.

(7)   But nothing in subsection (6) stops a person—

    (a)   providing life-sustaining treatment, or

    (b)   doing any act which he reasonably believes to be necessary to prevent a serious deterioration in P's condition,

while a decision as respects any relevant issue is sought from the court.

7 Payment for necessary goods and services

(1)   If necessary goods or services are supplied to a person who lacks capacity to contract for the supply, he must pay a reasonable price for them.

(2)   "Necessary" means suitable to a person's condition in life and to his actual requirements at the time when the goods or services are supplied.

8 Expenditure

(1)   If an act to which section 5 applies involves expenditure, it is lawful for D—

    (a)   to pledge P's credit for the purpose of the expenditure, and

    (b)   to apply money in P's possession for meeting the expenditure.

(2)   If the expenditure is borne for P by D, it is lawful for D—

    (a)   to reimburse himself out of money in P's possession, or

    (b)   to be otherwise indemnified by P.

(3)   Subsections (1) and (2) do not affect any power under which (apart from those subsections) a person—

    (a)   has lawful control of P's money or other property, and

    (b)   has power to spend money for P's benefit.

Lasting powers of attorney

9 Lasting powers of attorney

(1)   A lasting power of attorney is a power of attorney under which the donor ("P") confers on the donee (or donees) authority to make decisions about all or any of the following—

    (a)   P's personal welfare or specified matters concerning P's personal welfare, and

    (b)   P's property and affairs or specified matters concerning P's property and affairs,

and which includes authority to make such decisions in circumstances where P no longer has capacity.

(2)   A lasting power of attorney is not created unless—

    (a)   section 10 is complied with,

    (b)   an instrument conferring authority of the kind mentioned in subsection (1) is made and registered in accordance with Schedule 1, and

    (c)   at the time when P executes the instrument, P has reached 18 and has capacity to execute it.

(3)   An instrument which—

    (a)   purports to create a lasting power of attorney, but

    (b)   does not comply with this section, section 10 or Schedule 1,

confers no authority.

(4)   The authority conferred by a lasting power of attorney is subject to—

    (a)   the provisions of this Act and, in particular, sections 1 (the principles) and 4 (best interests), and

    (b)   any conditions or restrictions specified in the instrument.

10 Appointment of donees

(1)   A donee of a lasting power of attorney must be—

    (a)   an individual who has reached 18, or

    (b)   if the power relates only to P's property and affairs, either such an individual or a trust corporation.

(2)   An individual who is bankrupt [or is a person in relation to whom a debt relief order is made] may not be appointed as donee of a lasting power of attorney in relation to P's property and affairs.

(3)   Subsections (4) to (7) apply in relation to an instrument under which two or more persons are to act as donees of a lasting power of attorney.

(4)   The instrument may appoint them to act—

    (a)   jointly,

    (b)   jointly and severally, or

    (c)   jointly in respect of some matters and jointly and severally in respect of others.

(5)   To the extent to which it does not specify whether they are to act jointly or jointly and severally, the instrument is to be assumed to appoint them to act jointly.

(6)   If they are to act jointly, a failure, as respects one of them, to comply with the requirements of subsection (1) or (2) or Part 1 or 2 of Schedule 1 prevents a lasting power of attorney from being created.

(7)   If they are to act jointly and severally, a failure, as respects one of them, to comply with the requirements of subsection (1) or (2) or Part 1 or 2 of Schedule 1—

    (a)   prevents the appointment taking effect in his case, but

    (b)   does not prevent a lasting power of attorney from being created in the case of the other or others.

(8)   An instrument used to create a lasting power of attorney—

    (a)   cannot give the donee (or, if more than one, any of them) power to appoint a substitute or successor, but

    (b)   may itself appoint a person to replace the donee (or, if more than one, any of them) on the occurrence of an event mentioned in section 13(6)(a) to (d) which has the effect of terminating the donee's appointment.

11 Lasting powers of attorney: restrictions

(1)   A lasting power of attorney does not authorise the donee (or, if more than one, any of them) to do an act that is intended to restrain P, unless three conditions are satisfied.

(2)   The first condition is that P lacks, or the donee reasonably believes that P lacks, capacity in relation to the matter in question.

(3)   The second is that the donee reasonably believes that it is necessary to do the act in order to prevent harm to P.

(4)   The third is that the act is a proportionate response to—
- (a)   the likelihood of P's suffering harm, and
- (b)   the seriousness of that harm.

(5)   For the purposes of this section, the donee restrains P if he—
- (a)   uses, or threatens to use, force to secure the doing of an act which P resists, or
- (b)   restricts P's liberty of movement, whether or not P resists,

or if he authorises another person to do any of those things.

(6)   . . .

(7)   Where a lasting power of attorney authorises the donee (or, if more than one, any of them) to make decisions about P's personal welfare, the authority—
- (a)   does not extend to making such decisions in circumstances other than those where P lacks, or the donee reasonably believes that P lacks, capacity,
- (b)   is subject to sections 24 to 26 (advance decisions to refuse treatment), and
- (c)   extends to giving or refusing consent to the carrying out or continuation of a treatment by a person providing health care for P.

(8)   But subsection (7)(c)—
- (a)   does not authorise the giving or refusing of consent to the carrying out or continuation of life-sustaining treatment, unless the instrument contains express provision to that effect, and
- (b)   is subject to any conditions or restrictions in the instrument.

12 Scope of lasting powers of attorney: gifts

(1)   Where a lasting power of attorney confers authority to make decisions about P's property and affairs, it does not authorise a donee (or, if more than one, any of them) to dispose of the donor's property by making gifts except to the extent permitted by subsection (2).

(2)   The donee may make gifts—
- (a)   on customary occasions to persons (including himself) who are related to or connected with the donor, or
- (b)   to any charity to whom the donor made or might have been expected to make gifts,

if the value of each such gift is not unreasonable having regard to all the circumstances and, in particular, the size of the donor's estate.

(3)   "Customary occasion" means—
- (a)   the occasion or anniversary of a birth, a marriage or the formation of a civil partnership, or
- (b)   any other occasion on which presents are customarily given within families or among friends or associates.

(4)   Subsection (2) is subject to any conditions or restrictions in the instrument.

13 Revocation of lasting powers of attorney etc

(1)   This section applies if—

(a)   P has executed an instrument with a view to creating a lasting power of attorney, or

(b)   a lasting power of attorney is registered as having been conferred by P,

and in this section references to revoking the power include revoking the instrument.

(2)   P may, at any time when he has capacity to do so, revoke the power.

(3)   P's bankruptcy[, or the making of a debt relief order (under Part 7A of the Insolvency Act 1986) in respect of P,] revokes the power so far as it relates to P's property and affairs.

(4)   But where P is bankrupt merely because an interim bankruptcy restrictions order has effect in respect of him [or where P is subject to an interim debt relief restrictions order (under Schedule 4ZB of the Insolvency Act 1986)], the power is suspended, so far as it relates to P's property and affairs, for so long as the order has effect.

(5)   The occurrence in relation to a donee of an event mentioned in subsection (6)—

(a)   terminates his appointment, and

(b)   except in the cases given in subsection (7), revokes the power.

(6)   The events are—

(a)   the disclaimer of the appointment by the donee in accordance with such requirements as may be prescribed for the purposes of this section in regulations made by the Lord Chancellor,

(b)   subject to subsections (8) and (9), the death or bankruptcy of the donee [or the making of a debt relief order (under Part 7A of the Insolvency Act 1986) in respect of the donee] or, if the donee is a trust corporation, its winding-up or dissolution,

(c)   subject to subsection (11), the dissolution or annulment of a marriage or civil partnership between the donor and the donee,

(d)   the lack of capacity of the donee.

(7)   The cases are—

(a)   the donee is replaced under the terms of the instrument,

(b)   he is one of two or more persons appointed to act as donees jointly and severally in respect of any matter and, after the event, there is at least one remaining donee.

(8)   The bankruptcy of a donee [or the making of a debt relief order (under Part 7A of the Insolvency Act 1986) in respect of a donee] does not terminate his appointment, or revoke the power, in so far as his authority relates to P's personal welfare.

(9)   Where the donee is bankrupt merely because an interim bankruptcy restrictions order has effect in respect of him, [or where the donee is subject to an interim debt relief restrictions order (under Schedule 4ZB of the Insolvency Act 1986),] his appointment and the power are suspended, so far as they relate to P's property and affairs, for so long as the order has effect.

(10)   Where the donee is one of two or more appointed to act jointly and severally under the power in respect of any matter, the reference in subsection (9) to the suspension of the power is to its suspension in so far as it relates to that donee.

(11)   The dissolution or annulment of a marriage or civil partnership does not terminate the appointment of a donee, or revoke the power, if the instrument provided that it was not to do so.

14 Protection of donee and others if no power created or power revoked

(1)   Subsections (2) and (3) apply if—

(a)   an instrument has been registered under Schedule 1 as a lasting power of attorney, but

(b)   a lasting power of attorney was not created,

whether or not the registration has been cancelled at the time of the act or transaction in question.

(2) A donee who acts in purported exercise of the power does not incur any liability (to P or any other person) because of the non-existence of the power unless at the time of acting he—

    (a)   knows that a lasting power of attorney was not created, or

    (b)   is aware of circumstances which, if a lasting power of attorney had been created, would have terminated his authority to act as a donee.

(3) Any transaction between the donee and another person is, in favour of that person, as valid as if the power had been in existence, unless at the time of the transaction that person has knowledge of a matter referred to in subsection (2).

(4) If the interest of a purchaser depends on whether a transaction between the donee and the other person was valid by virtue of subsection (3), it is conclusively presumed in favour of the purchaser that the transaction was valid if—

    (a)   the transaction was completed within 12 months of the date on which the instrument was registered, or

    (b)   the other person makes a statutory declaration, before or within 3 months after the completion of the purchase, that he had no reason at the time of the transaction to doubt that the donee had authority to dispose of the property which was the subject of the transaction.

(5) In its application to a lasting power of attorney which relates to matters in addition to P's property and affairs, section 5 of the Powers of Attorney Act 1971 (c 27) (protection where power is revoked) has effect as if references to revocation included the cessation of the power in relation to P's property and affairs.

(6) Where two or more donees are appointed under a lasting power of attorney, this section applies as if references to the donee were to all or any of them.

General powers of the court and appointment of deputies

15 Power to make declarations

(1) The court may make declarations as to—

    (a)   whether a person has or lacks capacity to make a decision specified in the declaration;

    (b)   whether a person has or lacks capacity to make decisions on such matters as are described in the declaration;

    (c)   the lawfulness or otherwise of any act done, or yet to be done, in relation to that person.

(2) "Act" includes an omission and a course of conduct.

16 Powers to make decisions and appoint deputies: general

(1) This section applies if a person ("P") lacks capacity in relation to a matter or matters concerning—

    (a)   P's personal welfare, or

    (b)   P's property and affairs.

(2) The court may—

    (a)   by making an order, make the decision or decisions on P's behalf in relation to the matter or matters, or

    (b)   appoint a person (a "deputy") to make decisions on P's behalf in relation to the matter or matters.

(3) The powers of the court under this section are subject to the provisions of this Act and, in particular, to sections 1 (the principles) and 4 (best interests).

(4) When deciding whether it is in P's best interests to appoint a deputy, the court must have regard (in addition to the matters mentioned in section 4) to the principles that—

    (a)   a decision by the court is to be preferred to the appointment of a deputy to make a decision, and

(b)   the powers conferred on a deputy should be as limited in scope and duration as is reasonably practicable in the circumstances.

(5)   The court may make such further orders or give such directions, and confer on a deputy such powers or impose on him such duties, as it thinks necessary or expedient for giving effect to, or otherwise in connection with, an order or appointment made by it under subsection (2).

(6)   Without prejudice to section 4, the court may make the order, give the directions or make the appointment on such terms as it considers are in P's best interests, even though no application is before the court for an order, directions or an appointment on those terms.

(7)   An order of the court may be varied or discharged by a subsequent order.

(8)   The court may, in particular, revoke the appointment of a deputy or vary the powers conferred on him if it is satisfied that the deputy—

(a)   has behaved, or is behaving, in a way that contravenes the authority conferred on him by the court or is not in P's best interests, or

(b)   proposes to behave in a way that would contravene that authority or would not be in P's best interests.

[16A Section 16 powers: Mental Health Act patients etc]

[(1)   If a person is ineligible to be deprived of liberty by this Act, the court may not include in a welfare order provision which authorises the person to be deprived of his liberty.

(2)   If—

(a)   a welfare order includes provision which authorises a person to be deprived of his liberty, and

(b)   that person becomes ineligible to be deprived of liberty by this Act,

the provision ceases to have effect for as long as the person remains ineligible.

(3)   Nothing in subsection (2) affects the power of the court under section 16(7) to vary or discharge the welfare order.

(4)   For the purposes of this section—

(a)   Schedule 1A applies for determining whether or not P is ineligible to be deprived of liberty by this Act;

(b)   "welfare order" means an order under section 16(2)(a).]

17 Section 16 powers: personal welfare

(1)   The powers under section 16 as respects P's personal welfare extend in particular to—

(a)   deciding where P is to live;

(b)   deciding what contact, if any, P is to have with any specified persons;

(c)   making an order prohibiting a named person from having contact with P;

(d)   giving or refusing consent to the carrying out or continuation of a treatment by a person providing health care for P;

(e)   giving a direction that a person responsible for P's health care allow a different person to take over that responsibility.

(2)   Subsection (1) is subject to section 20 (restrictions on deputies).

18 Section 16 powers: property and affairs

(1)   The powers under section 16 as respects P's property and affairs extend in particular to—

(a)   the control and management of P's property;

(b)   the sale, exchange, charging, gift or other disposition of P's property;

(c)   the acquisition of property in P's name or on P's behalf;

(d)   the carrying on, on P's behalf, of any profession, trade or business;

(e)   the taking of a decision which will have the effect of dissolving a partnership of which P is a member;

(f)   the carrying out of any contract entered into by P;

(g)   the discharge of P's debts and of any of P's obligations, whether legally enforceable or not;

(h)   the settlement of any of P's property, whether for P's benefit or for the benefit of others;

(i)   the execution for P of a will;

(j)   the exercise of any power (including a power to consent) vested in P whether beneficially or as trustee or otherwise;

(k)   the conduct of legal proceedings in P's name or on P's behalf.

(2)   No will may be made under subsection (1)(i) at a time when P has not reached 18.

(3)   The powers under section 16 as respects any other matter relating to P's property and affairs may be exercised even though P has not reached 16, if the court considers it likely that P will still lack capacity to make decisions in respect of that matter when he reaches 18.

(4)   Schedule 2 supplements the provisions of this section.

(5)   Section 16(7) (variation and discharge of court orders) is subject to paragraph 6 of Schedule 2.

(6)   Subsection (1) is subject to section 20 (restrictions on deputies).

19 Appointment of deputies

(1)   A deputy appointed by the court must be—

(a)   an individual who has reached 18, or

(b)   as respects powers in relation to property and affairs, an individual who has reached 18 or a trust corporation.

(2)   The court may appoint an individual by appointing the holder for the time being of a specified office or position.

(3)   A person may not be appointed as a deputy without his consent.

(4)   The court may appoint two or more deputies to act—

(a)   jointly,

(b)   jointly and severally, or

(c)   jointly in respect of some matters and jointly and severally in respect of others.

(5)   When appointing a deputy or deputies, the court may at the same time appoint one or more other persons to succeed the existing deputy or those deputies—

(a)   in such circumstances, or on the happening of such events, as may be specified by the court;

(b)   for such period as may be so specified.

(6)   A deputy is to be treated as P's agent in relation to anything done or decided by him within the scope of his appointment and in accordance with this Part.

(7)   The deputy is entitled—

(a)   to be reimbursed out of P's property for his reasonable expenses in discharging his functions, and

(b)   if the court so directs when appointing him, to remuneration out of P's property for discharging them.

(8)   The court may confer on a deputy powers to—

(a)   take possession or control of all or any specified part of P's property;

(b)   exercise all or any specified powers in respect of it, including such powers of investment as the court may determine.

(9)   The court may require a deputy—

(a)   to give to the Public Guardian such security as the court thinks fit for the due discharge of his functions, and

(b)   to submit to the Public Guardian such reports at such times or at such intervals as the court may direct.

20 Restrictions on deputies

(1) A deputy does not have power to make a decision on behalf of P in relation to a matter if he knows or has reasonable grounds for believing that P has capacity in relation to the matter.

(2) Nothing in section 16(5) or 17 permits a deputy to be given power—

(a)   to prohibit a named person from having contact with P;

(b)   to direct a person responsible for P's health care to allow a different person to take over that responsibility.

(3) A deputy may not be given powers with respect to—

(a)   the settlement of any of P's property, whether for P's benefit or for the benefit of others,

(b)   the execution for P of a will, or

(c)   the exercise of any power (including a power to consent) vested in P whether beneficially or as trustee or otherwise.

(4) A deputy may not be given power to make a decision on behalf of P which is inconsistent with a decision made, within the scope of his authority and in accordance with this Act, by the donee of a lasting power of attorney granted by P (or, if there is more than one donee, by any of them).

(5) A deputy may not refuse consent to the carrying out or continuation of life-sustaining treatment in relation to P.

(6) The authority conferred on a deputy is subject to the provisions of this Act and, in particular, sections 1 (the principles) and 4 (best interests).

(7) A deputy may not do an act that is intended to restrain P unless four conditions are satisfied.

(8) The first condition is that, in doing the act, the deputy is acting within the scope of an authority expressly conferred on him by the court.

(9) The second is that P lacks, or the deputy reasonably believes that P lacks, capacity in relation to the matter in question.

(10) The third is that the deputy reasonably believes that it is necessary to do the act in order to prevent harm to P.

(11) The fourth is that the act is a proportionate response to—

(a)   the likelihood of P's suffering harm, [and]

(b)   the seriousness of that harm.

(12) For the purposes of this section, a deputy restrains P if he—

(a)   uses, or threatens to use, force to secure the doing of an act which P resists, or

(b)   restricts P's liberty of movement, whether or not P resists,

or if he authorises another person to do any of those things.

(13) ...

21 Transfer of proceedings relating to people under 18

[(1)] The [Lord Chief Justice, with the concurrence of the Lord Chancellor,] may by order make provision as to the transfer of proceedings relating to a person under 18, in such circumstances as are specified in the order—

(a)   from the Court of Protection to a court having jurisdiction under the Children Act 1989 (c 41), or

(b)   from a court having jurisdiction under that Act to the Court of Protection.

[(2) The Lord Chief Justice may nominate any of the following to exercise his functions under this section—

   (a)   the President of the Court of Protection;

   (b)   a judicial office holder (as defined in section 109(4) of the Constitutional Reform Act 2005).]

[Powers of the court in relation to Schedule A1]

[21A Powers of court in relation to Schedule A1]

[(1) This section applies if either of the following has been given under Schedule A1—

   (a)   a standard authorisation;

   (b)   an urgent authorisation.

(2) Where a standard authorisation has been given, the court may determine any question relating to any of the following matters—

   (a)   whether the relevant person meets one or more of the qualifying requirements;

   (b)   the period during which the standard authorisation is to be in force;

   (c)   the purpose for which the standard authorisation is given;

   (d)   the conditions subject to which the standard authorisation is given.

(3) If the court determines any question under subsection (2), the court may make an order—

   (a)   varying or terminating the standard authorisation, or

   (b)   directing the supervisory body to vary or terminate the standard authorisation.

(4) Where an urgent authorisation has been given, the court may determine any question relating to any of the following matters—

   (a)   whether the urgent authorisation should have been given;

   (b)   the period during which the urgent authorisation is to be in force;

   (c)   the purpose for which the urgent authorisation is given.

(5) Where the court determines any question under subsection (4), the court may make an order—

   (a)   varying or terminating the urgent authorisation, or

   (b)   directing the managing authority of the relevant hospital or care home to vary or terminate the urgent authorisation.

(6) Where the court makes an order under subsection (3) or (5), the court may make an order about a person's liability for any act done in connection with the standard or urgent authorisation before its variation or termination.

(7) An order under subsection (6) may, in particular, exclude a person from liability.]

Powers of the court in relation to lasting powers of attorney

22 Powers of court in relation to validity of lasting powers of attorney

(1) This section and section 23 apply if—

   (a)   a person ("P") has executed or purported to execute an instrument with a view to creating a lasting power of attorney, or

   (b)   an instrument has been registered as a lasting power of attorney conferred by P.

(2) The court may determine any question relating to—

   (a)   whether one or more of the requirements for the creation of a lasting power of attorney have been met;

   (b)   whether the power has been revoked or has otherwise come to an end.

(3) Subsection (4) applies if the court is satisfied—

(a)   that fraud or undue pressure was used to induce P—

   (i)   to execute an instrument for the purpose of creating a lasting power of attorney, or

   (ii)   to create a lasting power of attorney, or

(b)   that the donee (or, if more than one, any of them) of a lasting power of attorney—

   (i)   has behaved, or is behaving, in a way that contravenes his authority or is not in P's best interests, or

   (ii)   proposes to behave in a way that would contravene his authority or would not be in P's best interests.

(4)   The court may—

(a)   direct that an instrument purporting to create the lasting power of attorney is not to be registered, or

(b)   if P lacks capacity to do so, revoke the instrument or the lasting power of attorney.

(5)   If there is more than one donee, the court may under subsection (4)(b) revoke the instrument or the lasting power of attorney so far as it relates to any of them.

(6)   "Donee" includes an intended donee.

23 Powers of court in relation to operation of lasting powers of attorney

(1)   The court may determine any question as to the meaning or effect of a lasting power of attorney or an instrument purporting to create one.

(2)   The court may—

(a)   give directions with respect to decisions—

   (i)   which the donee of a lasting power of attorney has authority to make, and

   (ii)   which P lacks capacity to make;

(b)   give any consent or authorisation to act which the donee would have to obtain from P if P had capacity to give it.

(3)   The court may, if P lacks capacity to do so—

(a)   give directions to the donee with respect to the rendering by him of reports or accounts and the production of records kept by him for that purpose;

(b)   require the donee to supply information or produce documents or things in his possession as donee;

(c)   give directions with respect to the remuneration or expenses of the donee;

(d)   relieve the donee wholly or partly from any liability which he has or may have incurred on account of a breach of his duties as donee.

(4)   The court may authorise the making of gifts which are not within section 12(2) (permitted gifts).

(5)   Where two or more donees are appointed under a lasting power of attorney, this section applies as if references to the donee were to all or any of them.

Advance decisions to refuse treatment

24 Advance decisions to refuse treatment: general

(1)   "Advance decision" means a decision made by a person ("P"), after he has reached 18 and when he has capacity to do so, that if—

(a)   at a later time and in such circumstances as he may specify, a specified treatment is proposed to be carried out or continued by a person providing health care for him, and

(b)   at that time he lacks capacity to consent to the carrying out or continuation of the treatment, the specified treatment is not to be carried out or continued.

(2)   For the purposes of subsection (1)(a), a decision may be regarded as specifying a treatment or circumstances even though expressed in layman's terms.

(3)   P may withdraw or alter an advance decision at any time when he has capacity to do so.

(4)   A withdrawal (including a partial withdrawal) need not be in writing.

(5)   An alteration of an advance decision need not be in writing (unless section 25(5) applies in relation to the decision resulting from the alteration).

25   Validity and applicability of advance decisions

(1)   An advance decision does not affect the liability which a person may incur for carrying out or continuing a treatment in relation to P unless the decision is at the material time—

  (a)   valid, and

  (b)   applicable to the treatment.

(2)   An advance decision is not valid if P—

  (a)   has withdrawn the decision at a time when he had capacity to do so,

  (b)   has, under a lasting power of attorney created after the advance decision was made, conferred authority on the donee (or, if more than one, any of them) to give or refuse consent to the treatment to which the advance decision relates, or

  (c)   has done anything else clearly inconsistent with the advance decision remaining his fixed decision.

(3)   An advance decision is not applicable to the treatment in question if at the material time P has capacity to give or refuse consent to it.

(4)   An advance decision is not applicable to the treatment in question if—

  (a)   that treatment is not the treatment specified in the advance decision,

  (b)   any circumstances specified in the advance decision are absent, or

  (c)   there are reasonable grounds for believing that circumstances exist which P did not anticipate at the time of the advance decision and which would have affected his decision had he anticipated them.

(5)   An advance decision is not applicable to life-sustaining treatment unless—

  (a)   the decision is verified by a statement by P to the effect that it is to apply to that treatment even if life is at risk, and

  (b)   the decision and statement comply with subsection (6).

(6)   A decision or statement complies with this subsection only if—

  (a)   it is in writing,

  (b)   it is signed by P or by another person in P's presence and by P's direction,

  (c)   the signature is made or acknowledged by P in the presence of a witness, and

  (d)   the witness signs it, or acknowledges his signature, in P's presence.

(7)   The existence of any lasting power of attorney other than one of a description mentioned in subsection (2)(b) does not prevent the advance decision from being regarded as valid and applicable.

26   Effect of advance decisions

(1)   If P has made an advance decision which is—

  (a)   valid, and

  (b)   applicable to a treatment,

the decision has effect as if he had made it, and had had capacity to make it, at the time when the question arises whether the treatment should be carried out or continued.

(2)   A person does not incur liability for carrying out or continuing the treatment unless, at the time, he is satisfied that an advance decision exists which is valid and applicable to the treatment.

(3) A person does not incur liability for the consequences of withholding or withdrawing a treatment from P if, at the time, he reasonably believes that an advance decision exists which is valid and applicable to the treatment.

(4) The court may make a declaration as to whether an advance decision—

    (a)   exists;

    (b)   is valid;

    (c)   is applicable to a treatment.

(5) Nothing in an apparent advance decision stops a person—

    (a)   providing life-sustaining treatment, or

    (b)   doing any act he reasonably believes to be necessary to prevent a serious deterioration in P's condition,

while a decision as respects any relevant issue is sought from the court.

Excluded decisions

27 Family relationships etc

(1) Nothing in this Act permits a decision on any of the following matters to be made on behalf of a person—

    (a)   consenting to marriage or a civil partnership,

    (b)   consenting to have sexual relations,

    (c)   consenting to a decree of divorce being granted on the basis of two years' separation,

    (d)   consenting to a dissolution order being made in relation to a civil partnership on the basis of two years' separation,

    (e)   consenting to a child's being placed for adoption by an adoption agency,

    (f)   consenting to the making of an adoption order,

    (g)   discharging parental responsibilities in matters not relating to a child's property,

    (h)   giving a consent under the Human Fertilisation and Embryology Act 1990 (c 37)

    [(i)   giving a consent under the Human Fertilisation and Embryology Act 2008].

(2) "Adoption order" means—

    (a)   an adoption order within the meaning of the Adoption and Children Act 2002 (c 38) (including a future adoption order), and

    (b)   an order under section 84 of that Act (parental responsibility prior to adoption abroad).

28 Mental Health Act matters

(1) Nothing in this Act authorises anyone—

    (a)   to give a patient medical treatment for mental disorder, or

    (b)   to consent to a patient's being given medical treatment for mental disorder,

if, at the time when it is proposed to treat the patient, his treatment is regulated by Part 4 of the Mental Health Act.

[(1A) Subsection (1) does not apply in relation to any form of treatment to which section 58A of that Act (electro-convulsive therapy, etc) applies if the patient comes within subsection (7) of that section (informal patient under 18 who cannot give consent).]

[(1B) Section 5 does not apply to an act to which section 64B of the Mental Health Act applies (treatment of community patients not recalled to hospital).]

(2) "Medical treatment", "mental disorder" and "patient" have the same meaning as in that Act.

29 Voting rights
(1) Nothing in this Act permits a decision on voting at an election for any public office, or at a referendum, to be made on behalf of a person.
(2) "Referendum" has the same meaning as in section 101 of the Political Parties, Elections and Referendums Act 2000 (c 41).

Research

30 Research
(1) Intrusive research carried out on, or in relation to, a person who lacks capacity to consent to it is unlawful unless it is carried out—
    (a)   as part of a research project which is for the time being approved by the appropriate body for the purposes of this Act in accordance with section 31, and
    (b)   in accordance with sections 32 and 33.
(2) Research is intrusive if it is of a kind that would be unlawful if it was carried out—
    (a)   on or in relation to a person who had capacity to consent to it, but
    (b)   without his consent.
(3) A clinical trial which is subject to the provisions of clinical trials regulations is not to be treated as research for the purposes of this section.
[(3A) Research is not intrusive to the extent that it consists of the use of a person's human cells to bring about the creation *in vitro* of an embryo or human admixed embryo, or the subsequent storage or use of an embryo or human admixed embryo so created.
(3B) Expressions used in subsection (3A) and in Schedule 3 to the Human Fertilisation and Embryology Act 1990 (consents to use or storage of gametes, embryos or human admixed embryos etc) have the same meaning in that subsection as in that Schedule.]
(4) "Appropriate body", in relation to a research project, means the person, committee or other body specified in regulations made by the appropriate authority as the appropriate body in relation to a project of the kind in question.
(5) "Clinical trials regulations" means—
    (a)   the Medicines for Human Use (Clinical Trials) Regulations 2004 (SI 2004/1031) and any other regulations replacing those regulations or amending them, and
    (b)   any other regulations relating to clinical trials and designated by the Secretary of State as clinical trials regulations for the purposes of this section.
(6) In this section, section 32 and section 34, "appropriate authority" means—
    (a)   in relation to the carrying out of research in England, the Secretary of State, and
    (b)   in relation to the carrying out of research in Wales, the National Assembly for Wales.

31 Requirements for approval
(1) The appropriate body may not approve a research project for the purposes of this Act unless satisfied that the following requirements will be met in relation to research carried out as part of the project on, or in relation to, a person who lacks capacity to consent to taking part in the project ("P").
(2) The research must be connected with—
    (a)   an impairing condition affecting P, or
    (b)   its treatment.

(3) "Impairing condition" means a condition which is (or may be) attributable to, or which causes or contributes to (or may cause or contribute to), the impairment of, or disturbance in the functioning of, the mind or brain.

(4) There must be reasonable grounds for believing that research of comparable effectiveness cannot be carried out if the project has to be confined to, or relate only to, persons who have capacity to consent to taking part in it.

(5) The research must—

    (a)   have the potential to benefit P without imposing on P a burden that is disproportionate to the potential benefit to P, or

    (b)   be intended to provide knowledge of the causes or treatment of, or of the care of persons affected by, the same or a similar condition.

(6) If the research falls within paragraph (b) of subsection (5) but not within paragraph (a), there must be reasonable grounds for believing—

    (a)   that the risk to P from taking part in the project is likely to be negligible, and

    (b)   that anything done to, or in relation to, P will not—

        (i)   interfere with P's freedom of action or privacy in a significant way, or

        (ii)   be unduly invasive or restrictive.

(7) There must be reasonable arrangements in place for ensuring that the requirements of sections 32 and 33 will be met.

32 Consulting carers etc

(1) This section applies if a person ("R")—

    (a)   is conducting an approved research project, and

    (b)   wishes to carry out research, as part of the project, on or in relation to a person ("P") who lacks capacity to consent to taking part in the project.

(2) R must take reasonable steps to identify a person who—

    (a)   otherwise than in a professional capacity or for remuneration, is engaged in caring for P or is interested in P's welfare, and

    (b)   is prepared to be consulted by R under this section.

(3) If R is unable to identify such a person he must, in accordance with guidance issued by the appropriate authority, nominate a person who—

    (a)   is prepared to be consulted by R under this section, but

    (b)   has no connection with the project.

(4) R must provide the person identified under subsection (2), or nominated under subsection (3), with information about the project and ask him—

    (a)   for advice as to whether P should take part in the project, and

    (b)   what, in his opinion, P's wishes and feelings about taking part in the project would be likely to be if P had capacity in relation to the matter.

(5) If, at any time, the person consulted advises R that in his opinion P's wishes and feelings would be likely to lead him to decline to take part in the project (or to wish to withdraw from it) if he had capacity in relation to the matter, R must ensure—

    (a)   if P is not already taking part in the project, that he does not take part in it;

    (b)   if P is taking part in the project, that he is withdrawn from it.

(6) But subsection (5)(b) does not require treatment that P has been receiving as part of the project to be discontinued if R has reasonable grounds for believing that there would be a significant risk to P's health if it were discontinued.

(7) The fact that a person is the donee of a lasting power of attorney given by P, or is P's deputy, does not prevent him from being the person consulted under this section.

(8) Subsection (9) applies if treatment is being, or is about to be, provided for P as a matter of urgency and R considers that, having regard to the nature of the research and of the particular circumstances of the case—

(a) it is also necessary to take action for the purposes of the research as a matter of urgency, but

(b) it is not reasonably practicable to consult under the previous provisions of this section.

(9) R may take the action if—

(a) he has the agreement of a registered medical practitioner who is not involved in the organisation or conduct of the research project, or

(b) where it is not reasonably practicable in the time available to obtain that agreement, he acts in accordance with a procedure approved by the appropriate body at the time when the research project was approved under section 31.

(10) But R may not continue to act in reliance on subsection (9) if he has reasonable grounds for believing that it is no longer necessary to take the action as a matter of urgency.

33 Additional safeguards

(1) This section applies in relation to a person who is taking part in an approved research project even though he lacks capacity to consent to taking part.

(2) Nothing may be done to, or in relation to, him in the course of the research—

(a) to which he appears to object (whether by showing signs of resistance or otherwise) except where what is being done is intended to protect him from harm or to reduce or prevent pain or discomfort, or

(b) which would be contrary to—

(i) an advance decision of his which has effect, or

(ii) any other form of statement made by him and not subsequently withdrawn,

of which R is aware.

(3) The interests of the person must be assumed to outweigh those of science and society.

(4) If he indicates (in any way) that he wishes to be withdrawn from the project he must be withdrawn without delay.

(5) P must be withdrawn from the project, without delay, if at any time the person conducting the research has reasonable grounds for believing that one or more of the requirements set out in section 31(2) to (7) is no longer met in relation to research being carried out on, or in relation to, P.

(6) But neither subsection (4) nor subsection (5) requires treatment that P has been receiving as part of the project to be discontinued if R has reasonable grounds for believing that there would be a significant risk to P's health if it were discontinued.

34 Loss of capacity during research project

(1) This section applies where a person ("P")—

(a) has consented to take part in a research project begun before the commencement of section 30, but

(b) before the conclusion of the project, loses capacity to consent to continue to take part in it.

(2) The appropriate authority may by regulations provide that, despite P's loss of capacity, research of a prescribed kind may be carried out on, or in relation to, P if—

(a) the project satisfies prescribed requirements,

(b) any information or material relating to P which is used in the research is of a prescribed description and was obtained before P's loss of capacity, and

(c) the person conducting the project takes in relation to P such steps as may be prescribed for the purpose of protecting him.

(3) The regulations may, in particular,—

    (a)   make provision about when, for the purposes of the regulations, a project is to be treated as having begun;

    (b)   include provision similar to any made by section 31, 32 or 33.

Independent mental capacity advocate service

35 Appointment of independent mental capacity advocates

(1) The [responsible authority] must make such arrangements as it considers reasonable to enable persons ("independent mental capacity advocates") to be available to represent and support persons to whom acts or decisions proposed under sections 37, 38 and 39 relate [or persons who fall within section 39A, 39C or 39D].

(2) The appropriate authority may make regulations as to the appointment of independent mental capacity advocates.

(3) The regulations may, in particular, provide—

    (a)   that a person may act as an independent mental capacity advocate only in such circumstances, or only subject to such conditions, as may be prescribed;

    (b)   for the appointment of a person as an independent mental capacity advocate to be subject to approval in accordance with the regulations.

(4) In making arrangements under subsection (1), the [responsible authority] must have regard to the principle that a person to whom a proposed act or decision relates should, so far as practicable, be represented and supported by a person who is independent of any person who will be responsible for the act or decision.

(5) The arrangements may include provision for payments to be made to, or in relation to, persons carrying out functions in accordance with the arrangements.

(6) For the purpose of enabling him to carry out his functions, an independent mental capacity advocate—

    (a)   may interview in private the person whom he has been instructed to represent, and

    (b)   may, at all reasonable times, examine and take copies of—

        (i)   any health record,

        (ii)   any record of, or held by, a local authority and compiled in connection with a social services function, and

        (iii)   any record held by a person registered under Part 2 of the Care Standards Act 2000 (c 14) [or Chapter 2 of Part 1 of the Health and Social Care Act 2008],

which the person holding the record considers may be relevant to the independent mental capacity advocate's investigation.

[(6A) In subsections (1) and (4), "the responsible authority" means—

    (a)   in relation to the provision of the services of independent mental capacity advocates in the area of a local authority in England, that local authority, and

    (b)   in relation to the provision of the services of independent mental capacity advocates in Wales, the Welsh Ministers.

(6B) In subsection (6A)(a), "local authority" has the meaning given in section 64(1) except that it does not include the council of a county or county borough in Wales.]

(7) In this section, section 36 and section 37, "the appropriate authority" means—

    (a)   in relation to the provision of the services of independent mental capacity advocates in England, the Secretary of State, and

    (b)   in relation to the provision of the services of independent mental capacity advocates in Wales, the National Assembly for Wales.

36 Functions of independent mental capacity advocates

(1) The appropriate authority may make regulations as to the functions of independent mental capacity advocates.

(2) The regulations may, in particular, make provision requiring an advocate to take such steps as may be prescribed for the purpose of—

    (a)   providing support to the person whom he has been instructed to represent ("P") so that P may participate as fully as possible in any relevant decision;

    (b)   obtaining and evaluating relevant information;

    (c)   ascertaining what P's wishes and feelings would be likely to be, and the beliefs and values that would be likely to influence P, if he had capacity;

    (d)   ascertaining what alternative courses of action are available in relation to P;

    (e)   obtaining a further medical opinion where treatment is proposed and the advocate thinks that one should be obtained.

(3) The regulations may also make provision as to circumstances in which the advocate may challenge, or provide assistance for the purpose of challenging, any relevant decision.

37 Provision of serious medical treatment by NHS body

(1) This section applies if an NHS body—

    (a)   is proposing to provide, or secure the provision of, serious medical treatment for a person ("P") who lacks capacity to consent to the treatment, and

    (b)   is satisfied that there is no person, other than one engaged in providing care or treatment for P in a professional capacity or for remuneration, whom it would be appropriate to consult in determining what would be in P's best interests.

(2) But this section does not apply if P's treatment is regulated by Part 4 [or 4A] of the Mental Health Act.

(3) Before the treatment is provided, the NHS body must instruct an independent mental capacity advocate to represent P.

(4) If the treatment needs to be provided as a matter of urgency, it may be provided even though the NHS body has not been able to comply with subsection (3).

(5) The NHS body must, in providing or securing the provision of treatment for P, take into account any information given, or submissions made, by the independent mental capacity advocate.

(6) "Serious medical treatment" means treatment which involves providing, withholding or withdrawing treatment of a kind prescribed by regulations made by the appropriate authority.

(7) "NHS body" has such meaning as may be prescribed by regulations made for the purposes of this section by—

    (a)   the Secretary of State, in relation to bodies in England, or

    (b)   the National Assembly for Wales, in relation to bodies in Wales.

38 Provision of accommodation by NHS body

(1) This section applies if an NHS body proposes to make arrangements—

    (a)   for the provision of accommodation in a hospital or care home for a person ("P") who lacks capacity to agree to the arrangements, or

    (b)   for a change in P's accommodation to another hospital or care home,

and is satisfied that there is no person, other than one engaged in providing care or treatment for P in a professional capacity or for remuneration, whom it would be appropriate for it to consult in determining what would be in P's best interests.

(2)   But this section does not apply if P is accommodated as a result of an obligation imposed on him under the Mental Health Act.

[(2A)   And this section does not apply if—

  (a)   an independent mental capacity advocate must be appointed under section 39A or 39C (whether or not by the NHS body) to represent P, and

  (b)   the hospital or care home in which P is to be accommodated under the arrangements referred to in this section is the relevant hospital or care home under the authorisation referred to in that section.]

(3)   Before making the arrangements, the NHS body must instruct an independent mental capacity advocate to represent P unless it is satisfied that—

  (a)   the accommodation is likely to be provided for a continuous period which is less than the applicable period, or

  (b)   the arrangements need to be made as a matter of urgency.

(4)   If the NHS body—

  (a)   did not instruct an independent mental capacity advocate to represent P before making the arrangements because it was satisfied that subsection (3)(a) or (b) applied, but

  (b)   subsequently has reason to believe that the accommodation is likely to be provided for a continuous period—

    (i)   beginning with the day on which accommodation was first provided in accordance with the arrangements, and

    (ii)   ending on or after the expiry of the applicable period,

it must instruct an independent mental capacity advocate to represent P.

(5)   The NHS body must, in deciding what arrangements to make for P, take into account any information given, or submissions made, by the independent mental capacity advocate.

(6)   "Care home" has the meaning given in section 3 of the Care Standards Act 2000 (c 14).

[(7)   "Hospital" means—

  (a)   in relation to England, a hospital as defined by section 275 of the National Health Service Act 2006; and

  (b)   in relation to Wales, a health service hospital as defined by section 206 of the National Health Service (Wales) Act 2006 or an independent hospital as defined by section 2 of the Care Standards Act 2000.]

(8)   "NHS body" has such meaning as may be prescribed by regulations made for the purposes of this section by—

  (a)   the Secretary of State, in relation to bodies in England, or

  (b)   the National Assembly for Wales, in relation to bodies in Wales.

(9)   "Applicable period" means—

  (a)   in relation to accommodation in a hospital, 28 days, and

  (b)   in relation to accommodation in a care home, 8 weeks.

[(10)   For the purposes of subsection (1), a person appointed under Part 10 of Schedule A1 to be P's representative is not, by virtue of that appointment, engaged in providing care or treatment for P in a professional capacity or for remuneration.]

39 Provision of accommodation by local authority

(1)   This section applies if a local authority propose to make arrangements—

  (a)   for the provision of residential accommodation for a person ("P") who lacks capacity to agree to the arrangements, or

  (b)   for a change in P's residential accommodation,

and are satisfied that there is no person, other than one engaged in providing care or treatment for P in a professional capacity or for remuneration, whom it would be appropriate for them to consult in determining what would be in P's best interests.

[(1A)   But this section applies only if—

(a)   in the case of a local authority in England, subsection (1B) applies;

(b)   in the case of a local authority in Wales, subsection (2) applies.]

[(1B)   This subsection applies if the accommodation is to be provided in accordance with—

(a)   Part 1 of the Care Act 2014, or

(b)   section 117 of the Mental Health Act.]

(2)   [This subsection applies] if the accommodation is to be provided in accordance with—

[(a)   Part 4 of the Social Services and Well-being (Wales) Act 2014; or]

(b)   section 117 of the Mental Health Act,

. . ..

(3)   This section does not apply if P is accommodated as a result of an obligation imposed on him under the Mental Health Act.

[(3A)   And this section does not apply if—

(a)   an independent mental capacity advocate must be appointed under section 39A or 39C (whether or not by the local authority) to represent P, and

(b)   the place in which P is to be accommodated under the arrangements referred to in this section is the relevant hospital or care home under the authorisation referred to in that section.]

(4)   Before making the arrangements, the local authority must instruct an independent mental capacity advocate to represent P unless they are satisfied that—

(a)   the accommodation is likely to be provided for a continuous period of less than 8 weeks, or

(b)   the arrangements need to be made as a matter of urgency.

(5)   If the local authority—

(a)   did not instruct an independent mental capacity advocate to represent P before making the arrangements because they were satisfied that subsection (4)(a) or (b) applied, but

(b)   subsequently have reason to believe that the accommodation is likely to be provided for a continuous period that will end 8 weeks or more after the day on which accommodation was first provided in accordance with the arrangements,

they must instruct an independent mental capacity advocate to represent P.

(6)   The local authority must, in deciding what arrangements to make for P, take into account any information given, or submissions made, by the independent mental capacity advocate.

[(7)   For the purposes of subsection (1), a person appointed under Part 10 of Schedule A1 to be P's representative is not, by virtue of that appointment, engaged in providing care or treatment for P in a professional capacity or for remuneration.]

[39A Person becomes subject to Schedule A1]

[(1)   This section applies if—

(a)   a person ("P") becomes subject to Schedule A1, and

(b)   the managing authority of the relevant hospital or care home are satisfied that there is no person, other than one engaged in providing care or treatment for P in a professional capacity or for remuneration, whom it would be appropriate to consult in determining what would be in P's best interests.

(2)   The managing authority must notify the supervisory body that this section applies.

(3)   The supervisory body must instruct an independent mental capacity advocate to represent P.

(4)   Schedule A1 makes provision about the role of an independent mental capacity advocate appointed under this section.

(5)   This section is subject to paragraph 161 of Schedule A1.

(6)   For the purposes of subsection (1), a person appointed under Part 10 of Schedule A1 to be P's representative is not, by virtue of that appointment, engaged in providing care or treatment for P in a professional capacity or for remuneration.]

[39B Section 39A: supplementary provision]

[(1)   This section applies for the purposes of section 39A.

(2)   P becomes subject to Schedule A1 in any of the following cases.

(3)   The first case is where an urgent authorisation is given in relation to P under paragraph 76(2) of Schedule A1 (urgent authorisation given before request made for standard authorisation).

(4)   The second case is where the following conditions are met.

(5)   The first condition is that a request is made under Schedule A1 for a standard authorisation to be given in relation to P ("the requested authorisation").

(6)   The second condition is that no urgent authorisation was given under paragraph 76(2) of Schedule A1 before that request was made.

(7)   The third condition is that the requested authorisation will not be in force on or before, or immediately after, the expiry of an existing standard authorisation.

(8)   The expiry of a standard authorisation is the date when the authorisation is expected to cease to be in force.

(9)   The third case is where, under paragraph 69 of Schedule A1, the supervisory body select a person to carry out an assessment of whether or not the relevant person is a detained resident.]

[39C Person unrepresented whilst subject to Schedule A1]

[(1)   This section applies if—

    (a)   an authorisation under Schedule A1 is in force in relation to a person ("P"),

    (b)   the appointment of a person as P's representative ends in accordance with regulations made under Part 10 of Schedule A1, and

    (c)   the managing authority of the relevant hospital or care home are satisfied that there is no person, other than one engaged in providing care or treatment for P in a professional capacity or for remuneration, whom it would be appropriate to consult in determining what would be in P's best interests.

(2)   The managing authority must notify the supervisory body that this section applies.

(3)   The supervisory body must instruct an independent mental capacity advocate to represent P.

(4)   Paragraph 159 of Schedule A1 makes provision about the role of an independent mental capacity advocate appointed under this section.

(5)   The appointment of an independent mental capacity advocate under this section ends when a new appointment of a person as P's representative is made in accordance with Part 10 of Schedule A1.

(6)   For the purposes of subsection (1), a person appointed under Part 10 of Schedule A1 to be P's representative is not, by virtue of that appointment, engaged in providing care or treatment for P in a professional capacity or for remuneration.]

[39D Person subject to Schedule A1 without paid representative]

[(1)   This section applies if—

    (a)   an authorisation under Schedule A1 is in force in relation to a person ("P"),

    (b)   P has a representative ("R") appointed under Part 10 of Schedule A1, and

  (c) R is not being paid under regulations under Part 10 of Schedule A1 for acting as P's representative.

(2) The supervisory body must instruct an independent mental capacity advocate to represent P in any of the following cases.

(3) The first case is where P makes a request to the supervisory body to instruct an advocate.

(4) The second case is where R makes a request to the supervisory body to instruct an advocate.

(5) The third case is where the supervisory body have reason to believe one or more of the following—

  (a) that, without the help of an advocate, P and R would be unable to exercise one or both of the relevant rights;

  (b) that P and R have each failed to exercise a relevant right when it would have been reasonable to exercise it;

  (c) that P and R are each unlikely to exercise a relevant right when it would be reasonable to exercise it.

(6) The duty in subsection (2) is subject to section 39E.

(7) If an advocate is appointed under this section, the advocate is, in particular, to take such steps as are practicable to help P and R to understand the following matters—

  (a) the effect of the authorisation;

  (b) the purpose of the authorisation;

  (c) the duration of the authorisation;

  (d) any conditions to which the authorisation is subject;

  (e) the reasons why each assessor who carried out an assessment in connection with the request for the authorisation, or in connection with a review of the authorisation, decided that P met the qualifying requirement in question;

  (f) the relevant rights;

  (g) how to exercise the relevant rights.

(8) The advocate is, in particular, to take such steps as are practicable to help P or R—

  (a) to exercise the right to apply to court, if it appears to the advocate that P or R wishes to exercise that right, or

  (b) to exercise the right of review, if it appears to the advocate that P or R wishes to exercise that right.

(9) If the advocate helps P or R to exercise the right of review—

  (a) the advocate may make submissions to the supervisory body on the question of whether a qualifying requirement is reviewable;

  (b) the advocate may give information, or make submissions, to any assessor carrying out a review assessment.

(10) In this section—

  "relevant rights" means—

   (a) the right to apply to court, and

   (b) the right of review;

  "right to apply to court" means the right to make an application to the court to exercise its jurisdiction under section 21A;

  "right of review" means the right under Part 8 of Schedule A1 to request a review.]

[39E Limitation on duty to instruct advocate under section 39D]

[(1) This section applies if an advocate is already representing P in accordance with an instruction under section 39D.

(2)   Section 39D(2) does not require another advocate to be instructed, unless the following conditions are met.

(3)   The first condition is that the existing advocate was instructed—

(a)   because of a request by R, or

(b)   because the supervisory body had reason to believe one or more of the things in section 39D(5).

(4)   The second condition is that the other advocate would be instructed because of a request by P.]

[40 Exceptions]

[[(1)]   The duty imposed by section 37(3), 38(3) or (4)[, 39(4) or (5), 39A(3), 39C(3) or 39D(2)] does not apply where there is—

(a)   a person nominated by P (in whatever manner) as a person to be consulted on matters to which that duty relates,

(b)   a donee of a lasting power of attorney created by P who is authorised to make decisions in relation to those matters, or

(c)   a deputy appointed by the court for P with power to make decisions in relation to those matters.

[(2)   A person appointed under Part 10 of Schedule A1 to be P's representative is not, by virtue of that appointment, a person nominated by P as a person to be consulted in matters to which a duty mentioned in subsection (1) relates.]]

41   Power to adjust role of independent mental capacity advocate

(1)   The appropriate authority may make regulations—

(a)   expanding the role of independent mental capacity advocates in relation to persons who lack capacity, and

(b)   adjusting the obligation to make arrangements imposed by section 35.

(2)   The regulations may, in particular—

(a)   prescribe circumstances (different to those set out in sections 37, 38 and 39) in which an independent mental capacity advocate must, or circumstances in which one may, be instructed by a person of a prescribed description to represent a person who lacks capacity, and

(b)   include provision similar to any made by section 37, 38, 39 or 40.

(3)   "Appropriate authority" has the same meaning as in section 35.

Miscellaneous and supplementary

42   Codes of practice

(1)   The Lord Chancellor must prepare and issue one or more codes of practice—

(a)   for the guidance of persons assessing whether a person has capacity in relation to any matter,

(b)   for the guidance of persons acting in connection with the care or treatment of another person (see section 5),

(c)   for the guidance of donees of lasting powers of attorney,

(d)   for the guidance of deputies appointed by the court,

(e)   for the guidance of persons carrying out research in reliance on any provision made by or under this Act (and otherwise with respect to sections 30 to 34),

(f)   for the guidance of independent mental capacity advocates,

[(fa)   for the guidance of persons exercising functions under Schedule A1,

(fb)   for the guidance of representatives appointed under Part 10 of Schedule A1,]

(g)   with respect to the provisions of sections 24 to 26 (advance decisions and apparent advance decisions), and

(h)   with respect to such other matters concerned with this Act as he thinks fit.

(2)   The Lord Chancellor may from time to time revise a code.

(3)   The Lord Chancellor may delegate the preparation or revision of the whole or any part of a code so far as he considers expedient.

(4)   It is the duty of a person to have regard to any relevant code if he is acting in relation to a person who lacks capacity and is doing so in one or more of the following ways—

(a)   as the donee of a lasting power of attorney,

(b)   as a deputy appointed by the court,

(c)   as a person carrying out research in reliance on any provision made by or under this Act (see sections 30 to 34),

(d)   as an independent mental capacity advocate,

[(da)   in the exercise of functions under Schedule A1,

(db)   as a representative appointed under Part 10 of Schedule A1,]

(e)   in a professional capacity,

(f)   for remuneration.

(5)   If it appears to a court or tribunal conducting any criminal or civil proceedings that—

(a)   a provision of a code, or

(b)   a failure to comply with a code,

is relevant to a question arising in the proceedings, the provision or failure must be taken into account in deciding the question.

(6)   A code under subsection (1)(d) may contain separate guidance for deputies appointed by virtue of paragraph 1(2) of Schedule 5 (functions of deputy conferred on receiver appointed under the Mental Health Act).

(7)   In this section and in section 43, "code" means a code prepared or revised under this section.

43 Codes of practice: procedure

(1)   Before preparing or revising a code, the Lord Chancellor must consult—

(a)   the National Assembly for Wales, and

(b)   such other persons as he considers appropriate.

(2)   The Lord Chancellor may not issue a code unless—

(a)   a draft of the code has been laid by him before both Houses of Parliament, and

(b)   the 40 day period has elapsed without either House resolving not to approve the draft.

(3)   The Lord Chancellor must arrange for any code that he has issued to be published in such a way as he considers appropriate for bringing it to the attention of persons likely to be concerned with its provisions.

(4)   "40 day period", in relation to the draft of a proposed code, means—

(a)   if the draft is laid before one House on a day later than the day on which it is laid before the other House, the period of 40 days beginning with the later of the two days;

(b)   in any other case, the period of 40 days beginning with the day on which it is laid before each House.

(5)   In calculating the period of 40 days, no account is to be taken of any period during which Parliament is dissolved or prorogued or during which both Houses are adjourned for more than 4 days.

44 Ill-treatment or neglect

(1)   Subsection (2) applies if a person ("D")—

  (a)   has the care of a person ("P") who lacks, or whom D reasonably believes to lack, capacity,

  (b)   is the donee of a lasting power of attorney, or an enduring power of attorney (within the meaning of Schedule 4), created by P, or

  (c)   is a deputy appointed by the court for P.

(2)   D is guilty of an offence if he ill-treats or wilfully neglects P.

(3)   A person guilty of an offence under this section is liable—

  (a)   on summary conviction, to imprisonment for a term not exceeding 12 months or a fine not exceeding the statutory maximum or both;

  (b)   on conviction on indictment, to imprisonment for a term not exceeding 5 years or a fine or both.

PART 2   THE COURT OF PROTECTION AND THE PUBLIC GUARDIAN

The Court of Protection

45 The Court of Protection

(1)   There is to be a superior court of record known as the Court of Protection.

(2)   The court is to have an official seal.

(3)   The court may sit at any place in England and Wales, on any day and at any time.

(4)   The court is to have a central office and registry at a place appointed by the Lord Chancellor[, after consulting the Lord Chief Justice].

(5)   The Lord Chancellor may[, after consulting the Lord Chief Justice,] designate as additional registries of the court any district registry of the High Court and any county court office.

[(5A)   The Lord Chief Justice may nominate any of the following to exercise his functions under this section—

  (a)   the President of the Court of Protection;

  (b)   a judicial office holder (as defined in section 109(4) of the Constitutional Reform Act 2005).]

(6)   The office of the Supreme Court called the Court of Protection ceases to exist.

46 The judges of the Court of Protection

(1)   Subject to Court of Protection Rules under section 51(2)(d), the jurisdiction of the court is exercisable by a judge nominated for that purpose by—

  (a)   the [Lord Chief Justice], or

  [(b)   where nominated by the Lord Chief Justice to act on his behalf under this subsection—

     (i)   the President of the Court of Protection; or

     (ii)   a judicial office holder (as defined in section 109(4) of the Constitutional Reform Act 2005)].

(2)   To be nominated, a judge must be—

  (a)   the President of the Family Division,

  (b)   the [Chancellor of the High Court],

  (c)   a puisne judge of the High Court,

  (d)   a circuit judge, . . .

  (e)   a district judge[,

  (f)   a District Judge (Magistrates' Courts),

  (g)   a judge of the First-tier Tribunal, or of the Upper Tribunal, by virtue of appointment under paragraph 1(1) of Schedule 2 or 3 to the Tribunals, Courts and Enforcement Act 2007,

  (h)   a transferred-in judge of the First-tier Tribunal or of the Upper Tribunal (see section 31(2) of that Act),

(i) a deputy judge of the Upper Tribunal (whether under paragraph 7 of Schedule 3 to, or section 31(2) of, that Act),

(j) the Chamber President, or Deputy Chamber President, of a chamber of the First-tier Tribunal or of a chamber of the Upper Tribunal,

(k) the Judge Advocate General,

(l) a Recorder,

(m) the holder of an office listed in the first column of the table in section 89(3C) of the Senior Courts Act 1981 (senior High Court Masters etc),

(n) a holder of an office listed in column 1 of Part 2 of Schedule 2 to that Act (High Court Masters etc),

(o) a deputy district judge appointed under section 102 of that Act or under section 8 of the County Courts Act 1984,

(p) a member of a panel of Employment Judges established for England and Wales or for Scotland,

(q) a person appointed under section 30(1)(a) or (b) of the Courts-Martial (Appeals) Act 1951 (assistants to the Judge Advocate General),

(r) a deputy judge of the High Court,

(s) the Senior President of Tribunals,

(t) an ordinary judge of the Court of Appeal (including the vice-president, if any, of either division of that court),

(u) the President of the Queen's Bench Division,

(v) the Master of the Rolls, or

(w) the Lord Chief Justice].

(3) The [Lord Chief Justice, after consulting the Lord Chancellor,] must—

(a) appoint one of the judges nominated by virtue of subsection (2)(a) to (c) to be President of the Court of Protection, and

(b) appoint another of those judges to be Vice-President of the Court of Protection.

(4) The [Lord Chief Justice, after consulting the Lord Chancellor,] must appoint one of the judges nominated by virtue of subsection (2)(d) [to (q)] to be Senior Judge of the Court of Protection, having such administrative functions in relation to the court as the Lord Chancellor[, after consulting the Lord Chief Justice,] may direct.

Supplementary powers

47 General powers and effect of orders etc

(1) The court has in connection with its jurisdiction the same powers, rights, privileges and authority as the High Court.

(2) Section 204 of the Law of Property Act 1925 (c 20) (orders of High Court conclusive in favour of purchasers) applies in relation to orders and directions of the court as it applies to orders of the High Court.

(3) Office copies of orders made, directions given or other instruments issued by the court and sealed with its official seal are admissible in all legal proceedings as evidence of the originals without any further proof.

48 Interim orders and directions

The court may, pending the determination of an application to it in relation to a person ("P"), make an order or give directions in respect of any matter if—

(a) there is reason to believe that P lacks capacity in relation to the matter,

(b) the matter is one to which its powers under this Act extend, and

(c) it is in P's best interests to make the order, or give the directions, without delay.

49 Power to call for reports

(1)   This section applies where, in proceedings brought in respect of a person ("P") under Part 1, the court is considering a question relating to P.

(2)   The court may require a report to be made to it by the Public Guardian or by a Court of Protection Visitor.

(3)   The court may require a local authority, or an NHS body, to arrange for a report to be made—

    (a)   by one of its officers or employees, or

    (b)   by such other person (other than the Public Guardian or a Court of Protection Visitor) as the authority, or the NHS body, considers appropriate.

(4)   The report must deal with such matters relating to P as the court may direct.

(5)   Court of Protection Rules may specify matters which, unless the court directs otherwise, must also be dealt with in the report.

(6)   The report may be made in writing or orally, as the court may direct.

(7)   In complying with a requirement, the Public Guardian or a Court of Protection Visitor may, at all reasonable times, examine and take copies of—

    (a)   any health record,

    (b)   any record of, or held by, a local authority and compiled in connection with a social services function, and

    (c)   any record held by a person registered under Part 2 of the Care Standards Act 2000 (c 14) [or Chapter 2 of Part 1 of the Health and Social Care Act 2008],

so far as the record relates to P.

(8)   If the Public Guardian or a Court of Protection Visitor is making a visit in the course of complying with a requirement, he may interview P in private.

(9)   If a Court of Protection Visitor who is a Special Visitor is making a visit in the course of complying with a requirement, he may if the court so directs carry out in private a medical, psychiatric or psychological examination of P's capacity and condition.

(10)   "NHS body" has the meaning given in section 148 of the Health and Social Care (Community Health and Standards) Act 2003 (c 43).

(11)   "Requirement" means a requirement imposed under subsection (2) or (3).

Practice and procedure

50 Applications to the Court of Protection

(1)   No permission is required for an application to the court for the exercise of any of its powers under this Act—

    (a)   by a person who lacks, or is alleged to lack, capacity,

    (b)   if such a person has not reached 18, by anyone with parental responsibility for him,

    (c)   by the donor or a donee of a lasting power of attorney to which the application relates,

    (d)   by a deputy appointed by the court for a person to whom the application relates, or

    (e)   by a person named in an existing order of the court, if the application relates to the order.

[(1A)   Nor is permission required for an application to the court under section 21A by the relevant person's representative.]

(2)   But, subject to Court of Protection Rules and to paragraph 20(2) of Schedule 3 (declarations relating to private international law), permission is required for any other application to the court.

(3) In deciding whether to grant permission the court must, in particular, have regard to—

    (a)   the applicant's connection with the person to whom the application relates,

    (b)   the reasons for the application,

    (c)   the benefit to the person to whom the application relates of a proposed order or directions, and

    (d)   whether the benefit can be achieved in any other way.

(4) "Parental responsibility" has the same meaning as in the Children Act 1989 (c 41).

51 Court of Protection Rules

[(1) Rules of court with respect to the practice and procedure of the court (to be called "Court of Protection Rules") may be made in accordance with Part 1 of Schedule 1 to the Constitutional Reform Act 2005.]

(2) Court of Protection Rules may, in particular, make provision—

    (a)   as to the manner and form in which proceedings are to be commenced;

    (b)   as to the persons entitled to be notified of, and be made parties to, the proceedings;

    (c)   for the allocation, in such circumstances as may be specified, of any specified description of proceedings to a specified judge or to specified descriptions of judges;

    (d)   for the exercise of the jurisdiction of the court, in such circumstances as may be specified, by its officers or other staff;

    (e)   for enabling the court to appoint a suitable person (who may, with his consent, be the Official Solicitor) to act in the name of, or on behalf of, or to represent the person to whom the proceedings relate;

    (f)   for enabling an application to the court to be disposed of without a hearing;

    (g)   for enabling the court to proceed with, or with any part of, a hearing in the absence of the person to whom the proceedings relate;

    (h)   for enabling or requiring the proceedings or any part of them to be conducted in private and for enabling the court to determine who is to be admitted when the court sits in private and to exclude specified persons when it sits in public;

    (i)   as to what may be received as evidence (whether or not admissible apart from the rules) and the manner in which it is to be presented;

    (j)   for the enforcement of orders made and directions given in the proceedings.

(3) Court of Protection Rules may, instead of providing for any matter, refer to provision made or to be made about that matter by directions.

(4) Court of Protection Rules may make different provision for different areas.

[52 Practice directions]

[(1) Directions as to the practice and procedure of the court may be given in accordance with Part 1 of Schedule 2 to the Constitutional Reform Act 2005.

(2) Practice directions given otherwise than under subsection (1) may not be given without the approval of—

    (a)   the Lord Chancellor, and

    (b)   the Lord Chief Justice.

(3) The Lord Chief Justice may nominate any of the following to exercise his functions under this section—

    (a)   the President of the Court of Protection;

(b)   a judicial office holder (as defined in section 109(4) of the Constitutional Reform Act 2005).]

53 Rights of appeal

(1)   Subject to the provisions of this section, an appeal lies to the Court of Appeal from any decision of the court.

[(2)   Court of Protection Rules may provide that, where a decision of the court is made by a specified description of person, an appeal from the decision lies to a specified description of judge of the court and not to the Court of Appeal.]

(3)   . . .

(4)   Court of Protection Rules may make provision—

(a)   that, in such cases as may be specified, an appeal from a decision of the court may not be made without permission;

(b)   as to the person or persons entitled to grant permission to appeal;

(c)   as to any requirements to be satisfied before permission is granted;

(d)   that where a . . . judge of the court makes a decision on an appeal, no appeal may be made to the Court of Appeal from that decision unless the Court of Appeal considers that—

(i)   the appeal would raise an important point of principle or practice, or

(ii)   there is some other compelling reason for the Court of Appeal to hear it;

(e)   as to any considerations to be taken into account in relation to granting or refusing permission to appeal.

Fees and costs

54 Fees

(1)   The Lord Chancellor may with the consent of the Treasury by order prescribe fees payable in respect of anything dealt with by the court.

(2)   An order under this section may in particular contain provision as to—

(a)   scales or rates of fees;

(b)   exemptions from and reductions in fees;

(c)   remission of fees in whole or in part.

(3)   Before making an order under this section, the Lord Chancellor must consult—

(a)   the President of the Court of Protection,

(b)   the Vice-President of the Court of Protection, and

(c)   the Senior Judge of the Court of Protection.

(4)   The Lord Chancellor must take such steps as are reasonably practicable to bring information about fees to the attention of persons likely to have to pay them.

(5)   Fees payable under this section are recoverable summarily as a civil debt.

55 Costs

(1)   Subject to Court of Protection Rules, the costs of and incidental to all proceedings in the court are in its discretion.

(2)   The rules may in particular make provision for regulating matters relating to the costs of those proceedings, including prescribing scales of costs to be paid to legal or other representatives.

(3)   The court has full power to determine by whom and to what extent the costs are to be paid.

(4)   The court may, in any proceedings—

(a)   disallow, or

(b)   order the legal or other representatives concerned to meet, the whole of any wasted costs or such part of them as may be determined in accordance with the rules.

(5) "Legal or other representative", in relation to a party to proceedings, means any person exercising a right of audience or right to conduct litigation on his behalf.

(6) "Wasted costs" means any costs incurred by a party—

    (a)   as a result of any improper, unreasonable or negligent act or omission on the part of any legal or other representative or any employee of such a representative, or

    (b)   which, in the light of any such act or omission occurring after they were incurred, the court considers it is unreasonable to expect that party to pay.

56 Fees and costs: supplementary

(1) Court of Protection Rules may make provision—

    (a)   as to the way in which, and funds from which, fees and costs are to be paid;

    (b)   for charging fees and costs upon the estate of the person to whom the proceedings relate;

    (c)   for the payment of fees and costs within a specified time of the death of the person to whom the proceedings relate or the conclusion of the proceedings.

(2) A charge on the estate of a person created by virtue of subsection (1)(b) does not cause any interest of the person in any property to fail or determine or to be prevented from recommencing.

The Public Guardian

57 The Public Guardian

(1) For the purposes of this Act, there is to be an officer, to be known as the Public Guardian.

(2) The Public Guardian is to be appointed by the Lord Chancellor.

(3) There is to be paid to the Public Guardian out of money provided by Parliament such salary as the Lord Chancellor may determine.

(4) The Lord Chancellor may, after consulting the Public Guardian—

    (a)   provide him with such officers and staff, or

    (b)   enter into such contracts with other persons for the provision (by them or their sub-contractors) of officers, staff or services,

as the Lord Chancellor thinks necessary for the proper discharge of the Public Guardian's functions.

(5) Any functions of the Public Guardian may, to the extent authorised by him, be performed by any of his officers.

58 Functions of the Public Guardian

(1) The Public Guardian has the following functions—

    (a)   establishing and maintaining a register of lasting powers of attorney,

    (b)   establishing and maintaining a register of orders appointing deputies,

    (c)   supervising deputies appointed by the court,

    (d)   directing a Court of Protection Visitor to visit—

        (i)   a donee of a lasting power of attorney,

        (ii)   a deputy appointed by the court, or

        (iii)   the person granting the power of attorney or for whom the deputy is appointed ("P"),

and to make a report to the Public Guardian on such matters as he may direct,

(e)   receiving security which the court requires a person to give for the discharge of his functions,

(f)   receiving reports from donees of lasting powers of attorney and deputies appointed by the court,

(g)   reporting to the court on such matters relating to proceedings under this Act as the court requires,

(h)   dealing with representations (including complaints) about the way in which a donee of a lasting power of attorney or a deputy appointed by the court is exercising his powers,

(i)   publishing, in any manner the Public Guardian thinks appropriate, any information he thinks appropriate about the discharge of his functions.

(2)   The functions conferred by subsection (1)(c) and (h) may be discharged in co-operation with any other person who has functions in relation to the care or treatment of P.

[(2A)   The Public Guardian also has the following functions—

(a)   establishing and maintaining a register of guardianship orders,

(b)   supervising guardians,

(c)   receiving security which the court requires a guardian to give for the exercise of the guardian's functions,

(d)   receiving reports from guardians,

(e)   reporting to the court on such matters relating to proceedings under the Guardianship (Missing Persons) Act 2017 as the court requires,

(f)   dealing with representations (including complaints) about the way in which a guardian is exercising the guardian's functions, and

(g)   publishing, in any manner the Public Guardian thinks appropriate, information about the exercise of his or her functions in connection with guardians and guardianship orders.]

(3)   The Lord Chancellor may by regulations make provision—

(a)   conferring on the Public Guardian other functions in connection with this Act [or the Guardianship (Missing Persons) Act 2017];

(b)   in connection with the discharge by the Public Guardian of his functions.

(4)   Regulations made under subsection (3)(b) may in particular make provision as to—

(a)   the giving of security by deputies appointed by the court [or guardians] and the enforcement and discharge of security so given;

(b)   the fees which may be charged by the Public Guardian;

(c)   the way in which, and funds from which, such fees are to be paid;

(d)   exemptions from and reductions in such fees;

(e)   remission of such fees in whole or in part;

(f)   the making of reports to the Public Guardian by deputies appointed by the court and others who are directed by the court to carry out any transaction for a person who lacks capacity;

[(g)   the making of reports to the Public Guardian by guardians].

(5)   For the purpose of enabling him to carry out his functions [in relation to lasting powers of attorney or deputies], the Public Guardian may, at all reasonable times, examine and take copies of—

(a)   any health record,

(b)   any record of, or held by, a local authority and compiled in connection with a social services function, and

(c)   any record held by a person registered under Part 2 of the Care Standards Act 2000 (c 14) [or Chapter 2 of Part 1 of the Health and Social Care Act 2008],

so far as the record relates to P.

(6)   The Public Guardian may also for that purpose interview P in private.

[(7)   In this section "guardian" and "guardianship order" have the same meaning as in the Guardianship (Missing Persons) Act 2017.]

59 ...

. . .

60 Annual report

(1)   The Public Guardian must make an annual report to the Lord Chancellor about the discharge of his functions.

(2)   The Lord Chancellor must, within one month of receiving the report, lay a copy of it before Parliament.

Court of Protection Visitors

61 Court of Protection Visitors

(1)   A Court of Protection Visitor is a person who is appointed by the Lord Chancellor to—

   (a)   a panel of Special Visitors, or

   (b)   a panel of General Visitors.

(2)   A person is not qualified to be a Special Visitor unless he—

   (a)   is a registered medical practitioner or appears to the Lord Chancellor to have other suitable qualifications or training, and

   (b)   appears to the Lord Chancellor to have special knowledge of and experience in cases of impairment of or disturbance in the functioning of the mind or brain.

(3)   A General Visitor need not have a medical qualification.

(4)   A Court of Protection Visitor—

   (a)   may be appointed for such term and subject to such conditions, and

   (b)   may be paid such remuneration and allowances,

as the Lord Chancellor may determine.

(5)   For the purpose of carrying out his functions under this Act in relation to a person who lacks capacity ("P"), a Court of Protection Visitor may, at all reasonable times, examine and take copies of—

   (a)   any health record,

   (b)   any record of, or held by, a local authority and compiled in connection with a social services function, and

   (c)   any record held by a person registered under Part 2 of the Care Standards Act 2000 (c 14) [or Chapter 2 of Part 1 of the Health and Social Care Act 2008],

so far as the record relates to P.

(6)   A Court of Protection Visitor may also for that purpose interview P in private.

PART 3   MISCELLANEOUS AND GENERAL

Declaratory provision

62 Scope of the Act

For the avoidance of doubt, it is hereby declared that nothing in this Act is to be taken to affect the law relating to murder or manslaughter or the operation of section 2 of the Suicide Act 1961 (c 60) (assisting suicide).

Private international law

63 International protection of adults

Schedule 3—

   (a)   gives effect in England and Wales to the Convention on the International Protection of Adults signed at the Hague on 13th January 2000 (Cm 5881) (in so far as this Act does not otherwise do so), and

   (b)   makes related provision as to the private international law of England and Wales.

General

64 Interpretation

(1) In this Act—

"the 1985 Act" means the Enduring Powers of Attorney Act 1985 (c 29),

"advance decision" has the meaning given in section 24(1),

["authorisation under Schedule A1" means either—

   (a)   a standard authorisation under that Schedule, or

   (b)   an urgent authorisation under that Schedule;]

"the court" means the Court of Protection established by section 45,

"Court of Protection Rules" has the meaning given in section 51(1),

"Court of Protection Visitor" has the meaning given in section 61,

"deputy" has the meaning given in section 16(2)(b),

"enactment" includes a provision of subordinate legislation (within the meaning of the Interpretation Act 1978 (c 30)),

"health record" has the meaning given in section 68 of the Data Protection Act 1998 (c 29) (as read with section 69 of that Act),

"the Human Rights Convention" has the same meaning as "the Convention" in the Human Rights Act 1998 (c 42),

"independent mental capacity advocate" has the meaning given in section 35(1),

"lasting power of attorney" has the meaning given in section 9,

"life sustaining treatment" has the meaning given in section 4(10),

"local authority"[, except in [section 35(6A)(a) and] Schedule A1,] means—

   (a)   the council of a county in England in which there are no district councils,

   (b)   the council of a district in England,

   (c)   the council of a county or county borough in Wales,

   (d)   the council of a London borough,

   (e)   the Common Council of the City of London, or

   (f)   the Council of the Isles of Scilly,

"Mental Health Act" means the Mental Health Act 1983 (c 20),

"prescribed", in relation to regulations made under this Act, means prescribed by those regulations,

"property" includes any thing in action and any interest in real or personal property,

"public authority" has the same meaning as in the Human Rights Act 1998,

"Public Guardian" has the meaning given in section 57,

"purchaser" and "purchase" have the meaning given in section 205(1) of the Law of Property Act 1925 (c 20), "social services function"[—

(a) in relation to England] has the meaning given in section 1A of the Local Authority Social Services Act 1970 (c 42),

[(b) in relation to Wales, has the meaning given in section 143 of the Social Services and Well-being (Wales) Act 2014 (anaw 4),]

"treatment" includes a diagnostic or other procedure,

"trust corporation" has the meaning given in section 68(1) of the Trustee Act 1925 (c 19), and

"will" includes codicil.

(2) In this Act, references to making decisions, in relation to a donee of a lasting power of attorney or a deputy appointed by the court, include, where appropriate, acting on decisions made.

(3) In this Act, references to the bankruptcy of an individual include a case where a bankruptcy restrictions order under the Insolvency Act 1986 (c 45) has effect in respect of him.

[(3A) In this Act references to a debt relief order (under Part 7A of the Insolvency Act 1986) being made in relation to an individual include a case where a debt relief restrictions order under the Insolvency Act 1986 has effect in respect of him.]

(4) "Bankruptcy restrictions order" includes an interim bankruptcy restrictions order.

[(4A) "Debt relief restrictions order" includes an interim debt relief restrictions order.]

[(5) In this Act, references to deprivation of a person's liberty have the same meaning as in Article 5(1) of the Human Rights Convention.

(6) For the purposes of such references, it does not matter whether a person is deprived of his liberty by a public authority or not.]

65 Rules, regulations and orders

(1) Any power to make rules, regulations or orders under this Act[, other than the power in section 21]—

(a) is exercisable by statutory instrument;

(b) includes power to make supplementary, incidental, consequential, transitional or saving provision;

(c) includes power to make different provision for different cases.

(2) Any statutory instrument containing rules, regulations or orders made by the Lord Chancellor or the Secretary of State under this Act, other than—

(a) regulations under section 34 (loss of capacity during research project),

(b) regulations under section 41 (adjusting role of independent mental capacity advocacy service),

(c) regulations under paragraph 32(1)(b) of Schedule 3 (private international law relating to the protection of adults),

(d) an order of the kind mentioned in section 67(6) (consequential amendments of primary legislation), or

(e) an order under section 68 (commencement),

is subject to annulment in pursuance of a resolution of either House of Parliament.

(3) A statutory instrument containing an Order in Council under paragraph 31 of Schedule 3 (provision to give further effect to Hague Convention) is subject to annulment in pursuance of a resolution of either House of Parliament.

(4) A statutory instrument containing regulations made by the Secretary of State under section 34 or 41 or by the Lord Chancellor under paragraph 32(1)(b) of Schedule 3 may not be made unless a draft has been laid before and approved by resolution of each House of Parliament.

[(4A) Subsection (2) does not apply to a statutory instrument containing regulations made by the Secretary of State under Schedule A1.

(4B) If such a statutory instrument contains regulations under paragraph 42(2)(b), 129, 162 or 164 of Schedule A1 (whether or not it also contains other regulations), the instrument may not be made unless a draft has been laid before and approved by resolution of each House of Parliament.

(4C) Subject to that, such a statutory instrument is subject to annulment in pursuance of a resolution of either House of Parliament.]

[(5) An order under section 21—

(a) may include supplementary, incidental, consequential, transitional or saving provision;

(b) may make different provision for different cases;

(c) is to be made in the form of a statutory instrument to which the Statutory Instruments Act 1946 applies as if the order were made by a Minister of the Crown; and

(d) is subject to annulment in pursuance of a resolution of either House of Parliament.]

66 Existing receivers and enduring powers of attorney etc

(1) The following provisions cease to have effect—

(a) Part 7 of the Mental Health Act,

(b) the Enduring Powers of Attorney Act 1985 (c 29).

(2) No enduring power of attorney within the meaning of the 1985 Act is to be created after the commencement of subsection (1)(b).

(3) Schedule 4 has effect in place of the 1985 Act in relation to any enduring power of attorney created before the commencement of subsection (1)(b).

(4) Schedule 5 contains transitional provisions and savings in relation to Part 7 of the Mental Health Act and the 1985 Act.

67 Minor and consequential amendments and repeals

(1) Schedule 6 contains minor and consequential amendments.

(2) Schedule 7 contains repeals.

(3) The Lord Chancellor may by order make supplementary, incidental, consequential, transitional or saving provision for the purposes of, in consequence of, or for giving full effect to a provision of this Act.

(4) An order under subsection (3) may, in particular—

(a) provide for a provision of this Act which comes into force before another provision of this Act has come into force to have effect, until the other provision has come into force, with specified modifications;

(b) amend, repeal or revoke an enactment, other than one contained in an Act or Measure passed in a Session after the one in which this Act is passed.

(5) The amendments that may be made under subsection (4)(b) are in addition to those made by or under any other provision of this Act.

(6) An order under subsection (3) which amends or repeals a provision of an Act or Measure may not be made unless a draft has been laid before and approved by resolution of each House of Parliament.

68 Commencement and extent

(1) This Act, other than sections 30 to 41, comes into force in accordance with provision made by order by the Lord Chancellor.

(2) Sections 30 to 41 come into force in accordance with provision made by order by—

(a) the Secretary of State, in relation to England, and

(b) the National Assembly for Wales, in relation to Wales.

(3) An order under this section may appoint different days for different provisions and different purposes.

(4) Subject to subsections (5) and (6), this Act extends to England and Wales only.

(5) The following provisions extend to the United Kingdom—

    (a) paragraph 16(1) of Schedule 1 (evidence of instruments and of registration of lasting powers of attorney),

    (b) paragraph 15(3) of Schedule 4 (evidence of instruments and of registration of enduring powers of attorney).

(6) Subject to any provision made in Schedule 6, the amendments and repeals made by Schedules 6 and 7 have the same extent as the enactments to which they relate.

69 Short title

This Act may be cited as the Mental Capacity Act 2005.

[SCHEDULE A1

HOSPITAL AND CARE HOME RESIDENTS: DEPRIVATION OF LIBERTY]

[PART 1 AUTHORISATION TO DEPRIVE RESIDENTS OF LIBERTY ETC]

[Application of Part

1

(1) This Part applies if the following conditions are met.

(2) The first condition is that a person ("P") is detained in a hospital or care home—for the purpose of being given care or treatment—in circumstances which amount to deprivation of the person's liberty.

(3) The second condition is that a standard or urgent authorisation is in force.

(4) The third condition is that the standard or urgent authorisation relates—

    (a) to P, and

    (b) to the hospital or care home in which P is detained.

Authorisation to deprive P of liberty

2

The managing authority of the hospital or care home may deprive P of his liberty by detaining him as mentioned in paragraph 1(2).

No liability for acts done for purpose of depriving P of liberty

3

(1) This paragraph applies to any act which a person ("D") does for the purpose of detaining P as mentioned in paragraph 1(2).

(2) D does not incur any liability in relation to the act that he would not have incurred if P—

    (a) had had capacity to consent in relation to D's doing the act, and

    (b) had consented to D's doing the act.

No protection for negligent acts etc

4

(1) Paragraphs 2 and 3 do not exclude a person's civil liability for loss or damage, or his criminal liability, resulting from his negligence in doing any thing.

(2) Paragraphs 2 and 3 do not authorise a person to do anything otherwise than for the purpose of the standard or urgent authorisation that is in force.

(3) In a case where a standard authorisation is in force, paragraphs 2 and 3 do not authorise a person to do anything which does not comply with the conditions (if any) included in the authorisation.]

[PART 2   INTERPRETATION: MAIN TERMS]

[Introduction

5

This Part applies for the purposes of this Schedule.

Detained resident

6

"Detained resident" means a person detained in a hospital or care home—for the purpose of being given care or treatment—in circumstances which amount to deprivation of the person's liberty.

Relevant person etc

7

In relation to a person who is, or is to be, a detained resident—
"relevant person" means the person in question;
"relevant hospital or care home" means the hospital or care home in question;
"relevant care or treatment" means the care or treatment in question.

Authorisations

8

"Standard authorisation" means an authorisation given under Part 4.

9

"Urgent authorisation" means an authorisation given under Part 5.

10

"Authorisation under this Schedule" means either of the following—
(a)   a standard authorisation;
(b)   an urgent authorisation.

11

(1)   The purpose of a standard authorisation is the purpose which is stated in the authorisation in accordance with paragraph 55(1)(d).
(2)   The purpose of an urgent authorisation is the purpose which is stated in the authorisation in accordance with paragraph 80(d).]

[PART 3   THE QUALIFYING REQUIREMENTS]

[The qualifying requirements

12

(1)   These are the qualifying requirements referred to in this Schedule—
(a)   the age requirement;
(b)   the mental health requirement;
(c)   the mental capacity requirement;

    (d)   the best interests requirement;

    (e)   the eligibility requirement;

    (f)   the no refusals requirement.

(2) Any question of whether a person who is, or is to be, a detained resident meets the qualifying requirements is to be determined in accordance with this Part.

(3) In a case where—

    (a)   the question of whether a person meets a particular qualifying requirement arises in relation to the giving of a standard authorisation, and

    (b)   any circumstances relevant to determining that question are expected to change between the time when the determination is made and the time when the authorisation is expected to come into force,

those circumstances are to be taken into account as they are expected to be at the later time.

The age requirement

13

The relevant person meets the age requirement if he has reached 18.

The mental health requirement

14

(1) The relevant person meets the mental health requirement if he is suffering from mental disorder (within the meaning of the Mental Health Act, but disregarding any exclusion for persons with learning disability).

(2) An exclusion for persons with learning disability is any provision of the Mental Health Act which provides for a person with learning disability not to be regarded as suffering from mental disorder for one or more purposes of that Act.

The mental capacity requirement

15

The relevant person meets the mental capacity requirement if he lacks capacity in relation to the question whether or not he should be accommodated in the relevant hospital or care home for the purpose of being given the relevant care or treatment.

The best interests requirement

16

(1) The relevant person meets the best interests requirement if all of the following conditions are met.

(2) The first condition is that the relevant person is, or is to be, a detained resident.

(3) The second condition is that it is in the best interests of the relevant person for him to be a detained resident.

(4) The third condition is that, in order to prevent harm to the relevant person, it is necessary for him to be a detained resident.

(5) The fourth condition is that it is a proportionate response to—

    (a)   the likelihood of the relevant person suffering harm, and

    (b)   the seriousness of that harm,

for him to be a detained resident.

The eligibility requirement

17

(1)   The relevant person meets the eligibility requirement unless he is ineligible to be deprived of liberty by this Act.

(2)   Schedule 1A applies for the purpose of determining whether or not P is ineligible to be deprived of liberty by this Act.

The no refusals requirement

18

The relevant person meets the no refusals requirement unless there is a refusal within the meaning of paragraph 19 or 20.

19

(1)   There is a refusal if these conditions are met—
- (a)   the relevant person has made an advance decision;
- (b)   the advance decision is valid;
- (c)   the advance decision is applicable to some or all of the relevant treatment.

(2)   Expressions used in this paragraph and any of sections 24, 25 or 26 have the same meaning in this paragraph as in that section.

20

(1)   There is a refusal if it would be in conflict with a valid decision of a donee or deputy for the relevant person to be accommodated in the relevant hospital or care home for the purpose of receiving some or all of the relevant care or treatment—
- (a)   in circumstances which amount to deprivation of the person's liberty, or
- (b)   at all.

(2)   A donee is a donee of a lasting power of attorney granted by the relevant person.

(3)   A decision of a donee or deputy is valid if it is made—
- (a)   within the scope of his authority as donee or deputy, and
- (b)   in accordance with Part 1 of this Act.]

[PART 4   STANDARD AUTHORISATIONS]

[Supervisory body to give authorisation

21

Only the supervisory body may give a standard authorisation.

22

The supervisory body may not give a standard authorisation unless—
- (a)   the managing authority of the relevant hospital or care home have requested it, or
- (b)   paragraph 71 applies (right of third party to require consideration of whether authorisation needed).

23

The managing authority may not make a request for a standard authorisation unless—
- (a)   they are required to do so by paragraph 24 (as read with paragraphs 27 to 29),
- (b)   they are required to do so by paragraph 25 (as read with paragraph 28), or
- (c)   they are permitted to do so by paragraph 30.

Duty to request authorisation: basic cases

24

(1) The managing authority must request a standard authorisation in any of the following cases.

(2) The first case is where it appears to the managing authority that the relevant person—

> (a) is not yet accommodated in the relevant hospital or care home,
>
> (b) is likely—at some time within the next 28 days—to be a detained resident in the relevant hospital or care home, and
>
> (c) is likely—
>
> > (i) at that time, or
> >
> > (ii) at some later time within the next 28 days,
>
> to meet all of the qualifying requirements.

(3) The second case is where it appears to the managing authority that the relevant person—

> (a) is already accommodated in the relevant hospital or care home,
>
> (b) is likely—at some time within the next 28 days—to be a detained resident in the relevant hospital or care home, and
>
> (c) is likely—
>
> > (i) at that time, or
> >
> > (ii) at some later time within the next 28 days,
>
> to meet all of the qualifying requirements.

(4) The third case is where it appears to the managing authority that the relevant person—

> (a) is a detained resident in the relevant hospital or care home, and
>
> (b) meets all of the qualifying requirements, or is likely to do so at some time within the next 28 days.

(5) This paragraph is subject to paragraphs 27 to 29.

Duty to request authorisation: change in place of detention

25

(1) The relevant managing authority must request a standard authorisation if it appears to them that these conditions are met.

(2) The first condition is that a standard authorisation—

> (a) has been given, and
>
> (b) has not ceased to be in force.

(3) The second condition is that there is, or is to be, a change in the place of detention.

(4) This paragraph is subject to paragraph 28.

26

(1) This paragraph applies for the purposes of paragraph 25.

(2) There is a change in the place of detention if the relevant person—

> (a) ceases to be a detained resident in the stated hospital or care home, and
>
> (b) becomes a detained resident in a different hospital or care home ("the new hospital or care home").

(3) The stated hospital or care home is the hospital or care home to which the standard authorisation relates.

(4) The relevant managing authority are the managing authority of the new hospital or care home.

Other authority for detention: request for authorisation

27

(1) This paragraph applies if, by virtue of section 4A(3), a decision of the court authorises the relevant person to be a detained resident.

(2) Paragraph 24 does not require a request for a standard authorisation to be made in relation to that detention unless these conditions are met.

(3) The first condition is that the standard authorisation would be in force at a time immediately after the expiry of the other authority.

(4) The second condition is that the standard authorisation would not be in force at any time on or before the expiry of the other authority.

(5) The third condition is that it would, in the managing authority's view, be unreasonable to delay making the request until a time nearer the expiry of the other authority.

(6) In this paragraph—

> (a)   the other authority is—
>
>> (i)   the decision mentioned in sub-paragraph (1), or
>>
>> (ii)   any further decision of the court which, by virtue of section 4A(3), authorises, or is expected to authorise, the relevant person to be a detained resident;
>
> (b)   the expiry of the other authority is the time when the other authority is expected to cease to authorise the relevant person to be a detained resident.

Request refused: no further request unless change of circumstances

28

(1) This paragraph applies if—

> (a)   a managing authority request a standard authorisation under paragraph 24 or 25, and
>
> (b)   the supervisory body are prohibited by paragraph 50(2) from giving the authorisation.

(2) Paragraph 24 or 25 does not require that managing authority to make a new request for a standard authorisation unless it appears to the managing authority that—

> (a)   there has been a change in the relevant person's case, and
>
> (b)   because of that change, the supervisory body are likely to give a standard authorisation if requested.

Authorisation given: request for further authorisation

29

(1) This paragraph applies if a standard authorisation—

> (a)   has been given in relation to the detention of the relevant person, and
>
> (b)   that authorisation ("the existing authorisation") has not ceased to be in force.

(2) Paragraph 24 does not require a new request for a standard authorisation ("the new authorisation") to be made unless these conditions are met.

(3) The first condition is that the new authorisation would be in force at a time immediately after the expiry of the existing authorisation.

(4) The second condition is that the new authorisation would not be in force at any time on or before the expiry of the existing authorisation.

(5) The third condition is that it would, in the managing authority's view, be unreasonable to delay making the request until a time nearer the expiry of the existing authorisation.

(6) The expiry of the existing authorisation is the time when it is expected to cease to be in force.

Power to request authorisation

30

(1) This paragraph applies if—

    (a)   a standard authorisation has been given in relation to the detention of the relevant person,

    (b)   that authorisation ("the existing authorisation") has not ceased to be in force,

    (c)   the requirement under paragraph 24 to make a request for a new standard authorisation does not apply, because of paragraph 29, and

    (d)   a review of the existing authorisation has been requested, or is being carried out, in accordance with Part 8.

(2) The managing authority may request a new standard authorisation which would be in force on or before the expiry of the existing authorisation; but only if it would also be in force immediately after that expiry.

(3) The expiry of the existing authorisation is the time when it is expected to cease to be in force.

(4) Further provision relating to cases where a request is made under this paragraph can be found in—

    (a)   paragraph 62 (effect of decision about request), and

    (b)   paragraph 124 (effect of request on Part 8 review).

Information included in request

31

A request for a standard authorisation must include the information (if any) required by regulations.

Records of requests

32

(1) The managing authority of a hospital or care home must keep a written record of—

    (a)   each request that they make for a standard authorisation, and

    (b)   the reasons for making each request.

(2) A supervisory body must keep a written record of each request for a standard authorisation that is made to them.

Relevant person must be assessed

33

(1) This paragraph applies if the supervisory body are requested to give a standard authorisation.

(2) The supervisory body must secure that all of these assessments are carried out in relation to the relevant person—

    (a)   an age assessment;

    (b)   a mental health assessment;

    (c)   a mental capacity assessment;

    (d)   a best interests assessment;

    (e)   an eligibility assessment;

    (f)   a no refusals assessment.

(3)   The person who carries out any such assessment is referred to as the assessor.

(4)   Regulations may be made about the period (or periods) within which assessors must carry out assessments.

(5)   This paragraph is subject to paragraphs 49 and 133.

Age assessment

34

An age assessment is an assessment of whether the relevant person meets the age requirement.

Mental health assessment

35

A mental health assessment is an assessment of whether the relevant person meets the mental health requirement.

36

When carrying out a mental health assessment, the assessor must also—

    (a)   consider how (if at all) the relevant person's mental health is likely to be affected by his being a detained resident, and

    (b)   notify the best interests assessor of his conclusions.

Mental capacity assessment

37

A mental capacity assessment is an assessment of whether the relevant person meets the mental capacity requirement.

Best interests assessment

38

A best interests assessment is an assessment of whether the relevant person meets the best interests requirement.

39

(1)   In carrying out a best interests assessment, the assessor must comply with the duties in sub-paragraphs (2) and (3).

(2)   The assessor must consult the managing authority of the relevant hospital or care home.

(3)   The assessor must have regard to all of the following—

    (a)   the conclusions which the mental health assessor has notified to the best interests assessor in accordance with paragraph 36(b);

    (b)   any relevant needs assessment;

    (c)   any relevant care plan.

(4)   A relevant needs assessment is an assessment of the relevant person's needs which—

    (a)   was carried out in connection with the relevant person being accommodated in the relevant hospital or care home, and

    (b)   was carried out by or on behalf of—

      (i)   the managing authority of the relevant hospital or care home, or

      (ii)   the supervisory body.

(5)   A relevant care plan is a care plan which—

    (a)   sets out how the relevant person's needs are to be met whilst he is accommodated in the relevant hospital or care home, and

    (b)   was drawn up by or on behalf of—

      (i)   the managing authority of the relevant hospital or care home, or

      (ii)   the supervisory body.

(6)   The managing authority must give the assessor a copy of—

    (a)   any relevant needs assessment carried out by them or on their behalf, or

    (b)   any relevant care plan drawn up by them or on their behalf.

(7)   The supervisory body must give the assessor a copy of—

    (a)   any relevant needs assessment carried out by them or on their behalf, or

    (b)   any relevant care plan drawn up by them or on their behalf.

(8)   The duties in sub-paragraphs (2) and (3) do not affect any other duty to consult or to take the views of others into account.

40

(1)   This paragraph applies whatever conclusion the best interests assessment comes to.

(2)   The assessor must state in the best interests assessment the name and address of every interested person whom he has consulted in carrying out the assessment.

41

Paragraphs 42 and 43 apply if the best interests assessment comes to the conclusion that the relevant person meets the best interests requirement.

42

(1)   The assessor must state in the assessment the maximum authorisation period.

(2)   The maximum authorisation period is the shorter of these periods—

    (a)   the period which, in the assessor's opinion, would be the appropriate maximum period for the relevant person to be a detained resident under the standard authorisation that has been requested;

    (b)   1 year, or such shorter period as may be prescribed in regulations.

(3)   Regulations under sub-paragraph (2)(b)—

    (a)   need not provide for a shorter period to apply in relation to all standard authorisations;

    (b)   may provide for different periods to apply in relation to different kinds of standard authorisations.

(4)   Before making regulations under sub-paragraph (2)(b) the Secretary of State must consult all of the following—

    (a)   each body required by regulations under paragraph 162 to monitor and report on the operation of this Schedule in relation to England;

    (b)   such other persons as the Secretary of State considers it appropriate to consult.

(5)   Before making regulations under sub-paragraph (2)(b) the National Assembly for Wales must consult all of the following—

    (a)   each person or body directed under paragraph 163(2) to carry out any function of the Assembly of monitoring and reporting on the operation of this Schedule in relation to Wales;

    (b)   such other persons as the Assembly considers it appropriate to consult.

43

The assessor may include in the assessment recommendations about conditions to which the standard authorisation is, or is not, to be subject in accordance with paragraph 53.

44

(1) This paragraph applies if the best interests assessment comes to the conclusion that the relevant person does not meet the best interests requirement.

(2) If, on the basis of the information taken into account in carrying out the assessment, it appears to the assessor that there is an unauthorised deprivation of liberty, he must include a statement to that effect in the assessment.

(3) There is an unauthorised deprivation of liberty if the managing authority of the relevant hospital or care home are already depriving the relevant person of his liberty without authority of the kind mentioned in section 4A.

45

The duties with which the best interests assessor must comply are subject to the provision included in appointment regulations under Part 10 (in particular, provision made under paragraph 146).

Eligibility assessment

46

An eligibility assessment is an assessment of whether the relevant person meets the eligibility requirement.

47

(1) Regulations may—

    (a)   require an eligibility assessor to request a best interests assessor to provide relevant eligibility information, and

    (b)   require the best interests assessor, if such a request is made, to provide such relevant eligibility information as he may have.

(2) In this paragraph—

    "best interests assessor" means any person who is carrying out, or has carried out, a best interests assessment in relation to the relevant person;

    "eligibility assessor" means a person carrying out an eligibility assessment in relation to the relevant person;

    "relevant eligibility information" is information relevant to assessing whether or not the relevant person is ineligible by virtue of paragraph 5 of Schedule 1A.

No refusals assessment

48

A no refusals assessment is an assessment of whether the relevant person meets the no refusals requirement.

Equivalent assessment already carried out

49

(1) The supervisory body are not required by paragraph 33 to secure that a particular kind of assessment ("the required assessment") is carried out in relation to the relevant person if the following conditions are met.

(2) The first condition is that the supervisory body have a written copy of an assessment of the relevant person ("the existing assessment") that has already been carried out.

(3) The second condition is that the existing assessment complies with all requirements under this Schedule with which the required assessment would have to comply (if it were carried out).

(4) The third condition is that the existing assessment was carried out within the previous 12 months; but this condition need not be met if the required assessment is an age assessment.

(5) The fourth condition is that the supervisory body are satisfied that there is no reason why the existing assessment may no longer be accurate.

(6) If the required assessment is a best interests assessment, in satisfying themselves as mentioned in sub-paragraph (5), the supervisory body must take into account any information given, or submissions made, by—

     (a)   the relevant person's representative,

     (b)   any section 39C IMCA, or

     (c)   any section 39D IMCA.

(7) It does not matter whether the existing assessment was carried out in connection with a request for a standard authorisation or for some other purpose.

(8) If, because of this paragraph, the supervisory body are not required by paragraph 33 to secure that the required assessment is carried out, the existing assessment is to be treated for the purposes of this Schedule—

     (a)   as an assessment of the same kind as the required assessment, and

     (b)   as having been carried out under paragraph 33 in connection with the request for the standard authorisation.

Duty to give authorisation

50

(1) The supervisory body must give a standard authorisation if—

     (a)   all assessments are positive, and

     (b)   the supervisory body have written copies of all those assessments.

(2) The supervisory body must not give a standard authorisation except in accordance with sub-paragraph (1).

(3) All assessments are positive if each assessment carried out under paragraph 33 has come to the conclusion that the relevant person meets the qualifying requirement to which the assessment relates.

Terms of authorisation

51

(1) If the supervisory body are required to give a standard authorisation, they must decide the period during which the authorisation is to be in force.

(2) That period must not exceed the maximum authorisation period stated in the best interests assessment.

52

A standard authorisation may provide for the authorisation to come into force at a time after it is given.

53

(1) A standard authorisation may be given subject to conditions.

(2)   Before deciding whether to give the authorisation subject to conditions, the supervisory body must have regard to any recommendations in the best interests assessment about such conditions.

(3)   The managing authority of the relevant hospital or care home must ensure that any conditions are complied with.

Form of authorisation

54

A standard authorisation must be in writing.

55

(1)   A standard authorisation must state the following things—

    (a)   the name of the relevant person;

    (b)   the name of the relevant hospital or care home;

    (c)   the period during which the authorisation is to be in force;

    (d)   the purpose for which the authorisation is given;

    (e)   any conditions subject to which the authorisation is given;

    (f)   the reason why each qualifying requirement is met.

(2)   The statement of the reason why the eligibility requirement is met must be framed by reference to the cases in the table in paragraph 2 of Schedule 1A.

56

(1)   If the name of the relevant hospital or care home changes, the standard authorisation is to be read as if it stated the current name of the hospital or care home.

(2)   But sub-paragraph (1) is subject to any provision relating to the change of name which is made in any enactment or in any instrument made under an enactment.

Duty to give information about decision

57

(1)   This paragraph applies if—

    (a)   a request is made for a standard authorisation, and

    (b)   the supervisory body are required by paragraph 50(1) to give the standard authorisation.

(2)   The supervisory body must give a copy of the authorisation to each of the following—

    (a)   the relevant person's representative;

    (b)   the managing authority of the relevant hospital or care home;

    (c)   the relevant person;

    (d)   any section 39A IMCA;

    (e)   every interested person consulted by the best interests assessor.

(3)   The supervisory body must comply with this paragraph as soon as practicable after they give the standard authorisation.

58

(1)   This paragraph applies if—

    (a)   a request is made for a standard authorisation, and

    (b)   the supervisory body are prohibited by paragraph 50(2) from giving the standard authorisation.

(2)   The supervisory body must give notice, stating that they are prohibited from giving the authorisation, to each of the following—

    (a)   the managing authority of the relevant hospital or care home;

    (b)   the relevant person;

    (c)   any section 39A IMCA;

    (d)   every interested person consulted by the best interests assessor.

(3) The supervisory body must comply with this paragraph as soon as practicable after it becomes apparent to them that they are prohibited from giving the authorisation.

Duty to give information about effect of authorisation

59

(1) This paragraph applies if a standard authorisation is given.

(2) The managing authority of the relevant hospital or care home must take such steps as are practicable to ensure that the relevant person understands all of the following—

    (a)   the effect of the authorisation;

    (b)   the right to make an application to the court to exercise its jurisdiction under section 21A;

    (c)   the right under Part 8 to request a review;

    (d)   the right to have a section 39D IMCA appointed;

    (e)   how to have a section 39D IMCA appointed.

(3) Those steps must be taken as soon as is practicable after the authorisation is given.

(4) Those steps must include the giving of appropriate information both orally and in writing.

(5) Any written information given to the relevant person must also be given by the managing authority to the relevant person's representative.

(6) They must give the information to the representative as soon as is practicable after it is given to the relevant person.

(7) Sub-paragraph (8) applies if the managing authority is notified that a section 39D IMCA has been appointed.

(8) As soon as is practicable after being notified, the managing authority must give the section 39D IMCA a copy of the written information given in accordance with sub-paragraph (4).

Records of authorisations

60

A supervisory body must keep a written record of all of the following information—

    (a)   the standard authorisations that they have given;

    (b)   the requests for standard authorisations in response to which they have not given an authorisation;

    (c)   in relation to each standard authorisation given: the matters stated in the authorisation in accordance with paragraph 55.

Variation of an authorisation

61

(1) A standard authorisation may not be varied except in accordance with Part 7 or 8.

(2) This paragraph does not affect the powers of the Court of Protection or of any other court.

Effect of decision about request made under paragraph 25 or 30

62

(1) This paragraph applies where the managing authority request a new standard authorisation under either of the following—

    (a)   paragraph 25 (change in place of detention);

    (b)   paragraph 30 (existing authorisation subject to review).

(2) If the supervisory body are required by paragraph 50(1) to give the new authorisation, the existing authorisation terminates at the time when the new authorisation comes into force.

(3) If the supervisory body are prohibited by paragraph 50(2) from giving the new authorisation, there is no effect on the existing authorisation's continuation in force.

When an authorisation is in force

63

(1) A standard authorisation comes into force when it is given.

(2) But if the authorisation provides for it to come into force at a later time, it comes into force at that time.

64

(1) A standard authorisation ceases to be in force at the end of the period stated in the authorisation in accordance with paragraph 55(1)(c).

(2) But if the authorisation terminates before then in accordance with paragraph 62(2) or any other provision of this Schedule, it ceases to be in force when the termination takes effect.

(3) This paragraph does not affect the powers of the Court of Protection or of any other court.

65

(1) This paragraph applies if a standard authorisation ceases to be in force.

(2) The supervisory body must give notice that the authorisation has ceased to be in force.

(3) The supervisory body must give that notice to all of the following—

    (a)   the managing authority of the relevant hospital or care home;

    (b)   the relevant person;

    (c)   the relevant person's representative;

    (d)   every interested person consulted by the best interests assessor.

(4) The supervisory body must give that notice as soon as practicable after the authorisation ceases to be in force.

When a request for a standard authorisation is "disposed of"

66

A request for a standard authorisation is to be regarded for the purposes of this Schedule as disposed of if the supervisory body have given—

    (a)   a copy of the authorisation in accordance with paragraph 57, or

    (b)   notice in accordance with paragraph 58.

Right of third party to require consideration of whether authorisation needed

67

For the purposes of paragraphs 68 to 73 there is an unauthorised deprivation of liberty if—

    (a)   a person is already a detained resident in a hospital or care home, and

    (b)   the detention of the person is not authorised as mentioned in section 4A.

68

(1) If the following conditions are met, an eligible person may request the supervisory body to decide whether or not there is an unauthorised deprivation of liberty.

(2) The first condition is that the eligible person has notified the managing authority of the relevant hospital or care home that it appears to the eligible person that there is an unauthorised deprivation of liberty.

(3) The second condition is that the eligible person has asked the managing authority to request a standard authorisation in relation to the detention of the relevant person.

(4) The third condition is that the managing authority has not requested a standard authorisation within a reasonable period after the eligible person asks it to do so.

(5) In this paragraph "eligible person" means any person other than the managing authority of the relevant hospital or care home.

69

(1) This paragraph applies if an eligible person requests the supervisory body to decide whether or not there is an unauthorised deprivation of liberty.

(2) The supervisory body must select and appoint a person to carry out an assessment of whether or not the relevant person is a detained resident.

(3) But the supervisory body need not select and appoint a person to carry out such an assessment in either of these cases.

(4) The first case is where it appears to the supervisory body that the request by the eligible person is frivolous or vexatious.

(5) The second case is where it appears to the supervisory body that—

    (a)   the question of whether or not there is an unauthorised deprivation of liberty has already been decided, and

    (b)   since that decision, there has been no change of circumstances which would merit the question being decided again.

(6) The supervisory body must not select and appoint a person to carry out an assessment under this paragraph unless it appears to the supervisory body that the person would be—

    (a)   suitable to carry out a best interests assessment (if one were obtained in connection with a request for a standard authorisation relating to the relevant person), and

    (b)   eligible to carry out such a best interests assessment.

(7) The supervisory body must notify the persons specified in sub-paragraph (8)—

    (a)   that the supervisory body have been requested to decide whether or not there is an unauthorised deprivation of liberty;

    (b)   of their decision whether or not to select and appoint a person to carry out an assessment under this paragraph;

    (c)   if their decision is to select and appoint a person, of the person appointed.

(8) The persons referred to in sub-paragraph (7) are—

    (a)   the eligible person who made the request under paragraph 68;

    (b)   the person to whom the request relates;

    (c)   the managing authority of the relevant hospital or care home;

    (d)   any section 39A IMCA.

70

(1) Regulations may be made about the period within which an assessment under paragraph 69 must be carried out.

(2)   Regulations made under paragraph 129(3) apply in relation to the selection and appointment of a person under paragraph 69 as they apply to the selection of a person under paragraph 129 to carry out a best interests assessment.

(3)   The following provisions apply to an assessment under paragraph 69 as they apply to an assessment carried out in connection with a request for a standard authorisation—

(a)   paragraph 131 (examination and copying of records);

(b)   paragraph 132 (representations);

(c)   paragraphs 134 and 135(1) and (2) (duty to keep records and give copies).

(4)   The copies of the assessment which the supervisory body are required to give under paragraph 135(2) must be given as soon as practicable after the supervisory body are themselves given a copy of the assessment.

71

(1)   This paragraph applies if—

(a)   the supervisory body obtain an assessment under paragraph 69,

(b)   the assessment comes to the conclusion that the relevant person is a detained resident, and

(c)   it appears to the supervisory body that the detention of the person is not authorised as mentioned in section 4A.

(2)   This Schedule (including Part 5) applies as if the managing authority of the relevant hospital or care home had, in accordance with Part 4, requested the supervisory body to give a standard authorisation in relation to the relevant person.

(3)   The managing authority of the relevant hospital or care home must supply the supervisory body with the information (if any) which the managing authority would, by virtue of paragraph 31, have had to include in a request for a standard authorisation.

(4)   The supervisory body must notify the persons specified in paragraph 69(8)—

(a)   of the outcome of the assessment obtained under paragraph 69, and

(b)   that this Schedule applies as mentioned in sub-paragraph (2).

72

(1)   This paragraph applies if—

(a)   the supervisory body obtain an assessment under paragraph 69, and

(b)   the assessment comes to the conclusion that the relevant person is not a detained resident.

(2)   The supervisory body must notify the persons specified in paragraph 69(8) of the outcome of the assessment.

73

(1)   This paragraph applies if—

(a)   the supervisory body obtain an assessment under paragraph 69,

(b)   the assessment comes to the conclusion that the relevant person is a detained resident, and

(c)   it appears to the supervisory body that the detention of the person is authorised as mentioned in section 4A.

(2)   The supervisory body must notify the persons specified in paragraph 69(8)—

(a)   of the outcome of the assessment, and

(b)   that it appears to the supervisory body that the detention is authorised.]

[PART 5 URGENT AUTHORISATIONS]

[Managing authority to give authorisation

74

Only the managing authority of the relevant hospital or care home may give an urgent authorisation.

75

The managing authority may give an urgent authorisation only if they are required to do so by paragraph 76 (as read with paragraph 77).

Duty to give authorisation

76

(1) The managing authority must give an urgent authorisation in either of the following cases.

(2) The first case is where—

  (a) the managing authority are required to make a request under paragraph 24 or 25 for a standard authorisation, and

  (b) they believe that the need for the relevant person to be a detained resident is so urgent that it is appropriate for the detention to begin before they make the request.

(3) The second case is where—

  (a) the managing authority have made a request under paragraph 24 or 25 for a standard authorisation, and

  (b) they believe that the need for the relevant person to be a detained resident is so urgent that it is appropriate for the detention to begin before the request is disposed of.

(4) References in this paragraph to the detention of the relevant person are references to the detention to which paragraph 24 or 25 relates.

(5) This paragraph is subject to paragraph 77.

77

(1) This paragraph applies where the managing authority have given an urgent authorisation ("the original authorisation") in connection with a case where a person is, or is to be, a detained resident ("the existing detention").

(2) No new urgent authorisation is to be given under paragraph 76 in connection with the existing detention.

(3) But the managing authority may request the supervisory body to extend the duration of the original authorisation.

(4) Only one request under sub-paragraph (3) may be made in relation to the original authorisation.

(5) Paragraphs 84 to 86 apply to any request made under sub-paragraph (3).

Terms of authorisation

78

(1) If the managing authority decide to give an urgent authorisation, they must decide the period during which the authorisation is to be in force.

(2) That period must not exceed 7 days.

Form of authorisation

79

An urgent authorisation must be in writing.

80

An urgent authorisation must state the following things—

    (a)   the name of the relevant person;

    (b)   the name of the relevant hospital or care home;

    (c)   the period during which the authorisation is to be in force;

    (d)   the purpose for which the authorisation is given.

81

(1) If the name of the relevant hospital or care home changes, the urgent authorisation is to be read as if it stated the current name of the hospital or care home.

(2) But sub-paragraph (1) is subject to any provision relating to the change of name which is made in any enactment or in any instrument made under an enactment.

Duty to keep records and give copies

82

(1) This paragraph applies if an urgent authorisation is given.

(2) The managing authority must keep a written record of why they have given the urgent authorisation.

(3) As soon as practicable after giving the authorisation, the managing authority must give a copy of the authorisation to all of the following—

    (a)   the relevant person;

    (b)   any section 39A IMCA.

Duty to give information about authorisation

83

(1) This paragraph applies if an urgent authorisation is given.

(2) The managing authority of the relevant hospital or care home must take such steps as are practicable to ensure that the relevant person understands all of the following—

    (a)   the effect of the authorisation;

    (b)   the right to make an application to the court to exercise its jurisdiction under section 21A.

(3) Those steps must be taken as soon as is practicable after the authorisation is given.

(4) Those steps must include the giving of appropriate information both orally and in writing.

Request for extension of duration

84

(1) This paragraph applies if the managing authority make a request under paragraph 77 for the supervisory body to extend the duration of the original authorisation.

(2) The managing authority must keep a written record of why they have made the request.

(3) The managing authority must give the relevant person notice that they have made the request.

(4)   The supervisory body may extend the duration of the original authorisation if it appears to them that—

- (a)   the managing authority have made the required request for a standard authorisation,
- (b)   there are exceptional reasons why it has not yet been possible for that request to be disposed of, and
- (c)   it is essential for the existing detention to continue until the request is disposed of.

(5)   The supervisory body must keep a written record that the request has been made to them.

(6)   In this paragraph and paragraphs 85 and 86—

- (a)   "original authorisation" and "existing detention" have the same meaning as in paragraph 77;
- (b)   the required request for a standard authorisation is the request that is referred to in paragraph 76(2) or (3).

85

(1)   This paragraph applies if, under paragraph 84, the supervisory body decide to extend the duration of the original authorisation.

(2)   The supervisory body must decide the period of the extension.

(3)   That period must not exceed 7 days.

(4)   The supervisory body must give the managing authority notice stating the period of the extension.

(5)   The managing authority must then vary the original authorisation so that it states the extended duration.

(6)   Paragraphs 82(3) and 83 apply (with the necessary modifications) to the variation of the original authorisation as they apply to the giving of an urgent authorisation.

(7)   The supervisory body must keep a written record of—

- (a)   the outcome of the request, and
- (b)   the period of the extension.

86

(1)   This paragraph applies if, under paragraph 84, the supervisory body decide not to extend the duration of the original authorisation.

(2)   The supervisory body must give the managing authority notice stating—

- (a)   the decision, and
- (b)   their reasons for making it.

(3)   The managing authority must give a copy of that notice to all of the following—

- (a)   the relevant person;
- (b)   any section 39A IMCA.

(4)   The supervisory body must keep a written record of the outcome of the request.

No variation

87

(1)   An urgent authorisation may not be varied except in accordance with paragraph 85.

(2)   This paragraph does not affect the powers of the Court of Protection or of any other court.

When an authorisation is in force

88

An urgent authorisation comes into force when it is given.

89

(1)   An urgent authorisation ceases to be in force at the end of the period stated in the authorisation in accordance with paragraph 80(c) (subject to any variation in accordance with paragraph 85).

(2)   But if the required request is disposed of before the end of that period, the urgent authorisation ceases to be in force as follows.

(3)   If the supervisory body are required by paragraph 50(1) to give the requested authorisation, the urgent authorisation ceases to be in force when the requested authorisation comes into force.

(4)   If the supervisory body are prohibited by paragraph 50(2) from giving the requested authorisation, the urgent authorisation ceases to be in force when the managing authority receive notice under paragraph 58.

(5)   In this paragraph—

> "required request" means the request referred to in paragraph 76(2) or (3);
> "requested authorisation" means the standard authorisation to which the required request relates.

(6)   This paragraph does not affect the powers of the Court of Protection or of any other court.

90

(1)   This paragraph applies if an urgent authorisation ceases to be in force.

(2)   The supervisory body must give notice that the authorisation has ceased to be in force.

(3)   The supervisory body must give that notice to all of the following—

> (a)   the relevant person;
> (b)   any section 39A IMCA.

(4)   The supervisory body must give that notice as soon as practicable after the authorisation ceases to be in force.]

[PART 6   ELIGIBILITY REQUIREMENT NOT MET: SUSPENSION OF STAN-
DARD AUTHORISATION]

[91

(1)   This Part applies if the following conditions are met.

(2)   The first condition is that a standard authorisation—

> (a)   has been given, and
> (b)   has not ceased to be in force.

(3)   The second condition is that the managing authority of the relevant hospital or care home are satisfied that the relevant person has ceased to meet the eligibility requirement.

(4)   But this Part does not apply if the relevant person is ineligible by virtue of paragraph 5 of Schedule 1A (in which case see Part 8).

92

The managing authority of the relevant hospital or care home must give the supervisory body notice that the relevant person has ceased to meet the eligibility requirement.

93

(1)   This paragraph applies if the managing authority give the supervisory body notice under paragraph 92.

(2)   The standard authorisation is suspended from the time when the notice is given.

(3)   The supervisory body must give notice that the standard authorisation has been suspended to the following persons—

> (a)   the relevant person;

    (b)   the relevant person's representative;

    (c)   the managing authority of the relevant hospital or care home.

94

(1)   This paragraph applies if, whilst the standard authorisation is suspended, the managing authority are satisfied that the relevant person meets the eligibility requirement again.

(2)   The managing authority must give the supervisory body notice that the relevant person meets the eligibility requirement again.

95

(1)   This paragraph applies if the managing authority give the supervisory body notice under paragraph 94.

(2)   The standard authorisation ceases to be suspended from the time when the notice is given.

(3)   The supervisory body must give notice that the standard authorisation has ceased to be suspended to the following persons—

    (a)   the relevant person;

    (b)   the relevant person's representative;

    (c)   any section 39D IMCA;

    (d)   the managing authority of the relevant hospital or care home.

(4)   The supervisory body must give notice under this paragraph as soon as practicable after they are given notice under paragraph 94.

96

(1)   This paragraph applies if no notice is given under paragraph 94 before the end of the relevant 28 day period.

(2)   The standard authorisation ceases to have effect at the end of the relevant 28 day period.

(3)   The relevant 28 day period is the period of 28 days beginning with the day on which the standard authorisation is suspended under paragraph 93.

97

The effect of suspending the standard authorisation is that Part 1 ceases to apply for as long as the authorisation is suspended.]

[PART 7   STANDARD AUTHORISATIONS: CHANGE IN SUPERVISORY RE-
SPONSIBILITY]

[Application of this Part

98

(1)   This Part applies if these conditions are met.

(2)   The first condition is that a standard authorisation—

    (a)   has been given, and

    (b)   has not ceased to be in force.

(3)   The second condition is that there is a change in supervisory responsibility.

(4)   The third condition is that there is not a change in the place of detention (within the meaning of paragraph 25).

99

For the purposes of this Part there is a change in supervisory responsibility if—

    (a)   one body ("the old supervisory body") have ceased to be supervisory body in relation to the standard authorisation, and

    (b)   a different body ("the new supervisory body") have become supervisory body in relation to the standard authorisation.

Effect of change in supervisory responsibility

100

(1)   The new supervisory body becomes the supervisory body in relation to the authorisation.

(2)   Anything done by or in relation to the old supervisory body in connection with the authorisation has effect, so far as is necessary for continuing its effect after the change, as if done by or in relation to the new supervisory body.

(3)   Anything which relates to the authorisation and which is in the process of being done by or in relation to the old supervisory body at the time of the change may be continued by or in relation to the new supervisory body.

(4)   But—

    (a)   the old supervisory body do not, by virtue of this paragraph, cease to be liable for anything done by them in connection with the authorisation before the change; and

    (b)   the new supervisory body do not, by virtue of this paragraph, become liable for any such thing.]

[PART 8   STANDARD AUTHORISATIONS: REVIEW]

[Application of this Part

101

(1)   This Part applies if a standard authorisation—

    (a)   has been given, and

    (b)   has not ceased to be in force.

(2)   Paragraphs 102 to 122 are subject to paragraphs 123 to 125.

Review by supervisory body

102

(1)   The supervisory body may at any time carry out a review of the standard authorisation in accordance with this Part.

(2)   The supervisory body must carry out such a review if they are requested to do so by an eligible person.

(3)   Each of the following is an eligible person—

    (a)   the relevant person;

    (b)   the relevant person's representative;

    (c)   the managing authority of the relevant hospital or care home.

Request for review

103

(1)   An eligible person may, at any time, request the supervisory body to carry out a review of the standard authorisation in accordance with this Part.

(2)   The managing authority of the relevant hospital or care home must make such a request if one or more of the qualifying requirements appear to them to be reviewable.

Grounds for review

104

(1)   Paragraphs 105 to 107 set out the grounds on which the qualifying requirements are reviewable.

(2)   A qualifying requirement is not reviewable on any other ground.

Non-qualification ground

105

(1)   Any of the following qualifying requirements is reviewable on the ground that the relevant person does not meet the requirement—

(a)   the age requirement;

(b)   the mental health requirement;

(c)   the mental capacity requirement;

(d)   the best interests requirement;

(e)   the no refusals requirement.

(2)   The eligibility requirement is reviewable on the ground that the relevant person is ineligible by virtue of paragraph 5 of Schedule 1A.

(3)   The ground in sub-paragraph (1) and the ground in sub-paragraph (2) are referred to as the non-qualification ground.

Change of reason ground

106

(1)   Any of the following qualifying requirements is reviewable on the ground set out in sub-paragraph (2)—

(a)   the mental health requirement;

(b)   the mental capacity requirement;

(c)   the best interests requirement;

(d)   the eligibility requirement;

(e)   the no refusals requirement.

(2)   The ground is that the reason why the relevant person meets the requirement is not the reason stated in the standard authorisation.

(3)   This ground is referred to as the change of reason ground.

Variation of conditions ground

107

(1)   The best interests requirement is reviewable on the ground that—

(a)   there has been a change in the relevant person's case, and

(b)   because of that change, it would be appropriate to vary the conditions to which the standard authorisation is subject.

(2)   This ground is referred to as the variation of conditions ground.

(3)   A reference to varying the conditions to which the standard authorisation is subject is a reference to—

(a)   amendment of an existing condition,

(b)   omission of an existing condition, or

(c)   inclusion of a new condition (whether or not there are already any existing conditions).

Notice that review to be carried out

108

(1)   If the supervisory body are to carry out a review of the standard authorisation, they must give notice of the review to the following persons—

(a)   the relevant person;

(b)   the relevant person's representative;

    (c)   the managing authority of the relevant hospital or care home.

(2) The supervisory body must give the notice—

    (a)   before they begin the review, or

    (b)   if that is not practicable, as soon as practicable after they have begun it.

(3) This paragraph does not require the supervisory body to give notice to any person who has requested the review.

Starting a review

109

To start a review of the standard authorisation, the supervisory body must decide which, if any, of the qualifying requirements appear to be reviewable.

No reviewable qualifying requirements

110

(1) This paragraph applies if no qualifying requirements appear to be reviewable.

(2) This Part does not require the supervisory body to take any action in respect of the standard authorisation.

One or more reviewable qualifying requirements

111

(1) This paragraph applies if one or more qualifying requirements appear to be reviewable.

(2) The supervisory body must secure that a separate review assessment is carried out in relation to each qualifying requirement which appears to be reviewable.

(3) But sub-paragraph (2) does not require the supervisory body to secure that a best interests review assessment is carried out in a case where the best interests requirement appears to the supervisory body to be non-assessable.

(4) The best interests requirement is non-assessable if—

    (a)   the requirement is reviewable only on the variation of conditions ground, and

    (b)   the change in the relevant person's case is not significant.

(5) In making any decision whether the change in the relevant person's case is significant, regard must be had to—

    (a)   the nature of the change, and

    (b)   the period that the change is likely to last for.

Review assessments

112

(1) A review assessment is an assessment of whether the relevant person meets a qualifying requirement.

(2) In relation to a review assessment—

    (a)   a negative conclusion is a conclusion that the relevant person does not meet the qualifying requirement to which the assessment relates;

    (b)   a positive conclusion is a conclusion that the relevant person meets the qualifying requirement to which the assessment relates.

(3) An age review assessment is a review assessment carried out in relation to the age requirement.

(4) A mental health review assessment is a review assessment carried out in relation to the mental health requirement.

(5)   A mental capacity review assessment is a review assessment carried out in relation to the mental capacity requirement.

(6)   A best interests review assessment is a review assessment carried out in relation to the best interests requirement.

(7)   An eligibility review assessment is a review assessment carried out in relation to the eligibility requirement.

(8)   A no refusals review assessment is a review assessment carried out in relation to the no refusals requirement.

113

(1)   In carrying out a review assessment, the assessor must comply with any duties which would be imposed upon him under Part 4 if the assessment were being carried out in connection with a request for a standard authorisation.

(2)   But in the case of a best interests review assessment, paragraphs 43 and 44 do not apply.

(3)   Instead of what is required by paragraph 43, the best interests review assessment must include recommendations about whether—and, if so, how—it would be appropriate to vary the conditions to which the standard authorisation is subject.

Best interests requirement reviewable but non-assessable

114

(1)   This paragraph applies in a case where—

    (a)   the best interests requirement appears to be reviewable, but

    (b)   in accordance with paragraph 111(3), the supervisory body are not required to secure that a best interests review assessment is carried out.

(2)   The supervisory body may vary the conditions to which the standard authorisation is subject in such ways (if any) as the supervisory body think are appropriate in the circumstances.

Best interests review assessment positive

115

(1)   This paragraph applies in a case where—

    (a)   a best interests review assessment is carried out, and

    (b)   the assessment comes to a positive conclusion.

(2)   The supervisory body must decide the following questions—

    (a)   whether or not the best interests requirement is reviewable on the change of reason ground;

    (b)   whether or not the best interests requirement is reviewable on the variation of conditions ground;

    (c)   if so, whether or not the change in the person's case is significant.

(3)   If the supervisory body decide that the best interests requirement is reviewable on the change of reason ground, they must vary the standard authorisation so that it states the reason why the relevant person now meets that requirement.

(4)   If the supervisory body decide that—

    (a)   the best interests requirement is reviewable on the variation of conditions ground, and

    (b)   the change in the relevant person's case is not significant,

they may vary the conditions to which the standard authorisation is subject in such ways (if any) as they think are appropriate in the circumstances.

(5)   If the supervisory body decide that—

    (a)   the best interests requirement is reviewable on the variation of conditions ground, and

    (b)   the change in the relevant person's case is significant,

they must vary the conditions to which the standard authorisation is subject in such ways as they think are appropriate in the circumstances.

(6) If the supervisory body decide that the best interests requirement is not reviewable on—

    (a)   the change of reason ground, or

    (b)   the variation of conditions ground,

this Part does not require the supervisory body to take any action in respect of the standard authorisation so far as the best interests requirement relates to it.

Mental health, mental capacity, eligibility or no refusals review assessment positive

116

(1) This paragraph applies if the following conditions are met.

(2) The first condition is that one or more of the following are carried out—

    (a)   a mental health review assessment;

    (b)   a mental capacity review assessment;

    (c)   an eligibility review assessment;

    (d)   a no refusals review assessment.

(3) The second condition is that each assessment carried out comes to a positive conclusion.

(4) The supervisory body must decide whether or not each of the assessed qualifying requirements is reviewable on the change of reason ground.

(5) If the supervisory body decide that any of the assessed qualifying requirements is reviewable on the change of reason ground, they must vary the standard authorisation so that it states the reason why the relevant person now meets the requirement or requirements in question.

(6) If the supervisory body decide that none of the assessed qualifying requirements are reviewable on the change of reason ground, this Part does not require the supervisory body to take any action in respect of the standard authorisation so far as those requirements relate to it.

(7) An assessed qualifying requirement is a qualifying requirement in relation to which a review assessment is carried out.

One or more review assessments negative

117

(1) This paragraph applies if one or more of the review assessments carried out comes to a negative conclusion.

(2) The supervisory body must terminate the standard authorisation with immediate effect.

Completion of a review

118

(1) The review of the standard authorisation is complete in any of the following cases.

(2) The first case is where paragraph 110 applies.

(3) The second case is where—

    (a)   paragraph 111 applies, and

    (b)   paragraph 117 requires the supervisory body to terminate the standard authorisation.

(4) In such a case, the supervisory body need not comply with any of the other provisions of paragraphs 114 to 116 which would be applicable to the review (were it not for this sub-paragraph).

(5) The third case is where—

    (a)   paragraph 111 applies,

    (b)   paragraph 117 does not require the supervisory body to terminate the standard authorisation, and

    (c)   the supervisory body comply with all of the provisions of paragraphs 114 to 116 (so far as they are applicable to the review).

Variations under this Part

119

Any variation of the standard authorisation made under this Part must be in writing.

Notice of outcome of review

120

(1) When the review of the standard authorisation is complete, the supervisory body must give notice to all of the following—

    (a)   the managing authority of the relevant hospital or care home;

    (b)   the relevant person;

    (c)   the relevant person's representative;

    (d)   any section 39D IMCA.

(2) That notice must state—

    (a)   the outcome of the review, and

    (b)   what variation (if any) has been made to the authorisation under this Part.

Records

121

A supervisory body must keep a written record of the following information—

    (a)   each request for a review that is made to them;

    (b)   the outcome of each request;

    (c)   each review which they carry out;

    (d)   the outcome of each review which they carry out;

    (e)   any variation of an authorisation made in consequence of a review.

Relationship between review and suspension under Part 6

122

(1) This paragraph applies if a standard authorisation is suspended in accordance with Part 6.

(2) No review may be requested under this Part whilst the standard authorisation is suspended.

(3) If a review has already been requested, or is being carried out, when the standard authorisation is suspended, no steps are to be taken in connection with that review whilst the authorisation is suspended.

Relationship between review and request for new authorisation

123

(1) This paragraph applies if, in accordance with paragraph 24 (as read with paragraph 29), the managing authority of the relevant hospital or care home make a request for a new standard authorisation which would be in force after the expiry of the existing authorisation.

(2) No review may be requested under this Part until the request for the new standard authorisation has been disposed of.

(3) If a review has already been requested, or is being carried out, when the new standard authorisation is requested, no steps are to be taken in connection with that review until the request for the new standard authorisation has been disposed of.

124

(1) This paragraph applies if—

   (a) a review under this Part has been requested, or is being carried out, and

   (b) the managing authority of the relevant hospital or care home make a request under paragraph 30 for a new standard authorisation which would be in force on or before, and after, the expiry of the existing authorisation.

(2) No steps are to be taken in connection with the review under this Part until the request for the new standard authorisation has been disposed of.

125

In paragraphs 123 and 124—

   (a) the existing authorisation is the authorisation referred to in paragraph 101;

   (b) the expiry of the existing authorisation is the time when it is expected to cease to be in force.]

[PART 9   ASSESSMENTS UNDER THIS SCHEDULE]

[Introduction

126

This Part contains provision about assessments under this Schedule.

127

An assessment under this Schedule is either of the following—

   (a) an assessment carried out in connection with a request for a standard authorisation under Part 4;

   (b) a review assessment carried out in connection with a review of a standard authorisation under Part 8.

128

In this Part, in relation to an assessment under this Schedule—

   "assessor" means the person carrying out the assessment;

   "relevant procedure" means—

      (a) the request for the standard authorisation, or

      (b) the review of the standard authorisation;

   "supervisory body" means the supervisory body responsible for securing that the assessment is carried out.

Supervisory body to select assessor

129

(1)   It is for the supervisory body to select a person to carry out an assessment under this Schedule.

(2)   The supervisory body must not select a person to carry out an assessment unless the person—

    (a)   appears to the supervisory body to be suitable to carry out the assessment (having regard, in particular, to the type of assessment and the person to be assessed), and

    (b)   is eligible to carry out the assessment.

(3)   Regulations may make provision about the selection, and eligibility, of persons to carry out assessments under this Schedule.

(4)   Sub-paragraphs (5) and (6) apply if two or more assessments are to be obtained for the purposes of the relevant procedure.

(5)   In a case where the assessments to be obtained include a mental health assessment and a best interests assessment, the supervisory body must not select the same person to carry out both assessments.

(6)   Except as prohibited by sub-paragraph (5), the supervisory body may select the same person to carry out any number of the assessments which the person appears to be suitable, and is eligible, to carry out.

130

(1)   This paragraph applies to regulations under paragraph 129(3).

(2)   The regulations may make provision relating to a person's—

    (a)   qualifications,

    (b)   skills,

    (c)   training,

    (d)   experience,

    (e)   relationship to, or connection with, the relevant person or any other person,

    (f)   involvement in the care or treatment of the relevant person,

    (g)   connection with the supervisory body, or

    (h)   connection with the relevant hospital or care home, or with any other establishment or undertaking.

[(2A)   In relation to England—

    <u>(a)</u>   the provision that the regulations may make in relation to a person's training in connection with best interests assessments includes provision for particular training to be specified by Social Work England or the Secretary of State otherwise than in the regulations;

    <u>(b)</u>   the provision that the regulations may make in relation to a person's training in connection with other assessments includes provision for particular training to be specified by the Secretary of State otherwise than in the regulations.

(2B)   The regulations may give Social Work England power to charge fees for specifying any training as mentioned in sub-paragraph (2A)(a).

(2C)   If the regulations give Social Work England power to charge fees, section 50(2) to (7) of the Children and Social Work Act 2017 apply for the purposes of sub-paragraph (2B) as they apply for the purposes of that section.]

(3)   [In relation to Wales] the provision that the regulations may make in relation to a person's training may provide for particular training to be specified by *the appropriate authority* [the Welsh Ministers] otherwise than in the regulations.

(4)   *In sub-paragraph (3) the "appropriate authority" means—*

    (a)   in relation to England: the Secretary of State;

(b)   in relation to Wales: the National Assembly for Wales.

(5)   The regulations may make provision requiring a person to be insured in respect of liabilities that may arise in connection with the carrying out of an assessment.

(6)   In relation to cases where two or more assessments are to be obtained for the purposes of the relevant procedure, the regulations may limit the number, kind or combination of assessments which a particular person is eligible to carry out.

(7)   Sub-paragraphs (2) to (6) do not limit the generality of the provision that may be made in the regulations.

Examination and copying of records

131

An assessor may, at all reasonable times, examine and take copies of—

(a)   any health record,

(b)   any record of, or held by, a local authority and compiled in accordance with a social services function, and

(c)   any record held by a person registered under Part 2 of the Care Standards Act 2000 [or Chapter 2 of Part 1 of the Health and Social Care Act 2008],

which the assessor considers may be relevant to the assessment which is being carried out.

Representations

132

In carrying out an assessment under this Schedule, the assessor must take into account any information given, or submissions made, by any of the following—

(a)   the relevant person's representative;

(b)   any section 39A IMCA;

(c)   any section 39C IMCA;

(d)   any section 39D IMCA.

Assessments to stop if any comes to negative conclusion

133

(1)   This paragraph applies if an assessment under this Schedule comes to the conclusion that the relevant person does not meet one of the qualifying requirements.

(2)   This Schedule does not require the supervisory body to secure that any other assessments under this Schedule are carried out in relation to the relevant procedure.

(3)   The supervisory body must give notice to any assessor who is carrying out another assessment in connection with the relevant procedure that they are to cease carrying out that assessment.

(4)   If an assessor receives such notice, this Schedule does not require the assessor to continue carrying out that assessment.

Duty to keep records and give copies

134

(1)   This paragraph applies if an assessor has carried out an assessment under this Schedule (whatever conclusions the assessment has come to).

(2)   The assessor must keep a written record of the assessment.

(3)   As soon as practicable after carrying out the assessment, the assessor must give copies of the assessment to the supervisory body.

135

(1)   This paragraph applies to the supervisory body if they are given a copy of an assessment under this Schedule.

(2)   The supervisory body must give copies of the assessment to all of the following—

- (a)   the managing authority of the relevant hospital or care home;
- (b)   the relevant person;
- (c)   any section 39A IMCA;
- (d)   the relevant person's representative.

(3)   If—

- (a)   the assessment is obtained in relation to a request for a standard authorisation, and
- (b)   the supervisory body are required by paragraph 50(1) to give the standard authorisation,

the supervisory body must give the copies of the assessment when they give copies of the authorisation in accordance with paragraph 57.

(4)   If—

- (a)   the assessment is obtained in relation to a request for a standard authorisation, and
- (b)   the supervisory body are prohibited by paragraph 50(2) from giving the standard authorisation,

the supervisory body must give the copies of the assessment when they give notice in accordance with paragraph 58.

(5)   If the assessment is obtained in connection with the review of a standard authorisation, the supervisory body must give the copies of the assessment when they give notice in accordance with paragraph 120.

136

(1)   This paragraph applies to the supervisory body if—

- (a)   they are given a copy of a best interests assessment, and
- (b)   the assessment includes, in accordance with paragraph 44(2), a statement that it appears to the assessor that there is an unauthorised deprivation of liberty.

(2)   The supervisory body must notify all of the persons listed in sub-paragraph (3) that the assessment includes such a statement.

(3)   Those persons are—

- (a)   the managing authority of the relevant hospital or care home;
- (b)   the relevant person;
- (c)   any section 39A IMCA;
- (d)   any interested person consulted by the best interests assessor.

(4)   The supervisory body must comply with this paragraph when (or at some time before) they comply with paragraph 135.]

[PART 10   RELEVANT PERSON'S REPRESENTATIVE]

[The representative

137

In this Schedule the relevant person's representative is the person appointed as such in accordance with this Part.

138

(1)   Regulations may make provision about the selection and appointment of representatives.

(2)   In this Part such regulations are referred to as "appointment regulations".

Supervisory body to appoint representative

139

(1) The supervisory body must appoint a person to be the relevant person's representative as soon as practicable after a standard authorisation is given.

(2) The supervisory body must appoint a person to be the relevant person's representative if a vacancy arises whilst a standard authorisation is in force.

(3) Where a vacancy arises, the appointment under sub-paragraph (2) is to be made as soon as practicable after the supervisory body becomes aware of the vacancy.

140

(1) The selection of a person for appointment under paragraph 139 must not be made unless it appears to the person making the selection that the prospective representative would, if appointed—

    (a)   maintain contact with the relevant person,

    (b)   represent the relevant person in matters relating to or connected with this Schedule, and

    (c)   support the relevant person in matters relating to or connected with this Schedule.

141

(1) Any appointment of a representative for a relevant person is in addition to, and does not affect, any appointment of a donee or deputy.

(2) The functions of any representative are in addition to, and do not affect—

    (a)   the authority of any donee,

    (b)   the powers of any deputy, or

    (c)   any powers of the court.

Appointment regulations

142

Appointment regulations may provide that the procedure for appointing a representative may begin at any time after a request for a standard authorisation is made (including a time before the request has been disposed of).

143

(1) Appointment regulations may make provision about who is to select a person for appointment as a representative.

(2) But regulations under this paragraph may only provide for the following to make a selection—

    (a)   the relevant person, if he has capacity in relation to the question of which person should be his representative;

    (b)   a donee of a lasting power of attorney granted by the relevant person, if it is within the scope of his authority to select a person;

    (c)   a deputy, if it is within the scope of his authority to select a person;

    (d)   a best interests assessor;

    (e)   the supervisory body.

(3) Regulations under this paragraph may provide that a selection by the relevant person, a donee or a deputy is subject to approval by a best interests assessor or the supervisory body.

(4) Regulations under this paragraph may provide that, if more than one selection is necessary in connection with the appointment of a particular representative—

    (a)   the same person may make more than one selection;

    (b)   different persons may make different selections.

(5)   For the purposes of this paragraph a best interests assessor is a person carrying out a best interests assessment in connection with the standard authorisation in question (including the giving of that authorisation).

144

(1)   Appointment regulations may make provision about who may, or may not, be—

- (a)   selected for appointment as a representative, or
- (b)   appointed as a representative.

(2)   Regulations under this paragraph may relate to any of the following matters—

- (a)   a person's age;
- (b)   a person's suitability;
- (c)   a person's independence;
- (d)   a person's willingness;
- (e)   a person's qualifications.

145

Appointment regulations may make provision about the formalities of appointing a person as a representative.

146

In a case where a best interests assessor is to select a person to be appointed as a representative, appointment regulations may provide for the variation of the assessor's duties in relation to the assessment which he is carrying out.

Monitoring of representatives

147

Regulations may make provision requiring the managing authority of the relevant hospital or care home to—

- (a)   monitor, and
- (b)   report to the supervisory body on,

the extent to which a representative is maintaining contact with the relevant person.

Termination

148

Regulations may make provision about the circumstances in which the appointment of a person as the relevant person's representative ends or may be ended.

149

Regulations may make provision about the formalities of ending the appointment of a person as a representative.

Suspension of representative's functions

150

(1)   Regulations may make provision about the circumstances in which functions exercisable by, or in relation to, the relevant person's representative (whether under this Schedule or not) may be—

- (a)   suspended, and
- (b)   if suspended, revived.

(2)   The regulations may make provision about the formalities for giving effect to the suspension or revival of a function.

(3)   The regulations may make provision about the effect of the suspension or revival of a function.

Payment of representative

151

Regulations may make provision for payments to be made to, or in relation to, persons exercising functions as the relevant person's representative.

Regulations under this Part

152

The provisions of this Part which specify provision that may be made in regulations under this Part do not affect the generality of the power to make such regulations.

Effect of appointment of section 39C IMCA

153

Paragraphs 159 and 160 make provision about the exercise of functions by, or towards, the relevant person's representative during periods when—
- (a)   no person is appointed as the relevant person's representative, but
- (b)   a person is appointed as a section 39C IMCA.]

[PART 11   IMCAS]

[Application of Part

154

This Part applies for the purposes of this Schedule.

The IMCAs

155

A section 39A IMCA is an independent mental capacity advocate appointed under section 39A.

156

A section 39C IMCA is an independent mental capacity advocate appointed under section 39C

157

A section 39D IMCA is an independent mental capacity advocate appointed under section 39D.

158

An IMCA is a section 39A IMCA or a section 39C IMCA or a section 39D IMCA.

Section 39C IMCA: functions

159

(1)   This paragraph applies if, and for as long as, there is a section 39C IMCA.

(2)   In the application of the relevant provisions, references to the relevant person's representative are to be read as references to the section 39C IMCA.

(3)   But sub-paragraph (2) does not apply to any function under the relevant provisions for as long as the function is suspended in accordance with provision made under Part 10.

(4)   In this paragraph and paragraph 160 the relevant provisions are—
- (a)   paragraph 102(3)(b) (request for review under Part 8);

(b) paragraph 108(1)(b) (notice of review under Part 8);

(c) paragraph 120(1)(c) (notice of outcome of review under Part 8).

160

(1) This paragraph applies if—

(a) a person is appointed as the relevant person's representative, and

(b) a person accordingly ceases to hold an appointment as a section 39C IMCA.

(2) Where a function under a relevant provision has been exercised by, or towards, the section 39C IMCA, there is no requirement for that function to be exercised again by, or towards, the relevant person's representative.

Section 39A IMCA: restriction of functions

161

(1) This paragraph applies if—

(a) there is a section 39A IMCA, and

(b) a person is appointed under Part 10 to be the relevant person's representative (whether or not that person, or any person subsequently appointed, is currently the relevant person's representative).

(2) The duties imposed on, and the powers exercisable by, the section 39A IMCA do not apply.

(3) The duties imposed on, and the powers exercisable by, any other person do not apply, so far as they fall to be performed or exercised towards the section 39A IMCA.

(4) But sub-paragraph (2) does not apply to any power of challenge exercisable by the section 39A IMCA.

(5) And sub-paragraph (3) does not apply to any duty or power of any other person so far as it relates to any power of challenge exercisable by the section 39A IMCA.

(6) Before exercising any power of challenge, the section 39A IMCA must take the views of the relevant person's representative into account.

(7) A power of challenge is a power to make an application to the court to exercise its jurisdiction under section 21A in connection with the giving of the standard authorisation.]

[PART 12   MISCELLANEOUS]

[Monitoring of operation of Schedule

162

(1) Regulations may make provision for, and in connection with, requiring one or more prescribed bodies to monitor, and report on, the operation of this Schedule in relation to England.

(2) The regulations may, in particular, give a prescribed body authority to do one or more of the following things—

(a) to visit hospitals and care homes;

(b) to visit and interview persons accommodated in hospitals and care homes;

(c) to require the production of, and to inspect, records relating to the care or treatment of persons.

(3) "Prescribed" means prescribed in regulations under this paragraph.

163

(1) Regulations may make provision for, and in connection with, enabling the National Assembly for Wales to monitor, and report on, the operation of this Schedule in relation to Wales.

(2)   The National Assembly may direct one or more persons or bodies to carry out the Assembly's functions under regulations under this paragraph.

Disclosure of information

164

(1)   Regulations may require either or both of the following to disclose prescribed information to prescribed bodies—

(a)   supervisory bodies;

(b)   managing authorities of hospitals or care homes.

(2)   "Prescribed" means prescribed in regulations under this paragraph.

(3)   Regulations under this paragraph may only prescribe information relating to matters with which this Schedule is concerned.

Directions by National Assembly in relation to supervisory functions

165

(1)   The National Assembly for Wales may direct a Local Health Board to exercise in relation to its area any supervisory functions which are specified in the direction.

(2)   Directions under this paragraph must not preclude the National Assembly from exercising the functions specified in the directions.

(3)   In this paragraph "supervisory functions" means functions which the National Assembly have as supervisory body, so far as they are exercisable in relation to hospitals (whether NHS or independent hospitals, and whether in Wales or England).

166

(1)   This paragraph applies where, under paragraph 165, a Local Health Board ("the specified LHB") is directed to exercise supervisory functions ("delegated functions").

(2)   The National Assembly for Wales may give directions to the specified LHB about the Board's exercise of delegated functions.

(3)   The National Assembly may give directions for any delegated functions to be exercised, on behalf of the specified LHB, by a committee, sub-committee or officer of that Board.

(4)   The National Assembly may give directions providing for any delegated functions to be exercised by the specified LHB jointly with one or more other Local Health Boards.

(5)   Where, under sub-paragraph (4), delegated functions are exercisable jointly, the National Assembly may give directions providing for the functions to be exercised, on behalf of the Local Health Boards in question, by a joint committee or joint sub-committee.

167

(1)   Directions under paragraph 165 must be given in regulations.

(2)   Directions under paragraph 166 may be given—

(a)   in regulations, or

(b)   by instrument in writing.

168

The power under paragraph 165 or paragraph 166 to give directions includes power to vary or revoke directions given under that paragraph.

Notices

169

Any notice under this Schedule must be in writing.

Regulations

170

(1) This paragraph applies to all regulations under this Schedule, except regulations under paragraph 162, 163, 167 or 183.

(2) It is for the Secretary of State to make such regulations in relation to authorisations under this Schedule which relate to hospitals and care homes situated in England.

(3) It is for the National Assembly for Wales to make such regulations in relation to authorisations under this Schedule which relate to hospitals and care homes situated in Wales.

171

It is for the Secretary of State to make regulations under paragraph 162.

172

It is for the National Assembly for Wales to make regulations under paragraph 163 or 167.

173

(1) This paragraph applies to regulations under paragraph 183.

(2) It is for the Secretary of State to make such regulations in relation to cases where a question as to the ordinary residence of a person is to be determined by the Secretary of State.

(3) It is for the National Assembly for Wales to make such regulations in relation to cases where a question as to the ordinary residence of a person is to be determined by the National Assembly.]

[PART 13   INTERPRETATION]

[Introduction

174

This Part applies for the purposes of this Schedule.

Hospitals and their managing authorities

175

(1) "Hospital" means—
    (a)   an NHS hospital, or
    (b)   an independent hospital.

(2) "NHS hospital" means—
    (a)   a health service hospital as defined by section 275 of the National Health Service Act 2006 or section 206 of the National Health Service (Wales) Act 2006, or
    (b)   a hospital as defined by section 206 of the National Health Service (Wales) Act 2006 vested in a Local Health Board.

[(3) Independent hospital"—
    (a)   in relation to England, means a hospital as defined by section 275 of the National Health Service Act 2006 that is not an NHS hospital; and
    (b)   in relation to Wales, means a hospital as defined by section 2 of the Care Standards Act 2000 that is not an NHS hospital.]

176

(1) "Managing authority", in relation to an NHS hospital, means—

(a)   if the hospital—

    (i)   is vested in the appropriate national authority for the purposes of its functions under the National Health Service Act 2006 or of the National Health Service (Wales) Act 2006, or

    (ii)   consists of any accommodation provided by a local authority and used as a hospital by or on behalf of the appropriate national authority under either of those Acts,

the . . . . . . Local Health Board or Special Health Authority responsible for the administration of the hospital;

[(aa)   in relation to England, if the hospital falls within paragraph (a)(i) or (ii) and no Special Health Authority has responsibility for its administration, the Secretary of State;]

(b)   if the hospital is vested in a . . . National Health Service trust or NHS foundation trust, that trust;

(c)   if the hospital is vested in a Local Health Board, that Board.

(2)   For this purpose the appropriate national authority is—

(a)   in relation to England: the Secretary of State;

(b)   in relation to Wales: the National Assembly for Wales;

(c)   in relation to England and Wales: the Secretary of State and the National Assembly acting jointly.

[177

"Managing authority", in relation to an independent hospital, means—

(a)   in relation to England, the person registered, or required to be registered, under Chapter 2 of Part 1 of the Health and Social Care Act 2008 in respect of regulated activities (within the meaning of that Part) carried on in the hospital, and

(b)   in relation to Wales, the person registered, or required to be registered, under Part 2 of the Care Standards Act 2000 in respect of the hospital.]

Care homes and their managing authorities

178

"Care home" has the meaning given by section 3 of the Care Standards Act 2000.

[179

"Managing authority", in relation to a care home, means—

(a)   in relation to England, the person registered, or required to be registered, under Chapter 2 of Part 1 of the Health and Social Care Act 2008 in respect of the provision of residential accommodation, together with nursing or personal care, in the care home, and

(b)   in relation to Wales, the person registered, or required to be registered, under Part 2 of the Care Standards Act 2000 in respect of the care home.]

Supervisory bodies: hospitals

180

(1)   The identity of the supervisory body is determined under this paragraph in cases where the relevant hospital is situated in England.

[(2)   If the relevant person is ordinarily resident in the area of a local authority in England, the supervisory body are that local authority.]

(3)   If [the relevant person is not ordinarily resident in England and] the National Assembly for Wales or a Local Health Board commission the relevant care or treatment, the National Assembly are the supervisory body.

(4)   In any other case, the supervisory body are [the local authority] for the area in which the relevant hospital is situated.

[(4A)   Local authority" means—

    (a)   the council of a county;

    (b)   the council of a district for which there is no county council;

    (c)   the council of a London borough;

    (d)   the Common Council of the City of London;

    (e)   the Council of the Isles of Scilly.]

(5)   If a hospital is situated in the areas of two (or more) [local authorities], it is to be regarded for the purposes of sub-paragraph (4) as situated in whichever of the areas the greater (or greatest) part of the hospital is situated.

181

(1)   The identity of the supervisory body is determined under this paragraph in cases where the relevant hospital is situated in Wales.

(2)   The National Assembly for Wales are the supervisory body.

[(3)   But if the relevant person is ordinarily resident in the area of a local authority in England, the supervisory body are that local authority.

(4)   "Local authority" means—

    (a)   the council of a county;

    (b)   the council of a district for which there is no county council;

    (c)   the council of a London borough;

    (d)   the Common Council of the City of London;

    (e)   the Council of the Isles of Scilly.]

Supervisory bodies: care homes

182

(1)   The identity of the supervisory body is determined under this paragraph in cases where the relevant care home is situated in England or in Wales.

(2)   The supervisory body are the local authority for the area in which the relevant person is ordinarily resident.

(3)   But if the relevant person is not ordinarily resident in the area of a local authority, the supervisory body are the local authority for the area in which the care home is situated.

(4)   In relation to England "local authority" means—

    (a)   the council of a county;

    (b)   the council of a district for which there is no county council;

    (c)   the council of a London borough;

    (d)   the Common Council of the City of London;

    (e)   the Council of the Isles of Scilly.

(5)   In relation to Wales "local authority" means the council of a county or county borough.

(6)   If a care home is situated in the areas of two (or more) local authorities, it is to be regarded for the purposes of sub-paragraph (3) as situated in whichever of the areas the greater (or greatest) part of the care home is situated.

[Supervisory bodies: determination of place of ordinary residence]

183

(1)   . . .

(2)   . . .

[(2A) Section 39(1), (2) and (4) to (6) of the Care Act 2014 and paragraphs 1(1), 2(1) and 8 of Schedule 1 to that Act apply to any determination of where a person is ordinarily resident for the purposes of paragraphs 180, 181 and 182 as they apply for the purposes of Part 1 of that Act.]

[(2B) Section 194(1), (2), (4) and (5) of the Social Services and Well-being (Wales) Act 2014 apply to a determination of where a person is ordinarily resident for the purposes of paragraphs 180, 181 and 182 as it applies for the purposes of that Act.]

(3) Any question arising as to the ordinary residence of a person is to be determined by the Secretary of State or by the National Assembly for Wales.

(4) The Secretary of State and the National Assembly must make and publish arrangements for determining which cases are to be dealt with by the Secretary of State and which are to be dealt with by the National Assembly.

(5) Those arrangements may include provision for the Secretary of State and the National Assembly to agree, in relation to any question that has arisen, which of them is to deal with the case.

(6) Regulations may make provision about arrangements that are to have effect before, upon, or after the determination of any question as to the ordinary residence of a person.

(7) The regulations may, in particular, authorise or require a local authority to do any or all of the following things—

    (a)   to act as supervisory body even though it may wish to dispute that it is the supervisory body;

    (b)   to become the supervisory body in place of another local authority;

    (c)   to recover from another local authority expenditure incurred in exercising functions as the supervisory body.

Same body managing authority and supervisory body

184

(1) This paragraph applies if, in connection with a particular person's detention as a resident in a hospital or care home, the same body are both—

    (a)   the managing authority of the relevant hospital or care home, and

    (b)   the supervisory body.

(2) The fact that a single body are acting in both capacities does not prevent the body from carrying out functions under this Schedule in each capacity.

(3) But, in such a case, this Schedule has effect subject to any modifications contained in regulations that may be made for this purpose.

Interested persons

185

Each of the following is an interested person—

    (a)   the relevant person's spouse or civil partner;

    [(b)   where the relevant person and another person are not married to each other, nor in a civil partnership with each other, but are living together as if they were a married couple: that other person;]

    (d)   the relevant person's children and step-children;

    (e)   the relevant person's parents and step-parents;

    (f)   the relevant person's brothers and sisters, half-brothers and half-sisters, and stepbrothers and stepsisters;

    (g)   the relevant person's grandparents;

    (h)   a deputy appointed for the relevant person by the court;

    (i)   a donee of a lasting power of attorney granted by the relevant person.

186

(1)   An interested person consulted by the best interests assessor is any person whose name is stated in the relevant best interests assessment in accordance with paragraph 40 (interested persons whom the assessor consulted in carrying out the assessment).

(2)   The relevant best interests assessment is the most recent best interests assessment carried out in connection with the standard authorisation in question (whether the assessment was carried out under Part 4 or Part 8).

187

Where this Schedule imposes on a person a duty towards an interested person, the duty does not apply if the person on whom the duty is imposed—

  (a)   is not aware of the interested person's identity or of a way of contacting him, and

  (b)   cannot reasonably ascertain it.

188

The following table contains an index of provisions defining or otherwise explaining expressions used in this Schedule—

age assessment	paragraph 34
age requirement	paragraph 13
age review assessment	paragraph 112(3)
appointment regulations	paragraph 138
assessment under this Schedule	paragraph 127
assessor (except in Part 8)	paragraph 33
assessor (in Part 8)	paragraphs 33 and 128
authorisation under this Schedule	paragraph 10
best interests (determination of)	section 4
best interests assessment	paragraph 38
best interests requirement	paragraph 16
best interests review assessment	paragraph 112(6)
care home	paragraph 178
change of reason ground	paragraph 106
complete (in relation to a review of a standard authorisation)	paragraph 118
deprivation of a person's liberty	section 64(5) and (6)
deputy	section 16(2)(b)
detained resident	paragraph 6
disposed of (in relation to a request for a standard authorisation)	paragraph 66
eligibility assessment	paragraph 46
eligibility requirement	paragraph 17
eligibility review assessment	paragraph 112(7)
eligible person (in relation to para- graphs 68 to 73)	paragraph 68
eligible person (in relation to Part 8)	paragraph 102(3)
expiry (in relation to an existing authorisation)	paragraph 125(b)
existing authorisation (in Part 8)	paragraph 125(a)
hospital	paragraph 175

supervisory body (except in Part 8)	paragraph 180, 181 or 182
supervisory body (in Part 8)	paragraph 128 and paragraph 180, 181 or 182
unauthorised deprivation of liberty (in relation to paragraphs 68 to 73)	paragraph 67
urgent authorisation	paragraph 9
variation of conditions ground	paragraph 107]

SCHEDULE 1

LASTING POWERS OF ATTORNEY: FORMALITIES

Section 9

PART 1   MAKING INSTRUMENTS

General requirements as to making instruments

1

(1) An instrument is not made in accordance with this Schedule unless—
 (a) it is in the prescribed form,
 (b) it complies with paragraph 2, and
 (c) any prescribed requirements in connection with its execution are satisfied.

(2) Regulations may make different provision according to whether—
 (a) the instrument relates to personal welfare or to property and affairs (or to both);
 (b) only one or more than one donee is to be appointed (and if more than one, whether jointly or jointly and severally).

(3) In this Schedule—
 (a) "prescribed" means prescribed by regulations, and
 (b) "regulations" means regulations made for the purposes of this Schedule by the Lord Chancellor.

Requirements as to content of instruments

2

(1) The instrument must include—
 (a) the prescribed information about the purpose of the instrument and the effect of a lasting power of attorney,
 (b) a statement by the donor to the effect that he—
  (i) has read the prescribed information or a prescribed part of it (or has had it read to him), and
  (ii) intends the authority conferred under the instrument to include authority to make decisions on his behalf in circumstances where he no longer has capacity,
 (c) a statement by the donor—
  (i) naming a person or persons whom the donor wishes to be notified of any application for the registration of the instrument, or
  (ii) stating that there are no persons whom he wishes to be notified of any such application,
 (d) a statement by the donee (or, if more than one, each of them) to the effect that he—
  (i) has read the prescribed information or a prescribed part of it (or has had it read to him), and

(ii)   understands the duties imposed on a donee of a lasting power of attorney under sections 1 (the principles) and 4 (best interests), and

(e)   a certificate by a person of a prescribed description that, in his opinion, at the time when the donor executes the instrument—

(i)   the donor understands the purpose of the instrument and the scope of the authority conferred under it,

(ii)   no fraud or undue pressure is being used to induce the donor to create a lasting power of attorney, and

(iii)   there is nothing else which would prevent a lasting power of attorney from being created by the instrument.

(2) Regulations may—

(a)   prescribe a maximum number of named persons;

(b)   provide that, where the instrument includes a statement under sub-paragraph (1)(c)(ii), two persons of a prescribed description must each give a certificate under sub-paragraph (1)(e).

(3) The persons who may be named persons do not include a person who is appointed as donee under the instrument.

(4) In this Schedule, "named person" means a person named under sub-paragraph (1)(c).

(5) A certificate under sub-paragraph (1)(e)—

(a)   must be made in the prescribed form, and

(b)   must include any prescribed information.

(6) The certificate may not be given by a person appointed as donee under the instrument.

Failure to comply with prescribed form

3

(1) If an instrument differs in an immaterial respect in form or mode of expression from the prescribed form, it is to be treated by the Public Guardian as sufficient in point of form and expression.

(2) The court may declare that an instrument which is not in the prescribed form is to be treated as if it were, if it is satisfied that the persons executing the instrument intended it to create a lasting power of attorney.

PART 2   REGISTRATION

Applications and procedure for registration

4

(1) An application to the Public Guardian for the registration of an instrument intended to create a lasting power of attorney—

(a)   must be made in the prescribed form, and

(b)   must include any prescribed information.

(2) The application may be made—

(a)   by the donor,

(b)   by the donee or donees, or

(c)   if the instrument appoints two or more donees to act jointly and severally in respect of any matter, by any of the donees.

(3) The application must be accompanied by—

(a)   the instrument, and

(b)   any fee provided for under section 58(4)(b).

(4)   A person who, in an application for registration, makes a statement which he knows to be false in a material particular is guilty of an offence and is liable—

(a)   on summary conviction, to imprisonment for a term not exceeding 12 months or a fine not exceeding the statutory maximum or both;

(b)   on conviction on indictment, to imprisonment for a term not exceeding 2 years or a fine or both.

5

Subject to paragraphs 11 to 14, the Public Guardian must register the instrument as a lasting power of attorney at the end of the prescribed period.

Notification requirements

6

(1)   A donor about to make an application under paragraph 4(2)(a) must notify any named persons that he is about to do so.

(2)   The donee (or donees) about to make an application under paragraph 4(2)(b) or (c) must notify any named persons that he is (or they are) about to do so.

7

As soon as is practicable after receiving an application by the donor under paragraph 4(2)(a), the Public Guardian must notify the donee (or donees) that the application has been received.

8

(1)   As soon as is practicable after receiving an application by a donee (or donees) under paragraph 4(2)(b), the Public Guardian must notify the donor that the application has been received.

(2)   As soon as is practicable after receiving an application by a donee under paragraph 4(2)(c), the Public Guardian must notify—

(a)   the donor, and

(b)   the donee or donees who did not join in making the application,

that the application has been received.

9

(1)   A notice under paragraph 6 must be made in the prescribed form.

(2)   A notice under paragraph 6, 7 or 8 must include such information, if any, as may be prescribed.

Power to dispense with notification requirements

10

The court may—

(a)   on the application of the donor, dispense with the requirement to notify under paragraph 6(1), or

(b)   on the application of the donee or donees concerned, dispense with the requirement to notify under paragraph 6(2),

if satisfied that no useful purpose would be served by giving the notice.

Instrument not made properly or containing ineffective provision

11

(1)   If it appears to the Public Guardian that an instrument accompanying an application under paragraph 4 is not made in accordance with this Schedule, he must not register the instrument unless the court directs him to do so.

(2)   Sub-paragraph (3) applies if it appears to the Public Guardian that the instrument contains a provision which—

    (a)   would be ineffective as part of a lasting power of attorney, or

    (b)   would prevent the instrument from operating as a valid lasting power of attorney.

(3)   The Public Guardian—

    (a)   must apply to the court for it to determine the matter under section 23(1), and

    (b)   pending the determination by the court, must not register the instrument.

(4)   Sub-paragraph (5) applies if the court determines under section 23(1) (whether or not on an application by the Public Guardian) that the instrument contains a provision which—

    (a)   would be ineffective as part of a lasting power of attorney, or

    (b)   would prevent the instrument from operating as a valid lasting power of attorney.

(5)   The court must—

    (a)   notify the Public Guardian that it has severed the provision, or

    (b)   direct him not to register the instrument.

(6)   Where the court notifies the Public Guardian that it has severed a provision, he must register the instrument with a note to that effect attached to it.

Deputy already appointed

12

(1)   Sub-paragraph (2) applies if it appears to the Public Guardian that—

    (a)   there is a deputy appointed by the court for the donor, and

    (b)   the powers conferred on the deputy would, if the instrument were registered, to any extent conflict with the powers conferred on the attorney.

(2)   The Public Guardian must not register the instrument unless the court directs him to do so.

Objection by donee or named person

13

(1)   Sub-paragraph (2) applies if a donee or a named person—

    (a)   receives a notice under paragraph 6, 7 or 8 of an application for the registration of an instrument, and

    (b)   before the end of the prescribed period, gives notice to the Public Guardian of an objection to the registration on the ground that an event mentioned in section 13(3) or (6)(a) to (d) has occurred which has revoked the instrument.

(2)   If the Public Guardian is satisfied that the ground for making the objection is established, he must not register the instrument unless the court, on the application of the person applying for the registration—

    (a)   is satisfied that the ground is not established, and

    (b)   directs the Public Guardian to register the instrument.

(3)   Sub-paragraph (4) applies if a donee or a named person—

    (a)   receives a notice under paragraph 6, 7 or 8 of an application for the registration of an instrument, and

    (b)   before the end of the prescribed period—

        (i)   makes an application to the court objecting to the registration on a prescribed ground, and

(ii) notifies the Public Guardian of the application.

(4) The Public Guardian must not register the instrument unless the court directs him to do so.

Objection by donor

14

(1) This paragraph applies if the donor—

    (a) receives a notice under paragraph 8 of an application for the registration of an instrument, and

    (b) before the end of the prescribed period, gives notice to the Public Guardian of an objection to the registration.

(2) The Public Guardian must not register the instrument unless the court, on the application of the donee or, if more than one, any of them—

    (a) is satisfied that the donor lacks capacity to object to the registration, and

    (b) directs the Public Guardian to register the instrument.

Notification of registration

15

Where an instrument is registered under this Schedule, the Public Guardian must give notice of the fact in the prescribed form to—

    (a) the donor, and

    (b) the donee or, if more than one, each of them.

Evidence of registration

16

(1) A document purporting to be an office copy of an instrument registered under this Schedule is, in any part of the United Kingdom, evidence of—

    (a) the contents of the instrument, and

    (b) the fact that it has been registered.

(2) Sub-paragraph (1) is without prejudice to—

    (a) section 3 of the Powers of Attorney Act 1971 (c 27) (proof by certified copy), and

    (b) any other method of proof authorised by law.

PART 3   CANCELLATION OF REGISTRATION AND NOTIFICATION OF SEVERANCE

17

(1) The Public Guardian must cancel the registration of an instrument as a lasting power of attorney on being satisfied that the power has been revoked—

    (a) as a result of the donor's bankruptcy [or a debt relief order (under Part 7A of the Insolvency Act 1986) having been made in respect of the donor], or

    (b) on the occurrence of an event mentioned in section 13(6)(a) to (d).

(2) If the Public Guardian cancels the registration of an instrument he must notify—

    (a) the donor, and

    (b) the donee or, if more than one, each of them.

18

The court must direct the Public Guardian to cancel the registration of an instrument as a lasting power of attorney if it—

(a)   determines under section 22(2)(a) that a requirement for creating the power was not met,

(b)   determines under section 22(2)(b) that the power has been revoked or has otherwise come to an end, or

(c)   revokes the power under section 22(4)(b) (fraud etc).

19

(1) Sub-paragraph (2) applies if the court determines under section 23(1) that a lasting power of attorney contains a provision which—

(a)   is ineffective as part of a lasting power of attorney, or

(b)   prevents the instrument from operating as a valid lasting power of attorney.

(2) The court must—

(a)   notify the Public Guardian that it has severed the provision, or

(b)   direct him to cancel the registration of the instrument as a lasting power of attorney.

20

On the cancellation of the registration of an instrument, the instrument and any office copies of it must be delivered up to the Public Guardian to be cancelled.

PART 4 RECORDS OF ALTERATIONS IN REGISTERED POWERS

Partial revocation or suspension of power as a result of bankruptcy

21

If in the case of a registered instrument it appears to the Public Guardian that under section 13 a lasting power of attorney is revoked, or suspended, in relation to the donor's property and affairs (but not in relation to other matters), the Public Guardian must attach to the instrument a note to that effect.

Termination of appointment of donee which does not revoke power

22

If in the case of a registered instrument it appears to the Public Guardian that an event has occurred—

(a)   which has terminated the appointment of the donee, but

(b)   which has not revoked the instrument,

the Public Guardian must attach to the instrument a note to that effect.

Replacement of donee

23

If in the case of a registered instrument it appears to the Public Guardian that the donee has been replaced under the terms of the instrument the Public Guardian must attach to the instrument a note to that effect.

Severance of ineffective provisions

24

If in the case of a registered instrument the court notifies the Public Guardian under paragraph 19(2)(a) that it has severed a provision of the instrument, the Public Guardian must attach to it a note to that effect.

Notification of alterations

25

If the Public Guardian attaches a note to an instrument under paragraph 21, 22, 23 or 24 he must give notice of the note to the donee or donees of the power (or, as the case may be, to the other donee or donees of the power).

[SCHEDULE 1A
PERSONS INELIGIBLE TO BE DEPRIVED OF LIBERTY BY THIS ACT]

[PART 1   INELIGIBLE PERSONS]

[Application

1

This Schedule applies for the purposes of—
   (a)   section 16A, and
   (b)   paragraph 17 of Schedule A1.

Determining ineligibility

2

A person ("P") is ineligible to be deprived of liberty by this Act ("ineligible") if—
   (a)   P falls within one of the cases set out in the second column of the following table, and
   (b)   the corresponding entry in the third column of the table—or the provision, or one of the provisions, referred to in that entry—provides that he is ineligible.

	Status of P	*Determination of ineligibility*
Case A	P is— (a) subject to the hospital treatment regime, and (b) detained in a hospital under that regime.	P is ineligible.
Case B	P is— (a) subject to the hospital treatment regime, but (b) not detained in a hospital under that regime.	See paragraphs 3 and 4.
Case C	P is subject to the community treatment regime.	See paragraphs 3 and 4.
Case D	P is subject to the guardianship regime.	See paragraphs 3 and 5.
Case E	P is— (a) within the scope of the Mental Health Act, but (b) not subject to any of the mental health regimes.	See paragraph 5.

Authorised course of action not in accordance with regime

3

(1)   This paragraph applies in cases B, C and D in the table in paragraph 2.

(2)   P is ineligible if the authorised course of action is not in accordance with a requirement which the relevant regime imposes.

(3)   That includes any requirement as to where P is, or is not, to reside.

(4)   The relevant regime is the mental health regime to which P is subject.

Treatment for mental disorder in a hospital

4

(1)   This paragraph applies in cases B and C in the table in paragraph 2.

(2)   P is ineligible if the relevant care or treatment consists in whole or in part of medical treatment for mental disorder in a hospital.

P objects to being a mental health patient etc

5

(1)   This paragraph applies in cases D and E in the table in paragraph 2.

(2)   P is ineligible if the following conditions are met.

(3)   The first condition is that the relevant instrument authorises P to be a mental health patient.

(4)   The second condition is that P objects—

> (a)   to being a mental health patient, or
>
> (b)   to being given some or all of the mental health treatment.

(5)   The third condition is that a donee or deputy has not made a valid decision to consent to each matter to which P objects.

(6)   In determining whether or not P objects to something, regard must be had to all the circumstances (so far as they are reasonably ascertainable), including the following—

> (a)   P's behaviour;
>
> (b)   P's wishes and feelings;
>
> (c)   P's views, beliefs and values.

(7)   But regard is to be had to circumstances from the past only so far as it is still appropriate to have regard to them.]

[PART 2   INTERPRETATION]

[Application

6

This Part applies for the purposes of this Schedule.

Mental health regimes

7

The mental health regimes are—

> (a)   the hospital treatment regime,
>
> (b)   the community treatment regime, and
>
> (c)   the guardianship regime.

Hospital treatment regime

8

(1)   P is subject to the hospital treatment regime if he is subject to—
- (a)   a hospital treatment obligation under the relevant enactment, or
- (b)   an obligation under another England and Wales enactment which has the same effect as a hospital treatment obligation.

(2)   But where P is subject to any such obligation, he is to be regarded as not subject to the hospital treatment regime during any period when he is subject to the community treatment regime.

(3)   A hospital treatment obligation is an application, order or direction of a kind listed in the first column of the following table.

(4)   In relation to a hospital treatment obligation, the relevant enactment is the enactment in the Mental Health Act which is referred to in the corresponding entry in the second column of the following table.

Hospital treatment obligation	Relevant enactment
Application for admission for assessment	Section 2
Application for admission for assessment	Section 4
Application for admission for treatment	Section 3
Order for remand to hospital	Section 35
Order for remand to hospital	Section 36
Hospital order	Section 37
Interim hospital order	Section 38
Order for detention in hospital	Section 44
Hospital direction	Section 45A
Transfer direction	Section 47
Transfer direction	Section 48
Hospital order	Section 51

Community treatment regime

9

P is subject to the community treatment regime if he is subject to—
- (a)   a community treatment order under section 17A of the Mental Health Act, or
- (b)   an obligation under another England and Wales enactment which has the same effect as a community treatment order.

Guardianship regime

10

P is subject to the guardianship regime if he is subject to—
- (a)   a guardianship application under section 7 of the Mental Health Act,
- (b)   a guardianship order under section 37 of the Mental Health Act, or
- (c)   an obligation under another England and Wales enactment which has the same effect as a guardianship application or guardianship order.

England and Wales enactments

11

(1)   An England and Wales enactment is an enactment which extends to England and Wales (whether or not it also extends elsewhere).

(2)   It does not matter if the enactment is in the Mental Health Act or not.

P within scope of Mental Health Act

12

(1)   P is within the scope of the Mental Health Act if—

    (a)   an application in respect of P could be made under section 2 or 3 of the Mental Health Act, and

    (b)   P could be detained in a hospital in pursuance of such an application, were one made.

(2)   The following provisions of this paragraph apply when determining whether an application in respect of P could be made under section 2 or 3 of the Mental Health Act.

(3)   If the grounds in section 2(2) of the Mental Health Act are met in P's case, it is to be assumed that the recommendations referred to in section 2(3) of that Act have been given.

(4)   If the grounds in section 3(2) of the Mental Health Act are met in P's case, it is to be assumed that the recommendations referred to in section 3(3) of that Act have been given.

(5)   In determining whether the ground in section 3(2)(c) of the Mental Health Act is met in P's case, it is to be assumed that the treatment referred to in section 3(2)(c) cannot be provided under this Act.

Authorised course of action, relevant care or treatment & relevant instrument

13

In a case where this Schedule applies for the purposes of section 16A—

    "authorised course of action" means any course of action amounting to deprivation of liberty which the order under section 16(2)(a) authorises;

    "relevant care or treatment" means any care or treatment which—

        (a)   comprises, or forms part of, the authorised course of action, or

        (b)   is to be given in connection with the authorised course of action;

    "relevant instrument" means the order under section 16(2)(a).

14

In a case where this Schedule applies for the purposes of paragraph 17 of Schedule A1—

    "authorised course of action" means the accommodation of the relevant person in the relevant hospital or care home for the purpose of being given the relevant care or treatment;

    "relevant care or treatment" has the same meaning as in Schedule A1;

    "relevant instrument" means the standard authorisation under Schedule A1.

15

(1)   This paragraph applies where the question whether a person is ineligible to be deprived of liberty by this Act is relevant to either of these decisions—

    (a)   whether or not to include particular provision ("the proposed provision") in an order under section 16(2)(a);

      (b)   whether or not to give a standard authorisation under Schedule A1.

(2)   A reference in this Schedule to the authorised course of action or the relevant care or treatment is to be read as a reference to that thing as it would be if—

      (a)   the proposed provision were included in the order, or

      (b)   the standard authorisation were given.

(3)   A reference in this Schedule to the relevant instrument is to be read as follows—

      (a)   where the relevant instrument is an order under section 16(2)(a): as a reference to the order as it would be if the proposed provision were included in it;

      (b)   where the relevant instrument is a standard authorisation: as a reference to the standard authorisation as it would be if it were given.

Expressions used in paragraph 5

16

(1)   These expressions have the meanings given—

         "donee" means a donee of a lasting power of attorney granted by P;

         "mental health patient" means a person accommodated in a hospital for the purpose of being given medical treatment for mental disorder;

         "mental health treatment" means the medical treatment for mental disorder referred to in the definition of "mental health patient".

(2)   A decision of a donee or deputy is valid if it is made—

      (a)   within the scope of his authority as donee or deputy, and

      (b)   in accordance with Part 1 of this Act.

Expressions with same meaning as in Mental Health Act

17

(1)   "Hospital" has the same meaning as in Part 2 of the Mental Health Act.

(2)   "Medical treatment" has the same meaning as in the Mental Health Act.

(3)   "Mental disorder" has the same meaning as in Schedule A1 (see paragraph 14).]

SCHEDULE 2

PROPERTY AND AFFAIRS: SUPPLEMENTARY PROVISIONS

Section 18(4)

Wills: general

1

Paragraphs 2 to 4 apply in relation to the execution of a will, by virtue of section 18, on behalf of P.

Provision that may be made in will

2

The will may make any provision (whether by disposing of property or exercising a power or otherwise) which could be made by a will executed by P if he had capacity to make it.

Wills: requirements relating to execution

3

(1) Sub-paragraph (2) applies if under section 16 the court makes an order or gives directions requiring or authorising a person ("the authorised person") to execute a will on behalf of P.

(2) Any will executed in pursuance of the order or direction—

  (a)   must state that it is signed by P acting by the authorised person,

  (b)   must be signed by the authorised person with the name of P and his own name, in the presence of two or more witnesses present at the same time,

  (c)   must be attested and subscribed by those witnesses in the presence of the authorised person, and

  (d)   must be sealed with the official seal of the court.

Wills: effect of execution

4

(1) This paragraph applies where a will is executed in accordance with paragraph 3.

(2) The Wills Act 1837 (c 26) has effect in relation to the will as if it were signed by P by his own hand, except that—

  (a)   section 9 of the 1837 Act (requirements as to signing and attestation) does not apply, and

  (b)   in the subsequent provisions of the 1837 Act any reference to execution in the manner required by the previous provisions is to be read as a reference to execution in accordance with paragraph 3.

(3) The will has the same effect for all purposes as if—

  (a)   P had had the capacity to make a valid will, and

  (b)   the will had been executed by him in the manner required by the 1837 Act.

(4) But sub-paragraph (3) does not have effect in relation to the will—

  (a)   in so far as it disposes of immovable property outside England and Wales, or

  (b)   in so far as it relates to any other property or matter if, when the will is executed—

    (i)   P is domiciled outside England and Wales, and

    (ii)   the condition in sub-paragraph (5) is met.

(5) The condition is that, under the law of P's domicile, any question of his testamentary capacity would fall to be determined in accordance with the law of a place outside England and Wales.

Vesting orders ancillary to settlement etc

5

(1) If provision is made by virtue of section 18 for—

  (a)   the settlement of any property of P, or

  (b)   the exercise of a power vested in him of appointing trustees or retiring from a trust,

the court may also make as respects the property settled or the trust property such consequential vesting or other orders as the case may require.

(2) The power under sub-paragraph (1) includes, in the case of the exercise of such a power, any order which could have been made in such a case under Part 4 of the Trustee Act 1925 (c 19).

Variation of settlements

6

(1) If a settlement has been made by virtue of section 18, the court may by order vary or revoke the settlement if—

    (a)   the settlement makes provision for its variation or revocation,

    (b)   the court is satisfied that a material fact was not disclosed when the settlement was made, or

    (c)   the court is satisfied that there has been a substantial change of circumstances.

(2) Any such order may give such consequential directions as the court thinks fit.

Vesting of stock in curator appointed outside England and Wales

7

(1) Sub-paragraph (2) applies if the court is satisfied—

    (a)   that under the law prevailing in a place outside England and Wales a person ("M") has been appointed to exercise powers in respect of the property or affairs of P on the ground (however formulated) that P lacks capacity to make decisions with respect to the management and administration of his property and affairs, and

    (b)   that, having regard to the nature of the appointment and to the circumstances of the case, it is expedient that the court should exercise its powers under this paragraph.

(2) The court may direct—

    (a)   any stocks standing in the name of P, or

    (b)   the right to receive dividends from the stocks,

to be transferred into M's name or otherwise dealt with as required by M, and may give such directions as the court thinks fit for dealing with accrued dividends from the stocks.

(3) "Stocks" includes—

    (a)   shares, and

    (b)   any funds, annuity or security transferable in the books kept by any body corporate or unincorporated company or society or by an instrument of transfer either alone or accompanied by other formalities,

and "dividends" is to be construed accordingly.

Preservation of interests in property disposed of on behalf of person lacking capacity

8

(1) Sub-paragraphs (2) and (3) apply if—

    (a)   P's property has been disposed of by virtue of section 18,

    (b)   under P's will or intestacy, or by a gift perfected or nomination taking effect on his death, any other person would have taken an interest in the property but for the disposal, and

    (c)   on P's death, any property belonging to P's estate represents the property disposed of.

(2) The person takes the same interest, if and so far as circumstances allow, in the property representing the property disposed of.

(3) If the property disposed of was real property, any property representing it is to be treated, so long as it remains part of P's estate, as if it were real property.

(4) The court may direct that, on a disposal of P's property—

    (a)   which is made by virtue of section 18, and

(b)   which would apart from this paragraph result in the conversion of personal property into real property,

property representing the property disposed of is to be treated, so long as it remains P's property or forms part of P's estate, as if it were personal property.

(5)   References in sub-paragraphs (1) to (4) to the disposal of property are to—

(a)   the sale, exchange, charging of or other dealing (otherwise than by will) with property other than money;

(b)   the removal of property from one place to another;

(c)   the application of money in acquiring property;

(d)   the transfer of money from one account to another;

and references to property representing property disposed of are to be construed accordingly and as including the result of successive disposals.

(6)   The court may give such directions as appear to it necessary or expedient for the purpose of facilitating the operation of sub-paragraphs (1) to (3), including the carrying of money to a separate account and the transfer of property other than money.

9

(1)   Sub-paragraph (2) applies if the court has ordered or directed the expenditure of money—

(a)   for carrying out permanent improvements on any of P's property, or

(b)   otherwise for the permanent benefit of any of P's property.

(2)   The court may order that—

(a)   the whole of the money expended or to be expended, or

(b)   any part of it,

is to be a charge on the property either without interest or with interest at a specified rate.

(3)   An order under sub-paragraph (2) may provide for excluding or restricting the operation of paragraph 8(1) to (3).

(4)   A charge under sub-paragraph (2) may be made in favour of such person as may be just and, in particular, where the money charged is paid out of P's general estate, may be made in favour of a person as trustee for P.

(5)   No charge under sub-paragraph (2) may confer any right of sale or foreclosure during P's lifetime.

Powers as patron of benefice

10

(1)   Any functions which P has as patron of a benefice may be discharged only by a person ("R") appointed by the court.

(2)   R must be an individual capable of appointment under section 8(1)(b) of the 1986 Measure (which provides for an individual able to make a declaration of communicant status, a clerk in Holy Orders, etc to be appointed to discharge a registered patron's functions).

(3)   The 1986 Measure applies to R as it applies to an individual appointed by the registered patron of the benefice under section 8(1)(b) or (3) of that Measure to discharge his functions as patron.

(4)   "The 1986 Measure" means the Patronage (Benefices) Measure 1986 (No 3).

Section 63

SCHEDULE 3

INTERNATIONAL PROTECTION OF ADULTS

PART 1 PRELIMINARY

Introduction

1

This Part applies for the purposes of this Schedule.

The Convention

2

(1)   "Convention" means the Convention referred to in section 63.

(2)   "Convention country" means a country in which the Convention is in force.

(3)   A reference to an Article or Chapter is to an Article or Chapter of the Convention.

(4)   An expression which appears in this Schedule and in the Convention is to be construed in accordance with the Convention.

Countries, territories and nationals

3

(1)   "Country" includes a territory which has its own system of law.

(2)   Where a country has more than one territory with its own system of law, a reference to the country, in relation to one of its nationals, is to the territory with which the national has the closer, or the closest, connection.

Adults with incapacity

4

[(1)]   "Adult" means [(subject to sub-paragraph (2)] a person who—

    (a)   as a result of an impairment or insufficiency of his personal faculties, cannot protect his interests, and

    (b)   has reached 16.

[(2)   But "adult" does not include a child to whom either of the following applies—

    (a)   the Convention on Jurisdiction, Applicable Law, Recognition, Enforcement and Co-Operation in respect of Parental Responsibility and Measures for the Protection of Children that was signed at The Hague on 19 October 1996;

    (b)   Council Regulation (EC) No 2201/2003 concerning jurisdiction and the recognition and enforcement of judgments in matrimonial matters and the matters of parental responsibility.]

Protective measures

5

(1)   "Protective measure" means a measure directed to the protection of the person or property of an adult; and it may deal in particular with any of the following—

    (a)   the determination of incapacity and the institution of a protective regime,

    (b)   placing the adult under the protection of an appropriate authority,

    (c)   guardianship, curatorship or any corresponding system,

(d)   the designation and functions of a person having charge of the adult's person or property, or representing or otherwise helping him,

(e)   placing the adult in a place where protection can be provided,

(f)   administering, conserving or disposing of the adult's property,

(g)   authorising a specific intervention for the protection of the person or property of the adult.

(2)   Where a measure of like effect to a protective measure has been taken in relation to a person before he reaches 16, this Schedule applies to the measure in so far as it has effect in relation to him once he has reached 16.

Central Authority

6

(1)   Any function under the Convention of a Central Authority is exercisable in England and Wales by the Lord Chancellor.

(2)   A communication may be sent to the Central Authority in relation to England and Wales by sending it to the Lord Chancellor.

PART 2   JURISDICTION OF COMPETENT AUTHORITY

Scope of jurisdiction

7

(1)   The court may exercise its functions under this Act (in so far as it cannot otherwise do so) in relation to—

(a)   an adult habitually resident in England and Wales,

(b)   an adult's property in England and Wales,

(c)   an adult present in England and Wales or who has property there, if the matter is urgent, or

(d)   an adult present in England and Wales, if a protective measure which is temporary and limited in its effect to England and Wales is proposed in relation to him.

(2)   An adult present in England and Wales is to be treated for the purposes of this paragraph as habitually resident there if—

(a)   his habitual residence cannot be ascertained,

(b)   he is a refugee, or

(c)   he has been displaced as a result of disturbance in the country of his habitual residence.

8

(1)   The court may also exercise its functions under this Act (in so far as it cannot otherwise do so) in relation to an adult if sub-paragraph (2) or (3) applies in relation to him.

(2)   This sub-paragraph applies in relation to an adult if—

(a)   he is a British citizen,

(b)   he has a closer connection with England and Wales than with Scotland or Northern Ireland, and

(c)   Article 7 has, in relation to the matter concerned, been complied with.

(3)   This sub-paragraph applies in relation to an adult if the Lord Chancellor, having consulted such persons as he considers appropriate, agrees to a request under Article 8 in relation to the adult.

Exercise of jurisdiction

9

(1) This paragraph applies where jurisdiction is exercisable under this Schedule in connection with a matter which involves a Convention country other than England and Wales.

(2) Any Article on which the jurisdiction is based applies in relation to the matter in so far as it involves the other country (and the court must, accordingly, comply with any duty conferred on it as a result).

(3) Article 12 also applies, so far as its provisions allow, in relation to the matter in so far as it involves the other country.

10

A reference in this Schedule to the exercise of jurisdiction under this Schedule is to the exercise of functions under this Act as a result of this Part of this Schedule.

PART 3   APPLICABLE LAW

Applicable law

11

In exercising jurisdiction under this Schedule, the court may, if it thinks that the matter has a substantial connection with a country other than England and Wales, apply the law of that other country.

12

Where a protective measure is taken in one country but implemented in another, the conditions of implementation are governed by the law of the other country.

Lasting powers of attorney, etc

13

(1) If the donor of a lasting power is habitually resident in England and Wales at the time of granting the power, the law applicable to the existence, extent, modification or extinction of the power is—

    (a)   the law of England and Wales, or

    (b)   if he specifies in writing the law of a connected country for the purpose, that law.

(2) If he is habitually resident in another country at that time, but England and Wales is a connected country, the law applicable in that respect is—

    (a)   the law of the other country, or

    (b)   if he specifies in writing the law of England and Wales for the purpose, that law.

(3) A country is connected, in relation to the donor, if it is a country—

    (a)   of which he is a national,

    (b)   in which he was habitually resident, or

    (c)   in which he has property.

(4) Where this paragraph applies as a result of sub-paragraph (3)(c), it applies only in relation to the property which the donor has in the connected country.

(5) The law applicable to the manner of the exercise of a lasting power is the law of the country where it is exercised.

(6) In this Part of this Schedule, "lasting power" means—

    (a)   a lasting power of attorney (see section 9),

    (b)   an enduring power of attorney within the meaning of Schedule 4, or

(c)   any other power of like effect.

14

(1)   Where a lasting power is not exercised in a manner sufficient to guarantee the protection of the person or property of the donor, the court, in exercising jurisdiction under this Schedule, may disapply or modify the power.

(2)   Where, in accordance with this Part of this Schedule, the law applicable to the power is, in one or more respects, that of a country other than England and Wales, the court must, so far as possible, have regard to the law of the other country in that respect (or those respects).

15

Regulations may provide for Schedule 1 (lasting powers of attorney: formalities) to apply with modifications in relation to a lasting power which comes within paragraph 13(6)(c) above.

Protection of third parties

16

(1)   This paragraph applies where a person (a "representative") in purported exercise of an authority to act on behalf of an adult enters into a transaction with a third party.

(2)   The validity of the transaction may not be questioned in proceedings, nor may the third party be held liable, merely because—

(a)   where the representative and third party are in England and Wales when entering into the transaction, sub-paragraph (3) applies;

(b)   where they are in another country at that time, sub-paragraph (4) applies.

(3)   This sub-paragraph applies if—

(a)   the law applicable to the authority in one or more respects is, as a result of this Schedule, the law of a country other than England and Wales, and

(b)   the representative is not entitled to exercise the authority in that respect (or those respects) under the law of that other country.

(4)   This sub-paragraph applies if—

(a)   the law applicable to the authority in one or more respects is, as a result of this Part of this Schedule, the law of England and Wales, and

(b)   the representative is not entitled to exercise the authority in that respect (or those respects) under that law.

(5)   This paragraph does not apply if the third party knew or ought to have known that the applicable law was—

(a)   in a case within sub-paragraph (3), the law of the other country;

(b)   in a case within sub-paragraph (4), the law of England and Wales.

Mandatory rules

17

Where the court is entitled to exercise jurisdiction under this Schedule, the mandatory provisions of the law of England and Wales apply, regardless of any system of law which would otherwise apply in relation to the matter.

Public policy

18

Nothing in this Part of this Schedule requires or enables the application in England and Wales of a provision of the law of another country if its application would be manifestly contrary to public policy.

PART 4   RECOGNITION AND ENFORCEMENT

Recognition

19

(1)   A protective measure taken in relation to an adult under the law of a country other than England and Wales is to be recognised in England and Wales if it was taken on the ground that the adult is habitually resident in the other country.

(2)   A protective measure taken in relation to an adult under the law of a Convention country other than England and Wales is to be recognised in England and Wales if it was taken on a ground mentioned in Chapter 2 (jurisdiction).

(3)   But the court may disapply this paragraph in relation to a measure if it thinks that—

  (a)   the case in which the measure was taken was not urgent,

  (b)   the adult was not given an opportunity to be heard, and

  (c)   that omission amounted to a breach of natural justice.

(4)   It may also disapply this paragraph in relation to a measure if it thinks that—

  (a)   recognition of the measure would be manifestly contrary to public policy,

  (b)   the measure would be inconsistent with a mandatory provision of the law of England and Wales, or

  (c)   the measure is inconsistent with one subsequently taken, or recognised, in England and Wales in relation to the adult.

(5)   And the court may disapply this paragraph in relation to a measure taken under the law of a Convention country in a matter to which Article 33 applies, if the court thinks that that Article has not been complied with in connection with that matter.

20

(1)   An interested person may apply to the court for a declaration as to whether a protective measure taken under the law of a country other than England and Wales is to be recognised in England and Wales.

(2)   No permission is required for an application to the court under this paragraph.

21

For the purposes of paragraphs 19 and 20, any finding of fact relied on when the measure was taken is conclusive.

Enforcement

22

(1)   An interested person may apply to the court for a declaration as to whether a protective measure taken under the law of, and enforceable in, a country other than England and Wales is enforceable, or to be registered, in England and Wales in accordance with Court of Protection Rules.

(2)   The court must make the declaration if—

  (a)   the measure comes within sub-paragraph (1) or (2) of paragraph 19, and

  (b)   the paragraph is not disapplied in relation to it as a result of sub-paragraph (3), (4) or (5).

(3)   A measure to which a declaration under this paragraph relates is enforceable in England and Wales as if it were a measure of like effect taken by the court.

Measures taken in relation to those aged under 16

23

(1)   This paragraph applies where—

(a)   provision giving effect to, or otherwise deriving from, the Convention in a country other than England and Wales applies in relation to a person who has not reached 16, and

(b)   a measure is taken in relation to that person in reliance on that provision.

(2)   This Part of this Schedule applies in relation to that measure as it applies in relation to a protective measure taken in relation to an adult under the law of a Convention country other than England and Wales.

Supplementary

24

The court may not review the merits of a measure taken outside England and Wales except to establish whether the measure complies with this Schedule in so far as it is, as a result of this Schedule, required to do so.

25

Court of Protection Rules may make provision about an application under paragraph 20 or 22.

PART 5   CO-OPERATION

Proposal for cross-border placement

26

(1)   This paragraph applies where a public authority proposes to place an adult in an establishment in a Convention country other than England and Wales.

(2)   The public authority must consult an appropriate authority in that other country about the proposed placement and, for that purpose, must send it—

(a)   a report on the adult, and

(b)   a statement of its reasons for the proposed placement.

(3)   If the appropriate authority in the other country opposes the proposed placement within a reasonable time, the public authority may not proceed with it.

27

A proposal received by a public authority under Article 33 in relation to an adult is to proceed unless the authority opposes it within a reasonable time.

Adult in danger etc

28

(1)   This paragraph applies if a public authority is told that an adult—

(a)   who is in serious danger, and

(b)   in relation to whom the public authority has taken, or is considering taking, protective measures,

is, or has become resident, in a Convention country other than England and Wales.

(2)   The public authority must tell an appropriate authority in that other country about—

(a)   the danger, and

(b)   the measures taken or under consideration.

29

A public authority may not request from, or send to, an appropriate authority in a Convention country information in accordance with Chapter 5 (co-operation) in relation to an adult if it thinks that doing so—

(a)   would be likely to endanger the adult or his property, or

(b) would amount to a serious threat to the liberty or life of a member of the adult's family.

PART 6   GENERAL

Certificates

30

A certificate given under Article 38 by an authority in a Convention country other than England and Wales is, unless the contrary is shown, proof of the matters contained in it.

Powers to make further provision as to private international law

31

Her Majesty may by Order in Council confer on the Lord Chancellor, the court or another public authority functions for enabling the Convention to be given effect in England and Wales.

32

(1) Regulations may make provision—
  (a) giving further effect to the Convention, or
  (b) otherwise about the private international law of England and Wales in relation to the protection of adults.
(2) The regulations may—
  (a) confer functions on the court or another public authority;
  (b) amend this Schedule;
  (c) provide for this Schedule to apply with specified modifications;
  (d) make provision about countries other than Convention countries.

Exceptions

33

Nothing in this Schedule applies, and no provision made under paragraph 32 is to apply, to any matter to which the Convention, as a result of Article 4, does not apply.

Regulations and orders

34

A reference in this Schedule to regulations or an order (other than an Order in Council) is to regulations or an order made for the purposes of this Schedule by the Lord Chancellor.

Commencement

35

The following provisions of this Schedule have effect only if the Convention is in force in accordance with Article 57—
  (a) paragraph 8,
  (b) paragraph 9,
  (c) paragraph 19(2) and (5),
  (d) Part 5,
  (e) paragraph 30.

SCHEDULE 4

PROVISIONS APPLYING TO EXISTING ENDURING POWERS OF ATTORNEY
Section 66(3)

PART 1   ENDURING POWERS OF ATTORNEY

Enduring power of attorney to survive mental incapacity of donor

1

(1)   Where an individual has created a power of attorney which is an enduring power within the meaning of this Schedule—

    (a)   the power is not revoked by any subsequent mental incapacity of his,

    (b)   upon such incapacity supervening, the donee of the power may not do anything under the authority of the power except as provided by sub-paragraph (2) unless or until the instrument creating the power is registered under paragraph 13, and

    (c)   if and so long as paragraph (b) operates to suspend the donee's authority to act under the power, section 5 of the Powers of Attorney Act 1971 (c 27) (protection of donee and third persons), so far as applicable, applies as if the power had been revoked by the donor's mental incapacity,

and, accordingly, section 1 of this Act does not apply.

(2)   Despite sub-paragraph (1)(b), where the attorney has made an application for registration of the instrument then, until it is registered, the attorney may take action under the power—

    (a)   to maintain the donor or prevent loss to his estate, or

    (b)   to maintain himself or other persons in so far as paragraph 3(2) permits him to do so.

(3)   Where the attorney purports to act as provided by sub-paragraph (2) then, in favour of a person who deals with him without knowledge that the attorney is acting otherwise than in accordance with sub-paragraph (2)(a) or (b), the transaction between them is as valid as if the attorney were acting in accordance with sub-paragraph (2)(a) or (b).

Characteristics of an enduring power of attorney

2

(1)   Subject to sub-paragraphs (5) and (6) and paragraph 20, a power of attorney is an enduring power within the meaning of this Schedule if the instrument which creates the power—

    (a)   is in the prescribed form,

    (b)   was executed in the prescribed manner by the donor and the attorney, and

    (c)   incorporated at the time of execution by the donor the prescribed explanatory information.

(2)   In this paragraph, "prescribed" means prescribed by such of the following regulations as applied when the instrument was executed—

    (a)   the Enduring Powers of Attorney (Prescribed Form) Regulations 1986 (SI 1986/126),

    (b)   the Enduring Powers of Attorney (Prescribed Form) Regulations 1987 (SI 1987/1612),

    (c)   the Enduring Powers of Attorney (Prescribed Form) Regulations 1990 (SI 1990/1376),

(d)   the Enduring Powers of Attorney (Welsh Language Prescribed Form) Regulations 2000 (SI 2000/289).

(3)   An instrument in the prescribed form purporting to have been executed in the prescribed manner is to be taken, in the absence of evidence to the contrary, to be a document which incorporated at the time of execution by the donor the prescribed explanatory information.

(4)   If an instrument differs in an immaterial respect in form or mode of expression from the prescribed form it is to be treated as sufficient in point of form and expression.

(5)   A power of attorney cannot be an enduring power unless, when he executes the instrument creating it, the attorney is—

(a)   an individual who has reached 18 and is not bankrupt [or is not subject to a debt relief order (under Part 7A of the Insolvency Act 1986)], or

(b)   a trust corporation.

(6)   A power of attorney which gives the attorney a right to appoint a substitute or successor cannot be an enduring power.

(7)   An enduring power is revoked by the bankruptcy of the donor or attorney [or the making of a debt relief order (under Part 7A of the Insolvency Act 1986) in respect of the donor or attorney].

(8)   But where the donor or attorney is bankrupt merely because an interim bankruptcy restrictions order has effect in respect of him [or where the donor or attorney is subject to an interim debt relief restrictions order], the power is suspended for so long as the order has effect.

(9)   An enduring power is revoked if the court—

(a)   exercises a power under sections 16 to 20 in relation to the donor, and

(b)   directs that the enduring power is to be revoked.

(10)   No disclaimer of an enduring power, whether by deed or otherwise, is valid unless and until the attorney gives notice of it to the donor or, where paragraph 4(6) or 15(1) applies, to the Public Guardian.

Scope of authority etc of attorney under enduring power

3

(1)   If the instrument which creates an enduring power of attorney is expressed to confer general authority on the attorney, the instrument operates to confer, subject to—

(a)   the restriction imposed by sub-paragraph (3), and

(b)   any conditions or restrictions contained in the instrument,

authority to do on behalf of the donor anything which the donor could lawfully do by an attorney at the time when the donor executed the instrument.

(2)   Subject to any conditions or restrictions contained in the instrument, an attorney under an enduring power, whether general or limited, may (without obtaining any consent) act under the power so as to benefit himself or other persons than the donor to the following extent but no further—

(a)   he may so act in relation to himself or in relation to any other person if the donor might be expected to provide for his or that person's needs respectively, and

(b)   he may do whatever the donor might be expected to do to meet those needs.

(3)   Without prejudice to sub-paragraph (2) but subject to any conditions or restrictions contained in the instrument, an attorney under an enduring power, whether general or limited, may (without obtaining any consent) dispose of the property of the donor by way of gift to the following extent but no further—

(a) he may make gifts of a seasonal nature or at a time, or on an anniversary, of a birth, a marriage or the formation of a civil partnership, to persons (including himself) who are related to or connected with the donor, and

(b) he may make gifts to any charity to whom the donor made or might be expected to make gifts,

provided that the value of each such gift is not unreasonable having regard to all the circumstances and in particular the size of the donor's estate.

PART 2 ACTION ON ACTUAL OR IMPENDING INCAPACITY OF DONOR

Duties of attorney in event of actual or impending incapacity of donor

4

(1) Sub-paragraphs (2) to (6) apply if the attorney under an enduring power has reason to believe that the donor is or is becoming mentally incapable.

(2) The attorney must, as soon as practicable, make an application to the Public Guardian for the registration of the instrument creating the power.

(3) Before making an application for registration the attorney must comply with the provisions as to notice set out in Part 3 of this Schedule.

(4) An application for registration—

(a) must be made in the prescribed form, and

(b) must contain such statements as may be prescribed.

(5) The attorney—

(a) may, before making an application for the registration of the instrument, refer to the court for its determination any question as to the validity of the power, and

(b) must comply with any direction given to him by the court on that determination.

(6) No disclaimer of the power is valid unless and until the attorney gives notice of it to the Public Guardian; and the Public Guardian must notify the donor if he receives a notice under this sub-paragraph.

(7) A person who, in an application for registration, makes a statement which he knows to be false in a material particular is guilty of an offence and is liable—

(a) on summary conviction, to imprisonment for a term not exceeding 12 months or a fine not exceeding the statutory maximum or both;

(b) on conviction on indictment, to imprisonment for a term not exceeding 2 years or a fine or both.

(8) In this paragraph, "prescribed" means prescribed by regulations made for the purposes of this Schedule by the Lord Chancellor.

PART 3 NOTIFICATION PRIOR TO REGISTRATION

Duty to give notice to relatives

5

Subject to paragraph 7, before making an application for registration the attorney must give notice of his intention to do so to all those persons (if any) who are entitled to receive notice by virtue of paragraph 6.

6

(1) Subject to sub-paragraphs (2) to (4), persons of the following classes ("relatives") are entitled to receive notice under paragraph 5—

(a) the donor's spouse or civil partner,

(b) the donor's children,

      (c)   the donor's parents,

      (d)   the donor's brothers and sisters, whether of the whole or half blood,

      (e)   the widow, widower or surviving civil partner of a child of the donor,

      (f)   the donor's grandchildren,

      (g)   the children of the donor's brothers and sisters of the whole blood,

      (h)   the children of the donor's brothers and sisters of the half blood,

      (i)   the donor's uncles and aunts of the whole blood,

      (j)   the children of the donor's uncles and aunts of the whole blood.

(2)   A person is not entitled to receive notice under paragraph 5 if—

      (a)   his name or address is not known to the attorney and cannot be reasonably ascertained by him, or

      (b)   the attorney has reason to believe that he has not reached 18 or is mentally incapable.

(3)   Except where sub-paragraph (4) applies—

      (a)   no more than 3 persons are entitled to receive notice under paragraph 5, and

      (b)   in determining the persons who are so entitled, persons falling within the class in sub-paragraph (1)(a) are to be preferred to persons falling within the class in sub-paragraph (1)(b), those falling within the class in sub-paragraph (1)(b) are to be preferred to those falling within the class in sub-paragraph (1)(c), and so on.

(4)   Despite the limit of 3 specified in sub-paragraph (3), where—

      (a)   there is more than one person falling within any of classes (a) to (j) of sub-paragraph (1), and

      (b)   at least one of those persons would be entitled to receive notice under paragraph 5,

then, subject to sub-paragraph (2), all the persons falling within that class are entitled to receive notice under paragraph 5.

7

(1)   An attorney is not required to give notice under paragraph 5—

      (a)   to himself, or

      (b)   to any other attorney under the power who is joining in making the application,

even though he or, as the case may be, the other attorney is entitled to receive notice by virtue of paragraph 6.

(2)   In the case of any person who is entitled to receive notice by virtue of paragraph 6, the attorney, before applying for registration, may make an application to the court to be dispensed from the requirement to give him notice; and the court must grant the application if it is satisfied—

      (a)   that it would be undesirable or impracticable for the attorney to give him notice, or

      (b)   that no useful purpose is likely to be served by giving him notice.

Duty to give notice to donor

8

(1)   Subject to sub-paragraph (2), before making an application for registration the attorney must give notice of his intention to do so to the donor.

(2)   Paragraph 7(2) applies in relation to the donor as it applies in relation to a person who is entitled to receive notice under paragraph 5.

Contents of notices

9

A notice to relatives under this Part of this Schedule must—

    (a)   be in the prescribed form,

    (b)   state that the attorney proposes to make an application to the Public Guardian for the registration of the instrument creating the enduring power in question,

    (c)   inform the person to whom it is given of his right to object to the registration under paragraph 13(4), and

    (d)   specify, as the grounds on which an objection to registration may be made, the grounds set out in paragraph 13(9).

10

A notice to the donor under this Part of this Schedule—

    (a)   must be in the prescribed form,

    (b)   must contain the statement mentioned in paragraph 9(b), and

    (c)   must inform the donor that, while the instrument remains registered, any revocation of the power by him will be ineffective unless and until the revocation is confirmed by the court.

Duty to give notice to other attorneys

11

(1) Subject to sub-paragraph (2), before making an application for registration an attorney under a joint and several power must give notice of his intention to do so to any other attorney under the power who is not joining in making the application; and paragraphs 7(2) and 9 apply in relation to attorneys entitled to receive notice by virtue of this paragraph as they apply in relation to persons entitled to receive notice by virtue of paragraph 6.

(2) An attorney is not entitled to receive notice by virtue of this paragraph if—

    (a)   his address is not known to the applying attorney and cannot reasonably be ascertained by him, or

    (b)   the applying attorney has reason to believe that he has not reached 18 or is mentally incapable.

Supplementary

12

Despite section 7 of the Interpretation Act 1978 (c 30) (construction of references to service by post), for the purposes of this Part of this Schedule a notice given by post is to be regarded as given on the date on which it was posted.

PART 4   REGISTRATION

Registration of instrument creating power

13

(1) If an application is made in accordance with paragraph 4(3) and (4) the Public Guardian must, subject to the provisions of this paragraph, register the instrument to which the application relates.

(2) If it appears to the Public Guardian that—

    (a)   there is a deputy appointed for the donor of the power created by the instrument, and

(b) the powers conferred on the deputy would, if the instrument were registered, to any extent conflict with the powers conferred on the attorney,

the Public Guardian must not register the instrument except in accordance with the court's directions.

(3) The court may, on the application of the attorney, direct the Public Guardian to register an instrument even though notice has not been given as required by paragraph 4(3) and Part 3 of this Schedule to a person entitled to receive it, if the court is satisfied—

(a) that it was undesirable or impracticable for the attorney to give notice to that person, or

(b) that no useful purpose is likely to be served by giving him notice.

(4) Sub-paragraph (5) applies if, before the end of the period of 5 weeks beginning with the date (or the latest date) on which the attorney gave notice under paragraph 5 of an application for registration, the Public Guardian receives a valid notice of objection to the registration from a person entitled to notice of the application.

(5) The Public Guardian must not register the instrument except in accordance with the court's directions.

(6) Sub-paragraph (7) applies if, in the case of an application for registration—

(a) it appears from the application that there is no one to whom notice has been given under paragraph 5, or

(b) the Public Guardian has reason to believe that appropriate inquiries might bring to light evidence on which he could be satisfied that one of the grounds of objection set out in sub-paragraph (9) was established.

(7) The Public Guardian—

(a) must not register the instrument, and

(b) must undertake such inquiries as he thinks appropriate in all the circumstances.

(8) If, having complied with sub-paragraph (7)(b), the Public Guardian is satisfied that one of the grounds of objection set out in sub-paragraph (9) is established—

(a) the attorney may apply to the court for directions, and

(b) the Public Guardian must not register the instrument except in accordance with the court's directions.

(9) A notice of objection under this paragraph is valid if made on one or more of the following grounds—

(a) that the power purported to have been created by the instrument was not valid as an enduring power of attorney,

(b) that the power created by the instrument no longer subsists,

(c) that the application is premature because the donor is not yet becoming mentally incapable,

(d) that fraud or undue pressure was used to induce the donor to create the power,

(e) that, having regard to all the circumstances and in particular the attorney's relationship to or connection with the donor, the attorney is unsuitable to be the donor's attorney.

(10) If any of those grounds is established to the satisfaction of the court it must direct the Public Guardian not to register the instrument, but if not so satisfied it must direct its registration.

(11) If the court directs the Public Guardian not to register an instrument because it is satisfied that the ground in sub-paragraph (9)(d) or (e) is established, it must by order revoke the power created by the instrument.

(12) If the court directs the Public Guardian not to register an instrument because it is satisfied that any ground in sub-paragraph (9) except that in paragraph (c) is

established, the instrument must be delivered up to be cancelled unless the court otherwise directs.

Register of enduring powers

14

The Public Guardian has the function of establishing and maintaining a register of enduring powers for the purposes of this Schedule.

PART 5   LEGAL POSITION AFTER REGISTRATION

Effect and proof of registration

15

(1)   The effect of the registration of an instrument under paragraph 13 is that—

    (a)   no revocation of the power by the donor is valid unless and until the court confirms the revocation under paragraph 16(3);

    (b)   no disclaimer of the power is valid unless and until the attorney gives notice of it to the Public Guardian;

    (c)   the donor may not extend or restrict the scope of the authority conferred by the instrument and no instruction or consent given by him after registration, in the case of a consent, confers any right and, in the case of an instruction, imposes or confers any obligation or right on or creates any liability of the attorney or other persons having notice of the instruction or consent.

(2)   Sub-paragraph (1) applies for so long as the instrument is registered under paragraph 13 whether or not the donor is for the time being mentally incapable.

(3)   A document purporting to be an office copy of an instrument registered under this Schedule is, in any part of the United Kingdom, evidence of—

    (a)   the contents of the instrument, and

    (b)   the fact that it has been so registered.

(4)   Sub-paragraph (3) is without prejudice to section 3 of the Powers of Attorney Act 1971 (c 27) (proof by certified copies) and to any other method of proof authorised by law.

Functions of court with regard to registered power

16

(1)   Where an instrument has been registered under paragraph 13, the court has the following functions with respect to the power and the donor of and the attorney appointed to act under the power.

(2)   The court may—

    (a)   determine any question as to the meaning or effect of the instrument;

    (b)   give directions with respect to—

        (i)   the management or disposal by the attorney of the property and affairs of the donor;

        (ii)   the rendering of accounts by the attorney and the production of the records kept by him for the purpose;

        (iii)   the remuneration or expenses of the attorney whether or not in default of or in accordance with any provision made by the instrument, including directions for the repayment of excessive or the payment of additional remuneration;

    (c)   require the attorney to supply information or produce documents or things in his possession as attorney;

(d) give any consent or authorisation to act which the attorney would have to obtain from a mentally capable donor;

(e) authorise the attorney to act so as to benefit himself or other persons than the donor otherwise than in accordance with paragraph 3(2) and (3) (but subject to any conditions or restrictions contained in the instrument);

(f) relieve the attorney wholly or partly from any liability which he has or may have incurred on account of a breach of his duties as attorney.

(3) On application made for the purpose by or on behalf of the donor, the court must confirm the revocation of the power if satisfied that the donor—

(a) has done whatever is necessary in law to effect an express revocation of the power, and

(b) was mentally capable of revoking a power of attorney when he did so (whether or not he is so when the court considers the application).

(4) The court must direct the Public Guardian to cancel the registration of an instrument registered under paragraph 13 in any of the following circumstances—

(a) on confirming the revocation of the power under sub-paragraph (3),

(b) on directing under paragraph 2(9)(b) that the power is to be revoked,

(c) on being satisfied that the donor is and is likely to remain mentally capable,

(d) on being satisfied that the power has expired or has been revoked by the mental incapacity of the attorney,

(e) on being satisfied that the power was not a valid and subsisting enduring power when registration was effected,

(f) on being satisfied that fraud or undue pressure was used to induce the donor to create the power,

(g) on being satisfied that, having regard to all the circumstances and in particular the attorney's relationship to or connection with the donor, the attorney is unsuitable to be the donor's attorney.

(5) If the court directs the Public Guardian to cancel the registration of an instrument on being satisfied of the matters specified in sub-paragraph (4)(f) or (g) it must by order revoke the power created by the instrument.

(6) If the court directs the cancellation of the registration of an instrument under sub-paragraph (4) except paragraph (c) the instrument must be delivered up to the Public Guardian to be cancelled, unless the court otherwise directs.

Cancellation of registration by Public Guardian

17

The Public Guardian must cancel the registration of an instrument creating an enduring power of attorney—

(a) on receipt of a disclaimer signed by the attorney;

(b) if satisfied that the power has been revoked by the death or bankruptcy of the donor or attorney [or the making of a debt relief order (under Part 7A of the Insolvency Act 1986) in respect of the donor or attorney] or, if the attorney is a body corporate, by its winding up or dissolution;

(c) on receipt of notification from the court that the court has revoked the power;

(d) on confirmation from the court that the donor has revoked the power.

PART 6   PROTECTION OF ATTORNEY AND THIRD PARTIES

Protection of attorney and third persons where power is invalid or revoked

18

(1)   Sub-paragraphs (2) and (3) apply where an instrument which did not create a valid power of attorney has been registered under paragraph 13 (whether or not the registration has been cancelled at the time of the act or transaction in question).

(2)   An attorney who acts in pursuance of the power does not incur any liability (either to the donor or to any other person) because of the non-existence of the power unless at the time of acting he knows—

(a)   that the instrument did not create a valid enduring power,

(b)   that an event has occurred which, if the instrument had created a valid enduring power, would have had the effect of revoking the power, or

(c)   that, if the instrument had created a valid enduring power, the power would have expired before that time.

(3)   Any transaction between the attorney and another person is, in favour of that person, as valid as if the power had then been in existence, unless at the time of the transaction that person has knowledge of any of the matters mentioned in sub-paragraph (2).

(4)   If the interest of a purchaser depends on whether a transaction between the attorney and another person was valid by virtue of sub-paragraph (3), it is conclusively presumed in favour of the purchaser that the transaction was valid if—

(a)   the transaction between that person and the attorney was completed within 12 months of the date on which the instrument was registered, or

(b)   that person makes a statutory declaration, before or within 3 months after the completion of the purchase, that he had no reason at the time of the transaction to doubt that the attorney had authority to dispose of the property which was the subject of the transaction.

(5)   For the purposes of section 5 of the Powers of Attorney Act 1971 (c 27) (protection where power is revoked) in its application to an enduring power the revocation of which by the donor is by virtue of paragraph 15 invalid unless and until confirmed by the court under paragraph 16—

(a)   knowledge of the confirmation of the revocation is knowledge of the revocation of the power, but

(b)   knowledge of the unconfirmed revocation is not.

Further protection of attorney and third persons

19

(1)   If—

(a)   an instrument framed in a form prescribed as mentioned in paragraph 2(2) creates a power which is not a valid enduring power, and

(b)   the power is revoked by the mental incapacity of the donor,

sub-paragraphs (2) and (3) apply, whether or not the instrument has been registered.

(2)   An attorney who acts in pursuance of the power does not, by reason of the revocation, incur any liability (either to the donor or to any other person) unless at the time of acting he knows—

(a)   that the instrument did not create a valid enduring power, and

(b)   that the donor has become mentally incapable.

(3)   Any transaction between the attorney and another person is, in favour of that person, as valid as if the power had then been in existence, unless at the time of the transaction that person knows—

(a)   that the instrument did not create a valid enduring power, and

(b)   that the donor has become mentally incapable.

(4)   Paragraph 18(4) applies for the purpose of determining whether a transaction was valid by virtue of sub-paragraph (3) as it applies for the purpose or determining whether a transaction was valid by virtue of paragraph 18(3).

PART 7   JOINT AND JOINT AND SEVERAL ATTORNEYS

Application to joint and joint and several attorneys

20

(1)   An instrument which appoints more than one person to be an attorney cannot create an enduring power unless the attorneys are appointed to act—

(a)   jointly, or

(b)   jointly and severally.

(2)   This Schedule, in its application to joint attorneys, applies to them collectively as it applies to a single attorney but subject to the modifications specified in paragraph 21.

(3)   This Schedule, in its application to joint and several attorneys, applies with the modifications specified in sub-paragraphs (4) to (7) and in paragraph 22.

(4)   A failure, as respects any one attorney, to comply with the requirements for the creation of enduring powers—

(a)   prevents the instrument from creating such a power in his case, but

(b)   does not affect its efficacy for that purpose as respects the other or others or its efficacy in his case for the purpose of creating a power of attorney which is not an enduring power.

(5)   If one or more but not both or all the attorneys makes or joins in making an application for registration of the instrument—

(a)   an attorney who is not an applicant as well as one who is may act pending the registration of the instrument as provided in paragraph 1(2),

(b)   notice of the application must also be given under Part 3 of this Schedule to the other attorney or attorneys, and

(c)   objection may validly be taken to the registration on a ground relating to an attorney or to the power of an attorney who is not an applicant as well as to one or the power of one who is an applicant.

(6)   The Public Guardian is not precluded by paragraph 13(5) or (8) from registering an instrument and the court must not direct him not to do so under paragraph 13(10) if an enduring power subsists as respects some attorney who is not affected by the ground or grounds of the objection in question; and where the Public Guardian registers an instrument in that case, he must make against the registration an entry in the prescribed form.

(7)   Sub-paragraph (6) does not preclude the court from revoking a power in so far as it confers a power on any other attorney in respect of whom the ground in paragraph 13(9)(d) or (e) is established; and where any ground in paragraph 13(9) affecting any other attorney is established the court must direct the Public Guardian to make against the registration an entry in the prescribed form.

(8)   In sub-paragraph (4), "the requirements for the creation of enduring powers" means the provisions of—

(a)   paragraph 2 other than sub-paragraphs (8) and (9), and

(b)   the regulations mentioned in paragraph 2.

Joint attorneys

21

(1) In paragraph 2(5), the reference to the time when the attorney executes the instrument is to be read as a reference to the time when the second or last attorney executes the instrument.

(2) In paragraph 2(6) to (8), the reference to the attorney is to be read as a reference to any attorney under the power.

(3) Paragraph 13 has effect as if the ground of objection to the registration of the instrument specified in sub-paragraph (9)(e) applied to any attorney under the power.

(4) In paragraph 16(2), references to the attorney are to be read as including references to any attorney under the power.

(5) In paragraph 16(4), references to the attorney are to be read as including references to any attorney under the power.

(6) In paragraph 17, references to the attorney are to be read as including references to any attorney under the power.

Joint and several attorneys

22

(1) In paragraph 2(7), the reference to the bankruptcy of the attorney is to be read as a reference to the bankruptcy of the last remaining attorney under the power; and the bankruptcy of any other attorney under the power causes that person to cease to be an attorney under the power.

[(1A) In paragraph 2(7), the reference to the making of a debt relief order (under Part 7A of the Insolvency Act 1986) in respect of the attorney is to be read as a reference to the making of a debt relief order in respect of the last remaining attorney under the power; and the making of a debt relief order in respect of any other attorney under the power causes that person to cease to be an attorney under the power.]

(2) In paragraph 2(8), the reference to the suspension of the power is to be read as a reference to its suspension in so far as it relates to the attorney in respect of whom the interim bankruptcy restrictions order has effect.

[(2A) In paragraph 2(8), the reference to the suspension of the power is to be read as a reference to its suspension in so far as it relates to the attorney in respect of whom the interim debt relief restrictions order has effect.]

(3) The restriction upon disclaimer imposed by paragraph 4(6) applies only to those attorneys who have reason to believe that the donor is or is becoming mentally incapable.

PART 8   INTERPRETATION

23

(1) In this Schedule—

"enduring power" is to be construed in accordance with paragraph 2,

"mentally incapable" or "mental incapacity", except where it refers to revocation at common law, means in relation to any person, that he is incapable by reason of mental disorder . . . of managing and administering his property and affairs and "mentally capable" and "mental capacity" are to be construed accordingly,

"notice" means notice in writing, and

"prescribed", except for the purposes of paragraph 2, means prescribed by regulations made for the purposes of this Schedule by the Lord Chancellor.

[(1A) In sub-paragraph (1), "mental disorder" has the same meaning as in the Mental Health Act but disregarding the amendments made to that Act by the Mental Health Act 2007.]

(2)   Any question arising under or for the purposes of this Schedule as to what the donor of the power might at any time be expected to do is to be determined by assuming that he had full mental capacity at the time but otherwise by reference to the circumstances existing at that time.

SCHEDULE 5

TRANSITIONAL PROVISIONS AND SAVINGS

Section 66(4)

PART 1   REPEAL OF PART 7 OF THE MENTAL HEALTH ACT 1983

Existing receivers

1

(1)   This paragraph applies where, immediately before the commencement day, there is a receiver ("R") for a person ("P") appointed under section 99 of the Mental Health Act.

(2)   On and after that day—

    (a)   this Act applies as if R were a deputy appointed for P by the court, but with the functions that R had as receiver immediately before that day, and

    (b)   a reference in any other enactment to a deputy appointed by the court includes a person appointed as a deputy as a result of paragraph (a).

(3)   On any application to it by R, the court may end R's appointment as P's deputy.

(4)   Where, as a result of section 20(1), R may not make a decision on behalf of P in relation to a relevant matter, R must apply to the court.

(5)   If, on the application, the court is satisfied that P is capable of managing his property and affairs in relation to the relevant matter—

    (a)   it must make an order ending R's appointment as P's deputy in relation to that matter, but

    (b)   it may, in relation to any other matter, exercise in relation to P any of the powers which it has under sections 15 to 19.

(6)   If it is not satisfied, the court may exercise in relation to P any of the powers which it has under sections 15 to 19.

(7)   R's appointment as P's deputy ceases to have effect if P dies.

(8)   "Relevant matter" means a matter in relation to which, immediately before the commencement day, R was authorised to act as P's receiver.

(9)   In sub-paragraph (1), the reference to a receiver appointed under section 99 of the Mental Health Act includes a reference to a person who by virtue of Schedule 5 to that Act was deemed to be a receiver appointed under that section.

Orders, appointments etc

2

(1)   Any order or appointment made, direction or authority given or other thing done which has, or by virtue of Schedule 5 to the Mental Health Act was deemed to have, effect under Part 7 of the Act immediately before the commencement day is to continue to have effect despite the repeal of Part 7.

(2)   In so far as any such order, appointment, direction, authority or thing could have been made, given or done under sections 15 to 20 if those sections had then been in force—

    (a)   it is to be treated as made, given or done under those sections, and

    (b)   the powers of variation and discharge conferred by section 16(7) apply accordingly.

(3)   Sub-paragraph (1)—

    (a)   does not apply to nominations under section 93(1) or (4) of the Mental Health Act, and

    (b)   as respects receivers, has effect subject to paragraph 1.

(4)   This Act does not affect the operation of section 109 of the Mental Health Act (effect and proof of orders etc) in relation to orders made and directions given under Part 7 of that Act.

(5)   This paragraph is without prejudice to section 16 of the Interpretation Act 1978 (c 30) (general savings on repeal).

Pending proceedings

3

(1)   Any application for the exercise of a power under Part 7 of the Mental Health Act which is pending immediately before the commencement day is to be treated, in so far as a corresponding power is exercisable under sections 16 to 20, as an application for the exercise of that power.

(2)   For the purposes of sub-paragraph (1) an application for the appointment of a receiver is to be treated as an application for the appointment of a deputy.

Appeals

4

(1)   Part 7 of the Mental Health Act and the rules made under it are to continue to apply to any appeal brought by virtue of section 105 of that Act which has not been determined before the commencement day.

(2)   If in the case of an appeal brought by virtue of section 105(1) (appeal to nominated judge) the judge nominated under section 93 of the Mental Health Act has begun to hear the appeal, he is to continue to do so but otherwise it is to be heard by a puisne judge of the High Court nominated under section 46.

Fees

5

All fees and other payments which, having become due, have not been paid to the former Court of Protection before the commencement day, are to be paid to the new Court of Protection.

Court records

6

(1)   The records of the former Court of Protection are to be treated, on and after the commencement day, as records of the new Court of Protection and are to be dealt with accordingly under the Public Records Act 1958 (c 51).

(2)   On and after the commencement day, the Public Guardian is, for the purpose of exercising any of his functions, to be given such access as he may require to such of the records mentioned in sub-paragraph (1) as relate to the appointment of receivers under section 99 of the Mental Health Act.

Existing charges

7

This Act does not affect the operation in relation to a charge created before the commencement day of—

> (a)   so much of section 101(6) of the Mental Health Act as precludes a charge created under section 101(5) from conferring a right of sale or foreclosure during the lifetime of the patient, or
>
> (b)   section 106(6) of the Mental Health Act (charge created by virtue of section 106(5) not to cause interest to fail etc).

Preservation of interests on disposal of property

8

Paragraph 8(1) of Schedule 2 applies in relation to any disposal of property (within the meaning of that provision) by a person living on 1st November 1960, being a disposal effected under the Lunacy Act 1890 (c 5) as it applies in relation to the disposal of property effected under sections 16 to 20.

Accounts

9

Court of Protection Rules may provide that, in a case where paragraph 1 applies, R is to have a duty to render accounts—

> (a)   while he is receiver;
>
> (b)   after he is discharged.

Interpretation

10

In this Part of this Schedule—

> (a)   "the commencement day" means the day on which section 66(1)(a) (repeal of Part 7 of the Mental Health Act) comes into force,
>
> (b)   "the former Court of Protection" means the office abolished by section 45, and
>
> (c)   "the new Court of Protection" means the court established by that section.

PART 2   REPEAL OF THE ENDURING POWERS OF ATTORNEY ACT 1985

Orders, determinations, etc

11

(1)   Any order or determination made, or other thing done, under the 1985 Act which has effect immediately before the commencement day continues to have effect despite the repeal of that Act.

(2)   In so far as any such order, determination or thing could have been made or done under Schedule 4 if it had then been in force—

> (a)   it is to be treated as made or done under that Schedule, and
>
> (b)   the powers of variation and discharge exercisable by the court apply accordingly.

(3)   Any instrument registered under the 1985 Act is to be treated as having been registered by the Public Guardian under Schedule 4.

(4)   This paragraph is without prejudice to section 16 of the Interpretation Act 1978 (c 30) (general savings on repeal).

Pending proceedings

12

(1)   An application for the exercise of a power under the 1985 Act which is pending immediately before the commencement day is to be treated, in so far as a corresponding power is exercisable under Schedule 4, as an application for the exercise of that power.

(2)   For the purposes of sub-paragraph (1)—

(a)   a pending application under section 4(2) of the 1985 Act for the registration of an instrument is to be treated as an application to the Public Guardian under paragraph 4 of Schedule 4 and any notice given in connection with that application under Schedule 1 to the 1985 Act is to be treated as given under Part 3 of Schedule 4,

(b)   a notice of objection to the registration of an instrument is to be treated as a notice of objection under paragraph 13 of Schedule 4, and

(c)   pending proceedings under section 5 of the 1985 Act are to be treated as proceedings on an application for the exercise by the court of a power which would become exercisable in relation to an instrument under paragraph 16(2) of Schedule 4 on its registration.

Appeals

13

(1)   The 1985 Act and, so far as relevant, the provisions of Part 7 of the Mental Health Act and the rules made under it as applied by section 10 of the 1985 Act are to continue to have effect in relation to any appeal brought by virtue of section 10(1)(c) of the 1985 Act which has not been determined before the commencement day.

(2)   If, in the case of an appeal brought by virtue of section 105(1) of the Mental Health Act as applied by section 10(1)(c) of the 1985 Act (appeal to nominated judge), the judge nominated under section 93 of the Mental Health Act has begun to hear the appeal, he is to continue to do so but otherwise the appeal is to be heard by a puisne judge of the High Court nominated under section 46.

Exercise of powers of donor as trustee

14

(1)   Section 2(8) of the 1985 Act (which prevents a power of attorney under section 25 of the Trustee Act 1925 (c 19) as enacted from being an enduring power) is to continue to apply to any enduring power—

(a)   created before 1st March 2000, and

(b)   having effect immediately before the commencement day.

(2)   Section 3(3) of the 1985 Act (which entitles the donee of an enduring power to exercise the donor's powers as trustee) is to continue to apply to any enduring power to which, as a result of the provision mentioned in sub-paragraph (3), it applies immediately before the commencement day.

(3)   The provision is section 4(3)(a) of the Trustee Delegation Act 1999 (c 15) (which provides for section 3(3) of the 1985 Act to cease to apply to an enduring power when its registration is cancelled, if it was registered in response to an application made before 1st March 2001).

(4)   Even though section 4 of the 1999 Act is repealed by this Act, that section is to continue to apply in relation to an enduring power—

(a)   to which section 3(3) of the 1985 Act applies as a result of sub-paragraph (2), or

(b)   to which, immediately before the repeal of section 4 of the 1999 Act, section 1 of that Act applies as a result of section 4 of it.

(5)   The reference in section 1(9) of the 1999 Act to section 4(6) of that Act is to be read with sub-paragraphs (2) to (4).

Interpretation

15

In this Part of this Schedule, "the commencement day" means the day on which section 66(1)(b) (repeal of the 1985 Act) comes into force.

SCHEDULE 6

MINOR AND CONSEQUENTIAL AMENDMENTS

Section 67(1)

Fines and Recoveries Act 1833 (c 74)

1

(1)   The Fines and Recoveries Act 1833 (c 74) is amended as follows.

(2)   In section 33 (case where protector of settlement lacks capacity to act), for the words from "shall be incapable" to "is incapable as aforesaid" substitute "lacks capacity (within the meaning of the Mental Capacity Act 2005) to manage his property and affairs, the Court of Protection is to take his place as protector of the settlement while he lacks capacity".

(3)   In sections 48 and 49 (mental health jurisdiction), for each reference to the judge having jurisdiction under Part 7 of the Mental Health Act substitute a reference to the Court of Protection.

Improvement of Land Act 1864 (c 114)

2

In section 68 of the Improvement of Land Act 1864 (c 114) (apportionment of rentcharges)—

(a)   for ", curator, or receiver of" substitute "or curator of, or a deputy with powers in relation to property and affairs appointed by the Court of Protection for,", and

(b)   for "or patient within the meaning of Part VII of the Mental Health Act 1983" substitute "person who lacks capacity (within the meaning of the Mental Capacity Act 2005) to receive the notice".

Trustee Act 1925 (c 19)

3

(1)   The Trustee Act 1925 (c 19) is amended as follows.

(2)   In section 36 (appointment of new trustee)—

(a)   in subsection (6C), for the words from "a power of attorney" to the end, substitute "an enduring power of attorney or lasting power of attorney registered under the Mental Capacity Act 2005", and

(b)   in subsection (9)—

(i)   for the words from "is incapable" to "exercising" substitute "lacks capacity to exercise", and

(ii)   for the words from "the authority" to the end substitute "the Court of Protection".

(3) In section 41(1) (power of court to appoint new trustee) for the words from "is incapable" to "exercising" substitute "lacks capacity to exercise".

(4) In section 54 (mental health jurisdiction)—

    (a)   for subsection (1) substitute—

"(1) Subject to subsection (2), the Court of Protection may not make an order, or give a direction or authority, in relation to a person who lacks capacity to exercise his functions as trustee, if the High Court may make an order to that effect under this Act.",

    (b)   in subsection (2)—

        (i)   for the words from the beginning to "of a receiver" substitute "Where a person lacks capacity to exercise his functions as a trustee and a deputy is appointed for him by the Court of Protection or an application for the appointment of a deputy",

        (ii)   for "the said authority", in each place, substitute "the Court of Protection", and

        (iii)   for "the patient", in each place, substitute "the person concerned", and

    (c)   omit subsection (3).

(5) In section 55 (order made on particular allegation to be conclusive evidence of it)—

    (a)   for the words from "Part VII" to "Northern Ireland" substitute "sections 15 to 20 of the Mental Capacity Act 2005 or any corresponding provisions having effect in Northern Ireland", and

    (b)   for paragraph (a) substitute—

"(a) that a trustee or mortgagee lacks capacity in relation to the matter in question;".

(6) In section 68 (definitions), at the end add—

"(3) Any reference in this Act to a person who lacks capacity in relation to a matter is to a person—

    (a)   who lacks capacity within the meaning of the Mental Capacity Act 2005 in relation to that matter, or

    (b)   in respect of whom the powers conferred by section 48 of that Act are exercisable and have been exercised in relation to that matter.".

Law of Property Act 1925 (c 20)

4

(1) The Law of Property Act 1925 (c 20) is amended as follows.

(2) In section 22 (conveyances on behalf of persons who lack capacity)—

    (a)   in subsection (1)—

        (i)   for the words from "in a person suffering" to "is acting" substitute ", either solely or jointly with any other person or persons, in a person lacking capacity (within the meaning of the Mental Capacity Act 2005) to convey or create a legal estate, a deputy appointed for him by the Court of Protection or (if no deputy is appointed", and

        (ii)   for "the authority having jurisdiction under Part VII of the Mental Health Act 1983" substitute "the Court of Protection",

    (b)   in subsection (2), for "is incapable, by reason of mental disorder, of exercising" substitute "lacks capacity (within the meaning of that Act) to exercise", and

    (c)   in subsection (3), for the words from "an enduring power" to the end substitute "an enduring power of attorney or lasting power of attorney (within the meaning of the 2005 Act) is entitled to act for the trustee who lacks capacity in relation to the dealing.".

(3)   In section 205(1) (interpretation), omit paragraph (xiii).

Administration of Estates Act 1925 (c 23)

5

(1)   The Administration of Estates Act 1925 (c 23) is amended as follows.

(2)   In section 41(1) (powers of personal representatives to appropriate), in the proviso—

  (a)   in paragraph (ii)—

  (i)   for the words from "is incapable" to "the consent" substitute "lacks capacity (within the meaning of the Mental Capacity Act 2005) to give the consent, it", and

  (ii)   for "or receiver" substitute "or a person appointed as deputy for him by the Court of Protection", and

  (b)   in paragraph (iv), for "no receiver is acting for a person suffering from mental disorder" substitute "no deputy is appointed for a person who lacks capacity to consent".

(3)   Omit section 55(1)(viii) (definitions of "person of unsound mind" and "defective").

National Assistance Act 1948 (c 29)

6

In section 49 of the National Assistance Act 1948 (c 29) (expenses of council officers acting for persons who lack capacity)—

  (a)   for the words from "applies" to "affairs of a patient" substitute "applies for appointment by the Court of Protection as a deputy", and

  (b)   for "such functions" substitute "his functions as deputy".

USA Veterans' Pensions (Administration) Act 1949 (c 45)

7

In section 1 of the USA Veterans' Pensions (Administration) Act 1949 (c 45) (administration of pensions)—

  (a)   in subsection (4), omit the words from "or for whom" to "1983", and

  (b)   after subsection (4), insert—

  "(4A)   An agreement under subsection (1) is not to be made in relation to a person who lacks capacity (within the meaning of the Mental Capacity Act 2005) for the purposes of this Act if—

  (a)   there is a donee of an enduring power of attorney or lasting power of attorney (within the meaning of the 2005 Act), or a deputy appointed for the person by the Court of Protection, and

  (b)   the donee or deputy has power in relation to the person for the purposes of this Act.

  (4B)   The proviso at the end of subsection (4) also applies in relation to subsection (4A).".

Intestates' Estates Act 1952 (c 64)

8

In Schedule 2 to the Intestates' Estates Act 1952 (c 64) (rights of surviving spouse or civil partner in relation to home), for paragraph 6(1) substitute—

"(1) Where the surviving spouse or civil partner lacks capacity (within the meaning of the Mental Capacity Act 2005) to make a requirement or give a consent under this Schedule, the requirement or consent may be made or given by a deputy appointed by the Court of Protection with power in that respect or, if no deputy has that power, by that court.".

Variation of Trusts Act 1958 (c 53)

9

In section 1 of the Variation of Trusts Act 1958 (c 53) (jurisdiction of courts to vary trusts)—

(a) in subsection (3), for the words from "shall be determined" to the end substitute "who lacks capacity (within the meaning of the Mental Capacity Act 2005) to give his assent is to be determined by the Court of Protection", and

(b) in subsection (6), for the words from "the powers" to the end substitute "the powers of the Court of Protection".

Administration of Justice Act 1960 (c 65)

10

In section 12(1)(b) of the Administration of Justice Act 1960 (c 65) (contempt of court to publish information about proceedings in private relating to persons with incapacity) for the words from "under Part VIII" to "that Act" substitute "under the Mental Capacity Act 2005, or under any provision of the Mental Health Act 1983".

. . .

11

. . .

Compulsory Purchase Act 1965 (c 56)

12

In Schedule 1 to the Compulsory Purchase Act 1965 (c 56) (persons without power to sell their interests), for paragraph 1(2)(b) substitute—

"(b) do not have effect in relation to a person who lacks capacity (within the meaning of the Mental Capacity Act 2005) for the purposes of this Act if—

(i) there is a donee of an enduring power of attorney or lasting power of attorney (within the meaning of the 2005 Act), or a deputy appointed for the person by the Court of Protection, and

(ii) the donee or deputy has power in relation to the person for the purposes of this Act.".

Leasehold Reform Act 1967 (c 88)

13

(1)   For section 26(2) of the Leasehold Reform Act 1967 (c 88) (landlord lacking capacity) substitute—

    "(2)   Where a landlord lacks capacity (within the meaning of the Mental Capacity Act 2005) to exercise his functions as a landlord, those functions are to be exercised—

        (a)   by a donee of an enduring power of attorney or lasting power of attorney (within the meaning of the 2005 Act), or a deputy appointed for him by the Court of Protection, with power to exercise those functions, or

        (b)   if no donee or deputy has that power, by a person authorised in that respect by that court.".

(2)   That amendment does not affect any proceedings pending at the commencement of this paragraph in which a receiver or a person authorised under Part 7 of the Mental Health Act is acting on behalf of the landlord.

Medicines Act 1968 (c 67)

14

In section 72 of the Medicines Act 1968 (c 67) (pharmacist lacking capacity)—

    (a)   in subsection (1)(c), for the words from "a receiver" to "1959" substitute "he becomes a person who lacks capacity (within the meaning of the Mental Capacity Act 2005) to carry on the business",

    (b)   after subsection (1) insert—

    "(1A)   In subsection (1)(c), the reference to a person who lacks capacity to carry on the business is to a person—

        (a)   in respect of whom there is a donee of an enduring power of attorney or lasting power of attorney (within the meaning of the Mental Capacity Act 2005), or

        (b)   for whom a deputy is appointed by the Court of Protection,

    and in relation to whom the donee or deputy has power for the purposes of this Act.",

    (c)   in subsection (3)(d)—

        (i)   for "receiver" substitute "deputy", and

        (ii)   after "guardian" insert "or from the date of registration of the instrument appointing the donee", and

    (d)   in subsection (4)(c), for "receiver" substitute "donee, deputy".

Family Law Reform Act 1969 (c 46)

15

For section 21(4) of the Family Law Reform Act 1969 (c 46) (consent required for taking of bodily sample from person lacking capacity), substitute—

    "(4)   A bodily sample may be taken from a person who lacks capacity (within the meaning of the Mental Capacity Act 2005) to give his consent, if consent is given by the court giving the direction under section 20 or by—

        (a)   a donee of an enduring power of attorney or lasting power of attorney (within the meaning of that Act), or

        (b)   a deputy appointed, or any other person authorised, by the Court of Protection,

    with power in that respect.".

Local Authority Social Services Act 1970 (c 42)

16

(1)   Schedule 1 to the Local Authority Social Services Act 1970 (c 42) (enactments conferring functions assigned to social services committee) is amended as follows.

(2)   In the entry for section 49 of the National Assistance Act 1948 (expenses of local authority officer appointed for person who lacks capacity) for "receiver" substitute "deputy".

(3)   At the end, insert—

"Mental Capacity Act 2005	
Section 39	Instructing independent mental capacity advocate before providing accommodation for person lacking capacity.
Section 49	Reports in proceedings.".

Courts Act 1971 (c 23)

17

In Part 1A of Schedule 2 to the Courts Act 1971 (c 23) (office-holders eligible for appointment as circuit judges), omit the reference to a Master of the Court of Protection.

Local Government Act 1972 (c 70)

18

(1)   Omit section 118 of the Local Government Act 1972 (c 70) (payment of pension etc where recipient lacks capacity).

(2)   Sub-paragraph (3) applies where, before the commencement of this paragraph, a local authority has, in respect of a person referred to in that section as "the patient", made payments under that section—

   (a)   to an institution or person having the care of the patient, or

   (b)   in accordance with subsection (1)(a) or (b) of that section.

(3)   The local authority may, in respect of the patient, continue to make payments under that section to that institution or person, or in accordance with subsection (1)(a) or (b) of that section, despite the repeal made by sub-paragraph (1).

Matrimonial Causes Act 1973 (c 18)

19

In section 40 of the Matrimonial Causes Act 1973 (c 18) (payments to person who lacks capacity) (which becomes subsection (1))—

   (a)   for the words from "is incapable" to "affairs" substitute "("P") lacks capacity (within the meaning of the Mental Capacity Act 2005) in relation to the provisions of the order",

   (b)   for "that person under Part VIII of that Act" substitute "P under that Act",

   (c)   for the words from "such persons" to the end substitute "such person ("D") as it may direct", and

   (d)   at the end insert—

"(2) In carrying out any functions of his in relation to an order made under subsection (1), D must act in P's best interests (within the meaning of that Act).".

Juries Act 1974 (c 23)

20

In Schedule 1 to the Juries Act 1974 (c 23) (disqualification for jury service), for paragraph 3 substitute—

"3

A person who lacks capacity, within the meaning of the Mental Capacity Act 2005, to serve as a juror.".

Consumer Credit Act 1974 (c 39)

21

For section 37(1)(c) of the Consumer Credit Act 1974 (c 39) (termination of consumer credit licence if holder lacks capacity) substitute—

"(c) becomes a person who lacks capacity (within the meaning of the Mental Capacity Act 2005) to carry on the activities covered by the licence.".

Solicitors Act 1974 (c 47)

22

(1) The Solicitors Act 1974 (c 47) is amended as follows.

(2) . . .

(3) In section 62(4) (contentious business agreements made by clients) for paragraphs (c) and (d) substitute—

"(c) as a deputy for him appointed by the Court of Protection with powers in relation to his property and affairs, or

(d) as another person authorised under that Act to act on his behalf.".

(4) In paragraph 1(1) of Schedule 1 (circumstances in which Law Society may intervene in solicitor's practice), for paragraph (f) substitute—

"(f) a solicitor lacks capacity (within the meaning of the Mental Capacity Act 2005) to act as a solicitor and powers under sections 15 to 20 or section 48 of that Act are exercisable in relation to him;".

Local Government (Miscellaneous Provisions) Act 1976 (c 57)

23

In section 31 of the Local Government (Miscellaneous Provisions) Act 1976 (c 57) (the title to which becomes "Indemnities for local authority officers appointed as deputies or administrators"), for the words from "as a receiver" to "1959" substitute "as a deputy for a person by the Court of Protection".

Sale of Goods Act 1979 (c 54)

24

In section 3(2) of the Sale of Goods Act 1979 (c 54) (capacity to buy and sell) the words "mental incapacity or" cease to have effect in England and Wales.

Limitation Act 1980 (c 58)

25

In section 38 of the Limitation Act 1980 (c 58) (interpretation) substitute—

    (a)   in subsection (2) for "of unsound mind" substitute "lacks capacity (within the meaning of the Mental Capacity Act 2005) to conduct legal proceedings", and

    (b)   omit subsections (3) and (4).

Public Passenger Vehicles Act 1981 (c 14)

26

In section 57(2)(c) of the Public Passenger Vehicles Act 1981 (c 14) (termination of public service vehicle licence if holder lacks capacity) for the words from "becomes a patient" to "or" substitute "becomes a person who lacks capacity (within the meaning of the Mental Capacity Act 2005) to use a vehicle under the licence, or".

Judicial Pensions Act 1981 (c 20)

27

In Schedule 1 to the Judicial Pensions Act 1981 (c 20) (pensions of Supreme Court officers, etc), in paragraph 1, omit the reference to a Master of the Court of Protection except in the case of a person holding that office immediately before the commencement of this paragraph or who had previously retired from that office or died.

[Senior Courts Act 1981] (c 54)

28

In Schedule 2 to the [Senior Courts Act 1981] (c 54) (qualifications for appointment to office in Supreme Court), omit paragraph 11 (Master of the Court of Protection).

Mental Health Act 1983 (c 20)

29

(1)   The Mental Health Act is amended as follows.

(2)   In section 134(3) (cases where correspondence of detained patients may not be withheld) for paragraph (b) substitute—

        "(b)   any judge or officer of the Court of Protection, any of the Court of Protection Visitors or any person asked by that Court for a report under section 49 of the Mental Capacity Act 2005 concerning the patient;".

(3)   In section 139 (protection for acts done in pursuance of 1983 Act), in subsection (1), omit from "or in, or in pursuance" to "Part VII of this Act,".

(4)   Section 142 (payment of pension etc where recipient lacks capacity) ceases to have effect in England and Wales.

(5)   Sub-paragraph (6) applies where, before the commencement of sub-paragraph (4), an authority has, in respect of a person referred to in that section as "the patient", made payments under that section—

    (a)   to an institution or person having the care of the patient, or

    (b)   in accordance with subsection (2)(a) or (b) of that section.

(6)   The authority may, in respect of the patient, continue to make payments under that section to that institution or person, or in accordance with subsection (2)(a) or (b) of that section, despite the amendment made by sub-paragraph (4).

(7) In section 145(1) (interpretation), in the definition of "patient", omit " (except in Part VII of this Act)".

(8) In section 146 (provisions having effect in Scotland), omit from "104(4)" to "section),".

(9) In section 147 (provisions having effect in Northern Ireland), omit from "104(4)" to "section),".

Administration of Justice Act 1985 (c 61)

30

In section 18(3) of the Administration of Justice Act 1985 (c 61) (licensed conveyancer who lacks capacity), for the words from "that person" to the end substitute "he becomes a person who lacks capacity (within the meaning of the Mental Capacity Act 2005) to practise as a licensed conveyancer.".

Insolvency Act 1986 (c 45)

31

(1) The Insolvency Act 1986 (c 45) is amended as follows.

(2) . . .

(3) In section 390 (people not qualified to be insolvency practitioners), in subsection (4)—

    (a)   omit the "or" immediately after paragraph (b),

    (b)   in paragraph (c), omit "Part VII of the Mental Health Act 1983 or", and

    (c)   after that paragraph, insert

    ", or

    (d)   he lacks capacity (within the meaning of the Mental Capacity Act 2005) to act as an insolvency practitioner.".

Building Societies Act 1986 (c 53)

32

In section 102D(9) of the Building Societies Act 1986 (c 53) (references to a person holding an account on trust for another)—

    (a)   in paragraph (a), for "Part VII of the Mental Health Act 1983" substitute "the Mental Capacity Act 2005", and

    (b)   for paragraph (b) substitute—

    "(b) to an attorney holding an account for another person under—

        (i)   an enduring power of attorney or lasting power of attorney registered under the Mental Capacity Act 2005, or

        (ii)   an enduring power registered under the Enduring Powers of Attorney (Northern Ireland) Order 1987;".

Public Trustee and Administration of Funds Act 1986 (c 57)

33

In section 3 of the Public Trustee and Administration of Funds Act 1986 (c 57) (functions of the Public Trustee)—

    (a)   for subsections (1) to (5) substitute—

    "(1)   The Public Trustee may exercise the functions of a deputy appointed by the Court of Protection.",

    (b)   in subsection (6), for "the 1906 Act" substitute "the Public Trustee Act 1906", and

(c)   omit subsection (7).

Patronage (Benefices) Measure 1986 (No 3)

34

(1)   The Patronage (Benefices) Measure 1986 (No 3) is amended as follows.

(2)   In section 5 (rights of patronage exercisable otherwise than by registered patron), after subsection (3) insert—

"(3A)   The reference in subsection (3) to a power of attorney does not include an enduring power of attorney or lasting power of attorney (within the meaning of the Mental Capacity Act 2005)."

(3)   In section 9 (information to be sent to designated officer when benefice becomes vacant), after subsection (5) insert—

"(5A)   Subsections (5B) and (5C) apply where the functions of a registered patron are, as a result of paragraph 10 of Schedule 2 to the Mental Capacity Act 2005 (patron's loss of capacity to discharge functions), to be discharged by an individual appointed by the Court of Protection.

(5B)   If the individual is a clerk in Holy Orders, subsection (5) applies to him as it applies to the registered patron.

(5C)   If the individual is not a clerk in Holy Orders, subsection (1) (other than paragraph (b)) applies to him as it applies to the registered patron."

Courts and Legal Services Act 1990 (c 41)

35

(1)   The Courts and Legal Services Act 1990 (c 41) is amended as follows.

(2)   In Schedule 11 (judges etc barred from legal practice), for the reference to a Master of the Court of Protection substitute a reference to each of the following—

(a)   Senior Judge of the Court of Protection,

(b)   President of the Court of Protection,

(c)   Vice-President of the Court of Protection.

(3)   In paragraph 5(3) of Schedule 14 (exercise of powers of intervention in registered foreign lawyer's practice), for paragraph (f) substitute—

"(f)   he lacks capacity (within the meaning of the Mental Capacity Act 2005) to act as a registered foreign lawyer and powers under sections 15 to 20 or section 48 are exercisable in relation to him;".

Child Support Act 1991 (c 48)

36

In section 50 of the Child Support Act 1991 (c 48) (unauthorised disclosure of information)—

(a)   in subsection (8)—

(i)   immediately after paragraph (a), insert "or",

(ii)   omit paragraphs (b) and (d) and the "or" immediately after paragraph (c), and

(iii)   for ", receiver, custodian or appointee" substitute "or custodian", and

(b)   after that subsection, insert—

"(9)   Where the person to whom the information relates lacks capacity (within the meaning of the Mental Capacity Act 2005) to consent to its disclosure, the appropriate person is—

> (a)   a donee of an enduring power of attorney or lasting power of attorney (within the meaning of that Act), or
>
> (b)   a deputy appointed for him, or any other person authorised, by the Court of Protection,

with power in that respect.".

Social Security Administration Act 1992 (c 5)

37

In section 123 of the Social Security Administration Act 1992 (c 5) (unauthorised disclosure of information)—

> (a)   in subsection (10), omit—
>
> > (i)   in paragraph (b), "a receiver appointed under section 99 of the Mental Health Act 1983 or",
> >
> > (ii)   in paragraph (d)(i), "sub-paragraph (a) of rule 41(1) of the Court of Protection Rules 1984 or",
> >
> > (iii) in paragraph (d)(ii), "a receiver ad interim appointed under sub-paragraph (b) of the said rule 41(1) or", and
> >
> > (iv)   "receiver,", and
>
> (b)   after that subsection, insert—

"(11)   Where the person to whom the information relates lacks capacity (within the meaning of the Mental Capacity Act 2005) to consent to its disclosure, the appropriate person is—

> (a)   a donee of an enduring power of attorney or lasting power of attorney (within the meaning of that Act), or
>
> (b)   a deputy appointed for him, or any other person authorised, by the Court of Protection,

with power in that respect.".

Judicial Pensions and Retirement Act 1993 (c 8)

38

(1)   The Judicial Pensions and Retirement Act 1993 (c 8) is amended as follows.

(2)   In Schedule 1 (qualifying judicial offices), in Part 2, under the cross-heading "Court officers", omit the reference to a Master of the Court of Protection except in the case of a person holding that office immediately before the commencement of this sub-paragraph or who had previously retired from that office or died.

(3)   In Schedule 5 (retirement: the relevant offices), omit the entries relating to the Master and Deputy or temporary Master of the Court of Protection, except in the case of a person holding any of those offices immediately before the commencement of this sub-paragraph.

(4)   In Schedule 7 (retirement: transitional provisions), omit paragraph 5(5)(i)(g) except in the case of a person holding office as a deputy or temporary Master of the Court of Protection immediately before the commencement of this sub-paragraph.

Leasehold Reform, Housing and Urban Development Act 1993 (c 28)

39

(1)   For paragraph 4 of Schedule 2 to the Leasehold Reform, Housing and Urban Development Act 1993 (c 28) (landlord under a disability), substitute—

"4

(1)   This paragraph applies where a Chapter I or Chapter II landlord lacks capacity (within the meaning of the Mental Capacity Act 2005) to exercise his functions as a landlord.

(2)   For the purposes of the Chapter concerned, the landlord's place is to be taken—

(a)   by a donee of an enduring power of attorney or lasting power of attorney (within the meaning of the 2005 Act), or a deputy appointed for him by the Court of Protection, with power to exercise those functions, or

(b)   if no deputy or donee has that power, by a person authorised in that respect by that court.".

(2)   That amendment does not affect any proceedings pending at the commencement of this paragraph in which a receiver or a person authorised under Part 7 of the Mental Health Act 1983 (c 20) is acting on behalf of the landlord.

Goods Vehicles (Licensing of Operators) Act 1995 (c 23)

40

(1)   The Goods Vehicles (Licensing of Operators) Act 1995 (c 23) is amended as follows.

(2)   In section 16(5) (termination of licence), for "he becomes a patient within the meaning of Part VII of the Mental Health Act 1983" substitute "he becomes a person who lacks capacity (within the meaning of the Mental Capacity Act 2005) to use a vehicle under the licence".

(3)   In section 48 (licence not to be transferable, etc)—

(a)   in subsection (2)—

(i)   for "or become a patient within the meaning of Part VII of the Mental Health Act 1983" substitute ", or become a person who lacks capacity (within the meaning of the Mental Capacity Act 2005) to use a vehicle under the licence,", and

(ii)   in paragraph (a), for "became a patient" substitute "became a person who lacked capacity in that respect", and

(b)   in subsection (5), for "a patient within the meaning of Part VII of the Mental Health Act 1983" substitute "a person lacking capacity".

Disability Discrimination Act 1995 (c 50)

41

In section 20(7) of the Disability Discrimination Act 1995 (c 50) (regulations to disapply provisions about incapacity), in paragraph (b), for "Part VII of the Mental Health Act 1983" substitute "the Mental Capacity Act 2005".

Trusts of Land and Appointment of Trustees Act 1996 (c 47)

42

(1)   The Trusts of Land and Appointment of Trustees Act 1996 (c 47) is amended as follows.

(2)   In section 9 (delegation by trustees), in subsection (6), for the words from "an enduring power" to the end substitute "an enduring power of attorney or lasting power of attorney within the meaning of the Mental Capacity Act 2005".

(3)   In section 20 (the title to which becomes "Appointment of substitute for trustee who lacks capacity")—

(a) in subsection (1)(a), for "is incapable by reason of mental disorder of exercising" substitute "lacks capacity (within the meaning of the Mental Capacity Act 2005) to exercise", and

(b) in subsection (2)—

(i) for paragraph (a) substitute—

"(a) a deputy appointed for the trustee by the Court of Protection,",

(ii) in paragraph (b), for the words from "a power of attorney" to the end substitute "an enduring power of attorney or lasting power of attorney registered under the Mental Capacity Act 2005", and

(iii) in paragraph (c), for the words from "the authority" to the end substitute "the Court of Protection".

Human Rights Act 1998 (c 42)

43

In section 4(5) of the Human Rights Act 1998 (c 42) (courts which may make declarations of incompatibility), after paragraph (e) insert—

"(f) the Court of Protection, in any matter being dealt with by the President of the Family Division, the Vice-Chancellor or a puisne judge of the High Court."

. . .

44

. . .

Adoption and Children Act 2002 (c 38)

45

In section 52(1)(a) of the Adoption and Children Act 2002 (c 38) (parental consent to adoption), for "is incapable of giving consent" substitute "lacks capacity (within the meaning of the Mental Capacity Act 2005) to give consent".

Licensing Act 2003 (c 17)

46

(1) The Licensing Act 2003 (c 17) is amended as follows.

(2) In section 27(1) (lapse of premises licence), for paragraph (b) substitute—

"(b) becomes a person who lacks capacity (within the meaning of the Mental Capacity Act 2005) to hold the licence,".

(3) In section 47 (interim authority notice in relation to premises licence)—

(a) in subsection (5), for paragraph (b) substitute—

"(b) the former holder lacks capacity (within the meaning of the Mental Capacity Act 2005) to hold the licence and that person acts for him under an enduring power of attorney or lasting power of attorney registered under that Act,", and

(b) in subsection (10), omit the definition of "mentally incapable".

Courts Act 2003 (c 39)

47

(1) The Courts Act 2003 (c 39) is amended as follows.

(2)   In section 1(1) (the courts in relation to which the Lord Chancellor must discharge his general duty), after paragraph (a) insert—
>   "(aa) the Court of Protection,".

(3)   In section 64(2) (judicial titles which the Lord Chancellor may by order alter)—
>   (a)   omit the reference to a Master of the Court of Protection, and
>   (b)   at the appropriate place insert a reference to each of the following—
>>   (i)   Senior Judge of the Court of Protection,
>>   (ii)   President of the Court of Protection,
>>   (iii)   Vice-president of the Court of Protection.

SCHEDULE 7

REPEALS

Section 67(2)

Short title and chapter	Extent of repeal
Trustee Act 1925 (c 19)	Section 54(3).
Law of Property Act 1925 (c 20)	Section 205(1)(xiii).
Administration of Estates Act 1925 (c 23)	Section 55(1)(viii)
USA Veterans' Pensions (Administration) Act 1949 (c 45)	In section 1(4), the words from "or for whom" to "1983".
Mental Health Act 1959 (c 72)	In Schedule 7, in Part 1, the entries relating to—
	section 33 of the Fines and Recoveries Act 1833,
	section 68 of the Improvement of Land Act 1864,
	section 55 of the Trustee Act 1925,
	section 205(1) of the Law of Property Act 1925,
	section 49 of the National Assistance Act 1948, and
	section 1 of the Variation of Trusts Act 1958.
Courts Act 1971 (c 23)	In Schedule 2, in Part 1A, the words "Master of the Court of Protection".
Local Government Act 1972 (c 70)	Section 118.
Limitation Act 1980 (c 58)	Section 38(3) and (4).
[Senior Courts Act 1981] (c 54)	In Schedule 2, in Part 2, paragraph 11.
Mental Health Act 1983 (c 20)	Part 7.
	In section 139(1) the words from "or in, or in pursuance" to "Part VII of this Act,".
	In section 145(1), in the definition of "patient" the words "(except in Part VII of this Act)".
	In sections 146 and 147 the words from "104(4)" to "section),".
	Schedule 3.
	In Schedule 4, paragraphs 1, 2, 4, 5, 7, 9, 14, 20, 22, 25, 32, 38, 55 and 56.
	In Schedule 5, paragraphs 26, 43, 44 and 45.

Enduring Powers of Attorney Act 1985 (c 29)	The whole Act.
Insolvency Act 1986 (c 45)	In section 389A(3)—
	the "or" immediately after paragraph (b), and in paragraph (c), the words "Part VII of the Mental Health Act 1983 or".
	In section 390(4)—
	the "or" immediately after paragraph (b), and in paragraph (c), the words "Part VII of the Mental Health Act 1983 or".
Public Trustee and Administration of Funds Act 1986 (c 57)	Section 2.
	Section 3(7).
Child Support Act 1991 (c 48)	In section 50(8)—
	paragraphs (b) and (d), and the "or" immediately after paragraph (c).
Social Security Administration Act 1992 (c 5)	In section 123(10)—
	in paragraph (b), "a receiver appointed under section 99 of the Mental Health Act 1983 or",
	in paragraph (d)(i), "sub-paragraph (a) of rule 41(1) of the Court of Protection Rules Act 1984 or",
	in paragraph (d)(ii), "a receiver ad interim appointed under sub-paragraph (b) of the said rule 41(1) or", and
	"receiver,".
Trustee Delegation Act 1999 (c 15)	Section 4.
	Section 6.
	In section 7(3), the words "in accordance with section 4 above".
Care Standards Act 2000 (c 14)	In Schedule 4, paragraph 8.
Licensing Act 2003 (c 17)	In section 47(10), the definition of "mentally incapable".
Courts Act 2003 (c 64)	In section 64(2), the words "Master of the Court of Protection".

Appendix B

STATUTORY INSTRUMENTS

B1 Lasting Powers of Attorney, Enduring Powers of Attorney and Public Guardian Regulations 2007

B2 Court of Protection Rules 2007

2007 No 1253

LASTING POWERS OF ATTORNEY, ENDURING POWERS OF ATTORNEY AND PUBLIC GUARD-IAN REGULATIONS 2007

PART 1 PRELIMINARY

B1

1 Citation and commencement

(1) These Regulations may be cited as the Lasting Powers of Attorney, Enduring Powers of Attorney and Public Guardian Regulations 2007.

(2) These Regulations shall come into force on 1 October 2007.

2 Interpretation

(1) In these Regulations—

"the Act" means the Mental Capacity Act 2005;

"court" means the Court of Protection;

"LPA certificate", in relation to an instrument made with a view to creating a lasting power of attorney, means the certificate which is required to be included in the instrument by virtue of paragraph 2(1)(e) of Schedule 1 to the Act;

"[person to notify]", in relation to an instrument made with a view to creating a lasting power of attorney, means a person who[, under Schedule 1, paragraph 2(1)(c)(i) of the Act,] is named in the instrument as being a person to be notified of any application for the registration of the instrument;

"prescribed information", in relation to any instrument intended to create a lasting power of attorney, means the information contained in the form used for the instrument which appears under the heading ["Section 8—Your legal rights and responsibilities"].

3 Minimal differences from forms prescribed in these Regulations

(1) In these Regulations, any reference to a form—

    (a)   in the case of a form set out in Schedules 1 to 7 to these Regulations, is to be regarded as including a Welsh version of that form; and

    (b)   in the case of a form set out in Schedules 2 to 7 to these Regulations, is to be regarded as also including—

        (i)   a form to the same effect but which differs in an immaterial respect in form or mode of expression;

(ii)   a form to the same effect but with such variations as the circumstances may require or the court or the Public Guardian may approve; or

(iii)   a Welsh version of a form within (i) or (ii).

4 Computation of time

(1)   This regulation shows how to calculate any period of time which is specified in these Regulations.

(2)   A period of time expressed as a number of days must be computed as clear days.

(3)   Where the specified period is 7 days or less, and would include a day which is not a business day, that day does not count.

(4)   When the specified period for doing any act at the office of the Public Guardian ends on a day on which the office is closed, that act will be done in time if done on the next day on which the office is open.

(5)   In this regulation—

"business day" means a day other than—

(a)   a Saturday, Sunday, Christmas Day or Good Friday; or

(b)   a bank holiday under the Banking and Financial Dealings Act 1971, in England and Wales; and

"clear days" means that in computing the number of days—

(a)   the day on which the period begins, and

(b)   if the end of the period is defined by reference to an event, the day on which that event occurs,

are not included.

PART 2 LASTING POWERS OF ATTORNEY

Instruments intended to create a lasting power of attorney

5 Forms for lasting powers of attorney

The forms set out in Parts 1 and 2 of Schedule 1 to these Regulations are the forms which, in the circumstances to which they apply, are to be used for instruments intended to create a lasting power of attorney.

6 Maximum number of [people to notify]

The maximum number of [people to notify] that the donor of a lasting power of attorney may specify in the instrument intended to create the power is 5.

7 . . .

. . .

Amendment

Revoked by SI 2015/899, regs 2, 6.

8 Persons who may provide an LPA certificate

(1)   Subject to paragraph (3), the following persons may give an LPA certificate—

(a)   a person chosen by the donor as being someone who has known him personally for the period of at least two years which ends immediately before the date on which that person signs the LPA certificate;

(b)   a person chosen by the donor who, on account of his professional skills and expertise, reasonably considers that he is competent to make the judgments necessary to certify the matters set out in paragraph (2)(1)(e) of Schedule 1 to the Act.

(2)   The following are examples of persons within paragraph (1)(b)—

(a)   a registered health care professional;

(b)   a barrister, solicitor or advocate called or admitted in any part of the United Kingdom;

(c)   a registered social worker; or

(d)   an independent mental capacity advocate.

(3) A person is disqualified from giving an LPA certificate in respect of any instrument intended to create a lasting power of attorney if that person is—

(a)   a family member of the donor;

(b)   a donee of that power;

(c)   a donee of—

    (i)   any other lasting power of attorney, or

    (ii)   an enduring power of attorney,

which has been executed by the donor (whether or not it has been revoked);

(d)   a family member of a donee within sub-paragraph (b);

(e)   a director or employee of a trust corporation acting as a donee within sub-paragraph (b);

(f)   a business partner or employee of—

    (i)   the donor, or

    (ii)   a donee within sub-paragraph (b);

(g)   an owner, director, manager or employee of any care home in which the donor is living when the instrument is executed; or

(h)   a family member of a person within sub-paragraph (g).

(4) In this regulation—

"care home" has the meaning given in section 3 of the Care Standards Act 2000;

"registered health care professional" means a person who is a member of a profession regulated by a body mentioned in section 25(3) of the National Health Service Reform and Health Care Professions Act 2002; and

"registered social worker" means a person registered as a social worker in a register maintained by—

[(a)   the Health and Care Professions Council;]

(b)   [Social Care Wales];

(c)   the Scottish Social Services Council; or

(d)   the Northern Ireland Social Care Council.

9 Execution of instrument

(1) An instrument intended to create a lasting power of attorney must be executed in accordance with this regulation.

(2) The donor must read (or have read to him) all the prescribed information.

(3) As soon as reasonably practicable after the steps required by paragraph (2) have been taken, the donor must—

(a)   complete the provisions of [Sections 1 to 7] of the instrument that apply to him (or direct another person to do so); and

[(b)   subject to paragraph (7), in the presence of a witness—

    (i)   sign Section 9 of the instrument if the instrument is intended to create a lasting power of attorney for property and financial affairs (Form LP1F); or

    (ii)   sign Sections 5 and 9 of the instrument if the instrument is intended to create a lasting power of attorney for health and welfare (Form LP1H)].

(4) As soon as reasonably practicable after the steps required by paragraph (3) have been taken—

(a)   the person giving an LPA certificate. . .

(b)   . . .

must complete the LPA certificate at [Section 10] of the instrument and sign it.

(5) As soon as reasonably practicable after the steps required by paragraph (4) have been taken—

    (a)   the donee, or

    (b)   if more than one, each of the donees,

must read (or have read to him) all the prescribed information.

(6) As soon as reasonably practicable after the steps required by paragraph (5) have been taken, the donee or, if more than one, each of them—

    (a)   must complete the provisions of [Section 11] of the instrument that apply to him (or direct another person to do so); and

    (b)   subject to paragraph (7), must sign [Section 11] of the instrument in the presence of a witness.

(7) If the instrument is to be signed by any person at the direction of the donor, or at the direction of any donee, the signature must be done in the presence of two witnesses.

(8) For the purposes of this regulation—

    (a)   the donor may not witness any signature required for the power;

    (b)   a donee may not witness any signature required for the power apart from that of another donee.

(9) A person witnessing a signature must—

    (a)   sign the instrument; and

    (b)   give his full name and address.

(10) Any reference in this regulation to a person signing an instrument (however expressed) includes his signing it by means of a mark made on the instrument at the appropriate place.

Registering the instrument

10 Notice to be given by a person about to apply for registration of lasting power of attorney

Schedule 2 to these Regulations sets out the form of notice [(Form LPA3)] which must be given by a donor or donee who is about to make an application for the registration of an instrument intended to create a lasting power of attorney.

[11 Application for registration]

[(1) An application to the Public Guardian for the registration of an instrument intended to create a lasting power of attorney that is in Form LP1F or LP1H must be made by completion of Sections 12 and 13, the relevant parts of Section 14 and Section 15 of that Form.

(2) An application to the Public Guardian for the registration of an instrument intended to create a lasting power of attorney that is in a pre-July 2015 form must be made by using Form LP2 set out in Schedule 3 to these Regulations.

(3) An application to the Public Guardian for the registration of an instrument intended to create a lasting power of attorney where the application is a repeat application ("a reduced fee repeat application") may only be made if—

    (a)   the initial application for the registration of a lasting power of attorney is made on or after 1st October 2011;

    (b)   the initial application was returned to the applicant as invalid;

    (c)   the reduced fee repeat application is submitted for registration within three months of the date on which the initial application was returned to the applicant as invalid; and

    (d)   the reduced fee for such applications applies.

(4) Where the initial application for the registration of the lasting power of attorney was made in accordance with paragraph (1) using Form LP1F or LP1H, a reduced fee

repeat application must also be made by the completion of Form LP1F or LP1H as appropriate, including completion of the repeat application option in Section 14 of that Form.

(5) Where the initial application for the registration of the lasting power of attorney was made in accordance with paragraph (2) using a pre-July 2015 form, a reduced fee repeat application must be made by the completion of Form LP1F or LP1H as appropriate, including completion of the repeat application option in Section 14 of that Form.

(6) Where the instrument to be registered which is sent with the application is neither—

(a) the original instrument intended to create the power; nor

(b) a certified copy of it,

the Public Guardian must not register the instrument unless the court directs the Public Guardian to do so.

(7) In this regulation—

(a) "pre-July 2015 form" means a valid instrument intended to create a lasting power of attorney that is not in Form LP1F or LP1H but that complies with these Regulations as they were in force immediately before 1st July 2015; and

(b) "certified copy" means a photographic or other facsimile copy which is certified as an accurate copy by—

(i) the donor; or

(ii) a solicitor or notary.]

12 Period to elapse before registration in cases not involving objection or defect

The period at the end of which the Public Guardian must register an instrument in accordance with paragraph 5 of Schedule 1 to the Act is the period of [4 weeks] beginning with—

(a) the date on which the Public Guardian gave the notice or notices under paragraph 7 or 8 of Schedule 1 to the Act of receipt of an application for registration; or

(b) if notices were given on more than one date, the latest of those dates.

13 Notice of receipt of application for registration

(1) Part 1 of Schedule 4 to these Regulations sets out the form of notice ("LPA 003A") which the Public Guardian must give to the donee (or donees) when the Public Guardian receives an application for the registration of a lasting power of attorney.

(2) Part 2 of Schedule 4 sets out the form of notice ("LPA 003B") which the Public Guardian must give to the donor when the Public Guardian receives such an application.

(3) Where it appears to the Public Guardian that there is good reason to do so, the Public Guardian must also provide (or arrange for the provision of) an explanation to the donor of—

(a) the notice referred to in paragraph (2) and what the effect of it is; and

(b) why it is being brought to his attention.

(4) Any information provided under paragraph (3) must be provided—

(a) to the donor personally; and

(b) in a way that is appropriate to the donor's circumstances (for example using simple language, visual aids or other appropriate means).

14 Objection to registration: notice to Public Guardian [to be given by the donee of the power or a named person]

(1) This regulation deals with any objection to the registration of an instrument as a lasting power of attorney which is to be made to the Public Guardian [by the donee of the power or a] [person to notify].

(2)   Where [the donee of the power or a] [person to notify]—
  (a)   is entitled to receive notice under paragraph 6, 7 or 8 of Schedule 1 to the Act of an application for the registration of the instrument, and
  (b)   wishes to object to registration on a ground set out in paragraph 13(1) of Schedule 1 to the Act,
he must do so before the end of the period of [3 weeks] beginning with the date on which the notice is given.

(3)   A notice of objection must be given in writing, setting out—
  (a)   the name and address of the objector;
  (b)   . . . the name and address of the donor of the power;
  (c)   if known, the name and address of the donee (or donees); and
  (d)   the ground for making the objection.

(4)   The Public Guardian must notify the objector as to whether he is satisfied that the ground of the objection is established.

(5)   At any time after receiving the notice of objection and before giving the notice required by paragraph (4), the Public Guardian may require the objector to provide such further information, or produce such documents, as the Public Guardian reasonably considers necessary to enable him to determine whether the ground for making the objection is established.

(6)   Where—
  (a)   the Public Guardian is satisfied that the ground of the objection is established, but
  (b)   by virtue of section 13(7) of the Act, the instrument is not revoked,
the notice under paragraph (4) must contain a statement to that effect.

(7)   Nothing in this regulation prevents an objector from making a further objection under paragraph 13 of Schedule 1 to the Act where—
  (a)   the notice under paragraph (4) indicates that the Public Guardian is not satisfied that the particular ground of objection to which that notice relates is established; and
  (b)   the period specified in paragraph (2) has not expired.

[14A Objection to registration: notice to Public Guardian to be given by the donor]
[(1)   This regulation deals with any objection to the registration of an instrument as a lasting power of attorney which is to be made to the Public Guardian by the donor of the power.

(2)   Where the donor of the power—
  (a)   is entitled to receive notice under paragraph 8 of Schedule 1 to the Act of an application for the registration of the instrument, and
  (b)   wishes to object to the registration,
he must do so before the end of the period of [3 weeks] beginning with the date on which the notice is given.

(3)   The donor of the power must give notice of his objection in writing to the Public Guardian, setting out—
  (a)   the name and address of the donor of the power;
  (b)   if known, the name and address of the donee (or donees); and
  (c)   the ground for making the objection.]

15 Objection to registration: application to the court
(1)   This regulation deals with any objection to the registration of an instrument as a lasting power of attorney which is to be made to the court.

(2)   The grounds for making an application to the court are—
  (a)   that one or more of the requirements for the creation of a lasting power of attorney have not been met;

    (b)   that the power has been revoked, or has otherwise come to an end, on a ground other than the grounds set out in paragraph 13(1) of Schedule 1 to the Act;

    (c)   any of the grounds set out in paragraph (a) or (b) of section 22(3) of the Act.

(3)   Where any person—

    (a)   is entitled to receive notice under paragraph 6, 7 or 8 of Schedule 1 to the Act of an application for the registration of the instrument, and

    (b)   wishes to object to registration on one or more of the grounds set out in paragraph (2),

he must make an application to the court before the end of the period of [3 weeks] beginning with the date on which the notice is given.

(4)   The notice of an application to the court, which a person making an objection to the court is required to give to the Public Guardian under paragraph 13(3)(b)(ii) of Schedule 1 to the Act, must be in writing.

16 Notifying applicants of non-registration of lasting power of attorney

Where the Public Guardian is prevented from registering an instrument as a lasting power of attorney by virtue of—

    (a)   paragraph 11(1) of Schedule 1 to the Act (instrument not made in accordance with Schedule),

    (b)   paragraph 12(2) of that Schedule (deputy already appointed),

    (c)   paragraph 13(2) of that Schedule (objection by donee or named person on grounds of bankruptcy, disclaimer, death etc),

    (d)   paragraph 14(2) of that Schedule (objection by donor), or

    (e)   regulation 11(2) of these Regulations (application for registration not accompanied by original instrument or certified copy),

he must notify the person (or persons) who applied for registration of that fact.

17 Notice to be given on registration of lasting power of attorney

(1)   Where the Public Guardian registers an instrument as a lasting power of attorney, he must—

    (a)   retain a copy of the instrument; and

    (b)   return to the person (or persons) who applied for registration the original instrument, or the certified copy of it, which accompanied the application for registration.

(2)   Schedule 5 to these Regulations sets out the form of notice ("LPA 004") which the Public Guardian must give to the donor and donee (or donees) when the Public Guardian registers an instrument.

(3)   Where it appears to the Public Guardian that there is good reason to do so, the Public Guardian must also provide (or arrange for the provision of) an explanation to the donor of—

    (a)   the notice referred to in paragraph (2) and what the effect of it is; and

    (b)   why it is being brought to his attention.

(4)   Any information provided under paragraph (3) must be provided—

    (a)   to the donor personally; and

    (b)   in a way that is appropriate to the donor's circumstances (for example using simple language, visual aids or other appropriate means).

(5)   "Certified copy" is to be construed in accordance with regulation 11(3).

Post-registration

18 Changes to instrument registered as lasting power of attorney

(1) This regulation applies in any case where any of paragraphs 21 to 24 of Schedule 1 to the Act requires the Public Guardian to attach a note to an instrument registered as a lasting power of attorney.

(2) The Public Guardian must give a notice to the donor and the donee (or, if more than one, each of them) requiring him to deliver to the Public Guardian—

    (a)   the original . . . instrument which was sent to the Public Guardian for registration;

    (b)   any office copy of that registered instrument; and

    (c)   any certified copy of that registered instrument.

(3) On receipt of the document, the Public Guardian must—

    (a)   attach the required note; and

    (b)   return the document to the person from whom it was obtained.

19 Loss or destruction of instrument registered as lasting power of attorney

(1) This regulation applies where—

    (a)   a person is required by or under the Act to deliver up to the Public Guardian any of the following documents—

        (i)   an instrument registered as a lasting power of attorney;

        (ii)   an office copy of that registered instrument;

        (iii)   a certified copy of that registered instrument; and

    (b)   the document has been lost or destroyed.

(2) The person required to deliver up the document must provide to the Public Guardian in writing—

    (a)   if known, the date of the loss or destruction and the circumstances in which it occurred;

    (b)   otherwise, a statement of when he last had the document in his possession.

20 Disclaimer of appointment by a donee of lasting power of attorney

(1) Schedule 6 to these Regulations sets out the form ("LPA 005") which a donee of an instrument registered as a lasting power of attorney must use to disclaim his appointment as donee.

(2) The donee must send—

    (a)   the completed form to the donor; and

    (b)   a copy of it to—

        (i)   the Public Guardian; and

        (ii)   any other donee who, for the time being, is appointed under the power.

21 Revocation by donor of lasting power of attorney

(1) A donor who revokes a lasting power to attorney must—

    (a)   notify the Public Guardian that he has done so; and

    (b)   notify the donee (or, if more than one, each of them) of the revocation.

(2) Where the Public Guardian receives a notice under paragraph (1)(a), he must cancel the registration of the instrument creating the power if he is satisfied that the donor has taken such steps as are necessary in law to revoke it.

(3) The Public Guardian may require the donor to provide such further information, or produce such documents, as the Public Guardian reasonably considers necessary to enable him to determine whether the steps necessary for revocation have been taken.

(4) Where the Public Guardian cancels the registration of the instrument he must notify—

(a)   the donor; and

(b)   the donee or, if more than one, each of them.

22 Revocation of a lasting power of attorney on death of donor

(1)   The Public Guardian must cancel the registration of an instrument as a lasting power of attorney if he is satisfied that the power has been revoked as a result of the donor's death.

(2)   Where the Public Guardian cancels the registration of an instrument he must notify the donee or, if more than one, each of them.

PART 3   ENDURING POWERS OF ATTORNEY

23 Notice of intention to apply for registration of enduring power of attorney

(1)   Schedule 7 to these Regulations sets out the form of notice ("EP1PG") which an attorney (or attorneys) under an enduring power of attorney must give of his intention to make an application for the registration of the instrument creating the power.

(2)   In the case of the notice to be given to the donor, the attorney must also provide (or arrange for the provision of) an explanation to the donor of—

(a)   the notice and what the effect of it is; and

(b)   why it is being brought to his attention.

(3)   The information provided under paragraph (2) must be provided—

(a)   to the donor personally; and

(b)   in a way that is appropriate to the donor's circumstances (for example using simple language, visual aids or other appropriate means).

24 Application for registration

(1)   Schedule 8 to these Regulations sets out the form ("EP2PG") which must be used for making an application to the Public Guardian for the registration of an instrument creating an enduring power of attorney.

[(1A)   The Public Guardian must not register an instrument where only a certified copy of the instrument is sent with the application, unless the applicant verifies that he cannot produce the original instrument because it has been lost or, as the case may be, destroyed.]

(2)   Where the instrument to be registered which is sent with the application is neither—

(a)   the original instrument creating the power, nor

(b)   a certified copy of it [in relation to which paragraph (1A) has been complied with],

the Public Guardian must not register the instrument unless the court directs him to do so.

(3)   "Certified copy", in relation to an enduring power of attorney, means a copy certified in accordance with section 3 of the Powers of Attorney Act 1971.

25 Notice of objection to registration

(1)   This regulation deals with any objection to the registration of an instrument creating an enduring power of attorney which is to be made to the Public Guardian under paragraph 13(4) of Schedule 4 to the Act.

(2)   A notice of objection must be given in writing, setting out—

(a)   the name and address of the objector;

(b)   if different, the name and address of the donor of the power;

(c)   if known, the name and address of the attorney (or attorneys); and

(d)   the ground for making the objection.

26 Notifying applicants of non-registration of enduring power of attorney

Where the Public Guardian is prevented from registering an instrument creating an enduring power of attorney by virtue of—

(a) paragraph 13(2) of Schedule 4 to the Act (deputy already appointed),

(b) paragraph 13(5) of that Schedule (receipt by Public Guardian of valid notice of objection from person entitled to notice of application to register),

(c) paragraph 13(7) of that Schedule (Public Guardian required to undertake appropriate enquiries in certain circumstances), or

(d) regulation 24(2) of these Regulations (application for registration not accompanied by original instrument or certified copy),

he must notify the person (or persons) who applied for registration of that fact.

27 Registration of instrument creating an enduring power of attorney

(1) Where the Public Guardian registers an instrument creating an enduring power of attorney, he must—

(a) retain a copy of the instrument; and

(b) return to the person (or persons) who applied for registration the original instrument, or the certified copy of it, which accompanied the application.

(2) "Certified copy" has the same meaning as in regulation 24(3).

28 Objection or revocation not applying to all joint and several attorneys

In a case within paragraph 20(6) or (7) of Schedule 4 to the Act, the form of the entry to be made in the register in respect of an instrument creating the enduring power of attorney is a stamp bearing the following words (inserting the information indicated, as appropriate)—

"THE REGISTRATION OF THIS ENDURING POWER OF ATTORNEY IS QUALIFIED AND EXTENDS TO THE APPOINTMENT OF .... (insert name of attorney(s) not affected by ground(s) of objection or revocation) ONLY AS THE ATTORNEY(S) OF .... (insert name of donor)".

29 Loss or destruction of instrument registered as enduring power of attorney

(1) This regulation applies where—

(a) a person is required by or under the Act to deliver up to the Public Guardian any of the following documents—

(i) an instrument registered as an enduring power of attorney;

(ii) an office copy of that registered instrument; or

(iii) a certified copy of that registered instrument; and

(b) the document has been lost or destroyed.

(2) The person who is required to deliver up the document must provide to the Public Guardian in writing—

(a) if known, the date of the loss or destruction and the circumstances in which it occurred;

(b) otherwise, a statement of when he last had the document in his possession.

PART 4   FUNCTIONS OF THE PUBLIC GUARDIAN

The registers

30 Establishing and maintaining the registers

(1) In this Part "the registers" means—

(a) the register of lasting powers of attorney,

    (b)   the register of enduring powers of attorney, and

    (c)   the register of court orders appointing deputies,

which the Public Guardian must establish and maintain.

(2)   On each register the Public Guardian may include—

    (a)   such descriptions of information about a registered instrument or a registered order as the Public Guardian considers appropriate; and

    (b)   entries which relate to an instrument or order for which registration has been cancelled.

31 Disclosure of information on a register: search by the Public Guardian

(1)   Any person may, by an application made under paragraph (2), request the Public Guardian to carry out a search of one or more of the registers.

(2)   An application must—

    (a)   state—

        (i)   the register or registers to be searched;

        (ii)   the name of the person to whom the application relates; and

        (iii)   such other details about that person as the Public Guardian may require for the purpose of carrying out the search; and

    (b)   be accompanied by any fee provided for under section 58(4)(b) of the Act.

(3)   The Public Guardian may require the applicant to provide such further information, or produce such documents, as the Public Guardian reasonably considers necessary to enable him to carry out the search.

(4)   As soon as reasonably practicable after receiving the application—

    (a)   the Public Guardian must notify the applicant of the result of the search; and

    (b)   in the event that it reveals one or more entries on the register, the Public Guardian must disclose to the applicant all the information appearing on the register in respect of each entry.

32 Disclosure of additional information held by the Public Guardian

(1)   This regulation applies in any case where, as a result of a search made under regulation 31, a person has obtained information relating to a registered instrument or a registered order which confers authority to make decisions about matters concerning a person ("P").

(2)   On receipt of an application made in accordance with paragraph (4), the Public Guardian may, if he considers that there is good reason to do so, disclose to the applicant such additional information as he considers appropriate.

(3)   "Additional information" means any information relating to P—

    (a)   which the Public Guardian has obtained in exercising the functions conferred on him under the Act; but

    (b)   which does not appear on the register.

(4)   An application must state—

    (a)   the name of P;

    (b)   the reasons for making the application; and

    (c)   what steps, if any, the applicant has taken to obtain the information from P.

(5)   The Public Guardian may require the applicant to provide such further information, or produce such documents, as the Public Guardian reasonably considers necessary to enable him to determine the application.

(6)   In determining whether to disclose any additional information [relating] to P, the Public Guardian must, in particular, have regard to—

    (a)   the connection between P and the applicant;

(b)   the reasons for requesting the information (in particular, why the information cannot or should not be obtained directly from P);

(c)   the benefit to P, or any detriment he may suffer, if a disclosure is made; and

(d)   any detriment that another person may suffer if a disclosure is made.

Security for discharge of functions

33 Persons required to give security for the discharge of their functions

(1)   This regulation applies in any case where the court orders a person ("S") to give to the Public Guardian security for the discharge of his functions.

(2)   The security must be given by S—

(a)   by means of a bond which is entered into in accordance with regulation 34; or

(b)   in such other manner as the court may direct.

(3)   For the purposes of paragraph (2)(a), S complies with the requirement to give the security only if—

(a)   the endorsement required by regulation 34(2) has been provided; and

(b)   the person who provided it has notified the Public Guardian of that fact.

(4)   For the purposes of paragraph (2)(b), S complies with the requirement to give the security—

(a)   in any case where the court directs that any other endorsement must be provided, only if—

(i)   that endorsement has been provided; and

(ii)   the person who provided it has notified the Public Guardian of that fact;

(b)   in any case where the court directs that any other requirements must be met in relation to the giving of the security, only if the Public Guardian is satisfied that those other requirements have been met.

34 Security given under regulation 33(2)(a): requirement for endorsement

(1)   This regulation has effect for the purposes of regulation 33(2)(a).

(2)   A bond is entered into in accordance with this regulation only if it is endorsed by—

(a)   an authorised insurance company; or

(b)   an authorised deposit-taker.

(3)   A person may enter into the bond under—

(a)   arrangements made by the Public Guardian; or

(b)   other arrangements which are made by the person entering into the bond or on his behalf.

(4)   The Public Guardian may make arrangements with any person specified in paragraph (2) with a view to facilitating the provision by them of bonds which persons required to give security to the Public Guardian may enter into.

(5)   In this regulation—

"authorised insurance company" means—

(a)   a person who has permission under Part 4 of the Financial Services and Markets Act 2000 to effect or carry out contracts of insurance;

(b)   an EEA firm of the kind mentioned in paragraph 5(d) of Schedule 3 to that Act, which has permission under paragraph 15 of that Schedule to effect or carry out contracts of insurance;

(c)   a person who carries on insurance market activity (within the meaning given in section 316(3) of that Act); and "authorised deposit-taker" means—

    (a)   a person who has permission under Part 4 of the Financial Services and Markets Act 2000 to accept deposits;

    (b)   an EEA firm of the kind mentioned in paragraph 5(d) of Schedule 3 to that Act, which has permission under paragraph 15 of that Schedule to accept deposits.

(6)   The definitions of "authorised insurance company" and "authorised deposit-taker" must be read with—

    (a)   section 22 of the Financial Services and Markets Act 2000;

    (b)   any relevant order under that section; and

    (c)   Schedule 2 to that Act.

35 Security given under regulation 33(2)(a): maintenance or replacement

(1)   This regulation applies to any security given under regulation 33(2)(a).

(2)   At such times or at such intervals as the Public Guardian may direct by notice in writing, any person ("S") who has given the security must satisfy the Public Guardian that any premiums payable in respect of it have been paid.

(3)   Where S proposes to replace a security already given by him, the new security is not to be regarded as having been given until the Public Guardian is satisfied that—

    (a)   the requirements set out in sub-paragraphs (a) and (b) of regulation 33(3) have been met in relation to it; and

    (b)   no payment is due from S in connection with the discharge of his functions.

[(4)   The Public Guardian must, if satisfied as to the matters in paragraph (3), provide written notice of that fact to S within 2 weeks of being given notification in accordance with regulation 33(3)(b) in relation to the new security.]

36 Enforcement following court order of any endorsed security

(1)   This regulation applies to any security given to the Public Guardian in respect of which an endorsement has been provided.

(2)   Where the court orders the enforcement of the security, the Public Guardian must—

    (a)   notify any person who endorsed the security of the contents of the order; and

    (b)   notify the court when payment has been made of the amount secured.

37 Discharge of any endorsed security

(1)   This regulation applies to any security given by a person ("S") to the Public Guardian in respect of which an endorsement has been provided.

(2)   The security may be discharged if the court makes an order discharging it.

[(3)   Otherwise the security may not be discharged—

    (a)   if the person on whose behalf S was appointed to act dies, until the end of the period of 2 years beginning on the date of his death; or

    (b)   in any other case, until the end of the period of 7 years beginning on whichever of the following dates first occurs—

        (i)   if S dies, the date of his death;

        (ii)   if the court makes an order which discharges S but which does not also discharge the security under paragraph (2), the date of the order;

        (iii)   the date when S otherwise ceases to be under a duty to discharge the functions in respect of which he was ordered to give security.]

[(3A)   Where S has replaced a security ("the original security") previously given by S and the Public Guardian has provided notice in accordance with regulation 35(4), the original security shall stand discharged 2 years from the date on which that notice was issued unless discharged by earlier order of the court upon application under paragraph (2).]

(4) For the purposes of paragraph (3), if a person takes any step with a view to discharging the security before the end of the period specified in that paragraph, the security is to be treated for all purposes as if it were still in place.

[(5) For the purposes of paragraph (3A), if a person takes any step otherwise than under paragraph (2) with a view to discharging the original security before the end of the period specified paragraph (3A), the security is to be treated for all purposes as if it were still in place.]

Deputies

38 Application for additional time to submit a report

(1) This regulation applies where the court requires a deputy to submit a report to the Public Guardian and specifies a time or interval for it to be submitted.

(2) A deputy may apply to the Public Guardian requesting more time for submitting a particular report.

(3) An application must—

    (a)   state the reason for requesting more time; and

    (b)   contain or be accompanied by such information as the Public Guardian may reasonably require to determine the application.

(4) In response to an application, the Public Guardian may, if he considers it appropriate to do so, undertake that he will not take steps to secure performance of the deputy's duty to submit the report at the relevant time on the condition that the report is submitted on or before such later date as he may specify.

39 Content of reports

(1) Any report which the court requires a deputy to submit to the Public Guardian must include such material as the court may direct.

(2) The report must also contain or be accompanied by—

    (a)   specified information or information of a specified description; or

    (b)   specified documents or documents of a specified description.

(3) But paragraph (2)—

    (a)   extends only to information or documents which are reasonably required in connection with the exercise by the Public Guardian of functions conferred on him under the Act; and

    (b)   is subject to paragraph (1) and to any other directions given by the court.

(4) Where powers as respects a person's property and affairs are conferred on a deputy under section 16 of the Act, the information specified by the Public Guardian under paragraph (2) may include accounts which—

    (a)   deal with specified matters; and

    (b)   are provided in a specified form.

(5) The Public Guardian may require—

    (a)   any information provided to be verified in such manner, or

    (b)   any document produced to be authenticated in such manner,

as he may reasonably require.

(6) "Specified" means specified in a notice in writing given to the deputy by the Public Guardian.

40 Power to require final report on termination of appointment

(1) This regulation applies where—

    (a)   the person on whose behalf a deputy was appointed to act has died;

    (b)   the deputy has died;

(c)   the court has made an order discharging the deputy; or

(d)   the deputy otherwise ceases to be under a duty to discharge the functions to which his appointment relates.

(2)   The Public Guardian may require the deputy (or, in the case of the deputy's death, his personal representatives) to submit a final report on the discharge of his functions.

(3)   A final report must be submitted—

(a)   before the end of such reasonable period as may be specified; and

(b)   at such place as may be specified.

(4)   The Public Guardian must consider the final report, together with any other information that he may have relating to the discharge by the deputy of his functions.

(5)   Where the Public Guardian is dissatisfied with any aspect of the final report he may apply to the court for an appropriate remedy (including enforcement of security given by the deputy).

(6)   "Specified" means specified in a notice in writing given to the deputy or his personal representatives by the Public Guardian.

41   Power to require information from deputies

(1)   This regulation applies in any case where—

(a)   the Public Guardian has received representations (including complaints) about—

(i)   the way in which a deputy is exercising his powers; or

(ii)   any failure to exercise them; or

(b)   it appears to the Public Guardian that there are other circumstances which—

(i)   give rise to concerns about, or dissatisfaction with, the conduct of the deputy (including any failure to act); or

(ii)   otherwise constitute good reason to seek information about the deputy's discharge of his functions.

(2)   The Public Guardian may require the deputy—

(a)   to provide specified information or information of a specified description; or

(b)   to produce specified documents or documents of a specified description.

(3)   The information or documents must be provided or produced—

(a)   before the end of such reasonable period as may be specified; and

(b)   at such place as may be specified.

(4)   The Public Guardian may require—

(a)   any information provided to be verified in such manner, or

(b)   any document produced to be authenticated in such manner,

as he may reasonably require.

(5)   "Specified" means specified in a notice in writing given to the deputy by the Public Guardian.

42   Right of deputy to require review of decisions made by the Public Guardian

(1)   A deputy may require the Public Guardian to reconsider any decision he has made in relation to the deputy.

(2)   The right under paragraph (1) is exercisable by giving notice of exercise of the right to the Public Guardian before the end of the period of 14 days beginning with the date on which notice of the decision is given to the deputy.

(3)   The notice of exercise of the right must—

(a)   state the grounds on which reconsideration is required; and

(b)   contain or be accompanied by any relevant information or documents.

(4)   At any time after receiving the notice and before reconsidering the decision to which it relates, the Public Guardian may require the deputy to provide him with such

further information, or to produce such documents, as he reasonably considers necessary to enable him to reconsider the matter.

(5)   The Public Guardian must give to the deputy—

    (a)   written notice of his decision on reconsideration, and

    (b)   if he upholds the previous decision, a statement of his reasons.

Miscellaneous functions

43 Applications to the Court of Protection

The Public Guardian has the function of making applications to the court in connection with his functions under the Act in such circumstances as he considers it necessary or appropriate to do so.

44 Visits by the Public Guardian or by Court of Protection Visitors at his direction

(1)   This regulation applies where the Public Guardian visits, or directs a Court of Protection Visitor to visit, any person under any provision of the Act or these Regulations.

(2)   The Public Guardian must notify (or make arrangements to notify) the person to be visited of—

    (a)   the date or dates on which it is proposed that the visit will take place;

    (b)   to the extent that it is practicable to do so, any specific matters likely to be covered in the course of the visit; and

    (c)   any proposal to inform any other person that the visit is to take place.

(3)   Where the visit is to be carried out by a Court of Protection Visitor—

    (a)   the Public Guardian may—

        (i)   give such directions to the Visitor, and

        (ii)   provide him with such information concerning the person to be visited,

    as the Public Guardian considers necessary for the purposes of enabling the visit to take place and the Visitor to prepare any report the Public Guardian may require; and

    (b)   the Visitor must seek to carry out the visit and take all reasonable steps to obtain such other information as he considers necessary for the purpose of preparing a report.

(4)   A Court of Protection Visitor must submit any report requested by the Public Guardian in accordance with any timetable specified by the Public Guardian.

(5)   If he considers it appropriate to do so, the Public Guardian may, in relation to any person interviewed in the course of preparing a report—

    (a)   disclose the report to him; and

    (b)   invite him to comment on it.

45 Functions in relation to persons carrying out specific transactions

(1)   This regulation applies where, in accordance with an order made under section 16(2)(a) of the Act, a person ("T") has been authorised to carry out any transaction for a person who lacks capacity.

(2)   The Public Guardian has the functions of—

    (a)   receiving any reports from T which the court may require;

    (b)   dealing with representations (including complaints) about—

        (i)   the way in which the transaction has been or is being carried out; or

        (ii)   any failure to carry it out.

(3)   Regulations 38 to 41 have effect in relation to T as they have effect in relation a deputy.

46 Power to require information from donees of lasting power of attorney
(1) This regulation applies where it appears to the Public Guardian that there are circumstances suggesting that the donee of a lasting power of attorney may—
  (a) have behaved, or may be behaving, in a way that contravenes his authority or is not in the best interests of the donor of the power,
  (b) be proposing to behave in a way that would contravene that authority or would not be in the donor's best interests, or
  (c) have failed to comply with the requirements of an order made, or directions given, by the court.
(2) The Public Guardian may require the donee—
  (a) to provide specified information or information of a specified description; or
  (b) to produce specified documents or documents of a specified description.
(3) The information or documents must be provided or produced—
  (a) before the end of such reasonable period as may be specified; and
  (b) at such place as may be specified.
(4) The Public Guardian may require—
  (a) any information provided to be verified in such manner, or
  (b) any document produced to be authenticated in such manner,
as he may reasonably require.
(5) "Specified" means specified in a notice in writing given to the donee by the Public Guardian.

47 Power to require information from attorneys under enduring power of attorney
(1) This regulation applies where it appears to the Public Guardian that there are circumstances suggesting that, having regard to all the circumstances (and in particular the attorney's relationship to or connection with the donor) the attorney under a registered enduring power of attorney may be unsuitable to be the donor's attorney.
(2) The Public Guardian may require the attorney—
  (a) to provide specified information or information of a specified description; or
  (b) to produce specified documents or documents of a specified description.
(3) The information or documents must be provided or produced—
  (a) before the end of such reasonable period as may be specified; and
  (b) at such place as may be specified.
(4) The Public Guardian may require—
  (a) any information provided to be verified in such manner, or
  (b) any document produced to be authenticated in such manner,
as he may reasonably require.
(5) "Specified" means specified in a notice in writing given to the attorney by the Public Guardian.

48 Other functions in relation to enduring powers of attorney
[(1)] The Public Guardian has the following functions—
  (a) directing a Court of Protection Visitor—
    (i) to visit an attorney under a registered enduring power of attorney, or
    (ii) to visit the donor of a registered enduring power of attorney,
  and to make a report to the Public Guardian on such matters as he may direct;
  (b) dealing with representations (including complaints) about the way in which an attorney under a registered enduring power of attorney is exercising his powers.

[(2) The functions conferred by paragraph (1) may be discharged in co-operation with any other person who has functions in relation to the care or treatment of P.]

Signed by authority of the Lord Chancellor
Cathy Ashton,
Parliamentary Under-Secretary of State,
Department for Constitutional Affairs
16th April 2007

SCHEDULE 1
FORM FOR INSTRUMENT INTENDED TO CREATE A LASTING POWER
OF ATTORNEY
Regulation 5

PART 1   FORM FOR INSTRUMENT INTENDED TO CREATE A PROPERTY
AND AFFAIRS LASTING POWER OF ATTORNEY
* * * *

PART 2   FORM FOR INSTRUMENT INTENDED TO CREATE A PERSONAL
WELFARE LASTING POWER OF ATTORNEY
* * * *

SCHEDULE 2
NOTICE OF INTENTION TO APPLY FOR REGISTRATION OF A LASTING
POWER OF ATTORNEY: LPA 001
Regulation 10
* * * *

SCHEDULE 3
APPLICATION TO REGISTER A LASTING POWER OF ATTORNEY: LPA 002
Regulation 11
* * * *

SCHEDULE 4
NOTICE OF RECEIPT OF AN APPLICATION TO REGISTER A LASTING
POWER OF ATTORNEY: LPA 003A AND LPA 003B
Regulation 13

PART 1   NOTICE TO AN ATTORNEY OF RECEIPT OF AN APPLICATION TO
REGISTER A LASTING POWER OF ATTORNEY
* * * *

PART 2   NOTICE TO DONOR OF RECEIPT OF AN APPLICATION TO REGIS-
TER A LASTING POWER OF ATTORNEY
* * * *

SCHEDULE 5
NOTICE OF REGISTRATION OF A LASTING POWER OF
ATTORNEY: LPA 004
Regulation 17
* * * *

SCHEDULE 6
DISCLAIMER BY DONEE OF A LASTING POWER OF ATTORNEY: LPA 005
Regulation 20
* * * *

SCHEDULE 7
NOTICE OF INTENTION TO APPLY FOR REGISTRATION OF AN ENDURING
POWER OF ATTORNEY
Regulation 23
* * * *

SCHEDULE 8
APPLICATION TO REGISTER AN ENDURING POWER OF ATTORNEY
Regulation 24
* * * *

2007 No 1744

COURT OF PROTECTION RULES 2007

PART 9   HOW TO START PROCEEDINGS

Initial steps

* * * *

Steps following issue of application form

* * * *

B2

67 Applications relating to lasting powers of attorney

(1)   Where the application concerns the powers of the court under section 22 or 23 of the Act (powers of the court in relation to the validity and operation of lasting powers of attorney) the applicant must serve a copy of the application form, together with copies of any documents filed in accordance with rule 64 and a form for acknowledging service—

> (a)   unless the applicant is the donor or donee of the lasting power of attorney ("the power"), on the donor and every donee of the power;
>
> (b)   if he is the donor, on every donee of the power; and
>
> (c)   if he is a donee, on the donor and any other donee of the power,

but only if the above-mentioned persons have not been served or notified under any other rule.

(2)   Where the application is solely in respect of an objection to the registration of a power, the requirements of rules 66 and 70 do not apply to an application made under this rule by—

> (a)   a donee of the power; or
>
> (b)   a person named in a statement made by the donor of the power in accordance with paragraph 2(1)(c)(i) of Schedule 1 to the Act.

(3)   The applicant must comply with paragraph (1) as soon as practicable and in any event within [14] days of date on which the application form was issued.

(4)   The applicant must file a certificate of service within 7 days beginning with the date on which the documents were served.

(5)   Where the applicant knows or has reasonable grounds to believe that the donor of the power lacks capacity to make a decision in relation to any matter that is the subject of the application, he must notify the donor in accordance with Part 7.

68 Applications relating to enduring powers of attorney

(1)   Where the application concerns the powers of the court under paragraphs 2(9), 4(5)(a) and (b), 7(2), 10(c), 13, or 16(2), (3), (4) and (6) of Schedule 4 to the Act, the applicant must serve a copy of the application form, together with copies of any documents filed in accordance with rule 64 and a form for acknowledging service—

> (a)   unless the applicant is the donor or attorney under the enduring power of attorney ("the power"), on the donor and every attorney of the power;
>
> (b)   if he is the donor, on every attorney under the power; or
>
> (c)   if he is an attorney, on the donor and any other attorney under the power,

but only if the above-mentioned persons have not been served or notified under any other rule.

(2)   Where the application is solely in respect of an objection to the registration of a power, the requirements of rules 66 and 70 do not apply to an application made under this rule by—

(a)   an attorney under the power; or

(b)   a person listed in paragraph 6(1) of Schedule 4 to the Act.

(3)   The applicant must comply with paragraph (1) as soon as practicable and in any event within [14] days of the date on which the application form was issued.

(4)   The applicant must file a certificate of service within 7 days beginning with the date on which the documents were served.

(5)   Where the applicant knows or has reasonable grounds to believe that the donor of the power lacks capacity to make a decision in relation to any matter that is the subject of the application, he must notify the donor in accordance with Part 7.

* * * *

PART 23   MISCELLANEOUS

* * * *

201 Objections to registration of an enduring power of attorney: request for directions

(1)   This rule applies in any case where—

(a)   the Public Guardian (having received a notice of objection to the registration of an instrument creating an enduring power of attorney) is prevented by paragraph 13(5) of Schedule 4 to the Act from registering the instrument except in accordance with the court's directions; and

(b)   on or before the relevant day, no application for the court to give such directions has been made under Part 9 (how to start proceedings).

(2)   In paragraph (1)(b) the relevant day is the later of—

(a)   the final day of the period specified in paragraph 13(4) of Schedule 4 to the Act; or

(b)   the final day of the period of 14 days beginning with the date on which the Public Guardian receives the notice of objection.

(3)   The Public Guardian may seek the court's directions about registering the instrument by filing a request in accordance with the relevant practice direction.

(4)   As soon as practicable and in any event within 21 days of the date on which the request was made, the court will notify—

(a)   the person (or persons) who gave the notice of objection; and

(b)   the attorney or, if more than one, each of them.

(5)   As soon as practicable and in any event within 21 days of the date on which the request is filed, the Public Guardian must notify the donor of the power that the request has been so filed.

(6)   The notice under paragraph (4) must—

(a)   state that the Public Guardian has requested the court's directions about registration;

(b)   state that the court will give directions in response to the request unless an application under Part 9 is made to it before the end of the period of 21 days commencing with the date on which the notice is issued; and

(c)   set out the steps required to make such an application.

(7)   "Notice of objection" means a notice of objection which is made in accordance with paragraph 13(4) of Schedule 4 to the Act.

* * * *

Appendix C

LASTING POWER OF ATTORNEY FORMS

Contents

LP1F: FINANCIAL DECISIONS

[C1]

Office of the
Public Guardian

Form

LP1F

Lasting power
of attorney

Financial decisions

**Registering
an LPA costs**

£82

This fee is means-tested:
see the application
Guide part B

Use this for:

- running your bank and savings accounts
- making or selling investments
- paying your bills
- buying or selling your house

How to complete this form

PLEASE WRITE IN CAPITAL LETTERS USING A BLACK PEN

☒ Mark your choice with an X

█ If you make a mistake, fill in the box and then mark the correct
choice with an X

Don't use correction fluid. Cross out mistakes and rewrite nearby.
Everyone involved in each section must initial each change.

Making an LPA online is simpler, clearer and faster

Our smart online form gives you just the right amount of help
exactly when you need it: **www.gov.uk/power-of-attorney**

**Before
you start...**

This form is also available in Welsh. Call the helpline on 0300 456 0300.

The people involved in your LPA

Helpline
0300 456 0300

You'll find it easier to make an LPA if you first choose the people you want to help you. **Note their names here now** so you can refer back later.

People you must have to make an LPA

Donor

If you are filling this form in for yourself, you are the donor. If you are filling this in for a friend or relative, they are the donor.

Attorneys

Attorneys are the people you pick to make decisions for you. They don't need legal training.

They should be people you trust and know well; for example, your husband, wife, partner, adult children or good friends.

Choose one attorney or more. If you have a lot, they might find it hard to make decisions together.

Certificate provider

You need someone to confirm that no one is forcing you to make an LPA and you understand what you are doing. This is your 'certificate provider'. They must either:

- have relevant professional skills, such as a doctor or lawyer
- have known you well for at least two years, such as a friend or colleague

Some people can't be a certificate provider. See the list in the Guide, part A10.

Witnesses

You can't witness your attorneys' signatures and they can't witness yours. Anyone else over 18 years old can be a witness.

People you might want to include in your LPA

Replacement attorneys

You don't have to appoint replacement attorneys but they help protect your LPA. Without them, your LPA might not work if one of your original attorneys stops acting for you.

People to notify

'People to notify' add security. They can raise concerns about your LPA before it's registered – for example, if they think you are under pressure to make the LPA.

This page is not part of the form

LP1F Property and
financial affairs (03.17)

Office of the
Public Guardian

Helpline
0300 456 0300

Lasting power of attorney for property and financial affairs

Section 1
The donor

You are appointing other people to make decisions on your behalf.
You are 'the donor'.

Restrictions – you must be at least 18 years old and be able to understand
and make decisions for yourself (called 'mental capacity').

Help?

For help with
this section,
see the
Guide, part A1.

**If you are filling this in for
a friend or relative** and
they can no longer make
decisions independently,
they can't make an LPA.
See the Guide 'Before you
start' for more information.

Title   First names

Last name

Any other names you're known by (optional – eg your married name)

Date of birth

Day   Month   Year

Address

Postcode

Email address (optional)

For OPG office use only

LPA registration date

OPG reference number

Day   Month   Year

Only valid with the official stamp here.

LP1F Property and financial
affairs (07.15)

1

Section 2
The attorneys

The people you choose to make decisions for you are called your 'attorneys'. Your attorneys don't need special legal knowledge or training. They should be people you trust and know well. Common choices include your husband, wife or partner, son or daughter, or your best friend.

You need at least one attorney, but you can have more.

You'll also be able to choose 'replacement attorneys' in section 4. They can step in if one of the attorneys you appoint here can no longer act for you.

To appoint a trust corporation, fill in the first attorney space and tick the box in that section. They must sign Continuation sheet 4. For more about trust corporations, see the Guide, part A2.

Restrictions – Attorneys must be at least 18 years old and must have mental capacity to make decisions. They must not be bankrupt or subject to a debt relief order.

Help?

For help with this section, see the Guide, part A2.

Title First names	Title First names
Last name (or trust corporation name)	Last name
Date of birth	Date of birth
Day Month Year	Day Month Year
Address	Address
Postcode	Postcode
Email address (optional)	Email address (optional)
☐ This attorney is a trust corporation.	

Section 2 – continued

Helpline
0300 456 0300

Title   First names

Last name

Date of birth

Day   Month   Year

Address

Postcode

Email address (optional)

Title   First names

Last name

Date of birth

Day   Month   Year

Address

Postcode

Email address (optional)

More attorneys – I want to appoint more than 4 attorneys. Use Continuation sheet 1.

Section 3
How should your attorneys make decisions?

Helpline
0300 456 0300

You need to choose whether your attorneys can make decisions on their own or must agree some or all decisions unanimously.

Whatever you choose, they must always act in your best interests.

☐ **I only appointed one attorney** (turn to section 4)

How do you want your attorneys to work together? (tick one only)

☐ **Jointly and severally**
Attorneys can make decisions on their own or together. Most people choose this option because it's the most practical. Attorneys can get together to make important decisions if they wish, but can make simple or urgent decisions on their own. It's up to the attorneys to choose when they act together or alone. It also means that if one of the attorneys dies or can no longer act, your LPA will still work.

If one attorney makes a decision, it has the same effect as if all the attorneys made that decision.

☐ **Jointly**
Attorneys must agree unanimously on every decision, however big or small. Remember, some simple decisions could be delayed because it takes time to get the attorneys together. If your attorneys can't agree a decision, then they can only make that decision by going to court.

Be careful – if one attorney dies or can no longer act, all your attorneys become unable to act. This is because the law says a group appointed 'jointly' is a single unit. Your LPA will stop working unless you appoint at least one replacement attorney (in section 4).

☐ **Jointly for some decisions, jointly and severally for other decisions**
Attorneys must agree unanimously on some decisions, but can make others on their own. If you choose this option, you must list the decisions your attorneys should make jointly and agree unanimously on Continuation sheet 2. The wording you use is important. There are examples in the Guide, part A3.

Be careful – if one attorney dies or can no longer act, none of your attorneys will be able to make any of the decisions you've said should be made jointly. Your LPA will stop working for those decisions unless you appoint at least one replacement attorney (in section 4). Your original attorneys will still be able to make any of the other decisions alongside your replacement attorneys.

Help?

For help with this section, see the Guide, part A3.

 If you choose 'jointly for some decisions...', you may want to take legal advice, particularly if the examples in part A3 of the the Guide, don't match your needs.

Section 4
Replacement attorneys

Helpline
0300 456 0300

This section is optional, but we recommend you consider it

Replacement attorneys are a backup in case one of your original attorneys can't make decisions for you any more.

To appoint a trust corporation, fill in the first attorney space below and tick the box in that section. They must sign Continuation sheet 4.

Reasons replacement attorneys step in – if one of your original attorneys dies, loses capacity, no longer wants to be your attorney, becomes bankrupt or subject to a debt relief order or is no longer legally your husband, wife or civil partner.

Restrictions – replacement attorneys must be at least 18 years old and have mental capacity to make decisions. They must not be bankrupt or subject to a debt relief order.

Help?

For help with this section, see the Guide, part A4.

Title	First names

Last name (or trust corporation name)

Date of birth

Day   Month   Year

Address

Postcode

This attorney is a trust corporation.

Title	First names

Last name

Date of birth

Day   Month   Year

Address

Postcode

More replacements – I want to appoint more than two replacements. Use Continuation sheet 1.

When and how your replacement attorneys can act

Replacement attorneys usually step in when one of your **original** attorneys stops acting for you. If there's more than one **replacement** attorney, they will all step in at once. If they **fully** replace your original attorney(s) at once, they will usually act jointly. You can change some aspects of this, but most people don't. See the Guide, part A4.

You should consider taking legal advice if you want to change when or how your replacement attorneys act.

I want to change when or how my attorneys can act (optional). Use Continuation sheet 2.

Only valid with the official stamp here.

LP1F Property and financial affairs (07.15)

5

Section 5
When can your attorneys make decisions?

Helpline
0300 456 0300

You can allow your attorneys to make decisions:
- as soon as the LPA has been registered by the Office of the Public Guardian
- only when you don't have mental capacity

While you have mental capacity you will be in control of all decisions affecting you. If you choose the first option, your attorneys can only make decisions on your behalf if you allow them to. They are responsible to you for any decisions you let them make.

Your attorneys must always act in your best interests.

Help?

For help with this section, see the Guide, part A5.

When do you want your attorneys to be able to make decisions?
(mark one only)

☐ **As soon as my LPA has been registered
(and also when I don't have mental capacity)**

Most people choose this option because it is the most practical.

While you still have mental capacity, your attorneys can only act **with your consent**. If you later lose capacity, they can continue to act on your behalf for all decisions covered by this LPA.

This option is useful if you are able to make your own decisions but there's another reason you want your attorneys to help you – for example, if you're away on holiday, or if you have a physical condition that makes it difficult to visit the bank, talk on the phone or sign documents.

☐ **Only when I don't have mental capacity**

Be careful – this can make your LPA a lot less useful. Your attorneys might be asked to prove you do not have mental capacity each time they try to use this LPA.

Only valid with the official stamp here.

LP1F Property and financial affairs (07.15)

6

567

Section 6
People to notify when the LPA is registered

Helpline
0300 456 0300

This section is optional

You can let people know that you're going to register your LPA. They can raise any concerns they have about the LPA – for example, if there was any pressure or fraud in making it.

When the LPA is registered, the person applying to register (you or one of your attorneys) must send a notice to each 'person to notify'.

You can't put your attorneys or replacement attorneys here.

People to notify can object to the LPA, but only for certain reasons (listed in the notification form LP3). After that, they are no longer involved in the LPA. Choose people who care about your best interests and who would be willing to speak up if they were concerned.

Help?

For help with this section, see the Guide, part A6.

Title	First names

Last name

Address

Postcode

Title	First names

Last name

Address

Postcode

Title	First names

Last name

Address

Postcode

Title	First names

Last name

Address

Postcode

☐ I want to appoint another person to notify (maximum is 5) – use Continuation sheet 1.

Only valid with the official stamp here.

LP1F Property and financial affairs (07.15)

7

Section 7
Preferences and instructions

Helpline
0300 456 0300

This section is optional

You can tell your attorneys how you'd **prefer** them to make decisions, or give them specific **instructions** which they must follow when making decisions.

Most people leave this page blank – you can just talk to your attorneys so they understand how you want them to make decisions for you.

Help?

Preferences

Your attorneys don't have to follow your preferences but they should keep them in mind. For examples of preferences, see the Guide, part A7.

For help with this section, see the Guide, part A7.

Preferences – use words like 'prefer' and 'would like'

☐ I need more space – use Continuation sheet 2.

Instructions

Your attorneys will have to follow your instructions exactly. For examples of instructions, see the Guide, part A7.

Be careful – if you give instructions that are not legally correct they would have to be removed before your LPA could be registered.

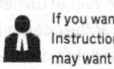

If you want to give instructions, you may want to take legal advice.

Instructions – use words like 'must' and 'have to'

☐ I need more space – use Continuation sheet 2.

Only valid with the official stamp here.

LP1F Property and financial affairs (07.15)

8

Section 8
Your legal rights and responsibilities

Helpline
0300 456 0300

! **Everyone signing the LPA must read this information**

In sections 9 to 11, you, the certificate provider, all your attorneys and your replacement attorneys must sign this lasting power of attorney to form a legal agreement between you (a deed).

By signing this lasting power of attorney, you (the donor) are appointing people (attorneys) to make decisions for you.

LPAs are governed by the Mental Capacity Act 2005 (MCA), regulations made under it and the MCA Code of Practice. Attorneys must have regard to these documents. The Code of Practice is available from www.gov.uk/opg/mca-code or from The Stationery Office.

Help?

For help with this section, see the Guide, part A8.

Your attorneys must follow the principles of the Mental Capacity Act:

1. Your attorneys must assume that you can make your own decisions unless it is established that you cannot do so.
2. Your attorneys must help you to make as many of your own decisions as you can. They must take all practical steps to help you to make a decision. They can only treat you as unable to make a decision if they have not succeeded in helping you make a decision through those steps.
3. Your attorneys must not treat you as unable to make a decision simply because you make an unwise decision.
4. Your attorneys must act and make decisions in your best interests when you are unable to make a decision.
5. Before your attorneys make a decision or act for you, they must consider whether they can make the decision or act in a way that is less restrictive of your rights and freedom but still achieves the purpose.

Your attorneys must always act in your best interests. This is explained in the Application guide, part A8, and defined in the MCA Code of Practice.

Before this LPA can be used:
• it must be registered by the Office of the Public Guardian (OPG)
• it may be limited to when you don't have mental capacity, according to your choice in section 5

Cancelling your LPA: You can cancel this LPA at any time, as long as you have mental capacity to do so. It doesn't matter if the LPA has been registered or not. For more information, see the Guide, part D.

Your will and your LPA: Your attorneys cannot use this LPA to change your will. This LPA will expire when you die. Your attorneys must then send the registered LPA, any certified copies and a copy of your death certificate to the Office of the Public Guardian.

Data protection: For information about how OPG uses your personal data, see the Guide, part D.

Only valid with the official stamp here.

LP1F Property and financial affairs (07.15)

9

Section 9
Signature: donor

By signing on this page I confirm all of the following:

• I have read this lasting power of attorney (LPA) including section 8 'Your legal rights and responsibilities', or I have had it read to me

• I appoint and give my attorneys authority to make decisions about my property and financial affairs, including when I cannot act for myself because I lack mental capacity, subject to the terms of this LPA and to the provisions of the Mental Capacity Act 2005

• I have either appointed people to notify (in section 6) or I have chosen not to notify anyone when the LPA is registered

• I agree to the information I've provided being used by the Office of the Public Guardian in carrying out its duties

Be careful

Sign this page (and any continuation sheets) before anyone signs sections 10 and 11.

Donor	Witness
Signed (or marked) by the person giving this lasting power of attorney and delivered as a deed.	The witness must not be an attorney or replacement attorney appointed under this LPA, and must be aged 18 or over.
Signature or mark	**Signature or mark**
Date signed or marked	**Full name of witness**
Day Month Year	
	Address
If you have used Continuation sheets 1 or 2 you must sign and date each continuation sheet at the same time as you sign this page.	
If you can't sign this LPA you can make a mark instead. If you can't sign or make a mark you can instruct someone else to sign for you, using Continuation sheet 3.	Postcode

Help? For help with this section, see the Guide, part A9.

Section 10
Signature: certificate provider

Helpline
0300 456 0300

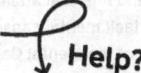

 Only sign this section after the donor has signed section 9

The 'certificate provider' signs to confirm they've discussed the lasting power of attorney (LPA) with the donor, that the donor understands what they're doing and that nobody is forcing them to do it. The 'certificate provider' should be either:

- someone who has known the donor personally for at least 2 years, such as a friend, neighbour, colleague or former colleague
- someone with relevant professional skills, such as the donor's GP, a healthcare professional or a solicitor

A certificate provider **can't** be one of the attorneys.

Help?

For help with this section, see the Guide, part A10.

Certificate provider's statement

I certify that, as far as I'm aware, at the time of signing section 9:

- the donor understood the purpose of this LPA and the scope of the authority conferred under it
- no fraud or undue pressure is being used to induce the donor to create this LPA
- there is nothing else which would prevent this LPA from being created by the completion of this instrument

By signing this section I confirm that:

- I am aged 18 or over
- I have read this LPA, including section 8 'Your legal rights and responsibilities'
- there is no restriction on my acting as a certificate provider
- the donor has chosen me as someone who has known them personally for at least 2 years **OR**
- the donor has chosen me as a person with relevant professional skills and expertise

Restrictions – the certificate provider must not be:

- an attorney or replacement attorney named in this LPA or any other LPA or enduring power of attorney for the donor
- a member of the donor's family or of one of the attorneys' families, including husbands, wives, civil partners, in-laws and step-relatives
- an unmarried partner, boyfriend or girlfriend of either the donor or one of the attorneys (whether or not they live at the same address)
- the donor's or an attorney's business partner
- the donor's or an attorney's employee
- an owner, manager, director or employee of a care home where the donor lives

Certificate provider

Title   First names

Last name

Address

Postcode

Signature or mark

Date signed or marked

Day   Month   Year

Only valid with the official stamp here.

LP1F Property and financial affairs (07.15)

11

Section 11
Signature: attorney or replacement

Helpline
0300 456 0300

 Only sign this section after the certificate provider has signed section 10

All the attorneys and replacement attorneys need to sign.
There are 4 copies of this page – make more copies if you need to.

 **Help?**

For help with this section, see the Guide, part A11.

By signing this section I understand and confirm all of the following:

- I am aged 18 or over

- I have read this lasting power of attorney (LPA) including section 8 'Your legal rights and responsibilities', or I have had it read to me

- I have a duty to act based on the principles of the Mental Capacity Act 2005 and to have regard to the Mental Capacity Act Code of Practice

- I must make decisions and act in the best interests of the donor

- I must take into account any instructions or preferences set out in this LPA

- I can make decisions and act only when this LPA has been registered and at the time indicated in section 5 of this LPA

Further statement by a replacement attorney: I understand that I have the authority to act under this LPA only after an original attorney's appointment is terminated. I must notify the Public Guardian if this happens.

Attorney or replacement attorney	Witness
Signed (or marked) by the attorney or replacement attorney and delivered as a deed.	The witness must not be the donor of this LPA, and must be aged 18 or over.
Signature or mark	Signature or mark
Date signed or marked	Full names of witness
Day Month Year	Address
Title First names	
Last name	Postcode

Only valid with the official stamp here.

LP1F Property and financial affairs (07.15)

12

Section 11
Signature: attorney or replacement

Helpline
0300 456 0300

 Only sign this section after the certificate provider has signed section 10

All the attorneys and replacement attorneys need to sign.
There are 4 copies of this page – make more copies if you need to.

 **Help?**

For help with this section, see the Guide, part A11.

By signing this section I understand and confirm all of the following:

- I am aged 18 or over
- I have read this lasting power of attorney (LPA) including section 8 'Your legal rights and responsibilities', or I have had it read to me
- I have a duty to act based on the principles of the Mental Capacity Act 2005 and to have regard to the Mental Capacity Act Code of Practice
- I must make decisions and act in the best interests of the donor
- I must take into account any instructions or preferences set out in this LPA
- I can make decisions and act only when this LPA has been registered and at the time indicated in section 5 of this LPA

Further statement by a replacement attorney: I understand that I have the authority to act under this LPA only after an original attorney's appointment is terminated. I must notify the Public Guardian if this happens.

Attorney or replacement attorney	Witness
Signed (or marked) by the attorney or replacement attorney and delivered as a deed.	The witness must not be the donor of this LPA, and must be aged 18 or over.
Signature or mark	Signature or mark
Date signed or marked	Full names of witness
Day Month Year	
Title First names	Address
Last name	
	Postcode

Only valid with the official stamp here.

LP1F Property and financial affairs (07.15)

13

574

Section 11
Signature: attorney or replacement

 Only sign this section after the certificate provider has signed section 10

All the attorneys and replacement attorneys need to sign.
There are 4 copies of this page – make more copies if you need to.

Help?

For help with this section, see the Guide, part A11.

By signing this section I understand and confirm all of the following:

- I am aged 18 or over

- I have read this lasting power of attorney (LPA) including section 8 'Your legal rights and responsibilities', or I have had it read to me

- I have a duty to act based on the principles of the Mental Capacity Act 2005 and to have regard to the Mental Capacity Act Code of Practice

- I must make decisions and act in the best interests of the donor

- I must take into account any instructions or preferences set out in this LPA

- I can make decisions and act only when this LPA has been registered and at the time indicated in section 5 of this LPA

Further statement by a replacement attorney: I understand that I have the authority to act under this LPA only after an original attorney's appointment is terminated. I must notify the Public Guardian if this happens.

Attorney or replacement attorney	Witness
Signed (or marked) by the attorney or replacement attorney and delivered as a deed.	The witness must not be the donor of this LPA, and must be aged 18 or over.
Signature or mark	Signature or mark
Date signed or marked	Full names of witness
Day Month Year	
Title First names	Address
Last name	
	Postcode

Only valid with the official stamp here.

LP1F Property and financial affairs (07.15)

14

575

Section 11
Signature: attorney or replacement

Helpline
0300 456 0300

 Only sign this section after the certificate provider has signed section 10

All the attorneys and replacement attorneys need to sign.
There are 4 copies of this page – make more copies if you need to.

 **Help?**
For help with this section, see the Guide, part A11.

By signing this section I understand and confirm all of the following:

- I am aged 18 or over
- I have read this lasting power of attorney (LPA) including section 8 'Your legal rights and responsibilities', or I have had it read to me
- I have a duty to act based on the principles of the Mental Capacity Act 2005 and to have regard to the Mental Capacity Act Code of Practice
- I must make decisions and act in the best interests of the donor
- I must take into account any instructions or preferences set out in this LPA
- I can make decisions and act only when this LPA has been registered and at the time indicated in section 5 of this LPA

Further statement by a replacement attorney: I understand that I have the authority to act under this LPA only after an original attorney's appointment is terminated. I must notify the Public Guardian if this happens.

Attorney or replacement attorney	Witness
Signed (or marked) by the attorney or replacement attorney and delivered as a deed.	The witness must not be the donor of this LPA, and must be aged 18 or over.
Signature or mark	Signature or mark
Date signed or marked	Full names of witness
Day Month Year	
Title First names	Address
Last name	Postcode

Now register your LPA

Before the LPA can be used, it **must** be registered by the Office of the Public Guardian (OPG). Continue filling in this form to register the LPA. See part B of the Guide.

People to notify

If there are any 'people to notify' listed in section 6, you must notify them that you are registering the LPA now. See part C of the Guide.

Fill in and send each of them a copy of the form to notify people – LP3.

When you sign section 15 of this form, you are confirming that you've sent forms to the 'people to notify'.

Register now

You do not have to register immediately, but it's a good idea in case you've made any mistakes. If you delay until after the donor loses mental capacity, it will be impossible to fix any errors. This could make the whole LPA invalid and it will not be possible to register or use it.

Register your lasting power of attorney

Section 12
The applicant

You can only apply to register if you are either the donor or attorney(s) for this LPA. The donor and attorney(s) should not apply together.

Who is applying to register the LPA? (tick one only)

☐ **Donor** – the donor needs to sign section 15

☐ **Attorney(s)** – If the attorneys were appointed jointly (in section 3) then they **all** need to sign section 15. Otherwise, only one of the attorneys needs to sign

Help?

For help with this section, see the Guide, part B2.

Write the name and date of birth for each attorney that is applying to register the LPA. Don't include any attorneys who are not applying.

Title | First names

Last name

Date of birth

Day | Month | Year

Title | First names

Last name

Date of birth

Day | Month | Year

Title | First names

Last name

Date of birth

Day | Month | Year

Title | First names

Last name

Date of birth

Day | Month | Year

Section 13
Who do you want to receive the LPA?

We need to know who to send the LPA to once it is registered. We might also need to contact someone with questions about the application.

We already have the addresses of the donor and attorneys, so you don't have to repeat any of those here, unless they have changed.

Who would you like to receive the LPA and any correspondence?

☐ **The donor**

☐ **An attorney** (write name below)

☐ **Other** (write name and address below)

Title   First names

Last name

Company (optional)

Address

Postcode

How would the person above prefer to be contacted?

You can choose more than one.

☐ **Post**

☐ **Phone**

☐ **Email**

☐ **Welsh** (we will write to the person in Welsh)

Help?

For help with this section, see the Guide, part B3.

Section 14
Application fee

There's a fee for registering a lasting power of attorney – the amount is shown on the cover sheet of this form or on form LPA120.

The fee changes from time to time. You can check you are paying the correct amount at www.gov.uk/power-of-attorney/how-much-it-costs or call 0300 456 0300. The Office of the Public Guardian can't register your LPA until you have paid the fee.

How would you like to pay?

☐ **Card** For security, **don't** write your credit or debit card details here. We'll contact you to process the payment.

Your phone number

☐ **Cheque** Enclose a cheque with your application.

Help?

For help with this section, see the Guide, part B4.

Reduced application fee

If the donor has a low income, you may not have to pay the full amount. See the Guide, part B4 for details.

☐ **I want to apply to pay a reduced fee**

You'll need to fill in form LPA120 and include it with your application. You'll also **need to send proof** that the donor is eligible to pay a reduced fee.

Are you making a repeat application?

If you've already applied to register an LPA and the Office of the Public Guardian said that it was not possible to register it, you can apply again within 3 months and pay a reduced fee.

☐ **I'm making a repeat application**

Case number

For OPG office use only

Payment reference

Payment date

Day   Month   Year

Amount

LP1F Register your LPA (07.15)

Section 15
Signature

 Do not sign this section until after sections 9, 10 and 11 have been signed.

The person applying to register the LPA (see section 12) must sign and date this section. This is either the donor or attorney(s) but not both together.

If the **attorneys** are applying to register the LPA and they were appointed to act **jointly** (in section 3), they must all sign.

By signing this section I confirm the following:

- I apply to register the LPA that accompanies this application
- I have informed 'people to notify' named in section 6 of the LPA (if any) of my intention to register the LPA
- I certify that the information in this form is correct to the best of my knowledge and belief

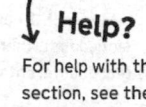 **Help?**

For help with this section, see the Guide, part B5.

Signature or mark	Signature or mark
Date signed	Date signed
Day Month Year	Day Month Year
Signature or mark	Signature or mark
Date signed	Date signed
Day Month Year	Day Month Year

If more than 4 attorneys need to sign, make copies of this page.

Check your lasting power of attorney

You don't have to use this checklist, but it'll help you make sure you've completed your LPA correctly.

Helpline
0300 456 0300

☐ The donor filled in sections 1 to 7.

☐ The donor signed section 9 in the presence of a witness. The donor also signed any copies of continuation sheets 1 and 2 that were used, on the same date as signing section 9.

☐ The certificate provider signed section 10.

☐ All the attorneys and replacement attorneys signed section 11, in the presence of witness(es).

☐ Sections 9, 10 and 11 were signed in order. Section 9 must have been signed first, then section 10, then section 11. They can be dated the same day or different days.

☐ The donor or an attorney completed sections 12 to 15. If the attorneys are applying and were appointed 'jointly' (section 3), they have all signed section 15 of this form.

☐ I've paid the application fee or applied for a reduced fee. If I've applied for a reduced fee, I've included the required evidence and completed form LPA120A.

☐ If there were any people to notify in section 6, I've notified them using form LP3.

☐ I've not left out any of the pages of the LPA, even the ones where I didn't write anything or there were no boxes to fill in.

Send to:

Office of the Public Guardian
PO Box 16185
Birmingham B2 2WH

This page is not part of the form

LP1F Property and financial affairs (07.15)

LP1H: HEALTH AND CARE DECISIONS

[C2]

Office of the
Public Guardian

Form

LP1H

Lasting power
of attorney

Health and care
decisions

**Registering
an LPA costs**

£82

This fee is means-tested:
see the application
Guide part B

Use this for:

- the type of health care and medical treatment you
  receive, including life-sustaining treatment
- where you live
- day-to-day matters such as your diet and daily routine

How to complete this form

PLEASE WRITE IN CAPITAL LETTERS USING A BLACK PEN

☒ Mark your choice with an X

If you make a mistake, fill in the box and then mark the correct
choice with an X

Don't use correction fluid. Cross out mistakes and rewrite nearby.
Everyone involved in each section must initial each change.

Making an LPA online is simpler, clearer and faster

Our smart online form gives you just the right amount of help
exactly when you need it: **www.gov.uk/power-of-attorney**

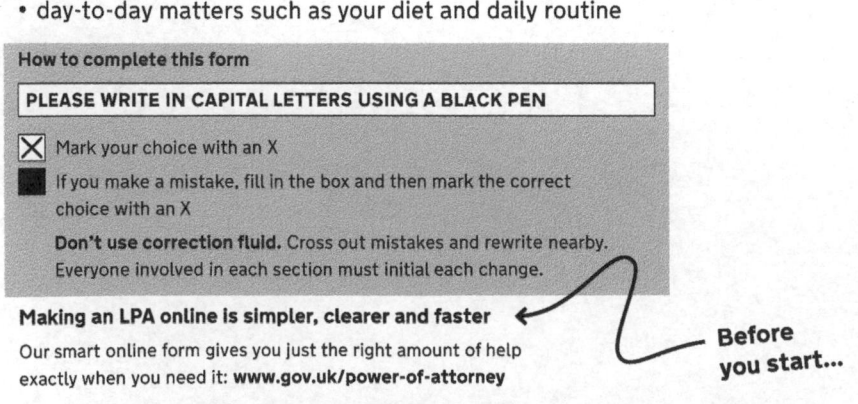

**Before
you start...**

This form is also available in Welsh. Call the helpline on 0300 456 0300.

The people involved in your LPA

You'll find it easier to make an LPA if you first choose the people you want to help you. **Note their names here now** so you can refer back later.

People you must have to make an LPA

Donor

If you are filling this form in for yourself, you are the donor. If you are filling this in for a friend or relative, they are the donor.

Attorneys

Attorneys are the people you pick to make decisions for you. They don't need legal training.

They should be people you trust and know well; for example, your husband, wife, partner, adult children or good friends.

Choose one attorney or more. If you have a lot, they might find it hard to make decisions together.

Certificate provider

You need someone to confirm that no one is forcing you to make an LPA and you understand what you are doing. This is your 'certificate provider'. They must either:

- have relevant professional skills, such as a doctor or lawyer
- have known you well for at least two years, such as a friend or colleague

Some people can't be a certificate provider. See the list in the Guide, part A10.

Witnesses

You can't witness your attorneys' signatures and they can't witness yours. Anyone else over 18 years old can be a witness.

People you might want to include in your LPA

Replacement attorneys

You don't have to appoint replacement attorneys but they help protect your LPA. Without them, your LPA might not work if one of your original attorneys stops acting for you.

People to notify

'People to notify' add security. They can raise concerns about your LPA before it's registered – for example, if they think you are under pressure to make the LPA.

LP1H Health and welfare (03.17)

585

**Office of the
Public Guardian**

Helpline
0300 456 0300

Lasting power of attorney for health and welfare

Section 1
The donor

You are appointing other people to make decisions on your behalf.
You are 'the donor'.

Restrictions – you must be at least 18 years old and be able to understand and make decisions for yourself (called 'mental capacity').

Help?

For help with this section, see the Guide, part A1.

If you are filling this in for a friend or relative and they can no longer make decisions independently, they can't make an LPA. See the Guide 'Before you start' for more information.

Title

First names

Last name

Any other names you're known by (optional – eg your married name)

Date of birth

Day   Month   Year

Address

Postcode

Email address (optional)

For OPG office use only

LPA registration date

OPG reference number

Day   Month   Year

Only valid with the official stamp here.

LP1H Health and welfare (07.15)

1

586

Section 2
The attorneys

The people you choose to make decisions for you are called your 'attorneys'. Your attorneys don't need special legal knowledge or training. They should be people you trust and know well. Common choices include your husband, wife or partner, son or daughter, or your best friend.

You need at least one attorney, but you can have more.

You'll also be able to choose 'replacement attorneys' in section 4. They can step in if one of the attorneys you appoint here can no longer act for you.

Restrictions – Attorneys must be at least 18 years old and must have mental capacity to make decisions.

Help?

For help with
this section,
see the
Guide, part A2.

Title First names	Title First names
Last name	Last name
Date of birth	Date of birth
Day Month Year	Day Month Year
Address	Address
Postcode	Postcode
Email address (optional)	Email address (optional)

Section 2 - continued

Helpline
0300 456 0300

Title	First names

Last name

Date of birth

Day   Month   Year

Address

Postcode

Email address (optional)

Title	First names

Last name

Date of birth

Day   Month   Year

Address

Postcode

Email address (optional)

More attorneys – I want to appoint more than 4 attorneys. Use Continuation sheet 1.

Only valid with the official stamp here.   LP1H Health and welfare (07.15)

3

Section 3
How should your attorneys make decisions?

Helpline
0300 456 0300

You need to choose whether your attorneys can make decisions on their own or must agree some or all decisions unanimously.

Whatever you choose, they must always act in your best interests.

- [ ] **I only appointed one attorney** (turn to section 4)

How do you want your attorneys to work together? (tick one only)

- [ ] **Jointly and severally**
  Attorneys can make decisions on their own or together. Most people choose this option because it's the most practical. Attorneys can get together to make important decisions if they wish, but can make simple or urgent decisions on their own. It's up to the attorneys to choose when they act together or alone. It also means that if one of the attorneys dies or can no longer act, your LPA will still work.

  If one attorney makes a decision, it has the same effect as if all the attorneys made that decision.

- [ ] **Jointly**
  Attorneys must agree unanimously on every decision, however big or small. Remember, some simple decisions could be delayed because it takes time to get the attorneys together. If your attorneys can't agree a decision, then they can only make that decision by going to court.

  Be careful – if one attorney dies or can no longer act, all your attorneys become unable to act. This is because the law says a group appointed 'jointly' is a single unit. Your LPA will stop working unless you appoint at least one replacement attorney (in section 4).

- [ ] **Jointly for some decisions, jointly and severally for other decisions**
  Attorneys must agree unanimously on some decisions, but can make others on their own. If you choose this option, you must list the decisions your attorneys should make jointly and agree unanimously on Continuation sheet 2. The wording you use is important. There are examples in the Guide, part A3.

  Be careful – if one of your attorneys dies or can no longer act, none of your attorneys will be able to make any of the decisions you've said should be made jointly. Your LPA will stop working for those decisions unless you appoint at least one replacement attorney (in section 4). Your original attorneys will still be able to make any of the other decisions alongside your replacement attorneys.

Help?

For help with this section, see the Guide, part A3.

 If you choose 'jointly for some decisions...', you may want to take legal advice, particularly if the examples in part A3 of the Guide don't match your needs.

Only valid with the official stamp here.

LP1H Health and welfare (07.15)

4

Section 4
Replacement attorneys

Helpline
0300 456 0300

This section is optional, but we recommend you consider it

Replacement attorneys are a backup in case one of your original attorneys can't make decisions for you any more.

Reasons replacement attorneys step in – if one of your original attorneys dies, loses capacity, no longer wants to be your attorney or is no longer legally your husband, wife or civil partner.

Restrictions – replacement attorneys must be at least 18 years old and have mental capacity to make decisions.

Help?

For help with this section, see the Guide, part A4.

Title	First names		Title	First names

Last name		Last name

Date of birth		Date of birth
Day Month Year		Day Month Year

Address		Address
Postcode		Postcode

☐ **More replacements –** I want to appoint more than two replacements. Use Continuation sheet 1.

When and how your replacement attorneys can act

Replacement attorneys usually step in when one of your **original** attorneys stops acting for you. If there's more than one **replacement** attorney, they will all step in at once. If they **fully** replace your original attorney(s) at once, they will usually act jointly. You can change some aspects of this, but most people don't. See the Guide, part A4.

You should consider taking legal advice if you want to change how your replacement attorneys act.

☐ I want to change when or how my attorneys can act (optional). Use Continuation sheet 2.

Only valid with the official stamp here.

LP1H Health and welfare (07.15)

5

Section 5
Life-sustaining treatment

! **This is an important part of your LPA.**

You must choose whether your attorneys can give or refuse consent to life-sustaining treatment on your behalf.

Life-sustaining treatment means care, surgery, medicine or other help from doctors that's needed to keep you alive, for example:
• a serious operation, such as a heart bypass or organ transplant
• cancer treatment
• artificial nutrition or hydration (food or water given other than by mouth)

Whether some treatments are life-sustaining depends on the situation. If you had pneumonia, a simple course of antibiotics could be life-sustaining.

Decisions about life-sustaining treatment can be needed in unexpected circumstances, such as a routine operation that didn't go as planned.

You can use section 7 of this LPA to let your attorneys know more about your preferences in particular circumstances (this is optional).

↓ Help?

For help with this section, including how your LPA relates to an 'advance decision', see the Guide, part A5.

Who do you want to make decisions about life-sustaining treatment? (sign only one option)

Option A – I give my attorneys authority	**Option B – I do not give my attorneys authority**
to give or refuse consent to life-sustaining treatment on my behalf.	to give or refuse consent to life-sustaining treatment on my behalf.
If you choose this option, your attorneys can speak to doctors on your behalf as if they were you.	If you choose this option, your doctors will take into account the views of the attorneys and of people who are interested in your welfare as well as any written statement you may have made, where it is practical and appropriate.

Signature or mark

Signature or mark

Date signed or marked

Day   Month   Year

Date signed or marked

Day   Month   Year

Witness
The witness must not be an attorney or replacement attorney appointed under this LPA, and must be aged 18 or over.

Signature or mark

Full name of witness

Address

Postcode

Only valid with the official stamp here.

LP1H Health and welfare (07.15)

6

591

Section 6
People to notify when the LPA is registered

Helpline
0300 456 0300

This section is optional

You can let people know that you're going to register your LPA. They can raise any concerns they have about the LPA – for example, if there was any pressure or fraud in making it.

When the LPA is registered, the person applying to register (you or one of your attorneys) must send a notice to each 'person to notify'.

You can't put your attorneys or replacement attorneys here.

People to notify can object to the LPA, but only for certain reasons (listed in the notification form LP3). After that, they are no longer involved in the LPA. Choose people who care about your best interests and who would be willing to speak up if they were concerned.

Help?

For help with this section, see the Guide, part A6.

Title	First names

Last name

Address

Postcode

Title	First names

Last name

Address

Postcode

Title	First names

Last name

Address

Postcode

Title	First names

Last name

Address

Postcode

☐ I want to appoint another person to notify (maximum is 5) – use Continuation sheet 1.

Only valid with the official stamp here.

LP1H Health and welfare (07.15)

7

Section 7
Preferences and instructions

This section is optional

You can tell your attorneys how you'd **prefer** them to make decisions, or give them specific **instructions** which they must follow when making decisions.

Most people leave this page blank – you can just talk to your attorneys so they understand how you want them to make decisions for you.

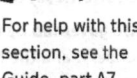
Help?

Preferences

Your attorneys don't have to follow your preferences but they should keep them in mind. For examples of preferences, see the Guide, part A7.

For help with this section, see the Guide, part A7.

> **Preferences** – use words like 'prefer' and 'would like'
>
>
>
> ☐ I need more space – use Continuation sheet 2.

Instructions

Your attorneys will have to follow your instructions exactly. For examples of instructions, see the Guide, part A7.

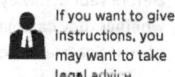 If you want to give instructions, you may want to take legal advice.

Be careful – if you give instructions that are not legally correct they would have to be removed before your LPA could be registered.

> **Instructions** – use words like 'must' and 'have to'
>
>
>
>
>
> ☐ I need more space – use Continuation sheet 2.

Section 8
Your legal rights and responsibilities

Helpline
0300 456 0300

 Everyone signing the LPA must read this information

In sections 9 to 11, you, the certificate provider, all your attorneys and your replacement attorneys must sign this lasting power of attorney to form a legal agreement between you (a deed).

By signing this lasting power of attorney, you (the donor) are appointing people (attorneys) to make decisions for you.

LPAs are governed by the Mental Capacity Act 2005 (MCA), regulations made under it and the MCA Code of Practice. Attorneys must have regard to these documents. The Code of Practice is available from www.gov.uk/opg/mca-code or from The Stationery Office.

Your attorneys must follow the principles of the Mental Capacity Act:

1. Your attorneys must assume that you can make your own decisions unless it is established that you cannot do so.
2. Your attorneys must help you to make as many of your own decisions as you can. They must take all practical steps to help you to make a decision. They can only treat you as unable to make a decision if they have not succeeded in helping you make a decision through those steps.
3. Your attorneys must not treat you as unable to make a decision simply because you make an unwise decision.
4. Your attorneys must act and make decisions in your best interests when you are unable to make a decision.
5. Before your attorneys make a decision or act for you, they must consider whether they can make the decision or act in a way that is less restrictive of your rights and freedom but still achieves the purpose.

Your attorneys must always act in your best interests. This is explained in the Application guide, part A8, and defined in the MCA Code of Practice.

Before this LPA can be used it must be registered by the Office of the Public Guardian (OPG). Your attorneys can only use this LPA if you don't have mental capacity.

Cancelling your LPA: You can cancel this LPA at any time, as long as you have mental capacity to do so. It doesn't matter if the LPA has been registered or not. For more information, see the Guide, part D.

Your will and your LPA: Your attorneys cannot use this LPA to change your will. This LPA will expire when you die. Your attorneys must then send the registered LPA, any certified copies and a copy of your death certificate to the Office of the Public Guardian.

Data protection: For information about how OPG uses your personal data, see the Guide, Part D.

Help?

For help with this section, see the Guide, part A8.

Only valid with the official stamp here.

LP1H Health and welfare (07.15)

9

594

Section 9
Signature: donor

Helpline
0300 456 0300

By signing on this page I confirm all of the following:

- I have read this lasting power of attorney (LPA) including section 8 'Your legal rights and responsibilities', or I have had it read to me

- I appoint and give my attorneys authority to make decisions about my health and welfare, when I cannot act for myself because I lack mental capacity, subject to the terms of this LPA and to the provisions of the Mental Capacity Act 2005

- I confirm I have chosen either Option A or Option B about life sustaining treatment in section 5 of this LPA

- I have either appointed people to notify (in section 6) or I have chosen not to notify anyone when the LPA is registered

- I agree to the information I've provided being used by the Office of the Public Guardian in carrying out its duties

Be careful

Sign this page and section 5 (and any continuation sheets) before anyone signs sections 10 and 11.

Donor	Witness
Signed (or marked) by the person giving this lasting power of attorney and delivered as a deed.	The witness must not be an attorney or replacement attorney appointed under this LPA, and must be aged 18 or over.
Signature or mark	Signature or mark
Date signed or marked	Full name of witness
Day Month Year	
You must also sign Section 5 (page 6) at the same time as you sign this page.	Address
If you have used Continuation sheets 1 or 2 you must sign and date each continuation sheet at the same time as you sign this page.	Postcode
If you can't sign this LPA you can make a mark instead. If you can't sign or make a mark you can instruct someone else to sign for you, using Continuation sheet 3.	**Help?** For help with this section, see the Guide, part A9.

Only valid with the official stamp here.

LP1H Health and welfare (07.15)

10

Section 10
Signature: certificate provider

Helpline
0300 456 0300

> **!** **Only sign this section after the donor has signed section 9**

The 'certificate provider' signs to confirm they've discussed the lasting power of attorney (LPA) with the donor, that the donor understands what they're doing and that nobody is forcing them to do it. The 'certificate provider' should be either:

* someone who has known the donor personally for at least 2 years, such as a friend, neighbour, colleague or former colleague
* someone with relevant professional skills, such as the donor's GP, a healthcare professional or a solicitor

A certificate provider **can't** be one of the attorneys.

Help?

For help with this section, see the Guide, part A10.

Certificate provider's statement

I certify that, as far as I'm aware, at the time of signing section 9:

* the donor understood the purpose of this LPA and the scope of the authority conferred under it
* no fraud or undue pressure is being used to induce the donor to create this LPA
* there is nothing else which would prevent this LPA from being created by the completion of this instrument

By signing this section I confirm that:

* I am aged 18 or over
* I have read this LPA, including section 8 'Your legal rights and responsibilities'
* there is no restriction on my acting as a certificate provider
* the donor has chosen me as someone who has known them personally for at least 2 years **OR**
* the donor has chosen me as a person with relevant professional skills and expertise

Restrictions – the certificate provider must not be:

* an attorney or replacement attorney named in this LPA or any other LPA or enduring power of attorney for the donor
* a member of the donor's family or of one of the attorneys' families, including husbands, wives, civil partners, in-laws and step-relatives
* an unmarried partner, boyfriend or girlfriend of either the donor or one of the attorneys (whether or not they live at the same address)
* the donor's or an attorney's business partner
* the donor's or an attorney's employee
* an owner, manager, director or employee of a care home where the donor lives

Certificate provider

Title   First names

Last name

Address

Postcode

Signature or mark

Date signed or marked

Day   Month   Year

Section 11
Signature: attorney or replacement

 Only sign this section after the certificate provider has signed section 10

All the attorneys and replacement attorneys need to sign.
There are 4 copies of this page – make more copies if you need to.

By signing this section I understand and confirm all of the following:

- I am aged 18 or over
- I have read this lasting power of attorney (LPA) including section 8 'Your legal rights and responsibilities', or I have had it read to me
- I have a duty to act based on the principles of the Mental Capacity Act 2005 and to have regard to the Mental Capacity Act Code of Practice
- I must make decisions and act in the best interests of the donor
- I must take into account any instructions or preferences set out in this LPA
- I can make decisions and act only when this LPA has been registered
- I can make decisions and act only when the donor lacks mental capacity.

Help?

For help with this section, see the Guide, part A11.

Further statement by a replacement attorney: I understand that I have the authority to act under this LPA only after an original attorney's appointment is terminated. I must notify the Public Guardian if this happens.

Attorney or replacement attorney	Witness
Signed (or marked) by the attorney or replacement attorney and delivered as a deed.	The witness must not be the donor of this LPA, and must be aged 18 or over.
Signature or mark	Signature or mark
Date signed or marked	Full names of witness
Day Month Year	
Title First names	Address
Last name	
	Postcode

Section 11
Signature: attorney or replacement

Helpline
0300 456 0300

 Only sign this section after the certificate provider has signed section 10

All the attorneys and replacement attorneys need to sign.
There are 4 copies of this page – make more copies if you need to.

By signing this section I understand and confirm all of the following:

- I am aged 18 or over
- I have read this lasting power of attorney (LPA) including section 8 'Your legal rights and responsibilities', or I have had it read to me
- I have a duty to act based on the principles of the Mental Capacity Act 2005 and to have regard to the Mental Capacity Act Code of Practice
- I must make decisions and act in the best interests of the donor
- I must take into account any instructions or preferences set out in this LPA
- I can make decisions and act only when this LPA has been registered
- I can make decisions and act only when the donor lacks mental capacity.

Help?

For help with this section, see the Guide, part A11.

Further statement by a replacement attorney: I understand that I have the authority to act under this LPA only after an original attorney's appointment is terminated. I must notify the Public Guardian if this happens.

Attorney or replacement attorney

Signed (or marked) by the attorney or replacement attorney and delivered as a deed.

Signature or mark

Date signed or marked

Day   Month   Year

Title   First names

Last name

Witness

The witness must not be the donor of this LPA, and must be aged 18 or over.

Signature or mark

Full names of witness

Address

Postcode

Only valid with the official stamp here.

LP1H Health and welfare (07.15)

13

Section 11
Signature: attorney or replacement

 Only sign this section after the certificate provider has signed section 10

All the attorneys and replacement attorneys need to sign.
There are 4 copies of this page – make more copies if you need to.

By signing this section I understand and confirm all of the following:

- I am aged 18 or over
- I have read this lasting power of attorney (LPA) including section 8 'Your legal rights and responsibilities', or I have had it read to me
- I have a duty to act based on the principles of the Mental Capacity Act 2005 and to have regard to the Mental Capacity Act Code of Practice
- I must make decisions and act in the best interests of the donor
- I must take into account any instructions or preferences set out in this LPA
- I can make decisions and act only when this LPA has been registered
- I can make decisions and act only when the donor lacks mental capacity.

Further statement by a replacement attorney: I understand that I have the authority to act under this LPA only after an original attorney's appointment is terminated. I must notify the Public Guardian if this happens.

Help?

For help with this section, see the Guide, part A11.

Attorney or replacement attorney	Witness
Signed (or marked) by the attorney or replacement attorney and delivered as a deed.	The witness must not be the donor of this LPA, and must be aged 18 or over.
Signature or mark	Signature or mark
Date signed or marked Day Month Year	Full names of witness
Title First names	Address
Last name	Postcode

Section 11
Signature: attorney or replacement

 Only sign this section after the certificate provider has signed section 10

All the attorneys and replacement attorneys need to sign.
There are 4 copies of this page – make more copies if you need to.

By signing this section I understand and confirm all of the following:

• I am aged 18 or over

• I have read this lasting power of attorney (LPA) including section 8 'Your legal rights and responsibilities', or I have had it read to me

• I have a duty to act based on the principles of the Mental Capacity Act 2005 and to have regard to the Mental Capacity Act Code of Practice

• I must make decisions and act in the best interests of the donor

• I must take into account any instructions or preferences set out in this LPA

• I can make decisions and act only when this LPA has been registered

• I can make decisions and act only when the donor lacks mental capacity.

Further statement by a replacement attorney: I understand that I have the authority to act under this LPA only after an original attorney's appointment is terminated. I must notify the Public Guardian if this happens.

Help?

For help with this section, see the Guide, part A11.

Attorney or replacement attorney	Witness
Signed (or marked) by the attorney or replacement attorney and delivered as a deed.	The witness must not be the donor of this LPA, and must be aged 18 or over.
Signature or mark	Signature or mark
Date signed or marked	
Day Month Year	Full names of witness
Title First names	Address
Last name	
	Postcode

Only valid with the official stamp here.

LP1H Health and welfare (07.15)

15

Now register your LPA

Before the LPA can be used, it **must** be registered by the Office of the Public Guardian (OPG). Continue filling in this form to register the LPA. See part C of the Guide.

People to notify

If there are any 'people to notify' listed in section 6, you must notify them that you are registering the LPA now. See Part B of the Guide.

Fill in and send each of them a copy of the form to notify people – LP3.

When you sign section 15 of this form, you are confirming that you've sent forms to the 'people to notify'.

Register now

You do not have to register immediately, but it's a good idea in case you've made any mistakes. If you delay until after the donor loses mental capacity, it will be impossible to fix any errors. This could make the whole LPA invalid and it will not be possible to register or use it.

Register your lasting power of attorney

Helpline
0300 456 0300

Section 12
The applicant

You can only apply to register if you are the donor or attorney(s) for this LPA.
The donor and attorney(s) should not apply together.

Who is applying to register the LPA? (tick one only)

☐ **Donor** – the donor needs to sign section 15

☐ **Attorney(s)** – If the attorneys were appointed jointly (in section 3)
then they **all** need to sign in section 15. Otherwise, only one of the
attorneys needs to sign

Help?

For help with this
section, see the
Guide, part B2.

Write the name and date of birth for each attorney that is applying to register
the LPA. Don't include any attorneys who are not applying.

Title	First names

Last name

Date of birth

| Day | Month | Year |

Title	First names

Last name

Date of birth

| Day | Month | Year |

Title	First names

Last name

Date of birth

| Day | Month | Year |

Title	First names

Last name

Date of birth

| Day | Month | Year |

LP1H Register your LPA (07.15)

17

Section 13
Who do you want to receive the LPA?

Helpline
0300 456 0300

We need to know who to send the LPA to once it is registered. We might also need to contact someone with questions about the application.

We already have the addresses of the donor and attorneys, so you don't have to repeat any of those here, unless they have changed.

Who would you like to receive the LPA and any correspondence?

☐ **The donor**

☐ **An attorney** (write name below)

☐ **Other** (write name and address below)

Title   First names

Last name

Company (optional)

Address

Postcode

Help?

For help with this section, see the Guide, part B3.

How would the person above prefer to be contacted?

You can choose more than one.

☐ Post

☐ Phone

☐ Email

☐ Welsh (We will write to the person in Welsh)

Section 14
Application fee

There's a fee for registering a lasting power of attorney – the amount is shown on the cover sheet of this form or on form LPA120.

The fee changes from time to time. You can check you are paying the correct amount at www.gov.uk/power-of-attorney/how-much-it-costs or call 0300 456 0300. The Office of the Public Guardian can't register your LPA until you have paid the fee.

How would you like to pay?

☐ **Card** For security, **don't** write your credit or debit card details here. We'll contact you to process the payment.

Your phone number

☐ **Cheque** Enclose a cheque with your application.

Help?

For help with this section, see the Guide, part B4.

Reduced application fee

If the donor has a low income, you may not have to pay the full amount. See the Guide, part B4 for details.

☐ **I want to apply to pay a reduced fee**

You'll need to fill in form LPA120 and include it with your application. You'll also **need to send proof** that the donor is eligible to pay a reduced fee.

Are you making a repeat application?

If you've already applied to register an LPA and the Office of the Public Guardian said that it was not possible to register it, you can apply again within 3 months and pay a reduced fee.

☐ **I'm making a repeat application**

Case number

For OPG office use only

Payment reference

Payment date

Day   Month   Year

Amount

LP1H Register your LPA (07.15)

19

Section 15
Signature

Helpline
0300 456 0300

 Do not sign this section until after sections 9, 10 and 11 have been signed.

The person applying to register the LPA (see section 12) must sign and date this section. This is either the donor or attorney(s) but not both together.

If the **attorneys** are applying to register the LPA and they were appointed to act **jointly** (in section 3), they must all sign.

By signing this section I confirm the following:

- I apply to register the LPA that accompanies this application

- I have informed 'people to notify' named in section 6 of the LPA (if any) of my intention to register the LPA

- I certify that the information in this form is correct to the best of my knowledge and belief

Help?

For help with this section, see the Guide, part B5.

Signature or mark	Signature or mark

Date signed	Date signed
Day Month Year	Day Month Year

Signature or mark	Signature or mark

Date signed	Date signed
Day Month Year	Day Month Year

If more than 4 attorneys need to sign, make copies of this page.

Check your lasting power of attorney

You don't have to use this checklist, but it'll help you make sure you've completed your LPA correctly.

Helpline
0300 456 0300

- [ ] The donor filled in sections 1 to 7.

- [ ] The donor signed both section 5 and section 9 in the presence of a witness. The donor also signed any copies of continuation sheets 1 and 2 that were used, on the same date as signing section 9.

- [ ] The certificate provider signed section 10.

- [ ] All the attorneys and replacement attorneys signed section 11, in the presence of witness(es).

- [ ] Sections 9, 10 and 11 were signed in order. Section 9 must have been signed first, then section 10, then section 11. They can be dated the same day or different days.

- [ ] The donor or an attorney completed sections 12 to 15. If the attorneys are applying and were appointed 'jointly' (section 3), they have all signed section 15 of this form.

- [ ] I've paid the application fee or applied for a reduced fee. If I've applied for a reduced fee, I've included the required evidence and completed form LPA120A.

- [ ] If there were any people to notify in section 6, I've notified them using form LP3.

- [ ] I've not left out any of the pages of the LPA, even the ones where I didn't write anything or there were no boxes to fill in.

Send to:

Office of the Public Guardian
PO Box 16185
Birmingham B2 2WH

This page is not part of the form

LP1H Health and welfare (07.15)

LPC: CONTINUATION SHEETS

[C3]

Office of the
Public Guardian

Form

LPC

Continuation sheets

Only use these continuation sheets if you are
told to in the lasting power of attorney (LPA)
form. Many people make an LPA without
needing to use a continuation sheet.

If you make two LPAs and you need to use
continuation sheets for both of them, use
separate sheets for each LPA.

Continuation sheets

Only use these continuation sheets if you are told to in the lasting power of attorney (LPA) form. Many people make an LPA without needing to use a continuation sheet.

If you make two LPAs and you need to use continuation sheets for both of them, use separate sheets for each LPA.

Continuation sheet 1 – Additional people

- Use this sheet if you need space to write more names for sections 2, 4 or 6 of the LPA form.

- You must sign and date this continuation sheet before you sign section 9 of the LPA, or on the same day.

Continuation sheet 2 – Additional information

- Use this sheet if you need more space to write information for sections 3, 4 or 7 of the LPA form.

- If you have to write extra information for more than one of those sections, use a fresh copy of the sheet for each one.

- You must sign and date this continuation sheet before you sign section 9 of the LPA, or on the same day.

Continuation sheet 3 – If the donor cannot sign or make a mark

- Use this sheet if you can't sign or make a mark yourself.

- You will need someone else to sign on your behalf and two people must witness their signature.

- If you're making an LPA for health and care decisions, the person signing for you must also sign section 5 of the LPA on the same day as they sign this sheet.

Continuation sheet 4 – Trust corporation appointed as an attorney

- Use this sheet if you appointed a trust corporation as an attorney or replacement attorney.

- Someone from the trust corporation must sign this sheet instead of signing section 11 of the LPA form.

- They must sign this sheet after your 'certificate provider' has signed section 10 of the LPA form.

This page is not part of the form

608

Continuation sheet 1
Additional people

Use this page if told to in section 2, 4 or 6 of the lasting power of attorney form.

If you use this page, you must sign it.

Help?

For help with this section, see the Guide, parts A2, A4 and A6.

☐ **Attorney** LPA section 2

☐ **Replacement attorney** LPA section 4

☐ **Person to notify** LPA section 6

Title   First names

Last name

Date of birth (not required for 'person to notify')

Day   Month   Year

Address

Postcode

Email address (optional)

☐ **Attorney** LPA section 2

☐ **Replacement attorney** LPA section 4

☐ **Person to notify** LPA section 6

Title   First names

Last name

Date of birth (not required for 'person to notify')

Day   Month   Year

Address

Postcode

Email address (optional)

Donor

You must sign here before you sign section 9 of the LPA, or on the same day.

Full name

Signature or mark

Date signed or marked

Day   Month   Year

Only valid with the official stamp here.

LPC Continuation sheet 1 (07.15)

Continuation sheet 1
Additional people

Use this page if told to in section 2, 4 or 6 of the lasting power of attorney form.

If you use this page, you must sign it.

Help?

For help with this section, see the Guide, parts A2, A4 and A6.

☐ **Attorney** LPA section 2	☐ **Attorney** LPA section 2
☐ **Replacement attorney** LPA section 4	☐ **Replacement attorney** LPA section 4
☐ **Person to notify** LPA section 6	☐ **Person to notify** LPA section 6

Title   First names

Title   First names

Last name

Last name

Date of birth (not required for 'person to notify')

Day   Month   Year

Date of birth (not required for 'person to notify')

Day   Month   Year

Address

Address

Postcode

Postcode

Email address (optional)

Email address (optional)

Donor

You must sign here before you sign section 9 of the LPA, or on the same day.

Full name

Signature or mark

Date signed or marked

Day   Month   Year

Only valid with the official stamp here.

Continuation sheet 1 (07,15)

Continuation sheet 2
Additional information

Helpline
0300 456 0300

Use this page if told to in section 3, 4 or 7 of the lasting power of attorney form.

If you use this page, you must sign it.

What additional information are you providing?

Use a fresh copy of this page for each type of additional information

☐	**Decisions attorneys should make jointly** LPA section 3
☐	**How replacement attorneys step in and act** LPA section 4
☐	**Preferences** LPA section 7
☐	**Instructions** LPA section 7

Help?

For help with this section, see the Guide, parts A3, A4 and A7.

Donor

You must sign here before you sign section 9 of the LPA, or on the same day.

Full name

Signature or mark

Date signed or marked

Day   Month   Year

Only valid with the official stamp here.

LPC Continuation sheet 2 (07.15)

611

Continuation sheet 2
Additional information

Helpline
0300 456 0300

Use this page if told to in section 3, 4 or 7 of the lasting power of attorney form.

If you use this page, you must sign it.

What additional information are you providing?

Use a fresh copy of this page for each type of additional information

☐ **Decisions attorneys should make jointly** LPA section 3

☐ **How replacement attorneys step in and act** LPA section 4

☐ **Preferences** LPA section 7

☐ **Instructions** LPA section 7

Help?

For help with this section, see the Guide, parts A3, A4 and A7.

Donor

You must sign here before you sign section 9 of the LPA, or on the same day.

Full name

Signature or mark

Date signed or marked

Day   Month   Year

Only valid with the official stamp here.

Continuation sheet 2 (07.15)

Continuation sheet 3
If the donor cannot sign or mark

Helpline
0300 456 0300

Only fill in this page if the donor cannot sign or make a mark in section 9 of the lasting power of attorney form

Donor

Full name

Witnesses

Witnesses must **not** be attorneys or replacement attorneys appointed under this LPA and must be aged 18 or over.

Signatory

You must:

- sign in the donor's presence and in the presence of 2 witnesses
- sign in your own name
- not also be a witness to this LPA
- sign any copies of Continuation Sheet 1 and 2 used in this LPA at the same time

If the LPA is for health and care decisions:

- you must also sign and date either Option A or Option B of Section 5, as directed by the donor
- your signature in Section 5 must be witnessed

Signed as a deed and delivered in the presence of and at the direction of the person giving this lasting power of attorney and in the presence of two witnesses.

Signature or mark

Full name of person signing

Date signed or marked

Day   Month   Year

Signature or mark of first witness

Full name of first witness

Address of first witness

Postcode

Signature or mark of second witness

Full name of second witness

Address of second witness

Postcode

Help? For help with this section, see the Guide, part A9.

Only valid with the official stamp here.

LPC Continuation sheet 3 (07.15)

613

Continuation sheet 4
Trust corporation appointed as an attorney

Helpline
0300 456 0300

Only use this page if the donor has appointed a trust corporation as an attorney or replacement attorney

By execution of this deed the trust corporation understands and confirms all of the following:

- It has read this lasting power of attorney (LPA), including section 8 'Your legal rights and responsibilities'.
- It has a duty to act based on the principles of the Mental Capacity Act 2005 and to have regard to the Mental Capacity Act Code of Practice.
- It can make decisions and act only when this LPA has been registered.
- It must make decisions and act in the best interests of the person giving this LPA.
- It is not going through winding-up proceedings.
- It can spend money to make gifts but only to charities or on customary occasions such as birthdays, and for reasonable amounts, with regard to size of the donor's estate.
- It has a duty to keep accounts and financial records and produce them to the Office of the Public Guardian or to the Court of Protection on request.
- It can make decisions and act regarding the donor's property and financial affairs only at the time indicated in section 5 of this LPA.

Further statement by a trust corporation acting as a replacement attorney: It has the authority to act under this LPA only after an original attorney's appointment is terminated. It must notify the Public Guardian if that happens.

Help? → For help with this section, see the Guide, part A11.

Company registration number

I/We are authorised to sign on behalf of the trust corporation acting as attorney whose details are given in this continuation sheet to this lasting power of attorney.

Signed as a deed and delivered by:

Signature of first authorised person

Full name of first authorised person

Date signed or marked

Day   Month   Year

Signature of second authorised person (if required)

Full name of second authorised person (if required)

Date signed or marked (if required)

Day   Month   Year

Only valid with the official stamp here.

LPC Continuation sheet 4 (07.15)

LP2: REGISTER YOUR LPA

[C4]

Office of the
Public Guardian

Form

LP2

**Registering
an LPA costs**

Register your lasting power of attorney

£82

This fee is means-tested:
see the application
Guide part B

Use this form if the LPA you want to register
was made using an LPA114, LPA117,
LP PA or LP PW.

How to complete this form

PLEASE WRITE IN CAPITAL LETTERS USING A BLACK PEN

 Mark your choice with an X

 If you make a mistake, fill in the box and then mark the correct
choice with an X

This form is also available in Welsh. Call the helpline on 0300 456 0300.

Before you start

Helpline
0300 456 0300

Before the lasting power of attorney (LPA) can be used, it **must** be registered by the Office of the Public Guardian (OPG). Fill in this form to register the LPA. See the Registration guide, part B.

People to notify

If there are any 'people to notify' (also called 'people to be told' or 'named people') listed in the LPA, you must notify them that you are registering the LPA now. See the Registration guide, part C.

Fill in and send each of them a copy of the form to notify people – form LP3.

When you sign section 5 of this form, you confirm that you've sent them the forms to the 'people to notify'.

Two lasting powers of attorney

If you are applying to register two LPAs, you must complete a copy of this form for each LPA.

Check your registration

When you've filled in this form you can use this checklist to help you make sure you have completed it correctly.

☐ I am either the donor or an attorney on the enclosed LPA form.

☐ I've completed sections 1 to 5 of this form.

☐ I used form LP3 to notify the 'people to notify' (also called 'people to be told' or 'named people'), if any were named on the LPA form.

☐ If the attorneys are applying to register the LPA and were appointed 'jointly' in the attached LPA, they have all signed section 5 of this form.

☐ (Optional) I've paid the application fee or applied for a reduced fee. If I've applied for a reduced fee, I've included form LPA120A and the required evidence.

☐ I've included all the pages of the LPA form in the envelope, even the ones where I didn't write anything or there were no boxes to fill in.

When completed send to:

Office of the Public Guardian
PO Box 16185
Birmingham B2 2WH

This page is not part of the form

LP2 Register LPA (03.17)

Register your lasting power of attorney

Section 1
About the lasting power of attorney

Donor

Title   First names

Last name

What type of lasting power of attorney (LPA) is being registered?
(tick one only)

If you are registering 2 LPAs, you must fill in one form for each LPA.

☐ Property and financial affairs

☐ Health and welfare

Help?

For help with this
section, see the
Guide, part B1.

617

Section 2
The applicant

Helpline
0300 456 0300

You can only apply to register if you are either the donor or attorney(s) for this lasting power of attorney (LPA). The donor and attorneys should not apply together.

Who is applying to register the LPA? (tick one only)

☐ **Donor** – the donor needs to sign section 5 of this form.

☐ **Attorney(s)** – If the attorneys were appointed jointly in the LPA then they **all** need to sign section 5 of this form. Otherwise, only one of the attorneys needs to sign.

Help?

For help with this section, see the Guide, part B2.

Write the name and date of birth for each attorney that is applying to register the LPA. Don't include any attorneys who are not applying.

Title	First names

Last name

Date of birth

Day	Month	Year

Title	First names

Last name

Date of birth

Day	Month	Year

Title	First names

Last name

Date of birth

Day	Month	Year

Title	First names

Last name

Date of birth

Day	Month	Year

Section 3
Who do you want to receive the LPA?

Helpline
0300 456 0300

We need to know who to send the LPA to once it is registered. We might also need to contact someone with questions about the application.

We already have the addresses of the donor and attorneys on the LPA form, so you don't have to repeat any of these here unless they have changed.

Who would you like to receive the LPA and any correspondence?

☐ The donor

☐ **An attorney** (write name below)

☐ **Other** (write name and address below)

Title   First names

Last name

Company (optional)

Address

Postcode

Help?

For help with this section, see the Guide, part B3.

How would the person above prefer to be contacted?

You can choose more than one.

☐ Post

☐ Phone

☐ Email

☐ **Welsh** (We will write to the person in Welsh)

If you need to update anyone else's address, use section 6.

Section 4
Application fee

There's a fee for registering a lasting power of attorney – the amount is shown on the cover sheet of this form and on form LPA120.

The fee changes from time to time. You can check you are paying the correct amount at www.gov.uk/power-of-attorney/how-much-it-costs or call 0300 456 0300. The Office of the Public Guardian can't register your LPA until you have paid the fee.

How would you like to pay?

☐ **Card** For security, don't write your credit or debit card details here. We'll contact you to process the payment.

Your phone number

☐☐☐☐☐☐☐☐☐☐☐☐☐☐☐☐☐

☐ **Cheque** Enclose a cheque with your application.

Help?

For help with this section, see the Guide, part B4.

Reduced application fee

If the donor has a low income, you may not have to pay the full amount. See the Guide, Part B4 for details.

☐ **I want to apply to pay a reduced fee**

You'll need to fill in form LPA120 and include it with your application. You'll also need to send proof that the donor is eligible to pay a reduced fee.

For OPG office use only

Payment reference

```
[                                                        ]
```

Payment date

☐☐ ☐☐ ☐☐☐☐

Day   Month   Year

Amount

```
[                        ]
```

LP2 Register LPA (07.15)

4

Section 5
Signature

Helpline
0300 456 0300

The person applying to register the lasting power of attorney (LPA) (see section 2) must sign and date this section. This is either the donor or attorney(s) but not both together.

If the **attorneys** are applying to register the LPA and they were appointed to act **jointly** they must all sign.

By signing this section I confirm the following:

- I apply to register the LPA that accompanies this application

- I have informed 'people to notify' named in the LPA (if any) of my intention to register the LPA

- I certify that the information in this form is correct to the best of my knowledge and belief

Help?

For help with this section, see the Guide, part B5.

Signature or mark	Signature or mark

Date signed	Date signed
Day Month Year	Day Month Year

Signature or mark	Signature or mark

Date signed	Date signed
Day Month Year	Day Month Year

If more than 4 attorneys need to sign, make copies of this page.

621

Section 6
Addresses

Use this page:
- if the LPA was made before 1 October 2009, to tell us **all** the attorneys' addresses
- if the LPA was made since 1 October 2009 and the donor or any attorney has changed address

Title	First names

Last name

Address

Postcode

Email address

Title	First names

Last name

Address

Postcode

Email address

Title	First names

Last name

Address

Postcode

Email address

Title	First names

Last name

Address

Postcode

Email address

LP3: FORM TO NOTIFY PEOPLE
[C5]

Office of the
Public Guardian

Form

LP3

Form to notify people

You only need to fill in this form if there are
'people to notify' (also called 'people to be
told' or 'named people') listed in the lasting
power of attorney.

How to complete this form

PLEASE WRITE IN CAPITAL LETTERS USING A BLACK PEN

☒ Mark your choice with an X

■ If you make a mistake, fill in the box and then mark the correct
choice with an X

This page is not part of the form   LP3 People to notify (07.15)

Office of the Public Guardian © Crown Copyright Published by LexisNexis 2015 under the Open Government Licence

Before you start

Helpline
0300 456 0300

You only need to fill in this form if there are 'people to notify' (also called 'people to be told' or 'named people') listed in the lasting power of attorney (LPA). See the Guide, part C.

A 'person to notify' is someone a person who makes an LPA (the 'donor') chooses to inform about the registration of their LPA. They don't have to choose anyone to notify, so if that section of the LPA is blank, you don't need to fill in this form.

When you apply to register the LPA you must tell the people to notify that the LPA will be registered.

You must send a copy of this form to each of the people to notify, before you send the LPA to be registered. You can send them this form or hand it to them in person.

You can save time by filling in pages 2 and 3 and making a photocopy to send to each person.

The donor's relatives are not entitled to be notified unless they have been named in the LPA.

Detach this cover sheet before sending the form to them.

Notice of intention to register a lasting power of attorney

Person to notify

Title

First names

Last name

Address

Postcode

Date

Day   Month   Year

You have received this notice because the person named on page 2 has made a lasting power of attorney.

A lasting power of attorney (LPA) is a legal document that lets someone (known as a 'donor') appoint people (known as 'attorneys') to make decisions on their behalf. It can apply to financial decisions or health and care decisions. An LPA can be used if the donor is unable to make their own decisions.

In other words, the person on page 2 is appointing the people on page 3 to make decisions on their behalf.

When they made the LPA, the donor decided you should be told about it before it's registered. This is so you can raise any concerns you may have. If you do have concerns, you can only object to the registration of the LPA for the reasons listed on page 4 of this form.

If you want to object, you must do so within 3 weeks of the date of this notice.

If you don't want to object you don't have to do anything.

Details of the lasting power of attorney

Helpline
0300 456 0300

About the donor – the person who made the LPA

Title

First names

Last name

Address

Postcode

About the lasting power of attorney

Who is applying to register the LPA?

☐ Donor

☐ Attorney(s)

What type of LPA is being registered?

☐ Property and financial affairs

☐ Health and welfare

When did the donor sign the LPA?

Day   Month   Year

626

About the attorneys

How are the attorneys appointed?

☐ There's only 1 attorney

☐ Jointly and severally

☐ Jointly

☐ Jointly for some decisions, jointly and severally for other decisions

Title	First names

Last name

Address

Postcode

Title	First names

Last name

Address

Postcode

Title	First names

Last name

Address

Postcode

Title	First names

Last name

Address

Postcode

If there are more than 4 attorneys, please make a copy of this page.
You don't need to list replacement attorneys appointed in the LPA (if any).

627

How to object

If you wish to object, you must do so within 3 weeks of being given this notice.

You can only object to an LPA for one of the reasons below.

Factual objections:

• the donor or an attorney has died

• the donor and an attorney were married or had a civil partnership but have divorced or ended the civil partnership (unless the LPA says the attorney can still act if that happens)

• an attorney doesn't have the mental capacity to be an attorney (they must be able to understand and make decisions for themselves)

• an attorney has chosen to stop acting (known as 'disclaiming their appointment')

• the donor or an attorney is bankrupt, interim bankrupt or subject to a debt relief order (LPA for financial decisions only)

• the attorney is a trust corporation and is wound up or dissolved (LPA for financial decisions only)

To make a factual objection, complete form LPA007 and send it to the Office of the Public Guardian. Get the form from www.gov.uk/power-of-attorney/object-registration or by calling 0300 456 0300.

Prescribed objections:

• the LPA isn't legally valid – for example, you don't believe the donor had mental capacity to make an LPA

• the donor cancelled their LPA when they had mental capacity to do so

• there was fraud or the donor was pressured to make the LPA

• an attorney is acting above their authority or against the donor's best interests (or you know that they intend to do this)

To make a prescribed objection:

• complete form COP7 and send it to the Court of Protection. Get the form from www.gov.uk/object-registration or by calling 0300 456 4000 **AND**

• complete form LPA008 and send it to the Office of the Public Guardian. Get the form from www.gov.uk/object-registration or by calling 0300 456 0300

If you are objecting to a specific attorney, it may not prevent registration if other attorneys or a replacement attorney have been appointed.

You can find out more about lasting powers of attorney at www.gov.uk/power-of-attorney or by calling 0300 456 0300.

LPA 003A: NOTICE TO AN ATTORNEY OF RECEIPT OF AN APPLICATION TO REGISTER A LASTING POWER OF ATTORNEY

[C6]

Office of the Public Guardian

Office of the Public Guardian
PO Box 16185
Birmingham B2 2WH

Tel: 0300 456 0300
Fax: 0870 739 5780

customerservices@publicguardian.gsi.gov.uk
www.gov.uk/opg

Notice to attorney: application to register a lasting power of attorney (LPA003A)

Date:

Case number:

To:

You have received this notice because:

- _____ (the 'donor') made a lasting power of attorney (LPA) for _____
- they named you as attorney in that LPA
- the person(s) named below has applied to register the LPA

Person(s) who applied to register the LPA
The following person(s) applied to register the LPA:

Your right to object
You can object to the proposed registration of the LPA.

You have 3 weeks from _____ to object. Page 2 of this notice tells you how to object.

How to object

If you wish to object, you must do so within 3 weeks of being given this notice.
You can only object to an LPA for one of the reasons below.

Factual objections:

- the donor or an attorney has died
- the donor and an attorney were married or had a civil partnership but have divorced or ended the civil partnership (unless the LPA says the attorney can still act if that happens)
- an attorney doesn't have the mental capacity to be an attorney (they must be able to understand and make decisions for themselves)
- an attorney has chosen to stop acting (known as 'disclaiming their appointment')
- the donor or an attorney is bankrupt, interim bankrupt or subject to a debt relief order (financial decisions LPA)
- the attorney is a trust corporation and is wound up or dissolved (financial decisions LPA)

To make a factual objection, complete form LPA007 and send it to the Office of the Public Guardian. Get the form from www.gov.uk/power-of-attorney/object-registration or by calling 0300 456 0300.

Prescribed objections:

- the LPA isn't legally valid – for example, you don't believe the donor had mental capacity to make an LPA
- the donor cancelled their LPA when they had mental capacity to do so
- there was fraud or the donor was pressured to make the LPA
- an attorney is acting above their authority or against the donor's best interests (or you know that they intend to do this)

To make a prescribed objection:

- complete form COP7 and send it to the Court of Protection. Get the form from www.gov.uk/object-registration or by calling 0300 456 4000 **AND**
- complete form LPA008 and send it to the Office of the Public Guardian. Get the form from www.gov.uk/object-registration or by calling 0300 456 0300

If you are objecting to a specific attorney, it may not prevent registration if other attorneys or a replacement attorney have been appointed.

You can find out more about lasting powers of attorney at www.gov.uk/power-of-attorney or by calling 0300 456 0300.

LPA003A (04.15)

LPA 003B: NOTICE TO DONOR OF RECEIPT OF AN APPLICATION TO REGISTER A LASTING POWER OF ATTORNEY

[C7]

**Office of the
Public Guardian**

Office of the Public Guardian
PO Box 16185
Birmingham B2 2WH

Tel: 0300 456 0300
Fax: 0870 739 5780

customerservices@publicguardian.gsi.gov.uk
www.gov.uk/opg

Notice to donor: application to register a lasting power of attorney (LPA003B)

Date:

Case number:

To:

You have received this notice because:

- You made a lasting power of attorney (LPA) for
- the person(s) named below has applied to register the LPA

Person(s) who applied to register the LPA
The following attorney(s) applied to register the LPA:

Your right to object
You can object to the proposed registration of the LPA.

You have 3 weeks from   to object.

How to object
Complete form LPA006 and send it to the Office of the Public Guardian – get the
form from www.gov.uk/object-registration or by calling 0300 456 0300.

LPA003B (04.15)

LPA 004: NOTICE OF REGISTRATION OF LASTING POWER OF ATTORNEY (PROPERTY AND FINANCIAL AFFAIRS)

[C8]

`LPA 004` `04.07`

Notice of registration of
Lasting Power of Attorney
(Property and Financial Affairs)

This notice is to confirm registration of a Lasting Power of Attorney.

Case no.

The donor

The attorney(s)

The lasting power of attorney was entered into the register on DD/MM/YYYY

Registration is confirmed as required in Schedule 1 Part 2 (15) of the Mental Capacity Act 2005 with regard to registration of this LPA.

LPA 005: DISCLAIMER BY A PROPOSED OR ACTING ATTORNEY
UNDER A LASTING POWER OF ATTORNEY

[C9]

Office of the
Public Guardian

Form

LPA005

Disclaimer by a proposed
or acting attorney under a
lasting power of attorney

1. Donor details (the person who made the lasting power of attorney)

Title   First names

Last name

Address

Postcode

To the donor

You have received this notice because:

- you made a lasting power of attorney (LPA)
- you chose the person named on page 2 (the 'disclaiming attorney') as an
  attorney for that LPA
- that person now wishes to give up their role as an attorney (this is called
  'disclaiming their appointment').

LPA005 (07.15)

1

2. About the lasting power of attorney (LPA)

What type of LPA is it?

☐ Property and financial affairs

☐ Health and welfare

When did the donor sign the LPA?
(To find out, look at Part A of the LPA if it was made before 1 July 2015 or section 9 if it was made on or after that date)

Date

☐☐ ☐☐ ☐☐☐☐

Day   Month   Year

Was the LPA registered by the Office of the Public Guardian?
(see page 1 of the LPA – the section marked 'OPG office use only')

☐ Yes

☐ No

When was the LPA registered?
Date

☐☐ ☐☐ ☐☐☐☐

Day   Month   Year

What is the 'OPG reference number'? (see page 1 of the LPA)

☐

3. Disclaiming attorney details (the person sending this notice)

Title   First names

☐ ☐

Last name

☐

Address

☐

☐

☐

Postcode ☐

Phone number

☐☐☐☐☐☐☐☐☐☐☐☐☐☐

4. Signature and date

I disclaim my appointment as attorney under the lasting power of attorney made by the donor named on this form. I will send copies of this form to any other attorneys named on the lasting power of attorney and to the Office of the Public Guardian:

Signature or mark

Date signed

Day   Month   Year

Notes for the person completing this form

When you have completed and signed this form:
- send the original form to the donor
- send a copy of this form to any other attorneys that were named in the LPA
- if you are the only attorney, send a copy of the form to any replacement attorneys named in the LPA

If the Office of the Public Guardian (OPG) has registered the LPA, you should also:
- send a copy of this form to OPG
- send any copies of the LPA that you have to OPG

Address: Office of the Public Guardian, PO BOX 16185, Birmingham, B2 2WH

If you have any queries call the OPG contact centre on 0300 456 0300.

LPA005 (07.15)

3

LPA 006: OBJECTION BY THE DONOR
[C10]

**Office of the
Public Guardian**

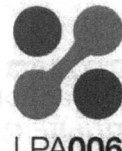

Objection by the donor to the registration of a lasting power of attorney(s)

LPA006

If you (the donor) **do not want** your lasting power of attorney(s) (LPA) to be registered, then you need to complete and sign this form and return it to the Office of the Public Guardian (OPG).

You can use this form to object to registration of up to two LPAs; please provide below the case number and LPA type for **each** LPA you want to object to.

Donor details

Title

First names

Last name

Address

Postcode

Date of birth

Day   Month   Year

LPA details

LPA case no (if known)

What type of LPA is it?

☐ Property and financial affairs

☐ Health and welfare

LPA case no (if known)

What type of LPA is it?

☐ Property and financial affairs

☐ Health and welfare

The reason(s) for your objection to registration of your LPA(s)

Note: OPG will suspend your LPA(s) when we receive this form. Your attorney(s) will then not be able to use the LPA(s), unless they apply to the Court of Protection and the court orders the LPA(s) to be registered.

LPA006 (03.17)
http://www.justice.gov.uk/global/forms/opg/index.htm. © Crown Copyright Published by LexisNexis 2017 under the Open Government Licence.

LPA 007: OBJECTION TO THE OFFICE OF THE PUBLIC GUARDIAN OF A PROPOSED REGISTRATION OF A LASTING POWER OF ATTORNEY ON FACTUAL GROUNDS

[C11]

LPA 007 | 06.16

Objection to the Office of the Public Guardian of a proposed registration of a lasting power of attorney on factual grounds

This form can only be used by the attorneys or people to notify

Donor's full name	
Date of birth (if known)	
Case no. (if known)	

On what grounds are you objecting to the registration?

You must place an 'X' in at least one box and provide evidence or proof of each ground to accompany this notice.

☐ The donor is bankrupt or interim bankrupt (property and financial affairs LPA only)

☐ The attorney is bankrupt or interim bankrupt (property and financial affairs LPA only)

☐ The attorney is a trust corporation that has been wound up or dissolved

☐ The donor is dead

☐ The attorney is dead

☐ There has been dissolution or annulment of a marriage or civil partnership between the donor and attorney (and the LPA does not provide for this event)

☐ The attorney lacks capacity to act

☐ The attorney has disclaimed appointment

Please list opposite the evidence on which your objection is based and attach a copy to this form.

Signed	☐ attorney
	☐ person to notify
Full name	
Dated	

Send your completed form and evidence to:
Office of the Public Guardian, PO Box 16185, Birmingham, B2 2WH

© Crown copyright 2016

http://www.justice.gov.uk/global/forms/opg/index.htm. © Crown Copyright Published by LexisNexis 2017 under the Open Government Licence.

LPA 008: NOTICE TO THE OFFICE OF THE PUBLIC GUARDIAN OF AN APPLICATION TO OBJECT TO REGISTRATION OF A LASTING POWER OF ATTORNEY MADE TO THE COURT OF PROTECTION

[C12]

LPA 008 `10.16`

Notice to the Office of the Public Guardian of an objection to registration of a lasting power of attorney

You use this form to tell the Office of the Public Guardian (OPG) about your objection to the Court of Protection ('the court') about a lasting power of attorney (LPA) registration. OPG and the court are different organisations. You need to tell OPG within three weeks of the date you are sent an 'LP3 form', which tells you an LPA is going to be registered. If you don't tell OPG, it may go ahead and register the LPA.

This notice confirms that I have applied to the court to object to the registration of the LPA(s) detailed below.

Which kind(s) of LPA are you objecting to?　　☐ Property and financial affairs　　☐ Health and welfare

Case no(s)
(if known)　[   ]

Details of the donor ─────────────────────────────

Name

[   ]

Address

[   ]

Phone no

[   ]

Postcode [ ][ ][ ][ ][ ][ ][ ]

Details of the person making the objection ─────────────

Your name

[   ]

Address

[   ]

Phone no

[   ]

Postcode [ ][ ][ ][ ][ ][ ][ ]

Why are you making the objection?

Please tick the reason(s) below you're objecting to registration of the LPA. **Note:** OPG won't suspend registration of an LPA for any other reason.

☐ The LPA(s) isn't legally correct (for example, you don't believe the donor had the mental capacity to decide to make an LPA)

☐ The donor cancelled their LPA(s) when they had capacity

☐ The donor was pressured to make the LPA(s)

☐ You suspect fraud (for example, someone faking the donor's signature)

☐ An attorney is acting against the donor's best interests

☐ If there is more than one attorney and you are objecting to a particular attorney, please name them here

I've sent my objection (form COP7) to the Court of Protection ☐

When did you send your objection to the court? | D | D | M | M | Y | Y | Y | Y |

Signature and date

Signed

Dated | D | D | M | M | Y | Y | Y | Y |

Send your completed form to:
Office of the Public Guardian
PO Box 16185
Birmingham
B2 2WH

Appendix D

ENDURING POWER OF ATTORNEY FORMS

Contents

EPA: PRESCRIBED FORM OF ENDURING POWER OF ATTORNEY
[D1]

STATUTORY INSTRUMENTS

2005 No. 3116

POWERS OF ATTORNEY, ENGLAND AND WALES

MENTAL HEALTH, ENGLAND AND WALES

The Enduring Powers of Attorney (Prescribed Form) (Amendment) Regulations 2005

Made - - - -	*8th November 2005*
Laid before Parliament	*10th November 2005*
Coming into force - -	*5th December 2005*

The Lord Chancellor makes the following Regulations in exercise of the powers conferred by section 2(2) of the Enduring Powers of Attorney Act 1985(**a**):

Citation, commencement and interpretation

1.—(1) These Regulations may be cited as the Enduring Powers of Attorney (Prescribed Form) (Amendment) Regulations 2005 and shall come into force on 5th December 2005.

(2) In these Regulations, a reference to the Schedule is a reference to the Schedule to the Enduring Powers of Attorney (Prescribed Form) Regulations 1990(**b**).

Amendments to the Enduring Power of Attorney (Prescribed Form) Regulations 1990

2. For the Schedule substitute the Schedule to these Regulations.

Transitional provision

3. A power executed in the form prescribed in the Schedule as though it had not been substituted by these Regulations and executed by the donor before 1st April 2007 shall be capable (whether or not seals are affixed to it) of being a valid enduring power of attorney.

Signed by authority of the Lord Chancellor

Cathy Ashton
Parliamentary Under Secretary of State,
8th November 2005   Department for Constitutional Affairs

(a) 1985 c.29.
(b) S.I. 1990/1376.

SCHEDULE   Regulation 2

ENDURING POWER OF ATTORNEY

Part A: About using this form

1. You may choose one attorney or more than one. If you choose one attorney then you must delete everything between the square brackets on the first page of the form. If you choose more than one, you must decide whether they are able to act:
- Jointly (that is, they must all act together and cannot act separately) or
- Jointly and severally (that is, they can all act together but they can also act separately if they wish).

On the first page of the form, show what you have decided by crossing out one of the alternatives.

2. If you give your attorney(s) general power in relation to all your property and affairs, it means that they will be able to deal with your money or property and may be able to sell your house.

3. If you don't want your attorney(s) to have such wide powers, you can include any restrictions you like. For example, you can include a restriction that your attorney(s) must not act on your behalf until they have reason to believe that you are becoming mentally incapable, or a restriction as to what your attorney(s) may do. Any restrictions you choose must be written or typed where indicated on the second page of the form.

4. If you are a trustee (and please remember that co-ownership of a home involves trusteeship), you should seek legal advice if you want your attorney(s) to act as a trustee on your behalf.

5. Unless you put in a restriction preventing it your attorney(s) will be able to use any of your money or property to make any provision which you yourself might expect to make for their own needs or the needs of other people. Your attorney(s) will also be able to use your money to make gifts, but only for reasonable amounts in relation to the value of your money and property.

6. Your attorney(s) can recover the out-of-pocket expenses of acting as your attorney(s). If your attorney(s) are professional people, for example solicitors or accountants, they may be able to charge for their professional services as well. You may wish to provide expressly for remuneration of your attorney(s) (although if they are trustees they may not be allowed to accept it).

7. If your attorney(s) have reason to believe that you have become or are becoming mentally incapable of managing your affairs, your attorney(s) will have to apply to the Court of Protection for registration of this power.

8. Before applying to the Court of Protection for registration of this power, your attorney(s) must give written notice, using a special form of notice, that that is what they are going to do, to you and your nearest relatives as defined in the Enduring Powers of Attorney Act 1985. You or your relatives will be able to object if you or they disagree with registration.

9. This is a simplified explanation of what the Enduring Powers of Attorney Act 1985 and the Rules and Regulations say. If you need more guidance, you or your advisers will need to look at the Act itself and the Rules and Regulations. You can obtain details of these from the Court of Protection.

10. Note to attorney(s)
After the power has been registered you should notify the Court of Protection if the donor dies or recovers.

11. Note to Donor
Some of these explanatory notes may not apply to the form you are using if it has been adapted to suit your particular requirements.

Please do not detach these notes. They are part of the Enduring Power of Attorney.
YOU CAN CANCEL THIS POWER AT ANY TIME BEFORE IT HAS TO BE REGISTERED

Part B: To be completed by the 'donor' (the person appointing the attorney(s))

Don't sign this form unless you understand what it means

Please read the notes in the margin which follow and which are part of the form itself.

Donor's full name and address.

I _____

of _____

Donor's date of birth.

born on _____

Attorney's full name and address.

appoint _____

of _____

See note 1 on the front of this form. If you are appointing only one attorney you should cross out everything between the square brackets. If appointing more than two attorneys please give the additional name(s) on an attached sheet.

• [and _____

of _____

Cross out the one which does not apply (see note 1 on the front of this form).

• jointly
• jointly and severally]

to be my attorney(s) for the purpose of the Enduring Power of Attorney Act 1985

Cross out the one which does not apply (see note 2 on the front of this form). Add any additional powers.

If you don't want the attorney(s) to have general power, you must give details here of what authority you are giving the attorney(s).

• with general authority to act on my behalf
• with authority to do the following on my behalf:

Cross out the one which does not apply.

in relation to
• all my property and affairs
• the following property and affairs:

Part B: continued

Please read the notes in the margin which follow and which are part of the form itself.

If there are restrictions or conditions, insert them here; if not, cross out these words if you wish (see note 3 on the front of this form).

If this form is being signed at your direction:-
• The person signing must not be an attorney or any witness (to Parts B or C).
• You must add a statement that this form has been signed at your direction.
• A second witness is necessary (please see below).

Your signature or mark.

Date.

Someone must witness your signature.

Signature of witness.

Your attorney(s) cannot be your witness.

• Subject to the following restrictions and conditions:

I intend that this power shall continue even if I become mentally incapable.

I have read or have had read to me the notes in Part A which are part of, and explain, this form.

I understand the purpose and effect of this document and the nature and extent of the powers I am granting my attorney(s).

Signed by me as a deed _____
and delivered

on _____

in the presence of _____

Full name of witness _____

Address of witness _____

_____

_____

A second witness is only necessary if this form is not being signed by you personally but at your direction (for example, if a physical disability prevents you from signing). Signature of second witness.

in the presence of _____

Full name of witness _____

Address of witness _____

_____

_____

YOUR ATTORNEY MUST NOW COMPLETE PART C

Part C: To be completed by the attorney(s)
Note: 1. This form may be adapted to provide for execution by a corporation.
2. If there is more than one attorney additional sheets in the form as shown below must be added to this Part C.

Please read the notes in the margin which follow and which are part of the form itself.

Don't sign this form before the donor has signed Part B or if, in your opinion, the donor was already mentally incapable at the time of signing Part B.

I understand that I have a duty to apply to the Court for the registration of this form under the Enduring Powers of Attorney Act 1985 when the donor is or is becoming mentally incapable.

If this form is being signed at your direction:-
• The person signing must not be an attorney or any witness (to Parts B or C);
• You must add a statement that this form has been signed at your direction;
• A second witness is necessary (please see below).

I understand that I am able to use the donor's money to make gifts, but only on specified occasions and for reasonable amounts in relation to the donor's money and property.

I also understand that I have a duty to keep proper accounts and records and produce them to the Court when requested.

I am not a minor.

Signature (or mark) of attorney.

Signed by me as a deed
and delivered

Date.

on

Signature of witness.

in the presence of

The attorney must sign the form and his signature must be witnessed. The donor may not be the witness and one attorney may not witness the signature of another.

Full name of witness

Address of witness

A second witness is only necessary if this form is not being signed by you personally but at your direction (for example, if a physical disability prevents you from signing).

Signature of second witness.

in the presence of

Full name of witness

Address of witness

EP1PG: NOTICE OF INTENTION TO APPLY FOR REGISTRATION OF AN ENDURING POWER OF ATTORNEY

[D2]

Form EP1PG

Mental Capacity Act 2005
Enduring Power of Attorney

Notice of intention to apply for registration
of an Enduring Power of Attorney

To...

Of..

This form may be adapted for use by three or more attorneys	**TAKE NOTICE THAT** I .... of .... and I .... of .... The attorney(s) of .... of .... intend to apply to the Public Guardian for registration of the enduring power of attorney appointing me (us) attorney(s) and made by the donor on the ....
Give the name and address of the donor	
The grounds upon which you can object are limited and are shown at 2 overleaf	1. You have the right to object to the proposed registration on one or more of the grounds set out below. You must notify the Office of the Public Guardian of your objection within five weeks from the day this notice was given to you. You may make an application to the Court of Protection under rule 68 of the Court of Protection Rules 2007 for a decision on the matter. No fee is payable for such an application. If you do not make such an application, the Public Guardian may ask for the court's directions about registration.

EP1PG – 09.11

Note: The instrument means the document used to make the enduring power of attorney made by the donor, which it is sought to register

The attorney(s) does not have to be a relative. Relatives are not entitled to know of the existence of the enduring power of attorney prior to being given this notice

Our staff will be able to assist with any questions you have regarding the objection (s). However, they cannot provide advice about your particular objection.

Note: Part 4 is addressed only to the donor

Note: This notice should be signed by every one of the attorneys who are applying to register the enduring power of attorney

Note:
The attorney(s) must keep a record of the date on which notice was given to the donor and to relatives. This information will be required from the attorney(s) when an application to register the EPA is made

2. The grounds on which you may object to the proposed registration are:

- That the power purported to be created by the instrument is not valid as an enduring power of attorney
- That the power created by the instrument no longer subsists
- That the application is premature because the donor is not yet becoming mentally incapable
- That fraud or undue pressure was used to induce the donor to make the power
- That the attorney is unsuitable to be the donor's attorney (having regard to all the circumstances and in particular the attorney's relationship to or connection with the donor).

3. If you object, you must notify the Office of the Public Guardian and state which of the grounds you are relying on within five weeks from the day this notice was given to you. You can obtain the necessary court forms to object by.
- Calling the court on 0300 456 4600
- Downloading the forms from www.justice.gov.uk/global/forms/hmcts/index.htm

4. You are informed that while the enduring power of attorney remains registered, you will not be able to revoke it until the Court of Protection confirms the revocation.

Signed: .... Dated: ....

Signed: .... Dated: ....

Please write to:
Office of the Public Guardian
PO Box 16185
Birmingham
B2 2WH

www.direct.gov.uk/mentalcapacity

EP1PG – 09.11

EP2PG: APPLICATION FOR REGISTRATION OF AN ENDURING POWER OF ATTORNEY

[D3]

Office of the Public Guardian
Mental Capacity Act 2005
Form EP2PG
Application for Registration of an Enduring
Power of Attorney

IMPORTANT: Please complete the form in **BLOCK CAPITALS** using a **black ball-point pen**. Place a clear cross 'X' mark inside square option boxes ☒ - do not circle the option.

Part One - The Donor

Please state the full name and present address of the donor. State the donor's first name in 'Forename 1' and the donor's other forenames in full in 'Other Forenames'. Company Name should be completed with the name of the nursing/care home or hospital where applicable.

Mr ☐ Mrs ☐ Ms ☐ Miss ☐ Other ☐
Place a cross against one option ☒

If Other, please specify here:

Last Name:

Forename 1:

Other Forenames:

Company Name:

Address 1:

Address 2:

Address 3:

Town/City:

County:

Postcode:

Donor Date of Birth: D D M M Y Y Y Y

If the exact date is unknown please state the year of birth

Please do not write below this line - For Office Use Only

Produced in association with the Office of the Public Guardian

© Crown Copyright 2010

Provider details

Page 1 of 7

651

	Part Two - Attorney One

Please state the full name and present address of the attorney. Professionals e,g, Solicitors or Accountants, should complete the Company Name field.

Mr   Mrs Ms Miss Other
☐   ☐   ☐   ☐   ☐   If Other, please specify here:
Place a cross against one option ☒

Last Name:

Forename 1:

Other Forenames:

Company Name:

Address 1:

Address 2:

Address 3:

Town/City:

County:

Postcode: DX No. (solicitors only):

DX Exchange (solicitors only):

Attorney Date of Birth: Daytime Tel No.:
D D M M Y Y Y Y   (STD Code):

Email Address:

Occupation:

Relationship to donor:

Civil Partner / Spouse   Child   Other Relation   No Relation   Solicitor   Other Professional   If 'Other Relation' or 'Other Professional', specify relationship:
☐   ☐   ☐   ☐   ☐   ☐
Place a cross against one option ☒

Part B of the Enduring Power of Attorney states whether the attorney is to act jointly, jointly and severally, or alone.

Appointment (*Place a cross against one option* ☒):   Jointly ☐

                                   Jointly and Severally ☐

                                   Alone ☐

Part Three - Attorney Two

Please state the full name and present address of the attorney. Professionals e.g. Solicitors or Accountants, should complete the Company Name field.

Mr   Mrs   Ms   Miss   Other
☐   ☐   ☐   ☐   ☐
Place a cross against one option ☒

If Other, please specify here:

Last Name:

Forename 1:

Other Forenames:

Company Name:

Address 1:

Address 2:

Address 3:

Town/City:

County:

Postcode:

DX No. (solicitors only):

DX Exchange (solicitors only):

Attorney Date of Birth:
D D M M Y Y Y Y

Daytime Tel No.:
(STD Code):

Email Address:

Occupation:

Relationship to donor:

Civil Partner / Spouse   Child   Other Relation   No Relation   Other Solicitor   Other Professional
☐   ☐   ☐   ☐   ☐   ☐
Place a cross against one option ☒

If 'Other Relation' or 'Other Professional', specify relationship:

Part Four - Attorney Three

Please state the full name and present address of the attorney. Professionals e.g, Solicitors or Accountants, should complete the Company Name field.

Mr   Mrs   Ms   Miss   Other
☐   ☐   ☐   ☐   ☐
Place a cross against one option ☒

If Other, please specify here:

Last Name:

Forename 1:

Part Four - Attorney Three cont'd

Other Forenames:	
Company Name:	
Address 1:	
Address 2:	
Address 3:	
Town/City:	
County:	
Postcode:	DX No. (solicitors only):
DX Exchange (solicitors only):	
Attorney Date of Birth:	Daytime Tel No.:
	D D M M Y Y Y Y (STD Code):
Email Address:	
Occupation:	

Relationship to donor:

Civil Partner / Spouse	Child	Other Relation	No Relation	Solicitor	Other Professional	If 'Other Relation' or 'Other Professional', specify relationship:
☐	☐	☐	☐	☐	☐	

Place a cross against one option ☒

If there are additional attorneys, please complete the above details in the 'Additional Information' section (at the end of this form).

Part Five - The Enduring Power of Attorney

I (We) the attorney(s) apply to register the Enduring Power of Attorney made by the donor under the Enduring Powers of Attorney Act 1985, the original, or if the original is lost or destroyed, a certified copy of which accompanies this application.

I (We) have reason to believe that the donor is or is becoming mentally incapable.

Date that the **Donor** signed the Enduring Power of Attorney.
You can find this in Part B of the Enduring Power of Attorney.

D D M M Y Y Y Y

To your knowledge, has the Donor made any other Enduring Powers of Attorney?: ☐ ☐
Yes No
Place a cross against one option ☒

If 'Yes', please give details below including registration date if applicable:

....
....

Part Six - Notice of Application to Donor

Notice must be given personally to the donor. It should be made clear if someone other than the attorney(s) gives the notice. The date on which the notice was given MUST be completed.

I (We) have given notice of the application to register in the prescribed form (EP1PG) to the donor personally,

on this date: ☐☐☐☐☐☐☐☐

    D D M M Y Y Y Y

If someone other than the attorney gives notice to the donor please complete the name and address details below. Please also complete the date above:

Full Name:	
Address 1:	
Address 2:	
Address 3:	
Town/City:	
County:	Postcode:

Part Seven - Notice of Application to Relatives

Please complete details of all relatives entitled to notice.

Please place a cross in the box ☒ if no relatives are entitled to notice: ☐

I (We) have given notice to register in the prescribed form (EP1PG) to the following relatives of the donor:

Full Name: _____   Relationship to Donor: _____
Address: _____   Date notice given: ☐☐☐☐☐☐☐☐
    D D M M Y Y Y Y

Full Name: _____   Relationship to Donor: _____
Address: _____   Date notice given: ☐☐☐☐☐☐☐☐
    D D M M Y Y Y Y

Full Name: _____   Relationship to Donor: _____
Address: _____   Date notice given: ☐☐☐☐☐☐☐☐
    D D M M Y Y Y Y

Full Name: _____   Relationship to Donor: _____
Address: _____   Date notice given: ☐☐☐☐☐☐☐☐
    D D M M Y Y Y Y

Full Name: _____   Relationship to Donor: _____
Address: _____   Date notice given: ☐☐☐☐☐☐☐☐
    D D M M Y Y Y Y

If there are additional relatives please complete the Relative Name, Relationship, Address and Date details in the 'Additional Information' section (at the end of this form).

Page 5 of 7

655

Part Eight - Notice of Application to Co-Attorney(s)

Do not complete this section if it does not apply. If there are additional co-attorneys please complete the Attorney Name, Relationship, Address and Date details in the 'Additional Information' section (at the end of this form).

Are all the attorneys applying to register?   Yes ☐ No ☐   *Place a cross against one option* ☒

If no, I (We) have given notice to my (our) co-attorney(s) as follows:

Full Name: [blank]   Relationship to Donor: [blank]

Address: [blank]   Date notice given:

D D M M Y Y Y Y

Full Name: [blank]   Relationship to Donor: [blank]

Address: [blank]   Date notice given:

D D M M Y Y Y Y

Part Nine - Fees

Guidelines on remission and postponement of fees can be obtained from the Office of the Public Guardian.

Have you enclosed a cheque for the registration fee for this application? Yes ☐ No ☐ *Place a cross against one option* ☒

Do you wish to apply for postponement, exemption or remission of the fee?   Yes ☐ No ☐ *Place a cross against one option* ☒

If yes, please complete the application for exemption or remission form.

Part Ten - Declaration

Note: The application should be signed by all attorneys who are making the application. This must not pre-date the date(s) when the notices were given.

I (We) certify that the above information is correct and that to the best of my (our) knowledge and belief I (We) have complied with the provisions of the Mental Capacity Act 2005.

Signed: [blank]   Dated: [blank]

D D M M Y Y Y Y

Signed: [blank]   Dated: [blank]

D D M M Y Y Y Y

Signed: [blank]   Dated: [blank]

D D M M Y Y Y Y

Page 6 of 7

656

Part Eleven - Correspondence Address

Solicitors please note: The address to which the correspondence should be sent **MUST** be entered here if this is different to the address of Attorney One. State the full name and present address. Insert the name of the Solicitor's Firm in the Company Name field, if appropriate, and the correspondence reference in the Company Reference field.

Mr   Mrs   Ms   Miss   Other

☐   ☐   ☐   ☐   ☐

Place a cross against one option ☒

If Other, please specify here:

Last Name:

Forename 1:

Other Forenames:

Company Name:

Company Reference:

Address 1:

Address 2:

Address 3:

Town/City:

County:

Postcode:

DX No. (solicitors only):

DX Exchange (solicitors only):

Daytime Tel No.:

(STD Code):

Email Address:

Part Twelve - Additional Information

Please write down any additional information to support this application in the space below. If necessary attach additional paper to the end of this form.

Appendix E
COURT FORMS

Contents

COP 7: APPLICATION TO OBJECT TO THE REGISTRATION OF A LASTING POWER OF ATTORNEY

[E1]

Court of Protection

Application to object to the registration of a lasting power of attorney (LPA)

For office use only
Date received
Case no.
Date issued

Seal

Name of the donor of the LPA (this is the person who made the LPA)

Please read first

- You can only object using this form if you are an intended attorney or a named person who received an LPA001 notice of intention to apply for registration of a lasting power of attorney.

- You may have to pay a fee when you make an application. Refer to the leaflet COP44 Court of Protection – Fees for details.

- An application to object must be made within three weeks from the day on which you received the LPA001 notice.

- If you are not one of the people who received the LPA001 notice but you wish to object, you can still do so but you need to file a COP1 application form and pay the specified fee. You need to notify the Public Guardian of your application. See note 1 at the end of this form for information on notifying the Public Guardian.

- An objection should be made to the Public Guardian (instead of the court) in the following circumstances:

    - if you are the donor, by using the form LPA006 objection by the donor to the registration of a lasting power of attorney; or
    - if you object on certain specified factual grounds, by using the form LPA007 objection to the Office of the Public Guardian of a proposed registration of a lasting power of attorney on factual grounds.

- You may need to pay for any costs you incur during the proceedings. If the court considers that you have acted unreasonably you can be ordered to pay the costs incurred by other parties.

- Please continue on a separate sheet of paper if you need more space to answer a question. Write your name, the name and date of birth of the person to whom the application relates, and the number of the question you are answering on each separate sheet.

- For assistance in completing the form please see guidance notes and website: www.gov.uk/court-of-protection

- Court of Protection staff cannot give legal advice. If you need legal advice please contact a solicitor.

COP 7: Application to object to the registration of a lasting power of attorney

Section 1 - Your details (the applicant)

1.1 Your details ☐ Mr ☐ Mrs ☐ Miss ☐ Ms ☐ Other [   ]

First name [   ]

Middle name(s) [   ]

Last name [   ]

1.2 Address (including postcode) [   ]

Telephone no. | Daytime | [   ]
| Evening | [   ]
| Mobile | [   ]

Email address [   ]

1.3 Is a solicitor representing you? ☐ Yes ☐ No

If Yes, please give the solicitor's details.

Name [   ]

Address (including postcode) [   ]

Telephone no. [   ] Fax [   ]

DX no. [   ]

Email address [   ]

1.4 Which address should official documentation be sent to?

☐ Your address

☐ Solicitor's address

☐ Other address (please provide details)

[   ]

1.5 Your description

☐ Attorney

☐ Other person entitled to be notified of the application to register the LPA

661

Section 2 - Objection to the registration of an LPA

2.1　Full name of the donor

☐ Mr.　　☐ Mrs.　　☐ Miss　　☐ Ms.　　☐ Other _____

First name _____

Middle name(s) _____

Last name _____

2.2　Full name of intended attorney(s)

☐ Mr.　　☐ Mrs.　　☐ Miss　　☐ Ms.　　☐ Other

First name _____

Last name _____

☐ Mr.　　☐ Mrs.　　☐ Miss　　☐ Ms.　　☐ Other

First name _____

Last name _____

2.3　Date donor signed the LPA

☐☐☐☐☐☐☐☐

2.4　Date you were given notice of the application to register the LPA

☐☐☐☐☐☐☐☐

2.5　You can only object to the court against the registration of the LPA on grounds which are prescribed in regulations under the Mental Capacity Act 2005.

Please indicate your grounds for objecting to the proposed registration:

☐ The power purported to be created by the instrument* is not valid as a LPA. (e.g. the donor did not have capacity to make an LPA).

☐ The power created by the instrument no longer exists (e.g. the donor revoked it at a time when he or she had capacity to do so)

☐ Fraud or undue pressure was used to induce the donor to make the power.

☐ The attorney proposes to behave in a way that would contravene his authority or would not be in the donor's best interests.

*The instrument means the LPA made by the donor.

2.6　Any evidence in support of your application must be filed with this application form. If you are attaching any written evidence please use the COP24 witness statement form.

☐ Evidence attached

2.7　You must have notified the Public Guardian of your intention to apply to the court to object to the registration of the LPA. **(See note 1)**

☐ I confirm that I have notified the Public Guardian

Page 3

Section 3 - Attending court hearings

3.1 If the court requires you to attend a hearing do you need any special assistance or facilities? **(See note 2)**   ☐ Yes   ☐ No

If Yes, please say what your requirements are. If necessary, court staff may contact you about your requirements.

Section 4 - Statement of truth

The statement of truth is to be signed by you, your solicitor or your litigation friend.

*(I believe) (The applicant believes) that the facts stated in this application form and its annex(es) are true.

Signed

*Applicant('s litigation friend)('s solicitor)

Name

Date

Name of firm

Position or office held

* Please delete the options in brackets that do not apply.

Now read note 3 about what you need to do next.

Sign and Lock >

COP 8: APPLICATION RELATING TO THE REGISTRATION OF AN ENDURING POWER OF ATTORNEY

[E2]

Court of Protection

Application relating to the registration of an enduring power of attorney (EPA)

For office use only
Date received
Case no.
Date issued

Seal

Name of the donor of the EPA (this is the person who made the EPA)

Please read first

- You need to complete and file this application form if you are the donor, an intended attorney or a relative of the donor entitled by Schedule 4 of the Mental Capacity Act 2005 (the Act) to be notified of the application to register the EPA and:
  - you wish to object to the registration of the EPA; or
  - you wish to seek the registration of the EPA where you have been notified that the registration has been suspended.

- If you are entitled to be notified then either you will have received an EP1PG notice of intention to apply for registration, or the Public Guardian will have notified you that the registration has been suspended.

- You may have to pay a fee when you make an application. Refer to the leaflet COP44 Court of Protection – Fees for details.

- Schedule 4 of the Act provides for the court to dispense with the requirement to give notice. If you are one of the people entitled by the Act to be notified then you can object to the court using this form even if you have not received an EP1PG notice but you find out about the application through other means.

- If you wish to apply to object to the registration of the EPA then you should do so as soon as reasonably possible after receiving the EP1PG notice. You should notify the Public Guardian of your application. If you do not make an application, the Public Guardian will ask for the court's directions on registration. See note 1 at the end of this form for information on notifying the Public Guardian.

- You may need to pay for any costs you incur during the proceedings. If the court considers that you have acted unreasonably you can be ordered to pay the costs incurred by other parties.

- If you are not one of the people entitled by the Act to be notified of the application to register the EPA but you wish to object you can still do so but you need to file a COP1 application form and pay the specified fee. You should notify the Public Guardian of your application. See note 1 in the separate guidance for information on notifying the Public Guardian.

- Please continue on a separate sheet of paper if you need more space to answer a question. Write your name, the name and date of birth of the donor, and the number of the question you are answering on each separate sheet.

- For assistance in completing the form please see guidance notes and website: www.gov.uk/court-of-protection

- Court of Protection staff cannot give legal advice. If you need legal advice please contact a solicitor.

Section 1 - Your details (the applicant)

1.1 Your details ☐ Mr ☐ Mrs ☐ Miss ☐ Ms ☐ Other [＿＿＿＿＿＿]

First name [＿＿＿＿＿＿＿＿＿＿＿＿＿＿＿＿＿]

Middle name(s) [＿＿＿＿＿＿＿＿＿＿＿＿＿＿＿＿]

Last name [＿＿＿＿＿＿＿＿＿＿＿＿＿＿＿＿＿]

1.2 Address (including postcode) [＿＿＿＿＿＿＿＿＿＿＿＿＿＿＿＿]

Telephone no.	Daytime	
	Evening	
	Mobile	

Email address [＿＿＿＿＿＿＿＿＿＿＿＿＿＿＿]

1.3 Is a solicitor representing you? ☐ Yes ☐ No

If Yes, please give the solicitor's details.

Name [＿＿＿＿＿＿＿＿＿＿＿＿＿＿＿＿＿]

Address (including postcode) [＿＿＿＿＿＿＿＿＿＿＿＿＿＿＿＿]

Telephone no. [＿＿＿＿＿＿＿＿＿] Fax [＿＿＿＿＿]

DX no. [＿＿＿＿＿＿＿＿＿＿＿＿＿＿＿＿＿]

Email address [＿＿＿＿＿＿＿＿＿＿＿＿＿＿＿]

1.4 Which address should official documentation be sent to?

☐ Your address

☐ Solicitor's address

☐ Other address (please provide details)

[＿＿＿＿＿＿＿＿＿＿＿＿＿＿＿＿＿＿]

1.5 Your description

☐ Donor (person making the EPA)

☐ Attorney

☐ Other person entitled to be notified of the application to register the LPA

Section 2 - Details of the EPA

2.1   Full name of the donor (if you are not the donor)

☐ Mr.   ☐ Mrs.   ☐ Miss   ☐ Ms.   ☐ Other _____

First name [   ]

Middle name(s) [   ]

Last name [   ]

2.2   Donor's address and telephone number (if you are not the donor)

Address
(including
postcode) [   ]

Telephone no.   Daytime [   ]
Evening [   ]
Mobile [   ]

Email address [   ]

2.3 Donor's date of birth   [| | | | | | |]

2.4   Full name of intended attorney(s)

☐ Mr.   ☐ Mrs.   ☐ Miss   ☐ Ms.   ☐ Other _____

First name [   ]

Last name [   ]

☐ Mr.   ☐ Mrs.   ☐ Miss   ☐ Ms.   ☐ Other _____

First name [   ]

Last name [   ]

☐ Mr.   ☐ Mrs.   ☐ Miss   ☐ Ms.   ☐ Other _____

First name [   ]

Last name [   ]

2.5   Date donor signed the EPA

[| | | | | | |]

2.6   Date you were given notice of the application to register the EPA

[| | | | | | |]

Section 3 - Your application

3.1   Please state the directions you are seeking.

3.2   If you object to the registration of the EPA you can only do so on grounds which are prescribed in the Mental Capacity Act 2005.

Please indicate your grounds for objecting to the proposed registration:

☐   The power purported to be created by the instrument* is not valid as an enduring power of attorney

☐   The power created by the instrument no longer subsists

☐   The application is premature because the donor is not yet becoming mentally incapable

☐   Fraud or undue pressure was used to induce the donor to make the power

☐   The attorney is unsuitable to be the donor's attorney (having regard to all the circumstances and in particular the attorney's relationship to or connection with the donor).

*The instrument means the EPA made by the donor.

3.3   I have notified the Public Guardian of my intention to apply to the court in relation to the registration of the EPA. **(See note 1)**   ☐ I confirm that I have notified the Public Guardian

3.4   If you seek registration please state your reasons for doing so.

3.5   Any evidence in support of your application must be filed with this application form. If you are attaching any written evidence please use the COP24 witness statement form.   ☐ Evidence attached

Section 4 - Attending court hearings

4.1   If the court requires you to attend a hearing do you need any special assistance or facilities? **(See note 2)**   ☐ Yes   ☐ No

If Yes, please say what your requirements are. If necessary, court staff may contact you about your requirements.

```

```

Page 4

667

Section 5 - Statement of truth

The statement of truth is to be signed by you, your solicitor or your litigation friend.

*(I believe) (The applicant believes) that the facts stated in this application form and its annex(es) are true.

Signed

*Applicant('s litigation friend)('s solicitor)

Name

Date

Name of firm

Position or office held

* Please delete the options in brackets that do not apply.

Now read note 3 about what you need to do next.

Sign and Lock >

Appendix F
GUIDANCE

Contents

MENTAL CAPACITY ACT 2005 CODE OF PRACTICE

7. WHAT DOES THE ACT SAY ABOUT LASTING POWERS OF ATTORNEY?

F1

This chapter explains what Lasting Powers of Attorney (LPAs) are and how they should be used. It also sets out:

- how LPAs differ from Enduring Powers of Attorney (EPAs)
- the types of decisions that people can appoint attorneys to make (attorneys are also called 'donees' in the Act)
- situations in which an LPA can and cannot be used
- the duties and responsibilities of attorneys
- the standards required of attorneys, and
- measures for dealing with attorneys who don't meet appropriate standards.

This chapter also explains what should happen to EPAs that were made before the Act comes into force.

> In this chapter, as throughout the Code, a person's capacity (or lack of capacity) refers specifically to their capacity to make a particular decision at the time it needs to be made.

Quick summary

Anyone asked to be an attorney should:

- consider whether they have the skills and ability to act as an attorney (especially if it is for a property and affairs LPA)
- ask themselves whether they actually want to be an attorney and take on the duties and responsibilities of the role.

Before acting under an LPA, attorneys must:

- make sure the LPA has been registered with the Public Guardian
- take all practical and appropriate steps to help the donor make the particular decision for themselves.

When acting under an LPA:

- make sure that the Act's statutory principles are followed

- check whether the person has the capacity to make that particular decision for themselves. If they do:
  - a personal welfare LPA cannot be used – the person must make the decision
  - a property and affairs LPA can be used even if the person has capacity to make the decision, unless they have stated in the LPA that they should make decisions for themselves when they have capacity to do so.

At all times, remember:

- anything done under the authority of the LPA must be in the person's best interests
- anyone acting as an attorney must have regard to guidance in this Code of Practice that is relevant to the decision that is to be made
- attorneys must fulfil their responsibilities and duties to the person who lacks capacity.

What is a Lasting Power of Attorney (LPA)?

7.1 Sometimes one person will want to give another person authority to make a decision on their behalf. A power of attorney is a legal document that allows them to do so. Under a power of attorney, the chosen person (the attorney or donee) can make decisions that are as valid as one made by the person (the donor).

7.2 Before the Enduring Powers of Attorney Act 1985, every power of attorney automatically became invalid as soon as the donor lacked the capacity to make their own decision. But that Act introduced the Enduring Power of Attorney (EPA). An EPA allows an attorney to make decisions about property and financial affairs even if the donor lacks capacity to manage their own affairs.

7.3 The Mental Capacity Act replaces the EPA with the Lasting Power of Attorney (LPA). It also increases the range of different types of decisions that people can authorise others to make on their behalf. As well as property and affairs (including financial matters), LPAs can also cover personal welfare (including healthcare and consent to medical treatment) for people who lack capacity to make such decisions for themselves.

7.4 The donor can choose one person or several to make different kinds of decisions. See paragraphs 7.21–7.31 for more information about personal welfare LPAs. See paragraphs 7.32–7.42 for more information about LPAs on property and affairs.

How do LPAs compare to EPAs?

7.5 There are a number of differences between LPAs and EPAs. These are summarised as follows:

- EPAs only cover property and affairs. LPAs can also cover personal welfare.
- Donors must use the relevant specific form (prescribed in regulations) to make EPAs and LPAs. There are different forms for EPAs, personal welfare LPAs and property and affairs LPAs.
- EPAs must be registered with the Public Guardian when the donor can no longer manage their own affairs (or when they start to lose capacity). But LPAs can be registered at any time before they are used – before or after the donor lacks capacity to make particular decisions that the LPA covers. If the LPA is not registered, it can't be used.
- EPAs can be used while the donor still has capacity to manage their own property and affairs, as can property and affairs LPAs, so long as the donor does not say otherwise in the LPA. But personal welfare LPAs can only be used once the donor lacks capacity to make the welfare decision in question.

- Once the Act comes into force, only LPAs can be made but existing EPAs will continue to be valid. There will be different laws and procedures for EPAs and LPAs.
- Attorneys making decisions under a registered EPA or LPA must follow the Act's principles and act in the best interests of the donor.
- The duties under the law of agency apply to attorneys of both EPAs and LPAs (see paragraphs 7.58–7.68 below).
- Decisions that the courts have made about EPAs may also affect how people use LPAs.
- Attorneys acting under an LPA have a legal duty to have regard to the guidance in this Code of Practice. EPA attorneys do not. But the Code's guidance will still be helpful to them.

How does a donor create an LPA?

7.6 The donor must also follow the right procedures for creating and registering an LPA, as set out below. Otherwise the LPA might not be valid. It is not always necessary to get legal advice. But it is a good idea for certain cases (for example, if the donor's circumstances are complicated).

7.7 Only adults aged 18 or over can make an LPA, and they can only make an LPA if they have the capacity to do so. For an LPA to be valid:

- the LPA must be a written document set out in the statutory form prescribed by regulations[1]
- the document must include prescribed information about the nature and effect of the LPA (as set out in the regulations)
- the donor must sign a statement saying that they have read the prescribed information (or somebody has read it to them) and that they want the LPA to apply when they no longer have capacity
- the document must name people (not any of the attorneys) who should be told about an application to register the LPA, or it should say that there is no-one they wish to be told
- the attorneys must sign a statement saying that they have read the prescribed information and that they understand their duties – in particular the duty to act in the donor's best interests
- the document must include a certificate completed by an independent third party,[2] confirming that:
  - in their opinion, the donor understands the LPA's purpose
  - nobody used fraud or undue pressure to trick or force the donor into making the LPA, and
  - there is nothing to stop the LPA being created.

---

[1] The prescribed forms will be available from the Office of the Public Guardian (OPG) or from legal stationers.

[2] Details of who may and who may not be a certificate provider will be available in regulations. The OPG will produce guidance for certificate providers on their role.

Who can be an attorney?

7.8 A donor should think carefully before choosing someone to be their attorney. An attorney should be someone who is trustworthy, competent and reliable. They should have the skills and ability to carry out the necessary tasks.

7.9 Attorneys must be at least 18 years of age. For property and affairs LPAs, the attorney could be either:

- an individual (as long as they are not bankrupt at the time the LPA is made), or
- a trust corporation (often parts of banks or other financial institutions).

If an attorney nominated under a property and affairs LPA becomes bankrupt at any point, they will no longer be allowed to act as an attorney for property and affairs. People who are bankrupt can still act as an attorney for personal welfare LPAs.

7.10 The donor must name an individual rather than a job title in a company or organisation, (for example, 'The Director of Adult Services' or 'my solicitor' would not be sufficient). A paid care worker (such as a care home manager) should not agree to act as an attorney, apart from in unusual circumstances (for example, if they are the only close relative of the donor).

7.11 Section 10(4) of the Act allows the donor to appoint two or more attorneys and to specify whether they should act 'jointly', 'jointly and severally', or 'jointly in respect of some matters and jointly and severally in respect of others'.

- Joint attorneys must always act together. All attorneys must agree decisions and sign any relevant documents.
- Joint and several attorneys can act together but may also act independently if they wish. Any action taken by any attorney alone is as valid as if they were the only attorney.

7.12 The donor may want to appoint attorneys to act jointly in some matters but jointly and severally in others. For example, a donor could choose to appoint two or more financial attorneys jointly and severally. But they might say then when selling the donor's house, the attorneys must act jointly. The donor may appoint welfare attorneys to act jointly and severally but specify that they must act jointly in relation to giving consent to surgery. If a donor who has appointed two or more attorneys does not specify how they should act, they must always act jointly (section 10(5)).

7.13 Section 10(8) says that donors may choose to name replacement attorneys to take over the duties in certain circumstances (for example, in the event of an attorney's death). The donor may name a specific attorney to be replaced, or the replacements can take over from any attorney, if necessary. Donors cannot give their attorneys the right to appoint a substitute or successor.

How should somebody register and use an LPA?

7.14 An LPA must be registered with the Office of the Public Guardian (OPG) before it can be used. An unregistered LPA will not give the attorney any legal powers to make a decision for the donor. The donor can register the LPA while they are still capable, or the attorney can apply to register the LPA at any time.

7.15 There are advantages in registering the LPA soon after the donor makes it (for example, to ensure that there is no delay when the LPA needs to be used). But if this has not been done, an LPA can be registered after the donor lacks the capacity to make a decision covered by the LPA.

7.16 If an LPA is unregistered, attorneys must register it before making any decisions under the LPA. If the LPA has been registered but not used for some time, the attorney should tell the OPG when they begin to act under it – so that the attorney can be sent relevant, up-to-date information about the rules governing LPAs.

7.17 While they still have capacity, donors should let the OPG know of permanent changes of address for the donor or the attorney or any other changes in circumstances. If the donor no longer has capacity to do this, attorneys should report any such changes to the OPG. Examples include an attorney of a property and affairs LPA becoming bankrupt or the ending of a marriage between the donor and their attorney. This will help keep OPG records up to date, and will make sure that attorneys do not make decisions that they no longer have the authority to make.

What guidance should an attorney follow?

7.18 Section 9(4) states that attorneys must meet the requirements set out in the Act. Most importantly, they have to follow the statutory principles (section 1) and make decisions in the best interests of the person who lacks capacity (section 4). They must also respect any conditions or restrictions that the LPA document contains. See CHAPTER 2 for guidance on how to apply the Act's principles.

7.19 Chapter 3 gives suggestions of ways to help people make their own decisions in accordance with the Act's second principle . Attorneys should also refer to the guidance in CHAPTER 4 when assessing the donor's capacity to make particular decisions, and in particular, should follow the steps suggested for establishing a 'reasonable belief' that the donor lacks capacity (see paragraphs 4.44–4.45).' Assessments of capacity or best interests must not be based merely on:

- a donor's age or appearance, or
- unjustified assumptions about any condition they might have or their behaviour.

7.20 When deciding what is in the donor's best interests, attorneys should refer to the guidance in CHAPTER 5. In particular, they must consider the donor's past and present wishes and feelings, beliefs and values. Where practical and appropriate, they should consult with:

- anyone involved in caring for the donor
- close relatives and anyone else with an interest in their welfare
- other attorneys appointed by the donor.

See paragraphs 7.52–7.68 for a description of an attorney's duties.

Scenario: Making decisions in a donor's best interests

Mr Young has been a member of the Green Party for a long time. He has appointed his solicitor as his attorney under a property and affairs LPA. But Mr Young did not state in the LPA that investments made on his behalf must be ethical investments. When the attorney assesses his client's best interests, however, the attorney considers the donor's past wishes, values and beliefs. He makes sure that he only invests in companies that are socially and environmentally responsible.

What decisions can an LPA attorney make?

Personal welfare LPAs

7.21 LPAs can be used to appoint attorneys to make decisions about personal welfare, which can include healthcare and medical treatment decisions. Personal welfare LPAs might include decisions about:

- where the donor should live and who they should live with
- the donor's day-to-day care, including diet and dress
- who the donor may have contact with
- consenting to or refusing medical examination and treatment on the donor's behalf
- arrangements needed for the donor to be given medical, dental or optical treatment
- assessments for and provision of community care services
- whether the donor should take part in social activities, leisure activities, education or training
- the donor's personal correspondence and papers
- rights of access to personal information about the donor, or

- complaints about the donor's care or treatment.

7.22 The standard form for personal welfare LPAs allows attorneys to make decisions about anything that relates to the donor's personal welfare. But donors can add restrictions or conditions to areas where they would not wish the attorney to have the power to act. For example, a donor might only want an attorney to make decisions about their social care and not their healthcare. There are particular rules for LPAs authorising an attorney to make decisions about life-sustaining treatment (see paragraphs 7.30–7.31 below).

7.23 A general personal welfare LPA gives the attorney the right to make all of the decisions set out above although this is not a full list of the actions they can take or decisions they can make. However, a personal welfare LPA can only be used at a time when the donor lacks capacity to make a specific welfare decision.

Scenario: Denying attorneys the right to make certain decisions

Mrs Hutchison is in the early stages of Alzheimer's disease. She is anxious to get all her affairs in order while she still has capacity to do so. She makes a personal welfare LPA, appointing her daughter as attorney. But Mrs Hutchison knows that her daughter doesn't always get on with some members of the family – and she wouldn't want her daughter to stop those relatives from seeing her.

She states in the LPA that her attorney does not have the authority to decide who can contact her or visit her. If her daughter wants to prevent anyone having contact with Mrs Hutchison, she must ask the Court of Protection to decide.

7.24 Before making a decision under a personal welfare LPA, the attorney must be sure that:

- the LPA has been registered with the OPG
- the donor lacks the capacity to make the particular decision or the attorney reasonably believes that the donor lacks capacity to take the decisions covered by the LPA (having applied the Act's principles), and
- they are making the decision in the donor's best interests.

7.25 When healthcare or social care staff are involved in preparing a care plan for someone who has appointed a personal welfare attorney, they must first assess whether the donor has capacity to agree to the care plan or to parts of it. If the donor lacks capacity, professionals must then consult the attorney and get their agreement to the care plan. They will also need to consult the attorney when considering what action is in the person's best interests.

Personal welfare LPAs that authorise an attorney to make healthcare decisions

7.26 A personal welfare LPA allows attorneys to make decisions to accept or refuse healthcare or treatment unless the donor has stated clearly in the LPA that they do not want the attorney to make these decisions.

7.27 Even where the LPA includes healthcare decisions, attorneys do not have the right to consent to or refuse treatment in situations where:

- **the donor has capacity to make the particular healthcare decision (section 11(7)(a))**
  An attorney has no decision-making power if the donor can make their own treatment decisions.
- **the donor has made an advance decision to refuse the proposed treatment (section 11(7)(b))**
  An attorney cannot consent to treatment if the donor has made a valid and applicable advance decision to refuse a specific treatment (see CHAPTER 9). But if the donor made an LPA after the advance decision,

and gave the attorney the right to consent to or refuse the treatment, the attorney can choose not to follow the advance decision.

- **a decision relates to life-sustaining treatment (section 11(7)(c))**
  An attorney has no power to consent to or refuse life-sustaining treatment, unless the LPA document expressly authorises this (See paragraphs 7.30–7.31 below.)
- **the donor is detained under the Mental Health Act (section 28)**
  An attorney cannot consent to or refuse treatment for a mental disorder for a patient detained under the Mental Health Act 1983 (see also CHAPTER 13).

7.28 LPAs cannot give attorneys the power to demand specific forms of medical treatment that healthcare staff do not believe are necessary or appropriate for the donor's particular condition.

7.29 Attorneys must always follow the Act's principles and make decisions in the donor's best interests. If healthcare staff disagree with the attorney's assessment of best interests, they should discuss the case with other medical experts and/or get a formal second opinion. Then they should discuss the matter further with the attorney. If they cannot settle the disagreement, they can apply to the Court of Protection (see paragraphs 7.45–7.49 below). While the court is coming to a decision, healthcare staff can give life-sustaining treatment to prolong the donor's life or stop their condition getting worse.

Personal welfare LPAs that authorise an attorney to make decisions about life-sustaining treatment

7.30 An attorney can only consent to or refuse life-sustaining treatment on behalf of the donor if, when making the LPA, the donor has specifically stated in the LPA document that they want the attorney to have this authority.

7.31 As with all decisions, an attorney must act in the donor's best interests when making decisions about such treatment. This will involve applying the best interests checklist (see CHAPTER 5) and consulting with carers, family members and others interested in the donor's welfare. In particular, the attorney must not be motivated in any way by the desire to bring about the donor's death (see paragraphs 5.29–5.36). Anyone who doubts that the attorney is acting in the donor's best interests can apply to the Court of Protection for a decision.

Scenario: Making decisions about life-sustaining treatment

Mrs Joshi has never trusted doctors. She prefers to rely on alternative therapies. Because she saw her father suffer after invasive treatment for cancer, she is clear that she would refuse such treatment herself.

She is diagnosed with cancer and discusses her wishes with her husband. Mrs Joshi knows that he would respect her wishes if he ever had to make a decision about her treatment. She makes a personal welfare LPA appointing him as her attorney with authority to make all her welfare and healthcare decisions. She includes a specific statement authorising him to consent to or refuse life-sustaining treatment.

He will then be able to consider her views and make decisions about treatment in her best interests if she later lacks capacity to make those decisions herself.

Property and affairs LPAs

7.32 A donor can make an LPA giving an attorney the right to make decisions about property and affairs (including financial matters). Unless the donor states otherwise, once the LPA is registered, the attorney is allowed to make all decisions about the donor's property and affairs even if the donor still has capacity to make the decisions for themselves. In this situation, the LPA will continue to apply when the donor no longer has capacity.

7.33 Alternatively a donor can state in the LPA document that the LPA should only apply when they lack capacity to make a relevant decision. It is the donor's responsibility to decide how their capacity should then be assessed. For example, the donor may trust the attorney to carry out an assessment, or they may say that the LPA only applies if their GP or another doctor confirms in writing that they lack capacity to make specific decisions about property or finances. Financial institutions may wish to see the written confirmation before recognising the attorney's authority to act under the LPA.

7.34 The fact that someone has made a property and affairs LPA does not mean that they cannot continue to carry out financial transactions for themselves. The donor may have full capacity, but perhaps anticipates that they may lack capacity at some future time. Or they may have fluctuating or partial capacity and therefore be able to make some decisions (or at some times), but need an attorney to make others (or at other times). The attorney should allow and encourage the donor to do as much as possible, and should only act when the donor asks them to or to make those decisions the donor lacks capacity to make. However, in other cases, the donor may wish to hand over responsibility for all decisions to the attorney, even those they still have capacity to make.

7.35 If the donor restricts the decisions an attorney can make, banks may ask the attorney to sign a declaration that protects the bank from liability if the attorney misuses the account.[3]

7.36 If a donor does not restrict decisions the attorney can make, the attorney will be able to decide on any or all of the person's property and financial affairs. This might include:

- buying or selling property
- opening, closing or operating any bank, building society or other account
- giving access to the donor's financial information
- claiming, receiving and using (on the donor's behalf) all benefits, pensions, allowances and rebates (unless the Department for Work and Pensions has already appointed someone and everyone is happy for this to continue)
- receiving any income, inheritance or other entitlement on behalf of the donor
- dealing with the donor's tax affairs
- paying the donor's mortgage, rent and household expenses
- insuring, maintaining and repairing the donor's property
- investing the donor's savings
- making limited gifts on the donor's behalf (but see paragraphs 7.40–7.42 below)
- paying for private medical care and residential care or nursing home fees
- applying for any entitlement to funding for NHS care, social care or adaptations
- using the donor's money to buy a vehicle or any equipment or other help they need
- repaying interest and capital on any loan taken out by the donor.

7.37 A general property and affairs LPA will allow the attorney to carry out any or all of the actions above (although this is not a full list of the actions they can take). However, the donor may want to specify the types of powers they wish the attorney to have, or to exclude particular types of decisions. If the donor holds any assets as trustee, they should get legal advice about how the LPA may affect this.

7.38 The attorney must make these decisions personally and cannot generally give someone else authority to carry out their duties (see paragraphs 7.61–7.62 below). But if the donor wants the attorney to be able to give authority to a specialist to make specific decisions, they need to state this clearly in the LPA document (for example, appointing an investment manager to make particular investment decisions).

7.39 Donors may like to appoint someone (perhaps a family member or a professional) to go through their accounts with the attorney from time to time. This might help to reassure donors that somebody will check their financial affairs when they lack capacity to do so. It may also be helpful for attorneys to arrange a regular check that everything is being done properly. The donor should ensure that the person is willing to carry out this role and is prepared to ask for the accounts if the attorney does not provide them. They should include this arrangement in the signed LPA document. The LPA should also say whether the person can charge a fee for this service.

3 See British Banking Association's guidance for bank staff on *'Banking for mentally incapaci-tated and learning disabled customers'*.

What gifts can an attorney make under a property and affairs LPA?

7.40 An attorney can only make gifts of the donor's money or belongings to people who are related to or connected with the donor (including the attorney) on specific occasions, including:

- births or birthdays
- weddings or wedding anniversaries
- civil partnership ceremonies or anniversaries, or
- any other occasion when families, friends or associates usually give presents (section 12(3)(b)).

7.41 If the donor previously made donations to any charity regularly or from time to time, the attorney can make donations from the person's funds. This also applies if the donor could have been expected to make such payments (section 12(2)(b)). But the value of any gift or donation must be reasonable and take into account the size of the donor's estate. For example, it would not be reasonable to buy expensive gifts at Christmas if the donor was living on modest means and had to do without essential items in order to pay for them.

7.42 The donor cannot use the LPA to make more extensive gifts than those allowed under section 12 of the Act. But they can impose stricter conditions or restrictions on the attorney's powers to make gifts. They should state these restrictions clearly in the LPA document when they are creating it. When deciding on appropriate gifts, the attorney should consider the donor's wishes and feelings to work out what would be in the donor's best interests. The attorney can apply to the Court of Protection for permission to make gifts that are not included in the LPA (for example, for tax planning purposes).

Are there any other restrictions on attorneys' powers?

7.43 Attorneys are not protected from liability if they do something that is intended to restrain the donor, unless:

- the attorney reasonably believes that the donor lacks capacity to make the decision in question, *and*
- the attorney reasonably believes that restraint is necessary to prevent harm to the donor, *and*
- the type of restraint used is in proportion to the likelihood and the seriousness of the harm.

  If an attorney needs to make a decision or take action which may involve the use of restraint, they should take account of the guidance set out in CHAPTER 6.

7.44 Attorneys have no authority to take actions that result in the donor being deprived of their liberty. Any deprivation of liberty will only be lawful if this has been properly authorised and there is other protection available for the person who lacks capacity. An example would be the protection around detention under the Mental Health Act 1983 (see CHAPTER 13) or a court ruling. Chapter 6 gives more guidance on working out whether an action is restraint or a deprivation of liberty.

What powers does the Court of Protection have over LPAs?

7.45 The Court of Protection has a range of powers to:
- determine whether an LPA is valid
- give directions about using the LPA, and
- to remove an attorney (for example, if the attorney does not act in the best interests of the donor).
  Chapter 8 gives more information about the Court of Protection's powers.

7.46 If somebody has doubts over whether an LPA is valid, they can ask the court to decide whether the LPA:
- meets the Act's requirements
- has been revoked (cancelled) by the donor, or
- has come to an end for any other reason.

7.47 The court can also stop somebody registering an LPA or rule that an LPA is invalid if:
- the donor made the LPA as a result of undue pressure or fraud, or
- the attorney behaves, has behaved or is planning to behave in a way that goes against their duties or is not in the donor's best interests.

7.48 The court can also clarify an LPA's meaning, if it is not clear, and it can tell attorneys how they should use an LPA. If an attorney thinks that an LPA does not give them enough powers, they can ask the court to extend their powers – if the donor no longer has capacity to authorise this. The court can also authorise an attorney to give a gift that the Act does not normally allow (section 12(2)), if it is in the donor's best interests.

7.49 All attorneys should keep records of their dealings with the donor's affairs (see also paragraph 7.67 below). The court can order attorneys to produce records (for example, financial accounts) and to provide specific reports, information or documentation. If somebody has concerns about an attorney's payment or expenses, the court could resolve the matter.

What responsibilities do attorneys have?

7.50 A donor cannot insist on somebody agreeing to become an attorney. It is down to the proposed attorney to decide whether to take on this responsibility. When an attorney accepts the role by signing the LPA document, this is confirmation that they are willing to act under the LPA once it is registered. An attorney can withdraw from the appointment if they ever become unable or unwilling to act, but if the LPA has been registered they must follow the correct procedures for withdrawing. (see paragraph 7.66 below).

7.51 Once the attorney starts to act under an LPA, they must meet certain standards. If they don't carry out the duties below, they could be removed from the role. In some circumstances they could face charges of fraud or negligence.

What duties does the Act impose?

7.52 Attorneys acting under an LPA have a duty to:
- follow the Act's statutory principles (see CHAPTER 2)
- make decisions in the donor's best interests

- have regard to the guidance in the Code of Practice
- only make those decisions the LPA gives them authority to make.

Principles and best interests

7.53 Attorneys must act in accordance with the Act's statutory principles (section 1) and in the best interests of the donor (the steps for working out best interests are set out in section 4). In particular, attorneys must consider whether the donor has capacity to make the decision for themselves. If not, they should consider whether the donor is likely to regain capacity to make the decision in the future. If so, it may be possible to delay the decision until the donor can make it.

The Code of Practice

7.54 As well as this chapter, attorneys should pay special attention to the following guidance set out in the Code:
- chapter 2, which sets out how the Act's principles should be applied
- chapter 3, which describes the steps which can be taken to try to help the person make decisions for themselves
- chapter 4, which describes the Act's definition of lack of capacity and gives guidance on assessing capacity, and
- chapter 5, which gives guidance on working out the donor's best interests.

7.55 In some circumstances, attorneys might also find it useful to refer to guidance in:
- chapter 6, which explains when attorneys who have caring responsibilities may have protection from liability and gives guidance on the few circumstances when the Act allows restraint in connection with care and treatment
- chapter 8, which gives a summary of the Court of Protection's powers relating to LPAs
- chapter 9, which explains how LPAs may be affected if the donor has made an advance decision to refuse treatment, and
- chapter 15, which describes ways to settle disagreements.

Only making decisions covered by an LPA

7.56 A personal welfare attorney has no authority to make decisions about a donor's property and affairs (such as their finances). A property and affairs attorney has no authority in decisions about a donor's personal care. (But the same person could be appointed in separate LPAs to carry out both these roles.) Under any LPA, the attorney will have authority in a wide range of decisions. But if a donor includes restrictions in the LPA document, this will limit the attorney's authority (section 9(4)(b)). If the attorney thinks that they need greater powers, they can apply to the Court of Protection which may decide to give the attorney the authority required or alternatively to appoint the attorney as a deputy with the necessary powers (see CHAPTER 8).

7.57 It is good practice for decision-makers to consult attorneys about any decision or action, whether or not it is covered by the LPA. This is because an attorney is likely to have known the donor for some time and may have important information about their wishes and feelings. Researchers can also consult attorneys if they are thinking about involving the donor in research (see CHAPTER 11).

Scenario: Consulting attorneys

Mr Varadi makes a personal welfare LPA appointing his son and daughter as his joint attorneys. He also makes a property and affairs LPA, appointing his son and his solicitor to act jointly and severally. He registers the property and affairs LPA straight away, so his attorneys can help with financial decisions.

Two years later, Mr Varadi has a stroke, is unable to speak and has difficulty communicating his wishes. He also lacks the capacity to make decisions about treatment. The attorneys apply to register the personal welfare LPA. Both feel that they should delay decisions about Mr Varadi's future care, because he might regain capacity to make the decisions himself. But they agree that some decisions cannot wait.

Although the solicitor has no authority to make welfare decisions, the welfare attorneys consult him about their father's best interests. They speak to him about immediate treatment decisions and their suggestion to delay making decisions about his future care. Similarly, the property and affairs attorneys consult the daughter about the financial decisions that Mr Varadi does not have the capacity to make himself.

What are an attorney's other duties?

7.58 An attorney appointed under an LPA is acting as the chosen agent of the donor and therefore, under the law of agency, the attorney has certain duties towards the donor. An attorney takes on a role which carries a great deal of power, which they must use carefully and responsibly. They have a duty to:

- apply certain standards of care and skill (duty of care) when making decisions
- carry out the donor's instructions
- not take advantage of their position and not benefit themselves, but benefit the donor (fiduciary duty)
- not delegate decisions, unless authorised to do so
- act in good faith
- respect confidentiality
- comply with the directions of the Court of Protection
- not give up the role without telling the donor and the court.
  In relation to property and affairs LPAs, they have a duty to:
- keep accounts
- keep the donor's money and property separate from their own.

Duty of care

7.59 'Duty of care' means applying a certain standard of care and skill – depending on whether the attorney is paid for their services or holds relevant professional qualifications.

- Attorneys who are not being paid must apply the same care, skill and diligence they would use to make decisions about their own life. An attorney who claims to have particular skills or qualifications must show greater skill in those particular areas than someone who does not make such claims.
- If attorneys are being paid for their services, they should demonstrate a higher degree of care and skill.

- Attorneys who undertake their duties in the course of their professional work (such as solicitors or corporate trustees) must display professional competence and follow their profession's rules and standards.

Fiduciary duty

7.60 A fiduciary duty means attorneys must not take advantage of their position. Nor should they put themselves in a position where their personal interests conflict with their duties. They also must not allow any other influences to affect the way in which they act as an attorney. Decisions should always benefit the donor, and not the attorney. Attorneys must not profit or get any personal benefit from their position, apart from receiving gifts where the Act allows it, whether or not it is at the donor's expense.

Duty not to delegate

7.61 Attorneys cannot usually delegate their authority to someone else. They must carry out their duties personally. The attorney may seek professional or expert advice (for example, investment advice from a financial adviser or advice on medical treatment from a doctor). But they cannot, as a general rule, allow someone else to make a decision that they have been appointed to make, unless this has been specifically authorised by the donor in the LPA.

7.62 In certain circumstances, attorneys may have limited powers to delegate (for example, through necessity or unforeseen circumstances, or for specific tasks which the donor would not have expected the attorney to attend to personally). But attorneys cannot usually delegate any decisions that rely on their discretion.

Duty of good faith

7.63 Acting in good faith means acting with honesty and integrity. For example, an attorney must try to make sure that their decisions do not go against a decision the donor made while they still had capacity (unless it would be in the donor's best interests to do so).

Duty of confidentiality

7.64 Attorneys have a duty to keep the donor's affairs confidential, unless:

- before they lost capacity to do so, the donor agreed that some personal or financial information may be revealed for a particular purpose (for example, they have named someone they want to check their financial accounts), or
- there is some other good reason to release it (for example, it is in the public interest or the best interests of the person who lacks capacity, or there is a risk of harm to the donor or others).
  In the latter circumstances, it may be advisable for the attorney to get legal advice. Chapter 16 gives more information about confidentiality.

Duty to comply with the directions of the Court of Protection

7.65 Under sections 22 and 23 of the Act, the Court of Protection has wide-ranging powers to decide on issues relating to the operation or validity of an LPA. It can also:

- give extra authority to attorneys
- order them to produce records (for example, financial accounts), or
- order them to provide specific information or documentation to the court.

Attorneys must comply with any decision or order that the court makes.

Duty not to disclaim without notifying the donor and the OPG

7.66 Once someone becomes an attorney, they cannot give up that role without notifying the donor and the OPG. If they decide to give up their role, they must follow the relevant guidance available from the OPG.

Duty to keep accounts

7.67 Property and affairs attorneys must keep accounts of transactions carried out on the donor's behalf. Sometimes the Court of Protection will ask to see accounts. If the attorney is not a financial expert and the donor's affairs are relatively straightforward, a record of the donor's income and expenditure (for example, through bank statements) may be enough. The more complicated the donor's affairs, the more detailed the accounts may need to be.

Duty to keep the donor's money and property separate

7.68 Property and affairs attorneys should usually keep the donor's money and property separate from their own or anyone else's. There may be occasions where donors and attorneys have agreed in the past to keep their money in a joint bank account (for example, if a husband is acting as his wife's attorney). It might be possible to continue this under the LPA. But in most circumstances, attorneys must keep finances separate to avoid any possibility of mistakes or confusion.

How does the Act protect donors from abuse?

What should someone do if they think an attorney is abusing their position?

7.69 Attorneys are in a position of trust, so there is always a risk of them abusing their position. Donors can help prevent abuse by carefully choosing a suitable and trustworthy attorney. But others have a role to play in looking out for possible signs of abuse or exploitation, and reporting any concerns to the OPG. The OPG will then follow this up in co-operation with relevant agencies.

7.70 Signs that an attorney may be exploiting the donor (or failing to act in the donor's best interests) include:

- stopping relatives or friends contacting the donor – for example, the attorney may prevent contact or the donor may suddenly refuse visits or telephone calls from family and friends for no reason
- sudden unexplained changes in living arrangements (for example, someone moves in to care for a donor they've had little contact with)
- not allowing healthcare or social care staff to see the donor
- taking the donor out of hospital against medical advice, while the donor is having necessary medical treatment
- unpaid bills (for example, residential care or nursing home fees)
- an attorney opening a credit card account for the donor
- spending money on things that are not obviously related to the donor's needs
- the attorney spending money in an unusual or extravagant way
- transferring financial assets to another country.

7.71 Somebody who suspects abuse should contact the OPG immediately. The OPG may direct a Court of Protection Visitor to visit an attorney to investigate. In cases of suspected physical or sexual abuse, theft or serious fraud, the person should contact the police. They might also be able to refer the matter to the relevant local adult protection authorities.

7.72 In serious cases, the OPG will refer the matter to the Court of Protection. The court may revoke (cancel) the LPA or (through the OPG) prevent it being registered, if it decides that:

- the LPA does not meet the legal requirements for creating an LPA
- the LPA has been revoked or come to an end for any other reason
- somebody used fraud or undue pressure to get the donor to make the LPA
- the attorney has done something that they do not have authority to do, or
- the attorney has behaved or is planning to behave in a way that is not in the donor's best interests.

    The court might then consider whether the authority previously given to an attorney can be managed by:

- the court making a single decision, or
- appointing a deputy.

What should an attorney do if they think someone else is abusing the donor?

7.73 An attorney who thinks someone else is abusing or exploiting the donor should report it to the OPG and ask for advice on what action they should take. They should contact the police if they suspect physical or sexual abuse, theft or serious fraud. They might also be able to refer the matter to local adult protection authorities.

7.74 Chapter 13 gives more information about protecting vulnerable people from abuse, ill treatment or neglect. It also discusses the duties and responsibilities of the various agencies involved, including the OPG and local authorities. In particular, it is a criminal offence (with a maximum penalty of five years' imprisonment, a fine, or both) for anyone (including attorneys) to wilfully neglect or ill-treat a person in their care who lacks capacity to make decisions for themselves (section 44).

What happens to existing EPAs once the Act comes into force?

7.75 Once the Act comes into force, it will not be possible to make new EPAs. Only LPAs can then be made.

7.76 Some donors will have created EPAs before the Act came into force with the expectation that their chosen attorneys will manage their property and affairs in the future, whether or not they have capacity to do so themselves.

7.77 If donors still have capacity after the Act comes into force, they can cancel the EPA and make an LPA covering their property and affairs. They should also notify attorneys and anyone else aware of the EPA (for example, a bank) that they have cancelled it.

7.78 Some donors will choose not to cancel their EPA or they may already lack the capacity to do so. In such cases, the Act allows existing EPAs, whether registered or not, to continue to be valid so that attorneys can meet the donor's expectations (Schedule 4). An EPA must be registered with the OPG when the attorney thinks the donor lacks capacity to manage their own affairs, or is beginning to lack capacity to do so.

7.79 EPA attorneys may find guidance in this chapter helpful. In particular, all attorneys must comply with the duties described in paragraphs 7.58–7.68 above. EPA attorneys can also be found liable under section 44 of the new Act, which sets out the new criminal offences of ill treatment and wilful neglect. The OPG has produced guidance on EPAs (see Annex A for details of publications and contact information).

PRACTICE DIRECTION 9H: APPLICATIONS RELATING TO THE REGISTRATION OF ENDURING POWERS OF ATTORNEY

F2

GENERAL

(1)   Rule 71 enables a practice direction to make additional or different provision in relation to specified applications.

APPLICATIONS TO WHICH THIS PRACTICE DIRECTION APPLIES

(2)   This practice direction applies where:
   (a)   an application has been made to the Public Guardian to register an instrument creating an enduring power of attorney; and
   (b)   the Public Guardian has received a notice of objection to registration which prevents him from registering the instrument except in accordance with the court's directions.

OBJECTIONS TO REGISTRATION

(3)   A notice of objection will prevent the Public Guardian from registering the instrument if the objection is made on one of the following grounds:[1]
   (a)   that the power purported to have been created by the instrument was not valid as an enduring power of attorney;
   (b)   that the power created by the instrument no longer subsists;
   (c)   that the application is premature because the donor is not yet becoming mentally incapable;
   (d)   that fraud or undue pressure was used to induce the donor to create the power; or
   (e)   that, having regard to all the circumstances and in particular the attorney's relationship to or connection with the donor, the attorney is unsuitable to be the donor's attorney.
(4)   This practice direction sets out the procedure to be followed by a person entitled to be given notice of the application to register the instrument who wishes to apply to the court for:
   (a)   directions that the instrument should be registered; or
   (b)   directions that the instrument should not be registered.
(5)   The persons who are entitled to receive notice of an application are the donor, certain of his relatives and any attorneys under the enduring power who are not making the application for registration.[2]

---

[1]   The grounds are set out in paragraph 13(9) of Schedule 4 to the Act. The Public Guardian is prevented from registering the instrument by paragraph 13(4) and (5) of that Schedule.

[2]   Paragraphs 5 to 11 of Schedule 4 to the Act set out who is entitled to receive notice.

PROCEDURE FOR APPLICATIONS TO WHICH THIS PRACTICE DIRECTION APPLIES

(6)   An application must be made using form COP8.

(Practice direction B accompanying Part 4 sets out more detailed requirements for statements of truth.)

(7) The application form must state:
   (a) what directions the applicant is seeking; and
   (b) if the applicant objects to registration, the grounds on which he does so; or
   (c) if the applicant is seeking registration, his reasons for doing so.

(8) The application form must be supported by evidence set out in either:
   (a) a witness statement; or
   (b) if it is verified by a statement of truth, the application form.

(9) As soon as practicable and in any event within 21 days of the application form being issued, the applicant must serve a copy of the application form, together with an acknowledgment of service using form COP5:
   (a) unless the applicant is the donor or an attorney, on the donor of the power and every attorney under the power;
   (b) if he is the donor, on every attorney under the power; or
   (c) if he is an attorney, on the donor and any other attorney under the power.

(10) Where the applicant knows or has reasonable grounds to believe that the donor of the power lacks capacity to make a decision in relation to any matter that is the subject of the application, he must notify the donor of the application in accordance with Part 7.

PRACTICE DIRECTION 23A: REQUEST FOR DIRECTIONS WHERE NOTICE OF OBJECTION PREVENTS PUBLIC GUARDIAN FROM REGISTERING ENDURING POWER OF ATTORNEY

F3

(1) Rule 201 provides for the Public Guardian to request the court's directions where a notice of objection prevents him from registering an instrument creating an enduring power of attorney. This practice direction makes provision about such requests.

(Practice direction H accompanying Part 9 deals with applications made by persons other than the Public Guardian who are seeking the court's directions about registration.)

(2) Time limits apply before the Public Guardian can request directions.[1] These are measured from the date (or the latest date) on which the attorney gave notice[2] to the donor's relatives of the attorney's intention to make an application for the registration of the instrument creating the enduring power. The Public Guardian cannot request directions until 5 weeks have expired beginning with the date of notification.

(3) However, this period is extended if it would otherwise expire less than 14 days after the Public Guardian receives the notice of objection which prevents him from registering the instrument. In this case, the Public Guardian may not request directions from the court until the end of the 14 day period which begins with the date on which he received the notice of objection.

(4) The request for directions must be made using form COP17. The Public Guardian must file the form and any document he considers may assist the court to give directions about the registration of the instrument.

(5) The Public Guardian will notify the donor in accordance with Part 7 that he has made a request within 21 days of the date on which he makes it. However, the Public Guardian is not required to serve the request on any other person or otherwise to notify them that a request has been made. He will participate in the proceedings only if the court requests him to do so.

(6) As soon as practicable after a request has been filed, notice of that fact[3] will be given by a court officer to:
(a) the person (or persons) who gave the notice of objection; and
(b) the attorney under the enduring power or, if more than one, each of them.

(7) If any person wishes to participate in the proceedings, he then has 21 days to file an application using form COP8. The application must be made in accordance with the detailed requirements for applications relating to the registration of enduring powers of attorney, which are set out in practice direction H accompanying Part 9. If no such application is received, the court will proceed to consider the matter in response to the Public Guardian's request and will give directions to the Public Guardian.

---

[1]   These time limits are imposed by rule 201(1)(b) and (2).

[2]   See paragraph 5 of Schedule 4 to the Act.

[3]   Rule 200(6) sets out what the notice must contain.

Appendix G

CASE REPORTS

Contents

[G1]

RE K; RE F (ENDURING POWERS OF ATTORNEY)

[1988] 2 FLR 15

CHANCERY DIVISION

HOFFMANN J 27 October 1987

Power of attorney – Mental incapacity – Enduring power of attorney executed by donors understanding nature and effect of power but lacking mental capacity to manage their affairs – Whether execution of power valid – Enduring Powers of Attorney Act 1985 s 6(5)(a)

In both cases enduring powers of attorney were executed under the Enduring Powers of Attorney Act 1985 at a time when those executing them were capable of understanding the nature and effect of the powers but were not capable by reason of mental disorder of managing their property and affairs. Applications were made to register the powers in accordance with s 4 of the 1985 Act. In the case of Miss K relatives objected to registration on the grounds that she had not had the necessary mental capacity at the time of execution and therefore that the power was not valid under s 6(5)(a). The Master rejected the application for registration and the applicant appealed. In the case of Mrs F, the Master referred to the court under the Court of Protection rules the question whether the power created by the instrument was valid if the donor understood the nature and effect of an enduring power of attorney notwithstanding that she was at the time of its execution incapable by reason of mental disorder of managing her property and affairs. The appeal and the reference were heard together.

Held – it was established at common law that an understanding of the nature and effect of a power was sufficient for its validity, but that a power could not longer be validly exercised if the donor had lost the mental capacity to be a principal. However, the fact that a power could not be validly exercised did not lead to the proposition that it was for all purposes invalid. Having regard to the purpose of the 1985 Act, which was to enable a power to be exercised notwithstanding that the donor did not have the mental capacity required by the common law, and taking into account further that the statutory safeguards for the donor built into the Act made it unnecessary to impose too high a standard of mental capacity for the valid execution of the power, it could be concluded that a power was valid for the purposes of s 6(5)(a) notwithstanding that the donor did not have the mental capacity which would make it exercisable, provided that she had understood the nature and effect of the juristic act conferring the power. Where there was mental incapacity at the time the power was executed the obligation of the attorney to register the power under s 4 arose immediately upon execution.

The appeal would be allowed and the reference answered in the affirmative.

Statutory provisions considered

Enduring Powers of Attorney Act 1985, ss 1, 2, 3, 4, 6 and 8

Cases referred to in judgment

Beaney (Deceased), Re [1978] 1 WLR 770; [1978] 2 All ER 595

Drew v Nunn (1879) 4 QBD 661; 40 LT 671; [1874–80] All ER Rep 1144, CA

Gibbons v Wright (1954) 91 CLR 423 (Aust. HC)

Re K:

Christopher McCall QC for Miss K;

John Morris Collins for the objectors;

Peter Rawson as amicus curiae.

Re F:

Christopher McCall QC for the Mrs F;

Cur. adv. vult.

HOFFMANN J:

There are before the court an appeal and a reference of a question of law from the Court of Protection. The appeal is from an order of the Master dismissing an application for the registration of an enduring power of attorney executed by Miss K under the Enduring Powers of Attorney Act 1985 ('the 1985 Act'). The question of law which is the subject of the reference has arisen in connection with an application for the registration of an enduring power of attorney executed by Mrs F. The appeal and the reference both raise the same point of law, and as it is of some importance for the future administration of the 1985 Act I am, at the request of counsel, giving this judgment in open court.

The 1985 Act was intended to provide an inexpensive method by which a person could confer power to manage his affairs upon a person of his own choice which would remain effective notwithstanding any change in his mental capacity. Before the Act the execution of a power of attorney, however expressed, was useless for this purpose because it would be revoked by the donor's loss of mental capacity.

Section 1(1)(a) of the 1985 Act provides that a power of attorney which is an 'enduring power' within the meaning of the 1985 Act shall not be revoked by any subsequent mental incapacity of the donor. Section 2(1) defines an 'enduring power' as one executed in the manner and form prescribed in regulations made by the Lord Chancellor. The current regulations require the instrument to be endorsed with certain explanatory information which is intended to tell the donor what the effect of executing the power will be.

Section 3 places certain restrictions on what an attorney under an enduring power can do. He may not benefit himself or persons other than the donor except to the extent that the donor might have been expected to provide for his or their needs. He may not make gifts except for presents of reasonable value at Christmas, birthdays, weddings and such like to persons related to or connected with the donor or charitable gifts which the donor might have been expected to make. Section 4 imposes on the attorney a duty to apply to the court for registration of the power as soon as practicable after he has reason to believe that the donor is or is becoming mentally incapable. For this purpose, 'mentally incapable' is defined in the same way as in s 94(2) of the Mental Health Act 1983:

' . . . in relation to any person, that he is incapable by reason of mental disorder of managing and administering his property and affairs.'

The incentive to register is that once mental incapacity has supervened, the attorney cannot (subject to narrow exceptions) validly exercise the power until it has been registered. Notice of an application for registration must be given to the closest relatives and they are entitled to object to registration on various grounds specified in s 6(5). These include:

'(a)   that the power purported to have been created . . . was not valid . . .
(d)   that fraud or undue pressure was used to induce the donor to create the power; and
(e)   that, having regard to all the circumstances and in particular the attorney's relationship to or connection with the donor, the attorney is unsuitable to be the donor's attorney.'

Once the power has been registered, it cannot be revoked by the donor without the confirmation of the court. Section 8 confers upon the court wide supervisory powers under which it may, for example, give directions to the attorney with respect to the management of the donor's property and affairs, demand that accounts be kept or documents and information supplied, and finally cancel the registration and revoke the power. In the case of Miss K, relatives objected to registration on the ground specified in s 6(5)(a), namely:

' . . . that the power purported to have been created by the instrument was not valid as an enduring power of attorney.'

The alleged cause of invalidity was that Miss K did not have the necessary mental capacity at the time of execution. The master received evidence of Miss K's mental capacity and made the following finding of fact:

'I accept the strong evidence that, on the particular date in question Miss K enjoyed a period during which she was able to understand that Mr K was to be her attorney under an enduring power of attorney and that she understood what an enduring power was; but that she was incapable by reason of mental disorder of managing her property and affairs.'

This finding raised the question of law which has been argued in this appeal, namely whether the power created by the instrument was valid if the donor understood the nature and effect of an enduring power of attorney notwithstanding that she was at the time to its execution incapable by reason of mental disorder of managing her property and affairs. The Master answered this question in the negative.

Shortly after she had given judgment in the case of Miss K, the Master heard an application for the registration of an enduring power which had been executed by Mrs F. She was a lady of 75 suffering from presenile dementia. Although she was at times lucid and capable of making decisions with full understanding of what she was doing, at other times she would become confused and suffer loss of memory. The medical evidence was that when she executed the power she fully understood its nature and effect, but that on account of her recurrent mental disability she could not in general terms be said to be capable of managing and administering her property. The case therefore presented the same question of law as the case of Miss K, and without giving a ruling the Master referred the question to this court under r 39 of the Court of Protection Rules 1984. The appeal in *Re K* and the reference in *Re F* were argued together in chambers, and I had not only the benefit of adversarial argument by Mr McCall for the applicants in both cases and Mr Collins for the objectors in *Re K*, but also the assistance as amicus curiae of Mr Rawson, instructed by the Official Solicitor.

The 1985 Act does not specify the mental capacity needed to execute an enduring power and the answer must therefore be found in the common law. It is well established that capacity to perform a juristic act exists when the person who purported to do the act had at the time the mental capacity, with the assistance of such explanation as he may have been given to understand the nature and effect of that particular transaction: see *Re Beaney* [1978] 1 WLR 770. In principle, therefore, an understanding of the nature and effect of the power was sufficient for its validity.

At common law there is, however, the further rule that a power can no longer be validly exercised if the donor has lost the mental capacity to be a principal. The way in which this rule is usually expressed is to say that mental incapacity revokes the power. What is meant by mental incapacity for this purpose has not been fully explored in the authorities. The question is plainly different from the usual question about capacity to perform a juristic act. It is hypothetical rather than factual. The donor did not in fact exercise the power and one cannot therefore ask whether he actually understood the nature and effect of what he was doing. One can only ask whether he would have understood, and this requires one first to decide what he must be supposed to have done and the circumstances in which he must be supposed to have done it. In the Australian case of *Gibbons v Wright* (1954) 91 CLR 423, 445, it was said that a power is revoked if the donor ceases to have the mental capacity to perform the acts authorized by the power. This would seem to mean that, at any rate in the case of a general power, there will be revocation if the donor no longer has the general capacity to manage and administer his property and affairs. It is not necessary for me to discuss the question further because I am content to assume, as did the Master, that the power executed by Miss K would at common law have been revoked, at latest, when she ceased to be able to manage and administer her property and affairs.

The main reason why the Master held that Miss K's power was invalid was because in her view a person suffering from mental incapacity which would have revoked a power could not validly create one. There is at first sight a compelling logic about this reasoning. It is, however, important to bear in mind that in the rule that a power is revoked by the onset of mental incapacity, the term 'revoke' is used as a metaphor. To revoke a power ordinarily means intentionally to perform a juristic act which terminates its legal effect. But the donor who becomes mentally incapable has not performed any act. What happens is that at least for some purposes the power ceased to have effect as if he had revoked it. As in the case of all rules expressed as metaphors or analogies, there are dangers in reasoning from the metaphor as if it expressed a literal truth rather than from the underlying principle which the metaphor encapsulates.

Brett LJ, after reserving judgment for more than 6 months in order to ponder the conceptual problems of revocation by incapacity, expressed the principle as follows in *Drew v Nunn* (1879) 4 QBD 661:

'When the principal, according to law, cannot act for himself, the person who represents him ceases to be able to act for him.'

The rule is therefore concerned with whether the power can be validly exercised rather than with its essential validity. Of course, for most purposes it will make no difference whether the one says that the power has ceased to be exercisable or has become invalid. But the fact that the power cannot be validly exercised does not commit one to the proposition that it is for all purposes invalid. For example, if it was the agent who lost mental capacity, the power would also not be exercisable, but one would not say that the power itself was invalid.

The question is therefore whether, as a matter of construction, a power in 'valid' for the purposes of s 6(5)(a) only if the donor had the mental capacity which would have made it exercisable. This must be decided by having regard to the purpose of the Act as a whole, which is to enable powers to be exercised notwithstanding that the donor does not have the mental capacity required by the common law. There seems to me no logical reason why the validity of the power for the purposes of s 6(5)(a) should be affected by considerations of whether it would have been exercisable. The court is not concerned with whether the power has been validly exercised but whether as a juristic act it should registered with a view to its future exercise notwithstanding the donor's loss of mental capacity.

The Master expressed her reasoning in a slightly different way when she said that she did not think that Miss K 'could validly pass to an attorney powers which she herself at the time did not possess'.

This proposition also requires further analysis. In one sense, Miss K did possess the powers to manage her property because she owned it. She could not exercise those powers on a regular basis because she lacked mental capacity. But there is no logical reason why, though unable to exercise her powers, she could not confer them upon someone else by an appropriate juristic act. The validity of that act depends upon whether she understood its nature and effect and not upon whether she would hypothetically have been able to perform all the acts which it authorized.

The Master also referred to s 4 of the 1985 Act, saying that as the obligation to register the instrument because the donor was or was becoming mentally incapable only arose after execution, if followed that at the time of execution the donor could not yet have been mentally incapable or even becoming mentally incapable. This appears to me fallacious. If the donor is already mentally incapable when he executes the power, there is no inconsistency with s 4. It only means that the obligation to register arises immediately upon execution.

Mr Collins, for the objectors in the appeal, founded a similar argument upon the long title of the 1985 Act:

'An Act to enable powers of attorney to be created which will survive any subsequent mental incapacity of the donor and to make provision in connection with such powers.'

He said that Act was concerned to protect the power against revocation by any subsequent mental incapacity and therefore contemplated that the donor would have full capacity at the time of execution. I think that this is reading too much into the words. The Act is intended to ensure that the power will continue to be exercisable notwithstanding mental incapacity. But for the reasons I have already given, I see no reason why the test for whether it was validly created should be the same as for whether it would have ceased to be exercisable. In principle they are clearly different.

I think that my conclusions are in accordance with what appears to be the general policy of the Act. In practice it is likely that many enduring powers will be executed when symptoms of mental incapacity have begun to manifest themselves. These symptoms may result in the donor being mentally incapable in the statutory sense that she is unable on a regular basis to manage her property and affairs. But, as in the case of Mrs F, she may execute the power with full understanding and with the intention of taking advantage of the Act to have her affairs managed by the attorney of her choice rather than having them put in the hands of the Court of Protection. I can think of no reason of policy why this intention should be frustrated.

The power does not amount to an outright disposition of assets like a gift, settlement or will. It is fiduciary and further limited as to gifts and payments to the attorney himself by the specific provisions of s 3. The obligation imposed upon the attorney to register under s 4 or run the risk that his exercise of the power will be invalidated by s 1(1)(b), provides the additional protection that the power will be brought to the attention of the court and the relatives to whom notice must be given. The application for registration gives the court an opportunity to consider the circumstances in which the execution of the power was procured and the suitability of the attorney. After registration, the court has its supervisory powers under s 8. The exercise of the power is thus hedged about on all sides with statutory protection for the donor. In these circumstances, it does not seem to me necessary to impose too high a standard of capacity for its valid execution.

Finally, I should say something about what is meant by understanding the nature and effect of the power. What degree of understanding is involved? Plainly one cannot expect that the donor should have been able to pass an examination on the provisions of the Act. At the other extreme, I do not think that it would be sufficient if he realized only that it gave cousin W power to look after his property. Mr Rawson, as amicus curiae, helpfully summarized the matters which the donor should have understood in order that he can be said to have understood the nature and effect of the power. First (if such be the terms of the power), that the attorney will be able to assume complete authority over the donor's affairs. Secondly (if such be the terms of the power), that the attorney will in general be able to do anything with the donor's property which he himself could have done. Thirdly, that the authority will continue if the donor should be or become mentally incapable. Fourthly, that if he should be or become mentally incapable, the power will be irrevocable without confirmation by the court. I do not wish to prescribe another form of words in competition with the explanatory notes prescribed by the Lord Chancellor, but I accept Mr Rawson's summary as a statement of the matters which should ordinarily be explained to the donor (whatever the precise language which may be used) and which the evidence should show he has understood.

As I read the Master's findings, Miss K understood the nature and effect of the enduring power to the extent which I have described. I therefore allow the appeal and direct that the instrument which she executed be registered. I answer the question of law referred to me in *Re F* in the affirmative. The costs of all parties in this court and before the Master will be paid on an indemnity basis from the estates of the respective donors.

Solicitors:

Re K:

Anthony Quinn Co. for Miss K;

Michael Dorsey Co., Leeds, for the respondents;

Official Solicitor.

Re F:

Withers for Mrs F;

Official Solicitor

P.H.

[G2]

RE R (ENDURING POWER OF ATTORNEY)

[1991] 1 FLR 128

CHANCERY DIVISION

VINELOTT J 13 December 1989

Power of attorney – Court of Protection – Application of donor's housekeeper for provision out of donor's estate – Donor incapable of managing her affairs – Court's jurisdiction to supervise donee's conduct – Whether court had power to grant provision – Enduring Powers of Attorney Act 1985, s 8(2)(b)(i)

The applicant, who was employed by R for over 20 years, initially as a cook and housekeeper but more recently as a companion, alleged that she had provided her services to R at far less than the wages she would ordinarily have expected to earn because of her close relationship with R and because of an expectation, encouraged by R, that she would provide for her for the rest of her life. When R was in her 80s she gave an enduring power of attorney to her nephew, with a general authority to act on her behalf (save for two restrictions) which was registered under the Enduring Powers of Attorney Act 1985. Soon afterwards, R was found by a visitor of the Court of Protection to be incapable of managing her affairs and was placed in a nursing home. R's attorney then gave the applicant notice terminating her employment and sought possession of the flat. The applicant applied to the Master of the Court of Protection seeking provision out of R's estate. The master dismissed the application and the applicant appealed.

Held – dismissing the appeal – the purpose and effect of the Enduring Powers of Attorney Act 1985 was to enable a person to give a power of attorney, which would endure despite a supervening incapacity, to a person of his choice, and to empower that person to deal with his property in the way that he thought fit. The scope of the attorney's authority was enlarged beyond that which it would bear under the general law by s. 3, subject to any express restrictions in the power.

The court's powers under the 1985 Act were primarily directed to the proper supervision of the attorney, and to giving consents and authorisations which were necessary to supplement the powers, but which were not inconsistent with restrictions imposed by the donor of the power. While s. 8 of the Act gave the court jurisdiction to supervise the conduct of an attorney in the exercise of his power, s 8(2)(b)(i), on its true construction, did not give the court unrestricted power to direct the disposal of the donor's property by way of gift, or in recognition of a moral obligation unaccompanied by any legal obligation; and that, accordingly, the court had no power to direct that provision be made for the applicant.

Statutory provisions considered

Mental Health Act 1983, ss 95, 96

Enduring Powers of Attorney Act 1985. ss 3, 8(2)(b)

APPEAL from the Master of the Court of Protection

Timothy Lyons for the applicant

Richard de Lacy for the attorney

VINELOTT J:

This is an appeal from the Master of the Court of Protection. It raises a short question concerning the construction and effect of the Enduring Powers of Attorney Act 1985.

I need say very little, and it is undesirable that I should say more than a very little, about the contentious matters which form the background for this appeal. The donor of the power of attorney, Mrs R, is now in her 80s. Not long after she had given the power of attorney she was found by a visitor of the Court of Protection to be incapable of managing her affairs. She is a widow and childless. She has for very many years lived in a flat in Ennismore Gardens and since, I think, 1967 she has had with her in the flat the applicant, who was initially employed as a cook and housekeeper. She says that in more recent years she has been more of a companion, and she says she has served in recent years at far less than the wages she would ordinarily have expected to earn because of her close relationship with Mrs R and, moreover, in the expectation which she was encouraged to form by Mrs R, that Mrs R would look after her and provide accommodation for her for the whole of her life. She says that it was in reliance on that expectation that in 1984 she declined an invitation by relatives to go to live with them in Luxembourg.

On 25 January 1988 Mrs R gave an enduring power of attorney to a nephew. That power was executed in the presence of her doctor and the family solicitor. It is on a printed form. She gave her attorney a general authority to act on her behalf, save that the power was not to extend to the management of her portfolio handled by Mr Raphael Zarn, a stockbroker, and was to be subject to the restriction that the attorney was not to make gifts to friends or relatives. That power was registered under the 1985 Act on 11 May 1988. No question is raised as to the validity of the power and, as I have said, a visitor has found that the donor of the power is now under an incapacity. She was taken first to a hospital following an accident in March, and then in mid-April moved to a nursing home in the country, where she now is.

There has been considerable hostility between the attorney and the applicant, which happily I need not enter into. As a result of the change in Mrs R's circumstances, the attorney gave the applicant notice terminating her employment and later sought possession of the flat, which has a very considerable value (of the order of £400,000) and a very considerable letting value; if improved, it would command a rent of about £800 a week. At the moment it is a drain on Mrs R's resources.

The applicant first applied under the 1985 Act for an order for the cancellation of the power on the ground that Mrs R was, and was likely to remain, mentally capable, or alternatively that fraud or undue pressure had been used to induce her to execute it. Following the report of the visitor, to which I have referred, the application was amended to seek provision out of Mrs R's estate. She asked for an order that such provision be made as the court deemed proper for her maintenance and accommodation, and for reimbursement of sums which she says she has disbursed. On that latter matter, there has been some reimbursement and I cannot, on the evidence before me, decide whether there are other sums in respect of which she has a valid claim. Any further claim will have to be put before the Master of the Court of Protection.

The grounds on which this application is founded are, as I have indicated, statements said to have been made by Mrs R that she would make financial provision for the applicant's future, and that she could trust her to make that provision. On that application being made, the attorney undertook not to restore proceedings he had taken for possession of the flat. The application came before the Master of the Court of Protection on 31 January 1989 when it was dismissed and the applicant appeals from that dismissal. I should perhaps add that the flat has been maintained in the meantime. The proceedings for possession are still pending and have been transferred to the county court. That is all I need say about the background.

The Enduring Powers of Attorney Act 1985 made a very remarkable change in the law. It created a regime for the administration of the affairs of somebody who becomes incapable of managing his affairs which is supplemental to that provided by the Mental Health Act 1983. In effect the Act permits a person, while capable of managing his affairs, to select somebody who will be responsible for managing his affairs if there is a supervening incapacity, so avoiding the expense and – I think, possibly, in the minds of some – the embarrassment of invoking the full jurisdiction of the Court of Protection. A power of attorney has very limited effect until it is registered. When registered, it takes effect according to its terms. The scope of the attorney's authority is enlarged beyond that which it would bear under the general law by s 3, subject to any express restrictions in the power, and the court is given wide powers of supervision under s. 8. Section 3(4) provides:

> 'Subject to any conditions or restrictions contained in the instrument, an attorney under an enduring power . . . may (without obtaining any consent) act under the power so as to benefit himself or other persons than the donor to the following extent but no further, that is to say—
>
> (a)   he may so act in relation to any other person if the donor might be expected to provide for his or that person's needs respectively; and
> (b)   he may do whatever the donor might be expected to do to meet those needs.'

That extension is then further extended by s 3(5), which gives the attorney power to 'dispose of the property of the donor by way of gift' in making gifts 'of a seasonal nature' or on a specified anniversary to 'persons . . . related to or connected with the donor' subject to the proviso that 'the value of each such gift is not unreasonable having regard to all the circumstances and in particular the size of the donor's estate'.

The role of the court is set out in s 8. Under s 8(2)(a) the court has power to determine questions as to the meaning or effect of the instrument. Under s 8(2)(b) the court has power to give directions with respect to:

> '(i)   the management or disposal by the attorney of the property and affairs of the donor;
> (ii)   the rendering of accounts by the attorney and the production of the records kept by him for the purpose;
> (iii)   the remuneration or expenses of the attorney, whether or not in default of or in accordance with any provision made by the instrument, including directions for the repayment of excessive or the payment of additional remuneration; . . . '

Section 8(2)(c) gives the court power to require the attorney to furnish information or produce documents, and s 8(2)(d) to give any consent or authorisation to act which the attorney would have to obtain from a mentally capable donor. Section 8(2)(e), I must read in full:

> '(2) The court may . . .
> (e)   authorise the attorney to act so as to benefit himself or
> other persons than the donor otherwise than in accordance with section 3(4) and (5) (but subject to any conditions or restrictions contained in the instrument); . . . '

Section 8(2)(f) gives the court power to relieve the attorney wholly or partly from any liability which he has or may have incurred on account of a breach of his duties as attorney.

It is quite plain, and it is not in dispute, that the only authority that the Court of Protection could have to give directions to the attorney, requiring him to make provision for the applicant, would have to be found, if at all, in s 8(2)(b)(i). The case put by the applicant's counsel is that that subparagraph does give the court unrestricted power to direct an attorney to dispose of any part of the property of the donor of the power, by way of gift or in recognition of some moral obligation unaccompanied by any legal obligation.

I find that an impossible view. Of course, the word 'disposal' is, in some contexts, capable of being given a very wide meaning, and could include a disposition by way of gift. But it seems to me that in the context of s 8 it cannot have been intended that it should bear that wide meaning. It comes in a paragraph, (b), which is plainly concerned with administrative matters: the management of the donor's property, the rendering of accounts and determination of the remuneration of the attorney. These are all part of the jurisdiction which the court is given to supervise the conduct of the attorney, and to see that he is exercising his powers of management and administration properly. It would be remarkable, in a paragraph directed to matters of that sort, to find an unrestricted power given to the court to dispose of the whole of the donor's property by way of gift.

The court, of course, has a very wide power, in the case of a patient within the jurisdiction of the Court of Protection. It is now conferred by ss. 95 and 96 of the Mental Health Act 1983. However, there the power of the court to direct dispositions of the patient's property is very clearly spelled out, and the rules provide for all persons potentially interested in the patient's estate to be represented, and for full consideration of the effect of any disposition of the patient's property.

Moreover, the construction which it is sought to put on s 8(2)(b)(i) brings that paragraph into conflict with s 8(2)(e) which gives the court a power which is supplemental to s 3(4) and (5); it is a power for the court to authorise gifts or dispositions of property which go beyond s 3(4) and (5). The power of the court to give that authority is, however, subject to any conditions or restrictions in the power of attorney itself. If the contentions made on behalf of the applicant were right, s 8(2)(b)(i) would enable the court to give directions for the gift or disposition of the property of the donor which are not subject to conditions or restrictions contained in the instrument. In my view that cannot possibly have been intended.

More generally, I think Mr de Lacy, counsel for the attorney, was right when he said that the purpose and effect of the Enduring Powers of Attorney Act 1985 is to enable somebody to give a power of attorney, which will endure despite a supervening incapacity, to a person of his choice, and to empower that person to deal with his property in the way that he thinks fit. It should be approached on the footing that the court's powers are primarily directed to the proper supervision of the attorney, and to giving consents or authorisations which are necessary to supplement the powers, but which are not inconsistent with restrictions imposed by the donor of the power. I find it unnecessary in these circumstances to consider the further question, whether the restriction in the power of attorney which I read would, in fact, put it outside the power of the court to authorise dispositions of the kind sought in favour of the applicant. In my judgment, therefore, this appeal fails and must be dismissed.

Solicitors:

Lithgow Pepper Eldridge for the applicant

Lovell White Durrant for the attorney

PATRICIA HOLLINGS

Barrister

[G3]

RE W (POWER OF ATTORNEY)

[1999] 2 FLR 1163

CHANCERY DIVISION

MR JULES SHER QC

(SITTING AS A DEPUTY JUDGE OF THE HIGH COURT)8 July 1999

Executors, administrators, wills and probate – Power of attorney

W, aged over 90, granted her eldest daughter, X, a power of attorney with general authority to act on her behalf in relation to all her property and affairs. W's other two children, who had an unrelated dispute with X, objected to registration of the enduring power of attorney. Their grounds were (1) that the power was invalid because W lacked capacity to grant it, and (2) that X was unsuitable because of the hostility between the siblings. The master of the court of protection refused to register the power of attorney on both grounds, taking into account in relation to X's unsuitability, an unauthorised gift which she had made to herself and her two siblings. X appealed.

Held – allowing X's appeal and making the order for registration of the power –

(1)   The onus was not on X to show that W had possessed the capacity to execute the power of attorney, but on the two objectors to show that W had lacked the capacity to do so. Therefore, even if there was insufficient evidence to satisfy the court that W had possessed the necessary understanding at the relevant time, if the court was not satisfied on the evidence that W had lacked the necessary understanding, it was bound by the Enduring Power of Attorney Act 1985 to register the power unless there was another valid ground of objection. The contemporary evidence from W's GP that W had the necessary mental capacity weighed more heavily with the court than evidence from a psychologist which was based on two interviews with W some months after the power was executed. The court was not satisfied that W lacked capacity.

(2)   If an estate was complex, hostility between siblings might well render all of them unsuitable as attorneys for the estate, because it would interfere with the smooth running of the administration of the estate, but where, as here, the estate was simple, such hostility need not impact adversely on the administration of the estate and the court should not interfere on the ground of unsuitability. In relation to the unauthorised gift, although the power of an attorney did not extend to the sort of inheritance tax planning which had been attempted by X, X had been scrupulously fair as between the three siblings, and had not behaved greedily or dishonestly. She was not unsuitable as attorney of W's estate.

Statutory provisions considered

Enduring Power of Attorney Act 1985, s 6(5)(a), (e), (6)

Cases referred to in judgment

K, Re; F (Enduring Powers of Attorney), Re [1988] Ch 310, [1988] 2 FLR 15, [1988] 2 WLR 781, [1988] 1 All ER 358, ChD

Adrian Jack for the appellant

David Rees for the respondent

JULES SHER QC:

This is an appeal from the decision of the master of the court of protection who refused to register an enduring power of attorney granted by Mrs W to her eldest child, Mrs X, on 4 July 1996 with general authority to act on her behalf in relation to all her property and affairs. As this judgment is being given in open court I shall restrict the recital of facts to the barest minimum necessary to identify the point at issue.

Mrs W is now over 90. Her husband died in 1979. They were hoteliers. The hotel was sold in 1987. In 1993 Mrs W moved to sheltered accommodation. On 29 August 1996 she moved to a residential home and in December 1997 she was transferred to a nursing home where she still resides.

She has three children: the donee of the power, Mrs X, now aged 61, another daughter Mrs Y now 60 and a son Mr Z, now aged 56. Much of the reason for what has turned out to be extremely wasteful litigation in relation to a relatively modest amount of property is due to a wholly unrelated dispute between Mrs X on the one hand and her brother and sister on the other. This dispute concerned two cottages in which the three siblings were, with one other person, in joint ownership as tenants in common. The brother and sister (as well as the other joint owner) wanted to sell at a price which had been offered. Mrs X wanted to hold out for a higher price. Her three joint owners sued her in the county court, causing both sides to run up expensive legal bills. Eventually higher offers came in and the properties were sold above the higher price for which Mrs X was holding out. Apparently even that did not settle the litigation as the plaintiffs continued to dispute the question as to who was to have conduct of the sale.

From the 275 pages in the bundle before me it is obvious that Mrs X, of the three siblings, is the most literary, in the sense at least of being given to committing her communications to writing. She also comes across as efficient in the recording of financial detail so far as her administration of the marketing and sale of the cottages was concerned. She appears from the evidence to be a businesswoman in her own right (unlike her siblings) and to have dominated family financial matters such as the obtaining of planning permission for the site and the campaign to achieve a sale. It is not surprising that she was chosen by her mother, Mrs W, to be her sole attorney.

Unfortunately, perhaps, Mrs X does not mince her words. Her letters are not only prolix but, it has to be said, unnecessarily vulgar. It is from one of these letters that the master quoted in his judgment and it is plain that such offensive letters to her siblings played an important role in persuading the master to reject the power of attorney.

I have had more extensive evidence than was before the master and I have come to a different conclusion. Ordinarily this judgment would be delivered in chambers. However, two points of principle emerge from my different treatment and that has led to this judgment being given in open court.

There survive in this court only two of the grounds put forward by the objectors (Mrs Y and Mr Z) who responded to Mrs X's notices dated 18 April 1998 of her intention to register the power. Those two grounds are the grounds in subparas (a) and (e) of s 6(5) of the Enduring Power of Attorney Act 1985. I quote those two subparagraphs below:

Section 6(5):

'For the purpose of this Act a notice of objection to the registration of an instrument is valid if the objection is made on one or more of the following grounds, namely—
(a)   that the power purported to have been created by the instrument was not valid as an enduring power of attorney;
        . . .
(e)   that, having regard to all the circumstances and in particular the attorney's relationship to or connection with the donor, the attorney is unsuitable to be the donor's attorney.'

I quote as well the next subsection (on which the first issue of principle in this appeal arises).

Section 6(6):

'If, in a case where subsection (4) above applies, any of the grounds of objection in subsection (5) above is established to the satisfaction of the court, the court shall refuse the application but if, in such a case, it is not so satisfied, the court shall register the instrument to which the application relates.'

This is a case, of course, in which 'subsection (4) above applies' because one of the occasions for the operation of subs (4) is that a valid notice of objection to the registration was timeously received: see s 6(4)(a) of the Act. There is no suggestion that this was not the case here.

The important point to notice is that the onus of establishing any of the grounds set out in subs (5) is firmly laid on the shoulders of the objectors. Under subs (6) it is only if the ground concerned is established to the satisfaction of the court that the court can refuse to register the power. Indeed, if the ground is so established the court must refuse. The contrary position is expressly made equally emphatic: if the court is not so satisfied it 'shall register the instrument to which the application relates'.

Very few cases in these days turn on the onus of proof. In ordinary civil litigation the judge is nearly always able to form a view on a balance of probabilities as to whether an event did or did not happen. But the state of a woman's mind some 3 years before the court hearing is inherently an issue in respect of which it is quite likely that the judge may not be satisfied either way.

The first ground: invalidity due to lack of capacity

In this case the essential facts were that at the time of the execution of the power (4 July 1996) Mrs W was 87 and by all accounts was physically well but suffering from a degree of memory impairment. Her GP, Dr H, had written a letter to her solicitor a fortnight before the execution of the power. The letter was dated 22 June 1996 and in it he said:

'I can confirm that I saw her recently with her daughter and found her to be suffering from a degree of memory impairment, however in my opinion she still has the necessary mental capacity to sign a power of attorney. I would add that her mental abilities are at their best in the early part of the day and tend to deteriorate as the day goes by.'

It seemed to me important for the court to see the doctor and ascertain precisely what he meant by the necessary mental capacity to sign a power of attorney and what tests he performed, if any, to reach this conclusion. However, I was told by Mr Jack, counsel for Mrs X, that the doctor had indicated that he could not now remember any detail whatsoever and that he was accordingly unable to help the court.

The hearing below proceeded in the total absence of Mrs X who, unfortunately, was not served appropriate notice of the hearing due to an error in the Public Trustee Office. That would of course have entitled Mrs X to have the proceedings below set aside as of right, but both counsel invited me, in the interest of saving costs, to treat the matter as effectively before me on the original as well as additional evidence put by Mrs X after the hearing before the master.

Against the doctor's evidence was the evidence of a chartered clinical psychologist to whom Mrs Y had taken Mrs W on 22 November and 13 December 1996. Mrs W had been taken from the residential home where she was then living to the psychologist without the knowledge of Mrs X, who first heard about the matter when the psychologist's report was produced in these proceedings.

As the master pointed out the psychologist's report was extensive and detailed. He concluded that:

' . . . the above detected severity of deterioration across a number of vital areas of cognitive functioning suggests strongly that for the past period running into a number of years, Mrs W has not been in a position to deal properly with the intangible (non-concrete) or hypothetical, or to correctly comprehend, interpret, see implications in, judge, or to direct any business or operation other than that which does not require weighing up the pros and cons, making comparisons, or seeing consequences of action beyond the immediate step.'

As the report did not specifically address the question whether or not Mrs W was capable of executing an enduring power of attorney, the psychologist wrote a supplemental note on 10 July 1998 in which he said:

> 'I believe that in no way was Mrs W in a condition on 4 July 1996 to execute an enduring power of attorney.'

The doctor's evidence has the inestimable advantage of being that of the patient's GP who saw her regularly, and of being more or less contemporaneous with the execution of the power. It would take a very strong opinion given as a result of an examination some 5 months later to persuade me positively that the patient did not have the necessary capacity. As it was the psychologist recognised in his report that medication could make an assessment of the kind he was making problematic. Yet there is no record in his report of the various forms of medication (including morphine) Mrs W was taking at the time. Mrs X has now given evidence of these: Dothiepin for depression, Inderalla for blood pressure, distalgesic co-proxamol for pain relief and Merellil to keep her calm. Moreover, on 16 January 1997 Mrs W was rushed to hospital and treated for anaemia. The effect of anaemia on her performance of the psychometric tests is unclear.

I have taken into account all the evidence, on both sides, as to various incidents showing a certain degree of confusion over the years. There is no point in recording all the detail here. It is worth noting, however, that Mrs X has for many years handled her mother's financial affairs. Mrs X had been made a signatory on her bank account with Lloyds Bank. Mrs X arranged for the payment of her bills. When it was apparent in April 1996 that Mrs W's mental faculties were getting weaker she wrote, in her own handwriting, to her solicitor, in a perfectly intelligible way in connection with her will, a codicil and the division of what she called her 'household goods'. Mrs W herself, I am told, had been the attorney under an enduring power of attorney for her elder sister so I can assume that she probably knew what an enduring power of attorney was.

I have further evidence before me in the shape of a statement by one of the directors of the nursing home in which Mrs W now lives who says that as late as 12 April 1998 when the notice of intention to register the power was served on her, Mrs W understood the arrangements with Mrs X as the attorney and Mrs W said, 'why would I want to change anything'. I have also been shown a letter written as late as April 1999 in a very shaky hand saying that she wanted the Public Trustee Office to stop interfering with her affairs. I must say that I was a little surprised at the coherence and vehemence of this letter and wondered to what extent it was influenced by others.

All in all, however, I am not satisfied that it has been established that Mrs W did not have the necessary understanding to execute an enduring power of attorney. That was the first ground put forward by the objectors, ie that the power was not valid as an enduring power because Mrs W did not understand the nature and effect of it. The degree of understanding and mental capacity necessary for this purpose has been laid down recently in Re K; Re F (Enduring Powers of Attorney) [1988] Ch 310, [1988] 2 FLR 15. The level of understand required is less than that required to enable an individual to manage her affairs generally. What is required is that she understood:

(a) that the attorney would be able to assume complete authority over her affairs;

(b) that the attorney could do anything with her property that she could have done;

(c) that that authority would continue if she became mentally incapable; and

(d) would in that event become irrevocable without confirmation by the court.

I am not satisfied on the evidence that Mrs W did not have this understanding. This does not mean that I am satisfied that she did have it. The point of this judgment is that this last issue is not the question before me. If, as is the case, I am not satisfied that she lacked the necessary understanding, it seems to me that I am bid by the Act to register the power, and that, subject to consideration of the second ground of objection, is what I propose to do.

In *Re K; Re F* Hoffmann J (as he then was) added, after describing the above four elements, the following sentence:

'I do not wish to prescribe another form of words in competition with the explanatory notes prescribed by the Lord Chancellor, but I accept Mr Rawson's summary as a statement of the matters which should ordinarily be explained to the donor (whatever the precise language which may be used) and which the evidence should show he has understood.'

This sentence forms no part of the reason for the decision. The judge was not concerned with an issue of onus or burden of proof. He inadvertently, in my judgment, turned the onus around so as to make it a requirement that the evidence should positively show the necessary understanding. The master concluded his judgment below thus:

'I must emphasise the final words of the passage I quoted earlier from Hoffmann J's judgment in *Re K; Re F* – "which the evidence should show that he has understood" – because they are often overlooked. The evidence in this case as it was presented to me prior to and at the hearing does not satisfy me that Mrs [W] understood the nature and effect of the enduring power of attorney she signed on 4 July 1996.'

In my judgment, the master went wrong in following this part of Hoffmann J's judgment. To sustain the power Mrs X did not have to satisfy him that Mrs W understood the nature of the power; the objectors had to satisfy him that she did not.

The second ground: unsuitability

This brings me to the second and only other surviving ground on which objection is made, and that is that having regard to all the circumstances, and in particular the attorney's relationship to or in connection with the donor, the attorney is unsuitable to be the donor's attorney.

The master decided that Mrs X was unsuitable for two reasons: first, because she had made unauthorised gifts to herself and her siblings of £20,000 each. The master said that he could not condone that. Secondly, and in my judgment more importantly, the master said this:

'In my opinion, the hostility and resentment between Mrs [W's] children renders any one of them unsuitable to be her attorney. The objectors clearly distrust the attorney, and the attorney obviously has no time for her brother and sister. Each party seems determined to thwart the actions and intentions of the other and, if need be, to air their family feud before the courts. Such contentiousness and bickering cannot possibly be in Mrs [W's] best interests, and it would be irresponsible of the court to allow either faction to gain the upper hand in terms of control over their mother. In the circumstances Mrs [W's] affairs should be managed by someone completely independent of the family.'

The gifts

I shall take these two points in turn. First, the gifts. It must be remembered that Mrs X was not at the hearing to defend herself. She did not even know that this criticism would be made. Before me and through her counsel, Mr Jack, she has made it quite

701

clear that now that she understands the law she will undertake to make retrospective application to approve the gifts and not make any further gifts without the court's permission.

The gifts have to be put into proper perspective. There is no suggestion that as between the three siblings Mrs X has not been scrupulously fair. Whatever she gave to herself she gave to each of her siblings. But it is more important to understand why the gifts were made in the first place. Plainly Mrs X is astute enough to have realised that there may be a case for sensible estate planning. She had, I gather from the evidence, sold the flat Mrs W owned and was living in sometime in mid-1996. That realised £100,000. There has been no criticism that this was not a sensible thing to do and the best price that could have been obtained. With Mrs W's other assets this figure put her well above the threshold at which inheritance tax is charged (currently some £231,000 I believe). To reduce the estate Mrs X made on behalf of Mrs W potentially exempt transfers of £20,000 each to the three siblings. Of course, Mrs W would have to survive for the requisite period for this to avoid the tax: but it was a perfectly rational thing to do. Whether it was the right thing to do in Mrs W's interests is another matter entirely and would be dependent upon the extent of her assets and her reasonable needs for the remainder of her lifetime. I say nothing about this aspect. It may have to be considered by the master at some other time.

What the master focused on, quite rightly in my opinion, was that the power of an attorney to make gifts of the donor's property is extremely limited, and certainly, without the authorisation of the court after the power is registered, does not extend to the making of gifts of this kind as part of inheritance tax planning.

But the evidence I have seen does not portray a picture of greed. At worst, Mrs X acted misguidedly in the interests of her siblings and herself and not, as she saw it, against the interests of her mother. The worst that can be said of her is that she ought to have known the law if she was to take on the responsibility of such an important fiduciary position, particularly as one of the few things expressly stated in part of the power itself is the following sentence:

'I also understand my limited power to use the donor's property to benefit persons other than the donor.'

Finally, of course, there is no indication that the two objectors ever complained about the gifts (from which they benefited as much as Mrs X did).

I do not think that the evidence concerning the gifts renders Mrs X unsuitable as an attorney.

Hostility

The second ground of unsuitability is the hostility between the three children. The master considered that that fact alone rendered any one of them unsuitable to be Mrs W's attorney. In my judgment such hostility may well have such consequences but it all depends upon the circumstances. For example, had the estate of Mrs W been complex and had it required strategic decisions in relation to its administration, one would expect the attorney to have had to consult and work with her siblings in relation to the administration. In such circumstances the evident hostility between them would impact adversely on the stewardship of the attorney, no matter who was at fault in creating the hostility in the first place.

But in this case the estate is simple. I asked counsel what the position was and was told that these are the following assets:

(1)   a portfolio of investments of a value (as at 23 December 1998) of £211,189;

(2)   £20,000 in premium bonds;

(3)   a life policy (written in trust) of £30,000.

As to the outgoings there is the cost of the nursing home at some £2000 a month, and then, simply, the need for a modest amount to cover a regular hairdo, telephone bills and the like. And, of course, on the income side there is the old age pension.

In other words there is nothing of any significance left to be done. The assets are under proper control. The income simply needs to be fed through to the nursing home. The evidence is that this has been done by Mrs X very efficiently. She had indicated more than once that she has never intended to charge for her services under the power of attorney and she does not intend to do so. Against this, if the public trustee were to come in, there would be an appointment fee and an annual fee of between £2350 and £3600 pa. If a solicitor were appointed the total cost would be likely to be somewhat less than that.

It seems to me that it is not right to say that (irrespective of the background) hostility of the kind we have seen in this case between the children renders any one of them unsuitable to be Mrs W's attorney. In this case the hostility will not impact adversely on the administration. It would, in my judgment, be quite wrong to frustrate Mrs W's choice of attorney in this way. Whether it is or is not a good idea for a parent in Mrs W's position, when such hostility exists, to appoint one child alone as attorney is another question. But Mrs W did so and, on the evidence, did so knowing of the hostility. That is her prerogative and in my judgment, when the hostility does not interfere with the smooth running of the administration, the court should not interfere on the ground of unsuitability.

That is not to say that this court approves of the strident tones in which Mrs X's correspondence is couched. It is earnestly to be hoped that after all this wasteful litigation she can find it in herself to conduct the family's affairs in a more congenial and co-operative manner.

I shall accordingly allow the appeal from the decision of the master and make the necessary order for the registration of the power.

Appeal allowed. Registration of power of attorney ordered.

Solicitors: Max Barford & Co for the appellant

Gaby Hardwicke Yearwood & Griffiths for the respondent

PHILIPPA JOHNSON

[G4]

RE W (ENDURING POWER OF ATTORNEY)

[2001] 1 FLR 832

COURT OF APPEAL

PETER   GIBSON   AND   ARDEN   LJJ   AND   SIR
CHRISTOPHER STAUGHTON11 December 2000

Power of attorney – Widow granting enduring power of attorney to eldest child – Child's siblings objecting on ground that instrument invalid through want of capacity of donor – Whether burden of proof on objectors or attorney – Enduring Power of Attorney Act 1985 ss 4, 6

In July 1996, a widow in her late eighties granted an enduring power of attorney to her eldest daughter. In April 1998, the daughter applied for it to be registered under the Enduring Power of Attorney Act 1985, having given notice of her intention to her siblings, the objectors. The objections were upheld by the Master in the Court of

Protection, but without the daughter being notified of the hearing. The matter was reconsidered on appeal. The Master upheld two grounds put forward by the objectors: (1) that the widow did not have the necessary capacity at the time the order was made, and (2) that having regard to all the circumstances, especially the attorney's relationship with the donor, the attorney was unsuitable. The Master's decision was reversed on those points. As regards the question of capacity he held that the objectors had not discharged the burden of proof which rested on them. He did not make an affirmative finding in respect of the attorney. The objectors appealed on ground (1). They contended also that the decision had been wrong on the facts. With the court's leave the objectors amended their notice of appeal to say that the burden of proof rested on the daughter as the attorney. Since the objection was valid the question to be decided was whether the ground of objection, that the power purported to have been created by the attorney was not valid, was established to the satisfaction of the court. If it was, then the court must refuse registration.

Held – dismissing the appeal – notwithstanding the dicta of Hoffmann J in Re K (Enduring Powers of Attorney); Re F and the principle of common law whereby the burden of proof was on the person seeking to uphold a deed or document on which the objectors had relied, s 6(6) of the Enduring Power of Attorney Act 1985 clearly provided that the grounds of objection had to be proved. The judge had been right to treat the burden of proof as resting throughout on the objectors, and, having found that the objectors had not discharged that burden, had been bound to register the instrument. He had not erred in law or on the facts in reaching his decision.

Statutory provisions considered

Law Commissions Act 1965, s 3(1)(e)

Mental Health Act 1983, Part 7

Enduring Power of Attorney Act 1985, ss 4, 6, 7, 8

Cases referred to in judgment

Beaney Dec'd, Re [1978] 1 WLR 770, [1978] 2 All ER 595, ChD

Brown v Pourau [1995] 1 NZLR 352, High Ct of NZ

K (Enduring Powers of Attorney), Re; Re F [1988] Ch 310, Court of Protection

Peters v Morris (CA 99/85) (unreported) 19 May 1987, CA (Wellington)

Waring v Waring [1848] VI Moore 342

David Rees for the appellant

Adrian Jack for the respondent

PETER GIBSON LJ:

(1) I will ask Sir Christopher Staughton to give the first judgment.

SIR CHRISTOPHER STAUGHTON:

(2) This appeal concerns the affairs of Mrs W, as I shall call her, a widow who is nearly 91 years of age. On 4 July 1996, she granted an enduring power of attorney to her eldest child, Mrs X. Two years later, on 27 April 1998, Mrs X applied for the enduring power of attorney to be registered under the Enduring Power of Attorney Act 1985. Meanwhile, she had given notice of intention to register on 18 April 1998 to the other two children of Mrs W: I will call them Mrs Y, who is now 61, and Mr Z, who is aged 57. They became the objectors. They had already, on 21 February 1997, obtained a report from a Mr C on Mrs W's mental health, but no action had been taken on that report in the ensuing year.

(3) On 13 May 1998, the objectors served notice of objection. That led to the present proceedings. The objections were upheld by Master Lush in the Court of Protection. However, his decision was reached in an unsatisfactory way in that Mrs X had not been notified of the hearing date and was not present. It seems to me, there having been real doubt as to whether she had been notified, that the Master would have been wiser not to proceed at that stage. In the event, we should disregard the conclusions of the Master. There might have been an order setting his decision aside and directing a fresh hearing before a new Master; but the parties instead agreed that on an appeal to a judge of the Chancery Division the matter should be reconsidered. That was done in order to save costs.

(4) The assets of the estate are not large. They are somewhat less now than they were before, no doubt, as the Master ordered the costs to come out of the estate. So did the judge. In the judge's decision it is said that the assets were a portfolio of investments valued in December 1998 at £211,000, £20,000 in premium bonds and a life policy written in trust of £30,000. At the time Mrs W was in a nursing home, which cost £2000 a month. She had some other simple and fairly modest requirements. Of course, she also had on the income side the old age pension.

(5) The grounds argued before the Master were these. First, that the power purported to have been created by the instrument was not valid as an enduring power of attorney. The reason put forward for that was that Mrs W did not have the necessary capacity and understanding at the time when she made it. Secondly, it was said that undue pressure was used to induce the donor to create the power. Thirdly, that having regard to all the circumstances, and in particular the attorney's relationship to or connection with the donor, the attorney was unsuitable as an attorney of the donor.

(6) The Master upheld the first and third grounds, that is to say lack of capacity and understanding and unsuitability, but not the second ground, which was undue pressure. The appeal came before Mr Julian Sher QC, sitting as a deputy judge of the Chancery Division. Before him only grounds one and three were argued, the ones upon which the objectors had succeeded before the Master. The deputy judge reversed the Master's decision on both points. He had, of course, additional evidence which was not before the Master.

(7) There is now an appeal to this court by permission of Walker LJ.

(8) The third ground, unsuitability, is no longer pursued by the objectors. So the only ground now is that the power of attorney was invalid through want of capacity.

(9) Before the judge the objectors had accepted that the burden of proof as to that rested on them. The judge accepted that, and there was no challenge to it in the notice of appeal. But now the objectors seek to amend their notice of appeal to say that the burden was on Mrs X, the attorney. There has been no objection to leave to amend the notice of appeal being granted; and we do grant it.

(10) The relevant provisions in the Enduring Power of Attorney Act 1985 are as follows. Section 4 provides:

> '(1) If the attorney under an enduring power has reason to believe that the donor is or is becoming mentally incapable subsections (2) to (6) below shall apply.
> (2) The attorney shall, as soon as practicable, make an application to the court for the registration of the instrument creating the power.'

(11) That, of course, was done in this case.

(12) Then s 6 says:

> '(1) In any case where—
>   (a) an application for registration is made in accordance with section 4(3) and (4), and

(b)   neither subsection (2) nor subsection (4) below applies,
the court shall register the instrument to which the application relates.'

(13) The provisions there referred to in subss (2) and (4) deal with two cases. Subsection (2) deals with the case where it appears to the court that there is in force under Part 7 of the Mental Health Act 1983 an order appointing a receiver. But that is not this case. In such a case the court can act of its own motion. Subsection (4) provides:

'If, in the case of an application for registration—
(a)   a valid notice of objection to the registration is received . . . [within a certain period], or
(b)   it appears from the application that there is no one to whom notice has been given under paragraph 1 of that Schedule, or
(c)   the court has reason to believe that appropriate inquiries might bring to light evidence on which the court could be satisfied that one of the grounds of objection set out in subsection (5) below was established,
the court shall neither register the instrument nor refuse the application until it has made or caused to be made such inquiries (if any) as it thinks appropriate in the circumstances of the case.'

(14) So that deals with two cases: first, whether there is a valid notice of objection; secondly, where the court has reason to believe that appropriate inquiries might bring to light evidence which was relevant.

(15) Then subs (5) sets out for the purposes of the Act what grounds may be included in the notice of objection. Ground (a) is that the power purported to have been created by the attorney was not a valid and enduring power of attorney. That is the case which now remains to be considered in this court.

(16) Then subs (6), which is critical for this case, provides:

'If, in a case where subsection (4) above applies, any of the grounds of objection in subsection (5) above is established to the satisfaction of the court, the court shall refuse the application but if, in such a case, it is not so satisfied, the court shall register the instrument to which the application relates.'

(17) In this case there was a valid objection under subs (4). The question is whether the ground of objection in subs (5)(a), that is to say that there was not a valid enduring power of attorney, is established to the satisfaction of the court. If it is, the court must refuse registration. If not, the court shall register the instrument.

(18) The law relating to this matter has been considered in two judgments to which we have been referred. First, there is the decision in *Re K (Enduring Powers of Attorney); Re F* [1988] Ch 310. In that case Hoffmann J said at 313:

'The Act does not specify the mental capacity needed to execute an enduring power and the answer must therefore be found in the common law. It is well established that capacity to perform a juristic act exists when the person who purported to do the act had at the time the mental capacity, with the assistance of such explanation as he may have been given, to understand the nature and effect of that particular transaction: see *In re Beaney, dec'd* [1978] 1 W.L.R. 770. In principle, therefore, an understanding of the nature and effect of the power was sufficient for its validity.'

(19) Later, Hoffmann J referred to what measures should be taken to achieve that. At 316:

'Finally, I should say something about what is meant by understanding the nature and effect of the power. What degree of understanding is involved? Plainly one cannot expect that the donor should have been able to pass an examination on the provisions of the Act. At the other extreme, I do not think that it would be sufficient if he realised only that it gave Cousin William power to look after his property. Mr Rawson helpfully summarised the matters which the donor should have understood in order that he can be said to have understood the nature and effect of the power. First, (if such be the terms of the power) that the attorney will be able to assume complete authority over the donor's affairs. Secondly, (if such be the terms of the power) that the attorney will in general be able to do anything with the donor's property which he himself could have done. Thirdly, that the authority will continue if the donor should be or become mentally incapable. Fourthly, that if he should be or become mentally incapable, the power will be irrevocable without confirmation by the court.'

(20) I would, for my part, agree that those four points are a sound indication of what the donor must understand if the power is to be valid.

(21) Hoffmann J went on to say (at 316):

'I do not wish to prescribe another form of words in competition with the explanatory notes prescribed by the Lord Chancellor, but I accept Mr. Rawson's summary as a statement of the matters which should ordinarily be explained to the donor (whatever the precise language which may be used) and which the evidence should show he has understood.'

(22) The last nine words have been relied on as showing that the burden of proof lies on the attorney for the purpose of showing that the instrument is valid. I am unable to reconcile that with the burden provided by s 6(6), which, as is accepted by Mr Rees for the objectors, at any rate imposes prime facie a burden on the objectors. With respect to Lord Hoffmann, I suspect that he did not have in mind the question of the burden of proof when he used those words in the form in which he did.

(23) We have also been referred to the case of *Re Beaney Dec'd* [1978] 1 WLR 770. There Mr Martin Nourse QC had something to say about how the requirement of understanding should be put to a donor. He said that the donor in that case was able to give an appearance of understanding that which was not simple, particularly if to the questions he was asked there could be given a yes or no answer, being the answer which was obviously wanted. That is more concerned with the way that understanding can be tested than with the requirement of understanding itself.

(24) The difficulty, as it seems to me, is that old people, as I happen to know, are reluctant to believe that senility is coming upon them and therefore are reluctant to release the powers which they have hitherto enjoyed: hence, I think, the two-stage approach of an enduring power of attorney; stage 1, when the proposed donor is still capable of understanding what she is doing; stage 2, when the attorney has reason to believe that she is no longer capable. An application must then be made for registration.

(25) For my part, I would not be inclined to rely on evidence of one interview, certainly not of the kind described by Mr Nourse. No doubt it is right to ask questions when it is contemplated that a donor shall execute an enduring power; but that is not by any means the final way of determining whether there is the necessary capacity.

(26) The argument for the objectors is that the burden of proof in such a case does not necessarily remain on them. It is put in this way in the outline argument on their behalf:

'19 The initial burden is upon the attorney. At common law the legal burden of proof lies upon the party seeking to establish the validity of a document. This burden of proof is therefore external to the provisions of section 6.

707

20 Section 6(6) supplements, but does not alter, the common law position by setting out the steps that the court must take once it has reached a decision as to whether a valid ground of objection exists. If it exists, the court must refuse registration. Otherwise, the court must register.

21 Section 6(6) does not reverse the burden of proof in relation to any particular ground of objection. If the objection is based on an allegation of fraud, then it is for the party alleging fraud to prove it. If it is based upon a contention that the document itself is invalid, then it is for the party seeking to rely on the document to prove it.'

(27) That was the way it was put in the outline argument. But before us it seemed to me that Mr Rees was not putting it quite in that way. He was prepared to acknowledge that s 6(6) put a burden in the first instance on the objectors; and if he was not prepared to acknowledge that, for my part I think it is perfectly clear in the section. To take an analogy with computer speak, the way to discover where the burden of proof lies, in my view, is to find the default setting. The default setting is stated quite clearly in s 6(6): if the court is not satisfied on the grounds of objection, then the court shall allow the power of attorney to be registered.

(28) The way that Mr Rees puts it now is that once evidence had been produced which tends to show that there was not the necessary capacity, then the burden shifts, and it lies with the attorney to show that there was capacity.

(29) In support of that he refers to *Halsbury's Commentaries on the Laws of England*, Vol 30, at para 1387:

'Every person is presumed to have mental capacity until the contrary is proven, and this presumption applies in civil as well as in criminal cases. However, it is for the executors or other people seeking to set up a will to show that the testator had capacity at the time.'

(30) Mr Rees submits that, just as with wills, so the same is true when somebody proposes an enduring power of attorney for registration. He also referred to a New Zealand case, *Brown v Pourau* [1995] 1 NZLR 352, and particularly to a passage at 363 where there is cited this passage from the earlier case of *Peters v Morris* (unreported) 19 May 1987:

'"The approach adopted to the matter of proof in all these cases is the same – that before a will can be admitted to probate it must be shown that the testator was a person of sufficient mental capacity; that in the absence of any evidence to the contrary it will be presumed that the document has been made by a person of competent understanding; that once a doubt is raised as to the existence of testamentary capacity an onus rests on the person propounding the will to satisfy the Court that the testator retained his mental powers to the requisite extent; that in the end the tribunal must be able to declare that it is satisfied of the testator's competence at the relevant time, but that a will will not be defeated merely because a residual doubt remains as to the matter."'

(31) If I may say so, Mr Rees' argument neatly encapsulates what was said in that passage. We were also referred to a case of considerable antiquity, *Waring v Waring* [1848] VI Moore 342.

(32) Where there is only one issue in the case and the burden of proof rests on one party, it seems to me wrong to say that the burden of proof shifts after one witness has been called and given evidence which, if believed, would discharge that burden. Courts do not make up their minds on an issue when they have heard only part of the evidence. Surely one can say, if one wishes, 'Well, the plaintiff is doing quite well. I wonder if there is going to be any evidence from the defendants?' But to say that the burden of proof has shifted seems to me to be wrong. One should make up one's mind on that issue having heard all the evidence on it; and I do not consider that in such a

case the burden of proof can be said to shift. At the end of the day, unless the burden as to that issue has been discharged, the person on whom it originally rested does not succeed.

(33) In this case, I think that the judge was right to treat the burden of proof as resting throughout upon the objectors. That is what he did. In the result, he did not feel able to conclude that the objectors had discharged that burden. But equally he did not make an affirmative finding in favour of the attorney, Mrs X. I reject the argument that he erred in law in that respect.

(34) The other ground which has been argued by Mr Rees is that the judge's decision was wrong on the facts. There were two principal witnesses, with other evidence as well. The first of the two principal witnesses was a Mr C, a chartered clinical psychologist. His evidence came in the form of a report of five pages. He had carried out tests on Mrs W's mental capacity on two occasions in November and December 1996. The conclusions that he reached in his report were these:

'As a final comment, the above detected severity of deterioration across a number of vital areas of cognitive functioning suggests strongly that for the past period running into a number of years, Mrs W has not been in a position to deal properly with the intangible (non-concrete) or hypothetical, or to correctly comprehend, interpret, see implications in, judge, or direct any business or operation other than that which does not require weighing up the pro's and con's, making comparisons, or seeing consequences of action beyond the immediate step.'

(35) Later, in a letter dated 10 July 1998, he said:

'I believe that in no way was Mrs W in a condition on the 4 July 1996 to execute an Enduring Power of Attorney.'

(36) There are comments that are made in respect of that evidence: first, that it was what one might call a theoretical discussion of the effect on comprehension, rather than a consideration of the actual things which had to be considered or the actual test for capacity to execute an enduring power of attorney. There was evidence that at the time of the tests by Mr C, Mrs W was taking drugs of several different kinds; and it was acknowledged that drugs might, not necessarily that they would, affect her capacity. There was also the lapse of time between the occasion in July when Mrs W executed the power of attorney and November and December when she was seen by Mr C.

(37) On the other hand, there is evidence from Mrs W's doctor who had treated her for some years. He had seen her quite regularly. He was not called as a witness because by the time the case came on for hearing before the judge he said, with admirable candour, that he could not now remember any detail whatsoever, and he was accordingly unable to help the court. But what was available was a letter that he wrote on 22 June 1996, that is to say about 2 weeks before the power of attorney was executed. It was written not to the proposed attorney or to Mrs W but to the solicitor who eventually witnessed the power of attorney. The letter said:

'Thank you for your letter about Mrs W. I can confirm that I saw her recently with her daughter and found her to be suffering from a degree of memory impairment. However in my opinion she still has the necessary mental capacity to sign a Power of Attorney. I would add that her mental abilities are at their best in the early part of the day and tend to deteriorate as the day goes by.'

(38) There is also evidence that Mrs W had seen her solicitor alone at some time previously; and it is said that she wished to have an enduring power of attorney.

(39) There are three letters which are relied on by the objectors as casting doubt on the capacity of Mrs W. In the first letter from Mrs X to her brother, and I take it her sister, dated 31 October 1994, there is this passage:

'Well, she is very confused and one has to organise her very carefully. She does not wake us up because she is used to coming here.'

(40) This was apparently in answer to the news that when staying with the brother Mrs W had woken them up in the night. That is October 1994. But, in a much later letter which was written to the Public Trust Office, Mrs X wrote this:

'My mother's mental health only started to deteriorate at a stage when she could no longer conduct her affairs when she came out of Eastbourne Hospital having had transfusions for severe anaemia at the end of January 1997.'

(41) Mr Rees points to the contrast of what was said there in a later letter dated July 1998 to what had been said in 1994.

(42) Thirdly there is another letter, dated 29 October 1998, again to the Public Trust Office. It says:

'As I have already stated, my mother was a little confused at times during late 1996. Most of the time she was very logical and she was very much aware of what was happening to her. That is why she previously had got her house in order and told both me and her solicitor what she wanted to happen in the future.'

(43) That is a brief summary of some points in the evidence. The judge, as I have said, was unable to conclude that it was shown that Mrs W had the necessary capacity. He also did not conclude that she was shown not to have the necessary capacity.

(44) I can see no ground for interfering with the judge's conclusions on those two points. It may be a simple view, but it seems to me that the general practitioner who saw Mrs W from time to time, and had done so for some time, was in as good a position as anybody to say whether or not she had the necessary understanding. At all events, if the judge reached that conclusion, I would see no reason to differ from him.

(45) Accordingly, I would dismiss this appeal.

ARDEN LJ:

(46) I agree. The Enduring Power of Attorney Act 1985 established a new mechanism whereby a person could give a power of attorney which would survive his or her incapacity. This was an important innovation because it enabled, among others, elderly people to give powers to attorneys to manage their affairs within the limits permitted by the Act. The Act was passed following a full law reform project by the Law Commission pursuant to the reference under s 3(1)(e) of the Law Commissions Act 1965. The final report is entitled *The Incapacitated Principal* ((1983) Law Com 122). Accordingly, the policy of the Act was very carefully considered; and it may therefore be taken to have been very carefully calibrated. In particular, it is evident that the Act provides a comprehensive set of provisions for registration of the power of attorney and indeed the effective registration is also dealt with in the Act: see in particular ss 7 and 8.

(47) Sir Christopher Staughton has already set out the prescribed procedure for registration. I agree with him that s 6(6) is the pivotal section. In my judgment that subsection clearly proceeds on the basis that the grounds of objection have to be proved. Accordingly, as I see it, the legal burden remains throughout on the objector, the person presenting the notice of objection. If the objector fails to establish his

objection, the instrument must be registered. The court has no residual discretion to refuse registration.

(48) Mr Rees has submitted that the position should apply as at common law so that the burden of proof is on the person seeking to uphold a deed or document. He draws an analogy with wills, as Sir Christopher Staughton has explained. But, as I see it, it is open to Parliament to change the common law rules for the purposes of this legislation. In addition Mr Rees accepts that the onus is on the objector when, for instance, there is a question as to the unsuitability of the attorney. As I see it, the Act must be construed as it stands.

(49) The learned Master relied on a passage in the judgment of Hoffmann J in *Re K (Enduring Powers of Attorney); Re F* [1988] Ch 310, namely the words 'and which evidence should show that he was understood' in the passage cited by Sir Christopher Staughton. I agree with what Sir Christopher has said about that passage.

(50) Mr Rees has submitted that the situation could arise in which an objector raises a doubt but fails to show lack of mental capacity. If the respondents to this appeal are correct and if the judge is correct, the court may then be in a position of registering instruments when it is not satisfied as to the donor's capacity. But the scheme of the Act does not require the court to be satisfied as to the donor's capacity. It has a discretion under subs (4) to conduct inquiries if the objection is made on statutory grounds. The Act does not require the court to carry out those inquiries. Indeed, the court may well take the view that where there are two parties contesting an issue, there is no need for it to make further inquiries. Accordingly, in my judgment, Parliament must have envisaged that a situation could arise in which a power of attorney would be registered where an objector had failed to discharge the onus of proof. But it should be taken into account that the Act contains other detailed safeguards for the donor, in particular the restriction on the attorney's capacity to make gifts on behalf of the donor without the court's consent.

(51) As respects the second ground of appeal (that the judge's conclusions on the facts were against the weight of the evidence), I agree that, for the reasons given by Sir Christopher Staughton, the appeal fails.

PETER GIBSON LJ:

(52) I agree with both judgments.

Appeal dismissed. Unsuccessful appellants shall pay costs of successful respondent, but on standard basis. We shall direct that there be interim payment on account of costs of £3000.

Solicitors: Gaby, Hardwicke, Yearwood & Griffiths for the appellant

Max Barford & Co for the respondent

PATRICIA HARGROVE

Barrister

[G5]

RE E (ENDURING POWER OF ATTORNEY)

[2000] 1 FLR 882

CHANCERY DIVISION

ARDEN J18 February 2000

Executors, administrators, wills and probate – Enduring power of attorney – Objection to registration – Revocation of power by conduct – Whether

execution of second power revoked first – Whether bad relations between family members meant some were unsuitable to act as attorneys

In 1992 Mrs E appointed two of her three daughters, Y and Z, jointly to be her attorneys for the purposes of the Enduring Powers of Attorney Act 1985, subject to a restriction that they did not have authority to sell, charge or lease land or other property in which Mrs E had an interest. In 1997 Mrs E executed a second power, appointing all three daughters, X, Y and Z, jointly as attorneys, with general authority to act without any restriction. This power included a provision that any two of the attorneys might sign documents. In 1998 X applied for the 1997 power to be registered, but registration was refused because an enduring power of attorney could only be created if the attorneys were appointed to act jointly or jointly and severally, and the provision permitting documents to be signed by only two of the three attorneys was inconsistent with that. The 1997 power therefore only took effect as an ordinary power of attorney, revoked by supervening mental incapacity. In 1999 Y and Z applied to register the 1992 power. X objected to registration on the basis that the 1992 power was revoked by the 1997 power, and that Y and Z were unsuitable to be Mrs E's attorneys because of the bad relations between X, Y and Z, who could not agree over management of the mother's affairs. The main area of disagreement was Y and Z's scheme to distribute some of the mother's assets for tax planning purposes, which X resisted. Mrs E, now in her eighties was living in a nursing home, having been diagnosed with a form of Alzheimer's disease. The master registered the 1992 power, ruling that the second power did not revoke the first, and that the attorneys were not unsuitable.

Held – dismissing X's appeal –

(1)   The 1997 power was capable of being used prior to the donor's mental incapacity, but did not revoke the 1992 power. Applying the general law of agency, revocation of a power of attorney by conduct required conduct which was unambiguously inconsistent with that power. The burden was on X to show that Mrs E must have intended, by her conduct in executing a second power, to revoke the first power; it was not enough to show that Mrs E must have forgotten about the first power. The two powers were not in fact inconsistent; Mrs E may have wanted to have several simultaneous powers, allowing her to safeguard against possible invalidity of a power, a legitimate and understandable wish.

(2)   Y and Z were suitable to be Mrs E's attorneys. Mrs E had appointed them to be attorneys in both of the powers which had been executed, and wherever possible the donor's wishes should be upheld. Hostility between family members did not automatically mean that a family member was unsuitable to act as attorney. The only controversial issue, the tax planning, would have to be decided by the court in any event, and once that matter had been resolved it was unlikely that any great degree of consultation between the daughters would be needed, as the estate was not complex. If a receiver were appointed, a third party would have to become involved, intervening between the donor and her family, and involving the estate in additional costs.

Statutory provisions considered

Enduring Powers of Attorney Act 1985, ss 3, 6, 8, 11

Cases referred to in judgment

Cousins v International Brick Co Ltd [1931] 2 Ch 90, CA

D (J), Re [1982] Ch 237, [1982] 2 WLR 373, [1982] 2 All ER 37, ChD

Goldsworthy v Brickell [1987] Ch 378, [1987] 1 All ER 853, sub nom *Goldsworthy v Brickell and Another* [1987] 2 WLR 133, CA

Heatons Transport (St Helens) Ltd v Transport and General Workers' Union; Craddock Brothers v Transport and General Workers' Union; Panalpina Services Ltd, Panalpina (Northern) Ltd v Transport and General Workers' Union [1973] AC 15, [1972] 3 WLR 431, [1972] 3 All ER 101, HL

Smith and Jenning's Case (1610) Lane 97, 145 ER 329

W (Power of Attorney), Re [1999] 2 FLR 1163, [2000] 1 All ER 175, ChD

Yaxley v Gotts and Gotts [1999] 2 FLR 941, sub nom *Yaxley v Gotts and Another* [1999] 3 WLR 1217, CA

Cases cited but not referred to in judgment

Tai Hing Cotton Mill Ltd v Liu Chong Hing Bank (No 1) [1986] AC 80, [1985] 2 All ER 947, sub nom *Tai Hing Cotton Mill Ltd v Liu Chong Hing Bank Ltd and Others* [1985] 3 WLR 317, CA

Ward v Van der Loeff [1924] AC 653, HL

Robert Pearce for the appellant/X

Piers Feltham for the respondents/Y and Z

ARDEN J:

Introduction

This is an appeal against the order of Master Lush, Master of the Court of Protection, dated 9 September 1999 whereby he dismissed objections of the appellant, Mrs X, and ordered that an instrument dated 24 November 1992 ('the 1992 power') be registered as an enduring power of attorney under the Enduring Powers of Attorney Act 1985 ('the 1985 Act'). This appeal is by way of rehearing. The discretion is that of the judge and the judge is not bound by the decision of the master (*Re D (J)* [1982] Ch 237, 245–247). Counsel appearing on this appeal did not appear before Master Lush.

As is well known, the 1985 Act in large measure implemented recommendations in The Incapacitated Principal (Law Com No 122 (1983) Cmnd 8977) and provides a means whereby powers of attorney ('EPAs') can be created so as to survive the subsequent mental incapacity of the donor. An EPA must be made in the prescribed form. When the attorney has reason to believe that the donor is, or is becoming, mentally incapable he must make an application to the Court of Protection for registration of the EPA. Before doing so, the attorney must give notice to the donor and the donor's relatives. Until registration, the powers of the attorney are limited. Thereafter, the attorney has the powers conferred by the EPA, which is not revoked by the supervening mental incapacity of the donor. Recourse may be had to the Law Commission's report to ascertain the defect in the law which the 1985 Act was intended to remedy, and in addition to help identify the policy behind the new legislation (*Yaxley v Gotts and Gotts* [1999] 2 FLR 941, 956–957 per Clarke LJ and 963–965 per Beldam LJ).

If a valid notice of objection to the registration of an enduring power of attorney is received by the court within a specified time, the court must neither register the instrument nor refuse the application until it has made or caused to be made such inquiries (if any) as it thinks appropriate in the circumstances of the case (s 6(4)). A notice of objection to the registration of an enduring power of attorney is valid if the objection is made on a number of specified grounds including (s 6(5)):

'(b)   that the power created by the instrument no longer subsists; . . .
. . .

(e)   that, having regard to all the circumstances and in particular the attorney's relationship to or connection with the donor, the attorney is unsuitable to be the donor's attorney.'

If any of these grounds of objection is established to the satisfaction of the court, the court must refuse the application for registration; in any other case the EPA must be registered (s 6(6)). Furthermore, the court must not register an EPA, or refuse the application for registration, until completion of appropriate inquiries if it considers that those inquiries might bring to light evidence that one of the grounds of objection is satisfied (s 6(4)). The 1985 Act makes provision for the revocation or cancellation of an EPA registration of which is refused (s 6(7), (8)). If, however, an EPA is registered it is irrevocable without the leave of the court. The attorney's authority to make gifts is strictly limited (s 3(5)). Accordingly, if an attorney wishes to enter into a scheme to minimise inheritance tax payable on the donor's death, the leave of the court will generally be needed.

The background facts relating to the 1992 power are as follows. Mr and Mrs E had three daughters, Mrs Y, Mrs Z and Mrs X. Mrs Y and Mrs Z are the respondents to this appeal. Mr E died in 1998 and Mrs E is in her eighties. She is living in a nursing home and she has been diagnosed as having a form of Alzheimer's disease.

On 24 November 1992 Mrs E executed the 1992 power. It appointed Mrs Y and Mrs Z jointly to be her attorneys for the purposes of the 1985 Act with general power to act on her behalf in relation to all her property and affairs. However, it was subject to a restriction or condition that 'My attorneys shall not have my authority to sell, charge or lease any land or other property in which I have an interest'.

On 9 April 1997 Mrs E executed a further power ('the 1997 power'). This appointed all three daughters jointly to be her attorneys for the purposes of the 1985 Act with general authority to act on her behalf in relation to all her property and affairs. The words 'save that any two of my attorneys may sign' were inserted in manuscript so as to follow the printed word 'jointly'. This appointment, unlike the 1992 power, was not expressed to be subject to any restriction or condition. The master's judgment states that these words were drafted on the spot by Mrs E's solicitor because it was felt that it could be inconvenient and time-consuming to have to send all documents to Mrs Y, who lived some distance away, for her signature, but I have not taken that factor into account as it is common ground that this finding is not supported by the evidence on this appeal.

On 3 December 1998 Mrs X applied for the 1997 power to be registered. The Public Trust Office rejected her application on the ground that the condition imposed by the power was contrary to the appointment. Mrs X has not appealed against this rejection. Master Lush in his judgment stated that the additional words 'save that any two of my attorneys may sign' were inconsistent with s 11(1) of the 1985 Act, which provides that 'An instrument which appoints more than one person to be an attorney cannot create an enduring power unless the attorneys are appointed to act jointly or jointly and severally' (see also The Law Commission's report, The Incapacitated Principal, paras 4.91–4.98). The 1997 power accordingly has effect at most only as an ordinary power of attorney and it is revoked by supervening mental incapacity.

On 5 February 1999 Mrs Y and Mrs Z applied to register the 1992 power. By a letter dated 10 February 1999, the donor's solicitors objected to the registration of the 1992 power on the grounds that it was revoked by the 1997 power and that the attorneys were unsuitable to be the donor's attorneys. From 26 March 1999 Mrs X objected to the registration of the 1992 power. Her grounds were those set out in the letter dated 10 February 1999. On 8 September 1999, following an oral hearing, Master Lush dismissed both grounds of objections and ordered that the 1992 power be registered forthwith. His reasons were as follows:

'The Enduring Powers of Attorney Act 1985 is silent on the question whether a later power revokes an earlier power, and I must admit that this is the first time I have been required formally to adjudicate on this particular issue.

The Law Commission's report, *The Incapacitated Principal*, which was published in 1983 and ultimately led to the 1985 Act, states, at paragraph 4.31:

"We would like to sound a note of caution about the drafting of the attorney's authority under the EPA. Subject to the exceptions mentioned above, the donor would in general be able to insert in the prescribed form of EPA whatever provisions he thought fit whether they related to the subject-matter of the power or to the authority conferred under it. And he could grant as many EPAs in favour of as many attorneys as he liked. This would merely reflect the general principle that people should be able to make such arrangements for the management of their affairs as they please. It will be important, however, for the donor to ensure that the authority bestowed under his EPA (or EPAs if several are granted) effectively covers the whole of his property and affairs. If he leaves a 'gap' so that part of his property and affairs is not covered by an EPA, it may be necessary for the Court to intervene and appoint a receiver. And whilst we would not wish to prevent the donor giving his attorney such limited authority as he thought fit, the fact remains that the less authority that is given to the attorney, the greater is the risk that he would be unable to act for the donor at a later date. If by that time the donor were incapable so that he could not create a new power, the Court might have to take over."

I should emphasise two particular sentences in this paragraph: "And he could grant as many EPAs in favour of as many attorneys as he liked. This would merely reflect the general principle that people should be able to make such arrangements for the management of their affairs as they please".

I imagine that the reason why the law is deliberately silent on the question as to whether or not a later power revokes an earlier power is because it was envisaged that a donor might create more than one power and that such powers might not be created simultaneously.

Paragraph 4.31 of *The Incapacitated Principal* appears mainly to contemplate the situation in which a donor might appoint one attorney to manage one aspect of his or her affairs, and a different attorney to manage another aspect. For example, a donor might in one instrument appoint an attorney to manage his property in England, and in another instrument appoint an attorney to manage his property in Wales.

Elsewhere in their report the Law Commissioners envisaged that a donor might create more than one power in order to achieve the effect of successive appointments. In footnote 214 on page 50 they said:

"We do not recommend that an instrument should be able to provide for successive EPAs; that is, one or more attorneys who would replace the original attorney or attorneys should he or they cease to act. Our main reason for this is that the benefit to be gained by including successive EPAs in our proposals would be out of all proportion to the complexity that such powers would create in relation to some of the more detailed areas of our scheme. In any event, successive EPAs are rendered largely unnecessary because a joint and several EPA would permit the continuation of the EPA in the event of one of the attorneys ceasing to act. It would, however, be possible to create the effect of successiveness by a donor granting EPAs in separate instruments so that the authority of an attorney under one power could commence only upon the termination of the authority of an attorney under another power."

So, for instance, a donor might sign one instrument appointing his wife as his sole attorney and another – perhaps later – instrument appointing his children to be his attorneys if his wife were to predecease him or become otherwise incapable of acting as attorney.

In the absence of any statutory provision to the effect that a later instrument revokes an earlier power, it is necessary to look to the common law for assistance. However, there are no decisions – either reported or unreported – which directly address this point.

There are a number of reported decisions on the revocation of wills, but they are mainly old authorities and are not always entirely consistent. In any event, wills and enduring powers are completely different types of document. To revoke an enduring power the donor must give notice of revocation to the attorneys.

However, some general principles do emerge in relation to the revocation of wills. They are as follows:

- whether a prior will or codicil has been impliedly revoked by a later will or codicil is a question of construction;
- there must be an intention to revoke (animus revocandi) on the part of the testator;
- extrinsic evidence of the testator's intention is admissible;
- where there is more than one instrument, the court should, if possible, construe them so that both may stand; and
- if the instruments are so inconsistent that they cannot stand together, neither can be admitted to probate.

If one applies these rules, so far as they are relevant, to enduring powers of attorney, the following principles emerge:

1. A later instrument does not automatically revoke an earlier instrument. This is because it was Parliament's intention that a donor should be able to create more than one enduring power of attorney, if he or she wished. It might be necessary to create more than one power in order to deal with different aspects of the donor's affairs or to take effect at different times or in different circumstances.
2. A later instrument which expressly revokes an earlier instrument will revoke the earlier instrument, but only when notice of the revocation is given to the attorney appointed in the earlier instrument. Where the instrument is registered, the revocation will only take effect when it is confirmed by the courts in accordance with s 8(3) of the Enduring Powers of Attorney Act 1985.
3. In the absence of express revocation, whether an earlier instrument is impliedly revoked by a later instrument is essentially a question of construction.
4. The donor must have intended to revoke the earlier instrument.
5. If there is more than one instrument, the court should attempt to construe them so that, wherever possible, both or all may stand. This reflects the general principle that people should be able to make such arrangements for the management of their affairs as they please.

In my judgment, Mrs E's intentions were as follows.

In 1992 she made a conscious decision to appoint her daughters [Mrs Y] and [Mrs Z], but not her daughter [Mrs X], jointly to be her attorneys.

In 1996 and 1997 there was closer contact and a reconciliation between [Mrs X] and her parents as a result of [Mr E's] illness.

In April 1997 both [Mr E] and Mrs E both decided to appoint [Mrs X] as an additional attorney for the purpose of the Enduring Powers of Attorney Act.

The most convenient way of appointing [Mrs X] as an additional attorney was to sign a new instrument appointing all three of their daughters as attorneys.

On 9 April 1997, when she signed the second power, [Mrs E's] intention was not to revoke the appointment of [Mrs Y] and [Mrs Z], but (a) to confirm their appointment and (b) to appoint [Mrs X] as an additional attorney. In other words, she did not have animus revocandi in respect of the earlier appointment.

. . .

The second ground on which [Mrs X] has objected to the registration of the 1992 power is that, having regard to all the circumstances, her sisters are unsuitable to be the donor's attorneys.

There are no reported decisions on the meaning of "unsuitable to be the donor's attorney" but Parliament's intention when including it as a ground of objection can be found in the Law Commission's report, *The Incapacitated Principal* (Law Com No 122), which was published in July 1983. At paragraph 4.29 the Commissioners said:

"This needs some explanation. It would amount in effect to a criticism of the donor's choice of attorney. But we would not wish this ground to be sustained merely because the attorney was not the sort of person that a particular relative would have chosen. It is our wish that the donor's choice of attorney should carry considerable weight. Thus, for example, a mother might be content to appoint her son as her EPA attorney despite being aware of a conviction for theft. We would not want her choice of attorney to be upset simply because a particular relative would not want the son to be his attorney. The question should be whether the particular attorney is suitable to act as attorney for the particular donor. In short, the Court should examine carefully all the circumstances – particularly the relationship between the donor and the attorney."

[Mrs X's] objection in this case was expressed by her solicitors in the following terms:

"The attorneys are unsuitable to be the donor's Attorneys. Relations between [Mrs E's] three daughters are not good because there is division of opinion as to how [Mrs E's] assets might be applied. It is believed that [Mrs Y] and [Mrs Z] favour some creative tax planning which [Mrs X] believes is inappropriate. We believe [Mrs E's] position would be best served and protected by the appointment by the court of a receiver.'"

The master then referred to *Re W (Power of Attorney)* [1999] 2 FLR 1163, to which I refer below.

Master Lush continued:

'In my judgment Mrs E must have been aware of the hostility between her daughters when she created the power in 1992, and she appointed [Mrs Y] and [Mrs Z] as her attorneys notwithstanding that hostility.
I am not convinced that the animosity between her daughters will have an adverse impact on the administration of her estate. The main bone of contention seems to have been the desirability or otherwise of entering into a scheme to mitigate the impact of inheritance tax on her death.
Attorneys have the very limited powers to make gifts of a donor's property contained in ss 3(4) and (5) of the Enduring Powers of Attorney Act 1985. Larger gifts, such as the kind of contemplated by [Mrs Y] and [Mrs Z], must be authorised by the court in accordance with the provisions of s 8(2)(e) of the Act.
If the attorneys wish to enter into some tax planning scheme, they must make a formal application to the court, and the court will then consider whether, having regard to all the circumstances, the proposed gifts are reasonable and will not impact adversely on [Mrs E's] present and future standard of living.
In the circumstances, I see no reason why the court should frustrate [Mrs E's] choice of attorneys and intervene on the ground of their unsuitability.'

There are two issues on this appeal, both of which were argued before Master Lush:

(1)   Is the 1992 power a subsisting power, or was it revoked by the 1997 power?
(2)   Are Mrs Y and Mrs Z unsuitable to be Mrs E's attorneys?

I will take these issues in turn.

Issue 1: was the 1992 power revoked by the 1997 power?

There are three differences between the 1992 power and the 1997 power. The first difference is that Mrs X is not an attorney under the 1992 power; she is however an attorney under the 1997 power. The second difference is that the 1992 power contains the restriction on the disposition of land and other property set out above, which is not present in the 1997 power. The third difference is that the 1997 power provides that any two attorneys may sign.

The appellant's submissions

The appellant submits that the 1992 power was revoked by the 1997 power and that Master Lush was wrong to hold otherwise. (The appellant did not argue that the 1992 power was invalid on any other ground as she had done before Master Lush.)

The appellant submits that although the 1997 power has not been registered as an enduring power of attorney, it was nonetheless valid as an ordinary power of attorney as soon as it was executed. As an ordinary power, however, it was revoked by Mrs E's supervening incapacity. The objection to the form of the power based on s 11(1) of the 1985 Act does not affect the validity of the 1997 power as an ordinary power. The power, on the appellant's submission, should be construed as a joint power which is enlarged in the particular respect that any two attorneys can sign. The appellant further submitted that the word 'sign' in the 1997 power should be construed narrowly and as referring only to signing to implement transactions which all three attorneys had decided on.

The appellant submits that as between donor and attorney an ordinary power of attorney is revoked by the doing of any act by the donor which is inconsistent with the continuation of the power and of which the donee has notice. In support of this submission, the appellant relies on *Bowstead and Reynolds on Agency*, arts 119, 122, especially at p 674, note 61, and *Heatons Transport (St Helens) Ltd v Transport and General Workers' Union; Craddock Brothers v Transport and General Workers' Union; Panalpina Services Ltd, Panalpina (Northern) Ltd v Transport and General Workers' Union* [1973] AC 15, 110C per Lord Wilberforce, delivering the joint opinion of their Lordships. The appellant also relied on the American Law Institute's Restatement of the Law of Agency (1958, 2nd edn), at pp 302–304. The relevant passage in *Bowstead and Reynolds* reads: ' . . . there may be implied revocation by an act which is inconsistent with the continuation of the agency, coming to the notice of the agent' and the authority cited for this at footnote 61 is *Smith and Jenning's Case* (1610) Lane 97; 145 ER 329. (Another example is *Cousins v International Brick Co Ltd* [1931] 2 Ch 90, where a shareholder who had appointed a proxy to vote for him could nonetheless vote in person.) Likewise the Restatement states that a principal can revoke the agency by conduct which is inconsistent with its continuance as where he authorises another agent to act on his behalf. The Restatement states that in such a case it is a question of construction whether the agent intends to terminate the authority of the first agent or merely authorise another agent also to act. The appellant relies particularly on a statement in the Restatement that the conduct will terminate an agent's authority 'if, reasonably understood', it indicates that the principal no longer consents to the agent acting for him. That the conduct must be such that it can be reasonably understood in this way is the issue for which the passage in the *Heatons* case was cited. In that particular case the withdrawal of authority had been equivocal. What happened in that case was that the principals had merely given advice to the agent and it was held that this did not amount to terminating their authority to act contrary to that advice. The appellant seeks to extend this principle by submitting that there is also a requirement that the conduct of the donor should also be reasonably construed in determining whether it was inconsistent with the continuation of the agency.

The appellant also submits that the execution of the 1997 power is inconsistent with the continuation of the 1992 power thereafter for the following reasons:

(i)   It would have been irrational for Mrs E not to have wished to express all the powers her daughters were to have in a single instrument.

(ii)   If the 1992 power continued after the execution of the 1997 power, Mrs Y and Mrs Z would thereafter have been simultaneously authorised to act jointly with Mrs X in all matters and to act independently of her in all matters save dealings in land. The effect of this would be that Mrs X's participation would be superfluous in all matters save dealings in land. If in 1997 it had been Mrs E's intention to make Mrs X's participation necessary only in relation to dealings in land, and to achieve this by two instruments rather than one, the obvious course for her to take would have been to grant a further power appointing her three daughters to be her joint attorneys solely in relation to matters falling within the restriction in the 1992 power.

(iii)   It is unlikely that Mrs E would have chosen to specify expressly in the 1997 power that any two of her attorneys may sign and to leave unstated that Mrs Y and Mrs Z could continue to act in all matters falling within the scope of the 1992 power independently of Mrs X if they saw fit.

(iv)   It is unlikely that Mrs E would have retained the word 'jointly' and deleted the alternative 'jointly and severally' in the 1997 power since if the 1992 power continued after the execution of the 1997 power the combined effect of both was more akin to a joint and several authority subject to restrictions.

There is no evidence as to Mrs E's intentions when she executed the 1997 power. The only evidence is that of Mrs X who states that the 1992 power was never mentioned and that she believes that Mrs E had forgotten about it. There is no suggestion that at the date of the execution of the 1997 power Mrs E was concerned to distinguish between dealings in land and other dealings. Mrs Y and Mrs Z both had express notice of the execution of the 1997 power as they countersigned it. The appellant contends that there is no justification for Master Lush's conclusion that in 1997 Mrs E did not intend to revoke the 1992 power.

The respondents' submissions

The respondents accept that the authority of an agent may be revoked by express notice given by the principal to the agent. They also accept that there can be revocation by conduct of the principal. They submit, however, that there has to be communication of revocation and in addition the conduct must be unequivocal, as in the case of promissory estoppel (see *Goldsworthy v Brickell* [1987] Ch 378, 410–411). Accordingly, it has to be shown that the 1997 power is inconsistent with the 1992 power. They submit that there is no inconsistency between the grant of the 1997 power and the continued subsistence of the 1992 power having regard to the following:

(i)   The 1992 power appoints Mrs Y and Mrs Z jointly and does not authorise them to sell, charge or lease any real property of Mrs E.

(ii)   The 1997 power is not so restrictive but requires the appellant and respondents to act jointly so that any two may sign.

The 1992 power and the 1997 power therefore overlap but are very far from co-extensive. The respondents also urge the court to take into account that the 1997 power did not take effect as an enduring power of attorney but only as an ordinary power of attorney. This meant that it could not operate after Mrs E became mentally incapable.

Accordingly, on the respondents' submission, no legal impasse was created by the coexistence of the powers side by side.

Conclusions

I accept the appellant's submission that the 1997 power takes effect as an ordinary power even if it cannot take effect as an EPA. The 1997 power is therefore capable of being used prior to the donor becoming mentally incapable. However, in my judgment, the 1992 power has not been revoked by the execution of the 1997 power and the reasons for my conclusion are as follows:

(1)   The general law of agency in my judgment shows that to amount to revocation by conduct, the conduct must be inconsistent with the continuation of the agency. Contrary to the appellant's submission, this in my judgment means more than that the conduct should be reasonably understood as amounting to revocation. To be inconsistent,

it must be unambiguous in its effect. I approach the question of revocation in this way rather than by applying presumptions as a matter of construction, which was the approach of Master Lush.

(2)   The onus is on the appellant to show that the 1992 power has been revoked. Accordingly, she has to show that the donor must have intended to revoke the 1992 power. It is not enough to show that the donor must have forgotten about the 1992 power or made no reference to it. Indeed if she had forgotten about it that would suggest that she did not intend to revoke it. As the passages cited by the master from the Law Commission's report show, it is not the policy of the 1985 Act to prohibit successive EPAs.

(3)   The 1997 power applies to land whereas the 1992 power does not. Had the 1997 power been limited to land it would have been clear that the two powers were not inconsistent. The present issue has arisen because there are some matters covered by both powers, for example the payment of bills.

(4)   There is no contemporaneous evidence as to the donor's intentions, or even any later evidence from her as to what she intended. All that is known is that she did not expressly revoke the 1992 power when she executed the 1997 power. On 4 January 1999 she wrote a letter saying that she agreed that her daughters could apply to register the 1992 power, but this does not inform the court about her intentions in 1997 and I must also bear in mind that the donor had previously objected to the registration of the 1992 power.

(5)   I do not consider that it is clear that the 1997 power revokes the 1992 power. There is no reason why the donor should not want to preserve the possibility that the 1992 power might be used if for some reason the 1997 power could not be used. She did not know that the 1997 power was not valid as an EPA when she signed it, but there is no reason why she should not have wanted to cover the situation that it might be invalid. To have several simultaneous powers would be a legitimate and understandable wish, and not an irrational one as suggested by the appellant.

(6)   The appellant contends that the 1997 power requires unanimity, ie that all three sisters had to agree on each transaction to be carried out by the attorneys and that the additional words added by the donor ('save that any two of my attorneys may sign') merely enabled two out of the three attorneys to sign if they had all agreed on a transaction. In my judgment, this interpretation involves adding words that are not expressed, preventing two only from signing unless all three sisters had agreed on the transaction to which the signature related. In my judgment those words cannot be read in. They are not a necessary implication. It is more likely that the donor wished to cover the possibility that one of the sisters was unable to act, for example because she was abroad or ill, or because she was unwilling to agree to something that two sisters approved. This is another situation for which the donor may have wanted to have a contingency plan. There is also some evidence to the effect that the appellant had not been on good terms with her parents prior to the execution of the 1992 power though the appellant contests this evidence. Be that as it may, the effect of the 1997 power as properly interpreted is not in my judgment

inconsistent with the 1992 power in any of the respects relied on by the appellant. Rather the 1997 power confirms the tenor of the 1992 power, that the donor was content that two only of the daughters should have power to act as her attorneys. The 1997 power should be seen as at one with the earlier power in this sense, and as an unsuccessful attempt to add the third daughter, Mrs X.

(7) The master based his conclusions on general principles applicable to wills. I do not think that it is necessary to invoke these principles as there is sufficient guidance in the general law of agency. However, I agree with him that a later instrument does not automatically revoke an earlier instrument. The donor must have intended to revoke the earlier power and this must also be the effect of the donor's words or conduct.

(8) I have considered whether it would be appropriate to make inquiries as to the donor's wishes as to who should be her attorney, and I refer to this below. I do not, however, consider that it would be appropriate to make inquiries from the donor as to the position regarding the 1992 power at the time of executing the 1997 power. If her medical condition means that she has a significant and persistent memory loss, she will not be able to assist the court. If her medical condition is satisfactory, she would of course have been able to revoke, or express a wish to revoke, the 1992 power since this dispute has arisen if she had wished to do so. Moreover, if her medical condition is satisfactory, it is likely that one of the parties could have obtained her evidence and have submitted it to the court. Finally, her intentions would not be conclusive by themselves. Revocation must be manifested and in my judgment that has not occurred.

Issue 2: suitability of the attorneys

The appellant's second ground of appeal is that the respondents are not suitable to be the donor's attorneys. The appellant says that the evidence shows that the relations between the three sisters have broken down, principally over the management of the donor's affairs. The appellant points out that there is more significance to be attached to the fact of disagreement where it relates to the affairs of the donor than if it relates to extraneous matters. The appellant says that there is a history of her being excluded by her sisters. She says that the donor wished all three daughters to be her attorneys: this is evident not only from the 1997 power but from a letter which the donor wrote to the court on 13 December 1998. In this letter the donor objected to the appellant applying for the registration of the 1997 power on the ground that 'the decision to make this application should be made by my three daughters, not by one acting alone'. Moreover, the appellant wishes to play an equal part.

The respondents for their part rely on the fact that they are mature and responsible women with no ill-will to the appellant. The only disagreement relates to tax planning. It is hoped to make potentially exempt transfers from the donor's assets among her children equally in order to avoid or mitigate inheritance tax. The appellant has expressed concern as to whether the donor will have sufficient assets left for her needs. It is accepted that the attorneys could not transfer any assets of the donor pursuant to a tax planning scheme without the approval of the court pursuant to s 8 of the 1985 Act.

The court could in theory appoint all three sisters as receivers and in that way seek to put the three sisters in the same position as if the 1997 power had been valid. But neither party seeks that and there is no indication that that would be a viable course.

(The appellant says in her evidence that at the present time she has no contact with either of her sisters.) The choice before the court is either to appoint a third party as a receiver or to register the 1992 power. It is against that background that the court is asked to hold, having regard to all the circumstances, the respondents are unsuitable to be the donor's attorneys.

The matters on which the appellant relies revolve around discussions about tax planning for the donor in June to December 1998 in which she was not involved culminating in the execution by the donor of a deed agreeing to an advancement of property out of her late husband's estate in favour of her three daughters in equal shares. I refer to this deed below. The advancement has not taken place because the appellant objected to it. She is one of the executrices of her late father's estate and the proposal cannot proceed without her concurrence.

There is evidence that prior to the death of Mr E both the donor and her late husband wanted to minimise the inheritance tax payable on their deaths by appropriate tax planning. For this purpose they had consulted Mrs Z's husband, Mr Z, who is an accountant. So it was natural that Mr Z should be asked to advise on the donor's estate. The donor's property now consists principally of a life interest in her late husband's estate, a 50% share in their house, other real property, cash on deposit and some investments. Mr Z produced plans to save up to £110,000 tax. The appellant was advised of these plans but she thought that the donor should keep £20,000 more than the scheme provided. This was agreed by the other sisters. In the course of preparing proposals, there was a meeting between Mr Z, the respondents and the donor's solicitor on 11 June 1998. The appellant was not invited to this, and the respondents at first said that they had not been present, contrary to what appears now to be the position. Likewise, it appears that Mrs E's solicitor wrote a letter giving advice so that all the sisters could read it, but it was not shown to the appellant.

In due course Mrs E's solicitors (acting on Mr Z's instructions) produced a draft deed to give effect to the advancement which it was desired that Mrs E should make. They sent it to Mr Z to obtain his instructions on one point. In order to save time, Mr Z arranged for Mrs E and Mrs Z (as executrix of Mr E) to sign it, notwithstanding that it had not been engrossed and notwithstanding that Mrs E had not received any independent legal advice on it. This was also before the appellant had been told about the proposals. The appellant says with some justification that if meetings were being held with Mrs E's solicitor, to which the other sisters were invited, she too should have had the opportunity to attend.

In my judgment Mr Z, Mrs Y and Mrs Z are to be criticised for obtaining the donor's signature to the draft deed, given her medical condition and given the fact that it was only a draft and the fact that she had no independent legal advice. There is medical evidence that Mrs E was not in a position to manage her affairs by December 1998. Mrs E had not received advice about the deed from her solicitor at the stage she was asked to sign.

The court had to consider an objection on the grounds of unsuitability in the recent case of *Re W (Power of Attorney)* [1999] 2 FLR 1163 to which the master referred. In that case, an elderly lady, W, gave one of her children, X, an EPA. Her two other children, who were hostile to X, objected to the registration of this power on the ground (among others) that X was unsuitable to be her attorney. X had made gifts on behalf of W without the consent of the court. The master held that he was not satisfied that W understood the nature and effect of the power and that the hostility between the children rendered them all unsuitable to be W's attorneys. On appeal Mr Jules Sher QC, sitting as a deputy judge of the High Court, held that the making of the gifts had been for sensible tax planning reasons and had been in favour of the three children equally. The other children did not object and there was some evidence that they had been in accordance with W's wishes expressed before she became incapable. Accordingly, he held that matter should be kept in perspective. On the issue of hostility, the court held that it all depended on the circumstances whether hostility made an attorney unsuitable. In that particular case there was little need for consultation and therefore no real likelihood that the hostility would impact adversely on the administration of the estate, as might happen if there was a need for a high degree of consultation between the children. If the Public Trustee were to be brought in, substantial fees would be incurred.

A number of relatives or friends of the donor in this case have written letters to the court giving their views on the suitability of the three sisters to be the donor's attorneys, but I have given these letters limited weight. There are two main reasons for this. First, there has been no challenge to the ability of Mrs Y and Mrs Z to discharge the function of attorneys. Secondly, some of the letters contain views on the personality of the appellant, but it is not necessary for me to decide where the responsibility for any breakdown in relations between the parties may lie.

Having considered the submissions made on this appeal, I do not, however, consider that the respondents are unsuitable to be the donor's attorneys for the following reasons:

(1)   Under both the 1992 power and the 1997 power, the donor appointed members of her family as act as her attorneys and her wishes in that regard should be upheld. It is part of the policy of the 1985 Act that the donor's wishes should if reasonably possible be upheld (see para 4.29 of *The Incapacitated Principal*, set out in the master's judgment). Thus for instance the 1985 Act does not give the court power to refuse to register an EPA except on one of a limited number of grounds. In addition, under s 6(5)(e) of the 1985 Act, the court has to be satisfied not as to the chosen attorney's suitability, but rather to his unsuitability.

(2)   To appoint a receiver would mean that a third party would have to be brought into the donor's affairs and between her and her family. This is not in principle a desirable outcome where members of the family have been caring for the donor for a substantial period of time already. Moreover, as I have said, in neither the 1992 power nor in the 1997 power did the donor appoint a third party. The appellant says that she does not think that her mother would be upset if a receiver were appointed. However, the most reliable indications of her wishes that I have are those in the deeds themselves

(3)   Mrs Z has had conduct of Mrs E's affairs for some time. Mrs Y and Mrs Z are more likely to know what the donor would want than a receiver, who may well be a stranger.

(4)   On the question of the hostility between the three sisters, I agree with Mr Sher QC that this does not automatically mean that the attorney should be some other person. It must depend on the facts. The tax planning issue has been the only matter of controversy in this case and it will have to be decided by the court in any event. It has not been suggested that once that matter is resolved there will have to be any great degree of consultation between the respondents and the appellant as to how the donor's affairs should be managed. Her estate, though presently not insubstantial, is not complex. It will consist mainly of a limited number of investments after the anticipated tax planning scheme has been implemented.

(5)   On 15 December 1998 the respondents made a sensible suggestion to submit the outstanding issues on the tax planning scheme to mediation by a solicitor. This offer has been refused by the appellant. They have also offered to consult the appellant on all decisions if she would abandon the present appeal. These suggestions demonstrate their willingness to try to resolve any difficulties with the appellant by negotiation and compromise. I have criticised them for obtaining Mrs E's signature to the draft deed of advancement, but there was no intention to act otherwise than in Mrs E's best interests and in accordance with her wishes. I also consider that it is regrettable that the appellant was not kept properly informed of the steps being taken. However, I do not consider that what has happened in those respects should be seen in isolation. Mrs Z in particular has given a considerable amount of time to managing her mother's affairs and there has been no complaint about that. I do not consider that, given all the circumstances of this case, either she or Mrs Y could be held to be unfit or unsuitable to act as attorneys for the donor in the future management of her affairs. Moreover, they clearly have access to legal and accountancy advice if that is needed.

(6)   Another issue is whether the appointment of two out of the three sisters is likely to be against the donor's interests because it will lead to disharmony among the family which will have an adverse effect on her. No one, however, has suggested that this will happen. The three sisters are all responsible and mature individuals: one is a finance manager for a large UK subsidiary of a French company, one is a schools inspector and one (the appellant) has recently been in the employment of a firm of solicitors as a legal accounts assistant. I would not expect any of them to cause any distress or anxiety to the donor because of any disharmony between themselves.

(7)   There would be significant costs involved in appointing a receiver which would not be incurred if Mrs Y and Mrs Z are attorneys.

(8)   I have considered whether the court should make inquiries from the donor as to whether she would be concerned if two of her daughters were to be her attorneys, but not the third. Counsel helpfully made suggestions as to the type of inquiries that could be made, such as whether the donor wanted the same people to continue to manage her affairs as at present. I do not however think that such inquiries would elicit significantly more information than I have at present and accordingly I do not consider that such inquiries would be appropriate. Moreover, the question is not what the donor would now prefer but whether Mrs Y and Mrs Z would be unsuitable to be her attorneys. I note that the Law Commission's report envisaged only a limited role for inquiries by the court and stated that the court would make independent inquiries of its own where there were suspicious circumstances or in cases where there were no relatives to be informed (see The Incapacitated Principal, paras 4.46 and 4.48). That is not to say that inquiries will only be appropriate in such circumstances: the court must form a view about the usefulness of inquiries based on all the circumstances of the particular case.

(9)   I do not consider that the attorneys under the 1992 deed should be treated as unsuitable simply because they do not include the appellant. Naturally if circumstances permitted it, it would have been desirable that she should have the same role as her sisters in relation to her mother's affairs but as I see it this is not open to the court because the donor chose to appoint her two sisters under the 1992 power. I hope that she will now accept that this was a decision which her mother (for whatever reason) was free to make, and abide by it, as best she can.

For the reasons given above, I dismiss the appeal and direct that the 1992 power be registered forthwith.

Order that the power be registered.

Solicitors: Ferguson Bricknell for the appellant/X

Darbys Mallam Lewis for the respondents/Y and Z

PHILIPPA JOHNSON

Barrister

[G6]

RE C (POWER OF ATTORNEY)

[2000] 2 FLR 1, CA

CHANCERY DIVISION

WALLER AND CHADWICK LJJ AND SIR CHRISTOPHER SLADE 21 December 1999

Enduring power of attorney – Registration – Objections – Inquiries – Terms – Report prepared by chartered accountant – Disclosure

The father, who was showing signs of memory loss, was advised by his doctor to execute a power of attorney in April 1998. In June 1998 he executed a power of attorney in favour of J, the woman he had been living with for many years, and M, a business associate who was also an old friend. The son opposed registration of the power on the basis that the father had not had capacity to grant the power in June 1998, that undue pressure had been used to induce the father to grant the power and that M was unsuitable to be the father's attorney. The son was particularly concerned about the transfer of substantial parts of the father's assets to J and to M. The judge took the view that the objections were without substance, and ordered registration of the power of attorney subject to certain conditions, including preparation by a chartered accountant of a report investigating all transactions over £25,000. The report was solely for the use and consideration of the Court of Protection and the attorneys, but the court had the power to disclose the report or any part of it to the family after 7 days' notice to the attorneys. The son sought disclosure of the report. The attorneys applied to the court for an order that the report should not be disclosed. The judge took the view that, although there was nothing on the face of the report to suggest that there was anything wrong with the relevant transactions, the report should not be disclosed, as disclosure would simply lead to further litigation. The son appealed against the registration of the power, and sought permission to appeal the judge's refusal to disclose the report.

Held – dismissing the appeal and refusing the application for permission to appeal – the first issue before the judge on an application to register the power of attorney was whether it was appropriate in the circumstances of the case to make inquiries into the question whether any of the grounds of objection were established. While there had been good reasons for registering the power, and the appeal therefore failed, there had been little or no express consideration of the issue of inquiries, and the judge's reasons for dismissing the objections should have been expressed in a way which left the objectors in no doubt that their concerns had been taken fully into account. The judge was entitled to reach the conclusion that there was no useful purpose to be served by disclosure of the report to the children, and much risk of distress to the father. There was also some risk of damage to the father's financial interests if the transactions were subject to hostile examination in litigation.

However, some further investigation into the suitability of M as an attorney was appropriate, in the light of a transaction in which, on the face of it, M took substantial benefit at the expense of the father. The matter should be remitted to the Court of Protection for consideration of its power to cancel registration on the ground of an attorney's unsuitability.

Statutory provisions considered

Enduring Powers of Attorney Act 1985, ss 4, 6, 8

Alastair Norris QC for the appellant

Hazel Williamson QC and Mark Cunningham for the respondents

CHADWICK LJ:

This is the judgment of the court. It is given in respect of two matters: first, an application for permission to appeal from an order made on 13 May 1999 by Jacob J, when sitting as a nominated judge of the Court of Protection in proceedings under the Enduring Powers of Attorney Act 1985; and, secondly, an appeal from an order made on 1 December 1999 by the same judge on a subsequent application in the same proceedings. The proceedings relate to a power of attorney executed by an elderly donor, to whom we shall refer as 'C', on 2 June 1998 in favour of the lady with whom he had long been living as his wife and a business associate who had been his friend for many years. We shall refer to the attorneys as 'Miss J' and 'M' respectively. Registration of the power, under s 6 of the Act, is opposed by the donor's son, to whom we shall refer as 'D', and other children of the donor.

The background to the proceedings

The circumstances in which the application for registration was made are unusual. They may be summarised as follows:

(1)   The suggestion that C should execute a power of attorney under the 1985 Act appears to have first come from his medical adviser, Dr Ian Perry, in the course of a telephone conversation with the donor's solicitor on 24 April 1998. That telephone conversation took place shortly after the donor, together with Miss J and the solicitor, had attended at Dr Perry's consulting rooms for the purpose of executing a will. A contemporary attendance note, confirmed by affidavit evidence from both Dr Perry and the solicitor, makes it clear that they were satisfied that he had testamentary capacity at that time.

(2)   The solicitor did not take the matter of an enduring power of attorney forward until 2 June 1998. On that day, at a meeting at the solicitor's offices which had been arranged for some other purpose and at which the donor, Miss J and M were present, the solicitor raised the suggestion with the donor. C expressed a wish to proceed immediately. The solicitor asked a colleague, also a solicitor, to come to his office. The power of attorney was executed by the donor, Miss J and M in the presence of the two solicitors on that day. There was no doctor present.

That was not surprising, given that the meeting had not been convened for that purpose and the donor's wish to proceed immediately. Both solicitors present had the question of capacity in mind. They have each sworn affidavits to the effect that they were satisfied that C knew and understood what he was doing.

(3) No steps were taken to register the power of attorney at that stage: or thereafter until 25 February 1999. But, in the meantime on 7 January 1999, D, the donor's son, had made application to the Court of Protection, under s 98 of the Mental Health Act 1983, for the appointment of a receiver in respect of his father's affairs. The application was supported by a medical certificate signed by Dr John Meadows on 6 November 1998. Although the certificate contains the statement that Dr Meadows was the medical attendant of the donor and had acted as such since 14 October 1996, it is not in dispute that Dr Meadows had seen the donor only on one occasion, that is to say on 14 October 1996 on referral from Dr Perry. Dr Meadows did not think it necessary to consult Dr Perry before signing the certificate on 6 November 1998; nor to inform him of what he had done.

(4) As a result of the application to which we have just referred, which was made without notice to C, Miss J, C's solicitor or Dr Perry, a receiver ad interim was appointed on 13 January 1999. The order was served personally on the donor on 21 January 1999. As may be imagined, it came as an unwelcome surprise to him.

(5) On 1 February 1999 the donor instructed his solicitor to apply to the Court of Protection to discharge the order of 13 January 1999. In making that application the solicitor disclosed the existence of the power of attorney which had been executed on 2 June 1998. The Court of Protection directed that one of the Lord Chancellor's Medical Visitors should make a report. Dr Ann Bailey visited C for that purpose on 12 February 1999. In the light of that report the Master of the Court of Protection directed that the interim receivership should continue: but he directed, further, that the attorneys should apply for registration of the power of attorney.

The attorneys applied for registration of the power by notice dated 25 February 1999. Notice of that application was given to the donor's five children. Objections were lodged by solicitors on behalf of D; and by the other children in person.

On 15 April 1999 the donor, through his solicitor, made application to the Court of Protection that the objections to the registration of the power should be summarily dismissed and that the power should be registered forthwith. That application was supported by the two attorneys, Miss J and M. On 22 April 1999 D applied for directions for the hearing of the objections; including, in particular, directions for the disclosure of documents relating to (i) instructions given by C to his solicitor since January 1998, (ii) all powers of attorney or contracts entered into between M and C (without limitation as to time), and (iii) details of all financial transactions between either of the attorneys and C since January 1996. The attorneys' application to register the power, C's application to dismiss the objections and D's application for directions came before Jacob J on 13 May 1999.

The proceedings so far

Jacob J took the view that the objections were without substance. He saw no need for directions preparatory to a hearing. He dismissed the objections summarily. He ordered registration of the power of attorney under the Act. But he did so upon terms set out in the schedule to his order, which required (amongst other things) that the attorneys should instruct a named chartered accountant to prepare a report for the Court of Protection. The report was to set out the nature and value of all transactions which had taken place since 1 June 1996 concerning the assets of the donor; being transactions in respect of which the value exceeded £25,000. Further, and for the future, the attorneys were to report to the Court of Protection, twice yearly, all transactions exceeding £5000 which had taken place in the preceding 6 months; and were to give notice to the Court of Protection, in advance, of their intention to effect any transaction which exceeded £25,000. That was to be accompanied by a certificate from the named chartered accountant that, having regard to the financial position and interests of the donor, the transactions appeared to him unobjectionable.

The order of 13 May 1999 contained, at paras 4 and 5 of the schedule, provisions as to use and disclosure of the report. The report was to be addressed and delivered to the Court of Protection. Three weeks after delivery to the court, it was to be copied to the two attorneys, Miss J and M. It was directed that the report was to be solely for the use and consideration of the court (to take such steps, if any, as it saw fit) and the attorneys. The Court of Protection might disclose the report, or any part of it, to members of the donor's family, but only after 7 days' notice to the attorneys so as to give them the opportunity to make such application to the judge as they might think fit.

The report was sent to the Master of the Court of Protection in the form of a letter dated 12 August 1999. The master raised a query, to which the named accountant responded on 24 August 1999. On the same day, solicitors instructed by D, who must have become aware that the report had been sent to the court, wrote 'to request the Court of Protection to exercise its discretion to release a copy of the report to [D] now, so that he can satisfy himself and his brothers and sisters that nothing untoward has occurred with his father's financial affairs and assets'. The master informed the attorneys' solicitors of that request. The attorneys applied to the judge – as, clearly, Jacob J had intended that they should have the opportunity to do – for an order that the report should not be disclosed to the children. That application was fixed for hearing before Jacob J on 1 December 1999. The judge acceded to the application. He directed that the report should not be disclosed. He gave leave to appeal against that order.

In the meantime, D has applied to this court for permission to appeal against the order of 13 May 1999. That application came before Evans LJ, with whom I was sitting, on 4 November 1999. That court took the view, first, that the then anticipated hearing before Jacob J might, in the light of the report that would be available to him at that hearing, provide an opportunity to resolve the issues that remained between the attorneys and the children, and, secondly, that, if there remained unresolved issues, then the Court of Appeal would be in a better position to decide whether this unfortunate litigation should proceed to an appeal if it knew what view Jacob J had taken of the report, and (if appropriate) were able to have sight of the report itself. Accordingly, the application for permission to appeal against the order of 13 May 1999 was adjourned so that it could come back before this court in the third week of December 1999. In the event, that application has been heard with the appeal against the order of 1 December 1999.

The statutory framework

The functions of the court on application for registration of an enduring power of attorney made under the 1985 Act are set out in s 6 of that Act. The court, in that context, is the Court of Protection – see s 13(1) of the Enduring Powers of Attorney Act 1985 and s 93(1) in Part VII of the Mental Health Act 1983. Section 6(1) of the 1985 Act requires that the court shall register the instrument provided that neither subss (2) or (4) of s 6 applies.

Section 6(2) requires that, where it appears to the court that there is in force an order under Part VII of the Mental Health Act 1983 appointing a receiver for the donor, then, unless it directs otherwise, the court shall refuse the application for registration. In the present case, the court had directed that the application for registration be made, notwithstanding the receivership ad interim. Before making that application the attorneys were required, by s 4(3) of the Act, to give notice to the persons described in Part I of Sch 1 to the Act. Those persons include the donor's children. Section 6(4) is in these terms, so far as material:

'If, in the case of an application for registration—
(a)   a valid notice of objection to the registration is received by the court before the expiry of the period of five weeks beginning with the date or, as the case may be, the latest date on which the attorney gave notice to any person under Schedule 1, . . .
the court shall neither register the instrument nor refuse the application until it has made such inquiries (if any) as it thinks appropriate in the circumstances of the case.'

Section 6(5) sets out the circumstances in which a notice of objection to the registration of an instrument is valid. They include, so far as material:

'(a)   that the power purported to have been created by the instrument is not valid as an enduring power of attorney;
        . . .
(d)   that fraud or undue pressure was used to induce the donor to create the power;
(e)   that, having regard to all the circumstances and in particular the attorney's relationship to or connection with the donor, the attorney is unsuitable to be the donor's attorney.'

Section 6(6) requires that, where s 6(4) applies and any of the grounds of objection in s 6(5) are established to the satisfaction of the court, the court shall refuse the application to register the instrument; but if the court is not so satisfied, it shall register the instrument to which the application relates.

Where an instrument has been registered under s 6 of the 1985 Act, the court has the functions prescribed by s 8 with respect to the power, the donor, and the attorney. Those functions include giving directions to the attorney with respect to the management or disposal by the attorney of the property and affairs of the donor (s 8(2)(b)(i)); requiring the attorney to furnish information or produce documents or things in his possession as attorney (s 8(2)(c)); and cancelling registration of the instrument registered under s 6 on being satisfied that fraud or undue pressure was used to induce the donor to create the power (s 8(4)(f)) or that, having regard to all the circumstances, the attorney is unsuitable to be the donor's attorney (s 8(4)(g)). In the case of an instrument creating joint attorneys – which this was – references in ss 6(5)(e) and 8(2) and (4) include references to any attorney.

The position, therefore, is that the court had power to register the instrument – notwithstanding the appointment of the receiver ad interim – and was required to do so unless it was satisfied that one or more of the grounds of objection set out in s 6(5) was or were established in respect of one or both attorneys. For that purpose the court was required to make or cause to be made 'such inquiries (if any) as it thinks appropriate in the circumstances of the case'. Once the instrument had been registered the court had the extensive powers of control over the attorneys conferred by s 8(2) of the Act. It was, as it seems to us, in the exercise of those powers that the judge gave the directions which are contained in the schedule to his order. This can be properly described as a registration subject to conditions as to an investigation of past transactions, and to restrictions as to the regulation of future transactions.

The objections

The 1985 Act required notice to be given to the donor's children – see s 4(2) and Sch 1, para 2(1)(b). The purpose of the requirement that notice be given is to enable the persons to whom notice is given to object to the registration of the instrument creating the power. In the present case the objections lodged by D were contained in a letter from his solicitors to the Public Trust Office dated 19 March 1999. They were: (i) that the donor did not have capacity to grant the power on 2 June 1998; (ii) that undue pressure was used to induce the donor to grant the power; and (iii) 'that M is unsuitable to be the [donor's] attorney, and that accordingly [Miss J] and [M] are unsuitable donees of a joint power'. Similar objections were lodged by the donor's daughters (by letters dated 10 March 1999 and 19 March 1999) and by his other two sons (by letters dated 16 March 1999 and 23 March 1999). In the form lodged, the objections could fairly be described as lacking in particulars; but, no doubt, it was the intention of the objectors to remedy this by the filing of evidence, for which purpose directions were sought in the application made on behalf of D dated 22 April 1999. In any event, there was before Jacob J a substantial skeleton argument, settled by counsel and dated 10 May 1999. Subsequently, in connection with the application in December 1999, D swore an affidavit; but this, understandably, is primarily directed towards the question whether the accountant's report should be disclosed rather than to the objections to registration.

The medical evidence

The judge treated the children's assertion that the donor lacked capacity on 2 June 1998 (the date on which he signed the instrument) as the principal objection. In our view he was right to do so. All the evidence before him suggested that C had been shrewd, successful and strong-willed in the course of a long life which had brought him substantial material rewards. If he knew and understood what he was doing in June 1998, it was inherently unlikely that he would have allowed his will to be overborne by undue pressure. Further, if he knew and understood what he was doing, he was likely to be a sound judge of the suitability of his chosen attorneys to look after his interests. He had known each of them for many years. He was likely to know whether they were of such integrity that they could be trusted with the powers which he was to confer upon them; and he was likely to know whether they would be competent to deal with the complexity of his business and financial affairs.

The medical evidence before the judge may be summarised as follows:

First, there is the medical certificate of Dr Meadows, given on 6 November 1998 on the basis of a single consultation which (although Dr Meadows describes it as having occurred 3 years earlier) had, in fact, taken place on 14 October 1996. Dr Meadows had written to Dr Perry on 15 October 1996:

'Thank you for referring this very pleasant gentleman who is seventy eight and failing intellectually, though he preserves all the social graces and has some insight. His memory is poor, calculation difficult, he is prone to confusion and he has some difficulty in finding words at times in running speech. There is nothing obviously wrong on the more physical front and the pattern is very much as one sees in idiopathic decline in intellectual function of the elderly.'

In his certificate, given some 2 years later, Dr Meadows diagnosed:

'Alzheimers disease/presenile dementia. Deteriorating memory, proneness to confusion, considerable word finding difficulty, inability to concentrate, impaired comprehension.'

He added the comment:

'My opinion is based upon consultation 3 years ago. It is inconceivable that there has been an improvement. I am told that his mental condition has deteriorated which is as expected.'

In a letter addressed to the Public Trustee Office and dated 11 May 1999, Dr Meadows confirmed that he stood by that certificate.

Secondly, there is the evidence of Dr Perry, a consultation physician who had known C for about 15 years and who had been his medical adviser since 1993. His opinion might be thought to be of particular relevance because, in April 1998, he had been asked to direct his mind to the question whether C had capacity to make a will; and it was he who had suggested to C's solicitor that consideration be given to C giving an enduring power of attorney. He had experience in the relevant field; he was consultant to the Wessex Alzheimer Society. He had referred C to Dr Meadows in October 1996 'because I wanted a neurological opinion to make sure that [he] did not have a brain tumour or other similar condition and that his presenting symptoms were only of an age onset (possibly early Alzheimer's disease)'. In his affidavit sworn on 27 January 1999 Dr Perry observed that he had never been convinced that C was suffering from Alzheimer's disease. His view was based on a perceived improvement in C's condition from 1997. He deposed:

'8 I see from my notes that on reviewing [him] on 21 October 1997 there had been a definite improvement in his memory and I was satisfied with that improvement when I saw him again on 28 January 1998 and 2 April 1998.'

Thirdly, there is the report of Dr Alice Parshall, a consultant psychiatrist approved under s 12 of the Mental Health Act 1983. She was asked to prepare a psychiatric report on C in connection with the application to discharge the receiver ad interim. She interviewed C for a period of over an hour on 2 February 1999. In her report, dated 3 February 1999, she expressed the view that:

'. . . the clinical picture which has emerged in [C] is not typical of progressive Alzheimer dementia . . . the picture now is more consistent with normal ageing complicated by a significant cerebral injury [suffered in 1995] from the latter of which some rehabilitation may have taken place . . . In summary however, while [C] does show "mental disorder" in the broad terms of the Act I have been presented with no evidence of recent decline and there would be no grounds to make a recommendation under the Act.'

Dr Parshall observed, in the final paragraph of her report, that C appeared to be aware of the responsibility of owning assets and showed no mental disorder likely to make him dispose of assets recklessly. She stated that it was not her view that he would readily be exploited financially.

Finally, and perhaps of the greatest significance, there is the report of the Lord Chancellor's Visitor, Dr Ann Bailey. She had seen Dr Meadows' certificate, Dr Perry's affidavit and Dr Parshall's report. She interviewed C on 12 February 1999, both in the presence of Miss J and alone. It is significant, in the present context, that she found no indication that either of Miss J or C dominated the other. As she put it, 'they were true partners'. Her diagnosis was of FOO.2 Atypical Alzheimer's disease; possibly precipitated by the accident in 1995. She went on, in the final paragraphs of her report:

'I consider that the mental disorder, particularly the impaired concentration, significant memory loss, a disinterest in current affairs and the fact that C has multiple business interests render him incompetent of fully managing his affairs. I feel he has insight into this problem.

731

Over the last year it would appear that [C] has taken steps to put his affairs in order. He has always been aware of his cognitive problems. It is my opinion that in June 1998 he would have had the capacity to create an enduring power of attorney.'

It is significant, also, that Dr Bailey formed the view that, on 12 February 1999, C understood the nature of a power of attorney (although perhaps not the special characteristics of an enduring power); that he knew that he had given powers of attorney to Miss J and M; and that he knew that those powers could be revoked.

The hearing on 13 May 1999

The first issue before Jacob J on 13 May 1999 was whether it was appropriate in the circumstances of the case, as they appeared from the material then available, to make or cause to be made inquiries into the question whether any of the three grounds of objection advanced by the donor's children were established. That was the issue raised by the donor's own application of 15 April 1999, seeking summary dismissal of the objections. It was also the issue raised by the legislation itself – see s 6(4) of the 1985 Act. If, but only if, he were satisfied that it was not appropriate to inquire beyond the material then available could the judge proceed to decide, there and then, whether to register the instrument of 2 June 1998 or to refuse registration. If he was not so satisfied, then he was bound to consider what inquiries should be made. That was what he was invited to do by the application for directions, dated 22 April 1999, which had been issued on behalf of D. If the judge thought that some inquiries should be made, it was for him to decide what those inquiries should be. He was not bound to make the directions sought if he did not consider them appropriate; but he was required to consider whether any, and if so what, directions were required in the circumstances.

It is clear that the judge formed a view, after hearing the submissions made by counsel instructed on behalf of the donor and before hearing counsel for D (or the other objectors in person), that a possible way forward was to register the instrument but to impose terms on the attorneys. He first expressed that view at pp 33–34 in the transcript of the proceedings on 13 May 1999. At p 36 (line 26) he gave a clear indication that the parties should work towards that solution, if they could: ' . . . I would much rather this did not end up in any kind of judgment if it is at all possible. It is always better if you can do without judgment, and as everybody is here now this is the time to try and sort something out briefly'. There was then a short adjournment to enable Mr Norris QC, instructed on behalf of D, to take instructions. He then sought to explain to the judge the concerns of his client and the other children. He said this, at p 37 of the transcript (lines 8–30):

'If I was asked to summarise what the real concerns on this side are, it is that over the last three years substantial parts of father's assets have been transferred to [Miss J] and to [M]. Over that period, father has, on all sides it is agreed, been vulnerable. The family would like some investigation into the transactions which have happened in the past three years. They involve giving away the patient's house of two flats which are worth about £1 million and a half share in a property development which is worth between £3–4 million. Those we know about. There are other transactions involving Liechtenstein anstalts, offshore bank accounts and so forth about which we simply know nothing at the moment. We would like somebody to look at those. Not in the sense that we want them set aside; we simply want them examined at the moment to see what actually happened . . . It is also the case that father has made a Bahamian Will. We do not know what that says, we do not particularly care what it says. Our concern is not what will happen to father's property another day but what is available for father now. That is the principal concern.'

These were the concerns which the judge sought to address by the order which he was to make. He observed (transcript, p 39, lines 29–31) that he was getting the very clear message that C did not want an outsider involved in his affairs; to which Mr Norris' response was that it was not a question of whether he wanted it or not, the question was whether it was for his benefit that that should be done.

The hearing continued in the form of a debate as to the details of the solution which the judge had in mind. There was little or no express consideration of the issue which the judge was required by the statute to address – namely, whether inquiries were appropriate before making a decision whether or not to register the instrument of 2 June 1998. But the following exchange (transcript, p 55, line 17 to p 56, line 9) is of significance:

'MR NORRIS: I hate this horse trading, my Lord, but it does seem that the family's concerns are simply not being addressed in this scheme.
MR JUSTICE JACOB: This is not a case about the family's concerns. At the moment there is an appointment of a power of attorney in these two people . . . I looked at the medical side of that and I came to the conclusion that the medical evidence was overwhelming in favour of the fact that the gentleman was compos mentis at the time he did it.
MR NORRIS: Your Lordship has not looked at the question of pressure. Your Lordship has not looked at the question of suitability.
MR JUSTICE JACOB: No, I have not. I thought the medical one was the strongest. Sometimes one takes the view that there are several points being run just because one of them is not a very strong one. If you want me to go through the whole lot, I will but I could just end up by confirming the whole thing. I am just trying to find a way to do it. I am not going to have the family having a look into all this when that was not what the donor wanted.
MR NORRIS: My Lord, this jurisdiction is all about the Court supervising the administration of the donor's assets. It is the very reason why the family is informed about the registration of the power and why the Law Commission called that notification of the family a keystone of the protective machinery.
MR JUSTICE JACOB: Of course it is, and the family does know about it and now the Court is going to be looking at it and the Court has taken control. It does not mean that the family can come barging in.
MR NORRIS: But, my Lord, the family is not seeking to come barging in, as I have endeavored to make plain.'

It is clear that the judge took the view that there was nothing to be gained by further inquiries, either into the question of capacity or into the related questions of undue pressure and unsuitability. It would, we think, have been helpful if he had explained why he reached that conclusion; but we are satisfied that his reasoning does emerge from the transcript of the proceedings before him. He was satisfied, from the medical evidence that was before him, that the donor had the necessary capacity at the time when he signed the instrument on 2 June 1998. He must have taken the view that there was little chance that oral evidence from the doctors – and the opportunity for cross-examination – would alter the conclusion which he had reached on that point; or, at the least, that such benefit as might be obtained from oral evidence did not justify the expense and delay that oral evidence would entail. There was really no evidence of pressure on the donor, other than the pressure inherent in his own perception of his failing intellect. There was a case for inquiry into the suitability of (at least) M; in the circumstances that there was, plainly, potential for a conflict of interest which M might have exploited in the past. But, clearly, the judge thought that the appropriate way to resolve that question was through the reporting procedure which he proposed to include in his order.

While recognising the reasons which led the judge to take the course which he did on 13 May 1999, we think there is much force in the criticism of his approach to the application which has been made to him. The 1985 Act gives objectors the right to have their objections considered by the court before an instrument creating an enduring power of attorney is registered. It is of particular importance, in a field as sensitive as this, that they are not left with the impression that those objections have been brushed aside. There is, we fear, a danger that that is the impression which was given by what occurred on 13 May 1999. We are satisfied that the judge had good reasons for taking the course which he did; but we are firmly of the view that those reasons could and should have been spelt out in a way which left the objectors in no doubt that their concerns had been taken fully into account.

The order of 1 December 1999

At the hearing on 1 December 1999 Jacob J had the benefit of the report from the named accountant. That would have satisfied him of two matters: (i) that the donor had more than enough assets to provide for his comfort and maintenance in his remaining years – a matter about which Mr Norris had expressed concern on behalf of the children at the hearing of 13 May 1999; and (ii) that there had been no transactions between the donor and either of the two attorneys other than those identified by Mr Norris at that earlier hearing. The judge had, also, the benefit of explanations – set out in confidential exhibits to affidavits sworn by Miss J and M – of their dealings with the donor.

The judge took the view that no useful purpose would be served by disclosure of the report to the children. He said this, at p 4F–H of the judgment which he gave on 1 December 1999:

'When I ordered this report I hoped, as I say, it would produce peace. I have no doubt whatever that if it is disclosed it will produce war. Almost every single one of the transactions will be the subject of further investigation. There is nothing on the face of the report to suggest there is anything wrong with these transactions, but from what I have seen of the material so far I can see nothing but continued litigation – speculative litigation at that.'

He went on, at p 6F–G:

'I am sorry that the procedure which I devised did not lead to peace. The Court has seen the report. Whilst, of course, one cannot say from the report that there is not behind the report something untoward, it is a pure matter of speculation whether there is or not. I can see no reason why the family should be allowed to indulge in that speculation to the distress of the patient.'

We have read the report and the other confidential material which was before the judge. Because it is confidential material we can say little about it. The appellant must be content that, having read that material, we can express our view that the judge was entitled to reach the conclusion that there was no useful purpose to be served by disclosure of the report to the children; and much risk of distress to their father. We would observe, also, that we are satisfied that there is some risk of damage to his financial interests if the other parties to transactions in which he is engaged came to the view that those transactions were to be the subject of hostile examination in the context of litigation.

The way forward

We are not persuaded that there is any purpose in an appeal against the order made on 13 May 1999. That order has been made and events have now moved on. We do not think that there is any real prospect that the Court of Appeal would think it sensible to set that order aside. There is ample power, if necessary, to deal with the situation which now exists under the provisions in s 8 of the 1985 Act.

Nor are we persuaded that the decision on 1 December 1999 to refuse disclosure of the report was flawed. It was, of course, a decision made by a judge of the Court of Protection in the exercise of his discretion. This court should not interfere with such a decision unless satisfied that the judge erred in principle. We can find no such error. Indeed, so far as our view is material, we think he reached the correct decision on 1 December 1999.

In those circumstances, and for the reasons which we have sought to give, we would dismiss the appeal against the order of 1 December 1999; and refuse the application for permission to appeal against the order of 13 May 1999.

We do not think it sufficient to leave the matter there. We think some further investigation into the suitability of M as an attorney is required. We think it appropriate to remit the matter to the Court of Protection, with a direction that express consideration be given to the question whether there is a case for the exercise by that court of its power under s 8(4)(g) of the 1985 Act on the ground that M's relationship to or connection with the donor make it suitable for him to remain the donor's attorney. The particular matter of concern to this court is the transaction evidenced by the letters of 28 and 29 October 1997 to which reference was made by Mr Norris in the court below. On the face of those letters the transaction is one from which M appears to have taken a substantial benefit at the expense of the donor. It is obvious that M is not, himself, a person who can inquire into the propriety of that transaction. We should make it plain that we have formed no view on that question. We think that should be left to the Court of Protection. But we are satisfied that the question needs to be addressed with more care than it appears to have received so far.

Order accordingly.

Solicitors: Charles Russell for the appellant

Nicholson Graham & Jones for the respondents

PHILIPPA JOHNSON

[G7]

RE F (ENDURING POWER OF ATTORNEY)

[2004] EWHC 725 (Ch)

CHANCERY DIVISION

PATTEN J 15 MARCH, 2 APRIL 2004 2 April 2004.

The following judgment was delivered.

PATTEN J:

[1] This is an appeal from the refusal of Master Lush, the Master of the Court of Protection, to register an enduring power of attorney dated 10 July 2000 which was made by the donor (Mrs F) in favour of her son (Mr A). The master upheld an objection to registration on grounds of the unsuitability of Mr A to be the donor's attorney, which was lodged by his sister (Mrs B).

[2] Mrs F was born in 1917. Her husband died in 1987. There were two children of the marriage (Mr A and Mrs B). Until 2002 Mrs F continued to live in a large house which she and her husband had purchased after the Second World War. The evidence before the master was that Mrs F was extremely attached to her home and was very reluctant to leave it. She had told her friends and family that she wished to remain there for the rest of her life. But by 2002 she had become unable to cope with the maintenance and upkeep of the property and its garden and was persuaded by her children to move into a nursing home. Even then she was unwilling to sell the house and had hoped that it might be let to provide her with an income.

[3] Mr A is a retired solicitor who was born in 1946 and continues to live close to his mother. His sister, Mrs B, who was born in 1950, lives abroad in Ireland. She has a

family of her own and is obviously unable to visit her mother with the same regularity as Mr A, but between her visits she maintains frequent contact with her mother by telephone. Both children are clearly concerned to do the best for their mother, but the difficulty which has arisen in this case is that Mr A and Mrs B have been at odds with each other for some time and the disagreements and animosity between them have spilled over into the question of whether effect should be given to the power of attorney executed in Mr A's favour.

[4] It is clear that the donor has in the past chosen to place her affairs in the hands of Mr A. The power of attorney was executed in July 2000, and in October 2001 Mrs F executed a will under which her son was appointed to be the sole executor. He is also, I believe, the executor of his father's will. One of the complications of this matter is that the family home was held by Mrs F and her late husband as joint tenants. On the advice of Mr A as part of what I am told was a scheme to minimise inheritance tax, his father served notice of severance on Mrs F, with the result that at his death the property was held by Mrs F as the surviving joint tenant on trust for herself and her husband as tenants in common in equal shares. Under their father's will Mr A and Mrs B are entitled to pecuniary legacies of £45,000 each, with the residue being held upon trust for Mrs F absolutely. In order to make title to the family home on a sale, it will be necessary for Mr A to appoint an additional trustee in order to give a good receipt. It seems to be common ground that the power of appointment would vest in him as Mrs F's attorney and that he could exercise the power on her behalf: see s 36(6A)–(6B) of the Trustee Act 1925. It would then be for him to arrange for the investment of his mother's share of the proceeds of sale, including the share of residue due to her under her late husband's will.

[5] The difficulties which have arisen are due to Mrs F's declining state of health. The medical evidence contained in a report by Dr X, the Lord Chancellor's medical visitor, based on a visit to Mrs F in October last year, is that she is suffering from arteriosclerotic dementia, which has led to some memory loss. She has also suffered a stroke, but her residence in the nursing home seems to have stabilised her condition and she is able to hold rational conversations. She is, however, disorientated in relation to dates and other historic details, and her mental condition will deteriorate with the passage of time. It is also clear that she can become confused. At one point in the interview, Mrs F asked Dr X why she had come and became distressed during the examination when she was asked to carry out a counting exercise.

[6] The importance of the evidence from the Lord Chancellor's medical visitor is that it forms the basis, and indeed the only evidence, upon which Mrs B's objection to registration is now sought to be maintained. During the course of her interview with Dr X, Mrs F expressed concern that her son and daughter were having disagreements. She would prefer them 'to live together and agree'. She also wanted Mr A to discuss things with his sister. She then went on to say that if they could not agree, it would be better for an independent receiver to be appointed.

[7] The master, in his judgment, interpreted Mrs F's wishes and feelings to be that:

'if the continued operation of the enduring power of attorney is likely to be a festering sore or a stumbling block that prevents her children from behaving in a civil manner towards one another, then she would rather an independent receiver be appointed. It is clear to me that the continued operation of the power is likely to be a stumbling block that prevents any prospect of reconciliation between her son and daughter. [Mr A] contends that his mother's views do not reflect an informed decision on the matter, that there would be considerable cost implications in appointing a receiver, and that there would be practical day-to-day difficulties over being reimbursed for small items of expenditure, such as purchasing items of clothing, giving Christmas or birthday presents, and treats such as going out for lunch. I agree that there are cost implications, but when [the house] is finally sold and the net proceeds are properly invested, there should be relatively little for the receiver to do, and it is unlikely that the costs would be substantial. In any event, [Mrs F] has a fairly substantial estate, and the costs should not be disproportionate, or cause any hardship or adversely impact on her standard of living. The practical day-to-day problems to which [Mr A] referred can be easily overcome.'

He therefore upheld the objection to registration on grounds of unsuitability.

[8] Before me Mr A has repeated his submission that his mother's expressed views are unreliable as an accurate account of her true wishes and feelings. To support this he has produced an undated letter in Mrs F's handwriting, in which she says that she wants Mr A to act for her in all her affairs and that she does not want anybody else. She says in the letter that he has acted as she has wished and that she wants this to continue. There is no evidence as to when and in what circumstances this letter came to be written and there is therefore little weight which I can attach to it. If Mr A is right and his mother's statement to Dr X is unreliable as an accurate statement of her wishes, it must also follow that this letter is subject to the same reservations.

[9] The master upheld Mrs B's objection to the registration of the power of attorney on the ground that Mr A was unsuitable by accepting at face value Mrs F's statement to Dr X that she would prefer an independent receiver to be appointed if her son and daughter could not agree. The likely continuation of bad relations between them due to the attorneyship was, in the master's judgment, the cause of her concern. She did not suggest that she regarded her son as unsuitable to be her attorney for any other reason, nor is there any evidence that he would fail to carry out his duties as attorney otherwise than in accordance with the law and in the best interests of his mother. In this connection some reference needs to be made to the history of these proceedings.

[10] On 21 January 2003 Mrs B applied to be appointed her mother's receiver under s 99 of the Mental Health Act 1983. In a letter to the Court of Protection enclosing the receiver's declaration and other documents, her solicitors referred to her concerns that Mr A would seek to use the power of attorney to sell Mrs F's property. The letter also states that Mrs B has had grave reservations about his conduct of her mother's affairs and that any communications between them are 'confrontational'. The solicitors refer to Mr A failing to provide information about investments and complain about losses incurred on the stock market. However, the principal cause of concern appears to have been the family house. Any sale of this was, they said, likely to cause Mrs F considerable distress.

[11] Mrs B's application to be appointed her mother's receiver led to Mr A applying for the registration of the power of attorney. In a letter of 3 April 2003, Mrs B's solicitors lodged her objection to this. This was made on the grounds of Mr A's unsuitability within the meaning of s 6(5)(e) of the Enduring Powers of Attorney Act 1985 and was based on a number of matters which can be summarised as follows: (i) Mr A's desire to sell the family home and the distress this has caused to Mrs F; (ii) Mr A's failure properly to secure and maintain the property following Mrs F's entry into a nursing home; (iii) the lack of information provided about Mr A's management of his mother's and father's affairs; and (iv) Mr A's own possible financial difficulties. There was then further lengthy correspondence between Mr A and Mrs B's solicitors, in which allegations and counter-allegations of various kinds were made and rebutted, but on 18 August 2003 the objection to registration was listed for hearing on 25 September.

[12] This led to discussions about a possible compromise. Mr A said that he was informed by the Public Guardianship Office (PGO) of the Court of Protection that his sister was willing to withdraw her objection, provided that Mr A produced an inventory of the current assets and liabilities of Mrs F's estate; agreed to produce annual accounts; and gave her written notice in advance of any steps taken in connection with the sale of the family home. He told the PGO that the conditions were acceptable. The conditions had been set out in a letter written by Mrs B's solicitors to the PGO on 19 September 2003, indicating that she had decided to withdraw her

objections, but inviting the master to embody the three conditions in directions under s 8(2)(b) of the 1985 Act. A copy of the letter was then sent to Mr A.

[13] Despite having indicated earlier his consent to the conditions, this provoked a hostile reaction. Mr A wrote to the Court of Protection stating that he objected to each of the directions sought. He told me that he was put out when he saw the terms of the letter sent to the PGO and that as an attorney he had no legal duty to keep relations informed, although it was common to do so. However, the objection seems to have been more one of form than of substance, because at the hearing on 25 September in front of the master, he indicated that he was willing to provide the information which his sister required. This caused events to take a new turn. Mr Sartin, who has appeared for Mrs B on this appeal and in front of the master, raised a new query about the circumstances in which the power of attorney came to be executed. Mr A had revealed that he had drawn it up himself, and Mr Sartin expressed concern about the possibility that undue pressure or influence had been used to obtain it. The hearing was therefore adjourned to 2 December 2003 to allow the Lord Chancellor's medical visitor to report. At the same time the master agreed that the family home would be placed on the market for sale, to avoid further deterioration in its condition.

[14] I have already referred to the principal finding set out in the medical visitor's report, which formed the basis of the master's decision that Mr A was not suitable to be Mrs F's attorney. The provision of this report put an end, however, to the suggestions of undue influence in connection with the execution of the power of attorney. On 17 October 2003 Mrs B's solicitors had written to the PGO indicating that, subject to the outcome of Dr X's visit and to an order being made under which Mr A would provide a schedule of Mrs F's estate and thereafter file accounts on a quarterly basis, Mrs B would not continue with her objections to Mr A's application for registration of the enduring power. On 12 November Mr A wrote to his sister's solicitors referring to that letter and confirming that he now had no objection to the suggested conditions. The letter also invited her agreement to the sale of the family home at a price of some £365,000, as advised by the selling agents. However, in a subsequent letter of 28 November to the PGO, Mrs B's solicitors stated that, following receipt of the medical visitor's report and in the light of Mrs F's expressed desire for the appointment of an independent receiver, Mrs B had confirmed that she did wish to maintain her objection, on grounds of suitability, to the registration of enduring power of attorney.

[15] It is important to bear in mind that the only question which I have to consider is whether Mr A is to be regarded as unsuitable to be his mother's attorney, in the light of her expressed preference for an independent receiver as a possible means of avoiding future strife between her children. There was no evidence before the master, nor is there any before me, to suggest that Mr A is unsuitable on any other grounds. Although complaints have in the past been made by Mrs B about his management of the property and his failure to communicate, none of these matters was pressed at the hearing before the master. Although this appeal takes the form of a rehearing, that does not entitle me to step outside the grounds of objection which have been pursued. Mrs B chose to put no evidence before the master or before me, but instead relied on the contents of the medical visitor's report. It is also relevant to restate that, in order to refuse registration of the power under s 6(5)(e) of the 1985 Act, the court has to be satisfied not of the chosen attorney's suitability, but rather that he is unsuitable to be the attorney: see *Re E, X v Y* [2000] 3 All ER 1004 at 1016, [2001] Ch 364 at 376.

[16] The hearing on 2 December 2003 added nothing in terms of evidence to the medical visitor's report and was largely confined to argument as to how to interpret Dr X's conclusions and whether they supported an objection to registration on grounds of unsuitability. The master in his decision cited two references to the meaning of the expression 'unsuitable to be the donor's attorney' in s 6(5)(e). The first was para 4.49

of the Law Commission's report, *The Incapacitated Principal* (Law Com no 122) published in 1983, which explains the policy behind the 1985 Act. Paragraph 4.49, so far as material, states as follows:

> 'This needs some explanation. It would amount in effect to a criticism of the donor's choice of attorney. But we would not wish this ground to be sustained merely because the attorney was not the sort of person that a particular relative would have chosen. It is our wish that the donor's choice of attorney should carry considerable weight. Thus, for example, a mother might be content to appoint her son as her EPA attorney despite being aware of a conviction for theft. We would not want her choice of attorney to be upset simply because a particular relative would not want the son to be his attorney. The question should be whether the particular attorney is suitable to act as attorney for the particular donor. In short, the Court should examine carefully all the circumstances – particularly the relationship between donor and attorney.'

[17] The second reference is to the judgment of Mr Jules Sher QC (sitting as a deputy judge of this Division) in the case of *Re W* [2000] 1 All ER 175, [2000] Ch 343, which was also a case in which there was hostility between the donor's children. The deputy judge said ([2000] 1 All ER 175 at 181–182, [2000] Ch 343 at 350–351):

> 'The second ground of unsuitability is the hostility between the three children. The master considered that that fact alone rendered any one of them unsuitable to be Mrs W's attorney. In my judgment such hostility may well have such consequences but it all depends upon the circumstances. For example, had the estate of Mrs W been complex and had it required strategic decisions in relation to its administration, one would expect the attorney to have had to consult and work with her siblings in relation to the administration. In such circumstances the evident hostility between them would impact adversely on the stewardship of the attorney, no matter who was at fault in creating the hostility in the first place. But in this case the estate is simple. I asked counsel what the position was and was told that there are the following assets: (1) a portfolio of investments of a value (as at 23 December 1998) of £211,189; (2) £20,000 in premium bonds; (3) a life policy (written in trust) of £30,000. As to the outgoings there is the cost of the nursing home at some £2,000 a month, and then, simply, the need for a modest amount to cover a regular hairdo, telephone bills and the like. And, of course, on the income side there is the old age pension. In other words there is nothing of any significance left to be done. The assets are under proper control. The income simply needs to be fed through to the nursing home. The evidence is that this has been done by Mrs X very efficiently. She has indicated more than once that she has never intended to charge for her services under the power of attorney and she does not intend to do so. Against this, if the Public Trustee were to come in, there would be an appointment fee and an annual fee of between £2,350 and £3,600 per annum. If a solicitor were appointed the total cost would be likely to be somewhat less than that. It seems to me that it is not right to say that (irrespective of the background) hostility of the kind we have seen in this case between the children renders any one of them unsuitable to be Mrs W's attorney. In this case the hostility will not impact adversely on the administration. It would, in my judgment, be quite wrong to frustrate Mrs W's choice of attorney in this way. Whether it is or is not a good idea for a parent in Mrs W's position, when such hostility exists, to appoint one child alone as attorney is another question. But Mrs W did so and, on the evidence, did so knowing of the hostility. That is her prerogative and in my judgment, when the hostility does not interfere with the smooth running of the administration, the court should not interfere on the ground of unsuitability.'

[18] The master did not uphold Mrs B's objection to the registration of the power on the ground that the hostility between her and her brother would make the administration of the estate difficult, if not impossible, and there is no evidence that, in my judgment, would support that conclusion. Now that the family house is to be sold using agents and solicitors, Mr A's duties will be confined to the investment of the proceeds in approved securities and the use of the income to pay for Mrs F's nursing home fees and to meet her other needs. Section 3 of the 1985 Act imposes restrictions on the power of the attorney to use the donor's estates so as to provide gifts or to meet the needs of anyone other than the donor herself: see s 3(4) and (5). The power is also

fiduciary in nature and has to be exercised in good faith for the benefit and in the interests of the donor. If there is any reason, following registration, to suppose that the attorney has or is likely to act otherwise than in accordance with this duty, the court has power to give directions under s 8(2) and may, in appropriate cases, cancel the registration under s 8(4) and appoint an independent receiver. No evidence was presented to the court to show that this was likely to be the consequence of registering the power of attorney in favour of Mr A.

[19] The sole objection to registration is Mrs F's apparent preference for the appointment of an independent receiver, if (as the master put it) the continued operation of the enduring power of attorney was likely to be a bar to her children behaving in a civilised manner to each other and hopefully becoming reconciled. It goes without saying that one hopes that an improvement in relations between Mr A and Mrs B will occur, but from what I have seen, it seems to me unlikely that the appointment of an independent receiver will actually heal the rift. If anything, it is just as (if not more) likely to add to Mr A's feelings that he has been unfairly criticised by his sister in relation to the management of his mother's affairs, which he has now carried out for many years. Unlike his sister, who lives in Ireland, he remains close to where his mother lives, visits her frequently and is trusted by her. He says that he is concerned about the possible effect on her of interposing a stranger to manage her affairs and considers that there is no necessity for it. It will only add expense and diminish his mother's assets and income unnecessarily.

[20] I am not satisfied that the appointment of an independent receiver would be justified in this case at this time. I accept from Dr X's report that Mrs F remains conscious of the disagreements between her children and would prefer them to cease. But she has lived with them for some time and it has not led to any apparent deterioration in her relationship with either of her children individually or in the trust she reposes in her son to manage her property and affairs. He may well have been chosen as the attorney because he lives close by and is in regular physical contact with her. There is no evidence that he has abused that trust or is likely in the future to do so. Unlike the master, I consider that the appointment of an independent receiver will not diminish the hostility between Mr A and Mrs B, but will simply increase it. In this case it will not achieve any useful purpose, but will merely add to expense. If, as the master found, Mrs F's acceptance of an independent receiver is only justified on the basis that it would heal the rift, then there can be no justification for departing from her earlier expressed desire to appoint Mr A as her attorney, and his lack of suitability is not made out. I do not read Dr X's report as indicating a preference by Mrs F for an independent receiver in any event, but rather as a reluctant acceptance of such, if no other way can be found of resolving her children's differences. It seems to me that to remove a chosen attorney because of hostility from a sibling or other relative, in the absence of any effective challenge to his competence or integrity, should require clear evidence either that the continuing hostility will impede the proper administration of the estate or will cause significant distress to the donor which would be avoided by the appointment of a receiver. Neither of these conditions is satisfied by the evidence in this case.

[21] I will therefore allow the appeal and order registration of the power of attorney. There will be no order as to the costs of the appeal. I will leave the master's order for costs undisturbed. As things stand, there are no grounds for making a s 8 direction in relation to the provision of an inventory and accounts. It is, however, very much in Mr A's interests to provide this information and to furnish accounts to Mrs B on a regular basis. If this is done, it will, one hopes, remove much of the ill-feeling between them and restore the position to what it would have been, had Mrs B adhered to the position she had reached prior to the medical visitor's report.

Appeal allowed.

[G8]

RE J (ENDURING POWER OF ATTORNEY)

[2009] EWHC 436 (Ch)

CHANCERY DIVISION

LEWISON J12 March 2009

Enduring Power of Attorney – Whether attorneys can be appointed in the alternative or in succession

J executed a form of enduring power of attorney (before the Mental Capacity Act 2005 came into force) which purported to appoint his wife as his sole attorney but provided that if she predeceased him or became unable to act or to continue to act then in the alternative he appointed A, B and C jointly and severally to be his attorneys. The Public Guardian contended that this was not a valid enduring power of attorney because the appointment of alternative or successive attorneys was prohibited.

Held – the enduring power of attorney was valid. Provided a power makes clear whether, in the event that they exercise the power, the attorneys must exercise it jointly or jointly and severally such a power may appoint attorneys in the alternative or in succession (see paras [25], [26]).

Statutory provisions considered

Powers of Attorney Act 1971, ss 1, 5

Enduring Powers of Attorney Act 1985

Mental Capacity Act 2005, ss 16–20, Sch 4

Enduring Powers of Attorney (Prescribed Form) Regulations 1990 (SI 1990/1376), regs 2(1)–(3), 4

Cases referred to in judgment

E (Enduring Powers of Attorney), Re [2001] Ch 364, [2000] 3 WLR 1974, [2000] 1 FLR 882, [2000] All ER 1004, ChD

Scottish & Newcastle plc v Raguz [2008] UKHL 65, [2008] 1 WLR 2994, [2009] 1 All ER 763, HL

Nicole Sandells for the applicant

David Rees for the respondent

Cur. Adv. Vult.

LEWISON J:

[1] On 9 February 2007 Mr J executed a document, the relevant parts of which read:

'I . . . appoint my wife [W] to be my Attorney for the purposes [of the] Enduring Powers of Attorney Act 1985 but if she shall have predeceased me or shall be unable to act or to continue to act as my Attorney whether registered or unregistered then in the alternative I appoint my son [A] and my son [B] and my son [C] jointly and severally to be my attorney(s) for the purpose of the Enduring Powers of Attorney Act 1985 with general authority to act on my behalf in relation to all my property and affairs.'

[2] This form was based on Form 147 in volume 31 of the Encyclopaedia of Forms and Precedents (LexisNexis). The short but difficult question is: is it a valid enduring power of attorney?

[3] The Public Guardian, represented before me by Mr David Rees, has taken the view that it is invalid because it purports to appoint attorneys in the alternative. Even if that is not prohibited, a valid enduring power of attorney cannot appoint successive attorneys where (as here) the power contemplates that one of the attorneys might begin to act before subsequently ceasing to act. Mr J's wife, W, represented before me by Ms Sandells, says that there is nothing wrong with the enduring power, and that now that Mr J has ceased to have mental capacity the power should be registered. She considers herself unable to act, and wishes the power to be registered so that her sons can act as Mr J's attorneys.

[4] At common law a power of attorney is an agency created by deed. The agency thus created was terminated by the subsequent loss of mental capacity of the donor of the power. This consequence of loss of mental capacity was widely perceived as a defect in the law; and the Law Commission proposed changing it. Following the publication of both a working paper and a report (*The Incapacitated Principal*, Law Com No 122 (HMSO, 1983)) the Enduring Powers of Attorney Bill was introduced into Parliament and was enacted as the Enduring Powers of Attorney Act 1985.

[5] Since 1 October 2007, when the Mental Capacity Act 2005 came into force, it has no longer been possible to create an enduring power of attorney. Now the way of creating a power of attorney which survives the mental incapacity of the donor of the power is by the creation of a lasting power of attorney. However, enduring powers of attorney created before that date continue to have effect. The law applicable to such powers is now contained in Sch 4 to the Mental Capacity Act 2005, which substantially re-enacts the Enduring Powers of Attorney Act 1985. The relevant parts of that Schedule are set out in Appendix 1 to this judgment. One of the main changes, however, is a change in procedure. Before 1 October 2007 the Court of Protection dealt with both the legal and administrative aspects of enduring powers of attorney. Since then the Court of Protection continues to deal with the legal aspects; but the Public Guardian deals with administrative aspects, and in particular the registration of powers.

[6] The essential features of an enduring power of attorney are these:

(i)   an enduring power of attorney is a subspecies of powers of Attorney-Generally (Sch 4, para 1). Thus it must comply with the formalities necessary to create a power of attorney. It follows from this that, unless qualified by a restriction in the instrument itself, an enduring power of attorney will take effect immediately;

(ii)   an enduring power of attorney must comply with additional formalities. These include a requirement that the instrument must be in a prescribed form; and that it must be executed not only by the donor of the power but also by the attorney (Sch 4, para 2);

(iii)   if an instrument appoints more than one person to be an attorney it must state whether they are appointed to act jointly, or jointly and severally (Sch 4, para 20);

(iv)   an enduring power of attorney may contain conditions or restrictions which limit the authority conferred on the attorney by the power (Sch 4, para 3);

(v)   there is no limit to the number of enduring powers that a donor can create; and they may exist concurrently or successively: *Re E (Enduring Powers of Attorney)* [2001] Ch 364, [2000] 3 WLR 1974, [2000] 1 FLR 882, 373E, 1983 and 892 respectively;

(vi)   if the formalities are complied with, an enduring power of attorney will not be revoked by any subsequent mental incapacity of the donor (Sch 4, para 1);

(vii)   as soon as an attorney under an enduring power of attorney has reason to believe that the donor is or is becoming mentally incapable, he must apply to the Public Guardian to register the power (Sch 4, para 4);

(viii) as soon as an attorney under an enduring power of attorney has reason to believe that the donor is or is becoming mentally incapable, he must apply to the Public Guardian to register the power (Sch 4, para 4);

(ix)   once the power has been registered it cannot be revoked without an order of the court; and the donor cannot extend or restrict the scope of the power or give instructions to the attorney (Sch 4, para 15).

[7] Some of these essential features of the scheme call for further comment at this stage. Firstly, the instrument creating the power must be made in the prescribed form. Various forms have been prescribed over the years. The operative parts of the form prescribed by the Enduring Powers of Attorney (Prescribed Form) Regulations 1990 are reproduced as Appendix 2 to this judgment. Regulation 2(1) of those regulations states:

> 'Subject to paragraphs (2) and (3) of this regulation and to regulation 4, an enduring power of attorney must be in the form set out in the Schedule to these Regulations and must include all the explanatory information headed "About using this form" in Part A of the Schedule and all the relevant marginal notes to Parts B and C. It may also include such additions (including paragraph numbers) or restrictions as the donor may decide.'

[8] Thus, subject to the specified provisions, reg 2(1) positively allows the donor to make additions to the prescribed form. Regulation 2(2) deals with certain other aspects of the form of the instrument. In particular there must be excluded one (and only one) of any pair of alternatives. One pair of alternatives is 'jointly' and 'jointly and severally' in Part A of the form. Thus, one of these alternatives must be omitted or deleted. Regulation 2(3) is not relevant for present purposes. Regulation 4 provides:

> 'Where more than one attorney is appointed and they are to act jointly and severally, then at least one of the attorneys so appointed must execute the instrument for it to take effect as an enduring power of attorney, and only those attorneys who have executed the instrument shall have the functions of an attorney under an enduring power of attorney in the event of the donor's mental incapacity or of the registration of the power, whichever first occurs.'

[9] Second, the power may contain conditions or restrictions. There is no limitation on the nature of the conditions or restrictions, except that they must not conflict with anything that the Act positively forbids. A condition may, for instance, be a condition precedent to the coming into operation of the power (eg 'This power shall not be exercisable unless two medical practitioners have certified that I lack mental capacity' or 'This power shall not be exercisable unless I have lacked mental capacity for more than three months'). It may be a restriction on the kind of asset with which the attorney may deal (eg 'This power does not extend to any sale charge or other disposition of land in which I have an interest'); or may place limitations on the manner in which the attorney may deal with a particular asset (eg 'My attorney may not sell or charge any dwelling in which I reside without the written consent of my spouse').

[10] Third, since there is no limit to the number of enduring powers of attorney that a donor may create a donor may create one enduring power of attorney governing his bank account and another governing his home; or one enduring power of attorney dealing with his property in England, and another dealing with his property in Wales. Given the ability to place temporal conditions or limitations on the operation of an enduring power of attorney it is also possible to create powers which will have alternative operation. Thus a donor may create one power in favour of his wife and

another in favour of his children, the latter being subject to a condition that it is not to come into operation unless his wife disclaims under the first power. The same technique may be used to create enduring powers of attorney that have successive operation. Thus a donor may create one power in favour of his wife and another in favour of his children, subject to a restriction that it is not to come into operation during his wife's lifetime.

[11] Fourth, the duty to apply for registration applies to every enduring power that a donor has created. Thus if the donor has created one power in favour of his wife, and another in favour of his children, the latter not to come into force during his wife's lifetime, both his wife and his children must apply to register their respective powers if they have reason to believe that the donor has become or is becoming mentally incapable. As mentioned, the Public Guardian must register the power unless one of the specified grounds of objection is made out. It is not a specified ground of objection that a condition precedent to the operation of the power has not yet been satisfied. In the case just mentioned, therefore, the Public Guardian must register both powers. The Act makes provision for what is called 'qualified registration'. This arises only under paras 20(6) and (7) of Sch 4. It applies only in the case of joint and several attorneys where a ground of objection is made out against one or more of them but not all. In such a case the entry in the register must be stamped with the words:

'The registration of this enduring power of attorney is qualified and extends to [name of attorney(s) not affected by the objection] only as the attorney(s) of [name of donor].'

[12] There is no other power to make a qualified registration. Once a power of attorney has been registered, the Public Guardian must keep a copy of it; and return the original to the person or persons who applied for registration.

[13] Fifth, because the duty to register only arises when the donor has become or is becoming mentally incapable, the power of attorney is likely to be scrutinised for the first time by the Public Guardian at a time when, if it is invalid as an enduring power of attorney because of some technical defect, it is probably too late for the donor to execute another one. This, in turn, means that the donor's affairs will have to be administered by a deputy, which is likely to be more cumbersome, more expensive and more public than administration by attorneys of the donor's choice. One of the important policies of the Mental Capacity Act 2005 is that, so far as possible consistent with his best interests, a protected person's wishes should be taken into account and respected.

[14] It is common ground that, as mentioned, a donor can achieve the effect of successive attorneyships by executing two or more separate enduring powers of attorney. If a donor can achieve a particular legal effect by two pieces of paper, why can he not achieve the same effect by one? The Public Guardian says that the answer to this question is that para 20(1) of the Schedule precludes that. Paragraph 20 says:

'(1)   An instrument which appoints more than one person to be an attorney cannot create an enduring power unless the attorneys are appointed to act—
(a)   jointly, or
(a)   jointly and severally.'

[15] The Public Guardian says that anyone named by the instrument as a present or future attorney (even if the power to act as attorney is contingent on satisfaction of a condition precedent) is an 'attorney' both for the purposes of the requirement to execute the instrument creating the enduring power of attorney and also for the purposes of para 20. Thus the instrument must state whether all those named are to act jointly or whether all those named are to act jointly and severally. There can be no mix and match, because one of the two alternatives must be deleted or omitted; otherwise the instrument will not satisfy the statutory requirement that it must be

made in the prescribed form. It, therefore, follows that a purported enduring power conferring power of attorney on W (acting alone) or failing her on A, B and C (acting jointly) or a purported power conferring power of attorney on W (acting alone) and subsequently to A, B and C (acting jointly and severally) fails to comply with para 20(1) and thus cannot be an enduring power of attorney.

[16] It is fair to say that opinions have differed over the years about whether this is the correct construction of the section. I was shown articles in legal publications by the Assistant Public Trustee which suggested that it was not; booklets issued for public guidance by the Public Trust Office and the Public Guardianship Office which also suggested that it was not. On the other hand, I was also shown extracts from textbooks which suggested that it was. None of these publications gave reasons for their conclusions so they were of limited assistance. I was also shown examples of powers of attorney in the form of that in the present case which the Court of Protection had registered as valid enduring powers of attorney. In those cases the registration was qualified by stamping the power of attorney with words to the effect that it took effect only as regards particular named attorneys.

[17] In support of the Public Guardian's submission Mr Rees relied on passages from the Law Commission's report that preceded the Enduring Powers of Attorney Act 1985. In para 4.92 of their report the Commission said:

'Thus the EPA donor might prefer to appoint not just, say, his spouse as attorney but his children as well. He might create a joint power so that all the attorneys would have to act together or a joint and several power which would be operated by all or any of them.'

[18] Footnote 214 to that paragraph said:

'We do not recommend that an instrument should be able to provide for successive EPAs; that is, one or more attorneys who would replace the original attorney or attorneys should he or they cease to act. Our main reason for this is that the benefit to be gained by including successive EPAs in our proposals would be out of all proportion to the complexity that such powers would create in relation to some of the more detailed areas of our scheme. In any event, successive EPAs are rendered largely unnecessary because a joint and several EPA would permit the continuation of the EPA in the event of one of the attorneys ceasing to act. It would, however, be possible to create the effect of successiveness by a donor granting EPAs in separate instruments so that the authority of an attorney under one power could commence only upon the termination of the authority of an attorney under another power.'

[19] There are two points to be made about this footnote. Firstly, it is only a footnote. It did not form part of the main text of the report, let alone the report's recommendations. Second, it is not a positive recommendation one way or another. Still less is it a firm prohibition. Nevertheless it deserves consideration, if only to try to see what complexities the Law Commission had in mind (which the report itself did not identify).

[20] Mr Rees summarised the difficulties or complexities as follows:

(i) The prescribed forms would have needed to be differently worded. This is, in essence, the point that the donor must choose between the two alternatives of 'joint' on the one hand or 'joint and several' on the other. There are, I think, at least two answers to this. Firstly, although regulations made under and contemporaneously with an Act of Parliament are part of the context, they cannot add to or detract from the proper interpretation of the Act. A recent example of a case in which the draftsman of a prescribed form misunderstood the Act under which the form was prescribed is *Scottish & Newcastle plc v Raguz*

[2008] UKHL 65, [2008] 1 WLR 2994. Second, reg 2(1) expressly permits additions to the prescribed form. I cannot see why that would prevent a donor of an enduring power of attorney from specifying two sets of attorneys, provided that it is made clear in relation to each set whether they are to act jointly on the one hand or jointly and severally on the other.

(ii)   There would be additional complexity in the registration process. Mr Rees put it thus.

'The legislation and rules would need to address the question of how such a power should be registered. If an instrument appoints A to act alone and then B and C to act jointly and severally, how is registration to be effected? Does the court simply register the instrument without qualification? If so, if an objector wishes to object to the registration of B as being unsuitable, does he need to object at this stage even though B cannot act whilst A is acting? If the registration is unqualified, how is a person dealing with B or C to know whether A's powers have come to an end?'

The answer to the first question is that since a qualified registration may only be made in very limited circumstances (of which this is not one) the registration must be unqualified. To that extent I can see no warrant for the practice developed by the Court of Protection of registering such powers as enduring powers of attorney but with qualifications. But the consequential problem that Mr Rees identifies is equally present if (as the Law Commission expressly contemplated) the donor executes two enduring powers of attorney, one in favour of A and the other a contingent power in favour of B and C. Both must be registered as soon as the donor loses mental capacity. An objector would have to object to the registration of the power in favour of B and C, even though B and C cannot act while A is acting. If the objection fails, then both enduring powers would be registered without qualification. So far as third parties are concerned, once again the same problem exists even if two powers are created by two separate instruments. Indeed the problem may be even worse for third parties, because there will be two separate original instruments, each bearing the Public Guardian's stamp. If there is only one instrument, the attorney acting for the time being will have the original. In addition, since non-fulfilment of a condition precedent contained in an instrument is not a valid ground for objection, a third party may still face the difficulty of knowing whether a conditional registered enduring power of attorney has come into operation, whichever construction of the Act is the right one.

(iii)   Mr Rees did suggest in oral argument that the fact that there was only one original stamped instrument might present a problem if the instrument purported to appoint successive attorneys. But that problem (if it is a problem) would exist in any case where more than one attorney is appointed to act concurrently, and (if it is a problem) would be particularly acute where the attorneys may act jointly and severally, because one attorney, acting alone, might not have the original instrument. And, as I have pointed out, the existence of only one original stamped instrument may itself guard against potential abuse of a registered enduring power of attorney where two or more powers would otherwise have been registered without qualification.

[21] I do not think that any other alleged complexities were identified. On examination they turn out either not to be complexities at all, or, to the extent that they are complexities they are complexities which are at any rate not increased by doing in one piece of paper what everyone accepts you can do in two. To the extent, then, that the Law Commission's view was based on complexities, it was not, in my judgment, a soundly based one. No other reason of policy was suggested for reaching the conclusion that what you can do by two pieces of paper you cannot also do by one. Such policy reasons as there are seem to me to point to the conclusion that it does not matter whether you use one piece of paper or two.

(i)   the principal policy objective of the 1985 Act was to abolish the common law rule that a power of attorney was revoked by the subsequent mental incapacity of the donor. The construction for which W contends does not undermine that policy;

(ii)   at common law, the appointment of successive attorneys is valid, and where the meaning of an Act is doubtful, Parliament is taken to have intended the least alteration of the common law;

(iii)   the Mental Capacity Act 2005, in which the current provisions are to be found, has as one of its policy objectives the encouragement of autonomy of protected persons. The Law Commission's report, on which the 1985 Act was based, also stressed the importance of the principle that people should be able to make such arrangements for the management of their affairs as they please;

(iv)   the Schedule should not be construed so as to leave technical traps for donors of powers, where the effect of falling into the trap may be irremediable once the problem has been identified;

(v)   there can be no doubt that a will appointing alternative or successive trustees would be valid to deal with the management of the affairs of a deceased person after his death. Why should it be any different for the management of his affairs during his lifetime?

[22] So it seems to me that the question is whether para 20 can be construed so as to permit the execution of an enduring power of attorney in the form of the one in this case.

[23] In addition to the general considerations that I have mentioned above, I am also struck by the clear prohibition contained in para 2(6) of the Schedule which says:

> 'A power of attorney which gives the attorney a right to appoint a substitute or successor cannot be an enduring power.'

[24] Given the clarity of this provision, it would be surprising if a similar prohibition applied to the donor of the power by the oblique and indirect drafting of para 20.

[25] The persons named in the instrument as actual or contingent attorneys are, I think, within the meaning of the word 'attorney' as used in para 20 of the Schedule. So para 20 is engaged where an enduring power purports to appoint successive attorneys. Ms Sandells, for W, submitted that para 20 should be construed as meaning that a valid enduring power of attorney must state whether, *in the event that they exercise the power*, the attorneys must exercise it jointly or jointly and severally. That, she said, was the correct meaning to be given to the phrase 'appointed to act'. Provided that an instrument makes this clear it complies with para 20. If and insofar as additional words need to be added to the prescribed form to repeat the designation of each set of attorneys, this is permitted by reg 2. In my judgment, this is a permissible reading of para 20, and I hold that it is the correct one. I further consider that this construction applies whether the power of attorney purports to appoint attorneys in the alternative

or in succession. What is important is that the power makes clear whether, while they are acting, the attorneys are to act jointly, or jointly and severally.

[26] I conclude, therefore, that the power of attorney in the present case is a valid enduring power of attorney and must be registered without qualification.

[27] My conclusion on this question makes it unnecessary for me to consider whether there is a power of severance and, if so, what limits (if any) there are upon its exercise. Since that is a difficult question, I prefer to leave it for a case in which it arises.

Order accordingly.

Solicitors: *Moody and Woolley* for the applicant
The Public Guardian

EASON RAJAH QC

Barrister

APPENDIX 1

Enduring power of attorney to survive mental incapacity of donor

1(1) Where an individual has created a power of attorney which is an enduring power within the meaning of this Schedule—

(a)   the power is not revoked by any subsequent mental incapacity of his,
(b)   upon such incapacity supervening, the donee of the power may not do anything under the authority of the power except as provided by subparagraph (2) unless or until the instrument creating the power is registered under paragraph 13, and
(c)   if and so long as paragraph (b) operates to suspend the donee's authority to act under the power, section 5 of the Powers of Attorney Act 1971 (c. 27) (protection of donee and third persons), so far as applicable, applies as if the power had been revoked by the donor's mental incapacity,

and, accordingly, s 1 of this Act does not apply.

Characteristics of an enduring power of attorney

2(1) Subject to subparagraphs (5) and (6) and paragraph 20, a power of attorney is an enduring power within the meaning of this Schedule if the instrument which creates the power—

(a)   is in the prescribed form,
(b)   was executed in the prescribed manner by the donor and the attorney, and
(c)   incorporated at the time of execution by the donor the prescribed explanatory information.

(2) In this paragraph, 'prescribed' means prescribed by such of the following regulations as applied when the instrument was executed—

(a)   the Enduring Powers of Attorney (Prescribed Form) Regulations 1986,
(b)   the Enduring Powers of Attorney (Prescribed Form) Regulations 1987,
(c)   the Enduring Powers of Attorney (Prescribed Form) Regulations 1990,

(d)   the Enduring Powers of Attorney (Welsh Language Prescribed Form) Regulations 2000.

(3) An instrument in the prescribed form purporting to have been executed in the prescribed manner is to be taken, in the absence of evidence to the contrary, to be a document which incorporated at the time of execution by the donor the prescribed explanatory information.

(4) If an instrument differs in an immaterial respect in form or mode of expression from the prescribed form it is to be treated as sufficient in point of form and expression.

(5) A power of attorney cannot be an enduring power unless, when he executes the instrument creating it, the attorney is—

(a)   an individual who has reached 18 and is not bankrupt, or
(b)   a trust corporation.

(6) A power of attorney which gives the attorney a right to appoint a substitute or successor cannot be an enduring power.

(7) An enduring power is revoked by the bankruptcy of the donor or attorney.

(8) But where the donor or attorney is bankrupt merely because an interim bankruptcy restrictions order has effect in respect of him, the power is suspended for so long as the order has effect.

(9) An enduring power is revoked if the court—

(a)   exercises a power under sections 16 to 20 in relation to the donor, and
(b)   directs that the enduring power is to be revoked.

(10) No disclaimer of an enduring power, whether by deed or otherwise, is valid unless and until the attorney gives notice of it to the donor or, where paragraph 4(6) or 15(1) applies, to the Public Guardian.

Scope of authority etc. of attorney under enduring power

3(1) If the instrument which creates an enduring power of attorney is expressed to confer general authority on the attorney, the instrument operates to confer, subject to—

(a)   the restriction imposed by subparagraph (3), and
(b)   any conditions or restrictions contained in the instrument,

authority to do on behalf of the donor anything which the donor could lawfully do by an attorney at the time when the donor executed the instrument.

Duties of attorney in event of actual or impending incapacity of donor

4(1) Subparagraphs (2) to (6) apply if the attorney under an enduring power has reason to believe that the donor is or is becoming mentally incapable.

(2) The attorney must, as soon as practicable, make an application to the Public Guardian for the registration of the instrument creating the power.

(3) Before making an application for registration the attorney must comply with the provisions as to notice set out in Part 3 of this Schedule.

(4) An application for registration—

(a)   must be made in the prescribed form, and
(b)   must contain such statements as may be prescribed.

Registration of instrument creating power

13(1) If an application is made in accordance with paragraph 4(3) and (4) the Public Guardian must, subject to the provisions of this paragraph, register the instrument to which the application relates.

(2) If it appears to the Public Guardian that—

(a)   there is a deputy appointed for the donor of the power created by the instrument, and
(b)   the powers conferred on the deputy would, if the instrument were registered, to any extent conflict with the powers conferred on the attorney,

the Public Guardian must not register the instrument except in accordance with the court's directions.

(3) The court may, on the application of the attorney, direct the Public Guardian to register an instrument even though notice has not been given as required by paragraph 4(3) and Part 3 of this Schedule to a person entitled to receive it, if the court is satisfied—

(a)   that it was undesirable or impracticable for the attorney to give notice to that person, or
(b)   that no useful purpose is likely to be served by giving him notice.

(4) Subparagraph (5) applies if, before the end of the period of 5 weeks beginning with the date (or the latest date) on which the attorney gave notice under paragraph 5 of an application for registration, the Public Guardian receives a valid notice of objection to the registration from a person entitled to notice of the application.

(5) The Public Guardian must not register the instrument except in accordance with the court's directions.

(6) Subparagraph (7) applies if, in the case of an application for registration—

(a)   it appears from the application that there is no one to whom notice has been given under paragraph 5, or
(b)   the Public Guardian has reason to believe that appropriate inquiries might bring to light evidence on which he could be satisfied that one of the grounds of objection set out in subparagraph (9) was established.

(7) The Public Guardian—

(a)   must not register the instrument, and
(b)   must undertake such inquiries as he thinks appropriate in all the circumstances.

(8) If, having complied with subparagraph (7)(b), the Public Guardian is satisfied that one of the grounds of objection set out in subparagraph (9) is established—

(a)   the attorney may apply to the court for directions, and

(b)   the Public Guardian must not register the instrument except in accordance with the court's directions.

(9) A notice of objection under this paragraph is valid if made on one or more of the following grounds—

(a)   that the power purported to have been created by the instrument was not valid as an enduring power of attorney,

(b)   that the power created by the instrument no longer subsists,

(c)   that the application is premature because the donor is not yet becoming mentally incapable,

(d)   that fraud or undue pressure was used to induce the donor to create the power,

(e)   that, having regard to all the circumstances and in particular the attorney's relationship to or connection with the donor, the attorney is unsuitable to be the donor's attorney.

(10) If any of those grounds is established to the satisfaction of the court it must direct the Public Guardian not to register the instrument, but if not so satisfied it must direct its registration.

(11) If the court directs the Public Guardian not to register an instrument because it is satisfied that the ground in subparagraph (9)(d) or (e) is established, it must by order revoke the power created by the instrument.

(12) If the court directs the Public Guardian not to register an instrument because it is satisfied that any ground in subparagraph (9) except that in paragraph (c) is established, the instrument must be delivered up to be cancelled unless the court otherwise directs.

Register of enduring powers

14 The Public Guardian has the function of establishing and maintaining a register of enduring powers for the purposes of this Schedule.

Effect and proof of registration

15(1) The effect of the registration of an instrument under paragraph 13 is that—

(a)   no revocation of the power by the donor is valid unless and until the court confirms the revocation under paragraph 16(3);

(b)   no disclaimer of the power is valid unless and until the attorney gives notice of it to the Public Guardian;

(c)   the donor may not extend or restrict the scope of the authority conferred by the instrument and no instruction or consent given by him after registration, in the case of a consent, confers any right and, in the case of an instruction, imposes or confers any obligation or right on or creates any liability of the attorney or other persons having notice of the instruction or consent.

Application to joint and joint and several attorneys

20(1) An instrument which appoints more than one person to be an attorney cannot create an enduring power unless the attorneys are appointed to act—

(a) jointly, or
(b) jointly and severally.

(2) This Schedule, in its application to joint attorneys, applies to them collectively as it applies to a single attorney but subject to the modifications specified in paragraph 21.

(3) This Schedule, in its application to joint and several attorneys, applies with the modifications specified in subparagraphs (4) to (7) and in paragraph 22.

(4) A failure, as respects any one attorney, to comply with the requirements for the creation of enduring powers—

(a) prevents the instrument from creating such a power in his case, but
(b) does not affect its efficacy for that purpose as respects the other or others or its efficacy in his case for the purpose of creating a power of attorney which is not an enduring power.

(5) If one or more but not both or all the attorneys makes or joins in making an application for registration of the instrument—

(a) an attorney who is not an applicant as well as one who is may act pending the registration of the instrument as provided in paragraph 1(2),
(b) notice of the application must also be given under Part 3 of this Schedule to the other attorney or attorneys, and
(c) objection may validly be taken to the registration on a ground relating to an attorney or to the power of an attorney who is not an applicant as well as to one or the power of one who is an applicant.

(6) The Public Guardian is not precluded by paragraph 13(5) or (8) from registering an instrument and the court must not direct him not to do so under paragraph 13(10) if an enduring power subsists as respects some attorney who is not affected by the ground or grounds of the objection in question; and where the Public Guardian registers an instrument in that case, he must make against the registration an entry in the prescribed form.

(7) Subparagraph (6) does not preclude the court from revoking a power insofar as it confers a power on any other attorney in respect of whom the ground in paragraph 13(9)(d) or (e) is established; and where any ground in paragraph 13(9) affecting any other attorney is established the court must direct the Public Guardian to make against the registration an entry in the prescribed form.

(8) In subparagraph (4), 'the requirements for the creation of enduring powers' means the provisions of—

(a)   paragraph 2 other than subparas (8) and (9), and
(b)   the regulations mentioned in para 2.

Joint attorneys

21(1) In paragraph 2(5), the reference to the time when the attorney executes the instrument is to be read as a reference to the time when the second or last attorney executes the instrument.

(2) In paragraph 2(6) to (8), the reference to the attorney is to be read as a reference to any attorney under the power.

(3) Paragraph 13 has effect as if the ground of objection to the registration of the instrument specified in subparagraph (9)(e) applied to any attorney under the power.

(4) In paragraph 16(2), references to the attorney are to be read as including references to any attorney under the power.

(5) In paragraph 16(4), references to the attorney are to be read as including references to any attorney under the power.

(6) In paragraph 17, references to the attorney are to be read as including references to any attorney under the power.

Joint and several attorneys

22(1) In paragraph 2(7), the reference to the bankruptcy of the attorney is to be read as a reference to the bankruptcy of the last remaining attorney under the power; and the bankruptcy of any other attorney under the power causes that person to cease to be an attorney under the power.

(2) In paragraph 2(8), the reference to the suspension of the power is to be read as a reference to its suspension insofar as it relates to the attorney in respect of whom the interim bankruptcy restrictions order has effect.

(3) The restriction upon disclaimer imposed by paragraph 4(6) applies only to those attorneys who have reason to believe that the donor is or is becoming mentally incapable.

APPENDIX 2

Part B: To be completed by the 'donor' (the person appointing the attorney(s))

Don't sign this form unless you understand what it means

Please read the notes in the margin which follow and which are part of the form itself.

Donor's name and address.

I _____

of _____

Donor's date of birth.

born on _____

appoint _____

See note 1 on the front of this form. If you are appointing only one attorney you should cross out everything between the square brackets. If appointing more than two attorneys please give the additional name(s) on an attached sheet.

of _____

● [and _____

of _____

Cross out the one which does not apply (see note 1 on the front of this form).

● jointly
● jointly and severally]

to be my attorney(s) for the purpose of the Enduring Powers of Attorney Act 1985

Cross out the one which does not apply (see note 2 on the front of this form). Add any additional powers.

● with general authority to act on my behalf
● with authority to do the following on my behalf:

If you don't want the attorney(s) to have general power, you must give details here of what authority you are giving the attorney(s).

in relation to

Cross out the one which does not apply.

● all my property and affairs:
● the following property and affairs:

Part B: continued

Please read the notes in the margin which follow and which are part of the form itself.
If there are restrictions or conditions, insert them here; if not, cross out these words if you wish (see note 3 on the front of this form).

• subject to the following restrictions and conditions:

If this form is being signed at your direction:-
• the person signing must not be an attorney or any witness (to Parts B or C).
• you must add a statement that this form has been signed at your direction.
• a second witness is necessary (please see below).

Your signature (or mark).

I intend that this power shall continue even if I become mentally incapable

I have read or have had read to me the notes in Part A which are part of, and explain, this form.

Signed by me as a deed _____
and delivered

Date.
Someone must witness your signature.
Signature of witness.

Your attorney(s) cannot be your witness. It is not advisable for your husband or wife to be your witness.

on _____

in the presence of _____

Full name of witness _____

Address of witness _____

_____

_____

A second witness is only necessary if this form is not being signed by you personally but at your direction (for example, if a physical disability prevents you from signing).
Signature of second witness.

in the presence of _____

Full name of witness _____

Address of witness _____

_____

_____

5

Part C: To be completed by the attorney(s)

Note:

1. This form may be adapted to provide for execution by a corporation

2. If there is more than one attorney additional sheets in the form as shown below must be added to this Part C

Part C: To be completed by the attorney(s)

Note: 1. This form may be adapted to provide for execution by a corporation
2. If there is more than one attorney additional sheets in the form as shown below must be added to this Part C

Please read the notes in the margin which follow and which are part of the form itself.

Don't sign this form before the donor has signed Part B or if, in your opinion, the donor was already mentally incapable at the time of signing Part B.

If this form is being signed at your direction:–
• the person signing must not be an attorney or any witness (to Parts B or C).
• you must add a statement that this form has been signed at your direction.
• a second witness is necessary (please see below).

Signature (or mark) of attorney.

I understand that I have a duty to apply to the Court for the registration of this form under the Enduring Powers of Attorney Act 1985 when the donor is becoming or has become mentally incapable.

I also understand my limited power to use the donor's property to benefit persons other than the donor.

I am not a minor

Signed by me as a deed _____
and delivered

Date.

on_____

Signature of witness.

The attorney must sign the form and his signature must be witnessed. The donor may not be the witness and one attorney may not witness the signature of the other.

in the presence of _____

Full name of witness_____

Address of witness _____

_____

_____

A second witness is only necessary if this form is not being signed by you personally but at your direction (for example, if a physical disability prevents you from signing).
Signature of second witness.

in the presence of _____

Full name of witness_____

Address of witness _____

_____

_____

6

756

RE FH; M V PUBLIC GUARDIAN

[2009] COPLR

COURT OF PROTECTION

SENIOR JUDGE LUSH22 June 2009

Property and affairs – Enduring power of attorney – Validity – Whether signatures of witnesses required if witnesses had given handwritten depictions of their names

The witnesses to the execution by the donor and attorney of an enduring power of attorney wrote their full names and addresses in their own handwriting but did not place their signatures above their names and addresses. An application was made to determine the validity of the enduring power of attorney.

Held: The handwritten depictions of the witnesses' names were sufficient proof of their identity and intent as to constitute signatures and the difference between a handwritten name and an actual signature was immaterial (see para [13]).

Per curiam: the court would have decided otherwise if the name and addresses of the witnesses had been typed (see para [13]).

Statutory provisions considered

Mental Capacity Act 2005

Court of Protection Rules 2007 (SI 2007/1744), r 89

Enduring Powers of Attorney (Prescribed Form) Regulations 1990 (SI 1990/1376), reg 3(1)

Cases referred to in judgment

J (Enduring Power of Attorney), Re [2009] EWHC 436 (Ch), [2010] 1 WLR 210, [2009] COPLR Con Vol 753, [2009] 2 All ER 1051, ChD

SENIOR JUDGE LUSH:

[1] This is an application to the court to determine a question as to the validity of an enduring power of attorney.

The facts

[2] H (the donor) was born in 1924 and lives in South Wales.

[3] On 7 September 2001 he executed an enduring power of attorney in which he appointed his son (the attorney) to be his attorney.

[4] A solicitor witnessed the donor's signature and another witness witnessed the attorney's signature on 14 October 2001.

[5] Both witnesses wrote their full names and addresses in their own handwriting but, unfortunately, omitted to place their signatures above their names and addresses.

[6] On 17 January 2008 the attorney applied to the Public Guardian to register the instrument, but the Public Guardian refused to register it because he regarded it as defective and technically invalid.

[7] On 23 July 2008 the solicitor who had acted as witness applied to the court 'to confirm the validity of the enduring power of attorney so that an application to register the same can be finalised'. A witness statement made by him on the same day accompanied the application.

[8] Following a directions order made by me on 6 October 2008, further statements were filed by the Public Guardian on 27 February 2009 and the attorney on 24 March 2009.

Decision

[9] The material regulation in this case is the Enduring Powers of Attorney (Prescribed Form) Regulations 1990, reg 3(1) of which provides that:

'an enduring power of attorney in the form set out in the Schedule to these Regulations shall be executed by both the donor and the attorney, although not necessarily at the same time, in the presence of a witness, but not necessarily the same witness, who shall sign the form and give his full name and address.'

[10] In this case, although the other formalities were properly complied with, the two witnesses did not sign the form as such, although they did write their full names and addresses in their own handwriting. Technically, the execution of the instrument was imperfect, but it seems harsh to make ruling that, as a consequence, the instrument is invalid.

[11] In my judgment, whenever possible, the donor should be given the benefit of the doubt when any question arises as to the construction of an enduring power of attorney or lasting power of attorney. In the recent case of *Re J (Enduring Power of Attorney)* [2009] EWHC 436 (Ch), [2010] 1 WLR 210, [2009] COPLR Con Vol 753, Lewison J observed, at para [13], that:

' . . . because the duty to register only arises when the donor has become or is becoming mentally incapable, the power of attorney is likely to be scrutinised for the first time by the Public Guardian at a time when, if it is invalid as an enduring power of attorney because of some technical defect, it is probably too late for the donor to execute another one. This, in turn, means that the donor's affairs will have to be administered by a deputy, which is likely to be more cumbersome, more expensive and more public than administration by attorneys of the donor's choice. One of the important policies of the Mental Capacity Act 2005 is that, so far as is possibly consistent with his best interests, a protected person's wishes should be taken into account and respected.'

[12] One of the common features between enduring powers of attorney and lasting powers of attorney is that the legislation provides that if an instrument differs in an immaterial respect in form or mode of expression from the prescribed form it is to be treated as sufficient in point of form and expression. The difference between the two regimes, however, is that, in the case of lasting powers of attorney the arbiter of immaterial differences is the Public Guardian, whereas in the case of enduring powers of attorney the arbiter is both the Court of Protection and the Public Guardian.

[13] Having regard to all the circumstances, I am satisfied that the handwritten depictions of the witnesses' names are sufficient proof of their identity and their intent as to constitute signatures, and that the difference between an autograph or handwritten name and an actual signature is immaterial. I would have decided otherwise if, as is sometimes the case, the full names and addresses of the witnesses had been typed. I am not satisfied that the power purported to have been created by the instrument is not valid as an enduring power of attorney, and accordingly I direct the Public Guardian to register the instrument.

[14] A separate order accompanies this judgment, which was made without holding an attended hearing. Pursuant to r 89 of the Court of Protection Rules 2007 any person who is aggrieved by my decision may apply within 21 days of the date on which the order was served, to have it set aside.

Order accordingly.

EASON RAJAH QC

Barrister

[G10]

RE A; D V B

[2009] COPLR

COURT OF PROTECTION

SENIOR JUDGE LUSH **21 July 2009**

Practice and procedure – Enduring power of attorney – When duty to consult regarding P's welfare arises – Whether failure by donee of unregistered EPA to consult sibling rendered her unsuitable to be attorney

P had three children; B, C, and D. P had granted B an enduring power of attorney (EPA). B applied to register the EPA. D opposed the registration on the ground that B was unsuitable to act as P's attorney as (a) she had failed to consult him about P's welfare pursuant to s 4(7)(b) of the Mental Capacity Act 2005; and (b) she had failed in a meaningful way to engage in a debate about the diagnosis of P's mental disorder.

Held – The EPA would be registered –

(1) It would not have been in P's best interests for B to consult D in circumstances where the consultation would have been unduly onerous, futile or would have served no useful purpose (see para [27]).

(2) B's authority under the EPA extended only to P's property and financial affairs and not to medical decisions, and she was consulted about medical decisions in her capacity as one of her mother's next of kin rather than as attorney under an EPA (see para [29]).

(3) Having regard to all the circumstances, the court was not satisfied that B was unsuitable to act as P's attorney. There was no effective challenge to B's competence or integrity. There was no evidence that hostility between B and D would impede the administration of P's estate or cause significant distress to her. There was relatively little for B to do as attorney and she was doing so perfectly competently. P's wishes, which carried considerable weight, were that B was to be her attorney. B was more likely to be aware of P's day to day needs than any third party and significant and disproportionate costs would be incurred if a professional deputy were appointed (see paras [31]–[34]).

Statutory provisions considered

Enduring Powers of Attorney Act 1985

Mental Capacity Act 2005, ss 4(7)(b), 42(4)(a), Sch 1, 4

Court of Protection Rules 2007 (SI 2007/1744), rr 89, 201, Part 9, PD 9H, 23A

Cases referred to in judgment

F (Enduring Power of Attorney), Re [2004] 3 All ER 277, [2004] EWHC 725 (Ch), ChD

W (Enduring Power of Attorney), Re [2000] Ch 343, [2000] 3 WLR 45, [1999] 2 FLR 1163, [2000] 1 All ER 175, ChD

W (Enduring Power of Attorney), Re [2001] Ch 609, [2001] 2 WLR 957, [2001] 1 FLR 832, [2001] 4 All ER 88, CA

SENIOR JUDGE LUSH:

[1] This is an application for the court to reconsider an order it made on 15 April 2009 without holding an attended hearing. The rule governing applications of this kind is r 89 of the Court of Protection Rules 2007.

The background

[2] Mrs A was born in 1921 and lives in Staffordshire. Her husband died in 1996. She has three children:

- a daughter, B, who was born in 1945, is a retired chemistry teacher and lives in the same town as Mrs A;
- a daughter C, who was born in 1953 and lives in Shrewsbury; and
- a son, D, who was born in 1949 and lives in Leicestershire.

[3] On 11 September 1996 Mrs A signed an enduring power of attorney (the EPA), in which she appointed her daughter, B, to be her sole attorney, with general authority to act on her behalf in relation to all her property and affairs. Lloyds & Cooper, Solicitors, Leominster, drew up the document, and a partner in that firm witnessed her signature.

[4] On 19 August 2008 B applied to the Office of the Public Guardian (the OPG) to register the EPA, having given notice of her intention to apply for registration, form EP1PG, to the donor personally, and to C and D.

The objection

[5] On 6 September 2008 D wrote to the OPG, although not to the Court of Protection, objecting to the registration of the EPA on the ground that, having regard to all the circumstances, the attorney is unsuitable to be the donor's attorney. He summarised his arguments as follows:

'In detail the evidence that B is unsuitable is that:
- B made decisions about mother's welfare without involving me. B decided that mother should go into a home and did not involve me in that decision. Also there is evidence that B had mother psychologically tested without involving me in the decision.
- B did not act in mother's best interests by not attempting to get a diagnosis from a private psychiatrist or psychotherapist in November 2005.
- B did not act in mother's best interests by failing to engage in a debate about a diagnosis. I repeatedly attempted to initiate a debate about diagnosis and B did not engage in the debate in a meaningful way.
- B did not act in mother's best interests by failing to act on information supplied by mother's community psychiatric nurse. In a meeting at mother's house the CPN agreed with me both that it is difficult to distinguish between dementia and depression and that depression is treatable. B knew this and did not act on this information and get an immediate diagnosis.
- B did not act in mother's best interests by failing to engage in a debate about dementia. I stated several times why I thought that dementia could not possibly be the reason mother needed constant attention.
- B did not respond to a letter from me reviewing various comments she had made. In my opinion this is not the act of a responsible and trustworthy person.'

Application by the Public Guardian under r 201

[6] Rule 201 of the Court of Protection Rules 2007 and Practice Direction 23A apply where (as in this case):

- the Public Guardian has received a notice of objection to the registration of an EPA, and is therefore prevented by para 13(5) of Sch 4 to the Act from registering the instrument except in accordance with the court's instructions; but

- no application has been made to the Court of Protection.

[7] After a specified period of time has elapsed, the Public Guardian can apply to the court for directions. The time limit is 5 weeks from the date, or the latest date, on which the attorney gave notice of his intention to apply for registration (form EP1PG) to the donor's relatives.

[8] If anyone wishes to participate in the proceedings, they have 21 days to file an application using form COP8. The application must be made in accordance with the detailed requirements for application relating to the registration of enduring powers of attorney, which are set out in Practice Direction 9H, accompanying Part 9 of the Rules. If no such application is made, the court will proceed to consider the matter in response to the Public Guardian's request and will give directions to the Public Guardian.

[9] On 15 March 2009 the Public Guardian made a request to the court on form COP 17 for directions relating to the registration of the power pursuant to r 201 of the Court of Protection Rules 2007 and on the following day the court sent D notice of the Public Guardian's application.

[10] There appeared to have been no response within 21 days from D, and on 15 April 2009 I made an order directing the Public Guardian to register the EPA as soon as was reasonably practicable. The Public Guardian registered the EPA on 7 May 2009.

[11] However, on 28 March 2009 D had, in fact, submitted to the court an application relating to the registration of an enduring power of attorney (form COP8) and a witness statement (form COP24). Neither of these documents had been placed on the court file when I made the order on 15 April 2009.

[12] In form COP8, D stated:

'B is not a suitable person to be appointed sole EPA because she failed to take action that might have led to a proper diagnosis and a treatment direction for Mrs A, and she has excluded me from decisions made about Mrs A.
I would like the children of Mrs A, B, C and D to be jointly appointed EPA in such a way that all three must agree on each and every decision concerning Mrs A, and that any financial transaction must bear all three signatures.'

[13] In his witness statement of 28 March 2009, which I do not propose to repeat here, D reiterated and elaborated upon the arguments he had put forward in his letter to the OPG dated 6 September 2008.

Application for reconsideration

[14] On 5 May 2009 D applied to the court to reconsider its decision of 15 April 2009. In the application form he said:

'The order directing the Public Guardian to register an enduring power of attorney is void because an application relating to the registration was received by the court within the 21 days stipulated and was not considered by the court when it should have been.'

[15] On 9 June 2009 I made a directions order setting out a timetable for the filing of evidence, and listing the application for hearing on 21 July 2009. In response to those directions two witness statements were filed: one from B, dated 7 July 2009, and the other from C, dated 8 July 2009. I shall quote C's statement, because it is both brief and to the point. She said:

'At a time when she was fully aware of her choices my mother, Mrs A, set up an enduring power of attorney in order to protect her best interests were she to become unable to so for herself.

Perhaps this court case is a reflection of why my mother chose to ask one of us to have enduring power of attorney and I believe my sister, as the eldest child, the person who has had most contact with my mother and whom my mother trusts, is a suitable choice.

My sister's attention to my mother's needs and more importantly her love and care have been constant and in abundant supply, particularly since the death of my father and my mother's move to Staffordshire, where my sister also lives. No mother could have asked for more and I have no hesitation in asking that my mother's wishes be adhered to.

To dispute this at this point is disrespectful and certainly not in my mother's best interests.'

[16] The hearing took place on Tuesday, 21 July 2009 and was attended by B and her husband; C, and D and his wife. It lasted from 2.00 to 3.40 pm.

Mrs A's estate

[17] Mrs A owns a half-share of her house in Staffordshire. Each of her three children owns a one-sixth share of the net proceeds of sale. The property is presently unoccupied and is said to be worth in the region of £360,000.

[18] She has a portfolio of investments, which is managed by Barclays and is worth approximately £100,000. Her total assets, excluding her share of the house, are said to be worth between £200,000 and £250,000.

The law relating to the unsuitability of an attorney

[19] This was an objection to the registration of the instrument on the ground that, having regard to all the circumstances, and in particular the attorney's relationship to or connection with the donor, the attorney is unsuitable to be the donor's attorney. This ground can be found in para 13(9)(e) of Sch 1 to the Mental Capacity Act 2005.

[20] The burden of proof in cases where there is an objection to the registration of an EPA was considered by Mr Jules Sher QC in *Re W (Enduring Power of Attorney)* [2000] 3 WLR 45, [1999] 2 FLR 1163. At 47G and 1165 respectively he said:

'The important point to notice is that the onus of establishing any of the grounds set out in subsection (5) is firmly laid on the shoulders of the objectors. Under subsection (6) it is only if the ground concerned is established to the satisfaction of the court that the court can refuse to register the power. Indeed, if the ground is so established the court must refuse. The contrary position is expressly made equally emphatic: if the court is not so satisfied it "shall register the instrument to which the application relates".'

[21] A brief explanation of the meaning of the expression 'unsuitable to be the donor's attorney' can be found in para 4.29 of the Law Commission's report, *The Incapacitated Principal* Cmnd 8977 (1983), which was published in 1983, and led to the enactment of the Enduring Powers of Attorney Act 2 years later. The Law Commissioners said:

'This needs some explanation. It would amount in effect to a criticism of the donor's choice of attorney. But we would not wish this ground to be sustained merely because the attorney was not the sort of person that a particular relative would have chosen. It is our wish that the donor's choice of attorney should carry considerable weight. Thus, for example, a mother might be content to appoint her son as her EPA attorney despite being aware of a conviction for theft. We would not want her choice of attorney to be upset simply because a particular relative would not want the son to be his attorney. The question should be whether the particular attorney is suitable to act as attorney for the particular donor. In short, the court should examine carefully all the circumstances, particularly the relationship between the donor and the attorney.'

[22] In *Re W (Enduring Power of Attorney)* [2000] 3 WLR 45, [1999] 2 FLR 1163, Jules Sher QC considered the concept of unsuitability in the context of hostility between various members of the donor's family. At 51–52 and 1169–1170 respectively he said as follows:

'The second ground of unsuitability is the hostility between the three children. The Master concluded that that fact alone rendered any one of them unsuitable to be Mrs W's attorney. In my judgment such hostility may well have such consequences but it all depends upon the circumstances. For example, had the estate of Mrs W been complex and had it required strategic decisions in relation to its administration, one would expect the attorney to have had to consult and work with her siblings in relation to the administration. In such circumstances the evident hostility between them would impact adversely on the stewardship of the attorney, no matter who was at fault in creating the hostility in the first place.

But in this case the estate is simple. I asked counsel what the position was and was told that there are the following assets:

(1)   a portfolio of investments of a value (as at 23 December 1998) of £211,189;

(2)   £20,000 in premium bonds;

(3)   a life policy (written in trust) of £30,000.

As to the outgoings there is the cost of the nursing home at some £2000 a month, and then, simply, the need for a modest amount to cover a regular hairdo, telephone bills and the like. And, of course, on the income side there is the old age pension.

In other words, there is nothing of any significance left to be done. The assets are under proper control. The income simply needs to be fed through to the nursing home. The evidence is that this has been done by Mrs X very efficiently. She has indicated more than once that she has never intended to charge for her services under the power of attorney and she does not intend to do so. Against this, if the Public Trustee were to come in, there would be an appointment fee and an annual fee of between £2,350 and £3,600 pa. If a solicitor were appointed the total cost would be likely to be somewhat less than that.

It seems to me that it is not right to say that (irrespective of the background) hostility of the kind we have seen in this case between the children renders any one of them unsuitable to be Mrs W's attorney. In this case the hostility will not impact adversely on the administration. It would, in my judgment, be quite wrong to frustrate Mrs W's choice of attorney in this way. Whether it is or is not a good idea for a parent in Mrs W's position, when such hostility exists, to appoint one child alone as attorney is another question. But Mrs W did so and, on the evidence, did so knowing of the hostility. That is her prerogative and in my judgment, when the hostility does not interfere with the smooth running of the administration, the court should not interfere of the ground of unsuitability.'

[23] Mr Sher's decision was subsequently upheld by the Court of Appeal, which was reported as *Re W (Enduring Power of Attorney)* [2001] 2 WLR 957. It was later applied by Arden J in *Re F (Enduring Powers of Attorney)* [2000] 3 WLR 1974, [2001] 1 FLR 832, and Patten J in *Re F (Enduring Power of Attorney)* [2004] EWHC 725 (Ch), [2004] 3 All ER 277. In *Re F*, at 284f, Patten J said:

'It seems to me that to remove a chosen attorney because of hostility from a sibling or other relative, in the absence of any effective challenge to his competence or integrity, should require clear evidence either that the continuing hostility will impede the proper administration of the estate or will cause significant distress to the donor which would be avoided by the appointment of a receiver. Neither of these conditions is satisfied by the evidence in this case.'

Decision

[24] There were two main themes to D's objections. First, that the attorney had failed to consult with him, but was under a duty to consult him, by virtue of s 4(7)(b) of the Mental Capacity Act 2005, as someone who is interested in his mother's welfare. And secondly, that the attorney had somehow made or got hold of the wrong diagnosis, as a result of which the donor had either been inappropriately treated, or had failed to receive the appropriate treatment at the material time.

[25] In support of his argument relating to his right to be consulted under s 4(7)(b), D quoted the following passages from the Mental Capacity Act 2005 Code of Practice: paras 5.13, 5.32, 5.37, 5.49, 5.51, 5.54, 5.61, 5.64, and 5.67. In para 5.54, for

example, the code states 'everybody's views are equally important – even if they do not agree with each other'. And para 5.61 says that decision-makers cannot simply impose their own views, 'They must have objective reasons for their decisions – and must be able to demonstrate them. They must be able to show they have considered all relevant circumstances and applied all elements of the best interests checklist'. D claims that the attorney fails to engage in any proper debate, and merely expresses an opinion, without justifying it or explaining the reasons for it.

[26] As I suggested to D at the hearing, whereas attorneys acting under a lasting power of attorney have a duty 'to have regard to' the Code of Practice (Mental Capacity Act 2005, s 42(4)(a)), attorneys acting under an enduring power of attorney do not, largely because it was considered inappropriate to impose the requirements of the new legislation retrospectively on them. Nevertheless, his arguments raise interesting issues regarding the extent to which any attorney should reasonably be expected to consult with someone who, in all reality, will treat every single issue upon which he is likely to be consulted as a bone of contention or stumbling-block. In such circumstances, the process of consultation would become both burdensome and futile.

[27] The first line of s 4(7) provides that any best interests decision-maker 'must take into account, if it is practicable and appropriate to consult them, the views of' various categories of individuals. In my judgment, where any attempt at consultation will inevitably be unduly onerous, futile, or serve no useful purpose, it cannot be in P's best interests, and it would be neither practicable nor appropriate to embark on that process in the first place.

[28] D's reference to para 5.32 demonstrates the other main strand of his argument. It says that, 'the decision-maker must consider the range of treatment options available to work out what would be in the person's best interests'. He asserts that his sister failed in a meaningful way to engage in a debate about the diagnosis of their mother's mental disorder.

[29] Again, as I suggested to D at the hearing, the authority of an attorney acting under an EPA extends only to property and financial affairs, and B would technically be acting ultra vires if she were to make any medical treatment decisions on her mother's behalf. She is, of course, entitled to be consulted by the health care professionals, but in her capacity as one of her mother's next of kin, rather than as the attorney acting under an EPA. Nor, of course, did she make any diagnosis herself, but was content to be guided in this respect by the health care professionals, such as Mrs A's GP, her community psychiatric nurse, and the consultant psycho-geriatrician. In a letter addressed 'to whom it may concern' dated 7 July 2009, the GP stated that:

> 'On review of her notes there are entries regarding memory loss as far back as 2001. It seems these became worse in 2003 and she was referred to the Community Mental Health Team who made an assessment of her mental state. She had a reasonably good score only indicating a mild deficit in short term memory and as this was not impeding her normal day to day functioning she was discharged from the clinic. She was subsequently referred back to the Community Mental Health Team in 2005 and from there she was referred to see a consultant psychiatrist specialising in elderly people. She was started on anti-dementia medication and this suggests that the diagnosis was an Alzheimer's type dementia. This is confirmed on a later letter from the Community Mental Health Team and they continued to follow up Mrs A with regular tests of her mental function.'

[30] Somewhat disingenuously D submitted that B should have obtained a second opinion from a clinician in the private sector. I say 'disingenuously' because it became patently clear during the hearing that Mrs A was unwilling to see any doctor, and that five or six people had to urge her to see an NHS doctor in the first place.

[31] In my judgment, there has been no effective challenge to B's competence or integrity, and I am satisfied with her general response to the objections that were

levelled against her by her brother. There is no evidence that any hostility between B and D will impede the proper administration of Mrs A's estate. Nor is there any evidence that the hostility between them is causing significant distress to Mrs A, which can only be alleviated by the appointment of an independent deputy. The evidence is that D has had very limited contact with his mother during the last 12 years, and has not visited her at all since November 2008.

[32] As in *Re W*, there is relatively little for B to do as attorney, other than keep the house tidy, secure and fully insured; pay any outgoings on it; liaise with the investment managers, and consider their advice; make sure that the nursing home bills are paid on time, and see that provision is made for new clothes and any additional comforts that Mrs A may require from time to time.

[33] If I were to uphold D's application, it would be necessary to appoint a deputy to act on his mother's behalf. This would be both unnecessary and undesirable because:

- it would mean that a third party would have to be brought into manage the donor's financial affairs, whereas her daughter has been managing them perfectly competently for a substantial period of time already;
- B visits her mother two or three times a week, and is more likely to know what she requires or needs on a day-to-day basis than any third party;
- as the Law Commission stated in *The Incapacitated Principal*, the donor's wishes in terms of her choice of attorney should carry considerable weight, and I was impressed by the manner in which C touched upon this important issue in her witness statement; and
- significant and disproportionate costs would be incurred if an independent third party, such as a solicitor, were to be appointed as deputy.

[34] Having regard to all the circumstances, therefore, I am not satisfied that the attorney is unsuitable to be the donor's attorney, and I confirm the order made on 15 April 2009 directing the Public Guardian to register the EPA.

[35] There is no need for me to adjudicate on costs because neither of the parties was legally represented.

Order accordingly.

EASON RAJAH QC

Barrister

[G11]

RE COLLIS

COURT OF PROTECTION

SENIOR JUDGE DENZIL LUSH 27 October 2010:

Property and affairs – Lasting Power of Attorney – capacity to grant a Lasting Power of Attorney

The court considered whether Mr Collis had the requisite mental capacity to make a lasting power of attorney. The certificate provider had been his solicitor, and gave time function specific evidence of his capacity, whereas a Court of Protection Medical Visitor had retrospectively assessed his capacity, which was not time specific. The court held the requisite capacity was as in *Re K Re F* [1988] 1 All ER 358, with some adaptation due to the change in type of power, and the donor would need to understand the power must be registered with the Public Guardian before use, it could be revoked at any time provided he had mental capacity, and his attorneys had to follow the principles as set out in s 1 and act in his best interests as set out in s 4 of the Mental Capacity Act 2005.

Statutory provisions considered

Mental Capacity Act 2005, ss 1(1), 1(3), 2, 3(1), 3(3), 3(4) and Schedule 1, paragraph 2(1)(a)

Cases referred to in judgment

Re K, Re F [1988] 1 All ER 358

Birkin v Wing (1890) 63 LT 80

Re W (Enduring Power of Attorney) [2000] 3 WLR 45

Re W (Enduring Power of Attorney) [2001] 1 FLR 832, CA

This was an application to the court to direct the Public Guardian to cancel the registration of a Lasting Power of Attorney ('LPA') on the ground that the power created by the instrument was not valid as an LPA because the donor lacked capacity to create an LPA. The following extract is taken from the judgment of the Senior Judge given on 27 October 2010:

The law relating to capacity to create an LPA

Section 1(2) of the Mental Capacity Act 2005 states that, 'A person must be assumed to have capacity unless it is established that he lacks capacity.'

Section 1(3) of the Act provides that, 'A person is not to be treated as unable to make a decision unless all practicable steps to help him do so have been taken without success.'

Section 2 defines 'people who lack capacity' as follows:

(1)   For the purposes of this Act, a person lacks capacity in relation to a matter if at the material time he is unable to make a decision for himself in relation to the matter because of an impairment of, or a disturbance in the functioning of, the mind or brain.

(2)   It does not matter whether the impairment or disturbance is permanent or temporary.

Section 3(1) sets out the following guidance on the meaning of the phrase 'unable to make a decision':

'For the purposes of section 2, a person is unable to make a decision for himself if he is unable:
(a)   to understand the information relevant to the decision,
(b)   to retain that information,
(c)   to use or weigh that information as part of the process of making the decision, or
(d)   to communicate his decision (whether by talking, using sign language or any other means).'

A person is not to be regarded as unable to understand the information relevant to a decision if he is able to understand an explanation of it given to him in a way that is appropriate to his circumstances (using simple language, visual aids or any other means) (s 3(2)).

The fact that a person is able to retain the information relevant to a decision for a short period only does not prevent him from being regarded as able to make the decision (s 3(3)).

The information relevant to decisions in general includes information about the reasonably foreseeable consequences of:

- deciding one way or another (s 3(4)(a)), or
- failing to make the decision (s 3(4)(b)).

Accordingly, in the context of creating an LPA, the relevant information should include information about the consequences of not executing an LPA.

The information specifically relevant to the execution of an LPA includes the prescribed information about the purpose of the instrument and the effect of LPA (Sch 1, para 2(1)(a)), which is contained in the prescribed form of LPA itself.

The degree of understanding required to create an enduring power of attorney was considered by Mr Justice Hoffmann (as he then was) in *Re K, Re F* [1988] 1 All ER 358. At page 363c–f, in the penultimate paragraph of his judgment, he said:

'Finally, I should say something about what is meant by understanding the nature and effect of the power. What degree of understanding is involved? Plainly one cannot expect that the donor should have been able to pass an examination on the provisions of the 1985 Act. At the other extreme I do not think it would be sufficient if he realised only that it gave cousin William power to look after his property. Counsel as amicus curiae helpfully summarised the matters which the donor should have understood in order that he can be said to have understood the nature and effect of the power: first, if such be the terms of the power, that the attorney will be able to assume complete authority over the donor's affairs; second, if such be the terms of the power, that the attorney will in general be able to do anything with the donor's property which the donor could have done; third, that the authority will continue if the donor should become mentally incapable; fourth, that if he should be or become mentally incapable, the power will be irrevocable without confirmation by the court. I do not wish to prescribe another form of words in competition with the explanatory notes prescribed by the Lord Chancellor, but I accept the summary of counsel as amicus curiae as a statement of the matters which should ordinarily be explained to the donor whatever the precise language which may be used and which the evidence should show he has understood.'

At page 362j Mr Justice Hoffmann said:

'I think that my conclusions are in accordance with what appears to be the general policy of the 1985 Act. In practice it is likely that many enduring powers of attorney will be executed when symptoms of mental incapacity have begun to manifest themselves. These symptoms may result in the donor being mentally incapable in the statutory sense that she is unable on a regular basis to manage her property and affairs. But, as in the case of Mrs F, she may execute the power with full understanding and with the intention of taking advantage of the Act to have her affairs managed by an attorney of her choice rather than having them put in the hands of the Court of Protection. I can think of no reason of policy why this intention should be frustrated.

However, in my judgment, the criteria in Re K, Re F are not entirely applicable to LPAs because of some fairly major differences between EPAs and LPAs, and would need to be adapted in several respects. For example:
- the donor would need to understand that the LPA cannot be used until it is registered by the Public Guardian. This is simply not the case with an EPA.
- one would expect to see a change of emphasis between the creation of an LPA for personal welfare and an LPA for property and affairs; and, in particular, the donor would need to understand that the attorney under an LPA for personal welfare can only make decisions that the donor is contemporaneously incapable of making for him- or herself.
- unlike an EPA, the donor can revoke an LPA at any time when he or she has the capacity to do so (section 19(2)), without the court having to confirm the revocation.

- the authority conferred by an LPA, unlike an EPA, is subject to the provisions of the Mental Capacity Act 2005 and, in particular, sections 1 (the principles) and section 4 (best interests) (section 9(4)).
- the statutory definition of capacity in section 3(4) of the Act specifically requires the donor to be aware of the foreseeable consequences of not executing an LPA, whereas in Re K, Re F Mr Justice Hoffmann did not include an understanding of the effect of not making an EPA in his summary of the matters which should ordinarily be explained to the donor.'

The burden of proof in cases where there is an objection that a power of attorney is not valid on account of the donor's incapacity was considered by Jules Sher QC in *Re W (Enduring Power of Attorney)* [2000] 3 WLR 45. At page 47G he said:

'The important point to notice is that the onus of establishing any of the grounds set out in subsection (5) is firmly laid on the shoulders of the objectors. Under subsection (6) it is only if the ground concerned is established to the satisfaction of the court that the court can refuse to register the power. Indeed, if the ground is so established the court must refuse. The contrary position is expressly made equally emphatic: if the court is not so satisfied it "shall register the instrument to which the application relates."'

Very few cases in these days turn on the onus of proof. In ordinary civil litigation the judge is nearly always able to form a view on a balance of probabilities as to whether an event did or did not happen. But the state of a woman's mind some three years before the court hearing is inherently an issue in respect of which it is quite likely that the judge may not be satisfied either way.

At page 49H he said this:

'I am not satisfied on the evidence that Mrs. W did not have this understanding. This does not mean that I am satisfied that she did have it. The point of this judgment is that this last issue is not the question before me. If, as is the case, I am not satisfied that she lacked the necessary understanding, it seems to me that I am bid by the Act to register the power.'

And, finally, at page 50D Mr Sher QC said:

'To sustain the power, Mrs. X did not have to satisfy [the Master] that Mrs. W understood the nature of the power; the objectors have to satisfy him that she did not.'

Mr Sher's decision was affirmed by the Court of Appeal on 11 December 2000, and is reported at *Re W (Enduring Power of Attorney)* [2001] 1 FLR 832, CA.

Decision

Essentially, the issue is whether I prefer the evidence of the certificate provider (Miss Spurgeon) that Mr Collis had the capacity to create the LPA to that of Dr Ananthanarayanan, the Court of Protection Special Visitor, who hazarded a guess that he may have lacked such capacity at the requisite time.

Mental capacity is 'issue-specific'. This means that the capacity required to create an LPA is not the same as the capacity to manage one's property and financial affairs generally, or the capacity to make a will or a gift or a loan, or the capacity to decide on a certain course of medical treatment, or the capacity to decide whether to live in a residential care home.

Capacity is also 'time-specific', focusing on the particular time when a decision is made or has to be made. The fact that, after just a few minutes, or on the following day, a person cannot recall having made a particular decision doesn't automatically mean that he or she lacked the capacity to make that decision, or that the decision is invalid.

In my judgment, the best evidence in this case is Miss Spurgeon's. I have described it as the 'best' evidence, not because it is of superlative quality (which it isn't), but simply because it is the best evidence that the circumstances of this case will allow. It is the only evidence that is both issue specific and time-specific, insofar as it addresses Mr Collis's specific ability to create an LPA, at a specific time, namely on 3 June 2010 and 9 June 2010.

Miss Spurgeon is an experienced solicitor of ten years' admission, and is familiar with the professional and ethical standards and safeguards that one needs to take into account when assessing whether an elderly person is capable of entering into a transaction of this kind. Her opinion is neither woolly nor equivocal. She was satisfied that Mr Collis understood the nature and effect of the LPA when he signed it. Dr Ananthanarayanan's opinion has the major disadvantage of being retrospective, and is thus neither time-specific nor issue specific.

I accept that it may seem unusual for the court to prefer the evidence of a solicitor to that of an experienced medical practitioner on what prima facie seems to be a clinical decision. However, this is not without precedent, and in *Birkin v Wing* (1890) 63 LT 80, for example, the judge preferred the evidence of a solicitor, who considered that his client was mentally capable of entering into a particular contract, to that of a doctor who said that he lacked capacity.

It is more than likely that Mr Collis was incapable of managing his property and affairs in a general sense in June 2009, but that doesn't mean that he was incapable of executing an LPA. This is precisely what Mr Justice Hoffmann envisaged when he said that:

> 'In practice it is likely that many enduring powers of attorney will be executed when symptoms of mental incapacity have begun to manifest themselves. These symptoms may result in the donor being mentally incapable in the statutory sense that she is unable on a regular basis to manage her property and affairs.'

In the circumstances, therefore, I am not satisfied that Mr Collis lacked the necessary understanding to create the LPA, and I dismiss the application.

For what it is worth, even if I had declared that the LPA was invalid for lack of capacity at the time of its creation, I would – without hesitation – have appointed [the attorney under the LPA instrument] as Mr Collis's deputy. There is clear evidence from various sources that it has been consistently Mr Collis's wish that [she] should manage his affairs whilst he is incapacitated. There is nothing irrational, impracticable or irresponsible about these wishes, and, as far as I can see, there would be no detrimental effect for him in implementing them.

[G12]

RE J

[2011] COPLR

COURT OF PROTECTION

HER HONOUR JUDGE HAZEL MARSHALL QC

(SITTING AS A NOMINATED JUDGE OF THE COURT OF PROTECTION)
6 December 2010

Property and affairs – Lasting Power of Attorney – Capacity of donor to execute – Power of joint and several attorneys to act independently of each other – Whether LPA should be revoked on the basis of conduct of attorney

E, 89, was the wife of H and the mother of G and SC. SC was married to C. There was a major family rift between (a) E and G who lived in the former family home and (b) SC, C, and H, who now lived in a private residential home. Several sets of proceedings were litigated between the parties during the course of 2009 and 2010. In January 2009 E executed a Lasting Power of Attorney (LPA) in favour of B and K who were partners in the firm of solicitors representing her. C applied for the appointment of a property and affairs deputy for E. He challenged the validity of the LPA on the grounds that E lacked capacity to make it at the time of its execution. In the alternative he asserted that the LPA should be revoked because the chosen attorneys were unfit to hold the appointment. This allegation was based on alleged unprofessional conduct by K in the conduct of proceedings on behalf of E, the allegedly excessive legal costs of the attorneys' firm, and alleged conflicts of interest arising in respect of such costs.

Held:

(1) The court was perfectly satisfied, and not just on the balance of probabilities, that E had capacity to execute the LPA at the time of its execution and that the LPA was valid (see paras [31], [55]).

(2) One of two joint and several attorneys could act alone even if the other attorney did not or could not act. The renunciation by B of his appointment as attorney under the LPA did not affect its validity as regards conferring powers on K (see paras [60]–[64]).

(3) In deciding whether to revoke a Lasting Power of Attorney under s 22(3)(b) of the Mental Capacity Act 2005, the court can consider any past behaviour or apparent prospective behaviour by the attorney, but, depending on the circumstances and gravity of any offending behaviour found, it can then take whatever steps it regards as appropriate in P's best interests (this only arising if P lacks capacity), to deal with the situation, whether by revoking the power or by taking some other course. In the circumstances of this case the court would not revoke the LPA and any lingering concerns the court had would be dealt with by giving appropriate directions to K (see paras [77], [176]–[177], [183]–[184]).

Per curiam: No one can be obliged to submit to a psychiatric examination under the Mental Capacity Act against their wishes: see Mental Capacity Act Code of Practice, at para 4.59. It is no part of a legal adviser's duty to seek to persuade or to pressurise his client to submit to a psychiatric examination against his wishes, nor to refuse to act if the client does not wish to do so. His duty is to explain to the client the relative advantages of doing or not doing so, and then to take, and act on, the client's instructions. If the client's wishes are known and clear, it may even be the legal adviser's duty to protect the client from the obvious pressure that the mere force of suggestion or request from the court may create.

Statutory provisions considered

Senior Courts Act 1981, s 9

Trusts of Land and Appointment of Trustees Act 1996

Mental Capacity Act 2005, ss 13(5)(b), (6)(a), (7)(b), 22(2)(a), (3)(a), (b), (4)(b), 23(2)(a), (3)(c)

Civil Procedure Rules 1998 (SI 1998/3132)

The applicant appeared in person

Dr Paul McCormick for the respondent

Cur. Adv. Vult.

HER HONOUR JUDGE HAZEL MARSHALL QC:

Introduction

[1] At the end of the hearing on 23 November I stated my intention, in the interests of speed, to produce an outline judgment only, and to give a fuller reasoned judgment to follow. In the event, I did not find it satisfactory to produce an outline judgment only. This judgment is therefore my final judgment. It has, however, been produced under some pressure for speed. Although, therefore, I have considered all the material before me and all the many points made to me by both parties, I have not mentioned them all in this judgment. The fact that I do not do so does not mean that I have not taken them into account. I have mentioned the most obvious matters which have brought about my decisions, and chosen examples where suitable.

[2] This matter concerns the J/C family. Central is E, aged 89, the respondent to this application and the subject of it. She is the wife of H a retired banker who is a year older. She is the mother of G and SC. The applicant is SC's husband, C.

[3] There is a major family rift between, on the one hand E and G (who now lives with her at what was formerly the long time family home) and on the other hand, H (who now lives in a private residential home) and C and SC.

[4] H and E are both frail. I understand that H is wheelchair bound, as is E, who is also doubly incontinent. The County Council provide home care assistance services for E. In addition, G has some mental health problems and, though currently stable, is attended by a community mental health nurse on visits at 3–4 weekly intervals for monitoring and support. There is a dispute as to whether G's diagnosis is more than merely a clinically recognised anxiety state; C contends that previous records show it to be more significant, namely Asperger's syndrome and a personality disorder.

History of the application

[5] C's application was issued in February 2009, although apparently not served on E at the time. He originally sought his own appointment as deputy for E in respect of both welfare matters and her property and affairs. The grounds of his application centre on E's conduct with regard to the family rift, and, in particular, her failure, in mid 2008, to support H when he took steps to require G to move out of the family house (owned by H and E), and instead to assert and carry through a wish to live with G rather than her husband of 65 years, thereafter refusing to see her daughter, son-in-law, and for the most part, her husband as well. This conduct is said by C to be so out of character and irrational that it shows either that E has lost capacity (having taken a succession of hugely unwise decisions) or that she is being manipulated or coerced by G as part of the family feud. Without access to see E, and in the light of previous records of complaints of G acting aggressively, and even violently, towards not only H and C and SC but also towards E herself, C says that he (and his wife and father-in-law) can only maintain their view that E must have lost capacity and that therefore a deputy needs to be appointed for E in her own best interests.

[6] The application for a welfare deputy has since been withdrawn. The application to appoint a property and affairs deputy has been amended to seek the appointment of an independent person to manage E's property and affairs on her behalf, rather than C himself.

[7] The entire application was opposed by E from the outset on the grounds that she did not lack capacity, and that there was no evidence to support any assertion that she did. An attempt by E to have the application struck out, relying on a psychiatric assessment which she had voluntarily undergone to demonstrate her capacity in relation to other proceedings by H concerning the occupation of the family home, failed before the district judge, in September 2009. The Official Solicitor had become involved in the matter and the district judge's order not only directed that the issue of capacity should go on to a full hearing, but also appointed the Official Solicitor as

E's litigation friend in yet other legal proceedings which she had by then brought. E appealed against the district judge's order. The appeal succeeded only on the peripheral point that the latter order exceeded the court's jurisdiction and was premature on any basis. The Official Solicitor was subsequently excused further involvement in the application, after his representatives had made attempts to assist the court by brokering directions between the parties.

[8] Towards the end of the proceedings before the district judge, it had been highlighted on behalf of E that on 7 January 2009, she had executed a Lasting Power of Attorney (the LPA) in favour, jointly and severally, of two partners in the firm of solicitors who were then acting for her, namely McDonald Law Associates, trading and known as Clereys. They were B and K. The LPA had been registered in June 2009. This would prima facie, therefore, render the appointment of a property and affairs deputy for E unnecessary.

[9] In response C sought permission (and was allowed) to amend his application:

(a)   to dispute the validity of the LPA by alleging E's lack of capacity to make one at the time of its execution, and alternatively;

(b)   to ask the court to revoke the LPA on the grounds (in paraphrase) that the chosen Attorneys were, on the evidence, unfit to hold the appointment.

This claim was founded on criticisms of K in particular, citing her alleged unprofessional conduct acting in legal proceedings on behalf of E (both as to the way in which these had been conducted and in 'allowing' E to engage in certain other legal proceedings at all) and the consequent excessive expense and liability to which E had become exposed in costs, and her alleged conflicts of interests with regard to E, in particular because of Clereys being a creditor of E in respect of such legal costs.

Circumstances of this hearing

[10] The application was listed for eventual hearing on 15 November before me for 4–5 days. It in fact took 7 days.

[11] By this time, C, who had originally instructed Mundays and counsel, had been forced by his own mounting costs bill to start to act in person. E, originally represented by Clereys and by counsel, Dr Paul McCormick, had recently dismissed Clereys and changed solicitors to Kingswell Berney Ltd. This was in fact the firm, two of whose partners had provided the necessary certificates of capacity for her when she executed the LPA – a fact which C submitted was further cause for suspicion. At the hearing, Dr McCormick still appeared for E, but with no solicitor in attendance.

[12] Shortly before the hearing there were three further developments. First, as a result of E's dismissal of Clereys, B felt obliged to disclaim his appointment under the LPA. (This decision may have been aided by his exasperation at a previous bizarre allegation from C that he had been told that the doctor who had provided a favourable psychiatric report on E had also been in chambers with a barrister daughter of B, when he had no such daughter.)

[13] Secondly, E's new solicitor took the view that her mental state had recently deteriorated, and it would consequently now be appropriate to seek the appointment of a litigation friend for her. K had not previously thought it appropriate to commence exercising her powers under the LPA, but she too now indicated that she would be minded to do so, but would await the determinations made by me at this hearing.

[14] Thirdly, some 10 days prior to the hearing, I myself visited E by previous arrangement and spoke with her, alone, for just over an hour.

The hearing

[15] C represented himself at the hearing and I record that he did so with commendable application, hard work, research, and resilience, albeit plainly under the disadvantage of having no legal training. He had managed to obtain some assistance in drafting documents from a direct access barrister, and it also emerged at the hearing that he had been able to discuss the presentation of his case with his former solicitors, and had derived some assistance from this.

[16] Dr McCormick represented E with tenacity and a determination to ensure that no point which ought to be made on her behalf was overlooked or glossed over. I also record that in doing so he was scrupulous to discharge the duty of an advocate who is appearing against a litigant in person to draw the attention of the court to points that might be raised on behalf of his opponent and which might otherwise be missed.

[17] At the start of the hearing Dr McCormick applied for the appointment of either K or N (a one time employee of Clereys, known to E but who had since moved on) as litigation friend for E. Both candidates had filed the necessary papers indicating their willingness to act and general ability to fulfil that role. In view of what I had observed on my visit to E, I considered such an application to be necessary and appropriate. I also took the view that because of the allegations against K which were part of the substance of the application hearing, it would be inappropriate to appoint her as E's litigation friend in these proceedings on any basis, and I therefore appointed N. In so doing I rejected the objection of C to either lady so acting, and for the Official Solicitor to be appointed, as being unrealistic, unnecessary and simply prone to cause yet more delay and cost, which was quite unacceptable in the light of the delay which had already regrettably occurred.

The live issues

[18] The remaining issues in the application were, accordingly, the following:

(i) Whether E had capacity to execute the Lasting Power of Attorney of 7 January 2009 at that time.

(ii) If so, whether the renunciation of the power by B nonetheless affected its validity as regards the purported appointment of K.

(iii) If the LPA remains technically valid in favour of K whether the court could and should revoke it on the grounds that K ought to be held to be unfit to be E's attorney on the grounds set out in s 22(3) of the Mental Capacity Act 2005 (which gives the court jurisdiction to revoke a Lasting Power of Attorney).

(iv) If the LPA is not valid as a result of want of capacity on E's part, whether K is a fit and appropriate person to be appointed property and affairs deputy for E, or whether, in the light of the evidence, some other independent person should be so appointed.

(v) Any further consequential orders or directions the court should give, consequent upon the above decisions.

The evidence

[19] I heard oral evidence on the applicant's side from C himself, who had also put in witness statements dated 17 February 2009 and 16 June 2010. I also granted him permission to call late oral evidence from D, a solicitor formerly employed by C's former solicitors, Mundays, with regard to evidence he wished to put forward about K. In the end, unsurprisingly, her oral evidence also extended to evidence of her perceptions of E.

[20] On behalf of E, I heard oral evidence from K, who has herself put in many witness statements in this application (this being indeed one of C's complaints about her

conduct; he says that this has been excessive). As a result of another application to call late evidence, I also heard from a JK, the registered Community Mental Nurse who attends G. He also meets E on his visits and was therefore able to give factual evidence of his perceptions. I admitted this evidence despite its late introduction because I felt it would be helpful to have such up to date evidence from a person both with recent contact with E and experience in the field of mental health, in view of the fact that by the time of the hearing most of the medical psychiatric evidence was historic.

[21] I have also treated what I observed on my visit to E herself as evidence in the matter. I therefore recounted to the parties, at the hearing, my notes of material observations made on my visit. Whilst accepting that I am not a trained psychiatrist, I found this visit to E extremely helpful in enabling me to evaluate the raft of other evidence which I have received. I also briefly encountered G in the course of arriving at and leaving the house, which again helped me place the evidence better in context.

[22] My brief views of the witnesses are as follows. I have no doubt that C, who is plainly an intelligent man, was an honest witness telling me the truth as he saw it. I am also satisfied that he has a genuine underlying affection for E. However, he comes to this application from an entrenched position in the family rift, of support for H (for whom he sees himself as champion) and for his own wife, and of antipathy towards G, and with the unswerving conviction that their views and attitudes are 'right'. Consequently, he struck me as being almost incapable of seeing the situation with any degree of detachment or objectivity. I therefore found it necessary to examine the basis for any assertion which he made very carefully. He was sometimes able to accept the inaccuracy, exaggeration, or just plain implausibility of some of the facts or propositions which he asserted or advanced when pressed for their justification. However, this recognition was sporadic and did not cause him to reconsider his basic attitude in any way. His evidence and argument was thus highly coloured by his mind-set and I approach it with much caution.

[23] I was not greatly impressed with the evidence of D either. It was admitted to introduce alleged recent evidence about K, itself largely hearsay on her part, but on which C wished to rely. However, first, the detail given in her statement turned out not to be entirely accurate, when examined. Secondly, whilst I accept that she was a sincere witness, I formed the view that her evidence was also coloured, first, by the fact that she had obviously formed a very firm pro-client views about the merits of the J/C side of the dispute, secondly, by the fact that she must inevitably have felt chagrined through having been involved in a breach of mediation privilege which had resulted in E successfully bringing High Court proceedings against her client, H, and thirdly, by the fact that she herself was involved in giving evidence to the SRA upon a complaint made by her former firm, Mundays, about K's conduct as solicitor on the opposite side of the various proceedings. D was thus hardly a disinterested witness. I also have some unease about her readiness to indulge, as far as she did, in the detailed and somewhat gossipy conversation with M of which she gave evidence, about a case in which she was no longer professionally involved, and which conversation she then passed on immediately to C and SC. I say this notwithstanding the fact that she had spoken to the ethics department at the SRA and been told (as I am willing to accept) that she had done nothing improper. D's views of K were plainly fixed and adverse, and the fact that they coloured her evidence is illustrated by her admission that she probably told C that K had been dismissed from Clereys for 'gross misconduct', which statement he then relied on as evidence to put to me, when that was not actually true, but somewhat of an embellishment of what had in fact been said. I must look at her evidence carefully in order to identify accurate facts, and must make any judgments about K for myself. D had already done so.

[24] On the other side, JK was an honest and patient witness, with no axe to grind. He was understandably wary, in the light of his medical relationship with G, but in the event, the questions put to him did not appear to pose him any professional difficulty.

He gave evidence in a firm but measured fashion, and I am satisfied that his evidence was reliable, so far as it could go. In regard to E herself, this was, however, rather limited, albeit of general circumstantial usefulness.

[25] K gave evidence in difficult circumstances, having been peripherally involved in a car accident on her way to attend court, in which she and her husband and baby had had a frighteningly narrow escape from injury. She gave evidence with dignity, restraint and courtesy even in the face of some inevitably offensive questions from C and probing questions from the court. She was asked to, and did, explain many of the numerous matters over which she was being criticised, not merely in the court but also in the investigation being currently held by the SRA. I am satisfied that her evidence to me was honest and sincere, and I am also confident that it has been conscientiously given as to accuracy. That does not mean, though, that it might not disclose facts which could either make it appropriate for the court to revoke the LPA or to decline to find her an appropriate deputy for E.

[26] I did not have any evidence oral or otherwise, from SC. This was somewhat surprising. SC's presence looms in the background throughout these proceedings, just as she actually sat in the background behind C throughout. There are many references to SC in the papers which I have seen, and she has certainly played a full and active part in the events of the family rift. Within this, there is evidence of a pattern of behaviour on her part, seeking to lobby, pressure, influence or cajole authorities round to her point of view, including the police, the social services, and (I can say from my own experience) the court, by sending emails direct to the judge without notice to the opposite side. I was told that it was C who had made this application rather than SC – who at first sight would seem more appropriate, as the blood relative – in order to protect her, presumably from cross-examination. At the end of the hearing, after all the evidence was already advanced, C suggested that perhaps I ought to hear from her. Since the decision not to call her originally had been a calculated one, I declined to do so.

[27] Less surprisingly, in view of his age and infirmity, I did not hear from H either. Neither did I receive any evidence from G. Since it was made apparent that he was not going to be called as a witness, I did not read statements by him which had been made in other proceedings and which had found their way into the court papers. Once again, there is a picture of him from the papers in the case, and also from the evidence of JK, which is consistent with his manner when I briefly met him. He is said to suffer from an acute anxiety state, which I infer makes it quite possible that he could behave extremely, or unpredictably, under stress or provocation. There is also strong evidence that he and SC do not get on and have not done for a long time. I am aware that he was convicted of assaulting her, although I am told that he regarded this as wrong and would have appealed, but for the stress that this would cause him and his mother. However, the independent evidence is clear that he has a strong bond with E, and she with him, and has for some time been a devoted carer for her. They also indicate that at present this is a stable situation. E herself told me that they 'understood each other' They had their 'tiffs' but would laugh about it afterwards.

[28] In addition to the oral evidence I had regard to written evidence, and to documents and materials previously introduced in this matter before the district judge and referred to on the appeal, and the further material introduced for the purpose of disposal of this final hearing. Most of the documents and materials are included in:

(a)   the Appeal Bundle previously prepared on behalf of E; and
(b)   the two bundles prepared for this hearing by C.

and reference should be had to these. I record that where it has been sought to place reliance on hearsay statements made in any such documents, I have accorded the statements such weight as I think appropriate, given that they have not been tested by cross-examination.

[29] The following are the most material items. Where the list may not be fully comprehensive, I have listed only the items which I have found most significant or of major impact for my reasoning or my decisions.

(i) Written witness statements comprising in particular:

(a)   statements from S, a community support worker employed by the County Council and who attends E, dated March 2009 and 5 June 2009.

[29A] These were to the broad effect that there was no perception that G was exercising any undue or malign influence over E, and that the living arrangements were apparently in accord with her wishes and were working satisfactorily:

(b)   a statement from W made on 26 March 2009 stating that she was an independent third party who had attended E at the request of K to satisfy herself (which she had done) that E was able to give instructions to solicitors, and that a statement made by E did record her true views.

[29B] It was noted by the County Council that the statement to W by E was less full than her own statement made with the assistance of K, and that therefore perhaps consideration should be given as to whether K had put words in her mouth. However, I am in the end satisfied that the more likely explanation is E's tendency to be reserved with strangers. I am also satisfied that the statement does contain her true views, which she has consistently expressed all along.

(c)   the above statement made by E herself on 25 March 2009, and a further statement made by E on 12 March 2010, in response to my direction that she submit evidence as to how she had come to execute the LPA and to choose the certificate providers for it.

[29C] This was the first time, in my acquaintance with the case, that I received a statement direct from E and not relayed by K.

(d)   a statement from Dr C, a consultant adult psychiatrist, Court of Protection Special Visitor, made on 21 June 2009.

[29D] I place this in the category of factual evidence because he was unable to meet and assess E at a pre-arranged visit on 27 May 2009, owing to her being kept out of the nursing home at which she was then resident by G, and being denied subsequent access. His report deals with these matters, but expressly states that he was unable to form any assessment of capacity whilst nonetheless reporting that in the circumstances, E needed to be regarded as being a vulnerable adult, whose care needs and capacity ought to be assessed. This report therefore goes to welfare matters, and is of only indirect relevance to the issues which I have to decide, as hearsay evidence of the facts which it records.

(e)   Statements from JW made on 15 June 2010 and V made on 16 June 2010.

[29E] These were the two solicitors who had provided certificates of E's capacity at the time of the execution of the LPA, in which, again by my order, they explained in detail how they came to be instructed to do so and the steps they took in order to be able to provide such certificates.

(ii) Written medical evidence as follows:

(f)   Two reports of Dr S, consultant psychiatrist with X Partnership, dated respectively 14 May 2008 and 26 June 2008.

[29F] In the former, Dr S had expressed the view that E had full capacity. In the latter, she had expressed some doubt as to E's then ability to manage her financial affairs.

(g)   A report of Dr A MD FRCP, dated 26 March 2009, which concluded that although E had some impairment of her higher cerebral functions, she had capacity with regard to certain specific matters comprising choice of living arrangements, contact, ability to make her views known, ability to instruct litigation solicitors and ability to appoint an attorney.

(h)   A report on E's capacity made by Professor H DM FRCP, Emeritus Professor of Geriatric Medicine, dated 12 April 2009, (and further answers to questions posed by both 'sides' later on, within these proceedings) obtained for the purpose of other proceedings, namely the proceedings ('the Family proceedings') brought by H in September 2008, seeking an occupation order to require G to leave the family home, and into which E had inevitably (but unwelcomely) been joined.

[29G] The original report considered the same questions as posed to Dr A and reached the same conclusions, with an additional comment that E had capacity to manage her own affairs. However, it, and the additional answers to questions posed, which were equally positive, had apparently not satisfied either His Honour Judge Rylance in the County Court or – and more importantly for present purposes – District Judge Jackson in this court, that there were no capacity issues regarding E, primarily because:

(a)   the report had not clearly addressed the provisions of the new Mental Capacity Act 2005 to the satisfaction of the district judge in principle; and

(b)   she had been concerned at the implications of K having been present when Professor H had interviewed E, both for the possible effect on E and for what she felt it said about Professor H.

[29H] It was apparently not intended to call Professor H, who had given evidence orally before District Judge Jackson. When I expressed my surprise at this, his attendance was lined up for the second or third day of the hearing. However, C indicated that he did not propose to question Professor H, and so he was stood down.

(iii) Papers from the County Council

(i)   Minutes of case conference meetings
        (1)   11 April 2006, 30 May 2006, 10 July 2006
        (2)   20 February 2008, 14 July 2008

[29I] C wished to introduce the Minutes of certain meetings of the adult safeguarding team of the County Council held during 2006 (three meetings) and 2008 (two meetings) which he wished to rely on as evidence showing variously:

(a)   doubt about E's capacity being expressed;

(b)   reports of inappropriate and aggressive behaviour by G; and

(c)   reports of E herself having complained at aggression and even violence by G.

[29J] These documents were lawfully in C's possession through his having been at the relevant meetings. However, E had been at only the very first such meeting. As the Minutes were marked as confidential, C very properly, therefore, made an application to me in advance of the trial to be allowed to use them. The County Council were served with the application, but made no objection if the court wished for production.

[29K] On behalf of E Dr McCormick did object, although mainly just on general principles of privacy. However, I concluded that since the issues with which I was concerned were E's capacity in 2009 and/or currently, the 2008 Minutes might well provide material of useful background relevance. I ordered that C could use those, but not the 2006 Minutes, as I regarded these as too historic to be of an real usefulness, not least because they even pre-dated E's suffering the stroke, in 2007, which was accepted to have caused deterioration in her mental and physical state. I nevertheless told C, who was particularly anxious that I should admit the 2006 Minutes, that if events at the hearing appeared to justify doing so, he could renew his application at the trial itself.

[29L] On the basis that comments made by (I think) JK contradicted comments made at one of the 2006 meetings, whereas JK claimed to have read the relevant files when giving his answers, C did renew that application at the trial. Pragmatically, Dr McCormick did not object again.

[29M] I gave C permission to introduce the relevant Minute, although he then used my permission to claim to introduce all three Minutes. Whilst this was not what I had intended, I was prepared to put this down to a misunderstanding and I admitted all three further documents.

[29N] I have, in consequence, read all five Minutes. I treat them as background material, but I find them to be of no real direct relevance. I should record, as C will otherwise regard it as a serious omission, that a reference to guns having been found in H's room at the care home he was staying at following a visit by E is not a matter to which I attach any relevance for the purpose of these proceedings. It was investigated by the County Council and the police and found to be inconclusive. Whether or not E played any knowing part in this, I would see it as no evidence of her incapacity to appoint an attorney.

[29O] C's eagerness that I should see the 2006 Minutes arises because it is only there that there is any apparently clear reference to any suggestion of E herself complaining of aggressive behaviour by G. However, I did not find these references to be of any great weight or relevance, first because they are reports which tend to refer to 'H and E' together, thus making it unclear how far any such complaint was really an independent complaint by E, secondly, they are untested hearsay, thirdly, they are historic, fourthly, they brought about no significant intervention by the County Council and were not treated as of any significance by them in later more relevant times, and fifthly, they are in any event relevant to welfare issues rather than management capacity, which is what I am concerned with.

(iv)   Independent report of JM

[29P] C also issued (with permission if this were required) a witness summons against the County Council to produce to the court for the purpose of the hearing an independent report into E's case commissioned by them from JM. Dr McCormick did not object to the introduction of this report, considering that it could be useful evidence. It appeared that the report itself must be quite recent.

[29Q] The summons was answered by the council by counsel on the first full day of the hearing. The council was prepared to act as the court directed, but as the report had been prepared for their own purposes, in order to enable them to review, assess and improve their own processes, they wished to redact out of it references to their own internal affairs, which had no bearing on the issues in this hearing. I directed that, on the council's assurance that this was the case, a suitably redacted version of the report should be copied and could be used in evidence.

[29R] The report, although written for the assistance of the County Council, has provided a useful overview from a relatively independent perspective, of the J case, its surrounding circumstances and history and of those involved although it was apparently composed rather earlier than anticipated, namely on 4 January 2010. It contains a good deal of chronological material, charting the material times of both H's and E's residence at the house and in various care homes and hospitals, and pertinent events. In order not to delay production of this judgment, and because of the length it would be, I have not included a chronology in this judgment, but commend JM's report as a useful source of chronological material, noting, but not as a criticism, that due allowance needs to be made for his use of layman's terminology in respect of some legal events.

[29S] Both C and Dr McCormick have drawn my attention to different comments made in it, and I was asked by Dr McCormick to have careful regard to the apparent source of any comment or information made in the Report, and indeed the earlier Minutes, when considering the weight I should attach to it.

(iv) Other documents

[29T] In addition to the above materials, I was shown various letters and communications which are either contained in the bundles to which I have referred (so that I do not propose to list them all) or, in the case of one or two documents, were produced at the hearing. (Particular examples of the latter are an internal court email between judges in the County Court, handed down to the parties in an interim hearing before (I think) His Honour Judge Sleeman in the Family proceedings, and a Position Statement produced on behalf of E by Dr McCormick in mid 2009 and given to those then acting for H).

[29U] I have read these and given them appropriate weight.

(v) Video/picture evidence

[29V] I received a short video of E taken by K for the purpose of demonstrating to District Judge Jackson, at one of the early hearings of this application in mid 2009, that E was expressing a wish not to attend court, and that the letter written to her by the court inviting her to attend had been received by her. It is notable that E is not particularly communicative in this video and it is composed almost entirely of leading questions put to her by K.

[29W] I was also shown photographs produced by C showing a happy picture of H and E on the occasion of their 65th wedding anniversary in June 2008, and on a visit by SC to her mother whilst E was in hospital also during 2008. These were produced in support of his assertion that E had formerly been a happy loving wife and mother to SC, such that her subsequent attitude of refusing to see them was not explicable on any normal basis.

(vi) Judgments

[29X] C wished to rely on judgments given by other judges in the course of other court proceedings. He wished to show me, in particular, criticisms of K's conduct made by:

(i)   District Judge Raeside upon a hearing in the Family proceedings in the County Court on 10 February 2009 in which an injunction was made against G, which had the effect of causing E also to leave the house;

(ii)   His Honour Judge Rylance on the appeal and final determination of the same application on 18 May 2009; and

(iii) District Judge Jackson in her judgment upon the application to strike out these proceedings already referred to, on 15 September 2009.

[29Y] Dr McCormick objected to references to judgments on the grounds that they were not evidence nor binding findings or determinations against either E or K.

[29Z] I had in fact already seen several of these judgments when considering papers in this case previously. I ruled that I would look at the relevant judgments, but made it plain (as I do now) that I apply the usual rules of procedure and evidence to them.

[29AA] I reject any submission that comments made by these judges in respect of K constitute any form of binding finding of fact or res judicata which I am obliged to follow, or even to take persuasive notice of. In my judgment, a comment or criticism made by a judge about a person's conduct, being (as it was in this case) at best a mere obiter dictum (ie not even a finding of fact upon which a judicial determination of a party's rights in issue in the relevant litigation is founded) is evidence only of the fact that that judge held that opinion on the basis of the material then available to him/her.

[29BB] The fact that such opinion has been expressed is therefore only evidence that there was material before the judge which provided a basis for such opinion to be held. In evidential terms the effect of that for present purposes is simply, in my judgment, to draw my attention to the underlying materials known to the judge which caused that opinion to be expressed. It is then for me to examine the evidence of those underlying facts and materials, along with all other relevant evidence available to me, and to form my own judgment of the correct conclusions to be drawn, with regard to the matters which I have to determine (and the other judge did not). This is the approach which I have adopted.

[29CC] As a result, I have looked, where requested by either party, at judgments in previous proceedings but always with the above approach. My conclusions are therefore my own, based on my findings as to underlying relevant facts.

My decisions

[30] Against the above background and on the basis of the above evidence and the arguments advanced by the parties, my decisions on the issues before me, in broad outline, are as follows:

(i) Did E have capacity to execute the Lasting Power of Attorney of 7 January 2009 when she purported to do so?

[31] The test here is whether I am satisfied, on balance of probability that she did. I am in fact perfectly satisfied that she did.

[32] The LPA is regular and regularly obtained on the face of it. Since this is the mechanism laid down by the Mental Capacity Act 2005 in order to guard against exactly the possibility of later question about the capacity of the donor of an LPA, this factor throws the burden onto the challenger, C, to prove on balance of probability that E lacked capacity.

[33] My two primary reasons for the conclusion that he fails to satisfy this burden are, first, the strong preponderance of the medical evidence and, secondly, the strength of the additional detailed evidence about how the LPA came to be executed, provided by K, E herself and the two certificate providers. I find this evidence compelling, and I see nothing in the other direction which goes anywhere near causing me to doubt it.

[34] As to medical evidence, there is none suggesting that E lacked the capacity to appoint an attorney at this time (January 2009) and good and direct evidence that she had this capacity only 2 or 3 months later (March/April 2009 – Dr A and Professor H). Criticisms that the latter, in particular, did not record that he followed the precise precepts of the Mental Capacity Act 2005 do not invalidate his conclusions, or rule them out, and go only to possible weight. In the context of the limited inquiry into E's capacity to appoint an attorney, I find them to carry strong weight. Professor H is, on any basis, an eminent and experienced medical expert in geriatrics.

[35] The only evidence suggesting any medical doubt about E's capacity is Dr S's second report, made much earlier in June 2008. I am told that this was at a time when E was likely to have been shaken by an unwelcome surprise encounter with

police wishing to question her. I accept this, as I find the evidence to be out of line with the other such evidence. In any event, even that evidence deals only with E's capacity to manage her financial affairs, which would require a higher level of capacity than that required to understand the implications of appointing an attorney and a decision to do so. This latter was not considered by Dr S.

[36] The factual evidence about the execution of the power of attorney is full, coherent and (I find) perfectly plausible. I say this in the light of both my own assessment of the evidence about E from relatively independent sources, the factual evidence of the situation in which she was at the time, and my own observations of E, albeit much later and at a time when she admittedly and plainly had some deterioration of capacity, but during which sparks of her behaviour and comments entirely chimed with the impression I had otherwise gained from the above.

[37] As arguments against capacity, C has invoked principally:

(i)   the generality of his own evidence that E had changed inexplicably in 2008 from her previous self;

(ii)   E's failure to submit to a further psychiatric examination after that performed by Professor H as evidence of lack of capacity – largely because of the adverse inference which he said could and should be drawn from the fact that this must (he contends) have involved a breach of the duty of her lawyers to the court to persuade her to do so;

(iii)   that the LPA contained specific directions about a wish to assist G by paying his legal fees in the family disputes, which was either irrational or suspicious;

(iv)   a series of allegedly unwise decisions by E in relation to use of her own money and throwing in her lot with G, and also the extent to which she had incurred fees on pursuing litigation which it was said she could ill afford; and finally

(v)   an assertion that there was a connection between JW, one of the Certificate Providers, and a charity run by Dr McCormick, thrown up by an internet search, which therefore cast suspicion on the independence of the certificate providers and hence the genuineness of the certificates.

[38] None of these points, in my judgment carries any serious weight or casts any real doubt on E's otherwise apparent capacity.

[39] (i) The first is mere general assertion. It does not, in my judgment, amount to any evidence of lack of capacity to make an LPA, but in any event, I do not find the change to be as incomprehensible as C submits.

[40] Dr McCormick points out that this change of attitude occurred just after the point where H, supported by SC and C, issued proceedings to force G out of the home, contrary to E's wishes. Once this, and the apparent importance to her of G's presence and company, is recognised her behaviour becomes entirely explicable as a response to having her wishes either ignored or overridden in something vitally important to her.

[41] I find this explanation entirely convincing. E struck me as a lady who had lived for most of her married life on the basis of deferring to the wishes of other, more forceful, members of her family, especially her husband, so that he, in particular, had become accustomed to assume (although perhaps perfectly benevolently) that she would simply fall in with his wishes. There came a point, however, where a particular matter, namely her dependence on G for care and companionship, became of such importance to her that she was prepared to assert herself to protect it.

[42] This has undoubtedly taken H and C and SC by surprise, an unpleasant surprise, such that they regard it as evidence of E's losing her faculties. As she has sought to assert her wish, and associated wishes, ever more forcefully to get notice taken of them (which is all she can do from her position of immobility and frailty) this has unfortunately simply been regarded by her husband, daughter and son-in-law as even stronger evidence of lack of capacity. I am satisfied, however, that it is no such thing.

[43] I add here, for completeness, that I have not overlooked the fact that it is agreed that as late as June 2009 E met H at one of the court hearings, and they held hands. This is said, by C and D, to be very significant, for showing either that E's antipathy towards living with H is out of character and evidence of incapacity, or that she was otherwise being coerced into that attitude by G. I do not accept this. It has been said by others, and I found support for this on my own visit to E, that whilst she is now almost implacably angry with her daughter and son-in-law for trying to control her life against her wishes, she has more sympathy for H, for whom she is sorry. She indeed said to me that she reckoned he was probably 'kicking himself' for what had happened. A residual affection for H may well therefore remain, but she has made her choice that it is, unfortunately more important to her to have the benefit of care and companionship from G, if she has to choose.

[44] (ii) The second objection is entirely misconceived, and serves to illustrate an underlying thread which I perceive in C's approach, namely that because it might be desirable for others or even objectively desirable in the abstract, that E should do something, her failure to do so must be evidence of lack of capacity.

[45] First, no one can be obliged to submit to a psychiatric examination under the Mental Capacity Act against their wishes: see *Mental Capacity Act Code of Practice*, at para 4.59. Furthermore, for obvious reasons it can be no evidence of incapacity to decline to do so. Anyone of full capacity could quite reasonably regard such a request as intrusive or impertinent.

[46] Secondly, C's conception of a legal adviser's 'first' duty to the court is misconceived. That duty is a duty not to mislead the court, nor to waste the court's, time, not to take bad or improper points, and to assist the court to deal with cases justly, and suchlike, but, subject to such rules of professional conduct towards the court, the legal adviser's duty is to carry out his client's instructions and to do so fully, fearlessly, and to the best of his ability. This is in fact recognised in para 1.02 of the Solicitors' Code of Conduct to which C himself refers elsewhere.

[47] It is no part of a legal adviser's duty to seek to persuade or to pressurise his client to submit to a psychiatric examination against his wishes, nor to refuse to act if the client does not wish to do so. His duty is to explain to the client the relative advantages of doing or not doing so, and then to take, and act on, the client's instructions. If the client's wishes are known and clear, it may even be the legal adviser's duty to protect the client from the obvious pressure that the mere force of suggestion or request from the court may create. Accordingly, the inference which C seeks to draw from E's failure or refusal to undergo another psychiatric examination, namely that this either demonstrates lack of capacity or submission to improper pressure by others, is not an inference which the court can draw.

[48] I add, at this point, that I have not overlooked the evidence of what occurred on the visits of, first, Dr C to E on 27 May 2009 and, secondly, Dr K to E, on 29 May 2009. Each was denied access to her, in the first case by (it is alleged) the expedient of G keeping her away from the nursing home in which she was then living, and in the second by the presentation to Dr K by K of a letter refusing him access to see E. This evidence has to be reviewed in the context of the state of the legal proceedings and suchlike known to E and her advisers at the time of these visits, and the above propositions. It suffices here to say that I am satisfied that what happened does not

support any inference of lack of capacity, relevant or otherwise on E's part, nor any inference of pressure or coercion on her.

[49] I am satisfied that these matters happened because of a genuine and reasoned decision on E's own part that she was not prepared to accede to an unexpected visit by either of these gentlemen, and the steps consequently taken by others, on her behalf, to ensure that her wishes were respected, and not subverted. I do not accept the proposition, which has been latched onto as a result of Dr C's comments, that it must have been G who irresponsibly kept E away from her nursing home at the known time of his visit until late. Having met E, I am satisfied that she would have been herself encouraging him on to do so. Equally, I am satisfied that her refusal to see Dr K, and deploying K to convey that message, was a perfectly rational decision. I remind myself that E was and is immobile, and quite literally unable to shut the door in any unwelcome visitor's face for herself, even if she might wish to.

[50] (iii) The third point – the direction as to payment of G's and her own legal fees – will not support the weight which C seeks to attach to it. I do not see it as irrational of E to have included such a direction, either at all, or without including other directions. The direction is only guidance for the attorney in any event. I see no force at all in C's suggestion that, if it were rational to include such a direction at all, one would also expect to see other directions such as a wish to provide a home for her son.

[51] (iv) The fourth point begs the entire question of whether the decisions referred to were unwise at all, and if so by whose standards? I have considered all the decisions referred to by C, including the allegations about the extent to which E has incurred fees on litigation and the way in which it has been conducted. I will consider these further later on, but I do not need to consider each element individually.

[52] The points listed by C amount to a single proposition that the way in which E has behaved, or been advised (or even 'allowed') to behave, with regard to litigation is so extraordinarily unwise as to prove a general lack of capacity on her part which must therefore include a lack of capacity to appoint an attorney. However, even if the former proposition were accepted, the latter simply does not follow. Capacity is decision specific.

[53] I am not, in fact, satisfied that the matters mentioned do demonstrate a lack of capacity even in general terms. The argument that they do must be examined against the context of how E appears to have seen her own position, and not that of how H, SC and C think she *ought* to have seen her own position. For present purposes, however, I am concerned only with evidence of a specific lack of capacity to appoint an attorney, at the time when E purported to do so in January 2009. In my judgment, none of the matters which C cites, when viewed in their proper context, and even in combination, supports any inference of a lack of such capacity on E's part at the relevant time (some of them even appear to post date this time), and they are certainly not sufficient to outweigh the considerable direct evidence the other way.

[54] (v) The fifth point is, in my judgment, fanciful to the point of virtual absurdity. This is not least because, whilst the stated internet link to a neutrally identified charity certainly appears when a search is carried out against the name of 'JW' (as I was invited to confirm), when this link itself is followed up, there seems to be no reference to JW on the charity's web page at all. How, therefore, the link came to be listed is a mystery. However, even if there were some connection between JW and Dr McCormick, it simply does not follow that this is any evidence that the certificate of capacity was somehow 'bent' – which is the least that would be necessary for this fact to suggest any doubt about E's relevant capacity. Moreover, this would have to involve the connivance or deception of the other certificate provider, and also some vestige of a plausible ulterior motive for the whole contrivance. On any balanced appraisal of the total situation, there is none.

[55] I am in fact *perfectly* satisfied, that E had the necessary capacity to execute a LPA on 7 January 2009, and that it is valid accordingly. For the avoidance of doubt, therefore I make this determination under s 22(2)(a) of the Mental Capacity Act 2005.

[56] I should add here that some of C's submissions began to move into an argument that the LPA was invalid, not for E's lack of capacity, but because it must have been executed under the undue influence, pressure or coercion of G, – or perhaps, I think, of K or even of Dr McCormick – over E. In legal analysis, this could be characterised as obtaining the LPA by fraud. Such an assertion, if proved, would either give rise to a claim that the LPA was invalid and ought to be set aside on general legal or equitable grounds (if E now still retained capacity to take that decision) or it would give rise to an application that the court should revoke the LPA under s 22(3)(a) and s 22(4)(b) of the 2005 Act, if she did not.

[57] Dr McCormick put down a marker, objecting to any such case being made on the grounds (which are correct) that it had not been included in C's amended application.

[58] I accept this. However, as C has been acting in person, I have borne in mind this possibility and asked myself whether there is any evidence in the case which suggests that it deserves further investigation or examination.

[59] I am quite satisfied that it does not.

(ii) Does the renunciation of the power by B affect the validity of the LPA as regards conferring powers on K?

[60] I conclude that it does not.

[61] Whilst I raised this point at the hearing so that it should not be overlooked, my immediate reaction was that it would not affect the position of K to 'act alone' under the terms of the power. Dr McCormick confirmed that this was his view and understanding after researching the matter.

[62] He submitted that this was a joint and several power and 'a disjunctive is not defeated by the failure of one of the disjuncts' in principle. The view that one of two joint and several attorneys could act alone even if the other attorney did not or could not act was also supported by s 10(7), and ss 13(5)(b), (6)(a) and (7)(b) of the 2005 Act.

[63] I accept this submission. C did not really seek to argue the contrary, and since the point was flagged up early, I conclude that if anything could have been argued in this regard, it would have been.

[64] I hold, therefore, that the LPA therefore remains prima facie valid in so far as K is willing to and does exercise it.

(iii) Can and should the court nonetheless revoke the Lasting Power of Attorney on the grounds that K ought to be held to be unfit to be E's attorney?

[65] This issue depends on the court's power to revoke an otherwise valid LPA contained in s 22(3)(b) of the 2005 Act.

[66] C's submissions, made, I understand, with some input from his former legal advisers, did not deal with this legal point, but simply raised various criticisms of K's behaviour as allegedly proving that she was not a suitable attorney for E. Indeed, he bluntly submits that K's behaviour is 'incompetent at best and criminal at worst'. In so doing, he is referring generally to K's conduct as E's litigation solicitor, as shown by his reliance on 'concerns' expressed by solicitors, counsel and the courts during the various proceedings in which the parties have been engaged, and his final comment that 'if she behaves in this way when she is regulated by the SRA and policed by the courts, how will she behave when she is not?'

[67] However, s 22 does not depend on a general or abstract notion of 'unsuitability', but is narrower and more focussed. The court may only revoke an LPA if it is satisfied:

'22(3)(b) that the donee . . . of a lasting power of attorney—
(i)   has behaved, or is behaving, in a way that contravenes his authority or is not in P's best interests, or
(ii)   proposes to behave in a way that contravenes his authority or would not be in P's best interests.'

[68] In addition, and in any case, the court can only revoke the power if it is not yet registered (which this is), or if the donor of the power lacks capacity to revoke it: see s 22(4)(b) to which the court's power under s 22(3) is subject. I assume without deciding, for present purposes, that this latter requirement would be met.

[69] It is therefore for C to satisfy me, in the first place, that K's conduct falls within one of the above limbs.

[70] This is not a case of exceeding a power, and therefore it is behaving, or proposing to behave contrary to E's best interests which is the relevant test. The first question is therefore the scope of such potentially disqualifying conduct, on the true construction of s 22(3)(b).

[71] Dr McCormick submits that the subsection is obviously intended to respect P's choice of attorney by being a safety net, and is therefore intended to be relatively narrow; otherwise it would have used some wider concept such as general unfitness. He then submits that it is only behaviour of the attorney *in his capacity as attorney* which is the subject of the subsection, and not behaviour in any other capacity. The point of this, he says, is that K's behaviour as E's litigation solicitor would not be within the scope of the subsection and would not give grounds for considering revoking the LPA. As all the criticisms of K are connected with her position as litigation solicitor, the application must, in effect, fall at this first hurdle.

[72] In support of this, Dr McCormick submits that the four elements of s 22(3)(b) must all relate to conduct of the same class, and since contravening authority can only apply to behaviour as (or at least purportedly as) P's attorney, behaving otherwise than in P's best interests must be limited in the same way.

[73] I am not inclined to accept this submission. It appears to me that the general thrust of s 22(3)(b) is that the court can revoke an LPA if it is satisfied that there is evidence that the attorney cannot be trusted to act in the manner and for the purposes for which the LPA was conferred upon him/her. This does not require limiting the 'behaviour' which can be considered to behaviour as, or in anticipation of acting as, P's attorney. Further, if there is sufficient evidence that the attorney is behaving contrary to P's interests even in a different context, then it seems to me that that might well quite reasonably provide a sufficient reason to revoke an LPA, perhaps because of conflict of interest.

[74] In addition, the construction of the subparagraph itself does not seem to me to lend the extent of support for his assertion that Dr McCormick claims. In the first place, the use of the very broad term 'behave' is not what one would expect if the subparagraph is concerned only with the actions taken or purportedly taken in exercise of the power of attorney. If so, it would, in my judgment, have been far more natural to use the expression 'exercise the power' rather than the word 'behave'. Secondly, it seems to me that Dr McCormick's argument does not fit at all well with the subpara (b)(ii) regarding prospective behaviour, where it is far more difficult to see why it should be limited to prospective behaviour as attorney, which might be very difficult to identify.

[75] In my judgment, the key to giving proper effect to the distinction between an attorney's behaviour as attorney and his behaviour in any other capacity lies in

considering the matter in stages. First, one must identify the allegedly offending behaviour or prospective behaviour. Secondly, one looks at all the circumstances and context and decides whether, taking everything into account, it really does amount to behaviour which is not in P's best interests, or can fairly be characterised as such, Finally, one must decide whether, taking everything into account including the fact that it is behaviour in some other capacity, it also gives good reason to take the very serious step of revoking the LPA.

[76] Dr McCormick reminds me, quite correctly, that the court is not obliged to revoke the power even if it finds behaviour or prospective behaviour by the attorney which can be so characterised. Subsection 22(4) is permissive ('may') and not mandatory, as to the revocation of the power of attorney. It is thus, in my judgment, at this last stage that the question whether the offending behaviour was as attorney or otherwise is relevant. It may be more likely that the court would feel it appropriate to revoke the power in the former situation, than in the latter.

[77] Having regard to this approach, and noting the court's powers with regard to directing an attorney under s 23 of the Act, I therefore hold that, on the true construction of s 22(3), the court can consider any past behaviour or apparent prospective behaviour by the attorney, but, depending on the circumstances and gravity of any offending behaviour found, it can then take whatever steps it regards as appropriate in P's best interests (this only arising if P lacks capacity), to deal with the situation, whether by revoking the power or by taking some other course.

[78] I therefore turn to the substance of C's criticisms of K, whether I find any of them proved, whether any so proved do, in my judgment, amount to behaviour contrary to E's best interests and if so, whether that behaviour ought to cause me to exercise my jurisdiction to revoke the LPA or to take some other steps and if so what.

[79] C makes his criticisms under seven headings, although these overlap.

SRA investigation

[80] I will set this criticism out as it appeared in C's final written submission on day 6 of the hearing, because it illustrates many points about his approach in this case.

> '(i) [K] accepted that she is currently under investigation by the SRA for between 50 and 80 breaches of the Code of Conduct. It is not clear whether they relate solely to this matter or to others as well. [D] gave evidence that the complaint to the SRA about [K] have been made by solicitors, Judges, Counsel and [K's] own employer. D also confirmed that they are investigating [K] for financial irregularity and that this investigation is a joint investigation between the SRA and the police.'

[81] There are the following inaccuracies in this submission, each gradually increasing the gravity of the attack on K's integrity.

[82] First, C accepted that in fact it was not '50–80 breaches' but 50–80 questions, put to K by the SRA, something rather different. K said, and I accept, that she did not know exactly what breaches, or how many, might be being alleged, but she agreed that she had been asked for her response to a large number of questions as a result of the complaint made by Mundays.

[83] Secondly, the conjecture that these might relate to 'other matters' appears to have been no more than speculative comment. K denied it and I see no reason to disbelieve this.

[84] Thirdly, the only 'solicitors' who have made complaints about K are Mundays; there is no evidence that I can see that any counsel has done so, there is no evidence that any judge has made a complaint to the SRA (as contrasted with criticisms expressed in judgments, which is not the same thing), and whilst it may be the case

that there is now some complaint about files from the owner of McDonald Law Associates, this is not entirely clear. The extent of alleged complainants is therefore exaggerated for dramatic effect.

[85] Fourthly, D did not confirm that K was being investigated for 'financial irregularity', which carries the obvious pejorative sense of embezzlement. She recorded only that M had apparently been complaining of her failure to render bills to E, (and perhaps also the extent of fees which had been earned by Dr McCormick) and as to her retention of client files, and specifically that she had 'spoken to' the SRA in relation to the latter. K, in her evidence confirmed that: (a) she was not aware of any complaint to the SRA against her regarding any matter of financial impropriety; (b) this included even any issue about rendering fees (as to which she stated that her fee rendering had been discussed openly in the firm and approved by B); (c) that there was indeed now an issue between her and Clereys, (which they had raised with the SRA although she had not seen any formal complaint) regarding her having retained client files in the J case which she had taken home to enable her to work on answers to the SRA questions, during her maternity leave, and (d) that she did not now expect that she would be returning to her job at Clereys.

[86] I am satisfied that the accusations made by C have, once again, been exaggerated and played up for all they could be worth. I accept K's evidence, which appears to me to be consistent with some kind of rift within Clereys as M, who is an investor and not a lawyer, has started to look critically at the return on his investment. (I understand, although the detail is not material, that M acquired Clereys by purchasing it from its former sole proprietor, R, who was subsequently bankrupted and was under investigation for alleged financial irregularities and mortgage fraud.)

[87] Fifthly, I can see no substantiation whatsoever for the allegation that K's conduct is being investigated by the police. This is neither stated by D nor is there any other evidence of this. It appears to be reckless invention.

[88] I have given this detailed account to illustrate why I have felt it necessary to check carefully just about every assertion made by C, and also why I am unable to give weight to his citings of evidence supposedly gathered from others. There is just too much room for misinterpretation, exaggeration or self-serving slant, even if not outright deliberate misrepresentation.

[89] The investigation by the SRA is just that, an investigation. It is not, at least not yet, a finding of any guilt against K. In evaluating it, I take account of the nature of it, namely a complaint by a firm of solicitors against the solicitor on the record for the opposite party in personally hostile litigation. Even if it subsequently results in some form of censure of K, that would not necessarily give grounds for revoking the LPA; it would depend on the actual substance of the matter.

[90] In fact, I am satisfied that this complaint or investigation, whether confined to 'litigation conduct', or extending to retaining files or rendering fees (if and insofar as the SRA might concern itself with either such matter, being more in the nature of an employment dispute), independently discloses no behaviour by K which is not in E's best interests, nor any evidence that she would propose to act otherwise than in E's best interests. Indeed, if anything it might be argued to have been provoked more by K's being over enthusiastic in pursuing E's best interests.

Costs

[91] There are two broad allegations under this head. The first is that K has failed in her duty, as a solicitor, to advise E as to the level of costs she was incurring in this and other litigation, and to render regular bills. C submits that E's costs now amount to in excess of £300,000, although Clereys have only billed her, on K's evidence, a rather modest £30,000.

[92] His second point is a submission that the evidence shows that E's litigation costs have been inflated. In support of this, C cites, for example, criticisms made by His Honour Judge Rylance in the family proceedings, of the 'wasted' costs of the High Court proceedings (ie the mediation privilege claim) and of 'absurd' and 'ludicrous' applications in the family proceedings. C points out that E's and G's combined costs in those proceedings have reached about £150,000. (There appears to be a dispute as to whether the majority of the costs are G's as Mundays or C have said, or E's, as Clereys have said.) C relies on D's evidence that in her experience a typical 'occupation order' application in such proceedings would cost about £5,000. He suggests that the huge discrepancy is because of 'spurious applications' made, for which, by implication, he is presumably saying K is responsible.

[93] As to the first broad point, K was not asked about whether she had given costs advice to E. C submitted that as she did not mention doing so, I should infer that she had not.

[94] I have some difficulty with this submission, since it seems to me to go behind E's legal professional privilege. The question of E's mounting costs bill has indeed been an aspect of this case which I have found very troubling. However, even if neither K nor B had given any such advice, it seems to me that this would be primarily a matter of professional conduct or negligence as between solicitor and client. If proved, it might be said to be have been behaviour which was not in E's best interests, but only in a very loose sense. I certainly would not regard that as sufficient grounds to cause me to exercise my jurisdiction to revoke the relevant power of attorney without considerably more proof that the attorney could not be trusted to use it in the best interests of E. It is, though, a point which I bear in mind.

[95] As to the criticism about levels of costs, this is far more wide ranging, with a myriad of points taken in respect of this and a similar point under 'litigation conduct and integrity' below. It will require more discussion.

[96] I was previously provided in May, at my insistence, with a list of E's costs incurred in six sets of proceedings – a superficially startling fact in itself. The information gave figures up to March 2010, in a total sum of about £295,000. Since then they will have increased, but largely because of her costs in this matter. Other cases have either been virtually concluded or were stayed then or shortly thereafter. The references below are to the March figures.

[97] Dr McCormick therefore accepted that E's bills were by now over £300,000, but submitted that on fair examination, this position was neither as apparently reckless as the first impression from that bald fact might suggest, nor, in fact unreasonable at all.

[98] First, he pointed out that the vast majority of E's costs have been incurred in proceedings where she was *defendant*, namely the Family proceedings (£127,000 for E and £26,000 in respect of G), and these proceedings (£72,000 up to March 2010). He suggests that it does not lie in the mouths of those who have taken a party to court to criticise or object to the costs which, as between that other party and her advisers, she then expends in her defence. It is entirely a matter for that party and her advisers to judge what expenditure is necessary or worthwhile to make such resistance, including the subjective importance to that party of success.

[99] The Family proceedings were discontinued at trial as against E thus in effect (it was submitted) making her successful, and were compromised on limited undertakings as regards G. H subsequently decided not to, or was unable to, return the family home. In view of the complex family background to the dispute the trial judge (District Judge Crichton) made no order as to costs. I understand there are no outstanding costs issues between the parties.

[100] As to the cases where E is claimant, Dr McCormick submitted that they could all be seen to have been necessary to protect E's interests or wishes, and had not been

launched either lightly, or hastily – except where the matter was urgent – and the level of costs was certainly not extravagant.

[101] The first, in time was the action in the High Court, brought in early 2009, to restrain breach of E's mediation privilege and prevent evidence about her when she attended the mediation from being put forward on behalf of H in the family proceedings in order to challenge her capacity. C claimed support for his criticism of launching this action, (and consequent criticism of K for being party to doing so) from the judgment of His Honour Judge Rylance in the County Court on 18 May 2009, lamenting the waste of cost in bringing such a separate case when he, His Honour Judge Rylance would (C submitted) have 'dealt with it for nothing'. Dr McCormick pointed out, however, that:

(a)   it was acknowledged that it was E's right to take separate proceedings if she wished;

(b)   there were in fact good reasons for doing so in that:

(i)   it would otherwise have meant His Honour Judge Rylance looking at the offending evidence, which in E's eyes would be unacceptable; and

(ii)   it was also desired to obtain a decision for all purposes and not just the Family proceedings;

(c)   the decision to do so had been vindicated by E's actual success in May 2009,

(d)   the deputy High Court judge who tried the fully contested interlocutory hearing on motion had made no adverse comment about her incurring costs, let alone a wasted costs order against her solicitors; and

(e)   E had obtained a costs order in her favour in those hearings, as yet unenforced. Thus, she stood to recover at least the bulk of her costs incurred to date, of about £39,000. (The remaining costs presently stand as costs in the case.)

[102] The remaining three cases were all launched in mid 2009. The first concerned an injunction against C which E had felt obliged to seek in the County Court, after he had been unacceptably persistent in trying to get to speak to her (upsetting her and causing, at its lowest, a scene). Discontinuance had been offered on the basis of an undertaking not to approach E to be given by C, but the matter had not been concluded (although an interim injunction was granted), because C disputes the allegations made against him and insists on going to trial to clear his name. E's unresolved costs position therefore stands at present at £11,000, which Dr McCormick submitted was quite reasonable.

[103] The second and third actions are two High Court cases launched by E against H. In the first, launched on 6 June 2009, E seeks the sale of the jointly owned house under the Trusts of Land and Appointment of Trustees Act 1996 and division of the proceeds between herself and H, (costs incurred £9,000). In the second, launched in July 2009, she claims the return of £106,000 from H, being money admittedly removed by him from their joint accounts in early 2008, which she claims was, as between them, hers (costs incurred £11,000). Each of those actions is now stayed, and has been transferred to me, sitting in my capacity as a deputy judge of the High Court, under s 9 of the Senior Courts Act 1981.

[104] I, in fact, requested such a transfer because of concerns I indeed held initially as to there being something in the suggestion that E was being subject to some undue influence or pressure, as to which only the High Court would have an inherent jurisdiction to take pro-active steps to protect a vulnerable person of capacity.

The Court of Protection, being a creation of statute, does not, and could in any event only act where a person apparently lacked capacity, rather than simply being overborne.

[105] C in effect submitted that the bringing of that action was so unnecessary, unreasonable in the context of E's circumstances or (I think) so plainly doomed to failure, that pursuing it is contrary to E's best interests, and it could therefore be seen that it had been launched for the benefit of the lawyers, (thus including K) for the purpose of obtaining and ramping up fees. He submits that bringing proceedings to sell the house is foolhardy to the point of madness when E has no other place to live and a costs bill which (he suggests) more than exceeds her assets, and is also inconsistent with her professed wish to continue living at the house with G. He submits, I think relying on reports of Mundays' views, that the other action is equally foolhardy as the moneys were lawfully drawn from a joint account by one joint signatory.

[106] Dr McCormick submits that, first, these actions have not been launched hurriedly, but are the almost inevitable consequence of the fact that E has been left stranded, financially, by various steps taken by H, with the assistance of SC and C, to starve her of access to any funds.

[107] As to the action claiming sale of the house, he points out that E's wish to stay there had been expressed rather in the context of her wish to live with G, with the house being the only practical place to do so at present. However, it is not ideal for her needs as there are no bathing facilities on the ground floor, to which she is confined. In addition, the house has been soured for E because of the upsetting introduction during her enforced absence, and at the behest of SC and H, of a security guard and dogs, who had dirtied the place unacceptably. (There is certainly evidence of her expressing this opinion.) Since the house is not best suited to her, she now has a need of cash, and her half-share in the house is in fact not the total extent of her resources, since she has not only her financial claim made in the other action, but also a claim on other matrimonial assets. The decision to seek a sale of the house is a perfectly sensible one.

[108] The action to recover money raises the question of the contentious financial transactions referred to above. Although I have looked at them, I do not have to go into the detail of them, and will not further lengthen this judgment by doing so. I only need to record a general summary, in order to illustrate how this is yet another aspect of the family dynamics in this case which needs to be taken into account in assessing, and in particular judging or castigating, anyone's conduct.

[109] In outline only, for this purpose, the salient features are that the matters in contention began as early as February 2008 (with an incident, I think, about the interception of the proceeds of some premium bonds which E claims were hers) and were followed by H's diverting to his own account (and latterly on to the control of SC) certain bank funds (£41,000 in April 2008) and the proceeds of bonds (£65,000 in June 2008) held in their joint names but, E says, agreed between them to be 'earmarked' for her as being owned in equal shares for each of them beneficially. In addition, during 2008, E's capacity had been put in question by SC or H to her bank manager, causing the freezing of her accounts, and H and SC had removed financial papers from the family house, preventing E from dealing with her affairs owing to lack of records.

[110] Much of the facts of this are accepted on C's part, but it is said that this had been done on advice and because of very genuine doubt and concern as to E's capacity, and the need to protect her from pressures or predations from G, who, it was alleged, had tried to obtain access to the accounts by forgery and/or undue influence. C pointed to sums totalling (I think) about £18,100 which it was said G had obtained from E through undue influence or unlawful means. In particular, he pointed to three contemporaneous cheques for £4,000 each (total £12,000) which G had been paid

after prevailing on E to sign them, in May 2008, it being suggested that she had been told this was for 'toiletries' (this also being used as evidence of E's lack of capacity with regard to financial matters).

[111] Once again this last submission turned out to be inaccurate in a major respect. Although the three cheques had been paid in, the payments had been stopped, and G had never received the money. Dr McCormick also submitted that I should have regard to the timing when considering this matter and what its significance might be, and the fact that this had taken place after the earliest two incidents of apparently joint moneys being appropriated to himself alone by H. I think I am invited to infer that it was a form of response, perhaps owing something to G's unpredictable nature.

[112] Whatever the precise position, and the rights and wrongs of who did what, I am not satisfied that the launching of these proceedings, over a year after the matters complained of, is any evidence of lawyers rushing to exploit fee earning potential.

[113] Dr McCormick also invited my attention to the following points, when considering the criticism that E is being exploited by having her litigation costs run up unnecessarily and unreasonably by unscrupulous lawyers. First, the suggestion that her billed costs now exceed her assets is hyperbole which does not survive examination. She has the benefit of costs orders, which will reduce her ultimate liability, and her overall assets are not confined to her one half interest in the house, as suggested, but would extend not merely to the moneys she is now claiming to recover from her husband, but, on the basis of a matrimonial division, to significant other assets currently held on H's side of the family.

[114] Secondly, whilst the current costs figures are high they are not exceptionally so given the various complicating matters in the matter, particularly in the Family proceedings in respect of which the bulk of them were incurred. Dr McComick put to C some 11 such complicating points which he suggested would tend to add to costs. Some of these were: the complexity of the background, the fact that H had pleaded a large number of allegations going back to 2004 which had therefore to be answered, the great importance of the matter for E, the number of interim hearings, disputes about whether evidence was manufactured, the extra time necessary to take instructions from an elderly lady such as E, supporting her appropriately to do so, and the need for legal advisers to go to see her rather than call her into the office. These points were in my judgment well made. C did, indeed accept many of them, and where he did not (such as refusing to accept that it was reasonable for lawyers to attend E rather than the other way round), I think this said more about C's intransigent mind-set than about the unreasonableness of any costs incurred by E.

[115] Thirdly, Dr McCormick reminded me that there were costs orders actually or potentially in E's favour to off-set the current apparent total – although it is not clear to me how far these costs may be recoverable.

[116] Fourthly, Dr McCormick pointed out that C had incurred such a significant bill in these proceedings (I think about £80,000) that he had been compelled to represent himself, but that this bill was comparable with E's own costs. I think C's response was rather to assert that Mundays, also, had been racking up costs unreasonably (he has not paid their bill) rather than simply ask himself whether his own judgment of the appropriate costs of litigation might be incorrect.

[117] Fifthly, Dr McCormick pointed out that although there were large potential bills for E, both Clereys, and indeed he himself, had refrained from rendering bills beyond a relatively modest £30,000, (confirmed by K) to date. He submitted that this was inconsistent with a suggestion that the lawyers were exploiting E. C submitted, in essence, that, on the contrary, this was suspicious, as it was so uncommercial, and it must therefore be evidence of a concerted plan to encumber E with a large debt which would be claimed out of her share of the house.

[118] Sixthly, Dr McCormick pointed out that, as a mere employee of Clereys, rather than an owner or equity partner, K would gain no benefit from the conduct alleged. In answer to this submission, C suggested that as employed solicitors had to meet targets of chargeable hours work, the benefit to K was that the great number of hours spent on E's matters would enable her to keep her job, a submission which I found unconvincing.

[119] Seventhly, Dr McCormick invited my attention to various matters which he suggested showed that, far from seeking to launch or prolong proceedings as a means of racking up fees, E's advisers, ie including K, had tried to keep them to the minimum possible, in her interests. He pointed out, first, that it was E who had proposed mediation in the Family proceedings, as soon as K and he had been instructed, in September/October 2008. He also drew my attention to a Position Statement, drafted by him on E's behalf and proposing a further attempt at a wide ranging mediation or negotiation, to resolve all the issues between all five family members at one time (rather than piecemeal) recognising the difficult and conflicting cross relationships between them and the legitimate wishes and interests of each of them, in about June 2009. This, he said, had been handed to Mundays or to counsel instructed by them at the trial in June 2009, but had received no response, they stating, no doubt on behalf of H, that he would prefer to await the outcome of this case.

[120] C believed that he had never seen this document, and I accept this, even though it has otherwise been perfectly clear that he and SC have, unsurprisingly, seen pretty well everything given to H in the court proceedings, even where this material would strictly be confidential to the parties. I record that I found the position statement to be a perceptive and sensitive document, framed in dispassionate language, and I find it to be support for Dr McCormick's submission.

[121] Dr McCormick also pointed out various explanations of points on which K had been criticised which he said showed that judicial criticism were misplaced and unfair. I am not going to deal with these individually, but will simply give examples, for flavour.

[122] Perhaps an initial important one is a possible inferential criticism by District Judge Jackson that K (and also, I supposed Dr McCormick) had not drawn the court's attention to the existence of the LPA until towards the end of the hearing on 20 August 2009, when Professor H's oral evidence was heard, then, apparently, producing it like a rabbit out of a hat. This has led to an implied, if not express, allegation and criticism that this had been deliberately suppressed. Dr McCormick submits that this is unfair. K's recent witness statement explains her thinking, and that it did not occur to her to produce the document earlier, bearing in mind the issue being considered. He also points out that there was no concealment of the document, as it was expressly referred to in Professor H's report. I accept that whilst it might have been, or appeared, more helpful if K or Dr McCormick had drawn attention to the LPA earlier, this is not evidence of improper conduct or deviousness on their part, and would, at its highest, be perhaps an error of judgment.

[123] An example in a different context is criticism by His Honour Judge Rylance that requests for further information, such as requests for receipts for flowers allegedly bought by H for E but which she denied, had been excessive to the extent of being 'ludicrous'. Dr McCormick submitted that this was misplaced and unfair, for in effect criticising the judgment of a legal adviser that it was not safe or sufficient, in his client's interest, merely to leave a point relied on by the other side to be determined on the basis of whose word is preferred, rather than to take it seriously and seek to elicit evidence (or even the absence of it) necessary to support his client's case. Once this point is made, it can be seen to be a question of professional judgment, and whilst one might not agree with the defence, and understand the judge's comments, it seems to me that this is a matter of judgment rather than misbehaviour.

[124] There had been criticism that K had not produced a medical report on E when 'requested' and had then absented herself from the court, so as not to be available when the court asked for information from her. This criticism said Dr McCormick, failed to take into account the fact that K's attendance on that day had only been to deliver documents, and she had not been required to sit behind him that day at the hearing. The judge perhaps also did not know that the medical report (Dr A's report) had been obtained with E's authorisation only for a different purpose, namely because K had asked for it for her own firm's benefit so that they could be sure that they were accepting valid instructions. He submitted that a legal adviser could not properly just produce it in such circumstances, simply because of a 'request' by the court. When the judge made an actual order, it had obediently been produced. The fact that the apparent non-co-operation really had been caused by concern for professional propriety and not an attempt to suppress adverse information had become apparent to the judge, when its contents were, contrary to his expectation, entirely favourable to E.

[125] It was submitted that judicial criticism of the absence of E and her advisers at a hearing of the Family proceedings before District Judge Raeside in February 2009 in the County Court was unfair and unreasonable, because it ignored that the hearing had been accelerated at the behest of Mundays on behalf of H from a date when K and Dr McCormick had arranged to be available, to a date when neither of them could be, and that the court had then refused to amend the date, so that consequently a decision had been taken to send in written submissions. Insofar as there was criticism of what was (I believe) an intimation that there would be an inevitable appeal if the court dealt adversely with the matter, for being inappropriate or arrogant, that was said to mischaracterise a mere courteous advance notification of intention.

[126] Dr McCormick drew my attention to K's own written evidence explaining why she had done various things, such as put in witness statements herself rather than obtain them from E, and in fact answering all the points of criticism actually made in C's application in terms of the reasons why she had thought it proper to take the steps she had done.

[127] A great number of individual points have been raised in the context of this topic, and I remind myself that the purpose of this general review of the way in which litigation, and other matters, has been conducted on E's behalf is to see if it discloses evidence which satisfies me that K has behaved, or proposes to behave, in a way that is not in E's best interests.

[128] Having considered carefully all the points that are made and all the matters of suspicion and criticism raised by C, whether his own criticisms or reports of other person's criticisms, I am satisfied that it does not.

[129] First, having been taken through the history of the litigation, with a view to seeing the context of steps taken at the time they were taken, I can find no evidence at all of any conspiracy between any lawyers, let alone one involving K, to commence extravagant proceedings or to inflate work or fees on existing proceedings, so as to exploit E.

[130] Secondly, I remind myself that I am concerned with K's behaviour. Many of the criticisms made of her involve acts carried out in the course of litigation, in which she had instructed counsel, and they are plainly steps which would appear to have been taken on the advice of counsel. Whilst instructing counsel does not absolve a solicitor from considering intelligently the advice received, and correcting or questioning any obvious errors or dubious points, the whole point of instructing counsel is to bring in an expert, and a solicitor who acts sincerely on counsel's advice can hardly be criticised. That appears to me to be what has been the position in respect of a great many of the criticisms which are now levelled at K, such as the making of apparently excessive requests for further information, or particular procedural statements. This is not the place to consider Dr McCormick's style or its impact on this litigation, because

that would on any basis be of no relevance. Dr McCormick's actions or conduct cannot, short of a conspiracy allegation, or some other extreme situation, be laid at K's door.

[131] Thirdly, many of the criticisms both made and imported by C, including the judicial ones, seem to me to have been made without the benefit of the underlying explanations and considerations, which have now been put to me. At their lowest, these satisfy me that there may well have been a genuine and legitimately held view that the relevant step or action was necessary or appropriate to protect the client's litigation interests, or carry out her instructions, rather than being professional misconduct, or part of any contrivance to inflate E's costs.

[132] Fourthly, whilst I do not agree with or accept every answer given by K, or argued by Dr McCormick in her favour, having seen her give evidence, I am inclined to accept a great majority. Even to the extent that I might have misgivings, I am satisfied that they could point to no more than a possible error of judgment on K's part, and even then maybe only in hindsight.

[133] For example C has criticised the video of E put before District Judge Jackson for the fact that it shows E answering leading questions, and giving the appearance, therefore, of being manipulated into giving the answers although these are said to be her own. This is a fair comment. It would certainly have been better if K had asked open questions (although I have no doubt that C would even then have argued that there must therefore have been a coaching session beforehand). However, this is an illustration of the kind of error of judgment which may not be good practice for a litigation solicitor, or might turn out to have been an error in hindsight, but is really no more heinous than that.

[134] I also bear in mind that all too many of C's criticisms, whilst they look serious because of the way they are expressed, turn out in practice to be inaccurate, exaggerated or simply misconceived. An example is his assertion that K 'ignored court orders', for example, about putting in evidence, which, on examination boil down to the all too commonplace missing of a time limit and consequent request for an extension of time.

[135] Fifthly, insofar as any criticisms of K are ones of 'discourtesy' or 'non-co-operation' or suchlike, they do not seem to me, even if substantiated, to amount at all to 'behaviour which is not in E's best interests' except on the loosest interpretation of that phrase, ie that they might bring her into disrepute with the court, or might indirectly cause some extra element of costs in the ordinary course of litigation. They come nowhere near matters with the kind of direct prejudicial effect on E's interests which I would find necessary in order to give grounds for revoking a validly granted power of attorney.

[136] Sixthly, as to any criticism that any costs charged to E had been unreasonably incurred or were unreasonable in amount, there is an obvious mechanism for resolving any question of this nature, namely a solicitor and own client taxation. It follows that it would only be the extreme case of an identifiable instance of perfectly obvious *improper* charging (of which there is no evidence here) that such complaints would, in my judgment, take the case outside the scope of the protection afforded by those mechanisms and into the ambit of what might fairly be characterised as 'behaviour not in E's best interests' within the meaning of s 22(3)(b) of the 2005 Act.

[137] My summary conclusion is therefore that I do not find the complaints under this heading of 'cost' to satisfy me that K has been guilty of behaviour which is not in E's best interests so as to suggest that the court should revoke the LPA.

[138] I should add, again for completeness, that since D had professed 'concerns' about K's conduct, I asked her, in evidence what these were. Apart from a rather condescending concern at K's lack of knowledge (later amended to 'experience') of the

workings of the family courts as contrasted with general litigation and a consequent tendency to resort to guidance in the CPR, (which would be only a matter of opinion) D's concerns duplicated matters cited by C, and I do not need, therefore, to deal with them separately.

Liabilities

[139] This is a criticism that K has 'put E's payment of litigation costs ahead of her payment of care fees owed to Social Services'. It has no doubt been prompted by K's evidence that because E had been largely starved of cash and for such a long period largely (I regret to say) whilst these proceedings have been coming to trial, she is now in arrears with her payment for care costs.

[140] There is nothing to support this accusation, which I find to be another example of an extravagant, unjustified, and even irresponsible accusation by C. E has not paid any litigation fees recently – a fact which, in another breath, C even seemed to use as a criticism of K for allowing a liability to accumulate. Furthermore, K has not been in control of E's finances. She had not exercised the power of attorney prior to the hearing before me. I therefore reject this assertion.

Client files

[141] This criticism is founded on the complaints reported second hand from M by the evidence of D, and the admission by K that she has indeed retained some of E's client files, and that this has been the subject of a dispute with M.

[142] In my judgment, this is not behaviour not in E's best interests, either in the relevant sense or indeed at all. C's final comment under this paragraph seeks to widen the criticism of K to one of general judgment. He alleges that 'she showed no insight into how wrong this was'. Whilst this patronising submission may have come from C, to me it smacks more of the rather self righteous D.

[143] The dispute about retention of client files is so recent, so lacking in detail and so unclear that I do not think it appropriate to express any comment about the rights and wrongs of it, still less to make any adverse judgment of K based upon it. It does not, in my judgment, even begin to qualify as evidence of a propensity to behave otherwise than in E's best interests.

Litigation conduct and integrity

[144] This is another section of narrative in which criticisms of K's conduct of the litigation between H and E are once again rehearsed, this time not so much with a focus on alleged unnecessary or unreasonable incurring of costs (see (ii) above) but with a focus on K's alleged lack of integrity and lack of proper professional responsibility towards the court and the proper approach to the conduct of litigation. As such, it would be even more indirect with regard to evidence of K's behaviour being otherwise than in E's best interests.

[145] This section is laced with supporting quotations from the judgment of District Judge Raeside of 10 February 2009, upon the accelerated hearing of the Family proceedings at which E's 'side' did not appear but sent written representations, the judgment of His Honour Judge Rylance of 18 May 2009, overturning the order of District Judge Raeside, which, he accepted, ought never to have been made (it had had the effect not merely of effectively turning G out of the house, probably prematurely, but also compelling E to move out as she could not, and did not want, to live in the house on her own without him), and of District Judge Jackson on her refusal to strike out this application.

[146] I have already indicated that I approach judicial criticism on the basis that I must look to the underlying facts, rather than the mere fact of the judicial criticism. I have also indicated that when I do so in the light of the further evidence and explanations given, I have come to the conclusion that Dr McCormick is broadly correct in his

submission that those criticisms were either made without taking cognisance of all the facts and without the benefit of submissions in answer to them, and that they fail to take account of the difficulties of a solicitor's duty to her client in the particular circumstances in which K has found herself.

[147] I can illustrate this with reference to the underlying criticisms of alleged obstructive behaviour by K with regard to E undergoing a test of her mental capacity in accordance with, at least, strong wishes expressed by the court, as a means of resolving the questions about her capacity which had been raised. To my mind, this illustrates the hugely difficult situation in which I am satisfied K has found herself.

[148] It is natural that with a dispute about mental capacity, the court will regard the obvious way of resolving it to be the obtaining of an expert report from either a specialist psychiatric expert instructed by the parties, or from a Court of Protection Special Visitor. The court will therefore seek to achieve this as a matter of good case management. Very often this will be uncontentious. However, even if the court does not order such a report (which, as already mentioned, it ultimately cannot compel) the mere fact that it may purport to do so, or make an order in indirect terms (eg that 'evidence be filed as to the capacity of P') or express a very strong desire that P should undergo assessment, puts huge pressure on P to go along with what the court obviously wants.

[149] In this case, it is quite apparent that throughout this matter, E has not been willing to undergo psychiatric examination, and this has been her instruction to K, who, as her legal adviser had a duty to assess whether E had the capacity to make that decision, and had concluded that she did. I add that this is a conclusion which I am satisfied was correct.

[150] It is also apparent that H has expressed the wish that his wife undergo a psychiatric test of her capacity, and that enabling H to achieve this wish is what C cares about. At one stage he said as much. It may be that he and H would accept the result of an independent (as they see it) assessment of E. But that requires her to go through an assessment for their benefit, not hers. Furthermore, H's and C's idea of an 'independent' psychiatrist is one whom they approve of.

[151] I ask myself how this will all have appeared to E. She would be being, in effect requested to submit herself to examination by a total stranger, whom she might well see as being effectively on the 'side' of those who were opposed to her wishes, and who would be assessing her by indications and standards not known to her, on the basis that if she did not 'pass' that assessment, the result would be that decisions very important to, her and by which she retained such control as she could of her own destiny, could well be removed from her. I bear in mind how important would seem the retaining of any such control to a frail person who is effectively immobile and utterly dependent on the willingness of others to do things for her and not just to overrule her wishes, even on a well-intentioned basis. She might well, and not without cause, have been concerned that any such psychiatrist would have been lobbied beforehand by SC.

[152] Given the importance to E of her expressed wish to be left to live with G and her understandable view that other members of her family were seeking to obtain evidence to enable them to subvert that wish, either directly, or at least indirectly (by depriving her of any resources which would help her to implement her wish), the prospect of submitting to such an examination and accepting a result which would not be in her control and even a remote risk that it might be adverse, would, I am sure be a terrifying one.

[153] The court may regard an independent psychiatric report as providing the obvious dispassionate answer. The other party may even be prepared to accept that answer for whatever it may be. But E does not want a dispassionate answer, she wants her wishes to be observed. To her, the risk of an examination must have appeared like the risks attached to a game of Russian roulette. It was therefore, in my judgment a

perfectly understandable and rational decision to refuse to see a psychiatric expert appointed either by the court, or with the agreement of H or C, whose motives she would suspect.

[154] E was persuaded to see psychiatric experts for the limited purpose of providing her own solicitor with the necessary assurance that she could give instructions, and she was eventually also persuaded that it would be in her own interests to see Professor H so as to put an end to questions about her capacity to give litigation instructions to resist H's claim. However, I can imagine that even that would have been difficult for her, and I can therefore understand and accept that she would not be prepared to go through yet another risky examination, especially as she would no doubt have had the feeling that the assessment by Professor H would finally conclude the dispute.

[155] Where would this leave K? In my judgment, in a position where she was obliged to do all she could to assist E to achieve her objective, and not to be pressured into taking the risk of yet another psychiatric examination, even at the risk of displeasing the court, always provided she could do so without breaking her duty not to mislead the court, nor to disobey a court order made with proper jurisdiction, and so forth. It appears to me that this is the line which K has been trying to tread, even at the cost of appearing to the court to be being 'difficult'.

[156] I find it unnecessary to review expressly all the individual criticisms of K's litigation conduct which have been put forward. I have already expressed my general view, which is that on full examination, most of them are very much misplaced, (and I make it clear that I am not making a finding that any of them is in fact justified) but more importantly for present purposes, none of them, to my mind, amounts to conduct which is not in E's best interests, very probably at all, but certainly not such that it ought to cause me to revoke the LPA.

[157] I must record the following further points. First, I have not overlooked the fact, which C reminded me of, that some previous judicial criticisms have even come from me, and indeed that I have made one order declaring an application on E's behalf to be 'totally without merit' ie, in effect vexatious. Suffice it to say, here, that my views and impressions of this case have changed as more of the facts have become known to me, and that in any event I do not find that the matters which have caused me to take the above critical stance were matters for which K was responsible.

[158] Secondly, I should mention two other points, first to illustrate an aspect of K which I think makes her very suitable to be E's attorney, and secondly, to illustrate the extraordinary lengths of fanciful criticism she has had to withstand and to deal with in E's interests, and which therefore add weight on the side of likelihood that her behaviour will not be contrary to E's best interests.

[159] I am perfectly satisfied from the evidence and from my own visit to E, that E likes and trusts K, greatly, appreciates what K has done for her, and wants her to continue to do so (although she feels even a bit guilty about asking her to). I am equally satisfied that K has developed a good relationship with E, which may not be easy to do, as E is quite a private person and somewhat reserved with strangers.

[160] One of C's criticisms of K is that she was was found at 10 pm one evening at the care home where E was then staying, sitting on E's bed, sharing a pizza with her. When asked what was the criticism of this, C said that it was unprofessional for a solicitor to be attending a client at that time of night, and in such an informal fashion, and to be buying the client a pizza. When pressed, he said that he believed she was there with the ulterior motive of preventing H or himself or SC from being able to see E.

[161] K was cross-examined about this incident. She explained that it was the day (I think 11 February 2009) when the injunction to make G leave the house was served, that she had been called in suddenly, to try to make emergency accommodation arrangements for E, who did not want to stay at the house without G. When

the County Council had found a place for E in a residential home, it had been late in the evening and the canteen was closed. She had therefore gone out and bought pizza, from her own money. When C asked her on what basis she thought it appropriate to be doing that, she said 'out of compassion'. C nonetheless persisted in his assertion that this was unprofessional conduct and should not have happened.

[162] K also disclosed that she had spent about £50 of her own money in buying a few clothes for E when she had nothing with her in the care home, and had on one occasion paid court fees out of her own pocket to enable an application on E's part to go ahead urgently – I think about £800 – which (she added ruefully) had been reimbursed by the court, but sent to Clereys and not to her, although she would, she hoped, recover it. Once again, C submitted that that was just not professional conduct, and was evidence of lack of judgment, or of some ulterior motive or conduct. I simply do not agree, even though it may be unusual.

[163] Secondly, K was further criticised for having presented Dr K with a letter, on his visit to E at the care home on 29 May 2009, politely telling him that E was not willing to see him and he should go away. When asked what was wrong with that, C's reply was that K should have let E do that herself in person. Given E's frailty and lack of mobility, and the feeling of impotence that that must give her in any confrontation with an able bodied person, I find that response breathtakingly insensitive.

[164] Thirdly, C submitted that, on the evidence, K has 'deliberately misled the court as to how the certificate providers were chosen'. The justification given for this assertion is that *if* D's evidence as to the supposed link between JW and the charity run by Dr McCormick is correct, then K's evidence as to how the certificate providers came to be chosen by E almost at random from the Yellow Pages, is 'clearly false'. The complete lack of logic in this submission is obvious, quite apart from the fact that K's evidence is supported by evidence from E herself and, from the other end of the transaction from JW and from V.

[165] Dr McCormick declined – perfectly properly – to provide any information to the court as to how the apparent web link which had provided the flimsy fuel for this accusation could have come to be recorded. He did so on the grounds that this might make him a witness in the case and prejudice his ability to represent E, and I have to respect this. In fact, of course, there is a perfectly obvious way in which an entirely independent link might have come about, as Dr McCormick is a barrister and JW is a solicitor. I do not need to speculate on this, however. I am simply citing this as an example of the personal attacks which K has had to put up with, and has stood up to, out of a loyalty for E, and a belief that she needs support.

[166] The final illustration is one of the lengths to which C is prepared to go in not merely assuming, but asking the court to find, improper conduct by K. In closing submissions he invited the court to disbelieve K's claim to have been late attending court because of being involved in a car accident. This, of course, had nothing to do with the substantive issues in the case, although it might have been mentioned with a view to founding a claim that it was a ploy to deprive C of time to cross-examine K, even though I had indicated that the court would sit as late as necessary that day, and C had eventually agreed that he had no more questions. No such challenge had been put to K. She was able, the following day, to fax to the court the police reference slip for the car accident which had been given to her. To my mind, this incident says far more about C, his lack of judgment and his intransigent mind set than it does about any criticism of K.

Conflict of interest

[167] Under 'conflict of interest' C submitted that K had a conflict of interest because she represented both G and E, and she ought therefore to cease to act for one side. The

actual submission went no further than this. To be material, it would of course have to found a further finding that this conflict either was, or was likely to become, behaviour contrary to E's best interests.

[168] Even assuming there is a conflict of interest between those two parties – and in view of the obvious bond between E and G that assumption might be questioned – the issue itself does not, in my judgment, arise in any practical sense. The proceedings in which G is involved are now largely over, but in any event, K is no longer acting as solicitor for E, and K is no longer, on her own evidence, expecting to return to her job at Clereys at the end of her maternity leave period even if they were continuing to act for G (which seems highly unlikely as the proceedings involving him are largely concluded).

[169] In any event, as K wearily said 'what possible motive do I have for putting G's interests before E's?'

[170] I agree. I find nothing in this point.

Independence

[171] Under this heading, C submitted that K had a conflict of interest because she was employed by E's main creditor, Clereys, and because E even owed K money personally, these being, I think, the sums for clothes and for the court fee referred to above.

[172] K was scornful of the suggestion that she would even ask to recover these from E. I find this to be sincere, and I say nothing further about it.

[173] However, the point of the implications arising from Clereys being owed fees by E, and whether this might place K in a difficult position, particularly if her duty to her employer required her to defend Clereys' bills to E when E's interests lay in reducing them, was a point which did concern me.

[174] I asked K about her views on this. She did not think it would cause her any difficulties. Dr McCormick submitted that this could all be dealt with by taxation of E's costs, and that the way in which taxations were conducted meant that no such difficulty could ever arise, as bills would be justified only by a costs draftsman. As I had no evidence on this point, though, I was not entirely convinced.

[175] However, two more points do allay any concerns I might otherwise begin to have about the effects of this fact and whether it might put K in difficulty as to behaving in E's best interests. First, K in effect assured me that she was no longer in effect working for Clereys and would not in reality be returning. This seems to me to make it clear that she will not in practice be placed in a position where her employment might require her to act in a manner which was in conflict with E's best interests in reducing her legal costs as far as she properly can.

[176] Secondly, although I do not, in the end, think that there is anything in the evidence before me which ought to cause me to revoke the LPA under my powers in that regard, or otherwise to be concerned about K's fitness to be E's attorney, I have a faint lingering concern about the level of E's costs liability notwithstanding all the very proper and forceful points made by Dr McCormick about this. He submits that if I have such concern, I can deal with this by giving a direction to K in respect of her attorneyship, for example, not to pay any legal bills of E without requiring them to be taxed or otherwise dealt with in accordance with the court's directions. He submits that I have jurisdiction to do this under s 23(2)(a) of the 2005 Act.

[177] I accept that submission, and this seems to me to be a proper way for me to ensure that any residual concerns I might entertain about protecting E's best interests can be met.

(iv) Is K a suitable deputy for E if the LPA is not valid?

[178] In the event, this question does not arise. However, I make it plain here that if I had not been satisfied of E's capacity at the time she executed the LPA, I would have been perfectly satisfied that K was not only a suitable deputy for E, but a most suitable appointee, in E's best interests.

[179] I say this both from the conclusions I have drawn as to K's character and her wish and ability to assist E out of goodwill, but also because there is ample evidence that her appointment would be E's wish (after she very realistically accepted that her wish that G should look after her affairs was impractical and inappropriate) and that it is overwhelmingly in E's best interests that her deputy should be someone she knows and has a good and trusting relationship with, rather than an impersonal stranger in the shape of a panel or local authority deputy.

[180] E is in need of a champion against the forceful and intrusive approach of her daughter and son-in-law, whether purportedly on behalf of her husband or not. I am confident that in a quiet, measured but firm way, K will provide her with this.

Conclusion – Order and other terms and conditions

[181] I will, therefore declare in favour of the validity of the LPA executed by E on 7 January 2009 in favour, jointly and severally, of K and B, and I will dismiss the application of C that the LPA be revoked.

[182] I will hear counsel for E on any further terms of the Order and I will hear C if, but only insofar as, I think it appropriate on such matters.

[183] I indicate provisionally that I am of the view that I can and should give certain directions under s 23 of the 2005 Act. I am of the view that I can do so, on the basis that at present, the evidence shows that on balance of probability E lacks capacity to do so. The pattern of s 23 is that the court can step in to make any decisions or give any directions that the donor of the power of attorney could give if s/he had capacity when s/he does not have such capacity, although it cannot do so if the donor retains capacity in that regard. I will therefore hear any submissions as to E's capacity in these limited respects, if appropriate.

[184] The directions I would be minded to make would be first, under s 23(3)(c), that K should receive her expenses of acting as E's attorney, but should not receive remuneration. K has offered to act for nothing, and I believe that also included expenses. I am of the view, however, that it is both in E's best interests and would be in accordance with her wishes that K should not be out of pocket for assisting her. This will encourage K not to stint on the contact she might have with E and the attention she will pay to her affairs, both of which will be of pleasure and value to E. However, I am of the opinion that it is in E's interests, and would also probably accord with her wishes and values as an old lady who is no one's fool, gratefully to accept K's kind offer to act for no remuneration.

[185] I would also be minded to direct, as I think I am entitled to do under s 23(3)(a) of the 2005 Act, that K should keep accounts in respect of E's affairs and render these to the Office of the Public Guardian annually in respect of each calendar year (2011 to include also any time in 2010).

[186] I am also minded to direct, under s 23(2)(a) of the 2005 Act, that K should seek a solicitor and client assessment of all legal fees to be billed to E by Clereys and not pay any such fees without such assessment, or without the permission of the court, as to which she should have permission to apply.

[187] Lastly, and with some regret, I think it necessary to give K an express permission to apply to the court for directions in case she should encounter any difficulty in discharging her duties to E or exercising her powers as E's attorney because of any interference from any third party.

[188] I am also minded, forthwith to order the lifting of the stay presently imposed on the two High Court cases which I have mentioned above, and which proceedings have been transferred to me.

[189] Finally, if necessary and unless there is reason not to do so, I will discharge N from her position as E's litigation friend for the purpose of these proceedings, with thanks to her for being willing to fulfil that function, and appoint K in her place.

Order accordingly.

Solicitors:

Kingswell Berney Ltd for the respondent

EASON RAJAH QC

Barrister

[G13]

RE PUTT

COURT OF PROTECTION

SENIOR JUDGE DENZIL LUSH 22 March 2011

Lasting power of attorney – eligibility of a certificate provider – delegation functions

The donor had made both types of LPA, which appointed a family member and two solicitors in XYZ Limited Liability Partnership (LLP) as attorneys. The certificate provider was an associate solicitor of the LLP. Regulation 8(3)(f) of the Lasting Powers of Attorney, Enduring Powers of Attorney and Public Guardian Regulations 2007, expressly disqualifies anyone who is a "business partner or employee" of the donor or donee from giving an LPA certificate. The issue for the court was whether the certificate provider was disqualified from acting as such. The effect of which would be that the instrument was not validly created.

Both LPAs also contained a delegation clause which purported to allowed the attorneys to delegate all their functions, and if this was so it would prevent the instruments from operating as valid LPAs and the clause would need to be severed.

Held

(1)   the wording of regulation 8(3)(f) cannot be construed as making any distinction between a partnership under the Partnership Act 1890 and the Limited Liability Partnership Act 2000 for the purpose of providing an LPA certificate and that the certificate provider was an employee of XYZ LLP and was ineligible to provide the certificate.

(2)   The delegation clause was very wide and authorised the attorney to delegate any of his functions. Theoretically, it would enable him to delegate all his functions, which certainly would be a substitution and was invalid and so severed.

Statutory provisions considered

Mental Capacity Act 2005, ss 10(8)(a), 22(2)(a), 22(4)(a), para 11(5)(a) of Sch 1, para 2(6) to Sch 4

The Lasting Powers of Attorney, Enduring Powers of Attorney and Public Guardian Regulations 2007, reg 8(3)(f)

Enduring Powers of Attorney Act 1985, s 2(9)

Limited Liability Partnerships Act 2000, s 1(2)

Cases referred to in judgment

Tiffin v Lester Aldridge [2010] UKEAT 0255_10_1611

Introduction

[1] This is an application by the Public Guardian regarding two Lasting Powers of Attorney ('LPAs') made by the same donor, and involves two points of law. The first is whether the person who provided the certificate in Part B of the LPAs was disqualified from doing so. And the second is whether clauses in both LPAs that allow the attorneys to delegate their functions prevent the instruments from operating as valid LPAs and need to be severed.

[2] On 5 August 2010 Mrs Putt ('the donor') executed an LPA for property and financial affairs and an LPA for health and welfare, in both of which she appointed a family member (A) and two solicitors (B and C), to be her attorneys. B and C are partners in XYZ LLP.

[3] The LPA for health and welfare contained the following clause permitting the attorneys to delegate their functions:

'My attorneys (or any of them) may delegate in writing any of his, her or their functions to any person and shall not be responsible for the default of that person (even if the delegation was not strictly necessary or expedient) provided that he, she or they took reasonable care in his, her or their selection and supervision.'

[4] The LPA for property and affairs contained the same clause, but with the additional words 'and my attorneys (or any of them) may vest my property in any person as nominee, and may place my property in the possession or control of any person'.

[5] D, an associate solicitor at one of the offices of XYZ LLP, witnessed the donor's signature and provided the certificate in Part B of both LPAs.

[6] It should be noted that regulation 8(3)(f) of the Lasting Powers of Attorney, Enduring Powers of Attorney and Public Guardian Regulations 2007 provides that:

'A person is disqualified from giving an LPA certificate in respect of any instrument intended to create a lasting power of attorney if that person is a business partner or employee of (i) the donor, (ii) a donee within sub-paragraph (b).'

[7] An application was made to the Office of the Public Guardian (OPG) to register the LPAs and there was subsequently correspondence between the OPG and XYZ LLP regarding:

(a)   whether an associate solicitor can be a Part B certificate provider when members of the Limited Liability Partnership that employs her are appointed as attorneys; and

(b)   whether the clause permitting the attorneys to delegate was too wide to be valid.

[8] As regards the eligibility of the certificate provider, XYZ LLP contends that:

'As this firm is an LLP, our view is that all employees are employees of the body corporate formed by incorporation, and not employees of individual partners (members). Our further view is that an associate solicitor could not be considered as a business partner of the partners. Our view is therefore than Regulation 8(3)(f) does not make the certificate provider ineligible.'

[9] As regards the clause authorising the attorneys to delegate their functions, XYZ LLP submits that:

'. . . although the default position is that an agent cannot delegate his function; this can be overridden by express authority granted by the donee of the Lasting Power of Attorney. We enclose, by way of authority, the Mental Capacity Act Code of Practice which sets out the default position, but allows for this to be expressly overridden.'

[10] This correspondence concluded with XYZ LLP's agreement that, at no cost to the donor, the OPG would make an application to the Court of Protection to determine both issues, and it did so on 10 March 2011.

The Public Guardian's submissions

[11] Jill Martin is a legal adviser at the OPG, and in a witness statement also dated 10 March 2011 she said as follows:

'(1) . . .
(2) The first matter which the Public Guardian wishes the court to consider is the eligibility of the certificate provider. The attorneys B and C are both partners at XYZ LLP, and the certificate provider in both instruments was D, an associate solicitor of this practice. Regulation 8(3) of the LPA, EPA and PG Regulations 2007 ('the Regulations') disqualifies a 'business partner or employee' of the donor or of an attorney under the instrument from being a certificate provider. If the firm had operated as a common law partnership, the certificate provider, being an associate solicitor at the same firm where two of the attorneys are partners, would be ineligible to act, as being the employee of the partners.
(3) However, the firm is an LLP (Limited Liability Partnership). Section 1(2) of the Limited Liability Partnerships Act 2000 states that: 'A limited liability partnership is a body corporate (with a legal personality separate from that of its members) which is formed by being incorporated under this Act.' The Public Guardian had at one time reluctantly accepted that regulation 8(3) did not apply where the practice was an LLP. This acceptance was reluctant because the purpose of regulation 8(3) is to ensure that the certificate provider should not feel obliged to provide the certificate because their employer, who is also the attorney, has requested it. If this is the rationale of regulation 8(3), it equally applies to LLPs and common law partnerships.
(4) The Public Guardian now considers that the decision of the Employment Appeal Tribunal in *Tiffin v Lester Aldridge LLP* [2010] UKEAT 0255_10_1611 (Exhibit JM3) may enable him to conclude that a solicitor certificate provider is ineligible even though the attorneys are members of an LLP.
(5) The decision just cited does not concern an LPA. The question there was whether a solicitor who was a salaried partner and then a fixed share partner in a firm which became an LLP was an 'employee' or a 'partner' for the purpose of his employment law rights.
(6) It is clear from the judgment of Mr Justice Silber that the status of 'partner' exists even though the practice operates as an LLP. The court is referred in particular to paragraphs 5, 6 and 12 of the judgment. The EAT held that the claimant was a 'partner' within the meaning of section 1(1) of the Partnership Act 1890, which provides that 'Partnership is the relation which subsists between persons carrying on a business in common with a view to profit.'
(7) So it appears to the Public Guardian that the attorneys B and C are partners in XYZ LLP and that D is an associate solicitor, and the website of the practice so describes them (Exhibit JM4), although their correspondence clearly states that 'Any reference to a partner in relation to XYZ LLP means a member of XYZ LLP.'
(8) However, regulation 8(3)(f) applies where the certificate provider is an employee of the attorney, and it may be that, in the case of an LLP, an associate solicitor is employed by the LLP rather than by the member/partners. That is the view of attorney C expressed in the correspondence (Exhibit JM5).
(9) If the court does not accept that regulation 8(3)(f) applies in relation to a practice which is an LLP, the court is asked to consider whether the certificate provider in this case was 'independent'. Part B includes the statement 'I confirm that I act independently of the attorneys and of the donor.' This is additional to the confirmation that she is not a business partner or paid employee of the donor or any of the attorneys.

(10) The other matter which the Public Guardian asks the court to consider is whether severance is necessary. In section 5 of the Property and Financial Affairs instrument the donor stated as follows: 'My attorneys (or any of them) may delegate in writing any of his, her or their functions to any person and shall not be responsible for the default of that person (even if the delegation was not strictly necessary or expedient) provided that he, she or they took reasonable care in his, her or their selection and supervision and my attorneys (or any of them) may vest my property in any person as nominee, and may place my property in the possession or control of any person.' (The donor then provided that the attorney should be authorised to view her will, which the Public Guardian does not ask the court to sever). The validity of the delegation provision is discussed in paragraphs 13 to 15 below. The Public Guardian does not seek severance of the direction that the attorneys may vest the donor's property in a nominee, but it is doubtful whether it is open to a donor to provide that attorneys may place her property in the possession and control of any person.

(11) In section 6 of the Health and Welfare instrument the donor stated as follows: 'My attorneys (or any of them) may delegate in writing any of his, her or their functions to any person and shall not be responsible for the default of that person (even if the delegation was not strictly necessary or expedient) provided that he, she or they took reasonable care in his, her or their selection and supervision.' (The donor then provided that the attorney should be authorised to view her will, medical records and other records, which the Public Guardian does not ask the court to sever).

(12) In section 6 of the Health and Welfare instrument the donor also directed that: 'I wish only A to make decisions relating to life-sustaining treatment and not B or C.' Although the attorneys were appointed to act jointly and severally, the Public Guardian does not ask the court to sever this provision because it is expressed as a wish and so may be treated as guidance only.

(13) The Public Guardian considers that the delegation provisions set out in paragraphs 10 and 11 above are too wide and need to be severed. They go beyond the limited delegation recognised by the MCA Code of Practice, which states (at paragraph 7.61): 'Attorneys cannot usually delegate their authority to someone else. They must carry out their duties personally. The attorney may seek professional or expert advice (for example, investment advice from a financial adviser or advice on medical treatment from a doctor). But they cannot, as a general rule, allow someone else to make a decision that they have been appointed to make, unless this has been specifically authorised by the donor in the LPA.'

(14) In this case the donor has specifically authorised delegation in the LPA, but the question is whether it is open to the donor to provide that, in effect, the entire function can be delegated. Section 10(8)(a) of the MCA provides that the instrument 'cannot give the donee (or, if more than one, any of them) power to appoint a substitute or successor.' It is submitted that the provisions set out in paragraphs 10 and 11 above do purport to give the attorneys power to appoint a substitute, either permanently or for an indeterminate period. Section 10(8)(a) does not say 'permanent substitute' and is, therefore, applicable to a provision purporting to authorise the attorney to delegate his or her entire function, whether or not this is expressed to be permanent.

(15) In a letter dated 20 October 2010 from XYZ LLP (please see Exhibit JM6) it is argued that the clause is delegation rather than substitution. The writer attaches precedent 148 from the Encyclopaedia of Forms and Precedents, which reads: 'My attorney[s] may appoint any agent to do any business which [he is (or) they are] unable to do [himself (or themselves] or which can more conveniently be done by an agent.' The Public Guardian submits that this precedent falls far short of a delegation of the whole function of the attorney. The Public Guardian, therefore, asks the court to sever the delegation provision in both instruments.

(16) The donor does not lack capacity. It is confirmed in a letter dated 30 November 2010 from her solicitors that she wishes the Public Guardian to apply to the court to seek a determination of the validity of the delegation clauses (Exhibit JM7). This letter does not refer to determination of the question whether the certificate provider was eligible to act because this issue was not being considered at that time. However, the letter from the donor's solicitors dated 2 March 2011 indicates that the donor is content for the Public Guardian to refer this matter to the court at no cost to her, and wishes to be informed of the outcome. As the donor and attorneys do not wish to be involved in the application the Public Guardian has not served it on them, but will do so if directed by the court.

(17) In summary, the Public Guardian requests the court to decide whether the certificate provider was eligible to act, either on the basis that she was employed by the attorneys

within regulation 8(3)(f) or, if not, that she was not acting independently of the attorneys, as required by the prescribed form. If the court decides that the certificate provider was not eligible to act, the court is requested to direct cancellation of the registered Property and Financial Affairs instrument and to direct the Public Guardian not to register the Health and Welfare instrument.

(18) If the court considers that the certificate provider was eligible to act, it is requested to sever the words set out in paragraph 10 above from 'My attorneys (or any of them' to 'supervision and' and the words 'and may place my property in the possession and control of any person' from the Property and Financial Affairs instrument. It is also requested to sever the words in inverted commas set out in paragraph 11 above from the Health and Welfare instrument pursuant to paragraph 11(5)(a) of Schedule 1 of the MCA.

(19) As the Property and Financial Affairs instrument has already been registered, the court is requested to direct severance under section 22(2)(a) of the MCA (if it wishes to sever the clause in question) and to direct that the instrument be returned to the Public Guardian to be stamped accordingly.'

Decision on the eligibility of the certificate provider

[12] In paragraph (2) of her witness statement, Jill Martin suggested that the purpose of regulation 8(3) was 'to ensure that the certificate provider should not feel obliged to provide the certificate because their employer, who is also the attorney, has requested it.' She may be right, but, having searched in vain through several consultation papers and the responses to them, I have failed to establish the precise legislative intent underlying regulation 8(3)(f), other than 'remedying the situation where a potentially vulnerable person with borderline capacity is asked to sign a power of attorney without proper safeguards,' which appears in Lasting Powers of Attorney – forms and guidance: Response to consultation, CP(R) 01/06, at page 25. Be that as it may, regulation 8(3)(f) expressly disqualifies anyone who is a 'business partner or employee' of the donor or donee from giving an LPA certificate.

[13] The words 'business partner or employee' are ordinary words of the English language and should be construed in the way that an ordinary sensible person would construe them. The choice of the word 'business' is designed to distinguish partnership as an economic relationship from partnership of a more personal and intimate nature. I assume that Parliament was looking at the substance rather than the form and intended to include all kinds of 'business partner' under this umbrella term – equity partner, salaried partner, fixed-share partner, and so on – and that, if it had intended to treat business arrangements under the Limited Liability Partnership Act 2000 any differently from those under the Partnership Act 1890, it would have expressly said so in the regulations. The word 'employee' probably denotes no more than a person who is employed and remunerated by the business and is generally, though not necessarily, of a junior or subordinate status to the attorney.

[14] On this broad analysis, it would seem that the wording of regulation 8(3)(f) is not entirely foolproof if the desired objective is to provide certain safeguards, and would allow, for example, an employee to be appointed as attorney and his or her employer or a fellow employee to act as the certificate provider. However, despite these shortcomings, the prescribed form itself requires the certificate provider to state, 'I am acting independently of the person making this LPA (the donor) and the person(s) appointed under the LPA,' in addition to confirming that he or she is not a person listed in regulation 8(3) who cannot provide a certificate. In paragraph 5 of his judgment in Tiffin v Lester Aldridge, Mr Justice Silber said it was 'common ground that the claimant was either a "partner" or an "employee" and that he could not be an independent contractor.' The same applies here. The certificate provider, D, was not an 'independent' contractor.

[15] In my judgment, the wording of regulation 8(3)(f) cannot be construed as making any distinction between a partnership under the Partnership Act 1890 and the Limited

Liability Partnership Act 2000 for the purpose of providing an LPA certificate and that, as D was an employee of XYZ LLP, she was ineligible to provide the certificates in Mrs Putt's LPAs.

[16] Accordingly, pursuant to section 22(2)(a) of the Mental Capacity Act 2005 the court determines that one the requirements for the creation of an LPA has not been met, and pursuant to section 22(4)(a) it directs that the instruments purporting to create the LPAs are not to be registered.

Decision on the delegation clause

[17] Strictly speaking, because of my finding above, there is no longer any need for me to consider the validity of the delegation clause. However, as Jill Martin on behalf of the Public Guardian has taken the trouble to set out her submissions, and as XYZ LLP has included this clause in other LPAs, as a matter of courtesy I shall address the issue.

[18] One of the basic rules of the law of agency is that an agent cannot delegate his authority. In the past this rule was expressed by the maxim delegatus non potest delegare and its application is based on the personal nature of the relationship which exists between a principal and an agent. A few exceptions to the general rule are permitted in the context of ordinary powers of attorney (those which do not continue to remain in force after the donor has lost capacity), such as:

(a)   where the act delegated is purely ministerial in nature and does not involve any confidence or discretion;
(b)   from the conduct of the parties;
(c)   where delegation is the usual practice in the trade, business or profession of one or both of the parties; and
(d)   through necessity of unforeseen circumstances.

[19] Delegation and substitution are not synonymous. A delegate merely deputises for the attorney, whereas a substitute completely replaces him, and in appointing a substitute the attorney irrevocably parts with his authority under the power.

[20] Section 10(8)(a) of the Mental Capacity Act 2005 provides that:

'An instrument used to create a lasting power of attorney - (a) cannot give the donee (or, if more than one, any of them) power to appoint a substitute or successor.'

[21] A similar provision applied to enduring powers of attorney under section 2(9) of the Enduring Powers of Attorney Act 1985, which has been re-enacted as paragraph 2(6) to Schedule 4 of the Mental Capacity Act 2005:

'A power of attorney which gives the attorney a right to appoint a substitute or successor cannot be an enduring power.'

[22] The origin of this prohibition can be found in the Law Commission's report, the Incapacitated Principal (1983), which led to the enactment of the Enduring Powers of attorney Act 1985. At paragraph 4.22 of that report the Law Commissioners stated:

'*Delegation and substitution.* As in the case of ordinary powers the EPA attorney would have implied power to delegate any of his functions which were not such that the donor would have expected the attorney to attend to them personally. Any wider power to delegate would have to be provided for expressly in the instrument. We would not wish, however, the attorney to be enabled to appoint a substitute or successor to himself. This would be contrary to the special relationship of trust subsisting between the EPA donor and attorney and would undermine some of the safeguards which we recommend in this Report. We accordingly propose that no power that enabled the attorney to appoint a substitute or successor should be capable of being an EPA.'

[23] The delegation clause in Mrs Putt's health and welfare LPA states that:

'My attorneys (or any of them) may delegate in writing any of his, her or their functions to any person and shall not be responsible for the default of that person (even if the delegation was not strictly necessary or expedient) provided that he, she or they took reasonable care in his, her or their selection and supervision.'

[24] This clause authorises the attorney to delegate any of his functions. Theoretically, it would enable him to delegate all his functions, which certainly would be a substitution. Even if this sub-delegation were not, strictly speaking, a substitution (because the clause implies that there could be ongoing supervision by the attorney), I consider that, as a matter of policy, the attorney's ability to delegate his functions in circumstances in which it is not strictly speaking necessary or expedient to do so, and the fact that he is exonerated from any default of the substitute or sub-delegate, so long as he took reasonable care in the selection and supervision of that person, are not simply contrary but almost repugnant to the special relationship of personal obligation and faith that one might reasonably expect to exist between a donor and the attorney of an LPA; particularly in a health and welfare power of attorney in which the donor (as is in Mrs Putt's case) has given the attorney authority to give or refuse consent to life-sustaining treatment on her behalf.

[25] Whereas the use of such a clause might be acceptable in a commercial agency agreement, it undermines some of the safeguards in the Mental Capacity Act 2005 and its inclusion in an LPA cannot really be in the donor's best interests.

[G14]

RE BUCKLEY: THE PUBLIC GUARDIAN V C

[2013] COPLR

COURT OF PROTECTION

SENIOR JUDGE DENZIL LUSH 22 January 2013

Property and affairs – Lasting Power of Attorney – Duties upon attorney in the management of P's monies

P signed an LPA for property and affairs appointing her niece, C to be her sole attorney. The Office of the Public Guardian (OPG) opened an investigation into P's affairs following a complaint. Following investigation the OPG asserted that C had used at least £87,682.53 of P's monies to fund C's reptile breeding business. C claimed this was an investment on behalf of P although the investment was made in C's name. The OPG also asserted that C had used a further £43,317.47 of P's monies for C's personal benefit. P lacked capacity to revoke the LPA. The public guardian applied for an order that the LPA be revoked.

Held – revoking the LPA –

A had behaved in a way that was not in P's best interests, P was unable to revoke the LPA herself, such a revocation was necessary and proportionate, and it was in P's best interests to do so.

Per curiam: the court gave guidance at paras [20]–[46] on the responsibilities of an attorney under an LPA when investing the donor's funds.

(1) Attorneys have fiduciary obligations similar to those of trustees. Until the OPG issues its own guidance, attorneys should comply with the provisions of the Trustee Act 2000 as regards the standard investment criteria and the requirement to obtain and consider proper advice. They should also have regard to the criteria in *Investing for Patients* (1998 edn), with allowance for updating as set out in para 37.

(2) Attorneys should keep the donor's money and property separate from their own or anyone else's. Investments should be made in the donor's name and if that is not possible the attorney should execute a declaration of trust or some other formal record acknowledging the donor's beneficial interest in the asset.

(3) Unless de minimis, an application must be made to the court for an order under s 23 of the Mental Capacity Act 2005 (the 2005 Act) if: (a) gifts exceeds the limited scope of the attorney's authority under s 12 of the 2005 Act; (b) a loan is to be made to the attorney or members of his or her family; (c) an investment is to be made in the attorney's business; (d) there is a proposed sale or purchase at an undervalue; (e) there is any other transaction where there is a conflict between the donor's interests and the interests of the attorney.

(4) Attorneys should know the law regarding their role and responsibilities. Ignorance is no excuse. They should at least be familiar with the 'information you must read' section on the LPA and the provisions of the Mental Capacity Act Code of Practice.

Statutory provisions considered

Trustee Act 2000, ss 4, 5

Mental Capacity Act 2005, ss 1(4), (5), 12, 22(3), (4)(b), 23, 42(4)(a), Sch 1

European Convention for the Protection of Human Rights and Fundamental Freedoms 1950, Art 8

Cases referred to in judgment

Harcourt: The Public Guardian v A, Re [2013] COPLR 69, CP

P (Statutory Will), Re [2009] EWHC 163 (Ch), [2010] Ch 33, [2009] COPLR Con Vol 906, [2009] WTLR 651, [2009] 2 All ER 1198, ChD

W (Enduring Power of Attorney), Re [2000] Ch 343, [2000] 3 WLR 45, [1999] 2 FLR 1163, [2000] 1 All ER 175, ChD

Wells v Wells; Thomas v Brighton Health Authority; Page v Sheerness Steel Co plc [1999] 1 AC 345, [1998] 3 WLR 329, [1998] 2 FLR 507, [1998] 3 All ER 481, HL

Marion Bowgen (Compliance Unit, OPG) for the public guardian

The respondent did not appear and was not represented

Cur. Adv. Vult.

SENIOR JUDGE DENZIL LUSH:

[1] This is an application by the public guardian for the court to revoke a lasting power of attorney (LPA) and to direct him to cancel the registration of the LPA.

The background

[2] Miss Buckley was born in 1931 and lives in Kent.

[3] Since July 2011 she has been a resident in a nursing home, at which the fees are £985 a week. She is fully self-funded and is not currently eligible for NHS continuing healthcare.

[4] On 7 September 2010 Miss Buckley executed an LPA for property and affairs, in which she:

- appointed her niece, C, who was born in 1954, to be her sole attorney;
- did not appoint a replacement attorney; and
- named her close friend, Shirley, as the only person who was to be notified when an application was made to register the LPA.

[5] Miss Buckley's solicitor witnessed her signature and was the Part B certificate provider.

[6] A month later an application was made to the Office of the Public Guardian (the OPG) to register the LPA, and it was registered on 17 January 2011.

The general visitor's report

[7] On 20 April 2012 the OPG received a complaint about the way in which the attorney was handling the donor's finances, and it opened a formal investigation into the matter.

[8] As is standard procedure in investigations of this kind, the OPG sent a Court of Protection General Visitor to see Miss Buckley. The visitor saw her on 6 August 2012 and concluded that she lacked the capacity to instruct the attorney to account for her dealings under the LPA, and that she also lacked the capacity to revoke the LPA. The visitor also commented as follows:

> 'We talked about her niece C (POA). She had a vague recollection of a niece and said she visited her home when she was ill and took everything she wanted and then did not bother with her any more. She said she only visited when she wanted money and indicated this by rubbing her fingers together. The manager was present during this conversation and believed the client's memory of some matters was quite reliable and that the client appeared to recollect her niece wanting money previously and no longer being bothered with her now. When asked whether she wanted the niece to manage her money she indicated very negatively. When asked if she had wanted her niece to use her money for anything special she said she didn't trust her and had only ever wanted her money.'

The application

[9] On 22 October 2012 Marion Bowgen, of the compliance unit at the OPG, applied to the court for the following interim orders:

(1)   The finance and property LPA registered on 17 January 2011 appointing C as the sole attorney to Miss Buckley to be suspended until further order.

(2)   C to be prohibited from dealing with or encashing any investment or other asset in the name of Miss Buckley, pending further orders from the court.

(3)   Miss Buckley's Nationwide Building Society accounts (*numbers*) and National Savings & Investments Premium Bonds (*numbers*) to be frozen, whereby access to her bank accounts should be limited to payment of her care home fees only.

(4)   C to be directed to provide a full account of her dealings under the LPA for the period 17 January 2011 to present, within 21 days of the date of service of this order. She is to provide explanations for all the transactions within all bank accounts held in the sole or joint name of Miss Buckley, and submit copies of receipts/invoices to support her explanations.

(5)   The public guardian to file and serve a further COP24 regarding his current investigation into these matters within 8 weeks of the date of this order.

[10] The application was accompanied by a witness statement made on 22 October 2012 by Yun Ding, an investigation officer with the OPG, which can be summarised as follows:

(1)   Miss Buckley's house had been sold for £279,000 on 28 April 2011.

(2)   Between 17 January 2011 and June 2012 the attorney had withdrawn £72,000 from Miss Buckley's funds to set up a reptile breeding business. The attorney claimed that this was a short-term investment which would generate a 20% return over a 2-year period.

(3)   The attorney admitted that she had used at least £7,650 of Miss Buckley's capital for her own personal benefit.

(4)   The attorney said she visited Miss Buckley once a week, but this was contradicted by the nursing home, who said that she had not visited her at all until 16 October 2012, when she appears to have obtained Miss Buckley's signature on some unknown documentation.

(5)   At one stage there had been daily cash withdrawals of £300 (the maximum amount) from Miss Buckley's Nationwide Building Society account.

(6)   The Special Investigation Department at the Nationwide had alerted Social Services in April 2012 and the matter was also referred to the police, who interviewed the attorney in July 2012.

(7)   Miss Buckley's estate may have incurred a total loss of approximately £150,000.

[11] On 23 October 2012 I made an order in the terms sought by the OPG, set a timetable for the filing of evidence, and listed the application for hearing on 19 December 2012.

The special visitor's report

[12] Although his report was unavailable when the OPG made its initial application to the court, on 21 October 2012 a Court of Protection Special Visitor, Dr Andrew Barker, examined Miss Buckley and prepared a report of his findings. He had been asked by the OPG specifically to assess Miss Buckley's capacity to make the following decisions:

(1)   to revoke or suspend the LPA;
(2)   to make a new LPA;
(3)   to manage her financial affairs;
(4)   to direct the attorney to make decisions on her behalf regarding the management of her financial affairs;
(5)   to instruct the attorney to provide an account of her dealings under the LPA; and
(6)   to choose or say who she would like to manage her affairs should she not be happy with the existing attorney.

[13] Dr Barker concluded his report as follows:

'Miss Buckley has a history of multiple strokes, leading her to be unable to look after herself, then needing residential and then nursing care. A hospital outpatient clinic letter following admission refers to a diagnosis of dementia. Her cognitive impairment leads her to need a rigid routine, suffer anxiety with sustained concentration, and have significant memory impairment. A general visitor found her to be generally confused, with a short concentration span, appearing disorientated, and could not participate in conversation beyond a very basic level.

My interview with Miss Buckley was time limited due to her increasing anxiety. I was told by Nurse Adams that she tended to get agitated if she had to concentrate very long. She also had some expressive and receptive dysphasia, making communication difficult. She was unable to recognise some simple words, and often unable to express herself fully. She was disorientated in time and place, had poor short and long term memory, impaired concentration and difficulties understanding even mildly complex abstract concepts.

Her documented history and my assessment are in keeping with Miss Buckley suffering with moderately severe vascular dementia. This is of a severity to affect her understanding of information, impair her recall and make her unable to weigh information in the balance, for any significant decision. She was unable to understand the nature and effects of an LPA to a sufficient degree or to choose an attorney, was not aware of her financial dealings and could not recall detail sufficiently well or concentrate long enough to weigh information in the balance to come to decisions about an attorney or to direct or instruct an attorney.'

Yun Ding's second witness statement

[14] On 13 December 2012 Yun Ding made a second witness statement, the primary purpose of which was to exhibit Dr Barker's report and to update the court on the OPG's investigation as required by the directions order of 23 October. She concluded the statement as follows:

'From the evidence gathered so far, I estimate that Miss Buckley has contributed at least £87,682.53 towards the reptile investment venture described by C. In the absence of any contrary evidence, the Public Guardian maintains that Miss Buckley's finances may have been used to heavily subsidize what appears to be a reptile breeding business, without any formal guarantee or security or her share of the alleged investment returns. C also appears to have misappropriated £43,317.47 of her aunt's estate without obtaining consent, contrary to what she had told the police. I have therefore re-referred this matter back to the police to conduct further inquiries.

In the light of the above and the content of my COP24 dated 22 October 2012, the Public Guardian believes that it would not be in Miss Buckley's best interests for C to continue as her finance and property attorney. Therefore, the Public Guardian would like to request the court to revoke and cancel the registered LPA executed by Miss Buckley under s 22(4)(b) of the Mental Capacity Act 2005. Should the court decide to appoint a deputy in the interests of Miss Buckley, the Public Guardian would like to highlight that the deputy may need to take action against the former attorney in order to restore Miss Buckley's estate to a more realistic level. The care manager of (*a named local authority*) has confirmed that the council is willing to consider applying to become Miss Buckley's property and affairs deputy.'

The attorney's response

[15] On 17 December 2012 C made a witness statement, in which she said:

'(1) I make this statement in connection with proceedings in the Court of Protection following the Office of the Public Guardian's (OPG) investigation into my actions under a Lasting Power of Attorney (LPA) over my aunt, Miss Buckley.

(2) The OPG has raised concerns that I may have been using my aunt's money for my own purposes and not acting in her best interests. They have made an application to the court, requesting that the LPA be revoked.

(3) I would like to say that I do not object to the LPA being revoked provided that my aunt's property and affairs will be looked after. However, I would like to make my position very clear that I have not acted contrary to my aunt's best interests and that in my view the investments I have made are in her best interests.

(4) I love my aunt and would never do anything to hurt her. I am very upset that these allegations have been made about me and would like to put forward my views for the benefit of the court and the OPG.

(5) I apologise that I have missed the deadline for filing this evidence and would be grateful if the court would consider this statement despite the fact that it has been filed out of time. I have only recently been able to obtain legal advice (6 December 2012) and was not previously aware that I had to file a statement as I had provided all the documentation I had to the OPG.

(6) I will set out the background to this matter briefly and my response to the statement made by Yun Ding dated 22 October 2012.

(7) My aunt executed an LPA in relation to her property and affairs appointing me as her attorney on 7 September 2010. This was done through her solicitors and I did not have any active involvement in that matter other than to agreeing to act as attorney and sign the necessary forms.

(8) My aunt has a close friend, Shirley, who has assisted her with her affairs for some time. She had been unable to continue to do so and it was her and four others that recommended I take over. I was reluctant to do so, but wanted to help my aunt as much as possible and therefore agreed to this.

(9) My aunt has been suffering with strokes, is incontinent and blind in one eye and nearly blind in the other. I was not aware of any formal diagnosis, however I note that the OPG has confirmed that she suffers from dementia.

(10) Myself and Shirley first became concerned about my aunt when she started wandering around and giving money to people she did not know. She would often think that she had run out of the things she needed and would ask people to get them for her. Shirley would look after her as I was unable to travel due to illness.

(11) I exhibit at C1 a letter from Shirley to myself dated 30 October 2010 in which she confirms that she was assisting with finding homes for my aunt and that the house would need to be sold. Shirley assisted my aunt with the sale of her house and solicitors were involved with this.

(12) I did state at this time that I would have my aunt living with me if I could, but due to space constraints in my home, which is a council property, I would not have been able to.

(13) The LPA was registered on 17 January 2011 and I began to assist my aunt with her affairs at that time. I had regular contact with my aunt through Shirley who visited her weekly.

(14) I was advised by Shirley that I should invest some of her money.

(15) I investigated this and found a company which specialises in breeding reptiles. I dealt with (name) who runs the company and felt that this would be a good investment for my aunt and was told that this would return her money plus 20% interest within 2 years. My aunt loves animals and I felt that this would be an investment which she would be happy with.

(16) It is stated that I did not provide evidence that the investment was made in the name of my aunt. I would like to state that I was not aware that the investment had to be made in her name and was concerned about signing on her behalf. I agree that perhaps I should have opened the investment in her name, but my intention has always been that the returns from the investment will go back to my aunt. The only reason that I transferred any money to my son's account was because I did not know how to transfer money abroad using 'CHAPS' and he did. I kept receipts for the transfers and provided these to the OPG.

(17) I agree that my aunt lacks capacity to manage her own financial affairs and in my view she has become increasingly confused and is unable to understand the information relevant to deciding how to handle her finances or retain that information.

(18) In relation to the withdrawals from my aunt's account, all the large amounts were invested in the reptile company and I admit that some of the money was used for my own benefit but only with my aunt's permission. She has given me money in the past and this was not unusual for her as we were very close.

(19) I have been investigated by the police who I understand have stated that I was naïve but that no crime had been committed. I only invested in the reptiles because I thought this would be what my aunt wanted.

(20) It is stated in para 8 that I wrote that I visited my aunt once per week, however, I would like to point out that the specific question I was asked was, 'how often do you or any other person visit Miss Buckley'. When I answered this question, I was referring to the fact that Shirley visits my aunt weekly and this is confirmed in the court visitor's report at exhibit YM2 to the OPG's statement.

(21) In relation to the question regarding my visit to my aunt, the only paperwork I signed was a form which the nurse had asked me to fill out and she had also asked me to discuss her funeral plans with her. I was very upset at this suggestion, but explained this to my aunt and did this for her. I exhibit at C2 a copy of a post-it note at the time when she wrote down her name and some details of funeral directors for me.

(22) I am very upset that my aunt has suggested that I was after her money. I do wonder whether she was confused and may have been referring to my cousin, Pam, who had

cleared her belongings from her house for her over two days. When I visited my aunt, she told me that in her will she has left her assets to a dogs home and donkey sanctuary as she 'did not want anyone else to get hold of it'.

(23) I am happy with my aunt's choice in relation to where her property should go and I know that she loves animals so I would support the choice.

(24) To conclude, I do not oppose the OPG's application to revoke the LPA. I am very upset at the allegations that have been made and did not intend to hurt my aunt in any way. While I maintain the view that the investment is a good one and that I had my aunt's interests at heart, I do feel that the responsibility is too much for me to continue with, especially as I am unwell myself.

(25) I have only ever had my aunt's interests at heart and would like the court to note that, while I agree to step down as attorney, I do not agree that I have done anything wrong by investing my aunt's money in this way.

(26) If a deputy is to be appointed by the court, I would be grateful if I could be notified so that I can arrange for any money coming in from the investment to be returned to my aunt as intended.'

The hearing

[16] The hearing took place on Wednesday, 19 December 2012, and lasted 1½ hours. Marion Bowgen attended on behalf of the OPG accompanied by Alan Eccles, the public guardian.

[17] Two days earlier, on 17 December 2012, C's solicitors had written to the court saying:

'We have been instructed to advise and assist C in this matter. C apologises for missing the deadline for filing her evidence as she did not realise she needed to do so and, unfortunately, she was only able to obtain our assistance on 6 December 2012.
C instructs us that she is unable to attend the hearing on 19 December 2012 due to illness. We are not instructed to represent C at any hearing and cannot go on record as acting for her, but please note our involvement as legal advisors.'

The law relating to applications of this kind

[18] In *Re Harcourt: The Public Guardian v A*, [2013] COPLR 69, an anonymised transcript of which can also be found on the OPG's website, I summarised the following areas of the law:

(1) the donor's capacity in the context of an investigation by the OPG;
(2) the public guardian's powers in relation to LPAs;
(3) the Court of Protection's powers in relation to LPAs;
(4) best interests;
(5) the law regarding compliance; and
(6) the donor's and the attorney's rights under Art 8 of the European Convention for the Protection of Human Rights and Fundamental Freedoms 1950.

[19] I do not propose to repeat what I said in *Re Harcourt: The Public Guardian v A* here, but I shall use this opportunity to discuss an issue which did not arise in that case, namely the responsibilities of an attorney acting under an LPA when investing the donor's funds.

The investment of funds by an attorney

[20] There are two common misconceptions when it comes to investments. The first is that attorneys acting under an LPA can do whatever they like with the donors' funds. And the second is that attorneys can do whatever the donors could – or would – have done personally, if they had the capacity to manage their property and financial affairs.

[21] Managing your own money is one thing. Managing someone else's money is an entirely different matter.

[22] People who have the capacity to manage their own financial affairs are generally not accountable to anyone and don't need to keep accounts or records of their income and expenditure. They can do whatever they like with their money, and this includes doing nothing at all. They can stash their cash under the mattress, if they wish and, of course, they are entitled to make unwise decisions.

[23] None of these options are open to an attorney acting for an incapacitated donor, partly because of their fiduciary obligations and partly because an attorney is required to act in the donor's best interests. Section 1(5) of the Mental Capacity Act 2005 (the 2005 Act) states that, 'an act done, or decision made, under this Act for or on behalf of a person who lacks capacity must be done, or made, in his best interests'.

[24] Mr Justice Lewison (as he then was) commented on this point in *Re P (Statutory Will)* [2009] EWHC 163 (Ch), [2010] Ch 33, [2009] COPLR Con Vol 906. At para [42], he said:

> 'I would add that although the fact that P makes an unwise decision does not on its own give rise to any inference of incapacity (s 1(4)), once the decision making power shifts to a third party (whether carer, deputy or the court) I cannot see that it would be a proper exercise for a third party decision maker consciously to make an unwise decision merely because P would have done so. A consciously unwise decision will rarely if ever be made in P's best interests.'

[25] Attorneys hold a fiduciary position, which imposes a number of duties on them. Like trustees and other fiduciaries, they must exercise such care and skill as is reasonable in the circumstances when investing the donor's assets and this duty of care is even greater where attorneys hold themselves out as having specialist knowledge or experience.

[26] Although it does not expressly apply to attorneys, s 4 of the Trustee Act 2000 requires trustees to have regard to what are known as the 'standard investment criteria' when exercising any power of investment. There are two standard criteria, namely:

(1)   the suitability of the investments; and
(2)   the need to diversify the investments, insofar as it is appropriate in the circumstances.

[27] Trustees are also required to review the investments from time to time and consider whether, having regard to the standard investment criteria, they should be varied.

[28] Section 5 of the Trustee Act 2000 requires trustees, before exercising any powers of investment or reviewing the investments, to obtain and consider proper advice about the way in which, having regard to the standard investment criteria, their power should be exercised. In this context, 'proper advice' means the advice of a person who is reasonably believed by the trustee to be qualified to give it by his ability in and practical experience of financial and other matters relating to the proposed investment. There is an exception to this general rule, and trustees need not obtain such advice if they reasonably conclude that it is unnecessary or inappropriate to do so.

[29] Before the 2005 Act came into force on 1 October 2007, both the Court of Protection and the antecedents of the Office of the Public Guardian (the Public Trust Office and later the Public Guardianship Office) were actively involved in the investment of patients' funds. There was a discrete Investments Branch, which issued in-house guidance for staff, *Investing for Patients*, and much of the discussion that follows has been taken from that guidance.

[30] The court used to set an investment code for every patient. There were four short-term (ST) codes and eight long-term (LT) codes, which were devised following consultation with the Lord Chancellor's Honorary Investment Advisory Committee (HIAC). HIAC, which was rebranded as the Strategic Investment Board in 2001 before finally being abolished in 2008, was a committee of six distinguished financial experts from the City who met with ex officio members from the Lord Chancellor's Department five times a year to consider issues relating to the investment of patients' funds including strategy, performance measurement and the setting of appropriate benchmarks.

[31] Two of the most important factors when considering the suitability of investments are the donor's age and life expectancy. Most donors are older people. Their average age is 80 years and 11 months and, in this respect Miss Buckley, who is 81½, is a typical LPA donor.

[32] Short-term investment codes are generally more appropriate where an individual has an anticipated life expectancy of 5 years or less, and the guidance to court staff suggested that, 'without clear medical evidence it would be prudent to consider a life expectancy of less than 5 years for new patients aged 80 or over'.

[33] There is no need for me to consider long-term investments for the purposes of this decision, but the short-term investment codes in *Investing for Patients* were as follows:

Investment Code	Approximate Value	Investment requirement	Usual investment strategy
ST1	£0–£50,000	Available quickly – safe	Special Account only
ST2	£50,001–£100,000	All or part available quickly – very little risk acceptable	Special Account with the option of purchasing short-dated gilts if the returns are more favourable
ST3	Over £100,000	All or part available quickly – very little risk acceptable	A portfolio based on short-dated gilts, provided their anticipated returns compare favourably with Special Account or accounts with building societies
ST4	Over £50,000 with existing portfolio	Aim to make all or part available quickly – reducing risk commensurate with the patient's requirements	Rationalisation and usually gradual reduction of longer-term investments in the portfolio within the scope of the annual CGT allowance and prudent investment advice

[34] It has never been possible for attorneys to keep funds on special account in the Court Funds Office, but a broadly similar outcome would be achieved from depositing the funds in an interest-bearing account offering instant access (or reasonably instant access) with a reputable bank or building society, or with National

Savings and Investments (NS&I), where there is a 100% guarantee from HM Treasury on all deposits.

[35] The last edition of Investing for Patients was drawn up 15 years ago in 1998 following the decision of the House of Lords in *Wells v Wells; Thomas v Brighton Health Authority; Page v Sheerness Steel Co plc* [1999] 1 AC 345, [1998] 3 WLR 329, [1998] 2 FLR 507. Circumstances have changed since then and the investment codes need to be revised.

[36] Generally speaking, attorneys acting under an LPA should ensure that any investment products or services they acquire on a donor's behalf are provided by individuals or firms who are regulated by the Financial Services Authority. One of the advantages of this course of action is that the donor's investments will be covered by the Financial Services Compensation Scheme (FSCS), in which eligible deposits are protected up to a maximum of £85,000.

[37] Accordingly, taking this and other factors into account, the short-term investment codes recommended in *Investing for Patients* could possibly be rewritten along the following lines:

Investment Code	Approximate Value	Investment requirement	Usual investment strategy
ST1	£0–£50,000	Available quickly – safe	Cash deposit that provides a competitive rate when compared with base rates and NS&I returns
ST2	Over £85,000	All or part available quickly – very little risk acceptable	Cash deposits with different financial institutions, including NS&I, which stay below the FSCS limits and/or a gilt portfolio to provide returns that compare favourably with base rates
ST3	Cash with an existing portfolio	Aim to make all or part available quickly – reducing risk commensurate with P's requirements	Depending on the nature of the portfolio, a liquidation process should be adopted using the annual CGT allowance.

Investment Code	Approximate Value	Investment requirement	Usual investment strategy
			The cash funds should be retained in cash deposits with different financial institutions, including NS&I, which stay within the FSCS limits and/or a gilt portfolio to provide returns that compare favourably with base rates

[38] *Investing for Patients* suggested a few other factors that may need to be considered, such as:

(a)   whether any major items of expenditure are anticipated or should be planned for;

(b)   whether any gifts or payments to dependants are likely to be made. This will usually involve an application to the Court of Protection for authorisation to make gifts in excess of the limits imposed by s 12 of the 2005 Act in order to reduce the impact of Inheritance Tax;

(c)   the type of return required. For example, whether a high income is needed from the investments, or whether the capital can be left to grow, or whether a mixture of the two would be more appropriate;

(d)   risk: whether absolute safety is required for the investment or whether some risk is acceptable in exchange for the possibility of getting a better return; and

(e)   whether there is an existing portfolio and, if so, the tax and cost considerations that may affect decisions about whether to change it and how quickly.

[39] The guidance also considered the interests of beneficiaries under the patient's will or intestacy, which included asking the following questions:

(a)   whether it is likely that the investments will be sold when the patient dies, or whether the beneficiaries of the patient's estate are likely to want the investments as they then stand; and

(b)   whether there are any provisions in the patient's will which affect the composition of the investments, such as a specific bequest of an investment or the creation of a trust in which income and capital go to different beneficiaries.

[40] In this respect, *Investing for Patients* concluded that:

'it will probably only be worthwhile to consider in depth the interests of those who will benefit on death if the following conditions all apply:
(a)   the capital available for investment is over £100,000;
(b)   there is no reason to believe that the patient's state of health is life-threatening; and
(c)   the capital, when invested, will adequately satisfy the patient's current and future income and capital requirements.'

[41] Until such time as the OPG issues its own guidance to attorneys and deputies on the investment of funds, I would suggest that, as they have fiduciary obligations that are similar to those of trustees, attorneys should comply with the provisions of the Trustee Act 2000 as regards the standard investment criteria and the requirement to obtain and consider proper advice. I would also recommend that attorneys and their financial advisers have regard to the criteria that were historically approved by the court and the antecedents of the OPG in *Investing for Patients*, albeit with some allowance for updating, as suggested in para [37] above.

[42] There are three further points I must mention relating to the fiduciary nature of the relationship between the donor and the attorney. The first is that attorneys should keep the donor's money and property separate from their own or anyone else's: Mental Capacity Act Code of Practice, para 7.68. This applies to investments and, wherever possible, all investments should be made in the donor's name. If, for any reason, it is not possible to register the investment in the donor's name, the attorney should execute a declaration of trust or some other formal record acknowledging the donor's beneficial interest in the asset.

[43] The second point is that, subject to a sensible de minimis exception, where the potential infringement is so minor that it would be disproportionate to make a formal application to the court, an application *must* be made to the court for an order under s 23 of the 2005 Act in any of the following cases:

(a)   gifts that exceed the limited scope of the authority conferred on attorneys by s 12 of the 2005 Act;
(b)   loans to the attorney or to members of the attorney's family;
(c)   any investment in the attorney's own business;
(d)   sales or purchases at an undervalue; and
(e)   any other transactions in which there is a conflict between the interests of the donor and the interests of the attorney.

[44] The final point is one that has been made in the past, but needs to be repeated. Attorneys should be aware of the law regarding their role and responsibilities. Ignorance is no excuse. I am not suggesting that attorneys should be able to pass an examination on the provisions of the 2005 Act, but they should at least be familiar with the 'information you must read' on the LPA itself and the provisions of the Mental Capacity Act 2005 Code of Practice. Section 42(4)(a) of the 2005 Act expressly stipulates that it is the duty of an attorney acting under an LPA to have regard to the code.

[45] Commenting on the conduct of an attorney in *Re W (Enduring Power of Attorney)* [2000] Ch 343, [1999] 2 FLR 1163, at 350 and 1169 respectively, Mr Jules Sher QC said:

'. . . . she ought to have known the law if she was to take on the responsibility of such an important fiduciary position, particularly as one of the few things expressly stated in part of the power itself is the following sentence: "I also understand my limited power to use the donor's property to benefit persons other than the donor".'

[46] Mr Sher was referring to an Enduring Power of Attorney. The declaration in Part C of Miss Buckley's LPA, which her attorney signed, is far more explicit. It says:

'By signing below, I confirm all of the following:
Understanding of role and responsibilities
I have read the section called "Information you must read" on page 2 of this lasting power of attorney.
I understand my role and responsibilities under this lasting power of attorney, in particular:

- I have a duty to act based on the principles of the Mental Capacity Act 2005 and have regard to the Mental Capacity Act Code of Practice
- I can make decisions and act only when this lasting power of attorney has been registered
- I must make decisions and act in the best interests of the person who is giving this lasting power of attorney
- I can spend money to make gifts but only to charities or on customary occasions and for reasonable amounts
- I have a duty to keep accounts and financial records and produce them to the Office of the Public Guardian and/or to the Court of Protection on request.'

Decision

[47] Subsections (3) and (4) of s 22 of the 2005 Act provide that the court may revoke an LPA if:

(1)   it is satisfied that the attorney has behaved or is behaving in a way that contravenes his or her authority or is not in the donor's best interests, or is proposing to behave in such a way; and

(2)   the donor lacks capacity to revoke the LPA.

[48] I am satisfied that C has contravened her authority and has acted in a way that is not in Miss Buckley's best interests.

[49] Even if one were to be generous and believe C and accept at face value her description of the way in which she has applied Miss Buckley's funds as an 'investment', it was a highly unsuitable investment to make and she broke almost every rule in the book in making it.

[50] She did not obtain and consider proper advice from someone who is qualified to give investment advice. One can hardly describe a man who runs a reptile breeding business as someone who is qualified to give investment advice by his ability in and practical experience of financial and other matters relating to investment.

[51] The investment was very high risk. When investing funds on behalf of older people, the perceived wisdom is that the investments should be safe and that very little risk is acceptable as can be seen from the short-term investment tables set out above. Even when investing funds long-term on behalf of a younger person, a hazardous and speculative investment of this kind would have been inappropriate for anyone in a fiduciary position to make.

[52] The attorney invested in her own business, which was in breach of her fiduciary duty. Paragraph 7.60 of the Mental Capacity Act Code of Practice states that:

'A fiduciary duty means attorneys must not take advantage of their position. Nor should they put themselves in a position where their personal interests conflict with their duties. They also must not allow any other influences to affect the way in which they act as an attorney. Decisions should always benefit the donor, and not the attorney. Attorneys must not profit or get any personal benefit from their position, apart from receiving gifts where the Act allows it, whether or not it is at the donor's expense.'

[53] The investment was also made in the attorney's name. This was in breach of the guidance to attorneys given in para 7.68 of the Code of Practice to keep the donor's money and property separate. The attorneys' admission in para 16 of her witness statement – 'I would like to state that I was not aware that the investment had to be made in her name and was concerned about signing on her behalf' – is no excuse.

[54] C's use of £43,317.47 (according to Yun Ding's second statement) of Miss Buckley's capital for her own personal benefit was way beyond the very limited authority to make gifts conferred on attorneys by s 12 of the 2005 Act. The attorney's comments paras 17 and 18 of her witness statement are no defence:

'I agree that my aunt lacks capacity to manage her own financial affairs and in my view she has become increasingly confused and is unable to understand the information relevant to deciding how to handle her finances or retain that information. . . . I admit that some of the money was used for my own benefit but only with my aunt's permission.'

[55] As regards Miss Buckley's capacity, I am satisfied that she is incapable of revoking the LPA herself. I accept the opinion of the Court of Protection Special Visitor, Dr Andrew Barker, who stated:

'She was unable to understand the nature and effects of an LPA to a sufficient degree or to choose an attorney, was not aware of her financial dealings and could not recall detail sufficiently well or concentrate long enough to weigh information in the balance to come to decisions about an attorney or to direct or instruct an attorney.'

[56] In deciding whether it is in Miss Buckley's best interests to revoke the LPA on her behalf, I am satisfied that:

(a)   it is unlikely that she will ever regain sufficient capacity to be able to manage her financial affairs and revoke the LPA herself, should she wish to do so; and

(b)   by engaging her in conversation, the Court of Protection General Visitor sought, so far as reasonably practicable, to permit and encourage Miss Buckley to participate as fully as possible in the decision-making process.

[57] It was Miss Buckley's past wish, when she had capacity, that her niece should be her attorney and manage her property and financial affairs. However, as far as her present wishes and feelings are concerned, the General Visitor reported that:

'When [Miss Buckley was] asked whether she wanted the niece to manage her money she indicated very negatively. When asked if she had wanted her niece to use her money for anything special she said she didn't trust her and had only ever wanted her money.'

[58] As regards the views of others who are engaged in caring for Miss Buckley or who are interested in her welfare, I have taken into account the views of her friend, Shirley, who visits her once a week and was the only person named by Mrs Buckley to receive notice of the attorney's application to register the LPA. In an email to Yun Ding dated 17 October 2012, in the context of the attorney's visit to Miss Buckley in her current nursing home on 16 October 2012, Shirley said:

'I am so worried that (Miss Buckley's) money will get stolen and that she won't be able to stay in the nursing home. I have been asked not to get in touch with C both by social services and by the police. I find this very difficult. I must have given two years of my full attention – selling her house for her – setting up the Nationwide to pay the (nursing home) monthly. Finding a decent retirement residence (from which she had to move for health reasons) then I found her the nursing home but it's nearly £1000 per week. She cannot afford for her money to be taken. She needs every penny.'

[59] Having regard to all the circumstances, therefore, I am satisfied that:

(a)   the attorney has contravened her authority and acted in a way that is not in Miss Buckley's best interests;

(b)   Miss Buckley is incapable of revoking the LPA herself;

(c)   the revocation of the LPA in order to facilitate the appointment of a deputy is both a necessary and proportionate response for the protection of Miss Buckley's right to have her financial affairs managed competently, honestly and for her benefit, and for the prevention of crime; and

(d)   it is in Miss Buckley's best interests that the court should revoke the LPA.

[60] Accordingly, I revoke the LPA under s 22(4)(b) of the 2005 Act and direct the public guardian to cancel the registration of the instrument under para 18 of Sch 1 to the 2005 Act.

Order accordingly.

EASON RAJAH QC

Barrister

Appendix H

DECISIONS MADE BY THE COURT

LASTING POWERS OF ATTORNEY CASES

H1 Re Parsonage (an order of the Senior Judge made on 1 April 2011)

The donor of an LPA inserted the following restriction: 'My replacement attorneys under this lasting power shall not have authority to do any act, or take any decision, under this lasting power except in those circumstances where I lack capacity or where the replacement attorneys reasonably believe that I lack capacity or when I have signed that I wish the lasting power to come into effect by signing the lasting power again.' On the application of the Public Guardian the words 'or when I have signed that I wish the lasting power to come into effect by signing the lasting power again' were severed on the ground that re-execution of the LPA by the donor after completion and registration would contravene the execution requirements for an LPA.

Re Batchelor (an order of the Senior Judge made on 2 April 2012)

The donor of a property and financial affairs LPA included the following provision: 'I would ask my attorneys to have regard to any separate guidance note which I may make from time to time and place with this Lasting Power of Attorney.' On the application of the Public Guardian the provision was severed on the ground that it contravened the requirements of reg 9 of the Lasting Powers of Attorney, Enduring Powers of Attorney and Public Guardian Regulations 2007, which do not permit additions to be made to an LPA.

Re Darlison (an order of the Senior Judge made on 9 July 2012)

The donor made an LPA for property and financial affairs. In the guidance section she stated: 'Oversee X's financial welfare. X is [my] daughter.' On the application of the Public Guardian the guidance was severed on the ground that the donor of an LPA cannot authorise the attorneys to act in relation to the financial affairs of another person.

Re Norris (an order of the Senior Judge made on 25 July 2012)

The donor made LPAs for property and financial affairs and for health and welfare and included the following guidance in both LPAs: 'At all times to make decisions in the best interests of [my wife] during her lifetime.' On the application of the Public Guardian the provision was severed as being potentially inconsistent with the requirement in s 1(5) of the MCA that any act done or decision made must be done or made in the donor's best interests. But see *Re JG(1), Re PG and Re CW* [2017] EWCOP 10 below.

Re Hart (an order of the Senior Judge made on 6 February 2013)

The donor made an LPA for property and financial affairs. He was also the sole attorney under an EPA made by his wife and registered. In his LPA he authorised his attorneys to have access to his will and medical records, and then continued as follows: 'This also applies to acting as Attorneys for my wife, whose EPA has been registered.' On the application of the Public Guardian this provision was severed because an LPA may not be used to add anything to someone else's EPA. (The donor appears to have wrongly assumed that his own attorneys could take over his role as attorney for his wife.)

Severance of restrictions incompatible with a Health and Welfare LPA

H2 Re Spaas (an order of the Senior Judge made on 2 April 2013)

The donor of a Health and Welfare LPA included the following provision: 'If I become completely mentally or physically incapable for example being unable to recognise my daughter then I wish steps to be taken to end my life as quickly and painlessly as possible. It that was not possible, I would wish the minimum medical intervention possible. I would not want my life unnecessarily prolonged.' On the application of the Public Guardian the words from 'steps to be taken' to 'I would wish' were severed. The donor may have been envisaging assisted suicide, which is unlawful (see *Re Gardner*, above) or even expressing a wish for her life to be terminated by others in circumstances which would involve a criminal offence.

Re Baxter (an order of the Senior Judge made on 10 April 2013)

The donor of a Health and Welfare LPA included the following provision: 'My attorneys shall have no power to act until they have reason to believe that I have become or that I am becoming mentally incapable of managing my own affairs or that I have become physically handicapped to such a degree that I cannot look after my affairs without significant inconvenience discomfort or difficulty.' On the application of the Public Guardian the words 'or that I am becoming' and 'or that I have become' to 'difficulty' were severed. Section 11(7)(a) of the MCA provides that decisions concerning the donor's health and welfare may not be made under an LPA 'in circumstances other than those where [the donor] lacks, or the donee reasonably believes that [the donor] lacks, capacity'. As previously held in *Re Azancot* (above), the donor may not provide for decisions to be made by the attorney when the donor lacks physical capacity but not mental capacity. The words 'or that I am becoming' were also inconsistent with sn 11(7)(a) because the donor must lack capacity (or be reasonably believed to lack capacity). It is not sufficient that the donor may be 'becoming' mentally incapable. The wording of s 11(7)(a) may be contrasted with para 4(1) of Sch 4 of the MCA, which imposes a duty to apply for registration on an attorney under an EPA when the donor 'is or is becoming' mentally incapable.

Re Azancot (an order of the Senior Judge made on 27 May 2009)

The donor of a personal welfare LPA inserted a restriction that her replacement attorneys 'may only act under this power in the event that the donor is physically or mentally incapacitated and there is written medical evidence to that effect'. The words 'physically or' were severed on the application of the Public Guardian, as the effect of s 11(7) of the MCA is that a personal welfare attorney may not make a decision unless the donor lacks mental capacity to make it.

Re Gardner (an order of the Senior Judge made on 6 July 2011)

The donor included the following statement in the guidance section of the instrument: 'If I am suffering from a terminal illness I would ask that my attorneys assist me in travelling to a country where it is legal for me to take my own life should I choose to do so.' On the application of the Public Guardian the court severed the guidance for the following reasons: (i) s 62 of the MCA 2005 provides that nothing in the Act is to be taken to affect the law relating to murder or manslaughter or the operation of s 2 of the Suicide Act 1961 (assisting suicide); (ii) the donor was purporting to authorise the attorneys to commit the criminal offence of assisting suicide, and the fact that a person who assists a suicide is not always prosecuted in England and Wales does not detract from the fact that it remains a criminal offence; (iii) although the statement appeared in the guidance section, it is not open to a donor to provide guidance to the attorneys relating to the commission of a criminal offence.

Re Stewart (an order of the Senior Judge made on 9 November 2011)

The donor included the following direction in the guidance section: 'I authorise my attorneys to refuse or consent to my deprivation of liberty.' The Public Guardian applied for severance on the ground that: 'The deprivation of the donor's liberty is only lawful if ordered by the court or done in accordance with the procedures prescribed by law under the Mental Capacity Act 2005 as amended by the Mental Health Act 2007. The donor does not have power to authorise her attorneys to consent to the deprivation of her liberty in the absence of a court order or going through the Deprivation of Liberty Safeguarding procedures.' The court determined that the direction was invalid for the reasons given by the Public Guardian.

Re McGregor (an order of the Senior Judge made on 16 November 2011)

The donor appointed attorneys to act jointly in some matters and jointly and severally in others, and directed as follows: 'Jointly – decisions on sale of house. Decisions on type of care received if no longer able to stay in own home. Severally – financial matters regarding bank accounts and general cash flow.' On the application of the Public Guardian the words 'decisions on sale of house' and 'Severally – financial matters regarding bank accounts and general cash flow' were severed because they purported to give Health and Welfare attorneys authority to make decisions regarding the donor's property and financial affairs. (The result would be that, by implication, the attorneys would be able to decide jointly and severally all matters other than the type of care the donor would receive if no longer able to stay in his own home.)

Re Kerron (an order of the Senior Judge made on 4 July 2012)

The donor made an LPA for health and welfare, and imposed the following restriction: 'If assessed as requiring nursing/residential care I would like to move promptly to a home jointly chosen by myself and my attorneys.' On the application of the Public Guardian the words 'jointly' and 'myself and' were severed on the ground that a health and welfare LPA can only be used when the donor lacks capacity, and if the donor lacked capacity she would not be able to choose a nursing or residential care home.

Re Sheppard (an order of the Senior Judge made on 25 July 2012)

The donor of a health and welfare LPA included the following guidance: 'My attorneys are to maintain the health and welfare needs of X.' On the application of the Public Guardian the provision was severed as it is not open to a donor to require attorneys to make health and welfare decisions on behalf of a third party.

Severance of restrictions relating to life-sustaining treatment

H3 Re Hodgkiss (an order of the Senior Judge made on 25 August 2011)

The donor of a Health and Welfare LPA selected Option B, which states that the attorneys have no authority to give or refuse life-sustaining treatment. He then directed as follows: 'Attorneys must consent to any life sustaining treatment if I am in a persistent vegetative state.' On the application of the Public Guardian this provision was severed as being incompatible with his selection of Option B. The court added that, if the donor had wished to give his attorneys authority to consent to life-sustaining treatment if he were in a persistent vegetative state, he should have selected Option A.

Severance of restrictions incompatible with a Property and Financial Affairs LPA

H4 Re Cranston (an order of the Senior Judge made on 18 February 2011)

The donor appointed attorneys to act jointly in some matters and jointly and severally in others. He included in the list of matters which should be decided jointly 'changing my will'. On the application of the Public Guardian these words were severed on the ground that an attorney has no authority to change a donor's will. An attorney may apply to the court for an order authorising the execution of a statutory will if a donor lacks testamentary capacity.

Re Wheeler (an order of the Senior Judge made on 25 July 2011)

The Public Guardian applied for the severance of an invalid clause in the LPA. The Senior Judge considered that another clause was also invalid, which was severed on the court's own initiative. The donor had provided the following guidance: 'My attorneys may act on the contents of my will.' The court's reason for severing the guidance was as follows: 'The court considers that the meaning of this guidance is unclear and that it is probably void for uncertainty. Potentially it authorises the attorneys to distribute the donor's estate during his lifetime as if he were dead, which would be not only contrary to public policy but also contrary to the provisions of s 12 of the Mental Capacity Act 2005. A will speaks from death, and it is not a function of an attorney to act as the executor of the donor's will.'

Severance of restrictions incompatible with a joint and several appointment

H5 Re Jenkins (an order of the Senior Judge made on 2 September 2008)

The donor had appointed the attorneys of a property and affairs LPA to act 'together and independently'. She then directed that they must act together in relation to any bills, payments or costs exceeding £2,000 in any one calendar month and in relation to any single payment greater than £1,000 in any calendar month. The donor had also appointed a replacement attorney, and directed that she should act if the original attorneys were 'not available through travel or living abroad or any other circumstances that may prevent or restrict their capacity to act on my behalf as attorneys'.

The court ordered the severance of both clauses, on the application of the Public Guardian. The directions in the first clause were incompatible with an appointment to act 'together and independently'. The directions in the second clause were invalid because a replacement attorney may only act on the occurrence of an event mentioned in s 13(6)(a) to (d) of the MCA, for example where an original attorney disclaims, dies or loses mental capacity.

Re P (an order of the Senior Judge made on 9 June 2009)

The donor appointed three attorneys to act jointly and severally, and imposed the following restriction: 'I require that two attorneys must act at any one time so that no attorney may act alone.' On the application of the Public Guardian the court severed the restriction on the ground that it was ineffective as part of an LPA.

Re Bratt (an order made by the Senior Judge on 14 September 2009)

The donor appointed two attorneys, A and B, to act jointly and severally, and directed that 'B is only to act as attorney in the event of A being physically or mentally incapable of acting in this capacity'. On the application of the Public Guardian this provision was severed as being inconsistent with a joint and several appointment. The Senior Judge added that, to have achieved the desired objective, the donor should instead have appointed B to be a replacement attorney.

Re D'Argenio (an order of the Senior Judge made on 9 June 2010)

The donor made a property and financial affairs LPA and a health and welfare LPA. In both she appointed six attorneys to act jointly and severally. In the property and affairs LPA she imposed the following restriction: 'My atorneys must act jointly in relation to decisions about selling my house. They may act jointly and severally in everything else.' In the health and welfare LPA she imposed the following restriction: 'My attorneys must act jointly in relation to decisions I have authorised them to make about life-sustaining treatment and where I live. They may act jointly and severally for everything else.' On the application of the Public Guardian the court severed both restrictions as being incompatible with a joint and several appointment.

Re P Crook (an order of the Senior Judge made on 2 July 2010)

The donor appointed one primary attorney and three replacement attorneys, the latter to act jointly and severally. He then imposed the following restriction: 'Provided I have more than two attorneys capable of acting under this power then any decision as to the exercise of any power or discretion reached by the majority of such attorneys (acting in their capacity as attorneys) shall bind all my attorneys to the extent that no attorney of mine can take issue with the decision reached by that majority.' On the application of the Public Guardian the court severed the restriction as being incompatible with a joint and several appointment.

Re Davies (an order of the Senior Judge made on 5 July 2010)

The donor appointed two attorneys, A and B, to act jointly and severally. He then imposed the following restriction: 'If in the unlikely event of A and B not being wholly in agreement, B is to defer to the wishes of A.' On the application of the Public Guardian the court severed the restriction as being incompatible with a joint and several appointment.

Re Cotterell (an order made by the Senior Judge on 3 August 2010)

The donor appointed two attorneys to act jointly and severally, and imposed the following restriction: 'My second named attorney may only act as my attorney if a general medical practitioner certifies that I am mentally incapable of managing my affairs and in this instance, if my first attorney is alive and mentally capable, may only act on my behalf in relation to a sale of the property which at that time is deemed to be my principal place of residence. If however my said first named attorney has passed away or is deemed by a general medical practitioner as incapable then my second named attorney may act generally on my behalf subject to no restrictions.' On the application of the Public Guardian the restriction was severed as being incompatible with a joint and several appointment.

Re Lan (an order of the Senior Judge made on 10 August 2010)

The donor appointed two attorneys to act jointly and severally. She then imposed the following restriction: 'Any major decisions should be discussed between my attorneys so that a joint agreement to the matter can be achieved.' On the application of the Public Guardian this restriction was severed as being incompatible with a joint and several appointment.

Re Ferguson (an order of the Senior Judge made on 26 October 2010)

The donor appointed three attorneys, A, B and C, to act jointly and severally. She then imposed the following restrictions: 'I wish my attorneys to act as follows: A to act independently. B and C to act only in the event that A is deceased or unable to act. In these circumstances B and C may act independently.' 'I wish my attorneys to act only when I lack capacity to act. A may judge for himself when I lack capacity to act. B and C must agree together that I lack capacity to act. Alternatively, should either of them wish, then at my expense they may seek medical and, if necessary, legal advice as to whether or not I have capacity to act.' On the application of the Public Guardian both restrictions were severed as being incompatible with a joint and several appointment.

Re Hartup (an order of the Senior Judge made on 28 October 2010)

The donor appointed two attorneys, A and B, to act jointly and severally, and two replacement attorneys. He then imposed the following restriction: 'My wife A is to take the lead in all decisions.' On the application of the Public Guardian the restriction was severed as being incompatible with a joint and several appointment. (See further under the heading 'Severance of invalid restrictions as to how a replacement attorney may act'.)

Re Wormsley (an order of the Senior Judge made on 24 October 2011)

The donor appointed two primary attorneys and two replacement attorneys, and directed them to act jointly and severally. He further directed as follows: 'If a replacement attorney is required to replace an original attorney, the two replacement attorneys shall decide which one of them shall serve as attorney.' On the application of the Public Guardian the court severed the provision as being inconsistent with the joint and several appointment of the replacement attorneys.

Re Wormsley, above, may be contrasted with Re Griggs (an order of the Senior Judge made on 17 June 2013)

In *Re Griggs* the donor appointed two primary attorneys and three replacements, to act jointly for some decisions and jointly and severally for other decisions. The donor directed that 'My Remaining attorney is to choose which replacement attorney is to act as my other attorney.' Although the provision could be viewed as incompatible with the manner of appointment, the court severed the provision for the reason given in the Public Guardian's application, which was that the donor should not leave it to the attorneys or replacement attorneys to decide which replacement is to act.

Re Williams (an order of the Senior Judge made on 16 November 2011)

The donor appointed three attorneys, A (the eldest), B and C, to act jointly and severally. He then directed as follows: 'If my attorneys shall disagree on any matter then the eldest attorney's decision shall be final. Priority of attorneys is therefore as follows: 1. A; 2. B; 3. C.' On the application of the Public Guardian the direction was severed as being incompatible with a joint and several appointment.

Re Dowden (an order of the Senior Judge made on 20 July 2012)

The donor made two LPAs in which she appointed a professional attorney and a lay attorney to act jointly and severally. She directed that the professional attorney should be paid fees 'in keeping with the charging rate in force at the time the work is undertaken'. She then directed that the lay attorney should be paid a reasonable hourly fee and stated that any sum paid 'must be with the approval of my Solicitor/Attorney' and 'will be at such rate as he feels is appropriate'. On the application of the Public Guardian the provision relating to the lay attorney's fees being approved and set by the professional attorney was severed as being incompatible with a joint and several appointment. The judge added that, to have achieved the desired objective, the donor should have appointed the attorneys to act jointly for some decisions (in this case on agreeing an appropriate level of remuneration for the lay attorney) and jointly and severally for other decisions.

Re Davies (an order of the Senior Judge made on 4 December 2012)

The donor appointed four attorneys, A, B, C and D, to act jointly and severally, and imposed the following restriction: 'The appointment of C and D shall not take effect unless I am mentally and/or physically incapable of managing my affairs and the appointment of C shall not take effect unless she has been in my employment within the period of one month preceding my loss of capacity to manage my affairs.' This restriction was severed on the ground that the appointments of co-attorneys cannot be activated at different times.

Re Black (an order of the Senior Judge made on 11 January 2013)

The donor, a solicitor, appointed A and B as attorneys, to act jointly and severally. She imposed the following restriction: 'A has been appointed solely to manage ABC Solicitors to enable continuing management of the Practice. B has been appointed to deal with all other financial matters both personal and business related, which do not specifically require a Solicitor of the Supreme Court.' On the application of the Public Guardian the restriction was severed because it was incompatible with a joint and several appointment.

Re Bishop (an order of the Senior Judge made on 28 February 2013)

The donor appointed attorneys to act jointly and severally and included the following provision: 'I direct that my attorneys shall endeavour to act jointly on decisions wherever possible. They must only act severally when all practicable steps to act jointly have been made without success. If an attorney must act severally then that attorney must consult the other before making the decision and keep the other informed of any decision made.' On the application of the Public Guardian the provision was severed as being incompatible with a joint and several appointment. Although in the guidance section, it was expressed in mandatory terms and was in substance a restriction.

Re SR [2017] EWCOP10

The Public Guardian sought severance of 'can act severally except on investment decisions of £50,000 or more where they should act jointly' in the preferences box within section 7 of the instrument because they were incompatible with the nature of the appointment of the attorneys to act jointly and severally. The judge refused to sever the words as they were merely guidance on how the donor wished the attorneys to act.

Re JF [2017] EWCOP10

The donor appointed three attorneys jointly and severally. The Public Guardian applied for the severance of 'my two daughters (if surviving) must always agree on any decision jointly before any actions regarding my estate can be implemented. OM may act as an attorney independently of my daughters,' included in the instructions box within section 7 of the instrument, because they were incompatible with the nature of the appointment of the attorneys to act jointly and severally. The judge noted that under the general law of agency, a principal may appoint co-agents, giving power to a quorum to act on her or his behalf. It seems virtually eccentric that a person must authorise (say) four attorneys to all act jointly or all separately and cannot specify anything in between. The aim should be a statutory scheme that gives as much flexibility to donors to set out how they wish their affairs to be dealt with as possible. However, he was bound by existing case-law in this area and so reluctantly severed the words as it was clearly contrary to the intention of the donor. See also *Re SH* and *Re GO* in the same judgment.

Severance of restrictions incompatible with a joint appointment

H6 Re Clarke (an order of the Senior Judge made on 18 November 2009)

The donor appointed three attorneys, A (his wife), B, and C, to be his attorneys. They were appointed to act jointly in some matters and jointly and severally in others. He then stated that the attorneys were to act independently for transactions not exceeding £5,000 'but together in respect of all other decisions subject to my wife A's opinion prevailing in the event that my attorneys are not unanimous in any decision involving property or expenditure exceeding £5,000'. On the application of the Public Guardian, the words 'subject to my wife A's opinion' onwards were severed on the ground that they purported to facilitate one of the three attorneys being able to act independently in relation to matters that had been specified as subject to the joint decision of the attorneys.

Re Warner (an order of the Senior Judge made on 31 August 2010)

The donor made an LPA appointing A as the original attorney and B and C as replacement attorneys, the latter to act jointly. She imposed the following restriction in relation to the replacement attorneys: 'If for any reason one of my replacement attorneys is unable or unwilling to act, the remaining replacement attorney is then permitted to act solely under my LPA'. On the application of the Public Guardian the restriction was severed as being incompatible with the joint appointment of the replacement attorneys.

Re Moore (an order of the Senior Judge made on 26 October 2010)

The donor appointed three attorneys to act jointly. She then imposed the following restriction: 'At least two attorneys to act on any transactions'. On the application of the Public Guardian the court severed the restriction as being incompatible with a joint appointment.

Re Pugh (an order of the Senior Judge made on 13 July 2011)

The donor appointed three replacement attorneys to act jointly. She then completed the box on page 5 of the form (which should be completed only if the attorneys are to act jointly in some matters and jointly and severally in others) and directed as follows: 'Where by this power I have appointed three replacement attorneys to act jointly on all occasions then I direct that if there is a dispute it is the majority decision of my three replacement attorneys that is to be followed and in the event that by reason of death or incapacity or other reason I only have two of my three replacement attorneys who are capable of acting then in the event of a dispute between my two continuing replacement attorneys it is the decision of the eldest that is to be followed.' On the application of the Public Guardian the court severed the restriction as being incompatible with a joint appointment.

Severance of restrictions incompatible with an appointment to act jointly in some matters and jointly and severally in others

H7 Re Weyell (an order of the senior Judge made on 2 December 2010)

The donor appointed three attorneys, A, B and C, to act jointly for some decisions and jointly and severally for others. He then imposed the following restrictions:

(1) 'Two out of three of my attorneys must act jointly in relation to any transaction with a value in excess of £5,000 and my attorneys may act jointly and severally in relation to everything else.'

(2) 'I direct that when acting jointly and severally where possible my attorneys are to act in the following order of priority: firstly A, then B and then C.'

On the application of the Public Guardian the first restriction was severed as being incompatible with the joint aspect of the appointment. In the application the Public Guardian submitted that, while a direction that attorneys appointed to act jointly and severally must act in an order of priority would normally be regarded as incompatible with a joint and several appointment, the addition of the words 'where possible' made the direction in effect a statement of wishes only. The court accepted this submission and did not sever the second restriction.

Re Warren (an order of the Senior Judge made on 10 December 2010)

The donor appointed four attorneys, A, B, C and D, to act jointly for some decisions and jointly and severally for others. She imposed the following restriction: 'All decisions will be made by my first attorney A unless and until such time that he no longer has the mental capacity to do so. Should A no longer have the mental capacity to make decisions the remaining attorneys will jointly make decisions regarding the house and property and jointly and severally make decisions concerning finance.' On the application of the Public Guardian the words preceding 'attorneys will jointly' were severed on the ground that, where attorneys were appointed to act jointly in some matters and jointly and severally in others, it was not open to the donor to provide that one attorney should act alone for so long as he was able to do so. The Senior

Judge added that, to have achieved the desired objective, the donor should have appointed A as the sole attorney and the three others as replacement attorneys.

Re Parker (an order of the Senior Judge made on 18 February 2011)

The donor of a Health and Welfare LPA appointed X and Y as attorneys to act jointly in some matters and jointly and severally in others. He then directed as follows: 'I wish the prime responsibility for decisions in respect of my health to vest in X. My attorneys need only act jointly in the event of serious and/or life threatening conditions. In this case X should endeavour to contact Y but if she is, for whatever reason, unable to do so she may act on her own (severally) despite the serious and/or life threatening condition.' On the application of the Public Guardian the last sentence of this direction was severed as being incompatible with the appointment to act jointly in some matters.

Re Freeman (an order of the Senior Judge made on 17 August 2011)

The donor appointed A and B as attorneys to act jointly in some matters and jointly and severally in others. He specified that they were to act as follows: 'Major capital expenses jointly. Day to day expenses A.' In his application the Public Guardian submitted that the donor had not specified any decisions to be made jointly and severally and so the words 'Day to day expenses A' should be severed, with the effect that decisions not specified to be taken jointly should by implication be taken jointly and severally. The court was also asked to sever the word 'Major' on the ground of uncertainty. The court accordingly severed these words so that the attorneys were appointed to act jointly for 'capital expenses' and (by implication) jointly and severally for everything else.

Re Ingham (an order of the Senior Judge made on 15 August 2011)

The donor appointed four attorneys to act jointly for some decisions and jointly and severally for others. She then directed as follows: 'A. While all attorneys are acting: 1. All may complete any transaction with a value not exceeding £2,500. 2. All must complete any transaction with a value exceeding £2,500. B. In the event that only two or three Attorneys remain capable of acting those Attorneys are bound by A1 and 2 above. C. In the event that only one Attorney remains capable of acting that Attorney has full powers to complete transactions of any value.' On the application of the Public Guardian directions B and C were severed on the ground that they were incompatible with the joint aspect of the appointment: if one attorney ceased to act, the matters to be decided jointly would not be able to be decided by the continuing attorneys.

Re Llewelyn (an order of the Senior Judge made on 2 May 2012)

The donor appointed attorneys including her husband to act jointly in some matters and jointly and severally in other matters. She stated that decisions were to be made jointly and severally apart from a list of specified decisions which were to be made jointly, but added a proviso to the effect that, provided her husband was able to act as one of her attorneys, all decisions could be made jointly and severally. On the application of the Public Guardian the proviso was severed as being incompatible with an appointment to act jointly in some matters and jointly and severally in others.

Re Edmonds (an order of the Senior Judge made on 12 November 2012)

The donor appointed a sole attorney and then two replacements, the latter to act jointly for some decisions and jointly and severally for others. She then directed as follows: 'I would like my replacement attorneys to act jointly as much as possible and always where any transaction is valued at more than £5,000.' On the application of the Public Guardian the words 'as much as possible and always' were severed on the ground that they were uncertain and incompatible with the appointment type.

Re MC [2017] EWCOP10

The donor had ticked the box on page 4 which stated that her attorneys were to act jointly and severally and included the following in the Instructions box, 'Any financial decisions up to the value of £150.00 can be made independently by my attorneys. However, any financial decisions over this amount must be agreed upon by both my attorneys.' The Public Guardian applied to have the words removed as they were inconsistent with a joint and several appointment. The judge noted that it was simply an error in completing the form and the donor's intention was not ambiguous. It would be wrong in principle to excise the condition or restriction in Section 7 when it was the box on page 4 which was the error. Instead of severance, the Judge made a declaration that the instrument was to be treated as if it was in the prescribed form and as if the donor had ticked the box on page 4 of the instrument to the effect that some decisions are to be made by her attorneys jointly and other decisions jointly and severally rather than the box on that page which states they are to act jointly and severally in all matters. Similar declarations were made in the cases of *Re JG2* and *Re JR*, which were part of the same judgment.

Severance of restrictions fettering an attorney's authority

H8 Re Begum (an order of the Senior Judge made on 24 April 2008)

On the application of the Public Guardian, the court directed the severance from a Property and Affairs LPA instrument of the following clauses, on the ground that they were ineffective as part of an LPA:

'All decisions about the use or disposal of my property and financial resources must be driven by what my Personal Welfare Lasting Power of Attorney(s) believe will support my long term interests.

Any decisions affecting assets (individually or together) worth more than £5,000 at any one time must be discussed and agreed with Dr X.

In the event of there being any disagreement between my Personal Welfare Lasting Power of Attorney(s) and/or Dr X this should be resolved by these parties appointing an independent advocate to adjudicate.'

Re Steiner (an order of the Senior Judge made on 17 October 2011)

The donor appointed two attorneys to act jointly. She then gave the following guidance: 'Should the need arise relating to the management of my financial affairs and my business interests, whoever at the time is acting for me personally as my accountant or solicitor shall adjudicate over my personal financial interests and whoever is acting professionally for me in respect of my business interests either my accountant or solicitor shall adjudicate over my business interests.' On the application of the Public Guardian the court severed the provision from the LPA on the ground that it could potentially oust the jurisdiction of the court.

Re Reading (an order of the Senior Judge made on 25 June 2009)

The donor appointed her husband and two of her children as original attorneys and a third child as replacement attorney. She added a restriction to the effect that, if her husband should predecease her, any decisions 'must be agreed by all four of my children'. The fourth child had not been appointed as attorney or replacement attorney. On the application of the Public Guardian the restriction was severed as being ineffective as part of an LPA, because it was not open to the donor to require that a person who was not an attorney should join in the making of decisions by the attorneys.

Re Scott (an order of the Senior Judge made on 11 January 2011)

The donor made an LPA for property and financial affairs, appointing A and B to act jointly and severally. She then imposed the following restriction: 'In the event of there being any disagreement between A and B (as the attorneys for property and financial affairs) and C (as the attorney for health and welfare) over expenditure on my health or welfare then C's decision is to prevail.' The Public Guardian applied for this restriction to be severed on the basis that *Re Reading* (above) showed that a donor could not require that a person who was not an attorney under the instrument should join in the making of decisions by the attorneys. The court dismissed the Public Guardian's application, considering that there was no reason in law why the donor of two separate LPAs should not be able to provide that, in the event of a disagreement between the attorneys for property and financial affairs and the attorney for health and welfare, the decision of the attorney for health and welfare should prevail.

Re Scragg (an order of the Senior Judge made on 1 February 2011)

The donor of a property and affairs LPA (who lived abroad) gave detailed instructions to his attorney relating to all of his assets in the event of a return to England, and added that these instructions were 'subject to the written consent of my daughter' (who was the replacement attorney and also the attorney under his Health and Welfare LPA). On the application of the Public Guardian the words 'subject to the written consent of my daughter' were severed because the requirement that the attorney should obtain the consent of a third party before exercising his powers imposed an unjustifiable fetter on his authority.

Severance of invalid restrictions as to when a replacement attorney may act

H9 Re Jenkins (an order of the Senior Judge made on 2 September 2008)

The donor had appointed the attorneys of a property and affairs LPA to act 'together and independently'. She then directed that they must act together in relation to any bills, payments or costs exceeding £2,000 in any one calendar month and in relation to any single payment greater than £1,000 in any calendar month. The donor had also appointed a replacement attorney, and directed that she should act if the original attorneys were 'not available through travel or living abroad or any other circumstances that may prevent or restrict their capacity to act on my behalf as attorneys'.

The court ordered the severance of both clauses, on the application of the Public Guardian. The directions in the first clause were incompatible with an appointment to act 'together and independently'. The directions in the second clause were invalid because a replacement attorney may only act on the occurrence of an event mentioned in s 13(6)(a) to (d) of the MCA, for example where an original attorney disclaims, dies or loses mental capacity.

Re Patel (an order of the Senior Judge made on 1 December 2008)

The donor appointed a replacement attorney to act if the original attorney should be 'mentally or physically incapable' or if the original attorney 'is not in England at any time that my personal or financial affairs require attention'. The words in bold were severed on the application of the Public Guardian on the ground that a replacement attorney may only act on the occurrence of an event mentioned in s 13(6)(a) to (d) of the MCA, for example where an original attorney disclaims, dies or loses mental capacity.

Re Bates (an order of the Senior Judge made on 3 December 2008)

The donor appointed two original attorneys and a replacement attorney, who would assume office in the following circumstances: 'She may act at any time at the election of either attorney'. These words were severed on the application of the Public Guardian on the ground that a replacement attorney may only act on the occurrence of an event mentioned in s 13(6)(a) to (d) of the MCA, for example where an original attorney disclaims, dies or loses mental capacity.

Re Noel (an order of the Senior Judge made on 31 January 2011)

The donor appointed two attorneys to act jointly in some matters and jointly and severally in others. He then appointed X as replacement attorney. He directed that a decision to sell a named property 'must be made jointly by all surviving attorneys including X'. On the application of the Public Guardian the words 'including X' were severed, as being incompatible with the manner in which the attorneys and replacement attorneys had been appointed. The court added that, to have achieved the desired objective, the donor should have appointed all three as attorneys (rather than two attorneys and a replacement) and directed them to act jointly in some matters and jointly and severally in others.

Re Hamilton (an order of the Senior Judge made on 25 October 2011)

The donor appointed one primary attorney and one replacement attorney. On page 5 of the LPA the donor inappropriately ticked the box indicating that the attorneys were appointed to act jointly for some decisions and jointly and severally for other decisions, and continued: 'My No 1 Attorney will make all decisions re my everyday expenses and decisions [and] will make joint decisions with the Replacement Attorney in reference to any large decisions re the selling of investments, property and the eventual need of a nursing home etc.' On the application of the Public Guardian the provision was severed on the ground that, having appointed the attorneys to act successively, the donor could not authorise them to make any decisions concurrently, whether jointly or jointly and severally.

Re Evans (an order of the Senior Judge made on 24 November 2011)

The donor appointed A (his wife) and B as attorneys, to act jointly and severally, and C as replacement attorney. He then directed as follows: 'My replacement attorney will replace both my attorneys and act alone if and when my wife becomes unable or unwilling to carry out her duties as my attorney.' On the application of the Public Guardian the direction was severed because the donor was attempting to provide for attorney B to be replaced even though one of the triggering events for his replacement listed in s 13(6)(a) to (d) of the MCA had not occurred.

Re Tucker (an order of the Senior Judge made on 9 December 2011)

The donor appointed one attorney and one replacement attorney and then directed as follows: 'My replacement attorney shall only act if my attorney is unable to act by virtue of: (a) the power to the attorney is revoked by me; or (b) the power is terminated by reason of the death, disclaimer or other incapacity of my attorney to act as my attorney; whichever shall first occur. For the avoidance of doubt my replacement attorney shall act alone if my attorney is not able to act.' On the application of the Public Guardian the words 'by virtue of: (a) the power to the attorney is revoked by me; or (b) the power is terminated' were severed because revocation of the attorney's appointment is not one of the events listed in s 13(6)(a) to (d) of the MCA that trigger the activation of the appointment of a replacement attorney.

Re SG [2017] EWCOP 10 (2017)

The donor appointed her son as her sole attorney for property and affairs and his wife, VVVE, as replacement attorney. In the instructions box of section 7 of the instrument, the donor wrote, 'Whereas I have appointed VVVE to be my Replacement Attorney in the event of my son TWG being unable to continue to act as my Attorney, I DIRECT that my Replacement Attorney VVVE shall only act as my Replacement Attorney if she remains legally married to my son TWG at the point he becomes unable to act as my Attorney.' The Public Guardian applied for the words to be severed because it is not in line with s 13(6)(a)–(d) of the MCA 2005. The dissolution or annulment of marriage between the attorneys is not one of the 5 reasons in which an attorney's appointment would cease. The judge refused to sever the words as it was a condition on the appointment and was not an attempt to extend the statutory grounds for terminating the appointment.

Attorney or replacement attorney under 18

H10 Re Mckenna (an order of the Senior Judge made on 1 February 2011)

The donor purported to appoint a replacement attorney who, at the date the donor signed the instrument, was 16 years old. The donor added the following restriction; 'My replacement attorney shall only act if she is over the age of 18.' On the application of the Public Guardian the appointment of the replacement attorney was severed as it contravened s 10(1)(a) of the MCA 2005, which provided that an attorney must have reached 18.

Re Brindley (an order of the Senior Judge made on 11 May 2011)

The donor appointed three attorneys, A, B and C, to act jointly and severally. She then imposed the following restriction: 'C does not attain the age of 18 until 21.12.2012 upon which date along with A and B she will act jointly and severally as attorney.' On the application of the Public Guardian the appointment of C was severed as invalid on the basis that it contravened s 10(1)(a) of the MCA.

Severance of invalid restrictions as to how a replacement attorney may act

H11 Re Hartup (an order of the Senior Judge made on 28 October 2010)

The donor made two LPAs, one for property and financial affairs and the other for health and welfare. In both instruments he appointed A (his wife) and B as primary attorneys, to act jointly and severally, and C and D as replacement attorneys. In the property and financial affairs instrument he imposed the following restriction: 'Should my wife be unable to continue to act severally as my attorney, then B and my two replacement attorneys are to act on my behalf. They must act jointly in relation to decisions about selling my house or they may act jointly and severally in everything else.' In the health and welfare instrument he imposed the following restriction: 'Should my wife be unable to continue to act severally as my attorney, then B and my two replacement attorneys are to act on my behalf. They must act jointly in relation to decisions I have authorised them to make about life-sustaining treatment and where I live. They may act jointly and severally for everything else.' On the application of the Public Guardian the court severed these restrictions on the ground that, where the original attorneys had been appointed to act jointly and severally, the donor could not change the nature of the appointment by directing that the surviving original attorney should act in a different manner when the other original attorney had been replaced.

Survivor of original joint appointment cannot act with replacement

H12 Re Druce (an order of the Senior Judge made on 31 May 2011)

The donor made LPAs appointing A and B as her attorneys, to act jointly, and C and D to be her replacement attorneys. She then imposed the following restriction: 'Both C and D should jointly replace the first attorney who needs replacing so that on the first replacement there will be 3 acting attorneys. No further replacements will be needed.' On the application of the Public Guardian the court severed the restriction. There is nothing in s 10(8)(b) of the MCA, which deals with the appointment of replacement attorneys, to displace the fundamental principle that the survivor of joint attorneys cannot act. Where one of the original joint attorneys can no longer act, the replacement(s) will step in and act alone, to the exclusion of the surviving original attorney. This ruling reflects what is stated to be the 'better view' in paragraph 4.44 of *Cretney and Lush on Lasting and Enduring Powers of Attorney* (6th edition).

Re Salter (an order of the Senior Judge made on 18 August 2011)

The donor appointed primary attorneys to act jointly in some matters and jointly and severally in others, and also appointed replacement attorneys. She then directed as follows: 'For decisions where my attorneys must act jointly, replacement attorney 1 should replace attorney 1, when he is unable to act and replacement attorney 2 should replace attorney 2 when he is unable to act.' On the application of the Public Guardian this provision was severed because the effect of one primary attorney ceasing to act would be that the other primary attorney could no longer act in the matters to be decided jointly, but the direction contemplated that the first replacement would act with the surviving primary attorney.

Re Krajicek (an order of the Senior Judge made on 12 July 2012)

The donor made two LPAs appointing two attorneys, A and B, and two replacement attorneys, C and D, and directed them to act jointly for some decisions and jointly and severally for other decisions. She provided that 'If either of the original attorneys is unable to act then C should step in. D is to step in if the second attorney is unable to act.' On the application of the Public Guardian the provision was severed because it appeared to provide for the replacement attorney to act jointly with the survivor of the original attorneys, which was incompatible with the appointment of the attorneys to act jointly for some decisions.

Miles v The Public Guardian and Beattie v The Public Guardian [2015] EWHC 2960 (Ch) (Judge Nugee)

The judge confirmed that a terminating event will result in a joint power ending, unless a replacement is appointed. However, there is nothing in the MCA 2005 which precludes the reappointment on a terminating event, of an originally appointed joint attorney. The MCA 2005 should be construed in a way which gives flexibility to donors to set out how they wish their affairs to be dealt. Provided that the wording is sufficiently clear and transparent that the donor, the attorneys and the Office of the Public Guardian (OPG) can see precisely how it is intended to operate.

Severance of invalid restrictions relating to gifts

H13 Re Sykes (an order of the Senior Judge made on 9 July 2009)

The donor of a property and affairs LPA imposed a restriction stating that no gifts of any of her assets should be made other than 'annual or monthly gifts already being made by me at the date of my signing this LPA by regular bank standing orders or direct debits'. On the application of the Public Guardian the court severed this restriction on the ground that the gifts envisaged by the donor exceeded the attorney's authority to make gifts as set out in s 12 of the MCA 2005.

Re Jass (an order of the Senior Judge made on 26 October 2010)

The donor of a property and affairs LPA included the following provision: 'I hereby authorise my attorneys to give gifts on my behalf at my attorneys' discretion up to the exempt amount permitted by ss 19 (Annual Exemption), 20 (Small Gifts) and 22 (Marriage/Civil Partnership Gifts) of the Inheritance Act 1984 (or such other legislation or provision as may supersede these sections) for the time being in force.' On the application of the Public Guardian the provision was severed on the ground that it contravened s 12 of the MCA 2005.

Re Baker (an order of the Senior Judge made on 12 November 2010)

The donor of a property and affairs LPA included the following provision: 'I authorise my Attorneys to make gifts from my assets on such terms and conditions as they think fit, for the purposes of inheritance tax planning, including but not restricted to the making of gifts in line with the annual lifetime gift allowance.' On the application of the Public Guardian the provision was severed on the grounds that it contravened s 12 of the MCA 2005.

Re Munn (an order of the Senior Judge made on 28 January 2011)

The donor of a property and affairs LPA included the following provision in the guidance section; 'My finances should be managed so that X can continue to live at [a named property] for as long as she wishes and receives income from all investments and holiday lettings.' On the application of the Public Guardian the provision was severed on the ground that it contravened s 12 of the MCA 2005. Although expressed as guidance, it was more in the nature of a direction.

Re Wheatley (an order of the Senior Judge made on 31 January 2011)

The donor of a property and affairs LPA included the following provision in the guidance section: 'My attorneys will continue to make contributions to my grandchildrens' Child Trust Funds and any other saving/pension plans that I fund for their benefit.' On the application of the Public Guardian the provision was severed on the ground that it contravened s 12 of the MCA 2005. Although expressed as guidance, it was more in the nature of a direction.

Re Careford (an order of the Senior Judge made on 16 February 2011)

The donor of a property and affairs LPA included the following provision in the guidance section: 'While my husband is my attorney, he may use my own money and property for his benefit in any way he wishes. My replacement attorneys may use my money and property for the benefit of my husband in any way they think fit. All of my attorneys may make gifts to my husband from my estate.' On the application of the Public Guardian the provision was severed on the ground that it contravened s 12 of the MCA 2005. Although the provision was expressed as guidance, it was not open to the donor to give guidance about gift making in terms going beyond the statutory power.

Re Knight (an order of the Senior Judge made on 18 February 2011)

The donor of a property and affairs LPA included the following provision in the guidance section: 'I wish my attorneys, if they think fit, to pay my sister by way of gift the sum of £3,000 annually and to pay by way of gift the sum of £250 annually to my brother in law, my nephew, his spouse and all my nieces including spouses (other than to X), my great nephew and great niece, all of whom are listed on page A2 being the amounts of gifts exempt from inheritance tax under the current inheritance tax laws or such other annual sums by way of gift as shall for the time being be exempt from inheritance tax or other tax payable on death.' On the application of the Public Guardian the provision was severed on the ground it contravened s 12 of the MCA 2005.

Although the provision was expressed as guidance, it was not open to the donor to give guidance about gift making in terms going beyond the statutory power, and although it might be possible for the attorneys to make the desired gifts on 'customary occasions', the donor did not appear to have been contemplating customary occasions at all.

Re Walker (an order of the Senior Judge made on 20 July 2011)

The donor of a property and affairs LPA included the following provision in the guidance section: 'To help my son X financially from my funds as and when he requires.' On the application of the Public Guardian the provision was severed on the ground that it contravened s 12 of the MCA 2005.

Re Fisher (an order of the Senior Judge made on 28 July 2011)

The donor included the following provision in his LPA: 'I direct that if I lack mental capacity or for any other reason am unable to deal with my day to day financial affairs then my Attorney is to pay from my business the sum of £4,000 per calendar month into the bank account of my wife.' On the application of the Public Guardian the provision was severed on the ground it contravened s 12 of the MCA 2005.

Re Jackson (an order of the Senior Judge made on 17 August 2011)

The donor of a property and affairs LPA included the following guidance: 'If my attorneys believe I lack mental capacity or am becoming mentally incapable of managing and administering my property and financial affairs then I wish them to realise all my stocks, shares and other investments and transfer the proceeds and the balances from all bank and other accounts in my sole name into a joint account in the names of myself and my wife to ensure that my wife has full access to all funds.' On the application of the Public Guardian the guidance was severed because it contravened s 12 of the MCA 2005.

Re Temple (an order of the Senior Judge made on 10 August 2011)

The donor of a property and affairs LPA included the following guidance: 'My attorney is authorised to grant gifts of up to £5,000 for family and also to provide interest free loans of up to £10,000 for extreme need. Where possible loans to be repaid within one year with flexibility of terms allowed at my attorney's discretion.' On the application of the Public Guardian the guidance was severed because it contravened s 12 of the MCA 2005.

Re Gee (an order of the Senior Judge made on 22 August 2011)

The donor of a property and affairs LPA included the following guidance: 'Although I authorise my Attorneys to make gifts of money to either grandchild in cases of extreme need (for which I rely on my Attorneys' discretion) no benefit directly or indirectly should go to my daughter. If my house has to be sold I authorise my Attorneys to distribute any furniture, household and personal effects to X, Y and my grandchildren as if I had died.' In making the application the Public Guardian referred the court to the view expressed by the Law Commission in its report on Mental Capacity (Law Com. No. 231) to the effect that an LPA attorney could provide for the needs of others as part of his duty to act in the donor's best interests, even in the absence of an express provision such as is conferred on EPA attorneys. The Public Guardian asked the court to consider whether the view of the Law Commission could be relied on in cases where the donor contemplated that the attorneys could provide for the needs of others in circumstances outside the statutory gifting power. However, the court severed the guidance on the ground that it contravened s 12 of the MCA 2005.

Re Dhir (an order of the Senior Judge made on 15 November 2011)

The donor set out eight restrictions, one of which was: 'My attorney must not sell any of my properties unless it is required for my wife's medical treatment.' On the application of the Public Guardian the restriction was severed on the ground that it authorised the attorneys to make gifts beyond the scope of the statutory power set out in s 12 of the MCA 2005.

Re Forrest (an order of the Senior Judge made on 2 March 2012)

The donor included the following guidance: 'I hereby express the wish that my Attorneys will continue to pay my contribution to the school fees of my granddaughters, A and B, as per my previous pattern of contributions.' On the application of the Public Guardian the guidance was severed on the ground that it contravened s 12 of the MCA 2005.

Re Bloom (an order of the Senior Judge made on 16 March 2012)

The donor of a property and financial affairs LPA included the following direction: 'I direct my attorneys to use such of my capital and income as they shall at their discretion deem necessary to make provision for my wife's maintenance and benefit.' The Public Guardian asked the court to sever either the entire direction or just the words 'and benefit'. The court severed only the words 'and benefit' on the ground that they contravened s 12 of the MCA 2005. The order recited that the donor had a common law duty to make provision for his wife's maintenance.

Re Strange (an order of the Senior Judge made on 21 May 2012)

The donor of a property and financial affairs LPA included the following guidance: 'I wish my attorneys to provide for the financial needs of my husband in the same manner that I might have been expected to do if I had capacity to do so.' The Public Guardian asked the court to consider whether the guidance needed to be severed as potentially contravening s 12 of the MCA 2005. In the application the Public Guardian referred to the case of Bloom (above), noting that a wife had no common law duty to maintain her husband and that the husband's common law duty would be abolished when s 198 of the Equality Act 2010 came into force, but noting also that various other legislation (see below) imposed a duty on a wife to maintain her husband. The court did not sever the guidance and explained the position in the following terms: 'In the context of clauses in an LPA in which the donor makes provision for the maintenance of his or her spouse, there should be no distinction between male and female spouses and, in principle, such clauses should be treated as valid on the basis of the specific maintenance obligations imposed by statutes such as National Assistance Act 1948, s 24(1)(b) and Social Security Administration Act 1992, s 105(3), and the absence of any distinction between husband and wife in other legislation, such as the Matrimonial Causes Act 1973 and the Inheritance (Provision for Family and Dependants) Act 1975.'

Re Drew (an order of the Senior Judge made on 4 April 2012)

The donor of a property and financial affairs LPA included the following guidance: 'If my father is still alive then my trustees should continue with my contributions to his care (my records make clear from which account) and assume my role in financial responsibility for him.' [The reference to 'trustees' should have been to 'attorneys'.] The court severed the provision on the ground that it contravened s 12 of the MCA 2005. The order recited that the case of *Bloom* (above) was distinguishable because in the present case the donor had no common law duty to make provision for her father's maintenance.

Re O'Brien (an order of the Senior Judge made on 18 May 2012)

The donor of a property and financial affairs LPA included the following guidance: 'My handicapped son should be adequately provided for.' On the application of the Public Guardian this provision was severed on the ground that it contravened s 12 of the MCA 2005.

Re Burdock (an order of the Senior Judge made on 2 July 2012)

The donor made an LPA for property and financial affairs and included the following guidance: '(1) If the house is sold I intend to pay off Z's student loan completely. (2) I also intend to give my three daughters, or their issue, as follows: X £30,000, Y £30,000, Z £50,000. (3) The remainder to be used for my care and needs.' On the application of the Public Guardian the provision was severed as it gave the attorneys greater gift making powers than are permitted under s 12 of the MCA 2005.

Re Barac (an order of the Senior Judge made on 20 February 2013)

The donor made an LPA for property and financial affairs which included the following provision: 'After having taken full regard for my financial welfare and security I want my attorneys to take sensible steps to protect my estate from the effects of taxation [eg Inheritance Tax] and be able to create Trusts where beneficial.' On the application of the Public Guardian the provision was severed on the ground that it contravened s 12 of the MCA 2005.

Re Rider (an order of the Senior Judge made on 20 February 2013)

The donor made an LPA for property and financial affairs which included the following provision: 'No political donations to be made other than to the conservative party.' On the application of the Public Guardian the provision was severed on the ground that it contravened s 12 of the MCA 2005. While s 12(2)(b) permits the making of gifts to charities (subject to certain conditions), donations to the conservative party, or any other political party, would not fall within that provision.

Re Buckley (an order of the Senior Judge made on 22 February 2013)

The donor made an LPA for property and financial affairs and included the following provision: 'Assets should be used firstly to ensure the well-being and comfort of [my wife] and secondly to meet any urgent need of the families of the Attorneys and thereafter managed until distributed in accordance with the terms of my will.' On the application of the Public Guardian the provision was severed. Although the attorneys would have power to maintain the donor's wife (see *Re Bloom* above), this should not be the priority of the LPA because s 1(5) of the MCA provides that 'An act done, or decision made, under this Act for or on behalf of a person who lacks capacity must be done, or made, in his best interests.' The attorneys had no authority to meet the needs of their families, as the donor was not under any legal obligation to maintain them. Any maintenance of the families would be a gift which would potentially fall outside s 12 of the MCA 2005.

Re JG(1), Re CW and Re PG [2017] EWCOP 10 (see Re Norris above)

In *Re JG(1)* the donor had included in the preference box the following, 'I would like my attorneys to consider Thomas G (my son) as my main priority when making decisions' and in *Re CW*, the donor had inserted in the preferences box, 'I wish that my attorney considers not only the use of my money for my own benefit but also to consider the use of my money for the benefit of my mother EJW and my daughter LAAW.' The judge refused to sever the guidance as the donor is entitled to make a written statement concerning their wishes and feelings (see s 4(6)(a)) which the donees must consider when deciding what decision is in the donor's best interests. The donor had done no more than exercise that right. Furthermore, there is a misunderstanding of the Act to take the view that acting in an incapacitated person's best interests in some way precludes giving any weight to the interests of other persons dear to them. In *Re PG*, the donor had included the following in the instruction's box, 'My attorneys must ensure that IBG [*the donor's daughter*] who is unable to make decisions for herself because of her disabilities that her needs are met.' The judge refused to sever the provision as was not per se contrary to PG's best interests that she exercised her right to impose a condition on her attorneys that they must ensure that her incapacitated child's needs continued to be met from her estate. See also *Re DH* and *Re MN* in the same judgment.

Severance of unreasonable, impractical or uncertain conditions

H14 Re Saunders (an order of the Senior Judge made on 30 March 2010)

The donor appointed two attorneys and a replacement attorney. He stated that the replacement should act only if the power given to the original attorneys 'is revoked by me' or terminated by death, disclaimer or incapacity. He further stated that the power of his attorneys 'shall only come into force only if and when my attorneys have presented medical evidence to the Court and the Court are satisfied that I am or am becoming incapable by reason of mental disorder of managing and administering my property and affairs'. On the application of the Public Guardian the condition requiring the attorneys to present medical evidence to the court was severed because, although it was not invalid, it imposed an unreasonable and impractical fetter on the attorneys. The words 'is revoked by me' were also severed as being incompatible with s 10(8)(b) of the MCA (revocation of an attorney's appointment is not an event upon which a replacement attorney may act).

Re Thrussell (an order of the Senior Judge made on 12 October 2010)

The donor directed her attorneys to consult with X 'in respect of any major decision'. On the application of the Public Guardian the court severed this provision on the grounds that it was so uncertain as to be unworkable.

Re XY v Public Guardian [2015] EWCOP 35

The Public Guardian had applied to the court to sever provisions in the donor's LPA on the basis that most of the conditions imposed were an unreasonable fetter on the attorneys' power to act and were ineffective as part of an LPA within the meaning of para 11, Sch 1 of the MCA and would prevent the instrument from operating as a valid LPA, in particular:

(i) A clause which provided that a psychiatrists' opinion must have been issued; and more than 60 days must have elapsed since the issue of the opinion; and the opinion must be an uncontested opinion; and if a contested opinion had been issued previously, at least six months must have elapsed since the issue of that contested opinion, was ineffective as it specified that there should be a time delay between an assessment of capacity and decision making authority given to the attorneys. This was opposed as the MCA test is decision specific.

(ii) All references to a 'protector' required severance as the person taking the role was not identified as someone with the expertise to assess the donor's capacity or overrule an expert opinion.

(iii) The protector was not an attorney, yet they were in a position to interfere with the attorneys' duty to act in the best interests of the donor. As the protector was not a party to the LPA they were not bound by the same duties as the attorneys.

(iv) The requirement to have 2 medical opinions was unworkable.

In the context of s 23 and para 11, Sch 1, of the MCA 2005 the phrase 'ineffective as part of a lasting power of attorney' clearly means 'not capable of taking effect, according to its legal terms as part of an LPA.' The judge refused to sever the words, as they were capable of taking effect. It was no part of the Public Guardian's statutory duties to police the practicality or utility of individual aspects of an LPA. Neither the court nor the Public Guardian are concerned with whether a restriction that does not contravene the terms of the MCA 2005 may pose practical difficulties in its operation.

Whether the instrument is in prescribed form

H15 Re Nazran (an order of the Senior Judge made on 27 June 2008)

The certificate provider had not completed the first two boxes in Part B of the 2007 prescribed instrument to confirm that he was acting independently of the donor, was not ineligible to provide a certificate, and was aged 18 or over. The attorneys applied to court for a declaration that the instrument was a valid LPA or, alternatively, that the instrument was to be treated as valid under MCA Sch 1, para 3(2). [Paragraph 3(2) provides that the court may declare that an instrument which is not in the prescribed form may be treated as if it were, if it is satisfied that the persons executing the instrument intended it to create a lasting power of attorney].

The court, in the exercise of its discretion under Sch 1, para 3(2), declared that the instrument was to be treated as if it were an LPA and registered accordingly. The Public Guardian does not have this discretion.

Re Ker (an order of the Senior Judge made on 21 September 2009)

The donor in Part A of the LPA form omitted to tick the box to confirm that he had chosen his certificate provider himself. The Public Guardian refused registration on the ground that the instrument was not in prescribed form. On the attorney's application, the court exercised its discretion under para 3(2) of Sch 1 to the MCA 2005 and declared that the instrument, although not in the prescribed form, was to be treated as if it were a lasting power of attorney. Registration was directed accordingly.

Re Murdoch (an order of the Senior Judge made on 30 October 2009)

The donor executed an instrument intended to be a personal welfare LPA. It contained the following defects: (i) the certificate provider had failed to tick the first two mandatory boxes in Part B, (ii) the attorney had failed to tick any of the boxes in Part C, although he had dated and executed it, and (iii) the replacement attorney had ticked the appropriate boxes in his Part C but had not dated or executed it. The Public Guardian refused to register the instrument, and the donor subsequently lost capacity. On the attorney's application, the court directed the Public Guardian not to register the instrument, because 'the errors in its execution are too fundamental'.

Re Helmsley (an order made by the Senior Judge on 30 November 2009)

The donor executed two instruments intended to be LPAs. In Part A of both instruments she omitted to tick the box to confirm that she gave her attorneys authority to act on her behalf in circumstances when she lacked capacity. The Public Guardian refused registration on the ground that the instruments were not in prescribed form. On the attorneys' application, the court exercised its discretion under para 3(2) of Sch 1 of the MCA 2005 and declared that the instruments, although not in prescribed form, were to be treated as if they were. Registration was directed accordingly.

Re Lane (an order of the Senior Judge made on 24 January 2012)

The donor made an LPA on 3 May 2011 using the 2007 prescribed form. The transitional provisions of the Lasting Powers of Attorney, Enduring Powers of Attorney and Public Guardian (Amendment Regulations) 2009, which introduced new prescribed forms, provide that an instrument executed by the donor before 1 April 2011 on the 2007 prescribed form is capable of being a valid lasting power of attorney. The Public Guardian made an application to the court for the severance of an invalid restriction, and drew the court's attention to the date of execution, submitting that the 'old' forms were not materially different from the 'new' forms. The court accepted that the 'old' forms differed from the 'new' forms in an immaterial respect and were accordingly within para 3(1) of Sch 1 of the MCA, which provides that an instrument which differs in an immaterial respect in form or mode of expression from the prescribed form is to be treated by the Public Guardian as sufficient in point of form and expression.

Re Gunn (an order of the Senior Judge made on 8 August 2012)

The donor made LPAs for property and financial affairs and for health and welfare. The donor's signature was witnessed in both LPAs, but in the health and welfare instrument the witness failed to state his address and registration of this LPA was refused by the OPG. On the attorney's application for an order that the instrument should be treated as if it were in the prescribed form, the court exercised its discretion under para 3(2) of Sch 1 of the MCA and declared that the instrument was to be treated as if it were an LPA for health and welfare. The court considered it relevant that the witness had stated his full address in the LPA for property and financial affairs which was executed on the same day.

Re SHH [2017] EWCOP 10

The person who witnessed the donor sign the Option A box of Section 5 in the donor's health and welfare LPA did not print her name and address next to her own signature in the space provided for the witness to do so. The witness did do so elsewhere on the LPA form, so her printed name and address was accurately recorded on the face of the instrument. The omission to print her name and address next to her signature in Section 5 was a defect in the prescribed form of the instrument. It was material given that it related to life-sustaining treatment but can be rectified by the court under para 3(2) of Sch 1 of the MCA given her clear intention. The judge also made a declaration under s 23 in terms of the meaning or effect of the instrument, and in particular, that Option A had effect.

Re RH [2017] EWCOP 10

The donor had signed Sections 5 (life-sustaining treatment) and 9 (donor's statement) on 24 May 2016 and the continuation sheet was signed on the 30 May 2016. The continuation sheet stated, 'My attorneys must act jointly in relation to decisions about where I live and may act jointly and severally for everything else.' The Public Guardian's sought severance of the continuation sheet on the basis it was invalid because it was executed by the donor six days after he had signed Sections 5 and 9 of the form. The effect would be that the donor had given no instructions as to which decisions were to be made jointly and which were to be made jointly and severally. The default statutory position is that donees act jointly. Therefore, the cross in the box in Section 3 of the form needed to be severed by the court because it indicated the donees are to act 'Jointly for some decisions, jointly and severally for other decisions'. Once severed, the form would take effect as a joint appointment. The judge noted that the continuation sheet does not require a witness, unlike Sections 5 and 9 and the donor signed the relevant sections on or before the date when certificate provider gave and signed his certificate. As such the intention of the donor was clear and so a declaration was made declare that the instrument which is not in the prescribed form was to be treated as if it were.

Appointment of office holder as attorney

H16 Re McGreen (an order of the Senior Judge made on 19 April 2012)

The donor appointed A as attorney and B as replacement attorney and then provided as follows on the A2 continuation sheet: 'If my Replacement Attorney is no longer a partner in the firm of XYZ Solicitors, I appoint in his place a suitably qualified partner of that firm or firm which has succeeded that firm and carries on its practice, to be my Replacement Attorney.' (Only A and B had signed Part Cs.) The Public Guardian applied for severance of the provision on the ground that it was not possible to appoint a replacement attorney to take over from a replacement attorney (see *Re Baldwin*, below, under the heading 'Replacement for replacement attorney'.) The court severed the provision for that reason and also for the following reason: 'Section 19(2) of the Mental Capacity Act 2005 states that, in respect of the appointment of deputies, "the court may appoint an individual by appointing the holder for the time being of a specified office or position". However, there is no comparable provision in the Act that permits the donor of an LPA to appoint an office holder to be his or her attorney. Section 10(1) states that the donee of an LPA must be an individual who has reached 18 or, if the power relates only to the donor's property and affairs, either such an individual or a trust corporation.'

Whether the instrument has been correctly executed

H17 Re Sporne (an order of District Judge S E Rogers made on 13 October 2009)

The instrument had two defects: (i) the certificate provider had failed to tick the first two mandatory boxes in Part B, and (ii) the attorney had executed Part C before the certificate provider had signed Part B, contrary to reg 9 of the LPA, EPA and PG Regulations 2007. The Public Guardian's normal practice in such a case is to request fresh Parts B and C, but the donor had lost capacity. The attorney applied to court for the determination of the validity of the instrument. The court order recorded that, while the court could have exercised its discretion under para 3(2) of Sch 1 of the MCA in respect of the defect in Part B of the instrument, it could not exercise any discretion to validate a significant procedural error in respect of the requirements for the completion and execution of Parts A, B and C. It further recorded that the errors could not now be rectified as the donor had lost capacity. The court, therefore, refused to direct registration of the instrument. [The terms of para 3(2) of Sch 1 of the MCA are set out in the summary of *Re Nazran* above].

Re M Crook (an order of the Senior Judge made on 16 July 2010)

The donor's Health and Welfare LPA included an invalid restriction. A further defect was that she had not entered the date on which she executed Part A of the instrument in Section 10, nor had she dated Section 5 when selecting Option A. The Public Guardian does not regard a failure to execute the Options section as invalidating the instrument, but a failure to date Part A will normally do so. However, in this case the Public Guardian was prepared to infer that both sections had been executed on 13 October 2009, as Continuation Sheet A1 had been signed on that date, and so was the Part B certificate. In addition, the certificate provider had witnessed the Part A signatures. When applying for severance of the invalid restriction, the Public Guardian requested the court to direct that Part A was to be treated as having been signed on 13 October 2009, to avoid any challenges by third parties. The court accordingly included a provision in the order to the effect that Sections 5 and 10 of Part A were to be treated as having been executed on 13 October 2009.

Re Hurren (an order of the Senior Judge made on 28 September 2011)

The Public Guardian refused to register the instrument as an LPA because the Part B certificate had been signed before the donor signed Part A, in contravention of reg 9 of the Lasting Powers of Attorney, Enduring Powers of Attorney and Public Guardian Regulations 2007. (The donor had subsequently lost capacity.) On the attorney's application, the court declared in the exercise of its discretion under para 3(2) of Sch 1 of the MCA 2005 that the instrument was to be treated as if it were in the prescribed form and directed registration. The Public Guardian applied to set aside the order on the ground that para 3(2) did not apply in the case of defective execution. The court set aside the order, and confirmed that the discretion given to the court under para 3(2) applies only to an instrument which is not in the prescribed form and does not apply to any prescribed requirements in connection with its execution.

Re Clarke (an order of the Senior Judge made on 19 September 2011)

The donor made an LPA for property and financial affairs, appointing her husband and daughter as attorneys and her other two daughters as replacement attorneys. She also made an LPA for health and welfare, appointing her husband and three daughters as attorneys. When an application was made to register the instruments, the husband objected on the ground that the instruments had not been properly witnessed. He alleged that the witness had not been in the house when the donor signed, but had added his signature later. The court preferred the evidence of the witness and one daughter, to the effect that the donor had signed at the dining room table and that the witness was in an adjacent room and could see her sign through glass doors separating the two rooms. Applying the old case *Casson v Dade* (1781), the court held that the instruments had been properly witnessed. (The husband also objected on the ground that the donor lacked capacity to make an LPA, but this was also dismissed. The donor's GP had acted as certificate provider and the court commented on the difficulties facing GPs who act as certificate providers within the time constraints of an appointment at the surgery).

Re H (an order of District Judge Ralton made on 24 January 2012)

The donor used the 2007 version of the LPA prescribed form and failed to tick the box to confirm that she had read (or had read to her) the prescribed information on pages 2, 3 and 4. On the attorney's application the court was unable to find on balance of probability that the donor had read (or had read to her) the prescribed information. This was a failure of execution and the court had no discretion to uphold it.

Re Smith (an order of the Senior Judge made on 1 March 2012)

The donor appointed two attorneys to act jointly and severally. The LPA was registered by oversight even though one attorney's signature had not been witnessed. The attorney applied for a declaration of validity, and the evidence was that the witness had been present when the attorney signed, but had not signed under the attorney's name. The court dismissed the application, holding that it had no jurisdiction to declare that the LPA was valid. The applicant was directed to return the instrument to the OPG so that his appointment could be marked as invalid in accordance with s 10(7) of the MCA 2005.

See *Re RH* [2017] EWCOP 10 above.

Attorney's date of birth missing

H18 Re John (an order of District Judge Ralton made on 14 October 2010)

The donor made an LPA using the 'old' form prescribed in 2007. She appointed an original attorney and a replacement attorney, but the replacement attorney's Part C omitted his date of birth, and it could not be inferred from the instrument that he was at least 18. The usual practice of the Public Guardian in such a case is to request a fresh Part C, but this could not be done because the donor had lost capacity (see *Re Sporne*, above). The instrument was registered, with registration being limited to the original attorney, but the attorney then applied to court to have the defective Part C 'reinstated'. The Public Guardian was joined as a party.

The court ruled that the LPA was not in the prescribed form because of the failure to include the replacement attorney's date of birth. As the court was satisfied on the evidence that the replacement attorney was in fact at least 18, it exercised its discretion under parah 3(2) of Sch 1 of the MCA (which is set out in the summary of *Re Nazran*, above) to declare that the LPA was to be treated as if it were in the precribed form.

(Note: in the case of LPAs made using the 2009 prescribed form, the attorney's date of birth must be included in Part A, so the practice of requesting a fresh Part C is not applicable, although limited registration may be possible if there is another attorney whose date of birth has been given.)

Re Dadd (an order of District Judge Hilder made on 17 November 2010)

The donor made an LPA using the 'new' form prescribed in 2009. She appointed two attorneys but provided no date of birth for either. The Public Guardian was willing to register in favour of one attorney because her title was given as 'Mrs', so that it could reasonably be inferred that she was at least 18. It was overlooked that the other attorney was described in the instrument as the donor's husband. On the attorney's application the court directed registration. As it could be inferred from the instrument that both attorneys were at least 18, the instrument differed from the prescribed form in an immaterial respect within para 3(1) of Sch 1 of the MCA 2005.

Re Cretney (an order of the Senior Judge made on 24 February 2011)

The donor made an LPA on the 2009 prescribed form but omitted the attorney's date of birth in Part A. The Public Guardian refused to register on the ground that the instrument differed materially from the prescribed form. On the application of the attorney (who was over 18) the court declared in the exercise of its discretion under para 3(2) of Sch 1 of the MCA that the instrument was to be treated as if it were in the prescribed form.

Donor's surname missing

H19 Re Baker (an order of the Senior Judge made on 4 February 2011)

In Part A of the instrument the donor put his middle name in the box for 'Last Name' and omitted his surname completely. As his middle name could have passed for a surname, this error was not noticed by anybody and the instrument was registered. The attorney applied for a declaration that the LPA was to be treated as valid under para 3(2) of Sch 1 of the MCA 2005, under which the court may declare that an instrument is to be treated as if it had been made in the prescribed form even though it differs in a material respect from the prescribed form. The court exercised its discretion under para 3(2) because, although the error was material, it was satisfied that the instrument was intended to be an LPA. The Public Guardian was directed to amend the register and attach a note to the instrument to this effect.

[Note: for a similar case concerning an EPA, see *Re Orriss*, under the 'Rectification' heading.]

Attorney or replacement attorney as a 'named person'

H20 Re Howarth (an order of the Senior Judge made on 29 July 2008)

The donor had named the replacement attorney as the only person to be notified of an application to register. MCA Sch 1, para 2(3) provides that a person who is 'appointed as donee under the instrument' may not be a named person. If there was no effective named person, the instrument could only be valid if it contained two Part B certificates, but it contained only one. On the application of the Public Guardian the court directed the severance of the appointment of the replacement attorney on the ground that a replacement attorney was a person 'appointed as donee under the instrument' who could not, therefore, be a named person. As the appointment of the replacement attorney was severed, the named person was not an attorney and so the instrument could be registered.

Re McAdam (an order of the Senior Judge made on 29 March 2010)

The donor had named X, one of two original attorneys (who had been appointed to act jointly and severally), as the only named person. On the application of the Public Guardian the court severed the appointment of X as attorney on the ground that the MCA does not permit an attorney to be a named person. The instrument was directed to be registered as an LPA appointing only the other attorney.

Eligibility of certificate provider

H21 Re Kittle (a judgment of the Senior Judge given on 1 December 2009)

Regulation 8(3) of the LPA, EPA and PG Regulations 2007 sets out categories of persons who cannot act as certificate provider. Included in the list is 'a family member' of the donor or of the attorney (or of the owner, director, manager or employee of any care home in which the donor is living when the instrument is executed). In this case the certificate provider was the donor's first cousin. The Public Guardian declined to register the instrument on the ground that a first cousin was a family member of the donor. The court ruled that a first cousin is not a family member, and so the LPA was valid.

Re Phillips (an order of the Senior Judge made on 16 May 2012)

The donor appointed three attorneys, A, B and C. She did not name any persons to be notified, and so there were two certificate providers. The Public Guardian refused to register on the ground that one certificate provider, X, was a member of the family of A. He was the unmarried partner of A but did not live at the same address. In his Part B certificate X said: 'I am the partner of A and have known the donor for 3 years.' The attorney applied to court for a direction to register and the Public Guardian was joined as respondent. The court decided that X was to be treated as a member of the family of A, and so the instrument could not be registered. The judge said: 'In my judgment, anyone who describes himself in this context as the attorney's partner is courting trouble and automatically disqualifies himself from being a person who can give an LPA certificate. This applies regardless of whether he describes himself as the attorney's partner intentionally or inadvertently, whether they live at the same address or at separate locations, whether the relationship is intimate or platonic, and whether the statement is true or false.' Although it was unnecessary to the decision, the judge added that, even if X were not to be treated as a family member, he was not independent of the attorney, as required by the prescribed LPA form.

Re Putt (an order of the Senior Judge made on 22 March 2011)

The donor appointed two partners of a firm of solicitors which was a Limited Liability Partnership (LLP) as attorneys in her property and affairs instrument and her health and welfare instrument. The certificate provider was an associate solicitor of the same LLP. Regulation 8(3)(f) of the Lasting Powers of Attorney, Enduring Powers of Attorney and Public Guardian Regulations 2007 disqualifies a person from acting as certificate provider if that person is 'a business partner or employee' of the donor or of an attorney under the instrument.

While this regulation clearly applies to a common law partnership, it does not expressly deal with LLPs. The Public Guardian made a severance application in relation to another matter (see below under the heading 'Appointment of substitute by an attorney') and asked the court also to consider whether the instrument was invalid on the ground that reg 8(3)(f) applied to LLPs as well as to common law partnerships. The court ruled that the instrument was not a valid LPA because the certificate provider was ineligible to act. (By a separate order made on 12 April 2011 the court directed that the health and welfare instrument should not be registered and that registration of the property and affairs instrument, which had been registered before the defect was noticed, should be cancelled.)

Replacement for replacement attorney

H22 Re Baldwin (an order made by the Senior Judge on 14 May 2009)

The donor appointed X as original attorney, Y as the replacement for X, and Z as the replacement for Y if Y was unable or unwilling to act. On the application of the Public Guardian the court directed the severance of the appointment of Z on the ground that the MCA does not permit a donor to appoint a person to take over as a second replacement attorney if the first replacement attorney starts to act and then becomes unable to act.

Re Martin (an order of the Senior Judge made on 14 February 2013)

The donor appointed two primary attorneys, A and B, to act jointly and severally, and three replacement attorneys, C, D and E. He included a valid provision to the effect that the D should replace B if B was unable to act, and then directed as follows: 'In the event of my first attorney being unable to continue, E should act as Assistant to C (1st Replacement Attorney), and in the event of C being unable to continue, he should assume the power of Attorney.' On the application of the Public Guardian this provision was severed because (applying *Re Baldwin*, above) the MCA does not permit a replacement attorney to be replaced, nor is it possible to direct an attorney or replacement attorney to act as assistant to another attorney or replacement attorney.

Re Boff (a judgment of the Senior Judge given on 16 August 2013)

The court subsequently confirmed in *Re Boff*, a contested application, that it is not possible to appoint a replacement for a replacement attorney.

Appointment of substitute by an attorney

H23 Re Swift (an order of the Senior Judge made on 30 March 2010)

The donor had been appointed to act as attorney under LPAs made by his wife. In his own LPA for property and financial affairs he stated as follows: 'In the event that I become incapacitated and am unable to take decisions in my role as Attorney to my wife, I appoint both my Attorneys as Guardians of my wife in order that they may, together, take decisions about her property and affairs.' He included an equivalent provision in his LPA for health and welfare. On the application of the Public Guardian the court severed these provisions as being ineffective because the MCA does not permit an attorney to appoint a substitute or successor to himself.

Re Williams (an order of the Senior Judge made on 1 December 2010)

The donor appointed three attorneys to act jointly. She then added: 'The attorneys are only to make decisions jointly and should any of the attorneys die within my lifetime I wish for their personal representative to take over as my attorney in their place.' On the application of the Public Guardian the court severed this provision on the ground that s 10(8)(a) of the MCA provided that an LPA instrument could not give the attorney power to appoint a substitute or successor.

[Note: The provision could also be viewed as incompatible with the nature of a joint appointment.]

Re Putt (an order of the Senior Judge made on 22 March 2011)

The donor appointed a family member and two solicitors in her property and affairs and health and welfare instruments. In both instruments she directed as follows: 'My attorneys (or any of them) may delegate in writing any of his, her or their functions to any person and shall not be responsible for the default of that person (even if the delegation was not strictly necessary or expedient) provided that he, she or they took reasonable care in his, her or their selection and supervision.' The Public Guardian applied for severance of the direction on the ground that it was too wide and in effect enabled the attorneys to appoint a substitute. The court ruled that the clause was invalid as being 'not simply contrary but almost repugnant to the special relationship of personal obligation and faith that one might reasonably expect to exist between a donor and the attorney of an LPA.' (The LPAs were in any event invalid: see above under the heading 'Ineligibility of certificate provider'.)

Re Clare (an order of the Senior Judge made on 8 September 2011)

The donor made two LPAs, each appointing an attorney and a replacement attorney. In each she directed as follows: 'My Attorney may at any time appoint a substitute to act as my Attorney and may revoke any appointment without giving a reason. Each appointment is to be in writing signed by my Attorney. Every substitute has full powers as my Attorney as if appointed by this Deed, except the power to appoint a substitute.' On the application of the

Public Guardian the provision was severed as being a plain breach of s 10(8)(a) of the MCA, which provides that an LPA cannot give the attorney power to appoint a substitute or successor.

Re Goodwin (an order of the Senior Judge made on 17 June 2013)

The donor appointed three attorneys and two replacements. Regarding the replacements, she directed that if one ceased to act the other could act alone, and added: 'She should also make every effort to find one or two replacement attorneys to take over her responsibilities in the event of her own death, or if she no longer has the mental capacity to carry on, so that there is a continuing "Lasting Power of Attorney" in place during the donor's lifetime.' On the application of the Public Guardian this provision was severed on the ground that s 10(8)(a) of the MCA invalidates any provision in an LPA giving an attorney power to appoint a substitute or successor.

Where attorney present when certificate provider interviews the donor

H24 Re Gibbs (an order of the Senior Judge made on 9 September 2008)

The certificate provider ticked the box to confirm that he had discussed the LPA with the donor and that the attorneys were not present, and also ticked the box to say that the LPA had been discussed with the donor in the presence of other persons, identified as the attorneys. The court directed that the LPA was valid (the certificate provider having confirmed by letter that he had interviewed the donor on her own as well as with the attorneys present).

Re Bullock (an order made by the Senior Judge on 15 December 2009)

The certificate providers did not tick the box to confirm that they had discussed the LPA with the donor and that the attorney was not present. The donor was in hospital and the certificate providers had discussed the LPA with the donor at his bedside, the attorney being present throughout. The Public Guardian refused registration on the ground that the instrument was not in prescribed form. The court, in the exercise of its discretion, declared under para 3(2) of Sch 1 of the MCA 2005 that the instrument, which was not in the prescribed form, should be treated as if it were. Registration was directed accordingly.

Note: There is no such requirement in the 2009 or 2015 LPA prescribed forms.

Capacity to make an LPA

H25 Re Collis (a judgment of the Senior Judge given on 27 October 2010)

An application was made to the court to direct the Public Guardian to cancel the registration of an LPA on the grounds that the instrument was not a valid LPA because the Donor lacked capacity to create an LPA at the date of execution. In the course of his judgment the Senior Judge set out the law relating to capacity to create an LPA.

A, B & C v X & Z (a judgment of Hedley J given on 30 July 2012)

The court was asked to make declarations as to whether X had capacity to do various things, including entering into marriage, litigating, making a will, managing his affairs, and making or revoking an enduring or lasting power of attorney. Paragraph 38 is of interest on the question of fluctuating or qualified capacity:

'Let me then turn to the question of revocation or creation of enduring or lasting powers of attorney. First, I am not satisfied that it has been established that X lacked capacity to revoke the power of attorney in favour of the Applicants, even indeed if that was still a live issue given that the revocation has been accepted and the registration has been cancelled. I found the issue of power to create a new enduring* power of attorney very much more difficult for all the reasons that apply in relation to testamentary capacity. In the end, I have reached exactly the same conclusion. I am unwilling to make, on the evidence, a general declaration that he lacks capacity, but qualify that immediately by saying that the exercise of such a power, unless accompanied by contemporary medical evidence of capacity, would give rise to a serious risk of challenge or of refusal to register. It seems to me, for exactly the same reasons as I endeavoured to set out in relation to testamentary capacity, that X's capacity is likely to diminish in the future and there will be times when undoubtedly he lacks capacity, just as there will be times when he retains it.'

[*The judge must have intended to refer to a lasting power of attorney, as new enduring powers of attorney may not now be made.]

ENDURING POWERS OF ATTORNEY CASES

Severance of restrictions incompatible with an LPA

Whether the instrument was validly executed

H26 Re Wealleans (an order of District Judge S E Rogers made on 8 May 2008)

The witness had not stated her address in the instrument, as required by reg 3(1) of the Enduring Powers of Attorney (Prescribed Form) Regulations 1990. On the application of the attorney the court declared pursuant to MCA Sch, 4 para 2(4) that the EPA was 'procedurally valid'. [Paragraph 2(4) provides that, if an instrument differs in an immaterial respect in form or mode of expression from the prescribed form it is to be treated as sufficient in point of form and expression].

Re Parker (an order of District Judge Keeley Bishop made on 22 December 2008)

This application concerned an EPA which had already been registered in 2007. The attorneys had signed the EPA on 25 December 1993 and the donor had signed later, on 13 January 1994. The court held that the EPA was valid, applying the unreported decision of Knox J in *Re R* dated 23 February 1988.

Re Harries (an order of the Senior Judge made on 22 June 2009)

The witnesses to the signatures of the donor and the attorney left the space for the signature of the witness blank, and wrote their names (and addresses) in capital letters in the space for the name and address of the witness. On the application of the attorney it was held that the instrument was a valid EPA. The judge added that the decision would have been otherwise if the names and addresses of the witnesses had been typed.

Re Lodge (an order of District Judge S E Rogers made on 6 August 2010)

Unfortunately by mistake the donor signed Part C and the attorney signed Part B of the EPA instrument. On the attorney's application the Court held that the donor's failure to execute the instrument correctly was a material defect and it was not a valid EPA.

The attorney applied for reconsideration of this order. By an order of the Senior Judge made on 14 March 2011 the previous order was affirmed.

Re Devine (an order of District Judge Eldergill made on 13 October 2010)

The attorney's signature in Part C was witnessed but the witness did not sign his name. On the application of the attorney the court declared that the instrument was defective in a material respect and did not take effect as an EPA.

Re Freeman (an order of District Judge Ralton made on 7 September 2010)

The donor signed Part B of the EPA instrument on 14 April 2006, but the attorney did not sign Part C until 3 October 2008. The Public Guardian refused to register on the ground that an instrument could not be a valid EPA unless the attorney had signed before 1 October 2007. Section 66(2) of the Mental Capacity Act 2005 provides that an EPA cannot be 'created' after commencement. On the attorney's application the court declared that the instrument was not a valid EPA. (The attorney applied for reconsideration but the Judge confirmed his earlier decision by an order made at a hearing on 28 February 2011.)

[Note: The Public Guardian will register an EPA appointing joint and several attorneys if at least one attorney signed before 1 October 2007 even though other(s) did not, in which case registration will be limited to the attorney(s) who signed before that date.]

Immaterial differences from the prescribed form

Re Newman (an order of the Senior Judge made on 30 July 2012)

The donor made an EPA in which, amongst other defects, he failed to select either of the following alternatives: 'with general authority to act on my behalf' or 'with authority to do the following on my behalf'. The court confirmed that this failure did not invalidate the EPA, because it was an immaterial difference from the prescribed form within para 2(4) of Sch 4 of the MCA.

Registration of uncertified copy

Re Vallet (an order of District Judge S E Rogers made on 27 January 2009)

The original EPA could not be produced, nor was there a certified copy in existence. Regulation 24(2) of the Lasting Powers of Attorney, Enduring Powers of Attorney and Public Guardian Regulations 2007 provides that, in such a case, the Public Guardian must not register without an order of the court. On the application of the attorney the court declared that it was satisfied that the copy was a copy of the original EPA, which had been lost but not revoked, and directed registration.

Delegation of trustee functions

Re Heartfield (an order of the Senior Judge made on 17 June 2008)

The donor stated in the EPA: 'I delegate all my trustee functions and powers whether conferred by statute, general law or a trust instrument to my attorneys'. On the application of the attorney the court determined that the provision was ineffective as part of an EPA and severed it.

Appointment by donor of substitute attorneys

Re J (an order of Lewison J made on 12 March 2009 in the High Court)

The judge decided that the donor of an EPA may validly appoint substitute attorneys in the same instrument. He also decided that the former practice of the Court of Protection before 1 October 2007 of registering some such powers with the 'qualified' stamp (which limits registration to a particular attorney) was wrong. The registration must be unqualified. The Court of Protection at Archway has ordered severance of the appointment of a substitute attorney on several occasions since 1 October 2007, but applications for severance are no longer necessary as a result of the High Court decision.

Re Ellis (an order made by the Senior Judge on 17 November 2009)

The donor appointed his wife as the original attorney and then appointed his two children as substitute attorneys to act in the event that the original attorney should be unable to act. However, the donor failed to specify whether the substitute attorneys should act jointly or jointly and severally. On the application of the attorneys, the appointment of the substitute attorneys was severed. Although the decision in *Re J* (above) confirmed that substitute attorneys may be appointed in an EPA, the appointment of two or more substitutes is invalid if the donor has not specified that they are to act either jointly or jointly and severally.

Re Bax (and order of District Judge S E Rogers made on 22 October 2009)

The donor appointed A and B to act jointly, and then provided that 'In the event A is unable or unwilling to act as my attorney then I appoint C.' On the attorneys' application the court severed the appointment of C. Although a donor may appoint a substitute attorney, the appointment must not be incompatible with a joint appointment of the original attorneys.

Re Farrow (an order of District Judge Eldergill made on 18 August 2010)

The donor appointed A to be her attorney and then appointed B to act in the event that A should be unable or unwilling to act or died. The donor then stated that A and B should act jointly and severally. On the application of the attorneys the court severed the words 'jointly and severally', so that the instrument could be registered as an EPA appointing A as primary attorney and B as substitute attorney.

Appointment of substitute by an attorney

Re Dickenson (an order of District Judge Hilder made on 12 November 2010)

The donor appointed two attorneys to act jointly and severally and imposed the following restriction: 'My professional Attorneys may at any time appoint a substitute to act as my attorney and may revoke the appointment without giving reason. Every appointment is to be in writing signed by my Attorney. Every substitute has full powers as my attorney, as if appointed by this Deed, except the power to appoint a substitute.' On the application of an attorney the court severed the restriction. Paragraph 2(6) of Sch 4 of the MCA 2005 provides that 'A power of attorney which gives the attorney a right to appoint a substitute or successor cannot be an enduring power.'

Severance of restrictions incompatible with an EPA

H27 Re Ditcham (an order made by the Senior Judge on 12 May 2009)

An EPA provided that 'my attorney(s) may take decisions on where I shall live provided that these decisions are made in my best interests and may negotiate with Social Services and any other relevant authorities to secure the best treatment and accommodation on my behalf that can be provided'. On the application of the attorneys the court severed this provision on the ground that it would be ineffective as part of an EPA.

Re King (an order of District Judge S E Rogers made on 14 July 2009)

An EPA provided that 'In case that I am unable to take part in decisions about my medical care then I appoint my Attorney to represent my views about them if I am unable to do so'. On the application of the attorney the court severed this provision on the ground that it would be ineffective as part of an EPA.

Re Viveash (an order of District Judge S E Rogers made on 21 September 2009)

An EPA provided that 'I grant to my attorneys the power to deal with all matters concerning my welfare health and matters of a personal nature to me and all other matters affecting me or my possessions.' On the application of the attorneys the court severed the restriction on the ground that it would be ineffective as part of an EPA.

Re Donegan (an order of the Senior Judge made on 6 January 2011)

The donor made an EPA including the following provision: 'All the while that I am practically and financially able to remain in my own home my Attorneys should ensure that I remain there. My Attorneys do not have power to sell my home.' On the application of the Attorneys the court severed the restriction on the ground that it was ineffective as part of an EPA because it sought to confer Personal Welfare decision making powers on the Attorneys.

Re Harris (an order of the Senior Judge made on 6 January 2011)

The donor made an EPA purporting to authorise the Attorneys to do the following: 'Making a choice on my behalf for any nursing/residential care needed for me in the future.' On the application of the Attorneys the court severed the provision on the ground that it would be ineffective as part of an EPA, because it sought to authorise Personal Welfare decision making.

Re Hollins (an order made by District Judge Jackson on 10 June 2009)

In Part B of the instrument, under the heading 'subject to the following restrictions and conditions', the donor wrote 'See attached supplement'. The attached supplement listed extended powers, including:

> '**Extended powers to deal with my affairs.** My Attorney may take decisions on where I shall live (if I have become mentally incapable of taking these decisions for myself) provided that these decisions are in my best interests. My Attorney may negotiate with Social Services and any other relevant authorities to secure the best treatment and accommodation on my behalf that can be obtained.
>
> **Power to consent to medical treatment.** My Attorney may give consent to medical treatment on my behalf provided that it is carried out to save my life or to ensure improvement or to prevent deterioration in my physical or mental health.
>
> **Extended power to make gifts.** My Attorney may make such gifts on my behalf as he sees fit to reduce the burden of Inheritance Tax on my estate provided that these are consistent with the provisions of my Will and provided that my lifestyle at the date of making the gift is in no way jeopardised by the making of the gift.'

The Public Guardian refused registration on the ground that the first two of the above provisions did not relate to the donor's property and affairs, and that the third was inconsistent with Sch 4, para 3(3) of the Mental Capacity Act. On the attorney's application, the court directed severance of the attached supplement and the reference to it in Part B of the instrument.

Re Robinson (an order of District Judge S E Rogers made on 18 September 2009)

An EPA provided that 'My Attorneys shall have power to deal with my affairs from time to time as may be necessary to reduce the incidence of Inheritance Tax at the date of my death provided that lump sum payments shall only be made to or on behalf of such persons who would otherwise receive the benefit of my estate as residuary beneficiaries (either original or substituted) of my Will.' On the application of the attorneys the court severed this restriction on the ground that it would be ineffective as part of an EPA (because it exceeded the statutory power to make gifts under Sch, 4 para 3 of the MCA).

Re Stevens (an order of District Judge Batten made on 11 January 2011)

The donor made an EPA including the following provision: 'The word "seasonal" in s 3(5) of the Enduring Powers of Attorney Act 1985 includes the end of one tax year and the beginning of another.' On the application of the attorneys the court severed the provision as being ineffective as part of an EPA.

Severance of restrictions incompatible with a joint and several appointment

H28 Re Blair (an order of the Senior Judge made on 1 October 2008)

The donor appointed two attorneys to act jointly and severally, and contained the following restriction: 'For single transactions of a value in excess of £500 (five hundred pounds) then I declare my attorneys shall act jointly as against jointly and severally.' On the application of the attorneys under para 4(5) of Sch 4 of the MCA to determine whether the power was valid, the court severed the restriction.

Re Wills (an order of District Judge S E Rogers made on 20 November 2008)

The donor appointed three attorneys to act jointly and severally. She then imposed the following restriction: 'Although I have appointed my Attorneys to act jointly and severally, I require that at least two of them shall sign any cheque on my behalf for a sum in excess of £500 or act in any transaction worth over £500.' On the application of the attorneys to determine whether the power was valid, the court severed the restriction.

See also *Re Newman*.

Re Bridge (an order of the Senior Judge made on 25 September 2009)

The donor appointed three attorneys to act jointly and severally. He imposed the following restriction: '2 of the 3 can deal with any household or every day expenses, but for any other issues I would like all 3 attorneys to be signatories. In particular I would not like my house to be sold or money to be invested without agreement and signatory from all 3. My money and assets are to be used to cover my care and living expenses in old age and ill health.' On the application of an attorney the court directed severance of the restriction as being ineffective as part of an EPA.

Re Akpabio (an order of the Senior Judge made on 15 March 2010)

The donor made an EPA appointing two attorneys to act jointly and severally. He included the following restriction: 'I want them to act jointly on important matters concerning my welfare including any future living arrangements and on any large financial decisions such as selling my property.' On the application of the attorneys the court severed the restriction as being incompatible with a joint and several appointment.

Re Candy (an order of the Senior Judge made on 18 March 2010)

The donor appointed two attorneys to act jointly and severally. She then imposed the following restriction: 'neither of my attorneys will act without the approval of the other'. On the application of the attorneys the court severed the restriction as being inconsistent with a joint and several appointment.

Re Dunningham (an order of District Judge S E Rogers made on 15 September 2009)

The donor appointed two attorneys, A and B, to act jointly and severally. She then imposed the following restriction: 'and the said B shall have no authority to act on my behalf unless the said A has died or is incapable of acting as my Attorney'. On the application of the attorneys for severance, the court severed the restriction as being inconsistent with a joint and several appointment.

[Note: compare *Re Taylor* (an order of District Judge Eldergill made on 7 December 2011) where, on similar facts, the court severed the words 'jointly and severally'.]

Re Porter (an order of District Judge S E Rogers made on 26 July 2010)

The donor appointed his wife and two children as attorneys, to act jointly and severally. He added the following restriction: 'My wife may act alone during her lifetime and whilst she is mentally capable. My children shall act jointly.' On the application of an attorney the court severed the restriction as being incompatible with a joint and several appointment.

Re Meaker (an order made by District Judge Ralton made on 16 June 2009)

The donor appointed two attorneys to act jointly and severally. She added the following restriction: 'My attorneys shall act jointly at all times unless the death, incapacity or bankruptcy of either one of them shall preclude her from acting, in which case the other Attorney shall continue to act alone'. On the application of the attorney the restriction was severed as being ineffective as part of an EPA.

Re Pattison (an order of District Judge Hilder made on 11 May 2010)

The donor appointed three attorneys, A, B and C, to act jointly and severally. A and B were her daughters. She then imposed the following restriction: 'I direct that not less than two of my attorneys shall act whilst there are two alive and capable of acting and that initially those two shall be my two daughters.' On the application of the attorneys the court directed severance of the restriction as being incompatible with a joint and several appointment.

Re Rayner (an order of District Judge S E Rogers made on 9 July 2009)

The donor appointed A and B as attorneys to act jointly and severally with general authority to act in relation to all her property and affairs. She then imposed a restriction, stating that A and B should not act in relation to properties jointly owned with the donor, and that C was appointed as attorney in relation to these properties. On the application of the attorney the restriction was severed, with the result that A and B could act in relation to all the donor's property and affairs and C could not act.

Re Furlow (an order made by District Judge SE Rogers on 1 October 2009)

The donor appointed X and Y to act jointly and severally. He included the following provision: 'X shall act with general authority on my behalf in relation to all my property and affairs. Y shall act with authority to do the following on my behalf: To deal with my bank accounts and savings and investments in relation to my bank accounts, savings accounts and investments.' He then added: 'Y may deal with my bank investments subject to my prior approval.' On the attorney's application, both provisions were severed. The first was incompatible with a joint and several appointment (as one attorney had more limited powers than the other), and the second was unworkable after the donor's loss of capacity.

Re Haworth (an order of District Judge Mainwaring-Taylor made on 20 December 2010)

The donor made an EPA appointing A and B to act jointly and severally. He then imposed the following restriction: 'B shall not, while A is alive and mentally capable, without A's consent (a) sell, mortgage, charge, lease, or otherwise dispose of any asset of mine or (b) enter into any transaction with a value of more than £2,000.' On the attorneys' application the court severed the restriction as being incompatible with a joint and several appointment.

Re Jarman (an order of District Judge Mainwaring-Taylor made on 8 August 2011)

The donor made an EPA appointing attorneys to act jointly and severally. He included the following restriction: 'While both of my Attorneys are alive and of capacity they are to act jointly and a certificate from a practising doctor will be sufficient evidence of capacity of either of my Attorneys.' On the application of the attorneys the court severed the restriction as being incompatible with a joint and several appointment.

Severance of restrictions incompatible with a joint appointment

H29 Re Bainbridge (an order of the Senior Judge made on 10 March 2009)

The donor appointed her three children to act jointly, adding the restriction 'PROVIDED THAT in the event that any one or more of my said children shall die or shall for any other reason be unable to act as my Attorneys then I appoint my remaining children to be my Attorneys for the purpose of the Enduring Powers of Attorney Act 1985 and in the event that only one of my said children shall be able to act as my Attorney then I appoint him/her as my sole Attorney for the purposes of the Enduring Powers of Attorney Act 1985.' On the application of the attorneys under para 4(5) of Sch 4 of the Mental Capacity Act 2005 to determine whether the power was valid, the court severed the restriction as being incompatible with a joint appointment.

Re Berg (an order of the Senior Judge made on 31 December 2010)

The donor made an EPA appointing A and B to act jointly. He then added: 'so long as neither Attorney dies or is incapacitated in which eventuality the other Attorney is empowered to act on his own'. On the application of the attorneys the court severed the restriction as being incompatible with a joint appointment.

Re Shepherd (an order of Judge Rogers made on 13 March 2009)

The donor appointed three attorneys to act jointly, adding the words 'Any two out of the three attorneys shall have power to sign jointly on my behalf'. The court severed these words as being incompatible with a joint appointment.

Re Williamson (an order of the Senior Judge made on 25 October 2010)

The donor appointed A, B and C to act jointly. He then imposed the following restriction: 'The said B and C shall not exercise their authority under this Power whilst my wife is alive and able to act as my attorney.' On the application of the attorneys the court severed the restriction as being incompatible with a joint appointment.

Severance of restriction fettering attorney's authority

H30 Re Corbett (an order of the Senior Judge made on 4 December 2008)

A restriction in an EPA which had been registered in 2006 contained the following restriction: 'No transaction with a value greater than £500 to be actioned without the written permission of my son SC.' The attorney applied for an order removing the restriction on the grounds that SC's whereabouts were unknown and had not been heard from for 12 months. The attorney wished to sell the donor's house to pay for care home fees. The court determined that, having regard to all the circumstances, the restriction was an unreasonable fetter on the scope of the attorney's authority, and was having an adverse impact on the management and administration of the donor's property and affairs. The restriction was accordingly severed and the Public Guardian was directed to register a note to that effect.

Re Johnston (an order of District Judge S E Rogers made on 15 October 2012)

The donor appointed two attorneys to act jointly and severally. The donor included the following restriction: 'The property at [address] shall not be disposed of without the agreement of A, B and C, as children of [the donor] in addition to the attorneys.' On the attorneys' application the restriction was severed as being ineffective as part of an EPA.

Rectification

Re Portues (an order made by District Judge S E Rogers on 6 January 2009)

In Part B of the instrument the donor appointed attorneys to act jointly and severally and struck out the words 'with general authority to act', leaving in place the words 'with authority to do the following'. She did not include any instructions under those words to indicate the scope of the attorneys' powers. On the application of the attorney for rectification of the instrument, the court was satisfied that it was the donor's intention to confer general authority on the attorneys and that the deletion of those words was a clerical error. The court declared that the EPA was to be read and construed as if the donor granted general authority to the attorneys and directed the Public Guardian to reconsider the registration of the EPA in the light of the declaration.

Re Sawyer (an order made by District Judge S E Rogers on 31 March 2009)

In Part B of the EPA the donor appointed four attorneys, but omitted to strike out either option 'jointly' or 'jointly and severally' in relation to how they should act. On the application of the attorneys, the court was satisfied that the donor had intended to appoint them to act jointly and severally, and directed that the EPA should be construed as if they had been appointed jointly and severally and the alternative option 'jointly' had been deleted. The Public Guardian was directed to attach a note to that effect to the registered EPA.

See also *Re Newman*.

Re Smith (an order made by District Judge Mainwaring-Taylor on 7 December 2009)

In Part C of the EPA the attorney had deleted the words 'I also understand my limited power to use the donor's property to benefit persons other than the donor'. On the attorney's application, the court was satisfied that the deletion was made in error, and directed that the instrument should be read as if the wording had not been deleted.

Re Orriss (an order of District Judge Ralton made on 20 October 2010)

By mistake the donor's surname was omitted from the instrument, which included only his first and second names. The EPA was registered without the mistake being discovered. On the application of the attorney the court directed the Public Guardian to attach a note to the EPA stating that the donor's surname had been omitted in error from Part B.

Capacity to revoke EPA: test is not the same as for creation of LPA

H31 Re Cloutt (an order of the Senior Judge made on 7 November 2008)

The donor made an EPA in October 2000 appointing NatWest Bank as attorney. This was registered in March 2008. In April 2008 the donor executed an instrument intended to be a Lasting Power of Attorney, appointing a different attorney, and executed a deed revoking the EPA. In the LPA the Part B certificate was provided by a medical practitioner, who had confirmed that he was satisfied that the donor was able to make an LPA. In June 2008 the LPA attorney applied to court for an order confirming the revocation of the EPA (as required by para 15 of Sch 4 of the MCA).

The Senior Judge made a directions order in August 2008 requiring the submission of further evidence on the ground that the revocation of an EPA is a different transaction from the creation of an LPA, and capacity to create an LPA is not necessarily the same as capacity to revoke an EPA. Thus a doctor's certification of an LPA is not of itself sufficient proof of capacity to revoke an EPA. On considering the further evidence subsequently provided by the doctor and the donor's solicitor, the court was satisfied that the donor had capacity to revoke the EPA. A final order was made confirming the revocation of the EPA and directing the Public Guardian to cancel its registration.

LAW SOCIETY PRACTICE NOTES

Contents

LASTING POWERS OF ATTORNEY

I1

7 June 2016

1 INTRODUCTION

1.1 Who should read this practice note?

Solicitors who advise clients on drawing up a lasting power of attorney (LPA), and solicitors who are acting as an attorney under an LPA.

1.2 What are the issues?

Any solicitor intending to give advice about an LPA or act as an attorney under an LPA must be aware of the provisions in the Mental Capacity Act 2005 (MCA 2005) and the Mental Capacity Act 2005 Code of Practice (Code of Practice). Solicitors should also be familiar with the relevant guidance produced by the Office of the Public Guardian (OPG).

The practice note provides an overview of LPAs and also covers the ongoing arrangements for enduring powers of attorney (EPA). It does not deal with situations with an international element, for example, using an LPA to sell a foreign property, or a non-UK individual who wishes to make an LPA.

2 POWERS OF ATTORNEY

2.1 Lasting powers of attorney

There are two current separate prescribed forms for LPAs available from the Ministry of Justice website:

- property and financial affairs LPA
- health and welfare LPA.

2.1.1 Property and financial affairs LPAs

A property and financial affairs LPA can be used to appoint attorneys to make a range of decisions, including:

- the buying and selling of property
- operating a bank account
- dealing with tax affairs
- claiming benefits.

See paragraphs 7.32-7.39 of the Code of Practice for more information.

2.1.2 Health and welfare LPAs

A health and welfare LPA can be used to appoint attorneys to make decisions on, for example:

- where the donor should live
- day-to-day care (including for example, diet and dress)
- whether to give or refuse consent to medical treatment.

See paragraphs 7.21-7.31 of the Code of Practice for more information.

All LPAs must be registered with the Office of the Public Guardian (OPG) before they can be used.

2.2 Enduring Powers of Attorney

The MCA 2005 repealed the Enduring Powers of Attorney Act 1985 and it is no longer possible to create a new EPA.

However, valid EPAs that were executed before the MCA 2005 came into force on 1 October 2007 will continue to be valid even if they have not been registered.

See section 16 Enduring Powers of Attorney for further information.

2.3 Ordinary powers of attorney

Section 10 of the Power of Attorney Act 1971 provides for the making of an ordinary power of attorney (OPA) to manage the donor's affairs. An OPA is usually made when it is difficult for the donor to manage their affairs, for example, because of a physical disability or when the donor is travelling abroad.

An OPA will cease when the donor becomes mentally incapable.

3 THE DONOR'S CAPACITY

3.1 Assessing capacity

You should be satisfied that the donor has the mental capacity to make a power of attorney. It is important that the donor is aware of the implications of their actions and should be alerted to possibilities of exploitation.

When assessing a client's capacity to create an LPA you should refer to sections 2 and 3 of the MCA 2005 and chapters 2-4 of the Code of Practice. See also the 2010 judgment of the senior judge of the Court of Protection in Re Collis (unreported), 27 October 2010, Court of Protection.

For further guidance, see Assessment of Mental Capacity: a practical guide for doctors and lawyers (Law Society 2015).

3.2 Where there is doubt about a donor's capacity

If there is doubt about the donor's capacity, a medical opinion should be considered. In cases where the LPA is being contested, for example by a family member, it may be necessary for the matter to be decided by the Court of Protection if the dispute cannot be resolved by other means.

You may want to ask the donor to give advance consent in writing authorising you to contact the donor's GP or any other medical practitioner if the need for medical evidence should arise at a later date to assess whether the donor has capacity to make a particular decision.

3.3 Incapacity: the functional and time-specific test

Unlike the EPA regime where registration demonstrates to a third party that the attorney has responsibility and the authority to make decisions relating to the donor's property and affairs, the MCA 2005 provisions for LPAs do not have such a readily identifiable point where the donor is deemed to lack capacity and the attorney is required to make best interest decisions rather than acting on the instruction of the donor.

This is because sections 2 and 3 of the MCA 2005 sets out a 'functional and time-specific' test of incapacity, which means capacity will vary according to the particular decision to be taken at a particular time.

For example, a donor may be able to make decisions about household spending but not about selling their home. One month later their capacity to make these decisions may have changed - either improving or becoming worse. There will not often be any one point where a person loses capacity to make all decisions.

Instead, the MCA 2005 sets out a joint approach where the attorney and the donor work together. The starting assumption must always be that a donor has the capacity to make a decision, unless it can be established that they lack capacity (section 1(2) MCA 2005).

A donor should not be treated as unable to make a decision unless all practical steps to help him or her to do so have been taken without success (section 1(3) MCA 2005). Involving the donor as fully as practicable could involve deferring a decision or setting up further assistance in order to enable the donor to make a decision.

This should be considered, particularly where the donor has elected that their property and affairs LPA should only become valid on their incapacity, and for health and welfare LPAs as these only operate where the person lacks capacity to make the decision.

Further guidance is provided in CHAPTERS 2 and 3 of the Code of Practice.

3.4 Acting in the donor's best interests

Where it is established that the donor lacks the capacity to make a particular decision, section 4 of the MCA 2005 requires the attorney to act in the donor's 'best interests', taking into account the relevant circumstances.

The MCA 2005 sets out a checklist of factors that should be considered by a person deciding what is in the best interests of a person who lacks capacity.

This includes, where practicable and appropriate to do so, consulting with the relatives, carers and others who have an interest in the donor's welfare.

It also includes, where reasonably practicable, permitting and encouraging the donor to participate as fully as possible or improving their ability to participate in making the decision.

Further guidance on best interests is provided in CHAPTER 5 of the Code of Practice.

4 RISK OF ABUSE

You should, when advising clients of the benefits of LPAs, also inform them of the risks of abuse, particularly the risk that the attorney(s) could misuse the power.

You should discuss with the donor appropriate measures to safeguard against the LPA being misused or exploited.

The donor may also wish to discuss with other family members or friends (who are not named persons to be notified of an application to register the LPA) of:

- the existence of the power
- why they have chosen the attorney(s)
- how the donor intends it to be used.

This may help to guard against the possibility of abuse by an attorney and may also reduce the risk of conflict between family members at a later stage.

4.1 Deputyships

There may be situations where a deputyship (once the person has lost capacity) could be viewed as being more appropriate and protective than the creation of an LPA. This may be advisable, for example:

- where the assets are more substantial or complex than family members are accustomed to handle and there is no suitable professional to appoint as attorney
- in cases where litigation may lead to a substantial award of damages for personal injury.

It is important to be aware, however, that the court will not approve a deputyship application as a matter of course and that, particularly for health and welfare matters, is likely to be reluctant to do so. See *G v E* [2010] EWHC 2512 (COP).

5 TAKING INSTRUCTIONS FOR AN LPA

Where you are instructed to prepare an LPA, the donor is the client. You should ensure that you have taken and recorded the instructions from the client.

You must not accept instructions where you have reasonable grounds to suspect that those instructions have been given by the client under duress or undue influence.

You must also not act on instructions until you are satisfied that the instructions represent the client's wishes (IB 1.28, see outcomes in CHAPTER 1 – Client care SRA Code of Conduct 2011).

5.1 Verifying instructions

You should be instructed by the client. When asked to prepare an LPA on written instructions alone, you should always consider carefully whether these instructions are sufficient, or whether you should see the client to discuss the instructions with them.

Where instructions for the preparation of an LPA are given by someone other than the client, you must not proceed without checking that the client agrees with the instructions given (IB 1.25, see outcomes in chapter 1 – Client care SRA Code of Conduct 2011).

If you have doubts you should try to see the client alone or take other appropriate steps to confirm:

- the instructions with the client personally after offering appropriate advice, and
- that the donor has the necessary capacity to make the power (see section 2 above).

5.2 Your duty to the donor after the LPA is registered

Once the LPA has been registered and the donor lacks the capacity to make the relevant decision, instructions may be accepted from the attorney(s) however your duties to the donor still remain in place.

It is important to obtain clear written instructions from the donor at the time of drafting the LPA as to whom and on what basis any copy of the registered LPA, or any other of the donor's documents (such as their will) can be released.

6 DRAFTING THE LPA

6.1 Choice of attorney(s)

The choice of attorney(s) is a personal decision for the donor, but it is important for you to advise the donor of the various options available and stress the need for the attorney(s) to be trustworthy.

The donor should be advised that the appointment of a sole attorney may provide greater opportunity for abuse and exploitation than appointing more than one attorney.

You should ask questions about the donor's relationship with the proposed attorney(s) including any replacement attorney. Depending on which type of LPA is being created, you should ask whether the attorney(s) has the skills required to manage the donor's property and financial affairs or to make decisions about the donor's health and welfare.

The donor should be advised to consider the suitability of appointing a family member, someone independent of the family, or a combination of both.

If the donor wishes to create both a property and financial affairs LPA and a health and welfare LPA you may wish to advise them to consider appointing different attorneys for each LPA.

6.2 More than one attorney

Where more than one attorney is to be appointed, they may be authorised to act 'jointly', 'jointly and severally', or 'jointly in respect of some matters and jointly and severally in respect of others' (section 10(4) MCA 2005).

If more than one attorney has been appointed and it is not stated whether they are appointed jointly or jointly and severally, they will be treated on the basis that they are appointed jointly when the LPA is registered.

This default position does not extend to EPAs and failure to specify on the prescribed form whether the attorneys should act jointly or jointly and severally would normally invalidate the instrument as an enduring power.

The differences between a joint and joint and several appointment should be explained to the donor. You should explain to your client that when making a joint appointment that:

- joint attorneys must all act together and not separately
- the LPA will terminate if any one of the attorneys disclaims, dies, becomes bankrupt (bankruptcy only applies to property and financial affairs LPAs), or lacks capacity unless the LPA specifically states otherwise it will also terminate with the dissolution or annulment of the marriage or civil partnership between the donor and the attorney, and
- joint appointments may provide a safeguard against possible abuse, since each attorney will be able to oversee the actions of the other(s).

You should explain to your client that when making a joint and several appointment:

- that joint and several attorneys can all act together but can also act independently if they wish, and
- the LPA will not be automatically terminated by the disclaimer, death, bankruptcy, dissolution/annulment of marriage/civil partnership (between the donor

and attorney), or incapacity of one attorney. In these circumstances the LPA would continue and the remaining attorney(s) can continue to act.

Your client may wish for their attorneys appointed under an LPA to act jointly in respect of some matters and jointly and severally in respect of others.

The donor may have to make difficult choices as to which member(s) of the family or others to appoint as their attorney. You may wish to inform the donor that it is possible to allow some flexibility.

One option could be that the donor appoints their spouse or civil partner as attorney, with their adult child(ren) appointed as replacement attorneys should the spouse or civil partner die or become incapacitated.

Alternatively, the donor could appoint everyone to act jointly and severally, with an informal understanding that the children will not act while the spouse or civil partner is able to do so.

The donor could appoint a family member and a professional to act jointly and severally. For example, the family member could deal with day-to-day matters, and the professional deal with more complex decisions. However, you may wish to highlight that the donor and the attorney(s) should consider the potential for conflict that could arise from this arrangement.

A professional attorney will have a higher duty of care and will usually be remunerated. This could create tension between the attorneys. Further problems could arise if, for example, the professional wishes to take a cautious approach and perhaps seek a court declaration or medical opinion, which would result in costs being incurred.

Extended time may be needed to explain the benefits and drawbacks of requiring specific decisions to be made jointly, and jointly and severally, as these areas can be confusing for the donor and attorneys.

6.3 Preferences, instructions and conditions

As well as allowing for the specification of instructions and conditions on the authority of attorney(s), the prescribed forms for LPAs also allow preferences to be provided to the attorney(s) when making decisions in the donor's best interests.

Any instructions or conditions, if deemed valid, will be automatically binding on the attorney(s) and can only be overturned by the court. Preferences, although clearly pertinent, are not binding on the attorney(s).

You should ensure that you make the distinction between instructions/conditions and preferences clear to the client. It is important that the drafting of this section reflects this distinction and that the language used does not suggest that any preferences are binding.

It is also important to inform the client that preferences within an LPA will be public and therefore visible to third parties. It also means that if the donor wishes to change their preferences, and do so in a side letter, for example, the previous preferences will remain in the LPA, apparently still valid, unless a new LPA is made.

You should explain to the client, and if practicable the attorney(s) that because preferences are not binding, the attorney(s) are entitled to act differently from suggestions within the preferences section of the LPA.

In this situation, the attorney(s) may conclude that, having used the 'best interests checklist' set out in section 4 of the MCA 2005, it would be in the overall best interests of the donor to act differently from the preferences stated.

However, it should also be stressed that the preferences must be considered in assessing the best interests of the donor.

Unless it states otherwise, a registered property and financial affairs LPA can be used while the donor retains capacity. Therefore, instructions that attempt to limit the attorney's power to use the LPA while the donor still has capacity are difficult to draft.

You should explain that this type of instruction may not be accepted by the court and might be rejected as unworkable by financial institutions.

If the donor does not trust the attorney to act only when appropriate, this may raise questions as to the appropriateness of their appointment.

7 CERTIFICATE PROVIDERS

A valid LPA must include a certificate completed by an independent third party known as the 'certificate provider' confirming that, in their opinion:

- the donor understands the purpose of the LPA and the scope of the authority conferred under it
- no fraud or undue pressure is being used to induce the donor to create the LPA, and
- there is nothing else that would prevent the LPA being created.

You should inform the donor that choosing a suitable certificate provider is an important safeguard and without the certificate the LPA cannot be registered and used. The choice of certificate provider is clearly a personal decision for the donor, but it is important you advise the donor of the various options available.

A certificate provider cannot be:

- under 18
- a member of the donor's or attorney's family
- a business partner or paid employee of the donor or attorney(s)
- an attorney appointed in this or another LPA or any EPA made by the donor
- the owner, director, manager or an employee of a care home in which the donor lives or their family member, or
- a director or employee of a trust corporation appointed as attorney in this LPA (this only applies to someone certifying a property and financial affairs LPA).

A person who signs an LPA as a certificate provider will also need to be able to demonstrate that they:

- understand what is involved in making an LPA
- understand the effect of making an LPA
- have the skills to assess that the donor understands what an LPA is and what is involved in making an LPA
- can assess that the donor also understands the contents of their LPA and what powers they are giving to the attorney(s)
- can verify that the donor is under no undue pressure by anyone to make the LPA, and
- have sufficient knowledge and understanding of the donor's affairs to able to be satisfied that no fraud was involved in the creation of the LPA.

It is important that the certificate provider is aware of the significance of making clear notes relating to the certification of the LPA. These notes should be kept for as long as is necessary and at least until the LPA is registered, in case there is a challenge against the validity of the LPA.

7.1 If you provide a certificate as a professional

Solicitors are one of the professional groups permitted to act as a certificate provider. However, you must ensure, on the facts of the particular case, that you do not fall into one of the excluded categories.

In particular, you cannot provide a certificate if you are:

- a business partner or paid employee of the attorney(s). This includes firms operating as limited liability partnerships or limited companies (despite being a separate legal entity), or
- an attorney appointed under any LPA or EPA made by the donor. This would mean, for example, that you could not provide a certificate if in the past the client executed an EPA in favour of you, even though the EPA was never used or registered or was revoked.

Before signing the certificate you should take a suitably detailed personal and financial history from the donor, and if necessary, insist on seeing them on their own to satisfy the requirements concerning undue pressure and fraud. This may have both time and cost implications.

You should also be aware that if, for example, a family member objects to the LPA during the registration process then the certificate provider may be called to the Court of Protection to account for their opinion.

You should retain any notes you have made in your role as a certificate provider for as long as is necessary and at least until the LPA is registered. You should provide these to the Court of Protection if they are relevant to any challenge regarding the LPA.

7.2 If you provide a certificate as a 'non-professional'

As a solicitor or retired solicitor, you may be approached by clients, former clients, friends or acquaintances asking you to provide a certificate on the basis that you have known them personally over the last two years. You should exercise considerable caution before providing a certificate on this basis.

The guidance given on the LPA instrument suggests that the requirement to know the donor 'personally' means the certificate provider should have known the donor 'for at least two years and as more than an acquaintance'.

A non-professional certificate provider may be called to the Court of Protection to account for their opinion if, for example, a family member objects to the LPA. The court may expect a higher standard of care and skill if the certificate has been provided by a solicitor and the donor is their client or former client.

If you have retired from practice you should consider why the donor has asked you to be their certificate provider. You should ensure that the donor has not specifically chosen you based on the skills and knowledge you have developed when practising as a solicitor, as opposed to you having known them personally for the last two years.

8 REGISTERING THE LPA

An LPA is not created unless the instrument purporting to confer authority has been registered by the Office of the Public Guardian (OPG).

You should explain to the donor and, where practicable, the attorney(s), that the LPA cannot be used until it has been registered. The LPA can be registered anytime after it has been completed and signed by all those who are required to sign.

It is important that you clearly explain to the donor the implications of not registering the LPA shortly after it has been made. For example, if the donor of an unregistered health and welfare LPA faced a medical emergency, their attorney(s) would not be authorised to act on their behalf until the power is registered, which would take approximately 10-13 weeks at the very least.

Refer to the health and incapacity law section of the GOV.UK website for current registration times.

You should inform the donor that a fee will be payable for the registration of the LPA and that a separate fee will be charged for a property and affairs LPA and for a personal welfare LPA, even if they have been made by the same donor.

Once registered, a property and financial affairs LPA can be used while the donor still has capacity, unless it specifies otherwise. A health and welfare LPA can only be used when the donor no longer has capacity to make the particular decision affecting their healthcare or personal welfare.

8.1 Time limits for registration

There is no time limit for making the application to register the LPA. The application can be made by the donor, all the attorneys if the LPA is a joint power, or if a joint and several power by any of the attorneys.

8.2 Notifying named persons of an application to register an LPA

You should explain to the donor that they can name up to five people to be notified when an application to register the LPA is made. An attorney or replacement attorney appointed in the LPA cannot be specified as a named person.

There is no requirement to have a named person, but you should advise the donor that including a named person may be a safeguard. You should do this particularly if the power is not registered shortly following execution, because if the donor lacks capacity at the time of registration they will be relying on these people to raise concerns. The OPG may raise concerns if the LPA has not been signed by all parties within 12 months.

You should advise the donor to make their named person(s) aware of the LPA, and what is required of them when an application to register is made, before the LPA is completed.

This will ensure that where a person does not wish to take on this role, someone else can be appointed. The donor may also tell their named person(s) who they have appointed as attorney(s). This allows the person(s) to raise any queries or concerns with the donor and may reduce objections when the application to register the LPA is made, avoiding extra costs and delays. You should give careful consideration as to who to advise the donor to notify as a named person.

The donor or the attorney(s) making the application to register must give notice using prescribed form (LPA001) to everyone named by the donor in the LPA as a person who should be notified of an application to register.

8.3 Verifying the registration

The registered LPA document will be stamped on every page by the OPG. You should check that each page has been stamped and that there are no missing pages, or unintentional additional pages attached.

8.4 The LPA register and disclosure of information

The OPG is responsible for maintaining a register of all LPAs, EPAs and court appointed deputies.

You should inform the donor that a registered LPA is a public document and certain information about their LPA will be available to anyone who applies to search the register.

9 ATTORNEYS

9.1 Duties and responsibilities of attorneys

An attorney has a duty to act within the scope of their powers set out in the LPA. The authority conferred by the LPA is also subject to the provisions of the MCA 2005, in particular section 1 (The principles) and section 4 (Best interests). Attorneys and anyone acting in a professional capacity in relation to the person who lacks capacity also have a specific obligation to have regard to the Code of Practice (section 42(4) MCA 2005).

In addition, attorneys have a duty:

- of care
- to carry out the donor's instructions
- not to take advantage of the position of the attorney
- not to delegate unless authorised to do so
- of good faith
- of confidentiality
- to comply with directions of the Court of Protection
- not to disclaim without notifying the donor, the other attorneys, and the Public Guardian, and
- to comply with the relevant guidance.

In relation to a property and financial affairs LPA there is also a duty to:

- keep accounts, and
- keep the donor's money and property separate from their own.

According to paragraph 7.59 of the Code of Practice:

'If attorneys are being paid for their services, they should demonstrate a higher degree of care and skill.

'Attorneys who undertake their duties in the course of their professional work (such as solicitors or corporate trustees) must display professional competence and follow their profession's rules and standards.

Further guidance on the duties and responsibilities of attorneys is provided in CHAPTER 7 of the Code of Practice.

9.2 Delegation by the attorney

It is a basic principle of the law of agency that an attorney cannot delegate their authority. Alternatively, this could be expressed as a duty on the part of an agent to perform their functions personally.

Such a duty is imposed because of the discretion and trust placed in the attorney(s) by the donor.

There are exceptions to this general rule and, like any other agent, an attorney acting under an LPA has an implied power in certain circumstances to delegate:

any functions which are of a purely administrative nature and do not involve or require the exercise of discretion

any functions which the donor would not expect the attorney to attend to personally, or

through necessity or unforeseen circumstances, although caution should be exercised before relying on this exception.

In Re Putt, (unreported), 22 March 2011, Court of Protection, the court rejected a delegation clause which authorised the attorney to delegate his functions where it was not strictly necessary or expedient to do so. Delegation and substitution are not interchangeable.

See 7.61 of the Code of Practice.

9.3 Replacement attorney

While an LPA cannot provide for an attorney to make a substitute or successor appointment, it can appoint a replacement attorney to act if any of the attorneys under a joint and several LPA cannot continue to act.

If the donor of an LPA wishes to appoint a replacement attorney(s), they should clearly state how replacements are to be appointed and how they are to act, for example solely or jointly.

If the donor has more than one attorney, he or she can specify who the replacement attorney can and cannot replace. The donor can only appoint a replacement attorney for the original attorneys.

In Re Druce, (unreported), 31 May 2011, Court of Protection, the court stated that 'there is nothing in section 10(8)(b) of the MCA 2005, which deals with the appointment of replacement attorneys, to displace the fundamental principle that the survivor of joint attorneys cannot act. Where one of the original joint attorneys can no longer act, the replacement(s) will step in and act alone, to the exclusion of the surviving original attorney'.

You should advise the donor that when considering whether a replacement attorney should be appointed, it is important that the donor chooses someone they know well and trust to make decisions in their best interests in the same way as would be the case for their first choice attorney(s).

Please refer to the OPG's current guidance on this matter as the law is currently under review.

9.4 Solicitor-attorneys and costs

Where you are appointed as the attorney of an LPA you should discuss with the donor your current terms and conditions of business (including charging rates and the frequency of billing) and have these approved by the donor at the time of granting the power.

You should ensure that the donor is aware that there is a likelihood that the costs provided may change with time. The donor should also be provided with sufficient information regarding the options for appointing a lay attorney, such as a family member.

The prescribed forms for LPAs include a section where the donor can confirm that they have agreed for their attorney to be paid a fee and set out the arrangements which have been agreed.

Decisions about payments should be recorded here with the appropriate level of detail, as necessary.

9.5 Disclaiming an appointment

An attorney or proposed attorney can disclaim their appointment by completing the prescribed form (LPA005) which must be sent to the donor and copied to the OPG and any other attorney(s) appointed under the power.

9.6 Retirement as attorney

Before agreeing to act as an attorney in your capacity as a professional solicitor, you should consider how matters will be dealt with if you retire from practice.

10 PROPERTY AND FINANCIAL AFFAIRS LPAS

10.1 Limiting the LPA

The donor can limit the power of the LPA by specifying that the LPA only grants authority to the attorney(s) to deal with certain specific assets.

10.2 Gifts

Section 12 of the MCA 2005 gives the attorney(s) limited authority to make gifts of the donor's money or property:

- The recipient of the gift must be either an individual who is related to or connected with the donor (including the attorney(s)), or a charity to which the donor actually made gifts or might be expected to make gifts if they had capacity.
- The timing of the gift must occur within the prescribed parameters, such as on customary occasions. The value of the gift must not be unreasonable having regard to all the circumstances and in particular the size of the donor's estate.
- The donor cannot confer wider authority on the attorney than that specified in section 12, but it is open to the donor to restrict or exclude the authority which would otherwise be available to the attorney(s) under that section.

The donor may include guidance in the power on the circumstances in which the attorney(s) may make gifts of money or property, but these should not exceed the limits specified in section 12.

Any attempt to expand or circumvent the scope of the provisions of section 12 is likely to be challenged by the Public Guardian. Circumventing section 12 by inserting what is in effect a restriction in the guidance section is also likely to be rejected by the court.

The Court of Protection can authorise the attorney(s) to act so as to benefit themselves or others, otherwise than in accordance with section 12, provided that there are no restrictions in the LPA itself and the court is satisfied that this would be in the donor's best interests (section 23(4) MCA 2005).

Solicitors must also take account of the professional rules concerning gifts from clients (IB 1.9, see outcomes in chapter 1 - Client care SRA Code of Conduct 2011).

10.3 Investment business

Unless the power is restricted to exclude investments as defined by the Financial Services and Markets Act 2000, the attorney(s) may need to consider the investment business implications of their appointment. If you are an attorney and conducting investment business you will need to be authorised under the Financial Services and Markets Act 2000.

In addition, you will need to consider whether the SRA Financial Services (Scope) Rules 2001 apply.

10.4 Trusteeships held by the donor

The solicitor should ask whether the donor holds:

- any trusteeships, or
- any property jointly with others.

In cases of jointly owned property you should exercise caution and consider any concerns or problems that may arise from your actions which affect the other joint owner.

Under the Trustee Delegation Act 1999 (the 1999 Act) the general rule is that any trustee functions delegated to an attorney must comply with the provisions of section 25 of the Trustee Act 1925, as amended by the 1999 Act.

However, section 1(1) of the 1999 Act provides an exception to this general rule. An attorney can exercise a trustee function of the donor if it relates to land, or the capital proceeds or income from land, in which the donor has a beneficial interest.

The transfer or deed must be made to two distinct trustees, not one person acting in two different capacities, subject to any provision to the contrary contained in the trust instrument or the power of attorney itself.

10.5 Disclosure of the donor's will

You are under a duty to keep your clients' affairs confidential (CHAPTER 4 - Confidentiality and disclosure SRA Code of Conduct 2011 as amended). However, the attorney(s) may need to know about the contents of the donor's will in order to avoid acting in a manner contrary to the testamentary intentions of the donor. An example would be the sale of an asset specifically bequeathed, when other assets that fell into residue could be disposed of instead.

The question of disclosure of the donor's will should be discussed at the time of making the LPA, and instructions should be obtained as to whether disclosure is denied, or the circumstances in which it is permitted. If no sufficient authority is available the attorney(s) should apply to the Court of Protection for a specific order for the contents of the will to be disclosed.

The attorney(s) also has a common law duty to keep the donor's affairs (including the contents of a will) confidential.

10.6 Money laundering

The preparation of an LPA for clients does not itself constitute a 'financial transaction' for the purposes of the Money Laundering Regulations 2007. However, a solicitor acting for property and financial affairs LPA attorney, or acting as an attorney themselves, is likely to be undertaking 'relevant business'.

For further advice see the Law Society's practice note on anti-money laundering.

10.7 Statutory wills

An attorney cannot execute a will on the donor's behalf because the Wills Act 1837 requires a will to be signed by the testator personally, or by someone in their presence and at their direction.

Where a person lacks testamentary capacity, the Court of Protection can order the execution of a statutory will on their behalf. The court's will-making jurisdiction is conferred by section 18 of the MCA 2005.

11 HEALTH AND WELFARE LPAS

11.1 Scope

An attorney appointed in a registered health and welfare LPA has no authority to make a decision which the donor has capacity to make for himself or herself. This is not the case for a registered property and financial affairs power and you should ensure that your client understands the difference.

Clients also need to know that, unless the donor adds restrictions or conditions, the attorney(s) of a health and welfare LPA will have authority to make almost all personal welfare and healthcare decisions. Important exceptions include:

- decisions relating to life-sustaining treatment, unless the LPA expressly authorises this
- cases where a valid and applicable advance decision made by the donor to refuse the proposed treatment takes precedence.

A health and welfare LPA is a powerful document because of the wide ranging decisions that can be made on behalf of the donor and therefore clients need to be in a position to make an informed decision about the scope of the power.

In addition to considering the scope of authority with you, clients may also want to discuss it with, for example, their prospective attorney(s) and, where appropriate, their GP or any relevant health or social care professionals.

A health and welfare LPA can be limited to specific decisions and it may be helpful to create a checklist of questions and a range of suggested clauses which the client might wish to consider when creating a health and welfare LPA.

The guidance box in section 7 of the prescribed form enables clients to set out their wishes and preferences for personal care, including healthcare, in a way that is not legally binding but which their attorney(s) will take into account in deciding best interests.

For example, the donor may wish to include guidance stating that the attorney should not accommodate the donor at another location without consulting specific members of the family.

When drafting the LPA you should ensure that the client's instructions are clear and comprehensible to any health or social care professional who enquires about the scope of an attorney's authority under the LPA.

11.2 Life-sustaining treatment

Decisions to give or refuse consent to life-sustaining treatment can only be made by the attorney(s) if the donor has specifically conferred this authority in section 5 of the prescribed form in the presence of a witness. The witness must be over 18 and cannot be an attorney appointed in the instrument.

Life-sustaining treatment is defined in section 4(10) of the MCA 2005 as 'treatment which in the view of a person providing health care for the person concerned is necessary to sustain life'.

Further guidance is provided in paragraphs 5.29–5.36 of the Code of Practice.

11.3 Relationship with advance decisions and advance statements

11.3.1 Advance decisions (living wills)

Some clients may ask about making a 'living will' – described in the MCA 2005 as an 'advance decision' – and whether they should make an advance decision, rather than a health and welfare LPA or vice versa.

An advance decision allows a person, provided they have capacity, to refuse medical treatment that might be given at a time in the future when they lack capacity to refuse that treatment. If an advance decision is both valid and applicable in the particular circumstances, it has the same effect as a contemporaneous refusal of treatment by a person with capacity. This means that the treatment specified in the decision cannot lawfully be given.

Further information and guidance is provided in CHAPTER 9 of the Code of Practice.

Possible points for the client to consider are as follows:

- A health and welfare LPA allows a donor to give general authority for the attorney(s) to give or refuse consent to life-sustaining treatment where option A, section 5, of the prescribed form is completed.

Unlike an advance decision, it is not necessary to specify a particular treatment or particular circumstances where treatment is refused. This of course requires a high degree of trust by the donor towards the attorney(s).

- Under a health and welfare LPA the attorney(s) must make decisions in the donor's best interests and follow the checklist in section 4 of the MCA 2005 which includes consultation with those close to the person who lacks capacity.

Where an advance decision is being followed, the best interests principle does not apply. If it is valid and applicable it must be respected, even if the healthcare professionals think it goes against the person's best interests.

- There are stringent requirements for completing and registering an LPA. The MCA 2005 does not impose any particular formalities concerning advance decisions, except for decisions relating to life-sustaining treatment.

This relative informality may be attractive for some clients, but it can also lead to uncertainty over whether an advance decision exists or is valid.

- In some cases when dealing with a seriously or terminally ill person, it may be prudent to consider with them whether to combine a health and welfare LPA with an advance decision. The LPA may take time to register, but the advance decision takes effect immediately and can be used before the LPA has been registered.

Clients should be made aware that where a person makes a health and welfare LPA (regardless of whether it provides authority to give or refuse consent to life-sustaining treatment) and subsequently makes an advance decision, which is valid and applicable in the circumstances, the advance decision takes priority.

A health and welfare LPA made after an advance decision will make the advance decision invalid if the LPA gives the attorney authority to make decisions about the same treatment.

If necessary, you may need to advise that the law relating to euthanasia and assisted suicide has not been changed, and the introduction of health and welfare LPAs and advance decisions does not legitimise euthanasia.

Clients may also want information about registering their decision in relation to organ donation. The NHS Organ Donor Register website has further information about signing-up online and carrying a donor card.

11.3.2 Advance statements

You should advise the donor that the MCA 2005 provides for creation of an 'advance statement' (distinct from an 'advance decision'), which enables a person with capacity to set out their wishes and feelings in writing about, for example, the care and treatment they would like to receive should they lose capacity in the future.

Advance statements are not legally binding but should be taken into account by decision makers - including attorney(s) - when making best-interest decisions under section 4(6) of the MCA 2005. A client could decide to make an advance statement as a separate exercise to providing guidance for their attorney in section 7 of the prescribed form.

Further information on advance statements is provided in paragraphs 5.37 - 5.45 of the Code of Practice.

12 USING THE PRESCRIBED LPA FORMS

The current prescribed LPA forms can be found on the Ministry of Justice website.

An LPA may be refused registration because of a defect in the form or the wording of the instrument. In some cases, registration may be possible after the filing of further evidence to overcome the defect.

Where you have assisted a donor in drawing up an LPA which is subsequently refused registration because of a material defect, you may find it alleged that you should be liable for the additional costs of deputyship, since at that point the donor may not have the capacity to execute a new LPA.

Once the LPA has been signed, any mistakes or errors cannot simply be corrected, even if the donor still has capacity. On occasion and for minor points the OPG may suggest this as a solution and accept the amended document.

13 EXECUTING THE LPA

An LPA must be executed by the donor, the certificate provider and the attorney(s) in the correct order. In Re Sporne, (unreported), 13 October 2009, Court of Protection, where part C of the LPA was signed before part B and the donor subsequently lost capacity, the Court of Protection refused to exercise its discretion to validate the LPA (under paragraph 3(2) of schedule 1 of the MCA 2005) as it was a significant procedural error.

Execution by the donor, certificate provider and attorney(s) need not take place simultaneously but the regulations require that each stage must take place as soon as reasonably practicable after the previous stage. Please be aware that the date for signing the registration element of the LPA form must be after or on the same date as the last attorney to sign.

(Note, that for section 5 'life-sustaining treatment' of a health and welfare LPA must be signed and witnessed at the same time).

13.1 Witnesses

Execution by the donor and the attorney(s) must take place in the presence of a witness (but not necessarily the same witness) who must sign part A and/or part C of the prescribed form as appropriate, and give their full name and address. There are various restrictions as to who can act as a witness, in particular:

- the donor and attorney/replacement attorney must not witness each other's signature
- it is not advisable for the donor's spouse or civil partner to witness the donor's signature because of the rules of evidence relating to compellability.

There are specific provisions in relation to a donor who is unable to sign. See the LPA form and supporting guidance for more information.

14 RELATIONSHIP BETWEEN PROPERTY AND FINANCIAL AFFAIRS AND HEALTH AND WELFARE LPAS

Depending on the decision to be made, an attorney may reasonably be expected to consult with the attorney(s) of any other LPA made by the donor, whenever the donor's best interests are being considered (section 4(7)(c), of the MCA 2005 and paragraph 5.55 of the Code of Practice). It is also likely that EPA attorney(s) would also be consulted.

Attorneys should also be aware that the demarcation between decisions made under a property and financial affairs LPA and a health and welfare LPA may not always be clear. For example, where the donor lives is a welfare decision which also has financial implications. If there are conflicts then an application can be made to the Court of Protection to resolve the issue but this should only be considered as a last resort.

15 REPORTING SUSPECTED ABUSE OF AN LPA

If you suspect that an attorney may be misusing an LPA or acting dishonestly you should immediately contact the Safeguarding Unit of the OPG on 0300 456 0300 or opg.safeguardingunit@publicguardian.gsi.gov.uk.

You should also contact the police if you suspect psychological, physical or sexual abuse, theft or fraud.

It may also be necessary, particularly in cases involving health and welfare LPAs, to refer the matter to the local authority adult protection unit.

Further guidance on addressing suspected abuse can be found at paragraph 5 of the Law Society's financial abuse practice note.

Further guidance is provided in paragraphs 7.69–7.74 and chapter 14 of the Code of Practice.

16 ENDURING POWERS OF ATTORNEY

The Enduring Powers of Attorney Act 1985 was repealed by the MCA 2005, but it was reintroduced almost in its entirety in schedule 4 of the MCA 2005. The amendments take account of the changes to the Court of Protection and the new role of the Office of the Public Guardian (OPG) in the registration process.

It is not possible to make new EPAs, although the operation of existing EPAs made before 1 October 2007 will fall under schedule 4 of the MCA 2005.

An EPA can only authorise attorneys to make decisions about the donor's property and financial affairs. EPA attorneys have no authority to make health and welfare decisions for the donor.

If the donor has full mental capacity an EPA does not have to be registered before you can use it, unless there is an express condition requiring registration.

The EPA must be registered with the OPG as soon as the donor starts to lose capacity.

Registration of an EPA may be cancelled on the donor's recovery.

16.1 Duties under an EPA

The principles of the MCA 2005 are specifically excluded from applying to an EPA attorney (schedule 4, paragraph1(1) MCA 2005). However under the law of agency, the EPA attorney has certain duties to the donor (some of these are indicated in section 10.1 above). Further guidance is available in paragraphs 7.58–7.68 of the Code of Practice.

According to paragraph 7.5 of the Code of Practice, EPA attorneys do not have a legal duty to have regard to the Code, but the Code's guidance will still be helpful to them.

16.2 Solicitors acting as an EPA attorney

If you are acting as an EPA attorney you may be considered to have a duty to have regard to the Code of Practice since you will be acting in a 'professional capacity' for the purposes of section 42(4)(e) of the MCA 2005.

This is not straightforward because under schedule 4 of the MCA 2005 the EPA must be registered when a person is becoming or has become incapable of managing their own affairs and from this point on it is the attorney who manages the donor's affairs.

This is different to the concept of incapacity used in the rest of the MCA 2005 which is both function and time-specific. It appears that the Code will therefore selectively apply to the professional EPA attorney as there will not be a requirement to assess capacity on each decision being made.

16.3 Acting in the donor's best interests

Under an EPA, an attorney has a common law duty to act in the donor's best interests. This duty is reinforced by paragraph 5.2 of the Code of Practice which states that the best interests principle 'covers all aspects of financial, personal welfare and healthcare decision-making and actions. It applies to anyone making decisions or acting under the provisions of the Act, including attorneys appointed under a Lasting Power of Attorney or registered Enduring Power of Attorney'.

However, paragraph 1(1) of schedule 4 of the MCA 2005 is somewhat ambiguous, stating:

'Where an individual has created a power of attorney which is an enduring power within the meaning of this schedule . . . and, accordingly, section 1 of this Act does not apply'.

You should therefore err on the side of caution and take into the account the best interests principle.

The attorney of an EPA is not specifically named as a person to be consulted when a decision maker is making a best interests determination under section 4 of the MCA 2005. However it is likely that in the majority of cases any EPA attorney appointed by the attorney will be considered to be a person who is 'interested in his welfare' for the purposes of section 4(7)(b) of the MCA 2005, and therefore would be consulted.

This appears to be confirmed in paragraph 5.55 of the Code of Practice.

16.4 EPA Register

The OPG is responsible for maintaining a register of EPAs which can be searched by any person on payment of a fee.

17 FURTHER INFORMATION

17.1 References

17.1.1 Legislation

- Mental Capacity Act 2005
- Enduring Powers of Attorney Act 1985
- Power of Attorney Act 1971
- Financial Services and Markets Act 2000
- Trustee Delegation Act 1999
- Trustee Act 1925
- Money Laundering Regulations 2007
- Wills Act 1837

17.1.2 Guidance

- Mental Capacity Act 2005 Code of Practice

17.1.3 Cases

- *Re Collis* (unreported), 27 October 2010, Court of Protection
- *G v E* [2010] EWHC 2512 (COP)
- *Re Sporne* (unreported), 13 October 2009, Court of Protection
- *Re Putt* (unreported), 22 March 2011, Court of Protection
- *Re Druce* (unreported), 31 May 2011, Court of Protection

17.1.4 Websites and publications

- Ministry of Justice website
- Directgov website
- Assessment of Mental Capacity: a practical guide for doctors and lawyers

17.2 Further products and support

17.2.1 Practice Advice

The Law Society provides support to solicitors on a wide range of areas of legal practice. The service is staffed by solicitors and can be contacted on 020 7320 5675 from 09:00 to 17:00 on weekdays.

Visit the Practice Advice Service website.

17.2.2 Professional Ethics Helpline

Solicitors Regulation Authority's Professional Ethics Helpline for advice on conduct issues.

17.2.3 Other Law Society practice notes

- Meeting the needs of vulnerable clients
- Trust corporations

17.3 Acknowledgements

The Law Society wishes to thank members of the Wills and Equity Committee for their assistance in drafting this practice note.

MEETING THE NEEDS OF VULNERABLE CLIENTS

I2

2 July 2015

1 INTRODUCTION

1.1 Who should read this practice note?

This practice note is essential reading for all solicitors, practice managers and legal support staff, particularly if you do not act for vulnerable clients on a regular basis.

1.2 What is the issue?

Some clients have difficulty accessing and using legal services. Research has concluded that solicitors need to adapt their practices to identify and meet the needs of vulnerable clients.

1.3 Who are vulnerable clients?

The terms vulnerable and vulnerability are used here as a shorthand to address a range of situations which could affect any client who is at a disadvantage because of factors that affect their access to, and use of, legal services.

Please note that this practice note does not provide specific advice in relation to children or the needs of vulnerable defendants in criminal proceedings.

The possibility of vulnerability should be considered whenever you are consulted or instructed by a client in any matter.

This practice note focuses on three broad categories of vulnerable clients.

They are:

- clients who have capacity to make decisions and provide you with instructions, but by reason of a range of mental and/or physical disabilities require enhanced support to engage your services and give you instructions - sections 2 and 3
- clients who lack mental capacity to make decisions and provide you with instructions, for whom a range of statutory and other safeguards must be followed - section 4
- clients who are vulnerable to undue influence or duress and who may or may not have mental capacity to make decisions and provide you with instructions - section 6

1.4 Compliance with regulatory and legislative obligations

Section 5 of this note discusses independent third party support for vulnerable clients which can often be crucial in assisting you in obtaining the best possible legal outcome for them.

1.4.1 There are ten mandatory principles which apply to all those the Solicitors Regulation Authority (SRA) regulates and to all aspects of practice. The principles can be found in the SRA Handbook. You should always bear these principles in mind and use them as your starting point. Failure to meet your professional duties within the SRA

Handbook may result in SRA sanctions or a referral to the Solicitors' Disciplinary Tribunal.

1.4.2 In addition, if you fail to meet the needs of a vulnerable client you could be at risk of:

- A discrimination claim or a claim for a failure to make reasonable adjustments under the Equality Act 2010, which could result in sanctions including damages.
- A claim for damages or compensation against you or your firm if you act on the instructions of a client lacking capacity to make relevant decisions, having failed to satisfy yourself as to the client's capacity to instruct you or failing to document your assessment of the client's capacity, leaving the validity of the transaction open to challenge.
- A complaint against you to the Legal Ombudsman, which could result in your name being published and/or you having to pay financial compensation. The ombudsman will refer complaints about discrimination to the SRA.
- Reputational risk - your practice's reputation is inextricably linked to the way in which you treat your clients. Conversely, a practice with an inclusive ethos will not only attract a wider group of clients but also a more diverse workforce bringing benefits to the business.
- Liability to other parties for breach of warrant of authority.[1]

1.4.3 This practice note will help you to recognise and meet your duties under the Mental Capacity Act 2005 and the Equality Act 2010.

2 IDENTIFYING THE VULNERABLE CLIENT

2.1 Vulnerability indicators

Risk factors may be short or long term, and can fluctuate over time depending on the circumstances. The following are offered as examples of risk factors and are not an exhaustive list:

- advanced age, children and young people
- physical disabilities or ill-health
- cognitive impairment
- loss of mental capacity to make relevant decisions
- mental health problems
- learning disabilities
- sensory impairment
- dementia
- acquired brain injury caused for example by a stroke or head injury
- severe facial or other disfigurement
- difficulty in accessing and/or understanding complex information, for example, because of psychological or emotional factors such as stress or bereavement
- communication difficulties, including no or limited speech, English as a foreign language, limited ability to read or write and illiteracy
- experience of domestic violence or sexual abuse
- heavy reliance on others (family or friends) for necessary care, support or accommodation
- long-term alcohol or drug abuse
- exposure to financial abuse

Some people may be affected by more than one risk factor - for example, many people with a learning disability have hearing and/or visual problems that can affect their communication and understanding.

Any one or more of these risk factors may mean that your client is vulnerable and may require your assistance to express their wishes, understand relevant advice and provide you with instructions, or that they may lack capacity to make relevant decisions and to give your instructions.

2.2 Signs of vulnerability: what to look out for

It may not always be easy to identify vulnerability. Some signs may be obvious while others are only just perceptible or hidden. You should not assume that your client will tell you of any difficulties. Simple observation will identify many mobility problems, physical or sensory disabilities or more severe impairment of mental capacity. It is important not to feel inhibited about asking for more information for fear of being intrusive - many clients will be open about any disability they have or specific assistance they require, or will be if asked, and will be glad to discuss how you can best meet their needs.

The Law Society practice note on financial abuse provides further guidance on the identification of adults at risk of financial abuse.

2.3 Identifying the needs of your client

Once you are aware that there are risk factors present, you can help your client to access your services and overcome any disadvantage caused by these risk factors. You should tactfully try to identify the needs of your client to find out whether they:

- have any requirements or preferences for communicating with you
- have any requirements to access your services, for example, to overcome mobility problems or hearing or sight difficulties
- have any requirements in terms of how services are provided, such as documents written in clear and simple language or information given orally
- understand and can act on the information and advice provided, or whether they may need support to do this, for example, from an advocacy service or interpreter.

Carers or family members may also be able to provide helpful information but in the first instance you should always seek to discuss these matters with the client alone, unless the client lacks capacity give you instructions (see Section 5).

3 ENABLING VULNERABLE CLIENTS TO ACCESS YOUR SERVICES

3.1 Areas to think about

Ensuring that your practice provides an accessible service to vulnerable clients will mean considering many different aspects of your practice including:

- Marketing/making use of local links: advertising the services that you offer and the ways in which you can assist vulnerable clients and their families and carers. Many vulnerable potential clients will not have access to the internet.
- Website accessibility: conversely, for many clients, your website will be an important source of information about your practice and the services that it offers. If your website is not easy to read or navigate or if its content is difficult to understand, you may put off potential clients[2].
- Accessibility to and around your premises: are your premises easy to find and to access? Would older clients and clients with sensory and mobility difficulties be able to access your building? Are the floors and corridors clear? Are your rooms well lit? This is particularly important for clients who may be lip reading. Do you have meeting rooms large enough to accommodate clients who may bring other family members, carers or advocates with them? The Centre for Accessible Environments can provide you with information about registered access audits.
- Ensuring compliance with your statutory obligations to make reasonable adjustments and avoidance of disability discrimination in charging for reasonable adjustments.

- Training for staff who may have contact with clients on accessibility, disability and deaf awareness, reasonable adjustments, mental capacity, recognising vulnerability, conflicts between clients and carers, safeguarding and financial abuse.
- Flexibility around appointment times, duration and location.
- Willingness to visit clients at home may put them at ease and aid communication, for example, where your clients have dementia or mental health problems.
- Accessibility of written communications, for example, client care letters, letters of advice, costs information, written clearly and free from 'legal jargon'.
- Anticipating accessibility issues that may arise at tribunal, hospital or court hearings.
- The use of support professionals or independent advocates who can assist, for example, clients with a learning disability, throughout the legal process, including at the initial advice stage.
- Appropriate safeguards when using semi-automated systems.
- Obtaining feedback from clients on how to improve the service you offer.

3.2 Tailored and appropriate communication

'He more or less explained a lot of it to me without some of the jargon that you would get with most. Some solicitors they go through all this jargon and you think 'what are they on about', you know, and he did explain a lot of it to me as well'.[3]

The 'reasonable adjustments' duty under the Equality Act 2010 is anticipatory: you must anticipate the needs of people with particular types of disability as well as making tailored reasonable adjustments for individuals. This means you need to be prepared: you should know, for example, how to find and engage a sign language interpreter.[4]

Types of adjustments that could aid communication with your clients include:

- allowing extra time for meetings with clients who may need longer to understand what you are explaining, or who have a speech impairment, or who are communicating through a third party
- explaining issues without using legal jargon
- enlisting the help of an appropriate third party
- providing information in large print, Braille, audio, DVD or easy-read format
- providing written text on a coloured rather than a white background; this can be particularly helpful for dyslexic clients or those with a visual impairment and they can advise you as to which colours to use
- providing a sign language interpreter, lip-speaker or deaf-blind communicator
- providing a reader for clients with visual impairments
- installing an induction loop or having a portable one available
- conducting conversations with clients using the text relay system
- providing a digital recorder, dictaphone or electronic notetaker, or
- not requiring the client to make complaints or other requests in writing.

3.3 Assisting vulnerable clients in the course of court proceedings

3.3.1 Criminal cases

Special considerations and measures apply to vulnerable defendants and witnesses in criminal and family cases. These are especially relevant if you are carrying out any advocacy on behalf of a vulnerable client or instructing counsel to do so. The Advocacy Training Council has developed specialist toolkits under the Advocates Gateway programme which provide valuable advice on supporting vulnerable clients throughout the trial or hearing process.

A range of 'special measures' apply to vulnerable and intimidated witnesses (but not defendants) in criminal cases pursuant to sections 16 to 33 of the Youth Justice and Criminal Evidence Act 1999, including screens to shield the witness from the defendant, use of a live link, exclusion of the public from the courtroom, and the removal of wigs and gowns in the Crown Court. The court may appoint an intermediary to assist a vulnerable witness to give their evidence at court and facilitate communication; the intermediary may explain questions or answers so far as is necessary to enable them to be understood by the witness or the questioner, without changing the substance of the evidence.

The Coroners and Justice Act 2009 extended intermediaries to the evidence of defendants, but this provision is not yet in force. However, the courts have a common law duty to appoint an intermediary to ensure that a vulnerable child defendant can have a fair trial (*see R(C) v Sevenoaks Youth Court* [2009] EWHC 465 (Admin); and *R (OP) v SS Justice, Cheltenham MC, and CPS* (Just for Kids Law intervening) [2014] EWHC 1944 (Admin)).

3.3.2 Family cases

Intermediaries have also been used in civil cases, in particular in the Family Court, for both children and vulnerable adults.

4 CLIENTS WHO MAY LACK MENTAL CAPACITY

4.1 What is capacity?

Mental capacity is the ability to make a decision - both day-to-day decisions and more significant decisions that may have legal consequences, such as buying property, entering into a contract, making a will, bringing or defending legal proceedings or seeking a divorce. Capacity is decision-specific, so a client may have capacity to make a simple decision but does not have capacity to make a complex decision or a decision that has significant consequences or carries significant risk.

If you reasonably entertain a doubt about your client's capacity to give proper instructions, it is your professional duty to satisfy yourself that the client either has or does not have the capacity to give instructions.[5] The statutory test of capacity to make a decision is contained in section 2(1) MCA 2005 which is set out at paragraph 4.3 below. There continues to be judicial debate as to the relationship between the statutory capacity test and common law tests of capacity although the High Court has clarified the position on the test for capacity to make a will and to make a lifetime gift (both of which are addressed at paragraphs 4.5.1 and 4.5.2 respectively).

The test of capacity to conduct proceedings is set out in paragraph 4.5.3 below.

4.2 Mental Capacity Act 2005 – the statutory principles

Section 1 MCA 2005 contains the first three principles that are the starting point for assessing capacity:

(1)   A person must be assumed to have capacity unless it is established that he lacks capacity.
(2)   A person is not to be treated as unable to make a decision unless all practicable steps to help him to do so have been taken without success.
(3)   A person is not to be treated as unable to make a decision merely because he makes an unwise decision.

The starting point is the presumption that an adult client has full legal capacity to make their own decisions. Where there is doubt as to a person's capacity, the burden of proof is on the person seeking to establish a lack of capacity, on the balance of probabilities.

A person must be given all appropriate help and support to enable them to make their own decisions or, in the event that they are assessed as lacking capacity to make the decision in question, to maximise their participation in any decision making process. An unwise decision should not, by itself be sufficient to indicate lack of capacity. However, doubt may be raised as to the person's capacity if, for example, their decision is out of character.

4.3 Mental Capacity Act – the legal test for capacity to make decisions

You should be aware that a lack of capacity cannot be established merely because of a person's age or appearance or their condition or an aspect of their behaviour. Section 2(1) of the MCA 2005 states that:

'. . . a person lacks capacity in relation to a matter if at the material time he is unable to make a decision for himself in relation to the matter because of an impairment of, or a disturbance in the functioning of, the mind or brain.'[6]

Capacity is therefore both decision specific and time specific and the inability to make the decision in question must be because of 'an impairment of, or a disturbance in the functioning of the mind or brain'.

Although there is one test of capacity, the statutory Code of Practice which supports the MCA 2005 identifies two elements: the 'diagnostic' and the 'functional' elements.

* Does the person have an impairment or disturbance that affects the way their mind or brain works?
* Does the impairment or disturbance mean that they are unable to make a specific decision at the time it needs to be made for one or more of the reasons set out in section 3 MCA 2005?

It is important to understand that a person is only considered to lack capacity for the purposes of the MCA 2005 if their inability to make a decision is because of an impairment or a disturbance in, the functioning of, the mind or brain.

Section 3 MCA 2005 defines what it means to be unable to make a decision.

In deciding whether the person is unable to make a decision the following four factors must be considered:

* Does the person understand the information relevant to the decision?
* Can the person retain the information?
* Can the person use or weigh up the information as part of the process of making the decision?
* Can the person communicate their decision (whether by talking, sign language, or any other means)?

Information relevant to a decision will include the particular nature of the decision in question, the purpose for which it is needed, the effect(s) of the decision and the likely consequences of deciding one way or another or of making no decision at all (MCA 2005 s.3(4)). You must provide an explanation of the relevant information in ways that are appropriate to the person's circumstances, using the most appropriate form of communication to help the person understand.

Retaining information for even a short time may be sufficient in the context of some decisions. It depends on what is necessary for the decision in question.

You can find further guidance about the MCA 2005 test of capacity in CHAPTER 4 of the MCA 2005 Code of Practice.

Section 6 of this practice note addresses the position where a client has capacity to make the material decisions but is vulnerable to the influence of those around them.

4.4 Capacity to instruct a solicitor to carry out specific instructions

You must be satisfied that your client has capacity to give you instructions on the matter in question. If you have any doubt as to whether a client has capacity to provide an instruction or instructions, you must undertake a capacity assessment before any instructions are acted upon. To do otherwise may place you at risk of the sanctions set out at paragraph 1.4.2 above.

Different levels of capacity are required for different transactions. For example, different considerations apply to making a gift than in conducting litigation. You must assess the client's understanding in the context of the transaction upon which you are instructed, applying the relevant legal test of capacity (see paragraph 4.5 below) and then consider whether the client is able to provide you with instructions on what they wish to do.

Even if you are satisfied that your client has the necessary mental capacity to make a specific decision, you may still need to be alert to the possibility of the client being subject to undue influence (see section 6).

If your client lacks capacity instruct you your role, your obligations and responsibilities are different from when you are acting for a client with capacity (see paragraph 4.7 below).

4.5 Other legal tests of capacity

4.5.1 Capacity to make a will

The High Court in *Walker v Badmin* [2014] All ER (D) 258 reviewed various conflicting decisions on whether the correct test of capacity is the MCA 2005 test or that established in the case of *Banks v Goodfellow* QBD 1870. It was concluded that the *Banks v Goodfellow* test is the correct test, although it is possible that an appellate court might reach a different conclusion. This test is set out below:

The testator must:

(a)   understand the nature of his act (of making a will) and its effects;
(b)   understand the extent of the property in his estate. be able to comprehend and appreciate the claims to which he ought to give effect; and
(c)   that no disorder of his mind 'shall poison his affections, perverse his sense of right, or his will in disposing of his property'.

4.5.2 Capacity to make a lifetime gift

As in the case of wills there has been uncertainty as to whether the common law test has been superseded by the MCA 2005 test. The High Court in *Kicks v Leigh* [2014] EWHC 3926 (Ch) reviewed the conflicting case-law and concluded that the common law test is the correct test. Again, it is possible that an appellate court might reach a different conclusion.

The common law test is set out in *Re Beaney* [1978] 2 All ER 595 which says that the degree of understanding required for the making of a valid lifetime gift is relative to the transaction which is to be carried out. If the subject matter and value of the gift is trivial in relation to the donor's other assets a low degree of understanding is sufficient. However, if the effect of the gift is to dispose of the donor's only asset of value and so pre-empt the devolution of his estate under his will or on his intestacy, the degree of understanding required is as high as that required for a will and the donor has to understand the claims of all potential donees and the extent of the property to be disposed of.

4.5.3 Capacity to conduct proceedings

(NB this section does not cover criminal proceedings)

Formally, the test of capacity to conduct proceedings will vary according to the type of court. However, as the Supreme Court has made clear in *Dunhill v Burgin* [2014] UKSC 18, there is unlikely to be any real difference whether the test is the statutory test applied under the MCA 2005 (as is applied in civil proceedings) or the common law.

The key question therefore remains as set out in the judgment of Chadwick LJ in *Masterman-Lister v Brutton* & Co [2003] All ER 162, namely whether:

'a party to legal proceedings is capable of understanding, with the assistance of such proper explanation (in broad terms and simple language) from legal advisers and other experts as the case may require, the matters on which their consent or decision was likely to be necessary in the course of those proceedings.'

This test applies to the proceedings as a whole and not at each step in the conduct of the proceedings.[7]

The test of lack of capacity to conduct proceedings is the statutory test under the MCA 2005. However, the principles that evolved under the common law continue to be of assistance in applying the statutory test.

Capacity depends on time and context and should not be determined in the abstract. The question is always whether the litigant has capacity to conduct proceedings in relation to the particular proceedings in which he is involved and not other proceedings or their ability to make decisions in general.[8]

The following are some of the factors that may be relevant, for example, in assessing a client's capacity to conduct civil proceedings:

- The client would need to understand how the proceedings were to be funded.
- The party would need to know about the chances of not succeeding and the risk of an adverse order as to costs.
- The client would need to have capacity to make the sort of decisions that arise in litigation.
- The client would need to have the capacity to give proper instructions for, and to approve the particulars of claim, and to approve a compromise.
- For a client to have capacity to approve a compromise, they would need insight into the compromise, an ability to instruct solicitors to advise them on it, and an understanding of the solicitor's advice and an ability to weigh that advice before making a decision.

The Supreme Court also made clear in *Dunhill v Burgin* that the test must be applied to the claim that the party in fact has, not to the claim as formulated by their lawyers.

If your client is a party to but lacks capacity to conduct proceedings in the County Court, High Court, Family Court or Court of Protection a litigation friend must be appointed to give instructions and otherwise conduct the proceedings on their behalf.[9] The rules that govern the procedures vary according to the court or tribunal that the party is before.

4.6 Assessing capacity

It is for you to decide whether a client has capacity to instruct you and whether you can accept and act on the client's instructions. Although the MCA 2005 guiding principle is the presumption of capacity you would not be acting in your client's best interests when you knew or should have known that there were grounds to doubt their capacity without first satisfying yourself that the client does indeed have the requisite capacity – see paragraph 1.4.2 above.

You must apply the relevant legal test in respect of each particular transaction at the time the decision needs to be made.

The assessment should be conducted whenever possible with the client alone. You should not assume that anyone accompanying the client (including a family member) has their genuine interests at heart.

It may be useful if you also observe how any relative or friend who has accompanied the client behaves towards the client and vice versa as that may identify whether there is the risk of undue influence or pressure.

If you are concerned about a client's capacity, especially in relation to a decision with serious consequences either for them or other people, it is advisable to seek the opinion of an appropriately qualified professional. Where possible, you should choose a professional who knows your client and has expertise relevant to your client's condition. You should explain to the professional the legal test of capacity and ask for an opinion as to how the client's medical condition may affect their ability to make the decision in question.

Testamentary capacity

Where a will is prepared for an elderly or seriously ill client, the courts have developed the '*golden rule*', which should be considered as guidance only. This provides that the will should be approved or witnessed by a medical practitioner, regardless of how tactless or difficult it may be to explain this precautionary measure to your client.[10] The aim of the rule is to minimise or avoid post-death disputes about the capacity of the testator.

Ultimately, you must satisfy yourself that your client has the requisite testamentary capacity. You should therefore make and retain detailed and contemporaneous attendance notes, which confirm the steps you have taken to explore their capacity, the evidence you have collated, the circumstances and the rationale for your decision.

If there is a doubt about whether a client has capacity to make a particular decision, it is advisable to see the client personally in order to satisfy yourself that your client has capacity to make the decision you are concerned with.

4.6.1 Techniques for assessing capacity

How and when you see the client may be important, for example, choosing the time of day when the client is most alert and seeing them in the place where they feel most comfortable. There may be times or intervals in the day when your client may be more lucid than others; it is important to recognise that capacity can fluctuate significantly during the course of one day.

To put your client at ease, you might first chat about matters other than the business that you intend to carry out. It is helpful to know from other sources (such as family or carers) something of the client's family background and career so that you can verify the client's recollection. You should also ask a few questions about current affairs and past events. You should prepare and retain detailed and contemporaneous notes of any attendances. It is also helpful to record the questions you ask the client and the client's response, using the client's own words if possible.

At any subsequent interview you should seek to discuss some of the same matters and see if there is consistency in what the client says. You should also seek detailed instructions again - if they are materially different there is a good chance that the client may lack capacity in respect of that particular transaction.

Remember that you are testing the client's understanding of the decision to be made at the time it is made, not whether you agree with the client.

See also the guidance on assessing capacity in the Law Society practice note, *Financial abuse*.

4.6.2 Obtaining a medical or other expert opinion

You should inform your client of any concerns that you have about their capacity, the purpose of any capacity assessment, and the implications if they are found to lack such capacity.

If your client is a party to proceedings you may require the permission of the court to obtain an expert opinion.

When obtaining a medical or other expert opinion you must provide the client's written consent or confirm that the client has agreed to be assessed: You will also need to:

- explain clearly the purpose of the assessment and appropriate test of capacity
- with the consent of the client, supply sufficient background information to enable the expert to make an informed assessment – the information the expert receives may well affect their opinion, which places the onus on you to provide the right information
- set out any concerns about the client, especially about the appropriateness of the proposed decision and whether the expert is in fact being asked to confirm your opinion
- ask the expert to set out how the client's condition may affect their ability to make the decision in question, giving reasons for their conclusions
- provide a timescale for any response, especially if the matter is urgent
- actively chase the expert for the report, if there is any delay, and
- let the expert know if and how they are to be paid for the opinion.

In some circumstances, it may be more relevant to obtain an opinion from a professional other than a medical practitioner, such as a social worker, clinical psychologist or speech and language therapist, depending on the client's particular condition and the decision in question. However, the same considerations apply in relation to all appropriately qualified professionals.

There may be occasions when the client objects to you obtaining a report. If you still have serious concerns that the client lacks capacity to provide you with instructions and you have taken all reasonable steps to encourage your client to obtain a report, you must explain to your client in writing that you are unable to act for him, or to continue to act for him without a report being obtained and explain the legal consequences.

If proceedings are being contemplated, or if you are concerned your client has lost capacity during the course of proceedings, an application can be made to the court for a determination of whether the client lacks capacity to conduct the proceedings. The court may then order an assessment. However, if the client refuses to undergo medical assessment then there is no power to order an individual to comply with an assessment of capacity. In some cases the judge will have to form a view as to capacity without the benefit of any external expertise, although the courts have emphasised that judges should be slow to do so because of the seriousness of the consequences for the person.[11]

The Official Solicitor has a standard form of report (Certificate of Capacity to Conduct the Proceedings) for recording the assessment of the mental capacity of an adult to conduct their own proceedings where that adult is a party or intended party to proceedings in the Family Court, the High Court, a county court or the Court of Appeal. The certificate has guidance notes for the assessor and can be sent with the letter of instruction.

4.7 What happens when a client lacks capacity to give you instructions?

If you consider that a potential client lacks capacity to give you instructions, you may be entitled to decline to act on their behalf. If you do wish to act on their behalf, you must first make sure that you are able to identify a person who has the requisite authority to give you instructions (see paragraph 4.7.1 below).

If you consider that an existing client has lost the capacity to continue to give you instructions, then the following considerations apply:

- generally a retainer terminates by operation of law when a client loses the capacity to give or confirm instructions
- however, there may be exceptions to this rule (in particular where the retainer has provided for the potential loss of such capacity).[12]

Where an existing client loses capacity to instruct you, you should as far as practicable take action to protect your client's interests. As set out below, if you are to continue to act, you need to make sure that you have identified a person who is able to give you instructions.

If you remain doubtful as to the correct course of action you should contact the SRA Ethics Helpline.

4.7.1 Taking instructions on behalf of a client who lacks capacity

Depending on the circumstances of the case, you may be able to act, or continue to act on behalf of a client lacking capacity to instruct you by obtaining your instructions from a litigation friend, attorney or court appointed deputy. For example:

- You may act under the instructions of an attorney (such as a family member) appointed under a registered enduring power of attorney (EPA) or lasting power of attorney (LPA), provided the decision in question is within the scope of their authority. You may act under the instructions of a court appointed deputy (depending upon the scope of the deputy's authority)
- You may continue to conduct legal proceedings on the client's behalf acting on the instructions of a litigation friend appointed by the court.
- Where there are no current proceedings, but where proceedings are contemplated, you may be able to identify a third party who can give instructions on the client's behalf, as a proposed litigation friend. The proposed litigation friend is able to sign an application for legal aid on behalf of the client: see Regulation 22 of the Civil Legal Aid (Procedure) Regulations 2012 and paragraph 3.12 of the Standard Civil Contract 2014.

You should also be aware that the new Rule 3A within the Court of Protection Rules allows the Court of Protection in some cases to appoint an accredited legal representative to act for a client without a litigation friend (assuming that a panel of representatives will have been created).

See paragraph 5.3 below for more detail about taking instructions from an agent.

5 THE ROLE OF CARERS AND OTHER THIRD PARTIES

5.1 Carers of vulnerable people

Carers can play a valuable role in supporting vulnerable people to access legal services and to make relevant decisions for themselves. Carers may also be able to assist with communication and help you to identify what reasonable adjustments could be made to assist the client. In practice, the definition of a carer has a wide meaning and includes informal carers such as relatives or friends providing personal care or supervision either full time or merely on a casual basis, as well as professional carers such as care workers, social workers and community nurses.

In the first instance, you should seek to obtain information and discuss matters with the client alone, being especially mindful of the principle of client confidentiality and the need for consent if confidentiality is to be waived.

It is important to be clear about who your client is, whenever relatives or other carers seek to give instructions on their behalf. As a general rule, you can act only on a client's instructions. No one, whether a family member or professional, has the right to give instructions or make decisions about another person's property, financial or legal affairs unless they have been given formal authority to do so either by the client or by a court (for example an attorney acting under and EPA or LPA, a litigation friend or deputy).

For further information please see the Law Society practice note, lasting powers of attorney.

5.3 Taking instructions from an agent

In some cases where the client lacks capacity to give instructions, you may be taking instructions from an agent such as an attorney (if it is within the scope of their authority) or a deputy (if it is within the scope of their authority). The person for whom the attorney or deputy is acting (the principal) is still your client and you must act in the client's best interests.

If you are concerned that the instructions you are given by the agent are not in your client's best interests or that there is a conflict of interest, you should inform the agent of your concerns. If necessary, you should decline to act on the instructions of the agent if you continue to believe that these are not in the client's best interests. You will have to decide whether you can continue to act for the client, or alternatively for the agent on the basis that another independent solicitor will be appointed to represent the principal.

In certain situations, you will be deemed to be acting for the agent rather than the principal. These include:

- where you have been instructed by an attorney to apply to the Office of the Public Guardian for registration of the EPA or LPA where a prospective deputy instructs you to apply to the Court of Protection for the appointment of a deputy
- where you represent the deputy, attorney or other party to Court of Protection proceedings when there is a conflict of interest – in such a situation, you may act for the party to the proceedings and the Court of Protection may, if no other party is available and in the last resort, appoint the Official Solicitor or another independent person to act as litigation friend to represent the interests of the principal
- where you believe there is a conflict of interest and that you must act for the agent rather than the principal (who should then be separately represented).

5.3.1 Attorneys

While they still have capacity to do so, adults aged 18 and over may make an LPA appointing their chosen attorney(s) to make specific decisions on their behalf. The attorney's role and powers will depend on the type of power of attorney made and whether the donor has specified any restrictions in the attorney's authority to act. In the case of a health and welfare LPA attorneys must always consider whether the donor can in fact make the decision themselves and should only act in their best interests if the donor is unable to. It is also important to note that attorneys are not entitled as of right to act as litigation friends and must be appointed in the normal way (see para 5.4.3 below).

Further information on the various forms of LPA and their effect please see the Law Society practice note on lasting powers of attorney.

5.3.2 Deputies

Where there is an ongoing need for decisions to be made on behalf of a person lacking capacity to make such decisions, and the person has not previously made an LPA or

EPA appointing an attorney to make the relevant decisions, the Court of Protection may appoint a deputy with authority to make those decisions.

Court appointed deputies can be given wide powers, including the power to conduct legal proceedings on behalf of a person lacking capacity if authorised by the court to do so. The scope of the deputy's authority will be specified in their order of appointment. Deputies can be appointed to make decisions either in respect of property and financial affairs or in respect of the health and welfare of the patient, or occasionally both. However, the court is required under the MCA wherever possible to make a single decision in preference to the appointment of a deputy, so the appointment of health and welfare deputies is rare.

Deputies must always act in the best interests of the person lacking capacity and in accordance with the MCA 2005 principles (see above) and must have regard to the guidance given in the MCA Code of Practice, in particular Chapter 8.

5.3.3 Litigation friends

People who lack capacity to conduct proceedings may become parties to proceedings in the High Court, the county courts and the Family Court, as well as in the Court of Protection. Litigation friends are appointed to give instructions and otherwise conduct the proceedings on their behalf. They will stand in the shoes of the individual lacking capacity and give instructions on their behalf. A litigation friend can be a family member or professional, but will not (save in exceptional circumstances) be the solicitor themselves.[13] The Official Solicitor is the litigation friend of last resort, and more detail about his role is available https://www.gov.uk/government/organisations/official-solicit or-and-public-trustee/about

5.4 Advocates

There are a range of independent advocates appointed under the MCA 2005, the Mental Health Act 1983 and also the Care Act 2014 who may be involved with vulnerable clients. Aside from statutory advocates many advocates are also appointed from the voluntary sector on a privately paid basis and often from personal care budgets. It is always important to check the basis upon which the advocate has been commissioned to provide the services to your client, because each will be providing a somewhat different function.

Advocates will often play a vital role in supporting vulnerable clients, and may well play a particularly important role in assisting the client to communicate with you for purposes of providing instructions. However, an advocate will never, by virtue of their role alone, be in a position to provide you with those instructions.

5.5 Appropriate Adults in criminal matters

Under the Police and Criminal Evidence Act 1984 (PACE) Codes of Practice, police custody sergeants must secure an Appropriate Adult (AA) to safeguard the rights and welfare of vulnerable people (children aged 10–17 and mentally vulnerable adults) who are detained and questioned by the police. The role includes:

- to support, advise and assist the detained person, particularly while they are being questioned
- to observe whether the police are acting properly, fairly and with respect for the rights of the detained person – and to tell them if they are not
- to assist with communication between the detained person and the police
- to ensure that the detained person understands their rights and that the AA has a role in protecting those rights.

An AA should be someone who is completely independent of the police and, where possible the vulnerable person (although parents often do act as AA for a child or young person). It is desirable that they should have a sound understanding of, and experience or training in, dealing with the needs of juveniles, vulnerable adults or mentally disordered people. An AA cannot, merely because of their position, give instructions to a solicitor on behalf of the individuals they are to assist.

6 INFLUENCE AND UNDUE INFLUENCE

There are a significant class of people who are unable to take their own decisions but whose inability to do so stems from the influence exercised over them by others (for example family members), rather than from an impairment of, or disturbance in, their mind or brain.

The law treats such vulnerable individuals differently to those lacking capacity for the purposes of the MCA 2005: because the person has capacity to make their own decision, no other person may take decisions on their behalf.

In these circumstances it is possible for any person or body concerned as to whether the individual is under duress to seek the assistance of the High Court to provide its protection under its inherent jurisdiction.[14] The High Court has the power to grant injunctive or other relief with the aim of putting in place a framework to enable the individual to make their own decisions.

In your first meeting with a vulnerable client, information may come from an intermediary, such as a family member, carer or concerned neighbour. In the majority of cases their assistance is well intentioned and they will be communicating on behalf of, and with the consent of, the client.

However, you should be aware of the possibility of conflicts of interest or, in some cases, undue influence. Your overriding duty is to your client and you must ensure that your instructions are from your client, free of undue influence of others. So, if your client has capacity to do so, you should confirm your instructions directly with the client by seeing them on their own, especially if detailed information has been provided by someone else.

Clients may seek legal advice (for example to make a will, an LPA or a significant gift) because they have been influenced or told by someone, such as a family member, that they ought to do so. Such 'influence' may be well-intentioned and sensible. However, if you suspect that a client's instructions are the result of coercion or pressure ('undue influence'), you need to exercise your professional judgment as to whether you can proceed or continue to act on the client's behalf.

Your duties in relation to assessing the possibility of undue influence bearing upon your client are underpinned by the indicative behaviours in CHAPTER 1 of the SRA Code. In particular IB 1.6 and IB 1.28 directly address the issue of undue influence:

- IB (1.6) 'in taking instructions and during the course of the retainer, [have] proper regard to your client's mental capacity or other vulnerability, such as incapacity or duress.'
- IB (1.28) 'acting for a client when there are reasonable grounds for believing that the instructions are affected by duress or undue influence without satisfying yourself that they represent the client's wishes' . . . would demonstrate that you have failed to comply with the Code.'

6.1 Presumption of undue influence

6.1.1 Gifts

Undue influence may be a factor even when there is no evidence of any coercion or pressure. If an individual is contemplating making a significant lifetime gift, undue influence is presumed where there is a relationship of trust and confidence between the client and the recipient of the gift, (for example, care giver and care receiver, patient and doctor, solicitor and client), and the proposed gift requires an explanation (for example, it is an absurdly generous gift, or a gift of their main asset, such as their home, perhaps to just one of their children).

Once the presumption of undue influence has arisen, it is not sufficient for the recipient to demonstrate that the individual had capacity to make the gift, and that there was no actual coercion or influence. It is important that the individual has their own independent legal advice, considering all the relevant information and risks, before making a free and fully informed decision to go ahead with the gift.

6.1.2 Testamentary dispositions

This 'presumption' of undue influence does not arise for testamentary dispositions. Persuading an individual to include a specific individual as a beneficiary in their will would not necessarily amount to undue influence. Coercive behaviour is usually required.

However, if the client is particularly elderly or frail, then less obviously aggressive methods might amount to undue influence.

6.2 No actual evidence of undue influence but concerns remain

Where there is no evidence of undue influence or pressure[15] but the client appears to want to continue with a transaction that you consider to be against their best interests, you should see the client alone (or with a neutral third party if the client wishes someone else to be present to support them or assist communication). In doing so you should explain the consequences of the instructions the client has given and get confirmation (preferably in writing) that the client wishes to proceed.

You should be mindful in circumstances such as these that a core principle of the MCA 2005 (and the common law) is that a decision you may consider to be unwise may nonetheless be a capacitous decision. It is therefore important that you probe carefully as to the driver for the decision where your suspicions are raised and keep a detailed note of your discussion.

It may be preferable to use an independent advocate or interpreter or other assistance from an independent source, rather than relying on a family member or carer to communicate the client's wishes.

7 CASE STUDIES FOR PRACTITIONERS

A. Working with disabled clients

Mrs Jones' marriage has broken down after forty years and she decides to seek legal advice about a divorce. She has a severe visual impairment but does not want anyone to know that she is thinking about a divorce, so she wants to meet with a solicitor on her own. She telephones a local solicitor's firm to book an appointment and is put through to the team secretary of the firm's family law department, Ms Clare Robinson.

Clare takes some details from her and explains that the first available appointment is the following Tuesday at 09:00. Mrs Jones asks if she could have a later appointment because, as a result of her visual impairment, she finds it easier to travel around when the streets are less busy. Clare asks if she would prefer a home visit. Mrs Jones is grateful for the offer but explains that she does not want her husband to know anything about the visit. She says that she is able to find her way to the office but asks if a member of staff can guide her into the building from the street as she is not familiar with the office. She also asks if any written documentation can be sent by e-mail or provided in large print format. Clare assures her that this will not be a problem. She also asks if the firm could provide a digital recorder for her to record any meetings so that she can remind herself of discussions and key points that are made. Clare says the firm would be happy to lend her a digital recorder for these purposes and can also let her use it to record instructions rather than e-mailing them if that would be easier for her, but will ask for it back when the matter is completed.

Clare makes the appointment for later on Tuesday and then explains Mrs Jones' needs to Mrs Temple, the solicitor who will be acting for Mrs Jones. She also speaks to the reception staff to make them aware of Mrs Jones' additional needs and Mary Baker, the lead receptionist, says she will wait outside the office to greet Mrs Jones.

On the morning of her appointment, Clare reminds the reception staff that Mrs Jones is coming in and discovers that Mary is off sick and that reception is short staffed as a result. She therefore waits outside for Mrs Jones herself, having checked that the reception area, toilets and meeting room are free from clutter and other trip hazards.

At the meeting Mrs Temple provides Mrs Jones with the digital recorder. She advises her about divorce proceedings and how to approach the division of money and assets. She discusses with her whether she will need additional support given that she will now be living on her own.

Mrs Jones is so impressed by the firm's service that she recommends the firm to her local support group for people who are visually impaired.

B. Working with clients who may lack capacity

Tom O'Sullivan was 38 years old when he was involved in a road traffic accident. On his way home from work as a graphic designer, he was knocked off his bicycle by a lorry turning left across the cycle lane he was travelling in. He suffered a severe closed head injury, a fractured shoulder and massive bruising to both legs. He was in hospital for nearly 6 months and then had several months attending out-patient appointments for physiotherapy and other forms of rehabilitation. When he returned to work over a year after the accident he was only able to perform routine clerical work. In order to keep up mortgage payments and provide for their two young children, Tom's wife returned to full-time work. After a few months of becoming increasingly frustrated with his mundane job, Tom resigned and has barely worked since then.

Shortly after the accident, with the help of his father and supported by his wife, Tom seeks advice from you about claiming damages against the lorry driver and the company that employed him. It took some time to gather together the medical reports and the information in relation to financial loss, but eventually the claim is issued almost three years after the accident. Although by that time Tom had largely recovered from his physical injuries, he complained that he continued to suffer from a complete loss of the senses of smell and taste, some hearing loss, forgetfulness, headaches, anxiety and mood swings. However, he seemed able to provide accurate information relating to the claim and to understand the advice given to him by you and counsel.

The defence denied liability and alleged contributory negligence as Tom had had an after-work drink before cycling home. Tom's counsel had advised that this could be assessed as high as 50 per cent. Following negotiations, the defence made a payment into court and Tom, accompanied by his wife, father and solicitor attended a conference at counsel's office to discuss the offer. During the course of the meeting Tom became increasingly angry, distressed and tearful, but continued to ask relevant questions and put forward cogent arguments for seeking a higher offer. Counsel expresses some concern about Tom's behaviour.

After the conference, you receive a phone call from Tom's wife, saying that she was concerned about personality changes since the accident and particularly his mood swings and depression which had got worse since the conference. She also let slip that he had talked about committing suicide, although he had asked her not to tell anyone for fear of upsetting the family. She asks you to speed up the negotiations and reach a settlement - any settlement - as soon as possible, even if they could not get the amount of damages they wanted, as she was worried about the effect of prolonged court proceedings on Tom's condition.

Points for consideration about litigation and settlement:

- You should ask to see Tom alone to make a careful assessment of Tom's capacity to give you instructions, and to consider whether the presumption of capacity continues to apply or was rebutted by the new information about Tom's condition and behaviour.
- You should notify counsel of your concerns and keep counsel apprised of the steps that are being taken to ascertain whether Tom has litigation capacity to conduct the proceedings.
- You will probably decide to seek an expert opinion, for example from a consultant in neuropsychiatric rehabilitation, to assess how Tom's brain injury may be affecting his ability to provide you with instructions. The letter of instruction to the expert should set out clearly the issues relating to his claim and the decisions required of him. The solicitor should also refer to the judgments in *Dunhill v Burgin* [2014] UKSC 18 and *Masterman-Lister v Brutton & Co (Nos. 1 and 2)* [2002] EWCA Civ 1889. You will need to seek Tom's consent to the examination by carefully explaining to him that any settlement could be invalid if he were later found to lack capacity to conduct the legal proceedings.
- If Tom refuses to consent to the medical examination, you will need to make your own assessment of Tom's capacity based on the available evidence. With or without a medical opinion you should keep a careful record of the assessment of capacity and the reasons for the conclusions reached.
- If you conclude that Tom continues to have capacity to conduct the proceedings, then you can continue to act on Tom's instructions. You should discuss with Tom his wife's concerns and the possible effect of the court proceedings and how Tom can best be supported during the process by you or a third party.
- If you conclude that Tom now lacks capacity to conduct the proceedings, a litigation friend must be appointed to conduct the proceedings on his behalf. The solicitor should discuss with Tom, his wife and his father who might be the most appropriate person to ask the court to be appointed as Tom's litigation friend.
- If you consider that there is no one among Tom's family or friends who is able to conduct the case and has no conflict of interest, you may wish to contact the Official Solicitor who is the last resort litigation friend. The Official Solicitor will require confirmation that Tom lacks litigation capacity to conduct the proceedings and information on how Tom's legal costs are to be paid.
- If you conclude that Tom now lacks capacity to conduct the proceedings and Tom continues to assert his own capacity to instruct you, you should inform the court hearing the claim and an application should be made to determine if Tom has lost capacity and, if so, for the appointment of a litigation friend.

C. Working with clients who may be vulnerable to undue influence

Mrs Bryan is 79 and has early onset dementia. Her previous solicitor acted for her and her late husband in the preparation of their wills.

Mrs Bryan's son Don has arranged an appointment for his mother at your offices to review her will, following the death of her husband. She is brought to the meeting by Don, who remains in the waiting room, while you see Mrs Bryan alone. She tells you during your meeting that she has recently rented out her own home and has moved in to live with Don, and his family. Neither Mrs Bryan nor her son Don are existing clients of your firm.

You receive a letter from Mrs Bryan shortly after the meeting, telling you that as she has decided to live with Don permanently, that she is selling her own house and would like you to handle the conveyancing. She further advises you that she is using the proceeds of sale to pay towards an extension, a conservatory and replacement windows and a new kitchen in Don's property.

Points for consideration:

As Mrs Bryan's arrangements and plans may result in some vulnerability, you should consider the following action:

- You should (with Mrs Bryan's authority) obtain a copy of her previous will, and discuss her reasons both for the change in solicitor and any substantive changes to the terms of her will.
- You should have a further face-to-face meeting with Mrs Bryan, to discuss her plans for her property and assess her mental capacity to provide instructions to you in relation to each of the proposed transactions. If you are in doubt, you should seek a medical opinion about her capacity to make the relevant decisions and to instruct you. Your instructions to the medical professional must set out the specific criteria to be considered for each transaction.
- Mrs Bryan will need advice (inter alia) on whether she should have a legal or beneficial interest in her son's house in exchange for her planned contribution, as she will need an 'exit plan' should the living arrangement break down for any reason.
- You should also consider whether Mrs Bryan may be at risk of undue influence, most obviously in relation to the money she is planning to 'gift' to Don to spend on his property, where the presumption of undue influence may arise. She may be dependent on Don and his family for her care and accommodation. She may not be entirely happy with the planned course of action but feel unable to express that to her family.
- You should endeavour to see Mrs Bryan alone, to enable her to explore fully the risks and benefits of the proposed transactions.

D. Working with clients with learning disability

John and Mary Smith need advice about possible care proceedings being taken in respect of their two year-old child. They have received a pre-proceedings letter from the local authority which urges them to take legal advice and which gives your firm's name (among others) as appropriate specialists. An appointment has been made, by telephone, by an independent advocate Mrs Jones, who said she was calling on behalf of the Smiths as they both have learning disabilities and find formal telephone conversations and correspondence problematic. She has left her contact number.

Although you are a very experienced care proceedings lawyer, you have not worked with clients with learning disabilities before, or with an independent advocate. Colleagues tell you that, in general terms, independent advocates help the people they work with to participate in decisions that affect their lives, to understand what they are being told and enable them to make their views, opinions and decisions known.

Your colleagues say that, similarly to working with intermediaries in court, having the assistance of an independent advocate is essential for ensuring that you can communicate effectively with your clients and that they can communicate effectively with you.

Points for consideration:

- Recent case-law involving parents with learning difficulties (for example *A Father v SBC & Others* [2014] EWFC 6) emphasises the need to ensure that the processes by which decisions about the children are made are fair and that the parents are sufficiently involved in that process. The Human Rights Act 1998 and the Equality Act 2010 are therefore likely to be particularly relevant for your clients.

- All aspects of this case, including the Smiths' contact with you and the local authority, how meetings and correspondence are managed, what services are offered, how decisions are reached, what adjustments have been made, will be pertinent when considering whether there has been compliance with the legislation.

Before the meeting

- Check if the advocate will be attending with the Smiths. Ask what you can do, at this stage, to ensure the Smiths will be able to participate fully. For example, normally, your new clients are asked to complete some paperwork while waiting for their appointment and they are given some generic information about the firm's client services and legal aid. Consider sending this paperwork to Mrs Jones, in advance of the meeting, together with a list of questions you will be asking the Smiths, expressed in plain English. You could also provide and Easyread version for the Smiths. This will give your clients an opportunity to think about their answers, before the meeting.
- Check the Working Together with Parents Network website for a wide range of information and resources relating to parents with learning disabilities.
- Start to consider likely case management issues that will arise in the office and at court including the Advocates Gateway resources and toolkits referenced at paragraph 3.3 above.

At the meeting

- Ensure the Smiths are happy for Mrs Jones to be present at the meeting.
- Check with the Smiths how you can make communication effective, for you both, during the meeting and with any follow up correspondence or actions.
- Consider whether there is any conflict of interest as between the Smiths or the potential for a conflict to arise.
- If you believe that the mental capacity of one or both of the Smiths to be at issue follow the relevant guidance contained within section 4 of this practice note.
- Without making assumptions about the degree of learning disability a client has, or how this impacts on their ability to engage with you, you know that the following steps are likely to be useful, and may be essential: you may need to repeat things several times, sometimes re-phrasing, but always using short sentences, one concrete idea at a time, in a logical and clear order; you may have to take into account a reduced ability to read, write, concentrate, process and recall information and a difficulty with organisational skills such as time-keeping.
- You will need to check understanding frequently – not by asking questions that only require a yes/no answer, but by asking short, simple, open questions designed to elicit from your client, for example: what they have understood to be happening, or what they will need to do, or what next steps you will be taking on their behalf.
- Explain to the Smiths the role of the different professionals such as the children's guardian.
- Check that the Smiths know where the court building is and how to get there for hearings.

8 FURTHER INFORMATION

8.1 Law Society

8.1.1 The Practice Advice Service for solicitors

The Law Society provides support for solicitors on a wide range of areas of practice. Practice Advice can be contacted on 0870 606 2522 from 09:00 to 17:00 on weekdays or email practiceadvice@lawsociety.org.uk.

8.1.2 Other Law Society practice notes

Lasting powers of attorney
Financial abuse
Providing services to D/deaf and hard of hearing people
Equality and diversity requirements
Gifts of assets
Legal professional privilege
Conflicts of interest

8.1.3 Law Society publications

Assessment of Mental Capacity, 3rd Edition
Equality Act 2010, A guide to the new law

8.2 SRA

8.2.1 Professional Ethics helpline

The SRA provides advice for solicitors on the SRA Handbook, call 0370 606 2577 (inside the UK), 09.00 to 17.00, Monday to Friday.

8.2.2 Reporting another professional

The SRA provides guidance reporting misconduct.

8.3 Other resources

8.3.1 Enabling access to your services for vulnerable clients

Various charities and other organisations have produced online guidance for professionals on assisting particular groups of clients. This is a selection:

Action on Hearing Loss
Advocates Gateway
Age UK
Alzheimer's Society
Business Disability Forum
Changing Faces
Disability Rights UK
Foundation for people with learning disabilities - criminal justice resources
General Medical Council - learning disability resources
Legal Services Consumer Panel
Mencap
Mind

National Autistic Society
RNIB
Sense

8.3.2 Mental Capacity Act practice and procedure

MCA 2005 Code of Practice
Social Care Institute for Excellence - MCA Directory
Court of Protection Handbook Guidance
British Medical Association MCA Toolkit
39 Essex Chambers - Mental Capacity Newsletter

8.4 General

Office of the Official Solicitor and Public Trustee

8.5 Acknowledgments

The Law Society kindly acknowledges the work of Jo Honigmann (Just Equality), Penny Letts and the Law Society's Mental Health and Disability Committee in developing this practice note.

The Law Society would also like thank Nadine Tilbury and Beth Tarleton at the Norah Fry Research Centre (Bristol University) for their assistance in reviewing the practice note and the provision of a case study in relation to clients with learning disability.

Footnotes

1. *Blankley v Central Manchester & Manchester Children's University Hospitals NHS Trust* [2015] EWCA Civ 18.
2. The World Wide Web Consortium produces recommendations for website accessibility.
3. Norah Fry Centre Research, What happens when people with learning disabilities access legal services?
4. The Law Society practice note on providing services to deaf/hard of hearing people provides more guidance.
5. *RP v Nottingham City Council and Official Solicitor* [2008] EWCA Civ 4.
6. *PC & Anor v City of York Council* [2013] EWCA Civ 478.
7. *Masterman-Lister v Brutton & Co* [2003] 3 All ER 162 confirmed in *Dunhill v Burgin* [2014] UKSC 18.
8. *Sheffield City Council v E and another* [2005] Fam 326 per Munby J at para 38.
9. Part 21 Civil Procedure Rules 1998, Part 15 Family Procedure Rules 2010, Part 17 Court of Protection Rules 2007.
10. *Templeman in Kenward v Adams* [1975] CLY 3591; *The Times*, 29 November 1975.
11. *Baker Tilly v Makar* [2013] EWHC 759 (QB).
12. See *Blankley v Central Manchester and Manchester Children's University Hospitals NHS Trust* [2015] EWCA Civ 18.
13. If a suitable panel is established, it may in due course be possible for solicitors to be appointed directly to represent the subject of proceedings before the Court of Protection as 'accredited legal representatives'.
14. See *Re L (vulnerable Adults with Capacity: Court's Jurisdiction)* [2012] EWC CIV 253.
15. See *A Local Authority v DL & Ors* [2011] EWHC 1022 (Fam).

ACCESS TO AND DISCLOSURE OF AN INCAPACITATED PERSON'S WILL

I3

Issued on 13 March 2017

This guidance has been drafted in conjunction with and approved by the following organisations that will also have regard to it when dealing with this issue: The Court of Protection, Office of the Public Guardian. Legal Ombudsman, The Law Society and the Society of Trust and Estate Practitioners.

PURPOSE OF GUIDANCE

The purpose of this guidance is to clarify when a solicitor can disclose a copy of a client's will to a property and financial affairs attorney or deputy appointed by the Court of Protection in circumstances where the client has lost mental capacity. The guidance applies to solicitors authorised to practise in England and Wales and regulated by the Solicitors Regulation Authority. The guidance may be used by other regulatory organisations if they wish to do so.

WHO IS YOUR CLIENT?

A solicitor can accept instructions given by someone else, where the person providing the instructions has the authority to do so on behalf of the client[1]. Where the client (also known as 'the donor') has made a power of attorney, he or she remains the client acting through their agent - the appointed attorney. A deputy appointed by the Court of Protection, will be acting on behalf of the person for whom they act, who lacks mental capacity, as a statutory agent[2]. Whether instructions come from an attorney or a deputy, (in that role) the solicitor's duty of care is to the person on whose behalf they act.

DUTY OF AN ATTORNEY OR DEPUTY

The Court of Protection has made it clear that property and financial affairs attorneys and deputies owe a duty when making financial decisions, so far as is reasonably possible, not to interfere with the succession plans made by the person for whom they act[3]. Having knowledge of the contents of the will and/or codicils(s), means that the attorney or deputy is in a position to act in the best interests of the person for whom them act and in particular may:

(i)   take and act upon appropriate professional advice;
(ii)   make appropriate investments;
(iii)   apply to the Court for an order to save a specific legacy (so far as possible), where disposal of the asset is required;
(iv)   apply to the Court for a statutory will to ensure that it reflects the intentions of the person who lacks mental capacity and the relevant circumstances; and

(v)   arrange for safekeeping and storage of the asset.

SCENARIOS OF POSSIBLE ADVERSE OUTCOMES WHICH CAN OCCUR WITHOUT KNOWING THE CONTENT OF THE WILL

Jack's case

Jack has made a will giving his house (currently worth £300,000) to his nephew, Paul, and the residue (about £20,000) to charity. He also made a Property and Financial Affairs Lasting Power of Attorney, without any restrictions in favour of Paul. This has been registered with the Office of the Public Guardian.

Jack subsequently has a stroke and is no longer able to live in his own home. Paul decides that he must sell the house to pay for Jack's care.

The effect of selling the house is that when Jack dies the gift in the will to Paul fails and he gets nothing. The charity benefits from the whole of the estate. This was not what Jack intended.

However, if Paul is aware of the contents of the will, he can apply to the Court of Protection for either a statutory will to be made so that Jack's wishes are followed or obtain an order for sale, which under the Mental Capacity Act 2005 ensures that the gift is saved[4].

June's case

June has made a will in which she gives her friend, Margaret her premium bonds. At the time of making the will these are worth £500. June's son, David is the sole residuary beneficiary. David is unaware of the contents of the will.

June has dementia and lacks mental capacity to manage her finances. David is appointed as June's deputy. He decides he should invest £49,500 of June's money in premium bonds.

June dies. David discovers that Margaret will now get £50,000 premium bonds (much more than his mother ever intended) and he gets less than intended.

Had David been aware of the will, he would have invested his mother's money differently, so as not to frustrate June's succession plans.

INSTRUCTIONS AT TIME OF MAKING A WILL AND A LASTING POWER OF ATTORNEY

Solicitors have a duty to act in their client's interests. The will forms part of the financial affairs belonging to the donor and so unless the donor provides contrary instructions, the attorney is entitled to a copy of the donor's will. To evidence compliance it is advisable for the question of disclosure of the donor's will to be discussed and recorded at the time of making the will and confirmed at the time of making the Lasting Power of Attorney (LPA). Having advised as to the consequences, instructions should be obtained as to whether disclosure is to be denied, or the circumstances in which it is permitted. This should be incorporated into the LPA or contained in a side letter. See the Law Society's Practice Note on Lasting Powers of Attorney (May 2016).

INSTRUCTIONS FOR NON-DISCLOSURE

If the client has made it clear that his or her will is not to be disclosed prior to his or her death, it should not be disclosed. If a specific court order has been obtained, requiring disclosure of the will, the solicitor must comply with the order and disclose the client's will. However, if the solicitor believes disclosure is not in the client's best interests, the solicitor will need to seek a variation of the order, by submitting a Witness Statement[5] to the Court of Protection which explains why the will should not be disclosed. The solicitor may also ask the Court of Protection for authority for payment of his or her costs to be paid out of the client's estate.

INCAPACITY RESTRICTION

If the LPA or Enduring Power of Attorney (EPA) contains a restriction, which prevents the attorney from acting until the donor lacks mental capacity to manage his or her property and financial affairs, the solicitor is advised to require of the attorney sufficient evidence to satisfy himself or herself that the attorney has authority to now act under the power. As an EPA must be registered by the attorney, with the Office of the Public Guardian, when the attorney believes the donor has become or is becoming unable to manage his or her property and financial affairs, a registered EPA will be sufficient evidence of the donor's mental incapacity. This assumption cannot be made with a registered LPA, as registration does not indicate incapacity. The attorney should provide sufficient evidence to confirm that the donor lacks capacity to consent to the disclosure of the will.

THE WILL IS THE CLIENT'S PROPERTY

The property and financial affairs attorney or deputy is the client's agent and the will forms part of the property and financial affairs, which the agent is authorised to manage. As such, if there is no instruction to the contrary within the LPA, EPA or the Court order, a full copy of the will can be disclosed to the attorney or deputy, unless the disclosing solicitor has cause for concern (see paragraph 7 below). The original will should be retained by the solicitor as part of the client's papers, in accordance with the original retainer, unless ordered otherwise by the Court of Protection.

CONCERNS ABOUT AN ATTORNEY OR DEPUTY

There may be occasions where the solicitor is aware or has reason to believe that the attorney or deputy has acted, is acting or proposes to act in breach of his or her statutory and/or fiduciary duties as set out in Chapter 7 of the Mental Capacity Act 2005 Statutory Code of Practice[6]. For example, where the solicitor has credible information which gives cause for reasonable concern that if the will were disclosed, there is a reasonable belief that the attorney or deputy may act or make a decision which is not in the best interests of the person for whom they act. In such circumstances, a solicitor may consider that it is not appropriate for the will to be disclosed, as it is not in the best interests of the client. In such case, the Refusal Notice in the Annex to this guidance should be given to the attorney or deputy. At the same time the solicitor should contact the Office of the Public Guardian and inform them of their concerns:

PO Box 16185
Birmingham
B2 2WH
opg.safeguardingunit@publicguardian.gsi.gov.uk
Telephone: 0300 456 0300

The nature of a concern raised to the Office of the Public Guardian will require disclosure of confidential information and is likely to be justified from a professional conduct perspective.

Examples of concerns include but are not limited to the following situations:

(i)   The attorney or deputy wishes to transfer or has transferred the client's assets to himself or herself or someone who is related or connected to them;

(ii) An indication of missing or converted assets;
(iii) The attorney or deputy has had a unexpected change in lifestyle or circumstance;
(iv) Care fees are not being paid;
(v) An investigation into and/or application for the attorney's or deputy's removal is in the process of being made;
(vi) The attorney or deputy refuses to disclose the residence of the client.

NOTIFICATION OF DISCLOSURE TO THE DONOR

It is both courteous and good practice to let the donor know in advance of sending the will to the attorney, that the attorney has requested a copy of the will and it is intended that it is to be provided to them. Letter 1 as set out in the Annex to this guidance should be sent to the donor, regardless whether or not the donor has mental capacity. The attorney should also personally inform the donor that he or she has requested a copy of the will. Letter 2 is a standard letter that can be used as a covering letter for sending the will to the attorney.

NOTIFICATION OF DISCLOSURE TO P BY THE DEPUTY

The Court of Protection appoints a deputy to make property and financial affairs decisions on a continuing basis, the wide terms of which enable the deputy to see a copy of will of the person for whom he or she has been appointed to act ('P'). However, incapacity is not a continuing state, so even where the Court has appointed a deputy, P is not prevented from making decisions, where the deputy knows or reasonably believes P has capacity in relation to that decision[7]. As such, it is for the deputy to ascertain whether P has sufficient capacity to make the decision for disclosure of the will or whether the deputy can rely on the Court order. It would be unduly onerous to require the deputy to provide medical evidence of capacity on each and every decision he or she makes, including capacity to consent to disclosure of P's will, and so the solicitor is able to rely on the deputy's request for disclosure. Letter 2 is a standard letter that can be used as a covering letter for sending the will to the deputy.

THE DUTY TO CONSULT THE CLIENT

Obtaining a copy of the will is a best interests decision, and where reasonably practicable, the attorney or deputy should involve the person for whom they act and let him or her know of any request sought to see a copy. Disclosure is a significant decision and as such, in the case of a deputy, would be expected to report this to the Office of the Public Guardian, when submitting his or her annual report.

ACKNOWLEDGEMENTS

The authors would also like to thank the following for their invaluable input: Angela Johnson of the Office of the Public Guardian, Senior Judge Denzil Lush from the Court of Protection, Richard Munden, barrister of 5RB and Caroline Bielanska, Solicitor of Caroline Bielanska Consultancy.

DISCLOSURE OF WILL: REFUSAL NOTICE

Date:

Request by an attorney or deputy for a copy of the will of the person for whom they act

Your request for disclosure of the will of the person for whom you act under an Enduring or Lasting Power of attorney or Deputyship Order has been denied at this time.

To obtain a copy of the will you will need to apply to the Court of Protection for a specific court order. Details of how to obtain an order can be found on www.gov.uk/courts-tribunals/court-of-protection, where the application forms can be downloaded.

FLOW CHART SETTING OUT THE PROCESS WHERE THE DONOR HAS NOT GIVEN EXPRESS PRIOR CONSENT TO DISCLOSE HIS/HER WILL

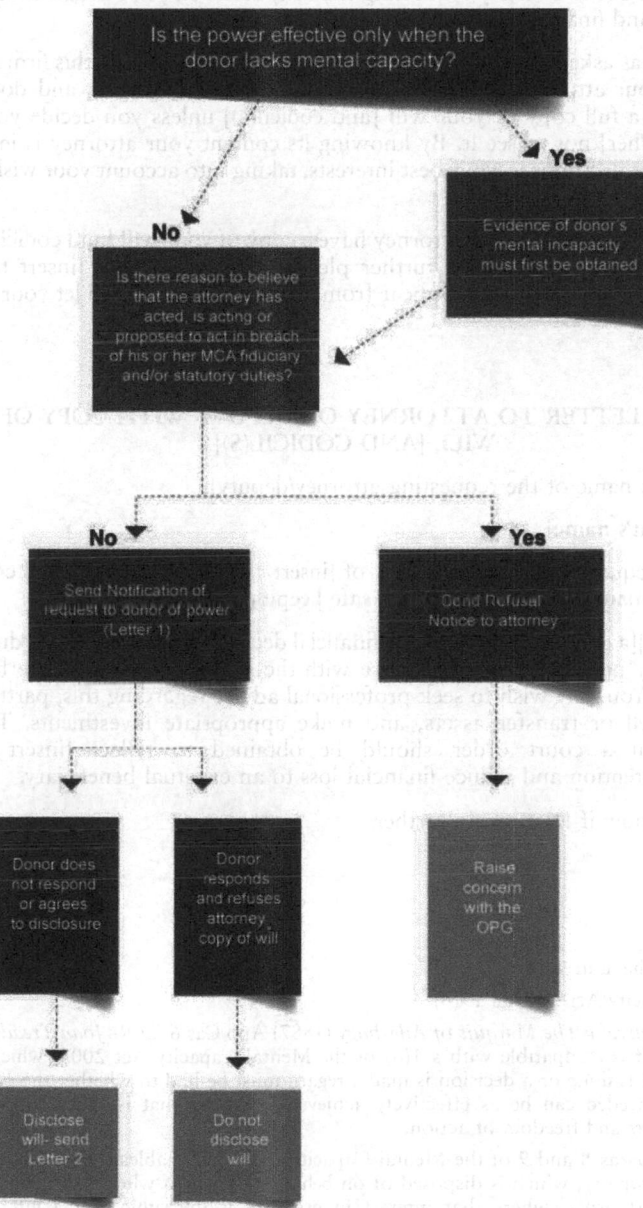

Is the power effective only when the donor lacks mental capacity?

Yes — Evidence of donor's mental incapacity must first be obtained

No — Is there reason to believe that the attorney has acted, is acting or proposed to act in breach of his or her MCA fiduciary and/or statutory duties?

No — Send Notification of request to donor of power (Letter 1)

Yes — Send Refusal Notice to attorney

Donor does not respond or agrees to disclosure

Donor responds and refuses attorney copy of will

Raise concern with the OPG

Disclose will- send Letter 2

Do not disclose will

LETTER 1: NOTIFICATION TO THE DONOR OF REQUEST BY ATTORNEY FOR A COPY OF THE DONOR'S WILL

Dear [insert the name of the donor]

You may recall that you made an [Enduring/Lasting] Power of Attorney and appointed [insert the name of the attorney requesting the will] to act on your behalf in relation to your property and finances.

Your attorney has asked for a copy of your will [and codicil(s] which this firm holds for safekeeping. Your attorney is allowed to see your financial papers and documents, which includes a full copy of your will [and codicil(s)] unless you decide you would prefer for [him/her] not to see it. By knowing its content your attorney is in a better position to make decisions in your best interests, taking into account your wishes as set out in your will.

If you do not want us to let your attorney have a copy of your will [and codicil(s)], and if you would like to discuss this further please telephone me on [insert telephone number] by [inset date[8]]. If I do not hear from you by that date I will let your attorney have a copy of your will.

Yours sincerely,

LETTER 2: LETTER TO ATTORNEY OR DEPUTY WITH COPY OF THE WILL [AND CODICIL(S)]

Dear [insert the name of the requesting attorney/deputy],

Re: [insert client's name]

As previously requested, I enclose a copy of [insert client's name] will [and codicil(s)]. The original remains within the firm for safe keeping.

As [an attorney][a deputy] when making financial decisions you are under a duty, so far as is reasonably possible, not to interfere with the succession plans made by [insert client's name]. You may wish to seek professional advice regarding this, particularly if you wish to sell or transfer assets, and make appropriate investments. There are occasions when a court order should be obtained to reflect [insert the client's name]'s intention and reduce financial loss to an eventual beneficiary.

Please let me know if I can assist further.

Yours sincerely,

Notes

[1]   Indicative behaviour 1.25.

[2]   Mental Capacity Act 2005, s 19(6).

[3]   *Attorney-General v The Marquis of Ailesbury* (1887) App Cas 672; *Re Joan Treadwell* (30th July 2013). It is compatible with s 1(6) of the Mental Capacity Act 2005, which requires before an act is done or a decision is made, regard must be had to whether the purpose for which it is needed can be as effectively achieved in a way that is less restrictive of the person's rights and freedom of action.

[4]   Schedule 2, paras 8 and 9 of the Mental Capacity Act 2005 enables the preservation of an interest in property, which is disposed of on behalf of a person who lacks mental capacity under a court order, where that interest in property is the subject of a gift under the person's will.

[5]   A witness statement should be made on form COP24 and can be obtained from https://form finder.hmctsformfinder.justice.gov.uk/cop024-eng.pdf

[6]   https://www.gov.uk/government/uploads/system/uploads/attachment_data/file/497253/Ment al-capacity-act-code-of-practice.pdf

7   Mental Capacity Act 2005, s 20(1).
8   Set a reasonable time scale, which should take into account statutory and bank holidays.

Index

A

Accountability
  precedents
    lasting power of attorney 15.32
Advance decision to refuse treatment
  precedents
    lasting power of attorney 15.49, 15.50
Advisers
  precedents
    lasting power of attorney 15.31
Advocates, certificate providers, as 6.40, 6.41
Annulment of marriage
  lasting power of attorney 4.42
Anticipatory decision-making 1.32
Applicable law
  precedents
    lasting power of attorney 15.1
Attorneys
  enduring power of attorney 16.14–16.20,
    21.34–21.38
  accounts 16.41
  acting for donor as administrator or executor 13.26
  alternative or successive attorneys 16.47
  appointment of more than one attorney 16.18, 16.19
  authority 18.1–18.3
    as administrator 18.12
    as executor 18.12
    at the onset of donor's incapacity 18.42–18.49
    conditions and restrictions 18.17, 18.18
    general 18.4–18.14
      donor's property and affairs 18.13, 18.14
      effect of conferring 18.4–18.6
      lawful actions 18.7–18.11
    gifts 18.30–18.41
    needs, provision for 18.20–18.29
    omission to delete general or specific authority 18.16
    restriction when mental incapacity established 18.47
    scope of 18.19
    specific 18.15

Attorneys – *cont.*
  enduring power of attorney – *cont.*
    bankruptcy 16.17, 21.15, 21.19, 21.20,
      21.34–21.37
    exclusion 16.17
    co-attorneys, liability for 21.39
    code 18.57
    common law of agency, excluded decisions 13.25
    Court of Protection
      breach of duty, relief from liability 11.48
      consent to act 11.40, 11.41
      directions on decisions 11.39
      remuneration and expenses, directions on 11.45–11.47
      report, accounts and records, rendering of 11.44
    death
      revocation of powers 14.34
    death as grounds for objection to registration 9.20
    decision-making 13.65–13.67
      consulting others 13.81–13.83
      donors
        assistance to 13.71, 13.72
        best interests 13.76–13.79
        capacity of, assessment 13.73–13.75
      exclusions 13.16–13.25
      principles 13.68–13.70
      treatment, life-sustaining 13.80
    disclaimer 14.10, 14.11, 20.21–20.23
      effect of 14.21–14.24
      form of 14.12–14.15
      issue to donor 14.16
      issue to other donees 14.17–14.20
      issue to Public Guardian 14.17–14.20
      mental incapacity, after onset 20.24
      preserved 20.25
      Public Guardian, notification 18.49
    disclaimer as grounds for objection to registration 9.26, 9.27
    disclaimers 21.38
    donors
      disclosure of will to 16.38, 16.39

913

Index

Index